Italy

a Lonely Planet travel survival kit

Helen Gillman
Damien Simonis

Italy

2nd edition

Published by
Lonely Planet Publications
Head Office: PO Box 617, Hawthorn, Vic 3122, Australia
Branches: 155 Filbert St, Suite 251, Oakland, CA 94607, USA
10 Barley Mow Passage, Chiswick, London W4 4PH, UK
71 bis rue du Cardinal Lemoine, 75005 Paris, France

Printed by
SNP Printing Pte Ltd, Singapore

Photographs by

Sonia Berto	Richard Stewart	Azienda di Promozione Turistica
Stefano Cavedoni	Helmuth Rier	(APT)
Greg Elms	Damien Simonis	Comitato Assistenza Italiani
Rob Flynn	Lauren Sunstein	(COASIT)
John Gillman	Tony Wheeler	Fotocolor ESIT-Cagliari

Front cover: Café near Piazza San Marco, Venice (Simon Rowe)

First Published
September 1993

This Edition
January 1996

National Library of Australia Cataloguing in Publication Data

Helen Gillman
Italy

2nd ed.
Includes index.
ISBN 0 86442 322 5.

1. Italy – Guidebooks. I. Simonis, Damien. II. Title.
(Series: Lonely Planet travel survival kit)

914.504929

text & maps © Lonely Planet 1996
photos © photographers as indicated 1996
climate charts compiled from information supplied by Patrick J Tyson, © Patrick J Tyson, 1996.

Helen Gillman

Helen works as a freelance journalist and editor, based in Italy. For many years she worked as a journalist in Australia (her country of birth), before deciding to 'retire' to Italy in 1990, at the age of 31. When not working on Lonely Planet guides, she coordinates the publications programme of the Community Forestry Unit within the Food & Agriculture Organisation of the United Nations, and occasionally writes magazine articles on scientific and agricultural topics. Helen lives in Rome with her husband, Stefano Cavedoni, and their two-year-old daughter Virginia.

Damien Simonis

Damien is a London-based journalist. With a degree in languages and several years' newspaper experience on, among others, the *The Australian* and *The Age*, he left Australia in 1989. He has worked and travelled widely in Europe, the Middle East and North Africa. In addition to this guide, he has worked on travel survival kits for *Jordan & Syria*, *Egypt & the Sudan*, *Morocco* and *North Africa*, as well as contributing to publications in the UK, Australia and North America. When not writing and travelling, Damien jumps the fence as a subeditor on *The Guardian* and other papers in London. He was last seen heading for Spain to co-write Lonely Planet's guidebook there.

From the Authors

Numerous organisations, friends and relatives contributed to the planning and research of the second edition of this travel survival kit. We would like to thank the directors and staff of the following tourist organisations for their valuable assistance: the Südtirol/Alto Adige Ufficio Provinciale per il Turismo (in particular Giovanna Buoninsegna); APT del Trentino; the Associazione Turistica Corvara (in particular Dr Damiano Dapunt); the Associazione Turistica Castelrotto/Siusi/Alpe di Siusi (in particular Tiziana Fata); Firenze APT (in particular Roberta Berni); Ente Sardo Industrie Turistiche (ESIT) (in particular Nino Manca); Venezia APT (in particular Cesare Battisti); Aosta APT; Bologna IAT; and the APTs of Udine, Parma, Modena, La Spezia, Matera, Ascoli Piceno, Macerata, Messina, Catania, Taormina and Syracuse. Aldo Cianci and colleagues at the Napoli Stazione Centrale counter of the EPT displayed enormous patience and good humour. Pierluigi and Fulvia at Enjoy Rome were a big help with the Rome chapter.

From Helen Gillman Helen would particularly like to thank Stefan Paungger, a patient and expert mountain guide who accompanied us on the trek in the Catinaccio group. Murena, our resident expert on Sardinia (and *sardo* through and through), was a great help. Thanks also to Rosita Castro and Daniela Cavedoni for their invaluable help; Michelle Gillman for her support and help with the baby; Beppe Culcasi, who was an indefatigable tour guide in Valle d'Aosta; Giovanni Cenacchi for his generous hospitality in San Candido; Anna Dondini and Flavio Boldrin for their hospitality on the Island of Elba, and Antonio Pezzinga for his inspiration in Rome and Lazio. The biggest thanks go to Stefano Cavedoni, who assisted with the research in Valle d'Aosta, Trentino-Alto Adige, Tuscany, Rome, Lazio and Sardinia. Without the influence of his explorer's spirit, sense of adventure and great appreciation of the rich history and natural beauty of his country, this would be a much lesser book. Of course it would be a great oversight not to thank Virginia who made it through some pretty long trips, went on quite a few mountain hikes, created havoc in numerous museums and art galleries, tested out more playgrounds than you can poke a stick at, and generally enriched our travelling experience.

From Damien Simonis Damien would like to thank Daniela Antongiovanni and friends in Milan, who showed hospitality well beyond the call of duty. Thanks also to John Glover for his culinary tips over a tipple. Francesco Melillo and Leonardo Poggi provided valuable information.

Vivi Giacco and Zia Cristina in Agrigento not only put me up, but went to great lengths, willingly helped by friends, to introduce me to as many delights of Sicilian gastronomy as was possible. I owe all a debt of gratitude for their forbearance during my Lampedusa adventures. *Alla prossima.*

Zia Maria, Zio Fortunato and the rest of the family in Chianche helped ensure a memorable Christmas and New Year while I shuttled in and out of Naples. The Fiore family in Avellino also helped out in a moment of crisis when we found ourselves trapped by storms without snow chains.

Ray Cassin lent a much appreciated hand with literary history.

A special thanks to my colleague Helen and the family, especially Stefano, Daniela and little Virginia for putting up with me in Rome and Bologna.

In London, a lot of people have kept my life ticking over or in boxes, including Michèle Nayman, Ian Jones, Caroline Dewhurst and Charles Gollop. Thanks also to Sue Quinn for her help between projects.

Above all, the results of my share of the toil around Italy are dedicated to Lucrezia and Ariana, who accompanied me when they could, put up with long separations and were unfailing in their support.

From the Publisher

This book was edited at the Lonely Planet office in Melbourne by Katie Cody, Anne Mulvaney and Ian Ward. Lynn McGaurr and Mary Neighbour proofread the text and Kerrie Williams produced the index. Maliza Kruh designed the book, and drew the maps with help from Sandra Smythe, David Kemp, Jane Hart, Jacqui Saunders, Marcel Gaston, Margaret Jung, Ann Jeffree and Chris Klep. Trudi Canavan produced new illustrations, black & white photographs are by Simon Bracken, and cover design is by Simon Bracken and Paul Clifton.

Thanks

All those involved in producing this book greatly appreciate the contribution of those travellers who put so much effort into writing and telling us of their experiences. These people's names appear at the back of the book.

Warning & Request

Things change – prices go up, schedules change, good places go bad and bad places go bankrupt – nothing stays the same. So if you find things better or worse, recently opened or long since closed, please write and tell us and help make the next edition better.

Your letters will be used to help update future editions and, where possible, important changes will also be included in a Stop Press section in reprints.

We greatly appreciate all information that is sent to us by travellers. Back at Lonely Planet we employ a hard-working readers' letters team to sort through the many letters we receive. The best ones will be rewarded with a free copy of the next edition or another Lonely Planet guide if you prefer. We give away lots of books, but, unfortunately, not every letter/postcard receives one.

Contents

Map Legend

BOUNDARIES

▪━▪━▪━▪━▪━▪━▪━▪ .... International Boundary

━▪━▪━▪━▪━▪━▪━ .... Regional Boundary

ROUTES

━━━━━━━━ .... Freeway

━━━━━━━━ .... Highway

━━━━━━━━ .... Major Road

━ ━ ━ ━ ━ ━ ━ .... Unsealed Road or Track

━━━━━━━━ .... City Road

━━━━━━━━ .... City Street

╈╈╈╈╈╈╈╈ .... Train Line

━━━━━━━━ .... Metro Line

━━━━━━━━ .... Tram

━ ━ ━ ━ ━ ━ ━ .... Walking Track

• • • • • • • • • • • • .... Walking Tour

━ ━ ━ ━ ━ ━ ━ .... Ferry Route

╫╫╫╫╫╫╫╫╫╫ .. Funicular, Funivia or Cable Car

AREA FEATURES

.... Park, Gardens

.... National Park

.... Built-Up Area

.... Pedestrian Mall

.... Market

+ + + + + + + ... Cemetery

.... Beach or Desert

⌒⌒ ⌒ .... Mountain Ranges

HYDROGRAPHIC FEATURES

.... Coastline

.... River, Creek

━ ━ ━ ━ ━ .... Intermittent River or Creek

.... Lake, Intermittent Lake

.... Salt Lake

.... Canal

.... Swamp

SYMBOLS

✪ CAPITAL	.... National Capital	⊕ ★	.... Hospital, Police Station
◉ Capital	.... Regional Capital	✈ ✝	.... Airport, Airfield
CITY	.... Major City	▭ ✿	.... Swimming Pool, Gardens
● City	.... City	❖ 🐘	.... Shopping Centre, Zoo
● Town	.... Town	◔ ♈	.....Embassy, Winery or Vineyard
● Village	.... Village	← A25	One Way Street, Route Number
▪	..........................Place to Stay	⁂	......Archaeological Site or Ruins
▼	.... Place to Eat	🏛	.. Palace or Stately Home, Castle
🍺 🍴	........................Pub, Café or Bar	♟ ▣	.... Monument, Tomb
✉ ☎	.....Post Office, Telecom Office	⌂	...... Cave, Hut, Shelter or Rifugio
🏛 ⑂	...........Gallery or Museum, Bank	▲ ❄	.... Mountain or Hill, Lookout
⬤ P	....................Transport, Parking	⚹ ⚐	.... Lighthouse, Shipwreck
❶ ⌂	.......Tourist Office, Youth Hostel	)(✕	.................Pass, Spot Height
🏕 ⚑	Caravan Park, Camping Ground		.... Ancient or City Wall
✝ ⛪	..................Church or Cathedral		.... Rapids, Waterfalls
✡ ✡	.................Temple, Synagogue		.....Cliff or Escarpment, Tunnel
Ⓜ ⛽	Metro Station, Petrol Station		..................................Train Station

Note: not all symbols displayed above appear in this book

Introduction

Since the days of the Grand Tour, travellers to Italy have speculated on the 'fatal spell' of the country. This special charm has been attributed to the flair of its people, the art, the history, even the air. What is it that makes Italy so seductive? The Italian writer, Luigi Barzini, had this to say on the question:

It made and still makes unwanted people feel wanted, unimportant people feel important and purposeless people believe that the real way to live intelligently is to have no earnest purpose in life.

This land of vibrant, expressive people has given the world pasta and pizza, Michelangelo and da Vinci, Dante and Machiavelli, Catholicism and a vast array of saints and martyrs, Verdi and Pavarotti, Fellini and Sophia Loren, not to mention the Mafia, a remarkable sense of style and {la dolce vita}. In Italy you can visit Roman ruins, study the art of the Renaissance, stay in tiny medieval hill towns, go mountaineering in the Alps and Apennines, feel romantic in Venice, participate in traditional festivals and see more beautiful churches than you imagined could exist in one country. Some people come simply to enjoy the food and wine.

Do your research before coming to Italy, but arrive with an open mind and you will find yourself agreeing with Henry James, who wrote on his arrival in Rome: 'At last, for the first time, I live'.

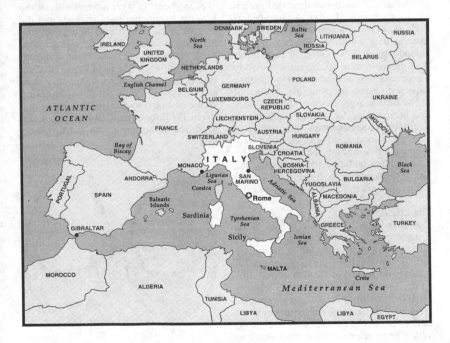

Facts about the Country

HISTORY

Italy's strategic position in the Mediterranean made it a target for colonisers and invaders, whose comings and goings over thousands of years have left a people with a diverse ethnic background. But it also gave the Romans, and later the Christian Church, an excellent base from which to expand their respective empires. Italy's history is thus a patchwork of powerful empires and foreign domination, and from the fall of the Roman Empire until the formation of the Kingdom of Italy in 1861, the country was never a unified entity.

Prehistoric Italy

The Italian peninsula has supported human life for thousands of years. Archaeological finds show that Palaeolithic Neanderthals lived in Italy about 70,000 years ago. By around 4000 BC, Neolithic, or New Stone Age, humans were no longer exclusively nomadic hunters and had started to establish settlements across the peninsula. At the start of the Bronze Age, around 1800 BC, Italy had been settled by several Italic tribes, which had frequent contact with eastern and other Mediterranean cultures until they were eventually absorbed into the Roman Empire. These tribes included the Ligurians, the Veneti, the Apulians, the Siculi, the Sardi, the Latins, the eastern Italics and many others.

The Etruscans

Historians differ on the exact origins of the Etruscan people and when they arrived in the Italian peninsula, although it is widely agreed they migrated from the Aegeo-Asian area around the end of the 12th century BC.

What is beyond doubt is that the Etruscans created a flourishing civilisation between the Arno and Tiber valleys, with other important settlements in Campania, Lazio and the Po valley. The earliest evidence of the Etruscan people in Italy was the Villanovan culture (around the 9th century BC) centred around present-day Bologna and characterised by the practice of cremating the dead and burying the ashes in urns.

From the 7th to the 6th century BC, Etruscan culture was at its height. The nation was based on large city-states, among them Caere (Cerveteri), Tarquinii (Tarquinia), Veii (Veio), Volsinii (believed to be either Bolsena or Orvieto), Felsina (Bologna), Perusia (Perugia), Volaterrae (Volterra), Faesulae (Fiesole) and Arretium (Arezzo), collectively known as the Etruscan League. The Etruscans were predominantly navigators and traders, competing for markets in the Mediterranean against the Phoenicians and Greeks.

A good deal of what is known about the Etruscan culture has been learned from the archaeological evidence of their tombs and religious sanctuaries. Their belief in life after death necessitated the burial of the dead with everything they might need in the afterlife, such as food and drink, clothing, ornaments and weapons. Painted tombs depicting scenes of everyday life, notably those discovered at Tarquinia, near Rome, provide an important document of how the Etruscans lived.

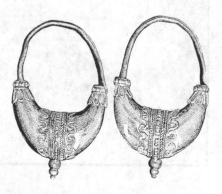

Etruscan earrings from the late 4th century BC

The long period of Etruscan decline began in the 5th century BC, when they began to lose control of their trade routes to the more powerful Greeks. By the 4th century BC, they had lost their northern territories to Gallic invaders and their settlements in Campania to the Samnites, confining Etruria to its original territories in central Italy. While Etruscan civilisation continued to flourish during this period, its development was by then greatly determined by its relationship with the growing power of Rome.

Rome had long been profoundly influenced by Etruscan culture and three of the seven kings who ruled Rome before the Republic were Etruscans, known as the Tarquins.

The Etruscan and Roman civilisations coexisted relatively peacefully until the defeat of Veii and its incorporation into the territory of Rome in 396 BC. During the ensuing century, Etruscan cities were either defeated or entered into peaceful alliance with an increasingly powerful Rome, although they maintained a fair degree of autonomy until 90 BC, when the Etruscans (as well as all the Italic peoples of the peninsula) were granted Roman citizenship. Thus absorbed into what was to become the Roman Empire, the separate Etruscan culture and language rapidly disappeared. Scholars of the day attached little importance to the need to preserve the Etruscan language, and few translations into Latin were made. No Etruscan literature survived and the only remaining samples of the written language are related to religious and funerary customs.

Greek Colonisation

The first Greek settlements in Italy were established in the early 8th century BC – first on the island of Ischia in the Bay of Naples, followed by other settlements along the peninsula's southern coast and in Sicily. What became known as Magna Graecia (Greater Greece) was, in fact, a group of independent city-states, established by colonists from the independent city-states of Greece itself. The founders of the colonies at Ischia and Cumae were from the island of Euboea; the Corinthians founded the great city of Syracuse; and exiled Spartans founded the wealthy city of Taranto.

The civilisation of Magna Graecia, which flourished in territories which had previously been colonised by Pheonicians or occupied by local peoples, spanned about six centuries. The ruins of magnificent Doric temples in Italy's south (at Paestum) and in Sicily (Agrigento, Selinunte and Segesta), and other monuments such as the Greek theatre at Syracuse, stand as testament to its splendour.

Syracuse became so powerful that Athens considered it enough of a threat to launch an attack on the city. In one of the great maritime battles in history, Syracuse managed to destroy the Athenian fleet in 413 BC. By the end of the 3rd century BC, Magna Graecia had succumbed to the might of the advancing Roman Republic, though not before playing a major role in introducing Hellenic culture to Rome.

The Roman Republic

The traditional date for the founding of Rome by Romulus is 21 April 753 BC, but the story of the first Roman Republic begins in 509 BC, after the phase of the seven kings. It is a complex, fascinating saga of a quest to create an intellectual and economic national entity from a fiercely independent, and primarily regionally focused, family and community-oriented people.

When Rome established its first Republic, it introduced a basic principle of political philosophy – that of the sovereign rights of the people. In modern Rome the initials SPQR, visible in carvings on ancient Roman monuments and stamped on municipal property to this day, stand as testimony to an ideal of continuity with the first Senate, *Senatus Populus Que Romanus*, the Senate & People of Rome.

More realistically though, during the period of the monarchy, there already existed a group of powerful families, known as the *patricii* (patricians), descendants of the *patres* (founding fathers), who wielded great influence over the rest of the population, known as the *plebeii* (plebeians). In the early years of the Republic, the patrician families managed to achieve a monopoly on public office. Hence the plebeians created their own movement, leading to what is known to scholars as the 'struggle of the orders'. The movement was successful to the extent that the Roman statesman Cato could assume in the 2nd century BC that there were no 'formal' barriers in the way of any Roman citizen achieving the highest office of the state. But, in reality, the control of the state always remained in the hands of the patricians and *equites* (the highest class of the non-noble rich), who constituted the vast majority of the 300 senators.

The politics of conquest favoured the patricians, but also permitted the compensation of plebeians, more specifically soldiers, with parcels of land from the newly conquered territories – a system of reward which enabled the Republic to avoid internal conflict. Other peoples allied with Rome also received concrete advantages. But, perhaps one of the main reasons for Rome's success was that its imperialistic exploits were based on a social system whereby every Roman citizen could participate according to his class, with the possibility to climb the social ladder.

The Punic Wars
The use of Latin became widespread as a result of the expansion of Rome, an expansion strongly opposed by Carthage, which controlled the Mediterranean's maritime traffic in competition with Greece. Carthage engaged in three long wars with Rome, called the Punic Wars, the first of which started in 264 BC and raged for 24 years.

In 264 BC Carthage was much more powerful than Rome. Originally one of several Phoenician trading posts at the narrow point of the Mediterranean opposite Sicily, in what is now Tunisia, Carthage had built up a colonial empire which extended to Morocco and included western Sicily, Corsica, Sardinia and even parts of Spain.

During the Punic Wars, the Romans were called upon for the first time to fight a war

across the sea against the greatest naval power of the age. The Greek historian Polybius claimed that the Romans had no idea even of how to construct a large warship until a Carthaginian vessel was grounded and they were then able to construct a replica.

The First Punic War (264-241 BC), which Rome won, was fought over control of Sicily. In the 20 years or so before the next war with Rome, Carthage extended its empire to Spain. In the meantime, Rome had managed to expel the Gauls from the Italian peninsula, consolidating the frontiers of Italy as we now know them.

With Spanish wealth and mercenaries, Hannibal launched his famous offensive, using elephants to cross the Alps, and sparking the Second Punic War in 218 BC. Hannibal crushed the Romans in bloody battles as he moved down the peninsula – around Lago di Trasimeno in what is now Umbria and at Cannae in what is now Apulia. He was ultimately defeated by the Roman general, Scipio, in 202 BC at Zama in North Africa, after being recalled to African soil by Carthage.

In the ensuing years, Rome added Macedonian Greece to its provinces, after decisively defeating Perseus, the son of Philip V of Macedon, in a three-year war. The Third Punic War (149-146 BC) dealt the final blow to Carthage. Vengeful in victory, Rome's destruction of Carthaginian civilisation was total; little knowledge of its culture remains and no known literature survives.

With Carthage destroyed, Rome incorporated Spain into its colonies and became the dominant power in the Mediterranean.

From Republic to Empire
Until 146 BC, the history of the Roman Republic was one of external warfare but relative peace at home. The constitution, with its government of two consuls who were elected annually, and its Senate representing the ruling class, worked efficiently. Roads and aqueducts were built to link the new estates of the Roman Republic. New cities were founded across the country. The Appian Way (Via Appia) had been started as

Linguistic Traditions

In the 4th century BC about 40 different languages were spoken in Italy and there were also several written languages. In addition to Latin, two languages were particularly widespread. The Umbrians, a civilised people who occupied roughly the region which now bears their name, left the world the *Eugubian Tables* written in Umbrian in about 200 BC, which are said to contain the largest body of religious ritual to have survived pre-Christian Europe. The other significant language, Oscan, was spoken widely throughout the south. It has been found inscribed on coins dating back to the 3rd and 4th centuries BC and was still used as graffiti on the walls of Pompeii in 79 AD. Almost all these languages gave way to Latin in the course of two or three centuries as the language of the Romans triumphed, first across Italy and then as the language of commerce throughout the empire, although Greek remained the language of the intellectuals. ■

early as 312 BC, when Rome was linked to Capua, and the road was extended to Brindisi in 244 BC. The Via Flaminia was built northwards over the Apennines to Fano in 220 BC and was subsequently extended to Rimini. The Via Aurelia hugged the west coast, eventually reaching Genoa, and is still in full use today, as are all the ancient consular roads.

As well as the great wealth gained from the conquest of the Carthaginian and Hellenic worlds, Italian society found itself changed by another spoil of war, the long-term effects of which were to prove less beneficial to the Republic. To achieve the visions of its rulers and satisfy its lifestyle, Rome needed slave labour. In its last years, the Roman Republic supported around two million slaves, about 35% of the population, all of whom were completely dependent on their masters for their existence.

The influx of slave labour ensured the growth of large estates for the select few at the expense of the many small freeholdings that had characterised pre-Punic War society. The demise of smaller holdings created an agrarian disaster which brought social disruption and human misery, resulting in the Social War of 91 BC. Recognised as a last attempt by the allied peoples of the peninsula to press their claims on Rome, the revolt was resolved by force, but it resulted in Rome offering citizenship to all the peoples of its colonies.

Another, more bloody social war was fought from 73 to 71 BC. In an attempt to

secure freedom for his fellow slaves destined for the ever-popular gladiatorial games, a Tracian slave named Spartacus escaped from a school for gladiators in Capua, taking with him 200 followers. About 78 of them remained with Spartacus, to form the nucleus of a force of some 70,000 runaway slaves and others. After initially repelling the Roman forces sent to suppress the uprising, Spartacus was killed and some 6000 of his followers were crucified, lining the Appian Way from Capua to Rome.

By then Rome's military greats – Gnaeus Pompeius (Pompey), Crassus (who was one of the wealthiest men in Rome), Julius Caesar, Mark Antony and Octavian – controlled the Senate and, in 60 BC, Pompey, with Caesar and Crassus, formed an unconstitutional triumvirate, effectively ending any semblance of government 'for and by the people'.

In 52 BC, Pompey finally took the title of sole consul and dictator, with the full support of Caesar, who, having secured command of the legions in Gaul, declared southern Britain part of Rome after two raids on the island Celts, in 55 and 54 BC. Caesar's flagrant disregard for the authority of the Senate, which had ordered him to disband his legions and return to Rome, gained him enormous popularity, particularly among his troops.

Following his defeat of Pompey in the battle of Pharsalus, and Pompey's murder in Egypt in 48 BC, Caesar returned to Rome and was made consul and dictator. His four-year reign was marked by intense activity both in Italy and throughout the territories under Roman control. He instigated land reforms which limited individual's holdings, and framed a uniform system of local government which extended throughout Italy and the outer provinces. He also introduced the Julian calendar, which was to be used throughout Europe for many centuries.

But Caesar continued to treat the political establishment of Rome with scant respect. He increased the number of senators to 900, effectively undermining and dissipating the Senate's power and, when he was murdered on 15 March 44 BC, it was said that among his murderers were more of his friends than his enemies – including Brutus, his adopted son.

Caesar's dictatorship paved the way for further domination by Rome's military imperialists, starting with Mark Antony (consul for the year 44 BC) and followed by Caius Octavian, who had been adopted by Caesar as his son and heir. Octavian became Rome's first emperor in 27 BC, adopting the title of Augustus, the Grand One.

Augustus ruled for 45 years, a period of great advancement in engineering, architecture, administration and military arts as well as literature. He often claimed that he found Rome a city of brick and left it a city of marble. The remains of his forum are still visible opposite the Roman Forum and his mausoleum is tucked away behind the Ara Pacis in Rome.

The Augustan age enabled the blossoming of Latin literature, the foundations of which had been laid by great writers and philosophers such as Cicero (106-43 BC) and the early humorous dramatists, Plautus (c 254-184 BC) and Terence (c 195-159 BC). Virgil and the two great poets of the Augustan era, Horace (65-8 BC) and Ovid (43 BC-c17 AD), had enormous influence on European thought and literature.

Rome's impeccable administrative system, giving great authority to institutions, and a rigorous military discipline promoting an efficient army, favoured the development of an empire which culturally and linguisti-

Julius Caesar, general, statesman, historian and dictator of the Roman Empire (49-44 BC).

cally unified many diverse peoples. By 100 AD, the city of Rome had more than 1.5 million inhabitants, and its wealth and prosperity were obvious in the rich floor mosaics, the marble temples, public baths, theatres, circuses, libraries, publishing houses, a postal service and even a telegraphic system based on light signals. Meanwhile, the empire boasted a 100,000 km network of roads and a complex system of aqueducts; and possessed the technology to drain large lakes and to develop sophisticated war machines.

Consolidation of Expansion

The succession of Augustus by his stepson Tiberius (14-37 AD) heralded an era which eventually was to disturb Roman imperialism, not because of any decline of military might but because of the rise of Christianity. Despite the efforts of many emperors to suppress the new religion, Christianity prospered. The Apostles and their followers travelled from Northumberland to Egypt, and from Portugal to Syria, spreading the Christian story.

Meanwhile the Empire continued to grow and flourish, with significant cultural expansion under emperors such as Claudius, who introduced major reforms to ministerial government, created a modern system of sanitation, shops and public baths, and built aqueducts on the massive Porta Maggiore. He also created an artificial harbour at Ostia (now known as Ostia Antica) at the mouth of the Tiber, the ruins of which are visible today.

The extravagant and obviously deranged Emperor Nero (ruled 54-68 AD) is best known for the burning of Rome and his persecution of the Christians.

After a short period of instability, Emperor Vespasian, the son of a civil servant from the Italian provinces and the first of the Flavian dynasty, carried out some of the most ambitious building projects of the Empire. He started the Colosseum, which was completed by his son Titus, who succeeded him as emperor in 78 AD. He is remembered in Roman architecture by the triumphal Arco di Tito (81 AD) where the Via Sacra enters the Roman Forum.

Trajan, a Roman general, was commanding his legions in Germany when he was appointed emperor by the Senate in 98 AD. He returned to Rome two years later to be crowned, but left soon after to conquer Dacia (present-day Romania), then Mesopotamia, Persia, Syria and Armenia. Under Trajan, the Roman Empire reached its point of greatest expansion: extending from present-day Kuwait to England, from the Caspian Sea to Morocco and Portugal and from North Africa to the Danube and Romania.

Trajan's architectural legacy included a new artificial harbour at Ostia to replace that built by Claudius (Trajan's harbour remains perfectly preserved in the private property of a Roman family) and the amphitheatre at Verona. The great architect Apollodorus of Damascus built a km-long wooden bridge over the Danube, to enable Trajan to invade new territories. He also designed Trajan's forum in Rome, where the emperor placed a magnificent marble column decorated with 2000 carvings depicting his Dacian campaign. The column, which later served as Trajan's tomb, remains today.

His successor, Hadrian (117-138 AD), was responsible for some of Rome's most famous landmarks: he rebuilt the Pantheon after a fire, and built the vast Villa Adriana at Tivoli, near Rome, as well as Hadrian's Wall in Britain. His tomb was converted into the fortress now called Castel Sant'Angelo, in Rome.

A terrible plague swept Europe during the 2nd century and, combined with the infiltration of Eastern religions and increasing pressure from Teutonic tribes on the Rhine and Danube frontiers, Rome began to lose its grip.

With the Edict of Milan in 313 AD, Emperor Constantine gave official recognition to Christianity after having first converted to Christianity himself. Rome was established as its headquarters. Formal recognition also sparked off a widespread building programme of cathedrals and churches throughout the land.

Division of the Empire

The Empire remained beset by civil wars as the once all-conquering Roman legions shifted their support from one would-be emperor to another. Tribes along the empire's borders took advantage of the power vacuum by grabbing ever-larger chunks of territory, and there was little Rome could do about it. The Empire was so large that it had become undefendable.

A section of Trajan's column (AD 113): Victory writing on a shield about Trajan's triumph.

Cutting his losses, and recognising the growing importance of the wealthy eastern regions of the empire, Emperor Constantine in 324 moved his capital city from Rome to Byzantium, a city on the northern shore of the Bosporus (now Turkey). He renamed it 'New Rome', but it became known as Constantinople (present-day Istanbul). Among the monuments left in Rome by Constantine are his triumphal arch between the Roman Forum and the Colosseum, and the imposing Basilica di Costantino (also known as the Basilica di Massenzio, in the forum).

The demise of the Roman Empire continued when the ruling brothers Valentian and Valens divided the empire into a western and eastern half in 364, a division that was formalised after the death of Emperor Theodosius I, in 395. His son Honorius ruled the Western Roman Empire, while his other son Arcadius ruled the Eastern Roman Empire.

Separated from its Roman roots, the Eastern Roman Empire embraced Hellenistic (Greek-Egyptian) culture and developed into the mighty Byzantine Empire, the most powerful Mediterranean state throughout the Middle Ages. It existed until the capture of Constantinople by the Turks in 1453.

The Early Middle Ages (400–600)

A population decline throughout the 2nd and 3rd centuries worsened in the 4th century through plague, famine and war.

The arrival of the Vandals in North Africa cut off Rome's corn supplies, while the western Teutonic tribe of Visigoths consolidated control of much of the northern Mediterranean coast and northern Italy. In 452, Attila the Hun, leader of a tribe from the central Asian steppes, invaded and, it is said, caused the people of Aquileia and Grado to found a city of refuge called Venice. This city was to become a great trading and seafaring centre and the birthplace, in 1254, of one of Italy's most well known adventurers, Marco Polo.

In 476, the year traditionally recognised as the end of the Roman Empire, the last Western Roman emperor, Romulus Augustulus, was deposed by a mutinous Germanic captain of mercenaries named Odovacar (476-93).

Gothic rule in Italy reached its zenith with the Ostrogothic emperor Theodoric (493-526). The greatest of the Ostrogothic rulers, Theodoric had spent several years as a hostage in Constantinople where he acquired great respect for Roman culture. When the Eastern Roman emperor Zeno put him in charge of Italy, Theodoric, ruling from Ravenna, brought peace and prosperity to the area.

After Theodoric's death, the Eastern Roman emperor Justinian (527-565) and his wife, Theodora, reconquered Italy and laid the groundwork for the Byzantine era. Among the early examples of Byzantine art in Italy are the mosaic portraits of Justinian and Theodora in the Basilica di San Vitale at Ravenna. Though the Justinian reconquest was soon rolled back by the Lombards, Byzantine emperors and empresses managed to hold on to parts of southern Italy until the 11th century.

During the middle years of the 5th century, Pope Leo I 'the Great' (440-461), known as the founder of Catholicism, had ensured the temporal power of the papacy by persuading Attila not to attack Rome. Using a document known as the *Donation of Constantine* (which made the Western Roman Empire a gift from Constantine to the papacy forever), Leo I secured the Western Roman Empire for the fledgling Catholic Church.

In 590, Pope Gregory I, son of a rich Roman family, returned from his self-imposed exile in a monastery, having given all his wealth to the poor. He set the pattern of Church administration which was to guide Catholic services and rituals throughout history.

Gregory oversaw the Christianisation of Britain, improved conditions for slaves, provided free bread in Rome and repaired Italy's extensive network of aqueducts, as well as leaving an enormous volume of writing on which much Catholic dogma was subsequently based.

Top Left: Sicilian man
Top Right: Pisciotta women, Campania
Bottom Left: Bergamasco men, Lombardy
Bottom Right: Baby during carnival, Rome

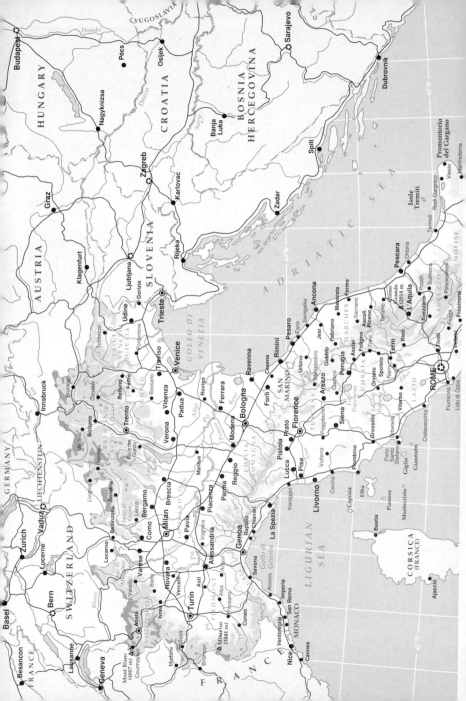

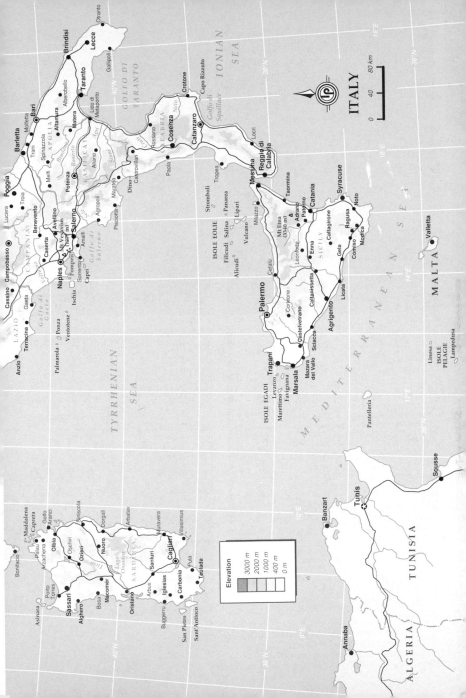

DAMIEN SIMONIS

JOHN GILLMAN

JOHN GILLMAN

DAMIEN SIMONIS

Top Left: Detail of Pomposa Abbey, Emilia Romagna
Top Right: Window sill in Gerace, Calabria
Bottom Left: Street scene in Camogli, Liguria
Bottom Right: Building on the Canale Grande, Trieste

Lombard Italy & the Papal States (600-800)

Even before Gregory became pope, the Lombard invasion of Italy had begun. The Lombards were a Swabian people who appear to have originally inhabited the lower basin of the Elbe; but as so often happened to conquerors of the Italian peninsula, rather than imposing their culture on the locals, they adopted the local culture. Their language did not last long after their arrival, and their culture too was almost completely integrated. Their more communal concept of land and property tenure was soon overthrown by the Romans' high regard for private property, either absolute or leased, and the Lombards, who mainly settled around Milan, Pavia and Brescia, soon became city dwellers, building many churches and public baths which still grace these cities. They eventually expanded their control farther down the peninsula – taking over the important duchies of Spoleto and Benevento – although they were unable to take Rome.

In an effort to unseat the Lombards, the pope invited the Franks to invade Italy, which they did in 754 and 756 under the command of their king, Pepin, disenfranchising the Lombards and establishing the Papal States, which were to survive until 1870. Using the *Donation of Constantine* as his precedent, Pepin issued the *Donation of Pepin* in 756, which gave land that was still nominally under the Byzantine Empire to Pope Stephen II and proclaimed the pope heir of the Roman emperors.

When Pepin's son and successor, Charlemagne, visited Rome in 774, he confirmed the *Donation of Pepin*. Charlemagne was crowned emperor by Pope Leo III on Christmas Day 800 in St Peter's Basilica, and the concept of the 'Holy Roman Empire' came into being. The bond between the papacy and the Byzantine Empire was thus forever broken, and political power in what had been the Western Roman Empire shifted north of the Alps, where it would remain for more than 1000 years. But, on Charlemagne's death his successors were unable to hold

A Goth (left) and a Swabian; these individuals represent just two of the different ethnic groups to invade the Italian peninsula.

together his vast Carolingian Empire. In 843, the Partition of Verdun divided the empire between his three nephews and Italy became a battleground of rival powers and states – the imperial crown being the prize of the most powerful man in the country, and the papacy fought over ruthlessly by Rome's aristocratic families.

An Oasis of Calm

Meanwhile, the Muslim Arabs had invaded Sicily and in 831 took Palermo as their capital, while Syracuse, an important city since the first Greek settlements, fell to them in 878. They established a splendid civilisation, restoring the fundamentals of Greek culture elaborated by Muslim scholars such as the philosopher Averroës, the physician and philosopher Avicenna, the astronomer and geographer Al Battani and the mathematician Al Kovarizmi. Cotton, sugar cane, oranges and lemons were introduced in the south, taxes there were lower, and the Sicilians lived relatively peacefully under their Arab lords for more than two centuries. Hundreds of mosques were built and the elegant,

architecture survived even after
was returned to the Christian fold.

malfi, which had secured independence
om Naples in the 840s, soon became a
major trading republic in the western Mediterranean, and, with the republics of Gaeta
and Naples along with Salerno, which was
still a Lombard principality, became a centre
of great cosmopolitan civilisation and learning. In the 11th century, Salerno was famous
for its medical school, where Greek,
Hebrew, Arab and Christian teachers worked
together.

While the south prospered under Arab
rule, the rest of Italy was not so calm. Following the end of the Carolingian Empire in
887, warfare broke out in earnest between
local Italian rulers who were divided in their
support of Frankish and Germanic claimants, all absentee landlords, to the imperial
title and throne. Italy became the battleground of Europe as rival factions fought for
ascendancy and refugees flooded safe cities
from the devastated countryside. Many of
Italy's medieval hill towns developed in this
period as easily defendable safe havens.

In 962, the Saxon Otto I was crowned
emperor in Rome and formally founded the
Holy Roman Empire. His son, Otto II, and
later his grandson, Otto III, also took the title
Holy Roman Emperor, cementing a tradition
that was to remain the privilege of Germanic
emperors until 1806.

In the early 11th century the fanatically
Christian Normans began arriving, first as
mercenaries in southern Italy where they
fought against the Arabs, but changing alle-
giances as profit dictated.

The Norman & Holy Roman Eras

The campaign of Hildebrand (who was to
become Pope Gregory VII in 1073) to
bring the world under the rule of Christianity was, in reality, a struggle for power
between Church and State. In order to be
legitimate, every new emperor had to be
sworn in and 'crowned' by the pope. The
papacy, based in Rome, and the Holy Roman
Empire, with its power base north of the
Alps, were compelled to agree in order to

reconstruct the political and cultural unity
which had been lost with the fall of the
Western Roman Empire. In reality, the two
powers were in perennial conflict and the
consequences of this dual leadership dominated the Middle Ages.

Both the Frankish and Germanic claimants to the crown were temporarily distracted
by the summons of Christendom to recapture
the Holy Land from the Muslims – the First
Crusade, a tragic disaster, moved primarily
from the regions which are today Germany
and France.

Having already established themselves
firmly in Apulia and Calabria, the Normans
moved into Sicily, which they progressively
managed to wrest from the Arab Muslims.
But, rather than banish the Arabs, the
Normans tended to assimilate Eastern traditions and systems and established what was
to be a long period of religious tolerance in
the south. When Roger II was crowned
king of Sicily in 1130, he established his
court at Palermo, which had been the
capital of the Arab emirate, and, before long,
church towers stood beside the domes of the
mosques.

The Normans brought with them a fine
appreciation of majestic spaces which are
characterised by Romanesque architecture,
but they liberally adapted Arab and Byzantine architectural features. The Chiesa di San
Giovanni degli Eremiti at Palermo might
equally pass as a mosque or a Greek or
Norman basilica. King Roger's magnificent
Cappella Palatina and the Cattedrale di
Monreale (just outside Palermo) are excellent examples of how the Normans
combined the vitality of Oriental influences
with the glory of Byzantine architecture and
the simple beauty of Romanesque.

Norman rule in the south gave way to
Germanic claims due to the foresight of Holy
Roman Emperor Frederick I (known as Barbarossa) who married off his son Henry to
Constance de Hauteville, heir to the Norman
throne in Sicily. Barbarossa's grandson,
Frederick II, became Holy Roman Emperor
in 1220. An enlightened ruler, Frederick,
who became known as Stupor Mundi

(Wonder of the World), was both a warrior and a scholar. A profound admirer of Arabic culture, he allowed freedom of worship to Muslims, as well as to Jews. He studied philosophy and magic, wrote laws and earned a place in Italian history as one of the country's earliest poets. In 1224, Frederick founded the University of Naples, with the idea of educating administrators for his kingdom. As a half-Norman southerner, Frederick rejected the tradition that Holy Roman Emperors lived north of the Alps. He moved his exotic, multi-cultural court (complete with Saracen guard) between Sicily and southern Italy, where he built several castles in Apulia – notably the superb octagonal Castel del Monte.

City-States & Comuni

Between the 12th and 14th centuries, government in Italy evolved into a new kind of political institution – the city-states or city-republics, whose political organisation became known as the *comune*, or town council.

The cities of northern Italy were highly favoured commercially by their position on the 'hinge' of the Mediterranean and the European continent – they were also a long way from both the pope and the emperor. With the resulting new wealth, some cities freed themselves from feudal control. Milan, Crema, Bologna, Florence, Pavia, Modena, Parma, Lodi and many other cities set themselves up as autonomous powers, but with the protection of either the pope or the emperor. The 'middle class' was born, composed of rich merchants and artisans who, very soon, passed from commercial rivalry to internal political struggles. These conflicts ended up favouring restricted oligarchies in which one family prevailed, charged by the city with exercising a form of government called the Signoria. The various Signorias were reinforced from within, persecuting rival families and opposers, while from without they expanded their territories at the expense of weaker neighbours.

The five great Italian regional divisions began to take shape: Veneto, Lombardy, Tuscany, the Papal States, and the Southern Kingdom.

In the south, Charles of Anjou, who had defeated and beheaded Conradin, Frederick II's 16-year-old grandson and heir, ousted Germanic rule. French dominion under Charles brought heavy taxes, particularly on rich landowners, who did not accept such measures graciously. Although always a hated foreigner, Charles supported much-needed road repairs, reformed the coinage, imposed standard weights and measures, improved the equipment of ports and opened silver mines.

Despite his grip on papal power and his subsequent conquests of Jerusalem and Constantinople, Charles of Anjou was to become infamous throughout Italy for a popular uprising, sparked off by the assault of a Sicilian woman by a French soldier in Palermo on 30 March 1282. A crowd gathered, killing the soldier, and a widespread massacre of the French ensued as communities throughout Sicily rose against their warlords. Known as the Sicilian Vespers, the events of this time led to the citizens of Palermo declaring an independent republic and endorsing Peter of Aragon as king, effectively separating themselves from the Neapolitan mainland and bringing themselves under Spanish rule.

The latter decades of the 13th century were marked by decreasing economic vitality as Europeans battled an invasion far more deadly than a mere army. The effects of plague (later to be known as the Black Death) or *la peste*, along with famine and deprivation from years of war, decimated over half the population of many major cities.

Meanwhile, in north and central Italy, the city-states were growing in importance. The Republic of Venice increased its possessions. Trading with its powerful fleet towards the Byzantine Orient, it securely managed its own independence in the ports of Dalmatia, Greece, Cyprus and the Aegean. Marco Polo, back from the court of the Great Khan after 25 years in China, wrote the *Million* at the end of the 13th century. The commercial traffic of Genoa, another 'maritime republic' and great rival of Venice, extended as far as the Black Sea.

The legal debate of this time and the ensuing changes to Italian society, together with the dawning of a new era of powerful literary and artistic expression, were to form the basis of the humanist culture which ushered in the Renaissance.

Humanism

The artist whose works signify the breakthrough from the Byzantine or Gothic style to the Renaissance was Giotto (see the following Arts section). In literature, Averroës, an Arabic philosopher born in Cordova in southern Spain, resurrected the influence of Aristotle's doctrine that immortality was gained through individual efforts towards universal reason. This emphasis on the autonomy of human reason, based on the theories of the classic philosophers instead of the increasingly self-serving dogmas of the Church hierarchy, was a revolutionary philosophical position that became known as humanism.

The church had chosen to embrace only those classical philosophers whose thinking fitted its theological purposes. Humanist thinkers were, instead, making incredible discoveries of ancient Roman and Greek works, which had been transcribed by religous orders during the Middle Ages and remained hidden away – even 'lost' – in monasteries throughout Europe. These classical works were not necessarily those which were accepted by the church and they inspired great debate among intellectuals of the day.

Translated into Latin, Averroës became a strong influence on another interpreter of Aristotelian thought, St Thomas Aquinas, who was educated at Monte Cassino by the Benedictines and at the University of Bologna, before joining the Dominicans in 1243. Aquinas bridged the gap between the Christian belief in God and Aristotle's respect for the validity of reason with his *Summa Theologica*. This had the effect that Italian Christianity never lost either its grip on the real world or its respect for good works.

The new era saw independent artisans flourish, and their guilds became influential in the power structure of the cities, particularly in Florence, which retained the trappings of the new republicanism until 1434, when the Medici family brought back a comparatively mild despotism.

The Florentine houses of Peruzzi and Bardi were the business moguls of Europe, minting some 400,000 units of their currency, the florence or florin, each year. Florentine prosperity was based on the wool trade, and on finance and commerce in general. Craft and trade guilds became increasingly powerful in the affairs of the city.

The Arte della Lana (wool guild) of Florence employed a workforce of more than 5000, but these workers were not citizens and could not take part in the elections of the Republic. In 1378, the poorest workers, the wool-carters or *ciompi*, revolted against their city fathers, taking power in the city-state for at least six weeks during which time they created new guilds to represent them.

But Europe's first working-class uprising was short-lived as a greater power struggle was taking place between the pope and the Holy Roman Emperor. This conflict formed the focal point of Italian politics in the late Middle Ages with a split into two camps – 'Guelph' (support of the pope) and 'Ghibelline' (support of the emperor).

Dante Alighieri, the great poet and writer who Italians see as the father of the Italian language, even of the Italian nation, was one of the casualties of the Guelph-Ghibelline battle. A dedicated Guelph supporter, Dante was exiled from his birthplace Florence in 1301 because he belonged to the wrong faction.

While the first decades of the 14th century were years of economic and cultural growth, not all cities employed the relatively liberal style of the government of Florence. Milan, like many of the Italian comuni, was still strictly dominated by Signorias. The Della Torre family, which represented the popular party of the city-state, came into dire conflict

The Borgia Family

It seems surprising, if not shocking, by today's standards, that the popes of 15th-century Italy fought wars to maintain their territories, had their enemies killed, kept mistresses and even had children by them.

But, if the church was to survive the effects of the Great Schism (1378-1417), when the popes resided at Avignon in France, it was necessary for the Pope to be noted more for his political and diplomatic skills, than for his spiritual and moral qualities. Thus he was chosen for his leadership abilities and capacity to compete with the various ferocious rulers of the peninsula at that time – in other words the popes of the period were no saints.

The Spaniard, Rodrigo Borgia, was elected Pope Alexander VI in 1492, in what is said to have been the most corrupt election in papal history. He went on to establish a notoriously corrupt and immoral court and throughout his papacy he maintained a mistress, Vannozza Catanei, who bore him the infamous Borgia family. It all seemed to make little difference to the Christian pilgrims who flocked to Rome to honour Alexander in the jubilee year of 1500.

Alexander's son, Cesare, who killed his own brother, terrorised Italy in a campaign to consolidate and expand the papal states. Ruthless and brilliant, he was at one point admired by Machiavelli. But, his sister, Lucrezia, has gone down in history as the embodiment of Borgia cruelty, lust and avarice. It is said that Pope Alexander was obsessed with his daughter almost to the point of incest. He ensured that she lived in incredible luxury and apparently no man was worthy of her – Lucrezia had several husbands, one of whom was assassinated by Cesare. Another of her husbands was publicly declared impotent by the Pope. ∎

with the Visconti family, which represented the Ghibelline nobility. Ottone Visconti had been made Archbishop of Milan in 1262, and his nephew, Matteo, was made imperial vicar by Henry VII. He subsequently destroyed the power of the Della Torre, extending Milanese control over Pavia and Cremona, and later Genoa and Bologna. Giangaleazzo Visconti (1351-1402) would turn Milan from a city-state into a strong European power, and although the Visconti were unappreciated as dictators, Milan managed to resist French attempts at invasion.

The government of the Visconti (up to 1450) and then of the Sforzas allowed Milan an economic and territorial development that extended the borders of the Signoria from Genoa to Bologna, and from Ticino in Switzerland to Lago di Garda. In those years of tireless labour the entire area of the Pianura Padana (the Po plain) was transformed. Massive hydraulic and irrigation projects (which included the participation of Leonardo da Vinci) converted the plain from a swampy woodland into an extremely productive agricultural collective with some of the most fertile farmland in Italy. Among other things,

the cultivation of rice and mulberry were introduced. In the 15th century parmesan cheese, a product of Parma, Reggio Emilia and Lodi, was among the most precious cheeses in Europe, and butter from the plains of Lombardy was exported as far as Rome.

The 'Babylonian Captivity'

Meanwhile, the Church was going through a profound crisis. The papacy's ongoing crusades against the Eastern infidels during the 13th century had turned into campaigns against European heretics in the 14th, campaigns which in Italy were thinly disguised grabs for wealth and prosperity by claimants from Italian ruling families and the related nobility of Europe.

Pope Boniface VIII (1294-1303) came from Italian nobility and his efforts were directed at ensuring his family's continuing wealth and power. His papal bull of 1302, *Unam Sanctum*, claimed papal supremacy in worldly and spiritual affairs – claims of temporal might which achieved its ends by eliminating heretics.

When the French pope John XXII (1316-34) chose to base the papacy in Avignon, the

Church of Rome, and indeed Rome in general, suddenly lost its raison d'être. Goats and cows grazed on the Capitoline Hill and in the Roman Forum, and residential support for the city's many churches and cathedrals disappeared. The city became a battleground for the struggles between the powerful Orsini and Colonna families. The ruling families challenged the papacy's ongoing claim to be temporal rulers of Rome and the Papal State began to fall apart.

There were seven popes in Avignon from 1305 to 1377, a period that became known as the 'Babylonian Captivity', a phrase coined by the Roman poet laureate Petrarch to castigate the evils of the French papal court.

After the failed attempt of Cola di Rienzo, a popular leader, to wrest the control of Rome from the nobility, Cardinal Egidio d'Albornoz managed to restore the Papal State with his *Egidian Constitutions*, enabling Pope Gregory XI to return to Rome in 1377. Finding a ruined and almost deserted city, Gregory made the Vatican his base because it was fortified and had the formidable Castel Sant'Angelo nearby.

When Gregory died a year after returning to Rome, Roman cardinals tried to ensure their continuing power by electing as pope the unpopular Urban VI, sparking off a renegade movement of cardinals, mainly French, who, a few months later, elected a second pope, Clement VII, who set up his claim in Avignon. So began the Great Schism, and the papacy was not to be reconciled with Rome until 1417.

The Renaissance

In the 15th century, the newly influential papacy initiated the transformation of Rome. Reduced during the Middle Ages to a conglomeration of majestic ruins and wretched dwellings, the city assumed a new elegance. In 1455, Bernardo Rossellino began construction of Palazzo Venezia; Sixtus IV initiated an urban plan which was to link the areas that had been cut off from one another during the Middle Ages; Donatello, Sandro Botticelli and Fra Angelico lived and worked in Rome at this time. At the beginning of the

16th century Pope Julius II opened Via del Corso and Via Giulia and gave Bramante the task of beginning work on the second St Peter's Basilica, which was to take more than a century to finish. In 1508, Raphael started his Vatican *Stanze di Raffaello*, while in 1512 Michelangelo began work on the vaults of the Sistine Chapel.

All the great artists of the epoch were influenced by the ever more frequent discoveries of marvellous pieces of classical art, such as the *Laocoön*, found in 1506 in the area of Nero's *Domus Aurea* (the sculpture is now in the Vatican Museums). Rome had 100,000 inhabitants at the height of the Renaissance and had become the major centre for Italian political and cultural life. Pope Julius II was succeeded by Pope Leo X, a Medici, and the Roman Curia (or Papal Court) became the meeting place for learned men such as Baldassar Castiglione and Ludovico Ariosto.

As the Renaissance dawned, Italians could no longer accept the papal domination of earlier times. A remarkable treatise by the humanist Lorenzo Valla (1407-57) revealed the *Donation of Constantine* as a forgery. Serious study of the Greek classics and the writings of others, such as Hebrew and Arabic scholars, pervaded the literary works of the later 15th century and highlighted the place of the individual in the universe.

The 15th and early 16th centuries showed unparalleled creativity and visionary accomplishments in all aspects of political, cultural and social life. In Florence, Cosimo de Medici, private citizen and wealthy merchant, took over the Signoria in 1434. His nephew, Lorenzo Il Magnifico (the Magnificent), is remembered in history as a great politician who counted very much on the economic and financial security of his Florence. In his refined diplomacy he focused on building the prestige of the city by enriching it with the presence, and the works, of the greatest artists of the time. This contribution, in the wake of the innovative concepts introduced by the humanists, would combine to make Lorenzo the greatest art patron of the Renaissance.

Fluctuating between the pope and the emperor, feudal lords such as Federico da Montefeltro in Urbino, a merchant as rich as the Medici, and Francesco Sforza, military commander of Milan, turned themselves into bankers and captains of adventure. In these and other cities, revitalised by the wealth of increased commerce, the princes competed with each other for the services of artists, writers, poets and musicians.

This phenomenal creativity was disrupted in Florence by the preaching of Savonarola, a Dominican monk who preached fire and brimstone against humanist thinking and who allied himself with the French King Charles VIII to overthrow the Medici family and declare a republic in Florence in 1494. Although the monk eventually met a gruesome end, he wielded tremendous power in Florentine politics in the later 15th century.

The Medici, briefly reinstated, could not regain their positive influence on the Florentines who eventually rejected them, setting up a second democratic republic in 1527. In 1530 this republic was in turn overthrown when Emperor Charles V, who had sacked Rome in 1527, brought back the Medici, whose rule over Florence for the next 210 years was, more typically, an unhappy oligarchy.

One public official of the first Florentine republic was Niccolò Machiavelli (1469-1527), whose short handbook, *The Prince*, outlined somewhat cynically the prerequisite skills for securing and retaining power. Machiavelli advocated the banishment of all foreign rule in Italy and urged the people to employ their native wit and cunning to achieve this end. He also wrote a history of Florence, in Italian rather than Latin, although his efforts were less original than those of his contemporary and friend, Francesco Guicciardini (1483-1532).

Not all Italian states experienced the great social blossoming of the Renaissance. In the south, continuing quarrels over rulership and landholdings by the Visconti family, in league with Alfonso V of Aragon against the house of Angevin, ensured repression of the liberty and free thinking which had inspired

a new sense of creativity and productivity in other parts of the country.

The Counter-Reformation

By the third decade of the 16th century, the broad-minded curiosity of the Renaissance had begun to give way to the intolerance of the Counter-Reformation. This was the response of the Church to the Reformation, a collective term for the movement led by Martin Luther, that aimed to reform the Church and led to the rise of Protestantism in its many forms. The transition was epitomised by the reign of Pope Paul III (1534-49), who promoted the building of the classically elegant Palazzo Farnese in Rome but who also, in 1540, allowed the establishment of Ignatius Loyola's order of the Jesuits and the organisation in 1542 of the Holy Office. This was the final (and ruthless) court of appeal in heresy trials which began to gather momentum with the increased activities of the Inquisition (1232-1820), the judicial arm of the Church whose aim was to discover and suppress heresy.

Pope Paul III's fanatical opposition to Protestantism and his purging of clerical abuse, as he saw it, resulted in a widespread campaign of torture and fear. In 1559, the Church published the *Index Librorum Prohibitorum*, the Index of Prohibited Books, and the Roman Church's determination to regain papal supremacy over the Christian churches set the stage for the persecution of intellectuals and free thinkers.

Two great Italian intellectuals who felt the brunt of the Counter-Reformation were Giordano Bruno (1548-1600) and Galileo Galilei (1564-1642). A Dominican monk, Bruno was forced to flee Italy for Calvinist Geneva, from where he travelled extensively throughout Europe before being arrested by the Inquisition in Venice in 1592. In 1870, the Kingdom of Italy erected a statue of him in Rome's Campo de' Fiori, where he had been burnt at the stake.

An advocate of Aristotelian science, Galileo was forced by the Church to renounce his approval of the Copernican astronomical system, which held that the earth moved round the sun rather than the reverse. But where Bruno had rejected the Catholic Church, Galileo never deviated from the faith which rejected him.

However, the latter years of the 16th century were not all counterproductive. Pope Gregory XIII (1572-85) replaced the Julian calendar with the Gregorian in 1582, fixing the start of the year on 1 January and adjusting the system of leap years to align the 365-day year with the seasons. The city of Rome was greatly embellished by the architectural and sculptural achievements of Giovanni Bernini (1598-1680).

Despite these exceptions, Italy no longer determined European cultural expression. Epidemics and wars, in particular the War of the Spanish Succession (1701-14), tossed the nation from Spanish domination in the 17th century to Austrian occupation in the 18th century, beginning with the conquest of Naples in 1707.

The Enlightenment

The Italy of the 18th century, although mainly ruled from abroad, was set to become part of an era which broke down many of the national barriers of Europe, a development which was as much due to the intermarriage of its monarchies as to new trading laws necessitated by bad harvests in many areas of the continent. The papacy became less influential, especially after the expulsion of the Jesuits from Portugal, France and Spain.

The 18th-century Enlightenment swept away the dark days of the Counter-Reformation, producing great thinkers and writers such as Cesare Beccaria (1738-94), whose masterpiece *Of Crimes & Punishments* attacked torture and capital punishment as barbarism, and advocated reform of the criminal code, a proposal taken up by Grand Duke Leopold of Tuscany, who abolished the death sentence.

Economic ideas advocating the liberalisation of trade laws were put forward by the influential writer Pietro Verri (1728-97) who, with his brother Alessandro, introduced reforms in schools and universities as well as in the government administration of Lombardy. Alessandro Volta (1745-1827), after whom the volt is named, invented the battery when he was professor of natural philosophy at the University of Bologna.

Napoleon

Italy had been the source of many enlightened political ideas, but the concept of national sovereignty had not been one of them. However, when the 27-year-old, Corsican-born French general Napoleon Bonaparte invaded Italy in 1796 and declared himself, quite unofficially, its dictator, a nationalist movement began in earnest. Inspired by the ideas of another Frenchman, Jean-Jacques Rousseau, the French leftist Jacobin movement gained significant support in Italy when, before the end of his first year of occupation, Napoleon used Italy as the base for his expedition into Egypt.

The Jacobin movement established a republic in Rome, renewing the debate about Italy as a nation and the sovereign rights of its people, dubbed the Risorgimento, or Revival, by Italian dramatist Vittorio Alfieri (1749-1803). But the mainly middle-class movement found itself unable to bring about social reforms quickly enough for the peasants, particularly the very poor of Naples. A peasant army sacked Naples, littering its streets with dead Jacobins.

Although having declared himself First Consul of Italy in 1799, Napoleon acceded to the calls of Italian deputies in the north to proclaim an Italian Republic and, for the first time in history, the political entity known as Italy came into being, albeit with Napoleon as its first, self-elected president.

When in 1804 Napoleon made himself emperor of France, he established the Kingdom of Italy and elected himself its first king, inviting Pope Pius VII to officially crown him in Paris. Pius delayed his visit, reluctant to give his endorsement to the power brokers of the French Revolution, which had greatly curtailed the power of the Catholic Church; nor was he keen on endorsing the marriage of Napoleon to the divorcee Josephine. When the pope finally arrived several days late, Napoleon was 'not amused'. As the pope raised the emperor's crown to his head, Napoleon took it and crowned himself.

Unification

During the final years of Napoleon's domination of Italy, hopes grew that his regime would be replaced with independence and constitutional rule. It was not to be: following Napoleon's demise at Waterloo in 1815, all of the peninsula's former rulers were reinstated by the Congress of Vienna. It was a backward step with terrible consequences for the country, but it ensured the rapid growth of secret societies made up in the main of disaffected middle-class intellectuals.

In the south, the republican Carbonari pushed hard and often ruthlessly to ensure a valid constitution, leading a revolutionary uprising in Naples in 1820. Another leading revolutionary figure of these secret societies was Filippo Buonarroti, who strove for independence from Austria and the establishment of a communist society devoid of private-property interests.

One of Italy's key proponents of nationhood and political freedom was a Genoan called Giuseppe Mazzini (1805-72). Having quit the Carbonari movement in 1830, Mazzini founded Young Italy, a society of young men whose aims were the liberation of Italy from foreign and domestic tyranny and its unification under a republican government. This was to be achieved through education and, where necessary, revolt by guerrilla bands.

Exiled from his homeland for his former activities with the Carbonari, Mazzini was responsible for organising a number of abortive uprisings throughout Italy during the 1830s and 1840s which left dead many of the young men who had flocked to join his Young Italy movement. Twice sentenced to death, Mazzini was to live out his days in England, from where he wrote articles and solicited as much support as he could from influential allies to raise the consciousness of Europeans about the 'Italian question'.

In 1848, there were revolutions in almost every major city and town of Europe. In their newspaper, *Il Risorgimento*, one of several publications to have sprung up as the Italian nationalist movement gained ground among Italians of all classes, Cesare Balbo, a nationalist writer, and Count Camillo Benso di Cavour of Turin pressed for a constitution. In 1848, they published their *Statuto*, advocating a two-chamber parliament with the upper chamber to be appointed by the crown and the lower chamber to be elected by educated taxpayers. In 1861, the *Statuto* was to become the constitutional basis of the Kingdom of Italy, but not before almost two more decades of warring between the European princes and their subjects had left a great many more Italians dead.

Count Camillo Benso di Cavour – among those who led the unification movement.

Returning to Italy in 1848 from his famous exploits in South America, where he is still remembered as a founding hero of Uruguay, Giuseppe Garibaldi (1807-82) was to become the hero Italians needed to lead them towards unification. Garibaldi's personal magnetism,

Garibaldi, in taking Sicily & Naples for Italy, won the imagination of the Italian people & made them realise independence was attainable.

minister, Cavour focused on forging an alliance with the French emperor Napoleon III, in a move destined to overthrow Austrian domination of Piedmont.

Meanwhile the unification movement was literally on the move, as Garibaldi led his Expedition of One Thousand, taking Sicily and Naples in 1860. The Kingdom of Italy was declared on 17 March 1861 and Victor Emmanuel II, the king of Sardinia-Piedmont from 1849, was proclaimed king. But Italy was still not completely united: Venice remained in the hands of the Austrians and Rome was held by France.

Cavour died within six months of achieving the first parliament of the Kingdom of Italy. He had been betrayed by his French allies when Napoleon III signed the armistice of Villafranca, ending the Franco-Austrian war (fought in Italy, largely by Italians). Venice was wrested from the Austrians in 1866 and it wasn't until the Franco-Prussian War of 1870 that Napoleon III's hold

the result of his respect for people rich and poor, drew more Italians into the fight for nationhood than ever before.

Despite significant personal animosity, Garibaldi and Cavour fought side by side, each in their chosen arena, to break the stranglehold of foreign domination. The brilliant diplomacy of Cavour, coupled with the independent efforts of Garibaldi and his 'people power', finally caught the attention of European communities, particularly the British, who become staunch supporters of a free and united Italy.

When the sympathetic Piedmontese monarch, King Carlo Alberto, granted a constitution based on the *Statuto* in March 1848, Cavour stood for election. In 1850 he was given three ministries – navy, commerce and finance – in the government headed by Massimo d'Azeglio. When Cavour's Centre-Left faction joined forces with the Centre-Right, headed by Urbano Rattazzi, behind d'Azeglio's back, the prime minister resigned and Cavour was asked by the king to take the top government post. As prime

Victor Emmanuel II became the first king of the Kingdom of Italy in 1861.

over Italy was broken. Needing all available troops, he withdrew his occupation of Rome, leaving the way clear for the Italian army to reclaim the capital.

The only resistance to the push on Rome came from the papal soldiers of Pope Pius IX who refused to recognise the Kingdom of Italy. The pope was eventually stripped of his remaining temporal powers as well as his palace, the Quirinale. The papacy regained some autonomy in the 1920s when the Fascist dictator Benito Mussolini restored the independent papal state, but in the interim, the papacy forbade Catholics to participate in the elections of their government.

As the 20th century dawned, the economic crisis of Europe was reflected in Italian politics by constant fluctuations as socialist democrats and right-wing imperialists gained and lost the support of the populace. When, in the general elections of 1894, Pope Pius X formally gave Catholics the right to vote (although many had already been doing just that), there was a widespread backlash against socialism. Giovanni Giolitti, one of Italy's longest serving prime ministers (heading five governments between 1892 and 1921), managed to bridge the extremes and was able to embark on parliamentary reforms which gave the vote to all literate men from the age of 21 and all illiterate men who had completed military service or were aged 30 or over. But while male suffrage had been achieved, Italian women were denied the right to vote until after WW II.

Fascism

When war broke out in Europe in July 1914, Italy, chose to remain neutral rather than become caught between old enemies. But soon senior politicians had allied themselves with the British, Russians and French, while the papacy spoke out against the 'atheist' French in favour of Catholic Austria.

In October 1914, the editor of the socialist newspaper *Avanti!* also came out strongly in favour of alignment with the Allied forces. For his views, young Mussolini was forced to resign. He started his own newspaper in November, the *Popolo d'Italia*, a propaganda publication financed by French, British and Russian interests.

In 1919 he founded the Fascist Party, with its hallmarks of the black shirt and Roman salute. These emblems were to become the symbols of violent oppression and aggressive nationalism for the next 23 years. In 1921, the party won 35 of the 135 seats in parliament. In October 1922, the king asked Mussolini to form a government, and thus began his domination of Italy. With an expedition of 40,000 Fascist militia, he began the famous March on Rome to 'free the nation from the Socialists'.

In April 1924, following a campaign marked by violence and intimidation, the Fascist Party won the national elections and Mussolini created the world's first Fascist regime. By 1925 the term 'totalitarianism' had entered the language. By the end of 1925 Mussolini had expelled opposition parties from parliament, gained control of the press and trade unions and had reduced the voting public by two-thirds. In 1929, Mussolini and Pope Pius XI signed the Lateran Pact, whereby Catholicism was declared the sole religion of Italy and the Vatican was recognised as an independent state. In return, the papacy finally acknowledged the united Kingdom of Italy.

In the 1920s, Mussolini embarked on an aggressive foreign policy, leading to skirmishes with Greece over the island of Corfu and to military expeditions against nationalist forces in the Italian colony of Libya. In 1935, Italy sought a new colonial conquest by invading Abyssinia (present-day Ethiopia) from the Italian base in Eritrea, only capturing Addis Ababa after seven months. The act was condemned by the League of Nations which imposed limited sanctions on Italy.

Fearful of international isolation, Mussolini formed the Rome-Berlin Axis with Hitler in 1936 – which was soon joined by Japan – and Italy entered WW II in June 1941 as an ally of Germany.

After a series of military disasters and the landing of the Allied armies in Sicily on 10 July 1943, Mussolini was faced not only with increasing discontent among Italians and diminishing support for Fascism, but also with Hitler's refusal to assign more troops to defend southern Italy. Two weeks after the Allied landing, the King of Italy, Victor Emmanuel III, led a coup against Mussolini and had him arrested.

In the confused period that followed, now known as the '45 days', Italy erupted in a series of massive demonstrations demanding an end to the war. The king signed an armistice with the Allies that amounted to an unconditional surrender and declared war on Germany, but it was too late to prevent the effective takeover of northern Italy by Nazi troops. As the Allies moved up through the south of the Italian peninsula, the Germans began their campaign of brutal suppression in the north, prompting the formation of the Resistance.

The Germans had rescued Mussolini from his prison on the Gran Sasso in the Abruzzi and installed him as head of the Republic of Salò in the north. By now completely demoralised, Mussolini was nothing more than a German puppet. He was eventually captured and shot, along with his mistress, Clara Petacci, by partisans in April 1945, and hung upside down from the roof of a petrol station in Milan's Piazzale Loreto.

The Resistance

Numbering more than 100,000 by conservative estimates in early 1945, members of the Resistance managed to gain control of small areas of the north and played a significant role in liberating Florence from the Germans in August 1944. The Nazi response to partisan attacks was savage. Whole villages were exterminated: in one of the most notorious reprisals, 1830 men, women and children were murdered by an SS battalion at Marzabotto, south of Bologna, on 1 October 1944. In Rome, in March 1944, urban partisans blew up 32 military police. In reprisal, the Germans shot 335 prisoners at the Fosse Ardeatine, just outside the city.

After Allied troops broke through German lines, northern Italy was finally liberated by the end of May 1945. The Resistance had suffered huge losses and its contribution to the Allied victory did not go unacknowledged. These people had fought not only against German and Fascist oppression, but also for an ideal of social and political change, and after the war they wanted to put change into action. The Allies, meanwhile, were wondering how to deal with what amounted to a massive, armed left-wing movement, whose leaders spoke often of 'insurrection'.

The Republic

The Resistance was disarmed, either voluntarily or by force, as Italy's political forces scrambled to regroup and the USA, through the Marshall Plan, was exerting a profound affect on the country both economically and politically. Immediately after the war there was a series of three coalition governments. The third was dominated by the newly formed Democrazia Cristiana (DC, Christian Democrats), led by Alcide de Gaspari, who remained prime minister until 1953.

In 1946, following a referendum, the constitutional monarchy was abolished and a republic established, with the DC winning the majority of votes at the first post-war elections. The Partito Comunista Italiano (PCI, Communist Party), led by Palmiro Togliatti, and the Partito Socialista Italiano (PSI, Socialist Party), led by Pietro Nenni, participated in the coalition governments until 1947, when de Gaspari formed a government which excluded the left.

Economic Recovery

By the early 1950s the country's economy had begun to show strong signs of recovery, although the more impoverished and less industrialised south lagged behind. To counter this, the government formed the Cassa per il Mezzogiorno (State Fund for the South) in 1950, which would eventually pour trillions of lire into development projects in the southern regions. When Italy became a founding member of the European Economic Community (ECC) in 1957, it signalled the beginning of the 'Economic Miracle', a period of significant economic growth which saw unemployment drop as industry expanded. A major feature of this period was the development of Italy's auto-mobile industry, and more particularly of Fiat in Turin, which sparked a massive migration of peasants from the south to the north in search of work.

The early 1950s also saw the formation of a new extreme right-wing party called the Movimento Sociale Italiano (MSI), also known as the Missini, which was basically neo-Fascist.

Although it was the only major party not to participate in the government of the country, the PCI nevertheless played a crucial role in Italy's social and political development well into the 1980s. The party steadily increased its share of the poll at each election and always had more 'card-carrying' members than the DC, but the spectre of European communism and the Cold War continued to undermine its chances of participating in government.

By the mid-1960s the Economic Miracle was waning and social unrest was becoming commonplace. Togliatti, the long-serving leader of the PCI, died in 1964. His policy of cooperation with the DC in the interests of national unity had played a significant role in avoiding serious social conflict. One year earlier Aldo Moro had been appointed prime minister, a position he held until 1968. It was Moro who invited the PSI into government in 1963 and more than a decade later was moving towards the Historic Compromise which would have seen the communists enter government for the first time, when he was kidnapped and murdered by the Red Brigades terrorist group.

Protest & Terrorism

The late 1960s were marked by student revolt in 1967-68. Influenced by similar events in France, university students rose up in protest, ostensibly against poor conditions in the universities, but in reality in broader protest against authority and what they saw as the impotence of the left. The movement resulted in the formation of many small rev-olutionary groups which attempted to fill what the students saw as an ideological gap in Italy's political left wing. The uprising was closely followed in 1969 by what has become known as the Autunno Caldo (Hot Autumn), when factory workers embarked on a series of strikes and protests which continued into 1971.

But, as the new decade began, a new phe-nomenon – terrorism – began to overshadow this turbulent era of protest and change. By as early as 1970, a group of young left-wing militants had formed the Brigate Rosse (BR, Red Brigades).

Neo-Fascist terrorists had already taken action. On 12 December 1969 a bomb exploded in a bank in Milan's Piazza Fontana, killing 16 people. Controversy and mystery shrouded this incident, but it is now certain it was an act of right-wing extremists directed by forces within the country's secret services. The bombing formed part of what was known as the 'Strategy of Tension', which culminated in the 1980 bombing of the Bologna Railway Station by right-wing terrorists, in which 84 people died.

The Red Brigades were by no means the only terrorists operating in the country during the Anni di Piombo (Years of Lead) from 1973-80, but they were certainly the most prominent. While many of the BR orig-inal members were dead or in prison by the mid-1970s, 1977 saw a major recruiting campaign give new life to the movement. The year was also marked by student pro-tests, sparked largely by their opposition to education reforms proposed by the govern-ment. As opposed to Sessantotto ('68), this was more an anti-political than an ideologi-cal movement. Universities were occupied in Rome, Bologna and Milan and the *centro sociale* – a type of left-wing cultural centre established by 'occupying' unused buildings – had its origin in this period.

In 1978, the Red Brigades claimed their most important victim – Aldo Moro, who was kidnapped to prevent the Historic Com-promise with the communists from taking place. During the 54 days Moro was held captive by the BR, his colleagues laboured over the question of whether to bargain with the terrorists to save his life, or to adopt a position of no compromise. In the end, they took the latter path and the BR killed Moro on 9 May 1978, leaving his body in the boot of a car parked in the centre of Rome, in a street equidistant from the headquarters of the DC and the PCI.

Finally, Carabinieri general, Carlo Alberto dalla Chiesa, was appointed to wipe out the terrorist groups. Using a new law which allowed *pentiti* (repentants) much-reduced prison sentences, he convinced key members of the groups to collaborate. In 1980, dalla Chiesa was appointed by the government to fight the Mafia in Sicily. He and his wife were assassinated in Palermo within a few months of his taking up the job.

The 1970s in Italy also produced much positive political and social change. In 1970, the country was divided into administrative regions and regional governments were elected. In the same year divorce became legal, and efforts by conservative Catholics to have the law repealed were defeated in a referendum in 1974. In 1978 abortion was legalised, following close on the heels of anti-sexist legislation which allowed women to keep their own names after marriage.

The Historic Compromise with the communists was never to eventuate, but in 1983, the DC government was forced by its diminishing share of the electoral vote to hand over the prime ministership to a socialist. Bettino Craxi became the longest-serving prime minister since De Gaspari, holding the post from 1983 to 1989. A skilled politician, Craxi continued to wield considerable power in government until he fled the country in 1993 after being implicated in the Tangentopoli national bribery scandal.

Italy enjoyed significant economic growth in the 1980s, during which it became one of the world's leading economic powers. However, the 1990s heralded a new period of crisis for the country, both economically and politically. High unemployment and inflation rates, combined with a huge national debt and an extremely unstable lira, led the government to introduce draconian measures to revive the economy.

In this period, the PCI reached a watershed. Internal ideological disagreements led to a split in the party in the early 1990s. The old guard now goes by the title Rifondazione Comunista, under the leadership of Fausto Bertinotti. The breakaway, more moderate wing of the old party reformed itself under the title Partito Democratico della Sinistra (PDS, Democratic Party of the Left), initially under the leadership of Achille Occhetto, who handed over in 1994 to Massimo d'Alema.

Tangentopoli

The Tangentopoli scandal broke in Milan in early 1992 when a functionary of the PSI was arrested on charges of accepting bribes in exchange for public works contracts. Tangentopoli literally means 'kickback cities'; the term probably originated in journalism and refers to the acceptance of bribes in return for public-works contracts. Led by Milanese magistrate Antonio di Pietro, dubbed the 'reluctant hero', investigations eventually implicated thousands of politicians, public officials and businesspeople.

Charges ranged from bribery, making illicit political payments and receiving kickbacks, to blatant thievery. It is ironic that few ordinary Italians were surprised that manypoliticians, at all levels of government, were entrenched in a system whereby they demanded secret payments as a matter of course. The corruption went to the very highest levels of government: Craxi was forced to resign as party secretary after he was served with five notifications that he was under investigation for corruption. He fled the country and took refuge in his villa in Tunisia.

In elections just after the scandal broke in 1992, voters expressed their discontent and the DC's share of the vote dropped by 5%. Umberto Bossi's Lega Nord (Northern League) made its first appearance as a force to be reckoned with at the national level, winning 7% of the vote on an anti-corruption, federalist platform. Following the elections, parliament elected the Christian Democrat Oscar Luigi Scalfaro, a man noted for his personal integrity, as President of the Republic. PSI deputy leader Giulio Amato was later appointed prime minister.

As Tangentopoli continued to unfold it was clear that few of the country's top politicians had escaped the taint of the scandal. The main parties – the DC and the PSI – were in tatters and the centre of the Italian political spectrum had effectively been demolished. A reform of the country's electoral system of proportional representation had resulted in the introduction of a predominantly first-past-the-post voting system, like that used in the UK, in both houses of parliament.

At the 1994 national elections, voters took the opportunity to express their disgust with the old order. The elections were won by a new right-wing coalition known as the Polo della Libertà (Freedom Alliance), whose members included the Neo-Fascist Alleanza Nazionale (National Alliance), as well as the federalist Northern League. Its leader, billionaire media magnate Silvio Berlusconi, who had entered politics only three months before the elections, was appointed prime minister. After a turbulent nine months in power, Berlusconi's volatile coalition government collapsed when Bossi, in an extremely controversial move, withdrew the support of his Northern League. In the meantime, Berlusconi himself had been notified that he was under investigation by the Milan 'Clean Hands' judges. He had also come under intense criticism for his failure to dissociate himself from his business empire, Fininvest, which included his ownership of three TV stations.

In the resulting chaos, Scalfaro appointed an interim government led by the former treasurer in Berlusconi's cabinet, Lamberto Dini, pending new elections in November 1995. Dini's government of 'technicians' immediately set about confronting the country's economic problems: it introduced pension reforms as well as measures aimed at reducing the public debt.

The new electoral system has resulted in a fairly clear division of the parties into two main groups: Centro-Destra (Centre-Right) and Centro-Sinistra (Centre-Left). Bossi's Northern League remained unaligned in mid-1995, although it was making overtures to the Centre-Left. Berlusconi's party, Forza Italia, remained aligned with the National Alliance, a repackaged and sanitised MSI, led by Gianfranco Fini. Their alliance, the Polo della Libertà, has gathered other small parties of the centre right under its umbrella.

The DC effectively no longer exists: the few members of the party who managed to hold on to their parliamentary seats have regrouped into various new parties, including the Centro Cristiano Democratico (CCD), which is aligned with Berlusconi's Polo della Libertà, and the Partito Poplar, which recently split over the question of whether or not to align with the Polo. The country's left-wing parties, particularly the PDS, showed through successes in 1995 regional elections that they were holding firm by polling approximately 50% of the vote. Although the Centre-Left had presented a new face, Romano Prod, as its front man, d'Alema had emerged as the group's driving force.

A referendum held in June 1995 posed important questions on TV ownership. Berlusconi's Polo was led a successful campaign to convince the public to vote 'No' to a proposal to limit the number of TV stations which could be owned by one person or organisation. Berlusconi, who owns three national stations, had stood to be dramatically affected by the outcome of the referendum if there had been a majority 'Yes' vote.

Anti-Mafia Action

The early 1990s saw the Italian government take on the Mafia. Prompted by the 1992 assassinations of the anti-Mafia judges Giovanni Falcone and Paolo Borsellino in separate car bomb attacks, the government sent troops to Sicily and, using the testimonies of pentiti, made several important arrests – most notably of the Sicilian godfather, Salvatore 'Toto' Riina, who went on trial in 1995. It is widely believed that four bombs which exploded in Milan, Florence and Rome in 1993, killing several people and damaging monuments and works of art, was the Mafia's response to the crackdown.

The most important development in the anti-Mafia fight was the bringing to trial in 1995 of Italy's leading postwar politician, Giulio Andreotti, on charges of having illegal connections with the Sicilian Mafia.

GEOGRAPHY

Italy's boot shape makes it one of the most recognisable countries in the world, with the island of Sicily appearing somewhat like a football at the toe of the boot and Sardinia situated in the middle of the Tyrrhenian Sea to the west of the mainland.

The country is bounded by four seas, all part of the Mediterranean Sea. The Adriatic Sea separates Italy from Slovenia, Croatia and Montenegro; the Ionian Sea laps the southern coasts of Apulia, Basilicata and Calabria; and to the west of the country are the Ligurian and Tyrrhenian seas. Coastal areas vary from the cliffs of Liguria and Calabria to the generally level Adriatic coast.

More than 75% of Italy is mountainous, with the Alps stretching from the Golfo di Genova (Gulf of Genoa) to the Adriatic Sea north of Trieste and dividing the peninsula from France, Switzerland, Austria and Slovenia. The highest Alpine peak is Mont Blanc (Monte Bianco) on the border with France, standing at 4807 metres, while the highest mountain in the Italian Alps (Le Alpi) is Monte Rosa (4634 metres) on the Swiss border.

The Alps are divided into three main groups – western, central and eastern – and undoubtedly are at their most spectacular in the Dolomites (Dolomiti) in the eastern Alps in Trentino-Alto Adige and the Veneto. There are more than 1000 glaciers in the Alps, remnants of the last Ice Age, which are in a constant state of retreat. The best known in the Italian Alps is the Marmolada glacier on the border of Trentino and the Veneto, a popular spot for summer skiers.

The Appenines (Apennini) form a backbone extending for 1220 km from Liguria, near Genoa, to the tip of Calabria and into Sicily. The highest peak is the Corno Grande (2914 metres) in the Gran Sasso d'Italia group in Abruzzo. Another interesting group of mountains, the Alpi Apuane (Apuan Alps), is found in north-western Tuscany and forms part of the sub-Apennines. These mountains are composed almost entirely of marble and, since Roman times, have been mined almost continuously. Michelangelo selected his blocks of perfect white marble at Carrara in the Alpi Apuane.

Lowlands, or plains, make up less than a quarter of Italy's total land area. The largest plain is the Po valley (Pianura Padana), bounded by the Alps, the Apennines and the Adriatic Sea. The plain is heavily populated and industrialised, and through it runs Italy's largest river, the Po, and its tributaries, the Reno, Adige, Piave and Tagliamento rivers. Other, smaller plains include the Tavogliere di Puglia and the Pianura Campana around Mt Vesuvius.

Italy has three active volcanoes: Stromboli (in the Aeolian islands), Vesuvius (near Naples) and Etna (Sicily). Stromboli and Etna are among the world's most active volcanoes, while Vesuvius has not erupted since 1944 – a source of concern for scientists, who estimate that it should erupt every 30 years. Etna's most recent major eruption occurred in 1992, when a trail of lava on its astern flank threatened to engulf the town of Zafferana Etnea. The lava flow stopped before it reached the town, but not before it had destroyed orchards and a house. Related volcanic activity produces thermal and mud springs, notably at Viterbo in Lazio and in the Aeolian Islands. The Phlegraean Fields near Naples are an area of intense volcanic activity, including hot springs, gas emissions and steam jets.

Central and southern Italy, including Sicily, are also subject to sometimes devastating earthquakes. Messina and Reggio di Calabria were devastated in 1908 by an earthquake which had its epicentre in the sea off the coast of Sicily. In November 1980 an earthquake south-east of Naples destroyed several villages and killed more than 3000 people.

ECOLOGY & ENVIRONMENT

Italy is a dramatically beautiful country, but since Etruscan times humans have left their mark on the environment. Pollution problems caused by industrial and urban waste exist throughout Italy, with air pollution proving a problem in the more industrialised north of the country and in the major cities such as Rome, Milan and Naples, where car emissions poison the atmosphere with carbon monoxide and lead. The seas, and therefore many beaches, are fouled to some extent, particularly on the Ligurian coast, in the northern Adriatic (where there is an algae problem resulting from industrial pollution) and near major cities such as Rome and Naples. However, it is possible to find a clean beach, particularly in Sardinia. Litter-conscious visitors will be astounded by the extraordinary Italian habit of discarding and dumping rubbish when and where they like.

The Italian government's record on ecological and environmental issues is not good. The Ministry for the Environment was only created in 1981, and many environmental laws are not adequately enforced. However, the Italian consciousness of environmental issues is growing and many environmental organisations exist, including the Lega Ambiente (Environment League), the World Wide Fund for Nature (WWF) and the Lega Italiana Protezione Uccelli (LIPU, the Italian Bird Protection League).

CLIMATE

Situated in the temperate zone and jutting deep into the Mediterranean, Italy is regarded by many tourists as a land of sunny, mild weather. The country's climate is, however, quite variable, because of the length of the peninsula and the fact that it is largely mountainous. In the Alps temperatures are lower and winters are long and severe. Generally the weather is warm from July to September, although rainfall can be high in September. While the first snowfall is usually in November, light snow sometimes falls in mid-September and the first heavy falls can occur in early October.

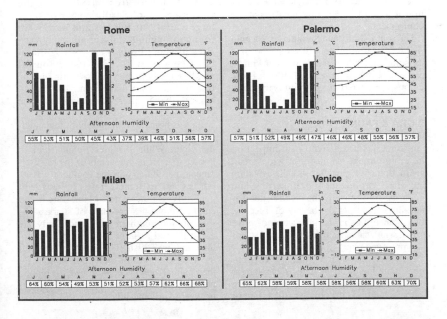

The Alps shield northern Lombardy and the Lakes area, including Milan, from the extremes of the northern European winter and Liguria enjoys a mild Mediterranean climate similar to southern Italy because it is protected by both the Alps and the Apennines.

Winters are severe and summers very hot in the Po valley. Venice can be hot and humid in summer and, although not extremely cold in winter, it can be unpleasant as the sea level rises and *acqua alta* (literally, 'high water') inundates the city.

Farther south, at Florence, which is encircled by hills, the weather can be extreme, but as you travel farther towards the tip of the boot, temperatures and weather conditions become milder.

Rome, for instance, has an average temperature in the mid-20s (Celsius) in July/August, although the impact of the sirocco, a hot, humid wind blowing from Africa, can produce stiflingly hot weather in August, with temperatures in the high 30s for days on end. Winters are moderate and snow is very rare in Rome, although winter clothing (or at least a heavy overcoat) is still a requirement.

The south, Sicily and Sardinia have a mild Mediterranean climate, with long, hot and dry summers, and moderate winters with an average temperature around 10°C. These regions are also affected by the sirocco in summer.

FLORA & FAUNA

The long presence of humans on the Italian peninsula has had a significant impact on the environment, resulting in widespread destruction of original forests and vegetation and their replacement with crops and orchards. Aesthetically the result is not displeasing – much of the beauty of Tuscany, for instance, lies in the interaction of olive groves with vineyards, fallow fields and stands of cypress and pine.

However, this alteration of the environment, combined with the Italians' passion for hunting *(la caccia)*, has led to many native animals and birds becoming extinct, rare or

endangered. Hunters are a powerful lobby group in Italy: they won the day in a recent referendum on whether hunting should be banned.

Under laws progressively introduced in this century, many animals and birds are now protected. The brown bear, which is protected in several national parks, and the lynx are now extremely rare and found only in isolated parts of the Alps and Apennines. Wolves and foxes are slightly more common and, in the Alps, you might come across marmots, chamois and deer. Among the native animals in Sardinia are wild boar, the mouflon sheep, fallow deer and a variety of wild cat. Commonly available maps in national parks in the Alps and Apennines detail the local wildlife and indicate areas where they might be found.

Hunters continue to denude the countryside of birds. However, enough remain to make bird-watching an interesting pastime. The golden eagle can still be seen in parts of the Alps, while a colony of griffon vultures survives on the western coast of Sardinia near Bosa. A large variety of falcons and hawks are found throughout Italy, as are many varieties of small birds. The irony is that it is often easier to spot the colourful smaller birds in city parks – among the few refuges they have from the Italian hunter – than in their natural habitats in the countryside.

Italy is home to remarkably little dangerous fauna. It has only one poisonous snake, the viper. While the great white shark is known to exist in the waters of the Mediterranean, particularly in the southern waters, attacks are extremely rare. Italians will generally respond with a blank stare if you enquire about the presence of sharks. The seas around southern Italy and Sicily are home instead to large numbers of blue-fin tuna and swordfish. The Egadi Islands, off the southern coast of Sicily, are famous for their annual *tonnara* or *mattanza*, the bloody netting and killing of tuna which occurs between April and July.

There are numerous national parks in Italy. The largest and most important include the Gran Paradiso in Valle d'Aosta, the Parco Nazionale dello Stelvio straddling Lombardy and Trentino-Alto Adige, and the Parco Nazionale d'Abruzzo.

GOVERNMENT

Italy is a parliamentary republic, headed by a president, who appoints the prime minister. The parliament consists of two houses – a Senate and a Chamber of Deputies – both with equal legislative power. Following a referendum in 1946, the Republic replaced the former constitutional monarchy and operates on the basis of a constitution which came into force on 1 January 1948.

The seat of national government is in Rome. The president resides in the Palazzo del Quirinale, the chamber of deputies sits in the Palazzo Montecitorio and the Senate in the Palazzo Madama, near Piazza Navona.

Until reforms were introduced in 1994, members of parliament were elected by what was probably the purest system of proportional representation in the world – which was the intent of the country's intensely democratic constitution. The reforms mean that 75% of both houses of parliament are elected on the basis of who receives the most votes in their district, basically the same as the first-past-the-post system in the UK. The other 25% are elected by proportional representation.

The Centre-Right were attempting to have another new electoral system, similar to that used in France, replace the first-past-the-post system. However, no action was expected to be taken before the elections due in November 1995. Italians are conscientious voters, with an average 88% turnout at the frequent elections.

The now-defunct right-of-centre DC consistently dominated government from the formation of the Republic until their devastating defeat in the 1994 elections. Italy's electoral system had generally forced them to form unstable coalition governments. Since the declaration of the Republic in 1946 there have been 54 governments, with an average lifespan of 11 months.

Political Scandals

The heritage of consistent one-party domination was a system which Italians called *partitocrazia* (partyocracy), which operated on the basis of *lottizzazione*, by which the major parties divided control of the country's public bodies and utilities. The resulting patronage system meant that

It's a Cat's Life

While animal rights are not a major consideration for the average Italian, the welfare of the country's huge cat and pigeon populations is a fascinating exception. In some cities the local government takes responsibility for feeding the pigeons. Where, for instance, would the Piazza San Marco in Venice be without those pesky birds that always seem to be under your feet or pooping on your head. Pick any statue in any piazza in the country and you are likely to find seven or eight pigeons sitting on its head – or at the very least, evidence that they were there. You are also very likely to find a cat or two draped across its feet.

Most of Italy's cat population is semi-wild, although it can be hard to pick the strays from the pets just out for a stroll. The strays are often just as well fed and contented, thanks to the army of women who give them leftover pasta. In Rome, there are an estimated 10,000 cat colonies, many located in archaeological areas, such as the Colosseum, Foro di Traiano and in Largo Argentina. Some 500 of these colonies are under veterinary supervision, either by private animal welfare groups or by the city's own services. Since the introduction of an extraordinarily humane law in 1988, Rome's stray cats are guaranteed the right to live where they're born – which means local people can't chase them away, whatever problems they cause. This right is also included in the model for national legislation. ■

government jobs and other positions of power and influence were handed out virtually as political favours, and that no government service was excluded from potential manipulation.

The *tangenti*, kickbacks or bribes to government officials and politicians, were another unfortunate offshoot of the system. These ranged from payments by companies wanting to secure government building contracts to payments by individuals wanting to speed up bureaucracy. The Tangentopoli scandal which erupted in 1992 dramatically changed the face of Italian politics, but it remains to be seen whether real change will filter through and result in an overhaul of the system.

The Regions

For administrative purposes Italy is divided into 20 regions which roughly correspond to the historical regions of the country. The regions are divided into provinces (*province*), which are further divided into town councils (*comuni*). Five regions (Sicily, Sardinia, Trentino-Alto Adige, Friuli-Venezia Giulia and Valle d'Aosta) are autonomous or semi-autonomous, with special powers granted under the constitution. Their regional assemblies are similar to parliaments and have a wider range of economic and administrative powers than the other 15 regions.

Elections for all three tiers of local government are held simultaneously every five years.

ECONOMY

At the end of WW II, Italy's economy was in ruins, but the country wasted little time in setting about repairing the damage. By the early 1950s much had been achieved and the country had regained prewar levels of production. The economic boom of the 1950s and early 1960s, known as the Economic Miracle, relied to a great extent on the masses of migrant workers moving from the poorer south of the country to the industrial north,

providing a more than ample but low-paid workforce.

Following spectacular economic growth during the 1980s, Italy became the fifth-largest economy in the world, made possible to a large extent by Italy's gift for producing entrepreneurs. There are the 'big ones' such as Agnelli (Fiat), De Benedetti (Olivetti) and Berlusconi (media), and then there are huge numbers of ordinary Italians who run their own small business. Some 90% of Italian firms have fewer than 100 workers and many of these are family businesses.

However, there remains much debate about Italy's ability to perform efficiently in a unified Europe. Following the country's severe economic crisis in 1992-93, draconian measures were introduced by the government to control public spending and reduce Italy's massive public debt. This was consuming a large proportion of the country's savings, keeping inflation high, stifling the entrepreneurial private sector and forcing the country to borrow even more to service the debt. The partial privatisation of the huge public sector has seen three major banks privatised: Banca Commerciale Italiano, Credito Italiano and Istituto Mobiliare Italiano. The national electricity commission (ENEL) is next on the list and there are long term plans to privatise the country's telecommunications monopoly.

The fact that in Italy the affluent, more industrialised northern regions continue to subsidise the generally poorer regions of the south remains a sore point for supporters of the Northern League. Overall, it is true to say there is a significant economic gap between north and south which continues to grow. Although the regions of Apulia, Abruzzo and Molise have experienced significant economic growth and continue to prosper, the fact remains that Italy's richest regions (Piedmont, Emilia-Romagna and Lombardy) are all northern, and its poorest (Calabria, Campania and Sicily) are all southern. Unemployment figures for the south generally are more than double those of the north, output per head in the south is only about half that of the north, and the southern regions are poorly served by economic infrastructure compared to the north.

Trillions of lire have been poured into the southern regions in the form of subsidies, grants, loans and tax incentives. The focus initially was on big, state-supported industrial ventures, many of which were abject failures. Private investment is now the target, although investors have been difficult to attract.

The impact of this economic gap is that, generally, things do not work as well in the south as they do in the north – notably in hospitals, banks and public services such as the post office.

POPULATION & PEOPLE

The population of Italy is 57.8 million. The country has the lowest birth rate in Europe (9.6 per thousand in 1987, compared with an EU average of 11.8), a surprising fact, considering the Italians' preoccupation with children and family. Demographers are predicting that the population will fall by about one million in the next 20 years. More children are born in the south than in the north – for instance, the birth rate in Emilia-Romagna is half that of Campania.

Population density can be high. The most heavily populated areas are around Rome, Milan and Naples, Liguria, Piedmont and parts of Lombardy, the Veneto and Friuli-Venezia Giulia. The most populous area of Italy – in fact the most populous in the world after Hong Kong – is Portici, a suburb of Naples located directly under Mt Vesuvius.

There is only a small minority of non-Italian-speaking people, which includes German-speakers in Alto Adige (in the province of Bolzano). Slovene is spoken by a small minority near Trieste and, in the south, there are small groups of Greeks and Albanians, descendants of immigrants in the 14th and 15th centuries.

Italy has traditionally been a country of emigrants, as Italians have left in search of work, travelling mainly to the USA, Argentina, Brazil, Australia and Canada. Southern Italians have also traditionally moved to the north of the country, to work in the factories of Piedmont and Lombardy.

In recent years, however, it has become a country of immigration. Minimal visa rules and a fairly relaxed attitude to enforcement of immigration laws by Italian authorities has made Italy an easy point of entrance into Europe, particularly for Africans. It is estimated that more than 1.5 million immigrants now live in Italy. Illegal immigrants are known in Italy as *extracomunitari*. Both African and Asian immigrants have become targets of racist attacks in Italy, although the incidence of such attacks remains limited.

Italians are far more concerned with the traditional hostility of northern Italians towards southerners. Many northerners are resentful that the richer north in effect subsidises the poorer south, and their concerns are finding a strong voice in the success of the Northern League, which has attracted considerable electoral support with its policies opposing the use of tax revenues to pay for public projects in the south. The League's leader, Umberto Bossi, has in the past also called for limitations on immigration of southern Italians to the north, as well as curbs on Third-World immigration to Italy.

EDUCATION

The Italian state-school system is free of charge and consists of several levels. Attendance is compulsory from the ages of six to 14 years, although children can attend a *scuola materna* (nursery school) from the ages of three to five years before starting the *scuola elementare* (primary school) at six. After five years they move on to the *scuola media* (secondary school) until they reach the age of 14.

The next level, the *scuola secondaria superiore* (higher secondary school), is voluntary and lasts a further five years until the student is 19 years old. It is, however, essential if young people want to study at university. At this level there are several options: four types of *liceo* (humanities-based school), four types of technical school, and teacher-training school.

The standards of education in the state-run system compare well with those in other countries, although the system does have its problems, compounded by relatively low standards in teacher-training and poor government management.

Private schools in Italy are run mainly by religious institutions, notably the Jesuits.

Italy has a long tradition of university education and can claim to have the oldest university in the world, at Bologna, which was established in the 11th century. Courses are usually from four to six years, although students are under no obligation to complete their courses within that time. Consequently, it is not uncommon for students to take many more years to complete their quota of exams and their final thesis. Attendance at lectures is not obligatory, and for scientific courses there are no practical experiments. Students therefore tend to study at home from books.

All state-school and university examinations are oral, rather than written.

ARTS

Italy has often been called a living art museum and certainly it is not always necessary to enter a gallery to appreciate the country's artistic wealth – it is all around you as you walk through Rome, Florence, or Venice, or visit a tiny church in a tiny medieval hill-town in Umbria. This evidence of the country's history is one of the most fascinating aspects of Italy. In Rome, for instance, the Roman Forum, the Colosseum and the Pantheon are juxtaposed with churches and palaces of the medieval, Renaissance and Baroque periods. Near Rome, at Tarquinia, you can visit 2000-year-old Etruscan tombs to see the vibrant funerary artwork of this ancient civilisation.

In the south of Italy and in Sicily, where Greek colonisation preceded Roman domination, there are some important Greek archaeological sites, including the temples at Paestum, south of Salerno, and at Agrigento in Sicily. Pompeii and Herculaneum near Naples, and Ostia Antica near Rome, give an idea of how ancient Romans actually lived.

Byzantine mosaics adorn churches throughout Italy, most notably at Ravenna, the Basilica di San Marco in Venice and Cattedrale di Monreale, near Palermo. In Apulia, you can tour the magnificent Romanesque churches, a legacy of the Normans, and their successors, the Swabians. However, in Sicily, where the Normans also held power, their art and architecture were heavily influenced by that of their predecessors, the Arabs.

A tour of Renaissance artworks would alone fill an extended trip to Italy. In Florence there is Italy's best-known art gallery, the Uffizi, which houses the extraordinary collection of the Medici family. Ten of its rooms trace the development of Florentine and Tuscan painting from the 13th to 16th centuries and works include Botticelli's *Birth of Venus* and *Primavera* (Spring) and da Vinci's *Annunciation*. In the Accademia is Michelangelo's *David*, while the Bargello houses Donatello's bronze *David*. At the Vatican in Rome there is Michelangelo's ceiling and *Last Judgment* in the Sistine Chapel and Raphael's frescoes in Pope Julius II's private apartment. In St Peter's Basilica is Michelangelo's *Pietà* and his *Moses* is in the Basilica di San Pietro in Vincoli.

Architecture

There is far too much to make a detailed architectural agenda worthwhile. There are 900 churches in Rome alone. Much of the character of Italian architecture, however, can be absorbed by simply wandering through the streets and admiring the richness and wealth on show.

Etruscan & Greek Little evidence remains of Etruscan civilisation, other than the numerous tombs of ancient Etruria, mainly concentrated in southern Tuscany and northern Lazio. However, it is known that the Etruscans invented the atrium, which became an important feature of Roman homes. They built their temples mainly from wood, on high stone bases, and decorated the façades with brightly coloured terracotta friezes. But much of what is known about the Etruscans has been learned from studying their tombs. Their *necropoli* (literally cities of the dead) range from the underground painted tombs of Tarquinia, to those carved into soft tufa rock (predominantly near Rome), and those of Cerveteri, the *tumoli*, huge mounds of earth atop tombs partially excavated and partially constructed.

Greeks colonised the south of the peninsula and Sicily from the 8th century BC and their architectural legacy is quite extensive, with some of the best preserved examples of Doric architecture to be found at Paestum, just south of Salerno. There are other Doric temples scattered around Sicily, at Agrigento in the spectacular Valley of the Temples, and at Segesta and Selinunte. Well-preserved Greek Theatres can be found at Syracuse, Segesta and Taormina (although the theatre at the latter was extensively rebuilt by the Romans).

Roman The ancient Romans were, as Horace wrote, captivated by Hellenist Greece and by the idealism of Greek art. For a time, they either copied or were heavily influenced by Greek painting, sculpture and architecture, but Roman art eventually developed its own distinct characteristics. In architecture the Romans liberally adapted the Greek orders, particularly Corinthian, but often built their temples on high podiums, as had the Etruscans, and began to use columns as decorative, rather than solely structural, devices. Their most important contribution to architecture was vaulting, a significant development which, combined with the use of concrete and arches, enabled them to span great spaces with no internal supports. Arches were used in another Roman invention, the aqueduct, which was built to carry water. One of the greatest of all Roman architectural achievements is the Pantheon in Rome. Its extraordinary dome remains one of the largest in existence.

Roman architects tended to construct buildings as part of a group, hence the development of Roman town centres which included temples, a forum or public area, market and other important buildings. Towns were generally laid out on a grid format and there was a significant degree of uniformity in the way buildings were constructed throughout the empire.

The Roman city of Pompeii, frozen in time, gives an excellent idea of how the ancient Romans lived. South-east of Naples, it was perfectly preserved in 79 AD, when Mt Vesuvius erupted violently and buried the entire city in a layer of ash. Its amphitheatre and thermal baths are among the earliest examples of these Roman structures. There is also a very early basilica, which was one of the most important types of Roman building. Pompeii's most interesting structures are the homes of the wealthy. These usually incorporated an entrance hall (vestibule), which led to the atrium and then the peristyle, an internal colonnaded courtyard, usually containing a garden and fountain. The family apartments opened onto the peristyle.

The best examples of how the average person lived can be found at Ostia Antica, where there are several very well-preserved *insulae*. These were multi-storey apartment houses, surprisingly similar to their modern-day successors. Examples of Roman *villas*, the country houses of the rich, can be found throughout Italy; that near Piazza Armerina in central Sicily, famous for its excellently preserved floor mosaics.

To accommodate their recreational needs the ancient Romans built thermae (*terme*), vast complexes of public baths, such as the Terme di Caracalla in Rome; theatres such as the Teatro Marcello in Rome; and amphitheatres, the most famous being the Colosseum.

During the Renaissance and especially the 18th century, when the towns of Pompeii and Herculaneum were being excavated, many architects turned to Roman heritage for inspiration, resulting in Roman-influenced structures which were referred to as 'classical'.

Early Christian & Byzantine The earliest examples of Christian architecture are the

Completed in 80 AD, the Colosseum, which could hold up to 87,000 spectators, was a venue for gladiator tournaments.

basic basilican style was used for centuries and can be seen in many churches, notably Santa Maria Maggiore and San Giovanni in Laterano in Rome.

The early Christians also adapted the classical central-plan building: a round structure with a dome. A good example is the Mausoleo di Santa Costanza in Rome. This style was later favoured by the Byzantines and was adapted for one of the most beautiful examples of Byzantine architecture in Italy, the Basilica di San Vitale in Ravenna.

The Byzantine style flourished in Italy, where architects were heavily influenced by developments at Constantinople. Major features of the style were the placement of domes on a square base, such as the crossing of the transept and nave in the basilican-style church. The mosaic was the main type of decoration. Ravenna harbours some of the best examples of the Byzantine style and mosaics in Italy. In Venice there is the fabulous Basilica di San Marco, modelled on the now destroyed church of the Holy Apostles in Constantinople, with a Greek-cross plan and five bulbous domes.

Romanesque The Romanesque style, characterised by round arches, blunt, heavy walls and the liberal use of stone sculpture in architectural features flourished throughout Europe in the 11th and 12th centuries.

Six main versions of Romanesque architecture can be identified in Italy, generally based on regional borders: that of the Lombard plain (best illustrated by the Duomo at Modena); Pisan Romanesque (the splendid group of cathedral, baptistry and bell tower in Pisa's Campo de Miracoli); Florentine Romanesque (characterised by San Miniato and the baptistry in Florence); Apulian Romanesque; and the unique mix of Romanesque with Norman, Byzantine and Arab influences in Sicily.

Gothic Spanning the 12th to the 14th century, the Gothic style originated in France and came to dominate architecture throughout Europe. Introduced into Italy by the Cistercian monks (Abbazia di Fossanova),

catacombs, the underground burial places of the Christians. These networks of galleries and rooms were carved into the soft tufa rock which is very common near Rome and were regularly used until Constantine legalised Christianity in 313 AD. Suddenly there was a need for buildings to meet the requirements of the new religion and churches sprang up in great numbers. Many were built adapting various Roman architectural forms, such as the basilica and the atrium.

The first great church of this period was the original St Peter's basilica in Rome, which was entered through a colonnaded atrium, leading to a vestibule (or narthex). The main body of the church consisted of a nave, side aisles, an apse and a transept. This the style was picked up by the Fransicans (Basilica di San Francesco at Assisi) and the Dominicans (Chiesa di Santa Maria Novella in Florence), but never really captivated Italians in the way it did other Europeans.

The Gothic style is a combination of pointed arch and flying buttress which together relieved the pressure of the heavy Romanesque wall and allowed the use of the pointed Gothic window. The tumultuous, spiky cathedral of Milan and the sumptuous cathedral of Siena highlight the Gothic style in Italy, as does the San Petronio basilica in Bologna, the cathedral at Orvieto and churches of the Frari and SS Giovanni e Paolo in Venice.

Italians were slightly more enthusiastic in the use of the Gothic style in public buildings and palaces. Examples include the Palazzo Pubblico in Siena and the Palazzo Ducale in Venice.

Holy Roman Emperor Frederick II's Castel del Monte near Bari in Apulia features an octagonal plan and elements derived from ancient Rome as well as French Gothic.

Renaissance The Renaissance was marked by innovation, a renewed interest in classical works and a rejection of dogmatic religious authority. The quattrocento or 15th century is the most important in the history of the arts in Italy. During this period many artists of genius emerged, most encouraged by the patronage of the ruling Medici family in Florence.

The two great architects of the early Renaissance are Filippo Brunelleschi (1377-1446) and Leon Battista Alberti (1404-72). Formerly a talented goldsmith and sculptor, Brunelleschi is said to have turned to architecture after losing the competition to make the doors for the baptistry in Florence. He is credited with having designed the first Renaissance building, Florence's Spedale degli Innocenti. An extraordinary engineer, his place in history was sealed when he designed the first major dome of the Renaissance over the Duomo in Florence, a beautifully proportioned structure whose design still baffles architects. A tradi-

tionalist when it came to building, Brunelleschi derived much of his inspiration from ancient sources and exhibited purity and elegance in works such as the Cappella dei Pazzi, the Chiesa di Santo Spirito and the Baslica di San Lorenzo, all in Florence.

A humanist, poet and theorist, Alberti was the first to place architecture within the context of town planning. He designed the

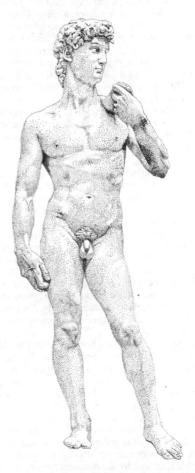

Michelangelo's *David*

Malatesta Temple in Rimini, and also constructed the churches of San Sebastiano and Sant'Andrea in Mantua and the Palazzo Rucellai in Florence. The wonderful façade of Florence's Chiesa di Santa Maria Novella is also his work.

Three men became known as the artistic triumvirate of the High Renaissance: Leonardo da Vinci (1452-1519), Michelangelo Buonarroti (1475-1564, usually known by his first name), and Raphael (1483-1520).

Da Vinci was a master of many forms – architect, weapons designer, musician, engineer, scientist and artist. He left behind more incomplete projects than finished objects, but still left a legacy of amazing achievements. Michelangelo's designs for the dome of St Peter's in Rome elevated Italian architecture to new heights.

Other notable architects working in the 16th century, or cinquecento, included Donato Bramante (1444-1514) who invented the 'rhythmic bay', a façade composed of alternating windows, pilasters (rectangular columns often attached to a wall) and niches. During this time the style of the Florentine palace emerged with its embossing, ringed columns, curved frontons or pediments and projecting cornices.

A leading figure of this period, Bramante worked in Milan and at the court in Urbino before developing the initial Greek-cross plan for the new St Peter's in Rome. Raphael succeeded Bramante as the architect of St Peter's and·was followed by Antonio da Sangallo and Michelangelo, who designed the dome while he was completing the city's Palazzo Farnese.

Andrea Palladio (1508-80) produced his work in the period between the Renaissance and the Baroque. He designed many palaces, villas and churches, including the Villa Rotunda at Vicenza and the Chiesa del Redentore in Venice. He also composed a series of architectural treatises, *Four Books on Architecture*, which helped to revive interest in classical Roman architecture. Palladio's work is characterised by the classical, central proportions of his buildings.

Mannerism Important examples of this style, known as the art of the Counter-Reformation, are the unusual Palazzo del Tè in Mantua, designed by Giuliano Romano, and the austere church of the Gesù in Rome, designed by Giacomo Barozzi da Vignola. Mannerism used the principles of the Renaissance, but altered them in an extreme or 'mannered' fashion.

Baroque The Baroque style was a reaction to the Mannerist period. Governed by irregular contours and generous forms, and characterised by sumptuous, often fantastic architecture, the Baroque style sought a combination of the theatrical and picturesque.

Carlo Maderna designed the façade of St Peter's Basilica in Rome in 1614. Francesco Borromini (1599-1667) was the most important High-Baroque architect, revolutionising architectural practice by emphasising the play of space and using light to enhance the effect of illusion.

Rome became the Baroque city it predominantly remains today, mainly as a result of the architectural achievements of Gian Lorenzo Bernini (1598-1680), whose work includes the immense colonnade of St Peter's Square. Sculptures such as the central fountain in the Piazza Navona are testament to Bernini's remarkable artistry. Rome's Trevi Fountain (1732) by Nicola Salvi is also one of the great Baroque fountains.

Other cities which were literally transformed during the Baroque period include Lecce in Apulia, Noto in Sicily, and Naples.

Later Styles The influence of the French led to the decorative Rococo style and the more imposing formalism of neoclassicism.

Antonio Sant'Elia, an architect of the early 20th-century Futurist movement made an important contribution to the development of modern Italian architecture with his unrealised plans for a high-tech, high-rise *Città Nuova*.

Fascist architecture, characterised by grandiose and often ill-advised town planning and building projects, is best illustrated by the work of Mussolini's favourite architect, Marcello Piacentini. His projects included the Stadio dei Marmi (at Rome's Stadio Olimpico) and the satellite city of Esposizione Universale di Roma (EUR), now a suburb of Rome.

Italy's role in the development of architecture has continued in the 20th century through the work of the modern and postmodern schools. Pier-Luigi Nervi and Gio Ponti were both experts in the use of reinforced concrete and plastics, and Ponti's Pirelli Tower, near Milan's main train station, is regarded as one of Europe's finest skyscrapers. Nervi was responsible for Florence's futurist soccer stadium and the Vatican's Pope Paul VI audience hall.

Painting & Sculpture

Etruscan Etruscan art is characterised by the strong colours and vigorous figures of the painted tombs at Tarquinia. Early wall paintings depict lively, joyous scenes reflecting the Etruscan view of death as a happy passing into another world. Later scenes are more subdued and reflect the increasingly strong influence of Greek culture on Etruscan civilisation.

Etruscan tombs have yielded a great wealth of sculpture in the form of stone and terracotta sarcophagi and funerary urns, as well as sculptured objects in clay and bronze. Among the most important pieces are the *Sarcophagus of the Married Couple*, dating from 6th-century BC Caere (Cerveteri), and the *Apollo of Veii*, a 6th-century BC terracotta statue which once adorned a temple at Veii (Veio). Both are now in the Museo Nazionale di Villa Giulia in Rome. Also significant are the 5th-century BC bronze *Chimera* found at Arezzo (now in the Museo Archeologico in Florence) and the famous *Capitoline Wolf*. The wolf itself is a fine example of Etruscan sculpture, while the suckling twins Romulus and Remus were added in the Renaissance. Now in Rome's Museii Capitolini, the statue was dedicated as the symbol of Rome in 296 BC.

Etruscan sculpture from the 6th century BC.

Roman The frescoes of Pompeii and Herculaneum are among the few surviving examples of Roman painting. Many of these are preserved in the Museo Nazionale in Naples, although some remain in their original locations, notably in the Villa dei Misteri at Pompeii. In Rome, frescoes known as the *Odyssey Landscapes*, dating from the 1st century BC, were taken from a Roman house on the Esquiline Hill and are now preserved in the Vatican Library.

The Romans were liberal in their adaptation of Greek artistic styles, but in both landscape painting and portrait sculpture, they developed strong individual styles. The idealism of Greek art captivated the Romans, and Greek sculptures were imported and copied by the hundreds – although many of these 'copies' are considered works of art in their own right. At the same time, Roman sculptors were developing a realistic portrait style, which concentrated on reflecting the character of the subject. The Musei Capitolini and the Vatican Museums, both in Rome, house many examples of Roman portrait sculpture.

Monumental relief sculpture was another important art form. Among the more famous examples are the Ara Pacis (Altar of Augustan Peace) and the Colonna di Traiana (Trajan's Column), both in Rome.

Early Christian & Byzantine Most examples of early Christian art are the frescoes which decorate catacombs. Constantine's official recognition of Christianity was followed by a period of intensive church building and mosaic was the preferred form of decoration. While early Christians tended to depict the life hereafter and were less concerned with the physical beauty of humans and nature, the style employed by artists didn't greatly differ from that of their pagan Roman contemporaries. The mosaics of the mausoleum of Santa Costanza in Rome, dating from the mid-4th century, are a good example. Early Christian artists used tesserae of reflective glass placed unevenly to catch and reflect the light and employed simple designs which could easily be understood.

Early Christians used the technique of sculptural relief, mainly to decorate sarcophagi, but they shunned free-standing statues, which could be too easily associated with pagan gods.

As the Eastern Roman Empire developed into the mighty Byzantine Empire, the early Christian style merged with the Byzantine, which flourished throughout the empire until well into the 12th century. This transition to the more abstract, symbolic Byzantine style is evident in the mosaics at Ravenna, dating from the 5th and 6th centuries. Byzantine mosaics are sumptuous works of ornamental splendour: those of the Basilica di San Vitale in Ravenna, which depict Emperor Justinian and his wife, Theodora, are probably the best examples of the style's early period. Later examples include the mosaics in the Basilica di San Marco in Venice, the cathedral at

Monreale in Sicily and at several churches in Rome. Hidden away in the apse of the cathedral, Santa Maria Assunta, on the Venetian island of Torcello, is one of the most striking mosaics of the later Byzantine period: a towering Madonna set against a gold background.

Romanesque Following the turn of the millennium, Romanesque emerged as the dominant style in Italian art, coming to prominence by the 12th century. Figurative sculpture was used to decorate churches, reviving the tradition of stone sculpture which had almost been lost in the 8th and 9th centuries. In a typical Romanesque church you'll find religious and fantastic figures decorating the portal and writhing around the capitals of the columns inside the church and in its cloister. Good examples of Romanesque sculpture can be seen in the various cathedrals of the period in Apulia, as well as in such cities as Pisa, Assisi and Modena.

Gothic & the Sienese School The first great Gothic sculptor in Italy, Nicola Pisano (c 1220-84), revived classical forms, while his son, Giovanni (1238-1314), introduced a vigorous and animated realism to Italian sculpture. Nicola Pisano's most important work is the pulpit in the Pisa baptistry. Among Giovanni Pisano's best works is the pulpit in the Pisa cathedral.

While northern Europe was preoccupied with the Gothic movement, artists in central Italy, notably throughout Tuscany, were using a combination of Gothic and Byzantine styles to produce a distinctive, stylised form of painting. Artists such as Duccio di

---

How to Recognize the Four Evangelists
The four evangelists, Matthew, Mark, Luke and John, who wrote the gospels recording events in the life of Christ, are very often represented in early Christian art with symbols. Matthew is depicted as an eagle, Mark as a lion, Luke as a bull and John as a man. Look for the symbols of the evangelists in mosaics, and in bas-relief decorations and on capitals in Romanesque churches. ∎

Buoninsegna (c 1255-1318) and Simone Martini (c 1284-1344) were prominent in the Sienese school. Duccio painted profoundly emotional religious subjects in the decorative Byzantine style. His great masterpiece is the *Maestà*, a massive altarpiece painted on both sides: the front depicting the Madonna enthroned and the reverse side depicting the life of Christ in a series of small panels. It is displayed in the Museo dell'Opera del Duomo in Siena. Ambrogio and Pietro Lorenzetti were the other main painters of the Sienese School.

Among Martini's most important works are the *Annunication* in the Uffizi Gallery, the *Life of St Martin* in the lower church of the Basilica di San Francesco in Assisi, and the stunning *Maestà* in the Palazzo Pubblico in Siena. Also in the Palazzo Pubblico is Ambrogio Lorenzetti's *Allegory of Good and Bad Government*.

The first evidence of a real break with the Byzantine manner was in the work of the late 13th-century artist, Pietro Cavallini, a contemporary of Duccio who worked in Rome. His masterpiece is the fresco cycle in the convent of Santa Cecilia in Trastevere, Rome. Like Pietro Cavallini, the Florentine painter, Giovanni Cimabue, was tending away from the rigidity of the Byzantine style towards naturalism, best illustrated by his frescoes in the upper church of the Basilica di San Francesco in Assisi.

Both artists influenced the work of Giotto di Bendone (1267-1337), known simply as Giotto, who, by introducing naturalism into his works, not only revolutionised painting but helped nurture the forces that spawned the Renaissance. Giotto, who studied under Giovanni Cimabue, brought passion, poignancy and depth to painting. Renowned as a humanist, Giotto overturned traditions and challenged the medieval world with his remarkable depictions of human dramas. His most famous frescoes narrating the lives of Mary and Christ are in the Capella degli Scrovegni in Padua. Giotto incorporated movement and light into his work, presenting the viewer with rounded figures who seem to move in three-dimensional space. His proportions and backgrounds are realis-

tic, and light, atmosphere and emotion are all featured. His *Death of St Francis* in the Cappella dei Bardi of the Chiesa di Santa Croce, Florence, is another good example of this. Also a sculptor and architect, Giotto designed the exquisite bell tower of the cathedral in Florence.

With the increase in communication between European countries in the 14th century, Italian artists such as Gentile da Fabriano (c 1370-1427) came into close contact with work being carried out in France, the so-called International Gothic style, which treated subjects in a more humanistic form even if it was largely unemotional and decorative. Andrea Orcagna and Andrea da Firenze were leaders of this period. Da Firenze, also known as Andrea di Bonaiuto, decorated the Capellone degli Spagnuoli (Spanish Chapel) in Chiesa di Santa Maria Novella in Florence and the main cemetery in Pisa.

Renaissance The 15th and early 16th centuries were a time of unparalleled creativity and visionary accomplishments in all aspects of political, cultural and social life. It was during the early stages of the Renaissance that artists overcame the problems of perspective, anatomy and movement and began painting their subjects in a realistic, convincing manner.

The artist Masaccio (1401-28) was the first to apply to painting the laws of perspective discovered by Brunelleschi. Masaccio used light, shadow and colour with rare skill. Some of his works, including the frescoes in the Cappella Brancacci in Florence's Chiesa di Santa Maria del Carmine, are arguably more dramatic and realistic in their depiction of human drama than Michelangelo was able to accomplish a century later.

Lorenzo Ghiberti (1378-1455), one of the most prominent of the early Renaissance sculptors, drew on Gothic influences to create the magnificent *Gates of Paradise*, the bronze doors of the baptistry in Florence. Creating the doors took decades and required the establishment of a workshop for students which eventually produced one of the most

The Art of Fresco Painting

The technique of fresco (which in Italian means 'fresh') painting was a welcome alternative for artists who laboured for months, and sometimes years, with the more time-consuming and complex medium of tempera. Frescoes forced painters to work fast. The technique basically involved painting in watercolour on wet plaster and the paint and plaster actually dried together. Colours which were not water-soluble were painted *a secco*, which means that they were painted on to the dry plaster (much of this paint eventually peeled off the frescoes).

Until the 15th century, fresco painters would first sketch their subjects on the walls with a brush dipped in ochre, then filled in the finer details with brushes dipped in red earth, a technique known as *sinopia*. Each day, the painter would apply the wet plaster, or *intonaco*, to a pre-determined area of the painting: he had to be able to complete that section of the painting before the plaster dried, although if some plaster was left over at the end of the day, he would scrape it off with a knife and bevel the edge to keep it from crumbling. The plaster covered that section of the sinopia drawing, meaning that the artists painted from memory, often making considerable changes to the original subject as they worked. In the 15th century, sinopia was replaced by *cartoons*, full-scale drawings on cardboard: holes were pricked around the outlines in the drawing and these were transferred on to the wall by dusting the cartoon with charcoal dust. During the High Renaissance, painters such as Raphael and Michelangelo did away with dusting and used metal points to prick the outlines directly on to the walls. ■

---

influential artists of the 15th century, Donatello (1386-1466).

While revering classical Roman forms, Donatello was an innovator and the first sculptor to give movement to niche statues. His bronze *David* in Florence's Museo Bargello was the first free-standing nude since antiquity. He also cast the first great equestrian statue since Roman times, the *Gattamelata*, which stands in Padua. A close study of anatomy inspired his sculpture which in turn inspired realism in subsequent Renaissance painters.

Luca della Robbia, a contemporary of Donatello, specialised in cherubs and developed a new art form in glazed terracotta, which his nephew, Andrea della Robbia, turned into a commercial industry.

At the end of the quattrocento, Florentine school sculptor Andrea del Verrocchio (1435-88) created his famous statue of Bartolomeo Colleoni in Venice.

Preserving the Gothic spirit but adopting the new style, Fra Angelico (1387-1455), a Dominican friar, created altarpieces and frescoes that were fresh, and combined purity of drawing and colour. His work can be seen in the Museo di San Marco in Florence. His beautiful paintings of the *Annunciation* are in Cortona's Museo Diocesano and in the tiny museum attached to the Duomo in San Giovanni Valdarno.

Paolo Uccello (1397-1475) was a master of perspective and foreshortening. In fact, Vasari records that Uccello was so absorbed by his study of perspective that he even refused to go to bed with his wife, saying 'What a sweet mistress is this perspective'. Ucello was far from being a prolific painter. The fresco known as the *Deluge*, in the Chiostro Verde in Florence's Santa Maria Novella, is considered his best work.

Fra Filippo Lippi (1406-98) displayed a sincere piety combined with pleasing composition and fine quality of drawing. Lippi also taught Sandro Botticelli (1444-1510), who drew on influences of classical art and pagan and Christian subjects and enjoyed the great patronage of the Medici. His *Birth of Venus* is a seminal work as is his *Spring*, both in Florence's Uffizi Gallery.

Other important painters working in this period were Domenico Ghirlandaio (1449-94), Andrea del Castagno (1423-57) and Benozzo Gozzoli (1420-97), whose work includes the vivid fresco cycle in San Gimignano's Chiesa di Sant' Agostino.

Piero della Francesca (c 1415-92) was trained in Florence by Domenico Veneziano, but spent most of his life working in Arezzo and Urbino. An expert in perspective and a skilled geometrician, della Francesca produced incredibly exact compositions. His masterpiece is the fresco cycle in the apse of the Chiesa di San Francesco in Arezzo.

Luca Signorelli (1441-1523), who painted the fresco of the Last Judgment in the Orvieto cathedral, was heavily influenced by the Florentine painter-sculptor, Antonio Pollaiuolo (c 1432-98), who made great advances in the development of figure painting.

Andrea Mantegna (1431-1506), the master of the *Dead Christ* now housed in Milan's Palazzo di Brera, taught his pupils and nurtured his passions for archaeology and anatomy at Mantua. In that city, he painted the famous fresco of the Camera degli Sposi in the Palazzo Ducale for the ruling Gonzaga family.

The Bellini family hailed from Venice, and consisted of Jacopo and his two sons, Gentile and Giovanni. Giovanni Bellini was the brother-in-law of Andrea Mantegna and displayed sensitivity and realism in his altarpiece compositions and landscapes.

Other important painters of the period were the Venetian, Giorgione (c 1476-1510), and Perugino (Pietro Vannucci, c 1450-1523), who was among the famous artists of the day summoned to Rome to paint frescoes on the walls of the Sistine Chapel. His most famous student was Raphael.

The High Renaissance The beginning of the cinquecento saw the focus of the Renaissance shift from Florence to Rome, where a series of powerful popes – Alexander VI, Julius II, Leo X and Clement VII – employed the greatest artists of the day to embellish their palaces and churches.

Da Vinci, Michelangelo and Raphael were the dominant artists of the High Renaissance.

The patronage of the Medici family helped Michelangelo develop his extraordinary talent. A painter and sculptor of incredible power, the ceiling of the Sistine Chapel is his great achievement in painting. After finishing it, he didn't paint again for 23 years, when he was recalled to the Sistine Chapel to paint the *Last Judgment*. In sculpture, he bequeathed many great works to the world: his *Pietà* in St Peter's in Rome, the virile *David* in the Galleria dell' Accademia in Florence, and *Moses*, a powerful work in Rome's San Pietro in Vincoli. After serving his apprenticeship in Florence, he came to Rome to design the tomb of Pope Julius II. He died in Florence after finishing the tombs of the Medici, in which his genius was allowed free rein.

Da Vinci, the 'universal man' was nothing if not diverse. He not only painted, but embarked on scientific endeavours and studies. His fresco the *Last Supper* in the Vinciano Refectory next to Milan's Chiesa di Santa Maria delle Grazie is a monumental work. This is the scene where Christ announces that one of his apostles has betrayed him. The fresco shows the range of emotions – rage, hatred, curiosity, pain – expressed by each. Da Vinci also set new

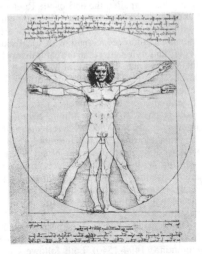

Leonardo da Vinci's study of proportions

standards for human proportional definition (helped by his anatomical studies), perfected aerial perspective, and was a virtuoso of *sfumato*, literally 'mist', a subtle technique used to glide from colour to colour. This revolutionised painting in Europe.

Known as the grand master of classicism, Raphael was prolific while striving for technical perfection. His accuracy, attention to detail and brilliant composition laid the foundations of modern painting. He invented the seated three-quarter-length portrait and the group portrait. His frescoes in the Vatican Museums (in the rooms known as the *Stanze di Rafaello*) are a must, as is his *Madonna* in Florence's Uffizi Gallery.

Titian (1490-1576), a disciple of Giovanni Bellini, was equally proficient with mythological or religious compositions and portraiture. His works are dotted around the country; Venice's Galleria dell'Accademia housing his *Presentation of the Virgin at the Temple*.

Other important painters of this period include Andrea del Sarto (1486-1531) and Correggio (Antonio Allegri, c 1489-1534).

Mannerism The Sack of Rome by Charles V in 1527 signalled the end of the Renaissance and the resulting disillusionment partly contributed to Mannerism, an art movement more concerned with idealised beauty and style rather than the naturalism of the Renaissance. The work of Mannerists – Michelangelo, Tintoretto and others – reflected feelings of tension, discord and violent emotion. Michelangelo's *Last Judgment* is crowded with writhing, agonised figures and is regarded as a reflection of the artist's tortured mind. Tintoretto (1518-94) used light to dramatic effect when working with religious subjects and his more unsettling secular works. *Paradise* in Venice's Doges' Palace is one of his masterpieces and is one of the world's largest paintings.

Other artists during this period were Jacopo Pontormo (1494-1556) and Rosso Fiorentino (1494-1540), both followers of Andrea del Sarto, and Bronzino (1503-72)

and Giorgio Vasari (1511-74), who is remembered more for his work as an art historian. Benvenuto Cellini (1500-71) and Giovanni da Bologna (1529-1608), known as Giambologna, was French by birth and is considered the most significant sculptor in Italy after Michelangelo.

Baroque Michelangelo da Caravaggio (1573-1610) emerged as Baroque Rome's pre-eminent painter later in the 16th century. Defining naturalism as the depiction of nature whether ugly or beautiful, Caravaggio led an outspoken, stormy existence scornful of those who feared ugliness. He invited controversy by framing his subjects with harsh lighting and portraying Christ's Disciples as labouring peasants. His dramatic work is exemplified by *The Descent from the Cross* in the Vatican Museums. Other painters of the period include Annibale Carracci (1560-1609) and Guido Reni (1575-1642). However, it was in sculpture and architecture that the Baroque style reached its highest expression, through artists including Bernini and Borromini who worked in Rome. (See the Architecture section).

The 18th century was unremarkable except for Giambattista Tiepolo (1696-1770), who was the last of the great Italian decorative painters. Using a bright palette, he created many vibrant frescoes. His *Virgin in Glory* in the Scuola dei Carmini in Venice displays his talent.

Later Styles Neoclassicism preceded the modern era, marked by the sculptor Antonio Canova (1757-1822), whose most noted work is the statue of Pauline Borghese in the Museo Borghese in Rome, and painter Appiani (1754-1817).

Early in the 20th century a group of young, educated Italians formed a movement called Futurism. Rebelling against all traditional art, the Futurists were heavily influenced by Cubism. They attempted to capture the different phases of movement and to discover a new world of art through the mechanical rhythms of machines. Futurism's major artists included Umberto Boccioni (1882-

1916), Giacomo Balla (1871-1958), Carlo Carrà (1881-1966) and Gino Severini (1883-1966). Their fascination with machines led many to join the army during WW I and the movement was profoundly affected by the death of Boccioni in the war.

The most prominent Italian artist of the 20th century was Amedeo Modigliani (1884-1920), a member of a banking family, who became addicted to drugs and alcohol. These indulgences, combined with tuberculosis and a poverty-stricken life in Paris, killed him at the age of 36. His major works are portraits, featuring oval faces with elongated necks and sloping shoulders.

Giorgio de Chirico (1888-1978), an Italian artist born in Greece, was a major influence on the surrealist movement. His eerie streetscapes and unsettling figures – often mysterious, threatening shapes – hovered on the edge of perception or moved in ambiguous space.

Literature

Roman The roots of ancient Latin literature lie in simple popular songs, religious rites and official documents. As Latin evolved and Rome came into direct contact with the Greek world, the emerging empire's upper classes began to acquire more sophisticated tastes. Plautus (259-184 BC) adapted classic Greek themes to create his own plays – a step forward from the translations of Greek literature that had come before.

Rome's classic period didn't occur until well into the 1st century BC. Cicero (106-43 BC) stands out in the early years of this period, as the Roman Republic collapsed into civil war and gave way to dictatorial government. Cicero's writing, infused with political *engagement*, explored new terrain in Latin prose with works such as *Brutus*. More concerned with affairs of the heart, particularly his own, Catullus (c 84-54 BC) devoted his creative power to passionate love poetry. Julius Caesar combined conquest with commentary in recording his campaigns in Gaul and the disintegration of the Republic.

The reign of Augustus marked the emergence of a new wave of intellectuals. Among the greats was Virgil, whose epic poem, *The Aeneid*, links the founding of Rome with the fall of Troy. Some years later, Ovid addressed love in his poems, *Amores*, annoyed Emperor Augustus with descriptions of lewd lifestyles in *Ars Amatoria* after the emperor's daughter had been banished for vice, and wrote about transformation myths in *Metamorphoses*. Horace toed the martial line while Livy chronicled the emergence of the new empire.

Seneca (4 BC-65 AD), a Spanish philosopher, introduced a more introspective, even existential note to Latin writing in the early years of the Christian era. Petronius (died 66 AD) conveyed the decadence of the age of Nero in his *Satyricon*, although only a fragment still exists. It is to Pliny the Younger (62-113 AD) that we owe first-hand descriptions of the disaster of Pompeii. The years following the downfall of Nero are detailed in the *Histories* of Tacitus (55-120 AD), while his *Annales* reveal the astounding court intrigues of the early emperors. Marcus Aurelius' *Meditations* were the musings of the last philosopher-king of the crumbling empire.

Middle Ages From before the final collapse of Rome until well into the Middle Ages, creative literary production declined, kept barely alive in western Europe by clerics and erudites who debated theology, wrote history, translated or interpreted classical literature and used Latin as their lingua franca.

Latin had, however, already ceased to be a living language. The genius of Dante, probably the greatest figure in Italian literature, confirmed the Italian vernacular (in its Florentine form) as a serious medium for poetic expression, culminating in his *Divina Commedia* (Divine Comedy) – an allegorical masterpiece that takes his protagonist on a search for God through Hell, Purgatory and Paradise. His Latin work *De Monarchia* reflects his preference for a return of imperial power and his vision of a world where the roles of pope and emperor complemented each other.

Another master of this time was Petrarch (Francesco Petrarca, 1304-74), son of a lawyer exiled from Florence at the same time as Dante. Petrarch was crowned poet laureate in Rome in 1341 after earning a reputation throughout Europe as a classical scholar. His epic poem, *Africa*, and the sonnets of *Il Canzoniere* are typical of his formidable lyricism, which has had a permanent influence on Italian poetry. His talent for self-examination in an individual, personal style was unprecedented.

Giovanni Boccaccio (1313-75) completes the triumvirate. Author of the *Decameron*, 100 short stories ranging from the bawdy to the earnest in chronicling the exodus of 10 young Florentines from their plague-ridden city, Boccaccio is considered the first Italian novelist.

Renaissance The 15th century produced several treatises on architecture and politics, but perhaps more important was the feverish study and translation of Greek classics and more recent Hebrew and Arabic scholars. The advent of the printing press accelerated the spread of knowledge. In Italy the industry was developed above all in Venice, where Aldo Manuzio (c 1450-1515) flooded the market with Greek classics from his famous Aldine Press. His Greek Academy published many great scholars. Manuzio introduced italic type in 1501 and also the octavo, half the size of a standard quarto page and more suitable for printed books.

Machiavelli's *Il Principe* (The Prince), although a purely political work, has proved the most lasting of the Renaissance works. Surprisingly for many, Machiavelli was also a fine playwright, whose *Mandragola* is a masterpiece. See the History section.

His contemporary Ludovico Ariosto (1474-1533) is arguably the star of the Italian Renaissance, his *Orlando Furioso* a subtle tale of chivalry in exquisite verse and laced with subplots. Torquato Tasso (1544-95) continued a tradition of narrative poetry with his *Gerusalemme Liberata*, for which he drew inspiration from Italy's increasingly precarious political situation towards the end of the century.

To the 19th Century At a time when French playwrights ruled the stage, the Venetian Carlo Goldoni (1707-1793) attempted to bring Italian theatre back into the limelight, combining realism and a certain literary discipline with a popular feel rooted in the *commedia dell'arte.*, the tradition of improvisational theatre based on a core of set characters.

The heady winds of Romanticism that prevailed in Europe in the first half of the 19th century did not leave Italy untouched. In the small Marches town of Recanati, Giacomo Leopardi began penning verses heavy with longing and melancholy, but equally crammed with his largely self-taught erudition. The best of them, the *Canti*, constitute a classic of Italian verse.

Poetry remained the main avenue of literary expression for much of the century, but the Milanese writer Alessandro Manzoni (1785-1873) changed all that with his *I Promessi Sposi* (The Betrothed), a historical novel on a grand scale. Manzoni laboured hard on the manuscript to establish a narrative language accessible to all Italians, lending it a barely disguised nationalist flavour lost on no-one when it appeared in the 1840s. In 1881, Giovanni Verga announced the arrival of the realist novel in Italy with *I Malavoglia*.

The 20th Century The turbulence of political and social life in Italy throughout most of this century has produced a wealth of literature, much of it available in translation for English speakers.

Theatre In Sicily, Luigi Pirandello (1867-1936) began his career writing novels and short stories along realist lines, but soon moved to theatre. With such classics as *Sei Personnagi in Cerca d'Autore* (Six Characters in Search of an Author) he threw into question every preconception of what theatre should be. A Nobel-prize winner in 1934, his influence continues to assert itself in the

West; from Brecht to Beckett, few modern playwrights could claim to have escaped his influence.

Modern Italian theatre is much the junior member of Italy's literary family. Its most enduring contemporary representative is Dario Fo (1926-), who from the 1950s to this day has written, directed and performed. Often a one-man show, but also in company, his work is laced with political and social critique. He has had a number of hits in London's West End, including *Accidental Death of an Anarchist, Can't Pay, Won't Pay* and *Mistero Buffo*.

Poetry Gabriele d'Annunzio (1863-1938) is in a class of his own. Ardent nationalist, his often virulent poetry was perhaps not of the highest quality, but his voice was a prestige tool to Mussolini's Fascists.

Giuseppe Ungaretti (1888-1970), whose creative and personal baptism of fire took place on the battlefields of WW I, produced a robust, spare poetry, far from the wordy complexity of his predecessors. The sum of his work is contained in *Vita d'un Uomo* (Life of a Man).

Two other 'hermetic' poets stand out, both Nobel-prize winners. Eugenio Montale (1896-1981) is less accessible than Ungaretti, and devoted much of his time after WW II to journalism. Sicilian poet Salvatore Quasimodo (1901-68) reached a high point after WW II, when he believed poetry could and should empathise with human suffering. The myth exploded; his later work is heavy with melancholy and nostalgia.

Fiction Italy's richest contribution to modern literature has been in the novel and short story. Turin especially has produced a wealth of authors. Cesare Pavese, born in a Piedmont farmhouse in 1908, took Walt Whitman as his guiding light. Involved in the intellectual and anti-Fascist circles of prewar Turin, his greatest novel, *La Luna e Il Falò* (The Moon and the Bonfire), was published in 1950, the year he took his life.

Like Pavese, the Turin doctor Carlo Levi experienced internal exile in southern Italy under the Fascists. The result was a moving account of a world oppressed and forgotten by Rome, *Cristo si è Fermato a Eboli* (Christ Stopped at Eboli).

Primo Levi, a Turin Jew, ended up in Auschwitz during the war. *Se Quest'è Un Uomo* (If This is a Man) is the dignified account of his survival, while *La Tregua* (The Truce) recounts his long road back home through eastern Europe. Born in 1919, he committed suicide in 1987.

Palermo-born Natalia Ginzburg (1916-) has spent most of her life in Turin. Much of her writing is semi-autobiographical. Tutti I Nostri Ieri, *Valentino* and *Le Voci della Sera* are just three novela among a palette of prose, theatre and essays. Swinging from light irony to a kind of worldly wisdom, her particular gift is in capturing the essence of gestures and moments in everyday life.

A writer of a different ilk is Italo Calvino. Born in Cuba in 1923, a resistance fighter and then Communist Party member until 1957, Calvino's works border on the fantastical, thinly veiling his main preoccupations with human behaviour in society. *I Nostri Antenati* (Our Ancestors), a collection of three such tales, is perhaps his greatest success.

Alberto Moravia (1907-90) describes Rome and its people in his prolific writings. Such novels as *La Romana* (A Woman of Rome) convey the detail of place and the sharp sense of social decay that make his story-telling so compelling.

Curzio Malaparte (1898-1957) concentrates on Naples and his native Tuscany, but with a polemical view, revealing the misery and corruption of post-Liberation Italy.

Unique is *Il Gattopardo* (The Leopard), the only work of lasting importance by Sicily's Giuseppe Tomasi di Lampedusa (1896-1957). Set at the time of Italian unification, it is a moving account of the decline of the virtually feudal order in Sicily, embodied in the slow ruin of Prince Fabrizio Salina, later played by Burt Lancaster in Luchino Visconti's 1963 film of the book.

Leonardo Sciascia, born in Agrigento in 1921, has dedicated most of his career to his native Sicily, attacking all facets of its past and present in novels and essays. His first great success was *Il Giorno della Civetta* (The Day of the Owl), a kind of whodunit illustrating the extent of the Mafia's power.

The novels of Rome's Elsa Morante (1918-), characterised by a subtle psychological appraisal of her characters, can be seen too as a personal cry of pity for the sufferings and troubles of individuals and society. Her 1948 novel *Menzogna e Sortilegio*, brought her to prominence. In it she recounts the slow decay of the southern Italian noble family.

The novelist of the moment is the Bologna intellectual Umberto Eco (1932-), who shot to popularity with his first and best known work, *Il Nome della Rosa* (The Name of the Rose), which was also made into a successful film with Sean Connery.

Music

The Italians have played a pivotal role in the history of music: they invented the system of musical notation in use today; a 16th-century Venetian printed the first musical scores with movable type; Cremona produced violins by Stradivari and others; and Italy is the birthplace of the piano.

The 16th century brought a musical revolution in the development of opera, which began as an attempt to recreate the drama of ancient Greece. The first successful composer, Claudio Monteverdi (c 1567-1643), drew from a variety of sources.

In the 17th and early 18th centuries, instrumental music started to become established, helped by the concertos of Arcangelo Corelli (1653-1713) and Antonio Vivaldi (1675-1741). Vivaldi, whose best known work is *The Four Seasons,* created the concerto in its present form while he was teaching in an orphanage in Venice. Domenico Scarlatti (1685-1757) wrote more than 500 sonatas for harpsichord, and Giovanni Battista Sammartini (1700-75) experimented with the symphony.

Verdi, Puccini, Bellini, Donizetti and Rossini, composers from the 19th and early 20th centuries, are all stars of the modern operatic era. Giuseppe Verdi (1813-1901)

was an icon midway through his life and his achievements include *Aïda* and one of the most popular operas of all, *La Traviata*. Rossini's *Barber of Seville* is an enduring favourite with a lively score, and *Madame Butterfly* ensures Puccini a firm place in musical history.

The composer Gian Carlo Menotti (1911-) is also famed for creating the Spoleto Festival of Two Worlds, at Spoleto in Umbria.

The opera season in Italy runs from December to June. The country's premier opera theatres include La Scala in Milan, San Carlo in Naples, the Teatro dell'Opera in Rome and La Fenice in Venice. Tenor Luciano Pavarotti (1935-) is today's luminary of Italian opera.

Canzone Napoletana If a great many rock and pop greats in the English-speaking world have their roots in the blues tradition. Italian popular music has much the same relation to the *canzone Napoletana* – Neapolitan song.

By the late 18th century, an annual pilgrimage in September to the Chiesa di Santa Maria di Piedigrotta, in Pozzuoli, had become an occasion for merriment and song. At a time when the Neapolitan dialect had the status of a language in its own right, bands played in impromptu competitions, that soon began to produce what could be considered the year's top hits. In 1840 came the first real classic, *Te Voglio Bene Assaje,* a song that remains enshrined in the city's musical imagination. But surely the best known Neapolitan song remains *O Sole Mio*.

Contemporary Music Few modern Italian singers or groups have made any impact outside Italy. The best vocalist to emerge since the war is probably Mina. During the 1960s she cut dozens of records. Many of her songs have been written by Giulio Rapetti, better known as Mogol, the unquestioned king of Italian songwriters.

The 1960s and 1970s produced various *cantautori* (singer songwriters), vaguely reminiscent of some of the greats of the UK and USA. Lucio Dalla, Vasco Rossi and Pino Daniele have been successfully hawking their versions of protest music since the early 1970s. While not of the stature of, say, Bob Dylan, the strength of their music lies in lyrics laced with venom portraying the shortcomings of modern Italian society. Daniele, whose Neapolitan roots are clearly on display, brings an unmistakeably bluesy flavour to his music.

Much softer and less inclined towards social critique, but highly popular since the end of the 1960s, is Lucio Battisti. Some of the early music will make your hair stand on end (*very* 1970s), but Battisti is highly regarded, even by younger generations.

Ivano Fossati is another well-established cantautore, but some of his most agreeable material is purely instrumental.

More recently arrived on the scene is Zucchero (Adelmo Fornaciari), who represents a phenomenon quite apart on the Italian music scene. Starting out as a session musician with the likes of Joe Cocker, he has aimed at both the Italian and international market in a way few other Italians have, earning a lot of sour grapes along the way. He sings many of his songs in Italian and English, and has become comparatively well known in the UK and USA as Sugar. Clever moves like doing *Senza una Donna* with Paul Young have also directed more attention his way.

Other names to look out for include Luca Carboni, Francesco de Gregori, Antonello Venditti, Fiorella Mannioa, Claudio Baglioni and the group RAF. In the early '90s, Eros Ramazzotti emerged as one of the country's top artists.

For what it's worth, Italian hip-hop and house productions are much appreciated by connoisseurs, including 99 Posse and Assalti Frontali.

Film

Born in Turin in 1904, the Italian film industry originally made an impression with silent spectaculars. By 1930 it was virtually bankrupt and Mussolini began moves to nationalise the industry. These culminated in 1940, when Rome's version of Hollywood, Cinecittà, was ceded to the state. Set up in 1937, this huge complex was fitted out with the latest in film equipment. Half the nation's production took place here – 85 pictures in 1940 alone.

Abandoned later in the war, Cinecittà only went timidly back into action in 1948 – its absence had not bothered the first of the Neo-Realist directors. In 1950 an American team arrived to make *Quo Vadis?*, and for the rest of the 1950s film-makers from Italy and abroad moved in to use the site's huge lots. By the early 1960s, however, this symbol of Italian cinema had again begun to wane as location shooting became more common.

Neo-Realism Even before the fall of Mussolini in 1943, those who were about to launch Italy's most glorious era of the silver screen were at work. Luchino Visconti (1906-76) came to cinema late, after meeting Jean Renoir, the French film-maker, in France in 1936. His first film, *Ossessione*, based on James Cain's *The Postman Always Rings Twice*, was one of the earliest examples of the new wave in cinema.

In the three years following the close of hostilities in Europe, Roberto Rossellini (1906-77) produced a trio of Neo-Realist masterpieces. The first, in 1945, was *Roma Città Aperta* (Rome Open City), set in German-occupied Rome and starring Anna Magnani. For many cinophiles the film marks the true beginning of Neo-Realism, uniting a simplicity and sincerity peculiar to Italian film-making; often heart-rending without ever descending into the bathos to which so many Hollywood products fall victim.

Paisà (1946) follows the course of war from Sicily to the Po river in a series of powerful vignettes, while *Germania Anno Zero* (Germany Year Zero, 1947) pulls no punches in looking at a country left crushed by the war it had launched.

Vittorio de Sica (1901-74) kept the Neo-Realist ball rolling with another classic in 1948, *Ladri di Biciclette* (Bicycle Thieves), the story of a man's frustrated fight to earn a crust and keep his family afloat. It is one of 10 films he made from 1939 to 1950.

1950s to the 1970s Schooled with the masters of Neo-Realism, Federico Fellini (1920-94) in many senses took the creative baton from them and carried it into the following decades. His disquieting filmic style is more demanding of audiences, abandoning realistic shots for pointed images at once laden with humour, pathos and double-meaning – all cleverly capturing not only the Italy of the day, but the human foibles of his protagonists. Fellini's greatest international hit was *La Dolce Vita* (1968), with Anita Ekberg and Marcello Mastroianni. Others include *8½* (1963), *Satyricon* (1969), *Roma* (1972) and *Amarcord* (1973). Fellini's wife, Giulietta Masina, starred in many of his pictures.

Luchino Visconti, meanwhile, continued to make movies until his death, one being the memorable adaptation of Tomasi di Lampedusa's *Il Gattopardo*.

Michelangelo Antonioni (1912-) began directing in 1950; his films explore existential themes and individual crisis, reaching a climax with *Blow-up* in 1967. Pier Paolo Pasolini's (1922-75) themes are altogether different, preoccupied at first with the condition of the subproletariat in films like *Accattone* (1961) and *Teorema* (1968), and later with human decay and death (*Decameron*, *I Racconti di Canterbury* and *Il Fiore delle Mille e Una Notte*).

In 1974, Lina Wertmüller (1928-) incurred the ire of feminists with her best known work, *Swept Away* (or in Italian, *Travolti Da Un Insolito Destino nell'Azzurro Mare di Agosto*). Bernardo Bertolucci (1941-) first made an international hit with *Last Tango in Paris* (1972).

1980 to the Present Bertolucci's foreign profile has continued to grow with blockbusters like *The Last Emperor* (1987) and *The Sheltering Sky* (1990). Another director who has done a lot of work outside Italy is Franco Zeffirelli (1923-), among whose better known films are *Othello* (1986), *Young Toscanini* (1988) and *Hamlet* (1990). He was also behind the TV epic *Jesus of Nazareth* (1977).

Paolo (1931-) and Vittorio Taviani (1929-) got started in the 1960s and in 1976 produced *Padre Padrone*, a heart-rending account of

---

Stars of the Screen

One of Italy's earliest international stars was Rudolph Valentino (actually Rodolfo Pietro Filiberto Guglielmi), whose brief career in Hollywood from about 1920 until his death in 1926 spanned 10 silent movies. A migrant from Apulia in southern Italy, he was a true American success story, arriving at the age of 18 and working as a waiter and professional dance partner before being 'discovered'.

Among Italy's greatest actors since WW II are: Marcello Mastroianni, who starred in *La Dolce Vita* and countless other films; including Robert Altman's *Prêt-à-Porter*; Anna Magnani, who won an Academy Award for *The Rose Tattoo*; Gina Lollobrigida *(Go Naked in the World* and *Come September)*; and, of course, Sophia Loren, whose films include *It Started In Naples*, *Houseboat* and *Boy On a Dolphin*.

The undisputed king of film comedy was long Totò, who until his death in 1967 was for Italy what Chaplin became for the Anglo-Saxon world. That he never achieved similar international recognition can perhaps be attributed to the special appeal for Italian audiences of his quick Naples wit, the kind of thing that does not translate well.

Who, however, has not seen at least one 'spaghetti western' with 160-kg Bud Spencer and his thin, blue-eyed counterpart, Terence Hill? The names are pseudonyms and these cowboys are all-Italian. From 1970, when *They Called Him Trinity* came out, until 1986, they kept Italy and much of the rest of the world in stitches with their version of how the West was won. They tried again in late 1994 with *Botte di Natale*, a box office flop. ∎

peasant life in Sardinia and one man's escape. Their biggest hits of the 1980s were *Good Morning Babilonia* (1986), an account of the creation of W D Griffiths' *Intolerance*, and *Kaos* (1984), inspired by stories by Luigi Pirandello.

A wonderful homage to film-making is *Nuovo Cinema Paradiso* (1988), by Giuseppe Tornatore (1956-). Nanni Moretti (1953-), who first came to the silver screen in the late 1970s, has proven a highly individualistic actor-director. *Caro Diario* (Dear Diary), his whimsical, self-indulgent, autobiographical three-part film won the prize for best director at Cannes in 1994.

CULTURE

It is difficult to define Italian culture without resorting to stereotypes, basically because Italians have only lived together as one nation for little over 100 years. Prior to unification, the inhabitants of the Italian peninsula were subject to a variety of masters – kings, popes, colonisers and conquerors – and cultures, in different periods influencing different areas of the peninsula. Consequently, the people absorbed and adapted diverse cultural influences, while maintaining their own dialects, traditions and customs. Even after unification, it was not until the advent of TV that all Italians began to speak standard Italian. Previously it was not unusual to find farmers and villagers who spoke only their local dialect.

While there exists a national identity and a sense of *patria* (homeland), it is more likely to find its expression at a World Cup soccer match than in a form of patriotism similar to the American style.

Regionalism remains a strong force in Italy and people identify far more strongly with their region, even their town, than with the concept of nationality. A person is therefore 'Apulian', 'Sicilian' or 'Tuscan' before they are Italian – and certainly their dialect, accent and even their culinary traditions define their own cultures. Others maintain an even further localised identity, being first and foremost Romano, Bolognese, Fiorentino or Napoletano.

But you can be sure that, confronted with a foreigner, Italians will energetically reveal a national pride that is difficult to detect in the relationship they have with each other.

Stereotypes

Foreigners may like to think of Italians as a land of passionate, animated people who gesticulate wildly when speaking, love to eat, drive like maniacs and don't like to work. However, it will take more than a holiday in Italy to understand its vigorous and remarkably diverse inhabitants.

The Italian journalist, Luigi Barzini, defined his compatriots as a hard-working, resilient and resourceful people, who are optimistic and have a good sense of humour. If there is a national stereotype, this is probably closer to the truth. They are also passionately loyal to their friends and families. Barzini noted that these were all-important qualities, since 'a happy private life helps people tolerate an appalling public life'.

Italians in general have a strong distrust of authority and, as Barzini observed, when confronted with a silly rule, an unjust law or a stupid order, they don't complain, nor do they try to change it, they simply ignore it and try to find the quickest way around it.

Family

In the end, the most important unit for the Italian is not country, state, region, town or even church, but the family. Unlike in many other Western countries, most young Italians tend to remain in the family home until they marry. In 1988 only 14% of Italians under the age of 25 lived away from home, although a lack of affordable housing for young single people is a major contributing factor.

Modern attitudes and practices have eroded the traditional institution of family to some extent. Statistics show that one in three married couples have no children and one in nine children is born out of wedlock. In Milan, more than one-third of families are headed by a single parent and two-thirds of these are headed by a woman.

Avoiding Offence

Italians tend to be very tolerant people, mainly concerned with their private lives, and are generally reluctant to become involved in other people's business.

They have a tendency towards prudishness which might seem strange, since every second billboard and TV advertisement uses semi-naked women to promote anything from laxatives to cars, and in public parks and parked cars you will find it difficult not to notice young couples engaged in physical activities that could have them arrested in another country.

On the other hand, if you walk around the streets of the Lido in Venice wearing only a bikini, you will be fined. And don't expect to be allowed into churches if you are wearing a miniskirt or shorts – in some churches you will be kicked out if you have bare arms.

Churches which are major tourist attractions, such as St Peter's in Rome and St Francis' in Assisi, are extremely strict in their enforcement of dress rules. Remember that churches are also places of worship, so if you want to visit one during a service, try to be as inconspicuous as possible.

In some parts of Italy, particularly in the south, women will be harassed if they wear skimpy or see-through clothing – in fact, one female traveller reported that she was hissed at, jeered and spat on by locals when she arrived in Assisi wearing a tight miniskirt.

Beach-goers will be likely to cause grave offence if they choose to sunbathe nude at beaches where no Italians are doing so. It is very common for women in Italy to sunbathe topless, but it is always best to check that you will not be alone before removing your own top.

You might find yourself in serious trouble if you offend a member of the police force. The police and carabinieri (see the Police information in the Dangers & Annoyances section of the Facts for the Visitor chapter) have the right to arrest you for 'insulting a state official' if they believe you have been rude or offensive to them.

THE MAFIA

It is quite an understatement to note that the Mafia knows no limits, but in Italy it is a reality which has led all to question just who runs the country – the government or the Mafia? And that is not an easy question to answer. As an English journalist noted, 'Everyone knows that the Mafia and the establishment are intertwined, and that this marriage is one of the pillars of political life in Italy. The Mafia is not only omnipotent, it is omnipresent'.

In Italy, the term 'Mafia' can be used to describe five distinct organised crime groups: the original Sicilian Mafia, also known as the Cosa Nostra; the Calabrian 'Ndrangheta; the Camorra of Naples; and two relatively new organisations, the Sacra Corona Unita (United Holy Crown) and La Rosa (the Rose) in Apulia. These groups operate both separately and together.

At a 1989 meeting in Nice, the Sicilian Mafia, the 'Ndrangheta and the Camorra met with representatives of the Colombian and Venezuelan drug cartels and carved up the world's heroin and cocaine markets. The Sicilians retained the heroin trade, with the Calabrians taking on an important role, and the Camorra emerged as the heroin specialists.

By the early 1990s, the combined estimated worth of the Italian mafia groups was around L100,000 billion, or about 12% of GNP. The EU shudders at the prospect of Mafia money being laundered legitimately as European borders break down.

Cosa Nostra

The Sicilian Mafia has its roots in the oppression of the Sicilian people and can claim a history extending back to the 13th century. Its complex system of justice is based on the code of silence known as *omertà*. Mussolini managed to virtually wipe out the Mafia, but from the devastation of WW II grew the modern version of the organisation, known as Cosa Nostra, which has spread its tentacles worldwide and is far more ruthless and powerful than its predecessor. It is involved in drug-trafficking and arms deals, as well as finance, construction and tourist development, not to forget public-sector projects and Italian politics. Few Italians doubt the claim that the Mafia's tentacles extend into almost every part of the country, and well beyond.

The early 1990s saw a virtual firestorm of Mafia violence in Sicily, seen by many as a push by the Cosa Nostra to once and for all wipe out its opposition. Two anti-Mafia judges were assassinated in Palermo in separate bomb blasts, and the murders were interpreted as messages from the Mafia that it could kill with impunity. The assassinations, however, had the opposite effect, as the Italian government, long lethargic and even reluctant in its efforts to combat the Cosa Nostra, was finally moved to take action.

One early result of this newly found, feverish anti-Mafia activity was the arrest of Salvatore 'Toto' Riina, the Sicilian godfather. Riina, head of the powerful Corleonese clan, had been the world's most wanted man since 1969. When he was arrested, it was discovered that he had never left Sicily and had, in fact, been living in the centre of Palermo with his family.

'Ndrangheta

Until the late 1980s, the 'Ndrangheta was a disorganised group of bandits and kidnappers; today it controls an organised crime network specialising in arms, drug-dealing and construction. In the 1970s, oil heir J Paul Getty III was kidnapped and held by the 'Ndrangheta, having his ear severed before his release. The organisation continues to kidnap for profit. With its base in the villages of Calabria, the 'Ndrangheta is notorious for its savage violence: in the early 1990s there was an average of one execution a day.

Camorra

This secret society grew to power in Naples in the 19th century. It was all but wiped out by severe repressive measures around the turn of the century, but managed to survive and enjoyed a renaissance in the post-WW II period, dealing mainly in contraband cigarettes. It took great advantage of the funds which poured into the region after the 1980 earthquake, diverting hundreds of millions of dollars meant for reconstruction projects to build an empire which has diversified into drugs, construction, finance and tourist developments. It has worked closely with the Sicilian Mafia.

Sacra Corona Unita & La Rosa

Apulia had managed to escape the clutches of the organised crime groups which had terrorised the rest of the south, but by the late 1980s the Mafia had arrived in the form of the Sacra Corona Unita in the south of the region and La Rosa in the north. As a natural gateway to Eastern Europe through its main ports of Bari and Brindisi, Apulia was a natural target following the collapse of communism. It quickly supplanted Naples as a base for the Mafia's smuggling activities, chiefly in contraband cigarettes, and an early consequence of its activities has been a massive upsurge in the number of heroin addicts in Bari, Brindisi and Taranto.

RELIGION

Some 85% of Italians professed to be Catholic in a census taken in the early 1980s. Of the remaining 15%, there were about 500,000 evangelical Protestants, about 140,000 Jehovah's Witnesses, and other, small groups, including a Jewish community in Rome and the Waldenses (Valdesi) – Swiss-Protestant Baptists living in small communities in Piedmont. There are also communities of orange-clad followers of the Bhagwan Rajneesh, known in Italy as the *arancioni*.

Strangely enough, while so many Italians are Catholic and the fabric of Italian life is so profoundly affected by Christian values, few Italians practise their religion. Church attendance is low – an average of only 25% attend Mass regularly – and many children are never baptised. But first communion remains a popular event, the majority of Italian couples prefer to be married in a church, and religious festivals never fail to attract a large turnout. Italians are also well acquainted with the saints and keenly follow the activities of the pope.

Pope John Paul II, the head of the Roman Catholic church, and resident of the Vatican.

LANGUAGE

Although many Italians speak some English because they study it in school, English is more widely understood in the north, particularly in major centres such as Milan, Florence and Venice, than in the south. Staff at most hotels, pensioni and restaurants usually speak a little English, but you will be better received if you at least attempt to communicate in Italian.

Italian is a Romance language related to French, Spanish, Portuguese and Romanian. The Romance languages belong to the Indo-European group of languages, which include English. Indeed, as English and Italian share common roots in Latin, you will recognise many Italian words.

Modern literary Italian began to develop in the 13th and 14th centuries, predominantly through the works of Dante, Petrarch and Boccaccio, who wrote chiefly in the Florentine dialect. The language drew on its Latin heritage and many dialects to develop into the standard Italian of today. Although many dialects are spoken in everyday conversation, standard Italian is the national language of schools, media and literature, and is understood throughout the country.

There are 58 million speakers of Italian in Italy; half a million in Switzerland, where Italian is one of the four official languages; and 1.5 million speakers in France, Slovenia and Croatia. As a result of migration, Italian is also widely spoken in the USA, Argentina, Brazil and Australia.

Visitors to Italy with more than the most fundamental grasp of the language need to be aware that many older Italians still expect to be addressed by the third person formal, ie *lei* instead of *tu*. Also, it is not considered polite to use the greeting *ciao* when addressing strangers, unless they use it first; it's better to say *buongiorno* (or *buonasera*, as the case may be) and *arrivederci* (or the more polite form, *arrivederla*). We have used the formal address for most of the phrases. The informal address appears in brackets.

Italian, like other Romance languages, has masculine and feminine forms. These two forms appear separated by a slash, the feminine form first.

See the Food Glossary in the Food section of the Facts for the Visitor chapter.

Pronunciation

Italian is not difficult to pronounce once you learn a few easy rules. Although some of the more clipped vowels, and stress on double letters, require careful practice for English speakers, it is easy enough to make yourself understood.

Vowels

Vowels are generally more clipped than in English:

a	as the second 'a' in 'cam**e**ra'
e	as in 'd**ay**' but a shorter sound
i	as in 'inn'
o	as in 'd**o**t'
u	as in 'c**oo**k'

Consonants

The pronunciation of many Italian consonants is similar to that of English. The following sounds depend on certain rules:

c	like 'k' before 'a', 'o' and 'u'. Like the 'ch' in 'choose' before 'e' and 'i'
ch	hard 'k' sound
g	hard, as in 'get' before 'a', 'o' and 'u'. As in 'job' before 'e' and 'i'.
gh	hard, as in 'get'
gli	as in 'million'
gn	as in 'canyon'
h	always silent
r	a rolled 'rrr' sound
sc	before 'e' and 'i', like the 'sh' in 'sheep'. Before 'h', 'a', 'o' and 'u', a hard sound as in 'school'
z	as the 'ts' in 'lights'. Like the 'ds' in 'beds' when the first letter of a word.

Note that when 'ci', 'gi' and 'sci' are followed by 'a', 'o' or 'u', the 'i' is not pronounced unless the accent falls on the 'i'. Thus the name 'Giovanni' is pronounced 'joh-**vahn**-nee'.

Stress
Double consonants are pronounced as a longer, often more forceful sound than a single consonant.

Stress often falls on the second-last syllable, as in *spa-**ghet**-ti*. When a word has an accent, the stress is on that syllable, as in *cit-**tà***, 'city'.

Language Problems
Please write it down.
Può scriverlo, per favore?
Can you show me (on the map)?
Me lo puo mostrare (sulla carta/ pianta)?
I (don't) understand.
(Non) Capisco.
Do you speak English?
Parla (Parli) inglese?
Does anyone speak English?
C'è qualcuno che parla inglese?
How do you say ... in Italian?
Come si dice ...in italiano?
What does ... mean?
Che vuole dire ...?

Paperwork
name	*nome*
nationality	*nazionalità*
date of birth	*data di nascita*
place of birth	*luogo di nascita*
sex (gender)	*sesso*
passport	*passaporto*
visa	*visto consolare*

Greetings & Civilities
Hello.	*Buongiorno/Ciao.*
Goodbye.	*Arrivederci/Ciao.*
Yes.	*Sì.*
No.	*No.*
Please.	*Per favore/Per piacere.*
Thank you.	*Grazie.*
That's fine/You're welcome.	*Prego.*
Excuse me.	*Mi scusi.*
Sorry (forgive me).	*Mi scusi/Mi perdoni.*

Small Talk
What is your name?
Come si chiama? (formal)
Come ti chiami? (informal)
My name is ...
Mi chiamo ...
Where are you from?
Di dove viene/Di dove sei?
I am from ...
Sono da .../Vengo da ...
How old are you?
Quanti anni ha (hai)?
I am ... years old.
Ho ... anni.
Are you married?
È sposata/o lei?
I'm (not) married.
(Non) sono sposata/o.
I (don't) like ...
(Non) Mi piace ...
Just a minute.
Un momento

Getting Around
I want to go to ...
Voglio andare a ...

What time does ... leave/arrive?	*A che ora · parte/arriva ...?*
the boat	*la barca*

the bus	*l'autobus*
the train	*il treno*
the aeroplane	*l'aeroplano*
the first	*il primo*
the last	*l'ultimo*
one-way ticket	*un biglietto semplice*
return ticket	*un biglietto di andata e ritorno*
1st class	*prima classe*
2nd class	*seconda classe*
platform number	*binario numero*
station	*stazione*
ticket office	*biglietteria*
timetable	*orario*
train station	*stazione*

The train is cancelled/delayed.
Il treno è cancellato/in ritardo.

I'd like to rent ...	*Vorrei noleggiare ...*
a car	*una macchina*
a bicycle	*una bicicletta*
a motorcycle	*una motocicletta*

Directions

Where is ...?	*Dov'è ...?*
Go straight ahead.	*Si va/(Vai) sempre diritto.*
Turn left.	*Gira a sinistra.*
Turn right.	*Gira a destra.*
at the next corner	*al prossimo angolo*
at the traffic lights	*al semaforo*
behind	*dietro*
in front of	*davanti*
far	*lontano*
near	*vicino*
opposite	*di fronte a*

Around Town

I'm looking for ...	*Cerco ...*
a bank	*un banco*
the church	*la chiesa*
the city centre	*il centro (città)*
the ... embassy	*l'ambasciata di...*
my hotel	*il mio albergo*
the market	*il mercato*

Useful Signs

CAMPEGGIO	CAMPING GROUND
OSTELLO PER LA GIOVENTÙ	YOUTH HOSTEL
INGRESSO/ENTRATA	ENTRANCE
USCITA	EXIT
COMPLETO	FULL/NO VACANCIES
PENSIONE	GUESTHOUSE
ALBERGO	HOTEL
INFORMAZIONE	INFORMATION
VIETATO FUMARE	NO SMOKING
APERTO	OPEN
CHIUSO	CLOSED
POLIZIA/ CARABINIERI	POLICE
QUESTURA	POLICE STATION
TELEFONO	TELEPHONE
GABINETTO/BAGNi	TOILETS

the museum	*il museo*
the post office	*la posta*
a public toilet	*un gabinetto/ bagno pubblico*
the telephone centre	*il centro telefonico*
the tourist infomation office	*l'ufficio di turismo/ d'informazione*

I want to exchange some money/travellers' cheques.
Voglio cambiare del denaro/degli assegni per viaggiatori

beach	*la spiaggia*
bridge	*il ponte*
castle	*il castello*
cathedral	*il duomo/la cattedrale*
church	*la chiesa*
island	*l'isola*
main square	*la piazza principale*
market	*il mercato*
mosque	*la moschea*
old city	*il centro storico*
palace	*il palazzo*
ruins	*le rovine*
sea	*il mare*

square	*la piazza*
tower	*il torre*

Accommodation

I'm looking for a ...	*Cerco un ...*
hotel	*albergo*
guesthouse	*pensione*
youth hostel	*ostello per la giovenù*

Where is a cheap hotel?
Dov'è un albergo che costa poco?
What is the address?
Cos'è l'indirizzo?
Could you write the address, please?
Può scrivere l'indirizzo, per favore?
Do you have any rooms available?
Ha camere libere/C'è una camera libera?

I would like ...	*Vorrei ...*
a bed	*un letto*
a single room	*una camera singola*
a double room	*una camera matrimoniale*
room with two beds	*una camera doppia*
a room with a bathroom	*una camera con bagno*
to share a dorm	*un letto in dormitorio*

How much is it per night/per person?
Quanto costa per la notte/ciascuno?
Can I see it?
Posso vederla?
Where is the bathroom?
Dov'è il bagno?
I am/We are leaving today.
Parto/Partiamo oggi.

Food

breakfast	*prima colazione*
lunch	*pranzo/colazione*
dinner	*cena*
restaurant	*ristorante*
grocery store	*un alimentari*

What is this?
Che cos'è?
I would like the set lunch.
Vorrei il menu turistico.
Is service included in the bill?
È compreso il servizio?
I am a vegetarian.
Sono vegetariana/o.

Shopping

I would like to buy ...
Vorrei comprare ...
How much is it?
Quanto costa?
I don't like it.
Non mi piace.
Can I look at it?
Posso dare un'occhiata?
I'm just looking.
Sto solo guardando.
Do you accept credit cards/travellers' cheques?
Accetta carte di credito/assegni per viaggiatori?
It's cheap.
Non è cara/o.
It's too expensive.
È troppo cara/o.

more	*più*
less	*meno*
smaller	*più piccola/o*
bigger	*più grande*

Time & Dates

What time is it?
Che ora è?/Che ore sono?

It is 8 o'clock ...	*Sono le otto...*
in the morning	*di mattina*
in the afternoon	*di pomeriggio*
in the evening	*di sera*
today	*oggi*
tomorrow	*domani*
yesterday	*ieri*

Monday	*lunedì*
Tuesday	*martedì*
Wednesday	*mercoledì*
Thursday	*giovedì*

Friday	*venerdì*	40	*quaranta*
Saturday	*sabato*	50	*cinquanta*
Sunday	*domenica*	60	*sessanta*
		70	*settanta*
January	*gennaio*	80	*ottanta*
February	*febbraio*	90	*novanta*
March	*marzo*	100	*cento*
April	*aprile*	1000	*mille*
May	*maggio*	one million	*un milione*
June	*giugno*		
July	*luglio*		
August	*agosto*	**Health**	
September	*settembre*	I am ill.	*Mi sento male.*
October	*ottobre*	It hurts here.	*Mi fa male qui.*
November	*novembre*		
December	*dicembre*		

Numbers

		I'm ...	*Sono ...*
0	*zero*	diabetic	*diabetica/o*
1	*uno*	epileptic	*epilettica/o*
2	*due*	asthmatic	*asmatica/o*
3	*tre*		
4	*quattro*	I'm allergic ...	*Sono allergica/o ...*
5	*cinque*	to antibiotics	*agli antibiotici*
6	*sei*	to penicillin	*alla penicillina*
7	*sette*		
8	*otto*	antiseptic	*antisettico*
9	*nove*	aspirin	*aspirina*
10	*dieci*	condoms	*preservativi*
11	*undici*	contraceptive	*anticoncezionale*
12	*dodici*	diarrhoea	*diarrea*
13	*tredici*	medicine	*medicina*
14	*quattordici*	sunblock cream	*crema/latte solare*
15	*quindici*		*(per protezione)*
16	*sedici*	tampons	*tamponi*
17	*diciassette*		
18	*diciotto*	**Emergencies**	
19	*diciannove*	Help!	*Aiuto!*
20	*venti*	Call a doctor!	*Chiama un*
21	*vent'uno*		*dottore/un*
22	*ventidue*		*medico!*
30	*trenta*	Call the police!	*Chiama la polizia!*
		Go away!	*Vai via!* (informal)

Facts for the Visitor

VISAS & EMBASSIES

Residents of the USA, Australia, Canada and New Zealand are not required to apply for visas before arriving in Italy, if they are entering the country as tourists only. (Citizens of the UK, France and other member countries of the European Union are subject to different regulations – see the separate EU Citizens section.) While there is an official three-month limit on stays in the country, border authorities rarely stamp the passports of visitors from Western nations.

But if you are entering Italy for any reason other than tourism (for instance, study) or if you plan to remain in the country for an extended period, you should insist on having the visa stamp. Without it you could encounter problems when trying to obtain a *permesso di soggiorno* – in effect, permission to remain in the country for a nominated period – which is essential for everything from enrolling at a language school to applying for residency in Italy.

While it is theoretically possible to officially extend a tourist visa in Italy, extensions are rarely granted in practice. In any case it would be extremely unlikely that you would encounter any problems with police or border guards if you happened to remain in Italy for longer than three months. Since the border guard probably didn't stamp your passport when you originally entered Italy, there is, in fact, no way of determining exactly how long you have been in the country anyway.

Tourists wanting to play it safe might find it easier to go to the nearest border post and ask for a new stamp in their passport.

Italian Consulates & Embassies

The following is a selection of Italian diplomatic missions abroad:

Australia
    Level 45, The Gateway, 1 Macquarie Place,

Sydney (☎ 02-392 7940)
    509 St Kilda Rd, Melbourne (☎ 03-867 5744)
Canada
    136 Beverley St, Toronto (☎ 416-977 1566)
    3489 Drummond St, Montreal (☎ 514-849 8351)
Croatia
    Medulicevaulica 22, 41000 Zagreb (☎ 051-427 182)
France
    47 Rue de Varennes, 73343 Paris (☎ 1-44.30.47.00)
Germany
    Karl Finkelnburgstrasse 49-51, 53173 Bonn 2 (☎ 0228-82 00 60)
Greece
    Odos Sekeri 2, Athens 106 74 (☎ 01-36 1 72 60)
New Zealand
    34 Grant Rd, Thorndon, Wellington (☎ 04-735 339)
Slovenia
    Snezniska ulica 8, 61000 Ljubljana (☎ 061-26 2194)
Switzerland
    Elfenstrasse 14, 3006 Bern (☎ 031-352 41 51)
Tunisia
    3 Rue de Russie, 1002 Tunis (☎ 01-34 1811)
UK
    14 Three Kings Yard, London (☎ 0171-312 2200)
USA
    12400 Wilshire Blvd, West Los Angeles (☎ 213-820 0622)
    690 Park Ave, New York (☎ 212-439 8600)
    2590 Webster St, San Francisco (☎ 415-931 4924)

Permesso di Soggiorno

By law, visitors to Italy must go to a *questura* (police station) if they plan to stay at the same address for more than one week, to receive a permesso di soggiorno. Tourists who are staying in hotels are not required to do this, because hotel-owners are required to register all guests with the police.

Obtaining a permesso di soggiorno only becomes a necessity if you plan to study, work or live in Italy. You can't live without one if you fit into any of these categories. Obtaining one is never a pleasant experience. It involves enduring long queues, rude police officers and the frustration of arriving at the counter (after a two-hour wait) to find that you don't have all the necessary documents.

The exact requirements, such as documents and official stamps *(marche da bollo)*, vary from city to city. In general you will need a valid passport, containing a visa stamp indicating your date of entry into Italy, a special visa issued in your own country if you are planning to study, four passport-style photographs and proof of your ability to support yourself financially.

It is best to go to the questura to obtain precise information on what is required. Sometimes there is a list posted, otherwise you will need to join a queue at the information counter.

The Rome questura, in Via Genova, is notorious for delays and best avoided if possible. This problem has been solved by decentralisation: in Rome it is now possible to apply at the questura closest to where you are staying.

Study Visas

Foreigners who want to study at a university in Italy must have a study visa. Australians and New Zealanders must also have a visa to study at a language school (citizens of the USA, Canada and EU countries do not need visas for this). These visas can be obtained from your nearest Italian embassy or consulate. It should be noted that you will normally require confirmation of your enrolment before a visa will be issued and the visa will then cover only the period of the enrolment. This type of visa is renewable within Italy, but again only with confirmation of ongoing enrolment and with proof that you are able to support yourself financially, such as a photocopy of your bank statement.

Work Permits

Non-EU citizens wishing to work in Italy will need to obtain a work permit *(permesso di lavoro)* in their own country. In order to qualify for a work permit they will need to have a guarantee from an employer for a position which could not be filled by an Italian.

A person with a genuine offer of work from an Italian company should ensure that the prospective employer organises the work permit. It is advisable to seek detailed information from an Italian embassy or consulate on the exact requirements before attempting to organise a legitimate job in Italy. Many foreigners, however, don't bother with such formalities, preferring to work 'black' in areas such as English-teaching, bar work and seasonal work. See the section on Work later in this chapter.

EU Citizens

Citizens of EU countries require only a passport or national identity card to stay in Italy for as long as they like. Danish, Irish and UK citizens need a valid passport, while citizens of other EU countries must have held a valid passport within the five years prior to entry into Italy. UK citizens may also use a British Visitor's Passport. In 1995, Italy had yet to meet all the requirements to be eligible to join the EU's Schengen Agreement, which allows free movement across the borders of the countries which are party to the agreement.

Legally EU nationals are required to obtain a permesso di soggiorno if they want to work. While EU citizens are legally allowed to work in Italy, they still need a letter from an employer promising a job. See the section on Work later in this chapter.

Foreign Diplomatic Missions in Italy

Foreign embassies are all based in Rome, although there are generally British and US consulates in other major cities. The following addresses and telephone numbers are for Rome (telephone area code 06):

Australia
    Via Alessandria 215 (☎ 85 27 21)
Austria
    Via Pergolesi 3 (☎ 855 82 41)
    Consulate: Viale Liegi 32 (☎ 855 29 66)
Canada
    Via G B de Rossi 27 (☎ 44 59 81)
    Consulate: Via Zara 30

Croatia
Via SS Cosma e Damiano 26 (☎ 33 25 02 42)
France
Palazzo Farnese (☎ 68 60 11)
Visas: Via Giulia 251 (☎ 68 80 21 52)
Germany
Via Po 25c (☎ 88 47 41)
Consulate: Via Francesco Siacci 2c
Greece
Via Mercadante 36 (☎ 855 31 00)
Consulate: Via Stoppani 10 (☎ 807 08 49)
Netherlands
Via Michele Mercati 8 (☎ 322 11 41)
New Zealand
Via Zara 28 (☎ 440 29 28)
Slovenia
Via L Pisano 10 (☎ 808 10 75)
Spain
Largo Fontanella Borghese 19 (☎ 687 81 72)
Consulate: Via Campo Marzio 34 (☎ 687 14 01)
Switzerland
Via Barnarba Oriani 61 (☎ 808 36 41)
Consulate: Largo Elvezia 15 (☎ 808 83 71)
Tunisia
Via Asmara 5-7 (☎ 860 30 60)
Consulate: Via Egadi 13 (☎ 87 18 31 59)
UK
Via XX Settembre 80a (☎ 482 54 41)
USA
Via Vittorio Veneto 119a-121 (☎ 4 67 41)

Note that the consulates for Australia, the UK and the USA are at the same addresses and telephone numbers as their embassies. For other foreign embassies in Rome and consulates in other major cities throughout Italy, look under 'Ambasciate' or 'Consolati' in the telephone book or, in Rome, in the English *Yellow Pages*. Tourist offices will also generally have a list.

DOCUMENTS

A passport is the only important document you will need in Italy if you want to stay as a tourist for up to three months. It is necessary to produce your passport when you register in a hotel or pensione in Italy. The proprietor, or desk clerk, is likely to want to keep the document long enough to copy out the necessary details. Some proprietors will want to keep your passport for the duration of your stay. This is not a legal requirement and you are entitled to have your passport returned to you if you request it. It is a legal requirement in Italy that everyone carry an identity card (or passport); however, in some parts of Italy, where bag-snatchers prey on tourists, it is probably safer to leave your passport at the hotel and carry a photocopy.

Vehicle Papers

If you want to rent a car or motorcycle, you will generally need to produce your driving licence. Certainly you will need to produce it if pulled over by the police or *carabinieri*, who, if it's a non-EU licence, may also want to see an Italian translation of the licence (available from the Italian State Tourist Office in your country, or its equivalent, ENIT, in Rome), although this is unlikely. An International Driving Permit, available from automobile clubs throughout the world and usually valid for 12 months, is an acceptable substitute in combination with your proper licence. If you are driving your own car in Italy you will need an International Insurance Certificate, also known as a Green Card (Carta Verde). Your third party insurance company will issue this. For further details, see the Car & Motorbike section in the Getting There & Away chapter.

Student & Youth Cards

In order to take advantage of the discounts offered to travelling students in Italy, get an International Student Identity Card (ISIC) before leaving home. Recognised in more than 70 countries worldwide, it is probably the safest student ID card to carry, although it might pay in Italy (where the bureaucrats are document-mad) to carry an additional form of student ID.

The cards are available from the following offices:

Australia
Student Services Australia, 1st Floor, 20 Faraday St, Carlton (☎ 03-348 1777)
Canada
Travel Cuts, 187 College St, Toronto (☎ 416-977 3703)
Voyages Campus, Université McGill, 3480 Rue McTavish, Montreal (☎ 514-398 0647)
UK
CTS, 33 Windmill St, London (☎ 071-580 4554)

USA

CIEE, 205 East 42nd St, New York (☎ 212-661 1414)

1093 Broxton Ave, Los Angeles (☎ 213-208 3551)

312 Sutter St, San Francisco (☎ 415-421 3473)

People who are aged under 26, but not students, can obtain an International Youth Card, issued by the Federation of International Youth Travel Organisations (FIYTO). The card entitles holders to a wide range of discounts on transport, accommodation, entrance fees to museums, car hire and in restaurants.

The head office of FIYTO is in Denmark, at Islands Brygge 81, DK-2300 Copenhagen S, where you can write to request a brochure. Otherwise, the student organisations listed above for the USA, UK and Canada will issue the cards. In Italy, any office of the Centro Turistico Studentesco e Giovanile (CTS) will issue them too, as long as you can prove that you are aged under 26. See the Useful Organisations section for more information.

Photocopies

Make photocopies of all your important documents, especially your passport. This will help speed up replacement if they are lost or stolen. Other important documents to photocopy might include your airline ticket and credit cards. It is also vital to record the serial numbers of your travellers' cheques (cross them off as you cash them in). All this material should be kept completely separate from your passport, money and other documents, and leave extra copies with someone reliable at home. Keep a small amount of emergency cash with this material. If your passport is stolen or lost, notify the police and obtain a statement, and then contact your embassy or consulate as soon as possible.

CUSTOMS

People from outside Europe can import, without paying duty, two still cameras and 10 rolls of film; a movie or TV camera with 10 cartridges of film; a portable tape recorder and 10 tapes; a CD player; a pair of binoculars; sports equipment, including skis; one bicycle or motorbike (not exceeding 50 cc); one portable radio and one portable TV set (both may be subject to the payment of a licence fee on entry to Italy); personal jewellery; up to 400 cigarettes; two bottles of wine and 375 mls liquor. Visitors who are residents of and entering from another EU country can import a maximum of 300 cigarettes, one bottle of wine and a half bottle of liquor. There is no limit on the amount of lire you can import.

MONEY
Currency

Italy's currency is the lira (plural: lire). The smallest note is L1000. Other denominations in notes are L2000, L5000, L10,000, L50,000 and L100,000. Coin denominations are L50, L100, L200 and L500. Although smaller coin denominations have been taken out of circulation, you will still often find a worthless L20 or even L10 coin in your change. Although also going out of circulation, you might occasionally find yourself in possession of *gettoni* (telephone tokens). They are legal tender and have the same value as a L200 coin.

Remember that, like other Continental Europeans, Italians indicate decimals with commas and thousands with points.

Exchange Rates

Australia	A$1	=	L1195
Canada	C$1	=	L1216
France	FF1	=	L323
Germany	DM1	=	L1142
Japan	Yen100	=	L18,250
New Zealand	NZ$1	=	L978
United Kingdom	UK£1	=	L2617
USA	US$1	=	L1653

Changing Money

Anything to do with money and banks is likely to cause significant time-wasting and frustration in Italy. As is the case at post offices and police stations, you will generally need to join long queues to exchange money or draw on your credit card. Banks are the most reliable places to exchange money and generally offer the best rates, but the best advice is to shop around for good rates and the lowest commission charges. Some places charge a flat fee of up to L8000 to exchange travellers' cheques and it may be best to locate institutions which instead charge a percentage commission.

Because of the high petty crime rate in major Italian cities it is unwise to carry large amounts of cash, so calculate your financial needs carefully before exchanging money. Note that your options for good rates might be limited during the weekend. It is advisable to obtain a small amount of lire (enough to cover transport, food and accommodation for the first night) before arriving in the country. In this way you can avoid the long queues and poor exchange rates at airports and most train stations.

Travellers' Cheques
These represent a safe and convenient way to carry money and are easily exchanged at banks and exchange offices throughout Italy. In order to avoid potential problems if your cheques are stolen, always keep the bank receipt listing the cheque numbers separate from the actual cheques and keep a list of the numbers of those you have already cashed.

Before deciding on which travellers' cheques to buy, check the provisions for replacement in the event of loss or theft. Travellers using the better known cheques, such as Visa, American Express and Thomas Cook, will have little trouble in Italy. American Express, in particular, has offices in all the major Italian cities and agents in many smaller cities.

Deciding which currency to buy will depend on current exchange rates and where you intend to travel. Study currency trends carefully before making your decision, taking into account the value of the lira against your own and other major currencies. In 1994/5 the country's ongoing political and economic crisis meant that the lira was very weak against the US dollar and the Deutschmark, but it's anybody's guess what the future will hold.

If you buy your travellers' cheques in lire, generally there should be no commission charge when cashing cheques.

Credit Cards & ATMs
Carrying a plastic card or two is an extremely convenient way to organise your holiday funds. You don't have large amounts of money or cheques to lose, you can get money after hours and on weekends, and the exchange rate is better than that offered for travellers' cheques or cash exchanges. By arranging for payments to be made into your card account while you are travelling, you can avoid paying interest. Even travellers on a shoestring budget should consider carrying a credit card for use in emergencies.

Major credit cards, such as Visa and MasterCard, are accepted throughout Italy in shops, restaurants and larger hotels. However, many trattorias, pizzerias and most pensioni and one-star hotels do *not* accept credit cards, particularly in the south of Italy. At large flea markets, such as the leather market around San Lorenzo in Florence, many stallholders accept Visa and MasterCard, but will bargain only if you pay cash.

Apart from the inevitable queuing, it is generally a simple procedure to obtain a cash advance on Visa and MasterCard. Simply go to the exchange counter *(cambio)* at the bank and present your card. Visa is probably the more convenient, since only a limited number of banks will honour MasterCard. The Banca Commerciale Italiana, the Cassa di Risparmio and Credito Italiano will all give cash advances on MasterCard.

If your credit card is lost or stolen, you can telephone toll-free to have an immediate stop put on its use. For MasterCard the number in Italy is ☎ 1678-6 80 86, or make a reverse-charges call to St Louis in the USA on ☎ 314-275 6690; for Visa, phone ☎ 1678-2 10 01 in Italy.

American Express is also convenient to use in Italy. It is widely accepted (though not as common as Visa or MasterCard) and it is possible to make payments on the card at

American Express offices in major Italian cities.

The full-service offices (such as in Rome and Milan) will issue new cards, usually within 24 hours and sometimes immediately, if yours has been lost or stolen. Some American Express offices have ATMs which you can use to obtain cash advances if you have made the necessary arrangements in your own country.

There is a toll-free emergency number to report a lost or stolen American Express card in Italy, but the number varies according to where the card was issued. Check with American Express in your country or contact American Express in Rome on ☎ 06-722 82.

Credit cards can also be used in automatic teller machines (ATMs), known as *bancomats*, to obtain cash 24 hours a day throughout Italy. You will need to get a PIN number from the bank issuing the credit card. Several travellers have reported having difficulties using ATMs, ranging from losing their cards in the machines, to simply having their cards rejected. Ensure that you obtain precise information about using ATMs in Italy, and how to replace your card quickly in the event that it is swallowed by the machine. Generally, if you stick to using ATMs at major banks in city centres, you should have less trouble.

Sending Money to Italy

The fastest and most reliable way to send money to Italy is by 'urgent telex' through the foreign office of a large Italian bank, or through major banks in your own country, to a nominated bank in Italy. It is important to have an exact record of all details associated with the money transfer, particularly the exact address of the Italian bank where the money has been sent. The money will always be held at the head office of the bank in the town to which it has been sent. Urgent-telex transfers should take only a few days, while other means, such as by telegraphic transfer, or draft, can take weeks. It is also possible to transfer money through American Express and Thomas Cook. You will be required to produce identification, usually a passport, in

order to collect the money. It is also a good idea to take along the details of the transaction. It is inadvisable to send cheques by mail to Italy, because of the unreliability of the country's postal service.

Costs

There are some basic guidelines to travelling in Italy which will be useful for everyone, from the backpacker to the luxury traveller. Those on a really tight budget will find Italy expensive – accommodation charges and high entrance fees for the major museums and monuments will keep daily expenditure high. A *very* prudent backpacker could get by on around L50,000 a day, but only by staying in youth hostels, eating one simple meal a day (at the youth hostel), making your own sandwiches for lunch and minimising the number of museums and galleries visited.

Mid-range travellers will find they can live reasonably for around L80,000 to around L100,000 per day (if you stay in a one-star, or low priced two-star hotel and still eat only one sit-down meal a day), although that only covers a visit to one museum per day.

If money is no object, you'll find your niche in Italy. There's no shortage of luxury hotels, expensive restaurants and shops. Realistically, a traveller with a flexible budget could live very well for around L200,000 to L250,000 a day, including the cost of two sit-down meals, and the shared cost of a three star hotel and a rental car.

A basic breakdown of costs per person during an average day for the low to middle-range traveller could be: accommodation L18,000 to L50,000; breakfast L2000 to L3000 (coffee and croissant); lunch (sandwich and mineral water) L3000 to L5000; bottle of mineral water L1500; public transport (bus or underground railway in a major town) L3500; entrance fee for one museum L6000 to L12,000; cost of long-distance train or bus travel (spread over three days) L15,000 to L20,000; and sit-down dinner L12,000 to L30,000.

Accommodation Budget travellers can save by staying in youth hostels (open to people of all ages) or camping grounds. If travelling with a group of friends and you plan to stay in pensioni or hotels, always ask for triples or quads: the cost per person diminishes dramatically the more people you have in a room. Travellers on a bigger budget should consider sticking to one and two or, at a stretch, three-star pensioni and hotels. Chosen carefully, they provide perfectly adequate accommodation. Avoid, where possible, pensioni and hotels which charge for a compulsory breakfast. A cappuccino and brioche at a bar could cost considerably less.

If you are planning to ski, it may be cheaper to organise accommodation as part of a skiing package known as White Week (Settimana Bianca). These package deals offer accommodation and meals, plus a ski pass.

Eating Remember that, in Italian bars, prices double (sometimes even triple) if you sit down. Stand at the bar to drink your coffee or eat a sandwich – or buy a sandwich or slice of pizza and head for the nearest piazza. Read the fine print on menus (usually posted outside eating establishments) to check the cover charge (coperto) and service fee (servizio). These can make a big difference to the bill and it is best to avoid restaurants which charge both. Shop in supermarkets and alimentari (grocery shops) for the makings of picnic lunches and for the odd meal in your room.

Travelling If travelling by train and you have time to spare, take a regionale or diretto: they are slower but cheaper than the Intercity trains, for which you have to pay a supplement. See the Getting Around chapter for information about these different types of trains and about various discounts on train travel.

In the cities, buy a daily tourist ticket for urban bus travel: costing around L4000, they are good value. When catching ferries (such as to Sardinia or Greece), consider travelling deck class (passaggio ponte) in summer where it is available.

Other Cost-Savers Instead of sending post-cards or normal letters by air mail, buy aerograms from the post office for L850. At museums, never hesitate to ask if there are discounts for students, young people, children, families or the elderly. When sight-seeing, buy a biglietto cumulativo where possible: a combined ticket that allows entrance to a number of associated sights for less than the cost of separate admission fees. Try to avoid buying food and drinks at service stations on the autostradas, where they can be up to 30 % more expensive. Petrol tends to be slightly more expensive on the autostradas.

Tipping & Bargaining

You are not expected to tip on top of restaurant service charges, but it is common (although not standard) practice among Italians to leave a small amount. If there is no service charge, the customer might consider leaving a 10% tip, but this is by no means obligatory. In bars, Italians will usually leave any small change as a tip, often only L100 or L200. Tipping taxi drivers is also not common practice, but, if staying in a higher class hotel, you should tip the porter.

Bargaining is common throughout Italy in flea markets, but not in shops. At the Porta Portese market in Rome, for instance, don't hesitate to offer half the asking price for any given item. Don't be deterred by stallholders who dismiss you with a wave of the arm: the person at the next stall will be just as likely to accept your offer after a brief (and obligatory) haggle. While bargaining in shops is not acceptable, you might find that the proprietor is disposed to give a discount if you are spending a reasonable amount of money. It is quite acceptable to ask if there is a special price for a room in a pensione if you plan to stay for more than a few days.

Consumer Taxes

Whenever you buy an item in Italy, you will pay value-added tax, known as IVA. Tourists who are residents of countries outside the EU are able to claim a refund on this tax if the item was purchased for personal use and cost more than a certain amount (around L400,000 at the time of writing). The goods must be carried with you and you must keep the fiscal receipt.

The refund only applies to items which were purchased at retail outlets affiliated to the system – these shops usually display a 'Tax-free for tourists' sign. Otherwise, ask the shopkeeper. You must fill out a form at the point of purchase and have the form stamped and checked by Italian customs when you leave the country, then return it by mail to the vendor within 60 days, who will then make the refund, either by cheque or to your credit card. At major airports and border points there are places where you can get an immediate cash refund.

Receipts

Laws introduced to tighten controls on the payment of taxes in Italy mean that the onus is on the buyer to ask for and retain receipts for all goods and services. This applies to everything from a litre of milk to a haircut. Although it rarely happens, you could be asked by an officer of the Fiscal Police (Guardia di Finanza) to produce the receipt immediately after you leave a shop. If you don't have it, you will have to pay a fine of up to L300,000.

WHEN TO GO

The best time to visit Italy is in the low season, from April to June and in September/October, when the weather is usually good, prices are lower and there are fewer tourists. The weather is warm enough for beach-goers in most of the country from June to September, but during August (high season) it is very hot, prices are inflated and the entire country swarms with holidaying foreigners and Italians.

Apart from the difficulty of maintaining a rigorous sightseeing schedule in the relentless August heat, tourists will find that a large number of businesses, including shops and restaurants, close down during that month, as most Italians abandon the cities to spend their annual holidays at the beach or in the mountains. Consequently this means it can be virtually impossible to find accommodation near a beach or mountain in August, unless you have booked months in advance.

July and September are the best months for people interested in hiking in the Alps and Apennines – walking trails and *rifugi* (mountain huts) are crowded in August. During these months the weather is generally good, although you should always allow for cold weather. Rifugi usually open from late June to the end of September for hikers and at Easter (March/April) for skiers.

A mild climate makes winter a reasonable time to visit Italy's southern regions and Sardinia. However, in recent years unusual weather patterns have brought extreme cold and snow to areas such as Apulia, Calabria and Sicily.

WHAT TO BRING

Certainly the best advice is to bring as little as possible; the second important consideration is what to carry it in. A backpack is a definite advantage in Italy: petty thieves prey on tourists who have no hands free because they are carrying too much luggage, and there are endless flights of stairs at most train stations and in many small medieval towns. Travellers with suitcases and portable trolleys will find themselves at a definite disadvantage under these circumstances. Otherwise, if you must carry a suitcase/bag, make sure it is lightweight and not too big. Pack a bag and test it out before leaving – could you carry it easily for a few km?

A small pack (with a lock) for day trips and for sightseeing is preferable to a handbag or shoulder bag, especially in the southern cities where motorcycle bandits are particularly active. A money belt is an unfortunate necessity in Italy, particularly in major cities and throughout the south of the country, where it is absolutely inadvisable to carry a purse or wallet in your pocket.

When choosing what to pack, remember that, except in the mountains, Italy is uniformly hot in summer, but the climate varies in winter. For example, in most areas you will need only a light jacket (in case of cool evenings) in July and August. In winter you will need a heavy coat, hat, gloves and scarf for the north of the country, while in Sicily a lined raincoat would be adequate. In Rome, which has a very mild climate, you will need to bring out the heavy woollens only if visiting in January/February.

Most importantly, bring a pair of hardy, comfortable walking shoes with rubber soles. Apart from the many km you will cover as a sightseer, pavements are uneven in many Italian cities and often made of cobblestones.

Clothing maintenance is an important consideration when travelling for long periods, and especially so in Italy where there is such an emphasis on style. Unless you plan to spend large sums of money in dry-cleaners and laundries, make sure you pack a portable clothesline at the very least. While many pensioni and hotels specifically ask guests not to wash clothes in the room, such rules are rarely enforced. Consider packing a light travel iron or crease-proof clothes.

People planning to hike in the Alps should ensure that they bring the necessary clothing and equipment, in particular a pair of hiking boots (lightweight and waterproof). Even in high summer you will need to carry warm clothing on long hikes, or if you plan to go to high altitudes on cable cars – even if its sweltering in the valley, it can be below zero at 3000 metres. Inexperienced hikers should check with a local mountaineering group for a list of essentials before leaving home. Otherwise, the list provided in the Dolomites section of the Trentino-Alto Adige chapter should be adequate.

Basic drugs such as headache pills are widely available. However, condoms are expensive in Italy at L30,000 for 12. If they are cheaper in your home country, bring a supply.

TOURIST OFFICES

The quality of the services offered by tourist offices throughout Italy varies dramatically. One office might have enthusiastic staff but no useful printed information, while another might have a gold mine of brochures kept hidden under the counter by indifferent and sometimes hostile staff.

There are three main categories of tourist office: regional, provincial and local. A reorganisation of the system means that the names of tourist boards vary throughout the country, but they all offer basically the same services.

Tourists shouldn't need to have anything to do with the regional offices, which are concerned with promotion, planning, budgeting and other projects far removed from the daily concerns of the humble tourist. Provincial offices are known as the Ente Provinciale per il Turismo (EPT) or, more commonly, as the Azienda di Promozione Turistica (APT) and usually have information on both the province and the town.

The Azienda Autonoma di Soggiorno e Turismo (AAST) offices usually have information only on the town itself. These offices are the places to go if you want specific information about bus routes, museum opening times etc.

In most of the very small towns and villages the local tourist office is called a Pro Loco. Run by local committees, in some towns these offices are similar to the AASTs, providing a good range of useful information. In others they are little more than a meeting place for the local elderly men.

Most offices of the EPT, APT and AAST will respond to both written and telephone requests for information about hotels, apartments for rent etc.

Tourist offices are generally open Monday to Friday from 8.30 am to 12.30 or 1 pm, and from 3 to around 7 pm. Hours are usually extended in summer, when some offices also open on Saturday afternoons or on Sundays.

There are tourist information booths at most major train stations and at many of the smaller stations. These tend to be open Monday to Saturday (and Sundays in summer) from 8.30 am to 12.30 pm and from 3 to 7 pm and can usually provide a map *(pianta della città)*, list of hotels *(elenco degli alberghi)* and information on the major sights *(informazioni sulle attrazioni turistiche)*. Many will help you find a hotel, either by making a few recommendations and marking them on a map, or by actually phoning to check for vacancies.

English, and sometimes French, is usually only spoken at offices in larger towns and in areas which attract large numbers of foreign tourists. In Alto Adige, staff also speak German. In major tourist areas, information is usually available in several languages: Italian, English, French, Spanish, sometimes German and occasionally Japanese. The best advice if you encounter lethargic, unhelpful or hostile staff is to be polite but insist that they provide you with the information you require.

If you are landing in Rome, you can obtain limited information about the major destinations throughout the country from the EPT office, Via Parigi 11, 00185 Rome, and at the headquarters of Italy's national tourist office, ENIT (Ente Nazionale Italiano per il Turismo), Via Marghera 2, 00185 Rome, both near Rome's central train station, Stazione Termini.

The addresses and telephone numbers of provincial and local tourist offices are listed under towns and cities throughout this book. Addresses are also included for regional offices which might be of assistance.

Tourist Offices Abroad

Information on Italy is available from the Italian State Tourist Office in the following countries:

Useful Organisations

ACI (Automobile Club Italiano)
Dial ☎ 116 for free roadside assistance to tourists driving cars with foreign number plates. ACI will also tow your car for free to the nearest garage. You may also have reciprocal rights through membership of your home-country organisation – enquire about this before you leave, and ask for a letter of introduction. The club has border offices on entry to Italy. The club has offices at Corso Venezia 43, Milan (☎ 02-7 74 51); Via Marsala 8, Rome (☎ 06-4 99 81); and throughout Italy.

AIG (Associazione Italiana Alberghi per la Gioventù)
The Italian youth hostel association, affiliated with Youth Hostelling International (HI), has its head office (☎ 06-487 11 52) at Via Cavour 44, Rome, where you can obtain a list of all hostels in Italy and buy a membership card if necessary. There are branch offices throughout the country.

CAI (Club Alpino Italiano)
CAI can provide information on trekking and skiing.

Sestante CIT (Compagnia Italiana di Turismo)
Italy's national tourist agency has offices throughout the country and abroad. You can book train, bus, air and sea travel and obtain information about guided tours of the cities and package tours of Italy.

CTS (Centro Turistico Studentesco e Giovanile)
This agency has offices all over Italy and specialises in discounts for students and young people. It is also useful for travellers of any age looking for cheap flights and sightseeing discounts (you will be required to pay a membership fee of around L39,000 if you don't have an ISIC card). CTS is linked with the International Student Travel Confederation and, with documents proving you are a student, you can get a student card at CTS offices.

TCI (Touring Club Italiano)
The head office (☎ 02-852 62 44) is at Corso Italia 10, Milan. It publishes useful trekking guides and maps, as well as an excellent series of sightseeing guides, the *Guide Rosse* (only in Italian), all available at major bookshops including Feltrinelli. ■

Australia
    Alitalia, Orient Overseas Building, Suite 202, 32
    Bridge St, Sydney (☎ 02-247 1308).
Canada
    1, Place Ville Marie, Suite 1914, Montreal, Que
    H3B 3M9 (☎ 514-866 7667)
UK
    1 Princes St, London W1R 8AY
    (☎ 0171-408 1254)
USA
    630 Fifth Avenue, Suite 1565, New York, NY
    10111 (☎ 212-245 4822)
    124000 Wilshire Blvd, Suite 550, Los Angeles
    CA 90025 (☎ 310-82 02977)
    401 North Michigan Ave, Suite 3030, Chicago,
    IL 60611 (☎ 312-644 0990)

Sestante CIT (Compagnia Italiana di Turismo), Italy's national travel agency, also has offices throughout the world (known as CIT outside Italy). It can provide extensive information on travelling in Italy and will organise tours, as well as book individual hotels. CIT can also make train bookings, including sector bookings (such as Rome-Naples), and sells Eurail passes and discount passes for train travel in Italy. Sestante CIT offices include:

Australia
    123 Clarence St, Sydney 2000 (☎ 02-299 4754)
    Suite 10, 6th Floor, 422 Collins St, Melbourne
    3000 (☎ 03-670 1322)
Canada
    1450 City Councillors St, Suite 750, Montreal,
    Que H3A 2E6 (☎ 514-954 8608)
    111 Avenue Rd, Suite 808, Toronto, Ont M5R 3J8
    (☎ 416-927 7712)
UK
    Marco Polo House, 3-5 Lansdowh Rd, Croydon,
    Surrey CR9 1LL(☎ 0181-686 0677)
USA
    242 Madison Ave, Suite 207, New York, NY
    10173 (☎ 212-697 2497) ·
    6033 Century Blvd, Suite 980, Los Angeles, CA
    90045 (☎ 310-338 8615)

Italian cultural institutes in major cities throughout the world have extensive information on study opportunities in Italy.

BUSINESS HOURS

Business hours vary from city to city, but generally shops are open Monday to Friday from 9 am to 1 pm and 3.30 to 7.30 pm (or

4 to 8 pm). In some cities, grocery shops might not reopen until 5 pm and, during the warmer months, they could stay open until 9 pm. They close on Thursday or Monday afternoons (depending on which town you're in) and often on Saturday afternoons. Shops, department stores and supermarkets also close for a half day during the week – it varies from city to city, but is usually either Monday morning or Thursday afternoon. Shops in smaller towns and on city outskirts often close on Saturday afternoons as well.

Banks tend to be open Monday to Friday from 8.30 am to 1.30 pm and 2.30 to 4.30 pm, although hours can vary. They are closed at weekends, but it is always possible to find an exchange office open in the larger cities and in major tourist areas.

Major post offices open Monday to Saturday from 8.30 am to 6 or 7 pm Monday to Saturday. Smaller post offices open Monday to Friday from 8.30 am to 2 pm and on Saturdays from 8.30 am to midday.

Pharmacies are usually open from 9 am to 12.30 pm and 3.30 to 7.30 pm. They are always closed on Sunday and alternatively on Saturday or Wednesday. Pharmacies with longer operating hours are listed where relevant; also, there is usually a list posted outside pharmacies.

Bars (in the Italian sense, ie coffee-and-sandwich places) and cafés generally open from 7.30 am to 8 pm, although many stay open after 8 pm and turn into pub-style drinking and meeting places. Discos and clubs might open around 10 pm, but often there'll be no-one there until around midnight. Restaurants open from midday to 3 pm and 7.30 to 11 pm (later in summer and in the south). Restaurants and bars are required to close for one day each week, which varies between restaurants.

Museum and gallery opening hours vary, although many close on Mondays and some close during religious holidays.

HOLIDAYS & FESTIVALS

Most Italians take their annual holidays in August, deserting the cities for the cooler seaside or mountains. This means that many

Festivals

February/March/April

Carnevale During the period before Ash Wednesday many towns stage carnivals and enjoy their last opportunity to indulge before Lent . The carnival held in Venice during the 10 days before Ash Wednesday is the most famous, but the more traditional and popular carnival celebrations are held at Viareggio on the north coast of Tuscany and at Ivrea, near Turin.

Sartiglia This event is the highlight of carnival celebrations at Oristano in Sardinia on the Sunday and Tuesday before Lent. It involves a medieval tournament of horsemen in masquerade.

Festival of the Almond Blossoms A traditional festival featuring a historical pageant and fireworks held at Agrigento, Sicily, in early March.

Le Feste di Pasqua Holy Week in Italy is marked by solemn processions and passion plays. At Taranto in Apulia on Holy Thursday there is the Procession of the Addolorata and on Good Friday the Procession of the Mysteries, when statues representing the Passion of Christ are carried around the town. One of Italy's oldest and most evocative Good Friday processions is held at Chieti in Abruzzo. The week is marked in Sicily by numerous events, including a Procession of the Mysteries at Trapani and the celebration of Easter according to Byzantine rites at Piana degli Albanesi, near Palermo. Women in colourful 15th-century costume give out Easter eggs to the public.

Scoppio del Carro (Explosion of the Cart) Held in Florence in the Piazza del Duomo at noon on Easter Sunday, this event features the explosion of a cart full of fireworks – a tradition dating back to the Crusades. If this works well, it is seen as a good omen for the city.

May

Feast of San Nicola On 2 and 3 May, the people of Bari, in Apulia, participate in a procession in traditional costume to re-enact the delivery of the bones of their patron saint to Dominican friars. The following day a statue of the saint is taken to sea.

Festival of Snakes Held at Cocullo in Abruzzo on May 5, this famous and still very traditional festival honours the town's patron, St Dominic. His statue is draped with live snakes and carried in procession.

Feast of San Gennaro Three times a year (the first Sunday in May, 19 September and 16 December) the faithful gather in Naples' Duomo to wait for the blood of the saint to liquefy – if the miracle occurs it is a good omen for the city.

Corsa dei Ceri (Race of the Candles) This exciting and intensely traditional event is held at Gubbio in Umbria on 15 May. Groups of men carrying huge wooden shrines race uphill to the town's basilica, dedicated to the patron saint, Ubaldo.

Cavalcata Sarda (Sardinian Cavalcade) Hundreds of Sardi wearing colourful traditional costume gather at Sassari on the second-last Sunday in May to mark a victory over the Saracens in the year 1000.

Palio della Balestra (Palio of the Crossbow) Held in Gubbio on the last Sunday in May this is a crossbow contest between men of Gubbio and Sansepolcro, who dress in medieval costume and use antique weapons. There is a rematch at Sansepolcro on the first Sunday in September.

Maggio Musicale Fiorentino A music festival held in Florence in May and June.

June

Historical Regatta of the Four Ancient Maritime Republics A procession of boats and a race between the four historical maritime rivals – Pisa, Venice, Amalfi and Genoa. The event rotates between the four towns.

Feast of Sant'Antonio Fans of St Anthony, patron saint of Padua and of lost things, might want to attend the procession of the saint's relics held annually on 13 June.

Infiorata To celebrate Corpus Domini on 21 June, some towns decorate a selected street with colourful designs made with flower petals. Towns include Genzano, near Rome, and Spello in Umbria.

Gioco del Ponte (Game of the Bridge) Two groups in medieval costume contend for the Ponte di Mezzo, a bridge over the Arno river, in Pisa.

Festival of Two Worlds (Festival dei Due Mondi) This major festival of the arts is held in June and July at Spoleto, a beautiful hill town in Umbria. Created by Gian Carlo Menotti, the festival features music, theatre, dance and art exhibitions.

July

Il Palio The pride and joy of Siena, this famous traditional event is held twice a year – on 2 July and 16 August – in the town's beautiful Piazza del Campo. It involves a dangerous bareback horse race around the piazza, preceded by a parade of supporters in traditional costume.

Ardia More dangerous than the Palio, this impressive and chaotic horse race at Sedilo in Sardinia on 6 and 7June celebrates the victory of the Roman Emperor Constantine over Maxentius in 312 AD (the battle was actually at the Ponte Milvio in Rome). A large number of horsemen race around the town while onlookers shoot guns into the ground or air.

Festa del Redentore (Feast of the Redeemer) Fireworks and a procession over the bridge to the Church of the Redeemer on Giudecca Island in Venice on the third weekend in July.

Umbria Jazz Held at Perugia in Umbria in July, this week-long festival features performers from around the world.

International Ballet Festival Held at Nervi, near Genoa, this festival features international performers.

August

Quintana This historical pageant features a parade of hundreds of people in 15th-century costume, followed by a spectacular jousting tournament. It is held at Ascoli Piceno in the Marches on the first Sunday in August.

I Candelieri (Festival of the Candelabra) Held on 14 August at Sassari in Sardinia, this festival features town representatives in medieval costume carrying huge wooden columns through the town. It celebrates the Feast of the Assumption to honour a vow made in 1652 to end a plague.

Il Palio This repeat of Siena's famous horse race is held on 16 August.

Festa del Redentore Held at Nuoro in Sardinia, this folk festival and parade is attended by thousands of people from all over the island, who dress in traditional regional costume.

International Film Festival Held at the Lido, Venice, the festival attracts the international film scene.

September

Living Chess Game The townspeople of Marostica in the Veneto dress as chess figures and participate in a match on a chessboard marked out in the town square. Games are held in even years on the first weekend in September.

Palio della Balestra A rematch of the crossbow competition between Gubbio and Sansepolcro is held at Sansepolcro.

Regata Storica (Historical Regatta) This race of gondolas along Venice's Grand Canal is preceded by a parade of boats decorated in 15th-century style. It is held on the first Sunday in September.

Giostra della Quintana A medieval pageant involving a parade and jousting event with horsemen in traditional costume. Held on the second Sunday in September.

Feast of San Gennaro On 19 September the faithful of Naples gather for the second time to await the miraculous liquefaction of the saint's blood. They gather again on 16 December.

October

Feast of San Francesco d'Assisi Special religous ceremonies are held in the churches of San Francesco and Santa Maria degli Angeli in Assisi on 3 and 4 October.

November

Feast of the Madonna della Salute Held in Venice on 21 November, this procession over a bridge of boats across the Canal Grande to the Chiesa di Santa Maria della Salute to give thanks for the city's deliverance from plague in 1630.

Feast of Santa Cecilia A series of concerts and exhibitions in Siena to honour the patron saint of musicians.

December

Feast of San Nicola Various religious ceremonies as well as traditional folk celebrations take place at Bari on the 6 December.

Christmas During the weeks preceding Christmas there are numerous processions, religious events etc. Many churches set up elaborate cribs or nativity scenes known as *presepi*. ■

businesses and shops close for at least a part of the month, particularly during the week around Ferragosto (Feast of the Assumption) on 15 August. Larger cities, notably Milan and Rome, are left to the tourists, who may be frustrated that many restaurants, and clothing and grocery shops are closed until early September.

National public holidays include the following: Epiphany (6 January); Easter Monday (March/April); Liberation Day (25 April); Labour Day (1 May); Feast of the Assumption (15 August); All Saints' Day (1 November); Feast of the Immaculate Conception (8 December); Christmas Day (25 December); and the Feast of Santo Stefano (26 December).

Individual towns also have public holidays to celebrate the feasts of their patron saints. Some of these are: the Feast of St Mark on 25 April in Venice; the Feast of St John the Baptist on 24 June in Florence, Genoa and Turin; the Feast of Saints Peter & Paul in Rome on 29 June; the Feast of San Genera (Janarius) in Naples on 19 September; and the Feast of St Ambrose in Milan on 7 December.

CULTURAL EVENTS

Italy has a full calendar of religious and cultural events, including colourful traditional festivals, either religious or historical, and festivals of the performing arts, including opera, music and theatre. Events range from the famous Venice Carnevale and Siena's Palio to festivals honouring patron saints, such as the Feast of San Gennaro in Naples and of San Nicola in Bari, and usually involve local people in full traditional costume. Festivals are particularly numerous in Sicily and Sardinia, notably Le Feste di Pasqua (Easter Week) in Sicily.

There are several important opera seasons, including those held at the Arena in Verona and La Scala in Milan. Major music festivals include Umbria Jazz in Perugia and Maggio Musicale Fiorentino in Florence, while the Festival of Two Worlds (Festival dei Due Mondi) in Spoleto is certainly worth including in your itinerary. As well as Carnevale,

Venice offers an international film festival and the Biennale visual arts festival, the latter held every odd year (previously every even year).

If you are interested in timing your visit to coincide with a particular festival, contact the Italian State Tourist office in your country or write to ENIT in Rome (see the preceding Tourist Offices Abroad

Siena's traditional Palio festival

section) for specific dates. The organisation publishes an annual booklet, *An Italian Year*, which lists most festivals, music, opera and ballet seasons, as well as art and film festivals.

The following are some of the more interesting and important festivals and events, although they represent only a small proportion of those held in a normal year. Since dates often change from year to year, the events are listed under the relevant month, and dates have been included only when they are fixed, such as for festivals of patron saints.

POST & TELECOMMUNICATIONS
Post
Sending Mail Italy's postal service is notoriously slow, unreliable and expensive. Don't expect to receive every letter sent to you, or that every letter you send will reach its destination. An air-mail letter will take up to two weeks to reach the UK or the USA, while a letter to Australia will take between two and three weeks. Postcards will take even longer because they are low-priority mail. The service within Italy is no better: local letters take at least three days and up to a week to arrive in another city, although instances of letters taking weeks to arrive are common. A 1988 survey on postal efficiency in Europe found that next-day delivery did not exist in Italy.

Sending letters express (*espresso*) can help, although you pay an extra L3000 for the service.

One way to avoid all of this frustration, but only if you are in Rome, is to use the Vatican post office in St Peter's Square, which has an excellent record for prompt and reliable delivery but doesn't accept poste restante (*fermo posta*) mail.

The cost of sending a letter air mail (*via aerea*) depends on its weight and where it is being sent. An average-size letter on air-mail paper will cost L1400 to send to Australia, L1100 to the USA and L750 to the UK. A postcard will cost around the same. Aerograms are a cheap alternative, costing only L850 to send anywhere. They can be purchased only at post offices.

Stamps (*francobolli*) are available at post offices and at authorised tobacconists (*tabacchi*), but since letters must be weighed it is best to go to the post office.

If you want to post more important items by registered mail (*raccomandato*) or by insured mail (*assicurato*), remember that they will take as long as normal mail. Raccomandato costs L3200 on top of the normal cost of the letter and assicurato is an extra L6000. Urgent mail can be sent by Express Mail Service (EMS), also known as CAI Post. A parcel weighing one kg will cost approximately L38,000 within Europe, L64,000 to the USA and Canada, and L90,000 to Australia and New Zealand. The service is not necessarily as fast as private services. It will take four to eight days for a parcel to reach Australia and two to four days to reach the USA. Ask at post offices for addresses of EMS outlets.

The international couriers DHL and UPS operate in Italy: both charge similar prices, although DHL has a handy low-cost option for packages weighing up to 500 grams. Look in the telephone book for addresses.

Receiving Mail Poste restante is known as fermo posta in Italy. Letters marked 'fermo posta' will be held at the counter of the same name in the main post office in the relevant town. Ask your friends to write your surname in block letters, and to address mail as follows: John SMITH, Fermo Posta, post code plus name of town or city (post codes of central-city areas are given throughout this book). You will need to pick up your letters in person and present your passport as identification.

Telephone
It is simple to make a telephone call in Italy, but the rates, particularly for long-distance calls are among the highest in Europe. A local call will cost L200 for around four minutes (you get less time for the same amount of money from 8 am to 1 pm). If you need to keep in touch with home by telephone, beware of the cost – even a call of less than five minutes to Australia after 11 pm will cost around L15,000. Travellers from countries

which offer direct dialling services paid for at home country rates (such as AT&T in the USA and Telecom in Australia) should think seriously about taking advantage of them.

There are four types of public telephones: increasingly rare old-style telephones which only accept telephone tokens *(gettoni)*, which have the same value as a L200 coin; normal pay telephones which accept gettoni as well as L100, L200 and L500 coins – many of these also accept phonecards *(carte telefoniche)* with a value of L5000, L10,000 or L15,000 (if one card starts to run out, you can insert another, as with coin telephones); pay telephones which accept only phonecards – these are increasingly common in Italy because they reduce the risk of vandalism, so it is a good idea to have a phonecard on hand; and metred telephones, either at Telecom offices (see below) or in a bar or shop in smaller towns – the cost of your call is recorded on a meter and you pay afterwards.

You can buy phonecards at post offices, tobacconists *(tabaccherie)*, newspaper stands and from vending machines in Telecom offices. To avoid the frustration of trying to find fast-disappearing coin telephones, always keep a phonecard on hand.

Public telephones are ubiquitous in Italy, both on the street and in bars. Otherwise you can go to a Telecom office in larger towns, where there are public telephones and usually telephone books for all of Italy. In many larger towns there are also Telecom (sometimes called Iritel) offices where you can make long-distance calls and pay afterwards. Addresses of telephone offices are listed throughout the book.

Direct international calls can easily be made from public telephones using phonecards. You need to dial 00 to get out of Italy, then the relevant country and city codes, followed by the telephone number. Useful country codes are: Australia 61, Canada and USA 1, New Zealand 64, and the UK 44. Codes for other countries in Europe include: France 33, Germany 49, Greece 30, Ireland 353, and Spain 34. Other codes are listed in Italian telephone books.

Note that it is always cheaper to telephone after 10 pm for long-distance calls within Italy, and after 11 pm for international calls. A toll-free number *(numero verde)* in Italy starts with the code 1678.

To make a reverse charges (collect) international call from a public telephone, dial ☎ 170. For European countries dial ☎ 15. All operators speak English. Otherwise, you can direct dial an operator in your own country and ask to make your collect call. Numbers for this service include: Australia ☎ 172 10 61; Canada ☎ 172 10 01; France ☎ 172 10 33; New Zealand ☎ 172 10 64; and USA (through AT&T) ☎ 172 1011.

Area codes are listed under cities and towns in this book. Important telephone area codes include: Rome 06, Milan 02, Florence 055, Naples 081, Cagliari 070, Venice 041 and Palermo 091.

Warning The telephone system in Italy seems to be in a constant state of overhaul, which means that telephone numbers change with alarming regularity. Often there will be a message giving you the new number, but only in Italian. You could try ringing ☎ 12, the Telecom information line for telephone numbers, but the operators usually speak only Italian and are often unhelpful. If a telephone number is going to change, the new number will often be listed in brackets after the existing number in the telephone book. It will be preceded by the word *prenderà*.

Fax & Telegraph

Faxes have become an extremely important mode of communication for Italian businesses. However, Italy's high telephone charges make faxes an expensive mode of communication. Charges to send a fax are generally around L2000 per page, plus the cost of the telephone call. If the fax is a slow machine the cost can be very high (at least L60,000 to send two or three pages to Australia). You will also pay between L1000 and L2000 per page to receive a fax. Public fax facilities are numerous throughout the country.

Telegrams are sent from post offices and are an expensive, but sure, way of having important messages delivered by the same or next day.

TIME
Italy operates on a 24-hour clock which will take getting used to for travellers used to a 12-hour clock. Daylight-saving time starts on the last Sunday in March, when clocks are put forward one hour. Clocks are put back an hour on the last Sunday in September. Ensure that when telephoning home you also make allowances for daylight-saving in your own country.

European cities such as Paris, Munich, Berlin, Vienna and Madrid have the same time as Italy. Athens, Cairo and Tel Aviv are one hour ahead. When it's noon in Rome, it's 11 pm in Auckland, 11 am in London, 6 am in New York, 7 pm in Perth, 3 am in San Francisco, 9 pm in Sydney, and 6 am in Toronto.

ELECTRICITY
The electric current in Italy is 220 V, 50 Hz, but make a point of checking with your hotel management because in some areas, for instance in parts of Rome, they still use 125 V.

Power points have two or three holes, and plugs have two or three round pins. The middle one is for earth, but since there is no earth in Italian electrical systems, many locals just pull out the middle pin (you'd be wise to seek information before following their example). Some power points have larger holes than others. Italian homes are usually full of plug adapters to cope with this anomaly. Power points do not have their own switches.

Travellers from the USA need a voltage converter (although many of the more expensive hotels have provision for 110 V appliances such as shavers). Make sure you bring plug adapters for your appliances. It is a good idea to buy these *before* leaving home as they are virtually impossible to get in Italy. If you do forget, there is always the option

of taking your appliance to an electrical store and having them replace the foreign plug with an Italian one.

LAUNDRY
Laundries in Italy are expensive, and coin laundrettes are few and far between. Most places charge by the kilo and do the laundry themselves, which can make it an expensive proposition. In larger towns, particularly where there are universities, there are more likely to be coin laundrettes, but a load will still cost around L8000. The best option is to wash your clothes in the basin of your hotel room and dry them on a portable clothesline.

Dry-cleaning is also expensive and the standard of service can be unreliable. Average charges are around L6000 for a shirt and L12,000 for a jacket.

WEIGHTS & MEASURES
Italy uses the metric system. Basic terms for weight include *un etto* (100 grams) and *un chilo* (one kg). Travellers from the USA will have to cope with the change from pounds to kg, miles to km and gallons to litres. A standard conversion table is at the back of this book.

Note that Italians indicate decimals with commas and thousands with points.

BOOKS
Most books are published in different editions by different publishers in different countries. As a result, a book might be a hardcover rarity in one country while it is readily available in paperback in another. Fortunately, bookshops and libraries search by title or author, so your local bookshop or library is best placed to advise you on the availability of the following recommendations.

History & People
For in-depth research there is Edward Gibbon's masterpiece, *History of the Decline and Fall of the Roman Empire* (available in six hardback volumes, or an abridged, single-volume paperback). Other, simpler

history books include: *The Oxford History of the Roman World* edited by John Boardman, Jasper Griffin & Oswyn Murray; *Daily Life in Ancient Rome* by Jerome Carcopino; *Italy: A Short History* by Harry Hearder; *Concise History of Italy* by Vincent Cronin; *History of the Italian People* by Giuliano Procacci; *The Oxford Dictionary of Popes* compiled by J N D Kelly; *Rome: Biography of a City* by Christopher Hibbert, and by the same author, *Venice: the Biography of a City* and *The Rise and Fall of the House of the Medici*. *A History of Contemporary Italy. Society and Politics 1943-1988* by Paul Ginsborg, is an absorbing and very well written book which will help Italophiles place the country's modern society in perspective.

For background on the Italian people and their culture, there is the classic by Luigi Barzini, *The Italians. Italian Labyrinth* by John Haycraft looks at Italy in the 1980s. *Getting it Right in Italy: A Manual for the 1990s* by William Ward aims with considerable success to provide accessible, useful information about Italy, while also providing a reasonable social profile of the people.

Art

The Penguin Book of the Renaissance by JH Plumb, *Painters of the Renaissance* by Bernard Berenson, and Giorgio Vasari's *Lives of the Artists* should be more than enough on the Renaissance. Other worthwhile books include *A Handbook of Roman Art*, edited by Martin Henig; *Roman Architecture* by Frank Sear; and *Art and Architecture in Italy 1600-1750* by Rudolf Wittkower (hardback).

There is also a series of guides to Italian art and architecture, published under the general title *World of Art*. They include: *Palladio and Palladianism* by Robert Tavernor; *Michelangelo* by Linda Murray; *Italian Renaissance Sculpture* by Roberta J M Oleson; *Roman Art and Architecture* by Mortimer Wheeler.

Travellers' Tales

There are endless books written by travellers to Italy. For a potted idea of how the great writers saw the country, it's worth reading *Venice: the Most Triumphant City* compiled by George Bull (hardback) and *When in Rome: the Humorists' Guide to Italy*.

Three Grand Tour classics are Johann Wolfgang von Goethe's *Italian Journey*, Charles Dickens' *Pictures from Italy*, and Henry James' *Italian Hours*. D H Lawrence wrote three short travel books while living in Italy, now combined in one volume entitled *D H Lawrence and Italy*.

Others include: *Venice* by James Morris; *The Stones of Florence* and *Venice Observed* by Mary McCarthy; *On Persephone's Island* by Mary Taylor Simeti; *Siren Land* by Norman Douglas; *Old Calabria* by Norman Douglas; *North of Naples, South of Rome* by Paolo Tullio; *The Golden Honeycomb* by Vincent Cronin (travels through Sicily); and, *A Traveller in Southern Italy* by H V Morton. Although written in the 1960s the latter remains a valuable guide to the south and its people. Morton also wrote *A Traveller in Italy* and *A Traveller in Rome*.

Travel Guides

The paperback Companion Guides are excellent and include *Rome* by Georgina Masson, *Venice* by Hugh Honour, *Umbria* by Maurice Rowdon, *Tuscany* by Archibald Lyall and *Southern Italy* by Peter Gunn. If you can read in Italian, you can't go past the excellent red guides of the Touring Club Italiano.

Lonely Planet publishes *Mediterranean Europe on a shoestring* and *Western Europe on a shoestring*; both books include chapters on Italy and are recommended for those planning further travel in Europe. Also by Lonely Planet, the *Mediterranean Europe phrasebook* lists the words and phrases you're likely to need when travelling in Italy and other countries in the area.

For information on hiking and climbing, try the guides published by Cicerone Press, Cumbria. Titles include *Walking in the Dolomites* and *Walking in the Central Italian Alps*, both by Gillian Price; *Classic Climbs in the Dolomites*, by Lele Dinoia and Valerio Casari (translated by Al Churcher);

and *Selected Climbs in Northern Italy*, by Al Churcher.

Literature

If you're serious, you might like to start with works of ancient literature, such as *Selected Works* of Cicero, Livy's *Early History of Rome*, Ovid's *Metamorphoses* and *Erotic Poems* and Virgil's *The Aeneid*.

You could then progress to Dante's *The Divine Comedy*, Giovanni Boccaccio's *The Decameron* and Niccolò Machiavelli's *The Prince*.

As far as modern literature is concerned, there are several books which you might like to put in your suitcase. They include: *The Leopard* by Giuseppe di Lampedusa; *Christ Stopped at Eboli* by Carlo Levi; and *The Name of the Rose* by Umberto Eco. Works by Italo Calvino, Alberto Moravia, Natalia Ginzburg, Primo Levi and Elsa Morante are also among the best Italy has produced.

The Mafia

The Honoured Society by Norman Lewis is an excellent introduction to the subject.

Food

The Food of Italy by Waverley Root is an acknowledged classic.

Bookshops

English-language books are expensive in Italy – expect to pay between L16,000 and L35,000 for novels, history books and translations of Italian writers. Consider swapping the books you've read with fellow travellers. There are several excellent bookshops in Italy which specialise in English-language books, including:

Rome
    The Corner Bookshop, Via del Moro 48, Trastevere
    The Anglo-American Bookshop, Via della Vite 27 & 57
    The Lion Bookshop, Via del Babuino 181
Florence
    The Paperback Exchange, Via Fiesolana 3r

Milan
    The American Bookstore, Via Camperio 16, at Largo Cairoli

Apart from these shops, Feltrinelli bookshops usually have a reasonable selection of English-language books. Other bookshops are listed under the individual towns.

MAPS

For maps of cities, you will generally find the maps in this book, combined with tourist office maps, adequate. However, if you want more detailed maps (such as for the larger cities), you can buy them at Feltrinelli bookshops or at newspaper stands. Excellent road and city maps are published by the Istituto Geografico de Agostini, the Touring Club Italiano and Michelin, and are available in all major bookshops. If you are driving around Italy, invest in de Agostini's *Atlante Stradale Italiano* (L35,000), a complete book of road maps for the country, including city maps for many places. See the Car & Motorbike section in the Getting There & Away chapter for further details.

Maps of walking trails in the Alps and Apennines are available in major bookshops, although you will find it easier to locate maps of specific zones once you are in the area. The best hiking maps are the 1:25,000 published by Tabacco.

MEDIA
Newspapers & Magazines

The major English-language newspapers available in Italy are the *Herald Tribune* (L2600), an international newspaper available from Monday to Saturday, and the *European* (L3500), available Fridays. The *Guardian* (L2800 on airmail paper), *The Times* (L4500) and the *Telegraph* (L3300), as well as the various tabloids, are sent from London, so, outside major cities such as Rome and Milan, they are generally a few days old. *Time*, *Newsweek* (both L5400) and the *Economist* (L7000) are available weekly.

Each major city has its own daily newspaper, which tends to have separate sections devoted to larger towns in the surrounding province. There is no 'national' newspaper as such, although Rome's *La Repubblica* and Milan's *Corriere della Sera* give extensive coverage of national and international events and have been 'adopted' as the two national newspapers; they're available throughout the country. Newspapers all have their own political slant, but as far as these two major papers are concerned probably no more so than those in the USA or the UK.

TV

Various news services are broadcast in English at various times of the day and night. However, the stations on which they are broadcast tend to change suddenly. In mid-1995 you could catch a half-hour Sky Channel news report from the UK at 6 am daily on TeleRoma 56 (also known as Odeon), on Channel 56. At 6.30 am on the same station, the ABC news with Peter Jennings was broadcast. On Channel 41, at some time between 7 and 10 pm Monday to Friday you could watch the American PBS McNeill Lehrer News Hour. Sky Channel and CNN are also available in many better hotels. CNN was broadcast on Telemontecarlo (TMC) nightly from 2 to 7.30 am, but this service had been suspended at the time of writing.

There are more than 600 TV channels in Italy, although some are obviously very local. There are three national public stations: RAI 1, 2 and 3. Before the Tangentopoli scandal brought down Italy's First Republic (the period from WW II) in 1994, control of these three was handed out to the three main political parties. These days the Radio Televisione Italiana radio stations RAI 1 and RAI 2 pretty well peddle the government line, while RAI 3 remains relatively 'independent'. There are five national private TV stations: Rete 4, Canale 5, Italia 1 (these three owned by Italy's billionaire former prime minister Silvio Berlusconi), TMC and a video music channel.

In a national referendum in 1995 voters rejected a proposal to limit the number of television stations to one per person. This move was a direct result of Berlusconi's rise to power in 1994 (he was forced to resign in early 1995. Many saw it is a conflict of interests that a Prime Minister could also be the owner of a media conglomerate incorporating the three TV stations. Berlusconi was negotiating in mid-1995 to sell portions of his business empire. Interested buyers hailed from the Middle East and the USA, and at one point included Rupert Murdoch.

There are numerous other local, private TV stations in Italy – about 600 licences were issued in early 1993 to 'solve' the world-record proliferation of pirate stations.

Radio

There are three public radio stations run by RAI. All of the rest are private and there are no pirates, since all may transmit until 1995 when about 1000 licences will be issued.

Vatican Radio (526 AM, 93.3 FM and 105 FM) broadcasts the news in English at 7 am, 8.30 am, 6.15 pm and 9.50 pm. Pick up a pamphlet at the Vatican information office. RAI (846 AM) broadcasts news in English from 1 to 5 am at three minutes past the hour. You can pick up the BBC World Service on medium wave at 648 kHz, short wave at 6195 kHz, 9410 kHz, 12095 kHz, 15575 kHz, and on long wave at 198 kHz, depending on where you are and the time of day. Voice of America (VOA) can be found on short wave at 15205 kHz.

FILM & PHOTOGRAPHY

A roll of 36 exposures 100 ASA Kodak film costs around L8000. It costs up to L23,000 to have 36 exposures developed and L16,000 for 24 exposures. A roll of 36 slides costs L10,000 and L6000 for development.

Outlets where you can buy films and have your photos processed are numerous. A roll of film is called a *pellicola* but you will be understood if you ask for 'film'. Many places claim to process films in one hour but you will rarely get your photos back that quickly – count on late the next day if the outlet has its own processing equipment, or three to four days if it doesn't.

Enthusiasts should note that the light changes quite markedly throughout Italy. In the south it is stronger and brighter, whereas the regions of Tuscany and Umbria in central Italy are noted for their soft light. As you go farther north the atmosphere is generally misty, a combination of natural effect and air pollution.

HEALTH

It is important to be aware that the quality of medical treatment in Italian public hospitals varies throughout Italy. Basically, the farther north you travel the better the standard of care. You will generally stand a better chance of good, prompt treatment, for instance, in Trentino-Alto Adige than you would in Rome at a public hospital, although standards can vary between hospitals.

Private hospitals and clinics throughout the country generally provide excellent and reliable services. They are, however, very expensive if you have no medical insurance, although if it is necessary to pay for treatment at a public hospital, costs can also be very high.

Your embassy or consulate in Italy will be able to provide a list of recommended doctors in major cities; however, if you have a specific health complaint, it would be wise to obtain the necessary information and referrals for treatment before leaving home.

The public health system is administered by local centres known as Unità Sanitaria Locale (USL), listed under 'U' in the telephone book. Each USL centre is responsible for about 15,000 people and therefore they can be very numerous in large cities. Opening hours are limited, from 8 am to 12.30 pm Monday to Saturday, although some also open in the afternoon. You will need to check with the individual centres for their aftrenoon opening hours.

For emergency treatment, it's better to go straight to the Casualty (*pronto soccorso*) section of a public hospital, where you'll also receive emergency dental treatment. In major cities you are likely to find doctors who speak English, or a volunteer translator service. Often, first aid is also available at train stations, airports and ports.

Medical Cover

Citizens of EU countries are covered for emergency medical treatment in Italy on presentation of an E111 form. It is necessary to obtain information about this from your national health service before leaving home. Note that treatment in private hospitals is not covered. Australia also has a reciprocal arrangement with Italy so that emergency treatment is covered, Medicare in Australia publishes a brochure with the details. The USA, Canada and New Zealand do not have reciprocal arrangements, and citizens of these countries will be required to pay for any treatment in Italy themselves. Advise medical staff of any reciprocal arrangements *before* they begin treating you.

Travel Health Guides

Most books on travel health are geared towards the tropics, where health is a major issue. This is not the case in Italy, although you might consider the following books:

Travellers' Health, Dr Richard Dawood. Comprehensive, easy to read, authoritative and also highly recommended, although it's rather large to lug around.
Travel with Children, Maureen Wheeler, Lonely Planet Publications. Includes basic advice on travel health for younger children.

Predeparture Preparations

Health Insurance A travel insurance policy to cover theft, loss and medical problems is a wise idea. There are a wide variety of policies and your travel agent will have recommendations. The international student travel policies handled by STA Travel or student travel organisations are usually good value. Some policies offer lower and higher medical expenses options but the higher one is chiefly for countries like the USA which have extremely high medical costs. Check the small print:

- Some policies specifically exclude 'dangerous activities' which can include scuba diving, motorcycling, even trekking. If such activities are on your agenda you don't want that sort of policy.

A locally acquired motor cycle licence may not be valid under your policy.

- You may prefer a policy which pays doctors or hospitals direct rather than you having to pay on the spot and claim later. If you have to claim later make sure you keep all documentation. Some policies ask you to call back (reverse charges) to a centre in your home country where an immediate assessment of your problem is made.
- Check if the policy covers ambulances or an emergency flight home. If you have to stretch out you will need two seats and somebody has to pay for them!

Medical Kit A small, straightforward medical kit is a wise thing to carry. A possible kit list includes:

- Aspirin or Panadol – for pain or fever.
- an antihistamine (such as Benadryl) – useful as a decongestant for colds, allergies, to ease the itch from insect bites or stings or to help prevent motion sickness.
- antiseptic and an antibiotic powder or similar 'dry' spray for cuts and grazes.
- calamine lotion to ease irritation from bites or stings.
  bandages and Band-aids for minor injuries.
  scissors, tweezers and a digital thermometer.
- insect repellent, sunscreen, suntan lotion and chap stick.

Other useful medications might include laxatives and antifungal skin ointments, Lomotil or Imodium for diarrhoea, and rehydration solution if travelling with children.

General Preparations

Given the potential problems with language, make sure you are healthy before you leave home. If you are embarking on a long trip, make sure your teeth are OK: dentists are particularly expensive in Italy.

If you wear glasses, take a spare pair and your prescription. If you lose your glasses, you will be able to have them replaced within a few days by an optician (*ottico*).

If you require a particular medication, take an adequate supply as well as the prescription, with the generic rather than the brand name, as it will make getting replacements easier.

No vaccinations are required for entry into Italy, unless you have been travelling through a part of the world where yellow fever or cholera may be prevalent.

Basic Rules

Care in what you eat and drink is the most important health rule; stomach upsets are the most likely travel health problem, but in Italy the majority of these upsets will be relatively minor and probably due to overindulgence in the local food.

However, it pays to be careful with certain foods in Italy. In recent years there have been incidences of salmonella poisoning throughout the country related to infected eggs. Therefore, raw eggs and foods containing them should be avoided. In 1994, there was an outbreak of cholera in Bari. The simplest way to avoid being affected if such an outbreak occurs is to drink bottled water and eat seafood only if it is well cooked.

Water Tap water should be drinkable throughout Italy. *Acqua non potabile*, is a sign seen in some camping grounds and in every train toilet, that means the water is not drinkable. Drinking water from drink fountains is safe unless there is a sign telling you otherwise.

Italians have developed the habit of drinking bottled mineral water, but if you are on a tight budget this can be an expensive proposition. As a rule, if you do drink tap water, you should have no problems apart from a temporary reaction to the change of water.

In the hotter climate of southern Italy, make sure you drink enough – don't rely on feeling thirsty to indicate when you should drink. Not needing to urinate or very dark yellow urine is a danger sign.

Nutrition Make sure your diet is well balanced. You will have little trouble finding good-quality fruit and vegetables in Italy.

Everyday Health A normal body temperature is 98.6°F or 37°C; more than 2°C higher is a 'high' fever. A normal adult pulse rate is 60 to 80 beats per minute (children 80 to 100, babies 100 to 140). You should know how to take a temperature and a pulse rate. As a general rule the pulse increases about 20 beats per minute for each °C rise in fever.

Respiration (breathing) rate is also an indicator of illness. Count the number of breaths per minute: between 12 and 20 is normal for adults and older children (up to 30 for younger children, 40 for babies). People with a high fever or serious respiratory illness (such as pneumonia) breathe more quickly than normal. More than 40 shallow breaths a minute usually means pneumonia.

Many health problems can be avoided by taking care of yourself. Avoid climatic extremes: keep out of the sun when it's hot, dress warmly when it's cold. You can avoid insect bites by covering bare skin when insects are around, by screening windows or beds or by using insect repellents. Seek local advice: if you're told the water is unsafe due to jellyfish (a common occurrence in some parts of the country) don't go in.

Climatic & Geographical Considerations
Sunburn In the south of Italy during summer or at high altitude in the Alps you can get sunburnt surprisingly quickly, even through cloud. Use a sunscreen and take extra care to cover areas which don't normally see sun – eg your feet. A hat provides added protection, and you could also use zinc cream or some other barrier cream for your nose and lips. Calamine lotion is good for mild sunburn.

Prickly Heat Prickly heat is an itchy rash caused by excessive perspiration trapped under the skin. It usually strikes people who have just arrived in a hot climate and whose pores have not yet opened sufficiently to cope with greater sweating. Keeping cool by bathing often, using a mild talcum powder or even resorting to air-conditioning may help until you acclimatise.

Heat Exhaustion Dehydration or salt deficiency can cause heat exhaustion. Take time to acclimatise to high temperatures and make sure you get sufficient liquids. Salt defi-

ciency is characterised by fatigue, lethargy, headaches, giddiness and muscle cramps and in this case salt tablets may help. Vomiting or diarrhoea can deplete your liquid and salt levels.

Anhidrotic heat exhaustion, caused by an inability to sweat, is quite rare. Unlike the other forms of heat exhaustion, it is likely to strike people who have been in a hot climate for some time, rather than newcomers.

Heatstroke This serious and sometimes fatal condition can occur if the body's heat-regulating mechanism breaks down and the body temperature rises to dangerous levels. Long, continuous periods of exposure to high temperatures can leave you vulnerable to heatstroke. You should avoid excessive alcohol or strenuous activity when you first arrive in a hot climate.

The symptoms are feeling unwell, not sweating very much or at all and a high body temperature (39°C to 41°C). Where sweating has ceased, the skin becomes flushed and red. Severe, throbbing headaches and lack of coordination will also occur, and the sufferer may become confused or aggressive. Eventually the victim will become delirious or convulse. Hospitalisation is essential, but meanwhile get patients out of the sun, remove their clothing, cover them with a wet sheet or towel and then fan them continually.

Fungal Infections Hot-weather fungal infections are most likely to occur on the scalp, between the toes or fingers (athlete's foot), in the groin (jock itch or crotch rot) and on the body (ringworm). You get ringworm (which is a fungal infection, not a worm) from infected animals or by walking on damp areas, like shower floors.

To prevent fungal infections, wear loose, comfortable clothes, avoid artificial fibres, wash frequently and dry carefully. If you do get an infection, wash the infected area daily with a disinfectant or medicated soap and water, and rinse and dry well. Apply an antifungal powder, like the widely available Tinaderm. Try to expose the infected area to air or sunlight as much as possible and wash all towels and underwear in hot water as well as changing them often.

Cold Too much cold is just as dangerous as too much heat, particularly if it leads to hypothermia. Cold combined with wind and moisture is particularly risky. If you are trekking at high altitudes or in a cold, wet environment, be prepared.

Hypothermia occurs when the body loses heat faster than it can produce it and the core temperature of the body falls. It is surprisingly easy to progress from very cold to dangerously cold through a combination of wind, wet clothing, fatigue and hunger, even if the air temperature is above freezing.

Symptoms of hypothermia are exhaustion, numb skin (particularly toes and fingers), shivering, slurred speech, irrational or violent behaviour, lethargy, stumbling, dizzy spells, muscle cramps and violent bursts of energy. Irrationality may take the form of sufferers claiming they are warm and trying to take off their clothes.

To treat hypothermia, first get the patient out of the wind and/or rain, remove their clothing if it's wet and replace it with dry, warm clothing. Give them hot liquids – not alcohol – and some high-kilojoule, easily digestible food. This should be enough for the early stages of hypothermia, but if it has gone further it may be necessary to place victims in warm sleeping bags and get in with them.

Altitude Sickness Acute Mountain Sickness or AMS occurs at high altitudes, where the lack of oxygen affects most people to some extent. There is no hard and fast rule as to how high is too high: AMS has been fatal at altitudes of 3000 metres, although 3500 to 4500 metres is the usual range. It is always wise to sleep at a lower altitude than the greatest height reached during the day. Very few treks or ski runs in the Alps reach heights of 3000 metres or more – Mont Blanc on the border with France is one exception – so it's unlikely to be a major concern.

Headaches, nausea, dizziness, a dry cough, insomnia, breathlessness and loss of appetite are all signs to heed. Mild altitude problems will generally abate after a day or so, but if the symptoms persist or become worse the only treatment is to descend – even 500 metres can help.

Motion Sickness Eating lightly before and during a trip will reduce the chances of motion sickness. If you are prone to motion sickness try to find a place that minimises disturbance – near the wing on aircraft, close to midships on boats, near the centre on buses. Fresh air usually helps, reading or cigarette smoke doesn't. Commercial anti-motion-sickness preparations, which can cause drowsiness, have to be taken before the trip commences; when you're feeling sick it's too late. Ginger is a natural preventative and is available in capsule form.

Diseases of Insanitation

Diarrhoea Despite all your precautions, you may still have a bout of mild travellers' diarrhoea, but a few rushed toilet trips with no other symptoms is not indicative of a serious problem. Moderate diarrhoea, involving half-a-dozen loose movements in a day, is more of a nuisance. Dehydration is the main danger with any diarrhoea, particularly for children, so fluid replenishment is the number one treatment. Weak black tea with a little sugar, soda water, or soft drinks allowed to go flat and diluted 50% with water are all good. With severe diarrhoea a rehydrating solution is necessary to replace minerals and salts, and you should see a doctor. Stick to a bland diet as you recover.

Infectious Diseases

Cholera Cholera vaccination is not very effective. The bacteria responsible for this disease are waterborne, so that attention to the basic rules of eating and drinking should protect the traveller.

Outbreaks of cholera are generally widely reported, so you can avoid such problem areas. The disease is characterised by a sudden onset of acute diarrhoea with 'rice water' stools, vomiting, muscular cramps and extreme weakness. You need medical help – but treat for dehydration, which can be extreme.

Viral Gastroenteritis This is caused not by bacteria but, as the name suggests, by a virus. It is characterised by stomach cramps, diarrhoea, and sometimes by vomiting and/or a slight fever. All you can do is rest and drink lots of fluids.

Hepatitis Hepatitis A (HAV) is a very common problem amongst travellers to areas with poor sanitation, so it really shouldn't be a concern in Italy. Protection is through the new vaccine Havrix or the antibody gammaglobulin. The antibody is short-lasting.

The disease is spread by contaminated food or water. The symptoms are fever, chills, headache, fatigue, feelings of weakness and aches and pains, followed by loss of appetite, nausea, vomiting, abdominal pain, dark urine, light coloured faeces, jaundiced skin and the whites of the eyes may turn yellow. In some cases you may feel unwell, tired, have no appetite, experience aches and pains and be jaundiced. You should seek medical advice, but in general there is not much you can do apart from rest, drink lots of fluids, eat lightly and avoid fatty foods. People who have had hepatitis must forego alcohol for six months after the illness, as hepatitis attacks the liver and it needs that amount of time to recover.

Hepatitis B (HBV) is spread through contact with infected blood, blood products or bodily fluids, for example through sexual contact, unsterilised needles and blood transfusions. Other risk situations include having a shave or tattoo in a local shop, or having your ears pierced. The symptoms of type B are much the same as type A except that they are more severe and may lead to irreparable liver damage or even liver cancer. Although there is no treatment for hepatitis B, an effective prophylactic vaccine is readily available in most countries. The immunisation schedule requires two injections at least a month

apart followed by a third dose five months after the second.

Hepatitis Non-A Non-B is a blanket term formerly used for several different strains of hepatitis, which have now been separately identified. Hepatitis C (HCV) is similar to B but is less common. Hepatitis D (HDV) is also similar to B and always occurs in concert with it; its occurrence is currently limited to IV drug users. Hepatitis E (HEV), however, is similar to A and is spread in the same manner, by water or food contamination.

Tests are available, but are very expensive. Travellers shouldn't be too paranoid about this apparent proliferation of hepatitis strains; following the same precautions as for Hepatitis types A and B should be all that's necessary to avoid them.

Rabies Rabies is still found in Italy, but only in isolated areas of the Alps. It is caused by a bite or scratch by an infected animal. Dogs are a noted carrier. Any bite, scratch or even lick from a mammal in an area where rabies does exist should be cleaned immediately and thoroughly. Scrub with soap and running water, and then clean with an alcohol solution. If there is any possibility that the animal is infected, medical help should be sought immediately. Even if the animal is not rabid, all bites should be treated seriously as they can become infected or can result in tetanus. A rabies vaccination is now available and should be considered if you are in a high-risk category – eg, if you intend to explore caves (bat bites could be dangerous) or work with animals.

Sexually Transmitted Diseases Sexual contact with an infected sexual partner spreads these diseases. While abstinence is the only 100% preventative, using condoms is also effective. Gonorrhoea and syphilis are the most common of these diseases; sores, blisters or rashes around the genitals, discharges or pain when urinating are common symptoms. Symptoms may be less marked or not observed at all in women. Syphilis symptoms eventually disappear completely but the disease continues and can cause severe problems in later years. The treatment of gonorrhoea and syphilis is by antibiotics.

There are numerous other sexually transmitted diseases, for most of which effective treatment is available. However, there is no cure for herpes and there is also no cure for HIV/AIDS.

HIV/AIDS HIV, the Human Immunodeficiency Virus, may develop into AIDS, Acquired Immune Deficiency Syndrome. HIV is a major problem in many countries and has become a considerable problem in Italy. Any exposure to blood, blood products or bodily fluids may put the individual at risk. Apart from abstinence, the most effective preventative is always to practise safe sex using condoms. It is impossible to detect the HIV-positive status of an otherwise healthy-looking person without a blood test.

HIV/AIDS can also be spread through infected blood transfusions and by dirty needles – acupuncture, tattooing and ear or nose piercing can potentially be as dangerous as intravenous drug use if the equipment is not clean. Needles used in Italian hospitals are reliable.

If you require treatment or tests for a suspected STD or for HIV/AIDS, head for the nearest USL or public hospital. Each USL area has its own Family Planning Centre (Consultorio Familiare) where you can go for contraceptives, pregnancy tests and information about abortion; these are listed under each USL office in the telephone book, otherwise ask at the USL office. See the Emergency section in the Rome chapter for further information.

Fear of HIV infection should never preclude treatment for serious medical conditions. Although there may be a risk of infection, it is very small indeed.

Cuts, Bites & Stings

Cuts & Scratches Skin punctures can easily become infected in hot climates and may be difficult to heal. Treat any cut with an antiseptic solution and Mercurochrome. Where possible avoid bandages and Band-aids, which can keep wounds wet.

Bites & Stings Bee and wasp stings are usually painful rather than dangerous. Calamine lotion will give relief, or use ice packs to reduce the pain and swelling.

Snakes There is only one dangerous snake in Italy – the viper, which is found throughout Italy (except in Sardinia). To minimise your chances of being bitten, always wear boots, socks and long trousers when walking through undergrowth where snakes may be present. Don't put your hands into holes and crevices, and be careful when collecting firewood.

Viper bites do not cause instantaneous death, and an antivenene is widely available in pharmacies. Keep the victim calm and still, wrap the bitten limb tightly, as you would for a sprained ankle, and attach a splint to immobilise it. Then seek medical help, if possible with the dead snake for identification. Don't attempt to catch the snake if there is even a remote possibility of being bitten again. Tourniquets and sucking out the poison are now comprehensively discredited.

Jellyfish Italian beaches are occasionally inundated with jellyfish. Their stings are rather painful, not dangerous. Dousing in vinegar will de-activate any stingers which have not 'fired'. Calamine lotion, antihistamines and analgesics may reduce the reaction and relieve the pain.

Lice All lice cause itching and discomfort. They make themselves at home in your hair (head lice), clothing (body lice) or in pubic hair (crabs). You catch lice through direct contact with infected people or by sharing combs, clothing and the like. Powder or shampoo treatment will kill the lice, and infected clothing should then be washed in very hot water.

Leeches & Ticks Leeches may be present in damp forest conditions; they attach themselves to your skin to suck your blood. Trekkers often get them on their legs or in their boots. Salt or a lighted cigarette end will make them fall off. Do not pull them off, as the bite is then more likely to become infected. An insect repellent may keep them away. Vaseline, alcohol or oil will persuade a tick to let go.

Always check your body if you have been walking through a tick-infested area. In recent years, there have been several reported deaths in Sardinia related to tick bites and health authorities have yet to pinpoint to cause.

Women's Health

Gynaecological Problems Poor diet, lowered resistance due to the use of antibiotics and even contraceptive pills can lead to vaginal infections when travelling in hot climates. Keeping the genital area clean, and wearing skirts or loose-fitting trousers and cotton underwear will help to prevent infections.

Yeast infections, characterised by a rash, itch and discharge, can be treated with a vinegar or even lemon-juice douche or with yoghurt. Nystatin suppositories are the usual medical prescription. Trichomonas is a more serious infection; symptoms are a discharge and a burning sensation when urinating. Male sexual partners must also be treated, and if a vinegar-water douche is not effective medical attention should be sought. Metronidazole (Flagyl) is the prescribed drug.

Pregnancy Most miscarriages occur during the first three months of pregnancy, so this is the most risky time to travel as far as your own health is concerned. Miscarriage is not uncommon, and can occasionally lead to severe bleeding. The last three months should also be spent within reasonable distance of good medical care. A baby born as early as 24 weeks stands a chance of survival, but only in a good modern hospital. Pregnant women should avoid all unnecessary medication, but vaccinations and malarial prophylactics should still be taken where possible. Additional care should be

taken to prevent illness and particular attention should be paid to diet and nutrition. Alcohol and nicotine, for example, should be avoided.

Women travellers often find that their periods become irregular or even cease while they're on the road. Remember that a missed period in these circumstances doesn't necessarily indicate pregnancy. There is a Consultorio Familiare attached to each USL (listed in the telephone book), where you can seek advice and have a urine test to determine whether you are pregnant or not.

Some women experience irregular periods when travelling, due to the upset in routine. If you use contraceptive pills, don't forget to take time zones into account, and beware that the pills may not be absorbed if you suffer intestinal problems. Ask your physician about these matters. If you think you've run into problems in Italy, contact the nearest Consultorio Familiare.

WOMEN TRAVELLERS

Italy is not a dangerous country for women, but women travelling alone will often find themselves plagued by unwanted attention from men. This attention usually involves catcalls, hisses and whistles and, as such, is more annoying than anything else. Lone women will also find it difficult to remain alone – you will have Italian men harassing you as you walk along the street, drink a coffee in a bar or try to read a book in a park. Usually the best response is to ignore them, but if that doesn't work, politely tell them that you are waiting for your husband (marita) or boyfriend (fidanzato) and, if necessary, walk away.

Avoid becoming aggressive as this almost always results in an unpleasant confrontation. If all else fails, approach the nearest member of the police or carabinieri.

Basically most of the attention falls into the nuisance/harassment category. However, women on their own should use their common sense. Avoid walking alone in deserted and dark streets, and look for hotels which are centrally located and within easy walking distance of places where you can eat at night (unsafe areas for women are noted throughout this book). Women should also avoid hitchhiking alone.

Women will find that, the farther south they travel, the more likely they are to be harassed. It is advisable to dress more conservatively in the south, particularly if you are travelling to small towns and villages. In cities where there is a high petty crime rate, such as Rome, Naples, Palermo, Syracuse and Bari, women on their own are regarded as prime targets for bag-snatchers and should be very careful about walking in deserted streets.

Rome is one of the worst cities when it comes to overattentive males. Watch out for men with wandering hands on crowded buses. Either keep your back to the wall or make a loud fuss if someone starts fondling your backside.

Recommended reading is the *Handbook for Women Travellers* by M & G Moss and the Rough Guide *Women Travel*.

TRAVEL WITH CHILDREN

Successful travel with children can require a special effort. Don't try to overdo things by packing too much into the time available, and make sure activities include the kids as well. Remember that visits to museums and galleries can be tiring even for adults. Children might also be more interested in some of the major archaeological sites, such as Pompeii, the Colosseum and the Forum in Rome, and Greek temples in the south and Sicily. If travelling in northern Italy, you might want to make a stopover at *Gardaland* the amusement park near Lago di Garda in Lombardy. Allow time for the kids to play, either in a park or in the hotel room; taking a toddler to a playground for an hour or so in the morning can make an amazing difference to their tolerance for sightseeing in the afternoon. Include older children in the planning of the trip – if they have helped to work out where they will be going, they will be much more interested when they get there.

Discounts are available for children (usually under 12 years of age) on public transport and admission to museums, galleries etc.

There are special sections on activities for families in the chapters on Rome, Florence and Venice, as well as in several other cities and towns. These include activities which might interest the kids and usually point out where you can find a playground for young children. Always make a point of asking at tourist offices if they know of any special family or children's activities and for suggestions on hotels which cater for kids. Families should book accommodation in advance where possible to avoid inconvenience.

Chemists (*farmacie*) sell baby formula in powder or liquid form as well as sterilising solutions, such as Milton. Disposable nappies are widely available at supermarkets, chemists (where they are more expensive) and sometimes in larger *cartolerie* (stores selling papergoods). A pack of around 30 Pampers costs around L18,000. Fresh cow's milk is sold in cartons in bars (which have a 'Latteria' sign) and in supermarkets. If it essential that you have milk, you should carry an emergency carton of UHT milk since bars usually close at 8 pm. In many out-of-the-way areas in southern Italy the locals use only UHT milk.

For more information, see Lonely Planet's *Travel with Children* by Maureen Wheeler.

SENIOR TRAVELLERS

Senior citizens are entitled to discounts on public transport and on admission fees at some museums in Italy. It is always important to ask. The minimum qualifying age is generally 60 years. You should also seek information in your own country on travel packages and discounts for senior travellers, through senior citizens' organisations and travel agents. Consider booking accommodation in advance to avoid inconvenience.

DISABLED TRAVELLERS

Italy has only recently started to make proper provisions for disabled people, but little is being done about the uneven pavements in most cities, or about the endless flights of stairs at train stations and in many medieval hill towns. If you have a physical disability, get in touch with your national support organisation to see if it has specific information on facilities in Italy. If not, it should at least be able to provide general travel advice. The Italian State Tourist Office in your country will provide advice on facilities for the disabled in Italy, as well as on Italian associations for the disabled.

The UK-based Royal Association for Disability & Rehabilitation (RADAR) publishes a useful guide called *Holidays & Travel Abroad: A Guide for Disabled People*, which gives a good overview of facilities available to disabled travellers throughout Europe. Contact RADAR (☎ 1-250 3222) 250 City Rd, London EC1V 8AS.

The Italian travel agency, CIT, can advise on hotels which have special facilities, such as ramps etc. By booking train travel in advance through CIT, you can also request that wheelchair ramps be provided on arrival of your train.

GAY & LESBIAN TRAVELLERS

Homosexuality is legal in Italy and is well tolerated in major cities and particularly in the north of the country. However, overt displays of affection by homosexual couples could attract a negative response in smaller towns and villages. Generally speaking, friendships between Italian men are very physical anyway, involving physical contact that most Anglo-Saxons would find excessive. As such, the sight of two men (or two women) walking down a street arm in arm is hardly unusual.

Cities such as Rome, Florence and Milan have several gay discos, which are generally listed in the Leisure sections of local newspapers. The national organisation for gay men is Arci Gay (☎ 051-43 67 00), which is affiliated with the Communist Party's youth section, at Piazza di Porta Saragozza 2, PO Box 691, 40100 Bologna. The corresponding organisation for lesbians is based in Rome: ARCI-Co-ordinamento Donne (☎ 06-325 09 21), Via F Carrara 24. The bimonthly newsletter for lesbians, *Bolletino delle Connessioni Lesbiche Italiane*, is available here.

Babilonia is the national gay magazine, published monthly, and *Guida Gay Italia* is published annually. Both provide extensive information and are available at newspaper stands. Further information about gay and lesbian discos can be found in the Entertainment section of the major city sections.

DANGERS & ANNOYANCES

Theft is the main problem for travellers in Italy. Pickpockets and bag-snatchers operate in most major cities and are particularly active in Naples and Rome. The best way to avoid being robbed is to wear a money belt under your clothing. You should keep all important items, such as money, passport, other papers and tickets in your money belt at all times. If you are carrying a bag or camera, ensure that you wear the strap across your body and have the bag on the side away from the road to deter snatch thieves, who often operate from motorbikes and scooters. Since the aim of young motorcycle bandits is often fun rather than gain, you are just as likely to find yourself relieved of your sunglasses – or worse, of an earring. Motorcycle bandits are very active in Naples, Rome, Syracuse and Palermo.

You should also watch out for groups of dishevelled-looking women and children. They generally work in groups of four of five and carry paper or cardboard which they use to distract your attention while they swarm around and riffle through your pockets and bag. Never underestimate their skill – they are lightning fast and very adept. Their favourite haunts are in and near major train stations, at tourist sights (such as the Colosseum) and in shopping areas. If you notice that you have been targeted by a group, either take evasive action, such as crossing the street, or shout *va via!* (go away!) in a loud, angry voice.

Pickpockets often hang out on crowded buses (the No 64 in Rome, which runs from Stazione Termini to the Vatican, is notorious) and in crowded areas such as markets. There is only one way to deter pickpockets: simply *do not* carry any money or valuables in your pockets, and be very careful about your bags.

Be careful even in hotels and don't leave valuables lying around your room. You should also be cautious of sudden friendships, particularly if it turns out that your new-found *amico* or *amica* wants to sell you something. Parked cars are also prime targets for thieves, particularly those with foreign number plates or rental company stickers. Try removing the stickers, or cover them and leave a local newspaper on the seat to make it look like a local car.

Never leave valuables in your car – in fact, try not to leave anything in the car if you can help it and certainly not overnight. It is a good idea to pay extra to leave your car in supervised car parks, although there is no guarantee tit will be completely safe. Throughout Italy, particularly in the south, service stations along the autostradas are favourite haunts of thieves, who can clean out your car in the time it takes to have a cup of coffee. If possible, park the car where you can keep an eye on it. When driving in cities, you also need to beware of snatch thieves when you pull up at traffic lights. Keep the doors locked, and if you have the windows open, ensure that there is nothing valuable on the dashboard. Car theft is a major problem in the regions of Campania and Apulia, particularly the cities of Naples, Bari, Foggia and Brindisi. Beware also of unofficial parking attendants, who say you can leave your car double-parked as long as you leave them your keys: you might return to find that both the attendant and your car have disappeared.

Horror tales abound about women being dragged to the ground by thieves trying to snatch their bags, about people losing wallets, watches and cameras on crowded buses or in a flurry of newspaper-waving children. The problem is that these things really do happen! Certainly even the most cautious travellers are still prey to expert thieves, but there is no need to be paranoid. By taking a few basic precautions, you can greatly lessen the risk of being robbed.

In case of theft or loss, always report the incident at the questura within 24 hours and ask for a statement, otherwise your travel insurance company won't pay out.

In case of emergency, you can contact the police throughout Italy on ☎ 113.

Traffic & Pedestrians

Italian traffic can at best be described as chaotic, at worst downright dangerous for the unprepared tourist. Drivers are not keen to stop for pedestrians, even at pedestrian crossings, and are more likely to swerve. Italians simply step off the sidewalk and walk through the (swerving) traffic with determination – it is a practice which seems to work, so if you feel uncertain about crossing a busy road, wait for the next Italian. In many cities, roads which appear to be for one-way traffic have special lanes for buses travelling in the opposite direction – always look both ways before stepping onto the road.

Pollution

Italy has a poor record when it comes to environmental concerns. Few Italians would think twice about dropping litter in the streets, illegally dumping household refuse in the country or driving a car or motorbike with a faulty or nonexistent muffler.

Tourists will be affected in a variety of ways by the surprising disregard Italians have for their country, which is of considerable natural and artistic beauty. Noise and air pollution are problems in the major cities, both caused mainly by heavy traffic. A headache after a day of sightseeing in Rome is likely to be caused by breathing carbon monoxide and lead, rather than simple tiredness. While cities such as Rome, Florence and Milan have banned normal traffic from their historic centres, there are still more than enough cars, buses and motorbikes in and around the inner city areas to pollute the air.

Periodically, particularly in summer, there are pollution alerts. The elderly, children and people with respiratory problems are warned to stay indoors. If you fit into one of these categories, keep yourself informed through the tourist office or your hotel proprietor.

When booking a hotel room it is a good idea to ask if it is quiet – although this might mean you will have to decide between a view and sleep.

One of the most annoying things about Rome is that the footpaths are littered with dog's poo – so be careful where you plant your feet.

Italy's beaches are generally heavily polluted by industrial waste, sewage and oil spills from the Mediterranean's considerable sea traffic. There are clean beaches in Sardinia, Sicily, the less populated areas of the south and around Elba.

Italian-Style Service

It requires a lot of patience to deal with the Italian concept of service. What for Italians is simply a way of life, can be horrifying for the foreigner – like the bank clerk who wanders off to have a cigarette just as it is your turn (after a one-hour wait) to be served, or the postal worker who has far more important work to do at a desk than to sell stamps to customers. Anyone in a uniform or behind a counter (including police officers, waiters and shop assistants) is likely to regard you with imperious contempt. Long queues are the norm in banks, post offices and any government offices.

It pays to remain calm and patient. Aggressive, demanding and angry customers stand virtually no chance of getting what they want.

Drugs

Drug laws in Italy are harsh, and anyone (including foreigners) found with even the smallest amount of drugs could find themselves hauled off to prison. The possession of any amount of drugs, including marijuana or hash, is illegal and penalties are harsh. Following a referendum in 1993, the Italian government is changing its 'zero tolerance' drug laws to make penalties less harsh for drug users, but the sensible option will still be to avoid drugs altogether.

Police

If you run into trouble in Italy, you're likely to end up dealing with either *la polizia* (police) or the *carabinieri* (military police). The police are a civil force and take their orders from the Ministry of the Interior, while the carabinieri fall under the Ministry of Defence. There is a considerable duplication of their roles, despite a 1981 reform of the police forces which intended to merge the two. Both forces are responsible for public order and security, which means that you can call either, in the event of a robbery, violent attack etc.

The carabinieri wear a dark-blue uniform with a red stripe and drive dark-blue cars with a red stripe. Many of them come from the south and they are the butt of 'dumb-jokes' (much like the Polish and Irish), although they are well trained and tend to be helpful. You are most likely to be pulled over by the carabinieri rather than the police when you are speeding etc. Their police station is called a *caserma*.

The police wear powder-blue pants with a fuchsia stripe and a navy-blue jacket and drive light blue cars with a white stripe, with 'polizia' written on the side. They are generally held to be arrogant and not very helpful. However, tourists who want to report thefts, and people wanting to get a residence permit, will have to deal with them. Their headquarters are called the questura, and addresses and telephone numbers are given in the Emergency sections throughout this book.

WORK

It is illegal for non-EU citizens to work in Italy without a work permit, but trying to obtain one is extremely difficult. EU citizens are allowed to work in Italy, but they still need to obtain a permesso di soggiorno from the main questura in the town where they have found work. See the Visas & Embassies section for more information about these permits. A letter from the prospective employer promising work is necessary.

'Black economy' work (for those without permits) is generally untaxed, but in Italy even illegal workers can pay their taxes. Some employers will be prepared to hire people without permits, but will require them to have a tax number *(codice fiscale)*, which means that you are registered as a taxpayer, even though you are working illegally. If you do need to get a codice fiscale, your prospective employer will explain how to go about it.

The easiest source of work for foreigners is teaching English, but even with full qualifications an American, Australian, Canadian or New Zealander might find it difficult to secure a permanent position. Most of the larger, more reputable schools will hire only people with work permits, but their attitude can become more flexible if demand for teachers is high and they come across someone with good qualifications. The more professional schools will require a TEFL (Teaching English as a Foreign Language) certificate. It is advisable to apply for work early in the year, in order to be considered for positions available in October (language school years correspond roughly to the Italian school year: late September to the end of June).

There are numerous schools throughout the country which hire people without work permits or qualifications, but the pay is usually low (around L15,000 an hour). It is more lucrative to advertise your services and pick up private students (although rates vary wildly, ranging from as low as L10,000 to up to L50,000 an hour). In a large city like Rome the average rate is around L30,000, while in smaller provincial towns, where the market is more limited, even qualified private teachers will have to charge as low as L15,000 to L20,000 in order to attract students. Although you can get away with absolutely no qualifications or experience, it might be a good idea to bring along a few English grammar books (including exercises) to help you at least appear professional.

Most people get started by placing advertisements in shop windows and on university notice boards, or in a local publication, such as *Wanted in Rome* or *Porta Portese* in Rome or *Secondamano* in Milan. All are available at newspaper stands.

Many foreigners also find illegal, untaxed work in bars, restaurants, or as babysitters. To find this type of work, ask around, or keep an eye on the employment columns in the publications just mentioned. Another option is au pair work. A useful guide is *The Au Pair and Nanny's Guide to Working Abroad* by S Griffith & S Legg (Vacation Work, paperback). By the same publisher is *Work Your Way Around the World* by Susan Griffith.

Busking is common in Italy, although theoretically buskers require a municipal permit. Although Italians tend not to stop and gather around street performers, they are usually generous. Selling goods on the street is also illegal unless you have a municipal permit, and you are likely to run into trouble unless you manage to find a spot at a flea market.

ACTIVITIES

If the museums, galleries and sights are not enough to occupy your time in Italy, there are numerous options for getting off the beaten tourist track. From mountaineering to courses in the history of art, Italy offers a wide range of outdoor and cerebral pursuits.

Hiking & Mountaineering

The Alps, in particular the spectacular Dolomites, offer well-marked trails and strategically placed rifugi for the long-distance hiker. With careful planning it is possible to walk for as many days as you want, without carrying large quantities of supplies, by staying and buying your food at the rifugi. However, hikers still need to be well prepared in the Alps – even at the height of summer the weather can change suddenly. Hikers planning to tackle longer and more difficult trails, particularly at high altitudes, should ensure that they leave basic details of their route with someone. They should also be well informed on weather predictions and prepared for cold weather, rain and snow (the first snow can fall in September). It is also a good idea to carry a lightweight thermal blanket in case you need to leave an injured person to get help, as help might not arrive until the next day. While there are many rifugi along the way, hikers should still carry lightweight, high-energy food, such as chocolate or muesli bars, and ensure that they have plenty of water.

Guided treks are a good idea for inexperienced walkers, although there are also guided treks along more difficult trails, These treks usually involve the use of ropes which means you need to have mountaineering skills and the correct equipment (see the Alpine sections of the northern Italy chapters for further information).

The Apennines also have good walking trails, and interesting areas include the Parco Nazionale d'Abruzzo and the Sila Massif in Calabria. The Alpi Apuane in Tuscany also have well-marked and challenging trails. In Sardinia the rugged landscape offers some spectacular hikes in the eastern ranges, such as Gennargentu, and the gorges near Dorgali. See the relevant sections for further information.

Downhill skiing *(lo sci)* is generally from December to late March

Skiing

There are numerous excellent ski resorts in the Italian Alps and, again, the Dolomites provide the most dramatic scenery. Options include downhill *(lo sci)* and cross-country *(sci di fondo)* skiing, as well as ski mountaineering *(sci alpinismo)* – only for the adventurous and advanced, where skiers head well away from the organised runs and combine their mountaineering and skiing skills.

Skiing is quite expensive because of the costs of ski lifts and accommodation, but a Settimana Bianca package can reduce the expense. It is not expensive, on the other hand, to hire ski equipment – and this factor should be weighed up against the inconvenience of bringing your own gear. Cross-country skiing costs less because you don't pay for the lifts.

The season in Italy generally extends from December to late March, although at higher altitudes and in particularly good years it can be longer. There is year-round skiing in areas such as the Marmolada glacier in Trentino-Alto Adige, and Mont Blanc (Monte Bianco)

and the Matterhorn (Monte Cervino) in the Valle d'Aosta.

The five major (read: most fashionable and expensive) ski resorts in Italy are Cortina d'Ampezzo in the Veneto, Madonna di Campiglio, San Martino di Castrozza and Canazei all in Trentino, and Courmayeur in the Valle d'Aosta. There are many other, less expensive resorts which also offer excellent facilities (see the Alpine sections of the northern Italy chapters for more information).

Water Sports

Windsurfing and sailing are extremely popular in Italy, and at most beach resorts it is possible to rent boats and equipment – generally for a hefty fee. There are also various diving schools, but the scenery above water is much more interesting. See the Things to See & Do and Activities sections throughout this book for boat and windsurfing equipment hire at water resorts.

Cycling

This is a good option for people who can't afford a car but want to see some of the more out-of-the-way places. The only problem is that more than 75% of Italy is mountainous or hilly, so you will need some stamina and a good bike. A mountain bike would be a good idea, enabling you to tackle some of the Alpine trails as well. Cycling and mountain biking are becoming increasingly popular in Italy and you'll find that most tourist offices will be able to offer information on bike hire, mountain bike trails and guided mountain bike rides. People planning to cycle around Italy could easily bring their own bikes, or might consider buying one once they arrive in Italy (see the Bicycle section of the Getting Around chapter for details). Bikes can be transported on aeroplanes for a surprisingly low fee and, within Italy, they can be transported free on ferries to Sicily and Sardinia, and relatively cheaply on trains. The hills of Tuscany are very popular for cycling, particularly around Florence and Siena, from where you could explore the hills around Fiesole, San Gimignano and Chianti, just to name a few possibilities. A bike would be particularly useful for exploring Sardinia. In Umbria, areas such as the Valnerina and the Piano Grande at Monte Vettore have beautiful trails and quiet country roads to explore. Serious cyclists will know where to go for the most challenging routes – the torturous, winding road up to the Passo Stelvio is one of the most famous. Mountain bikers have endless possibilities and are well catered for by tourist offices throughout the country with information, and maps of trails.

Courses

Travelling to Italy to study the language is becoming increasingly popular. Courses are offered by private schools and universities throughout Italy and are a great way to learn Italian, while enjoying the opportunity to live in an Italian city or town.

The cheapest option is the Università per Stranieri in Perugia, where the cost per month is L240,000 (compared to an average of L600,000 at a private school in Florence). Individual schools and universities are listed under the relevant towns throughout this

book. Accommodation can usually be arranged through the school.

Many schools also offer courses in painting, art history, sculpture, architecture and cooking; however, all these courses can be expensive at an average of L600,000 a month.

It is also possible to undertake serious academic study at an Italian university, although obviously only if you have a very good command of the language.

Italian cultural institutes will provide information about study in Italy, as well as enrolment forms. Otherwise, check with travel agencies in your country for organised study tours to Italy. In England, an organisation called Italian Study Tours (☎ 0171-482 3767), 35 Murray Mews, London NW1 9RH, organises small groups to study the language in a Tuscan farmhouse for one week.

The more adventurous traveller might want to take a course in rock climbing, ski mountaineering, or hang-gliding, just to name a few of the possibilities. Mountain guide groups offering courses are listed in the Alpine sections of the northern Italy chapters, or you can always get information from local tourist offices in the relevant areas.

HIGHLIGHTS

Being a serious tourist in Italy can be a mind-numbing experience. There are so many important churches, museums, galleries and archaeological sights – far too many to take in during the average holiday. Overzealous sightseers will find that after the first two or three major museums they might start to resent the sight of another sculpture or painting. Constant visits to archaeological sites and churches will start to seem like marathon runs and you will find yourself yearning for an armchair and TV.

The secret is not to overdo it. Try to do some research beforehand to determine which museums, galleries, churches etc you particularly want to see – while allowing enough time in your schedule for detours and surprises. Also make time for some long lunches and allow a few hours here and there to enjoy a coffee or wine in one of the country's beautiful piazzas. Instead of making a whirlwind tour of every archaeological site, choose some of the better ones and take along a picnic.

Following are a few of the highlights and 'musts' of a trip to Italy, including some lesser known, out-of-the-way places to visit. Don't take it as a definitive list of things to see, but rather as a start for your own further research.

Museums & Galleries

The Vatican Museums in Rome and the magnificent Uffizi Gallery in Florence are absolutely not to be missed, but try to take your time. The Museo Nazionale del Bargello in Florence, with its excellent sculpture collection, is another must, as is the Galleria dell' Accademia, which houses Michelangelo's *David*. In Venice the Peggy Guggenheim Gallery of Modern Art is well worth a visit. The Museo Archeologico Nazionale in Naples houses one of the most important archaeological collections in the world (although large sections of the museum are usually closed). A visit to the Museo Nazionale di Villa Giulia in Rome to see its collection of Etruscan treasures will make a tour of the Etruscan sites in Lazio (see the following section) more enjoyable.

Archaeological Sites

The Colosseum, the Roman Forum and the Palatine Hill are obvious musts in Rome, but also take a look at the Baths of Caracalla and at least one of the catacombs. Near Rome, at Tivoli, is the Villa Adriana, the massive villa of the Roman emperor Hadrian.

The best Etruscan sites are also near Rome and include the painted tombs of Tarquinia and the *tumuli*, tombs under huge mounds of earth, at Cerveteri. Both towns also have small Etruscan museums worth a look.

In Campania, the excavations at Pompeii should not be missed. Travelling farther south, at Paestum, are the first important relics of Magna Graecia, a group of well-preserved temples.

Other temples well worth a visit are at Agrigento, Selinunte and Segesta in Sicily. The backdrop to the Greek theatres at Segesta and at Taormina makes them particularly evocative. The archaeological park in Syracuse is also recommended. Still in Sicily, visit the imperial Roman villa at Casale, just out of Piazza Armerina, to see the fabulous mosaics.

Also visit the nuragic site, Su Nuraxi, at Barumini in Sardinia.

Churches

The phenomenal number of churches in Italy should satisfy even the most obsessive lover of religious architecture. A few highlights include the cathedrals in Florence, Milan, Siena and Orvieto, and that at Monreale, near Palermo, for its beautiful mosaics. There is also Pisa's stunning Romanesque cathedral, which stands in the Campo dei Miracoli with the Leaning Tower and baptistry. The Basilica di San Marco in Venice is one of the world's great churches, with its dazzling mosaics and decorations. The Basilica di San Vitale in Ravenna is notable both for its mosaics and for the design of the church. Apulia has several Romanesque churches worth a visit, the most beautiful being undoubtedly the cathedral at Trani. The Romanesque Cattedrale di Santa Maria Annunziata in Otranto, Apulia, is worth a visit to see the extraordinary 12th-century mosaic of *The Tree of Life* which covers its floor. Most tourists will eventually make their way to St Peter's Basilica in Rome, and you can even attend a mass said by the pope.

Historic Towns

There are so many fascinating and beautiful medieval towns in Italy that it seems a shame to confine your travels to the major cities. In Tuscany you could visit San Gimignano, Volterra and Arezzo, and in Umbria make a tour of the medieval hill towns, many still surrounded by their walls and crowned with ruined castles. The more interesting towns include Assisi, Spoleto, Gubbio and Orvieto, but also try to visit the villages of Spello and Narni. In the Marches, visit the beautiful town of Urbino, birthplace of Raphael. Ravenna, with its extraordinary Byzantine churches and mosaics, is one of the great highlights of a visit to Italy.

In Liguria walk along the coast of the Riviera di Levante to visit the Cinque Terre, five tiny villages linked by a walking track. One of the most fascinating towns in Italy is Matera in Basilicata. Wandering around its famous stone houses *(sassi)* is an experience not easily forgotten. Positano is the most beautiful town on the Amalfi coast, but it's also worth visiting Ravello.

National Parks

If you want to take a break from your grand tour of the tourist sights, head for the Dolomites, in particular the stunning park, Fanes-Sennes-Braies. Near Madonna di Campiglio is one of the more beautiful Alpine valleys, the Val di Genova in the Parco Nazionale Adamello-Brenta. The Parco Nazionale di Gran Paradiso, straddling the Valle d'Aosta and Piedmont, and the Parco Nazionale d'Abruzzo are also worth putting on the itinerary. There are some spectacular locations in Sardinia, including Capo Testa near Santa Teresa di Gallura; the long sandy beaches of the Costa Verde, notably the isolated Piscinas; and the Codula di Luna and the Gola di Gorroppu near Dorgali.

For an unforgettable experience, go on a tour of Sicily's volcanoes. Climb Vulcano and Stromboli in the Lipari Islands, and Mt Etna, one of the world's largest active volcanoes.

General Sights

In every part of the country you will come across monuments, works of art, views and special places which have the capacity to surprise even the most world-weary traveller. Here are a few of the better ones: Michelangelo's *Pietà* in St Peter's Basilica, Rome; the Grand Canal in Venice; the *Pala d'Oro* (gold altarpiece) in Basilica di San Marco, Venice; the view of Tuscany from the top of the town hall tower in San Gimignano; Giotto's frescoes in the Capella degli Scrovegni, Padua; Siena's Piazza del Campo (Il Campo) and Pisa's Campo dei Miracoli; the ruined Chiesa di San Galgano near Siena in Tuscany; the strange meadow named Piano Grande at Monte Vettore, near Castelluccio at the border of Umbria and the Marches; your first view of the Dolomites' spiky peaks, especially from up at around 2000 metres.

ACCOMMODATION

Prices for accommodation are intended as a guide only. There is generally a fair degree of fluctuation in hotel prices throughout Italy, depending on the season and whether establishments raise prices when they have the opportunity. It is not unusual for prices to remain fixed for years on end, and in some cases they even go down: but it is more common that they rise by around 5 % or 10_20% annually. Always check room charges before putting your bags down.

Camping

Facilities range from major complexes with swimming pools, tennis courts, restaurants and supermarkets, to simple camping grounds. Prices at even the most basic camping grounds can be surprisingly expensive once you add up the various charges for each person, a site for your tent or caravan and a car, but they generally still work out cheaper than a double room in a one-star hotel. Average prices are L8000 to L10,000 per adult, L4000 to L6000 for children aged under 12 years, and L8000 to L10,000 for a site. There is sometimes a charge for use of the showers, usually around L1000, and for electricity, usually between L2000 and L3000.

Locations are usually good, ranging from beach or lakeside, to valleys in the Alps. In major cities, camping grounds are often a long way from the historic centres, and the inconvenience, plus the additional cost of needing to use public transport, should be weighed up against the price of a hotel room.

Free camping is generally not permitted in Italy and you might find yourself disturbed during the night by the carabinieri. But out of the main summer tourist season, free campers who choose spots not visible from the road, don't light fires, and who try to be inconspicuous, shouldn't have too much trouble. Always get permission from the landowner if you want to camp on private property. Camper vans are very popular in Italy, particularly in Sardinia (see the Getting Around chapter for details on renting them) where they are a useful mode of transport, as well as accommodation, for travellers to the island's more isolated and beautiful spots.

Full lists of camping grounds in and near cities and towns are usually available from local tourist offices. In Sicily and Sardinia the regional tourist boards publish annual booklets listing all facilities throughout the islands. The Touring Club Italiano publishes an annual book listing all camping grounds in Italy, *Campeggi e Villagi Turistici in Italia* (L22,000), and the Istituto Geografico de Agostini publishes the annual *Guida di Campeggi in Europa* (L20,000), both available in major bookshops in Italy.

Hostels

Hostels in Italy are called *ostelli per la gioventù* and are run by the Associazione Italiana Alberghi per la Gioventù (AIG), which is affiliated with Hostelling International (HI). An HI card is not always required, but it is recommended that you have one. Membership cards can be purchased at major hostels, from CTS (student and youth travel centre) offices, from AIG (youth hostel association) offices throughout Italy, and of course from a HI-affiliated office in your home country. Pick up a booklet on Italian hostels, with details of prices, locations etc, from the AIG national head office (☎ 06-487 11 52), Via Cavour 44, Rome.

Many Italian hostels are beautifully located, some in castles and villas. Many have bars and with few exceptions they have restaurants, or kitchens (to cook your own meals), or both. Nightly rates vary from L12,000 to L22,000 and the cost per night often includes breakfast. If not, breakfast will cost around L2000. In some hostels there is an extra charge for use of heating and hot water, usually around L1000. A meal will cost L12,000.

Accommodation is in segregated dormitories, although some hostels offer family rooms (at a higher price per person).

Hostels are generally closed from 9 am to 3.30 pm, although there are many exceptions. Check-in is from 6 to 10.30 pm, although some hostels will allow you a morning check-in, before they close for the day (it is best to check beforehand). Curfew is 10.30 or 11 pm in winter and 11.30 pm or midnight in summer. It is usually necessary to pay before 9 am on the day of your departure, otherwise you could be charged for another night.

Pensioni & Hotels

Hotel prices in Italy were deregulated by the government in 1992, but establishments are still required to notify local tourist boards of prices for the coming year and by law must then adhere to those prices (although they do have two legal opportunities each year to increase charges). If tourists believe they are being overcharged they can make a complaint to the local tourist office. The best advice is to confirm hotel charges before you put your bags down, since many proprietors employ various methods of bill-padding. These include charges for showers (usually around L2000), a compulsory breakfast (up to L14,000 in the high season) and compulsory half or full board (although this can often be a good deal in some towns).

There is often no difference between a *pensione* and an *albergo*; in fact, some hotels use both titles. However, a pensione will generally be of one to three-star quality, while an albergo can be awarded up to five stars. *Locande* (similar to pensioni) and *alloggi*, also known as *affittacamere*, are generally cheaper, but not always. Locande and affittacamere are not included in the star classification system, although in some areas (such as the Lipari Islands and in the Alps) the standard of affittacamere is very high.

While the quality of accommodation can vary a great deal, one-star hotels/pensioni tend to be very basic and usually do not have private bathrooms attached to rooms. Standards at two-star places are often only slightly better, but rooms will generally have private bathrooms. Once you arrive at three stars you can assume that standards will be high, although quality still varies dramatically. Four and five-star hotels are usually part of a group of hotels and offer facilities such as room service, laundry and dry-cleaning. For the average traveller it is really an unnecessary expense to go above three-star hotels.

Overall, prices are higher in Rome, Florence, Milan and Venice, and at other major tourist destinations. They also tend to be higher in northern Italy than in the south, and prices can skyrocket in the high season at beach resorts and during the ski season in the Alps.

A single room (camera singola) is uniformly expensive in Italy, costing from L25,000 to well over L100,000, and many of the cheaper establishments do not even bother to cater for the single traveller. A double room (camera doppia) for a room with twin beds, and camera matrimoniale for a double bed, ranges from around L40,000 to upwards of L250,000. It is much cheaper to share with two or more people. In most parts of Italy, proprietors will charge no more than 15% of the cost of a double room for each additional person.

Tourist offices have booklets listing all pensioni and hotels, including prices (although they might not always be up to date). Ask for lists of locande and affittacamere. It is also possible to telephone many tourist offices to obtain information in advance.

Rental Accommodation

Finding rental accommodation in the major cities can be difficult and time-consuming, but not impossible. There are rental agencies which will assist for a fee (some agencies are listed in the major city sections). Prices are higher for short-term rental. A small apartment anywhere near the centre of Rome will cost around L1,800,000 a month and it is usually necessary to pay a bond (generally at least one month in advance). Apartments and houses (villas) for rent are listed in local publications such as the weekly Porta Portese in Rome. You will find that many owners want to rent to foreigners because it is short term, or because they intend to charge a high rent. Another option is to answer an advertisement in any of the local publications to share an apartment.

In major resort areas, such as the Lipari Islands and other parts of Sicily, the coastal areas of Sardinia and in the Alps, the tourist offices have lists of local apartments and villas for rent. Most offices will be more than cooperative if you telephone beforehand for information on how to book an apartment.

People wanting to rent a villa in the countryside can seek information from specialist travel agencies in their own country, or contact an organisation in Italy directly. One of the major companies in Italy, which has villas in Tuscany, Umbria, the Veneto, Sicily and near Rome, is Cuendet. This reliable company publishes a booklet listing all the villas in its files, many with photos. Prices for a villa for two or three people range from around US$500 a week in winter to up to US$2000 a week in August.

For details, write to Signora N Cuendet, Località Il Cereto/Strove, 53035 Monteriggioni, Siena (☎ 0577-30 10 12, fax 0577-30 11 49), and ask them to send you a copy of their catalogue (US$15).

In London, Cuendet operates through International Chapter (☎ 071-722 9560), 102 St John's Wood Terrace, London NW8 6PL. In the USA it operates in partnership with Destination Italia (☎ 0201-327 2333), 165 Chestnut St, Allendale, NJ 07401. Another agency in the USA which handles bookings for Cuendet is Rentals in Italy (☎ 800-726 6702), 1742 Calle Corva, Camarillo, California 93010-8428.

CIT offices throughout the world also have lists of villas and apartments available for rent in Italy. In Australia, try an organisation called Cottages & Castles (☎ 03-862 1142), 11 Laver St, Kew 3101.

Don't expect to land in Italy and find an apartment or villa immediately – unless you are staying for an indefinite period, you might find that your holiday is taken up with flat-hunting.

Other Accommodation

Agriturismo This is a holiday on a working farm and is becoming increasingly popular in Italy. Traditionally the idea was that families rented out rooms in their farmhouses, and it is still possible to find this type of accommodation. However, more commonly it is a restaurant in a restored medieval farm complex, with rooms available for rent. All *agriturismo* are operating farms and you will usually be able to sample the local produce.

Agriturismo is well organised in Trentino-Alto Adige, Tuscany, Umbria and parts of Sardinia, and local tourist offices will usually have information. For detailed information on all facilities in Italy, contact Agriturist (☎ 06-6 85 21), Corso Vittorio Emanuele 89, 00186 Rome. It publishes a book with all agriturismo listings throughout the country (L35,000), available at the office and in selected bookshops.

Rifugi If you are planning to hike in the Alps, Apennines or other mountains in Italy, obtain information on the network of rifugi. There are various kinds of rifugi, which are detailed in the relevant Alpine sections of the northern Italy chapters. The average price per person for an overnight stay plus breakfast is from around L18,000 to around L40,000. Accommodation is generally in dormitories and meals are available. The locations of rifugi are marked on good hiking maps and it should be noted that most are open only from July to September. Some are close to chair lifts and cable-car stations, which means they are usually expensive and crowded with tourists. Others are at high altitude, involving hours of hard walking or climbing from the nearest village or another rifugio. These tend to be cheaper and, in general, are used by serious trekkers and mountaineers. It is a good idea, particularly during August, to book a bed in advance.

Additional information, including telephone numbers, can be obtained from local tourist offices.

Religious Institutions Known as *casa religione di ospitalità*, these institutions offer accommodation in major cities and often in monasteries in the country. The standard is usually good, but prices are no longer low. You can expect to pay about the same as for a one-star hotel, if not more. Information can be obtained through local tourist offices, or through the archdiocese of the relevant city. Associazione Cattolica al Servizio della Giovane (or Protezione della Giovane) can organise accommodation for women in hostels. The organisation has offices in most major towns, and often at major train stations, although these can be open at irregular hours.

Student Accommodation People planning to study in Italy can usually organise accommodation through the school or university they will be attending. Options include a room with an Italian family, or a share arrangement with other students in an independent apartment. Some Italian universities operate a *casa dello studente*, which houses Italian students throughout the school year and lets out rooms to others during the summer break (July to the end of September). It can be very difficult to organise a room in one of these institutions. The best idea is to attempt to book a room through your own university, or contact the relevant Italian university directly.

Landmark Trust If you fancy staying in the building where the poet Keats died, one of Palladio's villas, or the poet Browning's house, contact the Landmark Trust in the UK. Established as a charity in 1965 by Sir John Smith, the trust restores and conserves a host of architectural marvels in the UK, as well as three in Italy: the third-floor apartment where Keats' died in Piazza di Spagna, Rome; the Casa Guidi in Florence where Browning lived; and the Villa Saraceno, near Vicenza, an early Palladio commission. For further information, contact The Landmark Trust (☎ 0628-825 925), Shottesbrooke Maidenhead, Berkshire SL6 3SW, UK. For information on Palladio's villa you can contact Lorella Graham directly at the Villa Saraceno (☎ 0444-89 13 17), Finale di Agugliaro, Vicenza.

FOOD

Eating is one of life's great pleasures for Italians. Be adventurous and never be intimidated by eccentric waiters or indecipherable menus and you will find yourself agreeing with the locals, who believe that nowhere in the world is the food as good as in Italy and, more specifically, in their own town.

What the world regards as Italian cooking is really a collection of regional cuisines (*cucine*). While the eating habits of Italians are now fairly homogeneous, cooking styles continue to vary notably from region to region and significantly between the north and south. In the north the food is rich and often creamy, while in Sicily, for example, it is spicier.

The regional specialities of Emilia-Romagna, including *tagliatelle al ragù* (and its adaptation, *spaghetti bolognese*), *lasagne* and *tortellini*, are among the best known Italian dishes, and the best *prosciutto* (cured ham) comes from Parma, which is also the home of *parmigiano reggiano*.

Liguria is the home of *pesto*, a delicious uncooked pasta sauce of fresh basil, garlic, oil, pine nuts and cheese, ground together with a mortar and pestle. Also try the *farinata*, a tart made with chick-pea flour, and the *focaccia*, a flat bread.

In Piedmont the cuisine is influenced to some extent by nearby France. It is often delicate and always flavoursome. *Tartufo bianco* (white truffle) is used in a wide variety of dishes. Traditional dishes make good use of game birds and animals, including chamois, pheasant and quail, as well as more unusual meats, such as horse, donkey and frog (there is even such a dish as frog risotto).

In Trentino-Alto Adige the cuisine has a heavy Austrian influence, and alongside minestrone and spaghetti, you will find *can-erdeli* (a soup with noodles in it), goulash soup and Wiener schnitzel. Local specialities include smoked meats, eaten with heavy, black rye bread.

In the Veneto, try the boiled meats and the bitter red lettuce *(radicchio trevisano)*, eaten baked, or in risotto or with pasta. Risotto comes in many varieties in the Veneto: with mushrooms, zucchini, sausage, quail, trout and other seafood, chicken, spring vegetables and, not to be missed, *risotto nero*, coloured and flavoured with the ink of squid.

In Tuscany and Umbria the locals use a lot of olive oil and herbs, and regional specialities are noted for their simplicity, fine flavour and the use of fresh produce.

In Tuscany, try *bistecca fiorentina*, a huge T-bone steak usually three to four cm thick. It is quite acceptable, and in fact advisable, to order one steak for two people. Among the staples of Tuscan cuisine are small white *cannellini* beans, although all types of beans are widely used. There is also a wide range of soups, from the simple *acquacotta*, which translates as 'cooked water', to the rich *minestrone alla fiorentina*, flavoured with pork and chicken giblets. Don't miss the incredibly rich *panforte*, Siena's famous Christmas fruitcake.

In Umbria both the *tartufo* (truffle) and the *porcini* mushrooms (like the French *cèpes*) are abundant and both turn up in pasta, rice and a large number of other dishes. While many Umbrian dishes are based upon vegetables, the locals eat more meat than any other Italians, and a local speciality is *porchetta*, a whole roast piglet stuffed with rosemary. Umbrian cakes and pastries are worth a try, as are the chocolates produced by the Perugina factory at Perugia, notably the famous *baci* (chocolate-coated hazelnuts).

In and around Rome, traditional pasta includes spaghetti *carbonara* (with egg yolk) and *alla matriciana* (with a sauce of tomato, and bacon). Offal is also popular in Rome – if you can stomach it, try the pasta *pajata*, made with the entrails of very young veal, considered a delicacy since they contain the congealed mother's milk.

Pasta al Dente

Cooking good pasta for an Italian is no mean feat. First the pasta has to be of the highest quality, second it has to be cooked for precisely the correct length of time, so that it is *al dente*, which means that it is firm, almost crunchy, an uninitiated eater might observe. Italians almost always add salt to the boiling water before adding the pasta and they never throw in *(buttare)* the pasta until everyone who is going to eat is present. Don't complain if your pasta takes a while to arrive in a restaurant – you'll need to wait the 10 to 12 minutes it takes to cook.

Italian pasta is infinitely varied. It comes in a dazzling variety of shapes and sizes, ranging from spaghetti and linguine, to tube pasta such as penne and rigatoni, shell-shaped *(conchiglie)*, bow-shaped *(farfalle,* which means butterflies), corkscrew-shaped *(fusilli)* and many others. Packet, or dried pasta, is made with high quality durum wheat and water. On the other hand, fresh egg pasta *(pasta all'uovo,* or *fatto a mano)* is made with eggs and flour and is used to make stuffed pasta such as tortellini and ravioli, or cut into strips called tagliatelle (thinner strips are also called *taglionini* or *tagliarini*). Egg pasta is usually served with richer, creamier sauces than those which usually accompany dried pasta, which are most likely to be tomato-based. Sampling the great variety of pasta sauces you'll find in Italy can make eating a lot of fun during your trip, particularly if you are adventurous enough to try traditional local recipes in the various regions or towns you visit. Pasta sauce ingredients traditionally vary quite dramatically between the north and south of the country. In the north they are richer, often creamy and often use red meat (such as the delicious *ragù* of Bologna, known outside Italy as *bolognese*), while as you head further south they tend to use more vegetables and, on the coast, lots of seafood. In Apulia, for instance, a typical pasta dish is *orecchiette con cime di rapa,* ear-shaped pasta served with turnip tops which have been sauteed in oil with chilli and garlic. In Sicily, eggplant is a popular addition to tomato-based pasta sauces. See the section on Food for some other traditional pasta dishes.

Freshly grated cheese is the magic ingredient for most pasta. Parmesan *(parmigiano)* is the most widely used, particularly in the north. Look for the name *Parmigiano Reggiano* on the rind to ensure you're getting the genuine parmesan, because there is also the similar, but lower quality *Grana Padano*. In Sardinia and around Rome there is a tendency to use the sharp *pecorino,* an aged sheep's cheese, while *ricotta salata* (salted ricotta), is widely used in the south and in Sicily. ∎

As you go farther south, the food becomes hotter and spicier and the *dolci* (cakes and pastries) sweeter and richer. Don't miss the experience of eating a pizza in Naples (where it was created), or the *melanzane parmigiana* (eggplant layered with a tomato sauce and mozzarella and baked), another classic Neapolitan dish. A favourite *dolce* in Naples is *sfogliatelle,* layers of fine pastry with a ricotta filling.

The food of Apulia is simple and hearty, featuring a lot of vegetables. Try the *orecchiette* (pasta in the shape of 'little ears' with a sauce of sautéed green vegetables). Another popular local dish is made from puréed broad beans topped with chicory. The Pugliesi also eat a lot of seafood.

In Sicily, try the *pesce spada* (swordfish, usually sliced into thick steaks and cooked on an open grill). *Pasta con le sarde* (pasta with sardines) is popular in Palermo. Eggplant is popular in Sicily, turning up in pasta or as *melanzane alla siciliana,* filled with olives, anchovies, capers and tomato.

The Sicilians are experts when it comes to their dolci. Don't leave the island without trying *cassata,* a rich sponge cake filled with a cream of ricotta cheese, liqueur and candied fruits. Another speciality is *cannoli,* tubes of sweet pastry filled with a rich cream, often made from a mixture of cream cheese, honey and almond paste with bits of candied fruit. Also try the assortment of *paste di mandorle* (almond pastries) and the *zabaione,* native to Marsala.

The *granita* is a drink made of crushed ice with fresh lemon or other fruit juices, or with coffee topped with fresh whipped cream. Another speciality is *marzapane* (marzipan), which Sicilian pastry chefs whip into every imaginable shape. Sicilian gelato is absolutely heavenly.

Sardinia's best known dish is *porcheddu*, baby pig roasted on a spit. Try also the *carte musica*, a thin, crisp bread eaten warm and sprinkled with salt and oil. *Pecorino sardo* is a sharp, aged sheep's cheese which the Sardi sprinkle on their pasta instead of parmigiano.

Vegetarians will have no problems eating in Italy. While there are very few restaurants devoted to them, vegetables are a staple of the Italian diet. Most eating establishments serve a good selection of *antipasti* and *contorni* (vegetables prepared in a variety of ways), and the farther south you go, the more excellent vegetable dishes you will find. Vegetarian restaurants and grocery shops are listed throughout this book.

Where to Eat

Eating establishments are divided into several categories. A *tavola calda* (literally 'hot table') usually offers cheap, pre-prepared meat, pasta and vegetable dishes in a self-service style. A *rosticceria* usually offers cooked meats, but often has a larger selection of takeaway food. A *pizzeria* will of course serve pizza, but usually also a full menu. An *osteria* is likely to be either a wine bar offering a small selection of dishes, or a small *trattoria*. A trattoria is basically a cheaper version of a *ristorante* (restaurant), which in turn generally has a wider selection of dishes and a higher standard of service. The problem is that many of the establishments that are in fact ristorantes call themselves trattorias and vice versa for reasons best known to themselves. It is best to check the menu, which is usually posted by the door, for prices.

Don't judge the quality of a ristorante or trattoria by its appearance. You are likely to eat your most memorable meal at a place with plastic tablecloths in a tiny back street, a dingy piazza or on a back road in the country.

And don't panic if you find yourself in a trattoria which has no printed menu: they are often the ones which offer the best and most authentic food and have menus which change daily to accommodate the availability of fresh produce. Just hope that the waiter will patiently explain the dishes and cost.

Most eating establishments have a cover charge, usually around L2000 to L3000, and a service charge of 10% to 15%. Restaurants usually open for lunch from 12.30 to 3 pm, but many are not keen to take orders after 2 pm. In the evening, opening hours vary from north to south. They eat dinner earlier in the north, usually from 7.30 pm, but in Sicily you will be hard-pressed to find a restaurant open before 8.30 pm. Very few restaurants stay open past 11.30 pm.

Numerous restaurants offer tourist menus, with an average price of L18,000 to L25,000 (usually not including drinks). Generally the food is of a reasonable standard, but choices will be limited and you can usually get away with paying less if you want only pasta, salad and wine.

After lunch and dinner, head for the nearest *gelateria* (ice-cream parlour) to round off the meal with some excellent *gelati*, followed by a *digestivo* (digestive liqueur) at a bar.

For a light lunch, or a snack, most bars serve *panini* (sandwiches), and there are numerous outlets where you can buy pizza by the slice *(a taglio)*. Another option is to go to one of the many alimentari and ask them to make a panino with the filling of your choice. At a *pasticceria* you can buy pastries, cakes and biscuits.

Fast food is becoming increasingly popular in Italy. There are McDonald's outlets throughout the country as well as numerous other chain restaurants and US-style hamburger joints.

Eating Customs

Italians rarely eat a sit-down breakfast *(colazione)*. The custom is to drink a cappuccino, usually *tiepido* (warm), and eat a brioche, *cornetto* (like the French croissant) or other type of pastry while standing at a bar.

Lunch *(pranzo)* is traditionally the main meal of the day and shops and businesses close for three to four hours each afternoon to accommodate the meal and siesta which generally follows.

A full meal will consist of *antipasto*, which can vary from *bruschetta*, a type of garlic bread with various toppings, to fried vegetables, or *prosciutto e melone* (cured ham wrapped around melon). Next comes the *primo piatto*, a pasta or risotto, followed by the *secondo piatto* of meat or fish. Italians often then eat an *insalata* (salad) or contorni, and round off the meal with fruit (occasionally with a sweet) and *caffè*, often at a bar on the way back to work.

The evening meal *(cena)* was traditionally a simpler affair, but habits are changing because of the inconvenience of travelling home for lunch every day.

Self-Catering

If you have access to cooking facilities, it is best to buy fruit and vegetables at open markets, and salami, cheese and wine at alimentari or *salumerie*, which are a cross between grocery stores and delicatessens. Fresh bread is available at a *forno* or *panetteria* (bakeries which sell bread, pastries and sometimes groceries) and usually at alimentari. There are also supermarkets in most towns and they are listed throughout this book.

Food Glossary

This is intended as a brief guide to some of the basics and by no means covers all of the dishes you are likely to encounter in Italy. Names and ingredients of dishes often vary from region to region, and even pizza toppings can change. Most travellers to Italy will already be well acquainted with the various Italian pastas, which include spaghetti, fettucine, penne, rigatoni, gnocchi, lasagne, tortellini and ravioli. The names are the same in Italy and no further definitions are given here.

Useful Words

bill/cheque	*il conto*
boiled	*bollito*
cooked	*cotto*
cooked over hot coals	*alla brace*
firm (as all good pasta should be)	*al dente*
fried	*fritto*
grilled	*alla griglia*
knife/fork/spoon/tea spoon	*cotello/forchetta/cucchiaio/cucchiaino*
menu	*menù*
plate	*piatto*
raw	*crudo*
restaurant	*ristorante*
roasted	*arrosto*
smoked	*affumicato*
waiter/waitress	*cameriere/a*
well done (cooked)	*ben cotto*

Staples

bread	*pane*
butter	*burro*
cheese	*formaggio*
chilli	*peperoncino*
cooked cornmeal	*polenta*
cream	*panna*
egg/eggs	*uovo/uova*
honey	*miele*
jam	*marmellata*

Stand or Sit?

Remember that as soon as you sit down in Italy, prices go up considerably, since you have to pay for the service. A cappuccino at the bar will cost around L1200 to L1500, but if you sit down you will pay anything from L2500 to L8000 and more than L12,000 in the Piazza San Marco in Venice. Italians rarely sit down in bars and, consequently, many do not even have seating. In some bars, where it is obvious that no-one is serving the tables, you can sometimes sit down without paying extra. ■

lemon	*limone*
oil	*olio*
olives	*olive*
pepper	*pepe*
rice	*riso*
rice cooked with wine and stock	*risotto*
salt	*sale*
sugar	*zucchero*
vinegar	*aceto*
wholemeal bread	*pane integrale*

Meat & Fish

anchovies	*acciughe*
beef	*manzo*
chicken	*pollo*
clams	*vongole*
cod	*merluzzo*
crab	*granchio*
cutlet or thin cut of meat, usually crumbed and fried	*cotoletta*
dentex (a type of fish)	*dentice*
lamb	*agnello or abacchio*
liver	*fegato*
lobster	*aragosta*
mackerel	*sgombro*
mussels	*cozze*
octopus	*polpo*
oysters	*ostriche*
prawns	*gamberi*
rabbit	*coniglio*
sardines	*sarde*
sausage	*salsiccia*
sole	*sogliola*
squid	*calamari*
steak	*bistecca*
swordfish	*pesce spada*
tripe	*trippa*
tuna	*tonno*
turkey	*tacchino*
veal	*vitello*

Vegetables

artichokes	*carciofi*
asparagus	*asparagi*
cabbage	*verza*
carrots	*carote*
chicory	*cicoria*
eggplant	*melanzane*
onion	*cipolla*
peas	*piselli*
peppers	*peperoni*
potatoes	*patate*
spinach	*spinaci*
string beans	*fagiolini*

Fruit

apples	*mele*
bananas	*banane*
cherries	*ciliegie*
grapes	*uva*
oranges	*arance*
peaches	*pesche*
pears	*pere*
strawberries	*fragole*

Soup & Antipasto

brodo	*broth*
carpaccio	*very fine slices of raw meat*
insalata caprese	*sliced tomatoes with mozzarella and basil*
insalata di mare	*seafood, generally crustaceans*
minestrina in brodo	*pasta in broth*
minestrone	*vegetable soup*
olive ascolane	*stuffed, deep-fried olives*
prosciutto e melone	*cured ham with melon*
ripieni	*stuffed, oven-baked vegetables*
stracciatella	*egg in broth*

Pasta Sauces

al ragù	*meat sauce (bolognese)*
arrabbiata	*tomato and chilli*
carbonara	*egg, bacon and black pepper*
matriciana	*tomato and bacon*
napoletana	*tomato and basil*
panna	*cream, prosciutto and sometimes peas*

pesto	*basil, garlic and oil, often with pine nuts*
vongole	*clams, garlic and oil, sometimes with tomato*

Pizzas

All pizzas listed have tomato and mozzarella.

capricciosa	*olives, prosciutto, mushrooms, artichokes*
frutti di mare	*seafood*
funghi	*mushrooms*
margherita	*oregano*
napoletana	*anchovies*
pugliese	*tomato, mozzarella and onions*
quattro formaggi	*with four types of cheese*
quattro stagioni	*the same as capricciosa, but sometimes with egg*
verdura	*mixed vegetables (usually zucchini, eggplant and sometimes carrot and spinach)*

DRINKS
Coffee

The first-time visitor to Italy is likely to be confused by the many ways in which the locals consume their caffeine. The Coffee information box is a basic guide, although there can be variations from north to south.

Tea

Italians don't drink a lot of tea *(tè)* and generally only in the late afternoon, when they might take a cup with a few *pasticcini* (small cakes). You can order tea in bars, although it will usually arrive in the form of a cup of warm water with an accompanying tea bag. If this doesn't suit your taste, ask for the water *molto caldo* or *bollente* (boiling). Good-quality packaged teas, such as Twinings tea bags and leaves, as well as packaged herbal teas, such as camomile, are often sold in alimentari and some bars. You can find a wide range of herbal teas in a herbalist's shop *(erboristeria)*, which sometimes also stocks health foods.

Wine & Spirits

Wine *(vino)* is an essential accompaniment to any meal, and digestivi are a popular way to end one. Italians are very proud of their wines, and find it hard to believe that anyone else in the world could produce wines as good as theirs. Many Italians drink alcohol only with meals, and the foreign custom of going out for a drink is still considered unusual, although in some parts of Italy, generally in the country and in Sardinia, it is common to see men starting their day with a grappa for breakfast, and to continue consuming strong drinks throughout the day.

Wine is reasonably priced and you will rarely pay more than L15,000 for a good bottle of wine, although prices range up to more than L30,000 for really good quality. There are two main classifications of wine, *(denominazione di origine controllata)* (DOC) and *vino da tavola* (table wine) – either classification will be marked on the label. A DOC wine is produced subject to certain specifications, although the label does not certify quality. *Denominazione d'origine controllata e garantita)* (DOCG) is subject to the same requirements as normal DOC but it is also tested by government inspectors. While there are table wines better left alone, there are also many which are of excellent quality, notably the Sicilian Corvo red and white.

Although some excellent wines are produced in Italy, most trattorias stock only a limited selection of bottled wines and generally only cheaper varieties. Most people tend to order the house wine *(vino della casa)* or the local wine *(vino locale)* when they go out to dinner.

The styles of wine vary throughout the country, so make a point of sampling the local produce in your travels. Try the famous Chianti in Tuscany, but also the Vernaccia of

Caffe Society

An *espresso* is a small amount of very strong black coffee. You can ask for a *doppio espresso*, which means double the amount, or a *caffè lungo* (although this can sometimes mean a slightly diluted espresso). If you want a long black coffee (as in a weaker, watered-down version), ask for a *caffè Americano*. If you are in an isolated village in Sardinia where they have no name for diluted coffee, try asking for an *espresso con molta acqua calda* (coffee with a lot of hot water). A *corretto* is an espresso with a dash of grappa or some other spirit, and a *macchiato* is espresso with a small amount of milk – on the other hand, *latte macchiato* is milk with a spot of coffee. *Caffè freddo* is a long glass of cold black coffee.

Then, of course, there is the *cappuccino*, coffee with hot, frothy milk – if you want it without the froth, ask for a *caffè latte* or a cappuccino *senza schiuma*. Italians tend to drink cappuccino only with breakfast and during the morning. They never drink it after meals or in the evening and, if you order one after dinner, don't be surprised if the waiter asks you two or three times, just to make sure that he or she heard correctly. You will also find it difficult to convince bartenders to make your cappuccino hot, rather than lukewarm. Ask for it *molto caldo* and wait for the same 'tut-tut' response that you attracted when you ordered a cappuccino after dinner. ∎

San Gimignano and the reds of Montalcino, notably the excellent Brunello di Montalcino; the Soave in Verona and Valpolicella around Venice. Piedmont and Trentino-Alto Adige both produce excellent wines, notably the Barolo in Piedmont. The wines of Orvieto in Umbria are good, and in Rome try the local Frascati and Est! Est! Est!. The wines of the Castelli Romani are reputed to be not as good as they once were, but they're still worth a try. In Sicily and Sardinia the wines are sweeter and heavier. Sicily is the home of Marsala.

Before dinner, Italians might drink a Campari and soda, or a fruit cocktail, usually pre-prepared and often without alcohol (*analcolico*). After dinner try a shot of grappa, a very strong, clear brew made from grapes, or an *amaro*, a dark liqueur prepared from herbs. If you prefer a sweeter liqueur, try an almond-flavoured *amaretto* or the sweet aniseed *sambuca*.

Beer

Italy produces its own beer (*birra*) and imports beers from throughout Europe and the world. All of the main German beers are, for instance, available in bottles or cans; English beers are often found on tap (*alla spina*) in *birrerie* (bars specialising in beer), and Australians might be pleased to know that you can even find a Foster's and a Castlemaine XXXX. The main local labels are Peroni, Dreher and Moretti, all very drinkable and cheaper than the imported varieties. If you want a local beer, ask for a *birra nazionale*, which will be either in a bottle or on tap.

Water

While tap water is reliable throughout the country, most Italians prefer to drink bottled mineral water (*acqua minerale*). It will be either sparkling (*frizzante*) or still (*naturale*) and you will be asked in restaurants and bars which you would prefer. If you want a glass of tap water, ask for *acqua dal rubinetto*, although simply asking for *acqua naturale* will also suffice.

ENTERTAINMENT

Whatever your tastes, there should be some form of entertainment in Italy to keep you amused, from the national obsession, soccer *(il calcio)*, to the opera, theatre, classical music concerts, rock concerts, traditional festivals and major entertainment festivals, such as the Festival of Two Worlds in June/July at Spoleto, Umbria Jazz in Perugia in July, and the Venice Biennale in every odd-numbered year (see the Cultural Events section in this chapter). Operas are performed in Verona and Rome throughout summer (for more information, see the Entertainment sections for both cities) and at various times of the year throughout the country, notably at the opera houses in Milan and Palermo.

The main theatre season is during winter, and classical music concerts are generally performed throughout the year. Nightclubs, indoor bars and discotheques are more popular during winter and, in fact, some close down for the summer months. Entrance charges to discos are high, usually starting at around L20,000. This usually covers the cost of the first drink, although after that you will pay up to L6000 just for a glass of wine. There are gay and lesbian discos and nightclubs in most cities. Entertainment listings are in the city and town sections. More detailed listings can be found in the entertainment sections of local newspapers. Tourist offices will also provide information on important events, festivals, performances and concerts.

THINGS TO BUY

Shopping in Italy is probably not what you are used to back home. The vast proportion of shops are small businesses, and large department stores and supermarkets tend to be very thin on the ground. If you need necessities such as underwear, pantyhose, pyjamas, T-shirts, toiletries, condoms etc, head for one of the large retail stores, such as Standa, Upim, Oviesse or Rinascente. Otherwise, you can pick up underwear, pantyhose and pyjamas in a haberdashery *(merceria)*, toiletries and condoms in a pharmacy *(farmacia)* or sometimes in an alimentari, and items such as T-shirts in a normal clothing store. All of these items can also be found in street markets. Hardware items can be purchased at a *ferramenta*, and

air-mail paper, note pads, pens, greeting cards etc at a paper-goods shop *(cartoleria)*.

Clothing

Italy is synonymous with elegant, fashionable and high-quality clothing. The problem is that most of the better quality clothes are very expensive. However, if you can manage to be in the country during the summer sales in July and August and the winter sales in December and January, you can pick up incredible bargains. By mid-sale, prices are often slashed by up to 60% and 70%. Generally speaking, Rome, Florence and Milan have the greatest variety of clothing, shoes and accessories. Main shopping areas are detailed under the relevant cities throughout this book. Fashions tend to be conservative and middle-of-the-range, and cheaper clothing can be downright boring for English, US and Australian travellers accustomed to a wide variety of styles and tastes.

The same applies to shoes. Expect to pay dearly (although still considerably less than at home) for the best quality at shops such as Beltrami and Pollini. Again, prices drop dramatically during the sales, but expect to have some difficulty finding shoes to fit if you take a larger size.

Italy is particularly noted for the quality of its leather goods, so plan to stock up on bags, wallets, purses, belts and gloves. At markets such as Porta Portese in Rome you can find some incredible second-hand bargains. The San Lorenzo leather market in Florence has a vast array of leather goods, including jackets, bags, wallets and belts, although the variety can be limited, and you should check carefully for quality before buying. At San Lorenzo, prices are usually half what you would pay in a shop. A few examples are: L70,000 for a bag, L15,000 for a belt, L15,000 for suede gloves, and L250,000 to L400,000 for a leather jacket.

Glassware & Ceramics

Some might call the famous and expensive Venetian glass grotesque – and it is certainly an acquired taste. Shops all over Venice are full of it and if you listen to the claims of the shop assistants, most of it (except for the glass in *their* shop) is not the real thing. If you want to buy Venetian glass, shop around and compare prices and quality. The merchandise at the larger factories is generally not cheaper, but you can be sure it is authentic. And remember you will probably have to pay customs duty on your purchase when you arrive home. For more information see the Things to Buy information in the Venice section of the Veneto chapter.

Ceramics and pottery are less costly and more rustic. There is a great diversity of traditional styles throughout Italy, associated with villages or areas, where designs have been handed down over the centuries. Major centres include: Deruta, near Perugia in Umbria; Faenza, in Emilia-Romagna; Vietri sul Mare, near Salerno at the start of the Amalfi coast; and Grottaglie, near Taranto in Apulia. Sicilian pottery is particularly interesting. Caltagirone and Santo Stefano di Canastra are two important ceramic producing towns.

Other Items

The beautiful Florentine paper goods, with their delicate flower design, and Venetian paper goods, with a marbled design, are reasonably priced and make wonderful gifts. Specialist shops are dotted around both cities, although it is possible to buy these paper goods in cartolerie throughout the country.

Popular jewellery tends to be chunky and cheap-looking, but if they can afford it, Italians love to wear gold. The best known haunt for tourists wanting to buy gold in Italy is the Ponte Vecchio in Florence, lined with tiny shops full of both modern and antique jewellery. Jewellery and ornaments carved from coral can be found at Torre del Greco just out of Naples, and on the west coast of Sardinia, although overharvesting and pollution threaten this once thriving industry.

Local handicrafts include lace and embroidery, notably on the Isola Maggiore in Lago de Trasimeno, Umbria, and the woodcarvings of the Val Gardena in Trentino-Alto Adige.

Getting There & Away

If you live outside Europe, flying is the easiest way to get to Italy. Competition between the airlines means you should be able to pick up a reasonably priced fare, even if you are coming from as far away as Australia. If you live in Europe, chances are you'll be going to Italy overland – by train, bus, car or hitchhiking.

Whichever way you are travelling, make sure that you take out travel insurance. This will cover you for medical expenses, luggage theft or loss, and for cancellation of and delays in your travel arrangements. Cover depends on your insurance and type of ticket, so ask both your insurer and ticket-issuing agency to explain where you stand. Ticket loss is also covered by travel insurance, but make sure you have a separate record of your ticket details (see the Photocopies information in the Documents section of the Facts for the Visitor chapter). Buy travel insurance as early as possible. If you buy it the week before you fly or hop on the bus, you may find, for example, that you are not covered for delays to your trip caused by strikes or other industrial action.

Paying for your ticket with a credit card often provides limited travel accident insurance, and you may be able to reclaim the payment if the operator doesn't deliver. Ask your credit card company what it will cover.

AIR

Always remember to reconfirm your onward or return bookings by the specified time – at least 72 hours before departure on international flights. Otherwise, there's a real risk that you'll turn up at the airport only to find you've missed your flight because it was rescheduled, or that you've been classified as a 'no show'.

Buying a Ticket

The plane ticket will probably be the single most expensive item in your budget, and buying it can be an intimidating business.

Start early: some of the cheapest tickets have to be bought months in advance, and some popular flights sell out early. Talk to recent travellers and look at the ads in newspapers and magazines (including the Italian press in your home country), consult reference books and watch for special offers. Then telephone travel agents for bargains. Find out the fare, the route, the duration of the journey and any restrictions on the ticket.

Official cheap tickets include advance-purchase tickets, budget fares, Apex and super-Apex and various other names thought up by the airlines. Unofficial discount tickets are released by the airlines through selected travel agents and it is worth shopping around to find them. Sometimes the discount 'special deals' have bonuses attached, such as a free flight within Europe, free accommodation for the first few nights, or a free stopover. Discounted tickets are available only from travel agents, although airlines can provide information on routes and timetables, and their low-season, student and senior citizens' fares can be very competitive.

Return tickets usually work out much cheaper than buying two one-way tickets (Italy is not the place to buy your ticket home, because cheap tickets, particularly one-way, can be difficult to find). If Italy is only one stop on your grand world tour, consider buying a Round-the-World (RTW) ticket, which is often an excellent deal. Official RTW tickets usually involve a combination of two airlines and permit you to fly anywhere you want on their route systems, as long as you don't backtrack. You are usually required to book the first sector in advance, and cancellation penalties then apply. There may be restrictions on how many stops you can make, and the tickets are usually valid for 90 days to one year. Prices start at about UK£900, A$1800 or US$1300, depending on the season.

Since RTWs can sometimes get a bit complicated, depending on how many stops you

Air Travel Glossary

Apex Tickets Apex stands for Advance Purchase Excursion fare. These tickets are usually between 30 and 40% cheaper than the full economy fare, but there are restrictions. You must purchase the ticket at least 21 days in advance and must be away for a minimum period and return within a maximum period. Stopovers are not allowed, and if you have to change your dates of travel or destination, there will be extra charges to pay. These tickets are not fully refundable – if you have to cancel your trip, the refund is often considerably less than what you paid for the ticket. Take out travel insurance to cover yourself in case you have to cancel your trip unexpectedly – for example, due to illness.

Baggage Allowance This will be written on your ticket; you are usually allowed one 20-kg item, plus one item of hand luggage. Some airlines which fly transpacific and transatlantic routes allow for two pieces of luggage (there are limits on their dimensions and weight).

Bucket Shops At certain times of the year and/or on certain routes, many airlines fly with empty seats. This isn't profitable and it's more cost-effective for them to fly full, even if that means having to sell a certain number of drastically discounted tickets. They do this by off-loading them onto bucket shops (UK) or consolidators (USA), travel agents who specialise in discounted fares. The agents, in turn, sell them to the public at reduced prices. These tickets are often the cheapest you'll find, but you can't purchase them directly from the airlines. Availability varies widely, so you'll not only have to be flexible in your travel plans, you'll also have to be quick off the mark as soon as an advertisement appears in the press.

Bucket-shop agents advertise in newspapers and magazines and there's a lot of competition so it's a good idea to telephone first.

Bumped Just because you have a confirmed seat doesn't mean you're going to get on the plane – see Overbooking.

Cancellation Penalties If you have to cancel or change an Apex or other discount ticket, there may be heavy penalties; insurance can sometimes be taken out against these penalties. Some airlines impose penalties on regular tickets as well, particularly against 'no show' passengers.

Check In Airlines ask you to check in a certain time ahead of the flight departure (usually two hours on international flights). If you fail to check in on time and the flight is overbooked, the airline can cancel your booking and give your seat to somebody else.

Confirmation Having a ticket written out with the flight and date on it doesn't mean you have a seat until the agent has confirmed with the airline that your status is 'OK'. Prior to this confirmation, your status is 'on request'.

Courier Fares Businesses often need to send their urgent documents or freight securely and quickly. They do it through courier companies. These companies hire people to accompany the package through customs and, in return, offer a discount ticket which is sometimes a phenomenal bargain. In effect, what the courier companies do is ship their freight as your luggage on the regular commercial flights. This is a legitimate operation – all freight is completely legal. There are two shortcomings, however: the short turnaround time of the ticket, usually not longer than a month; and the limitation on your luggage allowance.

Discounted Tickets There are two types of discounted fares – officially discounted (such as Apex – see Promotional Fares) and unofficially discounted (see Bucket Shops). The latter can save you more than money – you may be able to pay Apex prices without the associated Apex advance booking and other requirements. The lowest prices often impose drawbacks, such as flying with unpopular airlines, inconvenient schedules, or unpleasant routes and connections.

Economy Class Tickets Economy-class tickets are usually not the cheapest way to go, though they do give you maximum flexibility and they are valid for 12 months. If you don't use them, most are fully refundable, as are unused sectors of a multiple ticket.

Full Fares Airlines traditionally offer first class (coded F), business class (coded J) and economy class (coded Y) tickets. These days there are so many promotional and discounted fares available that few passengers pay full fare.

Lost Tickets If you lose your airline ticket, an airline will usually treat it like a travellers' cheque and, after inquiries, issue you with a replacement. Legally, however, an airline is entitled to treat it like cash, so if you lose a ticket, it could be forever. Take good care of your tickets.

MCO An MCO (Miscellaneous Charges Order) is a voucher for a value of a given amount, which resembles an airline ticket and can be used to pay for a specific flight with any IATA (International Air Transport Association) airline. MCOs, which are more flexible than a regular ticket, may satisfy the irritating onward ticket requirement, but some countries are now reluctant to accept them. MCOs are fully refundable if unused.

No Shows No shows are passengers who fail to show up for their flight. Full-fare no shows are sometimes entitled to travel on a later flight.

Open Jaw Tickets These are return tickets which allow you to fly to one place but return from another, and travel between the two 'jaws' by any means of transport at your own expense. If available, this can save you backtracking to your arrival point.

Overbooking Airlines hate to fly with empty seats, and since every flight has some passengers who fail to show up, they often book more passengers than they have seats available. Usually the excess passengers balance those who fail to show up, but occasionally somebody gets bumped. If this happens, guess who it is most likely to be? The passengers who check in late.

Promotional Fares These are officially discounted fares, such as Apex fares, which are available from travel agents or direct from the airline.

Reconfirmation You must contact the airline at least 72 hours prior to departure to 'reconfirm' that you intend to be on the flight. If you don't do this, the airline can delete your name from the passenger list and you could lose your seat.

Restrictions Discounted tickets often have various restrictions on them, such as necessity of advance purchase, limitations on the minimum and maximum period you must be away, restrictions on breaking the journey or changing the booking or route etc.

Round-the-World Tickets These tickets have become very popular in the last few years; basically, there are two types – airline tickets and agent tickets. An airline RTW ticket is issued by two or more airlines that have joined together to market a ticket which takes you around the world on their combined routes. It permits you to fly pretty well anywhere you choose using their combined routes as long as you don't backtrack, ie keep moving in approximately the same direction east or west. Other restrictions are that you (usually) must book the first sector in advance and cancellation penalties then apply. There may be restrictions on how many stopovers you are permitted. The RTW tickets are usually valid for 90 days up to a year.

The other type of RTW ticket, the agent ticket, is a combination of cheap fares strung together by an enterprising travel agent. These may be cheaper than airline RTW tickets, but the choice of routes will be limited.

Standby This is a discounted ticket where you only fly if there is a seat free at the last moment. Standby fares are usually only available directly at the airport, but sometimes may also be handled by an airline's city office. To give yourself the best possible chance of getting on the flight you want, get there early and have your name placed on the waiting list. It's first come, first served.

Student Discounts Some airlines offer student-card holders 15% to 25% discounts on their tickets. The same often applies to anyone under the age of 26. These discounts are generally only available on ordinary economy-class fares.

Tickets Out An entry requirement for many countries is that you have an onward or return ticket, in other words, a ticket out of the country. If you're not sure what you intend to do next, the easiest solution is to buy the cheapest onward ticket to a neighbouring country or a ticket from a reliable airline which can later be refunded if you do not use it.

Transferred Tickets Airline tickets cannot be transferred from one person to another. Travellers sometimes try to sell the return half of their ticket, but officials can ask you to prove that you are the person named on the ticket. This may not be checked on domestic flights, but on international flights, tickets are usually compared with passports.

Travel Periods Some officially discounted fares, Apex fares in particular, vary with the time of year. There is often a low (off-peak) season and a high (peak) season. Sometimes there's an intermediate or shoulder season as well. At peak times, when everyone wants to fly, both officially and unofficially discounted fares will be higher, or there may simply be no discounted tickets available. Usually the fare depends on your outward flight – if you depart in the high season and return in the low season, you pay the high-season fare. ■

want to make and where, ensure that your travel agent has made your bookings correctly and has filled you in on all of the ticket's restrictions and conditions. If you are travelling to Italy from the USA or South-East Asia, or you have decided to fly home from London in the hope of finding a cheaper fare there, you will probably find that the cheapest flights are being advertised by obscure agencies whose names haven't yet reached the telephone directory. Many such firms are honest and solvent, but there are a few rogues who will take your money and disappear, to reopen elsewhere a month or two later under a new name. If you feel suspicious about a firm, don't give them all the money at once – leave a deposit of 20% or so and pay the balance when you get the ticket. If they insist on cash in advance, go somewhere else. And once you have the ticket, ring the airline to confirm that you are actually booked on the flight.

Many travellers will prefer to pay more than the rock-bottom fare in order to fly with a major airline, or to avoid 'milk-run' flights which have several stopovers before finally landing in Rome. However, few travellers want to pay full airline fares, and there are numerous better known travel agents which offer bargain fares. Firms such as STA Travel, which has offices worldwide, Council Travel in the USA, Travel CUTS in Canada, and Flight Centres International in Australia, are not going to disappear overnight, leaving you clutching a receipt for a nonexistent ticket.

Use the fares quoted in this book as a guide only. They are approximate and based on the rates advertised by travel agents at the time of writing, and are likely to have changed by the time you read this.

Travellers with Special Needs

If you have broken a leg, you're a vegetarian or require a special diet, are travelling in a wheelchair, taking a baby or your dog, you are terrified of flying or have some other special need, let the airline know as soon as possible so that they can make arrangements accordingly. You should remind them when you reconfirm your booking (at least 72 hours before departure) and again when you check in at the airport. It may also be worth ringing round the airlines before you make your booking to find out how they can handle your particular needs. Some airlines publish brochures on the subject. Ask your travel agent for details.

Children aged under two travel for 10% of the standard fare (or free on some airlines), as long as they don't occupy a seat. They don't get a baggage allowance either. 'Skycots', baby food and nappies (diapers) should be provided by the airline if requested in advance. Children aged between two and 12 can usually occupy a seat for half to two-thirds of the full fare, and do get a baggage allowance. Pushchairs (strollers) can often be taken as hand luggage.

To/From the USA

The North Atlantic is the world's busiest long-haul air corridor and the flight options are bewildering. Several airlines fly direct to Italy, landing at either Rome or Milan. These include Alitalia, TWA and Delta. However, if your trip will not be confined to Italy, consult your travel agent on whether cheaper flights are available to other European cities. The *New York Times*, *LA Times*, *Chicago Tribune* and *San Francisco Chronicle Examiner* all have weekly travel sections with plenty of travel agents' ads.

Standard fares on commercial airlines are expensive and probably best avoided. However, travelling on a normal scheduled flight can be more secure and reliable, particularly for older travellers and families, who might prefer to avoid the potential inconveniences of the budget alternatives.

Discount and rock-bottom options from the USA include charter flights, stand-by and courier flights. Stand-by fares are often sold at 60% of the normal price for one-way tickets. Airhitch (☎ 212-864 2000), Suite 100, 2790 Broadway, New York, NY 10025, specialises in this sort of thing. You will need to give a general idea of where and when you want to go, and a few days before your departure you will be presented with a choice of two or three flights.

Courier flights are where you accompany freight or a parcel to its destination. A New York-Rome return on a courier flight can cost about US$300 to US$400 in the low season (more expensive from the US west coast). Generally courier flights require that you return within a specified period (sometimes within one or two weeks, but often up to one month). You will need to travel light, as luggage is usually restricted to what you can carry on to the plane (the parcel or freight you carry comes out of your luggage allowance), and you may have to be a US resident and apply for an interview before they will take you on. Most flights depart from New York.

A good source of information on courier flights is Discount Travel International in New York (☎ 212-362 3636), and Way to Go Travel in New York (☎ 212-947 1242) Los Angeles (☎ 213-466 1126) and San Francisco (☎ 415-292 7801). Call two or three months in advance at the beginning of the calendar month.

Charter flights tend to be significantly cheaper than scheduled flights. Reliable travel agents specialising in charter flights, as well as budget travel for students, include STA Travel and Council Travel, both of which have offices in major cities. Agencies specialising in cheap fares include:

STA Travel
48 East 11th St, New York, NY 10003 (☎ 212-477 7166)
914 Westwood Blvd, Los Angeles, CA 90024 (☎ 213-824 1574)
166 Geary St, Suite 702, San Francisco, CA 94108 (☎ 415-391 8407)
Council Travel
148 West 4th St, New York, NY 10011 (☎ 212-254 2525)
205 East 42nd St, New York, NY 10017 (☎ 212-661 1450)
1093 Broxton Ave, Los Angeles, CA 90024 (☎ 213-208 3551)
312 Sutter St, Suite 407, San Francisco, CA 94108 (☎ 415-42 3473)

To/From Canada

Both Alitalia and Air Canada have direct flights to Rome and Milan from Toronto and Montreal. Travel CUTS, which specialises in discount fares for students, has offices in all major cities. Otherwise scan the budget travel agents' ads in the *Toronto Globe & Mail*, the *Toronto Star* and the *Vancouver Province*. See the previous section for information on courier flights. For courier flights originating in Canada, contact FB on Board Courier Services (☎ 514-633 0740 in Toronto or Montreal, or ☎ 604-338 1366 in Vancouver). Airhitch (see the To/From the USA section) has standby fares to/from Toronto, Montreal and Vancouver.

To/From Australia

STA Travel and Flight Centres International are major dealers in cheap airfares, although heavily discounted fares can often be found at your local travel agent. The Saturday travel sections of the Melbourne *Age* and the *Sydney Morning Herald* have many advertisements offering cheap fares to Europe, but don't be surprised if they happen to be 'sold out' when you contact the agents – they are usually low-season fares on obscure airlines with conditions attached.

Discounted return airfares on mainstream airlines through reputable agents can be surprisingly cheap, with low-season fares around A$1600 to A$1800 return and high-season fares up to A$2500.

Qantas flies from Melbourne and Sydney to Rome twice a week and Alitalia has flights three times a week. Asian airlines such as Cathay Pacific, Singapore Airlines and Thai Airways all fly from Melbourne and Sydney to Rome. Flights from Perth are generally a few hundred dollars cheaper.

The following are some addresses for agencies offering good-value fares:

STA Travel
224 Faraday Street, Carlton, Vic 3053 (☎ 03-347 6911)
1st Floor, 732 Harris Street, Ultimo, NSW 2007 (☎ 02-281 9866)

Hackett Hall, University of Western Australia, Crawley, WA 6009 (☎ 09-380 2302)

Flight Centres International
Bourke Street Flight Centre, 19 Bourke Street, Melbourne, Vic 3000 (☎ 03-650 2899)
Martin Place Flight Centre, Shop 5, State Bank Centre, 52 Martin Place, Sydney, NSW 2000 (☎ 02-235 0166)
City Flight Centre, 25 Cinema City Arcade, Perth, WA 6000 (☎ 09-325 9222)

CIT
123 Clarence St, Sydney, NSW 2000 (☎ 02-29 4754)
Suite 10, 6th Floor, 442 Collins St, Melbourne, Vic 3000 (☎ 03-670 1322)
2nd Floor, 43 Ventnor Ave, Perth, WA 6000 (☎ 09-322 1096)

To/From New Zealand

STA Travel and Flight Centres International are popular travel agents in New Zealand. The cheapest fares to Europe are routed through the USA, and a RTW ticket may be cheaper than a return. Otherwise, you can fly from Auckland to pick up a connecting flight in Melbourne or Sydney. Air New Zealand can fly you to Bangkok to connect with a Thai Airways flight to Rome, to Singapore to connect with a Singapore Airlines flight, or to Hong Kong to connect with a Cathay Pacific flight. Garuda flies from Auckland to Rome via Jakarta.

Useful addresses include:

Flight Centres International
Auckland Flight Centre, Shop 3A, National Bank Towers, 205-225 Queen St, Auckland (☎ 09-309 6171)
STA Travel & International Travellers Centre
10 High St, Auckland (☎ 09-309 0458)
Campus Travel
Gate 1, Knighton Rd, Waikato University, Hamilton (☎ 07-856 9139)

To/From the UK

London is the discount flight capital of Europe, and finding a cheap fare to Italy should be no problem. The main airlines flying this route are British Airways (☎ 081-897 4000) and Alitalia (☎ 071-602 7111), which operate regular flights (usually several a day) to Rome, Milan, Venice, Turin, Naples and Pisa, as well other cities, including Palermo, during the summer. Normal fares on a scheduled flight are around £260 one way and £524 return on Alitalia, and £260 and £409 respectively on British Airways. However, Apex and other special fares are a better option and can cost as little as £180 return.

Bucket shops abound in London. They generally offer the cheapest tickets, usually with restricted validity. The magazines *Time Out* and *City Limits*, the Sunday newspapers, and the *Evening Standard* and *Exchange & Mart* carry ads for cheap fares. Also look out for the free magazines and newspapers widely available in London, especially *TNT* (recommended) and *Southern Cross* – you can usually pick them up outside the main train and tube stations.

The Trailfinders head office in west London is a good place to go for budget airfares and also has a travel library, bookshop, visa service and immunisation centre. STA Travel also has branches in the UK. Trailfinders can organise open-jaw return fares, whereby you can fly to one city in Italy and out of another. STA Travel has good-value fares as low as £280 return in the high season. Campus Travel is helpful and offers many interesting deals for students.

Another option is to take a direct charter flight from London to Rome or Milan. Italy Sky Shuttle in London, part of the Air Travel Group, specialises in charter flights, but also organises scheduled flights, to 22 destinations in Italy from London, Birmingham, Manchester, Glasgow and Edinburgh. An open return in August from London to Milan was £239. They can also organise a one week fly/drive deal which, in high season, costs £209 for the return flight and £185 for a small car. Cheaper fares can be found, for example an open-jaw ticket to Rome and out of Milan, valid for two months, costs from £194: it's just a matter of shopping around. Italy Sky Shuttle also has offices in Italy, from where you can buy tickets for charter flights to Britain. If you're booking a charter flight, remember to check what time of the day or night you'll be flying; many charter flights arrive very late at night. If you're flying in to Rome by charter, you will probably land at

Ciampino airport, from where there is no public transport into the city centre after about 11 pm.

There are two other organisations in the Air Travel Group: Magic of Italy, which organises resort holidays, and Italian Escapades, which puts together package deals.

Addresses of these and other agencies include:

Campus Travel
52 Grosvenor Gardens, SW1W OAG (☎ 0171-730 3402) tube: Victoria
Council Travel
28A Poland St, London W1 (☎ 0171-437 7767) tube: Oxford Circus
Italia Tours Ltd
205 Holland Park Ave, London W11 4XBT (☎ 0171-371 1114)
Air Travel Group (Italy Sky Shuttle)
227 Shepherd's Bush Rd, London W6 7AS (☎ 0181-748 1333)
STA Travel
74 Old Brompton Rd, London SW7 (☎ 0171-937 9921) tube: South Kensington
Trailfinders
194 Kensington High St, London W8 (☎ 0171-938 3232) tube: High St Kensington

Most UK travel agents are registered with the Association of British Travel Agents (ABTA). If you have paid for your flight to an ABTA-registered agent who then goes out of business, ABTA will guarantee a refund or an alternative. Unregistered bucket shops are obviously more risky.

The Globetrotters Club (BCM Roving, London WC1N 3XX) publishes a newsletter called *Globe* which contains useful information for travellers and can help you find a travelling companion.

To/From Continental Europe
Air travel between Italy and other places in Continental Europe is worth considering if you are pushed for time. Although relatively short hops can become extremely expensive, for longer journeys you can sometimes find airfares that beat on-the-ground alternatives in terms of cost.

If you want to fly from Greece to Italy, shop around the travel agents in the back-streets of Athens between Syntagma Square and Omonia Square. Cheap flights can also be found easily in Amsterdam – another major bucket shop centre.

Across Europe many travel agents have ties with STA Travel. Outlets include: Voyages et Découvertes (☎ 1-42 61 00 01), 21 Rue Cambon, 75001 Paris; SRID Reisen (☎ 069-43 01 91), Berger Strasse 118, Frankfurt; and Student Youth & Travel Service (☎ 01-323 3767), Nikis 11, Athens.

Several airlines, including Alitalia, Qantas and Air France, offer cut-rate fares on legs of international flights between European cities. These are usually very cheap, but the catch is that they are usually during the night, or very early in the morning, and the days on which you can fly are severely restricted. Some examples of cheap one-way fares, at the time of writing, were: Rome-Paris L136,000 (L272,000 return); Rome-London L179,000 (L295,000 return); Rome-Amsterdam L204,000 (L304,000 return).

Departure Tax
The departure tax payable when you leave Italy is factored into your airline ticket.

BUS
International bus travel in Europe tends to take second place to going by train. While buses can sometimes be cheaper, they are generally slower, less comfortable and more cramped. Eurolines (☎ 0171-730 0202), 52 Grosvenor Gardens, Victoria, London SW1, is the main international carrier, with representatives in Italy and across Europe. In summer 1995, buses were leaving for Rome three days a week (Monday, Wednesday and Friday) at 9.30 am and arriving in Rome at 6.15 pm the following day. (Timetables change, so check with Eurolines). Other destinations include Milan, Turin, Genoa, Florence, Rimini and Ancona. An example of fares in 1995 were: London-Rome £77 (one-way), £119 (return).

The bus companies operating the Eurolines service in Italy are: Lazzi in Florence (☎ 055-21 51 55), Piazza Adua, and Rome (☎ 06-884 08 40), Via Tagliamento

27r. In Turin go to the bus station at Corso Inghilterra 3 (☎ 011-433 25 25), and in Milan go to Autostradaleviaggi (☎ 02-72 00 13 04), Piazza Castello 1. Buses leave from Rome, Florence, Milan, Turin, Venice and Naples, as well as numerous other towns, for major cities throughout Europe, including Paris, London, Vienna, Prague, Barcelona, Athens, Amsterdam and Istanbul. Another option is to buy an explorer ticket which includes Rome as part of a series of European destinations.

For bookings and information on Eurolines elsewhere in Europe contact: Eurolines/Budget Bus (☎ 020-94 56 31) Amstelstation Zuidingang, Amsterdam; Eurolines (☎ 1-49 72 51 51), 3/5 Ave C de Gaulle Bagnolet, Paris; Eurolines Estacion Autobuses de Sants, Barcelona (☎ 3-490 40 00).

More examples of one-way ticket prices are: Rome-Paris L154,000, Venice-Barcelona L166,000 and Rome-London L205,000. Considering the small difference in price and the big difference in comfort, it really is preferable to take a train. Most fares carry a L10,000 to L15,000 supplement in July and August. Information and tickets can be obtained from the above companies, or from any Sestante CIT office within Italy.

TRAIN

Train travel is a convenient and simple means of travelling from most parts of Europe to Italy. It is certainly a popular way of getting around for backpackers and other young travellers, and even the more well-heeled travellers will find European trains a comfortable and reliable way to reach their destination.

If you plan to travel extensively by train in Europe it might be worth getting hold of the *Thomas Cook European Time-table*, which gives a complete listing of train schedules and indicates where supplements apply or where reservations are necessary. It is updated monthly and is available from Thomas Cook offices and agents worldwide.

EuroCity (EC) trains run from major destinations throughout Europe – includ-

ing Paris, Geneva, Zürich, Frankfurt, Vienna and Barcelona – direct to major Italian cities. On overnight hauls you can book a *cuccetta* (known outside Italy as a *couchette* or sleeping berth) for around US$18 for most international trains. In 1st class there are four bunks per cabin and in 2nd class there are six bunks. Sleepers are more expensive, but also much more comfortable.

It is always advisable to book a seat on EuroCity trains, or for any long-distance train travel to/from Italy. Trains are often extremely overcrowded, particularly during the summer months, and you could find yourself standing in the passageway for a six-hour trip or longer.

When crossing international borders on overnight trips, train conductors will usually collect your passport before you go to sleep and hand it back the following morning.

Travelling from the UK, you have the choice of train tickets which cover the channel crossing by ferry, on the faster Seacat, or you can take the new Eurostar train through the Channel Tunnel, which speeds up the initial part of the journey.

Examples of prices for normal one-way, 2nd-class fares from Italy are: Rome-London L210,000, Rome-Paris L160,000, and Rome-Barcelona L178,000. Examples of fares from the UK are: London Victoria-Rome £120 (one-way), £192 (return); London Victoria-Milan £103 (one-way) £159 (return).

Rail Passes

Eurail These passes can be bought by residents of non-European countries and are supposed to be purchased before arriving in Europe. If you have been resident in Europe for more than six months, you are entitled to buy an Inter-Rail pass, which is a better buy if you are aged under 26 (see the following section).

If you are planning to travel only within Italy, forget about buying a Eurail pass, since the relatively modest cost of train travel in Italy would make it difficult to justify the cost of the pass. The pass starts to become good value if you plan to do a reasonable amount of travelling within a short space of time – Eurail itself reckons that its passes only start saving money after 2400 km of travel within a two-week period – a long distance in Europe. Eurail Passes are valid for unlimited travel in 20 European countries, including Italy, but not including the UK, and are also valid for travel on ferries between Italy and Greece (and other European ferry routes). Note that, in Italy, you have to pay the supplement on Intercity and EuroCity trains (see the Getting Around section).

A Eurail Youthpass, for people aged under 26, is valid for unlimited 2nd-class travel for 15 days (US$398), one month (US$578) or two months (US$768). The Youth Flexipass, also for 2nd class, is valid for freely chosen days in a two-month period: five days for US$255, 10 days for US$398 or 15 days for US$540. A journey commencing after 7 pm counts as the next day's travel. The traveller must fill out in ink the relevant box in the calendar before starting the day's travel. If you don't fill in the boxes, or tamper with the pass in any way, there are hefty fines. Corresponding passes for people aged over 26 are available in 1st class only. The Flexipass is available for five, 10 or 15 freely chosen days in a two-month period, which cost US$348, US$560 or US$740 respectively. The standard Eurail pass (which has five versions) costs from US$498 for 15 days of unlimited travel up to US$1398 for three months. (See the Getting Around chapter for an idea of train fares within Italy.) Two or more people travelling together (minimum of three people from 1 April to 30 September) can get good discounts on a Saverpass, which works like the standard Eurail pass. Eurail passes for children are also available.

Lost or stolen Eurail passes can only be reissued in certain circumstances, so make sure you read the fine print and keep handy a copy of the Eurail Traveller's Guide which comes with the pass.

Europass This is a new rail pass for non-Europeans, which gives between five and 15 days' unlimited travel within a two-month period. Youth (aged under 26) and adult passes are available and can be purchased at the same outlets as for Eurail passes. They are bit cheaper than Eurail, but travel is limited to fewer countries, Italy included. Chosen countries must be adjacent.

Inter-Rail These passes are available to residents of European countries. Terms and conditions vary from country to country, but it is always the case that in the country of origin there is only a discount of 50% on normal fares. Therefore, if you're planning to travel only in Italy, it certainly isn't worth buying one there. Inter-Rail cards should be treated like cash, as you can make no claims in the event of loss or theft. There are two main types of pass: for travellers over 26 and for travellers under 26. The pass for travellers over 26, the Inter-Rail 26+, is not valid for travel in Italy. The pass for those under 26 has been split into zones. Italy is in zone G, with Greece, Turkey and Slovenia. A 15-day pass for travel in one zone costs £179. Multi-zone passes are better value and are valid for one month: two zones costs £209, three zones £229 and all zones £249.

Euro-Domino These passes (known as Freedom Pass in the UK) are valid for the country of your choice for three, five or 10 days. All of the countries covered by the zonal Inter-Rail pass (including Italy) are covered. For 2nd-class travel for three/five/10 days in Italy, the pass costs £105/£131/£219; for people under 26, the pass costs £79/£99/£164.

Italy Rail Passes These are valid for 3000 km of travel and can be shared by up to five people. They cost £90.

Other Cheap Tickets Travellers aged under 26 can buy Billet International de Jeunesse tickets (BIJ, also known in Italy as BIGE), which cut fares by up to 50% throughout Europe, although you can't always bank on a substantial reduction. Examples of one-way fares are Rome-Paris L122,000 (L244,000 return), Florence-Amsterdam

L173,000 (L346,000 return), and Milan-Vienna L77,000 (L144,000 return). These tickets are valid for two months and, although you must specify your destination, their great advantage is that you can make as many stopovers as you like within the period of validity. BIJ tickets can be purchased at Transalpino offices at most major train stations, at other agencies, including Campus Travel (☎ 0171-730 3402), 52 Grosvenor Gardens, SW1W OAG), or from any CTS or Sestante CIT office in Italy.

For people aged over 26 there are Rail Inclusive Tour (RIT) tickets. These are for either 1st or 2nd class and carry a discount of 20%. They must be purchased in conjunction with other tourist services, such as a reservation for a minimum of three nights' accommodation at the city of arrival. CTS and Sestante CIT can also provide information about these tickets.

People aged over 60 should investigate the special Rail Europe Senior Card.

For information about train discounts within Italy, see the Getting Around chapter.

Security

Travellers' horror stories about being robbed during train journeys range from whole carriages being gassed through the ventilation system by bandits and the occupants being divested of their belongings, to individual travellers being drugged and robbed. This sort of thing can happen, but it is not nearly as widespread as some people make out. Nevertheless it pays to take basic precautions. Don't leave your belongings unattended, and make sure you lock your compartment doors overnight. If it is necessary to leave your belongings, at least ensure that suitcases or packs are locked and, if possible, secured to the luggage rack.

CAR & MOTORBIKE

Travelling with your own vehicle is the best way to get to more remote places and gives you the most flexibility. An added bonus is that compared to Australia and North America it is not necessary to spend very long on the road between places of interest.

In Italy, the drawbacks are that cars can be inconvenient in larger cities, where you will have to deal with heavy traffic and parking problems. In southern Italy car theft is a major problem in some cities, so make sure you are well insured. Also bear in mind that *benzina* (petrol) is expensive in Italy and that you must pay tolls on the autostradas (see the Car & Motorbike section of Getting Around chapter for further details).

The main points of entry to Italy are the Mont Blanc tunnel from France at Chamonix, which connects with the A5 for Turin and Milan; the Grand St Bernard tunnel from Switzerland, which also connects with the A5; and the Brenner Pass from Austria, which connects with the A22 to Bologna. Mountain passes in the Alps are often closed in winter and sometimes in autumn and spring, making the tunnels a less scenic, but more reliable way to arrive in Italy.

Paperwork & Preparations

Proof of ownership of a private vehicle should always be carried (Vehicle Registration Document for British-registered cars) when driving through Europe. A British or other European driving licence is acceptable for driving throughout Europe, although in Italy the carabinieri may require an Italian translation or International Driving Permit for non-EU licences, or for the old-style green UK licences (see the Documents section in the Facts for the Visitor chapter). You are unlikely to have any problems without a translation, but in a tight spot it might prove useful.

Third party motor insurance is a minimum requirement in Italy and throughout Europe. Most UK insurance policies automatically provide this for EU countries and some others. It is compulsory to have a Green Card, an internationally recognised proof of insurance, which can be obtained from your insurer. Also ask your insurer for a European Accident Statement form, which can simplify matters in the event of an accident. Never sign statements you can't read or understand – insist on a translation and sign that only if it's acceptable.

A European breakdown assistance policy is a good investment, such as the AA Five Star Service or the RAC Eurocover Motoring Assistance. In Italy, assistance can be obtained through the national automobile club, Automobile Club Italiano (ACI). See the Getting Around chapter for details. ACI has a free breakdown service, including emergency tow-truck service, to foreign tourists driving cars with non-Italian number plates. See the Useful Organisations section in the Facts for the Visitor chapter.

Every vehicle travelling across an international border should display a nationality plate of its country of registration. A warning triangle (to be used in the event of a breakdown) is compulsory in Italy and throughout Europe. Recommended accessories are a first-aid kit, a spare bulb kit and a fire extinguisher.

In the UK, further information can be obtained from the RAC (☎ 0345-33 1133) or the AA (☎ 0256-20123).

Rental

There is a mind-boggling variety of special deals and terms and conditions attached to car rental. However, there are a few pointers to help you through. Multinational agencies – Hertz, Avis, Budget and Europe's largest rental agency, Europcar – will provide a reliable service and good standard of vehicle.

However, if you walk into an office and ask for a car on the spot, you will always pay high rates, even allowing for special weekend deals. National and local firms can sometimes undercut the multinationals, but be sure to examine the rental agreement carefully (although this might be difficult if it is in another language).

Planning ahead and prebooking a rental car through a multinational agency before leaving home will enable you to find the best deals. Prebooked and prepaid rates are always cheaper, and there are fly/drive combinations and other programmes that are worth looking into. You will simply pick up the vehicle on your arrival in Italy (or other European city) and then return it to a nominated point at the end of the rental period.

Ask your travel agent for information, or contact one of the major rental agencies. Holiday Autos has good rates for Europe, for which you need to prebook; it has offices in England (☎ 0171-491 11 11) and the USA (☎ 0909-949 1737).

No matter where you rent, make sure you understand what is included in the price (unlimited km, tax, insurance, collision damage waiver etc) and what your liabilities are. The minimum rental age in Italy is 21 years, while in other European countries it can be as high as 23 years. A credit card is usually required.

Motorbike and moped rental is common in Italy and there are specialist rental agencies in most cities (see the Getting Around chapter).

Purchase

It is illegal for nonresidents to purchase vehicles in Italy and some other European countries. The UK is probably the best place to buy, as second-hand prices are good. Whether buying privately or from a dealer, if you are English speaking, the absence of language difficulties will help you to establish exactly what you are getting for your money. Bear in mind that you will be getting a left-hand drive car (ie steering wheel on the right) if you buy in the UK. If you want a right-hand drive car and can afford to buy new, prices are relatively low in Belgium, the Netherlands and Luxembourg. Paperwork can be tricky wherever you buy, and many countries, including Italy, have compulsory roadworthiness checks on older vehicles which can add considerably to initial purchase costs.

Camper Van

A popular way to tour Europe is for three or four people to band together and buy a camper van. This mode of holidaying is extremely popular in Italy. London is the usual embarkation point. Look at the adverts in London's free magazine *TNT* if you want to form a group or buy a van. Private vendors gather on a daily basis at the Van market in Market Rd, London N7 (near Caledonian Rd tube station). Some second-hand dealers offer a 'buy-back' scheme for when you return from Europe but, if you have the time, buying and reselling privately is more advantageous. A great advantage of travelling in a camper van is the flexibility, but a disadvantage is that they can be difficult to manoeuvre around towns.

Motorcycling

Europe is made for motorcycle touring and Italy is no exception. Motorcyclists literally swarm into the country in summer to tour the winding, scenic roads, particularly in mountainous areas. Wearing crash helmets is compulsory in Italy, as throughout Europe. It is worth noting that motorcyclists rarely have to book ahead for ferries. You will be able to enter restricted traffic areas in Italian cities without any problems and Italian traffic police generally turn a blind eye to motorcycles parked on footpaths.

Anyone considering a motorcycle tour from the UK might benefit from joining the International Motorcyclists Tour Club (£19 per annum plus £3 joining fee). It organises European (and worldwide) bike jaunts, and members meet regularly to swap information. Contact Ken Brady, membership Secretary, Cornerways, Chapel Rd, Swanmore, Southampton, 303 2QA, UK.

SEA

Ferries connect Italy to Greece, Turkey, Tunisia and Malta. There are also services to Corsica, Toulon and Marseille in France, Durras, Albania and Barcelona in Spain. Ticket prices vary according to the time of year and are at their most expensive during summer. Prices for cars, camper vans and motorbikes vary according to the size of the vehicle, and bicycles can sometimes be taken

free of charge. Eurail pass and Inter-Rail pass holders pay only a supplement on the Italy-Greece route, but must travel with approved companies. Ticket prices are very competitive on the heavily serviced Brindisi-Greece route, and travellers wanting to pick up the best deals can shop around in Brindisi.

For detailed information, see the Getting There & Away sections for Brindisi and Bari (ferries to/from Greece), Ancona (to/from Greece and Turkey), Naples and Trapani (to/from Tunisia), Naples and Syracuse (to/from Malta), Porto Torres (to/from Marseille and Toulon), Livorno and Santa Teresa Gallura (to/from Corsica), Livorno and the Lipari Islands (to/from Barcelona), and Trieste (to/from Albania).

TOURS

See the Getting Around chapter for information about tours to/from Italy.

WARNING

The information in this chapter is particularly vulnerable to change: prices for international travel are volatile, routes are introduced and cancelled, schedules change, special deals come and go, and rules and visa requirements are amended. Airlines and governments seem to take a perverse pleasure in making price structures and regulations as complicated as possible. You should check directly with the airline or a travel agent to make sure you understand how a fare (and ticket you may buy) works. In addition, the travel industry is highly competitive and there are many lurks and perks.

The upshot of this is that you should get opinions, quotes and advice from as many airlines and travel agents as possible before you part with your hard-earned cash. The details given in this chapter should be regarded as pointers and are not a substitute for your own careful, up-to-date research.

Getting Around

AIR

Travelling by plane is expensive within Italy and it makes much better sense to use the efficient and considerably cheaper train and bus services. The domestic airlines are Alitalia and Meridiana. The main airports are in Rome, Pisa, Milan, Naples, Catania and Cagliari, but there are other, smaller airports throughout Italy. Domestic flights can be booked either directly through the airlines or through agencies such as Sestante CIT, CTS and normal travel agencies.

Alitalia offers a range of discounts for students, families, the elderly and weekend travel, as well as during off-peak periods. For instance, in 1995, you could travel from Rome to Milan for almost 50% off from 11 am to 3 pm on weekdays. The types and conditions of discounts vary from year to year and it is best to check with travel agents when buying your ticket. It should be noted that airline fares fluctuate, and that special deals sometimes only apply when tickets are bought in Italy. The Airfares Chart will give you an idea of return fares at the time of writing. Barring special deals, a one-way fare is generally half the cost of the return fare.

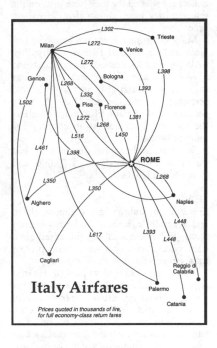

Italy Airfares

Prices quoted in thousands of lire, for full economy-class return fares

BUS

Bus travel within Italy is provided by numerous companies, and services vary from local routes linking small villages, to those making major intercity connections, which are fast and reliable. It is generally slightly cheaper to travel by bus than by train and, by utilising the local services, it is possible to arrive in just about any location throughout the country. However, services connecting small villages to each other or to larger provincial towns are provided for the local people and are usually not geared to tourist needs. Therefore, while it might be possible to arrive in a tiny village, it might not be possible to leave until the next day.

It is usually not necessary to make reservations on buses, although it is advisable in high season for overnight or long haul trips. Phone numbers and addresses of major bus companies are listed throughout this book.

Buses can be a cheaper and faster way to get around if your destination is not on major train lines, for instance from Umbria to Rome and Florence, and in the interior areas of Sicily and Sardinia.

It is usually possible to get bus timetables for the provinces and for intercity services from local tourist offices. If not, staff will be able to point you in the direction of the main bus companies. In larger cities most of the main intercity bus companies have ticket offices or operate through agencies, and buses leave from either a bus station (*autostazione*) or from a particular piazza or street. Details are provided in the individual towns and city sections. In some smaller towns and villages tickets are sold in bars – just ask for *biglietti per il pullman* – but often tickets are sold on the bus. Note that, unlike trains in Italy, buses almost always leave on time.

Major companies which run long-haul services include Marozzi (Rome to Brindisi); SAIS and Segesta (Rome to Sicily); Lazzi and SITA (from Lazio, Tuscany and other regions to the Alps – Lazzi also runs international services). See the Getting There & Away sections of Rome and Florence as well as the Getting There & Away chapter for more information.

Some price examples for intercity bus travel are: Palermo-Rome L70,000 and Rome-Siena L20,000.

TRAIN

Travelling by train in Italy is simple, cheap and generally efficient. The Ferrovie dello Stato (FS) is the partially privatised state train system and there are several private train services throughout the country.

There are several types of trains: *regionale*, which usually stops at all stations and can be very slow; *interregionale*, which runs between the regions; *diretto*, which indicates that you do not need to change trains to reach the final destination; *espresso*, which stops only at major stations; Intercity (IC) which services only the major cities; EuroCity (IC), which connect major European cities, but can also be used to get from Rome to Milan, for example; and the ETR450, known as the Pendolino a new express service between Rome, Florence, Bologna and Milan.

Travellers should note that a new ticket validation system has been introduced by the FS, whereby tickets must be punched by machines installed at the entrance to all train platforms. The machines are yellow and easy to find. The rule does not apply to tickets purchased outside Italy.

Costs

To travel on the Intercity and EuroCity trains, you are required to pay a *supplemento*, an additional charge determined by the distance you are travelling. For instance, on the Intercity train between Rome and Florence you will pay an extra L12,000. On the ETR 450, it is obligatory to make a booking, since they don't carry standing room passengers. The cost of the ticket includes the supplement and booking fee. The one-way fare from Rome to Florence on the Pendolino is L42,800 in 2nd class and L67,600 in 1st class. If you buy the 2nd-class fare, the difference in price between the Pendolino (1½ hours) and the Intercity (around 2 hours) is only L8000. For the extra money you get a faster, much more comfortable service, with an airline-type snack thrown in. The Pendolino always takes priority over other trains, so there's no risk of long delays in the middle-of-nowhere.

Always check whether the train you are about to catch is an Intercity, and pay the supplement before you get on, otherwise you will pay extra.

On overnight trips within Italy it can be worth paying extra for a *cuccetta* (L30,000 in a compartment with four bunks, L21,000 in a compartment with six bunks).

Some price examples for one-way train fares (not including supplements) are: Rome-Florence L38,000 (1st class) and L22,800 (2nd class); Venice-Milan L33,100 (1st class), L19,500 (2nd class); Turin-Reggio di Calabria L129,500 (1st class), L76,200 (2nd class).

Discounts

It is not worth buying a Eurail pass or Inter-Rail pass if you are going to travel only in Italy, since train fares are reasonably cheap (see the Rail Passes section in the Getting There & Away chapter). The FS offers its own discount passes for travel within the country. These include the Carta Verde for young people aged 12 to 26 years. It costs L40,000, is valid for one year and entitles you to a 20% discount on all train travel, but you'll need to do a fair bit of travelling to get your money's worth. Children aged between four and 12 years are automatically entitled to a 50% discount, and under four years they can travel for free. The Carta d'Argento entitles people aged 60 years and over to a 20% discount on 1st and 2nd-class travel for one year. It also costs L40,000. You can buy a kilometric ticket *(biglietto chilometrico)*, which is valid for two months and allows you to cover 3000 km, with a maximum of 20 trips. It costs L186,000 (2nd class) and you must pay the supplement if you catch an Intercity train. Its main attraction is that it can be used by up to five people, either singly or together.

Timetables & Reservations

Train timetables are posted at all train stations. There often are information booths (generally with long queues), or computerised information facilities. Tourist offices can also usually provide some information about trains. You can get timetable information and make train bookings at most travel agents, including CTS and Sestante CIT. You can make bookings for the Pendolino at travel agents, or at special booking offices at the relevant train stations. If you are doing a reasonable amount of travelling, it is worth buying a train timetable. There are several available, including the official FS timetables, which are available at newspaper stands in or near train stations for around L5000.

There are also several private train lines in Italy, which are noted throughout this book. There are also left-luggage facilities at all train stations. They are often open for 24 hours a day, but if not, they usually close only for a couple of hours after midnight. They open seven days a week and charge L1500 for each piece of luggage.

TAXI

Taxis in Italy are very expensive (even the shortest taxi ride in Rome will cost around L10,000) and it is generally possible to catch a bus instead. If you need a taxi, you can usually find them on taxi ranks at train and bus stations or you can telephone (radio-taxi phone numbers are listed throughout this book in the Getting Around sections of the major cities). However, if you book a taxi by

phone, you will be charged for the trip the driver makes to reach you. Taxis will rarely stop when hailed on the street, and generally will respond to telephone bookings only if you phone from a rank, or you phone from a house, office, hotel etc.

Rates vary from city to city. A good indication of the average is Rome, where taxis charge L6400 flagfall (for the first three km), then L1200 per km. There is a L3000 supplement from 10 pm to 7 am and L1000 from 7 am to 10 pm on Sunday and public holidays. After three km, the rate is L300 for every 250 metres. If you are stationary for more than nine minutes, the meter will start to tick over L300 every 50 seconds. The limit on the number of people is four or five depending on the size of the taxi.

Beware of the Rome airport supplement – L15,000 on travel to and from the airport, because it is outside the city limits. Watch out also for taxi drivers who take advantage of new arrivals and stretch out the length of the trip, and consequently the size of the fare.

CAR & MOTORBIKE

Trains and buses are fine for travelling through most of Italy, but if you want to get off the beaten track, renting a car or motorbike is a good idea, particularly in Sicily and Sardinia, where some of the most interesting and beautiful places are difficult to reach by public transport. See the Getting There & Away chapter for details on preparation, insurance and paperwork.

Roads & Maps

The Istituto Geografico de Agostini publishes detailed road maps for all of Italy. Its book *Atlante Stradale Italiano* has road maps as well as town maps and is available at bookshops throughout Italy. You can also buy individual maps of regions. TCI maps are excellent, including their *Atlante Stradale*. Other good options are AA's *Big Road Atlas* and the *Michelin Motoring Atlas*. All include a good number of town maps, which are indispensable if you plan to tackle Rome, Milan, Florence or Naples. See the Bookshops information in the Books section of the Facts for the Visitor chapter.

Roads are generally good throughout the country and there is an excellent network of autostradas. The main north-south link is the Autostrada del Sole, which extends from Milan to Reggio di Calabria (called the A1 from Milan to Naples and the A3 from Naples to Reggio di Calabria). Drivers usually travel at very high speed in the left-hand fast lane on the autostradas, so remain in that lane only to pass other cars. The only problem with the autostradas is that they are toll roads and the fees are increasingly expensive: for example Rome-Bologna L32,000; Rome-Orvieto L8000; Venice to Florence L20,500. Travellers with time to spare could consider using the system of state roads *(strade statali)*, which are often multi-lane dual carriageways and toll-free They are represented on maps as 'SS'. Provincial roads *(strade provinciali)* are sometimes little more than country lanes, but provide access to some of the more beautiful scenery and myriad towns and villages. They are represented as 'SP' on maps.

Road Rules

In Italy, as throughout Continental Europe, people drive on the right side of the road and overtake on the left. Unless otherwise indicated, you must give way to cars coming from the right. It is compulsory to wear seat belts if fitted to the car (front seat belts on all cars, rear seat belts on cars produced after 26 April 1990), and carabinieri spend a lot of time looking for those who break the law. If caught, you will be required to pay a L50,000 fine on the spot, although this doesn't seem to deter Italians, many of whom use them only on the autostradas.

Random breath tests are now made in Italy, but generally only near discos at closing time and after road accidents. If you're involved in an accident while under the influence of alcohol, the penalties can be severe. The limit on blood-alcohol content is 0.08%.

Speed limits, unless otherwise indicated by local signs, are: on autostradas 130 km/h

for cars of 1100cc or more, 110 km/h for smaller cars and for motorcycles under 350cc; on all main, non-urban highways 110 km/h; on secondary, non-urban highways 90 km/h; and in built-up areas 50 km/h. Speeding fines follow EU standards and are L50,000 for up to 10 km/h over the limit, L200,000 for up to 40 km/h, and L500,000 for more than 40 km/h. Driving through a red light will cost L100,000.

You don't need a licence to ride a moped under 50cc, but you should be aged 14 years or over, and a helmet is compulsory up to age 18; you can't carry passengers or ride on autostradas. A new law is being considered to make a helmet and licence compulsory for anyone riding a moped – check this when you arrive. The speed limit for a moped is 40 km/h. To ride a motorcycle or scooter up to 125cc, you must be at least 16 years old and have a licence (a car licence will do). Helmets are compulsory. Over 125cc you need a motorcycle licence and, of course, a helmet. There is no lights-on requirement for motorcycles during the day – in fact, this practice is officially illegal in Italy!

City Driving

Driving in Italian towns and cities is quite a 'different' experience and may well present the unprepared with headaches. The Italian attitude to driving bears little comparison to the English concept of traffic in ordered lanes (a normal two-lane road is likely to carry three or four lanes of traffic), and the farther south you travel, the less drivers seem to pay attention to road rules. Instead, the main factor in determining right of way is whichever driver is more forceful, or *prepotente*.

If you must drive in an Italian city, particularly in Rome or Naples, remain calm, keep your eyes on the car in front of you and you should be OK. Most roads are well signposted, and once you arrive in a city or village, follow the *centro* signs. Be extremely careful where you park your car. In the major cities it will almost certainly be towed away and you will pay a heavy fine if you leave it in an area marked with a sign reading *Zona Rimozione* (Removal Zone) and featuring a tow truck. A stopover in a medieval hill town will generally mean leaving the car in a car park some distance from the town centre.

Some Italian cities, including Rome, Siena, Perugia, Milan and Turin, have introduced restricted access to motorists (both private and rental cars) in their historical centres. The restrictions, however, do not apply to vehicles with foreign registrations, to allow tourists to reach their hotels. If you are stopped by a traffic police officer, you will need to name the hotel where you are staying and produce a pass (provided by your hotel) if required. Motorcyclists with large bikes might be stopped, but mopeds *(motorini)* and scooters (such as Vespas) are able to enter without any problems.

Parking

It is probably a good idea to leave your car in a supervised car park if you have luggage, but even then it's probably unwise to leave your belongings in an unattended car. Car parks are indicated in major city sections in this book. Car parks are denoted throughout Italy by signs with a white 'P' on a blue background.

At supervised car parks you'll usually pay from L2000 to L4000 for the first hours and around L2000 to L3000 per hour after that. Open air carparks are usually only supervised during business hours. Undercover ones close from around midnight to 7 am.

Petrol

The cost of petrol in Italy is very high, at around L1500 per litre (slightly less for unleaded petrol). Petrol is called *benzina*, unleaded petrol is *benzina senza piombo* and diesel is *gasolio*. If you are driving a car which uses LPG (liquid petroleum gas), you will need to buy a special guide to service stations which have *gasauto* or GPL. By law these must be located in nonresidential areas and are usually in the country or on city outskirts. GPL costs around L890 per litre.

Rental

It is cheaper to rent a car or camper van before leaving your own country, for instance through some sort of fly/drive deal. Most major firms, including Hertz, Avis and Budget, will arrange this, and you simply pick up the vehicle at a nominated point when you arrive in Italy. Foreign offices of Sestante CIT, can also help to organise car or camper van rental before you leave home (see the section on Rental in the Getting There & Away chapter).

You will need to be aged 21 years or over (23 years or over for some companies) to rent a car in Italy, and you will find the deal far easier to organise if you have a credit card. Most firms will accept your standard licence, sometimes with an Italian translation (which can usually be provided by the agencies themselves) or International Driving Permit.

At the time of writing, Avis offered a special weekend rate which compared well with rates offered by other firms: around L180,000 for a Fiat Uno or Renault Clio, from Friday 9 am to Monday 9 am. The cost for a week was around L850,000. Avis offered a deal on camper van rental, to be organised before you left home, from around US$106 a day for a four-berth van, but does not rent camper vans in Italy itself. Details are available through Sestante CIT offices abroad. Local operators aren't necessarily cheaper, and none can compete against fly/drive deals organised beforehand.

Rental motorbikes come in two versions: mopeds under 50cc, and scooters, such as a Vespa. The average cost for a Vespa is around L60,000 per day and L380,000 per week. For a small moped you will pay from around L50,000 per day and L300,000 per week. A 50cc Vespa will cost you from around L60,000 per day to L360,000 per week. To rent a Vespa or moped of 50cc you must be aged 14 years or over and no licence is required. With mopeds and scooters over 125cc you need a licence and must be 16 years old or more. Note that many places require a sizeable deposit, and that you could be responsible for reimbursing part of the cost of the bike if it is stolen. Always check the fine print in the contract. See the Road Rules section for age, licence and helmet requirements.

Rental agencies are listed under the major cities in this book. Most tourist offices can provide information about where to rent a car or motorbike, otherwise look in the local Yellow Pages (Pagine Gialle).

Purchase

Car It is not possible for foreigners to buy a car in Italy, as the law requires that you must be a resident to own and register one. The only way to get around this is to have a friend who is a resident of Italy buy one for you.

It is possible to buy a cheap, small 10-year-old car, for as little as L1,500,000, ranging up to around L7,000,000 for a decent five-year-old Fiat Uno, and up to L10,000,000 for a two-year-old Fiat Uno. The best way to find a car to buy is to look in the classified section of local newspapers. If you buy a car in another country and need any assistance or advice in Italy, contact the ACI (see the Useful Organisations section in the Facts for the Visitor chapter).

Motorbike The same laws apply to owning and registering a motorbike. The cost of a second-hand Vespa ranges from L500,000 to L1,500,000, and a moped will cost from L300,000 to L1,000,000. Prices for more powerful bikes start at L1,500,000.

BICYCLE

Bikes are available for rent in most Italian towns (see Getting Around in each city section), but if you are planning to do a lot of cycling, consider buying a bike in Italy. If you shop around, bargain prices range from L190,000 for a woman's bike without gears to L300,000 for a mountain bike with 16 gears, but you will need to pay a lot more for a very good bike. Rental costs for a bicycle range from L10,000 a day to around L40,000 per week. If you plan to bring your own bike, check with your airline for any additional

costs. The bike will need to be disassembled and packed for the journey.

A primary consideration on a cycling tour is to travel light, but you should take a few tools and spare parts, including a puncture repair kit and a spare inner tube. Panniers are essential to balance your possessions on either side of the bike frame. A bike helmet is a very good idea, as is a very solid bike lock and chain, essential to prevent your bike from being stolen.

One organisation that can help you plan your bike tour is the Cyclists' Touring Club (CTC ☎ 01483-417 217), Cotterell House, 69 Meadrow, Godalming, Surrey GU7 3HS, Britain. It can supply information to members on cycling conditions, itineraries and cheap insurance. Membership costs £24 per year or £12 for people aged under 18.

If you get tired of pedalling and want to put your feet up on a train, you can organise for your bike to be transported by train. It is quite cheap, although bikes will usually only be accepted as luggage on the slower local trains. Fast trains (IC, EC etc) will generally not accommodate bikes and they must be sent as registered luggage. This can take a few days and will probably mean that your bike won't be on the same train that you travel on. It might be an idea to send your bike in advance, if possible. During certain off-peak periods (April-June and September-October) it is possible to take your bike on as normal luggage – but only on two trains, the EC 54 and the EC 55 between Zurich and Rome (which also means between Milan, Florence and Rome). Travelling internationally, it costs L45,000 to carry the bike, and L10,000 for travel within Italy. Check with the FS or a travel agent that the service still operates.

The European Bike Express is a coach service where cyclists can travel with their machines. It runs in summer from north-east England to Italy or Spain, with pick-up/drop-off points en route. The return fare is £135 (£125 for CTC members); phone ☎ 01642-251 440 in England for details. See the Activities section in the Facts for the Visitor chapter for suggestions on places to cycle.

HITCHING

Hitching is never safe in any country, and we don't recommend it. Travellers who decide to hitchhike should understand they are taking a small but potentially serious risk. People who do choose to hitchhike will be safer if they travel in pairs and let someone know where they are planning to go.

It is illegal to hitchhike on Italy's autostradas, but quite acceptable to stand near the entrance to the toll booths. It is not a major pastime in Italy, but Italians are friendly people and you will generally find a lift. A man and a woman travelling together is probably the best combination. Two or more men must expect some delays, while two women together will make good time, although it is not a good idea for women, even in pairs, to hitchhike in some parts of Italy, particularly in the south, Sicily and Sardinia. Women travelling alone should be extremely cautious about hitching anywhere in Italy.

Hitching on smaller roads where there is less traffic can be very time-consuming, and don't try to hitchhike from city centres: take public transport to suburban exit routes or to the nearest point to Autostrada entrances. Never hitchhike where drivers can't stop in good time or without causing an obstruction. You could also approach drivers at petrol stations and truck stops. Look presentable, carry as little luggage as possible and hold a sign in Italian, indicating your destination. It is sometimes possible to arrange lifts in advance – scan student notice boards in colleges and universities, or ask around at youth hostels. Dedicated hitchhikers might like to get Simon Calder's *Europe – a Manual for Hitch-hikers*.

BOAT

Large ferries *(navi)* service the islands of Sicily and Sardinia, and smaller ferries *(traghetti)* and hydrofoils *(aliscafi)* service areas such as the Lipari Islands, Elba, the Tremiti Islands, Capri and Ischia. The main embarkation points for Sardinia are Genoa, Livorno, Civitavecchia and Naples; for Sicily the main points are Naples and Villa San Giovanni in Calabria. The main points of arrival in Sicily are Palermo and Messina; in Sardinia they are Cagliari, Arbatax, Olbia and Porto Torres.

Tirrenia Navigazione is the major company servicing the Mediterranean and it has offices throughout Italy. The FS also operates ferries to Sicily and Sardinia. Travellers can choose between cabin accommodation (men and women are usually segregated in 2nd class, although families will be kept together) or a *poltrona*, an airline-type armchair. Deck class is available only in summer and only on some ferries, so ask when making your booking.

Detailed information is provided in the Getting There & Away sections of the Sicily and Sardinia chapters. Many services are overnight and all ferries carry vehicles (generally it is possible to take a bicycle free of charge). Restaurant, bar and recreation facilities, including cinemas, are available on the larger, long-haul ferries.

LOCAL TRANSPORT

All major cities have good transport systems, including bus and underground train systems, although in Venice your only options are by boat or on foot. Efficient bus services also operate between neighbouring towns and villages. Tourist offices will provide information on urban public transport systems, including bus routes and maps of the subway systems.

In the cities, bus services are usually frequent and reliable. You must always buy bus tickets before you board the bus, and validate them once aboard. It is common practice among Italians and many tourists to ride buses for free by not validating their tickets – just watch how many people rush to punch their tickets when an inspector boards the bus. However, if you get caught with an un-validated ticket, you will be fined up to L50,000 on the spot. While in the past many foreigners pleaded ignorance and got away with it, today inspectors are less likely to accept your story, particularly since, in many cities, the signs telling people to punch their tickets are in English as well as Italian.

Tickets are sold at most tobacconists, at many newspaper stands and at ticket booths at bus stations (for instance, outside Stazione Termini in Rome where many of the urban buses stop). Tickets are different from city to city and generally cost from L1000 to L1600, although most cities offer 24-hour tourist tickets for around L4000.

On the subways in Milan (MM), Rome and Naples (Metropolitana) you must buy tickets and validate them before getting on the train. They are different from bus tickets, and you can usually get them at tobacconists and newspaper stands.

TOURS

People wanting to travel to Italy on a fully organised tour have a wide range of options, and it is best to discuss these with your travel agent. Foreign offices of CIT (see the Tourist Offices section in the Facts for the Visitor chapter) can provide information and organise package tours. Student or youth travel agencies will be able to recommend companies which specialise in tours for young people. In London these include: Contiki Travel Ltd (☎ 0171-637 0802), Royal National Hotel, Bedford Way WC1H ODG (tube: Russell Square), Tracks (☎ 0171-937 3028), 12 Abingdon Rd W8 6SH and Top Deck (☎ 0171-370 4555), 131 Earls Court Rd, London SW5 9RH.

For people aged over 60, Saga Holidays offers holidays ranging from cheap coach tours to luxury cruises. You will find offices in Britain (☎ 0800-300 500), Saga Building, Middelburg Square, Folkstone, Kent CT20 1AZ; the USA (☎ 0617-451 6808), 120 Boyleston St, Boston, MA 02116; and Australia (☎ 02-957 4222), Level 4, 20 Alfred St, Milsons Point, Sydney 2061.

Being in a tour group removes most of the hassles associated with travelling – such as where to sleep and eat and how to get around. However, it also takes away your independence and opportunities to make interesting detours or to take your time savouring the sights, so make sure you weigh up the pros and cons carefully before deciding on a guided tour.

Once in Italy, it is often less expensive and usually more enjoyable to see the sights independently, but if you are in a hurry or prefer guided tours, go to the CIT office (in all major cities). Apart from package tours of Italy, they organise city tours for an average price of L40,000. Local tourist offices sometimes offer cheap guided tours and can generally assist with information on other local agencies which offer tours.

Numerous mountain guide groups throughout the Alps offer guided hikes, ranging from nature walks to demanding week-long treks which may or may not require some mountaineering skills. Information about mountain guides can always be obtained from tourist offices throughout the Alps: many are also listed in the Alpine sections of the northern Italy chapters.

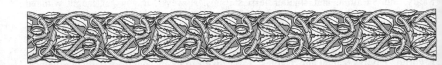

Rome (Roma)

'I now realise all the dreams of my youth,' wrote Goethe on his arrival in Rome in the winter of 1786. Perhaps Rome (Roma) today is more chaotic, but certainly no less romantic or fascinating. In this city a phenomenal concentration of history, legend and monuments coexists with an equally phenomenal concentration of people busily going about everyday life. It is easy to pick the tourists, because they are only the only ones to turn their heads as the bus passes the Colosseum.

In Rome, there is visible evidence of the two great empires of the Western world: the Roman Empire and the Christian Church. From the Roman Forum and the Colosseum to St Peter's Basilica and the Vatican and in almost every piazza, lies history on so many levels, that the saying 'Rome, a lifetime is not enough' must certainly be true.

It is generally agreed that Rome had its origins in a group of Etruscan, Latin and Sabine settlements on the Palatine, Esquiline and Quirinal hills – these and surrounding hills are the now-famous seven hills of Rome. Ancient Romans put the date of their city's foundation as 21 April 753 BC and, indeed, archaeological discoveries have confirmed the existence of a settlement on the Palatine in that period. It is, however, the legend of Romulus & Remus which prevails. The twin sons of Rhea Silvia and the war god Mars, they were raised by a she-wolf after being abandoned on the banks of the Tiber (Tevere) river. The myth says Romulus killed his brother during a battle over who should govern, and then established the city of Rome on the Palatine. Romulus, who had established himself as the first king of Rome, disappeared one day, enveloped in a cloud which carried him back to the domain of the gods.

From the legend grew an empire which eventually controlled almost the entire world known to Europeans at the time, an achieve-ment described by a historian of the day as 'without parallel in human history'. The 18th-century historian, Edward Gibbon, wrote that Rome comprised the most beautiful part of the earth and its most civilised people. He further wrote that the most prosperous and happy period of human existence took place between the death of Emperor Domitian in 96 AD and the ascent of Emperor Commodus in 180 AD. Perhaps Gibbon neglected to consider the lives of the thousands of slaves who served the Roman aristocracy.

Rome has always inspired wonder and awe in its visitors. Its ruined, but still imposing monuments represent a point of reference for a city which, through the imperial, medieval, Renaissance and Baroque periods, has undergone many transformations. As such, the cultured and well-to-do Europeans who, from the mid-17th century onwards rediscovered Rome, found in the 'Eternal City' a continuity from the pagan to the Christian worlds. In fact, from the time of the Roman Empire, through the development of Christianity to the present day – a period of more than 2500 years – Rome has produced an archaeological archive of Western culture.

The bronze She-Wolf is most probably Etruscan; the wolf as totemic animal of Rome also has links to Etruscan mythology. Romulus and Remus were added during the Renaissance.

The historical sites of Rome are the tip of the iceberg. Tourists wandering around the city with their eyes raised to admire its monuments, should know that about four metres under their feet exists another city, with traces of other settlements deeper still. St Peter's Basilica stands on the site of an earlier basilica built by Emperor Constantine in the 4th century over the necropolis where St Peter was buried. Castel Sant'Angelo was the tomb of Emperor Hadrian before it was converted into a fortress. The form of the Piazza Navona suggests a hippodrome and, in fact, it was built on the ruins of Emperor Domitian's stadium. To know all this can help you interpret and understand this chaotic and often frustrating city.

To see Rome, it is best to assume the attitude of an explorer and look for traces of its many levels – sometimes as simple as a broken piece of ancient sculpture set into the wall of a medieval church or palace.

Modern-day Rome is a busy city of about four million residents and, as the capital of Italy, it is the centre of national government. Tourists usually spend their time in the historic centre, thereby avoiding the sprawling and architecturally anonymous suburbs.

While the look of central Rome is most obviously defined by the Baroque style of the many fountains, churches and palaces, there are also ancient monuments, beautiful churches and buildings of the medieval, Gothic and Renaissance periods, as well as the architectural embellishments of the post-Risorgimento and Fascist eras.

Realistically, a week is probably a reasonable amount of time to explore the city. Whatever time you devote to Rome, put on your walking shoes, buy a good map and plan your time carefully, and the city will seem less overwhelming than it first appears. Remember it is best to avoid Rome during August, when the weather is suffocatingly hot and humid, making sightseeing a very unpleasant pastime. Most Romans head for the beaches or mountains at this time to take their summer holidays, leaving half the city closed down.

ORIENTATION

Rome is a vast city, but the historic centre is quite small. Most of the major sights are within a reasonable distance of the central railway station, Stazione Termini. It is, for instance, possible to walk from the Colosseum, through the Roman Forum and the Palatine, up to the Spanish Steps and across to the Vatican in one day, although such a crowded itinerary is hardly recommended even for the most dedicated tourist. One of the great pleasures of being in Rome is wandering through the many beautiful piazzas, stopping now and again for a caffè and *pasta* (cake). All the major monuments are west of the train station, but make sure you use a map. While it can be enjoyable to get off the beaten track in Rome, it can also be very frustrating and time-consuming.

It can be difficult to plan an itinerary if your time is limited, but generally it is best to head for museums in the morning, as most close by 2 pm. Sights such as the Colosseum, the Roman Forum and St Peter's Basilica are open in the afternoon, although the forum closes by 2 pm in winter and 5 pm in summer.

Most new arrivals in Rome will end up at Stazione Termini, the terminus for all international and national trains. The area around the train station is commonly referred to as Termini. The main city bus station is in the Piazza dei Cinquecento, directly in front of the station. Many Intercity buses depart from and arrive at Piazzale Tiburtina, in front of Stazione Tiburtina, accessible from Termini on the Metropolitana Linea B. Buses serving towns in the region of Lazio depart from various points throughout the city, usually corresponding to stops on the subway lines. See the following section on Lazio for information.

The main airport is Leonardo da Vinci, also known as Fiumicino airport, at Fiumicino – about half an hour by the special airport-Termini train, or 45 minutes to one hour by car from the city centre.

If you're arriving in Rome by car, invest in a good road map of the city beforehand so as to have an idea of the various routes into the city centre: easy access routes from the

Grande Raccordo Anulare (the ring road encircling Rome) include Via Salaria from the north, Via Aurelia from the north-west and Via Cristoforo Colombo from the south. Normal traffic is not permitted into the city centre, but tourists are allowed to drive to their hotels (you will need a booking and your hotel will give you a special pass.) Otherwise, there are numerous small, supervised car parks around the periphery of the historic centre. The main car park is at the Villa Borghese. See the Getting Around section in this chapter.

The majority of cheap hotels and pensioni are concentrated around Stazione Termini, but if you are prepared to go the extra distance, it is only slightly more expensive and definitely more enjoyable to stay closer to the city centre. The area around the train station, particularly to the west, is seedy and can be dangerous at night, but the sheer number of hotels makes it the most popular area for budget travellers and tour groups.

While Rome is nowhere near as chaotic as Naples, many drivers, particularly motorcyclists, do not stop at red lights. Don't expect them to stop at pedestrian crossings either. The accepted mode of crossing a road is to step into the traffic and walk at a steady pace. If in doubt, follow a Roman.

INFORMATION
Tourist Offices

There is an EPT branch office opposite platform No 2 at Stazione Termini which is open from 9 am to 7 pm. Here you can get a map, a full list of hotels and other information. The staff can also book accommodation. The hotel list gives addresses and telephone numbers, but only a vague idea of the location of hotels and pensioni in relation to the train station, so ask the staff to point you in the right direction. The office also has an indecipherable brochure on city bus routes, issued by the bus company ATAC – forget it and invest L5000 in the very good street map and bus guide simply titled *Roma*, with a red-and-blue cover, which is published by Editrice Lozzi in Rome; it is available at any newspaper stand in Termini. It lists all

streets, with map references, as well as all bus routes, and provides a simple guide to the major sights, in English, French, German and Italian.

The main EPT office (☎ 06-48 89 92 28) is at Via Parigi 11 and is open Monday to Saturday from 8.15 am to 7 pm. Walk northwest from Stazione Termini through Piazza dei Cinquecento and Piazza della Repubblica; Via Parigi runs north-east from the top of the piazza and is about five minutes walk from the train station. The office has a reasonable range of brochures, including *Here's Rome*, an introduction to the city which lists useful addresses and telephone numbers (the problem is that it hasn't been updated in years). The office has up-to-date information on the opening hours and admission fees of museums and monuments. Staff can also provide information on provincial and Intercity bus services, but you need to be specific about where and when you want to go. Brochures and, sometimes, maps and hotel lists for other Italian cities are available at this office.

Enjoy Rome (☎ 445 18 43; fax 445 0734), Via Varese 39 (a few minutes walk north-east of the train station) is a privately run tourist office which offers a free-of-charge hotel reservation service. Staff can also organise alternative accommodation, such as rental apartments, and have extensive practical information about Rome. The owners speak English and are keen to help: in fact you'll find them generally much more helpful than the staff at the EPT. The office is open Monday to Friday from 8.30 am to 1 pm and 3.30 to 6 pm and on Saturdays from 8.30 am to 1 pm.

ENIT (☎ 06-4 97 11) is at Via Marghera 2, where you can pick up information on most towns in Italy.

Money

Banks are open Monday to Friday from 8.30 am to 1.30 pm and 2.45 to 3.45 pm. You will find a bank and several exchange offices at Stazione Termini – the one in the main arrival area and another near the exit to Piazza dei Cinquecento are both open until

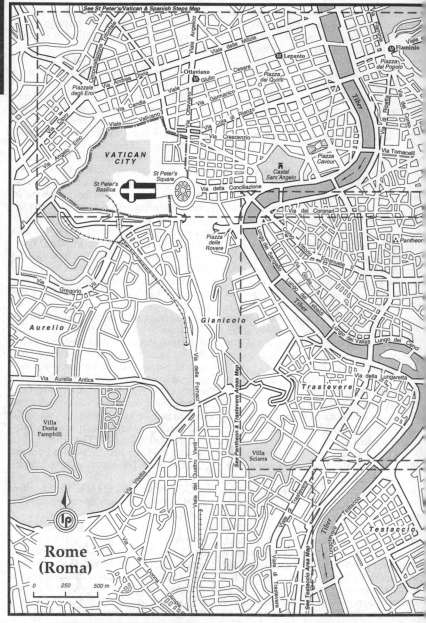

VATICAN
CITY

St Peter's
Basilica

St Peter's
Square

Piazzale
degli Eroi

Piazzale
degli Eroi

Via Andrea Doria

Via Candia

Viale   Vaticano

Via   Cipro

Via   Angelo   Emo

Circonvallazione Trionfale

Viale   Angelico

Viale   delle   Milizie

Ottaviano

Giulio

Cesare

Piazza
dei Quinti

Via Germanico

Via Ottaviano

Via Cola di Rienzo

Via Crescenzio

Lepanto

Flaminio

Piazza
del Popolo

Tiber

Via di Ripetta

Via di Ripetta

Via del Corso

Via Tomacelli

Piazza
Cavour

Castel
Sant'Angelo

Via della Conciliazione

Via del Coronari

Corso Vittorio Emanuele

Lungo del Sangallo

Via Giulia

Lungo dei Tebaldi

Lungo dei Vallati

Lungo dei Cenci

Pantheon

Piazza
delle
Rovere

Gianicolo

Via   Gregorio   VII

Aurelio

Via   Aurelia   Antica

Villa
Doria
Pamphili

Via delle Fornaci

Via Vitellia

Viale del Quattro Venti

Villa
Sciarra

Trastevere

Via della Lungaretta

See Pantheon & Trastevere Areas Map

Viale di Trastevere

Tiber

Tiber

Lungotevere Testaccio

Testaccio

See Testaccio Area Map

Rome
(Roma)

0   250   500 m

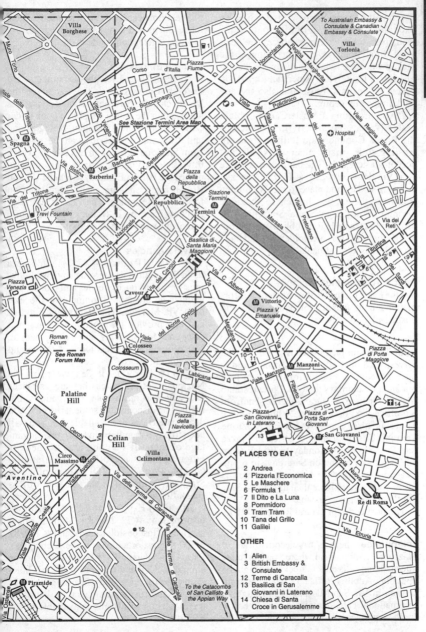

To Australian Embassy & Consulate & Canadian Embassy & Consulate

Villa Borghese

Villa Torlonia

Piazza Fiume

Corso d'Italia

Via Boncompagni

Viale del Policlinico

See Stazione Termini Area Map

Hospital

Spagna

Via Sistina

Barberini

XX Settembre

Via Barberini

Viale dell'Università

Piazza della Repubblica

Trevi Fountain

Repubblica

Stazione Termini

Termini

Via Marsala

Via dei Reti

Basilica di Santa Maria Maggiore

Piazza Venezia

Via Nazionale

Via del Cavour

Via C. Alberto

Cavour

Via del Monte Oppio

Vittorio Piazza V Emanuele

Piazza di Porta Maggiore

Roman Forum

See Roman Forum Map

Colosseo

Colosseum

Via Labicana

Manzoni

Palatine Hill

Celian Hill

Piazza della Navicella

Piazza San Giovanni in Laterano

Piazza di Porta San Giovanni

Villa Celimontana

San Giovanni

Circo Massimo

Aventino

Re di Roma

Via Appia Nuova

Via Etruria

Piramide

To the Catacombs of San Callisto & the Appian Way

Via delle Terme di Caracalla

PLACES TO EAT

2 Andrea
4 Pizzeria l'Economica
5 Le Maschere
6 Formula 1
7 Il Dito e La Luna
8 Pommidoro
9 Tram Tram
10 Tana del Grillo
11 Galilei

OTHER

1 Alien
3 British Embassy & Consulate
12 Terme di Caracalla
13 Basilica di San Giovanni in Laterano
14 Chiesa di Santa Croce in Gerusalemme

5 pm. Banco di Santo Spirito has an exchange office at Fiumicino airport. Numerous other exchange offices are scattered throughout the city, including at the main post office (where they charge a commission of L2000) and American Express in Piazza di Spagna. You could also try any bank in the city centre.

If you are using a MasterCard to obtain cash advances, go directly to a branch of the Banca Commerciale Italiana to avoid wasting time (many other banks do not accept MasterCard). The bank's head office is at Via del Corso 226, at Piazza Venezia, which is also a good place to receive money transfers; the closest branch to Stazione Termini is at Largo Santa Susanna 124, through Piazza della Repubblica, just before Via Barberini. Visa card holders should have no problems at most banks.

Post & Telecommunications

See the Facts for the Visitor chapter for information about making telephone calls and posting mail in Italy.

Post The main post office is at Piazza San Silvestro 28, just off Via del Tritone, and is open Monday to Friday from 8.30 am to 8 pm and on Saturdays to noon. Poste restante is available here. Telegrams can be sent from the office next door (open 24 hours a day). There is also a post office at Stazione Termini. The Vatican post office in Piazza San Pietro is open Monday to Friday from 8.30 am to 7 pm and on Saturdays to 6 pm. Legend has it that the service from here is faster and more reliable than anywhere else, but there's no poste restante.

The post code for central Rome is 00100.

Telephones There is a Telecom office at Stazione Termini, from where you can make international calls either direct or through the operator. Another office is near the train station, in Via San Martino della Battaglia. International calls can also be made easily (with a phonecard) from any public telephone. Phonecards can be purchased at most tobacconists and newspaper stands.

Rome's telephone code is 06.

Foreign Embassies

For addresses and telephone numbers, see Foreign Embassies in the Facts for the Visitor chapter. All embassies and consulates are listed in the Rome telephone book under 'Ambasciate'. The Australian, New Zealand and Canadian embassies can be reached from Stazione Termini on bus No 36, which travels along Via Nomentana. This bus also passes the British Embassy. Both the US and British embassies are easily accessible on foot from the station. The French Embassy and consulate are in Rome's historic centre and also easily reached on foot.

Travel Agencies

There is a CIT office (☎ 479 41) in Piazza della Repubblica where you can make bookings for trains, buses, ferries and planes, and another at Stazione Termini near the exit onto Via Marsala. The staff speak English and can provide information on fares and discounts for students and young people. The office also handles tours of Rome and surrounding areas.

CTS (☎ 4 67 91), Via Genova 16, off Via Nazionale, offers much the same services and will also make hotel reservations, but focuses on discount and student travel. Good deals on airfares are available, but you will need to pay a membership fee to take advantage of them. It's a good idea to check if other agencies are offering similar discounts. There is a CTS branch office at Stazione Termini. The staff at both offices speak English.

American Express (☎ 6 76 41 for travel information; ☎ 72 282 for 24 hour client service for lost or stolen cards; and ☎ 167-87 20 00 for lost or stolen travellers' cheques), Piazza di Spagna 38, has a travel service similar to CIT and CTS, as well as a hotel reservation service, and can arrange tours of the city and surrounding areas. A list of all travel agencies in Rome is available at the EPT office.

Bookshops

The Corner Bookshop, Via del Moro 48, Trastevere, has an excellent range of English-language books and travel guides (including the Lonely Planet series) and is run by a helpful Australian woman, Claire Hammond. The Anglo-American Bookshop, Via della Vite 102, off Piazza di Spagna, also has an excellent range of literature, travel guides (also including Lonely Planet) and reference books and is the Thomas Cook agent for Italy. The Lion Bookshop, Via del Babuino 181, also has a good selection. Feltrinelli, Via V E Orlando 83, just off Piazza della Repubblica, has mainly classics and an excellent choice of guidebooks and maps for Rome and Italy. The Economy Book & Video Center, Via Torino 136, also has a good selection of books, as well as second-hand paperbacks.

There are also English-language libraries at the British Council Library (☎ 482 66 41), Via delle Quattro Fontane 20, and the United States Information Service (USIS) (☎ 4 67 41), Via Veneto 119a.

Medical Services & Emergency

Emergency medical treatment is available in the casualty sections of public hospitals, including: Policlinico Umberto I (☎ 4 99 71), Viale del Policlinico 255, near Stazione Termini; and Policlinico A Gemelli (☎ 33 01 51), Largo A Gemelli 8 (some distance from the centre). There is a venereal diseases clinic at Ospedale San Gallicano (☎ 588 23 90), Via San Gallicano, in Trastevere. You can also go there for dermatological problems. For HIV/AIDS treatment, contact Ospedale Spallanzani (☎ 58 23 76 39), Via Portuense 332. For information about abortion, go to the free clinic at Ospedale San Camillo (☎ 5 87 01), Circonvallazione Gianacolense. There is a gynaecological clinic, known by its acronym AIED (☎ 884 0661), at Via Salaria 58, where foreign women can seek medical assistance. English-speaking doctors work there twice a week: phone for appointments.

The Rome American Hospital (☎ 2 25 51), Via E Longoni 69, is private and you should use its services only if you have health insurance and have consulted your insurance company. Rome's paediatric hospital is Bambino Gesù (☎ 68 59 23 51) on the Gianicolo (Janiculum Hill) at Piazza Sant'Onofrio.

Your embassy will also be able to recommend where to go for medical treatment. For an ambulance, call ☎ 51 00, and for first aid, call ☎ 115.

There is a pharmacy in Stazione Termini, open daily from 7 am to 11 pm (closed in August). For recorded information (only in Italian) on 24-hour pharmacies in Rome, call ☎ 19 21. Otherwise, closed pharmacies often post a list in their windows of others open nearby.

The questura (☎ 46 86) is at Via San Vitale 15. The Ufficio Stranieri (Foreigners' Bureau ☎ 46 86 29 87) is around the corner at Via Genova 2. It is open 24 hours a day and thefts should be reported here. You need to go here if you want to apply for a permesso di soggiorno. For immediate police attendance, call ☎ 112 or 113.

Other Information

If you need a wash when you arrive in Rome, there are public baths downstairs at Stazione Termini (follow the 'diurno' signs) open from 6.40 am to 8 pm. Showers cost L10,000. To wash your clothes, there is a coin laundrette, Onda Blu, at Via Principe Amedeo 70b, near the train station. A load costs L6000, plus L6000 for drying.

The Italian Youth Hostels Association (☎ 487 11 52), Via Cavour 44, will provide information about all youth hostels in Italy. You can also join HI here.

Dangers & Annoyances

Thieves are very active around Stazione Termini, at major sights such as the Colosseum and Roman Forum, and in the city's more expensive shopping streets, such as Via Condotti. Pickpockets like to work on crowded buses (the No 64 from Stazione Termini to St Peter's is notorious and the No 27 from Stazione Termini to the Colosseum is not much better). For more comprehensive

ROME

information on how to avoid being robbed see the Dangers & Annoyances section in the Facts for the Visitor chapter.

THINGS TO SEE & DO

It would take years to explore every corner of Rome, months to even begin to appreciate the incredible number of ancient monuments, and weeks for a thorough tour of the city. Most travellers usually have only a matter of days, but it is possible to cover most of the important monuments in five days, three at a minimum.

Suggested Itineraries

One Day St Peter's and the Vatican Museums in the morning; Piazza del Campidoglio, Roman Forum, Palatine Hill, Via dei Fori Imperiali and the famous Colosseum in the afternoon (the Roman Forum closes at 2 pm in winter and 5 pm in summer).

Two Days As above for the first day; then on the second day, a visit to one of the catacombs (such as San Callisto) on the Appian Way (Via Appia) in the morning and, in the afternoon, a wander around the historic centre of Rome to see the Spanish Steps, Trevi Fountain, the Pantheon and Piazza Navona, where you can stop for a well-earned coffee before planning the evening's activities.

Mosaics in Rome

Few tourists know that 'hidden' in Rome's medieval churches are some of the most beautiful Byzantine-style mosaics in Italy. Most of these mosaics decorate the apses of the city's important churches, such as Santa Maria Maggiore, Santa Maria in Trastevere and San Clemente. The oldest mosaics date from the 4th century (Mausoleo di Costanza and Chiesa di Santa Pudenziana), the period in which the Roman art of mosaic-making was evolving into the early-Christian and Byzantine styles. Those depicting Santa Costanza retain some characteristics of Roman mosaics: a white background, geometric composition and ornamental motifs.

During the reign of Emperor Constantine, who had legalised the Christian religion, many churches were being built and ornamental mosaic became the main form of decoration. Often used to cover vast areas of walls inside these new churches, they were a form of architectural tapestry which, with their uneven tesserae of coloured glass and gold, brilliantly reflected light to create strong effects and sharp contrasts of colour.

Rome's early-Christian mosaics also illustrate the progression from the naturalism of Roman art to the symbolism of Christian art, reflected, for example, in the various ways in which Jesus Christ was represented. A very early Christian mosaic, in a mausoleum under St Peter's Basilica, shows Christ in the form of Apollo. In Chiesa di Santa Pudenziana (390 AD) he is represented enthroned between the apostles, but his magisterial air is reminiscent of Jupiter and the apostles are dressed as Roman senators. By the 9th century, as in Chiesa di Santa Prassede, he has become the 'Lamb' and the faithful his 'flock'.

The mosaics of Rome's medieval churches are a fascinating and often overlooked treasure for the tourist who might not have time to visit Ravenna or Monreale. The following is a suggested itinerary of some of the lesser known churches. The mosaics in major churches are detailed in the Things to See section.

The **Mausoleo di Santa Costanza** was built in the mid-4th century by Costantia, daughter of Constantine, as a mausoleum for herself and her sister Helen. This round church is in the same grounds as **Basilica di Sant'Agnese Fuori le Mura**, on Via Nomentana, a few km north of the centre (catch bus No 60 from Piazza Venezia). The fascinating paleochristian mosaics on the barrel-vaulting of the ambulatory are mentioned above. Take a look also at the 7th-century mosaic of St Agnes and the popes Symmachus and Honorius I in the apse of the basilica.

Tradition says that **Chiesa di Santa Pudenziana**, one of the oldest churches in Rome, was founded in the late 4th century on the site of a house where St Peter was given hospitality. The structure actually incorporated the internal thermal hall of the house. As mentioned earlier, the mosaic in the apse dates from 390 AD and is the earliest of its kind in Rome, unfortunately partially destroyed by a 16th-century restoration. The church is in Via Urbana.

Three Days As above for the first two days; then on the third day, visit some of Rome's more interesting churches (see the tour outlined in the Mosaics information box) but adding Santa Maria Maggiore and San Giovanni in Laterano.

One Week All of the above, plus visits to some of the following: the Musei Capitolini, the Galleria Borghese (and a walk through the Villa Borghese), the Museo Nazionale di Villa Giulia and the Terme di Caracalla, as well as a day trip out of Rome, to one or more of the following – Tivoli (Villa Adriana and Villa d'Este), Ostia Antica or Tarquinia (painted Etruscan tombs). Or, if you want a break, take time out to wander around the Aventine or Celio hills, where you can picnic in a park.

Try not to overdo it if you have only a short time in Rome, and remember there is much more to the city than Roman ruins – it's worth making the time to have at least one long lunch at a little trattoria or pizzeria in one of the many piazzas.

Piazza del Campidoglio

Designed by Michelangelo in 1538, the piazza is on the Capitoline Hill (Campidoglio), and is bordered by three palaces: the Palazzo dei Conservatori on the south side, the Palazzo dei Senatori at the rear, and the

---

Basilica di SS Cosma e Damiano, on Via dei Fori Imperiali, harbours magnificent 6th-century mosaics on the triumphal arch (Christ as the Lamb enthroned, surrounded by candlesticks and angels, as well as the symbols of the Evangelists) and in the apse (saints Cosmas and Damian being presented to Christ by saints Peter and Paul and, underneath, Christ as the Lamb, with the 12 apostles also represented as lambs. Bethlehem and Jerusalem are represented on either side).

The 9th-century **Chiesa di Santa Prassede**, in Via Santa Prassede, was founded in honour of St Praxedes, sister of St Pudenziana, by Pope Paschal I, who transferred there from the catacombs the bones of 2000 martyrs. The rich mosaics of the apse date from the 9th century and feature Christ in the centre of the semi-dome, surrounded by saints Peter, Pudenziana and Zeno (to the right) and saints Paul, Praxedes and Paschal (to the left). Underneath is Christ the Lamb and his flock. The **Cappella di San Zenone** (Chapel of St Zeno), inside the church, is the most important Byzantine monument in Rome, built by Paschal I as a mausoleum for his mother. Known as the Garden of Paradise, the chapel has a vaulted interior completely covered in mosaics, including the *Madonna with Saints, Christ with Saints* and, in the vault, *Christ with Angels*. The pavement of the chapel is one of the earliest examples of opus sectile (polychrome marble), and in a small niche on the right are fragments of a column brought from Jeruselum in 1223, said to be the column at which Christ was scourged.

Across the Tiber river, in the Piazza dei Mercanti, is the **Basilica di Santa Cecilia in Trastevere,** built in the 9th century by Paschal I over the house of St Cecilia, where she was martyred in 230. The impressive mosaic in the apse was executed in 870 and features Christ giving a blessing. To his right are saints Peter, Valerian (husband of St Cecilia) and Cecilia. To his left are Saints Paul, Agatha and Paschal. The holy cities are depicted underneath. The baldacchino over the main altar was carved by Arnolfo di Cambio, and the statue of St Cecilia in front of the altar is by Stefano Maderno. This finely carved statue depicts with considerable compassion the body of the saint as she was found when her tomb was opened in 1599. Of great interest are the excavations of Roman houses, one of which was perhaps the house of St Cecilia, underneath the church. They are accessible from the room at the end of the left aisle, as you enter the church. In the convent there is a 13th-century fresco of the *Last Judgment* by Pietro Cavallini, which can be seen only on Tuesday and Thursday from 10 to 11.15 am and on Sunday from midday to 12.30 pm.∎

Palazzo Nuovo. The palace façades were also designed by Michelangelo. It was on this hill, which was the seat of the ancient Roman government and is now the seat of the city's municipal government, that Brutus spoke of the death of Julius Caesar and that Nelson hoisted the British flag in 1799 as a prelude to preventing Napoleon entering the city. For the greatest visual impact, approach the piazza from the Piazza d'Aracoeli and ascend the *cordonata*, a stepped ramp also designed by Michelangelo.

A bronze equestrian statue of Emperor Marcus Aurelius once stood in the centre of the piazza. The statue was removed for restoration in 1981 after being badly damaged by pollution. It is on display in the ground floor portico of the Palazzo del Museo Capitolino and it is planned that a copy be placed in the piazza.

Musei Capitolini (Capitoline Museums) is the title used to describe the two museums in the Palazzo del Museo Capitolino and the Palazzo dei Conservatori opposite. The most famous piece is the *Capitoline Wolf*, an Etruscan bronze statue from the 6th century BC. Romulus and Remus were added in 1509. It stands in the Sala della Lupa on the 1st floor of the Palazzo dei Conservatori. Also of interest in this wing are the *Spinario*, a statue of a boy taking a thorn from his foot, dating from the 1st century BC, and a bronze bust of Julius Caesar's assassin, Brutus. Both are in Room 3 on the 1st floor.

The inner court of the ground floor contains the fascinating remains of a colossal statue of Emperor Constantine – the head, a hand and a foot – which were removed from the Basilica of Constantine in the Roman Forum. You can look at these without having to pay for admission into the museum.

Major works in the **Museo Nuovo** in the Palazzo del Museo Capitolino, include the impressive *Dying Gaul* in Room 1 on the 1st floor, and the *Capitoline Venus*, a Roman copy of a 3rd-century BC Greek original, in Room 7. Well worth a look is the collection of busts of Roman emperors and other famous people of the day.

The museum is open Tuesday to Saturday from 9 am to 1.30 pm (also on Tuesday and Saturday from 5 to 8 pm) and Sunday from 9 am to 1 pm. Admission is L10,000.

If you walk to the right of Palazzo del Senato on Via del Campidoglio you'll see one of the best views in Rome – a panorama of the Roman Forum. To the left of the palace is Via di San Pietro in Carcere, and the ancient Roman **Carcere Mamertino** (Mammertine Prison), where prisoners were put through a hole in the floor to starve to death. St Peter was believed to have been imprisoned here and to have created a miraculous stream of water to baptise his jailers. It is now the site of Chiesa di San Pietro in Carcere.

Chiesa di Santa Maria d'Aracoeli is between the Piazza del Campidoglio and Monumento Vittorio Emanuele II at the highest point of the Capitoline Hill. It is accessible either by a long flight of steps from the Piazza d'Aracoeli, or from behind the Palazzo del Museo Capitolino.

Built on the site where legend says the Tiburtine Sybil told Augustus of the coming birth of Christ, it features frescoes by Bernardino Pinturicchio in the first chapel of the south aisle, and a statue of the baby Jesus said to have been carved from the wood of an olive tree from the garden of Gethsemane. The statue, in a chapel to the right of the altar, was an object of pilgrimage and was placed in a Nativity scene at the church each Christmas. It was stolen in 1994.

Piazza Venezia

The piazza is overshadowed by one of the world's more unusual monuments, dedicated to Victor Emmanuel II. Often referred to by Italians as the *macchina da scrivere* (typewriter) – because it resembles one – the monument was built to commemorate Italian unification. It incorporates the **Altare della Patria** (Altar of the Fatherland) and the tomb of the unknown soldier. Considered out of harmony with its surroundings, there have been many calls to demolish the monument. On the west side of the piazza is the Renaissance **Palazzo Venezia**. Mussolini used it as

SIMON BRACKEN

Monument to Victor Emmanuel II, Piazza Venezia, with Fiat Bambino in the foreground.

his official residence and made some of his famous speeches from the balcony. Major exhibitions are held here.

The **Palazzo Doria Pamphili** is just north of the piazza on the corner of Via del Corso and Via del Plebiscito. Inside is the **Galleria Doria Pamphili**, containing the private collections of the Doria and Pamphili families, including paintings by Titian, Tintoretto and Caravaggio, as well as sculptures. It's open Tuesday, Friday and weekends from 10 am to 1 pm. Admission is from Piazza del Collegio Romano 1 and costs L10,000 for the gallery and L5000 for the apartments.

Linking Piazza Venezia with the Colosseum is the Via dei Fori Imperiali, an unfortunate project of Mussolini's which saw many 16th-century buildings destroyed and part of the Velia Hill levelled. The road, which runs over part of the Foro di Traiano, was opened in 1933 after only superficial

excavations and studies had been undertaken. It has been proposed that the road should be closed between Via del Cavour and Piazza Venezia. At present, traffic is limited and the entire stretch from the Colosseum to Piazza Venezia becomes a pedestrian zone on most Sundays in summer.

Trajan's Forum (Foro di Traiano)

Designed by Apollodorus of Damascus for Emperor Trajan and constructed at the beginning of the 2nd century AD, Trajan's was the last of the forums. It was a vast complex, 300 by 185 metres, extending from what is now the Piazza Venezia, and comprised a basilica for the judiciary, two libraries – one Greek and one Latin – a temple, a triumphal arch in honour of the emperor, and the **Colonna di Traiano** (Trajan's Column). Restored in the late 1980s, the column was erected to mark the victories of Trajan over the Dacians, who lived in what is now Romania. It was built to house the ashes of the emperor, which were contained in a golden urn placed on a marble slab at the base of the column. The urn, along with the ashes, disappeared during one of the barbarian sacks of Rome.

The column is decorated with a spiral series of reliefs depicting the battles between the Roman and Dacian armies, which are regarded as among the finest examples of ancient Roman sculpture. A golden statue of Trajan once topped the column, but it was lost during the Middle Ages and replaced with a statue of St Peter. Apart from the column, all that remains of the grand imperial forum are some of the pillars which once formed part of Basilica Ulpia, the largest basilica built in ancient Rome.

By comparison, the **Mercati di Traiano** (Trajan's Markets) are well preserved. Also designed by Apollodorus, the markets were constructed on three levels, comprising six floors of shops and offices in a semicircle. You can get an idea of their grandeur from the high vaulted roofs. It's worth paying the admission fee if only to reach the high levels of the market, from where there are spectacular views across to the Roman Forum. The markets and forum are open Monday to Saturday from 9 am to 1.30 pm and Sunday to 1 pm. On Tuesdays and Thursdays in summer they are also open from 4 to 7 pm. Admission is L4000. The entrance to the markets is at Via IV Novembre 94.

Next to Trajan's forum and markets are the forums of Augustus and Nerva, although very little remains of either complex. The

30-metre-high wall behind the Foro d'Augusto was built to protect the area from the fires which frequently swept through the area known as the Suburra (suburb). There is a delightful walkway beneath the loggia of the Casa dei Cavalieri di Rodi (ancient seat of the Knights of St John of Jerusalem), which is between the forums of Trajan and Augustus and accessible from either Via dei Fori Imperiali or Piazza del Grillo. In summer the three forums are illuminated at night.

Across the Via dei Fori Imperiali is the Foro di Cesare, built by Julius Caesar at the foot of the Capitoline Hill. Again, very little remains to give an idea of the original structure.

Roman Forum & Palatine Hill (Foro Romano & Palatino)

The commercial, political and religious centre of ancient Rome, the Roman Forum stands in a valley between the Capitoline and Palatine hills. Originally marshland, the area was drained during the early Republican era and became a centre for political rallies, public ceremonies and senate meetings. The forum was constructed over 900 years, with later emperors erecting buildings next to those from the Republican era. Its importance declined along with the Roman Empire after the 4th century AD, and the temples, monuments and buildings constructed by successive emperors, consuls and senators fell into ruin, eventually leading to the site being used as pasture land; in the Middle Ages the area was known as the Campo Vaccino (cow field), an interesting example of history repeating itself, since the valley in which the forum stood was used as pasture land in the earliest days of the city's development.

During medieval times the area was extensively plundered for its stone and precious marbles. Many temples and buildings had been converted to other uses and other monuments lay half revealed. Ironically, the physical destruction of ancient Rome can be blamed not on the invading barbarians or natural disasters such as earthquake, but on the Romans themselves. Over the centuries,

The Roman Basilica
This type of building was introduced into the Roman Forum in the 2nd century BC. A large covered space devoted to public meetings and legal and administrative activities, a basilica usually had an apse, a long hall and two aisles. The design was adapted for the first Christian basilicas.■

in the name of progress, they literally dismantled the ancient city brick by brick and marble block by marble block to build palaces, churches and monuments.

During the Renaissance, with the renewed appreciation of all things classical, the forum provided inspiration for artists and architects. The area was systematically excavated in the 18th and 19th centuries, and excavations are continuing. You can watch archaeological teams at work in several locations.

You can enter the forum from Via dei Fori Imperiali. Opening hours vary according to the season; in summer from 9 am to 6 pm, to 3 pm in winter, and on Sundays and Tuesdays to 1 pm. Admission is L12,000 and covers both the forum and the Palatine Hill.

As you enter the forum, to your left is the **Tempio di Antonino e Faustina**, erected by the Senate in 141 AD and dedicated to the Empress Faustina and later, after his death,

to the Emperor Antontinus Pius. It was transformed into Chiesa di San Lorenzo in Miranda in the 8th century. To your right is **Basilica Aemilia**, built in 179 BC. The building was 100 metres long and its façade was a two-storey portico lined with shops. Destroyed and rebuilt several times, the basilica was almost completely demolished during the Renaissance, when it was plundered for its precious marbles. The Via Sacra, which traverses the forum from north-west to south-east, runs in front of the basilica. Continuing along Via Sacra in the direction of the Campidoglio (Capitoline Hill), you will reach the **Curia**, just after Basilica Aemelia on the right. Once the meeting place of the Roman Senate, it was rebuilt successively by Julius Caesar, Augustus and Domitian and converted into a Christian church in the Middle Ages. The church was dismantled and the Curia restored in the 1930s. The bronze doors are copies – the Roman originals were moved by Borromini to San Giovanni in Laterano.

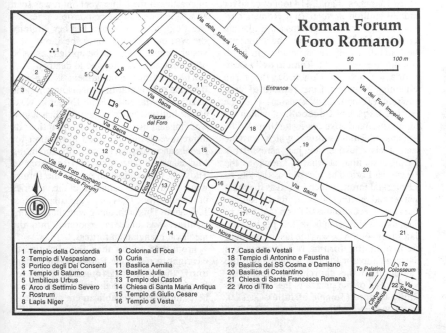

Roman Forum (Foro Romano)

1 Tempio della Concordia
2 Tempio di Vespasiano
3 Portico degli Dei Consenti
4 Tempio di Saturno
5 Umbilicus Urbus
6 Arco di Settimio Severo
7 Rostrum
8 Lapis Niger
9 Colonna di Foca
10 Curia
11 Basilica Aemilia
12 Basilica Julia
13 Tempio dei Castori
14 Chiesa di Santa Maria Antiqua
15 Tempio di Giulio Cesare
16 Tempio di Vesta
17 Casa delle Vestali
18 Tempio di Antonino e Faustina
19 Basilica dei SS Cosma e Damiano
20 Basilica di Costantino
21 Chiesa di Santa Francesca Romana
22 Arco di Tito

In front of the Curia is the famous **Lapis Niger**, a large piece of black marble which covered a sacred area legend says was the tomb of Romulus. Down a short flight of stairs (rarely open to the public), under the Lapis Niger, is the oldest known Latin inscription, dating to the 6th century BC.

The **Arco di Settimo Severo** (Arch of Septimus Severus) was erected in 203 AD in honour of this emperor and his sons and is considered one of Italy's major triumphal arches. A project to renovate the arch left it exactly half cleaned in 1988 when the money ran out. To the south is the Rostrum, used in ancient times by public speakers and once decorated with the rams of captured ships. A circular base stone, the *umbilicus urbis*, beside the arch marks the symbolic centre of ancient Rome.

South along the Via Sacra lies the **Tempio di Saturno** (Temple of Saturn), inaugurated in 497 BC and one of the most important temples in ancient Rome. It was used as the city's treasury and during Caesar's rule contained 13 tonnes of gold, 114 tonnes of silver and 30 million *sesterzi* (the Roman currency). Eight granite columns are all that remain. Behind the temple and backing onto the Capitoline Hill are (roughly from north to south) the ruins of the **Tempio della Concordia** (Temple of Concord), the three remaining columns of the **Tempio di Vespasiano** (Temple of Vespasian) and the **Portico degli Dei Consenti**, of which 12 columns remain (five are restorations). The remains of **Basilica Julia**, which was the seat of civil justice, are just across from Basilica Aemilia, at what is known as the Piazza del Foro. The piazza was the site of the original forum, which served as the main market and meeting place during the Republican era. The **Colonna di Foca** (Column of Phocus), which stands in the piazza and dates from 608 AD, was the last monument erected in the forum. It honoured the Eastern Emperor Phocus who donated the Pantheon to the church. At the southeastern end of the piazza is the **Tempio di Giulio Cesare** (Temple of Julius Caesar), which was erected by Augustus in 29 BC on the site where Caesar's body was burned and Mark Antony read his famous speech. Back towards the Palatine Hill is the **Tempio dei Castori** (Temple of Castor & Pollux), built in 489 BC to mark the defeat of the Etruscan Tarquins and in honour of the Heavenly Twins, or Dioscuri, who miraculously appeared to the Roman troops during an important battle. The temple was restored during the 1980s.

In the area south-east of the temple is **Chiesa di Santa Maria Antiqua**, the oldest Christian church in the forum. Inside the church are some early Christian frescoes. The area, including the church, has been closed to the public since 1992. Back on the Via Sacra is the **Casa delle Vestali** (House of the Vestals), home of the virgins who tended the sacred flame in the adjoining **Tempio di Vesta**. The six virgin priestesses were selected from patrician families between the ages of six and 10 years. They had to serve in the temple for 30 years and during this time they were bound by a vow of chastity. If the flame went out it was seen as a bad omen and the responsible priestess was flogged. If a priestess lost her virginity she was buried alive, since the blood of a vestal virgin could not be spilled, and the offending man was flogged to death.

The next major monument is the vast **Basilica di Constantino**, also known as the Basilica di Maxentius. The Emperor Maxentius initiated work on the basilica and it was finished in 315 AD by Constantine. Its impressive design provided inspiration for Renaissance architects, possibly including Michelangelo. The **Arco di Tito** (Arch of Titus), at the Colosseum end of the forum, was built in 81 AD in honour of the victories of the emperors Titus and Vespasian against Jerusalem. This arch, along with that of Constantine, was once incorporated into the medieval Frangiapani fortress.

From here, follow the Clivio Palatino to the right to reach the **Palatine Hill** (Palatino), the mythical founding place of Rome. Wealthy Romans built their homes here during the Republican era and later it became the realm of the emperors. Like those of the forum, the temples and palaces of the Palatine fell into ruin and in the Middle Ages a few churches and castles were built over the remains. During the Renaissance, wealthy families established their gardens on the hill, notably Cardinal Alessandro Farnese, who had his **Orti Farnesiani**, Europe's first botanical gardens, laid out over the ruins of the Domus Tiberiana. Excavations are being carried out at the site. South-west of the gardens is the **Tempio della Magna Mater**, also known as the Temple of Cybele, built in 204 BC to house a black stone connected with the Asiatic goddess of fertility, Cybele. East of here is the **Casa di Livia**, thought to have been the house of the wife of the Emperor Augustus, and decorated with frescoes. Farther east are the remains of the **Domus Flavia**, the residence of Domitian, and the vast **Domus Augustana**, which was the private residence of the emperors. Continuing east is the **Stadio**, probably used by the emperors for private games and events, and next to it are the ruins of the **Terme di Settimo Severo**.

Opening hours are the same as for the forum.

Basilica di SS Cosma e Damiano & Chiesa di Santa Francesca Romana

East towards the Colosseum along Via dei Fori Imperiali, past the Roman Forum entrance, is the 6th-century Basilica di SS Cosma e Damiano. The church once incorporated a large hall which formed part of Vespasian's Forum of Peace. In the apse are 6th-century mosaics, among the most beautiful in Rome, which were restored in 1989. Past the Basilica of Constantine there is a small stairway leading to Chiesa di Santa Francesca Romana. Built in the 9th century over an earlier oratory, the church incorporates part of the temple of Venus and Rome. It has a lovely Romanesque bell tower. There is a 12th-century mosaic in the apse of the Madonna and child and saints, as well as a 7th-century painting of the Madonna and child above the high altar. During restoration works in 1949, another painting of the Madonna and child was discovered beneath the 7th-century work. Dating from the early 5th century and probably taken from Chiesa di Santa Maria Antiqua in the Roman Forum, this precious painting is now in the sacristy.

Colosseum (Colosseo)

Originally known as the Flavian Amphitheatre, construction of the Colosseum was started by Emperor Vespasian in 72 AD in the grounds of Nero's private Golden House. It was inaugurated by his son Titus in 80 AD. The massive structure could seat more than 80,000, and the bloody gladiator combat and wild beast shows held there, when thousands of wild animals were slashed to death, give some insight into Roman people of the day.

Gladiators

These men, who fought to the death in bloody battles at the Colosseum, were usually prisoners-of-war or young slaves who had been offered the chance to become a gladiator because of their physical strength or prowess in battle. While the risks were great, so were the potential rewards: successful gladiators were considered heroes. Trained in military-style gladiator schools, their standard of living was usually much higher than that of the average slave. Battles between gladiators, and between gladiators and wild animals, were often great spectacles enhanced by elaborate scenery. The animals were brought into the arena from cages in the rooms below by a system of rope-pulled elevators: as many as 100 animals could appear at once. If it happened that a gladiator managed to disarm his opponent, he would turn to the public (or to the Emperor if he was present) for the verdict. The famous thumbs-down meant death. Thumbs-up meant a particular appreciation of the valour of the vanquished and so he was saved. ■

SIMON BRACKEN

The Colosseum, built of travertine marble, is now suffering from the effects of traffic and pollution.

The games held to mark the inauguration of the Colosseum lasted for 100 days and nights, during which some 5000 wild animals were slaughtered. The Emperor Trajan once held games which lasted for 117 days, during which 9000 gladiators fought to the death.

In the Middle Ages the Colosseum became a fortress, occupied by two of the city's warrior families: the Frangipane and the Annibaldi. Its reputation as a symbol of Rome, the eternal city, also dates to the Middle Ages when Christian pilgrims are said to have predicted that when the Colosseum fell, Rome also would fall. Damaged several times by earthquake, it was later used as a quarry for travertine and marble for the Palazzo Venezia and other buildings. Pollution and the vibrations caused by traffic and the Metro have also taken their toll. Restoration works have periodically been

carried out, the latest starting in 1992. Partly financed by the Banco di Roma, the project is expected to take 10 years and every effort will be made to keep the Colosseum open to the public during this time.

Opening hours in winter are from 9 am to 3 pm, in summer to 7 pm, and on Sunday, Wednesday and holidays to 1 pm. General admission to the Colosseum is free, but it costs L8000 to go to the upper levels.

Arch of Constantine (Arco di Costantino)

On the west side of the Colosseum is the triumphal arch built to honour Constantine following his victory over Maxentius at the battle of the Milvian Bridge (near the present-day Zona Olimpica, north-west of the Villa Borghese) in 312 AD. Its decorative reliefs were taken from earlier structures. Incorporated into the Frangiapani fortress, the arch was 'liberated' in 1804. Major restoration was completed in 1987.

Walk back towards Via dei Fori Imperiali and turn left into the Via Sacra, towards the Arch of Titus and one of the Roman Forum exits. Just before the gate, head uphill to the left for another panoramic view of the forum.

Esquiline Hill (Esquilino)

The Esquiline Hill covers the area stretching from the Colosseum across Via del Cavour, which links Via dei Fori Imperiali with Stazione Termini. Not the best known of Rome's seven hills, it incorporates the Parco del Colle Oppio, now a haunt of homeless people and drug users, but once the site of part of Nero's fabled **Domus Aurea** (Golden House). Nero had the palace built after the fire of 64 AD. It was a vast complex of buildings covering an area of some 50 hectares, stretching from the Colle Oppio to the Celian Hill and the Palatine. The gardens, which contained a lake and game animals, occupied the valley where the Colosseum now stands. After Nero's death in 68 AD, his successors were quick to destroy the complex, which had occupied a major part of ancient Rome's centre. Vespasian drained the lake to build the Colosseum, Domitian demolished the buildings on the Palatine and Trajan built his baths over the buildings on the Oppian Hill. During the Renaissance, artists descended into the ruins of the wing of the Domus Aurea on the Colle Oppio to study its architectural features and the rich paintings which adorned its walls. Unfortunately, the ruins have been closed indefinitely for conservation reasons.

From the Colle Oppio, follow the Via Terme di Tito and turn left into Via del Monte to reach the **Basilica di San Pietro in Vincoli**, built in the 5th century by the Empress Eudoxia, wife of Valentinian III, to house the chains of St Peter. Legend has it that when a second part of the chains was returned to Rome from Constantinople, the two pieces miraculously joined together. The presence of the chains makes the church an important place of pilgrimage, however, the church offers another great treasure –

Michelangelo's unfinished tomb of Pope Julius II, with his powerful *Moses* and unfinished statues of *Leah* and *Rachel* on either side. Michelangelo was frustrated for many years by his inability to find time to complete work on the tomb. In the end, Pope Julius was buried in St Peter's Basilica without the great tomb he had envisioned and the unfinished sculptures which were to have adorned it are in the Louvre and the Galleria dell'Accademia in Florence. A flight of steps through a low arch leads down from the church to Via del Cavour – make sure you turn around to see the balcony, so reminiscent of that featured in Shakespeare's *Romeo and Juliet*.

Basilica di Santa Maria Maggiore

One of Rome's four patriarchal basilicas (the others are St Peter's, San Giovanni in Laterano and San Paolo Fuori Le Mura), Santa Maria Maggiore was built on one of the summits of the Esquiline Hill in the 5th century, during the time of Pope Sixtus III. Its main façade was added in the 18th century, preserving the 13th-century mosaics of the earlier façade. The interior is Baroque and the bell tower Romanesque. The basilican form of the vast interior, a nave and two aisles, remains intact and the most notable feature is the cycle of mosaics dating from the 5th century which decorate the triumphal arch and nave. They depict biblical scenes, in particular events in the lives of Abraham, Jacob and Isaac (to the left), and from the lives of Moses and Joshua (to the right). Note also the Cosmatesque pavement, dating from the 12th century. The sumptuously decorated Cappella Sistina, last on the right, was built in the 16th century and contains the tombs of popes Sixtus V and Pius V. Opposite is the Cappella di Borghese, erected in the 17th century by Pope Paul V and also sumptuously decorated. The *Madonna and Child* above the altar is believed to date from the 12th-13th centuries.

Basilica di San Giovanni in Laterano

Head south from Basilica di Santa Maria

Maggiore along Via Merulana to reach Basilica di San Giovanni in Laterano, which is Rome's cathedral. The original church was founded by Constantine in the 4th century. It has been destroyed by fire twice and rebuilt several times. Borromini was commissioned to transform its interior into the Baroque style in the mid-17th century. The church was the first Christian basilica to be constructed in Rome and remains one of the most important in the Christian world. The bronze main doors were moved here by Borromini from the Curia in the Roman Forum and the beautiful 13th-century **cloister** was decorated by the Cosmati family. The **baptistry** was also built by Constantine. The heads of saints Peter and Paul are contained in a tabernacle over the papal altar.

Celian Hill (Celio)
The Celian Hill is accessible either from Via di San Gregorio or, from the other side, the Via della Navicella. The **Villa Celimontana** is a large public park on top of the hill, perfect for a quiet picnic. There is also a children's playground. The 4th-century **Chiesa di SS Giovanni e Paolo**, in the piazza of the same name on Via di San Paolo della Croce, is dedicated to two Romans, saints John and Paul, who had served in the court of Emperor Constantine II and were beheaded by his anti-Christian successor, Emperor Julian, for refusing to serve as officers in his court. The church was built over their houses. Downhill, along a pretty road under a series of brick arches, is the 8th-century **Chiesa di San Gregorio Magno**, built in honour of Pope Gregory the Great on the site where he dispatched St Augustine to convert the people of Britain to Christianity. The church was remodelled in the Baroque style in the 17th century.

The fascinating **Chiesa di Santo Stefano Rotondo** is on Via di S Stefano Rotondo, just across Via della Navicella from the Villa Celimontana. Inside are two rings of antique granite and marble columns. The circular wall is lined with frescoes depicting the various ways in which saints were martyred. The vivid scenes are quite grotesque and you might not make it through all 34 of them. Watch out for a little priest pointing to your shoes – he is worried you will dirty the polished wooden floor.

At the base of the Celian Hill, near the Colosseum, is **Chiesa di San Clemente** in Via San Giovanni in Laterano. Dedicated to one of the earliest popes, the church defines how history in Rome exists on many levels. The 12th-century church at street level was built over a 4th-century church which was, in turn, built over a 1st-century Roman house containing a late 2nd-century temple to the pagan god, Mithras (imported to Rome by soldiers returning from the East). Further, it is believed that foundations from the Republican Rome era lie beneath the house. It is possible to visit the first three levels. In the medieval church, note the marble choir screen, originally in the older church below, and the early Renaissance frescoes by Masolino in the Capella di Santa Caterina, depicting the life of St Catherine of Alexandria. The stunning mosaics in the apse date from the 12th century. On the triumphal arch are Christ and the symbols of the four Evangelists. In the apse itself is depicted the Triumph of the Cross, with 12 doves symbolising the apostles. Figures around the cross include the Madonna and St John, as well as St John the Baptist and other saints encircled by a vine growing from the foot of the cross.

While little remains of the church below (it was destroyed by Norman invaders in the 11th century), some Romanesque frescoes remain. Descend farther and you arrive at the Roman house and temple of Mithras.

Caracalla Baths (Terme di Caracalla)
This huge complex is on Via delle Terme di Caracalla, south of the Celian Hill, and is accessible by bus No 118 from the Colosseum. Covering 10 hectares, the baths could hold 1600 people and had shops, gardens, libraries and entertainment. Begun by Antonius Caracella and inaugurated in 217 AD, the baths were used until the 6th century AD. From the 1930s until 1993 they were an atmospheric venue for opera performances

in summer. These have now been banned to prevent further damage to the ruins. The baths are open in summer from 9 am to 6 pm and in winter to 3 pm (1 pm on Sundays and Mondays). Admission is L6000.

At the foot of the Palatine Hill is the **Circo Massimo** (Circus Maximus). There is not much to see here: only a few ruins remain of what was once a chariot racetrack big enough to hold more than 200,000 people.

Aventine Hill (Aventino)
South of the Circo Massimo is the Aventine Hill, best reached from Via di Circo Massimo by either Via di Valle Murcia or Clivo dei Pubblici to Via di Santa Sabina. (It is also easily accessible by bus No 27 from Stazione Termini and the Colosseum, or on the Metro Linea B, disembarking at the Circo Massimo train station). Along the way, you will pass the **Roseto Comunale**, a beautiful public rose garden, best seen obviously when the roses are in bloom from Spring into Summer, and the pretty, walled **Parco Savello**, planted with orange trees. There is a stunning view of Rome from the park. Next to the park is the 5th-century **Basilica di Santa Sabina**. Of particular note is the carved wooden door to the far left as you stand under the 15th-century portico facing the church. Also dating from the 5th century, it features panels depicting biblical scenes and the crucifixion scene is one of the oldest in existence. Farther south along Via Santa Sabina is the Piazza Cavalieri di Malta and the **Priorato di Malta**. Look through the keyhole in the central door of the entrance for a surprising view of the property's private garden.

Towards the Jewish Ghetto
The recently refurbished **Chiesa di Santa Maria in Cosmedin**, in the Piazza Bocca della Verità, is regarded as one of the finest medieval churches in Rome. It has a 12th-century seven-storey bell tower and its interior was heavily decorated with inlaid marble by the Cosmati family, including the beautiful floor. There are 12th-century frescoes in the aisles. Under the portico is the famous **Bocca della Verità** (Mouth of Truth), a large disk in the shape of a mask which probably once served as the cover of an ancient drain. Legend says that if you put your right hand into the mouth while telling a lie, it will snap shut. Opposite the church are two tiny Roman temples: the round Tempio di Ercole Vincitore and the Tempio di Portunus. Both were consecrated as churches in the Middle Ages.

Off the piazza, towards the Palatine Hill, is the Arco di Giano, a four-sided Roman arch which once covered a crossroads, and the medieval **Chiesa di San Giorgio in Velabro**. The church's portico was destroyed in a 1993 bomb attack attributed to the Mafia, and it is now being restored.

From Piazza Bocca della Verità, follow Via Petroselli to reach the **Teatro di Marcello**, built around 13 BC to plans by Julius Caesar and dedicated by Emperor Augustus. It was converted into a fortress and residence during the Middle Ages, and a palace built on the site in the 16th century preserved the original form of the theatre. In recent years open air concerts have been held there nightly in summer.

From the theatre, head north along Via Montanara to Piazza Campitelli and then take Via dei Funari to Piazza Mattei. In the piazza is the **Fontana delle Tartarughe**, a fountain designed by Giacomo della Porta and sculpted in bronze by Taddeo Landini in the 16th century. The tortoises were added in the 17th century and are thought to be by Bernini.

The area just south of here, around Via del Portico d'Ottavia, is known as the Jewish Ghetto. In the 16th century Pope Paul IV ordered the confinement of Jewish people in this area, marking the beginning of a period of intolerance which continued well into the 19th century. Follow Via del Portico d'Ottavia to the river and the 19th-century **synagogue**. Along the way note the medieval houses. There is a 15th-century house at No 1 which incorporates pieces of ancient Roman sculpture in its façade.

From the ghetto area, you can reach the **Isola Tiberina** (Tiber Island) across the

Ponte Fabricio, which was built in 62 BC and is Rome's oldest standing bridge. The island has been associated with healing since the 3rd century BC when the Romans adopted Aesculapius, the Greek god of healing, as their own and erected a temple to him on the island. Today it is the site of the Ospedale Fatebenefratelli. The Chiesa di San Bartolomeo was built in the 10th century on the ruins of the Roman temple. It has a Romanesque bell tower and a marble well-head, believed to have been built over the same spring which provided healing waters for the temple. The **Ponte Cestio**, built in 46 BC, connects the island to Trastevere. It was rebuilt in the late 19th century. The remains of a bridge to the south of the island are part of the **Ponte Rotto** (Broken Bridge), which was ancient Rome's first stone bridge.

Trastevere

The settlement at Trastevere was, in early times, separate from Rome. Although it was soon swallowed by the growing city, this sense of separation continued during medieval times, when the area, on the other side of the river, developed its own identity. It is said that even today many of the old people of Trastevere will rarely cross the river to the city. In recent years it has become a fashionable place to live and is always very busy on weekends and during summer, when tourists and Romans alike flock there to eat in the many trattorias or drink at the numerous bars.

Visit **Chiesa di Santa Maria in Trastevere**, in the lovely piazza of the same name, believed to be the oldest place of worship dedicated to the Virgin in Rome. Although the first basilica was built on this site in the 4th century AD, the present structure was built in the 12th century and features a Romanesque bell tower and façade, with a mosaic of the Virgin from the 12th century. The impressive interior features 21 ancient Roman columns. Of particular interest are the 17th-century wooden ceiling and the vibrant 12th-century mosaics in the apse and on the triumphal arch. Note the richly patterned dress of the Madonna in the apse.

There is a badly deteriorated painting of the Madonna and angels dating from the Byzantine era, displayed in a room to the left of the altar.

Also well worth visiting is **Chiesa di Santa Cecilia in Trastevere** and the **ex Istituto San Michele a Ripa**, which flanks the Tiber, to see a selection of paintings from the Galleria Borghese. The gallery, in the Villa Borghese, has been closed to the public for more than a decade as interminable restoration works proceed.

Via Giulia

This street, running parallel to the Tiber river, was designed by Donato Bramante, who was commissioned by Pope Julius II to create a new approach to St Peter's. It is lined with Renaissance palaces, antique shops and art galleries.

Palazzo Spada

South of the Campo de' Fiori on Via Pettinari, this 16th-century palace has an elaborately decorated façade. It was restored by Borromini a century later, after Cardinal Bernardino Spada had acquired the palace. Note the optical illusion created by Borromini's trompe l'oeuil colonnade, which he built to give an idea of greater space in linking two courtyards within the palace. The **Galleria Spada** contains the private collection of the Spada family, which was acquired by the state in 1926 and features works by Titian, Andrea del Sarto, Guido Reni and Caravaggio. It is open Tuesday to Saturday from 9 am to 7 pm and Sunday to 1 pm. Admission is L4000.

Campo de' Fiori

This is a lively piazza where a flower and vegetable market is held every morning except Sunday. Now lined with bars and trattorie, the piazza was in fact a place of execution during the Inquisition. The monk Giordano Bruno was burned at the stake for heresy in the piazza in 1600 and his statue now stands at its centre.

Nearby is the **Palazzo Farnese**, in the piazza of the same name. A magnificent

Renaissance building, it was started in 1514 by Antonio da Sangallo with work carried on by Michelangelo and completed by Giacomo della Porta. Built for Cardinal Alessandro Farnese (later Pope Paul III), the palace is now the French Embassy. The piazza has two fountains, which were enormous granite baths taken from the Terme di Caracalla.

Piazza Navona

This is a vast and beautiful piazza, lined with Baroque palaces. It was laid out on the ruins of Domitian's stadium and holds three fountains, including Bernini's masterpiece, the **Fontana dei Fiumi** (Fountain of the Rivers), in the centre, depicting the Nile, Ganges, Danube and Plate. The piazza is a popular gathering place for Romans and tourists alike. Take time to relax on one of the stone benches and watch the artists who gather in the piazza to work, have your tarot cards *(tarocchi)* read, or pay top prices to enjoy a drink at one of the outdoor cafés, such as Tre Scalini. Facing the piazza is the Chiesa di Sant'Agnese in Agone, its façade designed by Bernini's bitter rival, Borromini. It is traditionally held that the statues of Bernini's Fontana dei Fiumi are shielding their eyes in disgust from Borromini's church – but the truth is that Bernini completed the fountain two years before his contemporary started work on the façade.

The Pantheon

This is the best-preserved building of ancient Rome. The original temple was built by Marcus Agrippa, son-in-law of Augustus, in 27 BC and dedicated to the planetary gods. Although the temple was rebuilt by Emperor Hadrian around 120 AD, Agrippa's name remained inscribed over the entrance, leading historians to believe it was the original building until excavations in the 1800s revealed traces of the earlier temple.

After being abandoned under the first Christian emperors, the temple was given to the church by the eastern emperor, Phocus, in 608 AD and dedicated to the Madonna and all martyrs. (A column was erected in honour of Phocus in the Roman Forum to mark the occasion.) Over the centuries the temple was consistently plundered and damaged. The gilded bronze roof tiles were removed by an emperor of the eastern empire and in the 17th century, the Barberini pope, Urban VIII, had the bronze ceiling of the portico melted down to make the canopy (baldachino) over the main altar of St Peter's and 80 cannons for Castel Sant'Angelo.

The height and diameter of the building's interior both measure 43.3 metres and the extraordinary dome is considered the most important achievement of ancient Roman architecture.

The Italian kings, Victor Emmanuel II and Umberto I, and Raphael are buried there. The Pantheon is in the Piazza della Rotonda and is open Monday to Saturday from 9 am to 2 pm and Sunday and holidays to 1 pm. Admission is free.

Chiesa di Santa Maria Sopra Minerva

This 13th-century Dominican church, in Piazza della Minerva just east of the Pantheon, was built on the site of an ancient temple of Minerva. It was heavily restored in the Gothic style in the 19th century. It contains a number of important art treasures, including Michelangelo's statue, the *Risen Christ*, to the left of the high altar, as well as vibrant frescoes by Filippo Lippi in the Cappella Caraffa (the last chapel in the south transept) depicting events in the life of St Thomas Aquinas, and a beautiful *Annunciation*. The body of St Catherine of Siena, minus her head (which is in the Chiesa di San Domenico in Siena) lies under the high altar. In the piazza in front of the church is a delightful Bernini statue of an elephant supporting an Egyptian obelisk.

Piazza Colonna

Just off Via del Corso near its intersection with Via del Tritone, the main feature of this piazza is the **Colonna di Marco Aurelio** (Column of Marcus Aurelius), erected around 190 AD and decorated with bas-relief sculptures depicting military victories by the emperor.

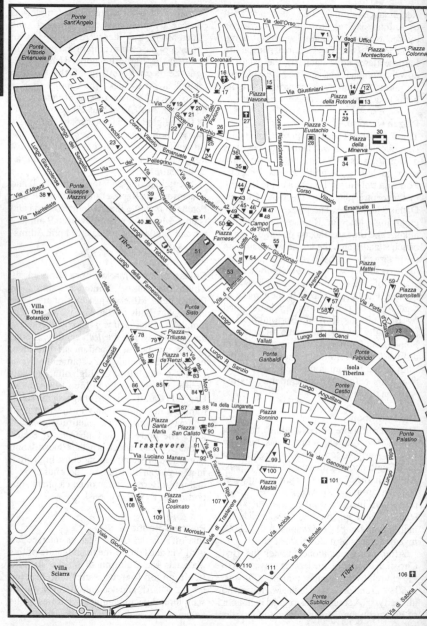

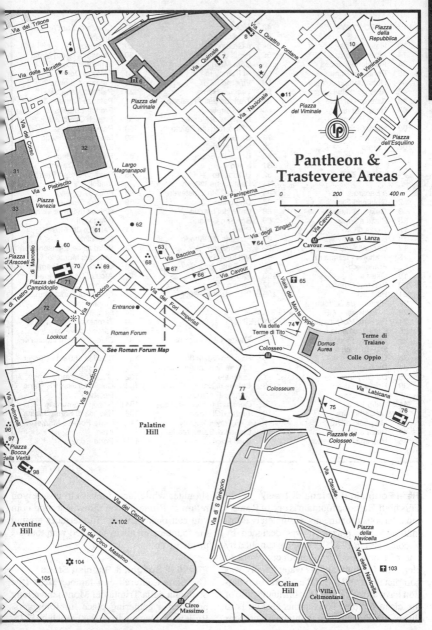

Pantheon & Trastevere Areas

0   200   400 m

ROME

PLACES TO STAY

13	Hotel Senato
14	Albergo Abruzzi
34	Pensione Mimosa
35	Pensione Primavera
46	Hotel Campo de'Fiori
47	Albergo della Lunetta
48	Albergo del Sole
63	Hotel Nerva
67	Hotel Forum
93	Hotel Cisterna
105	Aventino
108	Carmel

PLACES TO EAT

1	Il Bacaro
2	Gelateria Giolitti
3	Gelateria della Palme
5	Pizza a Taglio
12	Tazza d'Oro
15	Bevitoria Navona
17	Bar della Pace
18	Trattoria Pizzeria da Francesco
19	Osteria
20	Pizzeria Corallo
21	Paladini
22	Pizzeria da Baffetto
23	Il Cardinale – GB
24	Pizzeria Montecarlo
25	Caffè Gardenia
26	Enoteca Piccolo
28	Bar Eustachio
36	Cul de Sac 1
37	Pierluigi
38	Da Giovanni
39	Hosteria Giulio
40	Bar la Penna
41	Caffè Peru
42	La Carbonara
43	Grappolo d'Oro
44	Pizza a Taglio
45	Hosteria Romanesca

49	Goldfinch
50	Vineria
54	Il Grottino
55	Filetti di Baccalà
56	Sora Margherita
57	Al Pompiere
58	Piperno
59	Vecchia Roma
64	Trattoria dell'Angeletto
66	Alle Carette
74	Hosteria di Nerone
75	Il Ristoro della Salute
78	Da Gildo
79	Suria Mahal
80	Bar della Scala
81	Mario's
82	D'Augusto
84	Pasticceria Valsari
85	Da Otello in Trastevere
86	Da Lucia
88	Caffè del Marzio
89	Bar San Calisto
90	Paris
91	Pizzeria da Vittorio
92	Pizzeria Ivo
95	McDonald's
99	La Fonte della Salute
100	Panattoni
107	Frontoni
109	Pizzeria Popi-Popi

OTHER

4	Fontana & Piazza di Trevi
6	Palazzo Quirinale
7	Chiesa di Sant'Andrea al Quirinale
8	Chiesa di San Carlo alle Quattro Fontane
9	Questura (Police Station)
10	Teatro dell'Opera
11	CTS Travel Agency
16	Chiesa di Santa Maria della Pace

27	Chiesa di Sant'Agnese in Agone
29	Pantheon
30	Chiesa di Santa Maria sopra Minerva
31	Palazzo Doria Pamphili
32	Palazzo Colonna
33	Palazzo Venezia
51	Palazzo Farnese & French Embassy
52	French Consulate
53	Palazzo Spada
60	Monumento Vittorio Emanuele II
61	Foro di Traiano
62	Mercati di Traiano
65	Basilica di San Pietro in Vincoli
68	Foro d'Augusto
69	Foro di Cesare
70	Chiesa di Santa Maria d'Aracoeli
71	Palazzo del Museo Capitolino
72	Palazzo dei Conservatori
73	Teatro di Marcello
76	Chiesa di San Clemente
77	Arch of Constantine
83	Corner Bookshop
87	Chiesa di Santa Maria in Trastevere
94	Hospital
96	Tempio di Fortuna Virile
97	Tempio di Vesta
98	Chiesa di Santa Maria in Cosmedin
101	Basilica di Santa Cecilia in Trastevere
102	Circo Massimo
103	Chiesa di Santo Stefano Rotondo
104	Roseto Comunale
106	Basilica di Santa Sabina
110	Porta Portese Market Area
111	Porta Portese

Trevi Fountain (Fontana di Trevi)

This high-Baroque fountain is one of Rome's most famous monuments. Completely dominating a tiny piazza, it was designed by Nicola Salvi in 1732. Its water is supplied by one of Rome's earliest aqueducts. Work to clean the fountain and its water supply was completed in 1991, but the effects of pollution have already dulled the brilliant white of the clean marble. The famous custom is to throw a coin into the fountain (over your shoulder while facing away) to ensure you return to Rome. If you throw a second coin you can make a wish. The terraces around the fountain are always packed with tourists throwing coins.

Piazza di Spagna & Spanish Steps

The piazza, church and famous steps (the Scalinata della Trinità dei Monti) have long provided a gathering place for foreigners. Built with a legacy from the French in 1725, but named after the Spanish Embassy to the Holy See, the steps lead to the French church, Trinità dei Monti.

In the 18th century the most beautiful women and men of Italy gathered here, waiting to be chosen as an artist's model. In May each year the steps are decorated with pink azaleas. To the right as you face the steps is the house where Keats died in 1821, now the **Keats-Shelley Memorial House**. It is open Monday to Friday from 9 am to 1 pm and 2.30 to 5.30 pm. Admission is L4000. In the piazza is the boat-shaped fountain called the **Barcaccia**, believed to be by Pietro Bernini, father of the famous Gian Lorenzo. One of Rome's most elegant shopping streets, **Via Condotti**, runs off the piazza towards Via del Corso. The famous **Caffè Greco** is at No 86, where artists, musicians and the literati used to meet, including Goethe, Keats, Byron and Wagner.

Piazza del Popolo

This vast piazza was laid out in the early 16th century at the point of convergence of the three roads – Via di Ripetta, Via del Corso and Via del Babuino – which form a trident at what was the main entrance to the city from the north. The two Baroque churches which divide the three roads are Santa Maria dei Miracoli (bordering Via di Ripetta) and Santa Maria in Montesanto. The piazza was redesigned in the neoclassical style by Giuseppe Valadier in the early 19th century. In the piazza's centre is an obelisk brought by Augustus from Heliopolis and moved to the piazza from its place in the Circo Massimo in the mid-16th century. To the east there is a ramp leading up to the **Pincio Hill**, which affords a stunning view of the city.

The **Chiesa di Santa Maria del Popolo**, next to the Porta del Popolo at the northern end of the piazza, was originally a chapel built in 1099 on the site where Nero was buried. It was enlarged in the 13th century and rebuilt during the early Renaissance. In the 17th century the interior was renovated by Bernini. The Cappella Chigi (the second chapel in the north aisle after entering the

church) was designed by Raphael for the famous banker, Agostino Chigi. Raphael died leaving the chapel unfinished. It was completed more than 100 years later by Bernini. The apse was designed by Donato Bramante and contains the tombs of Cardinal Ascanio Sforza and Cardinal Girolamo Basso della Rovere, both signed by the Florentine sculptor, Andrea Sansovino. The frescoes in the vault are by Bernardino Pinturicchio. In the first chapel to the left of the high altar are two paintings by Caravaggio, the *Conversion of St Paul* and the *Crucifixion of St Peter*.

Villa Borghese

This beautiful park, just north-east of the Piazza del Popolo, was once the estate of Cardinal Scipione Borghese. The main entrance is from Piazzale Flaminio, from Piazza del Popolo, although it is also accessible through the park at the top of the Pincio Hill. Take a picnic to the park if the tourist trip starts to wear you down and certainly take the kids there for a break. The cardinal's 17th-century villa houses the **Museo e Galleria Borghese**, which has been under restoration for almost a decade (work is expected to continue into the 21st century). Only the sculpture section on the ground floor is open Tuesday to Saturday from 9 am to 7 pm and Sunday to 1 pm. Admission is L4000. The collection features numerous important classical works and several sculptures by Bernini and Canova. In Room 1 is Canova's famous statue of Pauline Borghese, wife of Camillo Borghese and sister of Napoleon Bonaparte. She is depicted as Venus Victrix. (Part of the museum's collection of paintings is temporarily displayed at the ex-Istituto di San Michele a Ripa in Trastevere.)

Also in the park are **Zoological Gardens**, north-west along Viale dell'Uccelliera from the museum. The animals are poorly housed and there are discussions underway on possible closure of the zoo. Just outside the park, on the Viale delle Belle Arti, is the **Galleria Nazionale d'Arte Moderna**, which houses an impressive collection of Italian art from the 19th century to the present day. It is open

Tuesday to Saturday from 9 am to 7 pm and Sunday to 1 pm. Admission is L8000.

Museo Nazionale Etrusco di Villa Giulia

Situated in the 16th-century villa of Pope Julius III at the top end of the Villa Borghese in the Piazzale di Villa Giulia, this museum houses the national collection of Etruscan treasures, many found in tombs at sites throughout Lazio. If you plan to visit Etruscan sites near Rome, a visit to the museum before setting out will give you a good understanding of Etruscan culture. Of particular note is the statue of Apollo found at Veio, and the *Sarcophagus of the Married Couple*, containing a husband and wife, in a tomb at Cerveteri. The museum is open Tuesday to Saturday from 9 am to 2 pm, Wednesday to 7 pm and Sunday to 1 pm. Admission is L8000.

Around Via Vittorio Veneto

This street was Rome's hot spot in the 1960s, where film stars could be seen at the expensive sidewalk cafés. It's still the city's most fashionable street, although the atmosphere of Fellini's *Roma* is long dead. **Chiesa di Santa Maria della Concezione** is an austere 17th-century church, but the Capuchin cemetery beneath (access is on the right of the church steps) features a bizarre display of the bones of some 4000 monks, used to decorate the walls of a series of chapels from 1528 to 1870.

In the centre of **Piazza Barberini**, at the southern end of Via Veneto, is the spectacular **Fontana del Tritone** (Triton Fountain), created by Bernini in 1643 for Pope Urban VIII, patriarch of the Barberini family. It features a Triton blowing a stream of water from a conch shell. He is seated in a large scallop shell which is supported by four dolphins. In the north-east corner of the piazza is another fountain created by the same artist for the Barberini, the **Fontana delle Api** (Fountain of the Bees). The Barberini family crest features three bees.

The 17th-century **Palazzo Barberini**, in Via delle Quattro Fontane, is well worth a visit, although it is partly closed for restoration. Carlo Maderno was commissioned by Pope Urban VIII to build the palace and both Bernini and Borromini worked on its construction for the Barberini family. Their family symbol, the bee, adorns many buildings throughout the city. The palace houses the **Galleria Nazionale di Arte Antica**. The collection includes paintings by Raphael, Caravaggio, Filippo Lippi and Holbein. It is open Wednesday and Friday from 9 am to 2 pm, Tuesday, Thursday and Saturday to 5 pm, and Sunday to 1 pm. Admission is from Via delle Quattro Fontane 13 and costs L8000. Note the ceiling of the main salon of the palace (part of the gallery), entitled the Triumph of Divine Providence; it was painted by Pietro da Cortona (the salon is often closed to the public).

From Palazzo del Quirinale to Piazza della Repubblica

The **Palazzo del Quirinale**, in the piazza of the same name, is the official residence of the President of the Republic. Built and added to from 1574 to the early 18th century, the palace was the summer residence of the popes until 1870, when it became the royal palace of the kings of Italy. The palace is open to the public on the last Sunday of each month, from 9 am to 1 pm. Arrive early, since it is usually not possible to join the queue after about 11.30 am. Admission is free.

Along Via del Quirinale are two excellent examples of Baroque architecture: the churches of **Sant'Andrea al Quirinale**, designed by Bernini, and **San Carlo alle Quattro Fontane**, designed by Borromini. Chiesa di Sant'Andrea is considered one of Bernini's masterpieces. He designed it with an elliptical floor plan, and with a series of chapels opening onto the central area. The interior is decorated with polychrome marble, stucco and gilding. Note the cherubs which decorate the lantern of the dome. Chiesa di San Carlo was the first church designed by Borromini in Rome and was completed in 1641. The small cloister was also designed by Borromini. The church stands at the intersection known as **Quattro Fontane**, after the late-16th-century fountains at its four corners.

From this intersection walk south-east along Via delle Quattro Fontane and turn left into Via Nazionale to reach Piazza della Repubblica. Formerly known as Piazza Esedra, it follows the line of the exedra of the adjacent Terme di Diocleziano. The fountain in its centre, the Fontana delle Naiadi, was erected at the turn of the century.

Terme di Diocleziano

Started by Emperor Diocletian, these baths were completed in the early 4th century. The complex of baths, libraries, concert halls and gardens was the largest in ancient Rome, covering about 13 hectares and with a capacity of 3000 people. The baths' calidarium (hot room) extended into what is now Piazza della Repubblica. After the aqueduct which fed the baths was destroyed by invaders in about 536 AD, the complex fell into disrepair. However, large sections of the baths were incorporated into Chiesa di Santa Maria degli Angeli, which faces onto Piazza della Repubblica, and the Museo Nazionale Romano, facing the Piazza dei Cinquecento. The baths are open Tuesday to Saturday from 9 am to 2 pm and Sunday to 1 pm. Admission is L12,000.

Baslilica di Santa Maria degli Angeli was designed by Michelangelo and incorporates what was the great central hall and tepidarium ('lukewarm room') of the original baths. During the following centuries his work was drastically changed and little evidence of his design, apart from the great vaulted ceiling of the church, remains. An interesting feature of the church is a double meridian in the transept, one tracing the polar star and the other telling the precise time of the sun's zenith, visible at midday (solar time). The church is open from 7.30 am to 12.30 pm and 4 to 6.30 pm. Through the sacristy is an entrance to a stairway which leads to the upper terraces of the ruins. A plaque near the stairway records the traditional belief that the baths were built by thousands of Christians slaves.

The **Museo Nazionale Romano**, which opened in 1889 and incorporated several halls of the ancient baths, houses a valuable collection of ancient art, including Greek and Roman sculpture. It also contains the Ludovisi Throne, a 5th-century BC Greek sculpture, and frescoes taken from the Villa of Livia at Prima Porta. Much of the museum has been closed for many years and only a fraction of its collection has been on public view. Fortunately, this situation is changing: the seat of the museum will be moved to the ex Collegio Massimo, diagonally across Piazza dei Cinquecento, although this is unlikely to happen within the next few years. The museum is open Tuesday to Saturday from 9 am to 2 pm and Sunday to 1 pm. Admission is L5000.

The Vatican

After unification, the Papal States of central Italy became part of the new Kingdom of Italy, causing a considerable rift between the church and state. In 1929, Mussolini, under the Lateran Treaty, gave the pope full sovereignty over what is now the Vatican City.

The city has its own postal service, currency, newspaper, radio station, train station and army of Swiss Guards, responsible for security. The corps was established in 1506 and its uniform was probably designed by Michelangelo.

Information & Services The tourist office, in Piazza San Pietro to the left of the basilica, is open daily from 8.30 am to 7 pm and has general information about St Peter's and the Vatican. Guided tours of the Vatican can be organised at the tourist office.

The Vatican post office, said to provide a much faster and more reliable service than the normal Italian postal system, is a few doors from the tourist office (there is another outlet on the other side of the piazza). Letters can be posted in Vatican post boxes only if they carry Vatican stamps.

Papal Audiences The pope usually gives a public audience every Wednesday at 10 or 11 am in the Papal Audience Hall. For permission to attend, go to the Prefettura della Casa Pontifica, through the bronze doors under the colonnade to the right of St Peter's as you

ROME

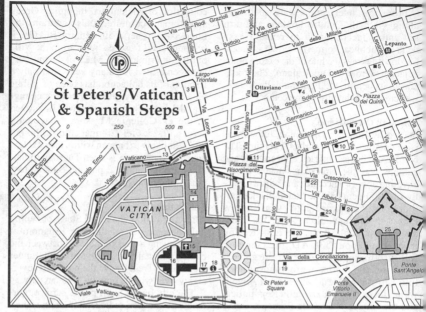

St Peter's/Vatican & Spanish Steps

VATICAN CITY

PLACES TO STAY		PLACES TO EAT		OTHER	
5	Pensione Valparaiso	1	Pizzeria Giacomelli	3	Alexanderplatz
6	Hotel Giuggioli, Pensione Lady & Pensione Nautilus	2	Osteria dell'Angelo	10	Castroni
		4	Il Tempio della Pizza	13	Entrance to Vatican Museums
7	Hotel Ticino	27	Caffè Rosati	14	Vatican Museums
8	Hotels Joli & Florida	28	Dal Bolognese	15	Sistine Chapel
9	Pensione San Michele	29	Caffè Sogo	16	St Peter's Basilica
11	Pensione Ottaviano	30	Paneformaggio	17	Vatican Post Office
12	Hotel Amalia	32	Margutta Vegetariano	18	Vatican Tourist Office
19	Hotel Columbus	34	Osteria Margutta	24	Il Castello
20	Hotel Bramante	37	Caffè Greco	25	Castel Sant'Angelo
21	Hotel Sant'Anna	38	Al 34	26	Chiesa di Santa Maria del Popolo
22	Hotel Prati	39	Fior Fiore		
23	Hotel Adriatic	40	Otello alla Concordia	41	Mausoleo d'Augusto
31	Albergo Fiorella	43	Il Convivio	42	Ara Pacis
33	Hotel Forte	44	La Campana	48	Main Post Office
35	Hotel Pensione Merano	45	M&M Volpetti	52	American Express Office
36	Hassler Villa Medici	46	El Toulà	54	Spanish Steps
53	Hotel Scalinata di Spagna	47	Pizzeria il Leoncino	57	US Embassy & Consulate
55	Hotel Gregoriana	49	Mario	60	Palazzo Barberini
56	Hotel Pensione Suisse	50	Sogo Asahi	64	Metropolis
58	Hotel Sistina	51	McDonald's	65	Trevi Fountain
61	Hotel Julia	59	Tullio	67	Palazzo del Quirinale
		62	Colline Emiliane	68	Chiesa di Sant'Andrea al Quirinale
		63	Golden Crown		
		66	Al Moro	69	Chiesa di San Carlo alle Quattro Fontane

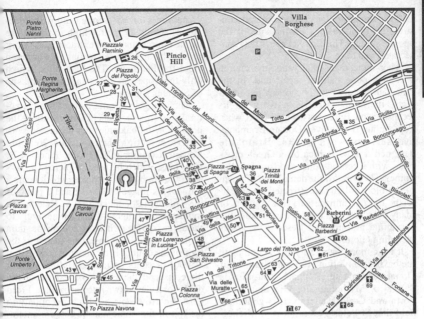

face the church. The office is open from 9 am to 1 pm and you can apply on the Monday or Tuesday before the audience. You can also apply in writing to the Prefettura della Casa Pontifica, 00120 Città del Vaticano. Individuals shouldn't have too much trouble obtaining a ticket to an audience at short notice. The pope also occasionally says mass at the basilica, and information can be obtained at the same office. You will be required to leave your passport with the Swiss Guards at the bronze doors. You can phone the Vatican (the operators always speak English) and ask for information.

People wanting to attend a normal mass at St Peter's can ask for the times of daily masses at the tourist office in the piazza. The most atmospheric service is conducted on Sundays, at 10.30 am during winter and 9.45 am in summer.

Piazza San Pietro Bernini's piazza is considered a masterpiece. Laid out in the 17th century as a place for the Christians of the world to gather, the immense piazza is bounded by two semicircular colonnades, each of which is made up of four rows of Doric columns. In the centre of the piazza is an obelisk brought to Rome by Caligula from Heliopolis in ancient Egypt. When you stand on the dark paving stones between the obelisk and either of the fountains, the colonnade on that side appears to have only one row of columns.

St Peter's Basilica (Basilica di San Pietro)
In the same area where the church now stands, there was once the Circo Vaticano, built by Nero. It was probably in this stadium that St Peter and other Christians were martyred between 64 and 67 AD. The body of the saint was buried in an anonymous grave next to the wall of the circus, and his fellow Christians built a humble 'red wall' to mark the site. In 160 the stadium was abandoned and a small monument erected on the grave.

In 315, Emperor Constantine ordered construction of a basilica on the site of the apostle's tomb. This first St Peter's was consecrated in 326.

After more than 1000 years, the church was in a poor state of repair and, in the mid-15th century Pope Nicholas V put architects, including Alberti, to work on its reconstruction. But it was not until 1506, when Pope Julius II employed Donato Bramante, that serious work began. Bramante designed a new basilica on a Greek cross plan, with a central dome and four smaller domes. He oversaw the demolition of much of the old basilica and attracted great criticism for the unnecessary destruction of many of its precious works of art – including Byzantine mosaics and frescoes by artists including Giotto.

It took more than 150 years to complete the basilica, involving the contributions of Donato Bramante, Raphael, Antonio da Sangallo, Michelangelo, Giacomo della Porta and Carlo Maderno. It is generally held that St Peter's owes most to Michelangelo, who took over the project in 1547 at the age of 72 and was responsible for the design of the dome. He died before the church was completed.

The façade and portico were designed by Carlo Maderno, who took over the project after Michelangelo's death. He was also instructed to lengthen the nave towards the piazza, effectively altering Donato Bramante's original Greek cross plan to a Latin cross.

The cavernous interior, decorated by Bernini and Giacomo della Porta, can hold up to 60,000 people. It contains treasures including Michelangelo's superb *Pietà*, at the beginning of the right aisle, sculpted when he was only 25 years old and the only work to carry his signature (on the sash across the breast of the Madonna). It is now protected by bulletproof glass after having been attacked in 1972 by a hammer-wielding vandal. The red porphyry disk just inside the main door marks the spot where Charlemagne and later emperors were crowned by the pope.

Bernini's huge Baroque canopy (baldacchino) stands 29 metres high in the centre of the church and is an extraordinary work of art. The bronze used to make it was taken from the Pantheon. The high altar, which only the Pope can use, stands over the site of St Peter's grave.

Michelangelo's dome, a majestic architectural masterpiece, soars 119 metres above the high altar. Its balconies are decorated with reliefs depicting the so-called Reliquie Maggiori (major relics) – the lance of St Longinus, which he used to pierce Christ's side; the cloth of St Veronica, which bears a miraculous image of Christ; and a piece of the True Cross, collected by St Helena, the mother of the Emperor Constantine. Entry to the dome is to the right as you climb the stairs to the atrium of the basilica. Access to the roof of the church is by elevator (admission L5000) or stairs (admission L4000). From there, ascend the stairs to the base of the dome for a view down into the basilica. From here, a narrow staircase leads eventually to the top of the dome and St Peter's lantern, from where you have an unequalled view of Rome. It is well worth the effort, but bear in mind it is a long and tiring climb. You can climb the dome from 8 am to one hour before the basilica closes.

To the right as you face the high altar is a famous bronze statue of St Peter, believed to a 13th-century work by Arnolfo di Cambio. The statue's right foot has been worn down by the kisses and touch of pilgrims.

The entrance to the **Vatican Grottoes**, the resting place of numerous popes, is next to the pier of St Longinus (one of four piers supporting the arches at the base of Michelangelo's cupola) to the right as you approach the papal altar. The tombs of many early popes were moved there from the old St Peter's, and later popes, including John XXIII, Paul VI and John Paul I, are buried there. The grottoes are open daily from 8 am to 6 pm (April to September) and 8 am to 5 pm (September to March).

The excavations beneath St Peter's, which began in 1940, have uncovered part of the original church, an early Christian cemetery and pagan tombs. Archaeologists believe they have also found the tomb of St Peter; the site of the empty tomb is marked by a shrine and a wall plastered with red. Nearby is another wall, scrawled with the graffiti of pilgrims, under which were found the bones of an elderly, strongly built man. Pope Paul VI declared these to be the bones of St Peter.

The excavations can be visited only by appointment, which can be made either in writing or in person at the Ufficio Scavi (☎ 698 53 18), in Piazza Braschi. They are open Monday to Saturday from 9 am to 5 pm. Small groups are taken most days between 9 am and midday and between 2 and 5 pm. It costs L10,000 to visit the excavations with a guide, which is recommended rather than the use of a tape and headset for L6000.

Dress regulations are stringently enforced at St Peter's. It is forbidden to enter the church in shorts (men included), or wearing a short skirt, or with bare shoulders.

Vatican Museums From St Peter's, follow the wall of the Vatican City north to the museums entrance. They are open Monday to Saturday from 8.45 am to 1 pm. In summer, and at Easter, they stay open Monday to Friday to 4.45 pm and Saturday to 1.45 pm. Admission is L13,000. The museums are closed on Sundays and holidays, but open on the last Sunday of every month from 9 am to 2 pm (free admission, but queues are always very long). A regular bus service runs from outside the Arco delle Campane (to the left of the basilica just near the tourist office) to the museum about every half-hour from 8.45 am to 12.45 pm. A ticket costs L2000 and it is certainly the easiest way to make the journey. The bus passes through an area of the Vatican City and gardens.

SIMON BRACKEN

St Peter's Basilica and Square in the Vatican, a city with its own services.

The Vatican Museums contain an incredible collection of art and treasures accumulated by the popes, and you will need several hours to see the most important areas and museums. One visit is probably not enough to appreciate the full value of the collections and it's worth trying to make at least two visits if you have the time. There are four 'one-way' itineraries which the Vatican has mapped out with the aim of simplifying visits and containing the huge number of visitors. It is basically compulsory that you follow the itineraries, but make some deviations if you want. •

Another point to note is that the Sistine Chapel comes towards the end of a full visit. If you want to spend most of your time in the chapel, or you want to get there early to avoid the crowds, it is possible to walk straight there and then walk back to the Quatro Cancelli to pick up one of the itineraries. Most tour groups (and there are many!) head straight to the chapel and it is almost always very crowded. It is also important to note that, while the museums don't officially close until 1 pm, the guards at the Sistine Chapel often refuse to let people in well before then. Of great assistance and well worth the L10,000 investment, is the *Guide to the Vatican Museums and City*, on sale at the Museii Vaticani. See the Sistine Chapel section.

The **Museo Gregoriano Egizio** contains many pieces taken from Egypt in Roman times. The collection is small, but there are interesting pieces.

The Vatican's enormous collection of ancient sculpture is contained in a series of galleries. The long corridor which forms the **Museo Chiaramonti** contains hundreds of marble busts, while the **Braccio Nuovo** (New Wing) contains important works, including a famous statue of Augustus, and a statue depicting the Nile as a reclining god with 16 babies playing on him, which are supposed to represent the number of cubits the Nile rose when in flood.

The **Museo Pio-Clementino** is in the Belvedere Pavilion and accessible through the Museum Egeziano. In the Cortile Ottagono (Octagonal Courtyard), which forms part of the gallery, is part of the Vatican sculpture collection: the Apollo Belvedere, a 2nd-century Roman copy in marble of a 4th-century BC Greek bronze, considered one of the great masterpieces of classical sculpture; and notably the *Laocoön*, depicting a Trojan priest of Apollo and his two sons in mortal struggle with two sea serpents. When discovered in 1506 on the Esquiline Hill (Michelangelo was said to be present), the sculpture was recognised from descriptions by the Roman writer, Pliny the Elder, and was purchased by Pope Julius II. In the Sala delle Muse (Room of the Muses) is the Belvedere Torso, a Greek sculpture of the 1st century BC, which was found in the Campo dei Fiori during the time of Pope Julius II and was much admired by Michelangelo and other Renaissahce artists. In the Sala a Croce Greca (Greek Cross Room) are the porphyry sarcophagi of Constantine's daughter, Constantia, and his mother St Helena.

Up the next flight of the Simonetti staircase is the **Museo Gregoriano Etrusco** (Etruscan Museum) which contains artefacts from Etruscan tombs of southern Etruria. Of particular interest are those from the Regolini-Galassi tomb, discovered in 1836 south of Cerveteri. Those buried in the tomb included a princess and among the finds on display are gold jewellery, and a funeral carriage with a bronze bed and funeral couch. There is also a collection of Greek vases and Roman antiquities in the museum.

Through the **Galleria degli Arazzi** (Tapestry Gallery) and the **Galleria delle Carte Geografiche** (Map Gallery) is the magnificent **Stanze di Rafaello**, the private apartment of Pope Julius II. Raphael painted the Stanza della Segnatura and the Stanza d'Eliodoro, while the Stanza dell'Incendio was painted by his students to his designs and the ceiling was painted by his master, Perugino. In the Stanza della Segnatura is one of Raphael's masterpieces, *The School of Athens*, featuring philosophers and scholars gathered around Plato and Aristotle. The lone figure on the steps is Diogenes, and is believed to be a portrait of Michelangelo, who was painting the Sistine Chapel at the time. Opposite is *Disputation on the Sacrament*, also by Raphael. In the Stanza d'Eliodoro is another Raphael masterpiece, *Expulsion of Heliodorus from the Temple*, on the main wall (to the right as you enter from the room of the Chiaroscuri), which depicts Julius' military victory over foreign powers. To the left is *Mass of Bolsena*, showing Julius II paying homage to the relic of a 13th-century miracle at Orvieto. Next is *Leo X Repulsing Attila*, by Raphael and his school, and on the fourth wall is *Liberation of St Peter*, which depicts St Peter being freed from prison, but is actually an allusion to Pope Leo's imprisonment after the battle of Ravenna (also the real subject of the Attila fresco)

From Raphael's rooms, go down the stairs to the **Appartamento Borgia**, but only to see the ceiling in the first room, decorated with frescoes by Bernardino Pinturicchio. It really isn't worth visiting the collection of modern religious art.

Sistine Chapel (Cappella Sistina) The private papal chapel, completed in 1484 for Pope Sixtus IV, the Sistine is used for some papal functions and for the conclave which elects the popes. But the chapel is best known for one of the most famous works of art in the world: Michelangelo's wonderful frescoes of the *Creation* on the barrel-vaulted ceiling, and the *Last Judgment* on the end wall. Both have been restored (the ceiling was unveiled after a 10 year-restoration project in 1990 and work on the *Last Judgment* was completed in 1994) and the rich, vibrant colours used by Michelangelo have been brought back to the surface. Michelangelo was commissioned by Pope Julius II to paint the ceiling and although very reluctant to take on the job (he never considered himself a painter), he started work on it in 1508. The complex and grand composition which Michelangelo devised to cover the 800 sq metres of ceiling took him four years to complete. He worked on scaffolding which the restorers believe was inserted into holes under the windows. The restorers

also learned much about the way in which the artist worked and how his painting skill developed as he progressed through the great project.

Vasari records Michelangelo's suffering and frustration, as well as his problems with an impatient Pope Julius and the fact that he did the work almost entirely alone, after dismissing in disgust the Florentine masters he had gathered to help.

Twenty-four years later Michelangelo was commissioned by Pope Clement VII to paint the *Last Judgment* (the pope died shortly afterwards and the work was executed under Pope Paul III). Two frescoes by Perugino were destroyed to make way for the new painting, which caused great controversy in its day. Criticism of its dramatic, swirling mass of predominantly naked bodies was summarily dismissed by Michelangelo, who depicted one of his greatest critics, Paul III's master of ceremonies, as Minos with ass's ears. As with the *Creation*, the *Last Judgment* was blackened by candle smoke and incense, but it had also been damaged by poor restorations and by the addition of clothes to cover some of the nude figures. One of Michelangelo's students, Daniele da Volterra, was commissioned by Pius IV to do the cover-up job.

The walls of the chapel were painted by famous Renaissance artists including Botticelli, Domenico Ghirlandaio, Bernardino Pinturicchio and Luca Signorelli. Even if you find it hard to drag your attention away from Michelangelo's frescoes, take time to appreciate these paintings, which were executed in the late 15th century and depict events in the life of Moses (to the right with your back to the *Last Judgment*) and of Christ (to the left). Note particularly Botticelli's *Burning Bush* on the right wall, as well as his *Cleansing of the Leper*, Domenico Ghirlandaio's *Calling of Peter and Andrew* and Perugino's *Christ giving the keys to St Peter*.

Castel Sant'Angelo
Originally the mausoleum of Emperor Hadrian, this building was converted into a

fortress for the popes in the 6th century AD. It was named Castel Sant'Angelo by Pope Gregory the Great in 590 AD, after a vision he saw of an angel above the structure heralded the end of a plague in Rome. It was linked to the Vatican palaces in 1277 by a wall and passageway, used often by the popes to escape to the fortress in times of threat. During the 16th-century sack of Rome by Emperor Charles V, hundreds of people lived in the fortress for months.

It is open daily from 9 am to 3 pm (closed the second and fourth Tuesday of the month). Admission is L8000.

Hadrian built the **Ponte Sant'Angelo** across the Tiber river in 136 AD to provide an approach to his mausoleum. It collapsed in 1450 and was subsequently rebuilt, incorporating parts of the ancient bridge. In the 17th century, Bernini and his pupils sculpted the figures of angels which now line the pedestrian-only bridge. It was being renovated in 1994/95.

Ara Pacis (Altar of Augustan Peace)

Cross the Ponte Sant'Angelo from the castle and turn left along the Lungotevere to reach the Ara Pacis, sculpted and erected during the four years after the victories of Augustus in Spain and Gaul. The marble altar is enclosed by a marble screen decorated with reliefs – historic scenes on the sides and mythological scenes on the ends. The structure is enclosed in a protective glass building. Of particular interest are the stories related to the discovery and eventual reconstruction of the Ara Pacis.

Sculpted marble panels were first unearthed in the 16th century and sections were acquired by the Medici, the Vatican and even the Louvre. More panels were unearthed in the early 19th century during excavations under a palace at the corner of Via del Corso and Via di Lucina. The Italian government began acquiring the various panels from all over the world and continued excavations until the surrounding palaces were in danger of collapse. It was not until Mussolini ordered the excavation to be

resumed that the remainder of the monument was unearthed and the Ara Pacis reconstructed at its present site.

The monument is open Tuesday to Sunday from 9 am to 1.30 pm. In summer it is also open Tuesday, Thursday and Saturday from 4 to 7 pm. Admission is L4000.

Beyond the monument is the **Mausoleo d'Augusto** (Mausoleum of Augustus), built by the emperor for himself and his family. It was originally faced with marble and was converted into a fortress during the Middle Ages. It then served various purposes until restored to its original state in 1936.

Other Basilicas & Churches

Chiesa di San Paolo Fuori le Mura is in Via Ostiense, some distance from the city centre (take Metro Linea B to San Paolo). The original church was built in the 4th century AD by Emperor Constantine over the burial place of St Paul and, until the construction of the present-day St Peter's Basilica, was the largest church in the world. The church was destroyed by fire in 1823 and the present structure was erected in its place. The beautiful cloisters of the adjacent Benedictine abbey, decorated with 13th-century mosaics, survived the fire.

Chiesa di Santa Croce in Gerusalemme, in the piazza of the same name (take Metro Linea A to San Giovanni) dates from the 4th century but was completely remodelled in Baroque style in the 18th century. A modern chapel inside the church contains what are said to be fragments of the cross on which Christ was crucified. The fragments were found by St Helena in the Holy Land.

Chiesa di San Lorenzo Fuori le Mura is dedicated to the martyred St Lawrence. The original structure was built by Constantine, but the church was rebuilt on many occasions. Of note are the 13th-century pulpits and bishop's throne. The remains of saints Lorenzo and Stefano are in the church crypt.

The opening hours of Rome's churches vary, but they are generally open from 7 or 8 am to midday, and then from around 4 to 7 or 8 pm.

Gianicolo Hill & Villa Doria Pamphili

Go to the top of the **Gianicolo Hill**, between St Peter's and Trastevere, for a panoramic view of Rome. This is a good place to take the kids if they need a break. At the top of the hill, just off Piazza Garibaldi there is a permanent merry-go-round and pony rides, and on Sundays there is often a Punch and Judy puppet show. In the piazza there is a small bar. Catch bus No 41 from Via della Conciliazione in front of St Peter's to reach Piazza Garibaldi, or walk up the steps from Via Mameli in Trastevere. Bus No 41 will also take you within easy walking distance of the nearby **Villa Doria Pamphili**, the largest park in Rome and a lovely quiet spot for a walk and a picnic. Ask for directions to the lake inside the park, which is home to a large population of ducks, a few herons and some strange little rodents known as *nutrie*. A short distance from the southern end of the lake is a children's playground. The villa was built in the 17th century for the Pamphili family and is now used for official government functions.

The Appian Way (Via Appia Antica)

Known to ancient Romans as the *regina viarum* (queen of roads), the Via Appia extends from the Porta San Sebastiano, near the Terme di Caracalla, to Brindisi on the coast of Apulia. It was started around 312 BC by the censor Appius Claudius Caecus, but did not connect with Brindisi until around 190 BC. The first 90 km of the road, to Terracina, was considered revolutionary in its day because it was almost perfectly straight – perhaps the world's first autostrada.

Along the road near Rome monuments include the catacombs and Roman tombs. The **Chiesa di Domine Quo Vadis** is built at the point where St Peter, as he was leaving Rome, is said to have met Jesus Christ. Peter consequently returned to Rome, where he was martyred.

Circo di Massenzio This circus, built around 309 AD by Emperor Maxentius, is better preserved than the Circo Massimo. In front of the circus is the **Tomba di Romolo**

(Tomb of Romulus), built by the same emperor for his son, and next to both are the ruins of the imperial residence. The circus is open Tuesday to Saturday from 9 am to 1.30 pm and Sunday until 12.30 pm.

Tomb of Cecilia Metella Farther along Via Appia is this famous tomb of a Roman noblewoman. The tomb was incorporated into the castle of the Caetani family in the early 14th century. It is open daily, except Monday, from 9 am to 1.30 pm. Admission is free.

Not far past the tomb is a section of the actual ancient road, excavated in the mid-19th century. It is very picturesque, lined with fragments of ancient tombs. Although it is an area where the rich have built their villas, the road is in a bad state – littered with rubbish and the ruins vandalised. It is advisable not to wander there alone after dark.

To get to Via Appia, catch bus No 118 from the Colosseum, or No 218 from Basilica di San Giovanni in Laterano.

Catacombs

There are several catacombs along and near Via Appia – km of tunnels carved out of the soft tufa rock, which were the meeting and burial places of early Christians in Rome from the 1st century to the early 5th century. People were buried, wrapped in simple white sheets, and usually placed in rectangular niches carved into the tunnel walls, which were closed with marble or terracotta slabs.

Catacombs of San Callisto These catacombs at Via Appia 110 are the largest and most famous and contain the tomb of the martyred St Cecilia (although her body was moved to Chiesa di Santa Cecilia in Trastevere). There is also a crypt containing the tombs of seven popes martyred in the 3rd century. In the 20 km of tunnels explored to date, archaeologists have found the sepulchres of some 500,000 people. The catacombs are open daily except Wednesday, from 8.30 am to midday and 2.30 to 5 pm. Admission is with a guide only and costs L8000. Catch bus No 218 from Piazza di

Porta San Giovanni (at Basilica di San Giovanni in Laterano) or Metro Linea A from Stazione Termini to the Colli Albani train station and then bus No 660.

Basilica & Catacombs of San Sebastiano

The basilica was built in the 4th century over the catacombs, which were used as a safe haven for the remains of saints Peter and Paul during the reign of the Emperor Vespasian, who repressed and persecuted the Christians. St Sebastian was buried here in the late 3rd century. Admission to the catacombs is with a guide only. They contain early Christian wall paintings and symbolic decorations. The church and catacombs, at Via Appia 136, just past the main entrance to the Catacombs of San Callisto, are open Friday to Wednesday from 9 am to midday and 2.30 to 5 pm. Admission is L8000.

Catacombs of San Domitilla

One of the largest and oldest catacombs in Rome, they were established on the private burial ground of Flavia Domitilla, niece of the Emperor Domitian and a member of the wealthy Flavian family. They contain Christian wall paintings and the underground Chiesa di SS Nereus e Achilleus. The catacombs are situated in Via delle Sette Chiese 283 (take bus No 218) and are open Friday to Wednesday from 8.30 am to midday and 2.30 to 5.30 pm. Admission is L8000.

Mausoleo delle Fosse Ardeatine

If you walk back to Via Ardeatine and turn right to reach the **Mausoleo delle Fosse Ardeatine**, you will come to the site of one of the most terrible atrocities carried out by the Nazis in Italy during WW II. After a brigade of Roman urban partisans blew up 32 German military police in Via Rasella, the Germans took 335 prisoners, who had no connection with the incident, to the Ardeatine Caves and shot them. The Germans used mines to explode sections of the caves and thus bury the bodies. After the war, the bodies were exhumed, identified and reburied in a mass grave at the site, now marked by a huge concrete slab and sculptures.

EUR

This acronym, which stands for Esposizione Universale di Roma, has become the name of a peripheral suburb of Rome, interesting for its many examples of Fascist architecture, including the **Palazzo della Civiltà del Lavoro** (Palace of the Workers), a square building with arched windows known as the Square Colosseum. Mussolini ordered the construction of the satellite city for an international exhibition to have been held in 1942. Work was suspended with the outbreak of war and the exhibition was never held; however, many buildings were completed during the 1950s.

The **Museo della Civiltà Romana**, Piazza G Agnelli, reconstructs the development of Rome with the use of models. It's open Tuesday to Saturday from 9 am to 1.30 pm and Sunday to 1 pm. On Tuesday and Thursday it is also open from 3 to 6 pm. Admission is L5000. Also of interest is the **Museo Nazionale Preistorico Etnografico Luigi Pigorini**, Piazza Marconi 14. Its Museo Preistorico covers the development of civilisation in the region, while its ethnographical collection includes exhibits from throughout the world. The museum is open Monday to Saturday from 9 am to 2 pm and Sunday to 1 pm. Admission is L8000.

EUR is accessible on the Metro Linea B.

FAMILY ACTIVITIES

Sightseeing in Rome will wear out adults – so imagine how the kids feel! If the weather isn't too hot, children of all ages should appreciate a wander through the Roman Forum and up to the Palatine Hill. Also take them to visit the port city, Ostia Antica. Another interesting, if not tiring, experience is the climb to the top of the dome of St Peter's Basilica for a spectacular view of the city. There is a Luna Park at EUR, as well as a couple of museums which older children might find interesting.

If you can spare the money, take the family on a tour of Rome by horse and cart. You'll pay through the nose at around L180,000 for what the driver determines is the 'full tour' of the city. Make sure you agree on a price and itinerary before you get in the cart – horror stories abound about trusting tourists who forgot to ask!

Fortunately the city has plenty of parks. Take a break for a picnic lunch and an afternoon in the Villa Borghese. Near the Porta Pinciana there are bicycles for rent, as well as pony rides, mini-train rides and a merry-go-round. In the Villa Celimontana, on the western slopes of the Celio Hill (entrance from Piazza della Navicella), there is a lovely public park and a children's playground. See the earlier section on Giancolo Hill & the Villa Doria Pamphili for more ideas on activities for small children.

ORGANISED TOURS

Vastours (☎ 481 76 24), Via Piemonte 34, operates half-day tours of Rome from L40,000 and full-day tours from L100,000. It also offers tours to Tivoli (L60,000), the Castelli Romani (L45,000) and to other Italian cities. You can pick up a brochure from most travel agents for information. American Express (☎ 6 76 41), Piazza di Spagna, also operates tours of the city. The CIT office at Stazione Termini offers guided tours.

FESTIVALS

Although Romans desert their city in summer, particularly in August, when the weather is relentlessly hot and humid, cultural and musical events liven up the place and many performances and festivals are held in the open. A summer festival, organised by the City of Rome and the EPT, features concerts, dance and folklore, including various events held in the city's many piazzas. Information is available from the EPT.

One of the more interesting and pleasant summer events is the jazz festival in the Villa Celimontana, a lovely park on top of the Celio Hill (entrance is from the Piazza della Navicella). Organised by Alexanderplatz, the festival doesn't feature big names but there are tables in the open and stalls serving cold beer.

The Festa de Noantri, in honour of Our Lady of Mt Carmel, is held in Trastevere in the last two weeks of July and, if you stick to Viale di Trastevere, is not much more than a line of street stalls. Head for the back streets, however, and you will find street theatre and live music. Locals eat their meals in the street.

The Festa di San Giovanni is held on 23 and 24 June in the San Giovanni area and features much dancing and eating in the streets. Part of the ritual is to eat stewed snails and suckling pig.

At Christmas the many churches of Rome each sets up its own Nativity scene, notably the 13th-century crib at Chiesa di Santa Maria Maggiore and the crib at Ara Coeli.

The focus is also religious during Holy Week and events include the famous procession of the cross between the Colosseum and the Palatine Hill on Good Friday, and the pope's blessing of the city and the world in St Peter's Square on Easter Sunday.

The Spanish Steps become a sea of flowers during the Spring Festival in April.

PLACES TO STAY

There are a vast number of pensioni and hotels in Rome. Even during summer, rooms can be found, although it is advisable to book ahead in this period. If you haven't already booked, go to the EPT office at Stazione Termini, the main EPT office or Enjoy Rome. You can check under Tourist Offices in the Information section of this chapter, although the choices listed here should offer ample choice.

A hotel booking service is available free-of-charge for new arrivals in Rome. Called HR Hotel Reservations, the service is offered by a consortium of Rome hotel owners and has booths at Fiumicinco airport in the International Arrivals Hall and at Stazione Termini opposite Platform 10. The service operates daily from 7 am to 10 pm. If the desk is unattended you can phone ☎ 699 10 00.

If you want to find your own room, either ring a hotel from the train station to check for vacancies, or check your bags in and walk the streets both to the left and right of the station. The EPT warns against people at the train station who claim to be tourism officials

ROME

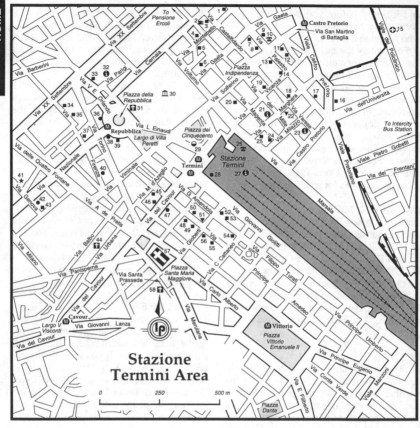

Stazione Termini Area

0   250   500 m

and offer to find you a room – ask them for identification.

The Associazione Cattolica Internazionale al Servizio della Giovane (also known as Protezione della Giovane), downstairs at Stazione Termini, is usually open from 9 am to 1 pm and 2 to 8 pm, and offers young women accommodation. If the office is closed, try contacting the head office (☎ 488 00 56) at Via Urbana 158, which runs parallel to Via del Cavour, off Piazza Esquilino.

Most of the budget pensioni and larger hotels catering for tour groups are located near Stazione Termini. The area south-west (to the left as you leave the station) can be noisy and unpleasant. It teems with pick-pockets and snatch thieves and women may find it unsafe at night. To the north-east there is accommodation in quieter and somewhat safer streets. However, the historic centre of Rome is far more appealing and the area around the Vatican much less chaotic; both areas are only a short bus or Metro ride away.

You'll often find three or four budget pensioni in the same building, although many are small establishments of 12 rooms or less which fill quickly in summer. The sheer

PLACES TO STAY

1 Hotel Montecarlo
3 Hotel Castelfidardo
4 Hotel Floridia
5 Albergo Mari 2
6 Papa Germano
7 Pensione Katty/
  Pensione Marini
8 Hotel Harmony
9 Pensione Gexim/Hotel
  Pensione Simonetta
11 Pensione Lachea/
  Hotel Pensione
  Dolomiti/Tre Stelle
12 Albergo Sandra
13 Hotel Positano
14 Pensione Restivo/
  Albergo Mari
16 Pensione Ester
17 Hotel Pensione
  Gabriella/Hotel Ventura
18 Hotel Venezia
19 Hotel Piemonte
20 Pensione Giamaica
24 Fawlty Towers
25 Hotel Rimini
33 Grand Hotel
34 Hotel Pensione Oceania

35 Hotel Pensione Seiler
37 Hotel Elide
39 Pensione Eureka/
  Pensione Arrivederci
43 Hotel Galatea
45 Hotel Giada
46 Argentina/
  Pensione Everest
48 Albergo Onella/
  Home Sweet Home
49 Hotel Acropoli
50 Hotel Dina
52 Hotel Goldoni
53 Hotel Rizzo
54 Hotel Kennedy
55 Hotel Igea
56 Hotel Palladium

PLACES TO EAT

2 Trimani
22 Da Gemma alla Lupa
51 Hostaria Angelo

OTHER

10 Telecom Office
15 Hospital
  (Policlinco Umberto I)

21 ENIT Tourist Office
  (Head Office)
23 Enjoy Rome
  Tourist Office
26 Telecom Office
27 EPT Tourist
  Branch Office
28 CIT Travel Agency
29 Urban Bus Station
30 Museo Nazionale
  Romano & Terme di
  Diocleziano
31 Chiesa di Santa Maria
  degli Angeli
32 EPT Tourist Office
36 CIT Travel Agency
38 Eurojet Travel Agency
40 Teatro dell'Opera
41 Questura
  (Police Station)
42 CTS Travel Agency
44 Chiesa di Santa
  Pudenziana
47 Italian Youth Hostels
  Association
57 Basilica di Santa Maria
  Maggiore
58 Chiesa di Santa
  Prassede

number of budget hotels in the area should, however, ensure that you find a room.

Most hotels will accept bookings in advance, although some demand a deposit for the first night. Many Roman pensioni proprietors are willing to bargain the price of a room. Generally prices go down if you stay for more than three days. Prices quoted here are for the high season (June to September). In many establishments, prices can drop by up to half in winter.

Bottom end

Unless otherwise stated, the prices quoted for hotels in this section are for rooms without a shower or bath. Many pensioni charge an extra L1000 to L2000 for use of the communal bathroom.

Camping All Rome's camping grounds are a fair distance from the centre. *Seven Hills* (☎ 30 31 08 26), Via Cassia 1216, charges L9500 per person, per day. It costs L8000 per

tent and L10,000 per person, an extra L5000 if you have a car. It is open from 15 March to 30 October. It's a bit of a hike from Termini: catch the Metro Linea A to Ottaviano, walk to Piazza Risorgimento and take bus No 907 (ask the driver where to get off). From Via Cassia it is a one-km walk to the camping ground. A good option is *Village Camping Flaminio* (☎ 333 26 04), Via Flaminia 821, which is about 15 minutes from the city centre by public transport. It costs L9500 per person and L4500 for your tent. Tents are available for rent at L22,000 a single, or L17,000 per person in a double. Caravans and bungalows are also available. From Stazione Termini catch bus No 910 to Piazza Mancini, then bus No 200 to the camping ground. At night, catch bus No 24N from Piazzale Flaminio (just north of Piazza del Popolo).

Hostels The HI *Ostello Foro Italico* (☎ 323 62 67) is at Viale delle Olimpiadi 61. Take

Metro Linea A to Ottaviano, then bus No 32 to Foro Italico. It has a bar, restaurant and garden and is open all year. Lockout is from 9.30 am to midday. Breakfast and showers are included in the price, which is L20,000 per night. A meal costs L12,000.

The Italian Youth Hostels Association (Associazione Italiana Alberghi per la Gioventù) will also assist with bookings to stay at universities during summer. See the Information section earlier this chapter.

Religious Institutions There are a number of religious institutions in Rome, including near Stazione Termini and the Vatican. However, they have strict curfews. If you want to stay in one, you can apply to the nearest Catholic archdiocese in your home town. Otherwise, try the *Domus Aurelia (delle Suore Orosoline)* (☎ 39 37 64 80), Via Aurelia 218 (about one km from San Pietro , which has singles/doubles with a bathroom for L58,000/85,000. From Stazione Termini catch bus No 64 to Largo Argentina, then No 46 to Via Aurelia. The *Padri Trinitari* (☎ 638 38 88), Piazza Santa Maria alle Fornaci, very close to St Peter's, has singles/doubles for L60,000/90,000 and triples for L111,000, with breakfast included.

Villa Bassi (☎ 581 53 29) is at the top of the Gianicolo Hill in the Monte Verde area at Via Giacinto Carini 24, very close to both Trastevere and the Vatican. Take bus No 75 from Stazione Termini. Clean, simple singles/doubles are L40,000/60,000.

North-East of Termini To reach the pensioni in this area, head to the right as you leave the train platforms, onto Via Marsala, which runs alongside the station. At Via Marghera 17 is the *Hotel Rimini* (☎ 446 19 91) with singles/doubles with a bathroom for L60,000/110,000. Off Via Vicenza, at Via Magenta 13, *Pensione Giamaica* (☎ 49 01 21) has OK singles/doubles for L40,000/55,000. *Fawlty Towers* (☎ 445 03 74), Via Magenta 39, offers hostel-style accommodation. A single is L22,000, or L25,000 with a shower.

Nearby in Via Palestro there are several reasonably priced pensioni. *Pensione*

Restivo (☎ 446 21 72), Via Palestro 55, has large singles/doubles for L50,000/80,000. There is a midnight curfew. *Albergo Mari* (☎ 446 21 37; fax 482 83 13) in the same building has rooms for L55,000/85,000, or L50,000/80,000 with a bathroom. *Hotel Positano* (☎ 49 03 60; fax 49 01 78) at No 49, has clean, but more expensive, rooms for up to L80,000/100,000 with a bathroom.

Pensione Katty (☎ 444 12 16), Via Palestro 35, has basic rooms for L45,000/60,000. In the same building is *Pensione Marini* (☎ 444 00 58) with doubles/triples for L55,000/65,000. Around the corner at Viale Castro Pretorio 25 is *Pensione Ester* (☎ 495 71 23) with large, comfortable doubles for L65,000 and triples for L85,000.

At Via San Martino della Battaglia 11, there are a number of pensioni. *Pensione Lachea* (☎ 495 72 56) has large, clean doubles/triples for L52,000/70,000. *Hotel Pensione Dolomiti* (☎ 49 10 58) has a helpful management and singles/doubles for L46,000/65,000 with breakfast included; a triple is L90,000. Downstairs is *Tre Stelle* (☎ 446 30 95) with singles/doubles for L65,000/100,000 and triples for L150,000.

Albergo Sandra (☎ 495 26 12), Via Villafranca 10 (which runs between Via Vicenza and Via San Martino della Battaglia) is clean with dark, but pleasant rooms. Singles/doubles cost L55,000/65,000, including the cost of a shower. Prices go down according to the length of your stay.

The *Pensione Gexim* (☎ 446 02 11), across Piazza dell'Indipendenza at Via Palestro 34, has singles/doubles for L45,000/70,000, and triples for L35,000 per person. In the same building is the *Hotel Pensione Simonetta* (☎ 444 13 02). Singles/doubles here cost L40,000/65,000 or up to L50,000/80,000 with a bathroom.

Albergo Mari 2 (☎ 474 03 71; fax 482 83 13), Via Calatafimi 38, has singles/doubles for L40,000/60,000 or up to L80,000/100,000 with a bathroom. *Papa Germano* (☎ 48 69 19), Via Calatafimi 14a, is one of the better budget places in the area and has singles/doubles for L35,000/55,000 and doubles with a bathroom for L70,000.

Nearby, at Via Montebello 45, is *Hotel Flori-dia* (☎ 481 70 64) with singles/doubles for L60,000/80,000. *Pensione Ascot* (☎ 474 16 75), Via Montebello 22, has singles/doubles with a bathroom for L55,000/75,000. Don't worry about the porn cinema opposite; the hotel itself is fine.

Hotel Castelfidardo (☎ 474 28 94), Via Castelfidardo 31, off Piazza dell'Indipendenza, is one of Rome's better one star pensioni. It has singles/doubles for L40,000/65,000, and triples for L25,000 per person. It costs L33,000 per person for a room with a private bathroom. Across Via XX Settembre, at Via Collina 48 (a 10-minute walk from the train station), is *Pensione Ercoli* (☎ 474 54 54) with singles/doubles for L35,000/ 50,000 and triples for L65,000. In the same building is *Pensione Tizi* (☎ 474 32 66) with singles/doubles for L35,000/60,000. Triples are L75,000 with a shower.

South-West of Termini This area is decid-edly seedier, but prices remain the same. As you exit the train station, follow Via Gioberti to Via G Amendola, which becomes Via Filippo Turati. This street and the parallel Via Principe Amedeo harbour a concentration of budget pensioni and you shouldn't have any trouble finding a room. The area improves as you head away from the train station and towards the Colos-seum and Roman Forum.

At Via del Cavour 47 there are two budget pensioni. The *Argentina* (☎ 488 32 63) is very clean with big rooms; singles/doubles cost L40,000/70,000 with a shower included. Downstairs is the *Pensione Everest* (☎ 488 16 29), also clean and simple, with rooms for L40,000/80,000. *Hotel Sandy* (☎ 488 45 85), Via del Cavour 136, has dormitory beds for L22,000 a night. Directly west of the train station, at Piazza della Repubblica 47, are the pensioni *Eureka* (☎ 482 58 06) and *Arrivederci* (☎ 48 03 34), run by the same management and with singles/doubles for L37,000/ 62,000, or L39,000/70,000 with a shower and breakfast included.

Off Via Nazionale is the *Hotel Elide* (☎ 488 39 77), Via Firenze 50, which has well-maintained rooms. Singles/doubles are L60,000/75,000 or L70,000/90,000 with a bathroom. Triples with a bathroom are L121,000. Ask for room No 18, which has an elaborate, gilded ceiling. *Hotel Galatea* (☎ 474 30 70), Via Genova 24, is through the grand entrance of an old palace. Its well-fur-nished singles/doubles are good value at L69,000/98,000 with a bathroom. A triple costs around L138,000.

City Centre Prices go up in the areas around the Spanish Steps, Piazza Navona, the Pan-theon and Campo de' Fiori, but you do have the convenience and pleasure of staying right in the centre of historic Rome. Budget hotels are few and far between, but there are some pleasant surprises. The easiest way to get to the Spanish Steps is on the Metro Linea A to Spagna. To get to Piazza Navona and the Pantheon area, take bus No 64 from Piazza dei Cinquecento, in front of Stazione Termini, to Largo di Torre Argentina.

One of the most centrally located lower-priced hotels is the *Pensione Primavera* (☎ 68 80 31 09), Piazza San Pantaleo 3, on Corso Vittorio Emanuele II, just south of Piazza Navona. A magnificent entrance leads to a pleasant, recently renovated establish-ment where a double costs L95,000 and triples are L60,000 per person, with break-fast included. *Albergo Abruzzi* (☎ 679 20 21), Piazza della Rotonda 69, overlooks the Pantheon. You couldn't find a better loca-tion, but the rooms can be very noisy until late at night when the piazza is finally deserted. Singles/doubles are L75,000 /100,000 and use of the communal shower is free. Bookings are essential throughout the year.

Pensione Mimosa (☎ 68 80 17 53) at Via Santa Chiara 61, off Piazza della Minerva, has singles/doubles for L65,000/95,000 and doubles with a bathroom for L125,000. Prices include breakfast.

Albergo della Lunetta (☎ 686 10 80), Piazza del Paradiso 68, on the north side of Campo de' Fiori, has doubles for L85,000 or L120,000 with a shower. Bookings are essen-tial. *Albergo Pomezia* (☎ 686 13 71), Via dei Chiavari 12, which runs off Via dei Giubbonari from Campo de' Fiori, is reasonably priced given its location, with doubles/triples for L80,000/120,000. Use of the communal shower is free.

Near the Spanish Steps is *Albergo Fiorella* (☎ 361 05 97), Via del Babuino 196, with very clean singles/doubles for L50,000/82,000, with breakfast included.

Near the Vatican & Trastevere Although there aren't many bargains in this area, it is comparatively quiet and still close to the main sights. Bookings are an absolute necessity because rooms are often filled with people attending conferences etc at the Vatican. The simplest way to reach the area is on the Metro Linea A to Ottaviano. Turn left into Via Ottaviano, and Via Germanico is a short walk away. Otherwise, take bus No 64 from Stazione Termini to St Peter's and walk away from the basilica, north along Via di Porta Angelica, which becomes Via Ottaviano after the Piazza del Risorgimento. This is a five-minute walk.

The best bargain in the area is *Pensione Ottaviano* (☎ 39 73 72 53), Via Ottaviano 6, near Piazza del Risorgimento. It has dormitory beds for L23,000 per person and the owner speaks English. *Hotel Giuggioli* (☎ 324 21 13), Via Germanico 198, is very small, but a delight. The woman owner, her dog and her cats make it seem like home. A double costs L90,000 or L120,000 with a bathroom. Rooms are well-furnished. There are other pensioni in the same building. *Pensione Lady* (☎ 324 21 12), on the 4th floor, has large, clean singles/doubles for L40,000/95,000. *Pensione Nautilus* (☎ 324 21 18), on the 2nd floor, has singles/doubles for L50,000/90,000 and triples/quads for L130,000/160,000.

Pensione San Michele (☎ 324 33 33), Via Attilio Regolo 19, off Via Cola di Rienzo, has average singles/doubles for L35,000/50,000. At Via Giulio Cesare 47, near the Lepanto Metro stop, is *Pensione Valparaiso* (☎ 321 31 84) with clean, simple singles/doubles for the bargain price of L35,000/50,000.

In Trastevere is the *Carmel* (☎ 580 99 21), Via Mameli 11, with singles/doubles for L50,000/70,000.

Middle
The establishments in this section are all hotels or pensioni, generally in the two-star category, but including some better quality one-stars. All rooms have private bathrooms unless otherwise stated.

Near Stazione Termini To the south of the train station, at Via Principe Amedeo 97, is the *Hotel Igea* (☎ 446 69 11). It has singles/doubles for L75,000/100,000 and triples for L130,000. *Hotel Acropoli* (☎ 488 56 85) in the same street at No 67 has singles/doubles for L90,000/110,000. *Hotel Dina* (☎ 474 06 94; fax 445 37 77), Via Principe Amedeo 62, is clean with a friendly management. Singles/doubles are L60,000/110,000. At No 47 is the *Hotel Sweet Home* (☎ 488 09 54), with singles without bathroom for L60,000 and doubles for L106,000, with breakfast included. In the same building is *Albergo Onella* (☎ 488 52 57), which has recently been renovated. Its singles/doubles cost up to L110,000/160,000.

Hotel Palladium (☎ 446 69 17; fax 446 69 37), Via Gioberti 36, has large double rooms for L140,000; singles are L110,000 and triples/quads cost L210,000/230,000. *Hotel Goldoni* (☎ 446 74 13), Via Filippo Turati 37, has comfortable rooms for L100,000/140,000. At the same address is *Hotel Rizzo* (☎ 446 73 26), with doubles/triples for L100,000/120,000.

Hotel Kennedy (☎ 446 53 73), Via F Turati 62, has very comfortable singles/doubles for L60,000/100,000. North-west of the train station, in Via Firenze, off Via Nazionale, there are a couple of good-value hotels. *Hotel Pensione Seiler* (☎ 488 02 04; fax 488 06 88) at No 48 has clean but basic rooms, although all have a TV and the price includes breakfast. Singles/doubles are L120,000/155,000. Triples/quads are also available. *Hotel Pensione Oceania* (☎ 482 46 96; fax 488 55 86) at No 38, is an ideal family hotel. Simply furnished singles/doubles are

L95,000/110,000, and triples/quads are L178,000/224,000. A room for five is L280,000. During winter the hotel offers a 20% discount and a 10% discount can be negotiated at other times.

North-east of the train station is *Hotel Harmony* (☎ 48 67 38), Via Palestro 13, which has singles/doubles for L80,000/ 100,000. The recently restored *Hotel Pensione Gabriella* (☎ 445 02 52), Via Palestro 88, has doubles for L120,000. In the same building is *Hotel Ventura* (☎ 445 19 51; fax 446 00 34), with recently renovated singles/doubles for up to L100,000/120,000.

City Centre *Albergo del Sole* (☎ 687 94 46), Via del Biscione 76, off Campo de' Fiori, has big rooms and a roof terrace. Singles/doubles cost L95,000/140,000 or L75,000/105,000 without a bathroom. *Hotel Campo de' Fiori* (☎ 688 68 65), Via del Biscione 6 is – as its name suggests – just off the Campo de' Fiori. It has nicely furnished rooms on its six floors (but there is no lift) and a roof garden. Singles/doubles are L120,000/130,000 or L85,000/90,000 without a bathroom.

Near Piazza di Spagna is *Hotel Pensione Suisse* (☎ 678 36 49), Via Gregoriana 56. It has good-quality singles/doubles without bathroom for L70,000/85,000; doubles with bathroom are L128,000, triples L165,000 and quads L200,000. Closer to Piazza del Popolo is *Hotel Margutta* (☎ 679 84 40), Via Laurina 34, off Via del Corso. It has spotless rooms, and prices, which are negotiable, include breakfast. There are no singles and a double costs up to L134,000, a triple L155,000 and a quad L180,000. *Hotel Forte* (☎ 320 76 25), Via Margutta 61 (parallel to Via del Babuino), is comfortable and quiet. Singles cost L100,000 and doubles up to L150,000.

Hotel Pensione Merano (☎ 482 17 96) is a lovely old place, well located at Via Vittorio Veneto 155. It has singles/doubles for L95,000/138,000 and triples for L175,000, with breakfast included. *Hotel Julia* (☎ 488 16 37), Via Rasella 29, off Via delle Quattro Fontane near Piazza Barberini, is a no-frills place but quiet and clean. Singles/doubles are

L120,000/ 170,000. The price includes breakfast and all rooms have TV.

Near the Vatican & in Trastevere Virtually next to the Vatican wall off Via de' Corridori is *Hotel Bramante* (☎ 654 04 26), Vicolo delle Palline 24. It has rooms of reasonable quality. Singles/doubles without a bathroom are L64,000/84,000. Doubles are L107,000, triples L145,000 and quads L182,000. *Hotel Prati* (☎ 687 53 57), Via Crescenzio 89, has singles/doubles for L79,000/108,000 and triples for L148,000. Singles/doubles without bathroom are L63,000/88,000. *Hotel Adriatic* (☎ 686 96 68), Via Vitelleschi 25 (the continuation of Via Porcari, off Piazza del Risorgimento), has modern rooms and is very good value with singles/doubles at L85,000/112,000; rooms without a bathroom are L64,000/85,000. A triple costs L150,000, or L120,000 without a bathroom.

At Via Cola di Rienzo 243 there are two good-quality hotels, both excellent value for their location and prices. *Hotel Joli* (☎ 324 18 54) is on the 6th floor. It has large rooms and is ideal for families. Singles/doubles are L70,000/90,000 and triples L120,000. *Hotel Florida* (☎ 324 18 72) is on the 2nd floor and has singles/doubles for L73,000/94,000 and triples for L150,000; without a bathroom, prices are L53,000/74,000 for singles/ doubles or L125,000 for a triple. Discounts are available out of the high season.

Hotel Ticino (☎ 324 32 51), Via dei Gracchi 161, has comfortable rooms and some are big enough for families. There are showeres but no toilets in the rooms, and prices include breakfast. Singles/doubles are L62,000/88,000 and triples are L122,000; without a bathroom, singles/doubles are L51,000/73,000 and L102,000 for triples. A room for four costs L156,000.

Hotel Amalia (☎ 31 45 19), Via Germanico 66, near the corner of Via Ottaviano, has a beautiful courtyard entrance and clean, sunny rooms. Singles/doubles are L50,000/90,000 with use of the communal shower; triples are L96,000. Singles/doubles with bathroom are L70,000/110,000, and triples are L135,000.

In Trastevere there is the *Hotel Cisterna* (☎ 581 72 12), Via della Cisterna 7-9, off Via San Francesco a Ripa. It has average, comfortable rooms. Singles/doubles L85,000/110,000 and triples are L140,000.

Top End

There is no shortage of expensive hotels in Rome, but many, particularly those near Stazione Termini, are geared towards large tour groups and, while certainly offering all conveniences, tend to be a bit anonymous. The following three and four-star hotels have been selected on the basis of their individual charm, as well as value-for-money and location.

Aventine Hill If you prefer quieter surroundings and don't mind being a bit out of the centre of town, try the *Aventino* (☎ 574 35 47), Via San Domenico 10. It has pleasant singles/doubles for up to L100,000/160,000.

Near Stazione Termini *Hotel Venezia* (☎ 445 71 01; fax 495 76 87), Via Varese 18, on the corner of Via Marghera, is beautifully furnished in antique style. Singles/doubles cost L174,000/242,000 and triples L320,000. Prices drop in the low season. At *Hotel Montecarlo* (☎ 446 00 00; fax 446 00 34)), Via Palestro 17a, singles/doubles cost L125,000/161,000, triples L210,000 and a quad L270,000. It also offers generous discounts on rooms in the low season. *Hotel Piemonte* (☎ 445 22 40; fax 445 16 49), Via Vicenza 34, has very pleasant singles/doubles for up to L150,000/210,000. On the other side of the train station is *Hotel Giada* (☎ 488 58 63), Via Principe Amedeo 9. It is a very pleasant establishment with singles/doubles for L160,000/190,000. Discounts are offered in the off season and during August.

At the end of Via del Cavour, in the area close to the Roman Forum, are two very good hotels. Both are in Via Tor de'Conti, which runs behind the Via dei Fori Imperiali and their location is hard to beat. *Hotel Nerva* (☎ 678 18 35), at No 3, can be expensive at up to L200,000/300,000 for singles/doubles.

Hotel Forum (☎ 679 24 46), at No 25, is a four-star hotel, with singles/doubles for up to L280,000/400,000.

City Centre Near the Spanish Steps are several of Rome's better hotels. The *Gregoriana* (☎ 679 42 69), Via Gregoriana 18, has long been an institution for the fashionable set. Its rooms are not numbered, but instead adorned with letters by the 1930s French fashion illustrator Erté. Singles/doubles cost up to L160,000/260,000 and triples cost L320,000. Magnificently located at the top of the Spanish Steps, at Piazza Trinità dei Monti 17, is *Hotel Scalinata di Spagna*, which has a roof terrace overlooking the city. It has singles/doubles for up to L130/380,000. Opposite is the high-class *Hassler Villa Medici* (☎ 678 26 51), another of Rome's top hotels. Doubles cost up to L650,000 per night. Around the corner at Via Sistina 136 is the small *Hotel Sistina* (☎ 474 41 76) with singles/doubles for L210,000/315,000.

Hotel Senato (☎ 678 43 43), Piazza della Rotonda 73, overlooks the Pantheon. Its comfortable rooms are L145,000/200,000. The rooms are also reasonably quiet, considering the hotel's position.

Near the Vatican *Hotel Columbus* (☎ 686 52 45), Via della Conciliazione 33, is in a restored 15th-century palace in front of St Peter's Basilica. It has singles/doubles for L200,000/270,000 and triples for L325,000. The elegant *Hotel Sant'Anna* (☎ 68 80 16 02), Borgo Pio 133, is also near the Vatican. It has doubles for L240,000 and triples for L300,000.

Rental Accommodation

Apartments near the centre of Rome are expensive and you can expect to pay a minimum of L1,500,000 a month. A good way to find a shared apartment is to buy *Wanted in Rome* or *Porta Portese* at newspaper stands. A room in a shared apartment will cost at least L600,000 a month, plus bills. There are also agencies, known as *agenzie immobiliari*, specialising in short-term

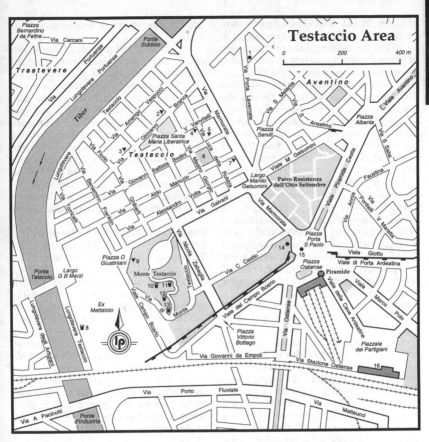

Testaccio Area

rentals in Rome, which charge a fee for their
services. They are listed in *Wanted in Rome*.

PLACES TO EAT

Rome offers a pretty good range of eating
places: there are some excellent establishments offering typical Roman fare to suit a
range of budgets, as well as some good, but
usually fairly expensive, restaurants offering
international cuisines such as Indian,
Chinese, Vietnamese and Japanese. The best
areas to look for good trattorie are Trastevere
and between Piazza Navona and the Tiber.
During summer these areas are lively and

1	Hotel San Domenico
2	Pizzeria Remo
3	Augustarello
4	Trattoria da Bucatino
5	Il Canestro
6	Piazza Testaccio & Market
7	Volpetti
8	Villaggio Globale
9	Checchino dal 1887
10	Radio Londra
11	Caffè Latino
12	Caruso Caffè
13	L'Alibi
14	Protestant Cemetery
15	Piramide di Cestio
16	Stazione Ostiense

atmospheric and most establishments have outside tables. Meal times are generally from 12.30 to 3 pm and from 8 to 11 pm, although in summer many restaurants stay open later. If you want to be sure of finding a table (especially if you want one outside), either drop into the restaurant during the day and make a booking or arrive before 9 pm.

Antipasto dishes in Rome are particularly good and many restaurants allow you to make your own mixed selection. Typical pasta includes: *spaghetti alla matriciana*, with a usually very salty sauce of tomato and pancetta (cured bacon); *penne all'arrabbiata*, which has a hot sauce of tomatoes and chilli; *spaghetti carbonara*, with pancetta, eggs and cheese. *Saltimbocca alla Romana* (slices of veal and ham) and *abbacchio* (roast lamb seasoned with rosemary) are classic meat dishes, which are followed by a wide variety of vegetables. During winter, try the *carciofi alla Romana* (artichokes stuffed with mint or parsley and garlic). Offal is also very popular in Rome, and a local speciality is the *pajata* (pasta with a sauce of chopped veal intestines).

Always remember to check the menu posted outside the establishment for prices, cover and service charges. Expect to pay under L25,000 per person at a simple trattoria, up to L50,000 at an average restaurant and around L100,000 or more at Rome's top eating places. These prices are for a full meal including entrée, main, dessert and wine. Eating only a pasta and salad and drinking the house wine at a trattoria can keep the bill down to around L15,000. If you order meat or, particularly fish, you will push up the bill substantially.

Good options for cheap, quick meals are at the hundreds of bars around the city, where panini costs L2500 to L5000 taken at the bar (al banco), or at takeaway pizzerias, where a slice of freshly cooked pizza, sold by weight, can cost as little as L2500. Bakeries are numerous in Piazza Navona and the Campo de' Fiori area and are another good choice for a cheap snack. Try a huge piece of pizza bianca, a flat bread resembling focaccia, which costs from around L1500 a slice.

See the Sandwiches & Snacks section for details.

For groceries and supplies of cheese, prosciutto, salami and wine, shop at alimentari. See under Alimentari in this section. For fresh fruit and vegetables there are numerous outdoor markets, notably the lively daily market in Campo de' Fiori. Cheaper food markets are held in Piazza Vittorio Emanuele near Stazione Termini, in Piazza Testaccio on the other side of the Aventine Hill from the Circo Massimo, and in Via Andrea Doria, near Largo Trionfale, north of the Vatican. The huge wholesale food markets in Via Ostiense, some distance from the city centre, are open Monday to Saturday from 10 am.

Restaurants, Trattorias & Pizzerias

Generally the restaurants near Stazione Termini are to be avoided if you want to pay reasonable prices for good-quality food. The side streets around Piazza Navona and Campo de' Fiori harbour many good-quality, low-priced trattorie and pizzerias, and the areas of San Lorenzo (to the east of Termini, near the university) and Testaccio (across the Tiber near the Piramide di Cestio mausoleum) are popular eating districts with the locals. Trastevere might be among the most expensive places to live in Rome, but it offers an excellent selection of rustic-style eating places hidden in tiny piazzas, and pizzerias where it doesn't cost the earth to sit at a table on the street.

City Centre – bottom end *Otello alla Concordia* (☎ 679 11 78), Via della Croce 81, between Via Babuino and Via del Corso, is a popular eating place for tourists and locals alike. You can eat a good Roman-style meal for around L25,000 to L30,000. Nearby at Via Margutta 82, which runs parallel to Via Babuino, is *Osteria Margutta* (☎ 320 77 13). It has good-quality food for around the same prices as Otello alla Concordia. *Pizzeria il Leoncino* (☎ 687 63 06), Via del Leoncino 28, across Via del Corso from Via Condotti, has good pizzas at low prices. You can eat and drink for under L15,000. *Pizzeria Montecarlo* (☎ 686 18 77), Vicolo Savelli

12, is a very traditional pizzeria, with paper sheets for tablecloths. The pizzas are fine and a meal of pizza and wine or beer will cost around L16,000. The *Pizzeria da Baffetto* (☎ 686 16 17), Via del Governo Vecchio 11, is a Roman institution. While its pizzas are extra large, they are by no means the best in Italy. However, expect to join a queue if you arrive after 9 pm and don't be surprised if you end up sharing a table. Pizzas cost around L8000 to L10,000, a litre of wine costs L8000 and the cover charge is only L1500. Farther along the street at No 18 is a tiny, nameless osteria (no telephone), run by Antonio Bassetti, where you can eat an excellent meal for under L20,000. The consistently good food and the low prices make it one of the best value eating places in Rome. There is no written menu, but don't be nervous: even when very busy, the owner/waiter will try to explain (in Italian) the dishes.

Trattoria Pizzeria da Francesco, Piazza del Fico 29 (take Via del Corallo from Via del Governo Vecchio), has good pasta for around L10,000, and a good range of antipasto and vegetables. Pizzas range in price from around L8000 to L12,000, and a full meal will cost around L30,000. *Pizzeria Corallo* (☎ 68 30 77 03), Via del Corallo 10, off Via del Governo Vecchio, has good pizzas and is open late. A meal will cost around L25,000.

In Piazza della Cancelleria, between Piazza Navona and Campo de' Fiori, is *Grappolo d'Oro* (☎ 686 41 18). It serves excellent quality, traditional Roman food for around L30,000 for a full meal.

There are several restaurants in the Campo de' Fiori. *Hosteria Romanesca* is tiny, so arrive early in winter, when there are no outdoor tables. A dish of pasta will cost L6000 to L10,000, and a full meal under L30,000. *La Carbonara*, also in the campo, is a popular spot where a full meal costs up to around L50,000. In Piazza de' Ricci, through Piazza Farnese and north along Via di Monserrato, is an excellent little restaurant, *Pierluigi*. A full meal here will cost around L50,000.

Hostaria Giulio (☎ 654 04 66), Via della Barchetta 19, off Via Giulia, is another good-value eating place. It has two or three tables outside in summer. Along Via Giubbonari, off Campo de' Fiori, is *Filletti di Baccalà* (☎ 686 40 18) in Largo dei Librari, off Via dei Cappellari, which serves only deep-fried cod fillets and wine. You can satisfy moderate hunger and thirst for under L10,000. *Il Grottino*, Via delle Grotte 27, off Via dei Giubbonari near Campo de' Fiori, serves reasonable pizzas for around L6000 to L9000, a litre of wine costs L5000 and the coperto is L1500. A full meal will cost under L25,000.

On the other side of Via Arenula, in the Jewish quarter, is *Sora Margherita* (☎ 686 40 02), Piazza delle Cinque Scole 30, which serves traditional Roman and Jewish food in simple surroundings. A meal will cost under L25,000. Also in the Jewish quarter is *Al Pompiere* (☎ 686 83 77), at Via Santa Maria de' Calderari 38. Its food is great – try the carciofi alla giudia (deep-fried artichokes) – and prices are reasonable. A full meal should cost around L30,000.

City Centre – middle The very popular *Mario* (☎ 678 38 18), Via della Vite 55, off Piazza di Spagna, offers Tuscan food for around L65,000 a full meal. Another good restaurant in the area is *Al 34* (☎ 679 50 91), Via Mario de' Fiori 34, which has a menu combining Roman cooking with regional dishes from throughout Italy. A full meal will cost around L55,000. Near the Fontana di Trevi is *Al Moro* (☎ 678 34 95), Vicolo delle Bollette 13, which runs between Via dei Crociferi and Via delle Muratte. A good-quality, traditional Roman meal will come to less than L60,000. *Tullio* (☎ 475 85 64), Via San Nicola da Tolentino 26, which runs off Piazza Barberini, serves Roman and Tuscan dishes. It is of a high standard and a full meal will cost between L60,000 and L70,000. Also near Piazza Barberini is *Colline Emiliane* (☎ 481 75 38), Via degli Avignonesi 22, a spartan-looking trattoria which serves superb Emilia-Romagnan food. A full meal will cost around L55,000.

At Via degli Spagnoli 27, a few streets north of the Pantheon, is *Il Bacaro* (☎ 686 41 10), a tiny trattoria whose menu reflects what is available fresh on any given day. A meal will cost around L50,000. *La Campana* (☎ 686 78 20), Vicolo della Campana 18, at the top end of Via della Scrofa, is believed to be Rome's oldest restaurant and is certainly a favourite. A full meal will cost around L60,000. *Il Cardinale – GB* (☎ 686 93 36), Via delle Carceri 6, which runs off Via Giulia, is another well-known restaurant with superb food. A full meal should come to less than L80,000.

Vecchia Roma (☎ 686 46 04), Piazza Campitelli 18, has a well-deserved reputation for good food. Its outside tables are extremely popular in summer. A full meal will cost around L70,000.

City Centre – top end The widely known *Dal Bolognese* (☎ 361 14 26), Piazza del Popolo 1, is in a prime position to attract tourists, but maintains high culinary standards and reasonable prices. You must book if you want a table outside in summer. A full meal will cost more than L70,000. *Andrea* (☎ 482 18 91), Via Sardegna 24-28, close to Via Vittorio Veneto, is one of Rome's most popular top restaurants. A full meal will be in the range of L100,000. *Il Convivio* (☎ 686 94 32), Via dell'Orso 44, a little north of Piazza Navona, is an elegant restaurant with a creative menu. A full meal will cost around L100,000. *El Toulà* (☎ 687 34 98), Via della Lupa 29, is one of Rome's most prestigious restaurants, which is reflected in the prices – around L130,000 for a full meal.

In the Jewish quarter is *Piperno* (☎ 654 27 72), Via Monte de' Cenci 9, which has a menu combining Roman and Jewish cooking and is considered one of Rome's better mid-range restaurants. A full meal will cost from L85,000.

West of the Tiber – bottom end The main concentration of good-value restaurants is in Trastevere and the Testaccio district. Most establishments around St Peter's and the Vatican are geared towards tourists and can

be very expensive. *Osteria dell'Angelo* (☎ 38 92 18), Via G Bettolo 24, is in the Trionfale area – walk along Via Leone IV from the Vatican. A hearty Roman meal can be had for around L30,000. *Pizzeria Giacomelli* (☎ 38 35 11), Via di Bruno Emilia Faà 25, is off Via della Giuliana past Largo Trionfale. The pizzas are good, big and cheap. *Il Tempio della Pizza* (☎ 321 69 63), Viale Giulio Cesare 91, is open late and the good-quality food is reasonably priced.

In Trastevere's maze of tiny streets there are any number of pizzerias and cheap trattorias. The area is beautiful at night and most establishments have outside tables. It is also very popular, so arrive before 9 pm unless you want to queue for a table.

Mario's (☎ 580 38 09), Via del Moro 53, is a local favourite for its cheap pasta (around L8000 to L10,000) but you can find better quality elsewhere. *D'Augusto* (☎ 580 37 98), nearby in Piazza dei Renzi 15, is another great spot for a cheap meal. Try the home-made fettucine. If you arrive early there is also a good selection of vegetables. A meal with wine will cost L15,000 to L20,000. *Da Otello in Trastevere*, Via della Pelliccia 47-53, has excellent antipasto. A hearty meal should cost between L25,000 and L30,000.

Da Giovanni (☎ 686 15 14), Via della Lungara 41, is a good 10-minute walk from the centre of Trastevere. It is a popular eating place and you will probably have to wait for a table. The food is basic but the prices are good. *Da Gildo* (☎ 580 07 33), Via della Scala 31, is a pizzeria/trattoria with a range of pizzas and good-quality food. A full meal will cost around L25,000. Nearby, at Vicolo del Mattinato 2, is *Da Lucia* (☎ 580 36 01), which offers an excellent range of antipasto and pasta. In summer it has outside tables. A full meal will cost around L40,000. *Pizzeria Ivo* (☎ 581 70 82), Via San Francesco a Ripa 158, has outdoor tables, but the pizza could be bigger for the price (from L7500 to L10,000). The bruschetta is an excellent start to the meal. The house wine comes in bottles and is not a bargain at L8000. *Pizzeria Popi-Popi*, Via delle Fratte di Trastevere, just off Piazza San Cosimato, is very popular among young people, who flock to its outside tables in summer. The pizzas are average but cheap. *Pizzeria da Vittorio*, Via San Cosimato 14a, is tiny and you have to wait if you arrive after 9 pm. A delicious bruschetta and pizza with wine will cost around L18,000. At Viale di Trastevere 53 is *Panattoni* (☎ 580 09 19); open late and always crowded, it is one of the more popular pizzerias in Trastevere. You can eat there for around L15,000.

You won't find a noisier, more popular pizzeria in Rome than *Pizzeria Remo* (☎ 574 62 70), Piazza Santa Maria Liberatrice 44, in Testaccio. A meal will cost around L16,000. *Augustarello* (☎ 574 65 85), Via G Branca 98, off the piazza, specialises in offal dishes. A full meal should cost around L20,000. *Trattoria da Bucatino*, Via Luca della Robbia 84, is a popular Testaccio eating place, with pasta from L7000 to L10,000 and pizzas for around the same prices. It also serves Roman fare. A full meal will cost around L30,000.

West of the Tiber – middle to top end
Paris (☎ 581 53 78), Piazza San Calisto 7, has developed a reputation for excellent cuisine. A meal will cost around L70,000.

In Testaccio is *Checchino dal 1887* (☎ 574 63 18), Via Monte di Testaccio 30, which serves superb Roman food – which means, of course, lots of offal. It was selected in 1994 as one of the best restaurants in Italy by the international newspaper, the *Herald Tribune*. A full meal will cost around L75,000.

San Lorenzo & from Stazione Termini to the Roman Forum As Rome's university district, eating places in San Lorenzo are influenced by the student population. One of the more popular places is, *Pizzeria l'Economica*, Via Tiburtina 44, serves local fare and good pizzas at prices students can afford. *Formula 1* (☎ 445 38 66), Via degli Equi 13, is another good-value pizzeria, as is *Le Maschere* (☎ 445 38 05), Via degli Umbri 8; both are popular with students. One of the area's more famous trattorias is *Pommidoro* (☎ 445 26 92), Piazza dei Sanniti 44; an excellent meal will cost around L40,000. *Tram Tram*, Via dei Reti 44, is a lively

hangout for trendy young Romans and has good pasta at low prices.

If you have no option but to eat near Stazione Termini, try to avoid the tourist traps offering overpriced full menus. There are many tavole calde in the area, particularly to the west of the train station, which offer panini and pre-prepared dishes for reasonable prices. There is a self-service in the station complex, *La Piazza*, where you can eat good food at reasonable prices. There are a few good-value restaurants in the area. *Da Gemma alla Lupa* (☎ 49 12 30), Via Marghera 39, is a simple trattoria with prices to match: a full meal will cost around L27,000. *Hosteria Angelo*, Via Principe Amedeo 104, is a traditional trattoria with very reasonable prices. *Galilei* (☎ 731 56 42), Via Galilei 12, between the train station and Basilica di San Giovanni in Laterano, is a good, cheap pizzeria. Towards the Colosseum, at Via delle Terme di Tito 96, is *Hostaria di Nerone* (☎ 474 52 07). Popular with tourists, it has good food and a full meal will cost under L25,000. Another decent pizzeria is *Alle Carrette* (☎ 679 27 70), Vicolo delle Carrette 14, off Via del Cavour near the Roman Forum; a pizza and wine will come to around L15,000. *Trattoria dell'Angeletto* is an excellent restaurant in the piazza of the same name, just off Via del Cavour. It has outside tables and, while the service can get a bit slow when they're busy, the food is good.

Going up the price scale, *Tana del Grillo* (☎ 731 64 41), Via Alfieri 4-8, off Via Merulana, a few streets north of Piazza San Giovanni in Laterano, offers examples of the cuisine of Ferrara, as well as the usual Roman fare. A full meal will cost from L35,000 to L40,000. *Il Dito e La Luna* (☎ 494 07 26), Via dei Sabelli 47-51, in the San Lorenzo district, serves hearty, good-quality meals for around L45,000.

Non-Italian Restaurants
These are not exactly abundant, but there are some very good restaurants in Rome which serve international cuisine. Chinese food is

very popular, but the food is often heavily salted and can leave a lot to be desired.

Golden Crown (☎ 678 98 31), Via in Arcione 85, between Via del Tritone and the Palazzo del Quirinale, is a good choice; a solid meal will cost up to L40,000. For an excellent Japanese meal, head for *Sogo Asahi* (☎ 678 60 93), Via di Propaganda 22, near the Spanish Steps. It is expensive, however, at around L70,000 a head. There's a sushi bar, for which you have to book. *Suria Mahal* (☎ 589 45 54), Piazza Trilussa, in Trastevere, is an Indian restaurant where a delicious meal will cost around L40,000.

If all you really want is a Big Mac, you'll find McDonald's outlets in Piazza della Repubblica (with outside tables), Piazza di Spagna and Viale di Trastevere (between Piazza Sonnino and Piazza Mastai).

Vegetarian Restaurants

All trattorie serve a good selection of vegetable dishes, but there are other options for vegetarians in Rome. *Centro Macrobiotico*, Via della Vite 4, requires a L8000 membership fee and dishes start at L10,000. At *Margutta Vegetariano* (☎ 678 60 33), Via Margutta 19, which runs parallel to Via del Babuino, décor and prices are up-market and a meal will cost no less than L40,000. *Il Canestro*, Via Luca della Robbia 47, Testaccio, is another good option. A full meal will cost around L35,000.

Cafés & Bars

Remember that prices skyrocket in bars as soon as you sit down, particularly near the Spanish Steps, where a cappuccino at a table can cost as much as L8000. The same cappuccino taken at the bar will cost only L1600. The narrow streets and tiny piazzas in the area between Piazza Navona and the Tiber offer a number of popular cafés and bars. For those on a tight budget, there is *Caffè Peru*, in Piazza di Santa Caterina della Rota, just down the street to the right as you face the Palazzo Farnese. Here, serious local drinkers mingle with bohemians and students and you can buy beer by the bottle at rock-bottom prices and sit at a table for no extra charge.

The *Vineria* in Campo de' Fiori, also known as *Giorgio's*, has a wide selection of wine and beers and was once the gathering place of the Roman literati. Today it is less glamorous but is still a good place to drink (although cheap only if you stand at the bar). *Goldfinch* is a good, cheap bar which stays open late and also stages theatre; it is near the Campo de' Fiori at Via Pollarola 31. *Caffè Gardenia*, Via del Governo Vecchio 98, has snacks for around L6000, and live jazz. *Enoteca Piccolo*, at No 75 in the same street, is a pleasant wine bar with snacks available. Off Via del Governo Vecchio, in Via della Pace, is the *Bar della Pace*, a popular place for the young 'in' crowd, but you pay high prices to drink there. *Cul de Sac*, Piazza Pasquino 73, just off Piazza Navona at the start of Via del Governo Vecchio, is a popular wine bar which also serves excellent food. The *Druid's Den*, Via San Martino ai Monti 28, is an Irish pub serving Guinness where you can meet other English speakers.

There are numerous cafés and bars (with outdoor tables in summer) in Piazza Navona, near the Spanish Steps, in Piazza della Rotonda and in Piazza Santa Maria in Trastevere, which are extremely popular with tourists. Expect to pay a lot of money to sit down and drink your coffee, wine or beer. The *Bevitoria Navona*, Piazza Navona 72, charges reasonable prices (around L2500 for a glass of average wine and up to L10,000 for better quality wine – although expect to pay higher prices to sit outside). *Trimani*, Via Cernaia 37, near Stazione Termini, is another good wine bar and serves good-quality food. *Cul de Sac 1* (☎ 654 10 94), Piazza Pasquino 73, just off Piazza Navona, is a wine bar with excellent light meals for around L30,000.

Those seeking the best coffee in Rome should go to the *Tazza d'Oro*, just off Piazza della Rotonda in Via degli Orfani, and *Bar Eustachio*, Piazza Sant'Eustachio, near the Pantheon. Fashionable (and expensive) places to drink coffee or tea are the *Caffè Greco*, Via Condotti 86, near Piazza di

Spagna, and *Caffè Rosati* in Piazza del Popolo.

In Trastevere there is the *Bar San Calisto* in the piazza of the same name, with tables outside. This bar is seedy, but cheap and you can sit down without paying extra. A much more comfortable place to drink is the *San Michele aveva un Gallo* in Via San Francesco a Ripa, across Viale Trastevere near the corner of the Piazza San Francesco d'Assisi. At *Caffè del Marzio*, Piazza Santa Maria in Trastevere, you will pay L5000 for a cappuccino if you sit down outside, but it's worth it as this is one of Rome's most beautiful and atmospheric piazzas.

Sandwiches & Snacks

Paladini, Via del Governo Vecchio 29, might look like a run-down alimentari but they make mouth-watering pizza bianca on the premises and fill it with whatever you desire for around L5000. Try the prosciutto and fig – an unusual combination but delicious. *Bar la Penna*, Via Giulia 21, is another place whose looks can be deceiving. It has good sandwiches for around L3500. In Via di Ripetta (which runs off Piazza del Popolo, parallel to Via del Corso) there are several bars and takeaways with good fare. *Caffè Sogo*, Via di Ripetta 242, has Japanese snacks, as well as coffee etc. Next door is a tiny Japanese grocery.

Paneformaggio, Via di Ripetta 7, and *M & M Volpetti*, Via della Scrofa 31, near Piazza Navona, are upmarket sandwich bars /rosticcerie where you can buy gourmet lunch snacks for above-average prices.

Among the more famous sandwich outlets in Rome is *Frontoni* in Viale di Trastevere, on the corner of Via San Francesco a Ripa, opposite Piazza Mastai. It makes its panini with both pizza bianca and bread and you can choose from an enormous range of fillings. Sandwiches are sold by weight and a generously filled one will cost around L6000. It also has excellent pizza by the slice.

Takeaway pizza by the slice is very popular in Rome and there are numerous outlets all over the city. Usually you can judge the quality of the pizza simply by

taking a look. Some good places are *Pizza Rustica* in Campo de' Fiori, *Pizza a Taglio*, Via Baullari, between Campo de'Fiori and Via V Emanuele II, and *Pizza a Taglio* in Via delle Muratte, just off the Piazza di Trevi. Near Piazza di Spagna, at Via della Croce 18, is *Fior Fiore*.

Gelati

Gelateria Giolitti, Via degli Uffici del Vicario 40, has long been a Roman institution. It was once the meeting place of the local art crowd and writers. Today it remains famous for its fantastic gelati. *Gelateria della Palma*, around the corner at Via della Maddalena 20, has a huge selection of flavours and some say the gelati is better than at Giolitti; a cone with three flavours costs around L2500. Both establishments also have cakes and pastries. *La Fonte della Salute*, Via Cardinal Marmaggi 2-6 in Trastevere, has arguably the best gelati in Rome. An atmospheric spot for a good gelati is *Il Ristoro della Salute* in the Piazza del Colosseo. Buy a cone or an excellent fruit drink *(frullato)* and wander across the road to the Colosseum.

Bread & Pastries

Bernasconi, Largo di Torre Argentina 1, is a reasonably good pasticceria. *Bella Napoli*, a bar/pasticceria that specialises in Neapolitan pastries, is at Via Vittorio Emanuele 246. *Valzani*, Via del Moro 37 in Trastevere, is one of Rome's best pasticcerie, as is *Antonini*, Via Sabotino 21-29, near Piazza Mazzini in Prati. *La Dolceroma*, Via del Portico d'Ottavia 20 (between the Teatro di Marcello and Via Arenula), specialises in Austrian cakes and pastries. In the same street at No 2 is kosher bakery *Il Forno del Ghetto*, a very popular outlet for cakes and pastries. You will need to look for the street number as there is no sign. Near Stazione Termini is *Panella l'Arte del Pane*, Largo Leopardi 2-10 (on Via Merulana), with a big variety of pastries and breads.

Grocery Shops

There are hundreds of small outlets in the

centre of Rome where you can buy cheese, salami, bread and groceries. The following are some of the better known gastronomic establishments.

Billo Bottarga, Via di Sant'Ambrogio 20, near Piazza Mattei, specialises in kosher food. It is famous for its bottarga (roe of tuna or mullet). *Castroni*, Via Cola di Rienzo 196, in Prati near the Vatican, has a wide selection of gourmet foods, packaged and fresh, including international foods (desperate Aussies will find Vegemite here). *Franchi*, in the same street at No 204, is a salumeria (delicatessen) as well as an excellent takeaway. *Gino Placidi*, Via della Maddalena 48, near the Pantheon, is one of central Rome's best alimentari. *Ruggeri*, Campo de' Fiori 1, has a good range of cheese and meats, and *Strega Cavour*, Via Marianna Dionigi 19, near Piazza Cavour in the Vatican area, combines a bar and well-stocked alimentari. *Volpetti*, Via Marmorata 47, in Testaccio, has high-quality cheese and meats.

Health Foods
Buying muesli, soy milk and the like can be expensive in Italy. The following outlets have a good range of products, including organic fruit and vegetables at relatively reasonable prices.

L'Albero del Pane, Via Santa Maria del Pianto 19, in the Jewish quarter has a wide range of health foods, both packaged and fresh. It has an outlet for organic fruit and vegetables at Via dei Baullari 112, just off the Campo de' Fiori. *Emporium Naturae*, Viale Angelico 2 (take Metro Linea A to Ottaviano), is a well-stocked health-food supermarket. *Il Canestro*, Via Luca della Robbia 47, in Testaccio near the market, also has a large selection of health food, as well as fresh fruit and vegetables and takeaway food.

ENTERTAINMENT
Rome's primary entertainment guide is *Trovaroma*, a weekly supplement in the Thursday edition of the newspaper *La Repubblica*. Considered the bible for what is happening in the city, it provides a comprehensive listing of music, cinema, theatre and other events. The newspaper also publishes a daily listing of cinema, theatre and concerts. All this information is in Italian, but it is pretty easy to understand. *This Week in Rome* is another excellent guide, in English, to what's happening in the city. *Metropolitan* is a fortnightly magazine in English (L1500) which reviews what is happening in Rome's English-speaking community. It also has entertainment listings, as well as details on bars, pubs etc. The magazine is available at various outlets, including the Lion Bookshop, the Economy Book & Video Center. See the Information section for Rome for addresses. It is also available at various newspaper stands in the city centre, including at Largo Argentina and at Piazza Santa Maria in Trastevere.

Exhibitions & Concerts
During June and July, Tevere Expo takes place on the banks of the Tiber, featuring an exhibition of regional crafts and products. Admission is free. Free jazz concerts are held during July at the Castel Sant'Angelo – check daily papers for listings.

The Comune di Roma coordinates a diverse series of concerts, performances and events throughout summer which are given the general title Estate Romana (Roman Summer). The series usually features major international performers. A series of concerts is performed in Piazza del Campidoglio during July and there are concerts of classical music in the ruins of the Teatro di Marcello, Via di Teatro Marcello 44, near Piazza Venezia, every evening at 9 pm from July to September. For information call ☎ 482 74 03.

There is a season of concerts in October and November at the Accademia di Santa Cecilia, Via della Conciliazione 4, and the Accademia Filarmonica, Via Flaminia 18. The opera season at the Teatro dell'Opera, Piazza Beniamino Gigli, starts in November. Ballet is also performed at the Teatro dell'Opera. Other musical events in this period feature performances by the RAI Symphonic Orchestra.

Rock concerts are held throughout the year and are advertised on posters plastered around the city. Concerts by major performers are usually held at the Palazzo dello Sport or Stadio Flaminia, both a good distance from the city centre. For information and bookings, contact the ORBIS agency (☎ 475 14 03) in Piazza Esquilino near Stazione Termini.

Nightlife

Nightclubs and discotheques are popular mainly during winter. Among the more interesting and popular Roman live music clubs is Radio Londra, Via di Monte Testaccio, in the Testaccio area. Admission is free, but you might find it hard to get in here because the bouncers tend to pick and choose. There are several other good nightclubs and bars in the same street, including Caruso Caffè Concerto at No 36 and Caffè Latino at No 96. In the same area is Villaggio Globale, Lungotevere Testaccio (accessible from Largo G B Marzi at the Ponte Testaccio), an alternative hangout for people who really know the meaning of 'angst'. This is one of several *centri sociale* in Rome, a type of squatters' club frequented by ageing hippies, new-age types and people who are still into punk and 'grunge' etc. Common throughout Italy, these places are often associated with extreme left-wing political activity, although in Rome they are principally places of entertainment.

Metropolis, Via Rasella 5, a few blocks west of Piazza Barberini, is a rock club which often stages live concerts by English, and even Australian, bands. Il Castello is a music club which often has live underground bands at Via Porta Castello 44, just near Castel Sant'Angelo. Circolo degli Artisti, Via Lamarmora 28, behind Stazione Termini towards the San Lorenzo area, is a lively club, popular among Rome's young 'cool' set. For jazz and blues, try Alexanderplatz, Via Ostia 9 (open nightly), Folkstudio, Via Frangipane 42 or Big Mama, Via San Francesco a Ripa 18, in Trastevere.

Roman discos are expensive. Expect to pay up to L30,000 to get in (although women

are sometimes allowed in free of charge), which may or may not include one drink. Hot spots include Alien, Via Velletri 13; Piper '90, Via Tagliamento 9; and Gilda-Swing, Via Mario de'Fiori 97.

Gay & Lesbian Venues Rome's best gay disco is L'Alibi, Via di Monte Testaccio 44. Women are allowed in only if accompanied by a man. Another choice for gays is the bar/disco L'Angelo Azzurro, Via Cardinal Merry del Val 13, in Trastevere.

Cinemas

The cinema Pasquino (☎ 580 36 22), Vicolo del Piede 19, in Trastevere, screens films in English. It is just off Piazza Santa Maria. On Monday nights you can see English-language films at Alcazar (☎ 588 00 99), Via Merry del Val, off Viale Trastevere. The Nuova Sacher (☎ 581 81 16) at Largo Ascianghi, between the Porta Portese area and Trastevere, shows films in their original language on Mondays and Tuesdays. A new cinema complex with three screens, the Greenwich (☎ 574 58 25), Via G B Bodoni 59, in Testaccio, also shows films in their original language from time to time.

A popular form of entertainment in the hot Roman summer is outdoor cinema. In July at the Castel Sant'Angelo, on the Tiber, two huge screens are erected to show films in Italian. Screens are also set up at other locations, but films are usually shown only in Italian. Check *Trovaroma* for details.

THINGS TO BUY

The first things that come to mind when thinking of shopping in Rome are clothing and shoes. But it can be difficult to find bargains here. The city's main shopping areas are not as compact as Florence, or as impressive as Milan, but although expensive, the quality is certainly there.

It is probably advisable only to window-shop in the expensive Ludovisi district, the area around Via Veneto. The major fashion shops are in the Via Sistina and Via Gregoriana, heading towards the Spanish Steps, as well as in Via Condotti and the parallel

ROME

streets heading from the Piazza di Spagna to Via del Corso. The big names are all here, including Gucci, Via Condotti 8; Giorgio Armani, Via del Babuino 140; Ferragamo, Via Condotti 73; and Valentino, Via Condotti 12. However, in these streets you will also find moderately priced clothing and footwear, as well as shops selling accessories. Via del Corso is also a major shopping street. It is cheaper, but not as interesting, to shop along Via del Tritone and Via Nazionale. There are some interesting second-hand clothes shops along Via del Governo Vecchio. West of the Tiber, near St Peter's, the best shopping street is Via Cola di Rienzo.

If clothes don't appeal to you, wander through the streets around Via Margutta, Via Ripetta, Piazza del Popolo and Via Frattina to look at the art galleries, artists' studios and antiquarian shops. There are antique shops in Via dei Coronari, between Piazza Navona and Tor di Nona.

Everyone flocks to the famous Porta Portese market every Sunday morning. Hundreds of stalls line the streets of Porta Portese, near Trastevere, selling anything you can imagine. Here you can pick up a genuine 1960s evening dress for L1000, an antique mirror for L10,000, or a second-hand leather jacket for L40,000. Take time to rummage through the piles of clothing and bric-a-brac and you will find some incredible bargains. The market extends for a few km along the side streets parallel to Viale Trastevere from the Trastevere station. The market becomes very crowded by 11 am. Hold on tight to your bag as the area is literally crawling with pickpockets: better still, wear a money belt.

The excellent market in Via Sannio, near Porta San Giovanni, sells new and second-hand clothes. It is open Monday to Saturday until around 1 pm. For prints, antiques and books, head for the market at Piazza Fontanella Borghese, held every morning except Sunday.

GETTING THERE & AWAY
Air
The main airport is Leonardo da Vinci

(☎ 6 01 21), also known as Fiumicino, after the town nearby. The other airport is Ciampino, where many national and some international, including charter, flights arrive. See the Getting Around section in this chapter for details on getting to/from the airports, and see the Getting There & Away chapter earlier in this book for information on flights to/from Rome.

All the airlines have offices in the departure hall at Fiumicino, but their main offices are located in the area around Via Veneto and Via Barberini, north of Stazione Termini. They include:

Alitalia
    Via Bissolati 13 (☎ 6 56 21)
Air France
    Via Veneto 93 (☎ 488 55 63)
Air New Zealand
    Via Bissolati 54 (☎ 488 07 61)
British Airways
    Via Bissolati 54 (☎ 47 99 91)
Cathay Pacific
    Via Barberini 3 (☎ 487 01 50)
Delta Airlines
    Via Bissolati 46 (☎ 47 73)
Qantas
    Via Bissolati 35 (☎ 48 64 51)
Singapore Airlines
    Via Bissolati 24-26 (☎ 481 89 43)
TWA
    Via Barberini 67 (☎ 4 72 11)

Bus
The main station for Intercity buses is in Piazzale Tiburtina, in front of Stazione Tiburtina. Catch the Metropolitana Linea B from Termini to Tiburtina. Buses connect with cities throughout Italy. COTRAL buses, which service Lazio, depart from numerous points throughout the city, depending on their destinations. The company is about to be linked with Rome's new public transport system, which is based on the purchase of single tickets for all modes of transport. It was not certain at the time of writing what this would mean for COTRAL services. Numerous companies, some of which are listed below, offer these services. For information about which companies go to which destinations, go to the EPT office or the

Enjoy Rome office for assistance (see Tourist Offices in this chapter), or to Eurojet, Piazza della Repubblica 54, where you can buy tickets for many bus services and get information about timetables.

Some useful bus lines are:

COTRAL
Via Ostiense 131 (☎ 591 55 51)
Services throughout Lazio. See under individual destinations in the Around Rome section

ARPA
Information at Eurojet (☎ 474 28 01)
Services to Abruzzo, including L'Aquila and Pescara

Bonelli
Bar Piccarozzi, Piazza della Republicca 62 (☎ 488 59 24)
Services to Emilia-Romagna, including Ravenna and Rimini

Lazzi
Via Tagliamento 27r (☎ 884 08 40)
Services to other European cities and the Alps

Lirosi
Information at Eurojet (☎ 474 28 01)
Services to Calabria

Marozzi
Information at Eurojet (☎ 474 28 01)
Services to Bari and Brindisi, via towns including Alberobello and Matera. Also services to Naples and the Amalfi coast

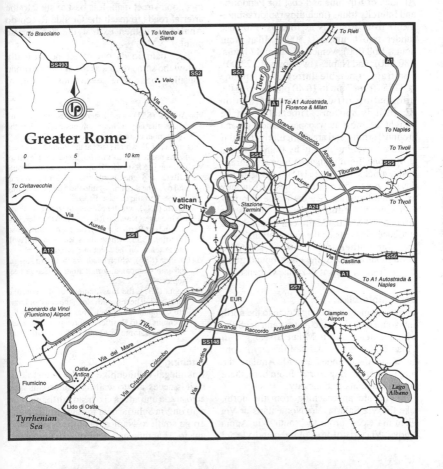

Greater Rome

SAIS & Segesta
   Piazza della Repubblica (☎ 482 50 66)
      Services to Sicily
Sena
   Information at Eurojet (☎ 474 28 01)
      Services to Siena
SULGA
   Information at Eurojet (☎ 474 28 01 or ☎ 075-500 96 41)
      Services to Perugia and Assisi

Train

Almost all trains arrive at and depart from Stazione Termini. There are regular connections to all major cities in Italy and Europe. An idea of trip time and cost for Pendolino and Intercity trains (including rapido supplement) from Rome is as follows: Florence (under two hours, L31,500); Milan (four hours, L68,000); Venice (six to eight hours, L80,000); and Naples (two hours, L27,000). For train timetable information, phone ☎ 4775 (from 7 am to 10.40 pm) or go to the information office at the train station (English is spoken). Timetables can be bought at most newspaper stands in and around Termini and are particularly useful if you are travelling mostly by train. Services at Stazione Termini include luggage storage beside tracks 1 and 22 (L1500 per item per day), a post office, telephones and money exchange facilities. See the Rome Information section for further details. Tickets for urban buses and the Metro can be purchased at tobacconists inside the train station. There are eight other train stations scattered throughout Rome. Some north-bound trains depart from or stop at Stazione Ostiense.

Car & Motorbike

The main road connecting Rome to the north and south of Italy is the Autostrada del Sole, which extends from Milan to Reggio di Calabria. On the outskirts of the city it connects with the Grande Raccordo Anulare, the ring road encircling Rome. From here, there are several exits into the city.

If you are approaching from the north, take the Via Salaria, Via Nomentana or Via Flaminia exits. From the south, Via Appia Nuova, Via Cristoforo Colombo and Via del Mare (which connects Rome to the Lido di Ostia) all provide reasonably direct routes into the city. The Grande Raccordo Anulare and all arterial roads in Rome are clogged with traffic on weekday evenings from about 5 to 7.30 pm, and on Sunday evenings, particularly in summer, all approaches to Rome are subject to traffic jams as Romans return home after weekends away.

The A12 connects the city to Civitavecchia and then along the coast to Genoa (it also connects the city to Fiumicino airport). Signs from the centre of Rome to the autostradas can be vague and confusing, so invest in a good street map. It is best to stick to the arterial roads to reach the Grande Raccordo Anulare and then exit at the appropriate point.

The main roads out of Rome basically follow the same routes as the ancient Roman consular roads. The seven most important are:

Via Aurelia (SS1), which starts at the Vatican and leaves the city to the north-east, following the Tyrrhenian coast to Pisa, Genoa and France;

Via Cassia (SS2), which starts at the Ponte Milvio and heads north-west to Viterbo, Siena and Florence;

Via Flaminia (SS3), which also starts at the Ponte Milvio, and goes north-west to Terni, Foligno and over the Apennines into the Marches, ending on the Adriatic coast at Fano;

Via Salaria (SS4), which heads north from near Porta Pia in central Rome to Rieti and into the Marches, and ends at Porto d'Ascoli on the Adriatic coast;

Via Tiburtina (SS5), which links Rome with Tivoli and Pescara, on the coast of Abruzzo;

Via Casilina (SS6), which heads south-east to Anagni and into Campania, terminating at Capua near Naples;

Via Appia (SS7), the most famous of the consular roads, which heads south along the coast of Lazio into Campania, and then goes inland across the Apennines into Basilicata, through Potenza and Matera to Taranto in Apulia and on to Brindisi.

Hitching

It is illegal to hitchhike on the autostradas, so it is necessary to wait on main roads near autostrada entrances. To head north, wait for a lift on Via Salaria, near the autostrada entry. To go south to Naples, take the Metropolitana to Anagnina and wait in Via Tuscolana.

Hitching is not recommended, particularly for women, either alone or in groups, as it can be dangerous.

GETTING AROUND
To/From the Airports

Fiumicino Access to the city is via the airport-Stazione Termini direct train (follow the signs to the train station from the airport arrivals hall), which costs L12,000. The train arrives at and leaves from Track No 22 at Termini. There is a ticket office at the platform. The first train leaves the airport for Termini at 7 am and the last at 10.50 pm. Another train makes stops along the way, including at Trastevere and Ostiense, and terminates at Stazione Tiburtina (L7000). A bus runs from Stazione Tiburtina (accessible at night by bus No 42N from Piazza Cinquecento in front of Termini and by day on Metro Linea B) to the airport. The airport is connected to Rome by an autostrada. Follow the signs for Rome out of the complex and exit from the autostrada at EUR. From there, follow the signs marked 'centro' to reach Via Cristoforo Colombo, which will take you directly into the centre.

Ciampino If you arrive at Ciampino airport, blue COTRAL buses (running between 5.45 am and 10.30 pm) will take you to the Anagnina Metropolitana stop, from where you can catch the subway to Stazione Termini. If you arrive late or very early, you have little option other than to catch a taxi.

The airport is connected to Rome by the Via Appia Nuova.

Bus

The city bus company is ATAC and most of the main buses terminate in Piazza dei Cinquecento at Stazione Termini. At the information booth in the centre of the piazza you can obtain a map detailing bus routes. The Lozzi map of Rome provides a good enough guide to bus routes. Generally, ATAC staff at the information booth are more than happy to provide information and advice on buses. See also the Rome Information section.

Another central point for the main bus routes is Largo di Torre Argentina, near Piazza Navona. Buses run from about 6 am to midnight, with limited services throughout the night on some routes.

Travel on Rome's buses, subway and suburban railways has now been linked and the same tickets are valid for all three modes of transport. This means individual tickets are now considerably more expensive, but if you manage to get the intended mileage out of them, the savings are high. Singles tickets cost L1500 for 75 minutes. They must be purchased *before* you get on the bus/train and then validated in the machine as you enter. The fine for travelling without a validated ticket is L50,000 and inspectors are tiring of the same old explanations from tourists that they 'didn't know'. Tickets are available in Piazza dei Cinquecento, at tobacconists and at newspaper stands. They can be purchased in blocks of 10. Daily tickets cost L5000, weekly tickets L25,000 and monthly tickets L50,000.

Useful buses include:

No 64, from Stazione Termini to St Peter's Basilica
No 27, from Stazione Termini to the Colosseum
No 44, from Piazza Venezia to Trastevere
No 118, from the Colosseum to the Terme di Caracalla, the Catacombs and Via Appia
No 3 or 910, from Stazione Termini to the Villa Borghese
No 36, from Stazione Termini along Via Nomentana (for foreign embassies)

Pickpockets are active on crowded buses, particularly those popular with tourists. The No 64, for example, is notorious and the No 27 is also a popular route for thieves.

Metropolitana

The Metropolitana (Metro) has two lines, Linea A and Linea B. Both pass through Stazione Termini. Take Linea A for Piazza di Spagna and Flaminio (the Villa Borghese), and for Ottaviano (the area near the Vatican). Linea B will take you to the Colosseum, Circo Massimo and Piramide (for Stazione

ROME

Ostiense and trains to the airport and the Lido di Ostia), as well as to EUR. See under the previous Bus section for information on tickets. Tickets can be purchased at ticket offices downstairs at Stazione Termini, from tobacconists or from vending machines at Metro stations. Trains run approximately every five minutes.

Taxi

Taxis are on radio call 24 hours a day in Rome. Cooperativa Radio Taxi Romana (☎ 3570) and La Capitale (☎ 4994) are two of the many operators. Major taxi ranks are at the airports and Stazione Termini and also at Largo Argentina in the historical centre. There are surcharges for luggage, night service, public holidays and travel to and from Fiumicino airport. The taxi flagfall is L6400 (for the first three km), then L1200 per km. There is a L3000 supplement from 10 pm to 7 am and L1000 from 7 am to 10 pm on Sunday and public holidays. There is a L15,000 supplement on travel to and from Fiumicino airport because it is outside the city limits. This means the fare will cost around L70,000. If you telephone for a taxi, the driver will turn on the meter immediately and you will pay the cost of travel from wherever the driver was when the call was received.

Car & Motorbike

Negotiating Roman traffic by car is difficult enough, but you may be taking your life in your hands if you ride a motorbike in the city. The rule in Rome is to look straight ahead to watch the vehicles in front, and hope that the vehicles behind are watching you!

Most of the historic centre of Rome is closed to normal traffic, although tourists are permitted to drive to their hotels. Traffic police control the entrances to the centre and should let you through if you have a car full of luggage and mention the name of your hotel. Once there, inform the hotel management that you have a car and they will provide a pass which allows you to drive and park in the centre. If you manage to enter without a pass, you are likely to return to find a brace on a wheel of your car or even that the car has been towed away. In the event that your car goes missing after it was parked illegally, always check first with the traffic police (☎ 6 76 91 or ☎ 676 98 38). You will have to pay about L180,000 to get it back.

Rather than having the hassle of driving around Rome, it is a much better idea to leave your vehicle in a car park (unless you are lucky enough to find a legal parking spot in the centre) and use public transport. There are numerous small car parks scattered around the centre on vacant blocks of land that are attended during the day, but for longer periods it's safer to use one of the larger, covered car parks.

The major parking area closest to the centre is at the Villa Borghese; entry is from Piazzale Brasile at the top of Via Veneto. There is also a supervised car park at Stazione Termini. Other car parks are at Piazzale dei Partigiani, just outside Stazione Ostiense and connected to the centre on the Metro nearby at Piramide, and at Stazione Tiburtina, from where you can also catch the Metro into the centre.

The EPT at Via Parigi 11 has a list of car parks in the suburbs of Rome, run by the ACI. All are accessible to the city centre by Metro or bus and are generally cheap (around L1000 an hour for those closer to the centre and as cheap as L2000 a day for those on the periphery of the city).

Car Rental To rent a car, you will need to be at least 21 years old and have a valid driving licence. It is cheaper to organise a car in advance if you want one for a long period. For a guide to rental costs, see the Getting Around chapter. The multinational operators in Rome (Avis, Europcar and Hertz) are slightly cheaper than the locals. The major companies are:

Avis: Fiumicino airport (☎ 65 01 15 79), Stazione Termini (☎ 470 12 19), Piazza Esquilino 1 (☎ 470 12 16) or toll-free ☎ 1678-6 30 63
Dollaroexpres: Viale delle Milizie 9d (☎ 37 51 59 44 or toll-free ☎ 1678-6 51 10)
Euronolo: Via Valle Vermiglio 21 (☎ 88 64 01 85)

Europcar: Fiumicino airport (☎ 65 01 08 79), Stazione Termini (☎ 488 28 54) or central phone ☎ 52 08 12 00

Hertz: Fiumicino airport (☎ 65 01 14 48), Stazione Termini (☎ 474 03 89) or toll-free 1678-2 20 99

Maggiore: Fiumicino airport (☎ 65 01 06 78), Stazione Termini (☎ 488 00 49) or toll-free ☎ 1678-6 70 67

Scooter & Bicycle Rental For scooters and bicycles, contact I Bike Rome (☎ 322 52 40), Via Veneto 156, in the underground Villa Borghese car park. A 50 cc motorbike costs L45,000 per day or L200,000 per week, with unlimited mileage. Bicycles cost L5000 an hour, L13,000 a day, L38,000 a week and L23,000 for a weekend. Bicycles are also available for rent in Piazza Sonnino, in Trastevere. For more information on rental costs, see the Getting Around chapter.

Lazio

Rome demands so much of your time and concentration that most tourists forget the city is part of the Lazio region. Declared a region in 1934, the Lazio area (also known as Latium in English) has, since ancient Roman times, been an extension of Rome. Through the ages, the rich built their villas in the Lazio countryside, and many towns developed as the fiefs of noble Roman families, such as the Orsini, Barberini and Farnese. Even today, Romans build their weekend and holiday homes in the picturesque areas of the region (the pope, for instance, has his summer residence at Castelgandolfo, south of Rome) and Romans continue to migrate from their chaotic and polluted city to live in the Lazio countryside. This means the region is relatively well-served by public transport, and tourists can take advantage of this to visit places of interest.

While the region does not abound in major tourist destinations, it does offer some worthwhile day-trips from the city. A tour of Etruria, the ancient land of the Etruscans, which extended into northern Lazio, is highly recommended. Visits to the tombs and museums at Cerveteri and Tarquinia provide a fascinating insight into Etruscan civilisation. The ruins of Hadrian's villa, near Tivoli, and of the ancient Roman port at Ostia Antica, are both easily accessible from Rome, as is the medieval town of Viterbo, north of the capital. In summer, tired and overheated tourists can head for the lakes north of Rome, including Bracciano and Vico, which are somewhat preferable to the polluted beaches near the city, or head south of Rome to Sabaudia or Sperlonga.

In general, the pickings south of Rome are more modest, but there are some hill-top towns well worth visiting, such as Anagni (and the remarkable frescoes in its Romanesque cathedral), Alatri and those of the Castelli Romani in the hills just past Rome's outskirts. People interested in Italy's involvement in WW II might want to visit Monte Cassino, the scene of a major battle during the dying stages of the war .

If you have your own transport, try to avoid day trips out of Rome on Sundays during summer. On your return in the evening you are likely to find yourself in traffic jams extending for many km, even on the autostradas.

OSTIA ANTICA

The Romans founded this port city at the mouth of the Tiber river in the 4th century BC and it became a strategically important centre of defence and trade. It was populated by merchants, sailors and slaves, and the ruins of the city provide a fascinating contrast to the ruins at Pompeii, which was populated by wealthy Romans. After barbarian invasions and the appearance of malaria it was abandoned, but Pope Gregory IV re-established the city in the 9th century AD.

Information about the town and ruins is available at the EPT office in Rome.

Things to See & Do

The ruins are quite spread out and you will need a few hours to wander through them. Admission to the city is through the **Porta Romana**, which leads you onto Ostia

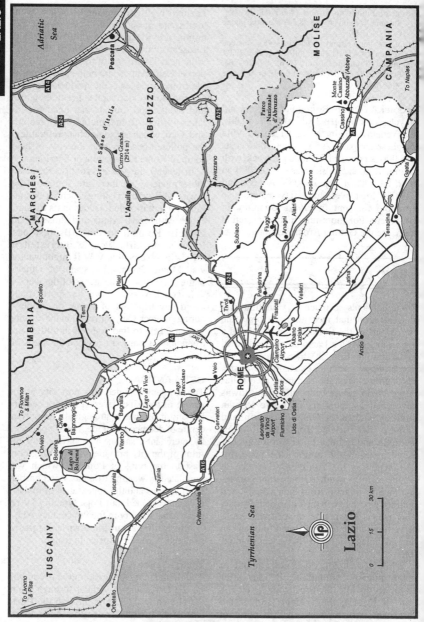

Antica's main thoroughfare, the **Decumanus Maximus**. The Porta Marina, at the other end of the road, once opened onto the seafront. Of particular note in the excavated city are the **Terme di Nettuno** (Neptune's Baths), to your right just after entering the city. Take a look at the black-and-white mosaic depicting Neptune and Amphitrite. Next is a **Roman theatre** built by Agrippa, which could hold 2700 people. It was restored in 1927 and is now used for staging classical performances and concerts. Behind the theatre is the **Piazzale delle Corporazioni**, where Ostia's merchant guilds had their offices, each distinguished by mosaics depicting their wares.

Returning to the Decumanus Maximus, you reach the **forum**, the **Tempio di Roma e Augusto**, dedicated to the goddess Rome, and the **Tempio Rotondo**. Follow the Vico del Pino and Via del Tempio Rotondo to the Cardo Maximus to reach the **Domus Fortuna Annonaria**, the heavily decorated home of one of Ostia's wealthier citizens. Opposite, in the area next to the **Grandi Horrea** (warehouses), are private houses, including the well-preserved **Casa di Diana**. Continue along the Via dei Dipinti to reach Ostia Antica's **museum**, which houses statues, mosaics and wall paintings found at the site (the museum has been closed because it is being moved to a new building: it could reopen in 1996). The ruins are open daily from 9 am to one hour before sunset year-round. Admission is L8000.

Getting There & Away

To get to Ostia Antica, take the Metro Linea B to Magliana and then the Ostia Lido train. Trains leave every half-hour and the trip takes about 20 minutes. Buy a ticket which covers both the Metro and the Ostia train. The ruins are also easy to reach by car from Rome. Take the Via del Mare, a fast superstrada which runs parallel to the Via Ostiense.

TIVOLI

Set on a hill by the Anio river, Tivoli was a resort town of the ancient Romans and became popular as a summer playground for the rich during the Renaissance. While the majority of tourists are attracted by the terraced gardens and fountains of the Villa d'Este, the ruins of the spectacular Villa Adriana, built by the Roman emperor Hadrian, are far more interesting.

The AAST office (☎ 0774-2 12 49) is in Largo Garibaldi, near the COTRAL bus stop. It is open in summer from 8 am to 6 pm and in winter to 2 pm.

Things to See & Do

The **Villa Adriana** was built in the 2nd century AD and was influenced by the classical architecture of the day. It was successively plundered by barbarians and Romans for building materials, and many of its original decorations were used to embellish the Villa d'Este. However, enough remains to give an idea of the magnificence of the villa, which was use by the emperor as a summer villa. You will need about four hours to wander through the vast ruins, and you'll find yourself exhausted before you've seen even half the place. Take a break for a picnic, or lunch at the bar in the visitors' centre before resuming your tour.

Highlights include **La Villa dell'Isola** (The Villa of the Island), where Hadrian is supposed to have spent his more pensive moments, the **Palazzo Imperiale** and its **Piazza d'Oro** (Golden Square) and the floor mosaics of the **Hospitalia**. Although very little remains of Hadrian's **Piccole e Grandi Terme** (Small and Large Baths), it is easy to work out their layout and imagine their former grandeur. Take a look at the model of the villa in the small visitors' centre to get an idea of the extent of the complex. The villa is open in the warmer months from 9 am to 7 pm (last admission at 6 pm) and in winter to around 5 pm. Admission is L8000.

The Renaissance **Villa d'Este** was built in the 16th century for Cardinal Ippolito d'Este, grandson of the Borgia pope, Alexander VI, on the site of a Franciscan monastery. The villa's beautiful gardens are decorated with numerous fountains, which are its main attraction. You will wander through the cardinal's villa on the way to the gardens. Rather than paying too much attention to the fairly drab rooms, take a look out of the windows for a bird's-eye view of the gardens and fountains. Opening hours are the same as for the Villa Adriana. Admission is L5000.

Getting There & Away
Tivoli is about 40 km east of Rome and accessible by COTRAL bus, which leaves from Via Tiburtina. Take Metro Linea B from Stazione Termini to Rebibbia; the bus leaves from outside the station every 15 minutes (L4600 return). The bus also stops at the Villa Adriana, about one km from Tivoli. Otherwise, from Tivoli's Piazza Garibaldi catch local bus No 4 to Villa Adriana. The fastest route by car is on the Rome-L'Aquila autostrada (A24).

ETRUSCAN SITES
There are several important Etruscan archaeological sites in Lazio, most within easy reach of Rome by car or public transport. These include Tarquinia (one of the major Etruscan League city-states), Cerveteri, Veio and Tuscania. The tombs and religious monuments discovered throughout the area yielded the treasures which can now be seen in museums including the Villa Giulia and the Vatican. The smaller museums at Tarquinia and Cerveteri are also well worth a visit.

The sheer number of tombs in the area has long supported the illegitimate industry of the *tombaroli* (tomb robbers), who have been plundering the sites for centuries and selling their 'discoveries' on the black market. It is said that, since many tombs are still to be excavated, a good number of tombaroli remain active. Prospective buyers of illicit Etruscan artefacts should, however, beware: another notorious activity of the tombaroli is the manufacture of fake treasures.

If you have the time, a few days spent touring at least Tarquinia and Cerveteri, combined with visits to their museums and the Villa Giulia, should constitute one of your more fascinating experiences in Italy. A useful guidebook to the area, *The Etruscans*, is published by the Istituto Geografico de Agostini and has a map. If you really want

to lose yourself in a poetic journey, take along a copy of D H Lawrence's *Etruscan Places* (published by Penguin in the compilation *D H Lawrence and Italy*).

Tarquinia
Believed to have been founded in the 12th century BC, and home of the Tarquin kings who ruled Rome before the creation of the republic, Tarquinia was an important economic and political centre of the Etruscan League. The town has a small medieval centre, with a good Etruscan museum, but the major attractions here are the painted tombs of its burial grounds.

Orientation & Information By car or bus you will arrive at the Barriera San Giusto, just outside the main entrance to the town. See Getting There & Away in this section. The AAST office (☎ 0766-85 63 84) is on your left as you walk through the medieval ramparts, at Piazza Cavour 1. It's open Monday to Saturday from 8.30 am to 12.30 pm and 4 to 6 pm. It is possible to see Tarquinia on a day trip from Rome, but if you want to stay overnight in the medieval town, it is advisable to make a booking.

Tarquinia's telephone code is 0766.

Things to See The 15th-century Palazzo Vitelleschi, in Piazza Cavour, houses the **Museo Nazionale Tarquiniese** and a significant collection of Etruscan treasures, including frescoes removed from the tombs. There is a beautiful terracotta frieze of winged horses, taken from the temple, **Ara della Regina**. Numerous sarcophagi found in the tombs are also on display. At any one time, sections of the museum are likely to be closed to the public. The museum is open Tuesday to Sunday from 9 am to 2 pm. Admission is L8000.

The same ticket admits you to the **necropolis**, also open from 9 am to 2 pm (ask for directions from the museum, a 15 to 20-minute walk). Almost 6000 tombs have been excavated, of which about 60 are painted, and only a handful are open to the public. Excavation of the tombs started in the 15th century and still

GREG ELMS

TONY WHEELER

ROB FLYNN

STEFANO CAVEDONI

Top Left: Fontana dei Fiumi, Piazza Navona, Rome
op Right: Spanish Steps, Rome
tom Left: Roman Forum, Rome
m Right: Detail of the Colonna di Traiana (Trajan's Column), Rome

DAMIEN SIMONIS

RICHARD STEWART

ROB FLYNN

Top Left: Nun outside St Peter's Basilica, Rome
Top Right: A boy and his grandmother, feeding the pigeons at St Peter's Square, Rome
Bottom: View of St Peter's Square from St Peter's Basilica, Rome

continues today. Unfortunately, exposure to air and human interference has led to serious deterioration in many tombs and they are now enclosed and maintained at constant temperatures. The painted tombs can be seen only through glass partitions. You must wait until a guide is available to open the tombs and it could be a long wait in summer, when thousands of tourists visit the necropolis daily.

D H Lawrence, who studied the tombs before measures were taken to protect them, wrote extensive descriptions of the frescoes he saw, and it is well worth reading his *Etruscan Places* before seeing the tombs of Tarquinia. Entering the famous Tomb of the Leopards, Lawrence noted how, despite the extensive destruction of the tombs through vandalism and neglect, the colours of the wall paintings were still fresh and alive:

The walls of this little tomb are a dance of real delight. The room seems inhabited still by Etruscans of the 6th century before Christ, a vivid life-accepting people, who must have lived with real fullness. On come the dancers and the music-players, moving in a broad frieze towards the front wall of the tomb, the wall facing us as we enter from the dark stairs, and where the banquet is going on in all its glory. Above the banquet, in the gable angle, are the two spotted leopards, heraldically facing each other across a little tree. And the ceiling of rock has chequered slopes of red and black and yellow squares, with a roof-beam painted with coloured circles, dark red and blue and yellow. So that all is colour, and we do not seem to be underground at all, but in some gay chamber of the past.

If you have a car, ask for directions to the remains of the Etruscan acropolis, on the crest of the Civita hill nearby. There is little evidence of the ancient city, apart from a few limestone blocks which once formed part of the city walls, since the Etruscans generally used wood to build their temples and houses. However, a large temple, the **Ara della Regina**, was discovered on the hill and has been excavated this century. It is enclosed by a wire fence because archaeological work is still underway, but it can be seen through the fence.

If you have time, wander through the pleasant medieval town of Tarquinia. There are several churches worth a look, including the late 13th-century Chiesa di San Francesco, in Via Porta Tarquinia, and the beautiful Romanesque Chiesa di Santa Maria di Castello, in the citadel at the north-west edge of the town.

Places to Stay & Eat There is a camping ground by the sea at Tarquinia Lido, *Tusca Tirrenia* (☎ 8 82 94), Viale Neriedi.

There are no budget options in the old town if you want to stay overnight, and it can be difficult to find a room if you don't book well in advance. The only moderately priced hotel in the medieval town, the *Hotel San Marco*, was closed for restoration at the time of writing. Check with the tourist office for details. Otherwise try the *Hotel all'Olivo* (☎ 85 73 18), Via Togliatti 15, in the newer part of town a 10-minute walk downhill from the medieval centre. Singles/doubles are L55,000/80,000. Closer to the centre, but more expensive, is *Hotel Tarconte* (☎ 85 65 85), Via Tuscia 23, with doubles costing more than L100,000, with breakfast included. At Tarquinia Lido is *Hotel Miramare* (☎ 8 80 20), Viale dei Tirreni 36, with single/doubles for L45,000/65,000.

There are few places to eat in Tarquinia, but for a good, cheap meal, go to *Trattoria Arcadia*, Via Mazzini 6. *Cucina Casareccia* is opposite at No 5.

Getting There & Away Buses leave approximately every hour for Tarquinia from Via Lepanto in Rome, near the Metro Linea A Lepanto stop, arriving at Tarquinia at the Barriera San Giusto, a few steps away from the tourist office. You can also catch a train from Rome, but Tarquinia's train station is at Tarquinia Lido, approximately three km from the centre. You will then need to catch one of the regular local buses to the Barriera San Giusto. Buses leave from the Barriera for Tuscania every few hours. If you are travelling by car, take the autostrada for Civitavecchia and then the Via Aurelia (SS1). Tarquinia is about 90 km from Rome.

Cerveteri

Ancient Caere was founded by the Etruscans in the 8th century BC and enjoyed a period of great prosperity as a commercial centre from the 7th to 5th centuries BC. The main attractions here are the tombs known as *tumoli*, great mounds of earth with carved stone bases. Treasures taken from the tombs can be seen in the Vatican Museums, the Villa Giulia Museum and the Louvre. The Pro Loco tourist office is at Via delle Mura Castellane.

The main necropolis area, **Banditaccia**, is open daily, except Monday, from 9 am to one hour before sunset. Admission is L8000. It's accessible by local bus in summer only from the main piazza in Cerveteri, otherwise it is a pleasant three-km walk west from the town. You can wander freely once inside the area, although it is best to follow the recommended routes to see the best-preserved tombs. One of the more interesting is the Tomba dei Rilievi, which is decorated with painted reliefs of household items. The tomb has been closed to avoid further damage to its paintings but it can be viewed through a glass window. Follow the signs also to the Tomba dei Capitali and the Tomba dei Vasi Greci. Signs detailing the history of the main tombs are in Italian only.

There is also a small **museum** in Cerveteri which contains an interesting display of pottery and sarcophagi. It is in the Palazzo Ruspoli and is open daily, except Monday, from 9 am to 2 pm. Admission is free.

Cerveteri is only about 40 minutes from Rome and accessible by COTRAL bus from Via Lepanto, outside the Lepanto stop on Metro Linea A. Otherwise, catch the Rome-Pisa train, which stops at Cerveteri. By car take either Via Aurelia or the Civitavecchia autostrada (A24).

Veio

Your visit to Etruria should include Veio, which is very close to Rome. This was the largest of the Etruscan League cities. Its proximity to Rome meant there was a traditional rivalry between the two cities, and, after a siege lasting 10 years, it finally fell

under Rome's dominion in 396 BC and was destroyed. It became a municipium under Augustus, but eventually declined in importance and was abandoned.

Little evidence remains of the city. The only things to see are the remains of a swimming pool and the lower section of a temple. However, important finds were made during excavations of the site in the 18th century, including the famous statue of Apollo, now in the Villa Giulia museum in Rome.

By car, leave Rome on the Via Cassia and exit at Isola Farnese. Signs will point you towards Veio. Otherwise, take bus No 201 (for Olgiata) from Piazza Mancini, near the Ponte Milvio, to Isola Farnese and ask the bus driver to let you off at the road to Veio (although, for the trouble of catching public transport, there is little to see at Veio).

CIVITAVECCHIA

There is little to recommend this busy port and industrial centre to tourists, other than the ferries which leave daily for Sardinia. Established by Emperor Trajan in 106 AD as the port town of Centumcellae, it was later conquered by the Saracens, but regained importance as a papal stronghold in the 16th century. The medieval town was almost completely destroyed by bombing during WW II. In 1995, the town hit the headlines when a 43-cm-high statue of the Madonna, located in the private garden of a local family, started crying tears of blood. Originally brought from Medgugori (part of the former Yugoslavia) the statue is now in the local Chiesa di Sant'Agostino. Tests revealed the tears were in fact human blood and the statue continues to attract crowds of pilgrims.

Orientation & Information

The port, and therefore the departure point for ferries, is a quick walk from the train station. As you leave the station, turn right into Viale Garibaldi and follow it along the seafront. The APT office (☎ 0766-2 53 48) is at Viale Garibaldi 42 and is open Monday to Friday from 8.30 am to 1 pm and 4 to 6.45 pm and Saturday from 9 am to 1 pm. From

June to September there is also an information booth at the port, open seven days a week.

The town's telephone code is 0766.

Places to Stay & Eat

There should be no need to spend the night in Civitavecchia. It is easily accessible from Rome and, to save time and money, it is better to catch a night ferry to Sardinia. If you get stuck, try *Hotel Traghetto* (☎ 2 59 20, Via Braccianese, just near the port.

For a meal, head for one of the pizzerias along the waterfront, or try *Trattoria da Vitale* at Viale Garibaldi 26. It is not overly expensive to eat on the ferry (full restaurant meals, as well as snacks, are available), but it is a good idea to bring supplies on board if you want to save money. There is a grocery shop near the station at Civitavecchia and a market every morning from Monday to Saturday in Via Doria.

Getting There & Away

Civitavecchia is on the main train line between Rome (1½ hours) and Genoa (2½ hours). By car it is easily reached from Rome on the A12. If arriving from Sardinia with your car, simply follow the A12 signs from the Civitavecchia port to reach the autostrada for Rome.

Ferries to/from Sardinia Tirrenia operates ferries to Olbia (seven hours), Arbatax (nine hours) and Cagliari (12 hours). Departure times and prices change annually and it is best to check with a travel agent, or with Tirrenia directly, for up-to-date information. At the time of writing, a one-way fare to Olbia was L40,700 for a seat (poltrona), L56,000 for a bed in a 2nd-class cabin, L77,800 for a bed in a 1st-class cabin and L116,000 for a small car. The company also operates fast boats which take only 3½ hours from Civitavecchia to Olbia. Tickets are considerably more expensive: about three times the price of a seat on the ferries. Tickets can be purchased at travel agents, including CIT, or at the Tirrenia office in Rome (☎ 06-474

20 41), Via Bissolati 41, and at Stazione Marittima in Civitavecchia.

The Ferrovie dello Stato (FS) also runs several ferries a day to Sardinia, docking at Golfo Aranci (about 20 km north of Olbia and accessible by bus or train). Tickets can be purchased at travel agents, at Stazione Termini in Rome, or Stazione Marittima in Civitavecchia.

VITERBO

Founded by the Etruscans and eventually taken over by Rome, Viterbo developed into an important medieval centre and in the 13th century became the residence of the popes.

Papal elections were held in the town's Gothic Palazzo Papale and stories abound about the antics of impatient townspeople who were anxious for a decision. In 1271, when the college of cardinals had failed to elect a new pope after three years of deliberation, the Viterbesi first locked them in a turreted hall of the palazzo, removed its roof and put the cardinals on a starvation diet. Only then did the cardinals manage to elect Gregory X.

Although badly damaged by bombing during WW II, Viterbo remains Lazio's best-preserved medieval town and it is a pleasant base for exploring northern Lazio. For travellers with less time, Viterbo is an easy day trip from Rome.

Apart from its historical appeal, Viterbo is famous for its therapeutic hot springs. The best known is the sulphurous Bulicame pool, mentioned by Dante in his *Divine Comedy*.

Orientation & Information

As with most historic centres in Italy, the town of Viterbo is neatly divided between newer and older sections. Hotels are in the newer part of town, and you must cross the Piazza del Plebiscito, with its 15th and 16th-century palaces, before reaching medieval Viterbo and the real reason for your visit. There are train stations north and south-east of the town centre; both are just outside the town walls. The station for intercity buses is

LAZIO

located somewhat inconveniently at Riello, a few km out of town.

The EPT office (☎ 0761-30 47 95) is at Piazza San Carluccio in the medieval quarter and is open Monday to Friday from 9 am to 5 pm and Saturday from 9 am to 1 pm.

The main post office is in Via F Ascenzi, just off Piazza del Plebiscito. The Telecom office is at Via Cavour 28, off the other side of the piazza.

Viterbo's post code is 01100 and its telephone code is 0761.

Things to See & Do
Piazza del Plebiscito The piazza is enclosed by 15th and 16th-century palaces, the most imposing of which is the **Palazzo dei Priori**, with an elegant 17th-century fountain in its courtyard. Many rooms are decorated with frescoes, notably the Sala Reggia, which is decorated with a late-Renaissance fresco depicting the myths and history of Viterbo.

Cattedrale di San Lorenzo & the Palazzo
Papale The 12th-century cathedral in Piazza San Lorenzo was rebuilt in the 14th century to a Gothic design, although the interior has just been restored to its original Romanesque simplicity. Also in the piazza is the **Palazzo Papale**, built in the 13th century with the aim of enticing the popes away from Rome. Its beautiful and graceful loggia is in the early Gothic style. The part facing the valley collapsed in the 14th century and you can see the bases of some of the columns. The hall in which papal conclaves were held is at the top of the steps. If it is not open, ask at the curia.

Head back to the Piazza della Morte and take Via Cardinale la Fontaine to **Piazza Santa Maria Nuova**. The Romanesque church of the same name was restored to its original form after sustaining bomb damage in WW II. The cloisters, which are believed to date from an earlier period, are worth a visit.

The Medieval Quarter Via San Pellegrino
takes you through the medieval quarter into **Piazza San Pellegrino**. The extremely well-preserved buildings which enclose this tiny piazza are considered the finest group of medieval buildings in Italy.

Other Sights The **Fontana Grande**, in Piazza Fontana Grande was built in the early 13th century and is the oldest and largest of Viterbo's Gothic fountains.

Back at the entrance to the town is **Chiesa di San Francesco**, in the piazza of the same name, a Gothic building which was restored after suffering serious bomb damage during WW II. The church contains the tombs of two popes: Clement IV (who died in 1268) and Adrian V (who died in 1276). Both tombs are lavishly decorated, notably that of Adrian, which features Cosmati work, a mosaic technique used in the 12th and 13th centuries.

The **Museo Civico** has reopened after a 10-year restoration project. It is housed in the convent of the Chiesa di Santa Maria della Verità, just outside the Porta della Verità on the north-east side of town. Among the works in the museum are the lovely *Pietà* by Sebastiano del Piombo and a Roman sarcophagus which is said to be the tomb of Galiana, a beautiful and virtuous woman murdered by a Roman baron after she refused his advances. The museum is open Tuesday to Saturday from 9 am to 6 pm. Admission is L6000.

Places to Stay & Eat
For budget accommodation try the *Hotel Roma* (☎ 22 64 87), Via della Cava 26, which runs off Piazza della Rocca. Singles/doubles are L39,000/59,000. For three-star accommodation there is *Hotel Tuscia* (☎ 34 44 00), Via Cairoli 41, with singles/doubles for L86,000/120,000.

For a reasonably priced meal try *All'Archetto*, Via San Cristoforo, off Via Cavour. A full meal will cost around L25,000. *Il Richiastro*, at Via della Marrocca 18, is slightly more expensive and has outside tables in summer. *Il Ciuffo* is a pizzeria in Piazza Capella, just off Piazza San Pellegrino.

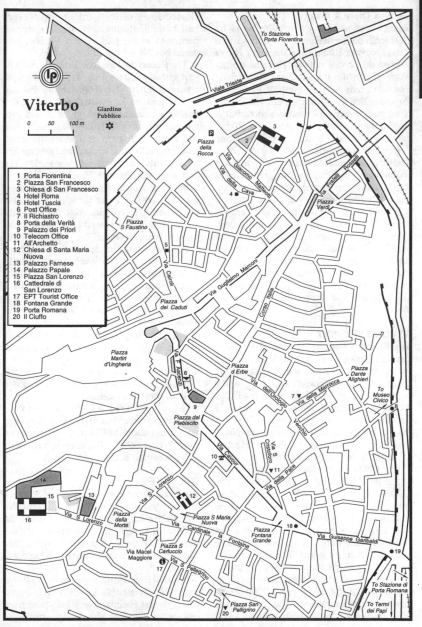

Viterbo

0   50   100 m

Giardino Pubblico

1 Porta Fiorentina
2 Piazza San Francesco
3 Chiesa di San Francesco
4 Hotel Roma
5 Hotel Tuscia
6 Post Office
7 Il Richiastro
8 Porta della Verità
9 Palazzo dei Priori
10 Telecom Office
11 All'Archetto
12 Chiesa di Santa Maria Nuova
13 Palazzo Farnese
14 Palazzo Papale
15 Piazza San Lorenzo
16 Cattedrale di San Lorenzo
17 EPT Tourist Office
18 Fontana Grande
19 Porta Romana
20 Il Ciuffo

Getting There & Away

The easiest way to get to Viterbo is by COTRAL bus from Rome. There are several a day, leaving Rome from the Saxa Rubra stop on the private railway, Ferrovia Roma-Nord. Catch the train to Saxa Ruba from Piazzale Flaminio (just north of Piazza del Popolo). You can catch a Ferrovia Roma-Nord train directly to Viterbo, although it is slower than the bus. By train from Rome, catch a normal FS train from Stazione Termini and get off in Viterbo at either Stazione di Porta Romana or Stazione Porta Fiorentina. The Intercity bus station is at Riello, a few km from the town centre. You can catch urban bus No 1 or 2 into Viterbo.

By car, the easiest way to get to Viterbo is on the Cassia-bis (about 1½ hours drive). Enter the old town through the Porta Romana onto Via G Garibaldi and follow the street as it becomes Via Cavour, through Piazza del Plebiscito. There are numerous public car parks scattered throughout the town, although the best is probably Piazza della Rocca.

AROUND VITERBO

Viterbo's **thermal springs** are about three km out of town. They were used by both the Etruscans and Romans, and the latter built large bath complexes, of which virtually nothing remains. Travellers wanting to take a cure or relax in the hot sulphur baths will find the Terme dei Papi (☎ 0761-25 00 93) the easiest to reach. Take urban bus No 2 from the bus station in Piazza Martiri d'Ungheria, near the EPT office.

If you have a car, follow the signs from the Terme dei Papi for the Etruscan necropoli at Castel d'Asso. The ancient tombs are interesting but in pretty poor shape. Work is underway to restore the archaeological zone.

At Bagnaia, a few km out of Viterbo, is the beautiful **Villa Lante**, a 16th-century villa noted for its fine gardens. The two, superficially identical, palaces are not open to the public, although you can wander in the large public park for free or pay L4000 for a guided tour of the gardens. The park is open daily from 9 am to one hour before sunset.

Guided tours of the gardens leave every half-hour. Unfortunately, picnics are not permitted in the park. From Viterbo, take urban bus No 6 from Piazza Caduti.

The **Parco dei Mostri** at Bomarzo will be particularly interesting for people with young children. The 16th-century Palazzo Orsini and park, created for the Orsini family, is scattered with gigantic and grotesque sculptures including an ogre, a giant and a dragon. Also of interest are the octagonal *tempietto* (little temple) and the crooked house, built without use of right angles. The park is open from 8.30 am to 7 pm in summer and until 4 pm in winter. Admission is L8000. To get there from Viterbo, catch the COTRAL bus, from the stop near Viale Trento, to Bomarzo, then follow the signs to Palazzo Orsini.

Another interesting detour from Viterbo is the tiny, hill-top medieval town of **Civita di Bagnoregio**, near its newer Renaissance counterpart, Bagnoregio. In a picturesque area of tufa ravines, Civita is known as the 'dying town' because continuous erosion of its hill has caused the collapse of many buildings. Eventually abandoned by its residents, who moved to Bagnoregio, most of the buildings were purchased by foreigners and artisans and, in recent years, Civita has been restored and developed into a minor tourist attraction.

Regular COTRAL buses connect Bagnoregio with Viterbo. From the bus stop, ask for directions to Civita, which has been recently connected to Bagnoregio's outskirts by a pedestrian bridge.

THE LAKES

There are three large lakes north of Rome – extremely popular recreational spots in summer for hot Romans. The shores of the lakes never seem to get as crowded as Lazio's beaches and their hilly, leafy environment makes them more attractive swimming destinations.

Lago di Bracciano is the closest to Rome and easily accessible by COTRAL buses, which depart roughly every half-hour from outside the Lepanto Metro stop, arriving in

Piazza Roma in the centre of the town of Bracciano. Walk to nearby Piazza Dante to catch one of the regular buses to the lake. For picnic supplies there is an alimentari in Piazza Roma, or you can dine at the excellent little trattoria *Da Regina* by the castle.

Closer to Viterbo is **Lago di Vico**, a nature reserve with various recreational facilities, including canoeing. There is a camping ground, *Natura* (☎ 0761-64 70 27), at the lakeside about four km from the town of Caprarola. It is open from June to December and bookings are essential in summer. The town is accessible by train from Rome's Trastevere station. Catch the Viterbo train and change at Capranica-Sutri. Otherwise catch a COTRAL bus from Viterbo to Caprarola.

Lago di Bolsena is too far from Rome to warrant a day trip for swimming; however, it is close to Viterbo, from where you can catch one of the regular COTRAL buses to the town of Bolsena. There are several camping grounds around the lake, including *La Pineta* (☎ 0761-79 90 81), Via A Diaz 48, open from April to October, and *Il Lago* (☎ 0761-79 91 91), Viale Cadorna 6, open from March to September.

SOUTH OF ROME
The Castelli Romani

Just past the periphery of the city are the Colli Albani (Alban Hills) and the 13 towns of the Castelli Romani. A summer resort area for wealthy Romans since the days of the Empire, its towns were mainly founded by popes and patrician families. Castel Gandolfo and Frascati are perhaps the best known: the former is the summer residence of the pope and the latter is famous for its crisp white wine. The other towns are Monte Porzio Catone, Montecompatri, Rocca Priora, Colonna, Rocca di Papa, Grottaferrata, Marino, Albano Laziale, Ariccia, Genzano and Nemi.

The area has numerous villas, including the 16th-century **Villa Aldobrandini** at Frascati, which was designed by Giacomo della Porta and built by Carlo Maderno, and with a beautiful garden. The ancient site of **Tusculum**, near Frascati, is preceded by a stretch of ancient Roman road. There is little to see here but you can take in the excellent view. At Grottaferrata is a 15th-century **Abbazia** and museum.

Nemi is worth a visit to see the pretty **Lago di Nemi**, in a volcanic crater. In ancient times there was an important sanctuary beside the lake, where the goddess Diana was worshipped. Today, very little remains of this massive temple complex, but it is possible to see the niched walls of what was once an arcaded portico. New excavations at the site have recently started. The incongruous-looking building at the edge of the lake, near the ruins of the temple, has an interesting story attached to it. It was built by Mussolini to house two ancient Roman boats (one 73 metres long, the other 71 metres), which were recovered from the bottom of the lake when it was partly drained in 1927-32. The official story is that retreating German troops burned the ships on June 1 1944. Locals tell a different story, but you'll have to go there to find out!

There is a delightful trattoria in the town of Nemi, the *Trattoria la Sirena del Lago*, located literally on the edge of a cliff and overlooking the lake. Signs will direct you there from the centre of town. A simple, but excellent meal will cost less than L30,000.

It is really best to tour this area by car: you could see most of the more interesting sights on an easy day trip from Rome. However, most of the towns of the Castelli Romani, including Nemi, are accessible by COTRAL bus from the Anagnina station on Metro Linea A. Trains also leave from Laziali platform at Stazione Termini for Frascati, Castelgandolfo and Albano Laziale, from where you could catch a bus to Nemi.

Palestrina

A town has existed on this site since as early as the 7th century BC, making it one of the oldest in the region. Known in ancient times as Praeneste, it is certainly worth visiting to see the massive **Santuario della Fortuna Primigenia**. Built by the ancient Romans on a series of terraces which cascade down the hill, the sanctuary was topped by a temple on

The Battle of Monte Cassino

'If you let me use the whole of our bomber force against Cassino we will whip it out like a dead tooth.' The US Major General was speaking of a key WW II German stronghold between Naples and Rome. This 'stronghold' was the ancient **Abbey of Montecassino**, a Benedictine monastery founded by St Benedict in 529. Destroyed and rebuilt three times – in 581, 883 and 1349 – each time on a grander scale, the abbey posed a formidable physical and psychological obstacle for the allied forces. For six long months in late 1943 and early 1944 the Germans used this position to prevent the Allies' Fifth Army from reaching Rome, with huge loss of life on both sides. Crowning the 518-metre-high Monte Cassino, the abbey, built of stone, with walls three metres thick and about 50 metres high, still housed members of the Benedictine order, as well as many refugees and a priceless collection of illustrated manuscripts and Latin literature. The Germans eventually ensured that most of these treasures were moved to safety at the Vatican. As the deadly stand-off continued into 1944, the plan to destroy the abbey was developed. Although there was strong opposition to the plan, on grounds that it was a precious part of Italy's cultural and religious heritage, the decision was made to bomb Monte Cassino in February 1944. About 300 monks and refugees died in the first attack, having been unable to evacuate the monastery despite allied warnings. The bombing, however, failed to destroy the massive structure and, just over one month later another 1000 tons of explosive were dropped on the abbey and the Cassino area. The abbey was destroyed, but the Germans held their position and what had been described as the 'greatest concentration of air power in the world' had failed. It was not until May 18, two months later, that Polish troops took the monastery and raised their flag there. Many of the 4000 Polish soldiers who died in the battle to take Monte Cassino are buried in a cemetery nearby. The monastery was rebuilt in medieval style and parts of it are open to the public.

Cassino is accessible from Rome on the Cassino-Caserta-Napoli train line. ■

the summit of the hill. The **Palazzo Colonna Barberini** now stands at this highest point and houses the **Museo Archeologico Nazionale Prenestino**. The view from the sanctuary is really special and alone would warrant a visit to the town.

Palestrina is accessible from Rome by COTRAL bus from the Rebibbia station on Metro Linea B.

Anagni & Alatri

These medieval towns are in an area about 40 minutes south of Rome, known as the Ciociaria. **Anagni**, birthplace of a number of medieval popes, is of particular interest for its lovely Lombard-Romanesque cathedral, built in the 11th century. Its pavement was laid by Cosmati marble workers of the Middle Ages. In the crypt is an extraordinary series of vibrant frescoes, painted by three Benedictine monks in diverse periods during the 13th century. Depicting a wide range of

subjects, the frescoes are considered a major example of medieval painting at the crucial stage of its transition from the Byzantine tradition to the developments which culminated in the achievements of Giotto. The frescoes were recently unveiled after a four-year restoration project and certainly warrant a day trip from Rome. The crypt's pavement was also laid by the Cosmati. Visits to the crypt can be made with a guide only, but you should need to wait no longer than 10 minutes.

Alatri has a couple of interesting churches, including the 13th-century Chiesa di Santa Maria Maggiore in its principal piazza. Its ancient **acropolis** is surrounded by massive 6th-century BC walls, built by the town's original inhabitants, the Ernici.

Anagni is easily accessible from Rome's Stazione Termini on the Cassino-Caserta-Napoli train line. For Alatri, catch the train to Frosinone and then a bus to Alatri.

Liguria, Piedmont & Valle d'Aosta

The north-western corner of Italy has long been a political, economic and intellectual engine room for the country. It was here that the movement for Italian unity took wing; Piedmont was the cradle of Italy's industrial success and birthplace of its labour movements, while the Piedmont capital, Turin, was for much of this century a hotbed of intellectual activity. A little farther south, Genoa was long a major port city, open to the rest of the world for centuries and today regaining importance.

Turin and Genoa resonate with past glories, but they are only one side of the coin. From the mountain ski pistes and walking trails of the Valle d'Aosta and northern Piedmont to the Ligurian coast and magic of the Cinque Terre (Five Lands), this corner of the country is a microcosm of the best Italy has to offer in natural beauty.

Liguria

The Ligurian coast was inhabited by Neanderthals about a million years ago, and many remains have been unearthed in the area. The locals say they were lured by the beaches, which still exert a hold over the hundreds of thousands of tourists who flock to this narrow coastal region each year. There is more to Liguria, however, than its beaches. Stretching from the French border in the west, to La Spezia in the east, the coast is dotted with resorts and medieval towns; the mountainous hinterland hides hill-top villages, the occasional ski piste and plenty of scope for walkers and climbers. Genoa, regional capital and one-time sea power, is still an important port and a much overlooked attraction in its own right.

Liguria has been ruled by the Greeks, Saracens, Romans, Venetians, Lombards and the French, and strong early trade influences from as far afield as Sicily, Northern Africa and Spain are evident.

Cuisine is marked by the products of the Mediterranean climate – fresh herbs, extra virgin olive oil and seafood. Among its culinary creations are pesto, focaccia and farinata, a chick pea flour bread. A visit to the Cinque Terre is not complete without trying its delicious but rare dessert wine, Sciacchetrà. The Riviera di Ponente is also well known for its wine.

A train line follows the coast from the French frontier to La Spezia and beyond, connecting all points along the way. By road you have the choice of good (and expensive) autostradas; the A10 west of Genoa, the A12 east or the Via Aurelia (SS1), an often congested but more picturesque state highway.

GENOA (GENOVA)

Travellers who write off Genoa as simply a dirty port town and bypass it for the coastal resorts do the city and themselves a disservice. Once a mighty maritime republic and the birthplace of Christopher Columbus, the city known as *La Superba* (the proud, haughty), has admittedly lost some of its gloss over the centuries, but none of its fascination. Genoa might have had a still greater story behind it had the town founders seen fit to lend an ear to Columbus' exploration ideas, but it was Spain that became a Renaissance superpower on the back of wealth discovered in the Americas. This didn't stop Genoa from celebrating the 500th anniversary of the discovery of America with an Expo in 1992. The Expo gave the city something of a facelift and economic heart-starter, although it ended up being a bit of a disaster when a serious flood devastated parts of the city.

The labyrinth of narrow alleys at the heart of the old city near the port is a scrappy zone of some ill-repute, but it is undeniably interesting; it is full of visiting sailors, prostitutes, delinquents and long-

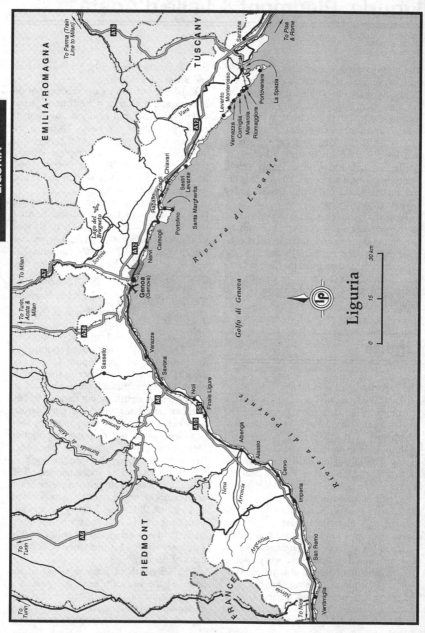

LIGURIA

EMILIA-ROMAGNA

To Parma (Train Line to Milan)

A15

TUSCANY

Sarzana

To Pisa & Rome

Portovenere

La Spezia

Levanto
Monterosso
Vernazza
Corniglia
Manarola
Riomaggiore

AT2

Vara

Chiavari

Rapallo
Zoagli
Sestri Levante
Santa Margherita
Portofino

Riviera di Levante

Camogli

A12

Nervi

Lago del Brugneto

Scrivia

To Milan

A7

To Turin, Aosta & Milan

Genoa (Genova)

A26

Sassello

Varazze

Savona

Golfo di Genova

Liguria

0   15   30 km

A6

Noli

Finale Ligure

SS1

A10

Albenga

Alassio

Bormida di Millesimo

Bormida

Riviera di Ponente

Cervo

Imperia

PIEDMONT

A6

To Turin

Neva

Arroscia

Argentina

San Remo

FRANCE

Nervia

To Turin

To Nice

Ventimiglia

time residents. Turn a corner and you stumble across medieval churches or well-to-do Renaissance residences converted into museums. During the day, the seamier side of Genoese life mixes it with the fashionable set. At night, however, central Genoa empties and becomes a decidedly uninviting neighbourhood.

History

Genoa was founded in the 4th century BC, and possibly derives its name from the Latin *ianua* (door). A key Roman port, it later became a mercantile power, although often subject to the domination of others. Genoa was occupied by the French in 774, the Saracens in the 10th century and even by the Milanese in 1353. A famous victory over Venice in 1298 led to a period of rapid growth, but quarrels between the noble families of the city – the Grimaldis, the Dorias and the Spinolas – caused much internal disruption.

Genoa reached its peak in the 16th century under the rule of imperial admiral Andrea Doria, and managed to benefit from Spain's American fortunes by financing Spanish exploration. Coinciding happily with the Renaissance, Genoa's golden age lasted into the following century and produced innumerable magnificent palaces and great works of art. The feverish activity attracted masters of the calibre of Rubens, Caravaggio and Van Dyck. Galeazzo Alessi (1512-72), who designed many of the city's splendid buildings, is ranked with Andrea Palladio. The age of exploration had left the writing on the wall, however, and as the importance of the Mediterranean declined, so too did Genoa's fortunes.

Already a participant in the Risorgimento – the process of Italian unification and independence in the 19th century – Genoa was the first northern city to rise against the Germans and the Italian Fascists towards the close of WW II, liberating itself before the arrival of Allied troops.

After the war, the city expanded rapidly along the coast and swallowed numerous villages along the way. But after the boom years of the 1960s it began to decline as big industry folded and port activity dropped. The waterfront and city centre were allowed to decay. The city may now have turned a corner. Vast amounts of money were poured into improvements for the Columbus Festival in 1992, and the largely privatised and restructured port operations are registering big increases in container business – a sign that Genoa may yet recover some of its glory as a trading port.

Orientation

Genoa stretches along the Ligurian coast for some 30 km and is served by 15 train stations. It can seem overwhelming on arrival, but the city centre is quite compact, tucked in between the two main train stations, Principe and Brignole. The main boulevard, Via XX Settembre, starts a short walk south of Stazione Brignole and spills into the city's focal point, Piazza de Ferrari. This stretch offers the better cheap accommodation. The APT office is on Via Roma, north of Piazza de Ferrari.

West towards the port and stretching around the waterfront towards Stazione Principe are the oldest Genoese quarters, within a maze of narrow lanes. Most of the city's monuments are here, but Genoa is no museum – a classic and somewhat weather-beaten port, the streets hum with activity, if not all of it salubrious. The Stazione Principe area, close to the port, is dodgy ground for newcomers – local buses run between it and Stazione Brignole.

It is easier to walk around the old city as most traffic is banned from the centre. Car parks are well signposted.

Information

Tourist Offices The main APT office (☎ 010-54 15 41) is on the 2nd floor at Via Roma 11 and is open Monday to Friday from 8 am to 1.30 pm and 2 to 5 pm and Saturday to 1.30 pm. There are branch offices at the airport and Stazione Principe, open Monday to Saturday from 8 am to 8 pm, and smaller offices in Nervi and Arenzano, which have irregular opening hours.

The APT produces a booklet of walking tours entitled *Genoa, The Old City*.

LIGURIA

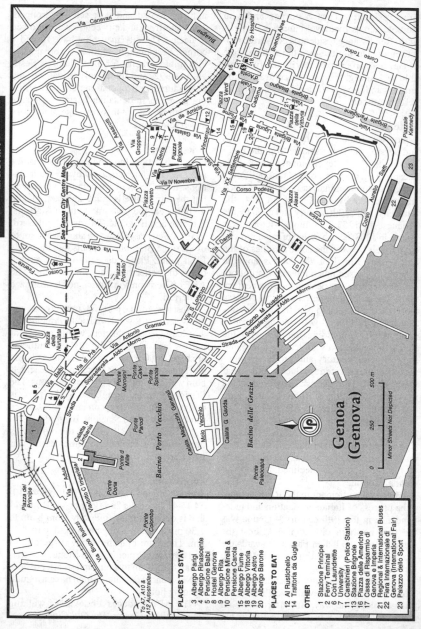

PLACES TO STAY
3   Albergo Parigi
4   Albergo Rinascente
5   Pensione Balbi
8   Hostel Genova
9   Albergo Rita
10 Pensione Mirella &
    Pensione Carola
15 Albergo Fiume
18 Albergo Vittoria
19 Albergo Astro
20 Albergo Barone

PLACES TO EAT
12 Al Rustichello
14 Trattoria da Guglie

OTHER
1   Stazione Principe
2   Ferry Terminal
6   Coin Laundrette
7   University
11 Carabinieri (Police Station)
13 Stazione Brignole
16 Piazza delle Americhe
17 Cassa di Risparmio di
    Genova e Imperia
21 Regional & International Buses
22 Fiera Internazionale di
    Genova (International Fair)
23 Palazzo dello Sport

Genoa
(Genova)

See Genoa City Centre Map

Minor Streets Not Depicted

0   250   500 m

Money Most banks will give cash advances and change travellers' cheques, and there are plenty of ATMs. The Cassa di Risparmio di Genova e Imperia, on Piazza delle Americhe near Stazione Brignole, is open from 8.20 am to 1.20 pm and 2.30 to 4 pm. The ATMs there are open from 6 am to 10 pm. Near Piazza de Ferrari, the Credito Italiano has similar opening hours and is also open Wednesday until 6 pm. American Express operates through Viatur travel agency (see the Travel Agencies section) and offers limited services.

Post & Telecommunications The main post office is in Via Dante, just off Piazza de Ferrari. It is open Monday to Saturday from 8.15 am to 7.40 pm. Genoa's post code is 16100.

The most convenient Telecom office is at the main post office and is open from 6 am to 10 pm. Other Telecom offices are at Stazione Brignole and Via XX Settembre 139, and are open daily from 8 am to 9.30 pm. The Brignole Telecom office is closed on Sunday. Genoa's telephone code is 010.

Foreign Consulates The British Consulate (☎ 56 48 33) is at Via XII Ottobre 2. The US Consulate (☎ 58 44 92) is at Via Dante 2, and the French Consulate (☎ 20 08 79) at Via Garibaldi 20.

Travel Agencies CTS (☎ 56 43 66) is at Via San Vincenzo 117. CIT (☎ 29 19 53) has an office at Via XXV Aprile 16.

Viatur (☎ 010-56 12 41) is at Piazza delle Fontane Marose 3.

Bookshops Bozzi, Via Cairoli 2, has a good selection of English and French-language books. Feltrinelli's store at Via Bensa 32r also has a reasonable range.

Gay & Lesbian Information Arci Gay (☎ 247 09 45) is at Via San Luca 11.

Emergency & Medical Services The carabinieri is at Via Diaz (☎ 5 36 61) or for immediate attendance, call ☎ 113. For an ambulance, call ☎ 570 59 51. The Ospedale San Martino (☎ 3 53 51) is at Via Benedetto XV. The Guardia Medica Regione Liguria (☎ 35 40 22) operates an after-hours, home-visit medical service from 8 pm to 8 am. Night pharmacies include Europa (☎ 38 02 39), Corso Europa 67r, and Ghersi (☎ 54 16 61), Corso Buenos Aires 74r.

Piazza de Ferrari

Flanked by the **Teatro Carlo Felice**, the imposing **Borsa** (former stock exchange) and **Palazzo Ducale**, Piazza de Ferrari, is the focal point of Genoa and an obvious starting point for exploration of the city. The palace, once the seat of the city's rulers, has been opened up for cultural exhibitions and houses a couple of good restaurants.

Cattedrale di San Lorenzo

A stone's throw west of Palazzo Ducale, whose main entrance faces Piazza Matteotti, is the city's cathedral. Its distinctively Genoese black and white striped Gothic marble façade is hard to miss. Construction and embellishment was carried out over several hundred years. Begun in the 12th century, its bell tower and cupola weren't erected until the 16th century. Inside, the **Cappella del Battista** once housed relics of St John the Baptist.

Look out for the museum, which houses the *Sacro Catino*, a cup allegedly given to Solomon by the Queen of Sheba and used by Jesus at the Last Supper. Other relics include the polished quartz platter upon which Salome is said to have received John the Baptist's head. It's open Tuesday to Saturday from 9.30 to 11.30 am and 3 to 5.45 pm.

Porta Soprana & Casa di Colombo

Head back south-east through Piazza Matteotti and you will find the impressive remains of Genoa's city walls. Porta Soprana was originally raised in 1155, although what you see is the restored version. In Genoa's heyday, the city was considered virtually impregnable on the landward side because of its walls.

In the gate's shadow, on Piazza Dante, is a much rebuilt house said to be the birthplace

The Ocean Blue

From an early age, Christopher Columbus (or Cristoforo Colombo to his compatriots) showed signs of having a bad case of what we might call the 'travel bug'. Steeped in Marco Polo's writings and Pliny's *Natural History*, he conceived an ambitious project to reach the Orient by sailing west instead of east. Adventurous as Genoa's rulers may have been, this was too much, so Columbus went off to Spain where he received a more sympathetic hearing. Cristóbal Colón, as the Spaniards know him, set off with the three ships *Niña, Pinta* and *Santa Maria* on 3 August 1492 and two months later landed in the Bahamas. In the following eight years, he discovered Cuba, Haiti, Jamaica and some of the Antilles, still convinced he was in Asia.

Sent back to Spain on charges of committing atrocities (although subsequent Spanish colonisers evidently developed a thicker skin in this regard), he made one last voyage in 1502-4, tracking the central American coast and reaching Colombia. When he died a forgotten and embittered man two years later in Valladolid, Spain, he still had no idea he had discovered a new world. Today, of course, he's everyone's hero, from Genoa to the USA and from Spain to Latin America. ∎

Christopher Columbus

of Columbus, or at least the spot where his father lived. There are conflicting opinions about the authenticity of the claims, so some healthy scepticism seems in order.

Via Garibaldi & Palazzi

Skirting the northern edge of what were then the city limits, Via Garibaldi clearly marks a break between the Middle Ages and the Renaissance, and equally between poor and rich. Lined with magnificent, if somewhat blackened and unkempt palazzi, it is the place to admire the pick of Genoa's museums.

The **Galleria di Palazzo Rosso** is open Tuesday to Saturday from 9 am to 7 pm (although it's likely to close around the middle of the day for a short period) and Sunday morning. Admission costs L4000. It boasts works from the Venetian and

Genoese schools and several canvasses by Van Dyck. The **Galleria di Palazzo Bianco** (same hours and admission fee as Palazzo Rosso) features works by Flemish, Spanish and Dutch masters, displaying Genoa's international cultural links, but there is plenty of home-grown material too, with the likes of Caravaggio and Antonio Pisanello. Look also for Dürer's *Portrait of a Young Boy*.

Many of the buildings on Alessi's grand boulevard house banks or other public facilities. Wander in if the gates are open. At No 9, the **Palazzo Doria Tursi**, Genoa's town hall since 1848, was built in 1564. It houses the relics of two famous Genoese – fragments of the skeleton of Christopher Columbus and one of Niccolò Paganini's violins, played occasionally at concerts. The **Palazzo Podestà**, Via Garibaldi 7, has magnificent frescoes in the courtyard.

Museums

Not far from Via Garibaldi, heading into the old town, is the **Galleria Nazionale di Palazzo Spinola**, Piazza Superiore di Pellicceria 1, a 16th-century mansion housing Italian and Flemish Renaissance works. It is open Tuesday to Saturday from 9 am to 7 pm and Sunday and Monday to 1 pm. Admission is L4000. The **Galleria di Palazzo Reale**, Via Balbi 10, also features Renaissance works. It is open from 9 am to 1 pm and admission is L4000.

The **Museo d'Arte Orientale**, set in gardens next to Piazzale Mazzini, has one of the largest collections of Oriental art in Europe. It is open Tuesday to Saturday from 9 am to 1.15 pm and 3 to 6 pm and Sunday to 12.45 pm. Admission is L4000. The city also boasts a **Museo d'Arte Moderna** at the suburb of Nervi, and a museum of pre-Columbian art, the **Museo Americanistico F Lunardi**, in the Villa Gruber on Corso Solferino.

Churches

The **Santissima Annunziata del Vestato**, Piazza della Nunziata, is a rich example of 17th-century Genoese architecture and is still being restored after virtually being destroyed in WW II bombing raids. Look up at the trompe l'oeuil in the dome. **Chiesa di San Siro**, Via San Siro, also badly damaged in WW II, dates to the 4th century, but was rebuilt in the 16th century.

Chiesa di San Donato, Strada S Agostino, was built in the 11th century in pure Romanesque style, but was enlarged in the 12th and 13th centuries. The church of the Doria family, **Chiesa di San Matteo**, in Piazza Matteotti, was founded in 1125. Doria's sword is preserved under the altar and his tomb is in the crypt. **Chiesa del Gesù**, also known as Chiesa di Sant'Ambrogio, is located nearby.

Old City

Medieval Genoa is a maze of twisting lanes and dank blind alleys, the core of which is bound by Porta dei Vacca on the waterfront, and vias Cairoli, Garibaldi, XXV Aprile and the Porta Soprana around the inland periph-ery. Beyond this it straggles along the coast in both directions, especially at the northern end with the seedy Via di Prè,

The best way to explore the area is simply to wander about. Most of the prostitution and lowlife seems to be concentrated in the zone west of **Via San Luca**, itself a hip thorough-fare full of cafés and bars which ends at its southern end at Piazza Bianchi. East off the piazza is Via degli Orefici, where you'll find market stalls, especially for second-hand books (there are some gems in the line of Fascist-era newspapers and mag-azines), more cafés and a couple of great restaurants and pasticcerie. As for Via di Prè, it is seedy but not really all that interesting.

As busy as it is in daylight, just about everything shuts at night, exceptions being some very good eateries and the 24-hour prostitution and drug trade.

Aquarium & Il Bigo

The 1992 Expo left the Genoese waterfront with some lasting attractions. Stars of the **aquarium** (Europe's biggest and well worth a visit) include sharks, dolphins and pen-guins. Located on Ponte Spinola, it's open weekdays from 9.30 am to 5.30 pm and on weekends and holidays until 7.30 pm. Admission is L10,000. A hundred metres south along the pier is **Il Bigo**, a kind of derrick built for the sole purpose of hoisting a cylindrical lift 200 metres into the air and allowing its occupants a bird's-eye view of the city. This costs L4000 and it operates Tuesday to Friday from 11 am to 1 pm and 3 to 6 pm. There is also a second session on weekends from 2 to 8 pm.

Spianata dell'Acquasole

This park beside Viale IV Novembre is a pleasant distraction from the chaos of the streets of central Genoa, and the swings and rides provide welcome relief for kids bored silly by museums.

Places to Stay – bottom end

Camping The camping grounds on the out-skirts of the city are all easily accessible by bus from Stazione Brignole. *Villa*

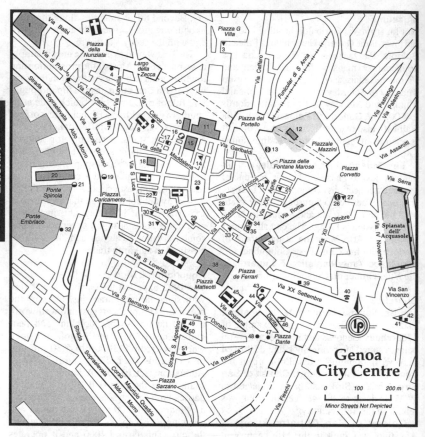

Genoa City Centre

0   100   200 m

Minor Streets Not Depicted

Doria (☎ 69 69 60 00), Via al Campeggio Villa Doria 15, on the way to Pegli, is open all year and can be reached by bus No 1, 2 or 3 from Piazza Caricamento, on the waterfront. Farther on is the *Caravan Park la Vesima* (☎ 63 57 72), Via Rubens 50r. Catch bus No 95 from Voltri (which you can reach on bus No 1).

Hostels & Hotels The HI *Hostel Genova* (☎ 242 24 57), Via Costanzi, is in the Righi area, north of Genoa's old centre. B&B is L19,000 and a meal costs L12,000. Catch bus No 35 from Stazione Principe or bus No

40 from Stazione Brignole. The hostel is closed from 16 December to 14 January.

The *Casa della Giovane* (☎ 20 66 32), Piazza Santa Sabina 4, is off Piazza Nunziata, a short walk east of Stazione Principe and usually has cheap beds for women.

Although the old city, Stazione Principe and the port areas have a fair smattering of budget places, you'll generally get better value and a greater feeling of security near Stazione Brignole and Via XX Settembre.

Near Stazione Brignole there are a couple of hotels in a lovely old building at Via

LIGURIA

PLACES TO STAY		31	La Santa	21	Port Tours
		33	Ristorante Bruno	23	Piazza Lavagna &
7	Albergo Rio				Flea Market
24	Hotel Metropoli	**OTHER**		26	APT Tourist Office
39	Bristol Palace			32	Il Bigo
41	Hotel Bel Soggiorno	1	Palazzo Reale	.34	CIT Travel Agency
42	Albergo Soana	2	Santissima Annunziata	35	Britannia Pub
			del Vestato	36	Teatro Carlo Felice
PLACES TO EAT		4	Feltrinelli Bookshop	37	Cattedrale di San
		5	Porta dei Vacca		Lorenzo
3	Rosticceria	8	Chiesa di San Siro	38	Palazzo Ducale
6	Trattoria Le Maschere	9	Bozzi Bookshop	40	Telecom Office
14	Trattoria Vittoria	10	Palazzo Bianco	43	Borsa
17	Trattoria Carletto	11	Palazzo Doria Tursi	44	US Consulate
22	Trattoria da Walter	12	Museo d'Arte Orientale	45	Chiesa del Gesù
25	Trattoria da Maria	13	Viatur (American Express)	46	Post Office
27	Mancini & C Pasticceria	15	Palazzo Rosso	47	Casa di Colombo
28	Café de Paris	16	French Consulate	48	Porta Soprana
29	Imperiale	18	Palazzo Spinola	49	Caffetteria Le Corbusier
30	A Ved Romanengo	19	AMT Bus Station	50	Chiesa di San Donato
	(Pastry Shop)	20	Aquarium	51	Teatro della Tosse

Groppallo 4. Turn right as you leave the train station and walk up Via de Amicis to Piazza Brignole. To your right is Via Groppallo. *Pensione Mirella* (☎ 89 37 22) has singles/doubles for L35,000/65,000. The *Pensione Carola* (☎ 839 13 40), on the 3rd floor, is better with clean, well-kept rooms for the same price. The doubles come with shower. Up the road at No 8, the *Albergo Rita* was shut for refurbishment at the time of writing, but may well be operating again when you read this, and the *Pesione Valle* was also closed.

Head east from the train station and you come across *Albergo Vittoria* (☎ 58 15 17) at Largo Archimede 1, just beyond Piazza G Verdi. Situated on the top floor and very quiet, the better rooms are large, and have character and a view. They cost L35,000/60,000. Down Via Fiume in front of the train station, *Albergo Fiume* (☎ 570 54 60) has immaculate rooms for L35,000/70,000. Single rooms with a shower are L65,000, and it's one of the few budget hotels to accept credit cards.

Head farther down Via Fiume and turn right into Via XX Settembre, and you'll come to *Albergo Astro* (☎ 58 15 33) at No 3, a simple but comfortable place on the 5th floor

with rooms for L40,000/70,000, breakfast included.

Virtually across the road at No 2, *Albergo Barone* (☎ 58 75 78) is good value at L40,000/60,000 and popular with travellers.

Closer to Piazza de Ferrari, at No 23 Via XX Settembre, *Albergo Soana* (☎ 56 28 14) offers quite decent singles/doubles, the latter with shower, for L45,000/65,000. Ear plugs are useful in some rooms because of street noise.

Near Stazione Principe is *Pensione Balbi* (☎ 28 09 12), Via Balbi 21-3, with singles/doubles for L30,000/45,000. Most of the singles are permanently occupied, but there are several hotels in a similar category on the same street.

If you want to mix it with prostitutes, sailors and so forth, head for Via di Prè. *Albergo Parigi* (☎ 25 21 72), Via di Prè 72, has secure rooms for L30,000/50,000. *Albergo Rinascente* (☎ 26 11 13), at No 59, costs the same but is not as good.

Places to Stay – middle

If you want to spend a little more money, you cannot go past *Hotel Bel Soggiorno* (☎ 58 14 18), Via XX Settembre 19. Singles are L55,000 and singles/doubles with a bathroom, TV and mini-bar are L65,000/90,000.

Albergo Rio (☎ 29 05 51), Via Ponte Calvi 5, charges L70,000/80,000 if you stay for a couple of nights.

The *Hotel Metropoli* (☎ 28 41 41) in Piazza delle Fontane Marose has rooms from L100,000/130,000, including breakfast. The rooms are spotless and the location hard to beat.

Places to Stay – top end

One of the grand old establishments of Genoese hospitality is the *Bristol Palace* (☎ 59 25 41; fax 56 17 56), Via XX Settembre 35. Rooms range from L140,000 to L350,000.

Places to Eat

The bulk of the good eating is to be done in the old city, although there are exceptions. Don't leave town without trying a pasta with *pesto genovese* (a sauce of basil, garlic, parmesan cheese and pine nuts), *torta pasqualina* (made with spinach, ricotta cheese and eggs), *pansoti* (spinach ravioli with a thick, creamy hazelnut sauce), *trenette* (a spaghetti with pesto and potato) and, of course, focaccia. If you're cooking your own meals, stock up in the Mercato Orientale on Via XX Settembre.

Some of the best and cheapest takeaways are at the *Rosticceria* on the corner of Spianata Castelletto and Piazza Goffredo Villa. You can take away a hot and filling serve of pasta, sold by weight, for a few thousand lire. Try the *trenette al pesto*.

Via San Vincenzo, near Stazione Brignole, is a short but busy food street. *Al Rustichello*, No 59r, is about the 'poshest' joint, where a main will cost L10,000 or more. For cheaper snacks try *Panificio Mario*, No 61, *Trattoria da Guglie*, No 64, or the focaccia at No 61a. You could finish with a delicious ice cream from the *Gelateria Biza*, at No 65.

The waterfront area around Piazza Caricamento is lined with cheap eateries and restaurants, including a couple of Chinese places. Less informal and wedged in at the corner of Via Sottoripa and Via Ponte Calvi is *Trattoria Le Maschere*.

A good place is *Trattoria da Maria*, Vico Testa d'Oro 14, off Via XXV Aprile, where a meal costs L12,000, including wine.

The *Gran Caffè Ducale* in the Palazzo Ducale on Piazza de Ferrari offers expensive coffee but great set menus, including several Ligurian specialities, for L20,000. It should not be confused with the more expensive joint upstairs.

Carlo Brusaca, the owner of *Trattoria da Walter* at Vico Colalanza 2r, concentrates on Genoese specialities. Pasta starts at L5000. The lane is off Via San Luca.

The *Imperiale*, Piazza Campetto 8, in the former Palazzo di Gio Vincenzo Imperiale, features magnificent frescoes and stucco, and a set menu for L25,000.

Hidden away in the nearby Vico degli Indoratori (No 5) just south of Via Orefici, *La Santa* is more expensive (set menu L30,000) but has a reputation for good regional cooking.

Seafood is inevitably a speciality in some restaurants. The *Trattoria Vittoria*, Vico del Duca 24, offers a limited but tasty range, and a full meal will cost around L30,000.

Looser purse strings will open up still more mouth-watering pleasures. The tiny *Trattoria Carletto*, Vico del Tempo Buono 5r, costs about L50,000 a head, but they know their fish – the family running this place lend it an atmosphere reminiscent of a Fellini film. *Ristorante Bruno*, Vico Casana 9, falls into a similar category, but the offerings are more limited.

Cafés Away from the waterfront, central Genoa all but shuts down in the evening – 'better to go home and sleep' was the advice of one local.

Mancini & C, on Via Roma at Piazza Corvetto, is renowned as Genoa's finest pasticceria. *A Ved Romanengo*, Via Orefici 31, has been serving scrumptious pastries since 1805. Nearby, Via San Luca and Campetto are good hunting grounds for cafés and snackbars during the day, but dead at night. *Café de Paris* on Vico Casana is pleasant, and the posh spot in the Borsa building opposite the post office is an experience on its own.

Entertainment

The Genoa Theatre Company performs throughout the year at the Politeama Genovese (☎ 89 35 89), Via Piaggio, and at the Teatro della Corte (☎ 570 24 72), Corte Lambruschini. The main season is from January to May.

The opera house, Teatro Carlo Felice (☎ 5 38 11), Piazza de Ferrari, opened in 1991 on the site of the original opera house (heavily bombed in WW II) and has a year-round programme.

The stage of Teatro della Tosse (☎ 29 57 20), Piazza Renato Negri, first saw action in 1702, when it was built as the Teatro Sant'Agostino. Some time later, Casanova walked the boards here.

Three cinema clubs show films in their original language on selected nights. They are: Cineclub Chaplin (☎ 88 00 69), Piazza Cappuccini 1; Fritz Lang (☎ 21 97 68), Via Acquarone 64; and Cineclub Lumière (☎ 50 59 36), Via Vitale 1. They cost L4000 to join and about L4000 to see a film.

If you like cocktails, you could try Caffetteria le Corbusier in Piazza San Donato, which is open until 1 am. If you're sick of lager, you could try the Britannia Pub on Vico Casana; the Guinness is L3500 a pint.

A popular disco is Mako, Corso Italia 28r.

You can find a few others, especially in summer, farther south-east along the waterfront in the Lido area.

Getting There & Away

Air The Cristoforo Colombo international airport at Sestri Ponente, six km west of the city, has regular domestic and international connections but, for the latter, Milan and Pisa have cheaper options. For flight information, ring ☎ 24 11 or the airline.

Bus Buses for international destinations leave from Piazza della Vittoria, as do limited interregional services and buses for other locations in Liguria.

Train Genoa is directly connected by train to Turin, Milan, Pisa and Rome, and it makes little difference which of the two train stations (Principe or Brignole) you choose, unless you have booked a hotel. Phone ☎ 28 40 81 for information.

Car & Motorbike The A12 connects Genoa with Livorno in Tuscany and with the A11 for Florence. The A7 goes to Milan, the A26 to Turin and the A10 to Savona and the French border. From the A7, take the exit marked 'Genova', which will take you into the centre. Hitchhikers should ask at Stazione Brignole for bus routes to autostrada on/off ramps, or at the APT office for main road maps. There may be more luck on

The Genius of Genoa

Born in 1782, Niccolò Paganini already knew just about all there was to know about the violin by his 13th year. Two years later, after learning composition in Parma, he launched his concert career, which in the following 40 years was to take him to every corner of Italy and to the great stages of Europe.

Paganini didn't just play a mean violin. He was a virtuoso on the guitar as well and from the violin extracted chords, harmonies, arpeggios and rhythms hitherto undreamed of. A prolific composer, he shared his genius with posterity, leaving behind six concertos, 24 quartets for violin, viola, guitar and other strings, 12 sonatas for violin and guitar and a long list of further sonatas. Liszt and Chopin applied much of what they learned from Paganini's genius to the piano. The virtuoso spent the last days of his restless life a little farther along the coast from his native Genoa, in Nice, where he died in 1840. He is buried in Parma. ■

the SS1 heading in either direction along the coast, or the SS35 heading north to Alessandria (and on to Turin). Drivers who hate tolls and are in no hurry should consider these roads.

Boat The city's busy port is an important embarkation point for ferries to Sicily, Sardinia, Corsica and Elba. Major companies are:

Corsica Ferries, Piazza Dante 1 (☎ 59 33 01)
    for Corsica, Sardinia and Elba.
Tirrenia, Pontile Colombo (☎ 25 80 41)
    for Sicily and Sardinia
Grandi Traghetti, Via Fieschi 17 (☎ 58 93 31)
    for Sardinia
Navarma Lines (☎ 58 77 53)

See the Getting There & Away sections for Sicily and Sardinia.

Ferries go to towns along the Riviera di Levante, including Camogli, Portofino, the Cinque Terre, Santa Margherita and San Fruttuoso. Cooperativa Battellieri del Porto di Genova (☎ 26 57 12) ferries leave from Ponte dei Mille, near the Stazione Marittima, and cost up to L33,000 return. Alimar (☎ 25 67 75), runs Marexpress, a catamaran service to Portofino and Monte Carlo. Frequency depends largely on demand. All these services run in July and August only.

Getting Around
To/From the Airport An airport bus service, the Volabus (☎ 59 94 14), leaves from Piazza Verdi, outside Stazione Brignole, and stops at Stazione Principe.

Bus AMT buses (☎ 599 74 14) operate services throughout the city. Main termini include the two train stations, Piazza della Vittoria and Piazza Caricamento. Buses No 33 and 37 link these stations. Full timetables are available at the tourist office.

Taxi For a taxi, call ☎ 26 96.

Tours It is possible to organise guided tours of the city or elsewhere in the region through travel agents such as Viatur.

In summer, the Cooperativo Battellieri del Porto di Genova runs tours of the port

from Ponte Spinola for L10,000, starting at 3.15 pm.

AROUND GENOA
Hidden behind the industrial wasteland of Genoa's west is **Pegli**, a victim of the city's growth. It lies in a sheltered harbour and offers magnificent views of the city and coastline. The Museo Navale is in the Villa Doria at Piazza Bonavino. The Museo Archeologico, Via Pallavicini, in the Villa Pallavicini, presents a comprehensive overview of Ligurian prehistory. The villa itself is set in a magnificent park modelled on the Genoese gardens of the Renaissance.

On Genoa's eastern edge, **Nervi** has also been absorbed by the growing city. Renowned for its outdoor International Ballet Festival at the Teatro ai Parchi in July, and an outdoor cinema in the rose garden (Cinema nel Roseto) at the same venue in August, Nervi still manages to retain its own identity.

Recco, a little farther east, is the scene of an enormous fireworks display in the first week of September. Take a train there, as traffic is so tight you could spend a whole evening looking for a parking spot.

RIVIERA DI LEVANTE
The coast east of the portside sprawl of Genoa is not as heavily developed as the western side of the capital and even rivals in beauty Campania's Amalfi coastline. A sprinkling of small resorts and villages, especially the Cinque Terre, retain a real charm despite their evident popularity, and the surrounding countryside is visually dramatic.

Camogli
Wandering through the alleyways and the long, cobbled streets of Camogli, it is hard not to be taken aback by the painstaking trompe-l'oeuil decoration – house after house sports meticulously painted columns, balustrades and even windows. Although a feature of many Ligurian towns, Camogli seems to take special pride in this genre of civic art. The esplanade, Via Garibaldi, is a colourful place for a stroll and really comes

to life on the second Sunday in May, when local fishermen celebrate the Sagra del Pesce, frying hundreds of fish for all and sundry in three-metre pans along the waterfront.

Camogli means 'house of wives' from the days when the women ran the town while their husbands were at sea. The town was also a strong naval base and at one stage boasted a fleet larger than Genoa's.

Information To the right when you leave the train station is the APT office (☎ 0185-77 10 66) at Via XX Settembre 33. It's supposed to be open Monday to Saturday from 8.40 am to 12.10 pm and 3.40 to 6.10 pm, but don't bet on it. Camogli's telephone code is 0185.

Activities Luigi Simonetti Nautica, Via Garibaldi 59, hires out canoes, pedal boats, rowing and motor boats. B&B Mare Sport (☎ 77 02 54), Via Garibaldi 197A, operates a diving centre.

Places to Stay & Eat The *Albergo la Camogliese* (☎ 77 14 02), Via Garibaldi 55, has singles/doubles from L50,000/70,000. The *Augusta* (☎ 77 05 92), Via P Schiaffino 100, has singles/doubles from L70,000/90,000 in high season, while the *Selene* (☎ 77 01 49), Via Cuneo 15, has singles/doubles for L50,000/80,000.

Like accommodation, eating out is expensive, with most waterfront restaurants charging high prices for ordinary food. Try *Il Faulo*, Via Garibaldi 98, which specialises in Genoese fare and has a vegetarian menu. Pasta starts at L10,000. Smaller, less expensive trattorie are tucked into the laneways away from the water, so you'll need to explore.

Getting There & Away Camogli is on the Genoa-La Spezia train line, and services are regular. Tigullio buses head for Rapallo, Santa Margherita and Portofino Vetta along a pretty drive known as La Ruta. Drivers can reach Camogli from the A12 or the Via Aurelia (SS1). In summer ferries connect Camogli with other towns on the Portofino

promontory and the Cinque Terre. See the Santa Margherita section.

Rapallo

Rapallo is a major resort, but often overlooked for the more illustrious Santa Margherita and Portofino. A bigger place, it has an air of bustle independent of tourists that the other towns farther down the promontory lack – all the more so on Thursday, which is market day at Piazza Cile.

Rapallo has Roman origins and even boasts a bridge supposedly used by Hannibal during the Carthaginian invasion of Italy in 218 BC.

More recently, Rapallo enjoyed a brief period of international popularity in the treaty-signing business. In 1920, the Italo-Yugoslav Treaty that defined the borders of the two countries was signed here, and two years later the Russians and Germans sealed a peace deal that lasted all of 19 years.

Information The IAT office (☎ 0185-5 45 73) is through the town centre at Via Diaz 9 and is open daily from 8.30 am to 12.30 pm and 2.30 to 5.30 pm. The telephone code for the area is 0185.

Things to See & Do A funivia (follow the signs from Corso Assereto) goes to **Montallegro**, a sanctuary built on the spot where the Virgin Mary reportedly appeared on 2 July 1557. A circuitous 10 km road also leads to the site. Just off the Lungomare Vittoria Veneto lies a 16th-century **castle**.

You can join up for PADI dive courses with Marco Maglia (☎ 26 04 98) or just call for advice on dive sites. Are submarines your thing? The Tritone 2 does underwater jaunts in summer. Get in touch with Portofino Coast (☎ 23 01 85), Via Lamarmora 17/6, but don't expect budget rates.

Places to Stay & Eat For the camping grounds in the hills near Rapallo take the Savagna bus from the train station. *Miraflores* (☎ 26 30 00), Via Savagna 12, is open from April to October, and *Rapallo* (☎ 26 20 18), Via San Lazzaro 4, is open only in summer. The cheap-end pick of the many hotels in Rapallo is *Bandoni* (☎ 5 04 23), Via Marsala 24, situated right on the waterfront with singles/doubles from L30,000/60,000. The *Duomo* (☎ 5 16 27), Via San Filippo Neri 12, has rooms from L35,000/60,000.

Vesuvio, Lungomare Vittorio Veneto 29, has pizzas from L7500, while *Da Monique*, at No 5 on the same street has a set seafood meal for L30,000. A slightly more intimate atmosphere makes the *Hostaria Vecchia Rapallo*, Via Fratelli Cairoli 24, a block farther back from the water, a pleasant alternative. A main will cost about L25,000.

Getting There & Away Regular buses connect Rapallo with Santa Margherita (every 20 minutes) and Camogli. The trip in both directions is more pleasant than by train. In summer, ferries connect Rapallo to other towns on the coast. See the following Santa Margherita section.

Santa Margherita

In a sheltered bay on the east side of the Portofino promontory on the Golfo di Tigullio, Santa Margherita is an attractive resort town and a comparatively affordable base for exploring the area. The old houses of the fishers face the port and you can admire the million-dollar yachts at their moorings.

Once home to a considerable coral-fishing fleet that roamed as far as Africa, Santa Margherita is now better known for its orange blossoms and lace. Surfers have supposedly tried their luck here, but the 'waves' are no more exciting than anywhere else in the Mediterranean.

From the train station, head downhill to the waterfront and then right along Via Gramsci to Piazza Caprera, from where most buses depart.

Information The IAT office (☎ 28 74 85), Via XXV Aprile 2b, just off Piazza Caprera, is open daily from 8.30 am to 12.30 pm and 2.30 to 5.30 pm. It's open from 9.30 am on

Sundays and holidays and has extended hours in summer.

The post office is at Via Roma 36 and is open Monday to Friday from 8.10 am to 5.30 pm and Saturday morning. The post code is 16038. There are telephones at the train station and around the city. The telephone code is 0185.

For the police, call ☎ 113 or the Carabinieri (☎ 28 71 21) in Via Vignolo. The Ospedale Civile di Rapallo (☎ 68 31) is at Rapallo in Piazza Molfino. For an ambulance call ☎ 28 70 19; for a night doctor (Guardia Medica) call ☎ 6 03 33.

Activities Santa Margherita is a sports playground, with the list headed by sailing, water-skiing and diving. Ask at the tourist office, the big hotels or on the waterfront – and have a fat wallet handy.

Places to Stay & Eat About the cheapest place is the *Albergo Lombardia e Bristol* (☎ 28 75 05), Via Palestro 26, where rooms start at L35,000/65,000. *Albergo Nuovo Riviera* (☎ 28 74 03), Via Belvedere 10, has singles/doubles from L45,000/70,000; full board (L80,000 per person) is compulsory in the high season. *Albergo Fasce* (☎ 28 64 35), Via L Bozzo 3, offers singles/doubles for L46,000/70,000. One of the town's best hotels is the *Grand Hotel Miramare* (☎ 28 07 13), Lungomare Milito Ignoto 30, but you will pay about L340,000 a double.

At *Trattoria San Siro*, Corso Matteotti 137 (15 minutes from the seashore), a full meal will cost around L20,000. Try the pansoti. *Trattoria da Pino*, Via Jacopo Ruffini, is quite cheap, while at *Ristorante da Alfredo*, Piazza Martiri della Libertà 38, near the water, pizzas start at L6000. It's one of several similar places on the esplanade. *Simonetti*, Via Bottaro 51, has good gelati.

Getting There & Away Santa Margherita is on the Genoa-La Spezia train line. By car, the A12 passes Rapallo before cutting inland towards Santa Margherita. Viale E Rainusso, which runs off Piazza Vittorio Veneto, joins the Via Aurelia (SS1), the secondary road to

Genoa, which is the best bet for hitchhikers. Buses leave Piazza Martiri della Libertà for Portofino.

In summer, Servizio Marittimo del Tigullio (☎ 28 46 70) operates ferries from near the bus stop to Portofino (L7000 return). Other ferries service San Fruttuoso (L15,000 return) and the Cinque Terre (L30,000 return). Some services begin in spring and run into October, but dry up in winter.

You can hire bicycles and motor scooters at Agrifogli, Piazza Martiri della Libertà 40, or from a place opposite the IAT office.

Paraggi

Two km short of Portofino, there's little here but a couple of hotels and one of the area's few slivers of white, sandy beach.

Portofino

Dubbed by the Italian press the 'richest promontory in Italy', Portofino and its environs is home (or holiday home) to the mega-rich and powerful. Anyone who is anyone has a villa here, and a host of movers and shakers wheels, deals and plays in Portofino. Entrepreneur and short-lived prime minister Silvio Berlusconi rents a villa he hardly ever visits (he prefers Sardinia, considered by many as rather brash).

For all this, a certain haughty disdain on the part of long-standing residents has given the town a healthy air of restraint, and the huddle of pastel-coloured houses around the modest port-side piazza are a delight. In summer the piazza, fronted by unassuming, but expensive, cafés and boutiques, is awash with glitterati as film stars flock to the most 'happening' spot in all Liguria.

Information The IAT office (☎ 0185-26 90 24), Via Roma 35, just back from the port, is open daily from 9 am to midday and 3 to 6 pm. It can advise on water sports and accommodation, which is scarce and expensive.

Things to See & Do Near the **Chiesa di San Giorgio** a flight of stairs leads up to the 16th-century **Castello di San Giorgio** of the same name. Built over an existing fort by the

Genoese, under some pressure from their Spanish allies, it occasionally saw action, particularly when occupied by Napoleon and taken by the English in 1814. It offers a great view, but for a still better outlook continue to the **lighthouse**, an hour's walk there and back.

Boats can be hired from Mussini Giorgio & C (☎ 26 93 27), Calata Marconi 39. The telephone code is 0185.

Places to Stay & Eat The cheapest lodgings are at *Eden* (☎ 26 90 91), Vico Dritto 18, set appropriately in a garden, for L180,000 a double. The cover charge alone at most restaurants would equal the daily meal allowance of some travellers. A cup of coffee at a table will cost L5000 or more at the waterfront cafés. Don't despair. *Pizzeria El Portico*, Via Roma 21, has pizzas from L7000 and the *Panificio Canale*, at No 30, has decent pastries for about L3000 a slice.

Getting There & Away Portofino can be reached by bus from Santa Margherita, and in summer ferries crisscross the gulf from most towns along the coast. Servizio Marittimo del Tigullio runs ferries to San Fruttuoso (L10,000 return), Rapallo (L9000 return) and Santa Margherita (L7000 return). Drivers must park at the entrance to the town (L6000 for the first hour) as cars are banned farther in.

San Fruttuoso

Accessible either by foot from Camogli or Portofino (an exhilarating cliffside walk that takes up to 2½ hours each way from either town), or by ferry, San Fruttuoso is a fascinating village dominated by the **Abbazia di San Fruttuoso di Capodimonte**, a Benedictine abbey with medieval origins. Built as a resting place for bishop St Fructuosus, martyred in Spain in 259 AD, the abbey was rebuilt in the mid-1200s with the assistance of the Doria family, who used it as a family crypt. It fell into decay with the decline of the religious community, and in the 1800s was divided into small living quarters by local fishermen. The Dorias donated the abbey and hamlet to the Italian Environmental Protection Foundation in 1983 and it was renovated three years later at a cost of L3.5 billion. It's open daily from 10 am to 4 pm in summer but otherwise opening hours are irregular. Admission is L5000.

Perhaps more fascinating is the bronze statue of Christ, *Il Cristo degli Abissi*, lowered 50 feet to the sea bed by locals in 1954 as a tribute to divers lost at sea and to bless the waters. You must dive to see it, but locals say if the waters are calm it can be viewed from a boat. A replica in a fish tank is on show in the church adjoining the abbey. A religious ceremony is held over the statue every August.

Chiavari to Levanto
The stretch of coast between the Portofino promontory and the Cinque Terre can come as a bit of a letdown, wedged as it is between two such beauty spots. It does have some of the Riviera di Levante's best beaches, but the resorts of Sestri Levante, Deiva and Levanto get predictably crowded in summer.

Cinque Terre
If you miss the five villages of the mountainside Cinque Terre – Monterosso, Vernazza, Corniglia, Manarola and Riomaggiore – you will have passed by some of Italy's most extraordinary country. But blink as the train zips between tunnels and miss them you will.

The mountains, covered wherever possible by terraced vineyards (the locals have set up ingenious monorail mechanisms to ferry themselves up and the grapes back down), drop precipitately into the Mediterranean, leaving little room for the tiny fishing villages that clutter the coves, are tucked into ravines or perched on top of sharp ridges. Fishing and viniculture have been the two main sources of income over the centuries, but tourism now plays a big role as well – the position of the villages has hopefully saved them from the thoughtless resort development that blights much of the Ligurian coast. Oddly, the area is popular more with foreign than Italian tourists, for whom it is still largely 'undiscovered'.

Ask at the IAT office in La Spezia and you may well be told all accommodation has been booked out in the Cinque Terre, but plenty of people rent out rooms on a more or less official basis – if you miss the telltale signs, 'camere' and 'affittacamere', ask around in the bars. Prices are not low but neither are they extortionate. Food is not cheap either, and often mediocre. Try to lay your hands on some local vintages, such as the nationally renowned white and dessert wines, Morasca, Chiaretto del Faro and the heavenly sweet Sciacchetrà.

You can drive to all five villages, but cars are not permitted beyond the entrance to each town. Note that some of the road between Vernazzo and Monterosso is in very poor condition – mules are much better transport. Occasional buses go close to the towns, but the local La Spezia-Genoa trains are regular and by far the most convenient way to get to and around the Cinque Terre.

Better than trains, buses or cars for those with the time is a scenic path reopened in late 1994 and connecting all the villages. There are a few slightly strenuous sections, but the dramatic views of the towns and coast more than compensate for any sweating you might do.

Monterosso Huge statues carved into the rocks overlook one of the few beaches in the Cinque Terre – a grey pebbly affair. Monterosso gets its name from the unusual red colouring of the nearby cliff faces, but it is the least attractive of the villages. It's expensive too. *Albergo Punta Mesco* (☎ 81 74 95), Via Molinelli 35 (just past the rail bridge), a few minutes walk from the beach, has singles/doubles for L65,000/80,000 in high season. The beachside hotels start at about L100,000 a single with breakfast in high season.

Vernazza Possibly the most fetching of the villages, Vernazza makes the most of the sea, with a promenade and piazza on the water. The road winding away from the centre is choked with tiny vineyards and patches of lemon grove. Head for the **Castello Doria**, which has sweeping views from the tower of the town and surrounding coast. *Del Capitano* (☎ 81 22 01), Piazza G Marconi 21 (ask at the bar) has singles/doubles in high season for L45,000/60,000. *Da Sandro* (☎ 81 22 23), Via Roma 62, is much the same. *Pensione Sorriso* (☎ 81 22 24), Via Gavino 4, offers half board only for L65,000 per person. All have restaurants. For waterside views you could try the immodestly priced restaurant and bar in the Belforte, a tower which dominates the sea. The train station is in the middle of town.

Corniglia Perched precariously on a ridge high above the sea, Corniglia is quite an uphill hike from the train station. Four-storey houses, narrow lanes and stairways are woven together on the hill, and topped by La Torre, a medieval lookout from which you can look south-east to Manarola.

On the path to Manarola, behind the train station, is the *Villaggio Marino Europa* (☎ 81 22 79), a row of self-contained bungalows sleeping up to six people. Open from June to the end of September, they can be rented for a minimum of three days and are cheaper in June and September. Local wine grower Domenico Spora (☎ 81 22 93) is just one of several people offering rooms – a quick walk around town will throw up several options. The Spora rooms start at L35,000 per person. *A Cantina de Mananan*, Via Carruggio 117, is a cosy little osteria where pasta starts at L10,000 and seafood at L11,000.

Manarola Perhaps lacking some of the atmosphere of Corniglia and Vernazza, Manarola is nonetheless a captivating village. If you're game for a good uphill hike, take the path off Via Rollandi, near Piazza Castello, through vineyards to the top of the mountain. On a clear day you can see all the villages. The affittacamere run by Gianni Capellini (☎ 2 23 68), Via Discovolo 6, near the church, has big, modern rooms with views for L50,000 a double. He also has an apartment with a kitchen and terrace overlooking the town for

L60,000 a day. There are several small restaurants by the water.

Riomaggiore The Via dell'Amore (Lovers' Lane) straggles the cliffside from Manarola to Riomaggiore – a mess of houses slithering down a ravine that forms the main street, with tiny fishing boats lining the shore and stacked in the small square. The older part of town is a few minutes walk south of the train station, through a long tunnel.

Up on the hillside is *Soggiorno Alle Cinque Terre* (☎ 92 05 87), Via de Gasperi 1. In high season rooms go for L40,000/70,000. The owners have other rooms in the town and an office on Via Colombo (you can't miss the 'camere/Zimmer/rooms' sign). Signora Anna Michielini (☎ 92 04 11) rents rooms at Via Colombo 143, and has apartments, each with a kitchen and bathroom, for L30,000 per person. A stroll down this street will reveal several similar deals. Most restaurants are along Via Colombo, which runs from the waterfront through the centre of the village. Try *Veciu Muin*, Via Colombo 83, for a good pizza. Or try *La Lanterna*, where a meal overlooking the cove will cost about L35,000 a head.

La Spezia
La Spezia sits at the head of the gulf of the same name – also known as the Gulf of Poets in deference to Byron, Dante, D H Lawrence, Shelley, George Sand and others who were drawn here by its beauty. A decision late last century to establish Italy's largest naval base in La Spezia propelled it from minor port to busy provincial capital; the street grid and venerable public buildings are largely a product of that time. It's still a navy town, with the ubiquitous blue sailor's uniform a constant reminder.

Orientation The city is sandwiched between the naval base to the west and the commercial port to the east. The main street and scene for the ritual passeggiata is the narrow Via Prione, running from the train station to the palm-lined Viale Italia on the waterfront.

LIGURIA

Information The IAT office (☎ 0187-77 09 00), Viale G Mazzini 45, is open Monday to Saturday from 9.30 am to 12.30 pm and 3.30 to 6.30 pm. There is another office (☎ 0187-74 37 17) at the train station.

The post office in Piazza Giuseppe Verdi is open Monday to Saturday from 8.30 am to 7.40 pm. La Spezia's post code is 19100. A Telecom office is at Via da Passano 30 and is open Monday to Friday from 9 am to 12.30 pm and 3.40 to 7 pm. There's also an unstaffed telephone booth at No 50 open until at least 10 pm. You'll find more telephones at the train station. The telephone code for La Spezia and much of the surrounding province is 0187.

Several banks have offices in the centre and most are open from 8 am to 1 pm and 2.30 to 4 pm. Quite a few have ATMs that take Visa and MasterCard.

For emergency police attendance, call ☎ 113. The questura (☎ 77 24 11) is at Via XX Settembre 4. For immediate medical attention, call ☎ 70 21 21 or, at night, ☎ 73 05 00.

Things to See The city's **Museo Navale**, Piazza Domenico Chiodo, is open Monday to Saturday from 9 am to midday, as well as Monday and Friday from 2 to 6 pm. Admission is L2000). Founded in 1870, following the transfer of the Genoese maritime museum to La Spezia, it hosts a phalanx of *polene*, the colourful busts or statuettes that graced the prows of vessels, and loads of model ships. The adjoining naval base is open to the public one day a year, 19 March, also the festival of the town's patron saint, San Giuseppe.

The most interesting part of the **Museo Civico**, Via Curtatone 9, off Corso Cavour, is the archaeology department, containing a hotchpotch of Bronze and Iron age objects and squat, ancient Ligurian *statue-stelae*. The **Museo Nazionale dei Trasporti**, about two km north-east of the city centre at Via del Canaletto 100, houses old buses for the urban transit nostalgic. It was closed at the time of writing.

Activities La Spezia has several walking clubs that offer information on medium to long walks around the coast and into the mountains. Natura Trekking (☎ 50 42 64), Via Sardegna, can help with maps and information; you could try the Università Verde (☎ 62 30 92), Via Paleocapa 19, although tourism isn't strictly its business.

The province, which takes in Calice, Luni and Varese Ligure, has more than a dozen horse riding clubs and many tracks. Ask the IAT or try the Associazione per l'Agriturismo e l'Ambiente (☎ 73 60 41), Via XXIV Maggio 69, for information on farms that organise horse riding; some offer accommodation, but you don't have to stay overnight.

Scuba diving is popular. The Federazione Italiana Pesca Sportiva (☎ 51 10 26), Via V Veneto 173, can advise on locations and hire places like Dyria Sub (☎ 52 05 09), Via Bosco 8, in the village of Cadimare (towards Portovenere). You could also try Spezia Sub (☎ 2 72 54).

Places to Stay You should have little trouble finding reasonably priced accommodation in La Spezia, unless you want a single room – seemingly in short supply. The town's proximity to the Cinque Terre, Portovenere and Lerici makes it a perfect base, especially as the limited accommodation in the surrounding area often fills up. There is no camping ground in La Spezia, but plenty in the surrounding towns. You might also want to ask at the IAT office about agriturismo options.

Albergo Giglio Rosso (☎ 3 13 74), Via Carpenino 31, has perfectly adequate, if slightly dingy, singles/doubles for L30,000/ 38,000 – most likely you'll be told there are no singles. The *Albergo Spezia* (☎ 73 51 64), Via Felice Cavallotti 31, is a block away and has singles/doubles from L30/42,000 – same problem here with snaring a single. Opposite the train station, *Albergo Terminus* (☎ 71 49 35), Via Paleocapa 21, has singles/doubles from L35,000/47,000. *Albergo Parma* (☎ 74 30 10), Via Fiume 143, has rooms from L40,000/56,000. *Hotel Diana* (☎ 2 51 20), Via Colombo 30, is near the naval base and has doubles only, from L60,000.

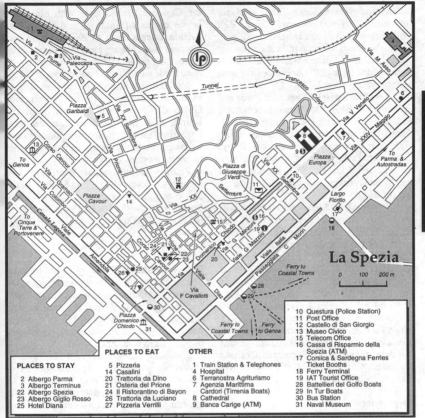

LIGURIA

La Spezia

0   100   200 m

10	Questura (Police Station)
11	Post Office
12	Castello di San Giorgio
13	Museo Civico
15	Telecom Office
16	Cassa di Risparmio della Spezia (ATM)
17	Corsica & Sardegna Ferries Ticket Booths
18	Ferry Terminal
19	IAT Tourist Office
28	Battellieri del Golfo Boats
29	In Tur Boats
30	Bus Station
31	Naval Museum

PLACES TO EAT

5	Pizzeria
14	Casalini
20	Trattoria da Dino
21	Osteria del Prione
24	Il Ristorantino di Bayon
26	Trattoria da Luciano
27	Pizzeria Verrilli

OTHER

1	Train Station & Telephones
4	Hospital
6	Terranostra Agriturismo
7	Agenzia Marittima Cardori (Tirrenia Boats)
8	Cathedral
9	Banca Carige (ATM)

PLACES TO STAY

2	Albergo Parma
3	Albergo Terminus
22	Albergo Spezia
23	Albergo Giglio Rosso
25	Hotel Diana

Places to Eat A produce market is held every day on Piazza Cavour, and there are plenty of restaurants, cafés and bars along Via Prione.

For a filling pizza, try *Pizzeria Verrilli* at Piazza Domenico Chiodi 32. It is one of a couple on the square and sells generous *pizzette* (good for one person) for about L7000. The pizzeria on Piazza Garibaldi isn't bad either.

The *Ristorantino di Bayon*, Via Felice Cavallotti 23, has a set menu including wine for L20,000. The *Trattoria da Luciano* Via Colombo 27, serves copious amounts of food for as little as L20,000. For good and reasonably priced seafood, head for the Tuscan *Trattoria da Dino*, Via Da Passano 17. Another locally recommended place, but some distance from the town centre, is *Da Francesco*, Via Pianazze 35. For bread or pastries, try *Casalini*, Via Prione 191.

Getting There & Away La Spezia is on the Rome-Genoa rail line, which follows the coast, and is also connected to Milan, Turin and other northern cities. The Cinque Terre and other coastal towns are easily reached by train, but other towns close to La Spezia, such as Portovenere, Sarzana and Lerici, are best reached by ATC buses (☎ 52 25 22), which leave from Piazza Domenico Chiodo. Some also leave from the train station.

Cyclists might like to know that most trains passing through the Apennines to Parma have bicycle storage.

The A12 runs past La Spezia to Genoa and Livorno, and the A15 to Parma also connects with the main north-south route, the A1. Hitchhikers can catch the Lerici bus along Viale San Bartolomeo and get off at Via Valdilocchi in the port area, a main access to the A12 and A15. The SS1 passes through the city and connects with the SS62 for Parma and the north.

Ferries leave La Spezia for coastal towns and Genoa during the summer months, and occasionally on pleasant weekends through the rest of the year. Navigazione Golfo dei Poeti (☎ 96 76 76; office in Lerici), Gruppo Battellieri del Golfo (☎ 77 03 69) at Banchina Revel off Passeggiata C Morin, In Tur (☎ 73 29 87), Viale Italia 2, and Baracco (☎ 96 69 55) all offer services. From April to October, Corsica Ferries (☎ 77 80 97), Largo Fiorillo, runs the occasional ferry to Bastia in Corsica. Tirrenia Navigazione runs summer services to Sardinia. Contact Marittima Cardori (☎ 77 02 50) at Via Francesco Crispi 39.

Portovenere

It is worth catching the bus from La Spezia for the razor-clam soup Portovenere has contributed to Ligurian fare. Rome founded Portus Veneris on the western shore of the Golfo di La Spezia as a base on the route from Gaul to Spain. From the brightly coloured houses along the waterfront narrow staircases and cobbled paths lead up the hillside towards the **Chiesa di San Lorenzo**, erected in the 12th century and subsequently altered. It lies in the shadow of **Castello Doria**, built in the 16th century on the site as part of the Genoese Republic's defence system. The views from its magnificent terraced gardens are superb.

At the end of the waterfront quay is the 13th-century **Chiesa di San Pietro**, built in the Genoese Gothic style with black and white bands of marble, and the **Grotta Arpaia**, once a haunt of Byron, with views towards the Cinque Terre. A plaque celebrates the poet's exploits as a swimmer – he once made a dash from Portovenere to Lerici.

Just off the promontory lie three tiny islands, Palmaria, Tino and Tinetto. Navigazione Golfo dei Poeti runs trips around the islands in summer, and you can hire local boats from the waterfront (haggling advised) to take you to Palmaria and the grottoes along its western shore.

Fishing is supposedly Portovenere's mainstay (a likely story). You can buy all the tackle and gear you want at Lucky Nautica Sport (☎ 90 21 98), Calata Doria 38. It hires out kayaks (L7000 an hour) and boats (L25,000 an hour).

Places to Stay & Eat Only 12 km from La Spezia, Portovenere is a straightforward day trip – a good thing as neither accommodation nor food is cheap. If you do want to stay, *Albergo Il Genio* (☎ 90 06 11), in a former castle at the start of the waterfront, has singles/doubles from L75,000/95,000.

Ristorante Miramare and *Taverna di Venere* are among the half-dozen or so restaurants along Calata Doria, by the sea. The former has a good seafood set meal for L30,000 including wine; the latter a less impressive set menu for L25,000. Or try *Bar al Naviglio*, Via Olive 73, away from the quay and a relatively cheap place for lunch. *Pizzaccia*, in Via Cappellini 94, the street leading from Albergo Il Genio to San Pietro, has takeaway pizza slices from L1500.

Lerici

At the southern end of the Riviera di Levante, 10 km from La Spezia, Lerici is an exclusive summer refuge for wealthy Italians, a town of villas with manicured gardens set into the surrounding hills and equally well-kept bathing boxes built into the cliffs along the beach. Make your way up to the 12th-century **Castello Lerici** for outstanding views of the town and the occasional art exhibition.

If you plan to stay in the area, jump off the bus at **San Terenzo**, a pleasant village (also dominated by a Genoese castle) half an hour's walk from Lerici. In 1822, Percy Bysshe Shelley set sail from here for Livorno (Leghorn), a fateful voyage that cost him his life on the return trip when his boat sank off the coast near Viareggio.

A pleasant four-km walk or bus ride from Lerici along the Fiascherino road takes you past some magnificent little bays towards Tellaro. The area was a haunt of D H Lawrence in the year before the outbreak of WW I. When you reach a huge illuminated sign reading 'Eco del Mare', make for the nearby *spiaggia libera*, the euphemism for a public beach – most others in the area are private.

Tellaro is a quiet fishing hamlet with pink and orange houses cluttered about narrow lanes and tiny squares. Weave your way to the Chiesa di San Giorgio, sit on the rocks and watch the world go by.

You can hire canoes and kayaks at Via Arpaia 8, quayside in Lerici, or call Gianni on ☎ 96 62 09.

Places to Stay & Eat Three camping grounds are based in the hills around Lerici. The *Gianna* (☎ 96 64 11), Via Fiascherino-Tellaro (just short of the village), is open from Easter to the end of September. *Maralunga* (☎ 96 65 89) at Via Carpanini 61, on the road from Lerici to Tellaro, and *Senato Park* (☎ 98 83 96), Via Senato 1, both open in May and close at the end of September. The camping grounds can be reached by bus from Piazza P G Garibaldi in Lerici.

Hotels include *Albergo delle Ondine* (☎ 96 51 31), Via Fiascherino 1, in a good spot at the top of Tellaro. Singles/doubles are L40,000/70,000. Outside Tellaro at Via Fiascherino 57 is the affittacamere *Armando Sarbia* (☎ 96 50 49), with doubles for L50,000, or L40,000 if you stay for several days. In San Terenzo, the *Pensione Pino* (☎ 97 05 95), Via Garibaldi 12, has singles/doubles from L50,000/70,000.

There are a few pleasant trattorias in San Terenzo. Try *La Palmira*, Via Angelo Trogu, where you can dine well for about L25,000. *Fuoco e Fiamme*, Piazza Brusacà, has pizzas from L7000.

Val di Magra

South-east of La Spezia, the Val di Magra forms the easternmost tongue of Ligurian territory before you reach Tuscany. **Sarzana**, a short bus ride from La Spezia, was once an important outpost of the Genoese republic. In the cathedral you can see the world's oldest crucifix, painted on wood. In the chapel is a phial said to have contained the blood of Christ. Nearby, the fortress of Sarzanello (also known as Castruccio Castracani) offers magnificent views. A pretty detour is to the hillside hamlet of **Castelnuovo Magra**, with a medieval castle.

Diehard fans of all things Roman may be interested in **Luni**, about six km south-east of Sarzana (one km off the SS1 towards the coast; it's not well signposted). Established as a Roman colony in 177 BC on the site of an Etruscan village, it thrived until the 13th century. Excavations have revealed the amphitheatre, forum, temple and other remnants of a classic Roman town, but the ruins are not in top condition. The site and a small museum are open daily from 9 am to 7 pm. Admission is L4000.

RIVIERA DI PONENTE

Stretching west from Genoa to France, this part of the Ligurian coast is more heavily developed than the eastern side and attracts package tour groups from northern Europe and Italian summer holiday-makers en masse. However, some of the resorts are not bad at all; several of Genoa's historical maritime rivals retain the architectural trappings of a more glorious past and the mountains, hiding a warren of hilltop villages, promise cool air and pretty walking and driving circuits.

Savona

From west or east, it is the sprawl of the port's facilities that first strikes you when

LIGURIA

approaching Savona, although with a population of only 70,000, it doesn't match the chaos of its long-time rival, Genoa. The two cities have been opponents since the Punic Wars, and the Genoese made their dominance clear in 1528 by destroying the town. Now a provincial capital and bishopric, Savona suffered heavy bombing raids during WW II. The small medieval centre, dominated by the Baroque **Cattedrale di Nostra Signora Assunta**, still survives.

Orientation The train station is in a newer part of town, south-east of the Letimbro river. Via Collodi, to the right of the train station as you walk out, and Via Don Minzoni, to the left, both lead across the river towards the leafy Piazza del Popolo (which serves as a drug-addicts' hang-out). From here, Via Paleocapa, Savona's elegant main boulevard, runs to the waterfront.

Information The APT office (☎ 019-82 55 44), Via Paleocapa 23, is open Monday to Saturday from 8 am to 1 pm and 3 to 6 pm. There is also an information booth on the river side of Piazza del Popolo. The telephone code for Savona is 019 and you'll find telephones on Piazza Mameli.

Places to Stay & Eat Savona has two youth hostels. The first is in the *Fortezza Priamar* (☎ 81 26 53), Corso Mazzini, on the waterfront which charges L28,000 for B&B and dinner. Take bus No 2 from the train station. The other, *Villa de' Franceschini* (☎ 26 32 22), Via alla Strà 29, Conca Verde, charges L14,000 for B&B; telephone on arrival in Savona for its private bus. Both hostels are open all year.

The *Albergo Cacciatori* (☎ 838 73 87), Via XX Settembre 7, has singles/doubles from L30,000/45,000. The *Nazionale* (☎ 85 16 36), Via Astengo 55, has rooms from L45,000/70,000.

A smattering of restaurants, trattorias and cafés can be found along Via Paleocapa and in the city centre. *Ristorante da Nicola*, Via XX Settembre 43, offers local specialities, with pasta from L8000.

Getting There & Away Apart from the trains, SAR and ACTS buses leave from Piazza del Popolo and the train station.

Around Savona

Noli For 600 years an independent republic, the seaside town of Noli has little of the Riviera di Ponente's made-to-measure resort atmosphere. Dominated by the ruined walls of the medieval republic, which run up a hill behind the old town and peak in a fort designed to watch for invaders from North Africa, the town sells itself as the original home of a Ligurian culinary singularity: *trofie* – tiny pasta shreds made from potato flour and eaten with pesto sauce. The claim is disputed by Recco, a town east of Genoa. Fishing remains one of Noli's mainstays, and the waterfront is often converted into an impromptu seafood market.

The APT office (☎ 019-74 89 31) is at Corso Italia 8, on the waterfront.

There are several decent places to stay where singles/doubles will cost about L40,000/60,000. They include *Albergo Romeo* (☎ 74 89 73), Via Colombo 83 and *Albergo Rini* (☎ 74 80 59), Via Cavalieri di Malta.

For meals, try *Puppy* on Piazza Garibaldi. Great gelatis are to be had at *Pappus*, Piazza Manin 12.

Buses run from Finale Ligure and Savona. For even better beaches, stop off in **Varigotti**, just past Noli on the way south to Finale Ligure.

Savonese Apennines About a 40-minute bus ride from Savona, **Sassello** is a tranquil mountain resort close to the regional boundary with Piedmont. A pleasant circuit from Savona to Genoa, if you have your own transport, takes you along winding mountain roads to Sassello and past several towns, including Rossiglione, just inside Piedmont. Sassello's modest monuments include the Bastia Soprano, a Doria family castle. **Acqui Terme**, 32 km farther north-east in Piedmont, is an ancient spa built around the ruins of a Roman water system. Enjoy a bath in the natural hot spring.

Finale Ligure

With a good beach and affordable accommodation, Finale Ligure is worth considering as a base for the Riviera di Ponente. If climbing rocks is your idea of fun, pack your ropes and head for the hinterland, where several areas offer good free climbing, and well-organised clubs produce maps of the best climbs.

Finale Ligure is divided into three areas. Finalborgo, away from the coast on the Pora river, is the original centre of the region. A clutter of twisting alleys behind medieval walls, it is the most interesting part of the Finale triad. Also atmospheric is the waterfront Finale Marina area, where most accommodation and restaurants can be found. Finale Pia, towards Genoa, runs along the Sciusa river and is rather suburban. The train station is at Piazza Vittorio Veneto, at the western end of Finale Marina. Walk straight down Via Saccone for the sea.

Information The APT office (☎ 019-69 25 81), opposite the beach at Via San Pietro 14, is open Monday to Saturday from 8.30 am to 1 pm and 3.30 to 6.30 pm. The telephone code for Finale Ligure is 019.

Activities Rock-climbing in the area immediately inland is popular. Rockstore in Via Nicotera, Finalborgo, hires out climbing gear and gives free advice. Another good place to seek information and meet other climbers is the nearby Caffè Centrale.

Places to Stay & Eat There are two camping grounds open all year: *La Foresta* (☎ 69 81 03) and *San Martino* (☎ 69 82 50), both in the same area about seven km north-east of town. ACTS buses run past from the centre. There's a *youth hostel* (☎ 69 05 15) at Via Caviglia 46. It costs L16,000 a night, including breakfast.

The APT can sometimes advise on private rooms or mini-apartments in private houses.

The town boasts 130 hotels. *Marita* (☎ 69 29 04), Via Saccone 17, is close to the train station with singles/doubles for about L30,000/50,000.

Pizzeria Forno a Legna, Via San Pietro 4, has specials galore and pizzas starting at L5000. *Trattoria la Tavernetta*, Via Colombo 42, does a great trofie with pesto.

Getting There & Away SAR buses along the coast leave from opposite the train station.

Getting Around Regular local buses link Finale Marina to Finalborgo. You can hire bicycles for L3500 an hour or L15,000 a day at Oddone, Via Colombo 20. They also have mountain bikes.

Albenga

Albenga's medieval centre sets it apart from many of the resorts farther west. Settled as far back as the 5th century BC, Albenga grew from its Roman roots to become an independent maritime republic in the Middle Ages, despite being destroyed several times by barbarian invaders. In the 13th century it threw in its lot with Genoa.

The Pro Loco tourist office (☎ 0182-55 90 58) is at Viale Martiri della Libertà 1, and is open Monday to Saturday from 9 am to midday and 3 to 6.30 pm. The telephone code is 0182.

Things to See Albenga's **Museo Diocesano**, featuring a painting by Caravaggio, is near the 5th-century **baptistry** and Romanesque **cathedral**. The baptistry is somewhat unusual, if only because the 10-sided exterior breaks with the usual octagonal shape that characterises its counterparts throughout northern Italy. The **Museo Navale Romano**, Piazza San Michele, has a collection of 1st-century amphoras, or wine urns, recovered in 1950 from the wreck of a Roman cargo vessel four km offshore. It is one of the oldest discovered shipwrecks.

Places to Stay & Eat There are some 20 camping grounds in the area around Albenga. The *Florida* (☎ 5 06 37) and *Delfino* (☎ 5 19 98), both on Via Aurelia (SS1), are reasonably close to the train station.

Albergo Italia (☎ 5 04 05), Viale Martiri della Libertà 8, is in a handy location. Rooms

LIGURIA

with breakfast cost L45,000/65,000. *Da Romano* (☎ 5 04 08), Piazza Corridoni 2, has doubles only for L50,000 or L60,000 with a bathroom – they are OK but not special.

Trattoria Bar la Bifora, Via delle Medaglie d'Oro 20, is in the historic heart of town and has pizzas starting at L5000. *Bar La Rocca*, Via Roma 74, does great things with swordfish and other seafood. If you don't want fish, try any of their pasta, with sauce 'alla Rocca'.

Getting There & Away Albenga is served by trains and SAR buses (main stop on Piazza del Popolo) along the coast.

Alassio

As well as three km of white beaches, Alassio boasts its own version of Baci, a delicious chocolate concoction that falls somewhere between a truffle and a biscuit. Not as well known as Perugia's version, Alassio's contribution is still money well spent – head for *Caffè Talmone*, Via Mazzini 107. One of the more pleasant beach resorts on this mountainous stretch of the Ligurian coast, there is no shortage of hotels should you decide to stay.

The IAT office (☎ 0182-64 03 46) is at Via Gibb 26, and a prominently placed billboard outside the train station lists accommodation and other information. The SAR Autolinee bus information office (☎ 64 05 96) at Piazza della Libertà can organise excursions around the Isola Gallinara nature reserve (you can't step onto the island), as well as day trips inland to Monte Carlo and other destinations. The telephone code is 0182.

Imperia

Dominated by lines of hothouses on the surrounding hillside, Imperia is the main city of the westernmost province of Liguria, commonly known as the Riviera dei Fiori because of the area's flower-growing industry – said to be among the most extensive in Europe. Imperia was founded in 1923 by Mussolini when he bridged the Impero river and unified the towns of Porto Maurizio (to

the west) and Oneglia (to the east), although they retain the air of separate towns.

Trains stop at Oneglia and Porto Maurizio stations, but the latter is the handiest. From the train station, head up the hill to Viale Matteotti, or through an underpass to the waterfront, which eventually leads to Corso Garibaldi. Buses connect both train stations, and bus No 3 runs through Porto Maurizio.

Information The APT office (☎ 0183-6 17 30) is at Viale G Matteotti 22. A post and Telecom office is at Via San Maurizio 13 and 15. Imperia's telephone code is 0183.

Things to See Porto Maurizio, the older of the two towns, is dominated by the **Cattedrale di San Maurizio**, a large neoclassical cathedral in Piazza del Duomo at the highest point on the hill. Across the square, the small **Museo Navale Internazionale del Ponente Liguria**, is open only for a couple of hours on Wednesday and Saturday evenings.

Places to Stay & Eat The camping grounds, *Eucalyptus* (☎ 6 15 34) and *La Pineta* (☎ 6 14 98) are just off the coast road (SS1) and can be reached by buses No 2 or No 3 from both train stations. There are several others in the area.

The *Pensione Paola* (☎ 6 29 96), Via Rambaldo 32, has simple singles/doubles from L21,000/42,000, while the nearby *Pensione Ambra* (☎ 6 37 15), at No 9, charges L30,000/50,000. They will probably insist on half or even full board. *Pensione Amo* (☎ 6 38 78), Via Aurelio Saffi 32, is near the cathedral and has singles/doubles for L20,000/40,000.

Pizzamania, Via XX Settembre 39, has pizza by the slice and is good for lunch. There are several restaurants and cafés along the esplanade, Via Scarincio. The poshest is the *Lanterna Blù* at No 32, with set menus starting at L45,000. Cheaper is the *Gambero*, virtually next door.

Getting There & Away Apart from the trains, buses for the coast stop virtually in front of the

Manarola village, Cinque Terre, Liguria

Top: Pastel-coloured houses of Portofino, Liguria
Bottom: Country around Corniglia, Cinque Terre, Liguria

tourist office. Tickets are sold in the café next door.

Around Imperia

Past Capo Cervo, heading east from Imperia, the small fishing village of **Cervo**, dominated by the ring of walls and towers around the medieval centre, makes for a pretty stop.

San Remo

San Remo gained prominence as a resort for Europe's social elite, and especially Britain and Russia, in the mid-to-late 1800s when the likes of Empress Maria Alexandrovna of Russia (mother of Nicholas II, the last tsar) held court here. Today, while a few hotels thrive as luxury resorts, many from that period are long past their prime and cut off from the beach by the railway line.

Orientation The old centre, La Pigna, is just north of Corso Matteotti, San Remo's main strip, where the wealthy take their evening stroll. Farther east, past Piazza Colombo and Corso Giuseppe Garibaldi is the seedier area. Corso Matteotti meets San Remo's other famous strip, Corso Imperatrice, at Piazzale Battisti and the train station.

Information The APT office (☎ 57 15 71) is at Largo Nuvoloni 1, just near the corner of Corso Imperatrice. It's open Monday to Saturday from 8 am to 7 pm and Sunday from 9 am to 1 pm. There are plenty of banks around, especially along Via Roma.

The main post office is at Via Roma 156 and is open Monday to Saturday from 8 am to 7.40 pm. The post code for central San Remo is 18038.

Public telephones are located at the train station and there is a Telecom office on the corner of Via Roma and Corso Mombello which is open from 8 am to 10 pm. San Remo's telephone code is 0184.

In an emergency, ring the police on ☎ 113. The questura (☎ 50 77 77) is at Via del Castillo 5. For medical assistance, head for the Ospedale Generale (☎ 53 61), Via Giovanni Borea 56.

Things to See The **Russian Orthodox Church** in Piazza Nuvoloni was built for the Russian community who followed Tsarina Alexandrovna to San Remo. The church, with its onion-shaped domes, was designed in 1906 by Josef Choussef, who 20 years later planned Lenin's mausoleum in Moscow. It is open daily from 7 am to 12.30 pm and 3.30 to 7 pm.

Italy's principal **flower market** is held in Corso Garibaldi from June to October, daily from 6 am to 8 am. Go along and watch the frenetic bidding.

Monte Bignone is a short drive from the centre, or a cable-car ride (if it's working) from Corso degli Inglesi, and offers views over San Remo and as far as Cannes.

The **Villa Nobel**, where the Swedish inventor of dynamite and originator of the Nobel prizes, Alfred Nobel, lived and died is at Corso Cavalotti 112, but is closed for restoration.

Activities Water-sport enthusiasts can hire windsurfing gear at Morgana (☎ 50 36 47), Corso Salvo d'Acquisto.

Festival In February, budding and established talents congregate for the Festival della Canzone Italiana. It is *the* music event, and although much of the music is depressingly middle-of-the-road, more than a few local success stories have emerged from the festival.

Places to Stay There are many hotels in San Remo, and with luck you may strike a reasonable deal. The tourist office has a full list, but don't take too much notice of the prices. Summer is difficult, and some places shut for holidays in September.

There are three camping grounds worth considering: *Blue Beach* (☎ 51 32 00), Via al Mare 183, five km east of town near the small town of Bussana; *La Vesca* (☎ 51 37 75), Corso Mazzini 74, a little closer to town; and *Villagio dei Fiori* (☎ 6 06 35), two km west at Via Tiro a Volo 3. All can be reached by bus from the train station.

The *Albergo al Dom* (☎ 50 14 60), Corso Mombello 13, is a homely place with singles/

LIGURIA

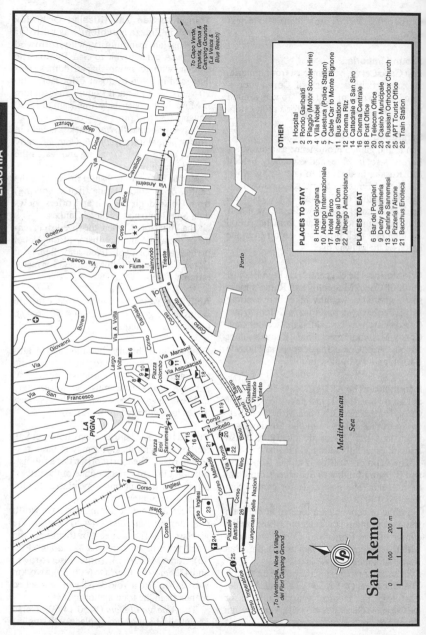

San Remo

PLACES TO STAY

8 Hotel Giorgiana
10 Albergo Internazionale
17 Hotel Parco
19 Albergo al Dom
22 Albergo Ambrosiano

PLACES TO EAT

6 Bar dei Pompieri
9 Derby Salumeria
13 Cantine Sanremesi
15 Pizzeria l'Airone
21 Bacchus Enoteca

OTHER

1 Hospital
2 Rondò Garibaldi
3 Piaggio (Motor Scooter Hire)
4 Villa Nobel
5 Questura (Police Station)
7 Cable Car to Monte Bignone
11 Bus Station
12 Cinema Ritz
14 Cattedrale di San Siro
16 Cinema Centrale
18 Post Office
20 Telecom Office
23 Casinò Municipale
24 Russian Orthodox Church
25 APT Tourist Office
26 Train Station

0   100   200 m

Mediterranean Sea

Porto

LA PIGNA

To Capo Verde, Imperia, Genoa & Camping Grounds (La Vesca & Blue Beach)

To Ventimiglia, Nice & Villaggio dei Fiori Camping Ground

doubles for L35,000/65,000. The doubles have shower and toilet. Not far off, the *Albergo Ambrosiano* (☎ 57 71 89), Via Roma 36, has OK doubles for L60,000. *Hotel Parco* (☎ 50 96 40), Via Roma 93, has decent if unspectacular rooms for L30,000/50,000.

Closer to Piazza Colombo, the *Hotel Giorgiana* (☎ 50 69 30), in a big block at Via San Francesco 37, has rooms for about L30,000/50,000. The *Hotel Gilda*, on the same floor, is closed. On Piazza Colombo, the *Albergo Internazionale* (☎ 50 45 50), has basic rooms starting at about L30,000/50,000.

Places to Eat Try the local cuisine at reasonable prices at *Cantine Sanremesi* at Via Palazzo 7, if it reopens. Many cheaper trattorie are around Piazza Colombo and Piazza Eroi Sanremesi. The *Pizzeria l'Airone*, at Piazza Eroi Sanremesi 11, feels tucked-away and offers a reasonable set menu for L18,000.

Another place with a cosy atmosphere, *Ivano*, just down from the Cattedrale di San Siro at Via Corradi 39, offers good-value meals. Another pleasant, if pricier, location is the *Pizzeria Vesuvio* at No 5. For modestly priced food and a few glasses of wine, you could try the *Bacchus Enoteca* at Via Roma 65. To make your own food, head for the *Derby Salumeria* on Piazza Colombo.

Entertainment With more than 20 clubs, San Remo jumps at night. First and foremost is the grand Casinò Municipale, Corso degli Inglesi 18, with its 'American Games', cabaret shows, roof garden and nightclub – bring your chequebook! The Odeon Music Hall, Corso Matteotti 178, is where all the groovy young things go to dance. The tourist office has a list of nightclubs and might be able to advise you on the most happening locations. More sedate are the cafés and bars lining Corso Matteotti.

Getting There & Away San Remo is on the Genoa-Ventimiglia train line and is easily accessible by regular trains from either city. Riviera Trasporti buses (☎ 50 20 30) leave from the train station and the main bus station near Piazza Colombo for the French border,

Imperia and inland. Other companies operate from the same bus station to destinations such as Turin and Milan. By car, you can reach San Remo quickly on the A10 or more scenically – and less expensively – by following the SS1 along the coast.

Getting Around The Piaggio agent, Bianchi Emilio (☎ 54 13 17), Corso Felice Cavalotti 39, hires out scooters and motorbikes. In summer, head down to Giardini Vittorio Veneto, by the old port, to hire bicycles.

Around San Remo
Valle Argentina The so-called 'silver valley' stretches away from **Taggia**, a charming little place a few km inland from the San Remo-Imperia road, into thickly wooded mountains that seem light years from the coastal resorts. Buses from San Remo go as far as **Triora**, 33 km from San Remo and 776 metres above sea level. This haunting medieval village, the scene of celebrated witch trials and executions in the 16th-century, dominates the surrounding valleys, and the trip alone is worth it. Those with their own transport can explore plenty of other villages, each seemingly more impossibly perched on hill crests than the one before.

Ventimiglia
Coming in from the splendidly rich end of the French Riviera, arrival in Ventimiglia can be a bit of a letdown. The town is jaded, the grey pebbly beach is nothing special and the limpid blue water of Nice is far away. But this is also its charm – none of the ritzy or package tour crowd hang about here. Typical of this frontier area, French almost seems to have equal level status with Italian.

The train station is at the head of Via della Stazione, which continues to the waterfront as Corso della Repubblica. Corso Genova, which runs past the Roman ruins, is the main eastern exit from the city, while its continuation to the west, Via Cavour, runs through the centre and heads to France.

Information The APT office (☎ 0184-35 11 83) is at Via Cavour 61. You can also get help at the train station. There are several banks (some with ATMs) and also an exchange booth at the train station. The telephone code is 0184.

Things to See Ventimiglia's **Roman ruins**, including an amphitheatre, date from the 2nd and 3rd centuries, when it was known as Albintimulium. The ruins straddle Corso Genova, a couple of km east of the train station, but are only for diehards. The train lines and traffic kill any atmosphere.

Squatting on a hill on the west bank of the Roia river is the medieval town. A 12th-century **cathedral** on Via del Capo rises above the surrounding lanes and neglected houses. There are some breath-taking views of the coast from Corso Giuseppe Verdi.

Places to Stay The camping ground, *Roma* (☎ 3 35 80), Via Peglia 5, is near the town centre and costs L9000 per person and tent and L7000 for a car. The *Albergo Cavour* (☎ 35 13 66), Via Cavour 3, has singles /doubles for L35,000/55,000 (add L10,000 for a room with a bathroom). *Albergo XX Settembre* (☎ 35 12 22), Via Roma 16, offers similar deals and has a popular restaurant downstairs. Near the waterfront on Corso della Repubblica 12 is *Hotel Villa Franca* (☎ 35 18 71), which offers reasonable rooms for L35,000/65,000 – considerably more if you take breakfast.

The *Hotel Posta*, Via Sottoconvento 15, is a step up in quality at L48,000/85,000.

Places to Eat A series of pizza restaurants lines the beach on Passeggiata G Oberdan. *Bar Il Corallo* offers pizza by the slice from L1200. Next door, the *Pizzeria 4 Assi* is not bad, offering a tourist set menu for L15,000. *Pizza 'al Giro'*, Via Cavour 56, sells pizza by the slice and focaccia for L1000. Several other down-to-earth places are located around Via Roma and Piazza della Libertà or along Via Cavour. For a cosier atmosphere, try the *Pergola* at Via Roma 6a. Ice-cream places abound – a popular one is *Gelatomania*, Via Cavour 50b.

Getting There & Away By bus, Riviera Trasporti (☎ 35 12 51), next to the tourist office, connects the city with towns along the coast and into France – frequency drops out of the high season; buy tickets in the office or at tobacconists. Trains connect the city with towns along the coast, including Genoa, Nice, Cannes and Marseilles. From Genoa you can make regular connections to Rome and Milan. The A10 connects the city with Genoa and Nice, the SS20 leaves the city to the north for France and the Via Aurelia (SS1) hugs the coast between the French border and Genoa.

Getting Around Eurocicli (☎ 35 18 79), Via Cavour 70b, hires out bicycles and tandems.

Around Ventimiglia
Bordighera A few km east of Ventimiglia, and easily reached by the bus to San Remo, is the built-up resort of Bordighera. Apart from being a one-time favourite haunt of rich British seaside lovers – the collection of charming and costly hotels attests to this – Bordighera's fame rests on a centuries-old monopoly on the Holy Week palm business. The Vatican selects its branches exclusively from the palms along the promenade, Lungomare Argentina. The views over the coast from the high reaches of Bordighera, like the Piazza del Capo, are magnificent. Tucked in, just to the north of the piazza, is the town's medieval kernel.

Balzi Rossi Right by the Ponte San Lodovico crossing into France, eight km west of Ventimiglia, is a stone age site, known as the Balzi Rossi ('red rocks'). To enter (with a guide only) the grottoes where Cro-Magnon people once lived, you must buy a ticket for the small **Museo Preistorico**, which features the Triple Burial (a grave of three Cro-Magnon), pots of weapons, and animal remains from the period. It is open daily from 9 am to 7 pm and admission is L4000, but the guided visits are infrequent and there is really not that much to see. While you're waiting you could have a dip at the small beach nearby. The Riviera Trasporti bus to

France which leaves from the bus office Via Cavour three times a day (except Sunday) drops you right there.

Villa Hanbury Overlooking the coast by the village of Mortola are the Giardini Botanici Hanbury. Established last century by Sir Thomas Hanbury, an English noble, the tumbledown gardens surround his Moorish-style mausoleum – the so-called villa under restoration since late 1993. It's open from 9 am to 6 pm in summer and closes at 4 pm in winter. Admission is L8500. You can get the No 1A bus from Via Cavour in Ventimiglia. The bus goes on to the Ponte San Luigi frontier post, from where you could walk down to the Balzi Rossi.

Piedmont (Piemonte)

Its position against the French and Swiss Alps has helped forge in Piedmont (Piemonte) an identity quite separate from the rest of Italy. The region's neat and tidy northernmost reaches could easily be Swiss, while Turin's grand squares, arcades and sophisticated café life owe more to French influence than anything 'typically Italian'.

The House of Savoy, which ruled Piedmont during the early 11th century, created in Turin one of Europe's grand cities. Victor Emmanuel II and the Piedmontese statesman Count Camillo Cavour, were instrumental in achieving Italian unification, and succeeded in making Turin the capital of Italy, albeit briefly, from 1861.

Much of Italy's industrial boom this century has its roots in the region, particularly in and around Turin, where Fiat started making cars. Today, Piedmont is second only to Lombardy in industrial production and is one of the country's wealthiest regions.

Piedmont cuisine is heavily influenced by French cooking and uses marinated meats and vegetables. *Bagna caoda* (meat dipped in oil, anchovies and garlic) is popular during winter, and the white truffles of Piedmont are considered the best in Italy. The region

accounts for two-thirds of Italy's rice production, so it comes as no surprise that risotto is popular in Piedmont. The crisp climate is no hindrance to wine-making, and you can find some good reds, notably those from the vineyards of Barolo and Barbera, and sparkling wines from Asti.

Centrally located, Turin is an ideal base for exploring the region. The area's main attraction is the Grande Traversata delle Alpi (GTA), a walk of more than 200 km through the Alps from the Ligurian border to Lago Maggiore in the north-east of the region.

Activities

Walking Allow yourself a couple of weeks to complete the Grande Traversata delle Alpi, or a couple of days for smaller sections. The walk starts in the area of Viozene, in the south of Piedmont, and follows a network of Alpine rifugi north through the province of Cuneo, the Valle di Susa and the Parco Nazionale del Gran Paradiso and across the north of the region before ending on the banks of Lago Maggiore at Cannobio.

The best months for walking are late June into September, although by the end of summer (officially September 21) the weather can be unpredictable.

A fold-out map entitled *Percorsi e Posti Tappa GTA* (Routes & Places to Stop), which lists names and locations of rifugi and emergency information, is available from the APT or the CAI in Turin. The information is in Italian only, but addresses and details are easily deciphered. All rifugi are open from July to September, and some remain open through winter for cross-country skiers – many are located in or near villages.

The paths described are clearly marked and generally within the grasp of moderately fit people, and in various places link with optional walks inside French territory.

In addition, readers of Italian can purchase a wide range of detailed guides to specific areas published by the CAI.

Emergency There is a 24-hour mountain rescue service. If you're in difficulty and you can get to a phone, call ☎ 118. In dire situations

PIEDMONT

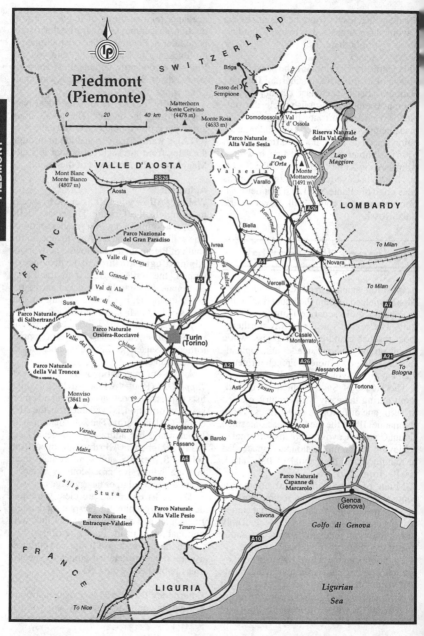

Piedmont
(Piemonte)

0   20   40 km

where a helicopter is sent in, signal for help by raising both arms above your head (one up and one down by your side means you don't need help).

Horse Riding The Alpitrek map, *A Cavallo Tra Val & Valsangone*, provides similar information for horse-riding tracks through the Piedmontese Alps. It is available from the Valle di Susa APT office in Oulx. A second map, *In Piemonte a Cavallo*, with routes starting at Albissola on the Ligurian coast, is available from the APT in Turin or the Associazione Nazionale Turismo Equestre Piemonte (☎ 54 74 55) in Turin, Via Bertola 39.

Quite a number of places organise horse-riding treks or less exacting rides through some of the region's valleys and national parks. A popular approach is to book places in an agriturismo or rifugio where horse riding is an option. Alpe Plane (☎ 0330-68 52 78), in Sauze di Cesana, down the southern slopes from Sestriere in the Valle del Chisone, is one such place. However, it is best to check the alternatives with individual tourist offices first.

Adventure Sports Several groups can organise a range of activities for the truly energetic. Adventure Office (☎ 011-822 20 80), Via Torino 112, San Mauro (between Turin and Vercelli), offers courses and excursions in canoeing, white water rafting, rock climbing, paragliding, mountain bike treks and even bungee jumping. Again, it's worth checking with the local tourist offices.

Skiing Skiing is possible in the north and west of Piedmont – consult skiing entries in this chapter for more details. The tourist offices in these areas have copious amounts of information on pistes, rifugi and ski hire.

TURIN (TORINO)

A gracious city of wide boulevards, elegant arcades and grand public buildings, Turin is built beside a pretty stretch of the Po river. Although much of the industrial and suburban sprawl, especially west and south of the

city centre, is predictably awful, the city is blessed with a green belt in the hills east of the river, with views to the snow-covered Alps west and north.

The Savoy capital from 1574, and for a brief period after unification the seat of Italy's parliament, Turin is also the birthplace of Italian industry. Giants like Fiat (Fabbrica Italiana di Automobili Torino) and Olivetti lured hundreds of thousands of impoverished southern Italians to Turin and housed them in vast company-built and owned suburbs, such as Mirafiori to the south. Fiat's owner, Gianni Agnelli, is one of the country's most powerful men, but Turin itself is a left-wing bastion. Industrial unrest on Fiat's factory floors spawned the Italian Communist Party under the leadership of Antonio Gramsci and, in the 1970s, the left-wing terrorist group, the Red Brigades.

History

Known as Taurisia, it is unclear whether the ancient city began as a Celtic or Ligurian settlement. Like the rest of northern Italy, it eventually came under the sway of Rome, which was succeeded by the Goths, Lombards and Franks.

When Turin became capital of the House of Savoy, it pretty much shared the dynasty's fortunes thereafter. The Savoys annexed Sardinia in 1720, but Napoleon virtually put an end to their power and occupied Turin in 1798. Turin suffered Austrian and Russian occupation before Victor Emmanuel I restored the House of Savoy and re-entered Turin in 1814. Nevertheless, Austria remained the true power throughout northern Italy until unification, when Turin became capital, an honour it passed on to Florence three years later.

Turin adapted quickly to its loss of political significance, becoming a centre for industrial production during WW I and later a hive of trade-union activity. Today, it is Italy's second-largest industrial city after Milan.

Orientation

The north-facing Stazione Porta Nuova is the point of arrival for most travellers. Trams and buses out the front of the station connect

PIEDMONT

PIEDMONT

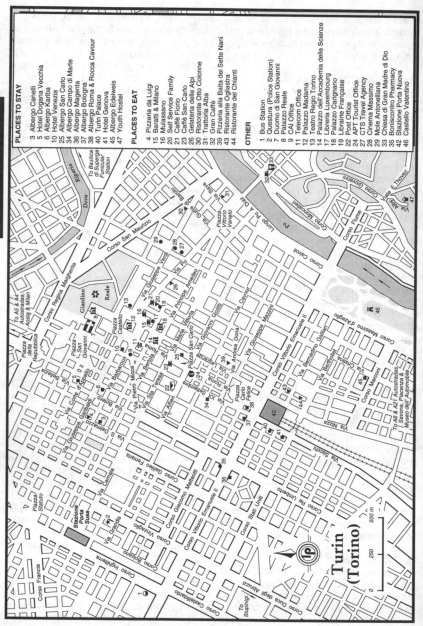

PLACES TO STAY

3 Albergo Canelli
5 Hotel Dogana Vecchia
6 Albergo Kariba
10 Hotel Venezia
25 Albergo San Carlo
34 Albergo Campo di Marte
36 Albergo Magenta
37 Albergo Bologna
38 Albergo Roma & Rocca Cavour
40 Turin Palace
41 Hotel Genova
45 Albergo Edelweis
47 Youth Hostel

PLACES TO EAT

4 Pizzeria da Luigi
15 Barati & Milano
16 Mulassano
20 Self Service Family
21 Caffè Fiorio
23 Caffè San Carlo
26 Gelateria delle Alpi
30 Ristorante Otto Colonne
31 Trattoria Alba
32 Gran Caffè
39 Pizzeria alla Baita dei Sette Nani
43 Ristorante Ogliastra
44 Ristorante del Chianti

OTHER

1 Bus Station
2 Questura (Police Station)
7 Duomo di San Giovanni
8 Palazzo Reale
9 CAI Office
11 Telecom Office
12 Palazzo Madama
13 Teatro Regio Torino
14 Palazzo dell'Accademia delle Scienze
17 Libreria Luxembourg
18 Palazzo Carignano
19 Librairie Française
22 Post Office
24 APT Tourist Office
27 CTS Travel Agency
28 Cinema Massimo
29 Mole Antonelliana
33 Chiesa di Gran Madre di Dio
35 Boniscontro Pharmacy
42 Stazione Porta Nuova
46 Castello Valentino

Turin
(Torino)

0   250   500 m

with most parts of the historic centre, which is quite spread out. From the station, walk straight ahead over the main east-west route, Corso Victor Emmanuel II, through the grand Piazza Carlo Felice and north along Via Roma until you come to the broad, café-lined Piazza San Carlo. Piazza Castello and the Duomo (which contains the Shroud of Turin) are farther north along Via Roma. The Mole Antonelliana dominates the horizon to the east, leading to Via Po (the student area), Piazza Vittorio Veneto and the mighty Po river.

Information
Tourist Office The APT office (☎ 011-53 51 81) is at Via Roma 226, under the colonnade at the south-west corner of Piazza San Carlo. There is a smaller office at Stazione Porta Nuova, and both are open Monday to Saturday from 9 am to 7.30 pm. Informa Giovani (☎ 011-57 65 49 76), Via Assarotti 2, publishes a magazine for young people, *Città di Torino Informa Giovani*, and has a range of information from travel to services for the disabled.

Money There is a bank with an ATM and an exchange booth at Stazione Porta Nuova. Banks are located along Via Roma and in Piazza San Carlo. Quite a few ATMs around the city accept Visa and MasterCard.

Post & Telecommunications The main post office is at Via Alfieri 10 and is open Monday to Saturday from 8.15 am to 2 pm. The Stazione Porta Nuova branch is open from 8.15 am to 7.30 pm. The post code for central Turin is 10100.

Telecom offices are located at Via Roma 18 and Stazione Porta Nuova. The telephone code for Turin is 011.

Emergency The questura (☎ 5 58 81) is at Corso Vinzaglio 10. Ring ☎ 113 in case of emergency. For an ambulance call ☎ 118. The Guardia Medica (☎ 57 47) makes house calls at night or on public holidays in emergencies; otherwise go to the Ospedale Mauriziano Umberto I (☎ 5 08 01), Largo

Turati 62. The Boniscontro pharmacy (☎ 53 82 71), Corso Vittorio Emanuele II 66, is open 24 hours a day.

Foreign Consulates The UK has a representative (☎ 650 92 02) at Corso d'Azeglio 60. The French consulate (☎ 83 52 52) is located at Via Bogino 8.

Bookshops Libreria Luxembourg, Via C Battisti 7, has a good range of English-language books and newspapers. For the French equivalent, try the Librairie Française, Via Bogino 4.

Other Information CTS travel agency (☎ 812 45 34) is at Via Montebello 2.

For gay and lesbian information, contact Arci Gay Maurice (☎ 650 98 60), Via O Moragari 17, or Informagay (☎ 436 50 00), Via Santa Chiara 1.

The CAI (☎ 53 92 60) is at Via Barbaroux 1.

Things to See & Do
Most of Turin's museums and monuments close on Monday and opening hours vary according to the season. Check at the APT office for the latest details.

Piazza Castello At the heart of Turin's historic centre and surrounded by museums, theatres, cafés and student quarters, this grand square is a logical place to start exploration of the city. Bordered by porticoed promenades, the piazza is dominated by **Palazzo Madama**, a part-medieval, part-Baroque 'castle'. Built in the 13th century on the site of the old Roman gate, Madama Reale Maria Cristina, the widow of Vittorio Amedeo I, made the castle her residence and so gave it its name in the 17th century; in the following century the rich Baroque façade was added. Today it houses the **Museo Civico d'Arte Antica**, at present closed for restoration.

In the north-western corner of the square is the Baroque **Chiesa di San Lorenzo**, designed by Guarino Guarini. The richly complex interior compensates for the spare façade.

Farther north, you pass through gates flanked by statues of the Roman deities, Castor and Pollux, to the **Palazzo Reale**. An austere, apricot-coloured building erected for Carlo Emanuele II around 1646, its lavishly decorated rooms house an assortment of furnishings, porcelain and other bits and pieces, including a collection of Chinese vases. The Giardino Reale (Royal Gardens), east of the palace, were designed by Andre le Noôtre in 1697, who created the gardens at Versailles. The **Armeria Reale**, the Savoy royal armoury, contains what some claim to be the best collection of arms in Europe. The palace is open from 9 am to 7 pm, but the armoury's timetable is all over the place. Admission to both costs L6000. The gardens are free.

Under Piazza Castello's porticoes you'll find the **Teatro Regio Torino** and a couple of Turin's more refined cafés.

Museums Perfect for a typical rainy day in Turin are the museums just south of Piazza Castello.

The Baroque **Palazzo Carignano**, Via Accademia delle Scienze 5, was the birthplace of Carlo Alberto and Victor Emmanuel II and the seat of Italy's first parliament, from 1861 to 1864. You can see the parliament as part of the **Museo Nazionale del Risorgimento Italiano**, which has an extensive display of arms, paintings and documents tracing the turbulent century from the revolts of 1848 to WW II. It is open Tuesday to Saturday from 9.30 am to 6.30 pm and Sunday from 9 am to 12.30 pm. It is one of the best museums in this genre in northern Italy but will be of limited interest to those who don't read Italian. Admission is L5000.

The **Palazzo dell'Accademia delle Scienze** on the street of the same name houses the **Museo Egizio**, established in the late 18th century and considered one of the best museums of ancient Egyptian art after those in London and Cairo. It is open Tuesday to Saturday from 9 am to 2 pm, and 3 to 7 pm and admission is L10,000. In the same building is the **Galleria Sabauda**, housing the Savoy collection, including

works by Italian, French and Flemish masters. It's open Tuesday to Saturday from 9 am to 2 pm and admission is L6000.

Farther afield is the **Galleria Civica d'Arte Moderna e Contemporanea**, Via Magenta 31, dedicated to 19th and 20th-century artists including Renoir, Courbet, Klee and Chagall. Opening times vary. Admission is L8000.

For modern art of a more metallic sheen, head for the **Museo dell'Automobile**, south along Via Nizza. Among its 400 masterpieces is one of the first Fiats and the Isotta Franchini driven by Gloria Swanson in the film *Sunset Boulevard*. It's open Tuesday to Sunday from 10 am to 6.30 pm. Admission is L9000. Bus No 34 goes there from beside Stazione Porta Nuova .

Back in central Turin, the **Museo della Marionetta**, Via Santa Teresa 5, contains puppets and costumes tracing the history of marionette theatre from the 17th century. If it's open (which seems to be a matter of chance), you may be lucky enough to see a performance as well.

Duomo di San Giovanni Turin's cathedral, west of the Palazzo Reale off Via XX Settembre, houses the **Shroud of Turin** in which Christ's body was supposedly wrapped after his crucifixion. Carbon dating in 1988 dated it to the 13th or 14th century, but current scientific research indicates that a fire in 1532 (in which the shroud caught alight) may have had an impact on the carbon dating, making it unreliable evidence. Despite the numerous tests that have been undertaken since the 19th century, no-one has been able to explain the images of the back and front of a man imprinted in the cloth. Certainly, the thousands who flock to see it don't seem to mind the continuing debate over it's authenticity.

The shroud is in the **Cappella della Santa Sindone** (Chapel of the Holy Shroud), topped by Guarino Guarini's honeycomb-like black marble dome, while a copy adorns the walls of a nearby chapel. Luigi Gagna's copy of da Vinci's *Last Supper*, above the doors, is considered the best ever produced. The chapel was closed for restoration at the time of writing.

Piazzas It is the great squares and elegant boulevards that lend Turin its air of reserved majesty. Via Roma, Turin's main shopping thoroughfare since 1615, heads south from Piazza Castello to the grandiose **Stazione Porta Nuova**, built by Mazzucchetti in 1865.

Walking south you first emerge in **Piazza San Carlo**, known as Turin's drawing room and home to several renowned cafés. Surrounded by the characteristic porticoes (central Turin boasts some 18 km of them), its southern end is capped by two Baroque churches, Chiesa di San Carlo and Chiesa di Santa Cristina. Farther down Via Roma you reach **Piazza Carlo Felice**, at once piazza and garden. The latter, like Via Nizza which continues south off the piazza past the train station, has seen better days. Now the main axis of Turin's seedier side of life, Via Nizza and the surrounding area is worth exploring but dodgy territory at night.

Via Po & Around The hip young scene, revolving around Turin's university, can be freely indulged in the cafés and trattorie along and around Via Po, which connects Piazza Castello and the river via Piazza Vittorio Veneto.

The single most remarkable sight in the area is the **Mole Antonelliana**, a couple of blocks north of Via Po on Via Montebello. Intended as a synagogue when it was started in 1863, this extraordinary structure comes as something of a shock when you first see it from the surrounding narrow streets. Capped by an aluminium spire, it is a display, in a similar vein perhaps to the Eiffel Tower, of engineering as an art form. Its chequered history can be studied at the small museum, but a trip to the highest platform, at 110 metres, is more rewarding for the view of the city and Alps. It's open Tuesday to Sunday from 9 am to 7 pm, and admission is L4000.

Walking south along the Po river, you will come to the **Castello del Valentino**, a mock medieval castle built in the 17th century. The carefully designed, French-style park around

it was first opened in 1856 and is one of the most celebrated in Italy.

East from Piazza Vittorio Veneto, across the Po, is the **Gran Madre di Dio** church, built between 1818 and 1831 to commemorate the return of Victor Emmanuel I from exile. Set into the hills, its dome is an unmistakable landmark, but the church is usually closed to the public.

Basilica di Superga In 1706, Vittorio Amedeo I promised to build a basilica to honour the Virgin Mary if Turin was saved from besieging French and Spanish armies. The city was saved and architect Filippo Juvarra built the church on a hill across the Po river to the north-east of central Turin. It became the resting place of the Savoys, whose lavish tombs make for interesting viewing.

The spot is now better known as a football shrine. The tomb of the Turin football team, all killed when their plane crashed into the basilica in 1949, is at the rear. The basilica is reached by No 15 tram. Take it to the end of the line and connecting funicular.

If you have a vehicle, the drive up through the thickly wooded Pino Torinese helps give the lie to the belief that Turin is little more than a polluted, industrial town.

La Palazzina di Caccia di Stupinigi A visit to the Savoys' sprawling hunting lodge, tucked away in manicured grounds beyond the Fiat plants and Mirafiori suburb, is a must. It is slowly being restored with Fiat money and many parts of the building are in original condition. Check with the APT because opening times vary. Take bus No 41 from Corso Vittorio Emanuele II, which runs along the north side of Stazione Porta Nuova.

Market Every morning until about midday, Piazza della Repubblica, north of the city centre, fills to the cries and smells of the main food and clothes market. On Saturdays Piazza d'Albera, on the north-eastern corner of Piazza della Repubblica, becomes an antique collector's heaven.

Places to Stay – bottom end

Finding a room can be difficult in Turin, and finding a cheap one even harder. Call the APT office in advance for a suggestion, although the staff won't make a reservation. The APT at Stazione Porta Nuova will provide a map and directions to your hotel.

Camping & Hostel The *Campeggio Villa Rey* (☎ 819 01 17), Strada Superiore Val San Martino 27, is away from the centre. Check with the APT for directions and opening times.

The youth hostel, *Ostello Torino* (☎ 660 29 39), Via Alby 1, is in the hills east of the Po river and can be reached by bus No 52 from Stazione Porta Nuova. Ask the driver for the right stop. B&B is L17,000 and a meal L12,000.

Hotels Near Stazione Porta Nuova, *Albergo Magenta* (☎ 54 26 49), Corso Vittorio Emanuele II 67, has rooms starting at L45,000/54,000.

Albergo Canelli (☎ 54 60 78), Via San Dalmazzo 7, off Via Garibaldi, has bare but serviceable rooms for L25,000/35,000. In the same pleasant area, *Albergo Kariba* (☎ 54 22 81), Via San Francesco d'Assisi 4, charges L35,000/50,000 for singles/doubles and L75,000 for a triple for slightly more comfortable digs.

Albergo Edelweis (☎ 669 01 17), Via Madama Cristina 34, will put you up for L45,000/55,000 a single/double. *Albergo San Carlo* (☎ 562 78 46), at No 197 on the piazza of the same name, has singles/doubles from L60,000/80,000 and L110,000 for a triple – the location is hard to beat. For the same price, *Albergo Distretto Antico* (☎ 521 37 13), Corso Valdocco 10, is OK. *Albergo Bologna* (☎ 562 01 91), Corso Vittorio Emanuele II 60, just across from Stazione Porta Nuova, is in a similar class but is often full.

Another good choice is *Albergo Campo di Marte* (☎ 54 53 61), Via XX Settembre 7, which also has singles/doubles from L60,000/80,000.

Places to Stay – middle to top end

With a little extra to spend, the *Hotel Dogana Vecchia* (☎ 436 67 52; fax 436 71 94), Via Corte d'Appello 4, has well kept rooms for L85,000/105,000 with breakfast. Mozart and Verdi were among its more distinguished guests.

The three-star *Albergo Roma & Rocca Cavour* (☎ 561 27 72), Piazza Carlo Felice 60, charges about L95,000 for a single and L135,000 for a double – all in sumptuous style. Weekend rates actually drop. *Hotel Genova* (☎ 562 94 00), Via Sacchi 14, is not much classier but charges L135,000/185,000.

Hotel Venezia (☎ 562 30 12), Via XX Settembre 70, has rooms from L150,000/185,000, but prices can come down in winter.

The city's most luxurious hotel is *Turin Palace* (☎ 562 55 11; fax 561 21 87), Via Sacchi 8, with singles/doubles starting at L268,000/291,000.

Places to Eat

Turin's cuisine is heavily influenced by the French, and the massive migration to the city of southern Italians brought traditions of cooking unmatched anywhere else in the north. Try *risotto alla piemontese* (with butter and cheese) or *zuppa canavesana* (turnip soup) and finish with a Savoy favourite, *panna cotta* (baked cream). The wines are largely from the Asti region or the Barolo vineyards.

Via Nizza near Stazione Porta Nuova is loaded with cheap eateries and takeaway joints. The area around Via Po is great for cheaper restaurants full of students.

One of the better self-service restaurants is *La Grangia*, Via Garibaldi 21, where you can eat a full meal for L11,000. Another is *Family*, Via Bogino 2, off Via Po, open for lunch only. There are a few others in a more takeaway line on Via Po itself.

Close to Stazione Porta Nuova, *Ristorante del Chianti*, Via Saluzzo 13 (parallel to Via Nizza), has a set menu for L11,000. Not far away, you can experiment with Sardinian cuisine at the *Ristorante Ogliastra* at Via B Galliari – a set menu with wine costs L17,500. A few doors down, at No 9, the *Bulldog* has spaghetti and beer.

Ristorante Peppino, Via Mercanti 7, is a popular and cheerful place with an extensive menu. A full meal will set you back around L25,000.

A cheap place to eat is *Ristorante Otto Colonne*, Via Guilia di Barolo 5, near Via Po, with pasta from L7000 and meat dishes from L10,000. *Trattoria Alba*, Via Bava 2, off Piazza Vittorio Veneto, is a busy, modestly priced restaurant offering solid serves of tasty food – a good meal with wine costs about L20,000.

Pizzeria alla Baita dei Sette Nani, Via A Doria 5, is said to be the best in Turin, with pizzas from L4500. Crowds queue for hours to get in. *Pizzeria da Luigi*, Via S Dalmazzo 1, off Via Garibaldi, is good value. *Pizzeria da Italo*, Via Botero 7, has scrummy pizzas, done in the Turinese style, and great salads.

Cafés & Bars Perhaps partly due to Turin's legacy of French and Austrian involvement, and maybe also as a result of the indifferent weather, the city has a flourishing and chic café life. Piazzas Castello and San Carlo are loaded with establishments patronised by the well-to-do (where a coffee can easily cost you L4000 or more) and there is a great choice along Via Po. Turin's long list of literary luminaries and political potentates have certainly not wanted for places to chat the day away.

Caffè Fiorio, Via Po 8, was a favourite haunt of Camillo Cavour; it's been operating since 1780. *Mulassano*, Piazza Castello, established in 1900, is a true belle époque relic and is popular with the theatre mob from the nearby Teatro Regio Torino. A couple of steps away is the slightly older and more elegant *Baratti & Milano*.

Caffè San Carlo, on Piazza San Carlo, once hosted a riotous gaggle of pre-unification patriots and other dangerous persons. Today it is more bankers' territory. *Gran Caffè*, just across the Po river at Piazza Gran Madre di Dio, makes for a tranquil change of atmosphere.

Gelati There are plenty of gelaterie to choose from. The *Gelateria delle Alpi*, Via Po 18, and *Gelateria Fiorio*, Via Po 8, are among the best; *Bar Blu* on the corner of Piazza Castello and Via Roma is also good.

Entertainment

On Fridays, the newspaper *La Stampa* has an entertainment insert, *Torino Sette*, which lists what's on around town. The city organises Punta Verdi – a series of summer concerts and films in various parks and theatres from June until August, and plenty of free music events in September – the APT has all the programmes. Free midday concerts are usually staged from February to April.

Theatre The cheapest tickets for the opera season at Teatro Regio Torino, Piazza Castello, sell for L25,000, but there is generally a queue. When they sell out, it is often possible to see the performance for free live on TV in the Teatro Piccolo Regio next door.

There are theatres throughout the city. Check *Torino Sette* and the APT office for programmes.

Cinema Cinema Massimo, on Via Massimo near the Mole Antonelliana, offers an eclectic mix of films, mainly in English, or with subtitles.

Nightclubs The nightclubs are among the country's best. Many require membership but you can often join temporarily. The scene changes quickly – pick up the free leaflet *Spettacolo News* at the APT office to get an idea of what's happening where. 'Ai Murazzi', the arcaded riverside area along the Po near Ponte Vittorio Emanuele I, is a popular place for late night entertainment. Riverside, Via Murazzi Po 35, puts on an alternative mix of jazz, blues and Latin music. Noisier stuff booms at Trionyx, Lungo Po Murazzi 53. Doctor Sax, Lungo Po Cadorna 4, near the river, is a nightclub and jazz venue. African Club, Via Principe Tommaso 5d, offers the kind of music the name suggests.

Getting There & Away

Air Turin is served by Caselle international

airport (☎ 567 63 61 for flight information), north-west of the city, which has connections to European and national destinations.

Bus Buses terminate at the bus station (☎ 433 25 25) at Corso Inghilterra 1. Buses serve the Valle d'Aosta, most towns and ski resorts in Piedmont, and major Italian cities.

Train The main train station (☎ 561 33 33) is Stazione Porta Nuova, Piazza Carlo Felice. Regular trains connect Turin with Milan, Aosta, Venice, Genoa and Rome.

Car & Motorbike Turin is a major autostrada junction. The A4 connects with Milan, the A5 with Aosta, the A6 with Savona and the Ligurian Coast and the A21 with Piacenza. If you're heading for Genoa, take the A21 and then the A7 rather than the expensive and sometimes dangerous A6. For hitchhikers, the SS29 heads for Asti, the SS24 for Susa and the SS11 east for Milan.

Getting Around
To/From the Airport The SADEM bus company (☎ 311 16 16) runs a service to the airport every half-hour from the bus station.

Bus & Tram The city boasts a dense network of buses and trams run by Trasporti Torinesi (☎ 53 83 76), which has an information booth at Stazione Porta Nuova. Day tickets (L9000) are available but would mean using a lot of buses to justify the investment.

The company also runs Navigazione sul Po (☎ 576 42 22), which operates boat rides on the river from June to September.

Taxi Call ☎ 57 37 or 57 30 if you need a cab.

Car Rental Major rental agencies include Avis (☎ 50 11 07), Corso Turati 15, and Europcar (☎ 650 36 03), Via Madama Cristina 72.

VALLE DI SUSA
West of Turin and easily accessible by car, bus and train, the Valle di Susa takes in the old town of Susa and several ski resorts, including the glamorous but overdeveloped

Sestriere. It is also known as Val. There are some beautiful spots and a few pleasant mountain villages, but they can be thronged in ski season and on weekends. The roads often get clogged with miles of traffic jams on Fridays and Sundays as Turin's weekend escapees pile in and out of the city. Walking possibilities are good, but better in the north and around the Parco Nazionale del Gran Paradiso. The area's telephone code is 0122.

Sacra di San Michele
Perched atop Monte Pirchiriano at the mouth of the Valle di Susa, high above the road from Turin, this brooding Gothic-Romanesque abbey dates to the 11th century. The closest town is Avigliana, a short train ride from Turin, which is connected to the abbey by bus (there are about three a day). A better route is to continue by train to Sant'Ambrogio, at the foot of the hill, and tackle the 90-minute walk up. Check opening times with the APT in Turin before setting out.

Susa
On the busiest route between Turin and France, Susa started life as a Celtic town (a Druid well remains as testimony) before falling under the sway of Rome. The modest Roman ruins make it a pleasant stop on the way to the western ski resorts.

In addition to remains of a Roman **acqueduct**, an **amphitheatre** still in use and the **Arco d'Augusto**, the early 11th-century **Duomo di San Giusto** is a rare Medieval survivor in Piedmont, and finally having some long overdue restoration.

Albergo Sole (☎ 62 21 92) in Piazza IV Novembre has doubles for under L50,000, but is not always open. *Albergo Stazione* (☎ 62 22 26), Corso Stati Uniti 2, is somewhat more expensive but more likely to be operating.

Sapar buses (☎ 62 20 15) connect Susa with Turin, Oulx and other valley destinations.

Exilles
Worth a brief look is the forbidding **fort** overlooking the quiet village of Exilles, 14

km west of Susa. Of obscure medieval origins, its military role only ended in 1943. It's generally open from 2 to 7 pm, but you should check with an APT office in the area before making a special trip. Sapar buses stop here.

Oulx

Nothing much in itself, Oulx is a good place to get information on skiing, hiking and other activities throughout the Valle di Susa. The APT office (☎ 83 15 96), Piazza Garambois 5, here is the main tourist office for the valley and can help with lodgings, Settimana Bianca packages and walking details. Regular trains run from Turin, and Sapar buses connect with destinations along the Susa and Chisone valleys.

Cesana Torinese

Eleven km from the resort of Sestriere, Cesana makes a much cosier base than its better known neighbour, and offers several cheaper accommodation possibilities. The APT office (☎ 85 80 09) is at Piazza V Amedeo 3. Three or four daily buses make the run up to Susa and back.

Sestriere

Conceived by Mussolini and built by the Agnelli clan (of Fiat fame), Sestriere is a cultural desert that has grown to become one of Europe's most fashionable ski resorts. The mountains here are pleasant indeed, and there are several villages on either side of Sestriere that could make more appealing bases, unless of course you feel a need to be seen here in your après-ski garb.

The APT office (☎ 75 54 44) is at Piazza Agnelli 5, and has information on skiing and accommodation. Summer activities include hiking, free climbing and mountain bike riding. Out of season, only a couple of three-star hotels remain open.

Buses connect the resort with Oulx, Susa and Turin.

SOUTHERN PIEDMONT

The roads south of Turin to Liguria mark the divide between the low hills and dull plains of most of eastern Piedmont from the slopes that rise in the west to the southern French Alps. It is an area little frequented by foreign tourists, where numerous valleys slice paths west towards France (only a few offer access across the border). Not as high as the mountains of the north, the area still provides good hiking opportunities, and skiing in winter.

Cuneo

Cuneo is a mildly interesting provincial capital and transport junction between Turin and Liguria. The old town lies in the northern wedge of the city, presenting a faded if pleasant picture, although there is not too much to delay the sightseer. Cuneo is useful as a base for exploring the southern valleys of Piedmont, especially for those without their own transport. If you have wheels, a better alternative is Saluzzo, 33 km north.

The bus station is handily located at the northern tip of the old town, which peters out at the vast central square, Piazza di Duccio Galimberti. The train station lies to the southwest on Piazzale Libertà.

Information The APT office (☎ 6 66 15), Corso Nizza 17, has extensive information about the province. The town's telephone code is 0171, and there are Telecom offices on Via Massimo d'Azegli and Via Carlo Emanuele III.

Places to Stay & Eat *Albergo Ciriegia* (☎ 69 27 03), Corso Nizza 11, has decent singles/doubles from L40,000/60,000 and triples from L80,000; *Albergo Cavallo Nero* (☎ 69 20 17), Via Seminario 8, charges the same, or L20,000 more with a bathroom.

This hotel also has a restaurant, or you could try a pizza at the cosy *Ristorante Capri* on the other side of Piazza Seminario. *Ristorante Tre Citroni*, Via Bonelli 2, is more formal, with set menus for L65,000. Piazza di Duccio Galimberti and Corso Nizza are the best places to look for cafés.

Getting There & Away Cuneo's big plus is transport. There are regular trains to Saluzzo, Turin, San Remo, Ventimiglia, and Nice in

France. There is a second train station for the Cuneo-Gesso line, serving small towns in the valley. Various bus companies run services to Saluzzo, Turin, Imperia, Savona and along the Valle Stura. By car, take the A6 from Turin towards Savona and exit at Fossano, or the SS20.

Around Cuneo

Among the valleys that radiate westwards from Cuneo, the **Valle Stura** (the longest) leads to the Colle della Maddalena crossing into France. The surrounding mountains offer skiing when snowfalls are good, and several rifugi for trekkers. The same can be said of the bare rock mountain slopes that feature along the **Valle Gesso**.

Another attractive option is the **Valle Maira**, which starts to the north-west of Cuneo. **Dronero**, a pretty medieval village with houses topped by precarious looking grey slate roofs, marks the start of the climb upwards and west.

Saluzzo

About 60 km south of Turin, Saluzzo warrants a one-day trip and is a good base for closer exploration of the valleys and castles of southern Piedmont. Once a feisty medieval stronghold, it maintained its independence until the Savoys won it by treaty with France in 1601. One of the town's better known sons was General Carlo dalla Chiesa, whose implacable pursuit of the Mafia lead to his assassination in 1982.

Information The APT office (☎ 0175-4 67 10), Via Griselda 6, has a range of information about the surrounding valleys. The telephone code is 0175.

Things to See Cobbled lanes twist upwards to La Castiglia, the sombre castle (now a prison) of the Marchesi, Saluzzo's medieval rulers. La Salita al Castello is lined with houses from the period. Commanding views over the old town's burnt-red tiled rooftops is the **Torre Civica**, a restored 15th-century tower that was part of the old *municipio* (town administration). Pass the contempo-

rary church and convent of San Giovanni on the same square and you reach the **Museo Civico di Casa Cavassa**, a fine example of a 16th-century noble's residence. It's open Wednesday to Sunday and admission is L4000.

Places to Stay & Eat *Albergo Luna* (☎ 4 37 07), Via Martiri della Liberazione 10, has singles/doubles from L25,000/40,000. Oddly, it closes on Sundays. *Albergo Persico* (☎ 4 12 13), Vicolo Mercati 10, has rooms for L55,000/70,000, and failing that the *Perpoin* (☎ 4 23 83), Via Spielberg 19, is decent.

The latter has its own restaurant, and there are plenty of little pizzerias scattered over the lower part of town. If you want to lash out, try *La Taverna di Porti Scür* (meaning 'dark porticoes'), Via A Volta, a dim, low-ceiling restaurant with medieval ambience. For a drink in style, head for the *Bistrot La Drancia*, in the shadow of La Castiglia's walls.

Getting There & Away There are regular bus and train connections from Turin and Cuneo. Buses also run up the Po valley.

Around Saluzzo

A few minutes drive south of Saluzzo is one of the more easily accessible castles in the region, that of **Manta** – enquire at the APT office for up-to-date information.

The Po river dog-legs north a few km west of Saluzzo, and the valley westward to its source, below **Monviso** (3841 metres) is an enticing excursion. Should you want to hike around the mountain, there are rifugi, and a few hotels in the nearby town of **Crissolo**. Take your passport in case you want to cross into France.

Alba

Solid red-brick towers rise above the heart of Alba, a wine town that has conserved enough of its medieval past to make it a worthwhile stop.

First settled in neolithic times, Alba's modern claims to fame includes cooking with truffles, and a Palio on donkey-back – inaugurated in 1932 as a snub to nearby Asti, eternal rival in all things including wine production.

Towards the end of the WW II, the town's citizens proclaimed Alba an independent republic for 23 days after partisans liberated it from the Germans.

Orientation & Information The tumbledown Piazza del Risorgimento, dominated by the 15th-century Cattedrale di San Lorenzo leads into Via Vittorio Emanuele II, Alba's main street and a busy pedestrian zone, which is in turn capped by the ample Piazza Savona, whose porticoed footpaths are lined with chic cafés.

The APT office (☎ 3 58 33), Piazza Medford, can help with suggestions on wineries to seek out in the region. They might be able to advise which of the many privately owned castles and medieval manors in the surrounding Langhe and Roero regions can be visited.

Places to Stay & Eat The cheapest place in town is *Albergo Rovej* (☎ 28 43 06), Via Silvio Pellico, where singles/doubles cost L35,000/50,000. *Albergo Piemonte* (☎ 44 13 54), Piazza Rossetti 6, has rooms for L40,000/60,000. There are several cafés and trattorias on Piazza Savona and along Via Vittorio Emanuele II.

Getting There & Away Alba can be reached by bus from Turin, Cuneo and Asti (30 km to the north-east).

Cin Cin

Only 10 km west of Alba, one of Italy's best known drinks, Cinzano, now has its own museum. At the Cinzano cellars in Santa Vittoria d'Alba you can inspect posters, photos and all sorts of artefacts chronicling the history of a company that started as a small distilling operation in the hills of Turin more than two centuries ago. The Cinzano family got into the vermouth-making business on an industrial scale in the mid-1800s, which really took off when the company's representatives started travelling the globe early this century. Publicity has been the key to world-wide success.

EASTERN PIEDMONT

Asti

On the third Sunday of every September, 21

PIEDMONT

Mushroom Magic

When autumn comes to Piedmont, it's time to *andare a funghi* – go mushroom-picking. Mushrooms, especially the popular *porcini* and the much harder to come by *tartufo* (truffle), also known as *tuber magnatum*, are considered something of a delicacy. So much so that the town of Alba celebrates the Fiera del Tartufo for a couple of weeks each mid-October. This is a delightful occasion for the palate, when Alba's best wines and rival vintages from Asti and the Langhe are brought out to accompany mouth-watering mushroom and truffle recipes that date to the 17th century. The markets overflow with great slabs of porcini – some as big as two kg have been found by avid pickers and that's a lot of mushroom. Porcini and other specimens sprout in the dark oak and chestnut forest floors on sunny days immediately following a good burst of rain. Truffles, on the other hand, incubate for several months, and those who know where to look often take specially trained truffle-sniffing dogs. If you head off mushroom picking yourself, it is well to let someone in the know examine them before you gobble them up – many species are dangerous. ■

jockeys spur their horses around a chaotic course in the regional wine centre of Asti; the prize a banner known as the Palio. The medieval horse race, revived in 1967 and dating back to the 13th century, comes at the end of a week-long wine festival. The largely flat lands around Asti produce grapes that make some of Italy's top sparkling wines.

Settled long before it was made a Roman colony in 89 BC, the town has had a more turbulent history than its subdued aspect might suggest. An independent city state in the 13th and 14th centuries, it subsequently was passed around between Spain, Austria, Napoleon's France and finally the Savoys, prior to unification.

Information The APT office (☎ 0141-53 03 57), Piazza Alfieri 34, in the centre of town, has information about the town and can assist with itineraries for the wine areas. The telephone code is 0141 and there's a Telecom office on the same square.

Things to See & Do The **cathedral**, Piazza Cattedrale, is a large 14th-century Gothic construction. The city's other noteworthy church is the **Chiesa di San Secondo**, Asti's patron saint. During the late 13th century, the region became one of Italy's wealthiest, and some 100 towers of the period stand as reminders of its glorious past.

Places to Stay & Eat September is a difficult time to find a place to stay. The nearest camping ground is *Campeggio Umberto Cagni* (☎ 27 12 38), Via Valmanera 78, off Corso Volta. *Albergo Antico Paradiso* (☎ 21 43 85), Corso Torino 329, has singles/doubles with shower from L40,000/55,000 and the *Cavour* (☎ 53 02 22), Piazza Marconi 12, has singles/doubles for L40,000/65,000, or L50,000/75,000 with a bathroom.

Asti is something of a culinary centre and has restaurants to suit most budgets; try on and around Piazza Alfieri or pick up a list from the APT office.

Getting There & Away Trains run to Turin and Genoa, and the region's bus station is just near the train station. By car, you can take the A21 Turin-Piacenza autostrada. It is also an easy drive from Genoa on good roads, starting with the SS35.

NORTHERN PIEDMONT

Head north-east from Turin towards Milan, and you'll pass through wide plains that largely typify eastern Piedmont – some of it so flat and wet it's good for growing rice, as is evident on the approaches to Vercelli. Take a left here and aim north; the landscape quickly changes as the lower slopes preceding the Swiss Alps come into view. Skiing (even in summer!), hiking and whitewater rafting are among the treats on offer among the valleys spreading west and north, while to the east you can get a taste of Lago Maggiore, the first of the string of lakes across northern Italy. See the Lombardy chapter for further information.

Varallo & the Valsesia

Varallo marks the beginning of the Valsesia, one of the less crowded Piedmontese valleys. The APT della Valsesia (☎ 0163-5 12 80), Corso Roma 38, has plenty of pamphlets on every conceivable aspect of the area. It's open daily (mornings only on Sunday and Monday). The telephone code for the area is 0163.

Albergo Monte Rosa (☎ 5 11 00), at Via Regaldi 4 in Varallo, is a delightful place and all the rooms face tree-covered hills. Immaculate singles/doubles cost L35,000/70,000.

Varallo makes sense as a starting point if only by virtue of being a railhead and bus line junction. A narrow winding road also links the valley directly with the pretty **Lago d'Orta**. Again, see the Lombardy chapter for further information.

The Valley to Monte Rosa From Varallo, at 450 metres, you can follow the valley up towards Monte Rosa and the Swiss frontier, where some peaks exceed 4000 metres. **Alagna** is the last town along the valley, and you can get detailed local skiing information there at Monterosa Ski. Some 20 rifugi dot the area, the Capanna Osservatorio Regina Mergherita at Punta Gnifetti being the highest at 4559 metres. A cable car at Alagna climbs to Punta Indren (3260 metres), from where it is possible (in summer at least) to hike to various of the several peaks. Get expert local advice on what can be safely undertaken before setting out, as some of the trails require expert Alpine skills and gear.

Some 25 Alpine guides are on the books at Alagna – enquire at the IAT tourist office (☎ 0163-92 29 88), Piazza Grober.

Domodossola

The last main stop before Switzerland, Domodossola might once have been an attractive pre-Alpine town, but the suburban spread and hotels have ruined the effect. Those intending to explore the surrounding valleys should make haste to do so and leave this place behind them.

Information The APT delle Ossola office (☎ 0324-48 13 08), Corso P Ferraris 49, has detailed information about walking and skiing. It's open Monday to Friday from 9 am to noon and 2 to 5 pm. Most resorts are well organised and offer Settimana Bianca packages. The Comunità Montane Valle Ossola (☎ 4 63 91) is also a useful place to get information. The telephone code in the area is 0324.

Places to Stay & Eat *Albergo Domus* (☎ 24 23 23), Via Cuccioni 12, is about the town's cheapest hotel, and very central, with singles/doubles from L30,000/50,000. *Albergo la Pendola* (☎ 24 37 04), is farther away from the centre and train station. It has singles for L32,000 or doubles with a bathroom for L70,000. Both have restaurants. Otherwise, the *Trattoria Romana*, Via Binda 16, is not unreasonable and specialises in French and Roman cuisine.

Getting There & Away Trains regularly run to Milan, and Novara for Turin. You can also board international trains to Switzerland, France, Germany and even Czechoslovakia from here.

The bus station is in front of the train

station. Milan is 125 km south-east, and Turin 168 km south-west of Domodossola.

Valle d'Aosta

Covering a mere 3262 square km and with a population of only 117,000, the Valle d'Aosta is the smallest of the Italian regions, but also one of the wealthiest. The Valdestans, as they are called, still speak the Franco-Provençal patois, and French is afforded equal rights with Italian. To the east of the region, villagers cling to the German dialect, Tich. The valley has always been an important passageway through the Alps and is lined with castles. The opening of the Monte Bianco (Mont Blanc) tunnel in 1965, which connects Courmayeur in the west to the French resort of Chamonix, turned what had been a quiet valley into a major road-freight thoroughfare and one of Europe's premier skiing areas. Unfortunately, overdevelopment and pollution soon followed, although you can certainly still 'get away from it all' in the valleys running off Valle d'Aosta.

Valle d'Aosta enjoys self-governing status, stemming from its binational origins, which means 90% of local taxes are spent in the province.

The region shares, with France, Europe's highest mountain, Monte Bianco (Mont Blanc, 4807 metres) and, with Switzerland, the Matterhorn (Monte Cervino, 4478 metres). It also takes in Monte Rosa (4638 metres) and the Gran Paradiso (4061 metres), which it shares with Piedmont. Its resort towns – Courmayeur, Breuil-Cervinia, La Thuile, Gressoney St Jean and Cogne – and valleys offer a feast of year-round activities. Some towns, such as Breui l-Cervinia, are anonymous, custom-built resort towns but others, such as Cogne, retain their mountain village character.

There is plenty of good hiking in areas such as the Parco Nazionale del Gran Paradiso. More adventurous (and expert) mountaineers might want to tackle Monte Bianco. It is possible to reach 3462 metres

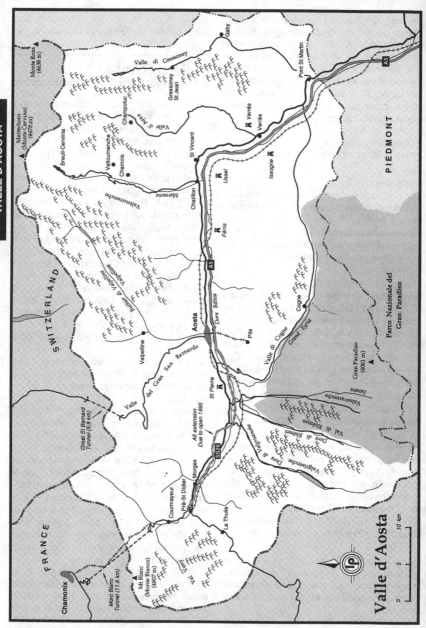

VALLE D'AOSTA

Valle d'Aosta

by cable car, from where trekkers can set off across the ice to the peak (4810 metres), although this is for expert climbers only – tourists should stay very close to the rifugio. Plenty of good information is available at the tourist offices in the region about walking trails and mountain rifugi and huts. Many trails will take you to high altitudes, so it is necessary to be well-prepared with the correct clothing and footwear, good maps and other essentials. For advice on what to take on long treks see the section on Trekking in the Dolomites in the Trentino-Alto Adige chapter.

Human settlement in the Valle d'Aosta dates to 3000 BC and Neolithic and early Bronze Age remains have been discovered. Early Roman sites dot the valley, and Aosta is known as the Rome of the Alps.

The cuisine of the Valle d'Aosta makes liberal use of the local cheese, Fontina, a curious cross between Gouda and Brie. Traditional dishes include *valpellineuntze*, a thick soup of cabbage, bread, beef broth and Fontina, and *carbonada con polenta*, traditionally made with the meat of the chamoix, although beef is now generally used. *Mocetta* (dried beef) is popular. The valley also boasts numerous small, government-subsidised cooperative vineyards, most producing whites, reds and *rosatos* (rosé). These wines are generally dry and fruity.

AOSTA

Aosta is the capital and only major city of the region, and has a population of about 37,000. It lies at the centre of the valley, with the Dora Baltea river on its southern boundary and the Buthier river on its eastern side, and is the transport hub for the region. It has limited attractions, but is a jumping-off point to the region's 11 valleys and their resorts.

Orientation

From Piazza Manzetti, outside the train station, Via G Carducci, to the west, and Via Giorgio Carrel, to the east, follow the Roman wall around the city. Viale della Stazione and Via Olletti lead from the train station into the town centre. The former goes to Piazza Narbonne, which houses the main post office and

bus station, and the latter to Piazza Chanoux, the main square.

The city is laid out on a grid following the Roman pattern and most of the historic centre is closed to traffic. Via de Tillier, west of Piazza Chanoux, is Aosta's main boulevard and has a good selection of restaurants, bars, cafés and fashion shops.

Information

Tourist Office The APT office (☎ 0165-23 66 27) is at Piazza Chanoux 8 and is open daily from 8 am to 1 pm and 3 to 8 pm. It is open on Sunday year-round from 8 am to 1 pm and also during the winter and summer high seasons from 3 to 8 pm. It has information on skiing conditions and cheap package deals and can assist with accommodation. The Valle d'Aosta APT has an office in Rome, at Via Sistina 3 (☎ 06-474 41 04).

Money Exchange booths are located in Piazza Chanoux and there are banks along Viale della Stazione.

Post & Telecommunications The main post office is on Piazza Narbonne and is open Monday to Friday from 8.15 am to 7.30 pm and Saturday to 1 pm. The post code for central Aosta is 11100.

There is a Telecom office at Viale della Pace 9 which is open Monday to Friday from 8.15 am to 12.15 pm and 2.30 to 6.30 pm, Saturday from 8.45 am to 12.15 pm and 3 to 6.30 pm and Sunday from 8 am to 3 pm. The telephone code is 0165.

Emergency Call ☎ 113 for immediate police attendance or contact the questura (☎ 2 37 11), Via Battaglione Aosta 169. For medical attention, call ☎ 30 41, or the Ospedale Regionale (☎ 4 14 00), Viale Ginevra. For an ambulance, call ☎ 30 44 51.

Things to See

The main attractions are the Roman ruins. The **Arco d'Augusto**, is placed in a straight axis between the Porta Pretoria (the main gate to the Roman city) and the Buthier river bridge at the end of Via Anselmo. The arch

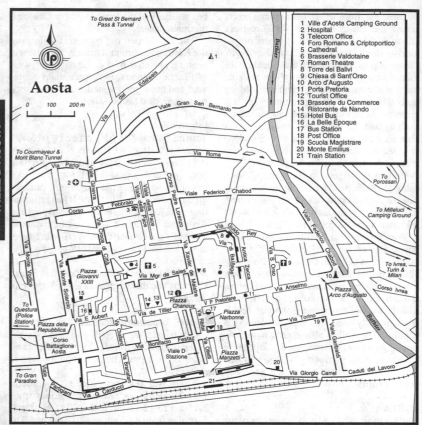

To Great St Bernard
Pass & Tunnel

Aosta

0   100   200 m

To Courmayeur &
Mont Blanc Tunnel

To
Porossan

To Milleluci
Camping Ground

To Ivrea,
Turin &
Milan

Piazza
Giovanni
XXIII

To
Questura
(Police
Station)

Piazza della
Repubblica

Corso
Battaglione
Aosta

To Gran
Paradiso

Piazza
Chanoux

Piazza
Narbonne

Piazza
Arco d'Augusto

Corso Ivrea

Piazza
Manzetti

Via Giorgio Carrel   Caduti del Lavoro

1   Ville d'Aosta Camping Ground
2   Hospital
3   Telecom Office
4   Foro Romano & Criptoportico
5   Cathedral
6   Brasserie Valdotaine
7   Roman Theatre
8   Torre dei Balivi
9   Chiesa di Sant'Orso
10 Arco d'Augusto
11 Porta Pretoria
12 Tourist Office
13 Brasserie du Commerce
14 Ristorante da Nando
15 Hotel Bus
16 La Belle Époque
17 Bus Station
18 Post Office
19 Scuola Magistrare
20 Monte Emilius
21 Train Station

bears a crucifix, added during medieval times. Walk the 300 metres westwards from the bridge to the gate and head north along Via di Baillage to the **Roman theatre**. Part of its 22-metre-high façade remains intact and performances are often held in the well-preserved lower section. All that remains of the **Foro Romano**, another couple of blocks westwards beneath the Piazza Giovanni XXIII, is a colonnaded walkway known as the **Criptoportico**. The **Torre dei Balivi**, at the corner of the Roman wall, was used until recently as a prison.

The **cathedral**, also in Piazza Giovanni XXIII, has a neoclassical façade which belies the impressive Gothic interior. The carved wooden choir stalls are particularly beautiful. Two floor mosaics in the church, dating from the 12th to 14th centuries, are also worth studying. The cathedral has a museum with religious treasures from throughout the region.

The **Chiesa di Sant'Orso** in Via Sant' Orso dates from the 10th century but was altered on several occasions, notably in the 15th century, when Giorgi di Challant of the ruling family ordered the original frescoes covered and a new roof installed. Remnants of the frescoes can be viewed by climbing up into the cavity between the original and

15th-century ceilings. Ask the church attendant for a tour. The interior and the magnificently carved choir are Gothic and recent excavations have unearthed the remains of an earlier church, possibly from the 8th century. The Romanesque cloister with ornately carved capitals representing biblical scenes is to the right of the church.

Activities
Rock climbing can be conducted on the rocks known as Adrénaline, Polyester and Lipstick. For information, call Up & Down (☎ 3 50 26) or Cooperativa Interguide (☎ 4 09 39), Via Monte Emilius 13. Centro Volo Valle d'Aosta (☎ 36 24 42) can set you up for hang-gliding or paragliding.

The tourist office can advise on walking trails or put you in contact with an Alpine guide if you prefer not to go it alone.

Festivals
Each October thousands of Valdestans come together to watch cow fights. Known traditionally as the Bataille des Reines (Battle of the Queens), the event is organised along the lines of a beauty contest. Knockouts start in March, when locals from across the region prime their best bovines for battle, and end with the finals on the third Sunday in October, when the queen of the cows is crowned. This might seem a bit strange, but it is a tradition from the days when cows returning from mountain fields would tussle with each other. The losing cow is not injured and the match ends when one pulls away. The queen sells for millions of lire.

The Foire de Sant' Orso, the annual wood fair held on 30-31 January in honour of the town's patron saint, brings together craftspeople from all over the valley who display their carvings and then present an item to the saint at Chiesa di Sant'Orso. It is held near the Porta Pretoria.

Places to Stay
Accommodation in Aosta is generally expensive and difficult to find, particularly during the high seasons around Christmas and Easter. Cheaper and more pleasant lodgings can be found in the hinterland, which is usually accessible by bus. Check with the APT. There are no hostels in the region.

There are camping facilities at *Ville d'Aosta* (☎ 3 28 78), Viale Gran San Bernardo 76, just north of the town. Another camping ground, *Milleluci* (☎ 4 42 74), is about one km east of Aosta and can be reached by bus No 11.

In Aosta, try the hotel *La Belle Époque* (☎ 26 22 76), Via d'Avise 18 (off Via E Aubert), which has singles/doubles for L32,000/ 60,000, with slightly cheaper rates in the low season. *Mochettaz* (☎ 4 37 06), about one km east of the town centre at Corso Ivrea 107, has singles/doubles for L27,000 /45,000. *Monte Emilius* (☎ 3 56 92), Via Giorgio Carrel 9, has singles/doubles for L28,000 /45,000. *Hotel Bus* (☎ 4 36 45), Via Malherbes 18, on the south side of Piazza Giovanni XXIII, is at the better end of the scale and has singles/doubles for L90,000/125,000; rates are cheaper in the low season. If you have a car, try *Hirondelle* (☎ 5 11 10), which is eight km into the hills from Aosta at Arpuilles and has great views of the city and mountains. Singles/doubles start at L40,000/70,000.

Almost all hotels in Aosta offer Settimana Bianca packages.

Places to Eat
At the cheaper end of the scale, Aosta has several self-service restaurants that are good and well-patronised. *Scuola Magistrare*, Viale Garibaldi, is open for lunch only.

For traditional food, *Ristorante da Nando*, Via de Tillier 41, is reasonably priced, as is *Brasserie du Commerce*, Via de Tillier 10. At the top end is *Brasserie Valdotaine*, Via Xavier de Maistre 8.

Boch, Piazza Chanoux, has Aosta's best gelati and is where the local youth hang out, while *Café Nazionale*, at the other end of the piazza, is where their parents drink coffee.

Things to Buy
Tradition has it that Sant'Orso gave carved shoes known as *sabo* to the city's poor. Valdestans continue to carve shoes, tiny houses and ceremonial pots which are still widely

used. Shops throughout the city, particularly along Via Porte Pretoriane, sell these goods.

Getting There & Away

Air Aosta has a small airport which services commuter flights. The airports at Turin and Geneva are both about an hour away by car.

Bus Buses to several major European cities leave from the bus station (☎ 26 20 27) in Via Carrel, in front of the train station. There is an extensive regional bus service connecting Aosta with most resorts in the region, although some services are considerably reduced out of season.

Train The town is serviced by trains from most parts of Italy, via Turin and Milan. Most travellers to and from Milan must change trains at Chivass. There is a limited train service from Aosta to Pré-St Didier, about five km from Courmayeur.

Car & Motorbike The A5 from Turin and Milan terminates east of the city and continues along its northern edge as Via Roma and then Via Parigi, which connects with the Mont Blanc (Monte Bianco) tunnel. Viale Gran San Bernardo, also to the north, connects Aosta with the Great St Bernard Tunnel and Switzerland. A continuation of the A5, bypassing Aosta to the south, is expected to open in late 1995, but only as far as Morgex, two towns before Courmayeur. Aosta has several large car parks, including one opposite the train station.

Hitching Hitchhikers should have no trouble on Viale Gran San Bernardo, Via Roma or Via Parigi, although hitchhiking is not recommended as it can be unsafe.

Getting Around

The town is quite small and all sites are easily reached on foot.

The SVAP bus No 1 connects the train station with Piazza Arco d'Augusto and Piazza Chanoux in the town centre. Coop Taxis can be reached on ☎ 4 43 55.

AROUND AOSTA

Apart from the slopes, the Aosta region is worth visiting for its impressive Romanesque and Gothic castles. The valley is virtually a living museum tracing the development of the Alpine castle, but seeing them really requires a car. At the few castles open to the public, you must visit in groups of about 25, which can mean waiting until more people turn up. For tickets and opening hours, enquire at the APT office.

Each castle is within view of the next, and messages used to be flagged along the valley. Heading east from Aosta is the magnificently restored **Castello di Fénis**, formerly of the Challant family and featuring rich frescoes, as well as period graffiti. The ruined **Castello d'Ussel** is close to the town of St Vincent, and past the town is the **Castello di Verrès**. About one km south of the Dora river, below the town of Verrès is the **Castello d'Issogne**, built in the 15th century and recently restored. Towards the Monte Bianco (Mont Blanc) tunnel from Aosta, near the village of Introd, is the **Castello di Saint Pierre**, which also houses a museum of natural history.

Probably the only reason to visit **St Vincent**, Valle d'Aosta's second-biggest city, is for its casino and as a stopping-off point for the Valle d'Ayas and Valtournenche, which leads to the Matterhorn.

PILA

This is the closest resort to Aosta (about 18 km south) and prices are quite reasonable. There is a village at Pila, but most services, such as the tourist office, police and medical services, are handled from Aosta. The telephone code is 0165.

Activities

Skiing Pila is among the largest ski areas in the valley, with more than 80 km of runs, including about 10 km for cross-country skiing. It is serviced by 15 lifts, including four cable ways, one of which connects the village with Aosta. It offers challenging and difficult black runs and has a competition slalom course, but also caters for beginners with many easy runs. The highest slope reaches 2700 metres, in the shadow of Gran Paradiso.

Hiking This is not one of the best areas for walking if you like high Alpine country, but the lower slopes leading down into the Dora Baltea valley provide picturesque and easy walks. There are only two rifugi in the Charvensod area a few km south of Aosta, with one open all year. Some of the lifts operate in summer for walkers or day trippers.

Places to Stay

It is cheaper to stay in Aosta than it is in Pila. There are camping facilities at *Soleil et Neige* (☎ 5 99 48), which is open all year, about seven km from the resort. *Hotel la Nouva* (☎ 0165-52 10 05) has singles/doubles from L55,000/80,000. *Chacaril*, (☎ 52 12 15) has rooms for L42,000/84,000. The best Settimana Bianca deals are in Aosta. See the Places to Stay section.

Getting There & Away

Two roads, one from Aosta and the other from Gressan, a town about six km west of Aosta, lead to Pila. A cable car connects Aosta with the village. SVAP buses Nos 4 and 5 go from Aosta to Charvensod and Gressan respectively, but there is no bus service to Pila.

COURMAYEUR & MONT BLANC (MONTE BIANCO)

With much of the original village intact and set against the backdrop of Mont Blanc, Courmayeur is one of the more picturesque of the skiing resorts in Valle d'Aosta. It is also one of the most expensive. Out of season, wealthy Milanese and Turinese women leave their fur coats in a local furrier's vault – minks and ermines too valuable to be worn in the streets of their home cities. The resort has more than 140 km of downhill and cross-country skiing runs and a feast of summer activities, including skiing, horse riding, hang-gliding, canoeing and 280 km of mountain walking trails. A cable-car service leaves from La Palud, near Courmayeur, and will

take you up to Punta Helbronner (3462 metres) on Mont Blanc. It is also possible to organise guided treks up the mountain. See the Activities section for details.

Information

Tourist Office The APT office (☎ 84 20 60) is at Piazzale Monte Bianco and is open Monday to Saturday from 9 am to 12.30 pm and 3 to 6.30 pm and Sunday from 9.30 am to 12.30 pm. The Associazione Operatori Turistici del Monte Bianco (☎ 84 23 70), Piazzale Monte Bianco 3, can assist with accommodation.

Emergency For police assistance, phone ☎ 113, or go to the questura (☎ 84 42 35) at Strada della Margherita. For medical attention and ambulance, phone ☎ 84 25 60 or go to the Pronto Soccorso at the Ospedale Regionale d'Aosta (☎ 4 14 00).

Activities

Skiing There is skiing year-round on Monte Bianco. The Ski Club Courmayeur Monte Bianco (☎ 84 24 41) is at Piazzale Monte Bianco, and there is a skiing school (☎ 84 24 77) at Strada Regionale 51. The best bet if you are skiing only is to book a Settimana Bianca package through an agent such as CIT. Most ski runs, chair lifts and ski lifts can be reached via the Courmayeur, Dolonne and Val Veny cable cars. For details, check with the APT or the cable-way station in Val Veny (☎ 84 35 66), or Cableways Mont Blanc in La Palud (☎ 8 99 25).

Walking, Trekking & Climbing A basic map of walking trails in the Valdigne and on Mont Blanc is available from the APT office and, if you plan to remain on the lower slopes, this is probably good enough. If you walk the higher trails on Monte Bianco, or want to walk on the glaciers, it is strongly recommended that you be properly prepared and equipped, or are accompanied by a guide. The cable car system, which starts at La Palud and brings skiers, climbers, trekkers, adventurers and tourists alike to Punta Helbronner means, you can reach very high altitude very easily. Many people are completely unprepared for what awaits them at almost 3500 metres. Even if the weather is sweltering in the valley, it could be minus 10° at Punta Helbronner: so be prepared with heavy winter clothes.

The best time to head up in the cable cars is very early in the morning because by early afternoon heavy weather usually descends on the summit area.

You can continue from Punta Helbronner down to Chamonix in France (remember to bring your passport and check if you need a visa to enter France). The return fare from La Palud to Punta Helbronner is L48,000. If you want to make the full trip to Chamonix, you can buy a ticket at Mont Blanc Tour Operator, Piazzale Monte Bianco 3, in Courmayeur. The return trip is by bus.

The Società guide di Courmayeur (mountain guide association) (☎ 84 20 64), Piazza Henry 2, organises activities including rock climbing courses and a seven-day guided trek up Mont Blanc. The Mountain & Alpine Guide Association can be contacted on ☎ 84 20 64.

There are many rifugi and huts located along walking trails in the mountains around Courmayeur. They are marked on all walking maps. Those offering hotel-style service and accommodation are usually only open during the summer months. Unattended huts, known as *bivacchi*, are open year-round. The APT publishes a guide to the different huts.

Mountain Biking To rent a bike, go to Noleggio Ulisse (☎ 84 22 55), in front of the Courmayeur chair lift, or Club des Sports (☎ 8 95 70), in Planpincieux.

Other Activities The Scuola di Canoa e Rafting Courmayeur (☎ 80 00 88) can advise on canoeing. If you want to go ballooning, contact the Club Aérostatique Mont Blanc (☎ 76 55 25).

Places to Stay & Eat
During peak seasons, accommodation in Courmayeur is very expensive if you aren't on a package deal, but the towns along the

valleys, of La Palud, Dolonne, Entrèves, La Saxe, Plan Ponquet, Val Ferret, Pré-St Didier and Morgex, offer reasonably priced rooms. Contact the APT office or the hotel association for assistance. See the Information section.

Campers can head for *Cai-uget Monte Bianco* (☎ 8 92 15) in Val Veny, and *Val Veny-Cuignon* (☎ 84 28 61), both within easy reach of Courmayeur. In Courmayeur, try the *Serena* (☎ 84 22 63), Via Villair 3, which has rooms from L40,000/54,000. In La Palud there is *La Quercia* (☎ 8 99 31), which has doubles from L54,000.

There are good food shops along Via Roma, through the old part of town, if you want to eat in your room or picnic. Most restaurants are also along Via Roma. *Café des Guides*, Viale Monte Bianco 2, is a popular spot for a snack.

Getting There & Away
Three trains a day from Aosta terminate at Pré-St Didier, with bus connections to the main bus station at Piazzale Monte Bianco, outside the tourist office. Courmayeur is serviced by long haul buses from Milan, Turin and Geneva. Local buses connect the resort with Aosta, as well as surrounding towns and villages. By car, Courmayeur is reached from Aosta on the SS26. The trip from Chamonix through the Mont Blanc tunnel for a small car costs L30,000.

VALTOURNENCHE
Stretching from the Valle d'Aosta to the Matterhorn, the Valtournenche takes in several smaller and reasonably priced skiing areas – Antey-St André, Chamois, La Magdeleine and Torgnon – and culminates in the resorts of Valtournenche and Breuil-Cervinia. The latter is the second-largest resort in Valle d'Aosta and is modern, purpose-built, expensive and basically pretty ugly, although it offers some of the best skiing in Europe.

Information
Tourist Office The Matterhorn Central Valley APT office (☎ 0166-4 82 66) is in Antey-Saint-André and the Breuil-Cervinia office (☎ 0166-94 91 36) is at Via Carrel 29. In the

town of Valtournenche, the APT office (☎ 0166-9 20 29) is at Via Roma. The telephone code for the valley is 0166.

Mountain & Alpine Guides For guides, contact the Società Guide del Cervino (☎ 0166-94 81 69), Via Carrel.

Activities

Skiing There are several resorts in the valley, all well equipped with downhill and cross-country runs. From Breuil-Cervinia, eight cable ways and 18 lifts take skiers into breathtaking terrain. Summer skiing is also possible as several cable ways and lifts continue to operate, taking skiers on to the Plateau Rosa. This resort introduced Valle d'Aosta to night skiing, in the Campetto area. For details, contact the tourist office or Ski-lift Crétaz (☎ 94 86 76). Breuil-Cervinia has two skiing schools, the Matterhorn Ski-School (☎ 94 84 51) and Ski-School Cielo Alto (☎ 94 84 51). For night skiing information, call Crétaz Val Furggen (☎ 94 86 76).

Hiking Basic walking maps are available at the tourist office, but if you want to tackle the Matterhorn, make sure you are equipped with a 1:25,000 walking map, as well as suitable clothing, shoes etc.

Places to Stay

There is a camping ground in Valtournenche, called the *Glair-Lago di Maen* (☎ 9 20 77). In Breuil-Cervinia, *Leonardo Carrel* (☎ 94 90 77) has rooms for L38,000/60,000, and *Hotel Sporting* (☎ 94 91 12) has doubles from L140,000. If you're heading there to ski, it is best to arrange a Settimana Bianca package.

Getting There & Away

Buses operate from Aosta to the resorts and most ski areas in the valley. SAVDA (☎ 0165-36 12 44) operates services from Courmayeur, Aosta and Breuil-Cervinia, and from Châtillon to Breuil-Cervinia. Dinotours (☎ 015-222 15) also operates bus services in the valley.

GRAN PARADISO NATIONAL PARK

The Parco Nazionale del Gran Paradiso was Italy's first national park, established in 1922 after Victor Emmanuel II gave his personal hunting reserve to the Italian state. The park incorporates the valleys around the Gran Paradiso (4061 metres), three of which are in the Valle d'Aosta: the Valsavarenche, Val di Rhêmes and the beautiful Valle di Cogne. On the Piedmont side of the mountain the park incorporates the valleys of Soana and Orco. An original priority of the park was the preservation of the ibex, which had been hunted almost to extinction. In 1945 there were only 419 ibex left in the park, but today there are almost 4000.

There are excellent cross-country trails in the Valle di Cogne, but the park is really devoted to summer activities. There are numerous well-marked trails and plenty of rifugi. The main point of departure for the Gran Paradiso mountain is Pont in the Valsavarenche.

If you are interested in a guided four-day trek in the park, which departs from Pont, contact the Società guide del Gran Paradiso-Valsavarenche (☎ 0165-90 57 34) or the tourist office for details. The tourist office in Cogne publishes a brief guide to walking in the Valle di Cogne.

If you are planning to spend some time in the area, the Valle di Cogne is the most picturesque and unspoiled valley and there are good accommodation possibilities in the village of Cogne.

Information

Tourist Offices The Gran Paradiso Mountain Community Tourist Office (☎ 0165-9 50 55) is at Loc Champagne 18, Villeneuve. There is an APT office in Cogne (☎ 0165-7 40 40). Both have excellent information about summer and winter activities. If you're looking for a mountain guide in Cogne, contact the Società guide di Cogne (☎ 0165-7 43 61), Via Cavagnet 10, Cogne. Les Amis du Paradis (the Friends of Paradise Association, ☎ 0165-7 48 35), in Cogne, offers reams of information about the area. The telephone code for the area is 0165.

Emergency For police attendance, call ☎ 113, or in Cogne call ☎ 7 40 26 , and in Villeneuve call ☎ 9 50 25 . First aid is available in Saint-Pierre (☎ 90 38 11) and Cogne (☎ 74 91 07).

Places to Stay

If you're camping, *Al Sole* (☎ 7 42 37) in the Lillaz area, Valle di Cogne, is open all year. In Valsavarenche, *Camping Pont Breuil* (☎ 9 54 58), at Pont, is open only during summer.

Hotels in Cogne include the *Albergo Stambecco* (☎ 7 40 68), Via Clementina 21, which charges around L40,000 per person and is open in summer only. *Du Soleil* (☎ 7 40 33), Viale Cavagnet 24, has singles/doubles from L48,000/92,000. *Hotel au Vieux Grenier* (☎ 7 40 02), Via Limnea Borealis, offers full board for up to L100,000 per person or half board for up to L90,000.

Getting There & Away

All the valleys are reached from Aosta or through the Monte Bianco (Mont Blanc) tunnel by car or a good network of buses. SAVDA (☎ 36 12 44) operates bus No 36 to Rhêmes-Notre-Dame, and Autoservizi Benvenuto (☎ 5 76 68) runs bus No 46 to Valgrisenche. SVAP (☎ 4 11 25) operates bus No 18 to Cogne and No 20 to Valsavarenche. Cogne can also be reached by cable car from Pila (☎ 7 40 08 in Pila).

AROUND MONTE ROSA

The Valle di Gressoney, the first of the Valle d'Aosta's eastern valleys, and the parallel Valle d'Ayas, are dominated by the massive Monte Rosa (4633 metres). Both valleys are picturesque and also very popular in both summer and winter. In Valle di Gressoney, stay in Gressoney-St-Jean, a pretty mountain village by a lake, which has retained its traditional atmosphere. Gressoney-La-Trinitè is higher up the valley and therefore closer to the main walking trails and ski runs, but is these days basically taken over by anonymous tourist facilities. In Valle d'Ayas, the main resort is Champoluc at the head of the valley, but Brusson is also a good option, particularly if you're interested in easy half or one-day walks.

Information

Tourist Offices APT offices are in Champoluc (☎ 0125-30 71 13), Brusson (☎ 0125-30 02 40), La Trinité (☎ 0125-36 61 43) and St Jean (☎ 0125-35 51 85). For information about mountain guides, contact the tourist offices, or the Società guide di Champoluc-Ayas (☎ 0125-30 89 60), at Champoluc, directly.

Telecommunications The telephone code in the lower valley is 0166, but higher up (including Champoluc, Brusson, La Trinité, St Jean and Verrès) it becomes 0125.

Emergency For police attendance call ☎ 113. In Brusson call ☎ 30 01 23, in St Jean call ☎ 35 53 04, and in Verrès call ☎ 92 90 10 .

Places to Stay

For camping, *Sole e Neve* (☎ 0125-30 66 10) in Morenex, Valle d'Ayas, is open all year. In the Valle di Gressoney, try *La Pineta* (☎ 0125-35 53 70) at Gressoney-Saint-Jean, also open all year.

Hotels in the Valle d'Ayas include *Albergo Cre-Forne* (☎ 0125-30 71 97) in Crest, with singles/doubles from L30,000/42,000 and the *Beau Site* (☎ 0125-30 01 44), Via Trois Villages 2, in Brusson.

In Valle di Gressoney, the *Grunes Wasser* (☎ 0125-35 54 03), Via Statale 14, has cheap singles/doubles for L45,000/60,000. *Lyskamm* (☎ 0125-35 54 36), Via Statale 1, has more up-market rooms from L65,000/100,000. At Gressoney-La-Trinitè, try the *Gasthaus Lysjoch* (☎ 0125-36 61 50), Loc. Fohre 4, which has singles/doubles for L60,000/110,000.

Getting There & Away

The train to Aosta stops in St Vincent and Verrès, from where you can catch a bus to either valley. SAVDA (☎ 0165-361244) operates bus No 33 along the Valle di Gressoney and bus No 35 from Verrès to Champoluc. Bus No 40 connects Aosta with Champoluc, via Col de Joux. Leave the A5, SS26 or Aosta-Turin/Milan train at Pont-St-Martin for the Valle di Gressoney, which is also accessible by SAVDA buses.

Lombardy & the Lakes

From the Alps to the lush plains of the Po river, Lombardy's often fractious political history is in part reflected in its geographical diversity. Beyond the financial metropolis of Milan, the region known to Italians as Lombardia is peppered with well-heeled towns that each conserve a distinct character inherited from the city-states period. Mantua, Cremona, Bergamo, Brescia and Pavia exude wealth and style, but the northern clime and perhaps a

degree of orderly self-satisfaction can leave the visitor feeling they are a little staid in comparison with cities farther south. The hard-working people of Milan have made this city Italy's economic and fashion capital; it's a businesslike place that more closely resembles the great cities of northern Europe than its southern Italian cousins.

Italy's richest and most developed region, Lombardy offers its sedulous populace numer-

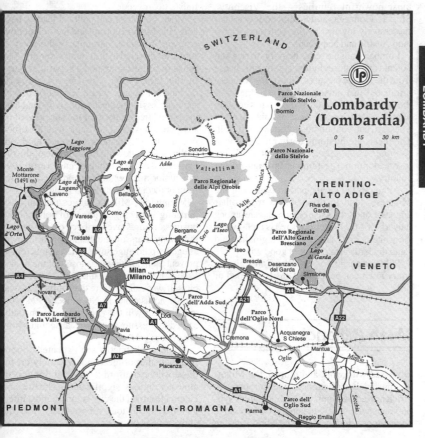

ous escape routes for letting off steam. The most popular of these is the string of enchanting lakes that stretches from Lago d'Orta in the west to Lago di Garda in the east and spills into the neighbouring Veneto.

Lombardy formed part of the Roman province of Gallia Cisalpina (Cisalpine Gaul) before it fell to barbarian tribes and later to the Germanic Lombards (Langobards). Interference by the Franks under Barbarossa in the 12th century came to an abrupt end when the region's cities united under the Lombard League and threw him out. Subsequently the League collapsed and Lombardy was eventually divided up among some of Europe's most powerful families – the Viscontis, Sforzas, Gonzagas and Scaligers. It was later successively invaded by the Venetians, Habsburg Austria and Napoleon.

Lombard cuisine relies heavily on rice and polenta and features butter, cream and cheese from the Alpine pastures. Gorgonzola cheese originated just outside Milan. The pasta of the region is fresh and usually stuffed with winter squash, meat, cheese or spinach or, as a dessert, can contain raisins or candied fruit. The meats are predominantly pork and veal – *cotoletta alla milanese* (fillet of veal fried in breadcrumbs) is famous throughout the country.

Although the locals, and in particular the Milanese, tend to drink wines from other regions, Lombardy's sparkling wines are among Italy's best – the Franciacorta red is mellow and the white is fruity and dry. The region around Lago di Garda also produces good wines.

Public transport is excellent and almost every town can be reached easily by road or rail.

Milan (Milano)

Obsessed with work and money, the Milanese run their busy metropolis with comparative efficiency and aplomb. Indeed, Milan is synonymous with style – the country's economic engine-room, the city is also the world's design capital and a leading fashion centre rivalling Paris.

Just as the Notre Dame cathedral in Paris is a symbol of the French capital, so is Milan's duomo this city's most striking image.

However much Milan feels it should be the country's leading city (and not a few Milanese have a healthy disregard for Rome) it is in fact smaller than the ancient imperial capital, whose population rapidly overtook Milan's after WW II. But Milan is home to Italy's stock market, most of the country's major corporations and the nation's largest concentration of industry. The city and surrounding zone generate almost a quarter of Italy's tax revenue.

Milan's business and political leaders have long railed against corrupt and inefficient government in Rome, particularly the river of subsidies directed to the country's south. The sense of protest spawned a separatist party in the late 1980s, the Lega Lombarda (Lombard League), which campaigned with some success for the creation of a federated Italy that would free the north of the shackles of its southern cousins. The Lega was absorbed into the larger Northern League which, out of the chaos following the collapse of the old parties and the first republic, ended up in 1994 as a junior member in the short-lived government of media magnate Silvio Berlusconi.

Meanwhile, Milan's judges remain busy pursuing a growing pantheon of political and business figures over bribery cases, including many stars of the fashion world, who allegedly paid huge sums to tax inspectors to prevent them looking too closely at the books. Where it will end is unclear – Berlusconi himself was called before the courts to answer similar accusations in November 1994. Any entrepreneur will tell you that everyone submitted to pressure to pay, because that's how the system worked.

Milan is distinctly sophisticated. Shopping, whether of the window variety or, for those who can afford it, the real thing, is of almost religious significance. Theatre and cinema flourish; the city is top on most international music tour programmes, and the club scene is busy.

Food is another of Milan's joys. Immigrants from the rest of Italy and abroad have introduced a surprisingly eclectic cuisine – it's not quite London or New York, but in precious few other Italian cities can you find Korean and African food, or Malaysian specialities side by side with Sicilian, Tuscan and Lombard dishes.

The Milanese are proud of their city, but it can seem daunting and uninviting to outsiders. Make yourself at home by spending a few days wandering the shopping arcades and back streets, the grimy student areas near the central train station, the exclusive boutique area of Monte Napoleone or groovy Navigli to the south. At all costs stay away in August – it is hot and stuffy and the city virtually shuts down as the population goes on holiday.

HISTORY

Milan is said to have been founded by Celtic tribes who settled along the Po river in the 7th century BC. In 222 BC, Rome's legions marched into the territory, defeated the Gallic Insubres and occupied the town, which they knew as Mediolanum ('middle of the plain'). Mediolanum's key position on trade routes between Rome and north-western Europe ensured its continued prosperity and it was here in 313 AD that Constantine I made his momentous edict granting Christians freedom of worship.

The city survived centuries of chaos ushered in by waves of barbarian invasions to form a *comune* in the 11th century. The city-state, governed by a council involving all classes, entered a period of rapid growth, but soon found itself squabbling with neighbouring towns. The Holy Roman emperor Frederick Barbarossa decided to exploit the local conflicts and besieged Milan in 1162. The city and its allies formed the Lega Lombarda and exacted revenge in 1176.

From the mid-13th century, the city was ruled by a succession of important families – the Torrianis, the Viscontis and finally the Sforzas. Under the latter two it enjoyed considerable wealth and power. It came under Spanish rule in 1535, and passed to Austria

under the Treaty of Utrecht of 1713, signed at the end of the War of the Spanish Succession. Legacies of the reign of Maria Theresa of Austria are still evident, particularly the dull-yellow (her favourite colour) façades of La Scala and the royal palace.

Napoleon made Milan the capital of his Cisalpine Republic in 1797, and five years later of his Italian Republic, crowning himself King of Italy and Milan there in 1805. Austria again occupied the town in 1814, but this time the occupation was to be short-lived. Troops of Victor Emmanuel II and Napoleon III crushed the Austrian forces at the Battle of Magenta in 1859 and Milan was incorporated into the nascent Kingdom of Italy.

Heavily bombed in WW II, the city was rebuilt and quickly grew to acquire its modern industrial prominence.

ORIENTATION

Milan is a sprawling metropolis, but most attractions are concentrated in the centre, between the duomo and the Castello Sforzesco. The duomo is an unmistakable focal point for your explorations, whether on foot or by public transport. The city is serviced by an efficient underground railway, the Metropolitana Milanese. It is easy to get lost, so a map is essential.

Apart from the centre, the main areas of interest for tourists are the Brera, immediately north of the duomo, which takes in many galleries and fashionable shopping streets, and Navigli to the south.

From Stazione Centrale (there is a Metropolitana station here), built in 1931 and a classic of the Fascist era, you emerge on Piazza Duca d'Aosta – the scruffy green patch in front of the station. (This is a junkies' hang-out and it's inadvisable to hang about here.) A good orientation point is the Pirelli building, a slender skyscraper to your right as you leave the train station. The area behind the station is occupied mainly by offices, and many of the better hotels are clustered here as well. To the south-east of Stazione Centrale, Via Dom Vitruvio leads to the main area for budget hotels. It meets Piazza Lima at the intersection of Corso Buenos Aires and becomes Via Plinio.

To get from Piazza Duca d'Aosta to the centre, walk south-west along Via Pisani, through the enormous park-lined Piazza della Repubblica, and along Via F Turati to Piazza Cavour. From here, take Via A Manzoni, which runs off the south-west side of the piazza. This takes you through the exclusive Monte Napoleone fashion district and on to Piazza della Scala, with its opera house. From there the glass-domed Galleria Vittorio Emanuele II leads to Piazza del Duomo. The APT office is at the south-east corner of this piazza.

To reach the city centre from the main budget hotel area east of Stazione Centrale, head south along the broad Corso Buenos Aires and its extension, Corso Venezia, and then veer right into Corso Vittorio Emanuele II from Piazza San Babila.

Via Orefici leads off the south-west corner of Piazza del Duomo, later becoming Via Dante as it approaches Castello Sforzesco, while Via Torino branches off southwards from the same corner towards Navigli.

INFORMATION
Tourist Office
The main branch of the APT (☎ 80 96 62) is at Via Marconi 1, in Piazza del Duomo, where you can pick up the useful *Milan is Milano* and *Milano Mese* brochures. It has a copy of the *Pagine Gialle – Turismo*, a bilingual Yellow Pages you can look through at leisure. The office is open Monday to Saturday from 8 am to 8 pm and on Sunday and holidays from 9 am to 12.30 pm and 1.30 to 5 pm. There is a branch office (☎ 669 05 32) at Stazione Centrale, also open seven days a week.

The Milan City Council operates an information office in Galleria Vittorio Emanuele II, just off Piazza del Duomo. It's especially good for finding out about cultural events and other activities in and around the city.

Money
Banks in Milan are open Monday to Friday from 8.30 am to 1.30 pm and for one hour in the afternoon, often from 2.45 to 3.45 pm.

Exchange offices at weekends include Banca Ponti, Piazza del Duomo 19, open Saturday from 9 am to 1 pm, and Banca delle Comunicazioni, Stazione Centrale, open Monday to Saturday from 8.35 am to 2.05 pm. There's a 24-hour cash changing machine as well. The Exact exchange booth at the station is open seven days a week from 7 am to 11 pm. There's a commission.

The Banca Commerciale Italiana has a 24-hour booth with a cash-changing machine inside on the corner of Via Manzoni and Piazza della Scala – you need a cash (or credit) card to get in, but the ATMs probably won't accept it for withdrawals. There are weekend exchange offices at both airports. The Sestante CIT office in Galleria Vittorio Emanuele II changes money. American Express (☎ 72 00 36 94) is at Viale Brera 3. It is open Monday to Friday from 9 am to 5 pm.

Post & Telecommunications
The main post office is at Via Cordusio 4, off Via Dante, and is open Monday to Friday from 8.15 am to 7.40 pm and Saturday to 5.40 pm. There are branches at Stazione Centrale and both airports. The post code for central Milan is 20100.

The main Telecom office is in Galleria Vittorio Emanuele II and is open daily from 8 am to 9.30 pm. There's another office at Stazione Centrale, open daily from 7 am to 7.45 pm, which also has telephone directories for the UK, Germany and France.

Telecom's drawn-out number-changing programme in Milan may yet cause confusion – if in doubt, directory enquiries is on ☎ 12 (but they speak Italian only). The telephone code for Milan is 02.

Foreign Consulates
Many countries have consulates in Milan, including the following:

Australia
    Via Borgogna 2 (☎ 76 01 33 30). Open Monday
    to Friday from 9 am to midday and 2 to 4 pm.
Canada
    Via Vittorio Pisani 19 (☎ 669 74 51, 66 98 06 00
    in emergency). Open Monday to Friday from
    9 am to 12.30 pm and 1.30 to 5 pm.

France
> Corso Venezia 42 (☎ 79 43 41)

UK
> Via San Paolo 7 (☎ 72 30 01). Open Monday to Friday from 9.15 am to 12.15 pm and 2.30 to 4.30 pm.

US
> Via P Amadeo 2-10 (☎ 29 03 51). Open Monday to Friday from 9 am to midday and 2 to 4 pm.

Travel Agencies

For student and budget travel, CTS has offices at Via S Antonio 2 (☎ 58 30 41 21) and Corso di Porta Ticinese 83 (☎ 837 26 74). Sestante CIT (☎ 86 66 61) is in the Galleria Vittorio Emanuele II.

Bookshops

The American Bookstore (☎ 72 02 00 30), Via Camperio 16, has a good selection. You could also try Feltrinelli, Via Manzoni 12, which has books in French and German, as well as English.

Gay & Lesbian Information

For information on gay activities, call Arci Gay/Centro d'Iniziativa Gay (☎ 58 10 03 99), Via Adige 11. The staff can advise on other associations in Milan. Babilonia (☎ 569 64 68) publishes several magazines for gays, including the monthly *Babilonia*, which is available at most newspaper stands.

Other Information

There are a few laundrettes *(lavanderie)* around the Stazione Centrale area, one on Via Petrella and another on Via Tadino – see the Around Stazione Centrale map.

For lost property *(oggetti smarriti)*, contact the Milan City Council (☎ 87 87 10), Linate airport (☎ 701 24 45) or Malpensa airport (☎ 74 85 42 15).

Emergency & Medical Services

For a police emergency, call ☎ 113. The questura (☎ 6 22 61) is at Via Fatebenefratelli 11. The staff speak English. For an ambulance, call ☎ 77 33, and for first aid, call the Italian Red Cross on ☎ 38 83.

The Ospedale Maggiore Policlinico (☎ 551 16 55) is at Via Francesco Sforza 35,

close to the city centre. All-night pharmacies include one at Stazione Centrale (☎ 669 07 35) and Ticinese (☎ 89 40 34 33), Corso S Gottardo 1.

Dangers & Annoyances

Milan's main shopping areas are popular haunts for pickpockets and thieves – including the kids-with-cardboard crowd, who operate in the same way as their confrères in Rome and other cities. The same streets are also patrolled by police, so don't hesitate to make a racket if you are hassled.

THINGS TO SEE

Since January 1994, an electronic Museumcard has been available that allows unlimited admission to some 20 museums and galleries for up to six months. It costs L37,000 and is good value if you intend to 'do' the sights thoroughly. Most museums close on Monday.

The Duomo

Milan's navel, Piazza del Duomo, is akin to London's Piccadilly Circus in atmosphere, the main difference being that the latter's statue of Eros doesn't quite compare as a famous meeting place with Milan's most visible monument, the duomo (MM1: Duomo). The world's fourth-largest church, it was commissioned by Gian Galeazzo Visconti in 1386.

The first glimpse of this late Gothic wonder is certainly memorable, with its marble façade shaped into pinnacles, statues and pillars, the whole held together by a web of flying buttresses. The Milanese pay a special tax to fund the ongoing works. Some 135 spires and 3200 statues have somehow been crammed onto the roof and into the façade, and masons add a new piece every few years.

The central spire is capped by a gilded copper statue of the Madonna, 108 metres above the ground. The forest of spires, statuary and pinnacles generally distracts observers from an interesting omission – Milan's duomo is one of very few churches of any importance without a bell tower. The huge brass doors at the front bear the marks of bombs that fell near the church during WW II.

Inside are 15th-century stained glass windows on the right and newer copies on the left. You will notice a definite contrast between the two. A nail stored high above the altar is said to have come from Christ's Cross and is displayed once a year, in September. Originally lowered using a device made by da Vinci called the *nigola*, it is now retrieved with more modern means. The nigola is stored near the roof on the right-hand side as you enter the church. Note the trompe l'oeuil ceiling. The 158-step climb to the roof of the duomo (L4000) is worth the effort – for some locals it serves as a sunbathing terrace. There's also a lift to the roof for L6000. The entrance is outside the church on the north flank.

Around the Duomo

At the **Museo del Duomo**, Piazza del Duomo 14, you can study more closely the church's six centuries of history, in addition to a rich collection of sculptures, some made for the duomo, from the 14th to the last century. It is open daily, except Monday, from 9.30 am to 12.30 pm and 3 to 6 pm. Admission is L7000.

The **Civico Museo d'Arte Contemporanea**, in the restored Palazzo Reale, south of the duomo, is dedicated to works by Italian futurists and lesser known modern Italian artists. It's open Tuesday to Sunday from 9.30 am to 5.30 pm.

Virtually destroyed in bombing raids during WW II and rebuilt afterwards, the cruciform **Galleria Vittorio Emanuele II** leads north off Piazza del duomo. The galleria, designed by Giuseppe Mengoni, was one of the first buildings in Europe to employ mainly iron and glass as structural elements. The four mosaics around the central octagon represent Europe, Asia, Africa and North America. The galleria became known as 'il salotto di Milano' (Milan's drawing room) thanks to elegant cafés like Savini (something of a contrast to the less exclusive hamburger joint opposite).

South-west of Piazza del Duomo, the **Pinacoteca Ambrosiana**, Piazza Pio XI 2 (MM1: Cordusio), is one of the city's finest galleries and contains Italy's first real still life, Caravaggio's *Fruit Basket*, as well as

works by Giovanni Tiepolo, Titian and Raphael. The library contains many protected da Vinci manuscripts. The gallery is due to reopen in early 1996. Behind lies the **Chiesa di San Sepolcro**, begun in 1030 and featuring a Romanesque crypt. It was dedicated to the Holy Sepulchre during the second crusade.

South of the duomo, and best viewed from the duomo roof, is one of Milan's more memorable skyscrapers, the **Torre Velasca**, a 20-storey building topped by a six-storey protruding block. A classic late-1950s design by Studio BBPR, this building should be seen. Apparently the duomo offered some inspiration.

La Scala & Around

Walk north through the Galleria Vittorio Emanuele II from Piazza della Duomo to Piazza della Scala, dominated by a monument dedicated to da Vinci, and **Teatro alla Scala**. La Scala, as it is most commonly known, opened on 3 August 1778 and was the venue for innumerable operatic first nights throughout the 19th and early 20th century. Heavily damaged in WW II, it was reopened in 1946 under the baton of Arturo Toscanini, who came from New York after a 15-year absence from Italy. The adjoining **Museo Teatrale alla Scala** boasts such curiosities as Verdi's death mask (complete with the maestro's facial hairs). You can wander into the opera house from the museum, which is open Monday to Saturday from 9 am to midday and 2 to 6 pm and Sunday from 9.30 am to midday from March to October only. Admission is L5000.

The **Palazzo Marino**, between Piazza della Scala and Piazza San Fedele, was begun in 1558 by Galeazzo Alessi and is a masterpiece of 16th-century residential architecture. For those who intend to explore Milan at greater length, it is worth bearing in mind that there are more than 60 grand *palazzi* scattered about the city centre – a far cry from the several hundred that were still standing at the end of the 19th century, but impressive enough.

North-east along Via Manzoni is the **Museo Poldi-Pezzoli**, a rich collection bequeathed to

LOMBARDY

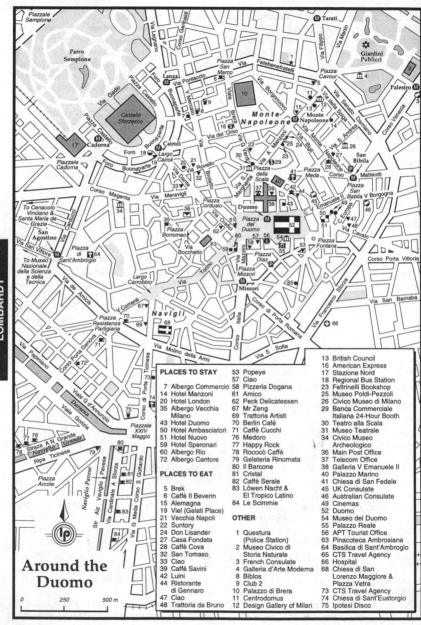

Around the Duomo

0 250 500 m

PLACES TO STAY

7 Albergo Commercio
14 Hotel Manzoni
20 Hotel London
35 Albergo Vecchia
    Milano
43 Hotel Duomo
50 Hotel Ambasciatori
51 Hotel Nuovo
59 Hotel Speronari
60 Albergo Rio
72 Albergo Cantore

PLACES TO EAT

5 Brek
6 Caffè Il Beverin
15 Alemagna
19 Viel (Gelati Place)
21 Vecchia Napoli
22 Suntory
24 Don Lisander
27 Casa Fondata
28 Caffè Cova
32 San Tomaso
33 Ciao
39 Caffè Savini
42 Luini
44 Ristorante
    di Gennaro
47 Ciao
48 Trattoria da Bruno

53 Popeye
57 Ciao
58 Pizzeria Dogana
61 Amico
62 Peck Delicatessen
67 Mr Zeng
69 Trattoria Artisti
70 Berlin Café
71 Caffè Cucchi
76 Medoro
77 Happy Rock
78 Rococò Caffè
79 Gelateria Rinomata
80 Il Barcone
81 Cristal
82 Caffè Serale
83 Löwen Nacht &
    El Tropico Latino
84 Le Scimmie

OTHER

1 Questura
   (Police Station)
2 Museo Civico di
   Storia Naturale
3 French Consulate
4 Galleria d'Arte Moderna
8 Biblos
9 Club 2
10 Palazzo di Brera
11 Centrodomus
12 Design Gallery of Milan

13 British Council
16 American Express
17 Stazione Nord
18 Regional Bus Station
23 Feltrinelli Bookshop
25 Museo Poldi-Pezzoli
26 Civico Museo di Milano
29 Banca Commerciale
    Italiana 24-Hour Booth
30 Teatro alla Scala
31 Museo Teatrale
34 Civico Museo
    Archeologico
36 Main Post Office
37 Telecom Office
38 Galleria V Emanuele II
40 Palazzo Marino
41 Chiesa di San Fedele
45 UK Consulate
46 Australian Consulate
49 Cinemas
52 Duomo
54 Museo del Duomo
55 Palazzo Reale
56 APT Tourist Office
63 Pinacoteca Ambrosiana
64 Basilica di Sant'Ambrogio
65 CTS Travel Agency
66 Hospital
68 Chiesa di San
    Lorenzo Maggiore &
    Piazza Vetra
73 CTS Travel Agency
74 Chiesa di Sant'Eustorgio
75 Ipotesi Disco

the city in 1881 by nobleman Giacomo Poldi-Pezzoli. Works by Raphael and Bellini figure among the paintings on display and there are collections of jewellery, sundials, tapestries and some bronzework. It is daily, except Monday, from 9.30 am to 12.30 pm and 2.30 to 6 pm (a little longer on Saturday). Admission is L8000.

Those wanting deeper insights into the history of Milan should make for the **Civico Museo di Milano**, Via Sant'Andrea 6 (MM1: San Babila). It is open daily, except Monday, from 9.30 am to 5.30 pm.

Castello Sforzesco

At the north end of Via Dante looms the imposing **Castello Sforzesco** (MM1: Cadorna or Cairoli, or MM2: Cadorna). Originally a Visconti fortress, it was entirely remodelled by Francesco Sforza in the 15th century, and da Vinci had a hand in designing the defences. Its modern museums hold excellent sculpture collections, including Michelangelo's *Pietà Rondanini*. Other collections include an applied arts display and a decent picture gallery that includes works by Bellini, Giovanni Tiepolo, Andrea Mantegna, Correggio, Titian and a Van Dyck. You can also visit a museum devoted to ancient Egyptian artefacts. The castle museums are open Tuesday to Sunday from 9.30 am to 5 pm. Admission is free. Behind the castle is the **Parco Sempione**, a 47-hectare park featuring a sadly neglected arena inaugurated by Napoleon. A fun park and (more discretely) drug dealers compete here for strollers' attention.

Palazzo di Brera

The sprawling 17th-century Palazzo di Brera, in the street of the same name east of the Castello Sforzesco, houses the **Pinacoteca di Brera** (MM2: Lanza). Its extensive treasure of paintings has continued to grow since the gallery was inaugurated at the beginning of the 19th century, and represents Milan's single most impressive collection. Andrea Mantegna's masterpiece, *The Dead Christ*, is just one of the better known works on display. Also represented are Raphael, Bellini (look for his *Madonna and Child*),

Giovanni Tiepolo, Rembrandt, Goya, Caravaggio, Van Dyck, El Greco and many more. There are also regular temporary exhibitions. It is open Tuesday to Saturday from 9 am to 5.30 pm and Sunday to 12.30 pm. Admission is L8000.

The Last Supper

An absolute must is da Vinci's *Last Supper*, in the Cenacolo Vinciano (Vinciano Refectory) next to the **Chiesa di Santa Maria delle Grazie** (MM1: Conciliazione, or MM2: Cadorna). Painted between 1495 and 1498 in the refectory of the Santa Maria delle Grazie convent, da Vinci's famous work is believed to capture the moment when Jesus uttered, 'One of you will betray me'. Recently, it has been argued that da Vinci believed Jesus had a twin. The basis for this contention can be seen in the painting, which depicts two virtually identical Christs.

Restoration of the *Last Supper* began in 1977 and is proceeding slowly, but centuries of damage from floods, bombing and decay have left their mark. It was the method employed by restorers last century that caused most damage – their alcohol and cotton wool removed a layer from the painting. A photo display shows an incredible post-WW II scene of the building virtually destroyed, with only the wall bearing the Cenacolo left standing. It was closed to visitors at the time of writing and due to reopen in mid-1995, after installation of a climate-control system.

South of Castello Sforzesco

The **Civico Museo Archeologico**, Corso Magenta 15 (MM2: Cadorna), features substantial Roman, Greek, Etruscan, Gandhara (ancient north-west Indian) and medieval sections. It is open daily, except Monday, from 9.30 am to 5.30 pm. Admission is free. It is housed in the Monastero Maggiore, which is attached to the Chiesa di San Maurizio and is adorned with frescoes by B Luini.

A short stroll south, the Romanesque **Basilica di Sant'Ambrogio** – dedicated to Milan's patron saint, St Ambrose, dominates the piazza of the same name. Founded in the 4th century by Ambrose, Bishop of Milan,

---

A Saint of the World

When the future Sant'Ambrogio was appointed Bishop of Milan in 374 AD, to great public acclaim, his credentials were hardly in order – he hadn't even been baptised. Small matter; this former governor of Liguria had impressed everyone with his skills in umpiring between Catholics and Arians, and so he received all the sacraments and the mitre in an unusually accelerated procedure.

At that time, Milan was the effective capital of the western half of the crumbling Roman empire, and Ambrogio became a leading figure in imperial politics. He and the Western emperor, Gratian, embarked on a crusade to eradicate paganism and the Arian heresy.

His influence became such that he was later able to challenge the authority of Theodosius – the Eastern emperor and guarantor of the western empire after Gratian's assassination – with impunity. In one incident, the emperor had ordered Christians responsible for burning down a synagogue to rebuild it. Ambrogio demanded the order be revoked and, threatening to thump the pulpit and stir popular feeling on the issue, convinced the emperor to see things his way.

Ambrogio, the public functionary who had never been a priest, turned out to be a powerful and charismatic bishop. He incarnated the triumph of spiritual over secular power, presaging the Church's future political role in European affairs and inspiring the composition of the *Te Deum*. He died in 397 AD. ∎

---

the church has been repaired, rebuilt and restored several times since and is a bit of a hodgepodge of styles. The shorter of the two bell towers dates to the 9th century, as does the remarkable ciborium under the dome inside. It is believed that at least parts of the columns inside date to St Ambrose's time. The saint is buried in the crypt.

The **Museo Nazionale della Scienza e della Tecnica**, Via San Vittore 21 (MM2 Sant'Ambrogio), is one of the world's largest technology museums and features a room dedicated to da Vinci's scientific work. The museum is open daily, except Monday, from 9.30 am to 4.50 pm. Admission is L10,000.

Around Piazza Cavour

The **Galleria d'Arte Moderna**, Via Palestro 16 (MM1: Palestro), in the 18th-century Villa Reale, which Napoleon temporarily called home, has a wide range of 19th-century works including works from the Milanese neo-classical period. It was closed at the time of writing. The nearby **Chiesa di San Babila** is said to have been built on the site of a paleo-Christian church dating to 46 AD.

The **Design Gallery of Milan**, at Via Manzoni 46, features exhibitions of local design works. The gallery is closed Tuesdays and admission is free.

Around Navigli

The **Chiesa di San Lorenzo Maggiore**, Piazza Vetra, an early Christian church built between 355 and 372 AD on the site of a Roman building, features several 3rd-century columns in front of the church. The **Chiesa di Sant'Eustorgio**, Piazza Sant'Eustorgio, was built in the 9th century and altered in the 11th century, and features a 15th-century Cappella Portinari (Chapel of St Peter Martyr). Donato Bramante designed the baptistry.

LANGUAGE COURSES

The Linguadue School of Italian (☎ 29 51 99 72), Corso Buenos Aires 43, offers individual or group courses in Italian. It is one of several language schools in Milan.

WORK

If you are so taken with Milan that you'd like to live there, one possible source of work is teaching English. There are many schools, but competition is stiff and pay unspectacular. The British Council (☎ 78 20 16), Via Manzoni 38, is not in the habit of employing people who simply walk in, but they might be able to point you in other directions.

ORGANISED TOURS

The Volontari Associati per i Musei Italiani

(VAMI, ☎ 76 02 21 52) organises free guided group visits to the duomo museum, Castello Sforza and other sites. English-speaking guides cannot be guaranteed. Call from 9 am to 1 pm. CIT organises day trips to lakes Maggiore and Como by bus and ferry.

FESTIVALS
If you needed any convincing of the special place that St Ambrogio, occupies in the city's iconography, a quick look around will reveal the omnipresence of the adjective *ambrosiano*, from banks to shops and advertising. See the Aside in this section. St Ambrose's Day, 7 December, is Milan's biggest feast day. Until late 1993, religious celebrations and a traditional street fair were held around the Basilica di Sant'Ambrogio, but it appears that from now on they will take place at the Fiera di Milano (MM1: Fiera), Milan's trade, conference and exhibition centre. La Scala also marks the occasion by opening its opera season on this day.

The first 10 days of June are devoted to the Festa del Naviglio, a smorgasbord of parades, music and other performances. Milan plays year-round host to fairs of all sorts – autumn seems the heaviest time for the fashion variety.

PLACES TO STAY
Milan's hotels are among the most expensive and heavily booked in Italy. The area around Stazione Centrale abounds with cheapish one and two-star joints, but quality varies and you'll be lucky to find singles/doubles for less than L45,000/65,000. The popularity of the city as a trade-fair and exhibition venue means hotel owners charge what they like – and get away with it.

The main tourist office will make recommendations but not bookings – the Stazione Centrale office is sometimes more helpful in this respect. Chiariva (☎ 48 00 71 21; fax 480 13 66) will book hotels of three-star rating and up.

The APT has lists of private rooms, student accommodation, religious institutions and boarding houses. Most are rented by the month. It also offers a deal called Weekend Milano –

discounted weekend packages in some of the better hotels.

Bottom End
Camping The *Campeggio Città di Milano* (☎ 48 20 01 34) is a fair distance from the centre at Via G Airaghi 61. Go to the MM1 De Angeli train station, west of the city centre, and take bus No 72. By car, exit the Tangenziale Ovest at San Siro-Via Novara. Otherwise, the nearest camping ground is in Monza (☎ 039-38 77 71), open April to September.

Hostels & Religious Institutions The HI youth hostel, *Ostello Pietro Rotta* (☎ & fax 39 26 70 95), is at Viale Salmoiraghi 1. B&B is L20,000, or L22,000 per bed for families. Take the MM1 in the direction of Molino Dorino and get off at QT8 (the name of the station and surrounding area) or take bus No 90 or 91. An HI card is compulsory, but you can buy a card and stamps there (effectively amounts to L30,000 for full membership).

The *Protezione della Giovane* (☎ 29 00 01 64), Corso Garibaldi 123, east of Parco Sempione, is for women aged between 16 and 25. Beds cost from L25,000.

The *Fondazione Sacro Cuore* (☎ 214 00 51), Via Rombone 78, near Stazione Centrale, is a religious hostel for men only. Rooms are usually rented long-term, but it's occasionally possible to get a room for the night for about L30,000.

Around Stazione Centrale & Corso Buenos Aires Most of the cheaper hotels near the station will not take bookings. One of the seriously nicest places is the Hotel Due Giardini (☎ 29 52 10 93), Via Settala 46. The rooms are simple and not rock bottom in price (starting at L50,000/65,000), but those at the back are separated from the outside world by a cheerful garden – you'd never know you were in a big city.

In Via Dom Vitruvio, to the left of Piazza Duca d'Aosta as you leave the train station, there are two cheaper options. The *Salerno* (☎ 204 68 70), at No 18, has singles/doubles for L40,000/60,000. The *Italia* (☎ 669 38

LOMBARDY

26), at No 44, has singles/doubles for L38,000/ 55,000 – but the rooms are pretty spartan.

Around the corner from the Salerno, in something of a red light area, is the *Hotel Paradiso* (☎ 204 94 48), Via Benedetto Marcello 85. It has singles/doubles for L40,000/60,000. Doubles with a shower are L80,000 and those with a bathroom are L90,000. You could also try *The Best* (sic) next door, which has a similar deal.

The *Hotel Valley* (☎ 669 27 77), Via Soperga 19, is not in a great location, but the rooms are reasonable and staff friendly. Singles/doubles with shower cost L55,000/75,000.

Just east of Corso Buenos Aires at Via Gaspare Spontini 6 is *Del Sole* (☎ 29 51 29 71), with singles/doubles for L45,000/60,000 and triples for L80,000.

A 10-minute walk south-east of the train station, *Hotel Nettuno* (☎ 29 40 44 81), Via Tadino 27, has singles for L42,000 and singles/doubles with a bathroom for L53,000/100,000.

Down near Piazza della Repubblica, *Hotel Casa Mia* (☎ 657 52 49), Viale Vittorio Veneto 30, has something of a family atmosphere. Singles/doubles come in at 50,000/70,000 and a triple is L80,000. The *Verona* (☎ 66 98 30 91), at Via Carlo Tenca 12 (also close to Piazza della Repubblica), has singles/doubles for L70,000/90,000 – this includes TV and breakfast. Up the road towards Stazione Centrale, *Hotel Boston* (☎ 669 26 35), Via Le Petit 7, has similar rooms for L75,000/135,000.

Two other possibilities are located in the one building at Viale Tunisia 6. *Hotel San Tomaso* (☎ 29 51 47 47), on the 3rd floor, has modest singles for L45,000. On the 6th floor, *Hotel Kennedy* (☎ 29 40 09 34) has better rooms for L50,000/100,000.

Closer to the city centre, in an interesting location near lots of restaurants and away from the seedy atmosphere of the train station, is *Hotel Tris* (☎ 29 40 06 74), Via Sirtori 26, with singles/doubles from L50,000/70,000 and triples from L90,000.

City Centre The *Albergo Commercio* (☎ 86 46 38 80), Via Mercato 1, has singles/doubles for L45,000/55,000 with shower, but it's often full. From Piazza Cordusio, walk up Via Broletto, which becomes Via Mercato. The entrance to the hotel is around the corner in Via delle Erbe. Within spitting distance of Piazza del duomo is *Hotel Speronari* (☎ 86 46 11 25), Via Speronari 4, with comfortable singles /doubles from L50,000/70,000. *Hotel Nuovo* (☎ 86 46 05 42), Piazza Beccaria 6, is also in a great location, to the south just off Corso Vittorio Emanuele II, and rooms cost the same as at the Speronari.

Around Navigli The *Albergo Cantore* (☎ 835 75 65), Corso Genova 25, is close to Milan's Bohemian zone. Singles/doubles are L45,000/65,000.

Middle to Top End
Around Stazione Centrale & Corso Buenos
Aires Singles at the five-star *Hotel Palace* (☎ 63 36; fax 65 44 85), on Piazza della Repubblica, start at L260,000 and soar skywards. The *Hotel Fenice* (☎ 29 52 55 41; fax 29 52 39 42), Corso Buenos Aires 2, in the upper three-star category, has singles/doubles from L160,000/210,000.

City Centre The *Albergo Vecchia Milano* (☎ 87 50 42), Via Borromei 4, near Piazza Borromeo, is a good two-star deal, offering singles/doubles with breakfast for L85,000/125,000 – all rooms have a bathroom. *Hotel London* (☎ 72 02 01 66; fax 805 70 37), Via Rovello 3 (off Via Dante), looks swanky but charges reasonable rates. Singles/doubles are L75,000/100,000, or L95,000/140,000 with a bathroom. *Albergo Rio* (☎ 87 41 14), Via Mazzini 8, in a great location just off Piazza del Duomo, has singles/doubles with breakfast for L105,000/175,000.

If you want to mix it with the big spenders, *Hotel Manzoni* (☎ 76 00 57 00; fax 78 42 12), Via Santo Spirito 20, is close to Armani & Co. A room here is L145,000/190,000.

The *Hotel Duomo* (☎ 88 33; fax 86 46 20 27) on the north side of the cathedral, is one of the city's better hotels and a room will set you back L310,000/410,000. The *Hotel Ambasciatori* (☎ 76 02 02 41; fax 78 27 00), Galleria del Corso 3, off Corso Vittorio

Emanuele II, is a little more modest, at L200,000/300,000.

PLACES TO EAT

Italians say Lombard cuisine is designed for people who don't have time to waste because they are always in a hurry to work. Fast-food outlets and sandwich bars are popular and cluttered around Stazione Centrale and the duomo.

The city has a strong provincial cuisine. Polenta (a cornmeal porridge similar to American grits) is served with almost everything, and risotto dominates the first course of the city's menus. Try cotoletta alla milanese or ossobuco (veal shank). Polenta also figures on the sweets menu, but torta di tagliatelle, a cake made with egg pasta and almonds, might be more inviting.

Via Speronari is one of the better areas to shop for bread, salami, cheese and wine. There is also a fresh produce market on weekends at Via Benedetto Marcello. The Super Sconto supermarket on Via Panfilo Castaldi, just off Corso Buenos Aires, is not a bad place for picking up supplies.

Bar snacks are an institution in Milan and most lay out their fare daily from 5 pm.

Around Stazione Centrale

For a decent American-style hamburger at around L5000, *Spontini Burger* on Via Spontini (technically Corso Buenos Aires 60) is a good bet. *Ciao*, Corso Buenos Aires 7, is part of a chain (there are others in Corso Europa and at Via Dante 5), but the food is good quality and relatively cheap, with pasta from L5000 and salads for around L3000. *Brek*, Via Roberto Lepetit 20 (turn left off Via Vitruvio if leaving the train station), has pasta from L5000. It's a chain too and you'll find one on Via Manzoni just off Piazza Cavour. Yet another chain of similar quality and price is *Amico*. There's one on the corner of Corso Buenos Aires and Via Vitruvio, and there's another on Piazza del Duomo.

LOMBARDY

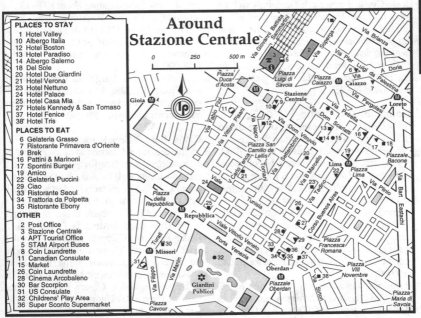

PLACES TO STAY
1 Hotel Valley
10 Albergo Italia
12 Hotel Boston
13 Hotel Paradiso
14 Albergo Salerno
18 Del Sole
20 Hotel Due Giardini
21 Hotel Verona
23 Hotel Nettuno
24 Hotel Palace
25 Hotel Casa Mia
27 Hotels Kennedy & San Tomaso
37 Hotel Fenice
38 Hotel Tris

PLACES TO EAT
6 Gelateria Grasso
7 Ristorante Primavera d'Oriente
9 Brek
16 Pattini & Marinoni
17 Spontini Burger
19 Amico
22 Gelateria Puccini
29 Ciao
33 Ristorante Seoul
34 Trattoria da Polpetta
35 Ristorante Ebony

OTHER
2 Post Office
3 Stazione Centrale
4 APT Tourist Office
5 STAM Airport Buses
8 Coin Laundrette
11 Canadian Consulate
15 Market
26 Coin Laundrette
28 Cinema Arcobaleno
30 Bar Scorpion
31 US Consulate
32 Childrens' Play Area
36 Super Sconto Supermarket

Around Stazione Centrale

0   250   500 m

Ristorante Primavera d'Oriente, Via Palestrina 13, offers a standard Chinese meal from L14,000.

Trattoria da Polpetta, near the Via V Veneto end of Via Tadino and on the corner of Via Panfilo Castaldi, is a small eatery where a full meal with wine will cost about L40,000. Virtually across the road, you have about the only chance you'll get in Italy to eat Korean.

The *Ristorante Seoul*, Via Tadino 1, serves a full meal for around L30,000. Around the corner at Via Panfilo Castaldi 42, you can have a taste of Africa at the *Ristorante Ebony*. A little walking in the back streets around here will turn up quite a few other little restaurants.

Heading west of Stazione Centrale towards Stazione Porta Garibaldi and Corso Como is the area haunted at night by a certain Milanese high society crew, all seemingly in search of the most expensive drink. You can find a couple of good places here.

At the unassuming *Trattoria da Tea*, Corso Como 3, you can eat and drink well for about L25,000 a head. For about double this, you too can munch where Ho Chi Minh once sampled the best of Lombard food, the *Antica Trattoria della Pesa*, Via Pasubio 10.

There are several self-service places along Via Pisani, including the often packed *Bar Scorpion* at No 28.

Around the City Centre

The *Alemagna*, Via Manzoni, on the corner of Via Croce Rossa, is an elegant, buffet-style restaurant, with main courses from L7000.

The first Milanese pizza was cooked at *Ristorante di Gennaro*, Via S Radegonda 3, east of Piazza alla Scala. They are a little more expensive than the average.

The *Trattoria da Bruno*, Via Cavallotti 15, off Corso Europa, is popular and has a set-price lunch for L16,000. *Pizzeria Dogana*, on the corner of Via Capellari and Via Dogana, near the duomo, has pasta and pizza for around L10,000.

Popeye, Via S Tecla 8 (just south of the duomo), is reputed to have the best pizza in Milan – for around L7000 to L10,000. *San Tomaso*, Via San Tomaso 5 (near Via Rovello), features live jazz and specialises in salads for up to L12,000. Close by is *Vecchia Napoli*, Via San Tomaso on the corner of Via Rovello, with pizzas from L10,000.

Particularly recommended for its Tuscan dishes is *Il Faro*, Piazzale San Materno 8. *Oscar* on Via Palazzi is the place to head to for cheap seafood – L20,000 should see you right.

One of the city's posher restaurants is *Don Lisander*, Via Manzoni 12A, which serves Milanese risotto and a host of Tuscan dishes. It is relatively expensive, with dishes starting at L18,000. But perhaps the city's most traditional restaurant is *Savini* in the Galleria Vittorio Emanuele II, with its chandeliers, plush red velvet and matching prices.

If Japanese is your thing, head to *Suntory*, Via Verdi 6. It's not cheap though.

Around Navigli

The *Berlin Café*, Via G Mora 5 (east of Piazza Resistenza Partigiana), has a limited menu, with dishes costing about L10,000, in an attempted Berlin '30s atmosphere.

Trattoria Artisti, Corso di Porta Ticinese 16, is a popular hang-out for Milanese bohemians. It serves a set-menu lunch for L18,000.

North towards Largo Carrobbio on the same road, *Mr Zeng* is a good Chinese restaurant, one of several in the area. You can eat well for less than L20,000.

Cafés, Bars & Snack Joints

In the Stazione Centrale area is *Pattini & Marinoni*, Corso Buenos Aires 53, which sells bread, as well as pizza by the slice for about L2000. The street is loaded with small cafés and places to grab a quick panino.

Close to the city centre is one of Milan's oldest fast-food outlets is *Luini*, Via S Radegonda 16, off Piazza del Duomo, which sells panzerotti (pizza dough stuffed with tomatoes, garlic and mozzarella) for L2500.

For gourmet takeaway, head for *Peck*. Its rosticceria is at Via Cesare Cantù 11 (just west of Piazza del Duomo), where you can buy cooked meats and vegetables; another outlet is at Via Spadari 9. There are several others, including a snack bar and restaurant at Via Victor Hugo 4.

Le Tre Marie, on the corner of Via Cesare Cantù and Via Armorai, has great bar snacks.

Cova, Via Monte Napoleone 8, in the Monte Napoleone shopping district, is an elegant but expensive tearoom where you can mix it with wealthy Milanese. Close by is the slightly less expensive *Sunflower Bar*, Via Pietro Verri, another haunt of the fashion-conscious.

Just south of Piazza San Marco, *Caffè Il Beverin* is a pleasant place for a drink, with tables spilling out onto the cobbled Viale Brera. They have food as well.

A good sandwich bar is *Quadronno*, on the corner of Via Quadronno and Porta Vigentina. It specialises in unusual concoctions.

South of the duomo, in and around Navigli, is a happening part of town, and there are plenty of cafés and bars to check out. *Cucchi*, at the northern end of Corso Genova, is a fine place for piazza-watching.

Head farther south still and you turn up the *Happy Rock* and *Rococó*, opposite each other on Via Casale as it runs into Alzaia Naviglio Grande. Around the corner on the latter street is *Medoro*, a similar bohemian locale.

Gelati

There are any number of places to pick up gelati. A popular one in the trendy Navigli area is *Gelateria Rinomata*, on Viale Gorizia (on the south side of Ripa di Porta Ticinese) by the Darsena.

Near Stazione Centrale, at Viale Andrea Doria, on the corner of Via Palestrina, is *Gelateria Grasso*, a fine tribute to 1970s architecture and an even better one to good gelati. If you'd like a crêpe as well, head for the *Gelateria Puccini*, Corso Buenos Aires 33.

A classic place is *Viel*, near the Castello Sforzesco and a favourite late-night haunt for young Milanese.

Perhaps best loved is the *Gelateria Marghera*, Via Marghera 33, west of the city centre (MM1: De Angeli).

ENTERTAINMENT

Milan has Italy's best clubs, a host of cinemas screening English-language films, and a fabulous year-round cultural calendar, topped by La Scala's opera season.

The tourist office has complete listings for the city's entertainment, as do most daily newspapers. Pick up *Milano Mese*, a monthly entertainment guide from the tourist office. For cinema and some clue to what's happening in the club scene, both *Corriere della Sera* and *La Repubblica* have entertainment liftouts on Thursdays – the latter publication is generally better.

Live in Italia is a free monthly you can sometimes dig up in the tourist office. It lists upcoming gigs, although these are mostly international acts.

Music & Theatre

La Scala's main opera season opens on December 7, but theatre, ballet and concerts are performed all year save the last week or two of July and all August. The box office (☎ 72 00 37 44) is in the portico in Via Filodrammatici, on the left-hand side of the building, and is open daily from midday to 7 pm and until 15 minutes after curtains on performance nights. Book well in advance, even from another city if you are travelling to Milan, as most performances sell out months before. Your only hope may be the 200 standing-room tickets that go on sale 45 minutes before the scheduled starting time at the entrance to the opera house museum. These can cost as little as L5000, depending on the performance. The best seats in the house on premier night can be as much as L1,500,000! CIT offices abroad will book tickets.

The Chiesa di San Maurizio in the Monastero Maggiore hosts concerts, usually involving small classical ensembles, throughout the year. Jazz festivals are held at various times of the year – check with the APT for the latest details. The summer months are usually full with musical and theatrical events.

The main season for theatre and concerts opens in October. The Conservatorio Giuseppe Verdi (☎ 76 00 17 55), Via Conservatorio 12, is the venue for many classical music concerts.

At least another 50 theatres are active in Milan – check the newspapers and ask at the tourist office.

Cinema

English-language films are shown at the following cinemas: Anteo (☎ 659 77 32), Via Milazzo 9 (MM2: Moscova); Arcobaleno (☎ 29 40 60 54), Viale Tunisia 11 (MM1: Porta Venezia); and Mexico (☎ 48 95 18 02), Via Savona 57 (MM2: Porta Genova).

Bars & Pubs

There are two areas in particular to search for a drink, some music and the madding crowd. The Brera (predictably located around Viale Brera) comes alive at night as crowds swirl through the narrow lanes and into watering holes where a beer will cost anything from L8000 to L20,000, depending on the bar and whether or not they have music (usually of the smoke-filled piano bar variety). Among the more popular of these places are Biblos, Via Madonnina 17, and Club 2, Via Formentini 2.

Alternatively you can head for Navigli, in particular Via A Sforza, which runs along a fairly slimy canal. There's plenty here. Starting south and moving up, you'll find Le Scimmie, No 49, a popular music bar, where you can sometimes hear good jazz. At No 41, El Tropico Latino comes equipped with a Mexican restaurant and Latin music bar. A German flavour is injected into Löwen Nacht next door. The Caffè Serale, No 29, is a more sedate and stylish place for a drink, while at Cristal you can sip an apéritif on a boat (in fact, most of these places have boats hitched to the side of the canal if crowds warrant the extra drinking space). Where the filthy dribble of water ends is an even bigger floating café, Il Barcone.

Another traditional meeting place for Milanese night owls is the Bar Magenta, Via Carducci 13, a short walk south of Castello Sforzesco.

Nightclubs

The club scene changes constantly and for some unknown reason comprehensive listings are in short supply, even in the appropriate newspaper liftouts.

Ipotesi is a popular disco on Piazzale XXIV Maggio, at the northern end of Navigli. At Bastioni di Porta Nuova 12, Shocking is practically always open, attracting different crowds with thematic changes in music each evening. Admission costs up to L25,000. Factory, Via Ricciarelli 11, has just about everything, including a speakers' corner and hair stylist. It roams from hip-hop and reggae to more classic rock and Goth nights. To get in you need a flier, which means being in the right bars nearby when they are handed out. Milano In, Via dei Missaglia 46/3, is a fairly posh place that often hosts cabaret-style acts, open until 2.30 am. Admission is around L20,000. If you want to hang out with designer types and sip cocktails to '60s music, Bar Metals, Corso di Porta Ticinese 58, might be the place for you.

Live music is the main emphasis at Rock Planet, Via Vittorio Veneto 32. Other venues for bands, including foreign acts, are City Square Club, Via Castelbarco 11, and Rolling Stone, Corso XXII Marzo 32.

Bigger concerts tend to be held at the Palatrussardi (☎ 33 40 43 68), Viale Elia 33, near the San Siro stadium, or the Forum di Assago, farther out of town.

Soccer

Milan's two teams, Inter and AC Milan, play on alternate Sundays during the football season, at San Siro stadium, also known as Meazza because it is in Piazza Meazza. Tram No 24 and buses Nos 95, 49 and 72 go direct. Or take the metro and get off at MM1: Lotto, from where a free shuttle bus runs to the stadium. Tickets are available at the stadium or for AC Milan matches, from Milan Point (☎ 79 64 81), Via Verri 8. For Inter matches, tickets are sold at Banca Popolare di Milano branches (or call ☎ 7 70 01). Cost ranges from L25,000 to L65,000.

Car Racing

The Italian Grand Prix is held at the Monza autodrome each September. The track is

Soccer is a national passion; two of the sport's stars are Diego Bortoluzzi and Giancarlo Marocchi.

several km out of town and can be reached along Viale Monza from Piazzale Loreto.

THINGS TO BUY

Every item of clothing you ever wanted to buy, but could never afford, is in Milan. The main streets for clothing, footwear and accessories are behind the duomo around Corso Vittorio Emanuele II, and between Piazza della Scala and Piazza San Babila.

For up-market and exclusive fashions, head for Via della Spiga, the boutique mecca Via Monte Napoleone or Via Borgospesso which runs between the two – all in an area known as the Quadrilatero d'Oro (Golden Quad), or Monte Napo to the in-crowd. Gianfranco Ferré is at Via della Spiga 11 and Krizia at No 23. Around the corner in Via Sant'Andrea you will find Armani, Trussardi and Kenzo. Versace, Valentino, Ungaro, Ferretti, Louis Vuitton and Cartier are cluttered along Via Monte Napoleone.

The areas around Via Torino, Corso XXII Marzo and Corso Buenos Aires are less expensive.

Markets are held around the canals, notably on Viale Papiniano on Tuesday and Saturday mornings. A flea market is held in Viale Gabriele d'Annunzio on Saturdays and a decent antique market is held in Brera at Via Fiori Chiari on every third Saturday of the month. Milan's version of Portobello Rd, a huge market where you can buy just about anything, is held on the last Sunday of each month on the Alzaia Naviglio Grande and Ripa di Porta Ticinese (tram No 19).

Design

Milan is the world's design capital, although you have to search it out as shops and galleries are spread throughout the city, and most products are made for export.

The magazine *Interni* publishes a fold-out guide called *Interni Annual* which lists the names and addresses of most design shops and galleries, as well as a list of upcoming design fairs and exhibitions (of which there are many). The magazine and supplement are on sale at newspaper stands or are available free from various furniture and other design-oriented shops and galleries. The *Milano Design Guide*, published by Abitare, is sold at most bookshops and contains 'design itineraries'.

GETTING THERE & AWAY
Air
International flights use Malpensa airport, about 50 km north-west of the city. Domestic and European flights use Linate airport, about seven km east. The city is served by an increasing number of flights from the US and from many cities in Europe.

Major airlines include Alitalia (☎ 26 8 51/2/3), Corso Como 15, and British Airways (☎ 80 90 41), Corso Italia 8.

Bus
Bus stations are scattered across the city, so unless you know exactly what you want and where you're going, you're better off with the train. Bear this in mind when deciding how to get to Milan as well. SAL, Autostradale and several other companies operate from Piazza Castello, in front of Castello Sforzesco (MM2: Cairoli) for some national and international destinations.

Train
You can catch a train from Stazione Centrale to all major cities in Italy, Western Europe and, increasingly, to Eastern Europe. Most trains from Rome are Intercities, for which you pay a supplement (plus a fine if you did not pay the supplement before embarkation). There are regular trains for Venice, Florence, Bologna, Genoa, Turin and Rome. The city has several stations, although most trains use Stazione Centrale. For information, phone ☎ 6 75 00.

Stazione Nord (☎ 851 16 08) in Piazzale Cadorna (MM1 and MM2) connects Milan with Como, Erba and Varese. Stazione Porta Garibaldi (☎ 655 20 78) connects Milan with

Lecco, Bergamo, Valtellina and the north-west.

Car & Motorbike
Milan is the major junction of Italy's motorways, including the Autostrada del Sole (A1) to Reggio di Calabria in southern Italy; the A4, also known as the Milano-Torino (west to Turin) and the Serenissima (east to Verona and Venice); the A7 south to Genoa; and the A8 and A9 north to the lakes and Swiss border. The city is also a hub for smaller national roads, including the SS7 (Via Emilia), which runs south through Emilia-Romagna, and the SS11, which runs east-west from Turin to Brescia.

All these roads meet with the Milan ring road, known as the Tangenziale Est and the Tangenziale Ovest. From here, follow the signs into the city centre. It should be noted that the A4 in particular is an extremely busy road, where numerous accidents can hold up traffic for hours. From October to April all roads in the area become extremely hazardous because of rain, snow and fog.

GETTING AROUND
To/From the Airports
The STAM airport bus service leaves from Piazza Luigi di Savoia, on the east side of Stazione Centrale. Buses run to Linate airport every 20 to 30 minutes from 5 am to 9 pm (L4000, 20 minutes), and to Malpensa airport every 30 to 60 minutes (L12,000, one hour) from 5 am to 8.45 pm (extra services from 9 pm to 5 am to coincide with flights). For Linate, you can also get local bus No 73 from Piazza San Babila (Corso Europa) for L1300.

Public Transport
Milan's public transport system (ATM ☎ 669 70 32) is efficient. Its Metropolitana consists of three underground lines (red MM1, green MM2 and yellow MM3). It is the most convenient way to get around, but you may find ATM buses and trams useful too. A Metropolitana ticket costs L1300 – good for one underground ride and/or up to 75 minutes on buses and trams. You can buy a book of 10 tickets for L12,000, a day ticket for L4000 or a

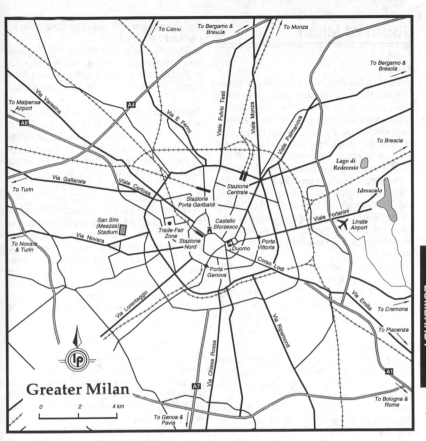

Greater Milan

0   2   4 km

LOMBARDY

weekly *tesserino* for L8000. Tickets are available at Metropolitana stations as well as authorised tobacconists and newspaper stands.

Free public transport maps are sometimes available from ATM offices at the duomo station and Stazione Centrale.

Taxi

Don't bother trying to hail a taxi, as it won't stop. Head for taxi ranks (marked with a yellow line on the road) which have telephones. A few of the radio-taxi companies are Radiotaxidata (☎ 53 53), Autoradiotaxi (☎ 85 85) and Esperia (☎ 83 88).

Car, Motorbike & Bicycle

Cars are banned (with some exceptions) from the city centre Monday to Friday from 7.30 am to 6 pm.

The city is dotted with expensive car parks (look for signs with a white P on a blue background). However, a cheaper alternative is to use one of the supervised car parks at the last stop on each Metropolitana train line.

Hertz, Avis, Maggiore and Europcar all have offices at Stazione Centrale.

To rent a bicycle, try Diego Seminari (☎ 738 48 80), Via Archimede 42.

South of Milan

PAVIA

Virtually a satellite of Milan, Pavia is none-theless a thriving industrial and agricultural centre on the banks of the Ticino river, perhaps best known for its prestigious university. Orig-inally the Roman Ticinum, Pavia later rivalled Milan as the capital of the Lombard kings until the 11th century. Like many cities of the north, Pavia became a pawn of power politics as the Renaissance dawned. Spain occupied it in the early 1500s and only relinquished control under the Treaty of Utrecht in 1713, upon which the Austrians promptly replaced them. Their rule, interrupted by a few years of Napoleonic French control from 1796, lasted until 1859.

Less than 30 minutes from Milan by train, Pavia warrants a visit in itself – the nearby Certosa di Pavia, a Carthusian monastery founded by the Visconti family, makes such a visit a must.

Orientation

From Piazzale Minerva, across from the main train station at the western edge of the city centre, go north along Viale Battisti for about 500 metres to the tourist office. Corso Cavour, which also runs off Piazzale Minerva, leads directly to Piazza Vittoria – the duomo is on your right.

Information

Tourist Office The IAT office (☎ 2 21 56), Via Filzi 2, produces two handy booklets, *Pavia in a Day* and *Pavia & its Province*. It is open Monday to Saturday from 8.30 am to 12.30 pm and 2 to 6 pm.

Money The Banca Nazionale del Lavoro on Via Mentana, near the university, has an ATM.

Post & Telecommunications The post office, Piazza della Posta 2, is open Monday to Satur-day from 8 am to 7 pm. The post code for central Pavia is 27100.

There is a Telecom office at Via Galliano, near the post office, which is open Monday to Friday from 9 am to 12.30 pm and 2.30 to 6 pm. The telephone code for Pavia is 0382.

Emergency For a police emergency, call ☎ 113. The questura (☎ 51 21) is at Piazza Italia 5. For medical assistance, go to the Ospedale San Matteo (☎ 50 11), Piazza Golgi 2; for emergencies, ring ☎ 47 23 51, and at night, ☎ 52 76 00.

Castello Visconti

Watching over the northern end of the medi-eval city, this forbidding castle (only two of its original four massive towers remain) was only ever used as a residence. It was built in 1360 for Galeazzo II Visconti and now houses the Museo Civico, Museo del Risorgimento and a small gallery of modern art. The castle is open Tuesday to Saturday from 9 am to midday and Sunday from 9.30 am to 12.30 pm. Admission is L6000.

University

On Corso Strada Nuova is the University of Pavia, which started life as a school in the 9th century and was elevated to university status in 1361. Among its notable graduates were Christopher Columbus (whose ashes are purportedly kept in a safe in the director's office) and the self-taught phys-icist Alessandro Volta, who discovered the electric volt.

Churches

The **duomo**, started in 1488, boasts the third largest dome in Italy, but it was only com-pleted last century. Both da Vinci and Donato Bramante contributed to the church's design. Parts of the duomo look the worse for wear, and in 1989 its bell tower simply fell over – killing four people.

The **Basilica di San Michele**, built on the site of a 7th-century church in 1090, was long a preferred location among European monarchs for coronations. Barbarossa was crowned Holy Roman emperor here in 1155.

The façade is in poor shape, despite restoration in the 1960s, and it appears they are having another shot at it now.

Medieval Towers

Pavia once boasted some 100 medieval watch towers. Most have been demolished, but a few remain – a group of three stands in Piazza di Leonardo da Vinci, just behind the post office.

Certosa di Pavia

Nine km north of Pavia, on the road to Milan, is the splendid Certosa di Pavia, a Carthusian monastery and one of the most notable buildings produced during the Italian Renaissance. Founded by Gian Galeazzo Visconti of Milan in 1396 as a private chapel for the Visconti family and a home for only 12 monks, the Charterhouse soon became one of the most lavish buildings in the country's north.

The interior is Gothic, although some Renaissance decoration is evident. Note the trompe l'oeuil high on the nave which gives the impression that people were watching the monks. In the former sacristy is a mammoth sculpture dating from 1409 and made from hippopotamus teeth, including 66 small bas-reliefs and 94 statuettes.

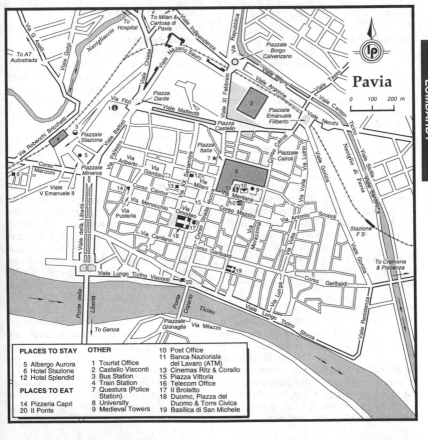

LOMBARDY

Pavia

0   100   200 m

PLACES TO STAY	OTHER	10 Post Office
5 Albergo Aurora	1 Tourist Office	11 Banca Nazionale del Lavaro (ATM)
6 Hotel Stazione	2 Castello Visconti	13 Cinemas Ritz & Corallo
12 Hotel Splendid	3 Bus Station	15 Piazza Vittoria
	4 Train Station	16 Telecom Office
PLACES TO EAT	7 Questura (Police Station)	17 Il Broletto
14 Pizzeria Capri	8 University	18 Duomo, Piazza del Duomo & Torre Civica
20 Il Ponte	9 Medieval Towers	19 Basilica di San Michele

Other features include inlaid-wood stalls dating from the 15th century, early plumbing devices and the tombs of the Viscontis.

The small cloisters to the right offer good photo angles of the church, particularly from behind the Baroque fountain. Behind the 122 arches of the larger cloisters are 24 cells, each a self-contained living area for one monk. Several are open to the public.

To get there by car from Milan, take the SS35 to Pavia and turn off at Torre del Mangano. The Certosa is well signposted. SGEA buses leave from Piazza Castello in Milan and from Via Trieste in Pavia, near the train station. The Certosa, a 10-minute walk from the bus stop, is also on the Milan-Pavia train line.

Places to Stay

It is better to stay in Milan and make the short trip to Pavia, as accommodation is in short supply.

Camping Ticino (☎ 52 53 62), Via Mascherpa 10, is open from April to September and charges L5000 per person and L5000 per tent. The *Hotel Stazione* (☎ 3 54 77), Via Bernardino de Rossi 8, is OK if you like the sound of passing trains, with adequate singles/ doubles from L40,000 /60,000. *Hotel Splen-did* (☎ 2 47 03), Via XX Settembre 11, is a better option and charges L5000 less than the Splendid for a single. The two-star *Albergo Aurora* (☎ 2 36 64), Viale Vittorio Emanuele II 25, charges L60,000/85,000, and is the last of the reasonably priced hotels in Pavia.

You could also stay out by the Certosa at *Hotel Certosa* (☎ 93 49 45; fax 93 30 04), Via Togliatti, which has comfortable singles/ doubles starting at L70,000/90,000.

Places to Eat

The province produces about one third of Italy's rice, so risotto is popular – try the favoured local version with small frogs. *Pizzeria Capri*, Corso Cavour 32, is a rea-sonable place for a pizza or a limited range of simple pasta and meat courses. Because the university has 22,000 students Pavia has a few good bars and a lively atmosphere, particularly around the campus. For some-

thing a little more elegant, you'll find a good choice of people-watching vantage points around Piazza della Vittoria. *Il Ponte*, Piazzale Ponte Ticino 1, is a busy student café/bar.

Getting There & Away

The city's bus station (☎ 30 20 20) is on Via Trieste, next to the train station. SGEA buses run to Milan and Certosa di Pavia. Trains leave hourly for Milan. The city can also be reached direct from Genoa, Piacenza, Cremona and Ventimiglia. To reach Pavia by car, take the A7 autostrada from Milan and exit at the Bereguardo or Gropello C turn-off. Follow the signs to the city centre. Alternatively, take the SS35 from Milan, a better bet for hitchhikers.

Getting Around

The town is small, almost grid-like and easy to navigate on foot. SGEA buses Nos 3 and 6 run from the train station through the main square, Piazza della Vittoria. Most cars are banned from the centre and there are car parks near the station.

East of Milan

BERGAMO

Virtually two cities, Bergamo's walled hilltop *città alta* (upper town) is surrounded by the *città bassa* (lower town), a sprawling modern addition to this magnificent former outpost of the Venetian empire. Although Milan's skyscrapers to the south-west are visible on a clear day, Bergamo's dialect and traditions echo more faithfully those of Venice, which controlled the city for 350 years until Napoleon arrived at the gates. Despite its wealth of medieval, Baroque and Renaissance architecture, the city is not a big tourist destination.

Orientation

Viale Papa Giovanni XXIII, which becomes Viale Roma and then Viale Vittorio Emanuele II uphill towards the old town, forms the principal axis of the city. It is capped at the southern end by the train and bus stations, and the main tourist, post and telephone offices and several banks are all located on or near this central boulevard. These services are duplicated in the upper town. Viale Vittorio Emanuele II swings east around the old town walls to enter the upper town at Porta di Sant'Agostino. You can also take a funicular up for the last leg.

Piazza Vecchia is the focal point of the upper town, and the main street is Via B Colleoni.

Information
Tourist Offices In the lower town, the APT is at Viale Papa Giovanni XXIII 106 (☎ 24 22 26), and in the upper town at Vicolo Aquila Nera 2 (☎ 23 27 30). Both are Monday to Friday from 9 am to 12.30 pm and 3 to 6.30 pm. The upper town office is open also at weekends.

Money There are several banks in the lower end of town. The Credito Italiano on Viale Roma has ATMs

Post & Telecommunications The main post office in the lower town is at Via Masone 2A, beyond Piazza della Libertà. It is open Monday to Friday from 8.15 am to 8 pm and Saturday from 8.30 am to 12.30 pm. A branch office on Via San Lorenzo in the upper town is open from 8 am to 1.30 pm. The post code is 24100.

The Telecom office is in Largo Porta Nuova, near Piazza Vittorio Veneto, and is open from 9 am to 12.30 pm and 2.30 to 7 pm. In the upper town, the Telecom office is just next to the Agnello d'Oro hotel on Piazzetta San Pancrazio.

Emergency For police emergency, call ☎ 113. The questura is on Via A Noli. The Ospedale Maggiore (☎ 26 91 11) is at the western edge of town, along Via Garibaldi and its continuation, Via Mazzini. For an ambulance, call ☎ 25 02 46.

Things to See
If you have limited time, head straight to the città alta. Bus No 1 from the train station goes to the funicular.

Piazza Vecchia The heart of medieval Bergamo is hard to miss. Whichever way you enter the walled hilltop town, you'll soon find yourself in this gracious square. The white porticoed building on Via Colleoni, which forms the north side of the piazza, is the 17th-century **Palazzo Nuovo**, now a library and the square's least interesting feature. Turn instead to the south and you will face the imposing arches and columns of the **Palazzo della Ragione**, first built in the 12th century, but largely reconstructed four centuries later. The lion of St Mark is a reminder of Venice's long reign. Note the sun clock in the pavement beneath the arches. The building occasionally hosts exhibitions, and on summer Sunday afternoons traditional puppeteers take over below. Their art dates to the 16th century and contributed much to the Venetian commedia dell'arte. Next to the palazzo, the **Torre Civica** still tolls the 10 pm curfew. For L2000 you can climb to the top for wonderful views of the city.

Tucked in behind these secular buildings is the core of Bergamo's spiritual life, the Piazza del Duomo. Oddly enough, the modest Baroque **duomo**, which is dedicated to Saint Alexander, very much plays second fiddle to the neighbouring **Chiesa di Santa Maria Maggiore**, an imposing Romanesque church begun in 1137 and whose weather-worn exterior hides a lavish Baroque interior. Gaetano Donizetti, a 19th-century composer and native son of Bergamo, lies buried here. The extravagant add-on is the **Cappella Colleoni**, built by the condottiere of the same name as a funeral chapel – he in fact was not buried here. A somewhat gawdy Renaissance gem, the interior was thickly covered with restorers' scaffolding at the time of writing. All churches are open from 9 am to midday and from 2 to 5 pm. Admission is free.

The octagonal **baptistry** was built inside Santa Maria Maggiore in 1340, but transferred outside late last century.

Viewpoints A stroll downhill along Via Colleoni and then Via Gombito, the latter marked by a 12th-century **tower** of the same

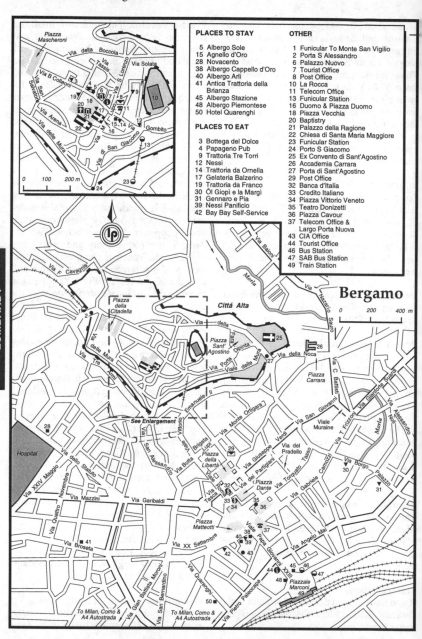

PLACES TO STAY

5 Albergo Sole
15 Agnello d'Oro
28 Novacento
38 Albergo Cappello d'Oro
40 Albergo Arli
41 Antica Trattoria della Brianza
45 Albergo Stazione
48 Albergo Piemontese
50 Hotel Quarenghi

PLACES TO EAT

3 Bottega del Dolce
4 Papageno Pub
9 Trattoria Tre Torri
12 Nessi
14 Trattoria da Ornella
17 Gelateria Balzerino
19 Trattoria da Franco
30 Öl Giopì e la Margì
31 Gennaro e Pia
39 Nessi Panificio
42 Bay Bay Self-Service

OTHER

1 Funicular To Monte San Vigilio
2 Porta S Alessandro
6 Palazzo Nuovo
7 Tourist Office
8 Post Office
10 La Rocca
11 Telecom Office
13 Funicular Station
16 Duomo & Piazza Duomo
18 Piazza Vecchia
20 Baptistry
21 Palazzo della Ragione
22 Chiesa di Santa Maria Maggiore
23 Funicular Station
24 Porto S Giacomo
25 Ex Convento di Sant'Agostino
26 Accademia Carrara
27 Porta di Sant'Agostino
29 Post Office
32 Banca d'Italia
33 Credito Italiano
34 Piazza Vittorio Veneto
35 Teatro Donizetti
36 Piazza Cavour
37 Telecom Office & Largo Porta Nuova
43 CIA Office
44 Tourist Office
46 Bus Station
47 SAB Bus Station
49 Train Station

Bergamo

LOMBARDY

name, takes you along Medieval 'main street' towards the funicular, and left to **La Rocca**, a fortress which houses the small **Museo Civico del Risorgimento e della Resistenza**. The views from the adjoining park are worth the effort. For more spectacular views, take the funicular to Monte San Vigilio from Porta di Sant' Alessandro, at the opposite end of the upper town.

Accademia Carrara Some time should be made for the art gallery of the Accademia Carrara, most pleasantly reached on foot from the upper town through the Porta di Sant'Agostino and down the cobbled Via D Noca. Founded in 1780, it contains an impressive range of Italian masters, particularly of the Venetian school. An early *St Sebastian* by Raphael is worth looking out for, and there are works by Botticelli, Lorenzo Lotto, Andrea Mantegna, Giovanni Tiepolo, Titian and Canaletto. It is open daily, except Tuesday, from 9.30 am to 12.30 pm and 2.30 to 5.30 pm. Admission is L3000.

Città Bassa If heading back to the station for a train to Milan, you could do worse than hover about the series of squares that make up the centre of the lower town. Piazza Matteotti was redesigned in 1924 by a Fascist favourite, Marcello Piacentini.

The **Teatro Donizetti**, near Piazza Cavour, was built in the shape of a horseshoe in the 18th century and dedicated to the composer in 1897, the centenary of his birth.

Activities
The CAI, Via Ghislanzoni 15, has details about winter sports, hiking and gentle walks in the Bergamo Alps, which rise to 1000 metres close to the town.

The tourist office also produces several maps of hiking trails in the Bergamo province, many of them numbered and quoted with approximate walking times. The Libreria Lorenzelli, Viale Papa Giovanni XXIII 72, has a range of hiking and cycling guidebooks in Italian devoted to the area.

Places to Stay
Bergamo is an easy day trip from Milan but if you want to stay, arrive early and/or telephone ahead – what hotels there are fill distressingly quickly.

A few cheaper hotels – often full with migrant workers from the south – are scattered about the lower town, but if you have a little extra, there are a few excellent options up the hill. The APT has a list of camping grounds and rifugi in the nearby Bergamo Alps, and agriturismo farms and houses throughout the province.

The *Ostello Bergamo* (☎ 34 23 49), Via Galileo Ferraris 1, is several km from the lower town. Take bus No 14 from the train station. It was closed for repairs in 1994.

Lower Town One budget hotel is *Novecento* (☎ 25 52 10), Via dello Statuto 23, near the corner of Via Damiano Chiesa, with singles/ doubles from L30,000/40,000. It's a bit of a hike from the train station. The *Antica Trattoria della Brianza* (☎ 25 33 38), Via Broseta 61a, is about 20 minutes walk west of the train station, opposite the Coop supermarket. It has modest, clean rooms for L25,000/ 45,000. Closer to the station, and a little more expensive, is *Hotel Quarenghi* (☎ 32 03 31), at Via Quarenghi 33. The nearby *San Giorgio* and *Sant'Antonino* are in much the same league.

A last-ditch option is *Albergo Stazione*, Piazzale Marconi 1, opposite the train station. The area is highly unpleasant at night and the same can be said of the hotel bar. The *Albergo Piemontese* (☎ 24 26 29), on the other side of the same square, is one of several three-star places in the area. If you're really out of luck, or have lire to burn, *Albergo Arli* (☎ 22 20 14), Largo Porta Nuova 12, has doubles for L85,000. Further up the scale again, *Albergo Cappallo d'Oro* (☎ 23 25 03), Viale Papa Giovanni XXIII 12, starts at L159,000 for a double and reaches upward.

Upper Town The *Agnello d'Oro* (☎ 24 98 83), Via Gombito 22, could almost pass for an antique shop. Just a short walk from the

LOMBARDY

funicular station, it has attractive rooms from L50,000/85,000. The *Albergo Sole* (☎ 21 82 38), Via Colleoni 1, just off Piazza Vecchia, has rooms from L70,000/100,000 and is also good.

Places to Eat
Like the Venetians, the Bergamaschi are fond of polenta and eat it as a side dish or dessert. They contributed casonsei, a ravioli stuffed with meat, to the Italian table, and the area is noted for its fine red wines, including Valcalepio.

Lower Town For a good, cheap lunch, *Bay Bay Self-Service*, Via Tiraboschi 73, is hard to beat. It's open Monday to Friday only. A hundred metres closer to Viale Giovanni XXIII in the same street, the *Nessi Panificio* is one of a chain of bakeries and pastry shops around the city. Here they do a popular takeaway pizza – all the school kids swarm in.

Gennaro e Pia, Via Borgo Palazzo 41, has pizzas from L5000. *Öl Giopì e la Margì*, Via Borgo Palazzo 25G, is expensive (L50,000 for a full meal) but the waiters wear traditional costume if that's important to you.

Upper Town Cheap food is in short supply here, but you can get good pieces of pizza sold by weight at the *Bottega del Dolce*, Via Colleoni 36. *Nessi* has a branch at Via Gombito 34, and they have a selection of local sweets, including polenta eösei, as well as pizza.

Trattoria da Franco, Via B Colleoni 8, has pizzas from L5000. *Trattoria da Ornella*, Via Gombito 15, offers traditional foods, and a full meal will cost around L45,000. A cosier spot offering Bergamesque specialities is the *Trattoria Tre Torri*, Piazza Mercato del Fieno, at the southern end of Via San Lorenzo. You'll need to book ahead.

Gelateria Balzerino, Piazza Vecchia, is the perfect spot for an ice cream or granita. There are a couple of watering holes and cafés along the main street. Try *Papageno Pub* at Via B Colleoni 2, or *Pasticceria Donizetti* for coffee under porticoes.

Getting There & Away
The bus station (☎ 24 81 50) in Piazzale G Marconi is serviced by SAB, which operates to the lakes and mountains from its own terminal, and a half dozen other lines that go to Milan, Brescia, Cremona, Como and Piacenza, to name a few.

The train station is also on Piazzale Marconi. There are frequent trains for the 50-minute run to Milan and less frequent trains to Brescia and Cremona.

To reach Bergamo by car, take the A4 autostrada from Milan or Venice, the SS11 from Milan or the SS42 from the south. On entering Bergamo note that the 'centro' signs refer to the lower town. If you want to head straight for the old city, follow the 'città alta' signs. Hitchhikers could try the SS11.

Getting Around
ATB buses serve the city, and you can get free route maps from the office on Largo Porta Nuova. Bus No 1 connects the train station with the funicular to the città alta. Bus No 3 runs from Porta Sant'Alessandro in the città alta to Via Pietro Paleocapa in the lower town. You can buy tickets valid for an hour's travel on buses and funiculars for L1200 or an all-day ticket for L4000. There are machines at the train and funicular stations.

AROUND BERGAMO
There are several small ski resorts in the Bergamo Alps, notably around the **Val Brembana**, reached from Bergamo along Via Nazario Sauro, and **Val Seriana**, reached by way of Via Santa Caterina from the lower town. Each valley boasts seven or eight Alpine rifugi for summer and winter activities (details from the Bergamo APT), many walking tracks and reasonably priced accommodation.

VALTELLINA
Covering the band of Alps across Lombardy's north, the Valtellina is one of Italy's least attractive Alpine regions, although it does have some acceptable skiing and is well set up for walking.

The APT Valtellina has offices in Bormio (☎ 0342-90 33 00), Via Stelvio 10; in Sondrio

(☎ 0342-51 25 00), Via C Battisti 12; in Aprica (☎ 0342-74 61 13), Corso Roma 161; in Madesimo (☎ 0343-5 30 15), Via Carducci 27; and in Livigno (☎ 0342-99 63 79), Via Dala Gesa 65. Pick up a copy of *Trekking in Valtellina*, which details walks and provides rifuge information for the area.

Trains leave Milan for Sondrio, a regional transport hub, and buses connect with the resorts and towns.

BRESCIA

With a population of 190,000, Brescia is a somewhat scruffy provincial capital, arms production centre and transport hub. Although rough around the edges, its student life gives the place a bit of jump noticeably lacking in some other Lombard towns, and there are a few sights worth stopping for.

When Rome took control of the Gallic town in 225 BC, Brescia (the name derives from a word meaning hill) already had hundreds of years of now obscure history behind it. Charlemagne and his successors ruled Brescia in the 9th century, and the following 1000 years brought a succession of outside rulers. As revolution swept Europe in 1848-49, Brescia was dubbed 'The Lioness' for its 10-day anti-Austrian uprising – an unsuccessful prelude to its participation in the movement towards Italian unification a decade later.

Orientation
From the train and bus stations on the southwestern edge, the city centre is a 10-minute walk along Viale della Stazione and Corso dei Martiri della Libertà towards Piazza della Vittoria.

Information
Tourist Office The APT (☎ 4 34 18) is at Corso Zanardelli 34. It is open Monday to Friday from 9 am to 12.30 pm and 3 to 6.30 pm and Saturday from 9 am to 12.30 pm.

Money There are plenty of banks in Brescia. The Banca San Paolo de Brescia on Corso Zanardelli and the Banca Credito Agrario Bresciano on Piazza Paolo VI both have fairly reliable ATMs.

Post & Telecommunications The main post office is in Piazza della Vittoria and is open Monday to Friday from 8.15 am to 5.30 pm and Saturday from 8.15 am to 1 pm. The post code for central Brescia is 25100.

The Telecom office is at Via Moretto 46 and is open Monday to Friday from 9 am to 12.30 pm and 2.30 to 6 pm. The telephone code for Brescia is 030.

Travel Agency CTS (☎ 4 18 89) is at Via Moretto 68b.

Emergency & Medical Services The questura (☎ 4 25 61) is on Via Botticelli. For emergencies call ☎ 113. The Ospedale Civile (☎ 3 99 51) is in Piazzale Ospedale at the northern edge of the city. You can get an ambulance on ☎ 200 25 22. There's an all-night pharmacy at Via Einaudi 9.

Colle Cidneo & Castle
Brescia's historic centre is dominated by the Colle Cidneo, surmounted by a rambling castle that has been the core of the city defences for centuries. Torre Mirabella, the main round tower, was built by the Viscontis in the 13th century; the rest is a hotchpotch of add-ons and alterations completed by Brescia's long series of outside overlords. The castle houses two museums. The **Museo delle Armi** and the **Civico Museo del Risorgimento** are open daily, except Monday, from 10 am to 12.30 pm and 3 to 5 pm. Admission to the latter, devoted to Italian unification history, is L2000. The former is said to contain one of Italy's most extensive weapons collections. You are free to wander the grounds and much of the castle walls, a smoochers' hang-out, from 8 am to 8 pm.

Cathedrals & Piazzas
The most compelling of Brescia's religious monuments is the **Duomo Vecchio**, or Rotonda, an 11th-century Romanesque basilica built over a 6th-century circular structure on Piazza Paolo VI. The form of the church is

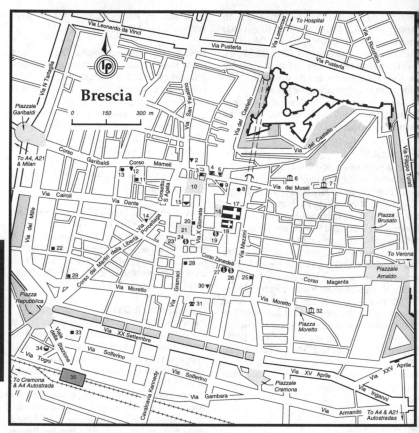

Brescia

0   150   300 m

PLACES TO STAY

9   Hotel Nuovo Orologio
11 Albergo Vellia
20 Hotel Vittoria
22 Servizio della Giovane
25 Albergo Regina
28 Albergo Italia
29 Albergo Rigamonti e
    Mansione
33 Albergo Solferino

PLACES TO EAT

2   I Chiostri
3   Manhattan

4   Caffetteria la Torre
5   Al Frate
12 Yo
14 Ciao
30 Don Rodriguez

OTHER

1   Colle Cidneo & Castle
6   Museo Romano
7   Museo dell'Età
    Cristiana
8   Il Broletto
10 Piazza della Loggia
13 Torre della Pallata
15 Post Office

16 Piazza Paolo VI
17 Duomo Nuovo
18 Duomo Vecchio
19 Banca Credito
    Agrario Bresciano
21 Piazza della Vittoria
23 Piazza del Mercato
24 Banca Commerciale
    d'Italia
26 Banca San Paolo di
    Brescia (ATM)
27 Tourist Office
31 Telecom Office
32 Pinacoteca
    Tosio–Martinengo
34 Bus Station
35 Train Station

LOMBARDY

hardly common, and there are hints, such as the mosaics, of an even earlier Roman presence on the site. Right next door, the Renaissance **Duomo Nuovo** dwarfs its elderly neighbour, but is of less interest. Also on the square is **Il Broletto**, a medieval town hall with an 11th-century tower.

North-west of Piazza Paolo VI is another square, Piazza della Loggia, dominated by the squat 16th-century **loggia**, in whose construction Palladio had a hand. The **Torre dell'Orologio**, with its exquisite astrological timepiece, is modelled on the one in Venice's Piazza San Marco.

Finally, the Fascist era **Piazza della Vittoria** is well worth a look. Laid out in 1932 by Piacentini, the square and its buildings (like the post office) are a perfect example of the period's monumentalism.

Roman Ruins & Museums

Evidence of the Roman presence in Brescia is still visible today. Along Via dei Musei, at the foot of the castle, are the remains of the **Capitolium**, a Roman temple built in 73 AD and now housing the modest **Museo Romano**. It is open Tuesday to Sunday from 10 am to 12.30 pm and 2 to 6 pm. Admission is L2000.

More interesting is the **Museo dell'Età Cristiana** (Museum of Christian Art), housed in the jumbled Monastero di Santa Giulia and Basilica di San Salvatore. It has the same hours as the Museo Romano and admission is free but there is a compulsory guided tour in Italian. Roman mosaics have been unearthed here as well. The star piece is the 8th-century Croce di Desiderio, a Lombard cross encrusted with hundreds of jewels.

The **Pinacoteca Tosio-Martinengo**, on Piazza Moretto, features works by artists of the Brescian school as well as Raphael. It is open Tuesday to Sunday from 9 am to 12.30 pm and 3 to 6 pm (a little later on weekends). Admission is L2000.

Organised Tours

A programme of free tours to specific sights is patronised by the Fondazione Credito Agrario Bresciano. Information can be obtained at Via Borgondio 29 or by calling

☎ 375 63 54. You'll need to understand Italian to get much out of the tours.

Places to Stay

There should be no problems finding accommodation, particularly in summer.

Among the better budget choices is *Hotel Nuovo Orologio* (☎ 377 28 78), Via Cesare Beccaria 17, just off Piazza Paolo VI. Some singles are pokey though, and they start at L35,000. Doubles start at L60,000. The hotel has a bar and TV room.

Albergo Regina (☎ 375 78 81), near the tourist office in Corso Zanardelli, charges the same rates, as does *Albergo Italia* (☎ 375 62 73), Via Gramsci 11.

Another reasonable choice in the same range is *Albergo Rigamonti e Mansione* (☎ 4 81 52), Contrada Mansione 6. *Albergo Solferino* (☎ 46 300), Via Solferino 1, is near the station and has basic singles/doubles from L30,000/50,000. Closer to the centre of town is the similar *Albergo Vellia* (☎ 375 64 72), Via Calzaveglia 5.

Places to Eat

The locals head for Piazza del Mercato for fresh produce on most days. Risotto and beef dishes are common in Brescia, as in most of Lombardy. The region offers many good wines, including those from the Botticino, Lugana and Riviera del Garda vineyards.

There is a collection of cheap snack places at the bus station, or you can try *Ciao*, Via Porcellaga 20, where pasta starts at about L4000. *Don Rodriguez*, Via Cavallotti 6, has moderately priced pizzas. *I Chiostri*, Via San Faustino 16, makes tramezzini (sandwiches) from L2000.

The happening area is along Corso Mameli and Via dei Musei. There are plenty of restaurants, cafés and bars, lent a bit of buzz by the student population.

If you're prepared to part with L40,000 plus, *Al Frate*, Via dei Musei 25, serves up well presented regional dishes – it's often full.

Caffetteria la Torre and the *Manhattan* bar are busy student haunts. For yoghurt gelato, go straight to *Yo*, Corso Mameli 63.

LOMBARDY

Entertainment

The International Piano Festival, held from early April until June, is staged in conjunction with nearby Bergamo, while the Estate Aperta festival of music and other activities occupy the summer months. The city's opera season is in October and November.

Getting There & Away

The main bus station (☎ 377 42 37) is near the train station, but most runs serve Brescia province and lakes Garda and Iseo. Only a few buses run to Milan and Bergamo.

If you're coming by train from Rome, change at Verona. From Milan, frequent trains take 50 minutes. There are quite a few to Cremona, Venezia, Verona and Bergamo.

By car, the A4 and SS11 go west to Milan and east to Lago di Garda and Verona, while the A21 and SS45 head south to Cremona.

CREMONA

Home of the Stradivarius violin, Cremona today jealously maintains its centuries-old status as premier exponent of the delicate art of making the perfect string instrument. All the great violin-making dynasties started here – Amati, Guarneri and Stradivari – and there are plenty of opportunities for getting better acquainted with the subject. Not that Cremona is Italy's only centre for violin-makers – rivals in nearby cities like Bologna will assure you the only thing better about the Cremonese product is the publicity. For centuries an independent city-state, Cremona also boasts a compact but impressive city centre, meriting a stopover if not necessarily an overnight stay. It is an easy daytrip from Milan, Mantua, Brescia and Piacenza.

Orientation

The town is small and easy to navigate. From the train station, walk straight south along Via Palestro to the central area around Piazza Cavour, Piazza della Pace and Piazza del Comune. Bus No 1 goes to Piazza Cavour from the train station, but you'll probably travel just as fast on foot.

Information

Tourist Office The APT office (☎ 2 32 33) is at Piazza del Comune 5, opposite the duomo and is open Monday to Friday from 9.30 am to 12.30 pm and 3 to 6 pm.

Money The Credito Romagnolo on Piazza della Libertá has an ATM.

Post & Telecommunications The post office is at Via Verdi 1, and it is open Monday to Friday from 8 am to 7 pm and Saturday to 1 pm. The post code for central Cremona is 26100.

The Telecom office is on Via Cadolini and is open Monday to Friday from 9 am to 12.30 pm and 2.30 to 6 pm. The telephone code for Cremona is 0372.

Emergency For police emergency, call ☎ 113. The questura (☎ 48 81) is at Via Tribunali 6. For an ambulance, call ☎ 43 44 45. The public hospital (☎ 40 51 11) is on Largo Priori.

Piazza del Comune

Even if violins do not ring your bell, the rust-red heart of Cremona, **Piazza del Comune**, makes at least a brief stop in this quiet town worthwhile. Quiet is the word – most museums are closed on Monday and city ordinances limiting traffic in the centre have so emptied the zone that shopkeepers groaning over the stay-away effect have told the authorities 'basta!' (enough!).

Medieval Cremona, like Lombard towns, was an indepedent *comune* until the 14th century, when the Viscontis of Milan added it to their growing collection. To keep clear the difference between the secular and the spiritual, buildings connected with the latter were erected on the east side of the square; those concerned with earthly affairs were constructed across the way.

The **duomo** started out as a Romanesque basilica but by the time it was finished in 1190 had been heavily overtaken by Gothic modishness – best demonstrated by its Latin cross-shaped ground plan. The façade, however, is largely faithful to the original concepts. Inside, partly hidden by restorers' scaffolding, there is plenty of

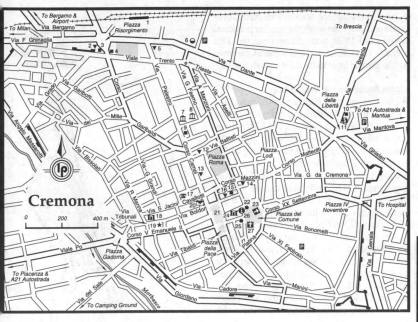

LOMBARDY

PLACES TO STAY		12	Pizzeria da Tonino	17	Telecom Office
		13	Ristorante Marechiaro	18	Palazzo di Giustizia
3	Albergo Bologna	14	Ristorante Centrale	19	Questura
4	Albergo Ideale	16	Ristorante Fou-Lú		(Police Station)
9	Albergo Touring			20	Post Office
10	Albergo Brescia	**OTHER**		21	Piazza Cavour
15	Hotel Astoria			22	Torrazzo
		1	Train Station	23	Duomo
PLACES TO EAT		6	Bus Station	24	Palazzo Comunale
		7	Museo Stradivariano	25	Loggia dei Militi
2	La Bersagliera	8	Museo Civico	26	APT Tourist Office
5	Taboga Fast Food	11	Credito Romagnolo (ATM)	27	Baptistry

artwork to admire – perhaps the most interesting are the partial frescoes uncovered in the early 1990s – some date to the cathedral's first days, including one of a winged harpy. Look for work by the Renaissance masters Boccaccino and Bembo. It's open daily from 7 am to 7 pm, with a three-hour break from midday.

The adjoining bell tower, or **Torrazzo**, is connected to the cathedral by a Renaissance loggia, the **Bertazzola**. At 111 metres, the Torrazzo is said to be the tallest tower of its ilk in Italy. It is open from 10.30 am to midday and 3 to 6 pm. Admission is L5000. To the south is the 12th-century **baptistry** which, like many Italian medieval baptistries, has an octagonal base. Alluding to renewal and hence baptism and resurrection, the figure eight appears in much religious decoration – its use in this kind of architecture is no coincidence.

Across the square are the **Palazzo Comunale** and, just to its south, the smaller porticoed **Loggia dei Militi**, both dating from the 13th century. The former was and remains the town hall, while the latter housed the town's militia.

Violin Museums & Workshop

While you're at the Palazzo Comunale, take a look at the violin collection, featuring two Amatis, two Guarneris and a 1715 Stradivarius. A local maestro occasionally plays the instruments to keep them in working order. To find out if and when he might do so, call the town hall switchboard (☎ 40 71) for an appointment. The collection can be viewed Monday to Saturday from 8.30 am to 6 pm and Sundays and holidays from 9.15 am to 12.15 pm and 3 to 6 pm. Admission is L5000.

As the name suggests, the **Museo Stradivariano**, Via Palestro 17, features items from the Stradivari workshop. It keeps the same hours as the Palazzo del Comune, and admission is L5000. Around the corner, the **Museo Civico** (same hours and admission fee) has more violins and various other odds and sods.

If you want to see violins being made, go to the 1st floor of the Torrazzo, where a functioning workshop has been installed. The APT also has a list of most of the 90 workshops scattered throughout Cremona today, where you may also be able to arrange visits.

Festivals

Violin-lovers flock to Cremona for the Triennale Internazionale degli Strumenti ad Arco (International String Instrument Expo). It's held every third October and the next time will be in 1997. Autumn and winter tend to be rich in music programmes and concerts – check with the APT.

Places to Stay

The *Camping Parco al Po* (☎ 2 71 37), Via Lungo Po Europa, has sites from L6000 per person, plus L5000 per tent. Head southwest from Piazza Cavour.

Albergo Bologna (☎ 2 42 58), at Piazza Risorgimento 7 near the train and bus stations, has about the cheapest beds in Cremona, with

A Stradivarius violin

small singles for L25,000. Not far off in Viale Trento e Trieste, *Albergo Ideale* (also known as *Rada*, ☎ 3 86 68) has singles/doubles for L35,000/45,000 and a pokey room for L25,000. Closer to the centre, *Albergo Touring* (☎ 3 69 76), Via Palestro 3, has singles/doubles for L30,000/50,000. If you're driving in, *Albergo Brescia* (☎ 43 46 15), Via Brescia 7, is handy. Decent singles/doubles cost L40,000/50,000. Located in a small lane near Piazza Cavour, *Hotel Astoria* (☎ 46 16 16), Via Bordigallo 19, has comfortable singles/doubles with three-star mod cons for L70,000/95,000.

Places to Eat

Cremona's gifts to Italian cuisine include bollito (boiled meats) – there are several varieties and cotechino served with polenta is the speciality. Mostarda is the odd item on the sweets list. Often served with your bollito, it consists of fruit in sweet mustardy goo. Sounds unpalatable, but it's really not bad at all.

For quick snacks, head for *Taboga Fast Food*, Via Palestro 51, near the train station. The *Ristorante Marechiaro*, Corso Campi 49, serves standard Italian fare, including pizzas for about L7000. *La Bersagliera*, Piazza Risorgimento 12, is similar. You can also get a decent pizza at *Pizzeria da Tonino*, Via Battisti.

With a little more money, you could head to the earthy and very good *Ristorante Centrale*, Via Pertusio 4, off Corso Mazzini. It's a popular no-nonsense spot where you can try cotechino, admire human-size jars of mostarda and drool over huge drums of fresh local cheese. You can eat well for about L35,000. If you need a change, go to *Ristorante Fou-Lú*, the Chinese establishment on Via Bordigallo, just north of Piazza Cavour.

Getting There & Away
The bus station is off Via Dante, east of the train station. Various companies run to Milan, Brescia and Bergamo, and occasionally long-distance buses heading for Genoa, Trieste and Venice call in here.

By train (☎ 2 22 37), the city can be reached from Milan via Treviglio, from Mantua, Pavia and Brescia, or from the south by changing at Piacenza.

If you're driving, the most direct road from Milan is the SS415 (Paullo exit); the A21 takes you to Brescia, where it joins with the A4.

MANTUA (MANTOVA)
On the shores of lakes Superiore, Mezzo and Inferiore (a glorified widening of the Mincio river), Mantua is a serene and beautiful city. However, industrial sprawl from its booming petrochemical industry has scarred the surrounding countryside and left the lakes heavily polluted. The city can be visited as a day trip from as far afield as Milan, but to do it justice, spend the night.

History
Mantua was settled by the Etruscans in the 10th century BC and later prospered under Roman rule. It passed to the House of Gonzaga in 1328, flourishing under one of the foremost Renaissance dynasties and attracting the likes of Petrarch, Antonio Pisanello, Andrea Mantegna, Giulio Romano and Rubens. The golden days of 'La Gloriosa' came to a mean end when Austria took control in 1708. Vienna's troops stayed in control (aside from the predictable Napoleonic interlude at the end of the 18th century) until 1866.

Orientation
The old part of the city is on a small peninsula at the southern edge of the three lakes, with the newer parts spread around their shores. From the train station in Piazza Don Leoni, head a short distance to the right for Largo di Porta Pradella. From there, take a

LOMBARDY

The Chaste & Royal Poet
Dryden called Virgil 'the chastest and royalest of poets'. Born 70 years before Christ on his parents' farm just outside Mantua, Virgil is that city's most illustrious son and one of Rome's greatest poets. Of the three works he left behind *The Aeneid* is the most exalted. An epic in the great tradition of the ancient Sumerian myth, Gilgamesh, and Homer's *Iliad* and *Odyssey*, the tale is a fantastic account of the foundation of Rome, loaded with symbolism and told with unsurpassed virtuosity. The inspiration of countless poets since, Virgil comes to life as Dante's 'sweet master' in the Florentine's *Divine Comedy*, 14 centuries after Virgil's death. ■

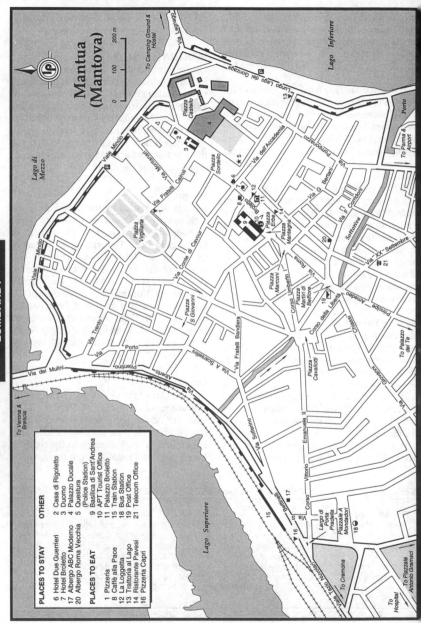

Mantua (Mantova)

Lago di Mezzo

Lago Inferiore

Lago Superiore

PLACES TO STAY
6 Hotel Due Guerrieri
7 Hotel Broletto
17 Albergo ABC Moderno
20 Albergo Roma Vecchia

PLACES TO EAT
1 Pizzeria
8 Caffè alla Pace
12 La Loggetta
13 Trattoria al Lago
14 Ristorante Pavesi
16 Pizzeria Capri

OTHER
2 Casa di Rigoletto
3 Duomo
4 Palazzo Ducale
5 Questura (Police Station)
9 Basilica di Sant'Andrea
10 APT Tourist Office
11 Palazzo Broletto
15 Train Station
18 Bus Station
19 Post Office
21 Telecom Office

sharp turn left up Corso Vittorio Emanuele II for a 10-minute walk to the city centre. The heart of the centre is a string of five piazzas, capped at the northern end by the sprawling complex of the Palazzo Ducale.

Information

Tourist Office The APT (☎ 32 82 53), Piazza Mantegna 6, produces a range of information about trips throughout the province. It is open Monday to Saturday from 9 am to midday and 3 to 6 pm.

Money Banks are located throughout the city centre and are open from 8.20 am to 1.20 pm and 3.20 to 4.20 pm. Some have extended hours on Thursdays.

Post & Telecommunications The main post office is on Piazza Martiri di Belfiore, along Via Roma south of Piazza Marconi. It is open Monday to Friday from 8.30 am to 7 pm and Saturday from 8.20 am to 1.20 pm. The post code for central Mantua is 46100.

There is a Telecom office on Via XX Settembre which is open Monday to Friday from 9 am to 12.30 pm and 2.30 to 6 pm. The telephone code for Mantua is 0376.

Emergency For police emergency, call ☎ 113. The questura (☎ 32 63 41) is at Piazza Sordello 46. For medical emergencies, call ☎ 33 73 37, or at night the Guardia Medica on ☎ 33 74 34. The public hospital (☎ 33 71) is on Via Albertoni, at the southern end of the old town.

Palazzo Ducale

Also known as the Reggia dei Gonzaga, after the longtime rulers of Mantua, the Palazzo Ducale occupies a great chunk of the north-eastern corner of the city. Its walls hide three piazzas, a park, a basilica and a total of 450 rooms – an imposing demonstration of the pride and wealth of the Gonzagas, although from Piazza Sordello you would never guess the extent of what lies behind. The centrepiece is the **Castello di San Giorgio**, which contains a museum. The Gonzagas were avid art collectors, as the visitor soon realises. The high point is Andrea Mantegna's Camera degli Sposi, a series of fine frescoes in one of the castle's towers. This part of the complex is open from 9 am to 12.30 pm and 2.30 to 4.30 pm. Admission is L12,000. You are free to wander the rest of the area at will. Occasionally other exhibitions are held in the cellars of the outer walls, so it is worth wandering outside the city gates and along the palazzo's lakeside walls.

Churches

The Baroque cupola of the **Basilica di Sant'Andrea**, Piazza Mantegna, looms majestically over the city in much the same way that St Paul's dominates east London. Designed by Leon Battisti Alberti in 1472, Mantua's principal place of worship houses a much disputed relic – containers said to hold the blood of Christ. They are paraded around the town in a grand procession on Good Friday. There is no dispute about the tomb of the painter Andrea Mantegna, also to be found inside the basilica.

East of the basilica across the 15th-century colonnaded Piazza delle Erbe is the **Rotonda di San Lorenzo**, sunk below the level of the piazza and believed to be on the site of a Roman temple dedicated to Venus.

The **duomo**, on Piazza Sordello, pales somewhat before the magnificence of the Basilica. Its origins lie in the 10th century, but there is little to see of them. The façade was erected in the mid-18th century, while the decoration inside was done by Giulio Romana after a fire in 1545.

Piazzas

Past the 13th-century Palazzo della Ragione on Piazza delle Erbe is the **Palazzo Broletto**, which dominates the neighbouring Piazza del Broletto. In a niche on the façade is a figure said to represent Virgil.

Enter Piazza Sordello from the south and on your left you have the grand house of the Gonzagas' predecessors, the Bonacolsi clan. Hapless prisoners used to be dangled in a cage from the tower – aptly known as the **Torre della Gabbia**. Behind the duomo lies the **Casa di Rigoletto**, which Verdi used as a set model for most of his operas.

Palazzo del Te

Mantua's other Gonzaga palace, at the southern edge of the centre along Via Roma and Via Acerbi, is a grand villa built by Giulio Romano with many splendid rooms, including the **Sala dei Giganti**, one of the most fantastic and frightening creations of the Renaissance. It also houses a modern art collection and an Egyptian museum. It is open daily, except Monday, from 9 am to 6 pm. Admission is L12,000.

Organised Tours

Boat tours of the lakes and downriver to the confluence with the Po are available. Enquire at Andes (☎ 32 38 75), Piazza Sordello 8. A couple of hours costs about L12,000.

Places to Stay

There is a hostel, the *Sparafucile* (☎ 37 24 65), east of the city centre off Strada Legnaghese. It is open from 1 April to 15 October. B&B is L15,000. Take APAM bus No 2M from the train station. There is also a *camping ground* on the site, with rates from L4000 per person.

Albergo Roma Vecchia (☎ 32 21 00), Via Corridoni 20, has singles/doubles from L40,000/55,000. It is closed in August and during the second half of December. *Albergo ABC Moderno* (☎ 32 23 29), Piazza Don Leoni 25, has a variety of rooms, ranging from pokey singles for L35,000 to reasonable doubles with a bathroom for L85,000.

If you have a little more money to burn, head for the centre and stay in *Hotel Due Guerrieri* (☎ 32 55 96), Piazza Sordello 52. The most expensive rooms have views over the square and cost L70,000/95,000. *Hotel Broletto* (☎ 32 67 84), Via dell'Accademia 1, also has good singles/doubles for L85,000/120,000.

Places to Eat

Over a million pigs are reared in the province of Mantua each year and many local dishes incorporate them. Try the salumi (salt pork), pancetta, prosciutto crudo or salamella (small sausages), or risotto with the locally grown vialone nano rice. Wines from the hills around Lago di Garda are much appreciated Try the red Rubino dei Morenici Mantovani

Pizzeria Capri, Via Bettinelli 8, opposite the train station, has good pizzas and other local dishes, with pasta from L6000. There's a small pizzeria across the park at Piazza Virgiliana.

Ristorante Pavesi, Piazza delle Erbe 13, is one of the city's better restaurants and inexpensive; a full meal could cost L30,000. In the same league is the restaurant at *Hotel Due Guerrieri*, which has L22,000 set meals for the tighter wallet. Check out the *Trattoria al Lago*, in a side street off Lungo Lago dei Gonzaga, a simple place that dishes up generous serves of local food – a full meal will come to about L30,000.

Caffè alla Pace, on Via Broletto facing the square of the same name, is an elegant old place for a late afternoon cappuccino. *La Loggetta*, on the square itself, is good for gelati. The most atmospheric place for a stiff drink is the *Taverna di Santa Barbara*, on Piazza di Santa Barbara inside the Palazzo Ducale.

Getting There & Away

APAM (☎ 23 01) operates bus services mainly to provincial centres from the bus station in Piazzale A Mondadori.

The easiest way to get from major cities to Mantua is by train (☎ 32 16 47). There are services to Milan, Verona, Modena, Pavia, Cremona, Padua and Ferrara.

By road, Mantua is close to the A22 autostrada – take either the Mantova Nord or Sud exits and follow the 'centro' signs. The SS236 runs direct to Brescia and the SS10 to Cremona; these are both alternative routes to Milan that intersect tollways and are worth taking if you're in a hurry.

Getting Around

The easiest way to get around the city is to walk – the centre is only 10 minutes from the train station. APAM buses Nos 2M and 4 will also get you from the station to the centre.

AROUND MANTUA
Sabbioneta

About 35 km south-west of Mantua, Sabbioneta was created in the second half of the 16th century by Vespasiano Gonzaga Colonna as an attempted Utopia, which promptly failed. You can only enter as part of a guided tour organised by the local tourist office (☎ 0375-52039), Via Vespasiano Gonzaga 1. Several buses run there from Mantua.

San Benedetto Po

The Benedictine abbey in the small Po valley town of Polirone, 21 km south-east of Mantua, was founded in 1007. Little remains of the original buildings, although the Chiesa di Santa Maria still sports a 12th-century mosaic. The star attraction is the Correggio fresco discovered in the refectory in 1984. There are buses from Mantua.

The Lakes

Where the Lombard plains rise into the Alps, northern Italy is pocked by a series of lakes, among the most beautiful of Italy's natural attractions. Unfortunately, the secret has been out for at least a century – the prices and summer crowds can detract from the pleasure. The lakes are not only the playground of the Milanese rich; tourists from all over northern Europe converge on their favourites – lakes Garda, Como and Maggiore especially, although even the minor lakes are hardly immune.

Most are within easy reach of Milan and provincial centres such as Bergamo and Brescia. There are plenty of camping grounds, some hostels and hotels in all budget categories, as well as many rifugi in the mountains.

LAGO MAGGIORE

The largest, and generally regarded as the most captivating of the lakes, Maggiore (also known as Lago Verbano) is indeed stunning in parts, although its shores are flatter and less spectacular than those of some of its pre-Alpine confrères. Fed principally by the Ticino and Tresa rivers, Lago Maggiore is about 65 km long. The area becomes stiflingly overcrowded in the high season, a good time to stay well away.

The lake's northern reaches are in Swiss territory, as are some of the better walking areas, so consult the Swiss Government Tourist Office (☎ Switzerland 093-31 03 33) for details, or write to the Ente Turistico di Locarno e Valli, Largo Zorzi, 6601 Locarno, Switzerland.

Stresa

Extremely popular with British and German tourists, mostly of the package tour variety, this resort town on the lake's western shore is like one great English tea-room – prim and not unattractive, but somehow insipid. Although commonly touted as a base for the Isole Borromee and the lake in general, the islands can be reached from other points around the lake.

Information The APT del Lago Maggiore (☎ 3 01 50) is at Via Principe Tomaso 70/72, and in summer is open seven days a week (mornings only on weekends; closed Sundays in winter). Other tourist offices are at Arona, Baveno and Verbania.

The telephone code for the area is 0323.

Things to See & Do Apart from the Isole Borromee, you could take a cable car west to the summit of Monte Mottarone, the highest peak in the vicinity (1491 metres). Modest skiing possibilities are an added attraction to the views, and the nearby **Parco del Mottarone** offers some pleasant walking. The cable car runs daily from about 9 am to 5 pm, or you can drive up through the park (L5000 per car for the round trip). The **Villa Pallavicino**, a huge garden with a zoo where the animals roam relatively freely, offers superb views of the lake and the surrounding mountains. Admission is L7500.

Places to Stay & Eat The nearest camping ground is the *Sette Camini Residence* (☎ 2 01 83), Via Pianezza 7, a few km from Stresa at Gignese. Check with the Stresa APT for other grounds in the area – there are some 40 camping grounds up and down the western shore of the lake. Hotels are plentiful in the area, but must be booked well in advance for summer or long weekends. *Orsola Meublé* (☎ 3 10 87), Via Duchessa di Genova 45, has singles/doubles from L35,000/50,000. *Albergo Vidoli* (☎ 3 11 76), Via G Leopardi 19, has singles/doubles from L30,000 /L45,000 or L55,000 for a double with a bathroom. There are 23 hotels in the three to five-star range. The *Speranza au Lac* (☎ 3 11 78), Piazza Imbarcadero, has rooms from L120,000/ 190,000.

Don't expect to find cheap eats in Stresa. Believe it or not, the *Shangri-La* Chinese restaurant at Via Principe Tomaso 74a has a good set menu for L12,000. *Bar Calypso*, Via Mazzini 17, does panini for about L5000. The *Irish Bar*, Via Principessa Margherita 11, offers Guinness and Harp lager on tap.

Getting There & Away Stresa lies on the Domodossola-Milan train line. Buses leave from the waterfront for destinations around the lake and elsewhere, including Milan, Novara and Lago d'Orta. By car, the A8 auto-strada connects Milan with Varese, south-east of Lago Maggiore. Exit at Legnano for the SS33 road, which passes the lake's west shore and continues to the Simplon pass. The A26 from Milan has an exit for Lago Maggiore, via Arona.

Navigazione Lago Maggiore (☎ 4 66 51) operates ferries and hydrofoils around the lake, connecting Stresa with Anora, Angera, Baveno, Cannobio, Pallanza, the islands and Locarno (Switzerland). A variety of day tickets (starting at L8200 and rising depending on destinations) are available for unlimited trips, but most unhurried visitors find normal single-trip tickets better value. Services are reduced in autumn and winter.

Isole Borromee (Borromean Islands)
The islands can be reached from various points around the lake, but Stresa and Baveno are the best step-off points. The four islands, Bella, Pescatori (or Superiore), Madre and San Giovanni, form the lake's most beautiful corner.

Isola Bella has long played host to famous holiday-makers – Wagner, Stendhal, Byron and Goethe among them. The **Palazzo Borromeo** is the main draw card. Built in the 17th century for the Borromeo family, the sumptuous palace contains works by Giovanni Tiepolo and Van Dyck, Flemish tapestries and sculptures by Canova. The gardens are magnificent and contain plants from around the world – although you must pay L11,000 to see it all. **Isola Madre** provides fertile ground for Italy's tallest palm trees, an 18th-century palace and even more lavish gardens than Isola Bella. Admission is L11,000.

Isola dei Pescatori retains some of its original fishing-village atmosphere. The *Albergo Belvedere* (☎ 3 00 47) on this island is open in summer only and charges L80,000 for a double with breakfast.

Western Shore to Switzerland
Stresa is not the only town on Lago Maggiore, and it is worth considering the alternatives. The choice depends a little on your tastes, and you will never really escape the feeling of being in a somewhat artificial environment. **Verbania**, the biggest town on the lake, offers plenty of accommodation in most classes, but it's the least inviting place to hang about. **Cannero Riviera**, farther north, is a small lakeside village and a good spot for a tranquil break. Just off the coast lie some tiny islets that, before being taken over by the Borromeo family in the 15th century, had served as a den for thieves who operated in the area in the 12th century. More interesting is **Cannobio**, five km short of the Swiss border – in fact the town's spotless cobblestone streets and the waves of Swiss day-trippers could just about leave you wondering if you haven't already crossed the frontier – Swiss francs are quite acceptable currency here.

Camp sites dot the coast and Cannero and Cannobio have about 20 hotels between them – check the APT in Stresa or branches in Arona, Baveno or Verbania for a list. A car ferry links Intra (Verbania) to Laveno on the east coast, and all the western shore towns are connected by ferry and bus.

LAGO D'ORTA

Only 15 km long and about 2.5 km wide, Lago d'Orta is one of the smaller of the Italian lakes. It is actually in the Piedmont region and is separated from its more celebrated eastern neighbour, Lago Maggiore, by Monte Mottarone. Its still waters are surrounded by lush woodlands and are not yet quite swarming with visitors like the big lakes, but it can still become congested on weekends and in summer.

Orta San Giulio

This is undoubtedly the prettiest of the lake's towns and suffers less than places like Stresa from the blandness born of over-tourism. It is difficult to beat a coffee over the morning paper in one of the cafés on the lakeside square. It is the obvious choice as a base, not only for Lago d'Orta but arguably for Maggiore as well (if you have a vehicle at any rate) – which you can reach via Monte Mottarone and its **national park**.

Information The APT del Lago d'Orta (☎ 90 354), Via Olina 9-11, can advise on hiking in the area. The telephone code is 0322.

Things to See & Do Regular launches make the short trip (L2500 a head return) to the **Isola San Giulio**, named after a Greek evangelist who earned his saintly status by ridding the island of an assortment of snakes and monsters late in the 4th century AD. A 12th-century basilica dominates the island. The **Sacro Monte**, behind Orta San Giulio, is dotted with a series of small chapels erected to St Francis of Assisi over a 200-year period from 1591 – it makes for a pleasant stroll above the town.

The small village of **Armeno**, at the foot of Monte Mottarone, is worth visiting, not least for its umbrella museum.

Places to Stay & Eat The hitch in Orta San Giulio can be finding a place to stay, espe-

cially in the high season and on weekends. *Camping Cusio* (☎ 9 02 90), Via G Bosco, is near the lake shore, and there are others in the area – ask the APT.

Taverna Antica Agnello (☎ 9 02 59) is an old establishment full of character, with fine singles/doubles from L30,000/50,000 and triples from L70,000. Try for room No 8, the only one with a lake view.

Pizzeria Campana, Via Giacomo Giovanetti 41, has about the cheapest food in town – which is not that cheap. The pizzas are great, but the pasta average.

The village of Armeno has one hotel, the *Madonna di Luciago* (☎ 90 01 92), which has singles/doubles from L40,000/L60,000. You may find cheaper rooms by asking the locals.

If all else fails, the APT has a list of places around the lake.

Getting There & Away Orta San Giulio is just off the Novara-Domodossola train line, and can also be reached by bus from Stresa. From the south, take the SS32 from Novara, in Piedmont, or the road to Borgomanero, also from Novara, which is not as interesting but much quicker.

LAGO DI COMO

Marie Henri Beyle first set foot on the shores of Lago di Como as a 17-year-old conscript under Napoleon. Years later, as Stendhal, he wrote in *La Chartreuse de Parme* that the blue-green waters of the lake and the grandeur of the Alps made it the most beautiful place in the world. Pliny the Elder and Pliny the Younger were born here, but are not known to have gushed about the area to the same degree as Stendhal. In any case, many people would no doubt consider Como's other famous son as having done quite a deal more for the world. Alessandro Volta, born in 1745, came up with, well, the battery.

Known also as Lago Lario, this immense body of water is enchantingly beautiful, as are its tiny waterside villages, some accessible only by boat. Today, the waters are murky and swimming, although permitted in parts, is inadvisable.

Como

Como gets a lot of bad press, but has the advantage over many other lakeside towns of being a real city (population about 90,000) with its own life. The people you mingle with in the streets just might be Italians – even locals – and not the usual crowd of package tourists crated in from northern Europe. The town offers a few attractions in its own right, and is a good base from which to make excursions around the lake.

Orientation From the main train station at Piazzale San Gottardo, walk east to Piazza Cacciatori delle Alpi, and continue along Via Garibaldi to Piazza Volta. The main square, Piazza Cavour, which overlooks the lake, is about 50 metres farther east along Via Fontana. Tourist boats depart from in front of the piazza, and regular ferries from along the shore. East of Piazza Cavour along Lungo Lario Trieste is the bus station and Stazione Ferrovia Nord Milano (FNM), a smaller train station running shuttles to Milan. The funicular for the mountain settlement of Brunate is farther along.

Information The APT office (☎ 27 40 64) is at Piazza Cavour 16 and is open Monday to Saturday from 9 am to 12.30 pm and 2.30 to 6 pm. There is a smaller office in the central train station.

The Credito Italiano just off Piazza Cavour is good for exchange.

The post office is at Via Gallio 6 and is open Monday to Friday from 8.15 am to 5.30 pm and Saturday from 8.15 am to 1 pm. The post code for central Como is 22100.

The Telecom office is on a small square off Via Albertolli, south of Piazza Cavour. It is open daily from 9 am to 12.30 pm and 2.30 to 6 pm. Como's telephone code is 031.

For police emergency, call ☎ 113. The questura (☎ 31 71) is at Viale Roosevelt 7. The Ospedale Sant'Anna (☎ 58 51 11) is at Via Napoleona 60.

Duomo From Piazza Cavour, walk along the arcaded Via Plinio to Piazza del Duomo and the marble-faced cathedral, built and repeat-edly altered from the 14th to the 18th centuries. The duomo combines elements of Romanesque, Gothic, Renaissance and Baroque design and is crowned with a high octagonal dome. Next to it, is the polychromatic **town hall**, altered in 1435 to make way for the cathedral.

Churches & Museums The **Basilica di San Fedele**, named after the saint who brought Christianity to the Como region, first went up in the 6th century. It has since undergone various changes, including those in the bell tower and façade this century – although the original lines of the basilica have been largely respected. It's on Via Vittorio Emanuele II, as are the Palazzo Giovio and Palazzo Olginati – the former housing the **Museo Archeologico Artistico**, with important prehistoric and Roman remains, and the latter the **Museo Civico del Risorgimento**, with relics from Garibaldi's period. Both are open daily from 9 am to midday and 2 to 5 pm, except Monday and Sunday afternoons. The **Pinacoteca Civica**, a small art gallery, is at Via Diaz 84.

Brunate East of Piazza Cavour along the waterfront is the funicular railway station for Brunate. Tickets are L3700 one way or L6500 return. Check the timetable for the last car before you leave. Brunate, at 720 metres, overlooks Como and the lake and offers a pleasant walk and excellent views from the small town of San Maurizio.

Hiking Around Como The tourist office has produced a hiking map of the area with a 50-km walk from Cernobbio, near Como, to Sorico, near the lake's northern edge. It can be broken into four stages. The map shows the location of rifugi and some camping grounds. Maps for other walks are available, but mostly in Italian. Try also the CAI (☎ 26 41 77), Via Volta 56.

Places to Stay Accommodation in the town is reasonably expensive, but the hostel in

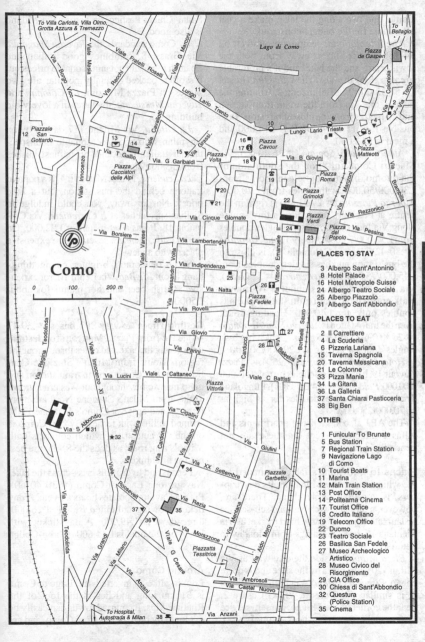

PLACES TO STAY

3 Albergo Sant'Antonino
8 Hotel Palace
16 Hotel Metropole Suisse
24 Albergo Teatro Sociale
25 Albergo Piazzolo
31 Albergo Sant'Abbondio

PLACES TO EAT

2 Il Carrettiere
4 La Scuderia
6 Pizzeria Lariana
15 Taverna Spagnola
20 Taverna Messicana
21 Le Colonne
33 Pizza Mania
34 La Gitana
36 La Galleria
37 Santa Chiara Pasticceria
38 Big Ben

OTHER

1 Funicular To Brunate
5 Bus Station
7 Regional Train Station
9 Navigazione Lago
  di Como
10 Tourist Boats
11 Marina
12 Main Train Station
13 Post Office
14 Politeama Cinema
17 Tourist Office
18 Credito Italiano
19 Telecom Office
22 Duomo
23 Teatro Sociale
26 Basilica San Fedele
27 Museo Archeologico
   Artistico
28 Museo Civico del
   Risorgimento
29 CIA Office
30 Chiesa di Sant'Abbondio
32 Questura
   (Police Station)
35 Cinema

Como, and two along the lake, make a visit affordable for the budget conscious.

The *International* camping ground (☎ 52 14 36), Via Cecilio, is away from both the town centre and the lake, and it's preferable to camp along the lake. The *Villa Olmo* hostel (☎ 57 38 00), Via Bellinzona 2, fronting the lake, is one km from the main train station and 20 metres from the closest bus stop. Take bus No 1, 6, 11 or 14. B&B is L14,000 and a meal is L12,000.

Albergo Teatro Sociale (☎ 26 40 42), Via Maestri Comacini 8, on the south side of the duomo, has dull but clean rooms from L30,000/50,000, with triples from L70,000. *Albergo Piazzolo* (☎ 27 21 86) is right in the centre at Piazzolo Terragni 6 (a tiny square along Via Indipendenza) with singles/doubles from L50,000/75,000. *Albergo Sant'Antonino* (☎ 30 42 77), Via Coloniola 10, is close to the bus station and has singles/doubles from L45,000/75,000. *Grotta Azzurra* (☎ 57 26 31), Via Borgovico 161, is about a 10-minute walk north of the main train station and has doubles only, for L40,000. Heading south from the train station is *Albergo Sant'Abbondio* (☎ 26 40 09), Via S Abbondio 7, which has basic singles/doubles starting at L20,000/30,000.

Hotel Metropole e Suisse (☎ 26 94 44), Piazza Cavour 19, has singles/doubles up to L150,000 /200,000. *Palace Hotel* (☎ 30 33 03), Lungolago Trieste 16 has singles/doubles for as high as L170,000/250,000.

The APT also has a list of apartments and villas available for rent but these are not generally cheap.

Places to Eat Como's fare, dominated by the whims of nearby Milan and its day-trippers, is good but rarely cheap. There are, however, many sandwich bars and self-service restaurants. There is a large food market at Via Mentana 15, open mornings from Monday to Saturday.

Pizza Mania, outside the city wall at Via Milano 20, sells pizza by the slice and is quite cheap. *Pizzeria Lariana*, Via Fiammenghino 4, is similar. *La Galleria*, Via G Cesare 2, near the corner of Via Milano, is a self-service restaurant with pizza slices from L3000.

Santa Chiara Pasticceria across Via Milano is also good.

By Como standards, the *Taverna Spagnola*, Via Grassi 8, combines good Italian and Spanish food with not unreasonable prices but it's often packed. Equally popular are two places on Piazza Mazzini, *Le Colonne* and *Taverna Messicana*, the latter in a lovely old building.

La Gitana, Via Milano 117, is run by an Egyptian who cooks reasonable if unspectacular Italian food and, on request, dishes from his homeland.

La Scuderia, Piazza Matteotti 4, is a popular trattoria behind the bus station, but a little pricey. Not far away, you could indulge in Sicilian specialities at *Il Carrettiere*, Via Coloniola 18. It has a set menu for L22,000. On the lakeside, there are several more expensive places with a view.

Some of Como's brighter young things hang about *Big Ben*, Via Leoni 10, for expensive British beer and hot panini for about L5000.

Getting There & Away SPT buses (☎ 30 47 44) leave from Piazza Matteotti for destinations along the lake and cities throughout the region. Trains from Milan's Stazione Centrale arrive at Como's main train station and go to many cities throughout Western Europe. Trains from Milan's Stazione Nord are more frequent and arrive at Como's Stazione FNM – timed to link with ferries. By car, Como is on the A9 autostrada, which connects with Milan's ring road, as does the SS35, the best bet for hitchhikers.

Ferries and hydrofoils criss-cross the lake. Navigazione Lago di Como (☎ 30 40 60), Piazza Cavour, operates boats all year. A day ticket allowing unlimited trips is L26,000; three days is L49,000. A day ticket with lunch on the boat is L44,600 (Como-Colico run).

Around Como

Looking like an inverted 'Y', Lago di Como is 51 km long and lies at the foot of the Rhetian Alps. Its myriad towns can easily be explored by boat, or bus from Como, and are worth at least a two-day visit. Highlights include the **Villa d'Este** at Cernobbio, a monumental 16th-century villa that is now a hotel; the **Isola Comacina**, the lake's sole island, where Lombard kings took refuge from invaders; and the **Villa Carlotta** near Tremezzo, with its magnificent gardens. The towns farther north are lesser tourist attractions.

There are two youth hostels on Lago di Como, numerous camping grounds and many reasonably priced hotels. The *Ostello La Primula* (☎ 0344-3 23 56), Via IV Novembre 38, at Menaggio, about halfway up the lake on the western side, is close to the bus stop on the route from Como. It charges L13,000 a night. Farther north is the *Ostello Domaso* (☎ 0344-9 60 94), Via Case Sparse 12, at Domaso, which is the same price and on the same bus route. Both are open from March to October/November. Check with the APT in Como for lists of the 50 or so camping grounds, hotels and agriturismo facilities along the lake.

Bellagio Considered the 'pearl' of the lake, Bellagio is indeed a pretty little town sitting more or less on the point where the western and eastern arms of the lake split and head south. The 30-km drive from Como is itself rewarding, but the trip down the east side towards Lecco is less so. The only drawback is the inevitable feeling you're sharing the pleasure with just a few too many other outsiders – would the real residents of Bellagio please stand up?

Albergo Roma (☎ 95 04 24) is neatly situated in the town and has singles/doubles starting at L30,000/45,000.

The lake's only car ferries connect the east and west shores in this area, stopping at Bellagio.

LAGO DI GARDA
The largest and most popular of the Italian lakes, Garda lies between the Alps and the Po valley, a position that lends it a temperate climate. At its northern reaches, Garda is hemmed in by craggy mountains and resembles a fjord. As it broadens towards the south,

the lake takes on the appearance of an inland sea.

There are many large villages around the lake, but most are heavily developed and unpleasant. The picturesque but Disneyland-like resort of Sirmione is worth visiting, as is Gardone Riviera on the lake's western edge. At the northern end, Riva del Garda is a good base for walking in the nearby Alps. If you are staying, a not entirely useless brochure to pick up for information is *Garda Doc*.

Getting There & Away
Buses leave Verona, Brescia, Mantua and Milan for the main towns on the lake. Desenzano del Garda is on the main Milan-Venice train line. By car, the A4 autostrada and the SS11, which connect Milan with Venice, pass the southern edge of the lake, and the A22 runs parallel with the lake's eastern shore, connecting Verona with Trento. Riva can be reached by exiting the A22 at Rovereto Sud.

Getting Around
Navigazione sul Lago di Garda (☎ 030-914 13 21), Piazza Matteotti, in Desenzano, operates ferries between most towns on the lake. It has offices or booths in all towns it serves and operates all year. Ask at tourist offices for timetables. Fares range from L2000 to L14,800, depending on the length of the trip.

Sirmione
Catullus, the Roman poet, celebrated Sirmione – a narrow peninsula jutting out from the southern shore of the lake – in his writings, and his name is still invoked in connection with the place. It is a popular bathing spot and is often jammed tight with tourists. In spite of this, Sirmione retains a comparatively relaxed atmosphere. The area of interest (watch for the castle) is an islet attached by a bridge to the rest of the peninsula.

Information The main tourist office (☎ 91 62 45), Viale Marconi 2, has information on hotels and activities such as walking, skiing, windsurfing and horse riding. There is a

Love's Labours

Gaius Valerius Catullus, born in Verona around 84 BC, hosted everyone – even Julius Caesar – to dinner at his family holiday home in Sirmione (then known as Sirmio). His dealings with Rome's upper classes gave Catullus ample material for his writings, mostly as a poet of love – both heterosexual and homosexual.

Our stereotype of the romantic poet as a tortured artist drifting from one obsessive relationship to another has its origins in the slightly satiric self-image Catullus presents in his verse. Of the many sexual partners he mentions, the most famous is 'Lesbia', or Clodia Metella, a notorious vamp who collected poets as Catullus apparently collected toy boys, and who allegedly poisoned her husband.

Reading Catullus is a window on decadent and pagan Rome. If you get past a nodding acquaintance with the poems, however, the world he describes begins to seem curiously familiar: Catullus and his friends, with their complex sexuality and jaded appetites, would not be too out of place among the characters of Fellini's *La Dolce Vita*.

The Poems of Catullus in paperback, World's Classics series (OUP, 1991) contains the Latin text and a fine modern English translation by Guy Lee.

Ray Cassin

Telecom office on Piazza Carducci. The telephone code is 030.

Things to See & Do The Roman villa and baths known as the **Grotte di Catullo** probably had nothing to do with the Roman poet, although Catullus and his family did have a villa in the area. The extensive ruins occupy a prime position on the northern, quieter end of the Sirmione island. The site is open Tuesday to Sunday from 9 am to 6.45 pm (5 pm in winter). Admission is L8000.

The **Castello Scaligero**, also known as the Rocca Scaligera, was built by Verona's ruling family, the Scaligeri, as a stronghold on the lake in 1250. There's not a lot inside, but the views from the tower are good. It's open daily from 9 am to 6.30 pm. Admission is L6000.

You can go for a watery spin around the island. Plenty of boats leave from near the castle – at about L25,000 per boat. All sorts of vessels will also make any manner of trip around the lake – at a price.

It is possible to swim at the small beaches on the town's eastern side and there is an array of water activities that can be arranged in the town. Windsurfers can try Grumelli (☎ 919 61 30) or Martini (☎ 91 62 08), while the Yachting Club Sirmione (☎ 919 60 72)

can assist with boating. There are several places that hire out pedalos and kayaks.

Places to Stay & Eat It is hard to believe there are close to 100 hotels crammed in here. Book ahead or stay away in summer and at long weekends. There are four camping grounds near the town and the APT can advise on others around the lake. *Campeggio Sirmione* (☎ 91 90 45), on the foreshore at Via Sirmioncino 9, is the largest.

Hotels include the *Albergo Regina* (☎ 91 60 52), Via Antiche Mura 11, east of the centre. It is cute and one of the cheapest, with singles/doubles from L35,000/45,000. The *Albergo degli Oleandri* (☎ 990 57 80), on Via Dante near the castle, is in a shady, pleasant location and has rooms for L50,000/70,000 including breakfast. The *Albergo Sirmione* (☎ 91 63 31), Piazza Castellò, has rooms from L95000/160,000.

The *Osteria al Pescatore*, Via Piana 20, is one of the better, reasonably priced restaurants and there is loads of takeaway food to be found, especially around Piazza Carducci. This is also where the bulk of the cafés and gelati joints are.

Around Sirmione

Sirmione is about five km east of Desenzano

del Garda, the lake's largest town and a main transport hub (but not really worth a visit). Farther north from Desenzano del Garda is Salò, which gave its name to Mussolini's puppet republic in 1943, after the dictator was rescued from the south by the Nazis. The CAI has an office in Salò, at Via San Carlo 17, with information on walks and Alpine rifugi in the surrounding mountains.

Heading east, kids will be excited to hear of **Gardaland**, Italy's equivalent of Disneyland. Adults and children over 10 years pay L27,000 to enter in the high season and get sick on the various rides. Only toddlers get in for free. The nearest train station is at Peschiera del Garda. The remaining two km are covered in a free bus. If that's not enough, you could try the **Parco Natura Viva**, a zoo and educational park a little farther north between Bussolengo and Pastrengo, but this time there's no free bus. Driving is really the only answer.

Gardone Riviera

On the western edge of the lake at the head of a small inlet, Gardone Riviera is a popular resort that retains a hint of its sophisticated past. Once the lake's most elegant holiday spot, Gardone Riviera has succumbed to development and the problems of being a group tourist destination.

The APT office (☎ 2 03 47) is at Corso Repubblica 35. The town's telephone code is 0365.

Things to See A visit to the town is a must to see **Il Vittoriale**, the exotic villa of Italy's controversial 20th-century poet and screeching nationalist, Gabriele d'Annunzio. He moved in here in 1922 because, he claimed, he wanted to escape the world, which made him ill. Protagonist of clamorous but ineffectual wartime stunts in WW I – he flew a lone raid to drop leaflets over Vienna – he died in 1938 and is buried near the villa among his wartime companions.

One of d'Annunzio's most triumphant and more bizarre feats was to capture, with a band of his soldiers, a battleship from the fledgling Yugoslavia shortly after WW I,

when Italy's territorial claims had been partly frustrated in postwar peace talks. The ship's bow protrudes from the villa's gardens and adds to the kitsch flavour of the residence. **D'Annunzio's villa** is at the north-eastern edge of town and is open Tuesday to Sunday from 9 am to 12.30 pm and 2.30 to 6 pm. Admission is L16,000 to both the grounds and house. The town also features **botanical gardens**, on the road to d'Annunzio's villa.

Some pleasant and easy walks can be undertaken from here heading inland to the rifuge at **Monte Spino** or **Monte Pizzicolo**. Ask at the APT for more details.

Places to Stay & Eat The *Albergo Nord* (☎ 2 07 07), Via Zanardelli 18, has singles/doubles from L35,000/60,000 and is in a good location. *Villa Fiordaliso* (☎ 20 158), Via Zanardelli 132, was a favourite of Mussolini's mistress, Clara Petacci. It is also one of the lake's most beautiful hotels and best restaurants. Rooms cost from L200,000 and food is expensive. For more modest food, try *Pizzeria Sans Souci*, near the tourist office, which has pizzas from L6000.

Gargnano & Villa

Gargnano is really just another lake resort town. It was here that Mussolini was based for the short life of his Repubblica Sociale Italiana (or Repubblica di Salò). He was heavily guarded by German SS units and indeed the republic was a fiction, as northern Italy was occupied territory after Italy signed an armistice with the Allies in September 1943. The republic lasted until 25 April 1945, when the last German troops were finally cleared from Italy. Mussolini and Petacci were lynched three days later near Lago di Como.

Just a couple of km south of Gargnano is Villa, an unremarkable place, but it may interest some to know that D H Lawrence spent a good deal of time here writing *Twilight in Italy*, commonly classed as travel writing but just as much a circuit through David Herbert's pelvic theories.

Riva del Garda

The most popular of the resort towns around Lago di Garda, Riva is at its northern edge. It has a pleasant old centre of cobbled laneways and squares and a nice position on the lake. The town's links with the Germanic world are evident not only in the bus and car loads of Germans and Austrians, but also in its history. Situated in Trentino-Alto Adige, Riva was part of Habsburg Austria until it was incorporated into Italy after WW I, and was annexed briefly by Nazi Germany in the closing years of WW II. While the likes of D H Lawrence were hanging about on the western shore, Central European luminaries such as Nietzsche, Kafka and Thomas Mann were wont to put their feet up in Riva.

Information The APT office (☎ 55 44 44) is in the Giardino di Porta Orientale, opposite the local 'castle'. It can advise on accommodation and sporting activities. The telephone code is 0464.

Things to See

A few km north of town is the **Cascata Varone**, a 100-metre waterfall fed by the Lago di Tenno. It costs L5000 to get in and access hours vary a lot – check with the APT.

Activities Riva is one of Italy's most popular spots for windsurfing and has four schools that hire out equipment. Try Bouwmeester Windsurfing Centre (☎ 55 42 30), c/o the Hotel Pier, or Nautic Club Riva (☎ 55 24 53), Viale Rovereto 132. They also run sailing classes.

The APT has a list of people who can help with information on free-climbing in the area. For mountain bike hire, try Centro Cicli Pederzolli (☎ 55 18 30), Viale Canella, or Girelli (☎ 55 66 02), Viale Damiano Chiesa 15/17. You're looking at L20,000 for a day.

Speedy Gonzales (☎ 55 20 89) runs boat excursions on the lake at L15,000 per person per hour. Boats leave from near the APT.

The town is a great starting point for walks around Monte Rocchetta, which dominates the northern end of Lago di Garda.

Places to Stay & Eat Several camping grounds dot the waterfront, including *Campeggio Bavaria* (☎ 55 25 24), Viale Rovereto 100. There is an HI youth hostel, the *Benacus* (☎ 55 49 11), at Piazza Cavour 10, in the centre of town. It charges L16,000 for B&B and is open from early March to mid-October.

Hotels are plentiful, but during summer it is advisable to book. *La Montanara* (☎ 55 48 57), Via Montanara 18, is one of the cheapest places and located in a narrow laneway in the centre. Singles/doubles are L25,000/48,000 and doubles with a bathroom L50,000. The hotel also offers half and full board and has a pleasant trattoria. The nearby *Albergo Vittoria* (☎ 55 43 98), Via Dante 39, has rooms for L35,000/70,000, although a few cheaper ones are available if you push. *Hotel Portici* (☎ 55 54 00) Piazza III Novembre 19, offers rooms for L63,000/100,000, although you may be obliged to take full board in the high season. *Hotel Sole* (☎ 55 26 86; fax 55 19 57), at No 35 overlooking the lake, was Nietzsche's favourite and has rooms starting at L170,000.

The town has many takeaway places and good delicatessens where you can pick up picnic supplies. *Leon d'Oro*, Via Fiume 26, has various Trentino dishes (including strangolapreti – 'strangle the priest') and prices are average. At *Speck Stube*, Piazza 3 Novembre 10, you can eat for about L20,000 per head and wash the meal down with German beer. Or try the *Bella Napoli* for pizza. There are plenty of lakeside cafés and pastry shops.

Getting There & Away The town's bus station is in Viale Trento, in the newer part of town, a 10-minute walk from the lake. Regular APT buses connect Riva with Verona, leaving Verona from the Porta Nuova bus station. Atesina buses connect Riva with Trento. Other buses serve stops around the lake.

LAGO D'ISEO & VALLE CAMONICA

Probably the least known of the large Italian lakes, Iseo is also arguably the least attractive. Although largely shut in by mountains, it is also scarred in the north-east (around Lovere and Castro) by industry and a string of tunnels.

Lying at the southern end of the Valle Camonica, the lake is fed by the Oglio river and marks the boundary between the provinces of Bergamo and Brescia – getting information about one side from the other tourist office is not easy! Farther south stretches the Franciacorta, a patch of rolling countryside known to produce a good drop of wine. The mountainous hinterland offers some decent walking possibilities. Check with the APT in the lake towns, or at Bergamo or Brescia, for more detailed suggestions.

Getting There & Around

Buses connect the lake with Brescia and Bergamo. There are also trains from Brescia to Iseo and several other towns on the lake. Navigazione sul Lago d'Iseo (☎ 035-97 29 70), based in Costa Volpino, operates ferries between (south to north) Sarnico, Iseo, Monte Isola, Lovere and Pisogne. The timetable is substantially reduced outside the summer season. Buses also connect towns around the lake.

Iseo

A pleasant, if somewhat dull, spot fronting the southern end of the lake, Iseo boasts the first monument erected to Garibaldi. The APT del Lago d'Iseo (☎ 98 02 09) is at Lungolago Marconi 2. The telephone code for the east (Brescia) side of the lake, starting with Iseo, is 030, and 035 on the other side (there are a couple of exceptions).

The area is well supplied with accommodation, particularly camping grounds. Iseo alone has 17 sites, including the Belvedere (☎ 98 90 48), Via Risorgimento. Albergo Il Cenacolo (☎ 98 01 36), Via Mirolte 13, is the cheapest place in Iseo with singles/doubles from L20,000/38,000.

Monte Isola

The best thing to do here is get a boat to Europe's biggest lake island, Monte Isola.

Few vehicles are allowed on the streets, leaving the fishing villages in something of their original peace. There are six hotels and a camping ground, Campeggio Monte Isola (☎ 982 52 21), Via Goce.

Eastern Shore

If Iseo seems a little empty and you want to stay on the mainland, a few smaller towns farther north are an option. **Sulzano** is small and quiet, and on the ferry run to Monte Isola. A little farther up the road is Marone, from which a side road winds up into the mountains to **Zone**. Walking is the attraction and there a few rifugi about – enquire at the APT.

Western Shore

The northern end of the lake you can forget, although some of the driving through the blasted rock face at the water's edge is vaguely enjoyable. **Riva di Solto** is a fairly unspoiled village on the western shore, although **Sarnico**, towards the southern end of the lake, is better set up with hotels and restaurants.

Valle Camonica

The Valle Camonica weaves its way from the north of Lago d'Iseo to the vast **Parco dell'Adamello** and farther north, to the **Parco Nazionale dello Stelvio**. The area borders on Trentino-Alto Adige and takes in the better parts of the Lombard Alps. The two national parks offer many walks of varying difficulty and are dotted with Alpine rifugi. See the Trentino-Alto Adige chapter.

About halfway between Darfo Boario Terme and Edolo, lovers of rock-carving will have a field day. The **Parco Nazionale delle Incisioni Rupestri** at Capo di Monte is a 30-hectare open air museum containing a representative spread of engravings going as far back as the Bronze Age. The valley is littered with such carvings. The park is open daily, except Monday, from 9 am to sunset.

The area from Edolo north offers some reasonable **skiing** in winter. This is particularly true around Ponte di Legno, at the northern end of the valley, and the nearby Passo del Tonale.

The area is part of the province of Brescia, and Brescia's APT is a good place to obtain walking, camping and rifuge information. In the valley there are tourist offices at Darfo Boario Terme (☎ 0364-53 16 09), Edolo (☎ 0364-7 10 65) and Ponte di Legno (☎ 0364-9 11 22).

Trentino-Alto Adige

This autonomous Alpine region, incorporating much of the spectacular limestone mountain range known as the Dolomites, is best thought of as two distinct areas. Its two provinces, Trentino and Alto Adige, are culturally, linguistically and historically separate. Alto Adige, or Südtirol (South Tyrol), in the north was part of the Tyrol area of Austria until 1918, when it was ceded to Italy. Its population is predominantly of Germanic descent and its first language is German, although there is also a section of the population which speaks Ladin, an ancient Latin-based language now confined mainly to the Val Badia (Gadertal) and the Val Gardena (Grödnertal): see the Aside in the Val Gardena section. Trentino, in the southern part of the region, was a reluctant part of the Austrian and Austro-Hungarian empires for about a century, until it was returned to Italy after WW I. The population here is strongly Italian and, although German is widely spoken, Italian is the preferred language.

The less than comfortable relationship of the two cultural groups has at times been characterised by extreme politics. The right-wing Italian party, the Alleanza Nazionale, has strong support in the region. Until recently known as the Movimento Sociale Italiano (MSI), the party was founded after WW II by Fascists closely associated with Mussolini. Now the party has attempted to distance itself from its Fascist past. Renamed the Südtiroler Volkspartei (SVP), it has strong support from the German and Ladin-speaking people of the Südtirol. While one of its primary aims is the preservation and development of the German and Ladin ethnic groups, it also encompasses a more extreme element which wants to secede from Italy. Terrorist bombings of railways, and electrical and military installations were associated with the more radical secessionists and shook the region in the 1950s, 1960s and again during the 1980s.

On the more positive side, tourism in Trentino-Alto Adige is highly organised and travellers will have little difficulty finding good-value accommodation, as well as extensive information on their choice of activity, including walking, trekking and skiing. You will find the types of accommodation are slightly different here than in other parts of Italy. While there are still hotels and pensioni (which tend to insist on half or full board), there are also garnis, which are basically B&Bs, and rifugi ranging from expensive hotel/restaurants at the top of cable car and chair lift routes, to simple bivacchi (mountain huts). Prices charged at all establishments can vary greatly according to the season and it should be noted that Alpine rifugi are generally open only from late June to late September. If you plan on walking in the mountains during August, it is best to book a bed at the rifugi before you set out, since they are often full.

The two provincial tourist offices are the APT del Trentino at Trent and the APT for Südtirol at Bolzano. Both are extremely helpful and have loads of information in English about the region. See town sections for details. There are also APT del Trentino offices in Rome (☎ 06-679 42 16), Via Poli 47, and in Milan (☎ 02-87 43 87), Piazza Diaz 5.

Trentino-Alto Adige has an excellent public transport network. The two main bus companies are SAD in Alto Adige and Atesina in Trentino. The main towns and many ski resorts are also accessible from major cities throughout Italy – including Rome, Florence, Bologna, Milan and Genoa – by a network of long-haul buses operated by three companies – Lazzi, SITA and STAT. Information about the services is available from tourist offices and bus stations throughout Trentino-Alto Adige, or from the following offices: Lazzi Express (☎ 06-884 08 40), Via Tagliamento 27B, Rome; SITA (☎ 055-21 47 21), Autostazione, Via Santa Caterina di Siena 17, Florence – go to Piazza Adua 1, Florence, for information about the Lazzi/SITA joint service, called ALPI Bus;

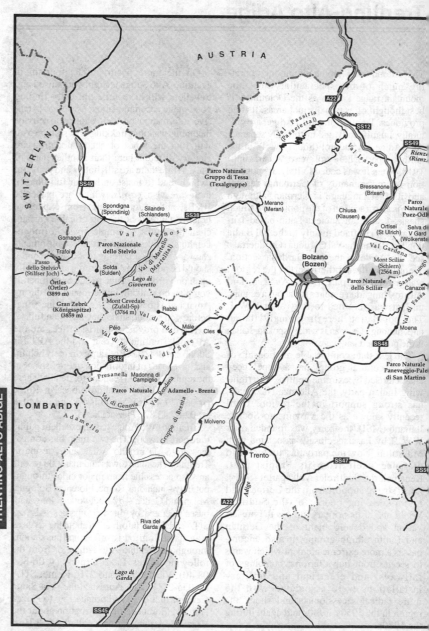

Trentino-Alto Adige

0   20   40 km

and STAT (☎ 0142-78 16 60, or 010-58 71 81), Piazza della Vittoria 30, Genoa.

TREKKING IN THE DOLOMITES

Without doubt, the Dolomites, stretching across Trentino-Alto Adige into the Veneto, provide the most spectacular opportunities for walkers in the Italian Alps – from a half-day stroll to walks/treks which you can plan for as many days as you like, as well as demanding treks which combine walking with mountaineering skills. There is a vast network of trails, which are generally well-marked with numbers on red-and-white painted bands (which you will find on trees and rocks along the trails), or by numbers inside different coloured triangles for the Alte Vie (High Routes). See the following Where to Go section. There are numerous rifugi where you can buy refreshments or spend the night. Tourist offices usually have maps which roughly mark out trails and are generally sufficient as a guide for short walks (less than a day), although we recommend that walkers planning anything more than the most basic itinerary should always use proper detailed maps. See the Preparations section below. Staff will also advise on the grade of difficulty of the various trails.

Preparations

If you plan to embark on a serious trek, it is recommended you invest in a good map. The best are the Tabacco 1:25,000 maps, which give extensive detail on trails, altitudes and gradients, as well as marking the locations of all rifugi and bivacchi. These maps are widely available throughout the Dolomites.

The season for walking is from the end of June to the end of September and, depending on weather conditions, sometimes into October – although it should be noted that rifugi will close by around 20 September. Trekkers should check weather predictions before setting out and ensure they are prepared for high-altitude conditions. Remember that, in the Alps, the weather can suddenly change from hot and sunny to cold and wet even in mid-August. Weather changes usually occur in the afternoon, so it is always best to

A Coral Reef 3000 Metres Above Sea Level
The Dolomites account for a vast portion of the eastern Alps and are divided between Trentino, Alto Adige and the Veneto. (These regions/provinces are now all part of Italy, but during WW I their borders marked the border between Italy and Austria and thus the front line of battle.) These spectacular, spiky peaks take their name from the French geologist De Dolomieu, who was the first to identify their composition of sedimentary limestone formed from calcium carbonate and magnesium. The realisation that the Dolomites are in fact ancient coral reefs, makes them seem all the more extraordinary. During the Triassic period, the entire zone was covered with tropical forest and a shallow, warm sea. After millions of years, the sea receded, while at the same time the Alps were being formed, raising what had once been the seabed to heights of 2000 and 3000 metres. During the Ice Age, the coral reefs and rocks were eroded by glaciers which, together with normal atmospheric erosion, shaped the fantastic formations we see today in the Dolomites. Among the pinnacles, towers and dramatic sheer drops of these mountains it is not unusual to find marine fossils. Coral reefs are always fascinating, but particularly so when reincarnated as Alpine peaks. ∎

set out early in the day. Even if you plan to walk a short distance, it is advisable to be prepared. And even on the shortest, most popular trails at the height of summer, it is recommended that you have good walking shoes, a warm jacket and plenty of water.

The following is a list of recommended items to carry on high-altitude treks of more than one day:

• Comfortable, waterproof walking/trekking boots (already worn in)
• Light, comfortable backpack
• Anorak (or pile/wind jacket)
• Change of T-shirt, underwear and socks (wool and cotton)
• Short and long pants
• Gloves, wool or pile hat, or headband, and scarf
• Water bottle with at least one litre per person
• Hooded raincoat or poncho
• Torch (flashlight) and batteries, a pocket knife, a lightweight thermal blanket (for emergencies), tissues, sunglasses and, if necessary, a sheet or sleeping bag. You could also bring along a pair of slippers or thongs to wear at the rifugio. And don't forget to carry some lightweight, energy-producing food.

Trekking Areas
The best areas to walk in the Dolomites include the following:

The Brenta group (Dolomiti di Brenta), accessible from either Molveno to the east or Madonna di Campiglio to the west.

The Val di Genova and the Adamello group, also accessible from Madonna di Campiglio (the Brenta and Adamello groups form the Parco Naturale Adamello-Brenta).

The Sella group, accessible from either the Val Gardena to the west or the Val Badia to the east.

The Alpe di Siusi, the Sciliar and the Catinaccio group, accessible from Siusi and Castelrotto.

The Pale di San Martino, accessible from San Martino di Castrozza.

The area around Cortina, which straddles Trentino and the Veneto and features the magnificent Parco Naturale di Fanes-Sennes-Braies, and, to the south, Monte Pelmo and Monte Civetta.

The Sesto Dolomites north of Cortina towards Austria.

There are four Alte Vie in the Dolomites – treks which can take from 10 days to two weeks to complete. The routes link up pre-existing trails and, in some places, have created new trails to make difficult sections easier to traverse.

Each route links a chain of rifugi and it is easy to walk only certain sections:

Alta Via No 1 crosses the Dolomites from north to south, from the Lago di Braies to Belluno.

Alta Via No 2 extends from Bressanone to Feltre and is known as the High Route of Legends, because it passes through Odle, the mythical kingdom of ancient Ladino fairy tales.

Alta Via No 3 links Villabassa and Longarone.

Alta Via No 4 goes from San Candido to Pieve di Cadore.

The Alte Vie are marked by numbers inside triangles – blue for No 1, red for No 2 and orange/brown for No 3 (No 4 is marked by the normal numbers on red and white bands). Booklets which map out the routes in detail are available at the APT di Belluno, in the Veneto, or ask at the APT in Trent.

People wanting to undertake guided treks, or who want to tackle the more difficult trails which combine mountaineering skills with walking (with or without a guide), can seek information at Alpine guide offices in most towns in the region. See under the particular town in this chapter.

A Three-Day Trek in Parco Naturale Fannes-Sennes-Braies

The following is a basic guide for a three-day trek, accessible from Cortina d'Ampezzo or Corvara, which incorporates a section of Alta Via No 1, starting from the Passo Falzarego and ending at the Passo Cimabanche. It should be used as an outline only and a detailed map should also be used. The best is the Tabacco 1:25,000 map No 03 for Cortina d'Ampezzo e Dolomiti Ampezzane. Estimated times are intended as a guide for walkers who maintain a steady pace. Those who tend to meander could double the time taken to complete each stage and this should be taken into account when aiming for specific rifugi. The trek is suitable for people with little trekking experience.

Day One This first stage will take you from the Passo Falzarego to the Rifugio Fanes (four to five hours). The Passo Falzarego (2105 metres) is easily accessible by public transport or car from Cortina. Bus services are run by Dolomiti Bus and three a day leave from the Cortina bus station; the trip takes 40 minutes. Buses also leave for the Passo Falzarego from Corvara. A cable car will then take you up to the Rifugio Lagazuoi (2752 metres). Enjoy the spectacular view across to the Marmolada glacier, because this is the highest altitude you will reach during the trek.

From the rifugio, head downhill into the wide valley, always following the

trail marked with a No 1 inside a blue triangle. On reaching the small Lago di Lagazuoi you will find, to the right, the beautiful but tiring ascent to the Forcella del Lago (2486 metres), from where you start the long descent into the Piano Grande, with a magnificent view of the Conturines mountains to your left. Once in the Piano Grande, a pretty valley of Alpine pastures, take the trail to the right. At the end of the Piano Grande, past Passo Tadega, follow the triangle signs along the dirt road to eventually reach the Lago di Limo (2159 metres) at the foot of the Col Bechei. Follow the trail to the left and you will descend to the picturesque *Rifugio Fanes* (2060 metres) or, slightly farther along the trail, the less expensive *Rifugio la Varella* (2042 metres). You can eat a meal and spend the night at either one. If you still have the energy, explore the beautiful Fanes high plain, taking trail No 12 to Lago Paron through enchanting scenery of limestone white and a thousand shades of green, dotted with the colours of Alpine flowers.

Day Two This stage will take you from Rifugio Fanes to Rifugio Biella (five to six hours). Again following the blue triangular Alta Via signs, head down into the small

Edelweiss; yellow flower heads in a dense cluster above woolly white leaves arranged in the form of a star.

valley of the San Vigilio river until you reach Lago Piciodèl on your right. Shortly after the lake, again on your right, is a trail that can be taken in preference to the Alta Via route, which, at this point, becomes a long descent to the Rifugio Pederù (1548 metres), from where you would have to ascend to 2000 metres following a road heavily used by 4WD vehicles ferrying tourist groups to the refuge. For those who want to finish their trek at this point, there is a road from the refuge that descends into the Val Badia. The detour, on the other hand, is an atmospheric route which, although tiring at times, is not

difficult. The trail, which is not numbered, heads off to the right just after a river of gravel and follows the lake before ascending into the heart of the semi-wilderness, Banc dal Se. You will arrive at the *Rifugio Fodara Vedla* (1966 metres), where you can relax on the terrace with a drink while enjoying the magnificent scenery. From here you rejoin the Alta Via route, heading in the direction of Rifugio Sennes (2116 metres). After a few hundred metres there is another recommended detour to your right, which crosses a high plain. It is not uncommon to encounter wild animals in this area.

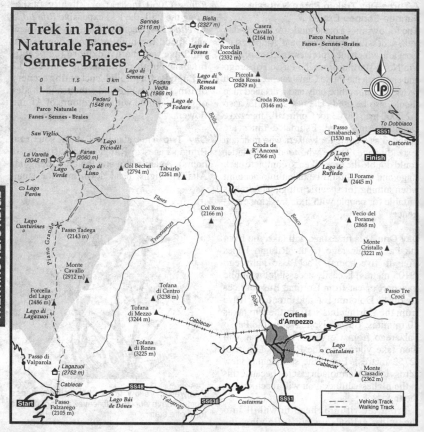

Once you rejoin the Alta Via route, follow it to the left until you reach Rifugio Sennes, situated by a lake of the same name, and surrounded by a small village of *malghe* (Alpine huts where graziers make butter and cheese in summer). From here, follow the Alta Via in the direction of Rifugio Biella, or take trail No 6, which crosses a beautiful high plain where it is not impossible to find pieces of twisted metal remaining from WW I. These mountains were the scene of some of the more ferocious battles along the Alpine front line. From trail No 6 you will descend to rejoin the Alta Via, within view of the old wooden *Rifugio Biella* (2327 metres), set in a fascinating and unforgettable lunar landscape. Here you can eat a meal and spend the night. If you have the energy, it's an easy climb up the Croda del Becco (two to three hours total).

Day Three This stage goes from Rifugio Biella to the Passo Cimabanche (five to six hours). Ascend trail No 28, which follows the crest above the rifugio. At this point the trek no longer follows the Alta Via route, which descends to the Lago di Braies, a short distance north. Our trek instead heads southeast towards the majestic Croda Rossa, a beautiful mountain inhabited by golden eagles. Trail No 28 follows the crest until it reaches the forcella Cocodain, a mountain pass at 2332 metres. From here you descend to the left, in a northerly direction on the slope of the Prato Piazza. After a short distance you will pick up trail No 3 and continue the descent until you reach an intersection with trail No 4. Continuing to follow No 3 to the right, you will reach the Casera Cavallo at 2164 metres. From here the trail starts to ascend, always towards the right. It follows the face of the Croda Rossa, where there's a narrow point with a sheer drop to one side. Here you will find a fixed iron cord to hold onto for security. This section might be a bit intimidating for those who are afraid of heights, but presents no technical difficulty. Continuing to follow trail No 3, you will descend towards the valley to meet trail No 18 (at this point ensure that you do not take

No 3A, which descends to the Prato Piazza). Follow the No 18 south, towards the Valle dei Canopi, where there is a slippery descent to the SS51 road and the Passo Cimabanche. Here there is a bar and bus stops for Cortina (to the right), which is only 15 km away, and Dobbiaco (to the left). It is also possible to hitch.

SKIING IN THE DOLOMITES

There are innumerable excellent ski resorts in the Dolomites, including the expensive and fashionable Cortina d'Ampezzo, Madonna di Campiglio, San Martino di Castrozza and Canazei, as well as the extremely popular resorts of the Val Gardena. Accommodation and ski facilities are abundant throughout the region and there are numerous opportunities to choose between downhill and cross-country skiing, as well as sci alpinismo, which combines skiing and mountaineering skills on longer ski excursions through some of the region's most spectacular territory.

Tourist offices throughout the region have extensive information on facilities. Probably the best offices to contact for brochures and general information are the APT del Trentino in Trent and the APT for Alto Adige/ Südtirol Dolomiti in Bolzano. See the Trent and Bolzano sections. Staff speak English at both offices and it is possible to write or phone requesting brochures which detail prices for accommodation, ski passes etc (addresses and telephone numbers are listed under the individual towns).

The high season is generally from Christmas to early January and then from early February to April, when prices go up considerably. A good way to save money is to buy a Settimana Bianca package. See the Skiing section in the Facts for the Visitor chapter.

If you want to go it alone, but plan to do a lot of skiing, it's worth investing in a ski pass. Most resort areas offer their own passes for unlimited use of lifts at several resorts for a nominated period (average price in the 1994/95 high season for a seven-day pass was around L230,000). However, the best value is the Superski Dolomiti pass which allows access to 450 lifts and more than 1100 km of ski runs. In the 1994/95 high season a Superski pass for seven days cost L258,000.

Ring Superski Dolomiti (☎ 0471-79 53 98) for information or pick up brochures at tourist offices throughout the region.

The average cost of ski and boot hire is from L17,000 to L25,000 a day for downhill skis and up to L14,000 for cross-country skis and boots. In an expensive resort like Cortina, however, prices jump to as high as L33,000 a day to rent downhill skis and boots.

There are ski schools at all resorts.

OTHER ACTIVITIES

Activities in the Dolomites include mountain biking, hang-gliding and rock climbing. Most tourist offices will provide information on mountain bike trails and where you can rent a bike. They will also help you find reputable hang-gliding schools.

There are Alpine Guides Groups in most towns and villages throughout the region and many are listed in this chapter. If no group is listed for a particular area, the local tourist office will be able to assist.

Through these groups you can go on guided treks (ranging from easy family nature walks to challenging treks of up to seven days at high altitudes), take rock climbing courses or even send the kids away for a few days of adventure. Many groups also offer guided mountain bike and horse riding tours.

Families are well catered for throughout the region, but particularly in Alto Adige. Many tourist offices organise special activities for kids in the summer and winter high seasons and some guides groups offer special courses and treks for youngsters. Most of the resort towns in Alto Adige have sports centres and playgrounds and many hotels are equipped for children (with cots, high chairs, special menus, playrooms etc).

Some information is given in this chapter, including some suggested family walks. Contact the individual tourist offices for more details.

Trentino

TRENT (TRENTO)

This calm, well-organised provincial capital is a good place to start any exploration of the province. Its tourist offices have extensive information, both about the town and about Trentino, and it is a convenient central point for public transport throughout the province.

Known as Tridentum under the Romans, Trent later passed from the Goths to the Lombards and was eventually annexed to the Holy Roman Empire, when it was known as Trent or Trient. For eight centuries from 1027 it was an episcopal principality, during a period marked by political and territorial conflict with the rulers of Tyrol. The famous Council of Trent (1545-63) considered the restructure of the Catholic Church here and launched the Counter-Reformation.

Orientation

The train station and adjacent bus station are close to Trent's compact historical centre, as well as to most accommodation. To get to the centre, turn right as you leave the train or bus station and follow Via Andrea Pozzo, which becomes Via Cavour, to Piazza del Duomo.

Information

Tourist Offices Cross the small park directly in front of the train station and turn right to reach the APT office (☎ 0461-98 38 80) at Via Alfieri 4. It's open Monday to Friday from 9 am to midday and 3 to 6 pm and on Saturday to midday. From mid-June to mid-September, it is open Sunday from 10 am to midday. The office has loads of information about the town, including maps and glossy brochures in English.

The provincial tourist office, the APT del Trentino (☎ 0461-90 00 00), Corso III Novembre 134, has extensive information on Trentino and can advise on skiing facilities, walking, trekking and climbing, as well as other activities, and has good road maps of the province, with suggested itineraries. It also has offices in Rome and Milan. See the introduction to this chapter.

Post & Telecommunications Trent's main post office is in Via Calepina, at Piazza Vittoria, east of Piazza del Duomo. The post code for central Trent is 38100.

There is a Telecom office in Piazza della Portella, on Via Torre Vanga, off Via Andrea Pozzo. Trent's telephone code is 0461.

Emergency In an emergency, call ☎ 113, or go to the questura (☎ 98 61 13), Piazza della Mostra, off Via San Marco near the Castello

del Buonconsiglio. Ospedale Santa Chiara (☎ 90 32 06) is in Largo Medaglie d'Oro, south-east of the centre, off Corso III Novembre.

Things to See & Do
The Piazza del Duomo is the natural place to start a tour of Trent. The piazza is flanked by the Romanesque **duomo** and the 13th-century **Palazzo Pretorio** and tower. The Council of Trent was held in the duomo (as well as in the Chiesa di Santa Maria Maggiore). Inside the cathedral, there are fragments of medieval frescoes in the transept, and two

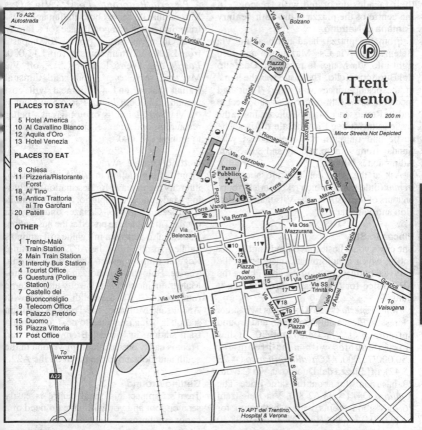

Trent (Trento)

0   100   200 m

Minor Streets Not Depicted

PLACES TO STAY
5   Hotel America
10 Al Cavallino Bianco
12 Aquila d'Oro
13 Hotel Venezia

PLACES TO EAT
8   Chiesa
11 Pizzeria/Ristorante Forst
18 Al Tino
19 Antica Trattoria ai Tre Garofani
20 Patelli

OTHER
1   Trento-Malè Train Station
2   Main Train Station
3   Intercity Bus Station
4   Tourist Office
6   Questura (Police Station)
7   Castello del Buonconsiglio
9   Telecom Office
14 Palazzo Pretorio
15 Duomo
16 Piazza Vittoria
17 Post Office

TRENTINO

colonnaded staircases flank the nave. The foundations of an early Christian church were discovered in the late 1970s beneath the cathedral. The area is open Monday to Saturday from 10 am to midday and 2.30 to 6 pm. Admission is L2500.

The ticket is also valid for admission to the **Museo Diocesano** in the Palazzo Pretorio, which houses paintings depicting the Council of Trent, as well as a collection of Flemish tapestries. Opening hours are 9.30 am to midday and 2.30 to 6 pm Monday to Saturday and entry is L5000.

On the other side of the piazza are two Renaissance houses, known as the **Case Rella**, their façades decorated with frescoes. In the centre of the piazza is the 18th-century **Fontana di Nettuno**.

From the piazza, head north along Via Belenzani or Via Oss Mazzurana and turn right into Via Manci to reach the **Castello del Buonconsiglio**. The castle was the home of the bishop-princes who ruled Trent and incorporates the 13th-century Castello Vecchio and the Renaissance Magno Palazzo. Inside the castle is the **Museo Provinciale d'Arte**. The castle and museum are open Tuesday to Sunday from 9 am to midday and 2 to 5 pm. Admission is L4000.

Ask at the APT del Trentino about the *trenini* (little trains) which take tourist groups on tours of the castles in the Valsugana, Val di Non and Vallagarina.

Places to Stay

The city's youth hostel has closed until further notice, which is unfortunate since it was the only real budget option in the city. Phone the APT office for the latest information on it status.

Hotel Venezia (☎ 23 41 14) has two street addresses, Piazza del Duomo 45 and around the corner at Via Belenzani 70. It has singles/doubles with a bathroom for L50,000/75,000. *Al Cavallino Bianco* (☎ 23 15 42), off Piazza del Duomo at Via Cavour 29, has rooms for about the same price. The *Aquila d'Oro* (☎ 98 62 82), Via Belenzani 76, has good rooms with a bathroom for L120,000/170,000. *Hotel America* (☎ 98 30 10), Via Torre Verde 50, is an excellent option if you don't mind the expense. It has comfortable singles/doubles for L120,000/150,000.

The APT office has information on agriturismo accommodation in the area.

Places to Eat

You will have no problem finding a decent place to eat in Trent: the town teems with pizzerias, trattorias and restaurants. *Al Tino*, Via SS Trinità 10, has pasta for around L9000 and salads for around L10,000. *Antica Trattoria ai Tre Garofani*, Via Mazzini, is a very simple place which also serves pizzas.

Pizzeria/Ristorante Forst, Via Oss Mazzurana 38, serves both Italian and Austrian dishes and is a good place for a family meal. It serves pizzas from L7000, pasta from L8000 and main courses from L11,000. *Patelli*, Via Dietro le Mura A 5, off Via Mazzini, serves very good and unusual Italian dishes, and a full meal will cost around L35,000. *Chiesa*, Parco San Marco, on Via San Marco, is one of Trent's better restaurants and an excellent meal will come to around L80,000.

Getting There & Away

From the bus station in Via Andrea Pozzo, intercity buses leave for destinations including Madonna di Campiglio, San Martino di Castrozza, Molveno, Canazei and Riva di Garda. Timetables are posted at the bus station. You can also pick up a full guide to Trentino's public transport from the APT del Trentino. Regular trains connect Trent with Verona, Venice, Bologna and Bolzano. The Trento-Malé train line connects the city along scenic routes with Cles in the Val di Non, and with Andalo and Molveno. The Trento-Malé train station is being relocated to next to the main train station, in Via del Brennero. By car, Trent is easily accessible from Verona in the south and Bolzano in the north on the A22.

Getting Around

Trent's compact historical centre is easily seen on foot and you will have no need of a car or city buses.

DOLOMITI DI BRENTA

This majestic group of jagged peaks is isolated from the main body of the Dolomites and provides good walking opportunities, but it is probably best suited to experienced trekkers wanting to test their mountaineering skills. North-west of Trent, and part of the Parco Naturale Adamello-Brenta, the group is easily accessible from either Molveno or Madonna di Campiglio. People should plan their routes, since many trails at higher altitudes incorporate *vie ferrate* (climbing trails with permanent steel cords) for which you will need harnesses and ropes to attach yourself to the cords. The group's most famous trail is the Via Bocchetta di Tuckett, opened up by 19th-century climber Francis Fox Tuckett, which runs from Molveno to Cima Brenta and includes sections of vie ferrate.

There are excellent skiing facilities at Madonna di Campiglio, and near Molveno is the well-equipped ski resort, Andalo.

Molveno

This village is in a very picturesque position by the Lago di Molveno, overshadowed by the towering Brenta group. It became famous in the 19th century as a base for the English and German mountaineers who came to open up trails into the group.

Information The APT office (☎ 0461-58 69 24) is at Piazza Marconi 7 and is open Monday to Saturday from 9 am to 12.30 pm and 3.30 to 7 pm and Sunday from 9 am to midday. The staff can help you find accommodation (although in August you should book in advance) and can advise on walking trails. Also in the piazza is the office of the Alpine Guides Group (☎ 0461-58 60 86).

There is a tourist medical service provided by the *comune* (☎ 58 60 45) during the day in the Palazzo Comunale. If a medical emergency occurs at night, phone the Guardia medica on ☎ 58 56 37.

The telephone code for the village is 0461.

Activities From the top of the village, a *cabinovia* (two-seater cable car) will take you up to the Rifugio Pradel (1400 metres),

from where you take trail No 340 to the Rifugio Croz dell'Altissimo (1430 metres), a pleasant and easy one-hour walk. Take trail No 340 to the Rifugio Selvata (1630 metres), then trail No 319 to the rifugi Tosa and Tommaso Pedrotti (2491 metres and about four hours walk).

From here most of the trails are difficult and you will need to be prepared for vie ferrate or for traversing glaciers. It is best to seek detailed information locally and take a carefully planned route using a good map.

For a less demanding walk, there is a path around the lake which starts at the camping ground. Making the entire circle of the lake will take about three and a half hours, but half the route is on the road, so it might be best to double back when the trail ends.

The Alpine Guides Group organises guided treks, some incorporating vie ferrate, as well as rock climbing courses and, in winter, ski-mountaineering. Of interest to families might be the five-day mountaineering courses for kids aged from eight to 15 years. The course is offered weekly from June to October.

Places to Stay & Eat The tourist office will provide a list of the mountain rifugi and their telephone numbers to help you plan your trek. If you want to stay in Molveno, there is *Camping Spiaggia Lago di Molveno* (☎ 58 69 78), which charges up to L9500 per person and L13,000 for a space.

Prices do not vary greatly among the various hotels in town and many require that you take full board. Average prices for full board are from L60,000 per person in May and June, and around L100,000 per person in the high season (July/August). Try the *Zurigo* (☎ 58 69 47), Via Rio Massò 2, or *Europa* (☎ 50 60 62), Via Nazionale 11. The *Hotel Ariston* (☎ 58 69 07) is right in the centre of town on Piazza San Carlo. The *Grand Hotel Molveno* (☎ 58 69 34) is in a lovely position out of town by the lake. Full board is around L140,000 in the high season.

Getting There & Away Molveno is accessible by FTM or Atesina bus from Trent. Atesina buses also connect Molveno with Milan in July and August, leaving from Piazza Castello in Milan every Saturday and Sunday (ring ☎ 02-80 11 61 in Milan for details).

Madonna di Campiglio

One of the top ski resorts in the Alps, Madonna di Campiglio (often simply called Madonna) is in the Valle Rendena, on the other side of the Brenta group. It is extremely well equipped with ski lifts and runs and there are excellent opportunities for cross-country and Alpine skiing.

Information The APT office (☎ 0465-44 20 00) is in the centre of the village, off Piazza Brenta Alta. It has loads of information about skiing and walking in the area and can advise on accommodation. It will mail out hotel lists and other information on request. The office of the Alpine Guides Group (☎ 0465-44 26 34) is across the street (open only after 4 pm) and brochures on its summer excursions are available at the tourist office.

A tourist medical service (☎ 480 16 00) operates during the winter and summer high seasons. Out of season, check the board posted beside the tourist office for information.

The telephone code for the village is 0465.

Activities A network of chair lifts and cable cars will take you from the village to the numerous ski runs or, in summer, to the walking trails. A few km out of the village at Campo Carlo Magno is a cable car (in two stages) up to the Passo Grosté, from where trekkers can set off into the Brenta group. (The return trip on the cable car will cost L22,000.) The Via delle Bocchette (trail No 305) leaves from the Rifugio Grosté at the cable car station. This is the via ferrata for which the Brenta group is famous and only experienced mountaineers with the correct equipment should attempt it. Otherwise, take trail No 316 to Rifugio del Tuckett and Rifugio Sella. From there, take trail No 328 and then No 318 (sentiero Bogani) to the Rifugio dei Brentei Maria e Alberto (4-5 hours from Grosté). All trails heading higher

into the group from here cross glaciers and special equipment is needed.

Near Madonna is the Val Genova, often described as one of the most beautiful valleys in the Alps. It is a perfect spot for walks and picnics, but can get very crowded in the summer high season. The valley extends up into the striking Adamello mountain range, where there are some challenging walking trails. Along the valley there are a number of spectacular waterfalls. There are four rifugi in the valley, each costing around L35,000 per person per night. During August the valley is closed to normal traffic and half-hourly buses ferry walkers and tourists to the Rifugio Adamello at the end of the road, from where you can take trail No 241 to the end of the valley (2000 metres) beneath a huge, receding glacier. The trail then climbs steeply to the Rifugio Caduti dell'Adamello (3020 metres) at the edge of the glacier.

Places to Stay & Eat There are numerous hotels and garnis in Madonna, none of which will suit the pockets of budget travellers. Most require that you pay for half or full board and in the high season may be reluctant to accept bookings for less than seven days. *Garni Bucaneve* (☎ 44 12 17) is south of the village, near Piazza Palù, and offers room and board from around L70,000 per person. The *Bellavista* (☎ 44 10 34), a very pleasant establishment uphill from the tourist office, near the Funivia Pradalago, charges from L80,000 to around L130,000 per person per day for full board, depending on the season. *La Fontanella* (☎ 44 13 98) is a few km out of town towards the Val di Genova and has a magnificent view of the Brenta group. Its prices are much lower, from around L70,000 to L95,000 per person per day for full board.

In the Val Genova, the *Rifugio Fontanabona* (☎ 5 11 75) and the *Rifugio Stella Alpina* are both in lovely settings. B&B costs around L40,000 and full board around L70,000 per person. Both have excellent restaurants and are open from July 1 to September 25.

In Madonna, try *Ristorante/Pizzeria Le Roi*, Via Cima Tosa, near Piazza Brenta Alta, where a full meal will cost from L25,000 to

L30,000. Around the corner is *Bar Dolomiti*, where hot sandwiches for L4500 should be sufficient for lunch. In the summer and winter high seasons you could try one of the malghe, such as *Malga Ritorto* (☎ 44 24 70), accessible by car in summer and by 'snow cat' service in winter.

Getting There & Away Madonna di Campiglio is accessible from Trent's bus station by regular Atesina bus. It is also accessible from cities including Rome, Florence and Bologna by Lazzi (in Rome and Florence) and SITA buses.

VAL DI NON

The Val di Non is a picturesque valley of apple orchards and castles accessible from Trent by Trento-Malé train or bus. The main town is Cles, dominated by the Castel Cles. The Pro Loco tourist office is in Corso Dante, just off the main road through town. If you want to stay here on your way north, try the *Antica Trattoria* (☎ 0463-2 16 31), Via Roma, which has singles/doubles for L38,000/52,000 with a bathroom. The *Cristallo* (☎ 0463-2 13 53), Corso Dante, has rooms for L60,000/92,000 with a bathroom.

SAN MARTINO DI CASTROZZA

East of Trent, this important ski resort is at the foot of the Pale di San Martino, an imposing group of Dolomite mountains, so stark and grey-white that they virtually glow in the dark. The mountains are part of the Parco Naturale Paneveggio-Pale di San Martino, noted for its Alpine vegetation and wildlife, including the roe deer, chamois, marmot, wildfowl and birds of prey such as the golden eagle. It is a magnificent area in which to ski or walk, and both San Martino di Castrozza and nearby Fiera di Primiero are well equipped for tourists.

Information

The APT office (☎ 0439-76 88 67) is at Via Passo Rollo 167. It has extensive information on accommodation, transport and skiing facilities, and can advise on walking trails. You can telephone or write to request infor-

mation about hotels or apartments. The office is open Monday to Saturday from 9 am to midday and 3 to 7 pm and Sunday from 9.30 am to 12.30 pm. Information about Alpine guides is also available at the office daily from 5 to 7 pm. A two-day trek with a guide costs L100,000 per person. Rock climbing and cord-trail courses are also offered.

San Martino's telephone code is 0439.

The nearest hospital is at Feltre, although a tourist medical service is available during summer and winter at San Martino and Primiero. Full details are available at the tourist office.

Activities

The area has excellent ski runs and is part of the extensive Superski Dolomiti; during winter a special ski bus connects the valley with the various runs. The Pale di San Martino has well-marked trails and a reasonable map is available at the tourist office. A chair lift and cable car will take you to the Rifugio Rosetta (2600 metres), from where you can choose between several relatively easy walks or treks requiring mountaineering skills.

Places to Stay & Eat

Prices vary according to the season and many places will require that you pay for half or full board. They may also be reluctant to accept bookings for less than seven days. The tourist office will advise on apartments to rent and has a full list of rifugi in the area.

The *Suisse* (☎ 6 80 87), Via Dolomiti 1, has singles/doubles for L40,000/80,000 (room only). *Biancaneve* (☎ 6 81 35) is nearby at No 14 and charges L44,000 per person for B&B. The newly renovated *Hotel Plank* (☎ 76 89 76), Via Laghetto, charges from around L115,000 per person for full board. Good Settimana Bianca deals are available.

For meals, try *Lo Sfizio*, a crêperie just off Via Passo Rollo, near the tourist office. Slightly out of town, along Via Fontanelle, are *Ristorante Le Fontanelle* and *Caffè Col*. Local food is served at the various malghe around San Martino, which have developed into proper restaurants. Try the traditional style *Malga Venegiota* (☎ 6 46 57), accessible by a short trail from the Malga Juribello near Passo Rolle.

Getting There & Away
San Martino is accessible directly from Florence and Rome (change at Florence) by the Alpi Bus service of Lazzi and SITA buses. From Bologna you can catch a Dolomiti Express bus from the bus station in Via XX Settembre. San Martino is also accessible from Trent by Atesina bus (leaving from the bus station in Via Pozzo, Trent) and from Canazei by SITA bus.

CANAZEI
This popular ski resort in the Val di Fassa is surrounded by the striking high mountains of the Gruppo di Sella to the north, the Catinaccio (Rosengarten) to the west and the Marmolada to the south-east. It is a fairly modern town and well equipped for tourists. Skiing possibilities include a range of downhill and cross-country runs, as well as some very challenging Alpine tours and the Sella Ronda network of runs. There is summer skiing on the Marmolada glacier. From the Val di Fassa walkers can approach the Catinaccio group from Vigo di Fassa, about 11 km south of Canazei. The best way to approach the Sella group from Canazei is from Passo Pordoi, where a cable car will take you up to almost 3000 metres. See the sections on the Catinaccio and Sella groups.

Information The Canazei AAST office (☎ 0462-6 11 13) has loads of information on ski runs, ski lifts and ski schools and can advise on accommodation and walking trails.

The telephone code for Canazei is 0462.

Places to Stay & Eat Hotels are numerous, but it is advisable to book in August and during the peak ski season. There are also rooms and apartments for rent and the tourist office can provide details.

The *Camping Marmolada* (☎ 6 16 60) is in the town centre and is open in both summer and winter. Prices are L9000 per person and L12,000 for a site.

Pensione Genzianella (☎ 6 11 43), Via Roma 15, charges L30,000 per person for B&B and L60,000 for half board. It closes in October and November. The *Stella Alpina* (☎ 6 11 27), Via Antermont 4, charges L42,000 per person for B&B and L54,000 for half board. *Pensione Rita* (☎ 6 12 19), Via Pareda, charges up to L90,000 per day and up to L600,000 per week half board in the high season.

There is a supermarket at Via Dolomiti 120, and numerous bars and panini shops. The *Osteria La Montanara*, Via Dolomiti 147, serves good meals for around L25,000. Opposite is the *Pizzeria/Ristorante Italia*, where pizzas cost from L7000 to L12,000 and a full meal under L25,000.

Getting There & Away Canazei can be reached by Atesina bus from Trent and by Servizi Autobus Dolomiti (SAD) bus from Bolzano and the Val Gardena. It should be noted that services do not cross the high mountain passes (such as Sella) in winter.

GRUPPO DI SELLA
The Sella group, in the western Dolomites, straddles the border between Trentino and Alto Adige, close to Cortina d'Ampezzo in the Veneto and the spectacular Parco Naturale di Fanes-Sennes-Braies. To the west is the spiky Sasso Lungo, which extends to the Alpe di Siusi in Alto Adige. To the east is the Val Badia and its main town, Corvara, while to the south is the Val di Fassa.

The entire zone is extremely well equipped for skiers, and, by following a network of runs known as the Sella Ronda, you can make a day-long skiing tour of the valleys surrounding the Sella group. Full details on the tour are available at all tourist offices in the area.

The walking trails of the Sella and Sasso Lungo are accessible from Canazei or from the resorts of the Val Gardena by SAD (Servizi Autobus Dolomiti) bus to Passo Sella or Passo Pordoi. At Passo Sella (2240 metres), where there is a magnificent view across the Alps, there is a cable car to the Rifugio T Demetz (2996 metres) on the Sasso Lungo. From here you can pick up trail No 525, which traverses the mountain's jagged peaks and will take you down to the Alpe di Siusi. From Passo Pordoi (2242 metres), take the cable car up to Sass Pordoi (2952 metres). Here you can take the Alta Via No 2, which crosses the group, heads down to the Passo Gardena and then continues into the breathtaking Parco Naturale Puez-Odle.

Alternatively you can take trail No 638 to the Rifugio Piz Fass on Piz Boé (3152 metres). Continuing along No 638 you will reach a combined chair lift and cable car service down to Corvara in the Val Badia. Note that both the cable car and chair lift are open from 8.30 am to 5.30 pm, with a break for lunch (from about 12.15 to 2 pm), and are closed all day Monday. As with all walks mentioned in this book, it is recommended that you use a 1:25,000 Tabacco map and plan your walk carefully.

The Sella also offers challenging walks, some incorporating vie ferrate, for people with mountaineering experience. For further information on the Sella, the Val Gardena and the Val Badia see the following section on Alto Adige.

Alto Adige (Südtirol)

BOLZANO (BOZEN)

The capital of the province of Alto Adige, Bolzano is unmistakably Austrian. Even though its inhabitants speak both German and Italian (both languages are compulsory subjects in school), and its street names, hotels and restaurants are identified in both languages, you will find little evidence of Italian influence here. The town's historic centre, with its Tyrolean architecture and arcaded streets, harbours numerous outdoor cafés and restaurants, making it a very pleasant place to spend a few days.

Settled in the Middle Ages, Bolzano was an important market town which became a pawn in the power battles between the bishops of Trent and the counts of Tyrol. During the first decades of the 19th century

it passed, with the rest of the Tyrol, from Bavaria, to Austria, to Napoleon's kingdom of Italy and, finally, again to Austria. Along with the Südtirol, Bolzano passed to Italy after WW I and was declared the capital of the province in 1927.

Orientation
The old-town centre is Piazza Walther (Waltherplatz), a few minutes walk along Viale Stazione from the train station on Via Garibaldi. The intercity bus station is on Via Perathoner, between the train station and the piazza.

Information
Tourist Offices The AST office (☎ 0471-97 56 56) is at Piazza Walther 8 and is open Monday to Friday from 8.30 am to 6 pm and Saturday from 9 am to 12.30 pm. The staff have extensive information on the town and accommodation.

The provincial tourist office for Alto Adige (☎ 0471-99 38 08) is at Piazza Parrocchia 11 and is open Monday to Friday from 9 am to midday and 3 to 5.30 pm. Here you can pick up information about accommodation, activities and transport, as well as walking and trekking possibilities. There is an Alpine information desk in the office, where you can get assistance in planning walks, treks, climbs etc.

Money Money can be changed at all banks in Bolzano. On weekends, from 7 am to 8 pm, there is an exchange office open at the train station.

Post & Telecommunications The post office is in Via della Posta, just off Piazza Walther. The Telecom office, Piazza Parrocchia, is open Monday to Saturday from 8.30 am to 12.15 pm and 3.30 to 7.45 pm and Sunday from 8 am to 1 pm. The post code for central Bolzano is 39100 and the telephone code is 0471.

Emergency For immediate police attendance, call ☎ 113. The questura (☎ 94 76 11) is in Via Marconi. The Ospedale Regionale San

ALTO ADIGE

Maurizio (☎ 90 81 11) is in Via Lorenze Böhler, some distance from the town centre off the road to Merano, and accessible on city bus No 8 from the train station.

Things to See & Do

While away a few hours at one of the many outdoor cafés in Piazza Walther or along the side streets which lead to Piazza delle Erbe (Obstplatz). Otherwise, rent a bike from Velosport, Via Grappoli 56 (Weintraubeng), near Piazza Walther.

The AST office offers a Visitor's Pass to tourists who spend at least three nights in town which includes free admission to some sights and a guided tour of the town.

Start with the Gothic **duomo** in Piazza Parrocchia and the nearby **Chiesa di Domenicani** with its cloisters and chapel featuring 14th-century frescoes of the Giotto school. Take a walk along the arcaded **Via dei Portici** (Lauben), through the Piazza delle Erbe, the daily fresh produce market

held there, to reach the 14th-century **Chiesa di Francescani** in Via dei Francescani. It features beautiful cloisters and a magnificent Gothic altarpiece in the Cappella della Beata Vergine (Virgin's Chapel), carved by Hans Klocker in 1500. There are two castles in the town: the 13th-century **Castel Mareccio** (Schloss Maretsch), along Via della Roggia from Piazza delle Erbe, and the **Castel Roncolo** (Schloss Runkelstein), out of town on the road to Sarentino (Sarnthein). A bike will come in handy for visiting both.

Places to Stay

There is a wide choice of accommodation in Bolzano, including hotels and pensioni, as well as rooms for rent and agriturismo – the AST office has full listings. There is a camping ground, *Moosbauer* (☎ 91 84 92), at Via San Maurizio 83, out of town towards Merano.

The *Croce Bianca* (☎ 97 75 52), Piazza del Grano 3, off Via Portici, charges up to

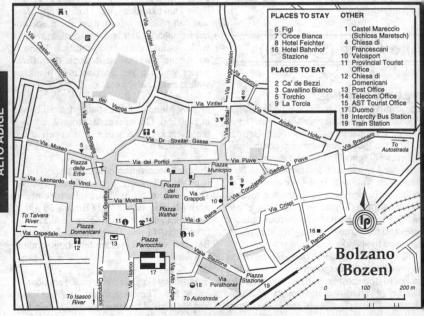

PLACES TO STAY
6 Figl
7 Croce Bianca
8 Hotel Feichter
16 Hotel Bahnhof Stazione

PLACES TO EAT
2 Ca' de Bezzi
3 Cavallino Bianco
5 Torchio
9 La Torcia

OTHER
1 Castel Mareccio (Schloss Maretsch)
4 Chiesa di Francescani
10 Velosport
11 Provincial Tourist Office
12 Chiesa di Domenicani
13 Post Office
14 Telecom Office
15 AST Tourist Office
17 Duomo
18 Intercity Bus Station
19 Train Station

Bolzano (Bozen)

L42,000 per person for B&B. The *Hotel Bahnhof Stazione* (☎ 97 32 91) is in a less pleasant position to the east of the train station, at Via Renon 23; it has singles/doubles with a bathroom for L27,500/54,000. The *Figl* (☎ 97 84 12), also in Piazza del Grano, has good rooms for up to L60,000 per person. *Hotel Feichter* (☎ 97 87 68), Via Grappoli 15, charges similar prices. Out of town at Colle (Kohlern), accessible by road or the Funivia del Colle, is *Klaushof* (☎ 97 12 94), which offers B&B for a more affordable L25,000 per person.

Places to Eat

You can pick up supplies of fruit and vegetables, bread and cheese etc from the open air market held every morning from Monday to Saturday at Piazza delle Erbe. In the same area are numerous bakeries, pastry shops and cafés, as well as a small supermarket. While you can eat pizza and pasta if you wish, Bolzano's best restaurants specialise in Tyrolean food. The *Cavallino Bianco*, Via Bottai, is extremely popular and the food is great, as well as reasonably priced at around L25,000 for a full meal. *La Torcia*, Via dei Conciapelli 25, is a cheap pizzeria, where you can also get reasonable pasta. *Torchio* (Torgglkeller), just off Piazza dell Erbe at Via Museo 2 (Museum Strasse) has excellent local specialities at reasonable prices. *Ca' de Bezzi*, Via Andrea Hofer 30 (Hofer Strasse), is one of the city's better restaurants. A full meal will cost L40,000 to L50,000.

Getting There & Away

Bus Bolzano is a major transport hub for Alto Adige. SAD buses leave from the bus terminal in Via Perathoner near Piazza Walther, for destinations throughout the province, including the Val Gardena, the Alpi di Siusi, Brunico, the Val Pusteria, and Merano (where you can change for destinations including the valleys leading up into the Parco Nazionale dello Stelvio). SAD buses also head for resorts outside the province, such as Cortina d'Ampezzo and Canazei (though it is necessary to make several changes). Full timetable details are available from the bus station or the AST office.

Train Regular trains connect Bolzano with Merano, Trent, Verona and Milan. You can also catch a train from Bolzano to Brunico and San Candido in the Val Pusteria.

Car & Motorbike The town is easily accessible from the north and south on the A22. The road connecting Bolzano and Merano is one long traffic jam in busy periods of tourism. There's no way to avoid it, so try driving at lunch or dinner time to at least miss the rush hours.

MERANO (MERAN)

Two words can be used to describe Merano: sedate and relaxing. The town's centre is clean, well tended and features characteristic Tyrolean architecture. The Terme di Merano, a large complex of therapeutic baths and treatments, is the town's main attraction and a majority of tourists tend to be of older age groups. Merano is close to the Parco Naturale Gruppo di Tessa (Texalgruppe), the Parco Nazionale dello Stelvio and the spectacular Ortles mountain range, so you might find yourself using the town as a stopover on your way to higher altitudes.

The train and intercity bus stations are in Piazza Stazione, a 10-minute walk from the centre of town. As you leave the train station, turn right into Via Europa and at Piazza Mazzini take Corso della Libertà to the town centre.

Information

The AAST office (☎ 0473-3 52 23) is at Corso della Libertà 45, where you can pick up a map of the town, an information brochure and advice on accommodation and restaurants.

The main post office and Telecom office are at Via Roma 2, on the other side of the river from the historic centre. The town's telephone code is 0473.

For police emergency, call ☎ 113. The Ospedale Provinciale (☎ 4 61 11) is at Via

Goethe 50, along Via O Huber from Corso della Libertà.

Things to See & Do

The historic centre of the town is around the arcaded Via Portici (Laubengasse) and the Piazza del Duomo – take any of the streets off Corso della Libertà near the tourist office (leading away from the river). As mentioned, the town's main attraction is the complex of **therapeutic baths**, which offers the full range of treatments, including thermal baths (cost L10,000), mud baths (cost L32,000), massages (cost L35,000) and physiotherapy. The complex is open all year from Monday to Saturday.

Beer lovers might be interested in a visit to the **Forst Brewery**, at Forst just out of Merano.

Places to Stay

Accommodation is abundant in Merano, including rooms and apartments for rent, hotels and guesthouses. Ask at the tourist office for assistance. The tourist office can also provide a list of hotels and pensioni equipped for children (with services such as baby cots, babysitting, playgrounds and playrooms). Many also offer reductions for children. Almost without exception, the establishments in and around the centre of town are expensive, although the *Albergo Dolomiten* (☎ 23 63 77), off Piazza del Duomo at Vicolo Haller 8, has reasonably priced rooms at L35,000 per person, including breakfast.

Villa Pax (☎ 23 62 90), Via Leichter 3, charges up to L27,000 per person. To reach it from Corso della Libertà, cross the river at Piazza D Rena and follow Via Cavour to Via Dante, turn right and then left into Via Leichter. *Pensione Tyrol* (☎ 4 97 19), Via XXX Aprile 8, has rooms for L37,000 per person. *Villa Fanny* (☎ 23 35 20), Winterpromenade 30, charges L50,000 per person for B&B. The *Conte di Merano* (☎ 23 21 81), Via delle Corse 78, is just near the Via dei Portici. Its lovely rooms, breakfast included, cost L60,000 to L70,000 per person.

Places to Eat

The *Ristorante Forsterbräu*, Corso della Libertà 90, has an internal garden/courtyard and serves typical Tyrolean food at reasonable prices. A full meal could cost under L25,000. *Picnic Grill*, Via delle Corse 26, is even more economical, with pizzas and pre-prepared food. Two restaurants in Via Portici serve excellent Tyrolean fare at higher prices: *Algunder Weinstube* at No 232 and *Terlaner Weinstube* at No 231. A full meal at either will cost at least L30,000.

Getting There & Away

Merano is easily accessible by bus or train from Bolzano (about 40 minutes). SAD buses also connect the town with Katharinaberg and other villages which give access to the Tessa group, as well as to Silandro and the valleys leading up into the Ortles range and the Parco Nazionale dello Stelvio. See the section on the Parco Nazionale dello Stelvio for bus information.

PARCO NAZIONALE DELLO STELVIO

If you can tear yourself away from the Dolomites, this major national park offers fantastic walking possibilities: at low altitudes in the pretty valleys, Val d'Ultimo (Ultental), Val Martello (Martelltal) and Val di Solda (Suldental); and at high altitudes on spectacular peaks such as the Gran Zebru (Königspitze) (3859 metres), Cevedale (3769 metres) and the breathtaking Ortles (Ortler) (3905 metres), all part of the Ortles range. There is a network of well-marked trails, including routes over some of the range's glaciers. The park actually incorporates one of Europe's largest glaciers, the Ghiacciaio dei Forni.

The glaciers mean that the park offers skiing year-round and there are well-serviced runs at Solda and the Passo Stelvio. The Passo Stelvio is the second highest pass in the Alps and is approached from Trafoi on one of Europe's most spectacular roads, a series of tight switchbacks with at times nerve-wrackingly steep gradients. The road is famous among cyclists, who flock to the park every summer to tackle the ascent.

The village of **Trafoi** marks the start of about 15 km of switchbacks up to the pass. If you want to stay here, there is a camping ground (☎ 0473-61 15 33) and several hotels including the *Hochleiten* (☎ 0473-61 17 91) at L32,000 for B&B, and the *Madatsch* (☎ 0473-61 17 67), with half board from L70,000.

A SAD bus operates to the pass in summer only. From Merano change at Spondigna (Spondinig).

The park straddles Alto Adige and Trentino and can be approached from Merano (from where you have easy access to the Val d'Ultimo, Val Martello, Val di Solda and the Passo Stelvio), or from the Val di Sole in Trentino, which gives easy access to the Valle di Péio and the Val di Rabbi and high trails up to the Forni glacier.

Male red deer live in wooded areas in sexually segregated herds, except when breeding.

Val di Solda (Suldental)

The village of Solda (Sulden), at the head of the valley, is a small ski resort and a base for walkers and climbers in summer. There are challenging walking trails which will take you to high altitudes, including the No 28, which crosses the Cima Madriccio (Madritschspitze) (3263 metres) into the Val Martello. The tourist office at Solda (☎ 0473-61 30 15) has information on accommodation and activities.

At Solda try *Pension Nives* (☎ 0473-61 32 20), which offers B&B for up to L30,000 per person, or half board for up to L50,000. *Parc Hotel* (☎ 0473-61 31 33), has lovely rooms and good food for up to L100,000 per person for half board. The village virtually closes down from October to Christmas.

Solda is accessible by SAD bus on weekdays during summer only. From Merano you need to change at Spondigna (Spondinig).

Val Martello

This very picturesque valley is a good choice for anyone wanting to walk at relatively low altitude, with spectacular views of the some of the park's high peaks. The real beauty of the valley is that there are no ski lifts or downhill runs, so the environment is unspoiled. The valley is a very popular base for mountaineers wanting to tackle the glaciers: guided treks can be organised through the valley's Pro Loco office (☎ 0473-74 45 98). Contact the Pro Loco for information on hotels and activities in the valley. In winter there is excellent cross-country skiing, and climbers can tackle the valley's frozen waterfalls from January to March. In spring the valley attracts ski mountaineers, since there is no danger of avalanches.

People with children might like to take trail No 20 up into the Val di Peder. It is an easy walk, with some lovely picnic spots along the way and the chance to see animals including chamois and deer.

To stay in the valley, try the *Schoenblick* (☎ 0473-7 04 76), which is situated high in the valley and offers half board from L44,000 per person.

The road into the valley is open year-round, but bus services operate to the head of the valley only during the summer. From Merano, change at Silandro (Schlanders).

Valle di Péio
From Péio (also spelt Péjo) Terme (1393 metres) there are chair lifts to the Rifugio Doss dei Cembri (2400 metres), from where you can pick up trail No 105 to the Rifugio Mantova al Vioz (3535 metres) at the edge of the Forni glacier. If you want to climb Monte Vioz (3645 metres) or continue onto the glacier, you will need the appropriate equipment. As with all walks mentioned in this book, carry a good map and plan your walk carefully.

The tourist office at Malé (☎ 0463-90 12 80), Piazza Regina Elena, has extensive information on these valleys, including accommodation, transport and sporting activities, and will advise on walking trails and ski facilities.

Ferrovia Trento-Malé buses connect Péio Terme with Madonna di Campiglio and with Malé in the Val di Sole. Malé is accessible on the Trento-Malé train line from Trent and from Cles.

VAL GARDENA (GRÖDENTAL)
This picturesque Alpine valley is surrounded by the towering peaks of the Parco Naturale Puez-Odle, the imposing Sella group and Sasso Lungo and the gentle slopes and pastures of the Alpi di Siusi, the largest high plain in the Alps. It is one of the more popular skiing areas in the Alps because of its relatively reasonable prices and excellent facilities. However, during the ski season its runs are packed and you may prefer to avoid the valley for this reason. It is also a great area for walking, since it provides easy access to trails at both high and low altitudes. See Activities in this section for details. Its main towns are Ortisei (St Ulrich), Santa Cristina (St Christina) and Selva (Wolkenstein), all offering lots of accommodation. Along with the Alpi di Siusi, the Val Gardena provides excellent facilities for families. The extremely well-organised tourist offices run activities for children in both summer and winter, and there are sports centres and well-equipped playgrounds.

The Val Gardena, as throughout the Dolomites, has a rich tradition of legends. It is also noted as one of the two valleys in the Dolomites which preserves the ancient Ladin language and culture -- the other is the Val Badia (Gadertal). See the information box in the Val Badia section later in this chapter. Woodcarving is an ancient tradition which is maintained in the valley. The wood-carvers of the Val Gardena are famous for their statues, figurines, altars and toys. If you plan to buy a woodcarving, choose carefully to ensure your purchase is handcrafted rather than mass-produced.

Information
There are tourist offices in each of the towns: Ortisei (☎ 471-79 63 28), Santa Cristina (☎ 0471-79 30 46) and Selva (☎ 0471-79 51 22). All have extensive information on accommodation, ski facilities and walking trails in the area. A guide book in English is available for each town detailing useful tourist information. Information on guided treks and rock climbing schools can also be obtained.

The telephone code for the valley is 0471.

Activities
There is an extensive and well-equipped network of downhill ski runs. The valley also forms part of the Sella Ronda, a network of runs connecting the Val Gardena, Val Badia and Val di Fassa. There is also excellent cross-country skiing in areas such as the Vallunga, near Selva. Alpine skiers should consult the tourist office for detailed information. There are some stunning trails in the areas of Forcella Pordoi and Val Lasties in the Sella group, and on the Sasso Lungo.

Walkers are in a virtual paradise in this area, surrounded by endless possibilities, from the challenging Alte Vie of the Sella group and the magnificent Parco Natural Puez-Odle (Naturpark Puez-Geisler), to picturesque walks in areas such as the Vallunga, a perfect place for a family walk. Just behind Selva, the valley is home to some over-

Top Left: Duomo, Piazza del Duomo, Milan
   Right: Inside the Galleria Vittorio Emanuele, Milan
Bottom: Detail of the Duomo, Milan

HELMUTH RIER

SONIA BERTO

Top: Mountain biking in the Alpe di Siusi, with the Denti di Terrarossa in the background
Bottom: The Dolomites, Trentino-Alto Adige

friendly horses who like to harass picnicking tourists. The walk to the end of the valley and back will take three to four hours. It is possible to continue from the end of the valley, along trail No 14, to pick up the Alta Via No 2. From here you can continue up into the Odle group, or double back into the Puez group and on to the Sella.

A Full Day Trek in the Puez-Odle This is a full day walk (about eight hours) at high altitude through the Alpe di Cisles, an extraordinarily beautiful landscape dominated by the Odle and Puez groups. As with all walks, make sure you carry a good map: the Tabacco 1:25,000 No 05 is recommended. Also ensure that you carry the correct items of clothing and plenty of water (see under Trekking in the Dolomites) and notify your hotel of your planned route.

From Ortisei (about 1250 metres) in the Val Gardena, take the funivia to Seceda (2456 metres). This is the highest point you will reach during the walk and there is a memorable view – one of the most spectacular in the Dolomites. Behind you is the Odle group, a series of spiky pinnacles. Take trail No 2a, which follows the slope and passes through what most people would consider a typical Alpine environment – lush green, sloping pastures dotted with wooden malghe, which herders use as summer shelters. This type of environment is in fact unusual at such high altitude. Following trail No 2a through the very scenic Alpe di Cisles, you will come to an area known as Prera Longia. Huge boulders with surreal forms dot landscape – who knows how long ago they fell from the mountains. It's highly likely that you'll see marmots, roe deer and certainly lots of birds here. Follow trail No 2a until you arrive in a valley: at this point you need to descend into the valley (continuing to follow trail No 2a and making sure you don't follow the signs for Rifugio Firenze) then go up the other side, following the sign for Forces de Sieles. It's a 200-metre descent and then a very tiring 400 metres uphill. At this point the trail becomes No 2 (there are several trails which branch off to the right – don't follow them),

which will bring you to the Forces de Sieles (2505 metres).

Continue on trail No 2: following it to the left you'll reach a short section of vie ferrate. Don't panic, you don't need any equipment; just hold onto the cord if you need help to cross this steep section. After a short distance, the trail joins the Alta Via No 2 (signed with the number 2 inside a triangle). Following the trail to the right, you'll pass a crest and then descend to a small high plain, almost like a rocky balcony above the Vallunga – you are directly beneath the Puez group at this point, the highest peak of which is the Cima Puez at 2913 metres. Continue along the trail, heading towards Rifugio Puez (Puezhutte) but, before you get there, you'll find trail No 4, which descends into a broad valley and eventually reaches the Vallunga and trail No 4-14. This is virtually a small road; follow it to the right and meander down the pretty Vallunga, with its Alpine vegetation. If you walk quietly, you should come across quite a few animals. The contrast between the majesty of the high mountains and the gentle environment of the valley creates a memorable effect and provides a fitting end to the walk. Once you arrive at the end of the valley, it will take another 15 minutes or so to reach the town of Selva, from where you catch a bus back to Ortisei.

Places to Stay

The valley has hundreds of hotels and pensioni, but it is still advisable to book in advance, particularly during August and at Christmas and Easter. Many places will require half or full board, but there are also plenty of B&Bs and affittacamere, as well as apartments for rent. The tourist offices have full lists, including photos and prices, so write or phone to request a booklet in advance.

Ortisei There are plenty of budget places, such as *Gran Cësa* (☎ 79 74 22), Via Zitadella-Str 67, which offers B&B for around L35,000 per person.

Panoramik (☎ 79 64 95), Via Vidalong-Str 9, has B&B for around L40,000 per person, while the *Rainell* (☎ 79 63 29), Via Vidalong-

Str 19, offers half board for L90,000 to L140,000 per person.

Santa Cristina Try *Affittacamere Desirée* (☎ 79 65 18), Via Chemun 60, which charges up to L26,000 for B&B. *Garni Cir* (☎ 79 33 58), Via Paul 22, charges around L30,000 per person for B&B. *Haus Walter* (☎ 79 33 37), Via Val 6, is very simple and charges up to L38,000 for B&B. *Pensione Bellavista* (☎ 79 20 39) is set back from the town at Via Plesdinaz 65 and offers half board for up to L65,000 per person, as well as B&B. In the centre of town is *Hotel Post* (☎ 79 20 79), which offers half board for up to L128,000 per person.

Selva *Villa Thëres* (☎ 79 54 65), back from the town at Via Rainel 47, charges around L30,000 per person with a bathroom and breakfast included. *Garni Katiuscia* (☎ 7 55 08) is near the Vallunga, a fair walk from the town, but in a lovely position, at Via Larciunëi 38. B&B is up to L45,000 a person. *Garni Zirmei* (☎ 79 52 12), Via Col da Lech 60, charges up to L50,000 for B&B.

Getting There & Away The Val Gardena is accessible from Bolzano by SAD bus, as well as from Canazei (only in summer). Regular buses connect the towns along the valley and you can reach the Alpi di Siusi either by bus or cable car. Full timetables are available at the tourist offices or from the SAD office in Antoniusplatz, Ortisei (☎ 79 61 06).

Information about long-distance bus services (Lazzi, SITA and STAT) to major cities throughout Italy can be obtained at Tourdolomiti Viaggi (☎ 79 53 24) in Selva, or in Ortisei (☎ 79 61 35).

ALPE DI SIUSI & PARCO NATURALE DELLO SCILIAR

There's something magical about the view across the Alpe di Siusi (Seiser Alm) to the Sciliar (Schlern): the green undulating pastures end dramatically at the foot of these towering peaks. It is a particularly spectacular scene in

an area which certainly doesn't lack in spectacle. The Alpe di Siusi (1700-2200 metres), the largest plateau in Europe, forms part of what is known as the Altipiano dello Sciliar, which also incorporates the villages of Castelrotto (Kastelruth) and Siusi (Seis), lower down at about 1000 metres.

There is something for walkers of all ages and expertise in this area. The gentle slopes of the Alpe di Siusi are perfect for families with young kids, and you won't need much more than average stamina to make it to the Rifugio Bolzano al Monte Pez (Schlernhaus) (2457 metres), just under Monte Pez, the Sciliar's summit. If you're after more challenging walks, the jagged peaks of the Catinaccio group and the Sassolungo (Langkofel) are nearby. These mountains are famous among climbers worldwide.

Information

Tourist Offices The area is popular in both summer and winter and its tourist offices are highly organised and efficient. All local offices will send out information, hotel lists and prices etc. There are three offices of the Associazione Turistica Sciliar: Castelrotto (☎ 0471-70 63 33), Piazza Kraus 1; Siusi (☎ 0471-70 71 34), Via Sciliar 8; and at Compatsch in the Alpe di Siusi (☎ 0471-72 79 04). Pick up the brochure which lists local services.

Emergency In a medical emergency phone ☎ 0471-70 65 55, or contact the Guardia Medica Turistica on ☎ 0471-70 54 44, which is based at Telfen, between Castelrotto and Siusi.

Activities

There's no shortage of organised activities or information about how to organise your own. In winter the area offers excellent skiing: downhill, cross-country and ski-mountaineering. It forms part of the Superski Dolomiti network. As in the Val Gardena, the area gets pretty crowded during peak periods. Ask at the tourist office about walking trails open during the snow season.

In summer, the trails of the Alpe di Siusi

are crowded with walkers, but as soon as you get to higher altitudes the crowds start to thin out. Using a good map and following the tourist office recommendations, you could spend days taking leisurely walks in the Alpe di Siusi, stopping for picnics or planning your walks to ensure that you reach a malgha for a lunch break. The tourist office organises low-priced guided walks of varying length and difficulty. There are also plenty of good trails for mountain bikers. Apart from the trek outlined in this section, there are plenty of challenging trails, including several vie ferrate. The Catinaccio group can also be approached from the Val di Fassa.

Activity Courses The *Scuola Alpina Dolomiten* (☎ 0471-70 53 43), Via Vogelweider 6, Castelrotto, has a summer programme which includes a seven-day guided trek that traverses the Dolomites from the Alpe di Siusi to the Tre Cime di Lavaredo. Also offered is a week of free-climbing (for experts), a rock climbing course for beginners, a mountain bike 'safari' from Bolzano to Sesto, and an expedition on horseback. In winter, a beginners' course in ski-mountaineering is on offer, as well as a 'Skisafari' for experts, both on and off runs, through the Alpe di Siusi, Val Gardena, Val Badia to Cortina, the Marmolada, the Val di Fassa and finishing at the Alpe di Siusi.

A Three-Day Trek in the Sciliar & Catinaccio This is a basic guide for a three-day trek through the Alpe di Siusi, up to the Sciliar and across to the Catinaccio d'Antermoia (Kessel-Kgl) and the famous Torri del Vajolet (Vajoletturme) and Cima Catinaccio (Rosengarten).

The walk starts and ends at Compatsch (Compaccio) (1820 metres), easily accessible by car or bus from the town of Siusi. It is an interesting walk, in particular for the contrasts between the gentle green slopes of the Alpe di Siusi and the Gothic pinnacles and rocky towers of the Catinaccio group, which give the impression of a fairy-tale castle.

As with all of the treks/walks detailed in this book, make sure you are correctly

dressed and equipped. The information here should be used as a guide only and you should use Tabacco 1:25,000 map No 05. (If this is not available, a different map, also produced by Tabacco, may be available at the Provincial Tourist Office in Bolzano.) The second day of the walk is demanding and may present some difficulties for walkers with no experience. However, if you are fit, healthy and cautious you should have no trouble. Note that you should book in advance to sleep at the small Rifugio Passo Santner.

Day One This first stage will take you from Compatsch to the Rifugio Bolzano (2450m) (three to four hours). From the big car park at Compatsch, take the trail marked No 10 and follow it until you reach the deviation to the left for Malga Saltner (Saltnerhutte) (trail No 5). You will be walking through the western part of the Alpe di Siusi, a vast and beautiful area of undulating green pastures, packed full of tourists in summer. Stop at the Saltnerhutte (1832 metres) for a drink before tackling the ascent to the Sciliar. Follow trail No 5, which becomes trail No 1, known as the Sentiero dei Turisti, which snakes its way up to the Sciliar high plain. The ascent is tiring, but by no means difficult, although you should watch out for falling rocks dislodged by chamois. There is a great view across the Alpe di Siusi to the Sasso Lungo, the Sella group and Le Odle (3025 metres at the highest peak). Once you arrive at Rifugio Bolzano (2450 metres), if you have the energy, climb the nearby Monte Pez (2563 metres). From its summit you have a 360° view: to the north you can see the Alps stretching into Austria; to the north-east you see Le Odle, Puez (2913 metres), and Sassongher (2665 metres); to the east is the Sella group (3152 metres), Sasso Lungo (3181 metres) and Sasso Piatto (2964 metres); south-east you can see the Catinaccio group, where you'll be heading on Day Two.

Day Two This tract will take you from Rifugio Bolzano to Rifugio Passo Santner (Santnerpasshutte) under the summit of the Rosengarten (a tough five to six hours). Head

Legend of the Red Roses

Over the centuries many popular legends were set in the Catinaccio group. One of the most famous is the *Legend of the Roses* which explains why the Rosengarten turns red at dusk, a common phenomenon in the Dolomites. It tells the story of the dwarf King Laurens, whose kingdom is a virtual garden of red roses, the *Rosengarten*. Peace-loving and wealthy, Laurens wants for nothing but the hand in marriage of Similda, a beautiful princess from a neighbouring kingdom. His request refused, Laurens uses magic to kidnap the princess and holds her prisoner for seven years – until her brother discovers her whereabouts and sets off with his men to rescue her. In the ensuing battles, Laurens is eventually defeated and taken prisoner. Only after many years does he manage to escape and return to his kingdom in the mountains where, on his arrival, he sees the beautiful rose garden. Realising that it was the roses which had led his enemies into his kingdom, Laurens casts a spell to turn the rose garden into stone: saying that the roses must not show themselves day or night. But Laurens forgot to include dusk in his spell, so every evening at sunset the enchanted garden becomes visible, casting a beautiful red glow over the Dolomites. 'And when the Rosengarten disappears and the roses again turn to stone, clear and cold, men are gripped by an inexplicable sadness as they return to their smoky huts.' If you're lucky, perhaps you will meet some elves, fairies or witches during the walk – at the very least you will have no trouble imagining them! ∎

back along trail No 1 for a short distance, then turn right onto trail No 3-4 which crosses the Sciliar high plain in the direction of the Catinaccio group, which completely dominates the landscape. You will pass the Cima di Terrarossa and the spectacular, jagged peaks of the Denti di Terrarossa. Keep to trail No 3-4 (don't take No 3 which heads to the right at a certain point) to reach the Rifugio Alpe di Tires (2440 metres), then go south on trail No 3a-554, ascend to the Passo Alpe di Tires and continue for the Passo Molignon 2596 (metres). From here you start the difficult and very steep descent on a *ghiaione* (river of gravel) into the lunar landscape of a valley. Before reaching the valley floor the trail forks. Keep to the left and stay on trail No 554, which will take you up to Rifugio Passo Principe (2599 metres), under the Catinaccio d'Antermoia (3200 metres). You can take a break at this tiny refuge. From here, descend into the valley along the comfortable trail No 584. You'll arrive at the rifugi Vajolet and Preuss (2243 metres), from where you take trail No 542s up to the Rifugio Re Alberto (2621 metres). This tract is better described as a climb and inexperienced mountaineers will find it quite challenging. There are plans to install an iron

cord for safety reasons, which would significantly reduce the excitement of the ascent.

Once at the top you will be in a wide valley with the Torri del Vajolet, famous amongst climbers, to your right and the peak of the Rosengarten to your left. Follow trail No 542s up to Rifugio Passo Santner, perched on a precipice under the Rosengarten, with an almost sheer drop down into the Val di Tires. It is one of the most spectacularly located rifugi in the Alps. The rifugio is tiny, with only two rooms, each with four beds. Climbers flock here in summer to tackle the Torri del Vajolet and the Rosengarten. The trail 542s becomes a vie ferrata where it descends from the rifugio. If you intend to tackle either the ferrata or a climb, make sure you are properly equipped.

Day Three The section from Rifugio Passo Santner back to Compatsch will take six to seven hours. Return down to Rifugio Vajolet along trail No 542s and return to Passo Principe. Instead of continuing for Passo Molignon, remain on trail No 584 to reach Passo d'Antermoia (2770 metres) and then descend to Lago d'Antermoia (2490 metres) and shortly afterwards the refuge of the same name. Here the trail becomes No

580 which heads east to the Passo Dona (2516 metres) and then descends towards the Alpe di Siusi. After a relatively short distance the No 580 veers to the right (east), but you will instead continue straight ahead and at the next fork, take trail No 555, which will take you in a westerly direction along the northern slopes of the Molignon group. At the base of the Molignon, the trail joins a dirt road (trail No 532) near the group of herder's shelters known as Malga Dòcoldaura (2046 metres). Follow No 532 to the Casa del TCI Sciliar, then go straight head along trail No 7, which will take you all the way down to Compatsch. (At Rifugio Molignon, the trail becomes a small road and some distance ahead it becomes trail No 7-12.)

Places to Stay

There are plenty of hotels and pensioni, but bookings are recommended during the summer and winter high seasons. There's a choice between places in the villages, or up on the Alpe di Siusi. If you choose to stay in the Alpe di Siusi, there is a regular bus service. In summer normal traffic is banned from the plateau. See Getting Around in this section.

Try *Albergo Zallinger* (☎ 72 79 47) at Saltria, at the foot of the Sassopiatto (Plattkofel). Half board per person per day costs up to L60,000. If you're travelling with kids, ask the tourist office for information on hotels which are equipped for, or offer special deals for, children. *Hotel Alpenflora* (☎ 70 63 26), just outside Castelrotto at Via Oswald von Wolkenstein 32, has children's menus, a playroom and a playground. Half board ranges from about L70,000 up to L110,000. The *Naturhotel Dolomitenhof* (☎ 70 61 28), Via Hauenstein 3, Siusi, offers a menu of organic and health foods. Half board costs from about L70,000 to L100,000 per person.

Getting There & Away

The Alipiano dello Sciliar is accessible by SAD bus from Bolzano, the Val Gardena and Bressanone. By car, you can exit the Brennero autostrada (A22) at Bolzano Nord or Chiusa.

Getting Around

From May to October the roads of the Alpe di Siusi are closed to normal traffic. Tourists with a booking at a hotel in the zone, who are staying for five days or more, can obtain a special permit from the tourist office at Compatsch to drive from 6 pm to 9 am. It is best to organise your pass before arriving in the area; ask your hotel owner for assistance. A regular bus service operates from Castelrotto and Siusi to Compatsch and from there on to the Alpe di Siusi. Tourists staying in hotels in the area will be given a special *Favorit* card which entitles them to free bus travel.

VAL BADIA (GADERTAL)

Along with the Val Gardena, this is one of the last strongholds of the ancient Ladin culture and language. Most local kids (as well as adults) are aware of the Ladin legends, richly peopled by giants, kings, witches, fairies and dragons. Many are centred on the nearby Fanes high plain, which forms part of the magnificent Parco Naturale Fanes-Senes-Braies. This is one of the most evocative places in the Dolomites and can be reached easily from the Alta Val Badia, either on foot or by funivia from Passo Falzarego. The towns in the valley include Colfosco (Colfosch), La Villa (La Ila), San Cassiano (San Ciascian) and Corvara.

Corvara

This ski resort is an excellent base for walkers wanting to tackle the peaks enclosing the Alta Badia. Corvara was the central town of the Ladin tribes and today is a pleasant little town, with a well-organised tourist office and plenty of accommodation.

The AAST tourist office (☎ 0471-83 61 76) is in the town's main street and open Monday to Saturday from 8 am to midday and 3 to 7 pm and Sunday from 10 am to midday. It has extensive information on ski facilities, walking trails, accommodation and transport.

For medical assistance, go to the *Croce Bianca* (☎ 83 64 44), set back from Corvara's main street just near the tourist office. In an

The Ladin Tradition

The Ladin language and culture traces its ancestry to around 15 BC, when the people of the Central Alps were forcibly united into the Roman province of Rhaetia. The Romans, of course, introduced Latin to the province, but the original inhabitants of the area, with their diverse linguistic and cultural backgrounds, modified the language to the extent that, by around 450 AD, it had evolved into an independent Romance language, known as raeto-romanic. At one point the entire Tirol was Ladin, but today the language and culture are maintained in the Val Gardena and the Val Badia, where about 90 per cent of the locals declared in the 1981 census that they belonged to the Ladin language group. Along with German and Italian, Ladin is taught in schools and the survival of the Ladin cultural and linguistic identity is protected by law.

The Ladin culture is rich in vibrant poetry and legends, set amid the jagged peaks of the fabulous Dolomites and peopled by fairies, gnomes, elves, giants, princesses and heroes. Passed on by word-of-mouth for centuries and often heavily influenced by Germanic myths, many of these legends were in danger of being lost. In the first decade of this century, journalist Carlo Felice Wolff, who had lived most of his life at Bolzano, undertook a major project: he spent 10 years gathering and researching the local legends, listening as the old folk, farmers and shepherds recounted the legends and fairytales. The originality of the legends he eventually published is that, instead of simply writing down what he was told, Wolff reconstructed the tales from the many different versions and recollections he gathered. ■

---

emergency, the nearest public hospital is in Brunico (☎ 0474-8 11 11).

Corvara's telephone code is 0471.

Activities Corvara is on the Sella Ronda ski trail and is part of the Superski Dolomiti network. From the town, you can reach the Passo Falzarego by SAD bus and then take the cable car up into the Fanes-Sennes-Braies park. See the section on Trekking in the Dolomites. Otherwise, you can pick up trail No 12 from near La Villa, or trail No 11, which joins Alta Via No 1, at the Capanna Alpina, a few km off the main road between Passo Valparola and San Cassiano. Either trail will take you up to the Alpe di Fanes and the two rifugi Lavarella and Fanes.

A combination of cabinovia and chair lift will take you from Corvara up into the Sella group at Vallon (2550 metres). On the way up, there is a spectacular view across to the Marmolada glacier. From Vallon you can traverse the Sella or follow the trail which winds around the valley at the top of the chair lift (about one hour). A good area for family walks is around Prelongiá (Prelungé) (2138 metres). Catch the funivia from La Villa and then take trail No 4 and trail No 23 to reach Prelongiá. Trail No 23 will take you down to Corvara. Horse riding, mountain biking and hang-gliding are also popular activities in the valley. The tourist office can provide information on trails, courses etc.

Places to Stay & Eat The tourist office will assist if necessary, but otherwise try the *Garni Laura* (☎ 83 63 40), back from the main road near the tourist office, which has B&B for up to L35,000 per person. *Ciasa Blancia* (☎ 83 62 96) offers half board for up to L78,000 per person per day. It is located on the hill overlooking Corvara at Via Pescosta 34. *La Tambra* (☎ 83 62 81), is a pleasant hotel which is 'children-friendly'. It offers full board for up to L135,000 per person per day. Full meals at *Ristorante/Pizzeria La Tambra* cost under L30,000.

Getting There & Away SAD buses connect Corvara with Bolzano, Merano, Brunico, the Val Gardena, the Passo Sella and Passo Pordoi, Canazei and the Passo Falzarego (note that buses do not cross the high passes in winter). Full timetables are available at the tourist office.

CORTINA D'AMPEZZO

Across the Fanes-Conturines mountains from the Val Badia is the jewel of the Dolomites, Cortina d'Ampezzo. Italy's most famous, fashionable and expensive ski resort, Cortina is actually situated in the region of Veneto, but has been placed here because of its central location in the Dolomites. It is one of the best equipped and certainly the most picturesque resorts in the Dolomites. If you are on a tight budget, the prices for accommodation and food will be prohibitive, even in the low season. However, camping grounds and Alpine rifugi (open only during summer) provide more reasonably priced alternatives.

Situated in the Ampezzo bowl, Cortina is surrounded by some of the most stunning mountains in the Dolomites, including Monte Cristallo, the Marmarole group, Monte Sorapiss and the Tofanes. To the south are Monte Pelmo and Monte Civetta. Facilities for both downhill and cross-country skiing are first class and the small town's population swells dramatically during the ski season, as the rich and famous pour in. The town is also busy during the summer months, since the area offers great possibilities for trekking and climbing, with well-marked trails and numerous rifugi.

Information

The main APT office (☎ 0436-32 31) is at Piazzetta San Francesco 8, in the town centre. It has information on accommodation, ski facilities and hiking trails. It can also provide a full listing of apartments and rooms for rent. There is a small information office at Piazza Roma 1.

Cortina's Alpine Guides Group (☎ 0436-47 40), based at Piazzetta San Francesco 5, is open from 8 am to midday and 4 to 8 pm. Apart from the usual rock climbing courses, guided treks and guided treks on vie ferrate, the guides group also offers special rock climbing courses for children from eight years of age (cost L265,000 in 1994), as well as guided one-day hikes for children.

Cortina's telephone code is 0436.

Activities

Apart from the three-day trek through Fanes-Sennes-Braies detailed in the Trekking in the Dolomites section, the Dolomites around Cortina offer a network of spectacular trails. A series of three cable cars (L52,000 return) will take you from Cortina up to the Tofana di Mezzo (3243 metres), from where all the trails are difficult and incorporate vie ferrate, for which you will need to be properly equipped. You can link up with the Alta Via No 1 either at the Passo Falzarego, or at the evocative Passo Giau, with the spiky Croda da Lago to the east and the Cinque Torri to the north-west. To get to the Passo Giau, you will need to catch a bus from Cortina to Pocol and then hitch a ride.

Another interesting possibility is to take the local bus from Cortina east to Passo Tre Croci (1805 metres) and take trail No 215 (which is a section of Alta Via No 3) up to the Rifugio A Vandelli (1928 metres) in the heart of the Sorapiss group. From here the Alta Via No 3 continues up to 2316 metres and then to the left, as trail No 242. This section incorporates a section of vie ferrate, as does trail No 215, which heads off to the right.

Not far from Cortina, and accessible by Dolomiti Bus in summer, are the Tre Cime di Lavaredo, one of the most famous climbing locations in the world and also a panoramic place to walk. The fact that you can arrive by bus literally at the foot of the Tre Cime means the area is crawling with tourists in the high season.

A Family Walk from Rifugio Ra Stua to Forcella Lerosa

This is a good walk for families because the climb is not too steep, is fairly short – around four hours up and back, including a picnic stop – and there are lots of animals and birds along the way. The area is easily accessible from either the Val Pusteria or Cortina, by car or public transport – from Cortina or Dobbiaco take the SS51.

Arriving from Cortina, take the small road to the left at the first switchback – if you are approaching from Dobbiaco it is the first switchback after Passo Cimabanche. During summer, from mid-June to mid-September, the road up to Ra Stua is closed to normal traffic. You can walk the two to three km from the car park (1420 metres) to Ra Stua (1670 metres), or use the reasonably priced minibus service which operates in summer from Albergo Fiàmes, a few km north of Cortina, to the Rifugio Ra Stua.

Use the Tabacco 1:25,000 map for Cortina d'Ampezzo e Dolomiti Ampezzane.

If you decide to walk, take the track which heads uphill from the eastern side of the switchback and follows the slope of the Croda de R'Ancona. The track doesn't have a number but is marked on the map.

Rifugio Ra Stua is at the beginning of the Val Salata, a lovely Alpine environment and perfect for a family walk. Before heading off for a walk in the valley, make sure you let the people running the rifugio know where you are going and check on the departure time of the last minibus.

More serious trekkers can walk to the end of the Val Salata, ascend to the Lago di Sennes (2116 metres) and pick up the walk through the Parco Naturale Fanes-Sennes-Braies which is detailed earlier in this chapter. However, for our walk, head along the Val Salata for about 150 metres and take the dirt road to your right, which ascends for about 250 metres, then turn right to take track No 8. Another 250 metres ahead the track forks – follow the track to the right: it is longer, but much easier and more scenic. There is a series of switchbacks winding uphill past ancient fir trees and at certain points there are panoramic views across the Fanes high plain. Always keep to the left. You will reach a small valley where, if you approach quietly, you might see the resident marmots, chamois and squirrels. Follow trail No 8 around the valley. In front of you now is the majestic Croda Rossa (3146 metres), one of the most beautiful peaks in the Dolomites. The trail will bring you to a wide valley, near the pass, Forcella Lerosa (2020 metres). There's a little wooden house and water fountain.

One option is to turn right, still following No 8, to reach the pass. Take the dirt road to the right (still No 8). After a picturesque walk of roughly four km you will reach the SS51,

closer to Dobbiaco and just before Passo Cimabanche.

Alternatively you can turn left at the wooden house and follow the trail back down to Rastua. This route is much shorter but less attractive than the ascent – so, there is always the option to return the way you came.

Once back at the Rifugio Ra Stua, make sure you stop for the fantastic hot chocolate topped with fresh cream that is served there.

Places to Stay

The *International Camping Olympia* (☎ 50 57) is a few km north of Cortina at Fiames. Open all year, it charges L8000 per person and from L9000 to L20,000 for a site, depending on the season. There are no budget hotels in Cortina and the lowest you can expect to pay is around L80,000 a double in the low season and L100,000 in the high season. *La Ginestrina* (☎ 86 02 55), Via Roma 55, charges up to L64,000 for B&B per person. *Albergo Cavallino* (☎ 26 14), Corso Italia 142, is in the heart of the town and charges up to L85,000 per person, with breakfast. *Albergo Villa Alpina Dolomiti* (☎ 21 18) is in Via Roma near La Ginestrina. Charges for full board range from L75,000 to L110,000 per day. *Fanes* (☎ 34 27), Via Roma 136, charges from L92,000 to L170,000 for full board.

Places to Eat

There are numerous good eating places in and around Cortina, though many are very expensive. The Standa supermarket in Via Franchetti is a good place to shop if you have access to a kitchen. For a good pizza, head for *Il Ponte*, Via Franchetti 8. The *Ristorante Croda Caffè*, Corso Italia 186, has reasonably priced meals. *Il Meloncino* overlooks Cortina on the road to Pocol and is one of the town's best known eating places. A full meal will cost up to around L80,000.

Getting There & Away

Cortina's bus station is in Via Marconi. Pick up a timetable at either the bus station or the tourist office. SAD buses connect Cortina with Bolzano, Brunico and Dobbiaco. Dolomiti Bus travels to Belluno, Pocol and Passo Falzarego. There are also bus services to Venice and Padua (ATVO), Bologna and Milan (Zani), and Florence and Rome (a combination of Lazzi and SITA). Local services connect the town with the camping ground at Fiames, and Pocol (from where you can hitch to Passo Giau).

As mentioned in the walk to Ra Stua, there is a minibus service from Fiames to the Malga Ra Stua daily from 8 am to 6 pm from mid-July to mid-September. A special bus service for mountain bikers and their bikes also operates from Fiames to various locations. Phone ☎ 86 70 88 for information.

VAL PUSTERIA (PUSTERTAL) & DOLOMITI DI SESTO

On the northern edge of the Dolomites, this valley is bordered by the magnificent Parco Naturale Fanes-Senes-Braies and, farther north, by the Parco Naturale delle Dolomiti di Sesto, which includes some of the area's most famous peaks – among them the Tre Cime di Lavaredo. The valley is easily reached from the Val Badia (Gadertal) and from Cortina d'Ampezzo along the spectacular Valle di Landro (Höhlensteintal). Its main town is Brunico (Bruneck), a pleasant market town with excellent transport connections which makes a good base for excursions into Fanes-Sennes-Braies. More picturesque options are San Candido (Innichen) and Sesto (Sexten) at the base of the Dolomiti di Sesto.

Information

The tourist office in Brunico (☎ 0474-55 57 22) is at the bus station in Via Europa. In San Candido, the tourist office (☎ 0474-91 31 49) is in Piazza del Magistrato, and in Sesto the office (☎ 0474-91 03 10) is in the main street, Via Dolomiti. All have plenty of information about ski facilities and walking possibilities and will send out brochures on accommodation etc.

There is an excellent public hospital at Brunico (☎ 8 11 11).

The telephone code for the valley is 0474.

Activities

Easy to get to from the Val Pusteria is the beautiful Lago di Braies, a perfect spot for a picnic, followed by a leisurely walk on the trail which circles the lake. More serious walkers might like to tackle part of the Alta Via No 1, which starts here. The Fanes-Sennes-Braies park is more easily approached from the Val Badia or from Passo Falzarego. At the other end of the valley, towards Austria, are the Dolomiti di Sesto, where there are some spectacular trails. Good areas for family walks are the Valle Campo di Dentro (Innerfeldtal), near San Candido, and the Val Fiscalina (Fischleintal), near Sesto. Both valleys are very popular spots for cross-country skiing in winter.

From Val Fiscalina, it is a long, but easy walk along trail No 102 to Rifugio Locatelli (Drei Zinnen-Htt.), from where there is a great view of the Tre Cime di Lavaredo (Drei Zinnen). You can continue to the Tre Cime along trail No 101 and then down to Rifugio Auronzo (2320 metres), from where you can catch a Dolomiti Bus down to the Valle di Landro. This is one of the highest rifugi in the Dolomites which can be reached by road.

All of the trails around the Tre Cime are easy enough for first-time walkers and for families. In fact, in July and August the trails here are more like autostradas; they are literally packed with tourists, since it is possible to get there by car or bus.

If you do want to walk here, don't be fooled by the crowded trails into thinking that you don't need suitable clothing, water etc. Remember you are walking at high altitude and the weather conditions can change dramatically at any time, so always carry a warm jacket and water and wear proper walking shoes.

Another option for serious walkers is to take trail No 103 from the Val Fiscalina up to Rifugio Comici (Zsigmondy-Htt) and then trail No 101 to Rifugio Pian di Cengia (Büllele-Joch-Htt) and then to Rifugio Locatelli.

Places to Stay

In Brunico, the *Krone-Corona* (☎ 8 52 67), Via

ALTO ADIGE

Out of Nowhere

While walking on a well-marked trail around the famous Tre Cime di Lavaredo near Cortina in early September we were side-tracked by the beautiful scenery and took a long break for a picnic and to let our 18-month-old baby play for a while – with the result that we arrived at the highest point of the walk quite late in the day. A very cold fog had set in and we were prepared with hats, gloves and pile jackets, unlike the fellow we encountered as we started our descent to the Rifugio Auronzo on the other side of the Tre Cime. He came running out of the mist, dressed in a T-shirt, a pair of shorts and runners, with no socks. In a panic he asked us if he and his daughter could walk down the mountain with us because, he said, he couldn't see the trail. Still panicking, he ran off into the ever-heavier fog, with his daughter trailing behind. We suppose he made it to Rifugio Auronzo! ■

Ragen di Sopra 8, is in the old town centre. It charges L45,000 per person for B&B and L61,000 per person for half board. In San Candido, *Residence Obermüllerhof-Fauster* (☎ 91 34 12), Via Castello 8, is in a picturesque position at the back of the town. It has rooms and apartments at reasonable prices, up to L30,000 per person per day. *Villa Waldheim* (☎ 91 31 87), Via Pascolo 1, offers half board for up to L80,000 per person per day.

Getting There & Away

By SAD bus you can reach Brunico and San Candido from Bolzano and Merano, the Val Badia and San Vigilio di Marebbe, the Val Gardena (on the Innsbruck bus) and Cortina. Catch a bus from Brunico or San Candido to Dobbiaco, from where you can catch a bus to the Lago di Braies. To get to the Rifugio Auronzo at the Tre Cime di Lavaredo, catch the Cortina bus from San Candido or Dobbiaco then, from Cortina, catch the bus for Misurina and the Tre Cime.

By train, you can reach the Val Pusteria from Bolzano, via Fortezza (where a change is necessary). By road, the valley is easily accessible from the Val Badia, from Cortina via the Valle di Landro, and from the A22.

ALTO ADIGE

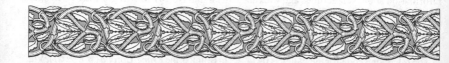

Veneto

Most travellers to the Veneto are so dazzled by Venice that they neglect to explore the rest of the region. Venice certainly deserves lots of time, but be sure to set aside extra days for Giotto's extraordinary frescoes at Padua, and to take in an opera at Verona's magnificent Roman Arena. Vicenza, was home town of the architect Palladio, and is also well worth a stopover, perhaps on your way to the northern reaches of the Veneto for a visit to Cortina,

one of the world's most famous ski resorts, and some trekking in the eastern Dolomites.

The region's cuisine is founded on rice and corn. Polenta is served with hearty game stews, is fried or turns up with other maincourse dishes across the region. Risotto is cooked with almost everything the countryside and lagoon have to offer, from baby peas to shellfish and game, although a local favourite is risotto flavoured with the ink of

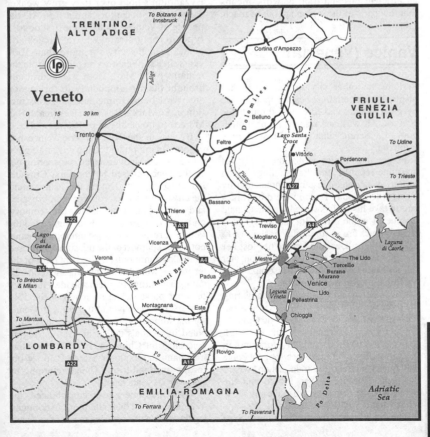

seppia (cuttlefish). One of the Veneto's best-known contributions to the Italian table is *tiramisù*, a rich dessert of mascarpone cheese, Marsala, sponge and chocolate. The wine list provides some of Italy's most popular brands, including the Soave, a fine white that is well known in the USA, the UK and Australia. The light, sparkling *prosecco* and the *bardolino* red wines are also known widely. Of course, the Bellini, a cocktail of prosecco and fresh peach juice, has come a long way since Giuseppe Cipriani first mixed one at Harry's Bar in Venice in the 1950s.

Getting around is easy. The A4, which runs from Turin to Venice, bisects the region, and an efficient bus and train network means that few parts of the region are out of reach.

Venice (Venezia)

Perhaps no other city in the world has inspired the superlatives heaped upon Venice by great writers and travellers through the centuries. It was, and remains, a phenomenon, 'La Serenissima', the Most Serene Republic.

Forget that Venice is no longer a great maritime republic, that its buildings are in serious decay and constantly threatened by rising tides. Today Byron would be reluctant to take his daily swim along the Canale Grande: it is too dirty. But the thoughts of Henry James are as true today as they were a century ago: 'Dear old Venice has lost her complexion, her figure, her reputation, her self-respect; and yet, with it all, has so puzzlingly not lost a shred of her distinction.'

The secret to really seeing and discovering the romance and beauty of Venice is to *walk*. Parts of Cannaregio, Dorsoduro and Castello are empty of tourists even in the high season. You could become lost for hours in the narrow, winding streets between the Ponte dell'Accademia and the train station, where the signs pointing to San Marco and the Ponte di Rialto never seem to make any sense – but what a way to pass the time!

The city's busiest months are June to September, during the Carnevale in February and at Easter, but it is always a good idea to make a hotel booking.

HISTORY

The barbarian invasions of the 5th and 6th centuries saw the people from the Roman towns of the Veneto and along the Adriatic coast flee to the marshy islands of the Venetian lagoon.

In the 6th century, the islands began to form a type of federation, with each community electing representatives to a central authority, though its leaders were subject to the Byzantine rulers in Ravenna. Byzantium's hold over Italy grew weaker early in the 8th century and in 726 AD the people of Venice elected their first doge, a type of magistrate whose successors would lead the city for more than 1000 years. In 828, Venetian merchants stole the remains of St Mark from Alexandria and brought them triumphantly to the lagoon city. Work began immediately on construction of St Mark's Basilica (Basilica di San Marco) to house the apostles remains.

By late in the 10th century, Venice had become an important trading city and a great power in the Mediterranean, prospering out of the chaos caused by the First Crusade, launched in 1095. During the 12th century the city continued to profit from the crusades and at the beginning of the 13th century, under Doge Enrico Dandolo, Venice led the Fourth Crusade to Constantinople. Venice not only kept most of the treasures plundered from Constantinople, it also kept most of the territories won during the crusade, consolidating a maritime might that made it the envy of other powers. During much of the 13th century, the Venetians struggled with Genoa for maritime supremacy, a tussle that culminated in Genoa's defeat in 1380 during an epic siege at Chioggia. In 1271, Venetian merchant and explorer Marco Polo set out for his overland trip to China, returning by sea over 20 years later.

Their maritime power consolidated, the Venetians turned their attentions to dominating the mainland, capturing most of the Veneto

Acque Alte

Venice can be flooded by high tides during winter. Known as *acque alte*, these occur mainly during the period November to April and flood low-lying areas of the city such as Piazza San Marco. The floods are announced by sirens and in some areas you can see the water rising up over the canal border: although most of the water actually bubbles up through drains. The best thing to do is buy a pair of gumboots, known in Italy as *stivali*, and continue sightseeing. Raised walkways are set up in Piazza San Marco and other major tourist areas of the city, but the floods usually last only a few hours.

Venice's flooding problems are compounded by the fact that the city is actually sinking: it sank by 26 cm in the first 80 years of this century. Another major concern is that the waters of the canals are incredibly polluted. Until 20 years ago, the Adriatic Sea's natural tidal currents flushed the lagoons and kept the canals relatively clean. But the dredging of a 14-metre-deep canal in the 1960s to allow tankers access to the giant refinery at Marghera changed the currents. Work is now underway to clean the sludge from the city canals.

A project to install three massive floodgates at the main entrances to the lagoon has been approved by the Italian Government, but work has been delayed by the country's seemingly endless political turmoil. The gates would be designed to protect the city from disaster-level floods (around 1.9 metres: the average incidence of aque alte is around 50 cm). As late as October 1994, the Association of Private Committees for the Safeguarding of Venice reminded the Italian Government of its unfulfilled commitment to this project. See the Saving Venice section for more information. ■

and portions of what is now Lombardy and Emilia-Romagna. But the increasing power of the Turks forced the Venetians to deploy forces to protect their interests elsewhere. When Constantinople fell to the Turks in 1453 and Morea in 1499, the Turks won control of access to the Adriatic Sea. The Portuguese Vasco da Gama's discovery of the sea route around the Cape of Good Hope in 1498 meant traders no longer needed to cart goods across land to the Venetian ports, thereby diminishing their importance.

But Venice remained a formidable power. At home, the doges, the Signory and the much-feared judicial Council of Ten, which was responsible for internal security, ruled with an iron fist. The Signory, also known as the Senate, was the main governing council, from which the members of all other governing committees were appointed. The doge was the only politician who could sit on all committees. Following a decree of 1297, only citizens whose ancestors had served on the Great Council (Maggior Consiglio) between 1172 and 1297 could serve on any of these committees, an act which virtually ensured that Venice's aristocracy had a firm hold on power. (For further information on the Great Council see the Palazzo Ducale section in this chapter.)

All Venetians were encouraged to spy for the security of the state, on other Venetians and in every city, port and country where the Venetian Republic had an interest. Acts considered to be against the state were punished swiftly and brutally: no public trial and execution, a body would just turn up on the street as an example to other potentially wayward citizens.

Venice was also a remarkably cosmopolitan city. Its strong links with the East and its position as one of the most important trading ports in the Mediterranean, meant the city was populated by people of all nationalities, races and creeds. While Venice created one of the original Jewish ghettos and limited the commercial and social activities of its Jewish community, it did nothing to stifle the Jewish religion. Similarly, the Armenians were permitted religious freedom for centuries and given protection during the Inquisition.

The incredible wealth of the city was obvious in the luxury goods which were traded and the fine goods produced there. The city had a monopoly in Europe on

VENETO

the making of the fine crystal glass now known as Murano glass; its merchants had also brought back from the East the art of making mosaics; and Venetian artisans made fine silks and lace. But, as the republic's fortunes declined, so its decadence increased.

Further successes by the Turks in the 16th century and a dispute with Rome in 1606 over papal jurisdiction damaged the republic's standing. In 1669, after a 25-year battle, Venice lost Crete, to the Turks, its last stronghold in the Mediterranean. The republic declined during the 18th century, and in 1797 its Great Council abolished the constitution and acceded to Napoleon, who in turn handed Venice to the Austrians during the signing of the Campo Formio Treaty that year. Napoleon returned in 1805, incorporating the city into his Kingdom of Italy, but it reverted to Austria after his fall. The movement for Italian unification spread quickly through the Veneto, and after several rebellions, the city was united with the Kingdom of Italy in 1866. The city was bombed during WW I but suffered only minor damage during WW II, when most attacks were aimed at the neighbouring industrial regions of Mestre and Marghera.

The city's prestige as a tourist destination grew during the 19th century, while its ports were surpassed in importance by those of Trieste. Today it is one of Italy's main tourist destinations. There is a permanent population of only about 75,000 people living in the historical city, less than half that of the 1950s, but the total population of the Comune di Venezia (municipality), including those living on the mainland in Mestre, is around 330,000. The city attracts more than 23 million tourists a year, most on day trips.

ORIENTATION

Venice is built on 117 small islands, has some 150 canals and more than 400 bridges. Only three bridges cross the Canale Grande (Grand Canal): the Rialto, the Accademia and the Scalzi. The city is divided into six sections (*sestieri*): Cannaregio, Castello, San Marco, Dorsoduro, San Polo and Santa Croce. A street is called a *calle* (sometimes shortened to *ca'*), *ruga* or *salizzada*; little side streets can be called *caletta* or *ramo*; a street beside a canal is called a *fondamenta*; a canal is a *rio*; and a street which follows the course of a filled-in rio is a *rio terrà*. A quay is a *riva* and where a street passes under a building (something like an extended archway) it is called a *sottoportego*. The only square in Venice called a piazza is San Marco – all the others are called a *campo*. On maps you will find the following abbreviations: Cpo for Campo, Sal for Salizzada, cl or C for Calle and Fond for Fondamenta.

Saving Venice

Floods, neglect, pollution and many other factors have contributed to the degeneration of Venice's monuments and artworks. But, since 1969, a group of private international organisations, in liaison with UNESCO, has been working to repair the damage. Known as the Joint UNESCO-Private Committees Programme for the Safeguarding of Venice, this unique international effort has raised millions of dollars for restoration work in the city: from 1969 to 1992 nearly 80 monuments and more than 800 works of art were restored. During the four years to 1995 alone, the programme was funding more than 70 restoration projects, including work on seven of Venice's churches. Major restoration projects which have been completed include the Chiesa di Madonna dell'Orto, the façade of the Chiesa di San Zulian, and the polyptych by Giovanni Bellini in the Basilica di SS Giovanni e Paolo. The programme is administered by UNESCO, and the funding is provided by the 24 private committees which represent 12 countries. Apart from restoration works, the programme also funds specialist courses for trainee restorers in Venice. ■

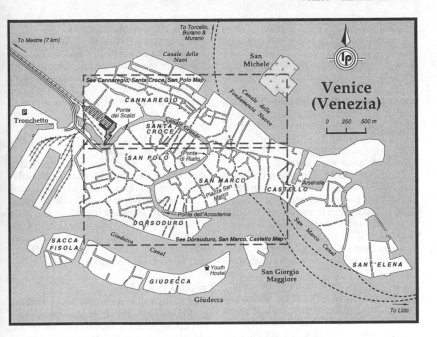

Venice (Venezia)

There are no cars on the islands, although ferries transport cars to the Lido, and all public transport is via the canals, on a *vaporetto* (small passenger boat/ferry). To cross the Canale Grande between the bridges, use a *traghetto* (ferry), a cheap way to get a short gondola ride, although there are only five operating. Signs will direct you to the traghetto points. The other mode of transportation is *a piedi* (on foot). To walk from the train station to Piazza San Marco along the main thoroughfare, initially called the Lista di Spagna (its name changes several times along the way), will take a good half-hour – follow the signs to San Marco.

From San Marco, the routes to other main areas, such as the Rialto, Accademia and the train station, are well signposted but can be confusing, particularly in the Dorsoduro and San Polo areas. The free map provided by the tourist office provides only a vague guide to the complicated network of streets. There are several good maps on sale in bookshops and

at newspaper stands, including the yellow FMB map, simply entitled *Venezia* (L8000), which lists all street names with map references.

Street Numbering System
If all that isn't confusing enough, Venice also has its own style of street numbering. Instead of a system based on individual streets, there is instead a long series of numbers for each sestiere. For instance a hotel might give its address as San Marco 4687, which doesn't help you much. This is really the postal address, so ask the hotel owner for the actual name of the street. As much as possible, we give actual street names, plus the sestiere numbers throughout the book.

INFORMATION
Tourist Offices
Venice's main APT office (☎ 041-529 87 30) is in the Palazzetto Selva in the ex Giardini Reali. From Piazza San Marco walk to the

waterfront and turn right. The office is about 100 metres ahead. The young staff will assist with information on hotels, transport and things to see and do in the city. The office opens Monday to Saturday from 9.30 am to 12.30 pm and 2 to 5 pm. In winter it closes one hour earlier in the afternoon. There is a smaller office at the train station (☎ 041-71 90 78), which opens Monday to Friday from 9 am to midday and 3 to 6 pm, and Saturday to 12.30 pm; and on the Lido (☎ 041-526 57 21) at Viale Santa Maria Elisabetta.

The useful booklet *Un Ospite di Venezia* (A Guest in Venice), published by a group of Venice hotel owners, is sometimes available at the tourist offices. If not, you can find it in most of the larger hotels. See the following Places to Stay section for details about the Venetian Hoteliers' Association office next to the APT at the train station, which will book you a room.

Take your passport and a colour photograph to the tourist office at the station and pick up the Rolling Venice card. It offers significant discounts on food, accommodation, entertainment, museums and galleries for a small charge.

Money

Most of the main banks have branches in the area around the Ponte di Rialto and San Marco. There is an exchange booth on Salizzada San Moisé, near San Marco, open Monday to Saturday from 9 am to 7 pm, and Sunday to 1 pm. The Thomas Cook exchange office, in Piazza San Marco, opens Monday to Saturday from 9 am to 7 pm, and Sunday to 5 pm. There is a bank with endless queues at the train station, and an Exact Change booth in the platform area offering good rates, which opens daily from 8 am to 10 pm. The American Express office (☎ 041-520 08 44) is at Salizzada San Moisé (exit from the western end of Piazza San Marco on to Calle Seconda dell'Ascensione). For American Express card holders there's also an express cash machine. The office is open Monday to Friday from 9 am to 5.30 pm, and Saturday to 12.30 pm.

Post & Telecommunications

The main post office is at Salizzada del Fontego dei Tedeschi, just near the Ponte di Rialto on the main thoroughfare between San Marco and the train station. It opens Monday to Saturday from 8.15 am to 7 pm. Stamps are available at windows No 11 and 12 in the central courtyard. There is a branch post office at the western end of San Marco. The address for poste restante mail is 30100 Venezia.

There is a staffed Telecom office next to the post office, open Monday to Saturday from 8 am to 7.45 pm. There is also a bank of telephones down a small lane opposite. The majority of public telephones take only phonecards, so it is a good idea to keep a few cards on hand. There is another Telecom office on the Strada Nova at the corner of Corte dei Pali. The telephone code for Venice is 041.

Foreign Consulates

The British Consulate (☎ 522 23 92) is in Palazzo Querini near the Accademia, Dorsoduro 1051. The French Consulate (☎ 522 19 78) is on the Fondamenta Zattere at Dorsoduro 1397. The closest US, Australian and Canadian consulates are in Milan, and New Zealanders should contact their embassy in Rome.

Travel Agencies

For budget student travel, contact CTS (☎ 520 56 60), Fondamenta Tagliapietra, near Campo Santa Margherita. Transalpino is near the train station, and CIT (☎ 504 00 33) is in Mestre at Via Mestrina 65.

Bookshops

A good selection of English-language guides and books on Venice is available at Studium, on the corner of Calle de la Canonica, on the way from San Marco to Castello. Il Libraio a San Barnaba, in Dorsoduro between Campo San Barnaba and Campo Santa Margherita has a good range of English-language books from the classics to contemporary literature and best sellers, as does San Giorgio, Calle Larga XXII Marzo 2087, west of San Marco.

Youth Information

There is an Informa Giovani office (☎ 041-534 62 68) at Mestre, Viale Garibaldi 155, which can provide a range of information, from assistance for the disabled to courses offered in the city.

Gay & Lesbian Information

Arci Gay Venezia (☎ 98 36 53) is in Mestre, Via Olivi 2. Call them for meeting-places, entertainment details or other information.

Lost Property

For property lost on trains call ☎ 78 52 38 or ☎ 71 61 22; for property left on vaporetti call ☎ 78 03 10. Otherwise call the municipal government (comune) on ☎ 520 88 44.

Medical Services

The Ospedale Civili Riuniti di Venezia (☎ 520 56 22) is at Campo SS Giovanni e Paolo. For an ambulance, call ☎ 523 00 00. Current information on all-night pharmacies is listed in *Un Ospite di Venezia*.

Emergency

For police emergencies, call ☎ 113. The questura (☎ 520 32 22), is at Fondamenta di San Lorenzo, in Castello.

THINGS TO SEE

Venice is a beautiful city and any visitor needs to allocate plenty of time just to wander through the narrow streets. The main tourist areas are Piazza San Marco, the Rialto and the souvenir shop-lined streets which connect the two, as well as the main thoroughfare connecting the train station and San Marco. This means that, year round, it is easy to escape the crowds. Head for the tranquil streets and squares of Dorsoduro and San Polo – while the hordes are cramming into the Basilica di San Marco, you will be virtually alone admiring Tintoretto's paintings in the Scuola San Rocco, or Titian's masterpieces in the adjacent Frari. If you go to the sestiere of Castello farther away from San Marco you'll discover relatively little-visited monuments such as the massive Gothic Chiesa di SS Giovanni e Paolo. In Cannaregio, keep away from the main thoroughfare and you will find this sestiere really worth exploring.

The monuments listed here are grouped roughly according to the sestieri. But, before organising yourself to visit the main monuments, churches and museums, catch the No 1 vaporetto along the Canale Grande, Venice's main 'street' (see the Canale Grande section for a description of the main palaces along the waterway).

The Comune di Venezia has produced the first in a series of walking itineraries, *Inside Venice*, designed to help tourists explore the city. The first itinerary covers Dorsoduro and Frari and copies are available in English and Italian at the tourist offices. Hopefully the other two planned itineraries will be published shortly. *A Day in Venice*, published by Bonechi, is available for L5000 at all the souvenir stands.

Opening Hours

Virtually all galleries and museums are closed on Mondays. Check with the APT for exceptions.

Special Tickets

The comune offers a special ticket for L16,000 that includes entry to the Doge's Palace, Ca' Rezzonico, Museo Correr and other civic museums. It can be purchased from any of the city's museums.

Canale Grande

Described by French writer Philippe de Commines in the 15th century as 'the finest street in the world, with the finest houses', the Canale Grande is a little dilapidated these days but still rivals the great boulevards of the world. It weaves for 3.5 km through the city like a huge, upside-down 'S', with a depth of about six metres and a width which ranges from 40 to 100 metres across. Taking a vaporetto is the only way to see the incredible parade of buildings, including more than 100 palaces, which date from the 12th to the 18th century. Board the vaporetto No 1 in Piazzale Roma and try to grab a seat on the deck at the back.

Not far past the train station and Canale di Cannaregio (the city's second largest canal) and just after the Riva di Biasio stop (to the right) is one of the most celebrated Veneto-Byzantine buildings, the **Fondaco dei Turchi**. Once a Turkish warehouse and now the Museo Civico di Storia Naturale (Natural History Museum), it was badly restored in the 19th century. It is recognisable by the three-storey towers on either side of its colonnade.

Continue past the Rio Terrà della Maddalena to the **Palazzo Vendramin Calergi** on the left. This fine example of Renaissance architecture is where Richard Wagner died in 1883, and it is now the winter home of Venice's casino. Farther on and to the right, just after the San Stae stop, is the **Ca' Pesaro**, the Baroque masterpiece of Baldassarre Longhena, which was built between 1679 and 1710. It is said the builder died worrying about the cost and it was completed after his death. The palace houses the city's Galleria d'Arte Moderna and Museo Orientale.

To the left, a short distance farther on at the Ca' d'Oro stop, is the magnificent **Ca' d'Oro** (Golden House), acclaimed as the most beautiful Gothic palace in Venice. (See the Ca' d'Oro information in the Cannaregio section later in this chapter.) To the right as the boat turns to approach the Ponte di Rialto (Rialto Bridge), is the **Pescheria** (fish market) on the Campo della Pescaria, built in 1907. Opposite the fish market is the **Palazzo Michiel dalle Colonne**, with its distinctive ground-floor colonnade.

On the right , just after the fish market, are the **Fabbriche Nuove di Rialto**, built in 1554 by Jacopo Sansovino as public offices for trade and commerce. Next door is the city's produce market and then the **Fabbriche Vecchie di Rialto**, built in 1522 as a courthouse. Just before the Ponte di Rialto, on the left bank, is the **Fondaco dei Tedeschi**, once the most important of the trading centres on the Canale Grande and rebuilt after a fire in 1505. Its façades were frescoed by Titian and Giorgione, but these have disappeared. The building now houses the main post office.

The stone **Ponte di Rialto** was built in the late 16th century by Antonio da Ponte, who won the commission in a public competition over architects including Palladio. The first palace of great interest after the bridge is the Renaissance **Palazzo Grimani**, on the left just before the Rio di San Luca. It was designed by Sanmicheli. Farther along, also on the left bank, is another Renaissance building, the **Palazzo Corner-Spinelli**, designed by Mauro Cordussi. On the right, as the canal swings sharply to the left, is the late-Gothic **Ca' Foscari**, commissioned by Doge Francesco Foscari, one of the finest palaces in the city. Farther on, to the left, is the 18th-century **Palazzo Grassi**. Now owned by Fiat, it is used as a cultural centre and as a venue for exhibitions. Opposite is the massive **Ca' Rezzonico**, designed by Baldassarre Longhena. It houses the city's collection of 18th-century art.

You are now approaching the last of the canal's three bridges, the wooden **Ponte dell' Accademia** (Accademia Bridge), built in 1930 to replace a metal 19th-century bridge. Past the bridge on the right is the unfinished **Palazzo Venier dei Leoni**,where American heiress Peggy Guggenheim lived until her death in 1979 and which is now home to her collection of modern art. Two buildings along is the delightful **Palazzo Dario**, built in 1487 and recognisable by the multi-coloured marble façade and its many chimneys. Note the leaning outside walls.

On the left bank, at the Santa Maria del Giglio stop, is **Palazzo Corner**, an imposing, ivy-covered palace also known as the Ca' Grande and designed in the mid-16th century by Jacopo Sansovino. On the right, before the canal broadens into the expanse facing San Marco, is the magnificent **Basilica di Santa Maria della Salute** by Baldassarre Longhena.

San Marco

Piazza San Marco One of the most famous squares in the world, San Marco was described by Napoleon as the finest drawing room in Europe. The piazza, enclosed by the basilica and the arcaded Procuratie Vecchie and Nuove, hosts flocks of pigeons and tourists, both competing for space in the high season. Stand and wait for the bronze *Mori* to strike the bell of the 15th-century Torre dell'Orologio, which rises above the entrance to the Mercerie, the main thoroughfare from San Marco to the Rialto. Or, sit and enjoy a coffee at Florian or Quadri, the two remaining 18th-century cafés, opposite each other on the piazza – expect to pay up to L12,000 (an extra L3000 if there is music).

Basilica di San Marco St Mark's Basilica is a magnificent blend of architectural and decorative styles, from Byzantine, through Romanesque to Renaissance – although its main inspiration is Byzantine. Built to house the body of St Mark the Evangelist, the church was richly embellished over centuries with mosaics, precious marble, porphyry and the booty of the crusades. The church is usually very crowded with tourists. There is too much to see in one visit, so try spreading your visits over a few days in order to really appreciate the incredible wealth of art works.

The Missing Body of St Mark
Legend has it that, during the rebuilding of the basilica in 1063, the body of St Mark was hidden and then 'lost' when its hiding place was forgotten. In 1094, when the church was consecrated, the body was miraculously found when it broke through the column in which it had been enclosed. St Mark was reburied in the church crypt. The body of the saint now lies beneath the basilica's high altar.■

Venetian merchants stole the body of St Mark from Alexandria, Egypt, in 828 AD and brought it to Venice for the Doge Giustiniano Participazio, who bequeathed a huge sum of money to build a basilica fitting for such a considerable relic. The merchants were fulfilling a portent – legend had it that, while on a journey from Acquilea to Rome, St Mark was anchored off Venice when he

Marble relief from the Basilica di San Marco

PLACES TO STAY

2	Domus G B Giustinian
3	Hotel al Gallo
4	Albergo & Trattoria da Bepi
5	Hotel dalla Mora
6	Albergo Casa Peron
14	Albergo Antico Capon
20	Antica Locanda Montin
23	Pensione Seguso
26	Albergo Accademia Villa Maravege
36	Gritti Palace
44	Locanda Sturion
51	Locanda San Salvador
55	Al Gambero

56	Serenissima
58	Locanda Casa Petrarca
61	Hotel Noemi
62	Astoria
63	Hotel ai do Mori
77	Hotel Riva
78	Locanda Silva
79	Hotel da Bruno
85	Foresteria Valdese
87	Locanda Piave
88	Albergo Corona
89	Hotel Bridge
92	Hotel Doni
93	Danieli
94	Albergo Paganelli
95	Londra Palace

101	La Residenza

PLACES TO EAT

9	Bar ai Nomboli
10	Crepizza
11	Da Silvio
15	Gelateria il Doge
16	L'Incontro
21	Gelati Nico
39	Vino Vino
42	Il Volto
43	Antica Carbonera
45	Trattoria alla Madonna
50	Osteria al Milion
53	Colussi il Fornaio

VENETO

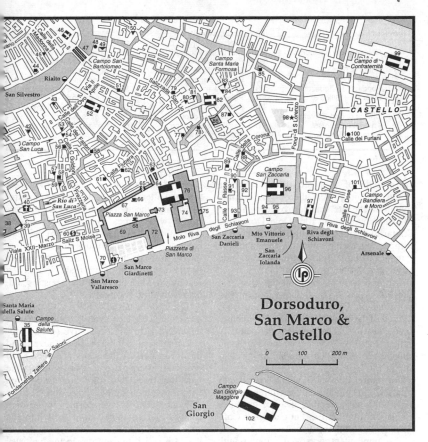

Dorsoduro, San Marco & Castello

0   100   200 m

54	Burghy	7	Scuola Grande di San Rocco
57	Zorzi	8	Frari
59	Ristorante da Ivo	12	Chiesa di San Pantalon
66	Caffè Quadri	13	Supermarket
68	Caffè Florian	17	Il Libraio San Barnarba
70	Harry's Bar	18	Scuola Grande dei Carmini
80	Osteria alle Testiere	19	Chiesa di San Sebastiano
81	Cip Ciap	22	Chiesa dei Gesuati
83	Osteria al Mascaron	24	Galleria dell'Accademia
84	Pizzeria da Egidio	25	Ponte dell'Accademia (Accademia Bridge)
90	Trattoria Rivetta	27	Ca' Rezzonico
91	Al Vecchio Penasa	28	Palazzo Grassi
		29	Ca' Foscari

30	Palazzo Corner-Spinelli
31	Chiesa di Santo Stefano
32	Palazzo Corner (Ca' Grande)
33	Palazzo Venier dei Leoni & Peggy Guggenheim Collection
34	Palazzo Dario
35	Basilica di Santa Maria della Salute
37	Chiesa di Santa Maria del Giglio
38	Teatro la Fenice
40	Chiesa di San Fantin
41	Palazzo Grimani

OTHER

1	Intercity Bus Station

continued on next page

had a vision of an angel who told him he would be laid to rest there. The original church on the site was destroyed by fire in 932 and rebuilt, but in 1063 Doge Domenico Contarini decided the building was poor in comparison to the splendid Romanesque churches being built in mainland cities, and had it demolished.

The new basilica, built on the plan of a Greek cross, with five bulbous domes, was modelled on Constantinople's (destroyed) Church of the Twelve Apostles and was consecrated in 1094. The basilica was actually built as the private chapel of the doges and remained so until it became Venice's cathedral in 1807.

For more than 500 years, the doges enlarged and embellished the church, adorning it with an incredible array of treasures plundered from the East, in particular Constantinople during the crusades.

The unusual **façade** is decorated with mosaics in the arches above the doorways. Take a look at the mosaic above the doorway at the left end of the façade. Made between 1260 and 1270, it depicts the arrival of the body of St Mark in Venice and features the oldest image in existence of the basilica. The three arches of the main doorway are decorated with Romanesque carvings, dating from around 1240.

On the balcony above the main door are copies of the famous gilded bronze horses: the originals, which are on display in the basilica's Museo Marciano, were stolen during the sack of Constantinople in 1204 during the Fourth Crusade. Napoleon removed them to Paris in 1797, but they were returned after the fall of the French Empire.

Through the doors is the **narthex**, or vestibule, with domes and arches decorated with mosaics, mainly dating from the 13th century. The oldest mosaics in the basilica, dating from around 1063, are in the niches of the bay in front of the main door. They feature the Madonna with the Apostles and, below, the four Evangelists.

The **interior** of the basilica is dazzling in its richness: the 12th-century antique marble pavement is highly decorative (it has subsided in places, making the floor uneven) and the lower part of the walls are lined with precious eastern marbles. Above the marble panelling, the walls of the church are covered with mosaics on a gilded background.

Work started on the mosaics in the 11th century and continued until well into the 13th century. Later mosaics were added in the 14th and 15th centuries in the baptistry and side chapels and as late as the 18th-century mosaics were being added or restored.

The following is a brief guide to some of the best mosaics: in the central dome is a 12th-century Ascension; those on the arch between the central and west domes date from the same period and include Christ's Passion, the Kiss of Judas and the Crucifixion; in the west dome are early 12th-century mosaics depicting Pentecost; in the lunette over the west door is Christ between the Virgin and St Mark (13th century); on the wall of the right aisle is a 13th-century Agony in the Garden; on the right-hand wall of the right transept is another 13th-century work depicting the miraculous rediscovery of the body of St Mark; in the dome of the left transept are early 12th-century mosaics of the life of St John the Evangelist; those in the east dome show the Religion of Christ as foretold by the Prophets (12th century); between the windows of the apse are the four patron saints of Venice, among the earliest mosaics in the basilica.

To the right of the high altar is the entrance to the **Sanctuary** (L3000). St Mark's body is contained in a sarcophagus beneath the altar. Behind the altar is one of the basilica's greatest treasures, the exquisite **Pala d'Oro**, a gold-enamel-and-jewel-encrusted altarpiece made in Constantinople for the Doge Pietro Orseolo I in 976. It was enriched and reworked in Constantinople in 1105 and enlarged by Venetian goldsmiths in 1209 and again reset in the 14th century. Among the precious stones adorning the Pala are emeralds, rubies, amethysts, sapphires and pearls.

The **Treasury** (L3000), accessible from the right transept, contains most of the booty from the 1204 raid on Constantinople, including a thorn said to be from the crown of thorns worn by Christ. Through a door at the far right end of the narthex is a stairway leading up to the **Museo Marciano**, which contains the original gilded bronze horses and the **Loggia dei Cavalli** (L3000). There is a great view of the piazza from the loggia.

Although the church opens longer hours, tourists are restricted to visiting Monday to Saturday between 9.30 am to 5.30 pm and Sunday and holidays from 2 to 5.30 pm. The best (but most crowded) times to go are when the mosaics are illuminated, Monday to Friday from 11.30 am to 12.30 pm, Saturday from 11.30 am to 5.30 pm, and all day Sunday.

The basilica's 99-metre-tall **bell tower** is in Piazza San Marco. It was built in the 10th century but suddenly collapsed on 14 July 1902 and was later rebuilt brick by brick. You can pay L2000 to climb it.

Procuratie Vecchie The former residence and offices of the Procurators of St Mark, who were responsible for the upkeep of the church, this building was designed by Mauro Codussi and occupies the entire north side of the Piazza San Marco.

On the south side of the piazza are the **Procuratie Nuove**, planned by Jacopo Sansovino and completed by Vincenzo Scamozzi and Baldassare Longhena. Napoleon converted this building into his royal palace and demolished the church of San Geminiano at the western end of the piazza to build the wing commonly known as the Ala Napoleonica, which housed his ballroom.

The Procuratie Nuove now houses the **Museo Correr**, dedicated to the art and history of Venice, but it can be a little dull compared to the city's other offerings. The building also houses the **Quadreria**, a picture gallery with several notable works by artists including Carpaccio. The **Museo del Risorgimento**, on the 2nd floor, has a good array of artefacts relating to the fall of the Venetian Republic and Italian unification.

Piazzetta di San Marco This is the area between Piazza San Marco and the waterfront and features the two columns bearing the statue of the Lion of St Mark and the statue of St Theodore, the two emblems of the city. Originally a marketplace, the area was later used by politicians as a place to gather before meetings. The area between the two columns was also used for public executions.

Palazzo Ducale The official residence of the doges and the seat of the republic's government, this palace also housed many government officials and the prisons. The original palace was established in the 9th century, but the building began to assume its present form in the 14th century, when the decision was taken to build the massive **Sala del Maggior Consiglio**. It was built to house the members of the Great Council, who ranged in number from around 1200 to as many as 1700, and was inaugurated in 1419.

The palace has two magnificent Gothic façades in white Istrian stone and pink

VENETO

Verona marble: the 14th-century main façade faces the water and the other façade, constructed in the same style in the early 15th century, lines the Piazzetta di San Marco. After much of the building was damaged by fire in 1577, a competition to rebuild the palace was held, attracting many of the day's celebrated architects. The winner was Antonio da Ponte, architect of the Ponte di Rialto, who restored the building to its 14th-century appearance.

The main entrance, the 15th-century **Porta della Carta** (Door of Paper), to which government decrees were fixed, was carved by Giovanni and Bartolomeo Bon. From the courtyard, the **Scala dei Giganti** (Giants' Staircase), by Antonio Rizzo, takes its name from the huge statues of Mars and Neptune by Sansovino, which flank the landing.

Up Sansovino's **Scala d'Oro** (Golden Staircase) are rooms dedicated to the various doges, including the **Sala delle Quattro Porte** on the 3rd floor, which was the waiting room for ambassadors. Its ceiling was designed by Palladio and the frescoes are by Tintoretto. Off the room is the **Anticollegio**, which features the *Rape of Europa* by Veronese and four paintings by Tintoretto. Through here is the splendid **Sala del Collegio**, with a ceiling by Francesco Bello which features a series of paintings by Veronese. Next is the **Sala del Senato** which has the superb paintings by Tintoretto.

The immense **Sala del Maggiore Consiglio** is on the 2nd floor and most easily accessible by the stairway at the southern end of the 3rd floor. The room features Tintoretto's *Paradise* on the entrance wall, one of the world's largest oil paintings, measuring 22 by seven metres. Among the many other paintings in the hall is a masterpiece, the *Apotheosis of Venice* by Veronese, in one of the central panels of the ceiling. Note the black space in the frieze of the first 76 doges of Venice. Doge Marin Falier would have appeared there, had he not been beheaded for treason in 1355.

The route through the palace takes you across the famous **Bridge of Sighs** (Ponte dei Sospiri) and into the prisons. The name of the bridge derives from the sighs released by prisoners crossing into the dungeons, including, no doubt, Casanova, who was condemned by the Council of Ten.

The palace opens daily from 9 am to dusk (up to 7 pm in summer and as early as 4 pm in winter) and admission is L8000. You can hire an infra-red radio receiver (which looks like a mobile telephone and picks up an audio-loop commentary in each room) in the first room after the Golden Staircase for L5000.

There are guided tours known as the *itinerari segreti* (secret itineraries) of the lesser known areas of the palace, including the original prisons. Check if the guide speaks English.

Libreria Sansoviniana Described by Palladio as the most sumptuous palace ever built, it was designed by Jacopo Sansovino in the 16th century and is considered his masterpiece. It takes up the entire west side of the Piazzetta di San Marco and houses the Libreria Marciana (also known as the Libreria Vecchia, or Old Library) and the Museo Archeologico. The library can only be visited with special permission from the director (call ☎ 520 87 88). The Archaeological Museum has an impressive collection of Greek and Roman sculpture. It opens Monday to Saturday from 9 am to 2 pm, Sunday to 1 pm, and costs L4000. Around the corner, facing the lagoon, is the **Zecca** (Mint), built in 1537, which now houses the Biblioteca Nazionale Marciana (National Library of St Mark),

San Marco to the Rialto The **Mercerie**, a series of streets lined with shops, is the main thoroughfare between Piazza San Marco and the Rialto. The **Chiesa di San Salvatore**, built on a plan of three Greek crosses laid end to end, features Titian's *Annunciation* and Bellini's *Supper in Emmaus*. North of the church and very close to the Ponte di Rialto is the bustling **Campo San Bartolomeo**.

San Marco to the Accademia The area immediately west of Piazza San Marco is a rabbit-warren of narrow shop-lined streets where, if you search hard enough, you might pick up some interesting gifts/souvenirs, such as watercolours of the city, marbled paper and carnival masks. Otherwise the shops in this area tend to be exclusive and expensive. On the way to the Ponte dell' Accademia, there are a couple of churches of interest. The Renaissance **San Fantin**, in the campo of the same name, has a domed sanctuary and apse by Jacopo Sansovino. Also in Campo San Fantin is the famous opera house, the **Teatro**

la Fenice, which opened in 1792. Several of Verdi's operas had their opening nights here. You can ask to be let in to see the plush interior.

Return to Calle Larga XXII Marzo and turn right to reach **Chiesa di Santa Maria del Giglio**, also known as Santa Maria Zobenigo. Its Baroque façade features maps of European cities as they were in 1678. Continue on to reach Campo Francesco Morosini (more commonly known as Campo Santo Stefano) and the Gothic **Chiesa di Santo Stefano**. Of particular note inside are three paintings by Tintoretto in the sacristy: the *Last Supper*, the *Washing of the Feet* and the *Agony in the Garden*.

Dorsoduro

Galleria dell'Accademia A visit to this gallery is an absolute must for visitors with even the most minor interest in Venetian art. Situated in the former church and convent of Santa Maria della Carità, which has additions by Palladio, the collection follows the progression of Venetian art from the 14th to

Façade of Baroque Santa Maria del Giglio, featuring maps of European cities in 1678.

the 18th centuries and is displayed in chronological order. The following is a brief guide to some of the highlights.

Room 1 contains works by the early 14th-century painter, Paolo Veneziano, including the *Coronation of the Virgin*. The main feature of Room 2, which contains works of the late 15th and early 16th centuries, is Carpaccio's altarpiece *The 10,000 Martyrs of Mt Ararat* and there are also works by Giovanni Bellini. Rooms 4 and 5 feature some of the collection's best work – Andrea Mantegna's *St George*, several paintings of the Madonna and Child by Giovanni Bellini and Giorgione's fabulous *La Tempesta*. Rooms 6 to 10 contain works of the High Renaissance and feature Tintoretto and Titian. One of the highlights of the collection is Paolo Veronese's *Christ in the House of Levi* in Room 10. Originally called *The Last Supper*, the painting's name was changed after leaders of the Inquisition objected to its depiction of characters such as drunkards and dwarfs. The room also contains one of Titian's last works, a *Pietà* and a number of paintings by Tintoretto. In Room 13 are a number of works by the 18th-century painter, Giambattista Tiepolo and Room 13 features several portraits by Tintoretto. The collection then returns to the art of the 15th and 16th centuries, with more works by Giovanni Bellini in Room 23, and works by Carpaccio in Rooms 19 and 21, which features his series depicting the *Legend of St Ursula*. The collection ends in Room 24 with Titian's beautiful *Presentation of the Virgin*.

The gallery is open Monday to Saturday from 9 am to 2 pm and Sunday to 1 pm. Entry costs L8000.

Peggy Guggenheim Collection This collection of modern art is housed in the unfinished Palazzo Venier dei Leoni, where Peggy Guggenheim lived for 30 years until her death in 1979. It is her personal collection and features pieces by her favourite modern artists, representing most of the major movements of the 20th century. Among the artists represented are Picasso, De Chirico, Kandinsky, Ernst, Chagall, Klee, Mirò, Dali,

Pollock, Rothko and Bacon. It is open daily except Monday, from 11 am to 6 pm, and entry costs L7000. Admission is free during special Saturday openings, usually held from 6 to 9 pm during winter. Take a wander around the sculpture garden, where Miss Guggenheim and many of her pet dogs are buried.

Santa Maria della Salute Dominating the entrance to the Canale Grande, this beautiful church was built in the 17th century to give thanks to the Virgin Mary, who was believed to have saved the city from an outbreak of plague which killed more than a third of the population. The octagonal church was designed by Baldassare Longhena. Inside, works of art include paintings by Titian and Tintoretto in the Great Sacristy. Every year, on 21 November, there is a procession from Piazza San Marco to the church to give thanks for the city's good health.

The Zattere The Fondamenta delle Zattere runs along the wide Canale della Giudecca from the Punta della Salute to the Stazione Marittima. It is a popular place among locals for the passeggiata and there is a good gelati place, Gelati Nico, at No 922. The main sight on the Zattere is the 18th-century Santa Maria del Rosario, known as **Chiesa dei Gesuati**, designed by Giorgio Massari. The frescoes on the ceiling of the church are by Tiepolo and tell the story of St Dominic. At the end of the Zattere, over Rio di San Basilio, is the **Chiesa di San Sebastiano**. This was the local church of Paolo Veronese who provided most of the paintings, including the ceiling panels which tell the story of Esther, the paintings in the choir and over the altar, and the ceiling of the sacristy. The artist is buried in the church. The church was under restoration in 1994 and most of the paintings were covered or removed.

Ca' Rezzonico This 17th/18th-century palace, its façade on the Canale Grande, houses the **Museo del Settecento Veneziano**. Designed by Baldassarre Longhena and completed by Massari, the palace was home to several notables over the years including the poet Robert Browning who died there. The museum houses a collection of 18th-century art and is worth visiting not only for the paintings, but also to see the magnificent 18th-century furnishings, the views over the Canale Grande and the fine ceiling frescoes by Tiepolo, notably the *Allegory of Merit* in the Throne Room. The museum is open daily, except Friday, from 9 am to 4 pm .

Scuola Grande dei Carmini There are more works by Tiepolo in this 16th-century building, which is beside the church of the same name, just west of the pleasant Campo di Santa Margherita. In the Salone, nine ceiling paintings depict the virtues surrounding the *Virgin in Glory.*

A short walk north of Campo Santa Margherita along Calle della Chiesa and over the bridge will bring you into Campo San Pantalon. In the campo is the **Chiesa di San Pantalon** with a stark, unfinished façade. It is worth a visit to see the ceiling painting by Gian Antonio Fumiani depicting events in the life of San Pantaleone. The artist was killed in a fall from the scaffolding as he was finishing the painting and he is buried in the church.

San Polo
Frari One of the highlights of a visit to Venice, this massive Gothic church is incredibly rich in art treasures. Properly known as Chiesa di Santa Maria dei Frari, the church was built for the Franciscans in the 14th and 15th centuries and was decorated by an illustrious line-up of artists. Titian, who is buried in the church, painted the dramatic *Assumption* over the high altar. Another of his masterpieces, the *Madonna di Ca' Pesaro*, hangs above the Pesaro altar (last on the left before the choir). Also of particular note is a beautiful triptych by Bellini in the apse of the sacristy; a statue of John the Baptist by Donatello in the first chapel to the right of the sanctuary, and a painting of St Mark and other saints by Vivarini, in the second last chapel to the left of the sanctuary.

Scuola Grande di San Rocco Built for the Confraternity of St Roch in the 16th century and decorated with more than 50 paintings by Tintoretto, this is one of the great surprises of Venice and under no circumstances should be missed. Tintoretto won a competition to decorate the school and spent 23 years painting the extraordinary series which adorn its walls and ceilings. The ground floor hall, which is the point of entry, was the last to be painted and features a series depicting events in the life of the Virgin Mary, starting on the left wall with the *Annunciation* and ending with the *Assumption* opposite. Up the grand staircase, designed by Scarpagnino, is the main hall. Tintoretto painted Old Testament scenes in the ceiling panels and a remarkable series of New Testament scenes around the walls. Pick up one of the hand-held mirrors so you can study the ceiling paintings without getting a sore neck. The small **Sala dell'Albergo**, off the main hall, contains the most striking paintings of the cycle. This room was the first to be painted by the artist and features the *Glorification of St Roch* in the centre of the ceiling, which Tintoretto painted for the competition. The magnificent *Crucifixion* occupies an entire wall of the room and is considered to be Tintoretto's masterpiece.

In summer the school is open Monday to Friday from 9 am to 5 pm (in winter from 10 am to 1 pm) and on Saturday and Sunday from 10 am to 1 pm and 3 to 6 pm. Entry costs L8000.

Towards the Rialto Following the signs for Ponte di Rialto from the Frari, you will soon arrive in the vast **Campo San Polo**, the largest square in the city after Piazza San Marco. Locals bring their children here to play, so if you are travelling with small kids they might appreciate some social contact, while you take a cappuccino break. The area around the **Ponte di Rialto** was one of the first places settled in Venice. Rialto, or *rivo alto* means high bank and it was considered one of the safest areas of the lagoon. The area is occupied by a busy market with lots of fruit and vegetable stalls and good grocery stores.

PLACES TO STAY

2 Hotel Canal
4 Hotel Abbazzia
7 Hotel Atlantide
8 Hotel Villa Rosa
9 Hotel Santa Lucia
10 Locanda Antica
    Casa Carettoni
11 Albergo Adua
12 Hotel Minerva &
    Nettuno
13 Alloggi Calderan
14 Hotel Rossi
16 Hotel al Gobbo
17 Hotel San
    Geremia
18 Alloggi Biasin
21 Arcadia
30 Ostello Santa
    Fosca

PLACES TO EAT

19 Pizzeria da Gigi
22 Trattoria alla
    Palazzina
24 Pizzeria all'Anfora
28 Paradiso Perduto
34 Osteria dalla Vedova
35 Trattoria Enoteca all
    Bomba
37 Cantina do Mori
38 Pizzeria Casa Mia

OTHER

1 Intercity Bus Station
3 Stazione Santa Lucia
    (Train Station) &
    Tourist Office
5 Chiesa dei Scalzi
6 Ponte dei Scalzi
    (Scalzi Bridge)
15 Park & Playground
20 Ghetto Nuovo &
    Jewish Museum

23 Chiesa di San
    Geremia
25 Chiesa di San Giacomo
    dell'Orio
26 Fondaco dei Turchi &
    Museo Civico di Storia
    Naturale
27 Palazzo Vendramin
    Calergi
29 Chiesa della
    Madonna dell'Orto
31 Ca' Pesaro
32 Chiesa di San
    Cassiano
33 Ca' d'Oro
36 Palazzo Michiel dalle
    Colonne
39 Chiesa dei
    Santissimi Apostoli
40 Gesuiti
41 Chiesa di Santa Maria
    dei Miracoli
42 Hospital
43 Chiesa dei SS
    Giovanni e Paolo

VENETO

Cannaregio,
Santa Croce &
San Polo

There has been a market in this area for almost 1000 years – the **Fabbriche Vecchie** along the Ruga degli Orefici and the **Fabbriche Nuove**, running along the Canale Grande, were built by Scarpagnino after a fire destroyed the old markets in 1514. Although there has been a bridge at the Rialto since the foundation of the city, the present stone bridge by Antonio da Ponte was completed in 1592.

Virtually in the middle of the market, off the Ruga degli Orefici, is the **Chiesa di San Giacomo di Rialto**. According to local legend it was founded on 25 March 421, the same day as the city.

Towards the Train Station Tintoretto fans will want to visit the **Chiesa di San Cassiano** in the campo of the same name, north-west of the Rialto. The sanctuary is decorated with three of his paintings, the *Crucifixion*, the *Resurrection* and the *Descent into Limbo*. The Renaissance **Ca' Pesaro**, its

façade facing the Canale Grande, houses the **Museo d'Arte Moderna** on the ground floor. Started in 1897, the collection comprises works mainly purchased from the Venice Biennale art festival held every even-numbered year, and is one of the largest collections of modern art in Italy. The gallery is open from 9 am to 2 pm and entry is L8000. The **Museo Orientale**, in the same building on the top floor, features a collection of Asian and Eastern oddments put together in the 19th century. It opens the same hours as the gallery, but entry is only L4000.

Continuing north-west, past the Chiesa di San Stae, and along Calle del Megio, is the **Fondaco dei Turchi**, a 12th-century palace used as a warehouse by Turkish merchants and is now **Museo Civico di Storia Naturale**. Take the kids there to see the 12-metre-long crocodile. It opens from 9.30 am to 1.30 pm. Entrance is L4000. Heading south, the 13th-century **Chiesa di San Giacomo dell'Orio**, near the square of

VENETO

the same name, is worth a visit. Of particular interest is the Old Sacristy, with its walls and ceilings decorated with a cycle of paintings depicting the *Mystery of the Eucharist* by Palma Giovane.

Cannaregio

The long main pedestrian thoroughfare connecting the train station and Piazza San Marco is usually crowded with tourists heading from the one to the other. What they don't realise is that this sestiere is really very peaceful and quite interesting; you only need to venture into back streets.

The Carmelite church of the **Scalzi** (literally 'barefoot') is next to the train station, and recognisable by the scaffolding covering its façade. There are damaged frescoes by Tiepolo in the vaults of two of the side chapels. A WW I bomb destroyed the fresco by Tiepolo which once decorated the main ceiling. Along the Lista di Spagna is the **Chiesa di San Geremia** in the campo of the same name. Built in the 18th century, it is of interest only because it contains the body of St Lucy, who was martyred in Syracuse in 304 AD. Her body was stolen by Venetian merchants from Constantinople in 1204 and moved to San Geremia after the Palladian church of Santa Lucia was demolished in the 19th century to make way for the train station.

Ghetto Nuovo Most easily accessible from the Fondamenta Pescaria, next to the Canale di Cannaregio, through the Sottoportico del Ghetto, this was the world's original **ghetto**. The area was originally a foundry and the word 'ghetto' possibly derives from the Venetian word for foundry, *'getto'*. The city's Jews were ordered to move to the small island, which became known as the Ghetto Nuovo, in 1516. The residents of the island were locked in at night by Christian soldiers and forced to follow a set of rules which limited their social and economic activities, but did not suppress their religion. Extreme overcrowding, combined with building regulations strictly limiting the height of buildings means that some apart-

ment buildings in the area have as many as seven storeys, but with very low ceilings. In 1797 Jews were allowed to leave the Ghetto to live wherever they chose. The **Jewish Museum** in Campo Ghetto Nuovo opens daily from 10 am to 4 pm, and entry costs L4000. Guided tours of the ghetto and three of its synagogues leave from the museum hourly between 10.30 am and 3.30 pm daily, except Saturday, and cost L10,000.

Cross the iron bridge from the Campo di Ghetto Nuovo to reach the Fondamenta degli Ormesini and turn right. This is a truly peaceful part of Venice, almost completely empty of tourists. There are some interesting bars and a couple of good restaurants along the fondamenta.

Madonna dell'Orto This 14th-century church was Tintoretto's parish church and contains many of his works, notably the *Last Judgement* and the *Making of the Golden Calf* in the choir and the *Vision of the Cross to St Peter* and the *Beheading of St Paul*, which flank an *Annunciation* by Palma Giovane in the apse. On the wall at the end of the right aisle is Tintoretto's *Presentation of the Virgin in the Temple*. The artist is buried in the church. Also of note is *St John the Baptist and Saints* by Cima da Conegliano over the first altar in the right aisle.

Gesuiti This Jesuit church (its proper name is Santa Maria Assunta) dates from the early 18th century. Its heavily decorated Baroque interior features walls with inlaid marble in imitation of curtains. There is a painting by Titian of the *Martydom of St Lawrence* on the first altar on the left, an *Assumption* by Tintoretto in the north transept, and the sacristy is decorated with paintings by Palma Giovane.

Santa Maria dei Miracoli This particularly beautiful Renaissance church, designed by Pietro Lombardo, features magnificent carvings and sculptures. Pietro and Tullio Lombardo executed the carvings on the choir.

Santi Apostoli This church, at the eastern end of the Strada Nuova, is worth visiting to see the 15th-century Cappella Corner by Mauro Codussi, which features a painting of St Lucy by Tiepolo (removed for restoration in 1994).

Ca' d'Oro Heading back towards the train station on the Strada Nuova, you will reach the Calle della Ca' d'Oro to the left, which will take you to the entrance of this magnificent Gothic palace. Built in the 15th century, it was named Ca' d'Oro (Golden House) for the gilding which originally decorated the sculptural details of the façade. Visible from the Canale Grande, the façade has been covered and under restoration for some years. The palace houses the **Galleria Franchetti** which has an impressive collection of bronzes, tapestries and paintings. It opens Monday to Saturday from 9 am to 2 pm and Sunday from 9 am to 1 pm. Entry costs L5000.

Castello

Santa Maria Formosa This church is in the middle of one of Venice's most appealing squares, Campo Santa Maria Formosa, a few minutes north-east of Piazza San Marco. It was rebuilt in the 15th century by Mauro Cordussi on the site of a 7th-century church, and the present building dates from 1492. Of interest is Palma Giovane's altarpiece depicting St Barbara, which has been said to represent an ideal of female beauty.

Palazzo Querini-Stampalia This 16th-century palace was donated to the city in 1868 by Count Gerolamo Querini. On its 2nd floor, the **Museo della Fondazione Querini-Stampalia** has a collection of paintings and Venetian furniture. It opens Tuesday to Sunday from 10 am to 12.30 pm.

SS Giovanni e Paolo This huge Gothic church, founded by the Dominicans, rivals the Franciscans' Frari in size and grandeur. Work started on the church in 1333, but it was not consecrated until almost a century later in 1430. Its vast and imposing interior is divided simply into a nave and two aisles, separated by graceful, soaring arches. There are beautiful stained glass windows, including that of the south transept, the largest in Venice, which was made in Murano to designs by Bartolomeo Vivarini and Girolomo Mocetto in the 15th century.

There are the tombs of 25 doges around the walls, many sculpted by famous Gothic and Renaissance artists. There are also several paintings of note, including Giovanni Bellini's polyptych of St Vincent Ferrer over the second altar of the right aisle. Still in its original frame, it also features an Assumption and Pietà. There are several paintings by Paolo Veronese in the Cappella del Rosario at the end of the north transept, including ceiling panels and an *Adoration of the Shepherds* on the west walls. They replaced paintings by earlier artists including Titian and Tintoretto which were lost when the chapel was destroyed by fire in 1867.

San Zaccaria The mix of Gothic and Renaissance architectural styles make this 15th-century church interesting. Most of the Gothic façade is by Antonio Gambello, while the upper part, in Renaissance style, is by Codussi. On the second altar of the north aisle is Giovanni Bellini's *Madonna with Saints and an Angel Musician*.

Riva degli Schiavoni Extending along the waterfront from the Palazzo Ducale to the area of the Arsenale at the far south-eastern end of Castello, this walkway has a number of very expensive and exclusive hotels and has long been a favourite place to stay for Venice's more affluent visitors. About halfway along is the church known as **La Pietà**, where concerts are held regularly. Vivaldi was concert-master there in the early 18th century. It is worth visiting to see the ceiling fresco by Tiepolo.

Scuola di San Giorgio degli Schiavoni The school was established by Venice's Slavic community in the 15th century and this building was erected in the 16th century. The walls of the ground floor hall are decorated with a series of superb paintings by Vittore Carpaccio, depicting events in the lives of the three patron saints of Dalmatia: George, Tryphone and Jerome.

San Francesco della Vigna Designed and built by Jacopo Sansovino, this 16th-century Franciscan church takes its name from the vineyard which originally stood on the site. Its façade was designed by Palladio. Inside, just to the left of the main door is a triptych of saints by Antonio Vivarini. The chapel to the left of the choir is decorated with sculpted reliefs by Pietro Lombardo and his school.

Arsenale The city's huge dockyards were founded in 1104 and at their peak were the base for some 300 shipping companies, employing up to 16,000 people, who could produce a new galley every 100 days. Covering some 32 hectares and completely enclosed by fortifications, the Arsenale was a symbol of the maritime supremacy of Venice. Napoleon destroyed the Arsenale in 1797, but it was rebuilt in the 18th century and remained in use until WW I, when ships were built there for the Italian army.

The Arsenale is entered through an imposing Renaissance gateway surmounted by the Lion of St Mark, with larger lions either side, brought to the city as spoils of war.

The **Museo Storico Navale**, back towards the San Marco Canal on the far side of the Rio dell'Arsenale, covers the republic's maritime history with a huge exhibition of paraphernalia, model boats, costumes and weapons, and is well worth visiting. Among the exhibits are Peggy Guggenheim's gondola, one of the oldest remaining in the city.

Most of the Arsenal is closed to the public, and some sections are derelict. Nevertheless, it is open Monday to Saturday, from 9 am to 1 pm and entry is L2000.

At the eastern edge of Venice, the islands of **San Pietro** and **Sant'Elena** are worth walking through to see how Venetians live.

Islands of the Lagoon

Giudecca Originally known as *spinalunga* (long spine) because of its shape, its present name probably derives from the Jewish community which lived here in the 13th century. Rich Venetians later built their villas on the island. Its main attraction is the **Redentore** church, built by Palladio in 1577 after the city was saved from a savage outbreak of plague, which killed more than one third of the population. On the third Saturday in July the doge paid a visit to the church, crossing the canal from the Zattere on a pontoon of boats. The tradition is maintained today and the festival of the Redentore is one of the

SIMON BRACKEN

Small canal near Chiesa di Santa Maria della Salute in the boat-building area of Dorsoduro.

Carnival mask, Venice

TONY WHEELER

RICHARD STEWART

AZIENDA DI PROMOZIONE TURISTICA (APT)

Top: Detail of the Basilica di San Marco, Venice
Bottom Left: Basilica di San Marco (St Mark's Basilica), Venice
Bottom Right: Domes of Basilica di San Marco, Venice

most important in Venice's calendar of events. The island can be reached on vaporetto No 82.

San Giorgio Maggiore Palladio's **Chiesa di San Giorgio Maggiore** has one of the most prominent positions in Venice and, although it inspired mixed reactions among the architect's contemporaries, it had a significant influence on Renaissance architecture. Built between 1565 and 1580, the church has an austere interior, an interesting contrast to its bold façade. Its art treasures include works by Tintoretto: a *Last Supper* and the *Shower of Manna* on the walls of the high altar, and a *Deposition* in the Cappella dei Morti (closed for restoration in 1994). Take the elevator to the top of the 60-metre-high bell tower for an extraordinary view.

Opening hours are from 9 am to 1 pm and 2 to 6 pm daily (one hour less in the afternoon in winter) and entry costs L2000.

San Michele The city's cemetery was established under Napoleon and is maintained by the Franciscans. **Chiesa di San Michele in Isola**, begun by Codussi in 1469, was among the city's first Renaissance buildings.

Murano The people of Venice have been making crystal glass since as early as the 10th century, when the secrets of the art were brought back from the East by merchants. The industry was moved to the island of Murano in the 13th century. Venice had a virtual monopoly on the production of what is now known as Murano glass and the methods of the craft were a well-guarded state secret. It was in fact considered treason for a glass worker to leave the city. The incredibly elaborate pieces produced by the artisans can range from beautiful to grotesque – it just depends on your taste. It is certainly interesting to visit the island and watch the glassmakers at work, especially if you have the kids in tow. But, these days the operation is heavily geared to tourism. Signs direct you to glass-blowing exhibitions.

If you plan to buy Murano glass in any quantity, it's possible to get it packed and sent home, although this can take some time. Check beforehand on the duty you will have to pay once it arrives in your own country.

Visit the **Museo Vetrario**, which contains some exquisite pieces and opens Monday to Saturday from 10 am to 4 pm, and on Sunday from 9 am to 12.30 pm. Entry is L4000.

The main attraction on the island is however the **Chiesa dei Santi Maria e Donato** a fascinating example of Venetian Byzantine architecture. Founded in the 7th century and rebuilt in the 12th century, it was originally dedicated to the Virgin Mary and was rededicated to St Donato after his bones were brought there from Cephalonia, along with those of a dragon he supposedly killed (four of the 'dragon' bones are hung behind the altar). The church has a magnificent mosaic pavement laid in the 12th century and an impressive mosaic of the Virgin Mary in the apse, from the same period.

The island can be reached on vaporetto No 12, 13, 23 or 52 from Fondamenta Nuove (Vaporetto Nos 23 and 52 also leave from San Zaccaria on the Riva degli Schiavoni).

Burano Famous for its lace industry, Burano is a pretty fishing village, its streets and canals lined with brightly painted houses. Although there are many shops filled with lace and souvenirs, the general impression is that the village remains unaffected by the tourist hordes. The **Consorzio Merletti di Burano** is a museum of lace-making and opens Tuesday to Saturday from 9 am to 6 pm, and Sunday from 10 am to 4 pm. Entry costs L5000. If you plan to buy lace on the island, choose with care and discretion. These days much of the lace is imported from China. Discerning buyers will be able to determine the local variety by the quality and the price, which is usually significantly higher than the imported stuff.

Take vaporetto No 12 from Fondamenta Nuove, or vaporetto No 14 from San Zaccaria which stops at the Lido on the way.

Torcello This delightful little island, with its overgrown main square and sparse, scruffy-looking buildings and monuments, was at its peak from the mid-7th century to the 13th century, when it was the seat of the Bishop of Altinum and home to some 20,000 people. Rivalry with Venice and malaria epidemics systematically reduced the island's splendour and its population. Today, fewer than 80 people call the island home.

The island's Veneto-Byzantine cathedral, **Santa Maria Assunta**, shouldn't be missed. Founded in the 7th century, it was Venice's first cathedral. It was rebuilt early in the 11th century and contains magnificent Byzantine mosaics.

On the west wall of the cathedral is a vast mosaic depicting the Last Judgement, but the cathedral's great treasure is the mosaic of the Madonna in the semi-dome of the apse. Starkly set on a pure gold background, the figure is one of the most stunning works of Byzantine art you will see in Italy.

The adjacent tiny **Chiesa di Santa Fosca** was founded in the 11th century to house the body of Santa Fosca. Across the square, in the Palazzo del Consiglio, is the **Museo di Torcello** with a history of the island. It opens Tuesday to Sunday from 10 am to 12.30 pm and 2 to 5.30 pm (closing one hour earlier in winter). Entry costs L3000.

Take vaporetto No 12 from Fondamenta Nuove. If you plan to visit all three islands, there is a special ticket which costs L5000 (one way only) for travel on vaporetto No 12.

The Lido The main draw here is the beach, but the water is heavily polluted and the public areas of the waterfront are unkempt and dirty. Alternatively, you can pay a small fortune (between L20,000 and L80,000) to rent a chair and umbrella in the more easily accessible and cleaner areas of the beach. The Lido forms a land barrier between the lagoon and the Adriatic Sea. For centuries, the doges trekked out here to fulfil Venice's Marriage to the Sea ceremony by dropping a ring into the shallows, to celebrate Venice's close relationship to the sea. It became a fashionable seaside resort around the turn of this century and its more glorious days are depicted in Thomas Mann's novel, *Death in Venice*. The rows of modern apartments and

hotels ensure the beaches are crowded particularly with holidaying Italians and Germans, but the Lido is far from fashionable these days.

The Lido's snappy **Palazzo del Cinema** hosts Venice's international film festival each September and the **casino** packs them in during the summer months. Apart from that, there is little to draw you here, unless you are passing through on your way to Chioggia. The Lido can be reached by vaporetto No 1, 6, 11, 52 or 82 and vehicle ferry No 17 from Tronchetto.

Chioggia Situated at the southern end of the lagoon, Chioggia is the second most important city in the lagoon after Venice. Always an ally of Venice, the town was invaded by the Venetian Republic's great rival, Genoa, in the late 14th century and was virtually destroyed in the ensuing battle, which resulted in Genoa's defeat.

The small medieval section is worth visiting, although the two-hour trip by ferry/bus from San Marco could bite heavily into your schedule. Chioggia remains one of Italy's main fishing ports, but its beach, the Sottomarina, is grubby and uninspiring. City bus No 1, 2, 6 or 7 connects Chioggia with the Sottomarina, saving you the 15-minute walk.

One highlight of the trip is the bus ride from the Lido, which takes you along the giant sea wall. Take bus No 11 (running every 30 to 60 minutes) from Gran Viale Santa Maria Elisabetta, outside the tourist office on the Lido, which boards the car ferry at Alberoni. It then connects with a steamer at Pellestrina which takes you to Chioggia. Another option is to take a bus from Piazzale Roma, which heads for Chioggia via Mestre. The APT (☎ 40 10 68) is on the waterfront at the Sottomarina and can assist with accommodation.

COURSES
The Società Dante Alighieri (☎ 528 91 27), Ponte del Purgatorio, Arsenale, offers intensive and longer Italian-language courses from

September to June. Monthly courses start at L330,000.

The Cini Foundation (☎ 528 99 00) runs seminars on subjects relating to the city, in particular music and art. From April to November, a local cultural association, Artfluence (☎ 524 17 68), arranges a slide show and talk called the 'Art & History of Venice', in the 18th-century Palazzo Ca' Favretto.

FAMILY ACTIVITIES

The kids will certainly enjoy a trip down the Canale Grande on vaporetto No 1. If you can't afford a gondola, at least treat them to a short trip across the canal on a traghetto. They will probably also enjoy a trip to the islands, particularly to see the glass-making demonstrations on Murano. Older kids might enjoy watching the big ships pass along the Canale della Giudecca, so take them to Gelateria Nico on the Fondamenta Zattere, where you can relax for half an hour or so.

Children of all ages will enjoy watching the mori strike the hour on the Law Courts'

The gondola represents the quintessential romantic Venice; if you have the money you shouldn't miss the experience.

clock tower in Piazza San Marco. In summer you could spend a few hours on the beach at the Lido, stopping for gelati on the way home.

There are public gardens at the eastern end of Castello, at the Giardini vaporetto stop. There is also a small playground tucked in behind the Lista di Spagna just before Campo San Geremia.

The Museo Civico di Storia Naturale, in the Fondaco dei Turchi, might also be of interest. Among its exhibits are dinosaurs and a 12-metre-long crocodile.

ORGANISED TOURS

A local group organises guided visits to St Mark's Basilica daily from Monday to Saturday at 11 am. Call ☎ 520 48 88 for information. Consult *Un Ospite di Venezia* for details of visits to other churches and sites in the city. The APT has an updated list of authorised guides, who will take you on a walking tour of the city. The going rate is L105,000 for a three-hour tour for 20 people.

Ital-Travel (☎ 522 91 11), San Marco 72B, under the colonnade at Piazza San Marco's western end, organises a variety of sightseeing trips, including Venice on Foot for L28,000, and a tour of the city by motorboat for L22,000. It also offers a half-day bus trip to the Venetian villas along the Brenta Riviera at a cost of L65,000.

FESTIVALS

The major event of the year is the famous Carnevale, held during the 10 days before Ash Wednesday, when Venetians don spectacular masks and costumes for what is literally a 10-day street party.

The APT publishes a list of annual events which includes the plethora of religious festivals staged by almost every church in the city. One of the main religious festivals is held in early July at the Chiesa del Redentore (see the Giudecca Island section), and another is celebrated at the Basilica di Santa Maria della Salute each November (see the San Marco to Dorsoduro section).

The city next hosts the Historical Regatta of the Four Ancient Maritime Republics in 1996. The former maritime republics of Genoa,

Pisa, Venice and Amalfi take turns to host this colourful event. The annual Redentore Regatta, held each July on the Canale Grande, is another celebration of the city's former maritime supremacy.

PLACES TO STAY

Venice can be expensive, with the average cost of a single/double room without a bathroom around L40,000/60,000. However, for budget travellers, the youth hostel on the Giudecca and the various religious institutions provide a cheaper alternative. If you're able to pay around L80,000 for a double room (without a bathroom) you'll have a few good options, but for good location, a bathroom and nice decor you'll be looking at L120,000 or more for a double. Hotel proprietors are inclined to pad the bill by demanding extra for a compulsory breakfast.

Most of the top hotels are around San Marco and along the Canale Grande, but it is possible to find some great bargains tucked away in tiny streets and on side canals in the heart of the city. Lots of hotels are near the train station, which is convenient for new arrivals, but remember that it is a good 20-minute walk to San Marco. The Dorsoduro area is quiet and relatively tourist-free.

It is advisable to book well in advance year-round in Venice, particularly in September, at Carnevale and on weekends.

The Associazione Veneziana Albergatori has offices at the train station, in Piazzale Roma and at the Tronchetto car park and will book you a room, but you must leave a small deposit. It opens from 8 am and does not accept reservations. New arrivals at the train station will be descended on by agents for many of the hotels nearby. They are generally legitimate, but it is always advisable to check with the APT before booking.

To avoid much frustration, and time wasting, make sure you get clear directions to your hotel and study a map before heading off. Also ask which vaporetto stop is closest.

Bottom End

Camping There are numerous camping grounds, many with bungalows, at Litorale del Cavallino, the coast along the Adriatic Sea, north-east of the city. The tourist office in San Marco has a full list, but you could try the *Marina di Venezia* (☎ 96 61 46), Via Montello 6, at Punta Sabbioni, which is open from May to the end of September.

Hostels The HI *Ostello Venezia* (☎ 523 82 11) is on Giudecca, at Fondamenta delle Zitelle 86. It's open to members only, although you can buy a card there. B&B is L21,000 and full meals are available for L12,000. Take vaporetto No 82 or 52 from the train station or Piazzale Roma (L3500 one way) and get off at Zitelle. The hostel is closed between 9.30 am and 1 pm. The *Istituto Canossiano* (☎ 522 21 57), nearby at Fondamenta del Piccolo 428, has beds for women only from L18,000 a night. Take vaporetto No 52 to Sant'Eufemia on Giudecca.

The *Foresteria Valdese* (☎ 528 67 97), Castello 5150, is in an old palace near Campo Santa Maria Formosa. Head east from the square on Calle Lunga. Cross the small bridge and the Foresteria is in front of you. It has a couple of dorms with beds for L25,000 per night, with breakfast included (less if you stay for a few nights). A bed in a private room is L32,000, with breakfast included. A great option for families are the two independent apartments costing up to L150,000 per day. Book well ahead.

Domus G B Giustinian (☎ 522 50 67), Santa Croce 326a is near the Rio Terrà dei Pensieri and has beds for L16,000 a night. The *Ostello Santa Fosca* (☎ 71 57 75), Cannaregio 2372, is about halfway between the train station and San Marco. Follow the signs for San Marco and you will see signs directing you to the hostel, which charges L16,000 for the first night and less for subsequent nights. Check-in is between 6 and 11.30 am.

Hotels & Pensioni – Cannaregio This is the easiest area to find a bed because of the sheer number of options. Many places are close to the train station, or on or near the busy main thoroughfare to San Marco.

Close to the train station is *Locanda Antica Casa Carettoni* (☎ 71 62 31), Lista di Spagna

130. Singles/doubles are L30,000/54,000 and there's no extra charge for use of the communal shower. The place is full of cats cared for by the pleasant and rather eccentric owner.

Just off the Lista di Spagna, at Calle Misericordia 358, is *Hotel Santa Lucia* (☎ 71 51 80), within a newish building with rooms for up to L55,000/80,000. Nearby is the *Hotel Villa Rosa* (☎ 71 65 69), Calle Misericordia 389, which has singles/doubles from L40,000/55,000 and triples from L85,000. All prices include breakfast. *Albergo Adua* (☎ 71 61 84), Lista di Spagna 233a, about 50 metres past Casa Carettoni, on the right, is a real find. Singles/doubles are L45,000/66,000 and triples are L84,000. The *Hotel Minerva & Nettuno* (☎ 71 59 68), Lista di Spagna 230, has rooms for L54,000/78,000.

The *Hotel Rossi* (☎ 71 51 64) is also near the train station in the tiny Calle delle Procuratie, off the Lista di Spagna. It is good value with pleasant singles/doubles for L48,000/70,000 and triples/quads for L95,000/115,000. In the low season singles/doubles are L35,000/55,000.

At *Hotel al Gobbo* (☎ 71 50 01), in Campo San Geremia, the compulsory breakfast bumps up the prices. Doubles/triples are L75,000/93,000.

Hotel San Geremia (☎ 71 62 45), in the same square, is a very pleasant establishment with friendly management. Small singles/doubles are L58,000/ 82,000, an extra L30,000 or so with a bathroom. There are bigger rooms for families and a few rooms with small balconies (usually heavily booked). The owner promises a 10% discount if you present this guide book.

Also in Campo San Geremia is *Alloggi Calderan* (☎ 71 53 61), with small, but clean singles/doubles for L35,000/50,000, or a bed in a four-bed dorm for L25,000. The *Hotel Marte* (☎ 71 63 51), Fondamenta Venier, at the Ponte Guglie, has singles/doubles from L45,000/80,000.

Alloggi Biasin (☎ 71 72 31), Fondamenta di Cannaregio 1252, across the Ponte delle Guglie, has singles/doubles for L30,000/60,000 and rooms for three or four are an extra L22,000 per person.

Hotels & Pensioni – San Marco Although this is the most heavily touristed part of Venice (and you might want to avoid staying there for this reason), it has some surprisingly good quality budget pensioni.

Just off Piazza San Marco is *Hotel ai do Mori* (☎ 520 48 17), Calle Larga 658. It has pleasant rooms, some with views of the basilica and one even has a terrace. Singles/doubles are L65,000/90,000.

Al Gambero (☎ 522 43 84), Calle dei Fabbri 4685, is in a great location, just off Piazza San Marco, and has been recommended by readers. Singles/doubles are L55,000/90,000 and triples are L120,000. Book well in advance.

Hotel Noemi (☎ 523 81 44), Calle dei Fabbri 909, has basic singles/doubles for L50,000/70,000 and a triple for L87,000. To get to these hotels from Piazza San Marco, take the sottoportego next to Caffè Quadri and then turn left into Calle dei Fabbri.

One of the nicest places to stay in this area is *Locanda Casa Petrarca* (☎ 520 04 30), San Marco 4386, with singles/doubles for L60,000/80,000. Extra beds in a room cost an additional 35 %. Doubles with a bathroom cost L100,000. The friendly owner speaks English. To get there find Campo San Luca, follow Calle dei Fuseri, take the second left and then turn right into Calle Schiavone. The *Locanda San Salvador* (☎ 528 91 47), San Marco 5264, is run by the same family and charges about the same. It is just off Campo San Bartolomeo in Calle del Galliazzo.

Hotels & Pensioni – Castello This area is to the east of San Marco, and though close to the piazza, is less heavily touristed. The easiest way to get there from the train station is to catch vaporetto No 1 and get off at San Zaccaria.

A stone's throw east of San Marco is a delightful little establishment, *Hotel Doni* (☎ 522 42 67), Fondamenta del Vin, off Salizzada San Provolo. It has clean, quiet rooms for L55,000/85,000 with breakfast included. *Hotel Bridge* (☎ 520 52 87), just off Campo SS Filippo e Giacomo in Calle Rimpeto la Sacrestia, has doubles/triples for L75,000/105,000, and breakfast is included. The *Albergo Corona* (☎ 522 91 74), north-east of Campo SS Filippo e Giacomo at Calle Corona 4464, has singles/doubles from L37,000/52,000 and triples from L75,000. An electric baggage carrier whisks luggage up the four flights. *Locanda Piave* (☎ 528 51 74) is just off Campo Santa Maria Formosa at Ruga Giuffa 4838/40. Doubles are L82,000, and breakfast is included. *Locanda Silva* (522 76 43), Fondamenta del Rimedio 4423, south of Campo Santa Maria Formosa towards San Marco, has pleasant, simple singles/doubles for L50,000/90,000.

Hotels & Pensioni – Dorsoduro, San Polo & Santa Croce The *Hotel al Gallo* (☎ 523 67 61) on Calle Amai, just off Campo Tolentini in the Santa Croce area is a couple of minutes walk from Piazzale Roma. Singles/ doubles cost L55,000/90,000, and all have showers. *Albergo da Bepi* (☎ 522 67 35), Fondamenta Minotto, just south of the Al Gallo, has singles/doubles from L55,000/ 75,000, breakfast included. Heading east, Fondamenta Minotto becomes Salizzada San Pantalon. At No 84 is the *Albergo Casa Peron* (☎ 528 60 38), which has singles/doubles for L50,000/75,000, with breakfast included. From the train station, cross the Ponte dei Scalzi and follow the signs to San Marco/Rialto until you reach the Rio delle Muneghette, then cross the wooden bridge.

Hotel dalla Mora (☎ 523 5703) is on a small canal just off Salizzada San Pantalon near the Casa Peron. It has clean, airy rooms, some with canal views, and there is a terrace. Singles/doubles are L50,000/80,000 with a shower. Triples/quads with a shower cost L115,000/150,000. Bookings are a must. The *Albergo Antico Capon* (☎ 528 52 92) on the lovely Campo Santa Margherita has singles/doubles from L50,000/65,000 or L70,000/90,000 with a bathroom. The *Antica Locanda Montin* (☎ 522 71 51), Fondamenta di Borgo, in Dorsoduro, is small and comfortable, with rooms for L40,000/70,000. It has a popular and pricey restaurant. A sign will direct you to the hotel from Fondamenta della Toletta.

Hotels & Pensioni – Chioggia The fishing-village atmosphere makes an alternative to the hustle and bustle of Venice. *Albergo Clodia* (☎ 40 08 13), Via Forno Filippini 876, has singles/doubles from L33,000/50,000. The *Val d'Ostriche* (☎ 40 05 27), Calle Sant'Andrea 763, is slightly more expensive.

Staying at Sottomarina, Chioggia's answer to the Lido, can be less expensive than its northern counterpart. The *Adige* (☎ 40 16 69), Via Adige 4, one block inland from the tourist office, has singles/doubles from L25,000/33,000.

Hotels & Pensioni – Lido *Pensione La Pergola* (☎ 526 07 84), Via Cipro 15, has pleasant doubles/triples for L70,000/90,000, with breakfast included. It is open all year and has a shady terrace. To get there, turn off the Gran Viale Santa Maria Elisabetta into Via Zara, then turn right into Via Cipro.

Hotels & Pensioni – Mestre Only 15 minutes away on the regular bus No 7 or by train, Mestre is an economical alternative to staying in Venice, especially if you are travelling by car. There are a number of good hotels, as well as plenty of cafés and places to eat around the main square. *Albergo Roberta* (☎ 92 93 55), Via Sernaglia 21, has good-sized, clean rooms for L60,000/80,000. The *Giovannina* (☎ 92 63 96), Via Dante 113, has singles/doubles for L35,000/55,000.

Middle

Hotels & Pensioni – Cannaregio The *Hotel Atlantide* (☎ 71 69 01), Calle della Misericordia 375a, has singles/doubles with bathroom for L100,000/155,000. The *Arcadia* (☎ 71 73 55), Rio Terrà San Leonardo 1333/d has been recently renovated. Its spic'n'span doubles are L120,000 with bathroom.

Hotels & Pensioni – San Marco The *Astoria* (522 53 81), Calle Fiubera 951, has very pleasant singles/doubles for L80,000 /105,000 or up to L105,000/150,000 with bathroom. Calle Fiubera runs between the Merceria and Calle dei Fabbri, just north of Piazza San Marco. The *Serenissima* (☎ 520 00 11), Calle Goldoni 4486, is tucked away in the area between San

Marco and the Ponte di Rialto. Singles/doubles are L93,000/120,000 or up to L131,000/170,000 with bathroom.

Hotels & Pensioni – Castello *Hotel Riva* (☎ 522 70 34), Ponte dell'Angelo 5310, is on a lovely side canal. Singles/doubles with breakfast and private bathroom are L80,000/110,000. From the Merceria just north of Piazza San Marco, turn right into the Calle Larga San Marco and then left into Calle Angelo. *Hotel da Bruno* (☎ 523 04 52), Salizzada San Lio 5726, just west of Campo Santa Maria Formosa, has singles/doubles from L120,000/160,000, including breakfast and showers.

An excellent deal, considering the prices of the other hotels along the waterfront, is the *Albergo Paganelli* (☎ 522 43 24), Riva degli Schiavoni 4182. Singles/doubles here are L110,000/170,000 and include both a bathroom and breakfast, and most rooms overlook the water. *La Residenza* (☎ 528 53 15), Campo Bandiera e Moro, is in a 14th-century palace and has delightful singles/doubles for L105,000/165,000. The price includes breakfast and a bathroom. It closes from January 6 to February 15 and from November 7 to December 6.

Hotels & Pensioni – Santa Croce, San Polo & Dorsoduro Although this area is not the most picturesque in Venice, the *Hotel Canal* (☎ 523 84 80), Fondamenta dei Tolentini, is a few minutes walk from Piazzale Roma and overlooks the Canale Grande. Singles/doubles with a bathroom and breakfast cost up to L120,000/180,000 and triples /quads are up to L225,000/270,000. Rooms cost considerably less in low season. In Dorsoduro, the *Albergo Accademia Villa Maravege* (☎ 521 01 88) on Fondamenta Bollani is set in lovely gardens, with views of the Canale Grande. This popular hotel has singles/doubles for up to L130,000/200,000.

The *Locanda Sturion* (☎ 523 62 43), Calle Sturion 679, is two minutes from the Ponte di Rialto. It has been a hotel on and off since the 13th century and, until a few years ago, its rooms with Canale Grande views were a

great bargain. A renovation and an upgrade have lifted prices to L150,000/220,000 for singles/doubles that include a private bathroom and breakfast. The *Pensione Seguso* (☎ 528 68 58), Fondamenta delle Zattere 779, facing the Giudecca Canal, is in a lovely quiet position, away from the tourist hordes. Singles/doubles cost up to L120,000/160,000 with a bathroom and breakfast. Full board costs up to L210,000 per person in high season, and drops to just over half in low season. Book well in advance.

Hotels & Pensioni – Mestre The three-star *Tritone* (☎ 93 09 55), Viale Stazione 16, is close to San Marco and the train station but does not have free parking. Singles/doubles cost up to L100,000/140,000.

Top end
Cannaregio The *Hotel Abbazzia* (☎ 71 73 33), is in a restored abbey in Calle Priuli 68, a one-minute walk from the train station. Many of the lovely rooms face on to a central garden. Singles/doubles cost up to L180,000/240,000, with a bathroom and breakfast . Prices drop considerably out of season.

San Marco The luxury *Gritti Palace* (☎ 79 46 11) is one of the most famous hotels in Venice – its façade fronting the Canale Grande. If you can afford to pay up to L738,000 a double, you'll be mixing with royalty.

Castello Some of the city's finest hotels are on the Riva degli Schiavoni. The four-star *Londra Palace* (☎ 5200533) has singles/doubles for up to L307,000/484,000 and most rooms have views over the water. The luxury class *Danieli* (☎ 522 64 80) next door has rooms for up to L450,000/660,000 and most of them look out over the canal.

Giudecca The *Cipriani* (☎ 520 77 44) is more like a resort set in lavish grounds on Giudecca, with unbeatable views across to San Marco. In high season you will need to hand over L990,000 for a double room. Prices drop by almost half in the low season. The Cipriani is recognised as one of Italy's

VENETO

finest hotels. Take the hotel's private boat from San Marco.

Torcello The *Locanda Cipriani* (☎ 73 07 57), Piazza Santa Fosca, is run by the owners of Harry's Bar and provides luxury accommodation in splendid isolation. The hotel generally offers packages that include meals.

PLACES TO EAT

If you've enjoyed the fine cooking of Tuscany and Emilia-Romagna and the basic 'down home' style of a Roman meal, you might find the fare in Venice a bit disappointing. It is best to search out the little trattorie tucked away in the side streets and squares, since most of the restaurants around San Marco and near the train station are tourist traps, where prices are high and the quality is low. Be careful to read the fine print if you want to eat seafood, as most fish is sold by weight.

The best areas to look for places to eat are in the side streets of Castello, and around Campo San Barnaba and Campo Santa Margherita in Dorsoduro. Many bars serve filling snacks with lunch-time and pre-dinner drinks. Most also have a wide range of Venetian panini, with every imaginable filling. *Tramezzi* (sandwich triangles) and huge bread rolls cost from L3000 to L5000 if you eat them standing up. A cheaper alternative can be the many *bacari*, also known as osterie, small bars serving local wines by the glass and snacks such as deep fried vegetables in batter, stuffed olives, pâté etc. Very popular with locals, they are a great way to experience a more down-to-earth side of Venice.

Regional Specialities

The staples of Veneto cuisine are rice and beans. Try the *risi e bisi* (risotto with peas), or *risotto nero* coloured and flavoured with the ink of cuttlefish (seppia). Seafood is very popular (but also expensive). Try *zuppa di pesce* (fish soup), or seppia with polenta. And don't miss a risotto or pasta dish with *radicchio trevisano* (red chicory). The rich mascarpone dessert, tiramisù, is a favourite here.

Self-Catering

There are fruit and vegetable stalls lining the main thoroughfare from the train station to San Marco, but the prices are inflated for tourists. The main markets are in the streets around the Ponte di Rialto (on the San Polo side). Grocery shops, for salami, cheese and bread, are concentrated around Campo Beccarie. There is a Standa supermarket on Strada Nova and a Mega 1 supermarket in Campo Santa Margherita.

Cannaregio

It is generally best to head for the side streets to look for little trattorie and pizzerie if you want value for money. However, there are a couple of OK spots on the main thoroughfare. *Trattoria alla Palazzina*, Cannaregio 1509, is just over the first bridge after Campo San Geremia. It has a garden at the rear and serves good pizza for L8000 to L10,000. There is a tourist menu for L18,000. *Pizzeria da Gigi*, next to the entrance to the Ghetto Nuovo on Fondamenta di Cannaregio, has basic, cheap fare and you can sit outside without paying extra.

On Fondamenta della Misericordia there are several trattorie and bars which are frequented mainly by locals. Young people will enjoy *Paradiso Perduto*, a restaurant/bar with live music and outside tables in summer. It's inexpensive, and attracts a young, lively, arty crowd. *Trattoria Enoteca alla Bomba*, Calle de l'Oca, parallel to Strada Nova near Campo SS Apostoli, is a good, reasonably priced place. A bit farther along is *Pizzeria Casa Mia*, which has good pizzas for up to L10,000, as well as pasta for around L8000 and main courses for around L18,000.

Around San Marco

If you really can't live without a hamburger and french fries, there is a *Burghy* outlet in Campo San Luca. In Calle Bembo, the continuation of Calle dei Fabbri, is *Antica Carbonera*, a small trattoria catering for the locals. Pasta starts at around L8000.

Noemi, beneath the hotel of the same name on Calle dei Fabbri, offers excellent food at reasonable prices. Pasta starts at L10,000 and main courses are from L15,000.

On Calle dei Fuseri, off Campo San Luca, is *Zorzo*, a vegetarian restaurant with main courses from L10,000. It also serves sandwiches and snacks. *Ristorante da Ivo*, farther along the same street beside a small canal, specialises in seafood and is recognised as one of Venice's best restaurants. Consequently it's not cheap: a full seafood meal will cost around L80,000 to L100,000.

Vino Vino, San Marco 2007, is a popular bar/osteria at Ponte Veste near Teatro la Fenice. The menu changes daily and the pre-prepared food is good quality. A pasta or risotto costs L8000, a main dish L13,000, and there is a good selection of vegetables. Wine is sold by the glass for L2000.

Castello

The *Trattoria Rivetta*, right next to the canal on Salizzada San Provolo, just before Campo San Provolo, serves Venetian dishes. Pasta costs around L9000, and a main dish around L15,000. Wine is expensive at L11,000 a litre.

Pizzeria da Egidio in Campo Santa Maria Formosa has pizzas from L8000 and you can sit in the piazza. Just west of the campo is *Cip Ciap*, at the Ponte del Mondo Nuovo. It serves fantastic, filling pizza by the slice, as well as *calzoni* and vegetable pies.

Santa Croce & San Polo

This is a great area for small, cheap places to eat. Locals say that the best pizza and pasta in Venice is served at *Pizzeria all'Anfora*, across the Canal Grande from the train station at Lista dei Bari 1223. It has a shady garden at the rear. Try the pizza ottombrina, with brie and spek (bacon). Pizzas cost from L8000 to L12,000, pasta is around L9000 and a main course from L9000 to L15,000. To get there, walk straight ahead from the bridge, turn left at the second street and follow the signs to the Rialto. *Trattoria da Bepi*, Fondamenta Minotto 159, is small and family-run and offers a good value set-price menu. The *Trattoria alla Madonna*, Calle della Madonna, two streets west of the Rialto,

off Fondamenta del Vin is an excellent trattoria specialising in seafood. Prices are reasonable, but a full meal will cost L60,000 or more.

Crepizza, Calle San Pantalon 3757, serves pasta, pizza and fantastic crêpes for L8000 to L10,000. Around the corner at Crosera San Pantalon 3817 is *Da Silvio*, a good value pizzeria and trattoria with outside tables in a garden setting. A full meal here will cost under L35,000.

Dorsoduro

Typical regional fare is served at *L'Incontro* along Rio Terrà Canal, between Campo San Barnaba and Campo Santa Margherita. The menu alters daily and a full meal will cost around L40,000. *Antica Locanda Montin*, Fondamenta di Borgo near Campo San Barnaba, has generally good food and a shady garden. A full meal is expensive for what you get at around L50,000. See the Hotels & Pensioni – Santa Croce, San Polo & Dorsoduro section for directions.

Giudecca

Harry's Dolci, Fondamenta San Biagio, is run by the Hotel Cipriani and has fantastic desserts. A meal in the restaurant will cost L60,000 or more. There is also a snack bar. *All'al Tanella*, Calle delle Erbe 269, is a cheaper alternative, where a meal will cost about L25,000.

Lido

The *Self Service Pilla*, Gran Viale Santa Maria Elisabetta, near the APT office, is cheap, with pasta from L4000. *Trattoria da Scarso*, Piazzale Malamocca 4, is one of the better restaurants near the beach, and offers a L15,000 set menu.

Murano

The *Osteria dalla Mora*, Fondamenta Manin 75, looks out over the island's canal and is worth considering for lunch or dinner. A meal will cost around L25,000.

Burano

Da Romano, Piazza Galuppi 221, is a family

run trattoria, widely known for its good food. A pasta costs L10,000 and a full meal will come to around L40,000.

Torcello

The Ponte del Diavolo and the Locanda Cipriani are both famous and expensive. For something simpler, try *Al Trono di Attila*, between the ferry stop and the cathedral, where a full meal will cost around L35,000.

Chioggia

La Plaza Pizza, Piazza XX Settembre, has good pizzas from L4500, and *Trattoria al Bersagliere*, Via Cesare Battisti, off Corso del Popolo, is recognised by the APT as serving typical Chioggia cuisine. Pasta starts at L5000 and main courses at L10,000.

Mestre

There is a *Brek* self-service restaurant at Via Carducci 54, where pasta starts at L4000 and main courses from L6000. *Da Bepi*, Via Sernaglia 27, serves some traditional dishes and a meal could cost L25,000.

Osterie

Venice's osterie are a cross between bars and trattorie, where you can sample wine by the glass while eating *cichetti*, finger-food such as stuffed olives and deep-fried vegetables in batter. Some also serve full meals. You'll find that most osterie are packed with locals. *Osteria al Mascaron*, on Calle Lunga, east of Campo Santa Maria Formosa, is a bar/osteria and trattoria. The cichetti are good, but a meal is overpriced. *Osteria alle Testiere*, on the other side of the campo on Calle del Mondo Nuovo, is another osteria/trattoria. Heading towards Cannaregio is *Osteria Al Milion*, in Corta Prima del Milion, just behind the Chiesa di San Giovanni Crisostomo. It is a very popular bar serving cichetti, and also has a good value trattoria. The *Osteria dalla Vedova* (also called Trattoria Ca d'Or), Calle del Pistor, off Strada Nova in Cannaregio, is one of the oldest osterie in Venice. It is also a good trattoria.

In the San Marco area, near Campo San Luca is *Il Volto*, in Calle Cavalli, which has an excellent wine selection and good snacks. On the San Polo side of the Ponte di Rialto is the *Cantina do Mori*, on Sottoportego dei do Mori, off Ruga Rialto, a small, very popular wine bar where you can grab a good panino for lunch, or a meal at night for about L25,000.

Bars, Snacks & Cafés

If you can cope with the idea of paying up to L15,000 for a cappuccino, spend an hour or so sitting at an outdoor table at Florian or Quadri, enjoying the atmosphere in Piazza San Marco, the world's most famous square. *Caffè Florian* is the most famous of the two – its plush interior was where Lord Byron, Henry James and friends took breakfast before crossing the piazza to *Caffè Quadri* for lunch. Both cafés have bars, where you will pay normal prices for a coffee or drink (taken on your feet) and still enjoy the elegant surroundings.

The world-famous *Harry's Bar*, Calle Vallaresso 1323, off Salizzada San Moisé is at the western edge of Piazza San Marco. The Cipriani family which started the bar claims to have invented many Venetian specialities, including the Bellini cocktail. A meal at the restaurant upstairs will cost you at least L100,000, but it is one of the few restaurants in the city to have been awarded a Michelin star.

Colussi il Fornaio, just off Campo San Luca, has pizza by the slice from L1500 as well as breads, and is good for lunch or a snack.

The *Black Jack Bar*, Campo San Luca, serves a decent Bellini for L3500 and is a great place for a cheap drink. *Nave de Oro*, Calle del Mondo Nuovo, off Salizzada San Lio, is open from 8 am to 1 pm and 5 to 8 pm and specialises in wines from the Veneto that are sold by the glass. In the market area at Campo Beccarie is *Vini da Pinto*, a small bar frequented by stall holders. In Calle delle Rasse, between Riva degli Schiavoni and Campo SS Filippo e Giacomo, is *Al Vecchio Penasa*, which offers an excellent selection of sandwiches and snacks at reasonable prices. *Bar Paradiso* in the Giardini della Biennale,

Castello 1260, faces the water and offers great views back towards San Marco.

In Campo Santa Margherita, in Dorsoduro, is *Bar la Sosta*, a student favourite. Panini cost from L2500 to L5000. The *Bar ai Nomboli*, between Campo San Polo and the Frari on the corner of Calle dei Nomboli and Rio Terrà dei Nomboli, has a great selection of gourmet sandwiches and tramezzini. If you can find a seat, it doesn't cost any extra to sit down.

Along the main thoroughfare between the train station and San Marco there are numerous bars serving sandwiches and snacks. The bar at the corner of Salizzada San Geremia just as you reach the Canale Cannaregio, has excellent tramezzini.

Gelati & Pastries

The best ice cream in Venice is at *Gelati Nico*, Fondamenta delle Zattere 922. The locals take their evening stroll along the fondamenta while eating their gelati. *Gelateria il Doge*, Campo Santa Margherita, also has excellent gelati. The *Boutique del Gelato*, Salizzada San Lio, is another good option. One of Venice's better cake shops is *Pasticceria Marchini*, just off Campo Santo Stefano, at Calle del Spezier 2769.

ENTERTAINMENT

The famous Venice Carnevale (see the Festivals section) is one of Italy's most famous festivals, but exhibitions, theatre and musical events continue throughout the year in Venice. Information is available in *Un Ospite di Venezia*, and the tourist office also has brochures listing events and performances for the entire year.

The Venice Biennale, a major exhibition of international visual arts, started in 1895 and has been held every even-numbered year since early this century. However, the 1992 festival was postponed until 1993 so there would be a festival on the Biennale's 100th anniversary in 1995. It is held from June to October in permanent pavilions in the Giardini Pubblici, as well as in other locations throughout the city. Major art exhibitions are held at the Palazzo Grassi and

you will find smaller exhibitions in various venues around the city throughout the year.

Concerts and opera are performed throughout the year at Teatro la Fenice (☎ 521 01 61), and concerts of symphony and chamber music are staged in the Chiesa di Santa Maria della Pietà. Tickets can be purchased from Agenzia Kele & Teo (☎ 520 87 22), Ponte dei Baratteri, San Marco, or from the church two days before the event. A Contemporary Music Festival is held annually in October at the Teatro Goldoni.

The Casino Municipale di Venezia has two locations. In winter it is at the Palazzo Vendramin Calergi, on the Canale Grande, and in summer it moves to the Palazzo del Casino at the Lido. Vaporetto No 2, the so-called Casino Express, takes you to both locations.

The Venice International Film Festival is also organised by the Biennale and is held annually in September at the Palazzo del Cinema on the Lido. The city doesn't have an English-language cinema. Summer Arena, a cinema-under-the-stars in Campo San Polo during July and August, features British and American films, but they are generally dubbed.

As far as nightclubs go, the city's spread is pretty dismal. In summer head for Paradiso Perduto (see under Places to Eat – Cannaregio). A drive to Mestre is the best bet, or a boat to the Lido, but clubs tend to close there during winter.

THINGS TO BUY

Who can think of Venice without a picture of its elaborately grotesque Venetian glass coming to mind? There are several workshops and showrooms, particularly in the area between San Marco and Castello, and on the island of Murano, designed mainly for large tourist groups. If you want to buy Venetian glass, shop around carefully, because quality and prices vary dramatically. The high number of shops around Piazza San Marco means that competition for tourist dollars is fierce. Remember to haggle, as the marked price is usually much higher than what the seller expects to get. If you do decide to buy Venetian glass, you can have the shop pack and ship it home for you.

Remember this can take a very long time, and you are likely to have to pay duty when it arrives in your country.

The famous Carnevale masks are beautiful souvenirs. Shop around because there are numerous shops which sell them, particularly in the side streets to the west of Piazza San Marco, and quality and price vary. A small workshop and showroom in a small street off Campo SS Filippo e Giacomo, towards San Marco, is worth a look, as is Mondo Nuovo, Campo Santa Margherita, which will design and make you a mask. Venice is also noted for its *carta marmorizzata* (marbled paper), sold at many outlets throughout the city. Many shops (and artists in the city's many squares) sell simple watercolours of typical Venetian scenes. They might not be great art, but carefully chosen, a few watercolours of gondolas, canals or Piazza San Marco, will make great gifts or mementos of your trip. Veneziartigiana, Calle Larga San Marco 412, is a collective selling works by Venetian artists.

The main shopping area for clothing, shoes, accessories and jewellery is in the narrow streets between San Marco and the Rialto, particularly the Merceria and the streets around Campo San Luca. The more upmarket shopping area is west of Piazza San Marco. Opening hours are roughly the same as in the rest of Italy, although many places open on Sundays during the tourist season.

GETTING THERE & AWAY
Air
Marco Polo airport (☎ 66 11 11) is just east of Mestre and is served by flights from most major Italian cities, most major European cities and New York.

Alitalia (☎ 521 63 33) is at San Marco, Fondamenta Orseolo 1166; the Padua office of British Airways (☎ 049-66 04 44) is the closest to Venice; Qantas, Canadian Airways and TWA are handled by Gastaldi Tours (☎ 98 97 55), Via Verdi 34 in Mestre.

Bus
ACTV buses (☎ 528 78 86) leave from Piazzale Roma for surrounding areas including Mestre and Chioggia. There are also bus connections to Padua and Treviso. Tickets and information are available at the ticket office in the piazza.

Train
The Stazione Santa Lucia (☎ 71 55 55), known in Venice as the *ferrovia*, is directly linked by train to Padua, Verona, Trieste, Milan and Bologna and thus is easily accessible from Florence and Rome. You can also leave from Venice for major points in Germany, Austria and the former Yugoslavia.

Orient Express The Venice Simplon Orient Express runs between Venice and London via Verona, Zürich and Paris twice weekly, although in winter there is only one service each week. Any travel agent in Venice can assist, or call the headquarters in London on ☎ 071-928 5100.

Car & Motorbike
The A4 passes through Mestre and is the quickest way to reach Venice. Take the Venezia exit and follow the signs for the city. The A4 connects Trieste with Turin, passing through Milan. From the south, take the A13 from Bologna, which connects with the A4 at Padua. A more interesting route is to take the SS11 from Padua to Venice. This is also the best road for hitchhikers.

Once you cross the bridge from Mestre, the Ponte della Libertà, cars must be left at one of the huge car parks in Piazzale Roma, or on the island of Tronchetto. Parking is not cheap and you will pay over L25,000 for every 24 hours. A cheaper alternative is to leave the car at Fusina near Mestre and catch vaporetto No 16 to Zattere and then the No 5 either to San Marco or the train station. Ask for information at the tourist office just before the bridge to Venice.

Avis (☎ 522 58 25) is in Piazzale Roma, and Europcar is at Marco Polo airport (☎ 541 50 92) and in Piazzale Roma (☎ 523 86 16).

Boat
Kompas Italia (☎ 528 65 45), San Marco

1497, operates some ferry and hydrofoil services to Croatia. Kompas also operates day trips to the towns of Porec, Rovinj and Pula on the Istrian peninsula, all L40,000 one way. Check on the current situation in ex-Yugoslavia before finalising your travel plans.

GETTING AROUND
To/From the Airport
The airport is accessible by regular *motoscafo* (motorboat) from San Marco and the Lido (L15,000), operated by the Cooperativa San Marco (☎ 522 23 03). There are also buses operated by the Società ATVO (☎ 520 55 30) from Piazzale Roma, which cost L5000, or you can take the regular ACTV city bus No 5, also from Piazzale Roma. A water taxi from San Marco will cost more than L87,000.

Local Transport
Vaporetto As already mentioned, there are no cars in Venice proper. Vaporetti are the city's mode of public transport. However, car ferry No 17 departs from Tronchetto, near Piazzale Roma, for the Lido, which enables you to take your car to the islands in the Adriatic Sea.

From Piazzale Roma or Tronchetto, vaporetto No 1 zigzags up the Canale Grande to San Marco and then the Lido. If you aren't in a hurry it is a great introduction to Venice. There are faster and more expensive alternatives if you are in a hurry. A ticket for vaporetto No 1 costs L2500, and L3500 for the other, faster vaporetti. A 24-hour ticket is good value at L14,000 for unlimited travel and a three-day ticket is a very good deal at L20,000, particularly if you will need to use the vaporetti regularly.

There is a special L5000 one-way ticket for the islands of the lagoon, which allows you to visit Murano, Burano and Torcello on vaporetto No 12. It is valid for a full day.

Tickets can be purchased at the ticket booth at most landing stations and should be validated in the machines at each landing station before you get on the boat.

A map of the vaporetto services is usually available at the landing stations at Piazzale Roma and at the train station, or at the APT office. It should be noted that routes change regularly, as do the numbers denoting the routes, so the following list of useful vaporetti should be taken as a guide only.

Useful vaporetti include:

No 1: Piazzale Roma, Ferrovia, Canale Grande, Lido
No 3: Tronchetto, Canale Grande, San Zaccaria
No 12: Fondamente Nuove, Murano, Torcello, Burano
No 17: Car ferry from Tronchetto to Lido
No 52: Circular route from San Zaccaria to Murano, the train station, Piazzale Roma, Zattere, Zitelle (HI hostel), San Zaccaria, Lido
No 82: San Zaccaria, San Marco, Canale Grande, Ferrovia, Piazzale Roma, Zattere, Giudecca, San Zaccaria, Lido.

Traghetto The cheap way to ride in a gondola, traghetti are used by locals to cross the Canale Grande when there isn't a bridge nearby. As they are unprofitable, they are slowly being phased out and only five remain. Signs direct you to the locations. They operate between Calle Traghetto, near San Marco, and Fondamenta della Salute; between Campo San Samuele, north of the Ponte dell' Accademia, and Calle Traghetto; between Calle Mocenigo, farther north, and Calle Traghetto; between Fondamenta del Vin and Riva del Carbon, near the Ponte di Rialto; and between Campo Santa Sofia and Campo Pescaria, near the produce market. The ride costs L500.

Water Taxis Water taxis are prohibitively expensive, with a set L27,000 charge for a maximum of seven minutes, an extra L8000 if you order one by telephone, and various surcharges which make a gondola ride seem cheap.

Gondola These represent the quintessential romantic Venice and, if you have the money, you shouldn't miss the experience. But at L80,000 for 50 minutes they aren't cheap and the price goes up to L100,000 after 8 pm. However, these prices are for a maximum of six people, which is less romantic but more affordable. Prices are set for gondola rides, so don't try to bargain. You can, however,

VENETO

negotiate fees for additional services, such as a singer to serenade you during the ride.

Gondolas are available near main canals all over the city, or can be booked in the following areas: San Marco (☎ 520 06 85), Rialto (☎ 522 49 04), Piazzale Roma (☎ 522 05 81) and the train station (☎ 71 85 43).

Porters Getting from the vaporetto stop to your hotel can be quite difficult if you are heavily laden with luggage. There are several porter stands around the city with baggage carriers who will escort you to your hotel. They charge L9000 for one or two items and L3000 for each subsequent item. They can be found at points including the Ponte dell' Accademia (☎ 522 48 91), the train station (☎ 71 52 72), Piazzale Roma (☎ 520 30 70), the Ponte di Rialto (☎ 520 53 08), and San Marco (☎ 523 23 85).

Around Veneto

THE BRENTA RIVIERA
Dotted along the Brenta river, which passes through Padua and spills into the Venetian lagoon, are more than 100 villas, built by wealthy Venetian families as summer homes, although most are closed to the public. The most outstanding are the **Villa Foscari** (1571), built by Palladio at Malcontenta, and the **Villa Pisani**, also known as the Villa Nazionale, at Strà. ACTV buses running between Padua and Venice stop at or near the villas. The one at Strà was built for Doge Alvise Pisani, was used by Napoleon and was the site of the first meeting between Hitler and Mussolini. See the Around Vicenza section for more Venetian villas.

The luxurious *Burchiello* barge plied the Brenta river between Venice and Padua in the 17th and 18th centuries. Today a reproduction barge ferries tourists for about L100,000, including lunch and short tours. Call ☎ 049-66 09 44 for information.

PADUA (PADOVA)
Although famous as the city of St Anthony and for its university, one of the oldest in Europe, Padua is often seen as merely a convenient and cheap place to stay while visiting Venice. The city, however, offers a rich collection of art treasures, including Giotto's incredible frescoed chapel, and its many piazzas and arcaded streets are a pleasure to explore.

The city's wealth grew during the 13th century when it was controlled by the counts of Carrara, who encouraged cultural and artistic prosperity and established the Stadium, the forerunner of the university.

Orientation
From the main train station it's an easy 10-minute walk to the centre of town: walk through the piazza in front of the train station and continue directly ahead along Corso del Popolo, which becomes Corso Garibaldi. Bus No 10 will also get you into the centre. Piazza della Frutta and the adjoining Piazza delle Erbe are the locations for daily fresh produce markets and form the lively heart of the old city. The Basilica del Santo and the vast piazza, the Prato della Valle (for parking) are at the southern end of the historical centre – a good 20-minute walk from the train station.

Information
Tourist Offices There is a tourist office at the train station (☎ 049-875 20 77), open Monday to Saturday from 9 am to 6 pm and Sunday from 9 am to midday. There is another small tourist office on Piazza Eremitani (☎ 049-875 11 53), at the entrance to the Cappella degli Scrovegni (Scrovegni Chapel). It opens Tuesday to Sunday, from 9.30 am to 4.30 pm. From March to October, another tourist office opens in Prato della Valle in the Ex Foro Boario (☎ 875 30 87). It is open Monday to Saturday from 9.30 am to 4.30 pm.

Post & Telecommunications The post office is at Corso Garibaldi 33, and the 24-hour Iritel telephone office is nearby at No 7. A Telecom office is at Riviera dei Ponti Romani 40, and is open daily from 8 am to 9.30 pm. Address poste restante mail to 35100 Padua. The city's telephone code is 049.

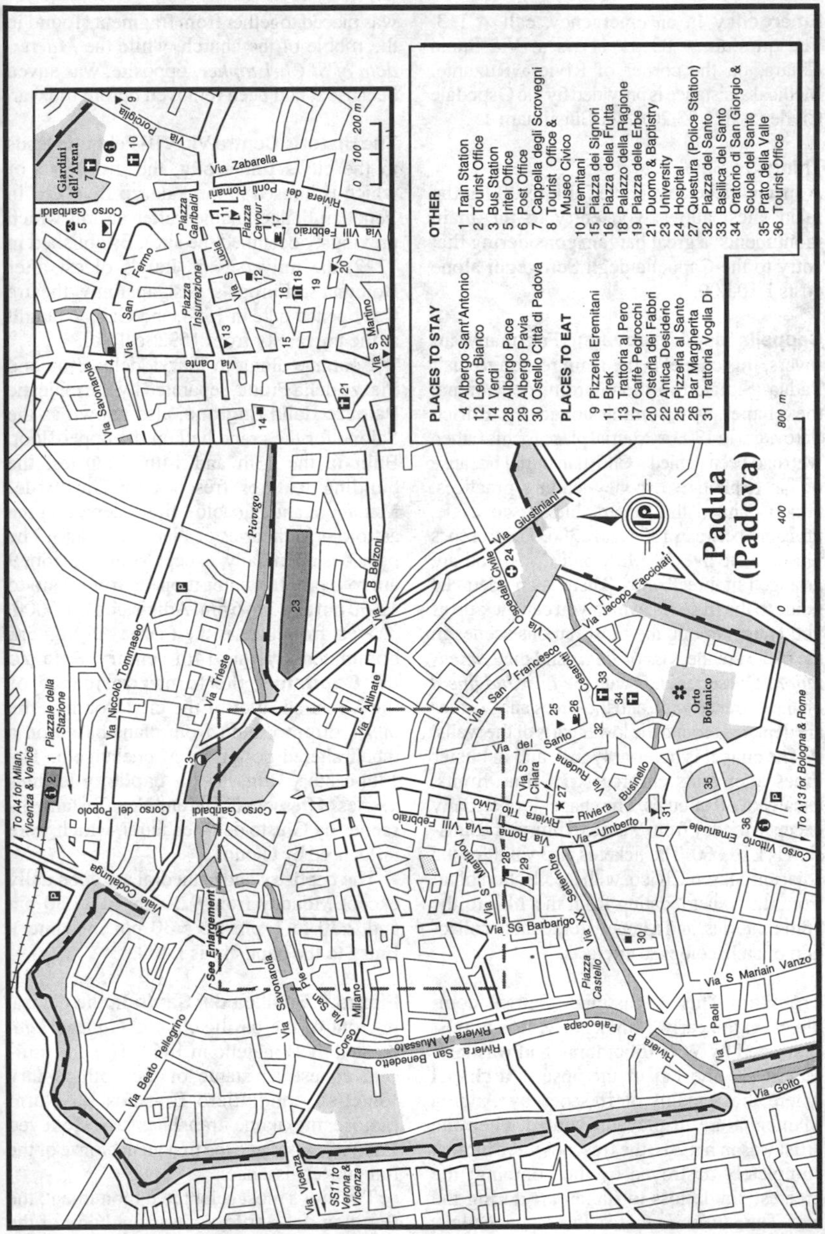

Padua (Padova)
0 400 800 m
0 100 200 m
PLACES TO STAY
4 Albergo Sant'Antonio
12 Leon Bianco
14 Verdi
28 Albergo Pace
29 Albergo Pavia
30 Ostello Città di Padova
PLACES TO EAT
9 Pizzeria Eremitani
11 Brek
13 Trattoria al Pero
17 Caffè Pedrocchi
20 Osteria dei Fabbri
22 Antica Desiderio
25 Pizzeria al Santo
26 Bar Margherita
31 Trattoria Voglia Di
OTHER
1 Train Station
2 Tourist Office
3 Bus Station
5 Iritel Office
6 Post Office
7 Cappella degli Scrovegni
8 Tourist Office & Museo Civico
10 Eremitani
15 Piazza dei Signori
16 Piazza della Frutta
18 Palazzo della Ragione
19 Piazza delle Erbe
21 Duomo & Baptistry
23 University
24 Hospital
27 Questura (Police Station)
32 Piazza del Santo
33 Basilica del Santo
34 Oratorio di San Giorgio & Scuola del Santo
35 Prato della Valle
36 Tourist Office
Giardini dell'Arena
Corso Garibaldi
Via Porciglia
Via Zabarella
Piazza Garibaldi
Piazza Insurrezione
Piazza Cavour
Via San Fermo
Via Savonarola
Via Dante
Via S Lucia
Via Ponti Romani
Riviera dei Ponti Romani
Via VIII Febbraio
Via S Martino
See Enlargement
To A4 for Milan, Vicenza & Venice
Piazzale della Stazione
Corso del Popolo
Viale Codalunga
Via Niccolò Tommaseo
Via Trieste
Piovego
Via G B Belzoni
Via Altinate
Via San Francesco
Via Ospedale Civile
Via Giustiniani
Via Jacopo Facciolati
Via Cesarotti
Via del Santo
Via S Chiara
Via Rudena
Riviera Tito Livio
Via Roma
Via Umberto I
Riviera Businello
Orto Botanico
Corso Vittorio Emanuele
To A13 for Bologna & Rome
Via SG Barbarigo
Via XX Settembre
Piazza Castello
Via Beato Pellegrino
Via San Pio X
Corso Milano
Riviera A Mussato
Riviera San Benedetto
Via Paleocapa
Riviera P Paleocapa
Via P Paoli
Via S Mariain Vanzo
Via Goito
Via Vicenza
SS11 to Verona & Vicenza

VENETO

Emergency In an emergency, call ☎ 113. The questura ☎ 83 31 11) is at Via Santa Chiara, on the corner of Riviera Ruzante. Medical assistance is provided by the Ospedale Civile (☎ 821 33 20), Via Giustiniani 1.

Things to See

A special ticket, available for L15,000 at the main sites, allows you entry to the main monuments; a great bargain considering that entry to the Cappella degli Scrovegni alone costs L10,000.

Cappella degli Scrovegni For many art lovers, this chapel is the main reason to visit Padua. Situated in the Giardini dell'Arena, the chapel was commissioned by Enrico Scrovegni in 1303 as a burial place for his father, who had been denied a Christian burial because of his exploitative money-lending practices. Giotto painted the remarkable fresco cycle, probably between 1304 and 1306. The frescoes illustrate the lives of Mary and Christ and are arranged in three bands. There is an adequate guide to the frescoes, which you can pick up as you enter. Among the most famous scenes in the cycle are the *Kiss of Judas* and the *Lamentation*. The series ends with the *Last Judgment* on the entrance wall, and the Vices and Virtues are depicted around the lower parts of the walls.

The chapel is invariably full, and in busier times attendants enforce strict time limits, usually of 30 minutes. The chapel is open daily except Monday from 9 am to 6 pm, and admission is L10,000. The ticket is also valid for the adjacent Museo Civico, with a collection of art from the Veneto, dating from the 14th to the 18th centuries, and a largely forgettable collection of archaeological artefacts.   .

Eremitani This Augustinian church, completed in the early 14th century, was almost destroyed by WW II bombing and was later rebuilt. To the left of the apse is a chapel where the remains of frescoes by Andrea Mantegna are displayed. Painted when the artist was in his 20s, the frescoes were almost completely destroyed by the bombing: the greatest single loss to Italian art during the war. The *Martyrdom of St James*, on the left, was pieced together from fragments found in the rubble of the church, while the *Martyrdom of St Christopher*, opposite, was saved because it had been removed before the war.

The Historic Centre Via VIII Febbraio leads to the city's **university**, the main part of which is housed in the Palazzo Bò ('Ox' in Venetian dialect, named after an inn which previously occupied the site). Established in 1222, the university is Italy's oldest after Bologna's. Europe's first anatomy theatre was opened here in 1594, and Galileo taught at the university from 1592 to 1610.

Continue along to Piazza delle Erbe and Piazza della Frutta, separated by the majestic **Palazzo della Ragione**, also known as the Salone for the grand hall on the upper floor. Built in the 13th and 14th centuries, the building features frescoes by Giusto de' Menabuoi and Niccolò Mireto depicting the astrological theories of Pietro d'Abano. The palace is open daily, except Monday, from 9 am to 6 pm. In winter it opens from 9 am to 12.30 pm and 3 to 6 pm. Admission is L5000.

West from here is the Piazza dei Signori, dominated by the 14th-century **Palazzo del Capitanio**, the former residence of the Venetian ruler of the city. South is the city's **duomo**, built from plans based on a much-altered design by Michelangelo. The 13th-century Romanesque **baptistry** features a series of frescoes of Old and New Testaments scenes by Giusto de' Menabuoi, which were influenced by Giotto.

The baptistry and cathedral are open daily except Monday from 9.30 am to 12.30 pm and 2.30 to 6 pm (to 5.30 pm in winter). Entry to the baptistry is L400.

Piazza & Basilica del Santo In the piazza, in front of the basilica, is the *Gattamelata*, created by Donatello in 1453. This magnificent equestrian statue of the 15th-century Venetian condottiere Erasmos da Narni (whose nickname translates as 'Honeyed Cat') is considered the first great bronze of the Italian Renaissance.

The city's most celebrated monument, the **Basilica del Santo**, houses the body of the saint and is an important place of pilgrimage. It is known to the people of Padua as Il Santo. The church was started in 1232 and was always intended as a sanctuary for the body of St Anthony, the town's patron, whose tomb is in the Cappella del Santo in the left transept. The sculptures and reliefs of the high altar are by Donatello.

On the south side of the piazza the **Oratorio di San Giorgio**, the burial chapel of the Lupi di Soranga family of Parma, with 14th-century frescoes. Next door is the **Scuola del Santo** containing works believed to be by Titian. The two open from 9 am to 12.30 pm and 2.30 to 6 pm (to 4.30 pm in winter), and entry is L2000.

The street next to the gallery leads to the **Orto Botanico**, the oldest botanical gardens in Europe. Both open from 9 am to 1 pm and 3 to 6 pm, with shorter hours in winter, and entry costs L3000.

Places to Stay

Padua has no shortage of budget hotels, but they fill quickly in summer with the overflow from Venice. University holidays can mean some cheaper accommodation in student quarters, but usually for a minimum of one week. Contact the Centro Universitario (☎ 65 42 99), Via Zabarella 82, or the Cattolici Popolari (☎ 828 31 11 ext 399).

The closest camping ground, *Camping Sporting Center* (☎ 79 34 00), is at Via Roma 123, at Montegrotto Terme, about 15 km from Padua and can be reached by city bus M. The non-HI *Ostello Città di Padova* (☎ 875 22 19), Via A Aleardi 30, offers B&B for L18,000. Take bus No 3, 8 or 12 from the train station to Prato della Valle and then ask directions. There is an HI youth hostel, the *Rocca degli Alberi*, about 40 km from Padua at Montagnana (see the Around Padua section for details).

The *Verdi* (☎ 875 57 44), Via Dondi dell' Orologio 7, has basic, clean singles/ doubles for L35,000/45,000. *Albergo Pavia* (☎ 66 15 58), Via dei Papafava 11, also has rooms for the same price. The *Albergo Pace* (☎ 875 15 66), a few doors down at No 3, has rooms for the same price. To reach Via Papafava,

follow Corso del Popolo until it becomes Via Roma, then turn right into Via Marsala.

The *Albergo Sant'Antonio* (☎ 875 13 93), Via San Fermo 118, at the northern end of Via Dante, has singles/doubles for L43,000/ 66,000 or L70,000/92,000 with a bathroom. The three-star *Leon Bianco* (☎ 65 72 25), Piazzetta Pedrocchi 12, near Piazza della Frutta, has rooms from L109,000/136,000.

Places to Eat

Daily markets are held in the piazzas around the Palazzo della Ragione, with fresh produce sold in the Piazza delle Erbe and Piazza della Frutta, and bread, cheese and salami sold in the shops under the porticoes.

For a snack, try the *Bar Margherita*, Via del Santo 169, near the Basilica del Santo, for good cheap panini. A cheap, but not very atmospheric, place to eat a meal is *Brek* in Piazza Cavour, a self-service restaurant with pasta from L5000 and main courses from L7000.

Pizzeria Eremitani, at the end of Via Porciglia near the bus station, has excellent pizzas from L7000. *Trattoria al Pero*, Via Santa Lucia 38, serves regional dishes and a full meal will come to around L20,000. *Osteria dei Fabbri*, Via dei Fabbri 13, is another good choice, although more expensive. In the area around Prato della Valle, the best choice is *Trattoria Voglia Di*, Via Umberto, just before the Prato. It serves an excellent meal for around L20,000, or you can eat a snack in the bar. *Pizzeria al Santo*, Via del Santo 63, has good pizzas from L7000.

The city's famous *Caffè Pedrocchi*, just off Via Cavour, was the meeting place for 19th-century liberals and one of Stendhal's favourite haunts. It warrants a visit, although it has lost most of its grandeur. A cheaper and equally atmospheric alternative is *Vescovi*, in the market building in Piazza delle Erbe.

Entertainment

The city hosts the Notturni d'Arte festival from July to September each year, featuring concerts and outdoor events, many for free. The tourist office has details. Each summer, Italian and some foreign films are shown from 8 pm at an outdoor cinema in the Giardini dell'Arena. Some opera and theatrical performances are held at the Teatro Comunale Verdi (☎ 3 94 79), Via Livello 32. If you want to go out dancing try New Lola-Lola, Riv. Ponti Romani.

Getting There & Away
Bus & Train Autotrasporti Padova (ATP) buses (☎ 820 68 11) depart from Piazzale Boschetti, 200 metres south of the train station, for Montegrotto, the Euganean Hills, Trieste, Venice, Este, Mantua, Piacenza and Genoa. By train (☎ 875 18 00), the city is connected to Milan, Venice and Bologna, and is easily accessible from most other major cities.

Car & Motorbike By car and motorcycle, the A4 (Turin-Venice) passes to the north, while the A13, which connects the city with Bologna, starts at the southern edge of town. The two autostradas are connected by a ring road. If you take the Padova Ovest exit, you will eventually end up near the train station, where there is parking available. From the Padova Sud exit you will reach Prato della Valle, where there are plenty of parking spaces. Driving from the autostrada into the historical centre is confusing and frustrating because of the lack of signs to point the way. If you get lost, the only option is stop and ask directions.

Getting Around
To reach the centre of town from the train station, take bus No 10. A 24-hour tourist bus ticket, allowing unlimited travel, is available for L3500.

AROUND PADUA
Just south-west of Padua, along the A13 or the SS16, are the **Colli Euganei** (Euganean Hills), dotted with vineyards and good walking trails: ask at the Padua tourist office for information about the trails and accommodation. The Consorzio Vini DOC dei Colli Euganei (☎ 049-521 18 96), Via Vescovi 35 in Luvigliano, can provide details of the vineyards.

If you are driving, follow the Strada dei Vini dei Colli Euganei (Euganean Hills Wine Road), identified by special signposts throughout the hills, which will take you on a tour of many vineyards. Pick up a map and itinerary from the APT in Padua. Most of the vineyards are open to the public and some offer accommodation.

The medieval town of **Montagnana** has a tourist office (☎ 0429-8 13 20), Piazza Trieste, which can assist with information about the region. The city also has a youth hostel, the *Rocca degli Alberi* (☎ 0429-81 07 62), Castello degli Alberi, housed in a former castle and open from April to October. B&B is L14,000 and it is close to the town's train station.

VERONA
Forever associated with Romeo and Juliet, Verona has much more to offer than the relics of a tragic love story. Known as *piccola Roma* (little Rome) for its importance as a Roman city, its golden era was during the 13th and 14th centuries under the rule of the della Scala family (also known as the Scaliger), a period noted for the savage family feuding on which Shakespeare based his play. It is one of Italy's most beautiful cities, and is definitely worth visiting.

Orientation
Old Verona is small, there is a lot to see and it is a popular base for exploring surrounding towns; it's easy to find your way around. Buses leave for the centre from outside the train station; otherwise walk to the right, past the bus station, cross the river and walk along Corso Porta Nuova to Piazza Brà, 15 minutes away. From the piazza, walk along Via Mazzini and turn left at Via Cappello to reach Piazza delle Erbe.

Information
Tourist Office The main tourist office (☎ 045-59 28 28) is at Via Leoncino 61, on the corner of Piazza Brà, facing the Roman arena. It opens Monday to Saturday from 8 am to 8 pm (closing one hour earlier in winter) and

Sundays from 8.30 am to 1.30 pm (in summer only). There is also a tourist office at the train station (☎ 045-800 08 61), which opens daily from 8 am to 7.30 pm in summer and 8.30 am to 2.30 pm during the rest of the year. In summer, a tourist office opens at Piazza delle Erbe 42 (☎ 045-803 00 86), daily from 9 am to 12.30 pm and 2.30 to 7 pm.

Money There are numerous banks around the town centre, including the Cassa di Risparmio at Piazza Brà 26A, which has an automatic exchange machine. Many other banks in Verona also have ATMs.

Post & Telecommunications The main post office is at Piazza Viviani 7. It opens Monday to Friday from 8 am to 5 pm , Saturday to 1 pm. Address poste restante mail to 37100 Verona. There are telephones at the train station, open Monday to Saturday from 8.15 am to 7.45 pm. Verona's telephone code is 045.

Emergency & Medical Services The city's Guardia Medica (☎ 91 32 22) provides medical services from 8 am to 8 pm and usually comes to you. Otherwise, the Ospedale Civile Maggiore (☎ 807 11 11) is at Piazza A Stefani, north-west from Ponte Vittoria.

In an emergency, call ☎ 113. The questura ☎ 809 05 05) is at Lungadige Porta Vittoria, near Via San Francesco.

Things to See & Do
Roman Arena This pink marble Roman amphitheatre, in the bustling Piazza Brà, was built in the 1st century AD and is now Verona's opera house. The third largest Roman amphitheatre in existence, it could seat around 20,000 people. It is remarkably well preserved, despite a 12th-century earthquake which destroyed most of its outside wall. The arena is open from 7.40 am to 6.30 pm and entry is L6000. See the Verona Entertainment section for information about opera and plays at the Arena.

Casa di Giulietta Along Via Mazzini, Verona's main shopping street, is Via Cappello

and 'Juliet's house' at No 23. Although the young lovers Romeo and Juliet were fictional, you can stand beneath the balcony and picture Shakespeare's love scene if you like, or rub the left breast of the bronze statue of Juliet by the entrance if you want a new lover. It is even doubtful there was ever a feud between the Cappello and Montecchi, the local families on which Shakespeare based the play. The house is open from 7.30 am to 6.30 pm and entry costs L5000.

Piazza delle Erbe Originally the site of a Roman forum, this piazza today remains the lively centre of the city, but the permanent market stalls in its centre detract from its beauty. The square is lined with some of Verona's most sumptuous palaces, including the **Palazzo Maffei**, at the northern end, with the adjoining 14th-century **Torre del Gardello** and the **Casa Mazzanti**, on the east side, a former palace of the della Scala, which has a fresco-decorated façade.

Separating the Piazza delle Erbe from the **Piazza dei Signori** is the **Arco della Costa.** Suspended in this archway is a whale's rib which legend says will fall on the first 'just' person to walk beneath it. In several centuries, it has never fallen, not even on the various popes who have paraded beneath it.

In the Piazza dei Signori, the 15th-century **Loggia del Consiglio**, the former city council building, is regarded as Verona's finest Renaissance building. It is attached to the **Palazzo degli Scaligeri**, the former residence of the della Scala. Ascend the 12th-century **Torre dei Lamberti** by elevator (L4000) or on foot (L3000) for a great view of the city. It is open daily, except Monday from 8.30 am to 6.30 pm.

Through the archway at the far end of the piazza are the fascinating **Arche Scaligeri**, the elaborate tombs of the della Scala. They were closed for restoration in 1994.

North from here is the Gothic Chiesa di Sant'Anastasia, started in 1290, but not completed until the late 15th century. Inside are numerous art works, including a lovely fresco by Pisanello in the sacristy of *St George Setting out to Free the Princess*. The 12th-

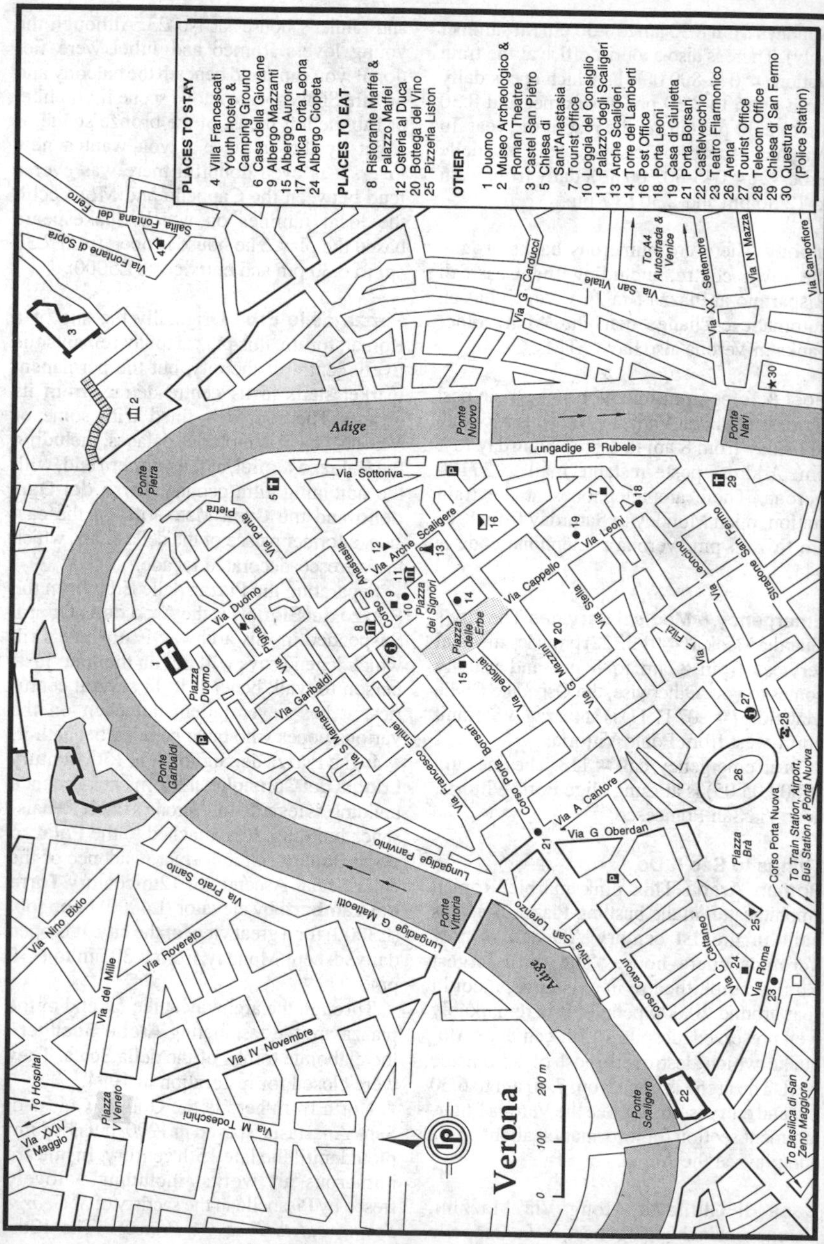

Verona
0
100
200 m
PLACES TO STAY
4 Villa Francescati Youth Hostel & Camping Ground
6 Casa della Giovane
9 Albergo Mazzanti
15 Albergo Aurora
17 Antica Porta Leona
24 Albergo Ciopeta
PLACES TO EAT
8 Ristorante Maffei & Palazzo Maffei
12 Osteria al Duca
20 Bottega del Vino
25 Pizzeria Liston
OTHER
1 Duomo
2 Museo Archeologico & Roman Theatre
3 Castel San Pietro
5 Chiesa di Sant'Anastasia
7 Tourist Office
10 Loggia del Consiglio
11 Palazzo degli Scaligeri
13 Arche Scaligeri
14 Torre dei Lamberti
16 Post Office
18 Porta Leoni
19 Casa di Giulietta
21 Porta Borsari
22 Castelvecchio
23 Teatro Filarmonico
26 Arena
27 Tourist Office
28 Telecom Office
29 Chiesa di San Fermo
30 Questura (Police Station)
Adige
Ponte Pietra
Ponte Garibaldi
Ponte Vittoria
Ponte Nuovo
Ponte Navi
Ponte Scaligero
Salita Fontana del Ferro
Via Fontane di Sopra
Via G Carducci
Via San Viale
To A4 Autostrada & Venice
Via XX Settembre
Via N Mazza
Via Campofiore
Lungadige B Rubele
Via Sottoriva
Via Ponte Pietra
Via Duomo
Piazza Duomo
Via Arche Scaligere
Corso S Anastasia
Piazza dei Signori
Piazza delle Erbe
Via Cappello
Via Leoni
Via Stella
Via Leoncino
Stradone San Fermo
Via F Filzi
Via G Mazzini
Via Pellicciai
Via Garibaldi
Via Pigna
Via S Mamaso
Via Emilei
Via Francesco
Corso Porta Borsari
Via A Cantore
Via G Oberdan
Piazza Brà
Corso Porta Nuova
To Train Station, Airport, Bus Station & Porta Nuova
Lungadige Panvinio
Lungadige G Matteotti
Riva San Lorenzo
Corso Cavour
Via C Cattaneo
Via Roma
Via Prato Santo
Via Nino Bixio
Via del Mille
Via Rovereto
Via IV Novembre
Via M Todeschini
Piazza V Veneto
Via XXIV Maggio
To Hospital
To Basilica di San Zeno Maggiore

VENETO

century **duomo** combines Romanesque (lower section) and Gothic (upper section) styles and has some very interesting features. Look for the sculpture of Jonah and the Whale on the south porch and the statues of two of Charlemagne's paladins, Roland and Oliver, on the west porch. In the first chapel of the left aisle is an *Assumption* by Titian, in an altar frame by Jacopo Sansovino.

Across the River Across Ponte Pietra is a **Roman theatre**, founded in the 1st century AD. Concerts and plays are staged here. Take the lift at the back of the theatre to the convent above, which houses the **Museo Archeologico**, an interesting collection of Greek and Roman pieces. On a hill high above the theatre and museum is the **Castel San Pietro**, built by the Austrians on the site of an earlier castle. Both the museum and theatre open daily, except Monday, from 8.30 am to 1.30 pm daily. Entrance is L6000, which covers both the theatre and museum.

Castelvecchio South-west from Piazza delle Erbe, on the banks of the Adige, is the 14th-century fortress of the Cangrande II (of the della Scala family). It was also used by subsequent rulers. The fortress was damaged by bombing during WW II and was restored in the 1960s. It now houses a museum with a diverse collection of paintings, frescoes, jewellery and medieval artefacts. Among the paintings are works by Pisanello, Giovanni Bellini, Tiepolo, Carpaccio and Veronese. Also of note is a 14th-century equestrian statue of Cangrande I. The museum opens daily except Monday from 8 am to 6.30 pm and entry costs L5000. The **Ponte Scaligero** spanning the Adige river was rebuilt after being destroyed by WW II bombing.

Basilica di San Zeno Maggiore A masterpiece of Romanesque architecture, this church in honour of the city's patron saint was built mainly in the 12th century, although its apse was rebuilt in the 14th century and its bell tower, a relic of an earlier structure on the site, was started in 1045. The basilica's magnificent rose window depicts the Wheel of Fortune. Before going inside, take a look at the sculptures on either side of the main doors. The doors themselves are decorated with bronze reliefs of biblical subjects. The highlight inside is Mantegna's triptych of the *Madonna and Saints*, above the high altar.

Other Sights Near Casa di Giulietta, in Via Leoni is the **Porta Leoni**, one of the gates to the old Roman Verona. The other is the **Porta Borsari** at the bottom end of Corso Porta Borsari. At the end of Via Leoni is the **Chiesa di San Fermo**, which is actually two churches: the Gothic church was built in the 13th century over the original 11th-century Romanesque structure.

Places to Stay
The beautifully restored HI youth hostel, the *Villa Francescati* (☎ 59 03 60), Salita Fontana del Ferro 15, should be your first choice. B&B is L18,000 a night. An HI or student card is necessary. Next door is a *camping ground*. To reserve a space, speak to the hostel management. Catch bus No 72 from the train station.

The *Casa della Giovane* (☎ 59 68 80), Via Pigna 7, off Via Garibaldi, is for women only and costs up to L28,000 for a bed in a small dormitory. Catch bus No 70 and ask the driver where to get off.

The *Volto Cittadella* (☎ 800 00 77), Via Volto Cittadella 8, has doubles/triples for L45,000/70,000. It is off Corso Porta Nuova, just before Piazza Brà. At Corso Cavour 43 is *Al Castello* (☎ 800 44 03), with rooms for L30,000/48,000. *Albergo Ciopeta* (☎ 800 68 43), Vicolo Teatro Filarmonico 2, near Piazza Brà, is a great little place, but you'll need to book well in advance. Its singles/doubles cost L50,000/75,000.

One of the best located hotels in the city is the *Albergo Aurora* (☎ 59 47 17), Piazzetta XIV Novembre 2. Its rooms are overpriced, at L75,000/110,000 for singles/doubles without bathroom. The *Albergo Mazzanti* (☎ 800 68 13), Via Mazzanti 6, just off Piazza dei Signori has singles/doubles for L50,000/73,000, or L77,000/115,000 with a bathroom. *Antica Porta Leona* (☎ 59 54 99),

Corticella Leoni 3, is an excellent hotel, just near Casa di Giulietta. Its lovely rooms cost L110,000/160,000.

Places to Eat

Known for its fresh produce, its crisp Soave (a dry white wine) and its boiled meat, Verona offers good eating at reasonable prices. The best bet for cheap meals is *Brek*, facing the Arena in Piazza Brà. Pasta starts at L5000 and the view across the piazza to the Arena is unbeatable. *Pizzeria Liston*, Via dietro Liston 19, near the Castelvecchio, has pizza with mascarpone cheese and rucola (rocket) for L8500.

The *Osteria al Duca*, Via Arche Scaligere 2, in the so-called Casa di Romeo (actually the former home of the Montecchi, one of the families on which Shakespeare's play is based), has a good set menu for L18,000. The *Bottega del Vino*, Vicolo Scudo di Francia 37, has pasta from L10,000. The frescoes are worth seeing. The excellent *Ristorante Maffei* in the Palazzo Maffei, Piazza delle Erbe 38, has pasta from L12,000 and main dishes from L20,000.

Try the small bar, *Birreria Mazzini*, Via Mazzini, near the Arena, which serves local wines for L1500 a glass and panini from L3000. Giovanni Zampieri's *wine bar* at Via Alberto Mario 23, near the Arena, has local wines from L800 a glass.

Entertainment

Throughout the year the city hosts musical and cultural events, culminating in the season of opera and drama from July to September at the Arena (tickets from L30,000). There is a programme of ballet and opera in winter at the 18th-century Teatro Filarmonico (☎ 800 28 80), Via dei Mutilati 4, just south of Piazza Brà, and Shakespeare is performed at the Roman theatre in summer. Information and tickets for these events are available at the Ente Lirico Arena di Verona (☎ 800 51 51), Piazza Brà 28.

Getting There & Away

Verona-Villafranca airport (☎ 51 30 39) is just outside the town and accessible by bus and train. Flights from all over Italy and some European cities arrive here. City buses depart for the airport from the bus station near Porta Nuova.

The main intercity bus station (☎ 800 41 29) is in the piazza in front of the train station, an area known as Porta Nuova. Buses leave for surrounding areas, Mantua, Ferrara and Brescia. By train, Verona is directly linked to Milan, Venice, Padua, Mantua, Modena, Florence, Rome, Austria and Germany. By car, the city is at the intersection of the Serenissima A4 (Milan-Venice) and Brennero A22 autostradas.

Getting Around

Buses No 11, 12, 13 and 72 (buses No 91 or 98 on Sundays and holidays) connect the train station with Piazza Brà, and bus No 70 with Piazza delle Erbe. Otherwise it's a 15 to 20-minute walk along Corso Porta Nuova. Cars are banned from the city centre in the mornings and early afternoon, but you will be given entry if you are staying at a hotel. If you do arrive by car, follow the 'Centro' signs, or the signs to your hotel. Free car parks are at Via Città di Nimes (near the train station), Porta Vescovo and Porta Palio, from where there are buses into the city centre. For a taxi, call ☎ 53 26 66.

VICENZA

This city is the centre for Italian textile manufacture and a leader in the development and production of computer components, making it one of the country's wealthiest cities. However, most tourists come to Vicenza to see the work of Andrea di Pietro della Gondola, better known as Palladio, whose designs have influenced architects worldwide. Vicenza flourished as the Roman Vicentia and in 1404 became part of the Venetian Republic, sharing the city's fortunes, as the many Venetian Gothic palaces demonstrate.

Orientation

From the train station, in the gardens of the Campo Marzo, walk straight ahead along Via Roma into Piazzale de Gasperi. From here, the main street, Corso Andrea Palladio, leads

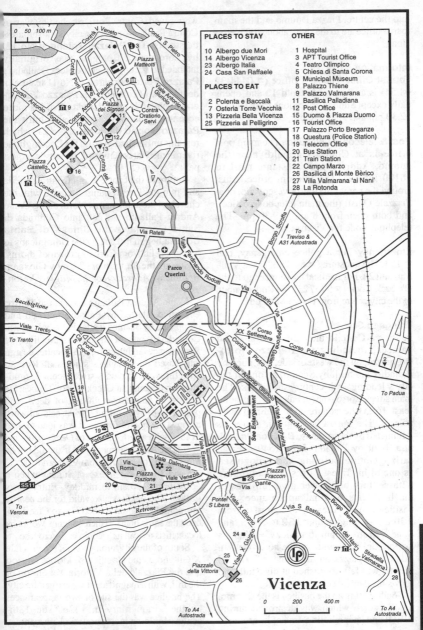

PLACES TO STAY

10 Albergo due Mori
14 Albergo Vicenza
23 Albergo Italia
24 Casa San Raffaele

PLACES TO EAT

2 Polenta e Baccalà
7 Osteria Torre Vecchia
13 Pizzeria Bella Vicenza
25 Pizzeria al Pelligrino

OTHER

1 Hospital
3 APT Tourist Office
4 Teatro Olimpico
5 Chiesa di Santa Corona
6 Municipal Museum
8 Palazzo Thiene
9 Palazzo Valmarana
11 Basilica Palladiana
12 Post Office
15 Duomo & Piazza Duomo
16 Tourist Office
17 Palazzo Porto Breganze
18 Questura (Police Station)
19 Telecom Office
20 Bus Station
21 Train Station
22 Campo Marzo
26 Basilica di Monte Bèrico
27 Villa Valmarana 'ai Nani'
28 La Rotonda

Vicenza

VENETO

into the centre. Piazza Duomo and the main tourist office are to the right, about 200 metres along.

Information

Tourist Office The APT office (☎ 0444-32 08 54) is at Piazza Matteotti 12 and opens daily except Sunday afternoons from 9 am to 12.30 pm and 2.30 to 6 pm.

Post & Telecommunications The main post office is at Contrà Garibaldi near the duomo. Address poste restante mail to 36100 Vicenza. The Telecom office is just around the corner in Contrà Vescovado, or at Piazzale Giusti (the main telephone office), and both open from 8 am to 9.30 pm. The telephone code for Vicenza is 0444.

Emergency For a police emergency, call ☎ 113. The questura (☎ 54 33 33) is at Viale Mazzini 24. For medical assistance, go to the Ospedale Civile (☎ 99 37 23), Via Rodolfi, north of the city centre from Piazza Matteotti.

Things to See

In Piazza Castello there are several grand palaces, including the **Palazzo Porto-Breganze**, on the western side, designed by Palladio and built by Scamozzi, one of the city's leading 16th-century architects. The main street, Corso Andrea Palladio, runs north-east from the square and is lined with palaces. The Piazza dei Signori, nearby, is dominated by the immense **Basilica Palladiana**, built by Palladio from 1549 over an earlier Gothic building and recognised as one of his finest works. The adjoining 12th-century bell tower gives an idea of the basilica's original appearance. The basilica is open Tuesday to Saturday from 9.30 am to midday and 2.30 to 5 pm, and Sunday from 10 am to midday. Palladio's **Loggia del Capitanio**, on the north-western side of the piazza on the corner of Via del Monte, was left unfinished at his death and shows his flair for colour.

South-west from the basilica is the **duomo**, a dull church which was destroyed during WW II and later rebuilt. Some of its artworks were saved. Contrà Porti, reached by way of Contrà Riale, is one of the city's most majestic streets. The **Palazzo Thiene** at No 12, by Lorenzo da Bologna, was originally intended to occupy the entire block. Palladio's **Palazzo Porto-Barbaran** at No 11 features a double row of columns. His **Palazzo Valmarana** at No 16 is considered one of his more eccentric creations, and he also built the **Palazzo Isoppo da Porto** at No 21, which remains unfinished. Across the Bacchiglione river is the **Parco Querini**, the city's largest park.

Return to the centre along Contrà Zanella and into the Piazza Santo Stefano, with the church of the same name. North along Corso Andrea Palladio and left into Contrada di Santa Corona is the **Chiesa di Santa Corona**, begun in 1261 by the Dominicans to house a relic from Christ's crown of thorns. Inside are the *Baptism of Christ* by Giovanni Bellini and *Adoration of the Magi* by Veronese.

Corso Andrea Palladio ends at the **Teatro Olimpico**, started by Palladio in 1580 and completed by Scamozzi after Palladio's death. Considered one of the purest creations of Renaissance architecture, the theatre design was based on Palladio's studies of Roman structures. Scamozzi's street scene is modelled on the ancient Greek city of Thebes. He created an impressive illusion of depth and perspective by slanting the streets upward towards the rear of the set. It was inaugurated in 1580 with a performance of *Oedipus Rex* and operas are still performed here. It should not be missed. It is open daily from 9.30 am to 12.30 pm and 3 to 5.30 pm, except Sunday when it opens from 9.30 am to midday. Entry costs L5000. The ticket is also valid for the nearby **Municipal Museum** in the Palazzo Chiericati, open the same hours, which contains works by local artists as well as Tiepolo and Veronese.

South of the city, along Via Dante or Viale X Giugno, is the **Basilica di Monte Bèrico** and the Piazzale della Vittoria, set on top of the hill, with a magnificent view over the city. The basilica was the site of two appearances by the Virgin Mary in 1426. The 18th-century building incorporates a 15th-century

Gothic church. An impressive 18th-century colonnade runs most of the way along Viale X Giugno to the church at the top of the hill. Catch city bus No 8.

A 10-minute walk back along Viale X Giugno is the **Villa Valmarana ai Nani**, featuring brilliant frescoes by Giambattista and Giandomenico Tiepolo. The 'ai nani' ('dwarves' in Italian) refers to the statues perched on top of the gates surrounding the property. The villa has very particular opening hours, which depend on the time of year. However, it is open every afternoon, except Monday, as well as Wednesday, Thursday, Saturday and Sunday mornings. Check at the tourist office for more information, or call ☎ 32 18 03. Entry costs L8000.

Signs mark the path to Palladio's Villa Capra, better known as **La Rotonda**. Considered one of the finest buildings ever constructed, the Rotonda is also one of the most copied, with architects using it as a base for Palladian buildings in Europe and the USA. The gardens are open Tuesday, Wednesday and Thursday from 10 am to midday and 3 to 6 pm, and the villa opens Wednesday from 10 am to midday and 3 to 6 pm. To visit on Friday, Saturday or Sunday call ☎ 32 17 93. Entry to the gardens is L5000, and L10,000 to the gardens and villa. Bus No 8 stops nearby.

Places to Stay

Many hotels close during the summer, particularly in August, so never arrive without a booking. At other times you should have no problems getting a room.

The closest camping, the *Campeggio Vicenza* (☎ 58 23 11), Strada Pelosa, is near the Vicenza Est exit from the A4. The city has a non-HI hostel, the *Madonna di Monte Berico* (☎ 54 38 30), Contrà San Marco 3. Bus Nos 4 and 9 will drop you off close by. A HI hostel is due to open by 1996. Check at the tourist office for details.

The *Albergo Italia* (☎ 32 10 43), Viale Risorgimento, near the train station, has singles/doubles with a bathroom for L50,000/80,000. The *Vicenza* (☎ 32 15 12), Stradella dei Nodari 5-7, near Piazza dei Signori, has rooms with a bathroom for L50,000/75,000. The *Albergo due Mori* (☎ 32 18 86), nearby at Contrà do Rode 26, has rooms for around the same price. One of the best choices is the *Casa San Raffaele* (☎ 32 36 63), Viale X Giugno 10, in a former convent behind the colonnade leading to Monte Berico, with singles/doubles with a bathroom for L52,000/75,000.

Places to Eat

A large produce market is held each Tuesday and Thursday in Piazza delle Erbe. *Vini al Chiampo*, Contrà Pescherie Vecchie near Piazza delle Erbe, is an old wine bar with cheap local wines. *Pizzeria Bella Vicenza*, Contrà dei Proti, has excellent pizzas from L8000, as does *Pizzeria al Pellegrino* at Piazzale della Vittoria. *Polenta e Baccalà*, Viale della Pace 7, is a trattoria where a meal could cost L25,000. *Osteria Torre Vecchia*, Contrà Oratorio dei Servi 23, serves good local dishes and a meal will cost over L35,000.

Entertainment

Concerts are held in summer at the Villa Valmarana ai Nani; check at the tourist office for details. For details about performances in the Teatro Olimpico, contact the APT or call ☎ 32 37 81.

Getting There & Away

FTV buses (☎ 54 43 33) leave from the bus station, just near the train station for Padua, Thiene, Asiago, Bassano, Verona and towns throughout the nearby Berici mountains. Trains (☎ 32 50 46) connect the city with Venice, Milan, Padua, Verona, Treviso and with smaller towns in the north. By car, the city is on the A4 connecting Milan with Venice. The SS11 connects the city with Verona and Padua, tand this is the best route for hitchhikers. There is a large car park near Piazza Castello and the train station.

Getting Around

The city is best seen on foot, but buses No 1, 2, 3 and 7 connect the train station with the city centre.

VENETO

AROUND VICENZA

As Venice's maritime power waned in the 15th century, the city's wealthy inhabitants turned their attention inland, acquiring land to build sumptuous villas (see also the Brenta Riviera section earlier in this chapter). Forbidden from building castles by the Venetian senate, which feared a landscape dotted with well-defended forts, the city's patricians set about building thousands of villas, of which about 3000 remain. Most are inaccessible to the public and many are run down.

The APT in Vicenza can provide reams of information about the villas, including a booklet entitled *Vicenza – the Villas*. The De Agostini map, *Ville Venete*, sells for about L7000 from newspaper stands and is one of the few complete maps. Drivers should have little trouble planning an itinerary. Otherwise, a good route is to take the FTV bus north from Vicenza to Thiene, passing through Caldogno and Villaverla, and then to continue on to Lugo.

The Villa Godi-Valmarana, now known as the **Malinverni**, at Lonedo di Lugo, was Palladio's first villa. A good driving itinerary is to take the SS11 through Montecchio Maggiore and continue south for Lonigo, Pojana Maggiore and then head north for Longare and back to Vicenza. A round trip of 100 km, the route takes in about a dozen villas.

There is an HI hostel a few km south of Pojana Maggiore at Montagnana, reached by bus from Vicenza, which enables you to plan a trip through the region (see the Around Padua section for details).

Check with the APT in Vicenza for details of the Concerti in Villa Estate, a series of classical concerts held in villas around Vicenza each summer. Also ask about accommodation, which is available in some villas.

TREVISO

A small, pleasant city with historical importance as a Roman centre, Treviso is worth a stopover when heading north for the Dolomites. However, the complete absence of one-star accommodation means there are no cheap rooms in the city. If you are able to pay higher rates, it can make a good base from which to see the smaller towns leading up into the Alps. It is an extremely prosperous town, and claims Luciano Benetton as its favourite son. The company's factories can be found around the city.

Information

The APT office (☎ 0422-54 76 32) is in the Palazzo Scotti, Via Toniolo 41, south of Piazza dei Signori along Via Santa Margherita. It opens Monday to Friday from 8.30 am to 12.30 pm and 3 to 6 pm, and Saturday to 1 pm. The telephone code is 0422.

Things to See & Do

The APT promotes Treviso as the *città d'acqua* (city of water) and compares it with Venice. While the Sile river, which weaves through the centre, is quite beautiful in parts, the city is not a patch on La Serenissima. Boat cruises on the *Silis* (☎ 78 86 63) and *Altino* (☎ 78 86 71) operate on the Sile between Treviso and the Venetian lagoon, but only in summer.

The city's other claim to fame as the *città dipinta* (frescoed city) is a little more worthy. Pick up a copy of *Treviso Città Dipinta* from the APT and follow the fresco itinerary, which takes in the **Cattedrale di San Pietro**, with frescoes by Pordenone, the **Chiesa di San Nicolò**, with frescoes by Tomaso da Modena, and the deconsecrated **Chiesa di Santa Caterina**, where there is a fresco cycle by Tomaso.

Places to Stay & Eat

The best accommodation options are at *Al Cuore* (☎ 41 09 29), Piazzale Duca d'Aosta, which has singles/doubles for L32,000/52,000, or L50,000/75,000 with a bathroom and also has a good, cheap restaurant, or the *Beccherie* (☎ 54 08 71), Piazza Ancillotto 10, with rooms for L35,000/60,000, or L70,000/95,000 with a bathroom. It also has a good restaurant, where a meal will cost around L40,000 per person. *Ristorante Al Dante*, Piazza Garibaldi 6, is one of the better budget options, with pasta from L8000.

Getting There & Away

The bus station (☎ 54 58 47) is at Lungosile Mattei, near the train station. Lamarca Trevigiani buses connect Treviso with towns throughout the province, while ACTV buses will get you to Venice. Trains (☎ 54 13 52) arrive at Piazzale Duca d'Aosta and connect the city with Venice, Belluno, Padua and major cities to the south and west. By car, the SS53 connects the city with Venice, Padua and the A27.

BELLUNO

Belluno is a beautiful little town at the foot of the Dolomites and makes a good base for exploring the mountains. It is worth a day trip from Venice either by train or bus and is also easily accessible from Treviso.

The tourist office, the Azienda di Promozione Turistica delle Prealpi e Dolomiti Bellunesi (☎ 0437-94 00 83), Via Rodolfo Psaro 21, produces a feast of information on walking, trekking, skiing and other sporting endeavours, and should be visited if you are planning to head into the Dolomites. The Comunità Montana Bellunese (☎ 0437-94 02 83), Via San Lucano 7, can assist with details on Alpine rifugi and mountain guides. The town's telephone code is 0437.

The *Camping Park Nevegal* (☎ 90 81 43), Via Nevegal 347, is about 10 km from the town at Nevegal and is reached by Autolinee Dolomiti bus from Belluno. The *Casa per Ferie Giovanni XXIII* (☎ 94 44 60), Piazza Piloni 11, near the centre of Belluno, has singles for L36,000 and only a few doubles for L62,000. The *Albergo Taverna* (☎ 2 51 92), Via Cipro 7, has singles/doubles for L30,000/60,000, while the three-star *Mirella* (☎ 94 18 60), Via Don Minzoni 6, has B&B for L55,000 per person or half board for L75,000 per person. Most of the town's restaurants are around the central Piazza dei Martiri.

Autolinee Dolomiti buses (☎ 94 12 37), Piazzale della Stazione, depart from the train station at the western edge of town for Agordo, Cortina d'Ampezzo, Feltre and smaller towns in the mountains and south of town. Trains (☎ 94 44 38) are less regular to northern towns but there are services to Cortina as well as to Treviso and Venice.

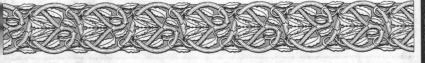

Friuli-Venezia Giulia

Made up of some of the last areas to join the Italian state after unification, Friuli-Venezia Giulia could be seen as a distant backwater – not a few of Rome's politicians see it just that way. The region marks the front line between the three great European cultural groupings, for it is here that the Latin, Slav and Germanic worlds have for centuries run

up against each other, more often than not violently.

Little more than a series of lagoons and flat wetlands along the Adriatic coast in the south, the Friulian plains and Giulian plateaux lead up to pine-covered Alps in the north. Roughly a square, the remaining three sides are sealed off by the Veneto in

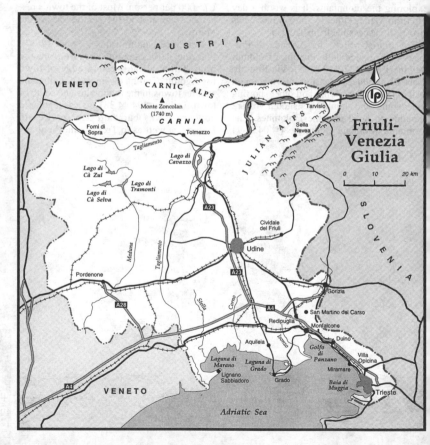

he west, Austria to the north and Slovenia n the east.

After Roman rule came the Visigoths, Attila's Huns, the Lombards and Charlemagne's Franks, each leaving their mark. The Patriarchate of Aquileia, formed in the second half of the 10th century, unified the local church and remained autonomous for several centuries. Parts of Friuli went to Venice in 1420, but he easternmost area, including Gorizia, was only briefly touched by the influence of La Serenissima (Venice). By 1797, the whole region had come under the Habsburg Austrians. Most of Friuli joined Italy in 1866, but it was not until after WW I that Gorizia, Trieste (in a roughly defined area known as the Giulia), Istria and Dalmatia were included – and at what cost. The Latin-Germanic-Slav triangle found its bloodiest expression in the trenches of WW I – Italy's 700,000 dead came from as far afield as Sardinia and Sicily, but they fell nearly to a man in what would subsequently become Friuli-Venezia Giulia.

After WW II Italy was obliged to cede Dalmatia and the Istrian peninsula to Tito's Yugoslavia in 1947, keeping Trieste. The Iron Curtain fell right through the frontier town of Gorizia. Road signs in the area around the town are even today in Italian and Slovene, and you can still stumble across the occasional Slovene monument to Yugoslav partisans along the back lanes of the province. The Slovene community is strong but feels, not without reason, that Rome pays little heed to its needs – for years there has been talk of bilingual education for Italian Slovenes, with no result. Relations between Italy and Slovenia are cordial at best, each side critical of the other's treatment of their respective Slovene and Italian minorities. Italy is also miffed that its eastern neighbour tends to turn north to Austria and Germany to expand trade rather than looking towards Rome.

Heading west from the frontier, the road signs are in Italian and Friulian. Udine is the heart of Friuli, and you can still hear the dialect spoken in some areas. The city itself bears the marks of Venetian intervention,

while Trieste is largely a neoclassical creation of Habsburg Austria.

The region is relatively unexplored, and its cities and towns are worth a few days of your time. You can mix urban culture with nature by heading for the Adriatic beaches, northern ski slopes or forest walking tracks.

TRIESTE

Sitting snugly between the Adriatic Sea and Slovenia, Trieste is an odd city. The faded grandeur of its largely homogeneous architecture is owed entirely to its days as the great southern port for the Austro-Hungarian empire in the 18th and 19th centuries. The city is a kind of microcosm of Western Europe's preoccupation – migrant pressure from east and south. What could be more incongruous, or more eloquent, than the sight of Croatian shoppers (bus and carloads flock to Trieste daily) bargaining fiercely with illegal Black African migrants hawking their wares in the streets?

Strangely attractive, although hardly strong on specific tourist sights, Trieste is not a bad place to end an Italian tour and embark on a foray into Eastern Europe – war in the former Yugoslavia permitting. The city closes down almost completely in August, including many restaurants and hotels.

History

Known in antiquity as Tergeste, a fortified settlement occupied by a succession of Venetian tribes, Gauls and Celts, Trieste grew to prominence under the Romans in the 2nd century BC as a port and trading centre. However, when the Romans founded Aquileia to the west, Trieste fell into an obscurity that was to last until the 18th century, when the Austrian empress Maria Theresa saw its potential as a port. Much of the city's medieval heart was levelled to make way for a new layer of neoclassical buildings. When Trieste became part of Italy in 1918, the government found the city no match for its ports to the south, and again it fell into decline.

Known as Trst to the Slavs, it has often been a bone of contention. Poet and ultranationalist Gabriele d'Annunzio launched some of his madcap escapades into Yugoslavia from here after WW I, and in 1945 the Allies occupied it pending settlement of Italy's border disputes with Belgrade. They only left in 1954. Today, traffic through the port is growing, although its main purpose is as an unloading point for the massive oil tankers supplying a pipeline to Austria.

Orientation
The train and bus stations are at the northern edge of Trieste's historic centre, in Piazza della Libertà. Head straight south along any main street and you'll be in the grid of the 18th-century Borgo Teresiano, where several budget hotels are located, as well as plenty of bars and restaurants. South of the grid (about a 20-minute walk from the train station) is the Castello di San Giusto on a hill dominating the city. The main museums are a little farther south-west, while the principal shopping boulevards stretch east off Via Giosue Carducci.

Information
Tourist Office The APT office (☎ 040-42 01 82) at the train station, is open Monday to Friday from 9 am to 7 pm and Saturday to 2 pm. The main tourist office is at Via San Niccolò 20, but its opening hours are shorter. There is also a small information booth at Stazione Marittima.

Money There is no shortage of banks. Branches of the Banca Nazionale del Lavoro have ATMs that accept Visa. There are exchange booths at the train and bus stations and Stazione Marittima. The former two are open daily from 9 am to 7 pm.

Post & Telecommunications The main post office is at Piazza Vittorio Veneto. It is open Monday to Saturday from 8 am to 7 pm. The post code is 34100.

The Telecom office is at Via Pascoli 9, near Piazza Garibaldi, and is open 24 hours a day. There is another telephone office at the train station. The telephone code for Trieste is 040.

Foreign Consulates The British Consulate (☎ 30 28 84) is at Vicolo delle Ville 16. The USA has a consular agency (☎ 66 01 77) at Via Roma 15. France (☎ 36 69 68) is represented at Via Einaudi 3. The Federal Republic of Yugoslavia (☎ 41 01 25) has a consulate at Strada Friuli 54 and Slovenia (☎ 63 61 61) is represented at Via Giosue Carducci 29.

Travel Agencies CTS (☎ 36 18 79), Piazza Dalmazia 3, can advise on travel to the former Yugoslavia.

Emergency & Medical Services For a police emergency, call ☎ 113. The questura (☎ 37 901) is at Via Tor Bandena 6.

The Ospedale Maggiore (☎ 3 99 11) is in Piazza dell'Ospedale, south-east of Via Giosue Carducci. Call ☎ 192 for the location of the nearest 24-hour pharmacy. For an ambulance, call ☎ 118.

Colle di San Giusto
With commanding views across the city and out to sea, this hill is topped by a rambling 15th-century **castle**, largely rebuilt over earlier fortifications by the city's Venetian rulers from 1470 on. Apart from wandering around the walls, you can visit the **museum**, which houses a small collection of arms and period paraphernalia. Entry to the castle site costs L1000, and it is open from 8 am to sunset. Entry to the museum costs L2000, and it is open Tuesday to Sunday from 9 am to 1 pm.

The **Basilica di San Giusto**, completed in 1400, is the synthesis of two earlier Christian basilicas and blends northern Adriatic and Byzantine styles. The interior contains 14th-century frescoes depicting St Justus, the town's patron saint. Down the road a little, the **Civico Museo di Storia e Arte** has religious artefacts and Egyptian oddments and opens daily except Monday from 9 am to 1 pm. Entrance is L2000. The **Orto Lapidario** (Stone Garden), behind the museum, has a collection of bits of classical statues and pottery.

Bus No 24 connects the hill with the Stazione Centrale train station, or you can

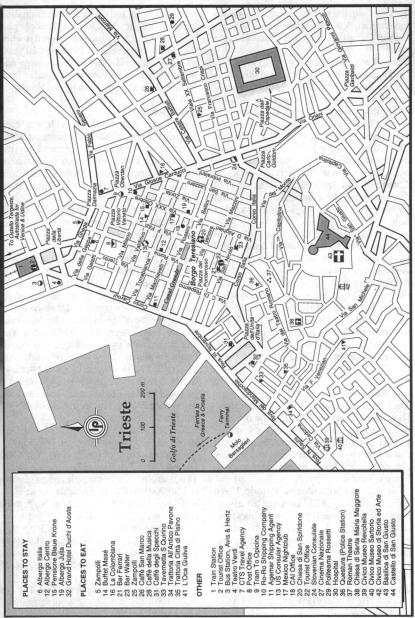

PLACES TO STAY
6 Albergo Italia
12 Albergo Centro
15 Pensione Blaue Krone
19 Albergo Julia
32 Grand Hotel Duchi d'Aosta

PLACES TO EAT
5 Zampolli
14 Buffet Masé
16 La Colombiana
21 Bar Ferrari
23 Bar Walter
25 Zampolli
26 Caffè San Marco
28 Caffè della Musica
31 Caffè degli Specchi
33 Tavernetta S Quirino
34 Trattoria All'Antico Pavone
35 Trattoria Città di Pisino
41 L'Oca Giuliva

OTHER
1 Train Station
2 Tourist Office
3 Bus Station, Avis & Hertz
4 Teatro Verdi
7 CTS Travel Agency
9 Post Office
10 Tram To Opicina
11 Ro-Ro Shipping Company
13 Agemar Shipping Agent
13 US Consular Agency
17 Mexico Nightclub
18 CAI Office
20 Chiesa di San Spiridone
22 Tourist Office
24 Slovenian Consulate
27 Cinema Nazionale
29 Politeama Rossetti
30 Hospital
36 Questura (Police Station)
37 Roman Theatre
38 Chiesa di Santa Maria Maggiore
39 Civico Museo Revoltella
40 Civico Museo Sartorio
42 Civico Museo di Storia ed Arte
43 Basilica di San Giusto
44 Castello di San Giusto

Trieste

Golfo di Trieste

Ferries to
Greece & Croatia

Ferry
Terminal

Molo
Bersaglieri

To Ostello Tergeste,
Autostrada for
Venice & Udine

Borgo Teresiano

0   100   200 m

walk up from the waterfront area, taking Via F Venezian, Via San Michele and Via San Giusto. Car access is by Via Capitolina.

Borgo Teresiano Area

Going back down Via Capitolina you come to Corso Italia, the main business thoroughfare. The area of straight boulevards to the north, known as the Borgo Teresiano, was designed by Austrian urban planners in the 18th century for Empress Maria Theresa. The rather pathetic-looking Canal Grande runs through this area and marks the northern end of the harbour. The Serbian Orthodox **Chiesa di San Spiridione**, on the street of the same name, was completed in 1868. With its glittering mosaics, it is one of a kind in Italy.

At its southern end, Corso Italia spills into the grand **Piazza dell'Unità d'Italia** edged by the most elegant buildings, the results of Austrian town-planning efforts.

Farther in from the waterfront, and also accessible off Corso Italia, is Via del Teatro Romano. Built under Emperor Trajan and only rediscovered in 1938, the **Roman theatre** is today in poor condition. The nearby Baroque **Chiesa di Santa Maria Maggiore** is one of Trieste's finest churches.

Museums

The city's chief museum, the **Civico Museo Revoltella**, is at Via Diaz 27. The museum and art gallery are worth seeing, but visits are guided. Technically open from 10 am to 1 pm and 3 to 6 pm (closed Tuesday and Sunday afternoon), the hours in fact seem erratic. Entry is L2000.

Nearby, the **Civico Museo Sartorio**, Largo Papa Giovanni XXIII, contains an assortment of 19th-century furnishings and decorative art of the period. It's open daily, except Monday from 9 am to 1 pm, and entry is L2000.

Risiera di San Sabba

This was a rice-husking plant at the southern end of Trieste on Via Valmaura. In 1943 the Germans built a crematorium here and turned it into Italy's only exterminatior camp. It is believed that 20,000 people perished here. Yugoslav partisans closed it wher they liberated the city in 1945, and 20 years later it became a national monument and museum. It is open Tuesday to Sunday from 9 am to 1 pm. You get there by bus No 10.

Activities

The APT runs a walking tour (in Italian) each Sunday starting at Stazione Marittima, Molo Bersaglieri 3 – check beforehand for the latest times and prices. Also on Sundays, local boat operators run harbour tours from just opposite Piazza dell'Unità d'Italia from L5000 a person.

The CAI (☎ 36 90 67), Via Machiavelli 17 can advise on walking and skiing in the region.

Places to Stay

Finding a room is generally easy, although in August many hotels close. Note that the cheaper places can fill with Croatians in town on shopping sprees. The closest camping ground to the city centre is *Obelisco* (☎ 2 16 55) on the SS58 in Villa Opicina. Take bus No 2 or No 4 from Piazza Oberdan. The *San Bartolomeo* (☎ 27 41 82), Lazzaretto di Punta Sottile, at Muggia, can be reached by bus No 7. The HI *Ostello Tergeste* (☎ 22 41 02), Viale Miramare 331, is five km from the train and bus stations towards Venice and can be reached by bus No 36. B&B is L17,000 and it opens all year.

The *Albergo Centro* (☎ 63 44 08), Via Roma 13, has rooms from L30,000/55,000. There are a couple of places along Via XXX Ottobre. The *Pensione Blaue Krone* (☎ 63 18 82), at No 12, offers simple rooms starting at L30,000/40,000. In much the same class is *Albergo Julia* (☎ 37 00 45) at No 5, with rooms for L29,000/46,000.

The two-star *Albergo Italia* (☎ 36 99 00), Via della Geppa 15, has rooms from L97,000/130,000. To do it in style, try the *Grand Hotel Duchi d'Aosta* (☎ 73 51 at Piazza dell' Unità d'Italia.

Ask at the APT about 'T For You', a weekend discount deal involving some of the city's better hotels.

Places to Eat

Friulian cuisine has been influenced by many cultures but poverty has contributed most. One typical dish, *brovada*, could see you eating turnips fermented with the dregs of pressed grapes. Otherwise gnocchi (potato, pumpkin or bread dumplings) is popular, as are polenta and boiled meats, eaten in restaurants called *buffets*. Wines from the eastern hills of Friuli, stretching from near the city on the border up into the Alps, are considered the region's best. Finish dinner with a *resentin*, coffee in a cup rinsed with grappa.

One restaurant with a deliberately Germanic ambience is the *Buffet Masé*, Via Valdirivo 32, where you can wash down a plate of German sausage with a huge mug of Munich lager. This cosy place is perfect on a freezing winter night.

If you get hungry when you're in the Castello area, head for *L'Oca Giuliva*, Via Venezian 27, where L20,000 should ensure a good feed. The *Trattoria All'Antico Pavone*, Via Cadorna 14a, has pasta from L10,000.

Closer to Piazza dell'Unità d'Italia, there are a few places worth a look. *Tavernetta S Quirino*, Via A Diaz 3B, has something of the atmosphere of a small English pub, and you can get cheap modest meals. The surrounding area is traditional fishers' territory, as some of the street names suggest. Try the *Osteria da Giulio*, Via del Pesce 1b, for seafood, or the nearby *Trattoria Città di Pisino*, Via Alberto Boccardi 7c.

Cafés & Bars Triestini take their coffee seriously. The elegant *Caffè San Marco*, Via Cesare Battisti 18, and *Caffè Tommaseo*, Piazza Tommaseo, take you straight into the elegant central European world of newspapers and *kaffeeklatsch* (a chat over coffee or tea). Or you could reflect instead in the *Caffè degli Specchi* on Piazza dell'Unità d'Italia 7. Coffee-lovers might want to head for *La Colombiana* on Via Giosue Carducci, where you can buy all kinds of the roasted bean to make your own coffee.

Bars are an odd mix, some reflecting a standard Italian model and others feeling more like the beer houses of Mitteleuropa. They are not bad for snacks – *Bar Walter* and *Bar Ferrari* on Via San Nicolò are decent.

For gelati, you can't go past *Zampolli*, Viale XX Settembre 25, which turns out ice-cream creations shaped like pasta and meat dishes. They look bad, but taste great. They have another outlet at Via Ghega 10.

Entertainment

The Teatro Verdi (☎ 36 78 16), Piazza Libertà, is the main venue for the city's opera, while the Politeama Rossetti (☎ 56 72 01), Viale XX Settembre 45, is the principal stage for drama. Most of the nightclubs are pretty tacky but the Mexico, Via XXX Ottobre 4, is bearable. The Buffet Masé (see the Places to Eat section) has live music on Saturday nights.

Getting There & Away

Air Some international flights and domestic flights to Rome, Genoa and southern Italy land at Ronchi dei Legionari international airport (☎ 0481-77 32 25) on Via Aquileia.

Bus All national and international buses operate from the bus station (☎ 37 01 60) at Via Gioia 2, off Piazza della Libertà. Autolinee Triestine (☎ 42 50 20) and Saita (☎ 42 50 01) operate services to Udine, Gorizia, Duino, Cividale del Friuli, Venice, Genoa and places in Slovenia and Croatia.

Train The train station (☎ 41 82 07) in Piazza della Libertà handles trains to Gorizia, Udine, Pordenone, Mestre and main cities to the east and in the south. There are regular trains to Zagreb (Croatia) and less regular trains to Slovenia and Budapest (Hungary).

Car & Motorbike Trieste is at the end of the A4 (to Venice and Milan) and connects with the A23 to Austria. The SS14 follows the coast and connects the city with Venice. It continues into Slovenia, as does the SS15.

Avis (☎ 42 15 21) and Hertz (☎ 42 21 22) have offices at the bus station if you want to rent a car.

Boat Agemar (☎ 36 40 64), Via Rossini 2, is a good place to enquire about ferries to Greece, Croatia and Albania. Anek Lines runs a summer service to Patras, Igoumenitsa and Corfu, leaving once or twice a week. Adriatica normally has twice-weekly runs to Durrés, Albania, but these may be suspended. When the ferries are running it costs L155,000 one way in high season. In summer, Adriatica runs motorboats to Lignano and Grado, as well as a couple of spots on the Croatian coast.

Getting Around

A bus runs from the bus station in Piazza della Libertà to the airport at regular intervals.

ACT (☎ 7 79 51) operates buses throughout the city. Bus No 30 connects the train station with Via Roma and the waterfront, while Bus No 24 goes to the Castello di San Giusto. There are services to Miramare and Villa Opicina.

Taxi Radio Trieste (☎ 30 77 30) or Autotassametri Cooperativa Alabarda (☎ 5 45 33) are the main taxi companies.

AROUND TRIESTE

About seven km north-west of Trieste is the **Castello Miramare**, a grand white castle in a commanding position on the coastline. It was ordered built by Archduke Maximilian of Austria in the mid-19th century, but he never occupied it. After a brief stint as emperor of Mexico for Napoleon III, he was executed by the Mexicans in 1867. His widow, Carlotta, who remained at the castle, went mad, and it was subsequently rumoured that anyone spending a night at Miramare would come to a bad end. In summer you can see a sound and light show (*suoni e lumi*) recreating all of this. Take bus No 36 from Trieste, or the train.

Villa Opicina, five km from Trieste, boasts the **Grotta Gigante**, the world's largest accessible cave. The interior is spotlit with coloured globes, and the 90-metre-high cavern is worth the effort it takes to get there. Take the Villa Opicina tram from Piazza Oberdan to Villa Opicina and then the No 45 bus. In summer buy a biglietto cumulativo for L11,000, which includes the bus and tram tickets and the entrance fee. Out of season you'll have to pay separately for the transport and admission to the cave. Opening hours in summer are daily from 9 am to noon and 2 to 7 pm; in winter opening hours are reduced.

Several monuments to soldiers who died in WW 1 were built in the Il Carso heights area in the 1930s. The **Redipuglia memorial** contains the remains of more than 100,000 dead and is as sobering a reminder of the idiocy of war as any of the WW I monuments littered across Europe. There is a museum there, and a couple of km north an Austro-Hungarian war cemetery. The area is sprinkled with other monuments, including one on **Monte di San Michele**, the scene of particularly bloody encounters (you can wander the battlefield today), and the **Sacrario di Olsavia**, north of Gorizia. Redipuglia can be reached by bus or train from Trieste. Your own transport is the best bet for the other sites, which are in any case of less interest.

GORIZIA

That strangely un-Italian feeling you may have picked up elsewhere in Friuli-Venezia Giulia is no more evident than in Gorizia – right on the frontier of the Latin and Slav worlds, and with a long history of Germanic/Austrian tutelage. Most locals speak Italian and Slovenian, many road signs are in both languages, Austrian-style café culture (lots of rustling newspapers) rules and not a few of the GO number plates are from Nova Gorica, that post-WW II creation over the border. Only a short train or bus ride from Trieste or Udine, it is an interesting and quirky place and a stop worth making.

History

Settled before the arrival of the Romans, the hilltop castle and surrounding town were always on the periphery of someone else's empire – Roman, Holy Roman and, from the early 16th century, that of the Austrian Habsburgs. Apart from a brief spell under Venice, Gorizia first came under Italian control after WW I. In the wake of the next war, Italy and Yugoslavia finally agreed to draw a line through the city in 1947, leaving most of the old city in Italian hands, and spurring Tito's followers to erect the soulless Nova Gorica on the other side.

Information
The helpful APT (☎ 0481-53 38 70) is at Via A Diaz 16. The main post office is on the corner of Corso Verdi and Via Oberdan. The Telecom office, at Via Crispi 7, is open daily from 9 am to 10 pm. The telephone code is 0481.

Borgo Castello
Gorizia's main sight is the castle itself, the original nucleus of the town. It has undergone several transformations and was restored in the 1920s after suffering serious damage in WW I. Occasional exhibitions are held there, and it makes a pleasant excursion.

It is open Tuesday to Sunday from 9.30 am to 12.30 pm and 2 to 5 pm. Entry costs L5000.

There is a small **war museum** about 50 metres away, downhill a bit, but you need Italian to benefit from the explanations. It opens Tuesday to Sunday from 10 am to 1 pm and 3 to 5 pm. Entrance is L3000.

Churches
The most outstanding of the churches is **Sant'Ignazio** on Piazza della Vittoria. You can't miss the onion-shaped domes – another sign that you're in Mitteleuropa. The little 14th-century **Chiesa di Santo Spirito**, by the castle, is also worth a quick look.

Nova Gorica
It's a hoot to hop across into Slovenia for a brief look at the post-Tito republic. There's nothing much to see, but the difference between the two places has its own fascination, and you may want to visit the **Kostanjevica monastery**, the burial place of the last of the French branch of the Bourbon royal family. You can walk or drive across at several points – formalities are minimal, but have your passport handy.

Places to Stay & Eat
The *Albergo Sandro* (☎ 52 08 03), Via Santa Chiara 18, has good singles/doubles with bathroom for L42,000/63,000. There are a couple of good little trattorie in the centre of the old town below the castle.

Getting There & Away
Trains and buses connect with Trieste and Udine. Buses also run to Nova Gorica, from

---

Italy in WW I
The wanton spilling of young blood in the fight for a few cm of ground during WW I was not restricted to the killing fields of France and Russia. From May 1915, Italy decided to join the massacre, hoping to end the campaign begun the century before by booting Austria off 'Italian' soil. The price of this folly to a nation barely 50 years old was 700,000 dead and more than a million wounded.

The main Italian front stretched from the Alps to the Adriatic Sea through Friuli and the Giulia, and Italy made substantial gains in its first offensive – approaching Gorizia (which did not fall until the following year) and advancing as far as Caporetto in the north (in modern Slovenia). From then on, typical trench warfare set in, with neither side making much progress. Some of the toughest fighting took place on the Carso Heights between Trieste and Gorizia, and the Isonzo river soon had the impact on the Italians that the Somme had on the Allies in France. In October 1917 disaster struck when the Austro-Hungarians crushed the Italians at Caporetto (Italians don't meet their Waterloo, they 'have a Caporetto'), pretty much throwing them back to their 1915 starting lines, where they hung on grimly until the collapse of the Central Powers the following year. ∎

where you can get buses all over Slovenia. The bus station is on Via IX Agosto, off Corso Italia, while the train station is about a km south-west of the centre at Piazzale Martiri Libertà d'Italia, at the end of Corso Italia.

A branch of the A4 starts just south of Gorizia. The SS56 connects the town to Udine. From Trieste you can take the SS14 and from Monfalcone the SS55 to avoid toll roads.

AQUILEIA

Once the fourth city of the Roman Empire, Aquileia was founded in 181 BC. Dubbed the 'Second Rome' within 100 years, the city was a major trading link between the imperial capital and the East. At the beginning of the Christian era, Aquileia was the richest market town in Italy and subordinate only to Rome, Milan and Capua. A patriarchate was founded here as early as the 4th century AD, and in spite of repeated assaults by Huns, Lombards and others, Aquileia's religious importance ensured it a privileged position until as late as the 14th century – the 4th-century mosaics in the town's Romanesque basilica are quite extraordinary.

What is a now a small town lies at the eastern end of the Venetian plains, and the local dialect is a good measure of the influence the expanding Venetian republic was to have on Aquileia. The modern town is tiny and easily navigated.

Information

The APT office (☎ 0431-9 10 87), Piazza Capitolo 4, opens daily from April 1 to November 1. The telephone code is 0431.

Things to See

Head straight for the **basilica**, largely rebuilt after the 1348 earthquake. Under the original floor was discovered that of its 4th-century predecessor – a precious and rare pictorial document of Christianity's early days, made up of mosaics depicting episodes in Christ's life, Roman notables and animal scenes. The basilica is open daily from 9 am to 12.30 pm and 2.30 to 5.30 pm. You can climb to the top of the bell tower, erected in 1030, for L1000.

There are various remains of the **Roman town**, including ruins of the one-time river port (*porto fluviale*), forum, houses and markets – don't get too excited though; the offerings are modest.

Visit the **Distilleria Aquileia**, Via Julia Augusta 87A, where you can sample local products (for free), and view the grappa-making process.

Places to Stay

Camping Aquileia (☎ 9 10 42 in summer and ☎ 9 10 37 in winter), at Via Gemina 10, is the most affordable. The *Albergo Aquila Nera* (☎ 9 10 45), Piazza Garibaldi 5, has rooms starting from L25,000/45,000.

Getting There & Away

The town is only a short distance from Trieste and Udine. There are regular buses (on the way to Grado) or trains to Cervignano to the north (local buses connect with the trains). The SS352 heads north towards Udine and south to Grado.

GRADO

About 14 km south of Aquileia, Grado is a not unpleasant Adriatic beach resort, spread out along a narrow island backed by lagoons. The small medieval town centre, criss-crossed by narrow calles (Venetian for lane), is a bright little spot dominated by a Romanesque **basilica** and surrounded by cheery, tumbledown houses. For centuries the townspeople have made their living by fishing, a vocation they have not yet abandoned in spite of beachside tourism.

The APT office (☎ 0431-89 91) is at Viale Dante Alighieri 72. Grado is a day trip by bus from Udine or Trieste, but if you want to stay in summer, book ahead. There are several camp sites and 86 hotels, many of which close in winter. *Albergo Zuberti* (☎ 0431-8 01 96), Piazza Carpaccio 25, is one of the cheapest hotels open all year. Rooms start at L35,000/70,000.

LIGNANO

Lignano is pure resort, dispensing with the trappings of old town centres. Lying on the tip of a peninsula facing the lagoon to the north and the Adriatic Sea to the south, Lignano Sabbiadoro is the main town of the area. The water here and in the neighbouring resorts is generally clean, and is about all there is of interest. The APT office (☎ 0431-7 18 21), Via Latisana 42, at Lignano Sabbiadoro, can assist with hotels and camping grounds, most of which fill during summer.

UDINE

The region's second-largest city, Udine's topsy-turvy history has left it heir to an oddly mixed Italian, Slavic and Germanic culture. At the heart of Friuli, some inhabitants still speak the local dialect.

Imperial Rome founded Udine as a way-station. By the early 15th century, when it first came under Venetian control, it had grown into a substantial city to rival nearby Cividale and Aquileia. It is the Venetian influence that most strikes the eye in the town's bright medieval centre. Napoleon's lieutenants briefly took control of Udine at the beginning of the 19th century, before it fell under an Austrian domination which lasted until 1866, when it joined the Italian kingdom. The city survived WW II intact, but an earthquake in 1976 caused heavy damage and cost hundreds of lives. The great Renaissance painter Giambattista Tiepolo lived in Udine for many years, leaving a number of works behind, notably in the Duomo.

Orientation

The train station is on Viale Europa Unità at the southern edge of the old city centre. Walk along Via Roma, through Piazza Repubblica and along Via Carducci for the Duomo. An alternative route from Piazza Repubblica is to veer to the left along Via Dante and continue to Piazza della Libertà. The massive Piazza I Maggio is to the north-east.

Information

Tourist Office The APT office (☎ 29 59 72), Piazza I Maggio 7, opens Monday to Friday from 9 am to 1 pm and 3 to 5 pm, and Saturday to noon. It produces a good city map and a booklet, *Udine Il Giracittà*, featuring walking-tour itineraries. It has lots of information on the rest of the region too.

Money The Banca Commerciale Italiana is centrally located in Piazza del Duomo, and there are plenty of other banks scattered through the city centre.

Post & Telecommunications The main post office is at Via Vittorio Veneto 42 and opens Monday to Saturday from 8.15 am to 7.30 pm. Poste restante mail can be addressed to 33100 Udine.

The Telecom office is at Via Savorgnana 15. It is open daily from 9 am to 9.30 pm, and staffed Monday to Friday from 9 am to 12.30 pm and 4 to 7.30 pm. The telephone code for Udine is 0432.

Gay & Lesbian Information Arci Gay (☎ 51 33 11) is at Via Manzoni 42.

Emergency For a police emergency, call ☎ 113. The castle (☎ 59 41) is at Via D Prefettura 16. For medical attention, go to the Ospedale Civile (☎ 55 21), north of the city centre in Piazza Santa Maria della Misericordia, or call an ambulance on ☎ 118.

Piazza della Libertà

A gem of the Renaissance, Piazza della Libertà lies at the heart of the old town, and most sights of historical interest are clustered on or near it.

The 15th-century Palazzo del Comune (town hall), also known as the **Loggia del Lionello** after its architect, is a clear reminder of Venetian influence, as is the **Loggia di San Giovanni** opposite, featuring a clock with Moorish figures that strike the hours – similar to the Mori of Venice's Torre dell'Orologio.

Clock tower of Loggia di San Giovanni

Castle

The **Arco Bollani** next to the Loggia di San Giovanni was designed by Palladio in 1556 and leads up to the **castle**, which was used by the Venetian governors. It now houses the **Galleria d'Arte Antica** with an extensive art collection including works by Caravaggio, Carpaccio and Tiepolo, and the **Museo Archeologico**. The complex is open Tuesday to Sunday from 9.30 am to 12.30 pm and 3 to 6 pm, and entrance is L4000. Also on the hill is the 12th-century **Chiesa di Santa Maria del Castello**, which originally stood within the walls of the medieval castle.

Duomo Area

Down Via Vittorio Veneto from Piazza della Libertà you reach the Piazza del Duomo and the 13th-century Romanesque-Gothic **Duomo**, with several frescoes by Tiepolo. The **Museo del Duomo**, in the bell tower, contains other frescoes by Viale da Bologna and opens Wednesday, Thursday and Saturday from 9 am to midday. To the right of the Duomo is the **Oratorio della Purità**, with a beautiful ceiling painting of the *Assumption* by Tiepolo. At the time of writing, the museum and much of the church were inaccessible due to restoration work.

North-east of Piazza del Duomo is the **Palazzo Arcivescovile** (Archbishop's Palace) on Piazza Patriarcato, where Tiepolo completed a remarkable series of frescoes depicting Old Testament scenes. The palace supposedly opens Monday to Friday from 9 am to midday, but check with the APT. Entry is free.

South of Piazza del Duomo on Via B Odorico, the 13th-century **Chiesa di San Francesco**, although once one of Udine's most striking churches, is now used as a gallery.

Galleries

The **Galleria d'Arte Moderna**, Piazzale P Diacono 22, features a wide selection of well-known 20th-century art and also displays works by modern Friulian artists. It opens from 9.30 am to 12.30 pm and 3 to 6 pm, but is closed Sunday afternoon and all day Monday. Entry is L4000, but free on Sunday mornings.

Places to Stay

Udine has no youth hostel or camping ground, and many cheap hotels can fill with workers. A map outside the train station pinpoints all hotels. The *Albergo da Brando* (☎ 50 28 37), Piazzale Cella 16, west of the station, is the cheapest, charging L20,000 per person. The *Albergo Al Vecchio Tram* (☎ 50 25 16), Via Brenari 32, near Piazza Garibaldi, has decent rooms from L30,000/50,000.

Pensione Al Fari (☎ 52 07 32), south of the train station at Via Melegnano 41, is more comfortable but in something of a residential backwater. Singles/doubles/triples cost L36,000/55,000/62,000.

More atmospheric is the *Albergo Piccolo Friuli* (☎ 50 78 17), Via Magrini 9, west of Piazza della Libertà, which has singles/doubles with bathroom and telephone in a centuries-old building for L50,000/70,000. *Albergo Clocchiatti* (☎ 50 50 47) is east of the city centre at Via Cividale 29, and charges the same.

The *Hotel Vienna* (☎ 29 44 46), Viale Europa Unita 47, is almost opposite the train station and has singles/doubles from

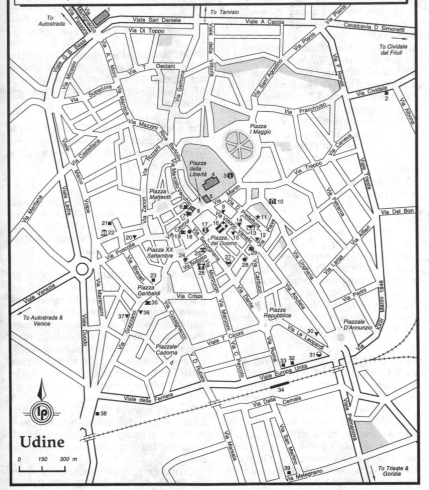

Udine

0   150   300 m

L80,000/100,000. The *Hotel Principe* (☎ 50 60 00) next door has singles/doubles starting from L85,000/120,000.

Places to Eat

Don't wait too late to eat out, as the city seems to shut down pretty early, especially during the week – no Latin excitement in the streets here. Things are generally pretty quiet by 9 pm.

The city has a vegetarian restaurant, the *Circolo ENDAS Risveglio* (☎ 29 72 43), Via Aquileia 103, open for lunch and dinner, although a reservation is required for dinner. *Ai Portici*, Via Veneto 10, behind the Duomo, is a snack bar/restaurant where pasta starts at L7000. The *Trattoria Vecchia Pescheria*, Piazza XX Settembre, is a weird combination of traditional pizzeria and Chinese restaurant.

Via Grazzano is not a bad place to look. The *Spaghetteria da Ciccio* at No 18 does cheap, filling meals in a cosy atmosphere. Another one along here is the almost hidden *All'Allegria*, at No 11, which stays open comparatively late and serves local cuisine – count on spending about L35,000 a head.

Otherwise, the *Enoteca Aquila Nera*, on the corner of Via Vittoria Veneto and Via Piave, does a cheap tavola calda that you can wash down with a broad selection of wine. Across Via Vittorio Veneto, the *Bar Odeon* is a popular place open for snacks and meals until quite late. Another cosy option is the *Trattoria al Lepre*, Via Poscolle 29b. A good lunch spot is the sandwich place at Via Vittorio Veneto 27.

Cafés & Bars The 'in' crowd hangs out at *Caffè Contarena*, Via Cavour 1a, but for an Austrian-style mood and a good read of the newspaper day or night, head to *Caffè Delser*, Via Cavour 18a. The Nuovo Caffè Commercio, across the road, is also popular. The Germanic influence is clearly visible in the city's sweets; for great cakes and a coffee, try *Pasticceria Carli di L Fogoletto*, Via Vittorio Veneto 36, in a building dating from 1392. For a tipple, you could do worse than *Bar Bubulco* on the corner of Vicolo Repetella and Via Grazzano.

Getting There & Away

Bus The bus station (☎ 50 69 41) is opposite the train station, slightly to the east. Ferrari (☎ 50 40 12) operates services to smaller towns in the north of the region and to Trieste and Lignano. Saita (☎ 50 24 63) also serves Trieste and Grado. More distant destinations include Belluno, Padua, Venice, Bolzano and even Taranto. CSAD runs buses to Bratislava in Slovakia via Tarvisio.

Train The train station (☎ 50 36 56) is on the main Trieste-Venice train line and services are regular. Connections can be made to Milan and beyond as well as to Vienna and Salzburg.

Car & Motorbike The A23 passes the city to the west. It connects the A4 with Austria. For hitchhikers, the SS56 leads to Trieste and the SS13 to Austria.

Getting Around

The train and bus stations are a few minutes from the city centre, but all ATM buses (☎ 50 30 45) pass outside it. Take bus No 1 or No 3 for Piazza del Duomo. Radiotaxi (☎ 50 58 58) serves the city all hours.

CIVIDALE DEL FRIULI

A trip to Cividale del Friuli is a must if you make it to Udine. One of the most picturesque towns in the region, Cividale has a well-preserved, if small, medieval centre, which has survived several devastating earthquakes. Julius Caesar founded the town in 50 BC and in the 6th century it became the seat of the first Lombard duchy. About 200 years later, its growing reputation drew the patriarch of Aquileia to the town.

The APT office (☎ 0432-73 13 98) at Largo Boiani 4 has information about the town, the Natisone valley and walking in several parks and the mountains to the north and east.

Cividale is at its most picturesque where the **Ponte del Diavolo** (Devil's Bridge) crosses the emerald green Natisone river. Take a walk through the cobbled lanes to the **Tempietto Longobardo**, on Borgo Brossano. This 'little temple', is also known as the Oratorio di Santa Maria in Valle, was rebuilt after a 13th-century earthquake, and is an exquisite example of Lombard artwork. It's open daily from 10 am to 1 pm and 3.30 to 5.30 pm (an hour longer in summer). Entry is L2000. The **Duomo**, to the west, is not the most engaging cathedral you'll ever see, but you can continue exploring the Lombard theme in the tiny museum – the centrepiece is the Altar of Ratchis, a magnificent example of 8th-century Lombard sculpture. Opening hours are 9.30 am to noon and 3 to 6 pm (7 pm in summer) daily.

The town has only three hotels, the cheapest of them the *Albergo Pomo d'Oro* (☎ 0432-73 14 89), Piazza San Giovanni 20, has singles/doubles for L50,000/80,000.

Trains and buses connect the town with Udine and Trieste, or you can drive the 17 km from Udine on the SS54.

CARNIA

North of Udine, the Friulian lowlands gradually give way to Alpine country on the way to Austria. Known generically as the Carnia which settled the region around the 4th century BC, its prime attractions are walking, hiking and skiing – and an agreeable, if only relative, absence of tourists.

The eastern half is characterised by forbidding and rocky bluffs along the valley to **Tarvisio**. This Alpine resort, seven km short of the Austrian border (heading for Villach) and 11 km from Slovenia, is not a bad base for skiing and walking. The town itself is a curiosity. The Saturday market especially attracts hordes of Austrians, and the bargains on everything from alcohol to clothes must be pretty good, because Vienna's visitors are joined by bargain-hunters from as far afield as Budapest, Zagreb and Ljubljana. A few km east are a couple of fairly peaceful lakes, from where you can set out on forest rambles.

For the more attractive, verdant western half of the Carnia, head off the main north-south road west for Tolmezzo, a small town surrounded by industry. Don't bother stopping but make for the west (Forni di Sopra) or north (Monte Zoncolan for instance). It's a pretty and comparatively undisturbed area.

Information

The AAST office has branches in the towns of Tarvisio (☎ 0428-21 35), Via Roma 10; at Forni di Sopra (☎ 0433-88 67 67), Via Cadore 1; and Piancavallo (☎ 0434-65 51 91). The Azienda Regionale delle Foreste (☎ 0432-29 47 11) at Via Manzini 41 in Udine can assist with maps and other information.

Activities

Skiing There are 18 skiing centres across northern Friuli-Venezia Giulia, the most important being (in a rough curve west to east) Piancavallo, Forni di Sopra, Ravascletto-Zoncolan, Sella Nevea and Tarvisio. Daily, weekly and season ski passes are available. A season ski pass (Cartaneve) is valid for the whole region and costs L460,000. The main centres have ski schools. There are some pretty decent downhill pistes, all starting at about 1700 metres or higher. Families tend to be attracted by these resorts and some effort is made to cater for children.

Walking & Hiking The Udine APT office produces *Rifugi Alpini*, a useful guide to rifugi in the region. It's in Italian, but you should be able to make out the salient details. Leaflets suggesting various walking routes are also available. There is plenty of scope; the Tarvisio APT alone has a brochure outlining some 70 walks in the area around the town, from one to seven hours duration. You can buy detailed walking maps in local newsagencies.

Bicycle FS and some of the northern mountain communities have put together a useful guide to eight bike itineraries in the Carnia. The rides are not too exacting and routes coincide with train stations for those who want to ease up on the way. Older kids can cope with at least one of the more laid-back rides. Ask at the Udine APT office or hunt around the main train stations for the booklet *La Pedemontana col Treno*. Although it is written in Italian, you can follow the routes in conjunction with a decent map.

Places to Stay

Camping grounds are sparse. You can try *Da Cesco* (☎ 0428-29 18) at Camporosso, outside Tarvisio, or *Tornerai* (☎ 0433-8 80 35) at Andreazza, a village near Forni di Sopra.

Most towns have at least a few hotels, a surprising number in the one-star bracket. At the height of the season you may well be advised to book ahead – the Udine APT has a full list of the region's accommodation.

Getting There & Away

Tarvisio is connected by up to 10 trains a day to Udine (1¾ hours), and is the most easily accessible town in the region. Without your own transport, you'll need to rely on the Olivo bus line which operates often infrequent services throughout the Carnia. Drivers heading north from Udine can take the A23 or the SS13 – possibly one of the most boring roads in Italy, at least until you pass the chain of supermarkets between Udine and Gemona. The A23 is faster but is a tollway.

Emilia-Romagna & San Marino

Despite its convenient location between the big tourist draw cards of Tuscany to the south and Lombardy and Veneto in the north, Emilia-Romagna is largely overlooked by the visiting masses. The regional capital, Bologna, was one of the most important Renaissance cities; its university is Europe's oldest and turned out the likes of Dante and Petrarch. Bologna has also long been regarded as Italy's culinary capital, drawing on produce from the fertile plains along the Po valley and adding Parmesan, prosciutto and Lambrusco wines to the Italian table. In short, it is a sophisticated city well worth several days visit, and makes a good base for short trips to Ferrara, Modena and Parma, all once important Renaissance towns.

The Adriatic towns of Ravenna, which boasts one of the world's best collection of Byzantine mosaics, and Rimini, with its beaches and nightlife, add to the region's diversity, as does the marshland of the Po delta, which Emilia-Romagna shares with Veneto.

A highlight for those interested in trekking is the Grand'Escursione Appenninica, a 25-day hike that cuts a path through the Apennines, taking in rifugi and many of the dozens of medieval castles dotting the range.

Emilia, which stretches west of Bologna, and Romagna to the east were joined on Italian unification. Both former papal states, they each retain their own identity: the Emilians are an industrious people while the Romagnoli are known for their blood feuds – perhaps more in memory than practice.

Settled by the Etruscans, the area only began to prosper after 187 AD, when the Romans built the Via Emilia. Apart from a period of Byzantine rule along the Adriatic coast, the real boom came with the Renaissance, when some of the country's most notable families ruled the various towns – the Farnese in Parma and Piacenza, the Este in Ferrara and Modena – and built opulent palaces and courts.

Transport along the Via Emilia is excellent and bus connections enable exploration into the mountains and north along the Po river. The region's prosperity means prices are relatively high, but thanks to several youth hostels even a budget traveller can see the entire region without too much trouble. Accommodation can be difficult to find, so it may be worth considering booking ahead.

Squeezed in between Emilia-Romagna and the Marches to the south is the tiny 'independent' republic of San Marino. Closer to Walt Disney's imagination than a real place, it is still worth a visit if you're in the area.

Bologna

They call it Red Bologna. Bastion of the former Italian Communist Party and home to its newspaper, *L'Unità*, this elegant porticoed city of half a million really does take on every conceivable hue of red with the changing light of day. As if to drive the point home, even the telephone boxes and litter bins are painted bright red – someone on the city council either had a strong sense of humour, or absolutely none at all!

Among the most expensive cities in Italy, Bologna retains its traditional political colouring. Left-wing parties rule and the university, one of Europe's oldest, is still a source of student agitation, albeit on a smaller scale than in the protest heyday of the 1970s. Together with one of the country's better organised gay communities, the students provide a dynamic air that is missing in smaller Emilian cities. The city administrators chip in with an unstinting cultural programme to keep even the most demanding well occupied.

Recent politics has, on occasion, taken a nasty turn in Bologna. The left-wing terrorist

EMILIA-ROMAGNA

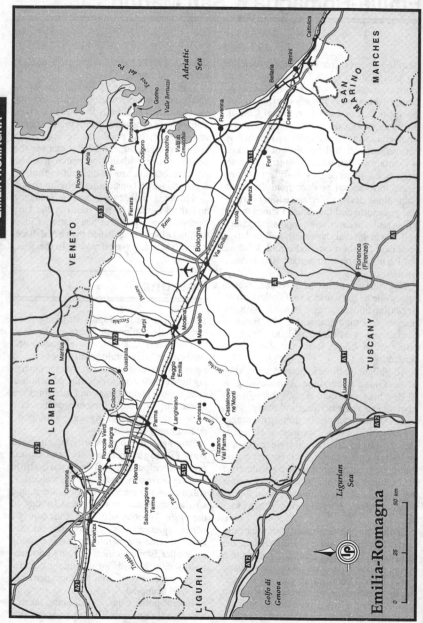

Emilia-Romagna

organisation, the Red Brigades, found support here and, in 1980, right-wing terrorists planted a bomb at the train station, killing 85 people and wounding 200.

HISTORY
Bologna started life in the 6th century BC as Felsina, for two centuries the capital of the Etruscan Po plains territories until tribes from Gaul waltzed in and renamed it Bononia. They lasted another couple of hundred years before ceding to Rome's northward march. As the Western Empire crumbled, Bologna became increasingly exposed to attack from the north, and was sacked and occupied by a succession of Visigoths, Huns, Goths and Lombards.

The city reached its apogee as an independent *comune* and leading European university in the 12th century. Wealth brought a building boom and every well-to-do family left its mark by erecting a tower – 180 of them in all, of which 15 still stand.

The endless tussle between the Papacy and Holy Roman Empire for secular control of the Italian north could not fail to involve Bologna. The city started by siding with the Guelphs (who backed the Papacy) against the Ghibellines, but went its own way in the 14th century. Papal troops took Bologna in 1506 and the city remained under Papal control until the arrival of Napoleon at the end of the 18th century, followed by the Austrians. In 1860, Bologna joined the newly formed Kingdom of Italy.

During heavy fighting in the last months of WW II, up to 40% of Bologna's buildings were destroyed. Today, the city is a centre for Italy's high-tech industries.

ORIENTATION
It would be a travesty not to explore Bologna on foot, and the compactness of the historical centre leaves few excuses for buses or taxis.

Via dell'Indipendenza leads south from the train and bus stations into the Piazza del Nettuno and Piazza Maggiore – a brisk 10-minute walk to the heart of the city.

Drivers should follow the 'centro' target symbol off the tangenziale, or ring road.

Much of the centre is off-limits to most traffic however, and parking can be a hassle.

INFORMATION
Tourist Office
The main Informazioni e Assistenza Turistica (IAT) office is on the western side of Piazza Maggiore (☎ 23 96 60) in the Centro di Informazione Comunale. It is open Monday to Saturday from 9 am to 7 pm and Sunday to 1 pm. Other offices are at the train station and airport. Staff will assist with finding rooms, but will not make bookings. They have stacks of information and such brochures as *A Guest in Bologna*. If the Piazza Maggiore office is closed, there is computerised information in the foyer.

Money
A booth at the train station gives reasonable rates and is open daily from 8 am to 7.45 pm. The Banca Nazionale del Lavoro branch at the bus station has an ATM that accepts Visa cards. Otherwise, branches of the major banks are on Via Rizzoli, the continuation of Via Ugo Bassi, and there is no shortage of ATMs.

Post & Telecommunications
The main post office is in Piazza Minghetti, south-east of Piazza Maggiore. It is open Monday to Friday from 8.15 am to about 7 pm and Saturday to 12.30 pm. Poste restante mail can be addressed to 40100 Bologna.

Telecom offices, with attendants, are at Piazza VIII Agosto 24 and open daily from 8 am to 10 pm. Another unstaffed office at the train station is open 24 hours. Bologna's telephone code is 051.

Gay & Lesbian Information
Arci Gay (☎ 657 01 00), Piazza di Porta Saragozza 2, arranges various events and provides information for gay people.

Other Information
The CIT travel agency (☎ 26 61 24) is at Piazza del Nettuno 2, and the CTS (☎ 22 76 46) is at Largo Respighi 2.

Feltrinelli has an Italian bookshop on Via

EMILIA-ROMAGNA

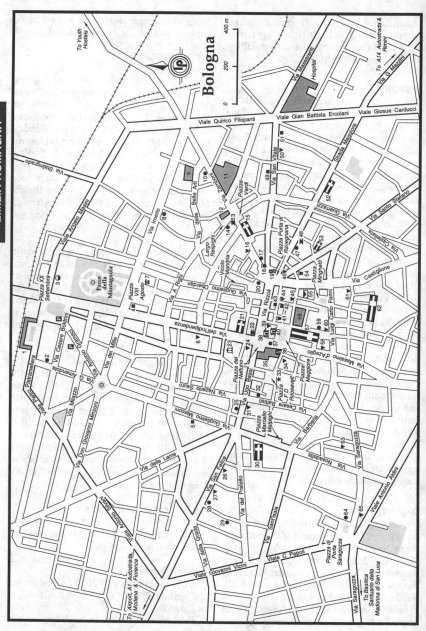

EMILIA-ROMAGNA

dei Giudei, near the two leaning towers, and an international one at Via Zamponi 7b.

There is a coin laundrette, Lava & Lava, at Via Irnerio 35b.

Emergency & Medical Services

For police emergency, call ☎ 113 or ☎ 23 33 33. The questura (☎ 640 11 11) is at Piazza Galileo 7. For an ambulance call ☎ 33 33 33 or ☎ 50 50 50. Ospedale Sant'Orsola (☎ 636 31 11) is on Via Massarenti, at the eastern edge of Via San Vitale. The Farmacia dalla Maddalena at Via Zamboni 62 operates 24 hours a day. The pharmacy at the train station is open until 11 pm on weeknights.

Dangers & Annoyances

The city is only just starting to have problems with street crime such as bag theft and pickpocketing. The area around the university, particularly Piazza Verdi, is a haunt for drug addicts and can be unsafe at night.

PIAZZAS MAGGIORE & NETTUNO

The centre of Bologna's old city, Piazza Maggiore and the adjoining Piazza del Nettuno to the north are lined by some of Bologna's most graceful Medieval and Renaissance monuments. Car-free but bustling nevertheless, the squares are a focal point of city life, with Bolognesi flocking to the cafés and often gathered around the mime artists and buskers that perform on the uneven stone pavement.

Fontana del Nettuno

In the area between the two piazzas stands a mighty bronze Neptune, sculpted in 1566 by a Frenchman known to posterity as Giambologna. The four angels represent the winds and the four sirens the then known continents.

Palazzo Comunale

Lining the western flank of two piazzas, the town hall sports an immense staircase, attributed to Bramante, to the 1st floor. It was wide enough for horse-drawn carriages so that the occupants could be chauffeured up from ground level. In one courtyard you'll see a bronze statue of Pope Gregory XIII, a native of Bologna and responsible for the Gregorian calendar. You can visit two art collections, the **Collezioni Comunali** (good views over Piazza Maggiore) and the new **Museo Morandi**, both open daily from 10 am to 6 pm. Admission to both is L8000, or L5000 to one. Note the huge panel outside the palazzo covered with photos of Italian partisans killed in the resistance to German occupation. Such displays are common in the cities and towns of Emilia-Romagna, which was a centre of fierce partisan activity.

Palaces
Across from the Palazzo Comunale, the **Palazzo del Re Enzo** is named after King Enzo of Sicily, who was confined here for 20 years from 1249. The **Palazzo del Podestà** next door is a fine example of Renaissance architecture. Beneath it and behind the cafés facing Piazza Maggiore are so-called whisper chambers. Stand diagonally opposite another person and whisper – the acoustics are amazing.

BASILICA DI SAN PETRONIO & AROUND
Named after the city's patron saint, Bologna's largest house of worship was started in 1392 to plans by Antonio di Vicenzo (who was in fact subordinated to Andrea da Faenza) but never finished.

Originally intended to be larger than the first St Peter's in Rome (the structure destroyed to make way for the present St Peter's Basilica), San Petronio was effectively truncated by the papacy, which decreed it could not be larger than St Peter's and decided that much of the land should be used for a university. Walk along Via dell'Archiginnasio along the eastern side of the basilica and you will see the beginnings of apses poking out oddly from the basilica and the incomplete façade. Even so, the basilica is one of the largest in the world and a fine example of Gothic architecture.

The central doorway, by Jacopo della Quercia, dates from 1425 and features carvings from the Old and New Testaments and a

beautiful Madonna & Child. The chapels inside contain frescoes by Giovanni da Modena and Jacopo di Paolo. A giant sundial, designed by Cassini in 1656, lines the floor of the north aisle.

Museo Civico Archeologico
Just east of the basilica along Via dell' Archiginnasio (entrance on Via de' Musei), this museum has impressive collections of Egyptian and Roman artefacts and one of Italy's best Etruscan displays, featuring two burial chambers unearthed near the city. It is open Tuesday to Friday from 9 am to 2 pm and Saturday and Sunday from 9 am to 1 pm and 3.30 to 7 pm. Admission is L5000.

Archiginnasio
Site of the city's first university and now its library, the Archiginnasio contains an anatomy theatre carved entirely from wood in 1647. It was destroyed during WW II and completely rebuilt. The theatre and the Sala della Stabat Mater, named after the hymn by Rossini first played here in 1842, can be visited for free. Just find the attendant.

NORTH OF PIAZZA DEL NETTUNO
Cattedrale di San Pietro
Dating from the 10th century but rebuilt many times since, this uninspiring cathedral is located in an oddly uncommanding position on Via dell'Indipendenza. Across the road on Via Manzoni is the **Museo Civico Medioevale e del Rinascimento**, housed in the Palazzo Ghislardi-Fava. Among the bronze statues and medieval coffin slabs, it contains some armour and a few frescoes by Jacopo della Quercia. It's open weekdays (closed Tuesday) from 9 am to 2 pm and weekends from 9 am to 1 pm and 3.30 to 7 pm. Admission is L5000.

LE DUE TORRI (LEANING TOWERS)
The two slender and highly precarious-looking towers that rise above Piazza di Porta Ravegnana are an unmistakable landmark. The area just north of the piazza, particularly around Vicolo Mandria and Via Tubertina, once the city's Jewish ghetto

and long derelict, is experiencing a resurgence as a trendy housing area.

The taller of the towers is the Torre degli Asinelli at 97.6 metres. Raised by the family of the same name in 1109, it has 498 steps which can be climbed for marvellous views of the city, in spite of the 1.3 metre lean. Admission is L4000.

The Garisenda family was even less cautious with foundations when erecting its tower, originally designed to compete with its neighbour, and later sized down to 48 metres because of its 3.2-metre lean.

UNIVERSITY QUARTER

North-east of the towers along Via Zamboni is the **Chiesa di San Giacomo Maggiore**, in Piazza Rossini. Built in the 13th century and remodelled in 1722, the church contains the Cappella Bentivoglio with frescoes by Lorenzo Costa. A little farther up the road is the **Teatro Comunale**, where Wagner's works were performed for the first time in Italy.

The university area is worth visiting just for the cafés and bars. The university has several museums open to the public, mostly

in the **Palazzo Poggi**, on the corner of Via Zamboni and Via San Giacomo, details of which can be obtained from the IAT office.

North of the university, at Via delle Belle Arti 56, is the **Pinacoteca Nazionale**, which concentrates on works by Bolognese artists from the 14th century on. The extensive exhibits include several works by Giotto and also Raphael's *Ecstasy of St Cecilia*. El Greco and Titian are also represented by comparatively little-known works. The gallery is open Tuesday to Saturday from 9 am to 2 pm and Sunday to 1 pm. Admission is L8000.

BASILICA DI SANTO STEFANO

From the two towers, head south-east along Via Santo Stefano, long a residential area for Bologna's well-off, a fact still visible in the elegant façades of the palazzi lining the street.

Where the street widens into what is more or less a piazza, you find yourself before the Basilica di Santo Stefano, actually a group of four churches (originally there were seven). On the right are the 11th-century Romanesque Chiesa del Crocefisso (Crucifix) and the octagonal Chiesa del San Sepolcro (Holy Sepulchre), whose shape suggests it started life as a baptistry. The 11th-century church houses the bones of St Petronius, Bologna's patron saint. The basin in the small courtyard has long been seen in the popular imagination as the one in which Pilate washed his hands after he condemned Christ to death. In fact it is an 8th-century Lombard artefact.

The city's oldest church, the San Vitale e Agricola, incorporates many recycled Roman ruins. The bulk of the building dates to the 5th century, and the tombs of the two saints, a hundred years older still, once served as altars in the side aisles. Only one remains. From the Chiesa della Santa Trinità you can pass to the modest medieval colonnaded cloister, off which a small museum contains a limited collection of paintings and frescoes. The complex is open from 9 am to midday and 3.30 to 6 pm.

BASILICA DI SAN DOMENICO

The basilica, south of the city centre, was erected in the early 16th century to house the remains of St Dominic, the founder of the Dominican order. St Dominic had only just opened a convent on the site when he died in 1221.

The Cappella di San Domenico contains the saint's elaborate sarcophagus, the reliefs of which illustrate scenes from his life. Designed by Nicolò Pisano in the late 13th century it was worked on by a host of artists over the following couple of centuries. The angel on the right of the altar was carved by Michelangelo when he was 19 and bears a resemblance to *David*, which he sculpted years later. The chapel is also decorated with several paintings of the saint, whose skull lies in a reliquary behind the sarcophogus. Ask an attendant to let you see the inlaid wood of the choir stalls behind the main altar of the church and the small museum.

When Mozart spent a month in the city's music academy, he had a tinkle on the church's organ.

CHIESA DI SAN FRANCESCO

At the western end of Via Ugo Bassi, at Piazza Marcello Malpighi, the Chiesa di San Francesco is fronted by the tombs of the *glossatori* (law teachers), elaborate constructions standing in the church grounds. Inside the church, one of the first in Italy to be built in the French Gothic style and completed in the 13th century, is the tomb of Pope Alexander V.

SANTUARIO DELLA MADONNA

The Basilica Santuario della Madonna di San Luca lies in the hills overlooking Bologna, about four km south-west of the city centre and connected for part of the way by a long portico with 666 arches. Built in the mid-18th century, the sanctuary houses a painting of the Virgin Mary supposedly painted by St Luke (hence the place's name) and transported from the Middle East to Bologna in the 12th century.

Each April a statue of the Virgin is carried from the church along the portico in an effort to stop the rains and bring on summer. Take bus No 20 from the city centre to Villa Spada, from where you can get a COSEPURI minibus (L2000 return) to the sanctuary.

WORK

There is no shortage of foreign language teachers in Bologna. If you want to try your luck, you could start with the British Council (☎ 22 51 42), Corte Isolani 8, or Inlingua (☎ 33 39 56), Viale XII Giugno 18.

FESTIVALS

Each summer, the city sponsors Bologna Sogna (Bologna Dreams), a three-month festival of events involving museums and galleries, the university and local and national performers. Torri da Estate is another summer programme and includes discos. Most events are free and a schedule is available at the tourist office.

PLACES TO STAY

Budget hotels in Bologna are in short supply and it can be hard to find a room for one person only, especially as students fill the bulk of the cheap accommodation. Bologna's booming trade-fair calendar usually fills most hotels for at least one week a month, so it may be wise to call ahead.

There are several camping grounds within driving distance of the city. Check with the IAT. You could also ask for student accommodation, but only during university holidays.

A group called SIAT (☎ 23 96 60), Piazza Maggiore 6, organises special all-in deals with discounted accommodation for weekends and holiday periods.

Hostels

The best options are the joint HI youth hostels, the *Ostello San Sisto* (☎ 51 92 02), Via Viadagola 14, and the *Ostello Le Torri-San Sisto 2* (☎ 50 18 10), in the same street at No 5. Both charge L17,000 for B&B and L12,000 per meal. Take bus No 93 from Via dei Mille (weekdays until 8.15 pm and Saturday mornings only), No 301 from the bus station (few on weekends) or No 20B from

Via dei Mille. Get off Via Salgari and you then have a 1.5 km walk. The hostels produce a series of walking-tour maps.

There is one other hostel option for groups. The *Centro Europa Uno* (☎ 625 83 52; fax 45 03 59) in San Lazzaro di Savena, about nine km south-east of Bologna at Via Emilia 297, offers sporting facilities and is aimed more at families and groups. It is open from mid-March to mid-November and bookings are essential. Bus No 94 runs into central Bologna.

Hotels
The pick of the city's cheaper hotels is *Albergo Garisenda* (☎ 22 43 69), Galleria del Leone 1, off Via Rizzoli, with rooms looking out over the leaning towers. Prices for singles/doubles start at L40,000/70,000. *Albergo Apollo* (☎ 22 39 55), Via Drapperie 5, also off Via Rizzoli, has rooms from L33,000 /60,000.

Albergo Perla (☎ 22 45 79), Via San Vitale 77, at the eastern edge of the city centre, has rooms from L40,000/69,000. Just up the road at No 94, *Albergo San Vitale* (☎ 22 59 66) is a reasonable alternative with rooms starting at L50,000/70,000.

On the opposite side of town, rooms at *Albergo Marconi* (☎ 26 26 52), Via Marconi 22, start at L40,000/65,000.

Albergo Panorama (☎ 22 18 02), Via Livraghi 1, off Via Ugo Bassi, has singles/doubles for L45,000/70,000.

The city is jammed with expensive hotels catering to business people, but standards are sometimes poor. *Albergo Donatello* (☎ & fax 24 81 74), Via dell'Indipendenza 65, has singles/doubles for L110,000/145,000, although they occasionally have rooms going more cheaply.

PLACES TO EAT
Some know Bologna as La Grassa (the Fat) and as the epithet suggests, the Bolognese are serious about food and fussy about their pasta. The best pasta is *tirata a mano*, hand-stretched and rolled with a wooden pin, not a machine. It is cooked in many ways and eaten with a multitude of sauces. Everyone knows spaghetti bolognese, but the Bolognesi call the meat sauce ragù. Mortadella, known sometimes as Bologna sausage or baloney, hails from the area. The hills nearby produce the Riesling Italico and a full, dry Sauvignon.

Fortunately it is cheap to eat in Bologna, particularly in the university district north of Via Rizzoli. The city has many good bars and osterias, where you can get cheap drinks and snacks. Some serve full meals and rarely levy a cover charge.

You can shop at the vast Mercato Ugo Bassi, Via Ugo Bassi 27, or the daily produce market just east of Piazza Maggiore, centred on speciality food shops along Via de' Fusari, Via Drapperie, Via Marchesana and Via Clavature.

Restaurants
McDonald's is on the corner of Via dell'Indipendenza and Via Ugo Bassi, if you feel that peculiar urge.

There are several self-service places about town. *La Mamma*, Via Zamboni 16, is open until 3 am and even has karaoke if you want to eat and sing. For a more classy version of the genre, head to *Tamburini*, Via Caprarie 1. Apart from selling some of Bologna's finest food products, it has a self-service restaurant where you can taste some of the goodies without having to cook yourself.

Osteria du Madon, Via San Vitale 75, at the road's eastern edge, serves mainly pasta and is quite cheap, with courses starting at L6000. *Osteria Senzanome*, Via Senzanome 42, is one of the best known osterie and a full meal could cost L20,000. *Osteria dei Poeti*, Via dei Poeti 1a, is more expensive but the food excellent. It's been in operation since 1600.

Local opinion is divided on the subject of Bologna's top pizza, but you won't go far wrong on price or quality at *Pizzeria Bella Napoli*, Via San Felice 40.

Vanes, Strada Maggiore 5C, near the two towers, specialises in pasta made at the restaurant. Pasta costs from L7000, pizzas from L5000 and the cover charge is L2500. Very popular with Bolognesi on a budget is the

Trattoria da Boni, Via Saragozza 88. Also recommended is the *Trattoria da Gianni*, Via Clavature 18.

Ristorante Torre de' Galluzzi, Piazza Galluzzi behind the Basilica di San Petronio, has a L48,000 set menu (the cheapest) featuring local specialities. But if you're aiming for the top, hit *Diana*, Via dell'Indipendenza, three blocks north of Piazza del Nettuno, considered the city's best restaurant, where a full meal will cost at least L60,000.

Cafés & Bars

The *Zanarini*, Via Luigi Carlo Farini 2, behind the Basilica di San Petronio, is one of the city's finest tearooms and specialises in unusual cakes. Some of its past glory is lost, but the grand décor makes a visit worthwhile, if a little expensive. In the past few years *Caffè Commercianti*, Strada Maggiore 23, has become something of a haunt for the city's intelligentsia, apparently inspired by Umberto Eco.

More modest and with plenty of student life is *Caffè al Teatro*, on the corner of Largo Respighi and Via Zamboni. Some places provide filling bar snacks – one is *Bar Canton de' Fiori*, Via dell'Indipendenza 1a.

Gelati

Gelateria Ugo, Via San Felice 20, is one of the city's best ice-cream places. Also well-established is *Gelateria la Torinese*, on Via Archiginnasio behind Palazzo del Podestà.

ENTERTAINMENT

The IAT office has several what's-on brochures, only available sometimes, including *VIP a Bologna* and *Bologna Spettacolo News*. They have plenty of information on theatre, cinema and night life.

Theatre & Music

The Teatro Comunale (☎ 52 99 99), Piazza Verdi, is the main venue for opera, theatre and concerts, and has a year-round programme. Other drama theatres include the Teatro Dehon (☎ 34 29 34), Via Libia

59, and the Teatro Duse (☎ 22 52 84), Via Castellata 7.

The Basilica di Santa Maria dei Servi boasts one of the largest organs in Italy, and is the place to go for recitals.

Cinema

English-language films are screened at Tiffany (☎ 33 07 57), Piazza di Porta Saragozza 5, and Lumière (☎ 52 35 39), Via Pietralata 55A. The latter shows a lot of arthouse movies in all languages. A similar place is the Adriano, Via San Felice 52. Those who would like to see Bologna on film should try to catch *Dichiarazioni d'Amore*, a somewhat wistful movie released by Pupi Avati in 1994, which is set in the city and beautifully shot (whatever you think of the plot).

Discos, Pubs & Nightclubs

Bologna has one of the healthiest night scenes in Italy, bolstered by an active student population and gay scene. For the latest info on what's on in club land, buy *Mongolfiera* (L3000), a bi-weekly magazine with a multilingual listings insert, *C'è*.

First opened for business in about 1400, Osteria del Sole, Via Ranocchi 1D, is the only place left in Bologna to maintain the centuries-old tradition of the osteria as watering hole only. It's also one of Bologna's few early openers. It is open from 8 am to 2 pm and 7 to 8.30 pm, although this is not set in stone. If you want to eat, arm yourself with goodies from the surrounding food shops.

Kinki, Via Zamboni 1, is a longtime favourite and goes lesbian and gay on Saturday nights. If techno, hip-hop and the very latest music trends are your thing, head for Matis, Via Rotta 10. Cover charges can range to L30,000 at both places. At the handily located Porto di Mano, Vicolo Sampieri 3b, you can eat, drink and dance until the wee hours. Music ranges from hip-hop to acid jazz; there is no cover charge and it's one of the better inner-city spots.

More standard Italian-style discos include Hobby One, Via Mascarella 2a, and Vertigo,

Via di San Luca 35. They all have a cover charge.

THINGS TO BUY
If you're intending to do any shopping in Bologna, don't come on a Thursday, as all shops shut for the afternoon that day. On weekends there's a flea market at the Parco della Montagnola.

GETTING THERE & AWAY
Air
Bologna's Guglielmo Marconi airport (☎ 31 15 78), north-west of the city on Borgo Panigale, is serviced by mainly European airlines and there are flights to Rome, Venice, southern Italy, Pisa, London, Paris and Frankfurt.

Bus
Buses to regional centres such as Ravenna, Ferrara and Modena depart from the depot (☎ 24 21 50) in Piazza XX Settembre, around the corner from the train station. There are buses to Ancona and Milan, and international services to London, Paris, Amsterdam, Brussels, Prague and Warsaw.

Train
Bologna is a major transport junction for northern Italy, and trains from most major cities stop here. The only hitch is that many are Intercity trains, which means you have to pay a supplement. The super-fast Pendolino (ETR 500) which runs between Rome and Milan stops here. Call ☎ 24 64 90 for information.

Car & Motorbike
The city is linked to Milan, Florence and Rome by the A1 Autostrada del Sole. The A13 heads directly for Venice and Padua, and the A14 for Rimini and Ravenna. The city is also on the SS9, which connects Milan with the Adriatic coast. The SS64 goes to Ferrara.

For car hire, all major companies are represented in the city and most have offices at the airport. Avis (☎ 55 15 28) is at Via Pietramellara, and Europcar (☎ 24 71 01) is at Via Boldrini 3B. Hertz (☎ 25 48 30) is at Via G Amendola 17.

GETTING AROUND
To/From the Airport
ATC bus No 91 connects the city with the airport. It leaves from in front of the train station.

Bus
Bologna has an efficient bus system, run by ATC (☎ 24 70 05), which has information booths at the train station, bus depot and on Via Marconi, near Via Ugo Bassi. Bus Nos 11, 25 and 27 are among the many connecting the train station with the city centre.

Taxi
For a taxi, call ☎ 37 27 27.

South of Bologna

PORETTA
About 50 km south of Bologna, in the Appenines, is the tiny thermal spring town of Porretta Terme. Traditionally a sleepy resort for people wanting to take advantage of the therapeutic mineral waters, the town has in recent years become a focal point for soul music lovers from across Europe. Each year, during the third weekend in July, the town hosts the Sweet Soul Music Festival, a tribute to Otis Redding and a celebration of the Memphis sound. If you happen to be in the region at the time, it really is worth making the trip to Porretta for the festival, held over three nights in the town's Rufus Thomas Park. In 1995 the headliner was Wilson Pickett. In 1996, tickets will cost L35,000 per night For information about the festival and about the town itself, contact the APT di Porretta (☎ 0534-22 02 1), Piazza della Libertà. Places to stay include the one-star *Trattoria Toscana* (☎ 22 20 8), in Piazza della Libertà, or the three-star *Hotel Santoli* (☎ 23 20 6), Via Roma. Trains leave hourly for Porretta from

Bologna. The town is also accessible from Florence, via Pistoia, by regular trains.

West of Bologna

MODENA

Some 40 km north-west of Bologna, Modena was one of a series of Roman garrison towns established along the Via Emilia in the 2nd century BC, in this case on the site of an already extant Etruscan settlement.

Modena remained an obscure little place until it became a free city in the 12th century and passed to the Este family late the following century. Prosperity finally came when it was chosen as capital of a much-reduced Este duchy in 1598, after the family had lost Ferrara to the Papal States. Apart from a brief Napoleonic interlude, the Este remained in control until Italian unification.

Modena is home to Italy's favourite tenor, Luciano Pavarotti, and car manufacturers such as Ferrari, Maserati, Bugatti and De Tomaso, all of whom do their bit to make this town of 200,000 one of the most well-off in the country.

Orientation

From the main train station in Piazza Dante, head west down Viale Crispi and turn right into Corso Vittorio Emanuele II, which leads to the Palazzo Ducale. Walk around the palace to Piazza degli Estensi, and then straight ahead along Via L C Farini for Via Emilia, the main drag. The duomo and Piazza Grande are south of Via Emilia, and the bulk of offices, banks, hotels and restaurants are within easy walking distance of the centre.

Information

Tourist Office The IAT office (☎ 22 24 82), Via Scudari 8, has been merged with Informa Giovani (☎ 20 65 83), which provides a range of information for young people. Opening hours are 10.30 am to 12.30 pm and 4 to 7 pm. There was talk at the time of writing of moving the office to another location on Piazza Grande. Ask for the *Week-End in Modena* brochure, detailing 11 itineraries for the city and surrounding province.

Post & Telecommunications The post office is at Via Emilia 86 and is open from 8.15 am to 7.40 pm. Poste restante mail can be addressed to 41100 Modena. The Telecom office is at Via L C Farini 26 and there's a smaller office on Via dell'Università. The telephone code for Modena is 059.

Emergency & Medical Services For the police, call ☎ 113. The questura (☎ 41 04 11) is at Viale della Rimembranza 14. You can call an ambulance on ☎ 118 or ☎ 22 22 08. The main hospital (☎ 20 51 11) is at Piazzale Sant'Agostino, opposite the Palazzo dei Musei. There is a night pharmacy nearby at Via Ramazzini 5.

Duomo

Dedicated to Modena's patron saint, St Geminiano, the duomo was started in 1099 and is one of the finest Romanesque cathedrals in Italy – even if it and its bell tower, the Torre Ghirlandina, are both sinking. Barricades erected around Piazza Grande fence off the church, but it is possible to enter the building. The façade is adorned with bas-reliefs depicting scenes from Genesis by the 12th-century sculptor Wiligelmo. Much of his work has been removed to the Museo Lapidario del Duomo, adjoining the duomo at Via Lanfranco 6. Ask the sacristan to let you in; admission by donation. Inside, the striking screen over the nave was carved in the 12th century and shows scenes from Christ's Passion.

The **Torre Ghirlandina** was started in 1269 and rises to 87 metres, culminating in a Gothic spire which has quite a lean. At its base is the almost standard Emilian memorial to the partisans who fell in WW II. It's open on Sundays and holidays only from 10 am to 1 pm and 4 to 7 pm. In winter the hours are 10 am to 4 pm. Admission is L1100.

Palazzo dei Musei

West along Via Emilia, **Palazzo dei Musei**,

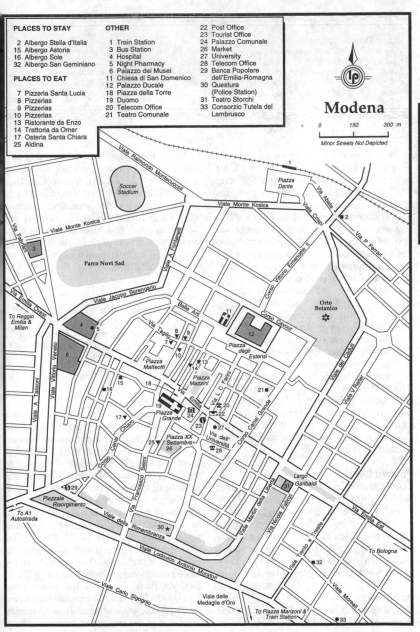

EMILIA-ROMAGNA

Modena

0   150   300 m

Minor Streets Not Depicted

PLACES TO STAY

2 Albergo Stella d'Italia
15 Albergo Astoria
16 Albergo Sole
32 Albergo San Geminiano

PLACES TO EAT

7 Pizzeria Santa Lucia
8 Pizzerias
9 Pizzerias
10 Pizzerias
13 Ristorante da Enzo
14 Trattoria da Omer
17 Osteria Santa Chiara
25 Aldina

OTHER

1 Train Station
3 Bus Station
4 Hospital
5 Night Pharmacy
6 Palazzo dei Musei
11 Chiesa di San Domenico
12 Palazzo Ducale
18 Piazza della Torre
19 Duomo
20 Telecom Office
21 Teatro Comunale

22 Post Office
23 Tourist Office
24 Palazzo Comunale
26 Market
27 University
28 Telecom Office
29 Banca Popolare
dell'Emilia-Romagna
30 Questura
(Police Station)
31 Teatro Storchi
33 Consorzio Tutela del
Lambrusco

EMILIA-ROMAGNA

> **Bucketing Bologna**
> Way back in 1325, Modena and Bologna fought one of the innumerable wars that periodically
> bled Italy's medieval city-states and the Bolognesi and Modenesi have loathed one another ever
> since. The greatest bone of contention still lies in the base of the Torre Ghirlandina (or rather a
> copy does) – a wooden bucket stolen from the red city during the war. Bologna, it is said, still
> wants its *secchia rapita* (stolen bucket) back. ∎

in the Piazzale Sant'Agostino, houses several galleries, including the city's art collection and the Biblioteca Estense. The **Museo Lapidario Estense** contains Roman stonework including sarcophagi. The **Galleria Estense** (admission L4000) features most of the Este family collection and comprises works by Cosimo Tura, Paolo Veronese, Antonio Correggio and Tintoretto. The **Biblioteca Estense** has one of Italy's most valuable collections of books, letters and manuscripts and includes the *Bible of Borso d'Este*, 1200 pages illustrated by Ferrarese artists and considered the most decorated Bible in existence. It can be seen, but you must leave your passport at the desk. The **Museo Civico del Risorgimento** is a standard display chronicling Italian unification, but may be still closed for restoration. The **Museo Civico Archeologico Etnologico** (admission L3000) presents a range of Bronze Age exhibits, as well as items from Africa, Asia, Peru and New Guinea. Opening times vary for each museum, so check first at the IAT.

Palazzo Ducale

Started in 1634 for the Este family, this grand edifice is now home to Modena's military academy, whose cadets wear fuchsia-coloured uniforms (looking like they've stepped off a Quality Street chocolate tin) and are considered Italy's crack soldiers. The doors of the palace are thrown open to the public once a year – on the Sunday nearest November 4.

Activities

If you're tiring of soaking up culture, the Apennines south of Modena offer lots of scope for outdoor activities, including walking, horse riding, canoeing and skiing. The CAI (☎ 24 31 30), Vicolo Caselline 11, and the tourist office have stacks of brochures, such as *Modena Altro Turismo*, *Modena Trekking*, *Modena's Apennine* and *Skiing on Modena's Mountains*, which are replete with details of clubs. About 12 rifugi are located in the mountains and there are many walking trails.

Festival

A summer event that has been successful recently but over whose future hangs a question mark is the Settimana Estense in July, a week of banquets, jousts and other early Renaissance fun, with lots of locals flitting about in period costume.

Places to Stay

Modena is close enough to Bologna to make it a short day trip, although the city does have reasonably cheap accommodation. *International Camping Modena* (☎ 33 22 52), Via Cave di Ramo 111, is a couple of km west of the city in Bruciata. Take bus No 19. It's open from April to the end of September.

Albergo Sole (☎ 21 42 45), Via Malatesta 45, west of Piazza Grande, has singles/doubles from L30,000/50,000 (look for the 'locanda' sign). *Albergo Astoria* (☎ 22 55 87), Via Sant'Eufemia 43, one block back from Via Emilia near the duomo, has rooms from the same price. *Albergo Stella d'Italia* (☎ 22 25 84), Via Paolo Ferrari 3, has rooms from L36,000/55,000, and *Albergo San Geminiano* (☎ 21 03 03), Viale Moreali 41, a 10-minute walk east of the city centre, has rooms from

L50,000/60,000 (one or two may go more cheaply). It also has free parking.

Places to Eat
Like Bologna and Parma, Modena produces excellent *prosciutto crudo* (cured ham). The city's gastronomic delight is *zampone* (stuffed pig's trotter). It also produces the bulk of Italy's balsamic vinegar, a rich aromatic vinegar using local wine that is sprinkled liberally over salads and meat dishes. Tortellini are a speciality and served only in broth, and the area produces Lambrusco, one of the more famous Italian sparkling reds, which should be drunk chilled and with everything. The city's Consorzio Tutela del Lambrusco, Via Schedone 39-41, can tell you about vineyards and advise on tastings and opening times. The fresh produce market is just south of Piazza XX Settembre.

At the trattoria *Aldina*, Via Albinelli 40, a meal could cost L20,000. *Pizzeria Santa Lucia*, Via Taglio, north of Piazza Matteotti, has pizzas from L6000 – it is one of four around here, so take your pick. *Trattoria da Omer*, Via Torre 33, serves local dishes, but a meal will cost over L35,000. *Ristorante da Enzo*, Via Coltellini 17, is one of the better restaurants, with main courses from L10,000. They make their own pasta on the premises. Try *Osteria Santa Chiara*, Via Ruggera 8, for local cuisine in a cosy old building.

Entertainment
The city's better bars are along Via Emilia, near the duomo, but check prices, as a beer could cost L10,000.

Sipario in Piazza, held during July and August, features outdoor concerts and ballet in Piazza Grande, with tickets starting at around L10,000. Posters advertise upcoming events.

The opera season each winter sometimes attracts Pavarotti to the Teatro Comunale (☎ 22 51 83), Corso Canal Grande 85. Check out the Teatro Storchi (☎ 22 32 44), Largo Garibaldi 15, for drama.

Cinema Embassy, Vicolo dell'Albergo 8, sometimes screens English-language films. Check with the tourist office for discos.

Things to Buy
On the last weekend of every month a big **antiques fair** is held in Parco Novi Sad, 500 metres north-west of the city centre.

Getting There & Away
The bus station (☎ 30 88 00) is on Via Fabriani. ATCM (☎ 30 80 11) and other companies connect Modena with most towns in the region and other cities including Cremona and Milan.

The main train station is in Piazza Dante (☎ 21 82 26). There are services to Bologna, Rome, Parma and Milan.

By car, the city is at the junction of the A1 Autostrada del Sole, which connects Rome with Milan, and the A22, which heads north for the Brenner pass.

Getting Around
ATCM's bus No 6 connects the train station with the city centre. For a taxi, call ☎ 37 42 42. Bicycles can be rented next to the train station.

AROUND MODENA
Galleria Ferrari
Enzo Ferrari, who died in 1989, reckoned the Modenese possess a rare combination of the boldness and hard-headedness needed to build racing cars. The nearby Bolognesi, who have long held Modena in strong disregard, would be considerably less complimentary, but what does Modena care? It has the racing cars. The factory is in Maranello, 23 km south of Modena (regular buses run from Modena). You may be able to organise a visit, but an easier task is a visit to the firm's museum, the Galleria Ferrari (☎ 0536-94 32 04), Via Dino Ferrari 43. It boasts one of the largest collections of Ferraris on show in the world and is open daily from 9.30 am to 12.30 pm and 3 to 6 pm (closed Mondays in winter). Admission is L10,000.

Fossoli
A small village about 40 km north of Modena, Fossoli was not only in the heart of partisan territory, it was also the site of a transit

EMILIA-ROMAGNA

concentration camp, the first step for Italian prisoners on the road to greater horrors in Germany. The crumbling barrack blocks are supposedly part of a project to maintain this memory of inhumanity, but little has been done except to throw up a fence to keep people from wandering around inside.

REGGIO EMILIA
Also known as Reggio nell'Emilia, this town started life in the 2nd century BC as a Roman colony along the Via Emilia, which splits it in two. Nothing remains of those days, and much of the present city was built by the Este family during the 400 years it was in control from 1406.

Although most of us know the cheese from this area as Parmesan (as in Parma), it is in fact called *parmigiano-reggiano*, reflecting the fact that it's produced across both provinces.

Few tourists bother to stop here, but Reggio has a pleasant centre and makes a functional base for exploring the Apennines to the south – it certainly merits a look-in if you're passing through.

Information
Tourist Office The IAT (☎ 45 11 52) in Piazza Camillo Prampolini is one km west of the train station, along Via Emilia San Pietro, and is open Monday to Friday from 8.30 am to 12.30 pm and 2.30 to 5.30 pm and Saturday morning.

Money There are several banks in the town centre and you can also change cash or cheques at the post office.

Post & Telecommunications The post office is at Via Sessi 3, and poste restante mail can be addressed to 42100 Reggio Emilia. The telephone code is 0522.

Emergency The questura (☎ 113 in emergency or ☎ 43 58 41) is at Via Dante Alighieri 6. For medical problems, the Ospedale Santa Maria Nuova (☎ 33 51 11) is at Viale Risorgimento 80, or call ☎ 118 in emergency.

Churches
The city's sights are concentrated around Piazza Cesare Battisti, and Piazza Prampolini and Piazza San Prospero to the south. The latter two are separated by the **duomo**, built in the 13th century in the Romanesque style and completely remodelled 300 years later. The 15th-century **Chiesa di San Prospero**, on the piazza of the same name, is fronted by lions of red marble and worth a quick look. Its striking octagonal bell tower was built in 1537.

Palazzo del Municipio
On the south side of Piazza Prampolini, the 14th-century town hall contains the Sala del Tricolore, the room where the Italian flag was devised during a conference that established Napoleon's Cispadane Republic in 1797.

Museums
North from Piazza Battisti, facing the Piazza Martiri del VII Luglio, are the four **Musei Civici**, with a collection of 18th-century artworks and archaeological discoveries. They are open Tuesday to Saturday from 9 am to midday and on Sunday from 3 to 6 pm as well. Admission is free.

The **Galleria Parmeggiani** at Corso Cairoli 2 contains some worthwhile Italian, Spanish and Flemish canvasses, including an El Greco, but remains closed (they say for the purpose of installing air conditioning!).

Places to Stay & Eat
The *Reggio Emilia* youth hostel (☎ 45 47 95), Via dell'Abbadessa 8, about 500 metres from the train station in the city centre, has B&B for L16,000. For a hotel, try *Albergo Stella* (☎ 43 22 80), Via Blasmatorti 5, near Piazza Roversi, which has singles/doubles from L30,000/60,000. *Albergo Morandi* (☎ 45 43 97), Via Emilia San Pietro 64, has rooms with a bathroom for L50,000/70,000, while *Albergo Cairoli* (☎ 45 35 96), Piazza XXV Aprile 2, near the bus station, has rooms for L38,000/58,000. *Albergo Brasil* (☎ 45 53 76), Via Roma 37, has rooms for much the same price and will discount for longer stays.

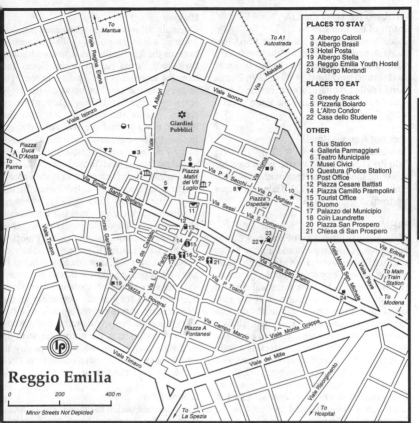

PLACES TO STAY

3 Albergo Cairoli
9 Albergo Brasil
13 Hotel Posta
19 Albergo Stella
23 Reggio Emilia Youth Hostel
24 Albergo Morandi

PLACES TO EAT

2 Greedy Snack
5 Pizzeria Boiardo
8 L'Altro Condor
22 Casa dello Studente

OTHER

1 Bus Station
4 Galleria Parmaggiani
6 Teatro Municipale
7 Musei Civici
10 Questura (Police Station)
11 Post Office
12 Piazza Cesare Battisti
14 Piazza Camillo Prampolini
15 Tourist Office
16 Duomo
17 Palazzo del Municipio
18 Coin Laundrette
20 Piazza San Prospero
21 Chiesa di San Prospero

Reggio Emilia

0   200   400 m

Minor Streets Not Depicted

For sheer luxury, try *Hotel Posta* (☎ 43 29 44; fax 45 26 02), Piazza Cesare Battisti 4.

There is a produce market each Tuesday and Friday in Piazza San Prospero. The hostel restaurant, the *Casa dello Studente*, is the best bet for budget meals. You can get reasonable takeaway pizza for L3000 from *Greedy Snack*, Via Raimondo Franchetti 1. Slightly more upmarket are *Pizzeria Boiardo*, Via San Rocco, and *L'Altro Condor*, Via Secchi 17.

Getting There & Away

ACT buses (☎ 51 44 22) serve the city and region from the station in Viale Allegri, while trains arrive at the eastern end of town on Piazza Marconi. There are plenty of the latter serving all stops on the Milan/Bologna line.

The city is on the Via Emilia (the SS9), and the A1 passes to the north. The SS63 is a tortuous but scenic route that takes you south-west across the Parma Apennines to La Spezia on the Ligurian coast.

Getting Around

You are unlikely to need the ACT's city buses. If you are in a blind hurry, you can call a taxi on ☎ 45 25 45.

AROUND REGGIO EMILIA
South of Reggio Emilia
South-west of the city along the SS63 is a national park spread along the province's share of the Apennines. The tourist office at **Castelnovo ne' Monti** (☎ 81 04 30), Piazza Martiri della Libertà 12b, can provide details of activities. For walkers, there are several rifugi along the trails.

North of Reggio Emilia
Guastalla's *youth hostel* (☎ 82 49 15), Via Lido Po 11, makes the town a good base for exploring the Po valley area north of Reggio Emilia. B&B costs L14,000. Trains and buses run from Reggio Emilia.

PARMA
Of the Emilian cities west of Bologna, Parma is the pick of the crop. Straddling the banks of a Po tributary – the 'Torrente Parma' – this well-off, orderly city should not be bypassed. The bicycle rules in the squares and cobbled lanes of the old town centre, and the surrounding countryside is home not only to Parmesan cheese and Parma ham (Italy's best prosciutto) but a smorgasbord of castles and walking tracks. The city itself is a little expensive, but the budget-conscious can stay at the hostel or camping ground.

Verdi and Toscanini composed many of their greatest works here, and Stendhal in some sense immortalised the city in *La Chartreuse de Parme*.

Prosciutto is one of the many delicacies you can sample in Parma.

History
Originally Etruscan, Parma achieved importance as a Roman colony on what would become the Via Emilia. As Rome's authority dwindled, Parma passed to the Goths and later the Lombards and Franks. In the 11th century, as the conflict between the Holy Roman Empire and the papacy gathered steam, Parma threw in its lot with the former, even furnishing two Anti-Popes. In the following centuries internal squabbling was largely responsible for the city's turbulent fate, as it fell to the Visconti family, the Sforzas, the French and finally the papacy.

The Farnese family ruled Parma in the Pope's name from 1545 to 1731, when the Bourbons took control, making Parma one of the pawns in European power games. Don Phillip of Bourbon, son of Spain's Philip V, and his wife Louise Elisabeth, daughter of France's Louis XV, nevertheless ushered in a period of peace and frenetic cultural activity. From the time of Napoleon's incursions into northern Italy at the beginning of the 19th century, Parma entered a period of instability that ended only with Italian unification. Some 60 years later, the barricades went up as Parma became the only Emilian city to oppose the infamous march on Rome in 1922 by Mussolini's blackshirts.

Orientation
From the train station in Piazzale dalla Chiesa, head south along Via Verdi for the huge Palazzo della Pilotta. Cross Via Garibaldi for the duomo area, or walk south for Piazza Garibaldi, the main square.

Information
Tourist Office The IAT office (☎ 23 47 35) is at Piazza del Duomo 5 and is open Monday to Friday from 9 am to 12.30 pm and 3 to 5 pm and Saturday to 12.30 pm. Informa Giovani (☎ 21 87 48), Viale Toscanini 2, has information on a range of issues, including for gay, lesbian and disabled travellers.

Post & Telecommunications The main post office is at Via Melloni, off Via Garibaldi, and is open Monday to Friday from 8.15 am to

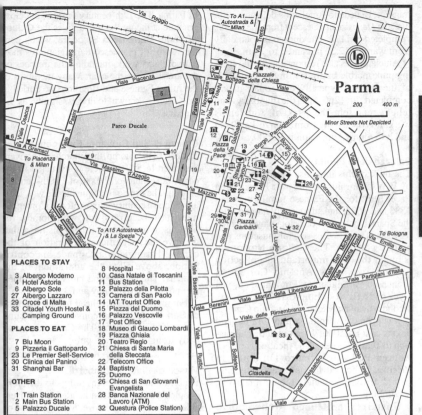

Parma

0   200   400 m

Minor Streets Not Depicted

PLACES TO STAY

3 Albergo Moderno
4 Hotel Astoria
6 Albergo Sole
27 Albergo Lazzaro
29 Croce di Malta
33 Citadel Youth Hostel &
   Camping Ground

PLACES TO EAT

7 Blu Moon
9 Pizzeria il Gattopardo
23 Le Premier Self-Service
30 Clinica del Panino
31 Shanghai Bar

OTHER

1 Train Station
2 Main Bus Station
5 Palazzo Ducale

8 Hospital
10 Casa Natale di Toscanini
11 Bus Station
12 Palazzo della Pilotta
13 Camera di San Paolo
14 IAT Tourist Office
15 Piazza del Duomo
16 Palazzo Vescovile
17 Post Office
18 Museo di Glauco Lombardi
19 Piazza Ghiaia
20 Teatro Regio
21 Chiesa di Santa Maria
   della Steccata
22 Telecom Office
24 Baptistry
25 Duomo
26 Chiesa di San Giovanni
   Evangelista
28 Banca Nazionale del
   Lavoro (ATM)
32 Questura (Police Station)

7 pm and Saturday to 12.30 pm. Poste restante mail can be addressed to 43100 Parma. The Telecom office is on Piazza Garibaldi; the telephones are down a flight of stairs in front of the office and are open daily from 7 am to midnight. The telephone code for Parma is 0521.

Emergency & Medical Services In a police emergency, call ☎ 113. The questura (☎ 21 94) is at Borgo della Posta. For an ambulance, call ☎ 118, or the Guardia Medica on ☎ 29 25 25.

The Ospedale Maggiore (☎ 9 67 20) is at Via Gramsci 14, west of the centre. To find a late-night pharmacy (farmacia di turno) call ☎ 192.

Piazza del Duomo

The **duomo** is a classic example of Po valley Romanesque design. It was begun in 1059 but largely rebuilt 60 years later after Parma was hit by an earthquake. Antonio Correggio's *Assunzione della Vergine* (Assumption of the Virgin) graces the inside of the cupola and took the painter six years to complete from 1524. Take time to look at the restored wood inlay work in the Sagrestia dei Consorziali (sacristy) and, in the south transept, Benedetto Antelami's delicate sculpture, the *Deposizione* (Descent from the Cross), completed in 1178. The duomo is open daily from 9 am to 12.30 pm and 3 to 7 pm.

Antelami was also responsible for the striking pink marble **baptistry** on the south side of the square. Typically octagonal, it was completed in 1260 and the baptistry and reliefs represent the peak of Antelami's work. It is open daily from 9 am to 12.30 pm and 3 to 6 pm. Admission is L3000.

Palazzo della Pilotta

The hulk of this immense palace, shattered by WW II air raids, looms over Piazza della Pace. Built for the Farnese family between 1583 and 1622, and supposedly named after the Spanish ball game of pelota played within its walls, it now houses several museums and picture galleries. The **Galleria Nazionale** is by far the most important. Its collection includes works by Antonio Correggio, Francesco Parmigianino, Fra Angelico, van Dyck and a figure of Empress Marie-Louise, second wife of Napoleon, by Antonio Canova.

It is open daily from 9 am to 1.45 pm and tickets cost L12,000, which includes admission to Teatro Farnese. The theatre, a copy of Andrea Palladio's Teatro Olimpico in Vicenza, is housed in the palace's fencing school. It was completely rebuilt after WW II bombing.

Upstairs, the **Museo Archeologico Nazionale** is devoted partly to Roman artefacts discovered around Parma and also hosts a display of Etruscan artefacts dug up in the Po plain. It is open daily, except Monday, from 9 am to 1.30 pm. Admission is L4000. The **Biblioteca Palatina**, first opened to the public in 1769, contains more than 700,000 volumes and 5000 manuscripts. The **Museo Bodoniano**, which can be visited only by appointment, is devoted to the life of Giambattista Bodoni, who designed the typeface that bears his name.

Piazza Garibaldi

Piazza Garibaldi, more or less on the site of the ancient Roman forum, is still the centre of Parma. The 17th-century Palazzo del Governatore at the northern end hides the **Chiesa di Santa Maria della Steccata**, which contains some of Francesco Parmigianino's most extraordinary work, including the frescoes on the arches above the altar. Many members of the ruling Farnese and Bourbons lie buried in this church, known to locals simply as La Steccata.

Chiesa di San Giovanni Evangelista

Just east of the duomo, this church and convent dedicated to St John were constructed in the early 16th century on the site of a 10th-century church. The ornate Baroque façade was actually added a century later. Antonio Correggio must have been on a roll with domes, for here, as in the duomo, it is to his hand that we owe the magnificent decoration of the cupola. Parmigiano also made his contribution, above all to the adornment of the chapels. The church and cloisters are open from 6.30 am to midday and 3.30 to 8 pm.

For more Correggio, head for the **Camera di San Paolo**, in the convent of the same name off Via Melloni. The Camera is open daily from 9 am to 1.45 pm.

Museo di Glauco Lombardi

Waterloo meant different things to different people. While Napoleon headed into miserable exile, his second wife, Marie-Louise of Austria, got off pretty lightly. After her heady few years as Empress of the French, she was left with the dukedom of Parma, Piacenza and Guastalla. She ruled until 1847, with a moderation and good sense uncommon for the time.

Various of her belongings, including a portrait of her great husband, ended up in the hands of town notable and collector Glauco Lombardi. An eclectic assortment of Lombardi's artworks and other objects illustrative of life in Parma over the past few centuries now fill the Museo di Glauco Lombardi, on Via Garibaldi. It is open Tuesday to Saturday from 9.30 am to 1 pm and 3 to 5 pm and Sunday mornings. Admission is free.

West Bank

On the west bank of the Parma (l'Oltretorrente) are spread the rambling gardens of the **Parco Ducale**, first laid out in 1560 around the Farnese family's **Palazzo Ducale**. The palace is now home to the local carabinieri, but groups can visit by calling ahead – ask at the tourist office. Admission is free, and the gardens are open from dawn to dusk, except in summer, when you can stroll until midnight.

Just south of the park, at Via R Tanzi, is the **Casa Natale di Toscanini**, the birthplace of one of Italy's greatest modern conductors, Arturo Toscanini (1867-1957). His career began almost by accident during a tour in Brazil, when he was asked to take the podium in Rio de Janeiro after the Brazilian conductor had stormed off. In 1908 he joined the New York Metropolitan, and from then on split his time between Italy and the US, where he died in 1957. The house contains a small museum dedicated to his life and music. While in a musical frame of mind, you could visit the tomb of Niccolò Paganini, a couple of km farther south in the Cimitero della Villetta.

Places to Stay

Cheap accommodation can be difficult to find most of the year, so bookings are advisable. Located within the walls of the giant former fortress, the city's youth hostel, the *Ostello Cittadella* (☎ 58 15 46), Parco Cittadella 5, charges L13,000 a night. It's open from the beginning of April to the end of October. Take bus No 6 or 9 from the train station or city centre and ask the driver for directions. There is a *camping ground* inside the fortress, run by the same management.

The *Albergo Sole* (☎ 99 51 07), Via Gramsci 15, has basic singles/doubles from L45,000/60,000. Take bus No 10 from the train station. *Albergo Lazzaro* (☎ 20 89 44), Via XX Marzo 16, the street leading away from the baptistry, has rooms from L35,000/60,000. The *Croce di Malta* (☎ 23 56 43), Borgo Palmia 8, south of Piazza Garibaldi, has simple rooms from L40,000/60,000. The location is great and they provide parking permits for the area. The two-star *Albergo Moderno*

(☎ 77 26 47), handy for the train station at Via A Cecchi 4, has rooms from L42,000/60,000 or L54,000/85,000 with a bathroom, but the area is a little unpleasant. The *Hotel Astoria* (☎ 27 27 17), Via Trento 9, has all the mod cons and is near the train station – rooms cost L95,000/140,000.

Places to Eat

There is a produce market in Piazza Ghiaia, near the river south of the Palazzo della Pilotta, that is open daily. For a cheap lunch, the self-service restaurant *Le Premier*, Borgo San Biagio 6, is open from midday to 2 pm only. Another decent snack place is the *Clinica del Panino*, Borgo Palmia 2d.

Il Gattopardo, Via M d'Azeglio 63, is one of the city's more popular pizzerias, with big pizzas from L8000 to L11,000. If you are staying at Albergo Sole, *Blu Moon*, a couple of doors towards the city centre on Via Gramsci, has everything from seafood to pizzas. Main courses start at about L10,000. The *Albergo Lazzaro* has a restaurant that does a L16,000 vegetarian menu. The *Croce di Malta*, in the hotel of the same name (see Places to Stay for location) is more upmarket. Parma has attracted plenty of Chinese chefs – the *Shanghai Bar* on Strada Farini is just one of the city's ubiquitous Oriental restaurants.

Piazza Garibaldi is as good a spot as any for sipping your Campari and reading the paper.

Entertainment

Parma's opera, concert and theatre season runs from about October to April. A rich music and opera programme is offered by the Teatro Regio (☎ 21 86 78), Via Garibaldi 16, while Teatro Due (☎ 23 02 42), Via Salnitrara 10, presents the city's top drama. In summer the city sponsors outdoor music programmes – enquire at the IAT.

Getting There & Away

Bus TEP (☎ 21 41) operates buses throughout the region, including into the Apennines and to Soragna and Busseto (see the following section) from just in front of the train station on Piazzale della Chiesa. Interregional services are more scarce, but do run to Mantova, Bologna, Milan, Trentino and Ancona.

Train By train (☎ 77 11 18), the city is connected by frequent services to Milan, Bologna, Brescia, La Spezia and Rome.

Car & Motorbike The city is just south of the A1 to Milan and east of the A15, which connects the A1 to La Spezia. It is on the Via Emilia (SS9), while the SS62 provides an alternative route parallel to the A15. There is a major car park at the Palazzo della Pilotta and plenty of metered parking near the station. Traffic is restricted in the centre, which is a labyrinth of one-way streets.

AROUND PARMA
Verdi Country

Head north-west of Parma along the Via Emilia and branch north at Fontevivo for Fontanellato and you will find one of the more interesting of Parma province's 25 castles. Sitting in its murky moat, the **Rocca di Sanvitale** was built in the 16th century by the family of the same name more as a pleasure dome than a military bastion, inclined as the Sanvitale clan was to more idle pursuits. Parmigianino had a part in the decoration. It is open from 9.30 to 11.45 am and 3 to 5 pm (longer in summer). Admission by guided tour costs L6000. Nine km farther on is Soragna, site of the **Rocca Meli Lupi**. It looks more like a stately home, but there

are Parmigianino works and a display of period furniture. Opening times are similar to those at Fontanellato, but both are closed on Monday. Admission is L8000.

Roncole Verdi, site of the humble home where Giuseppe Verdi came into the world, is 10 km on. The **Casa Natale di Giuseppe Verdi** is open from 9.30 am to midday and 2.30 to 5 pm (longer in summer). Admission costs L4000 if you don't have a L8000 cumulative ticket to all the Verdi sights.

Next stop is Busseto, a couple of km farther on. The **Teatro Verdi** is closed but you can visit a small **museum** dedicated to Verdi in the run-down Villa Pallavicino and, a few km outside Busseto, his villa at **Sant'Agata**.

TEP buses from Parma run along this route up to six times a day on weekdays.

South into the Apennines

You could take several routes south of Parma to cross the Apennines into north-western Tuscany, stopping at a castle on the way or hiking through the hills and around several glacial lakes.

One route roughly follows the Parma river towards Langhirano (a town of 6th-century Lombard origin). About five km short of the town rises the majestic **Castello di Torrechiare**, one of many built or rebuilt by Pier Maria Rossi in the 15th century. Here he romped with his lover Bianca Pellegrino in the Camera d'Oro (Golden Room), where he could look at a map of all his castles on the ceiling.

The Small World of Don Camillo

If postwar Italy was dominated by the squaring off between the church-backed Christian Democrat party and the communists, no-one captured the essence of that conflict better than humorist Giovanni Guareschi. Emilia-Romagna, the stronghold of Italian communism, became the scene of Guareschi's village scraps between Don Camillo, the local curate with a direct line to God, and Peppone, the town mayor with a striking resemblance to Stalin. Their antics in what became known as Guareschi's Piccolo Mondo, published weekly in satirical magazines and later collected in several volumes (eg *Don Camillo* and *Don Camillo e il Suo Gregge*), were a clever balance between comedy and political satire – so successful that several of the stories ended up on film.

A free exhibition dedicated to Guareschi's Piccolo Mondo in the Sala delle Damigiane at Roncole Verdi is scheduled to remain open until the year 2000. ∎

From Langhirano, follow the road down the west bank of the Parma, crossing the river at Capoponte and proceeding to **Tizzano Val Parma**, a charming Apennine town that offers pleasant walking in summer and skiing in winter (five km farther on at Schia). Farther south still, the heights around **Monchio delle Corti** offer views to La Spezia on a good day. It's a possible base for exploring some of the 20 **glacial lakes** that dot the southern corner of the province, bordering on Tuscany.

The mountains are in fact riddled with walking and cycling tracks and rifugi. If you'd prefer to be carried, the Centro Turismo Equestre at Tarsogno (☎ 0525-8 93 00), south of Salsomaggiore Terme (ask for Berni Sergio), hires out horses and arranges riding excursions. There are several similar organisations in the province – the Parma IAT can point you to some of them. An interesting challenge is to follow the Romea, an ancient route for pilgrims heading to Rome. The IAT in Parma has an excellent trekking brochure for this route and can advise on appropriate maps.

Of the other 20 or so castles in the province, **Castello Bardi**, about 60 km south-west of Parma (not on the above route), is also worth a mention. Soaring above the surrounding town, it dates to 898 AD, although most of the present structure was built in the 15th century.

Getting There & Away

TEP runs buses from Parma to most destinations throughout the province. On weekdays there are four a day to Bardi for instance, and at least as many to Monchio delle Corti via Langhirano. On weekends the La Spezia -Parma train service guarantees space for transporting bicycles.

PIACENZA

At the north-western corner of Emilia, just short of the Lombard frontier, Piacenza is another prosperous town generally overlooked by tourists. Its few noteworthy monuments certainly make a stop worthwhile, but probably don't warrant an enormous effort to go out of your way.

Orientation

The train station is at the eastern edge of town, about a 15-minute walk from the central square, Piazza dei Cavalli. A couple of cheapish hotels lie between the two.

Information

The IAT office (☎ 2 93 24) in Piazzetta dei Mercanti is open from 9.30 am to 12.30 pm and 4 to 6 pm but is closed on Thursday afternoons and Sundays. Poste restante mail can be addressed to 29100 Piacenza, and the telephone code for Piacenza is 0523.

Things to See

Piazza dei Cavalli is dominated by the impressive brick and marble 13th-century town hall, also known as **Il Gotico**. In front of the building, the two equestrian statues of the Farnese dukes Alessandro and his son Ranuccio, by Francesco Mochi, date from 1625 and are masterpieces of Baroque sculpture.

The **duomo**, on Via XX Settembre, was started in 1122 and is a sombre Romanesque building with frescoes by Guercino. The nearby **Basilica di Sant'Antonino** was built in the 11th century on the site of an earlier church. Its octagonal tower is claimed to be the oldest of its type in Italy.

The **Palazzo Farnese** in Piazza Cittadella was started in 1558 but never finished. It houses three little museums, of which the main one, the Civico Museo, is home to the Etruscan Fegato di Piacenza, a bronze liver which was used for divining the future. The other two are devoted to carriages and Italian unification memorabilia. All are open Tuesday to Sunday from 9 am to 12.30 pm, and on Thursday and Sunday afternoons as well.

A few blocks south of Piazza dei Cavalli, the **Galleria d'Arte Moderna**, Via San Siro 13, contains a fairly decent collection of 18th and 19th-century Italian art and sculpture. It's open from 10 am to midday and 3 to 5 pm (2 to 4 pm in winter).

Places to Stay & Eat

Budget accommodation is not one of Piacenza's strong points. *Albergo Corona* (☎ 2 09 48), Via Roma 141, has singles/doubles

EMILIA-ROMAGNA

Piacenza

0   100   200 m

OTHER
1 Palazzo Farnese
3 Il Gotico
4 Tourist Office
8 Telecom Office
10 Pasta Store
11 Politeama Cinema
12 Galleria
     d'Arte Moderna
13 Basilica di Sant'
     Antonino & Piazza
14 Post Office
15 Chiesa di San
     Francesco
17 Duomo
20 Train Station

PLACES TO STAY
2 Grande Albergo Roma
18 Albergo & Ristorante
     Corona
19 Hotel Moderno

PLACES TO EAT
5 Balzer
6 Gelateria
7 The Bonnie Prince
     Charles
9 Il Pizzaio
16 Pizzeria da Pasquale

from L40,000/50,000, but call ahead. *Hotel Moderno* (☎ 38 50 41), Via Tibini 31 (there's no sign) is nearest the train station and costs L40,000/60,000 – it's nothing special. If for some reason you want to spend big in Piacenza, you could try the overpriced *Grande Albergo Roma* (☎ 32 32 01), Via Citadella 14, where singles start at L135,000.

If you're just passing through, *Il Pizzaio*, Corso Vittorio Emanuele II, has pizza by the slice from about L2000, or else grab one at the *Ristorante Corona*, beneath the hotel, for about L6000. The *Pizzeria da Pasquale* on Piazza del Duomo does a similar deal. More adventurous takeaway can be had in the nameless pasta store across the road from Il Pizzaio. The *Balzer* café, on Corso Vittoria Emanuele II where it runs into Piazza dei Cavalli, is popular, although the monumental interior is somewhat over the top. For an expensive ale, you could pretend you're somewhere else at *The Bonnie Prince Charles*, a pub and restaurant around the corner on Vicolo Perestrello.

Getting There & Away
The easiest way to get to Piacenza is by train. There are direct services from Milan, Turin,

Cremona, Bologna and Ancona. If you're driving, Piacenza is just off the A1 from Milan and the A21 (and SS10) from Brescia or Turin. The SS9 (Via Emilia) runs past Piacenza across the line of the region's main cities to the Adriatic.

East of Bologna

FERRARA

Lucrezia Borgia found marriage into the Este family brought several disadvantages, not least among them the move to this Po valley city, just south of the modern frontier with Veneto. Close to the river and wetlands, Ferrara in winter can be cold and grey, shrouded in cloying banks of fog. Used to a warmer climate, Borgia's feelings were perhaps understandable, but Ferrara (especially on a sunny day) retains much of the austere splendour of its Renaissance heyday, when it was strong enough to keep Rome and Venice at arm's length.

History
The Este dynasty ruled Ferrara from 1260 to 1598, and their political and military prowess was matched by an uninterrupted stream of cultural activity. Petrarch, Titian, Antonio Pisanello and the poets Torquato Tasso and Ludovico Ariosto are just some of the luminaries who spent time here under the patronage of the Este dukes.

When the House of Este collapsed in 1598, Pope Clement VIII claimed the city and presided over its decline. It recovered some importance during the Napoleonic period when it was made chief city of the lower Po river, and the local government has carefully restored much of the centre since the end of WW II.

Orientation
From the train station in Piazza Stazione at the western edge of the centre, head north along Via Felisatti and turn right into Viale Cavour, the main street. Turn right again at the Castello Estense (impossible to miss) for

Piazzetta del Castello. Corso Martiri della Libertà, at the east side of the castle, runs into Piazza Cattedrale and Piazza Trento Trieste, the centre of town. The centre can also be reached along Via Cassoli and Via Garibaldi, a more direct route from the station.

Information
Tourist Office The main IAT office (☎ 20 93 70), Corso della Giovecca 21, is open Monday to Saturday from 9 am to 7 pm and Sunday from 9 am to 1 pm and 2.30 to 5.30 pm. There is a second office at Via Kennedy 2.

Post & Telecommunications The post office is at Viale Cavour 27, near the castle. It's open Monday to Saturday from 8.10 am to 7.20 pm. Poste restante mail can be addressed to 44100 Ferrara.

The Telecom office is in Largo Castello 30 and is open until 7.30 pm. The telephone code for Ferrara is 0532.

Emergency The questura (☎ 29 43 11) is at Corso Ercole I d'Este 26, and the staff speak English. In an emergency dial either ☎ 113 or ☎ 20 01 11. For an ambulance, call ☎ 20 31 31. The Ospedale Sant'Anna (☎ 29 51 11) is at Corso della Giovecca 203.

Things to See
The IAT publishes a guide called *Ferrara*, which lists six itineraries, taking in the medieval and Renaissance aspects and the city wall, which extends around the centre for nine km and is worth a look, especially in the north of the city.

Castello Estense The imposing castle in the centre of town was started in 1385 for Nicolò II d'Este, primarily to defend the family from riotous subjects who at one point rebelled over tax increases. By the middle of the following century, the Este family had begun to expand the fortress. Under Ercole I it became the dynasty's permanent residence.

Although sections are now used for government offices, many of the rooms, including the royal suites, are open for viewing. Highlights are the Sala dei Giganti

EMILIA-ROMAGNA

Ferrara

0   250   500 m

Minor Streets Not Depicted

(Giants' Room) and Salone dei Giochi (Games' Salon), with frescoes by Camillo and Sebastiano Filippi, the Cappella di Renée de France, and the dungeon. Here, in 1425, Duke Nicolò III d'Este had his young second wife, Parisina Malatesta, and his son, Ugo, beheaded after discovering they were lovers, providing the inspiration for Robert Browning's *My Last Duchess*. The castle is open daily, except Monday, from 9.30 am to 5.30 pm. Admission is L6000.

Palazzo Municipale Linked to the castle, the town hall once also contained Este family

apartments. The grand staircase by Pietro Benvenuti degli Ordani is worth seeing. Although closed to the public, you can see some of the rooms if you ask the attendant.

Cathedral Consecrated early in the 12th century, the cathedral features a mixture of Renaissance and Gothic styles. Note also the array of columns along its south façade. For many years, all or part of the façade and its remarkable reliefs have been covered up for restoration, but in 1995 it appeared the cathedral would at last be freed of all scaffolding. The **Museo**

PLACES TO STAY		OTHER		20	Palazzo Municipale
				21	Piazzetta del Castello
4	Albergo Bergamasco	1	Porta degli Angeli	23	Piazza Municipio
13	Albergo Tre Stelle	2	Certosa	24	Piazza Cattedrale &
22	Albergo Annunziata	3	Museo Civico d'Arte		Cathedral
30	Albergo Nazionale		Moderna e	25	Piazza Trento Trieste
31	Casa degli Artisti		Contemporanea	27	Credito Romagnolo (ATM)
		5	Pinacoteca Nazionale	28	Ghetto
		6	Museo del Risorgimento e	29	Parking (Foreign Cars)
PLACES TO EAT			della Resistenza	33	Casa Romei
		7	Questura (Police Station)	34	Monastero del Corpus
11	Trattoria da Giacomino	8	Train Station		Domini
18	Al Postiglione	9	Stadium	35	Palazzina di Marfisa
19	Al Brindisi	10	Post Office	36	Hospital
26	Ristorante Royal	12	Bus Station	37	Piazzale Medaglie d'Oro
32	Le Grazie	14	Market	38	Palazzo Schifanoia
39	Il Cucco	15	Telecom Office	41	Tourist Office
40	Gelateria Borsellin	16	Castello Estense	43	Palazzo di Lodovico il
42	Antica Trattoria del Volano	17	Tourist Office		Moro

EMILIA-ROMAGNA

della Cattedrale contains a superb collection of Renaissance pieces including 15th-century illustrated missals, and works by Jacopo della Quercia and other Renaissance masters. It is open daily from 10 am to midday and 3 to 5 pm and admission is by donation. The bell tower was started in 1412 by the Florentine architect, Leon Battista Alberti.

The city's former **ghetto** is centred on Via Vignatagliata south of the cathedral.

Museums & Galleries Heading north along Corso Ercole I d'Este from the castle is Palazzo dei Diamanti (Palace of the Diamonds), named after the shape of its rusticated façade and built for Sigismondo d'Este late in the 15th century by Biagio Rossetti. Regarded as the family's finest palace, the building now houses the **Pinacoteca Nazionale**, in which are hung works by artists of the Ferrarese and Bolognese schools, and a series of prints by Andrea Mantegna.

The gallery is open on Sunday from 9 am to 1 pm, Tuesday, Wednesday and Saturday to 2 pm and Thursday and Friday to 6 pm. Admission is L8000. Next door at No 19 is the **Museo del Risorgimento e della Resistenza,** a fairly standard display of decrees, letters and other memorabilia tracing Italian political history from the mid-19th century to WW II.

The **Museo Civico d'Arte Moderna e Contemporanea** is located in the Palazzo Massari at Corso Porta Mare 9, east of the Pinacoteca. It is open from 9 am to 1 pm and 3 to 6 pm. Admission is L8000.

The **Palazzina di Marfisa d'Este**, Corso della Giovecca 170, went up in 1559 and is worth a look for its decoration and furnishings. It is open daily from 9 am to 12.30 pm and 3 to 6 pm. Admission is L3000.

Lucrezia Borgia spent many of her Ferrara days in what is now the **Casa Romei**, on the corner of Via Praisolo and Via Savonarola, a typical Renaissance-style house. It is open daily, except Monday, from 8.30 am to 2 pm. Admission is L4000. She is buried in the nearby Monastery of Corpus Domini, along with several Este family members, but the tombs are closed for restoration.

Via Borgo di Sotto leads to the 14th-century **Palazzo Schifanoia**, a sumptuous Este residence on Via Scandiana. The Salone dei Mesi (Room of the Months), featuring frescoes by Francesco del Cossa, ranks as the finest example of Ferrarese Renaissance mural painting. The palace is open daily from 9 am to 7 pm. Admission is L8000.

South of the palace, on the corner of Via Porta d'Amore and Via XX Settembre, is the

Palazzo di Ludovico il Moro, housing the Museo Archeologico Nazionale. The palace was built by local architect Biagio Rossetti for the Duke of Milan. If it's not closed for renovations, take a look at the collection of Etruscan artefacts.

City Walls Although not terribly impressive, most of the nine km of ancient city walls are partly intact and a tour makes a pleasant walk. Start with the Porta degli Angeli in the north of the city – the surrounding area is leafy and tranquil, apart from the odd jogger or cyclist.

Festivals
On the last Sunday of May each year, the eight *contrade* (districts) of Ferrara compete in the Palio, a horse race that momentarily turns Piazza Ariostea into medieval bedlam. Claimed to be the oldest such race in Italy, the first official competition was held in 1279.

The Ferrara Buskers' Festival, held late each August, attracts buskers from around the globe, primarily because the city pays travel and accommodation expenses for 20 of the lucky performers. Entry forms are available from the festival organisers (☎ 24 93 37; fax 75 41 91), or write c/o the Istituto di Cultura, Casa G Cini, Via Boccacanale di Santo Stefano 24.

Places to Stay
Accommodation is usually easy to find although many hotels close during August. The city's only camping ground is *Estense* (☎ 75 23 96), Via Gramicia, north of the centre outside the wall. Take bus No 3 from the train station.

The best hotel deal is at *Casa degli Artisti* (☎ 76 10 38), Via Vittoria 66, a few minutes walk south of the cathedral, with singles/doubles for L24,000/38,000. Book ahead. *Albergo Bergamasco* (☎ 20 49 56), Corso Porta Po 170 (next to the Chinese restaurant), is near the train station and has rooms from L25,000/40,000. *Albergo Tre Stelle* (☎ 20 97 48), Via Vegri 15, is central and charges L25,000/35,000. *Albergo Nazionale* (☎ 20

96 04), Corso Porta Reno 32, has rooms from L48,000/65,000. For well-located luxury, head to the four-star *Albergo Annunziata* (☎ 20 11 11), Piazza della Repubblica 5. Rooms start at L180,000.

Places to Eat
Ferrara's cuisine is typical of the region, incorporating meats and cheeses. One of the local specialities is *cappelacci di zucca*, a pasta pouch filled with pumpkin that looks vaguely like a small, floppy hat. Another traditional dish is *tigella*, a mixture of cheeses and meats served with bread.

For simple snacks, *Al Postiglione*, tucked away at Vicolo Chiuso del Teatro 4, does decent panini and the like. A bright place to eat pizza is *Ristorante Royal*, Via Vignatagliata 11.

A good value place, popular with locals, is the *Trattoria da Giacomino*, Via Garibaldi 135. A meal with wine will cost about L20,000. A little more expensive, and perhaps a little better as well, is the *Antica Trattoria del Volano*, Viale Volano 20. Try the cappelacci di zucca and rabbit. More upmarket still is *Il Cucco*, Via Voltacasotto, where you'll be looking at L40,000 for a meal. *Le Grazie*, Via

Vignatagliata 61, in the ghetto, specialises in Jewish dishes. Main courses start at about L10,000. *Al Brindisi*, Via Adelardi 11, next to the cathedral, dates from 1435 and serves a salami-and-red-wine dish. This restaurant is quite expensive.

Entertainment

There are a few cinemas about town, but Ferrara is otherwise pretty quiet. Ferrara Musica (☎ 20 24 00) organises a limited spring and autumn season of classical music.

Getting There & Away

Bus The bus station is at Via Rampari di San Paolo. ACFT buses (☎ 24 06 79) operate services within the city and to surrounding towns such as Comacchio as well as the Adriatic beaches (some of these leave from the train station).

Train By train (☎ 24 64 90 for information) there are frequent services to Bologna, Venice, Ravenna and other towns in the region.

By car, the city is close to the A13, which connects Bologna with Padua. A branch running south of the city goes to Comacchio.

Car & Motorbike The SS16 runs directly to Ravenna, Rimini and down the coast into the Marches. The A13 from Padua to Bologna lies west of the city.

Getting Around

Most traffic is banned from the city centre, but there is a small parking area for foreigners' cars on Corso Porta Reno. There are parking stations at the southern end of the centre on Via Bologna and the eastern edge near Piazzale Medaglie d'Oro. ACFT runs buses Nos 1, 2 and 9 from the train station to the city centre.

THE PO DELTA

Considering the incredibly polluted state of the Po river, the Po delta, which straddles Emilia-Romagna and Veneto, should be an unpleasant place. However, the stretch of coast where the river spills into the Adriatic Sea is strangely alluring, particularly because the wetlands surrounding its two large lagoons – the Valli di Comacchio in the south and the Valle Bertuzzi in the north – have been designated nature reserves. The area provides some of Europe's best bird-watching, and after years of neglect by tourist authorities is now drawing quite a crowd. Despite this, swimming is banned, and many beaches have perennial problems with sludge-like algae plagues caused by the dumping of phosphates upstream. The only other problem is that the area is plagued by mosquitoes in summer, so be sure to have repellent, if not mosquito nets, on hand.

Information

Most towns in the area have tourist offices, although many are open in summer only. Those at Comacchio (☎ 0533-31 28 44), Via Buonafede 12, and the Pomposa Abbey (☎ 0533-71 01 00) near Codigoro are open year-round. They produce a wealth of information, including cycling itineraries, walking and horse-riding details, and tips on boat excursions, which are the best way to see the delta.

Things to See & Do

The **Abbazia di Pomposa**, 50 km east of Ferrara, near Codigoro, is one of the oldest Benedictine abbeys in Italy, with a church dating from the 7th century. It is believed the monk Guido d'Arezzo invented the musical scale here, and from the turn of the millennium it was one of Italy's supreme cultural centres. It's decline began in the 14th century, and in 1652 the abbey was closed. Inside, the church is adorned with frescoes from the 14th-century Rimini school and works by Vitale di Bologna, and it contains a small museum with free admission. The complex is open daily from 9 am to 6 pm. Musica Pomposa is a music festival staged at the abbey each July (☎ 0533-72 95 85 for information). Sporadic buses connect with Ravenna and Comacchio, but plan carefully or you'll end up stranded there.

Comacchio is a small fishing village that has but one attraction – the Trepponti (Triple Bridge) built in 1635, which crosses three canals. Don't stop unless you must, as the city's claim to be a mini-Venice is a trifle exaggerated.

The delta's information office at Ca' Vecchia (☎ 0544-44 68 66), a wildlife guardians' centre at Via Fossatone in the Stazione Pineta San Vitale park north of Ravenna, produces a map detailing the types of birds likely to be found in that part of the delta's Riserva Naturale, and the sanctuaries at Punte Alberete and Valle Mandriole. You can pick up the same map at the Ravenna IAT. The World Wide Fund for Nature in Ferrara (☎ 0532-6 00 09), Viale Alfonso I d'Este 7, can provide information about the wildlife.

For boat trips, try the boat *Delfinus* (☎ 0533-38 12 65), which leaves from Lido degli Scacchi east of Comacchio, or the *Principessa* (☎ 0533-99 98 15), which leaves from Gorino.

Places to Stay
If you want to stay in the area, a cheap option is the *Albergo Luciana* (☎ 0533-71 21 40), Via Roma 66, in Codigoro, which charges L29,000/42,000 for a single/double.

Getting There & Away
Moving around the area with public transport is difficult. From Ferrara to the Pomposa, for instance, there is virtually nothing. You can get as far as Codigoro, but from there you're on your own. This makes a day trip from Ferrara without your own transport a frustrating prospect.

RAVENNA
Celebrated for the early Christian and Byzantine mosaics that adorn its churches and monuments, Ravenna was in fact capital of the Byzantine Empire's western regions during the reign of Emperor Justinian and Empress Theodora.

The city had been the capital of the Western Roman Empire from 402 AD, when the ineffectual Emperor Honorius moved his court from Rome because Ravenna's surrounding malarial swamps made it easier to defend from northern invaders. The latter, however, simply walked around him and marched into Rome in 410. Honorius was unable, or unwilling, to react, preferring to

vegetate in Ravenna until his death in 423 – the city finally succumbed 50 years later. The Byzantines arrived in 540 and ruled until 752, when the city was conquered by the Lombards. Venetians controlled the city from 1441 to 1509, at which time it was incorporated into the Papal States.

Under the Romans, Goths and Byzantines, Ravenna gradually rose to become one of the most splendid cities in the Mediterranean, and its mosaics are matched only by those of Istanbul; in his *Divine Comedy*, Dante described them as a symphony of colour. The city is close to Adriatic beaches but, especially when effluent from the Po is a threat, they are hardly attractive.

Orientation
From the train station, on the eastern edge of town in Piazza Farini, it's a short walk along Viale Farini and its continuation, Via Diaz, into the central Piazza del Popolo. Nearly everything of interest is within easy walking distance of here. A few of the cheaper hotels are near the train station.

Information
Tourist Offices The IAT (☎ 3 54 04) is at Via Salara 8, off Via Cavour. It is open daily from 9 am to 1 pm and 3 to 6 pm. A second office (☎ 45 15 39) is open from March to September at the Mausoleo di Teodorico, Via delle Industrie 14.

Post & Telecommunications The main post office is in Piazza Garibaldi, just south of Piazza del Popolo, and is open Monday to Saturday from 8 am to 7 pm. Poste restante mail can be addressed to 48100 Ravenna.

The Telecom office is in Via G Rasponi 22 and is open from 8 am to 11 pm. The telephone code for Ravenna is 0544.

Emergency For police call ☎ 113. The questura (☎ 54 41 11) is in Piazza del Popolo. For an ambulance call ☎ 118 or for home attendance by the Guardia Medica call ☎ 3 30 11. The Ospedale Santa Maria delle Croci (☎ 40 91 11) is at Via Missiroli 10.

EMILIA-ROMAGNA

PLACES TO STAY

11 Albergo Centrale Byron
14 Albergo al Giaciglio
15 Albergo Ravenna

PLACES TO EAT

6 Scai'
7 Pizzeria Altero
9 La Gardela
10 Free Flow Bizantino
12 Caffè Roma
24 Guidarello
30 Ca' Vèn

OTHER

1 Mausoleo di Teodorico
2 Tourist Office
3 Mausoleo di Galla Placidia
4 Basilica di San Vitale
5 Museo Nazionale
8 Tourist Office
13 Battistero degli Ariani &
   Chiesa dello Spirito Santo
16 ATM Bus Ticket Office
17 Train Station
18 Regional Bus Station
19 Basilica di Sant'Apollinare
   Nuovo
20 Banca Nazionale del Lavoro
21 Piazza Garibaldi
22 Questura (Police Station)
23 Post Office
25 Telecom Office
26 Piazza del Duomo
27 Battistero Neoniano
28 Duomo
29 Museo Arcivescovile
31 Tomba di Dante
32 Piazza Caduti per la Libertà
33 Piazza di San Francesco
34 Chiesa di San Francesco
35 Hospital

Ravenna

0   100   200 m

Minor Streets Not Depicted

Things to See

A biglietto cumulativo allows you into the six main monuments for L9000. If you intend to view the Museo Internazionale delle Ceramiche in Faenza as well, buy the ticket for L10,000. Opening times given below are summer times, which tend to be longer than opening times through the rest of the year.

Basilica di San Vitale Just in off the street of the same name and a few minutes walk north-west of the tourist office, the Basilica di San Vitale was consecrated in 547 by Archbishop Maximian. Its sombre exterior hides a dazzling internal feast of colour, dominated by the mosaics around the chancel, which was constructed between 521 and 548. The mosaics on the side and end walls represent scenes from the Old Testament; to the left, Abraham and the three angels and the sacrifice of Isaac are depicted; and on the right are the death of Abel and the offering of Melchizedek. Inside the chancel, the finest mosaics of the series depict the Byzantine emperor Justinian with St Maximian and Empress Theodora. It is open in summer from 9 am to 7 pm. Admission is L5000 (if you don't have the L9000 ticket).

Mausoleo di Galla Placidia In the same grounds as the basilica lies the mausoleum erected by Galla Placidia, the half-sister of Emperor Honorius, who initiated construction of many of Ravenna's grandest buildings. The light inside, filtered through the alabaster windows, is dim but good enough to illuminate the city's oldest mosaics (same opening hours and ticket as the basilica).

Museo Nazionale Ravenna's main museum is also here; monks began the collection of prehistoric, Roman, Christian and Byzantine artefacts in the 18th century and various items from later periods have been added. It is open in summer from 8.30 am to 7.30 pm. Admission is L8000 and is not covered by the cumulative ticket.

Duomo The town's cathedral, in Via G Rasponi, was built in 1733 after its 5th-century predecessor was destroyed by earthquake. Although the cathedral itself is unremarkable, the small adjoining **Museo Arcivescovile** (Episcopal Museum) contains an exquisite 6th-century ivory throne of St Maximian and some beautiful mosaics. More mosaics, of Christ's Baptism and the apostles, can be seen in the neighbouring **Battistero Neoniano**. Thought to have started life as a Roman bathhouse, it was converted into a baptistry in the 5th century. They are open from 9.30 am to 5.30 pm. Admission to both is L4000.

Tomba di Dante As Dante showed in the *Divine Comedy* (much of it written in Ravenna), politics is a dodgy business. Having been exiled from Florence in 1302, Dante finally went to live in Ravenna, where he died in 1321. His tomb is next to the Chiesa di San Francesco, and there is a small **museum** (admission L3000). A mound placed over his sarcophagus during WW II to protect it from air raids is proudly marked and the area around the tomb has been declared a *zona di silenzio*. Opening hours seem flexible – ring the bell and see what the custodian has to say. To continue on a literary

note, Lord Byron lived in a house on Piazza di San Francesco in 1819.

Other Churches Those appreciative of mosaics will want to visit the **Basilica di Sant'Apollinare Nuovo**, off Via di Roma, originally built by the Goths in the 6th century. The high walls in the nave are covered with mosaics – on the right depicting a procession of 26 martyrs and opposite a procession of virgins. It is open from 9 am to 5.30 pm. Admission is L4000. The Gothic **Battistero degli Ariani** is behind the Chiesa dello Spirito Santo, in Via Diaz.

Five km south-east of the city centre is the **Basilica di Sant'Apollinare in Classe** (take bus No 4 or the train to Classe). Built in the 6th century on the burial site of Ravenna's patron saint, St Apollinaris, who converted the city to Christianity in the 2nd century, the basilica features a brilliant mosaic over the altar.

Mosaic Courses
The Centro Internazionale di Studi per l'Insegnamento del Mosaico runs a series of two-week mosaic courses during June, July and August, starting at L450,000. Contact CISIM (☎ 48 23 78), Via Corrado Ricci 29, for information.

Places to Stay
The city is an easy day trip from Bologna, but its hostel and a few cheap hotels make staying overnight no problem, except in summer. The IAT office can provide a list of the hundreds of hotels lining the beaches near Ravenna. If you're interested in staying on a farm in the province, ask the IAT for its agriturismo brochure. The closest camping ground is at Marina di Ravenna on the beach (take the ATM bus or follow the SS67). *Camping Piombino* (☎ 53 02 30), Viale della Pace 42, and *Campeggio Riva Verde* (☎ 53 04 91), Viale della Nazione 301, have reasonably priced sites.

The HI youth hostel, the *Ostello Dante* (☎ 42 04 05), Via Aurelio Nicolodi 12, is one km from the train station towards the beach, and is served by bus No 1. Here B&B is

L16,000 and a meal L12,000. They have family rooms.

Albergo al Giaciglio (☎ 3 94 03), Via Rocca Brancaleone 42, is one of the cheaper alternatives, with rooms starting at L30,000/43,000. Handy to the train station is *Albergo Ravenna* (☎ 21 22 04), Via Maroncelli 12, which has rooms for L37,000/48,000. They also have parking. Those with looser purse strings could do worse than the centrally located *Albergo Centrale Byron* (☎ 3 34 79), on Piazza Andrea Costa, which has doubles starting from L75,000.

Places to Eat
The city's fresh-produce market (Mercato Coperto) in Piazza Andrea Costa, north of Piazza del Popolo, is the best bet for budget food, while the self-service *Free Flow Bizantino*, in the same piazza, is very cheap. *Pizzeria Altero*, Via Cavour 31, has pizza by the slice from L1500, and the hamburger fast-food restaurant *Burghy*, in Piazza del Popolo, has a great view and cheap beers.

The *Ca' Ven* enoteca, Via Corrado Ricci 24, has a good selection of local wines and serves traditional food at reasonable prices in a very nearly medieval atmosphere. At *La Gardela*, Via Ponte Marino 1, and *Scai'*, Via Maggiore 2, you can eat a meal for about L30,000, while *Guidarello*, Via Gessi 9, specialises in local dishes and charges from L8000 for main courses.

Entertainment
The Ravennati let it all hang out for the annual blues festival in July, which attracts big US names. There is also a busy summer concert calendar, including jazz and opera, with many of the churches as venues. Enquire at the IAT.

Things to Buy
To see local artisans constructing mosaics in the traditional way, visit **Studio Il Mosaico** (☎ 3 60 90), next to the museum at Via Benedetto Fiandrini 14, which specialises in copies of the city's finer works. Most are for sale.

Getting There & Away
Bus ATM buses (☎ 3 52 88) depart from behind the train station for towns along the coast and north, in the Po delta area.

Train Frequent trains (☎ 3 64 50) connect the city with Bologna, Ferrara (where you can change for Venice), Faenza, Rimini and the south coast.

Car & Motorbike Ravenna is on a branch of the A14 Bologna-Rimini autostrada. Otherwise, the SS16 (Via Adriatica) heads south from Ravenna to Rimini and on down the coast. There are car parks at the train station and near the Basilica di San Vitale.

Getting Around
Ravenna is easy to cover on foot. To see the city by bicycle, hire one at Coop San Vitale in Piazza Farini to the left of the station for L2000 an hour or L15,000 a day.

AROUND RAVENNA
Bicycle Tour
The Ravenna IAT produces a slim brochure detailing a three-day tour beginning and ending in Cervia, on the coast south of the city, which takes you through pine forests and past lagoons in the coastal area up towards the Valli di Comacchio.

Faenza
This Romagnola town has been producing high-grade ceramics for hundreds of years, and gave us the word faïence. A half-hour train ride from Ravenna, the Museo Internazionale delle Ceramiche is worth a visit. It's open daily in summer from 9 am to 7 pm. Admission is L6000.

You can get a L10,000 ticket in Ravenna for six monuments within the town as well as the Museo Faenza. There's a tourist office (☎ 0546-2 52 31) at Piazza del Popolo 1.

Mirabilandia
This huge amusement park, about 10 km south of Ravenna, could be one for the kids. Free buses connect with local trains at the

---

Remembering Il Duce

It may seem a little odd that Italy's great dictator, Benito Mussolini, should have been born and raised in the red territory of the Romagna. Predappio, a village overloaded with monumental buildings erected by its most infamous son, is also the Fascist leader's final resting place. His remains were buried here in 1957. About 15 km south of Forlì (a dull town 45 km north-west of Rimini along the Via Emilia), Predappio is the scene of pro-fascist celebrations each year, when the faithful few mark October 31, the anniversary of the day Mussolini became prime minister in 1922. Many of the young skinheads and older faithful probably forget that their beloved icon, prior to donning the black shirt, started his political life as a card-carrying socialist and journalist who rarely missed a chance to wave the red rag. ■

Savio station. For information, call free-phone ☎ 1678-15 082.

RIMINI

Originally Umbrian, then Etruscan and Roman, Rimini sits at the centre of the Riviera del Sole and is now inhabited by beach-goers. The city continued to change hands through the Middle Ages, knowing Byzantine, Lombard and papal rule before ending up in the hands of the Malatesta family in the 13th century. Two centuries later Cesare Borgia added it to his list of short-lived conquests, until it was ruled by Venice and finally, again, by the Papal States. It joined the Kingdom of Italy in 1860.

Little is left of the old city centre, and what remained was badly damaged or destroyed during 400 bombing raids in WW II. The town's main attraction is its frenetic nightlife – John Paul II in the early 1990s let loose a few papal broadsides at what he considers the limitless immorality of the place. In summer, Rimini fills with Italian and, increasingly, foreign holiday-makers in search of a scrap of beach and nocturnal fun and games – they have more than 100 discos and clubs to choose from, and the spectacle of a booming transsexual prostitution trade. In spite of all this, it is for many Italians a ritual family holiday destination.

Orientation

The main train station is in Piazzale Cesare Battisti, at the northern edge of the old city centre. Via Dante becomes Via IV Novembre and leads to Piazza Tre Martiri. Corso d'Augusto heads north-west from here to the city's other main square, Piazza Cavour. To get to the beach, walk to the north-western edge of Piazzale Cesare Battisti and turn right into Viale Principe Amedeo di Savoia, which broadens into the Parco di Federico Fellini at the waterfront.

Information

Tourist Offices The main IAT office (☎ 5 11 01) is at Piazzale di Federico Fellini 3 and is open daily from 8 am to 8 pm (to 2 pm in winter). There is a second office (☎ 5 13 31) at Via Dante 86, near the train station. It is open from 8.30 am to 12.30 pm and 4 to 6 pm. The Comune di Rimini (☎ 70 41 10) operates the Centro di Informazione at Corso d'Augusto 156, which opens Monday to Friday from 8 am to 1 pm and 2 to 7 pm and Saturday to 1 pm. They all provide an array of brochures, including the *Book Istantaneo*, a useful guide to the city.

Money There are plenty of banks where you can change money. The Banca Nazionale del Lavoro and Cassa di Risparmio di Rimini, both on Corso d'Augusto, have ATMs that accept Visa and several other cards.

Post & Telecommunications The main post office is at Largo Giulio Cesare and is open Monday to Friday from 8.10 am to 5.30 pm and Saturday to 1 pm. There's a branch at Via

Gambalunga. Poste restante mail can be addressed to 47037 Rimini.

The Telecom office is at Via Trieste 1 and is open from 8 am to 9.30 pm. The telephone code is 0541.

Emergency & Medical Services For police attendance, call ☎ 113. The questura (☎ 5 10 00) is at Corso d'Augusto 152. In medical emergencies, call ☎ 38 70 01 for an ambulance or the Guardia Medica. The Ospedale Infermi (☎ 70 51 11) is at Viale Luigi Settembrini 2, south-east of the city centre along Viale Roma and Viale Ugo Bassi.

The city offers cut-price medical attention for tourists during summer months, usually near Piazzale di Federico Fellini.

Castel Sigismondo

Brooding over the south-west corner of the old town, the castle takes its name from one of the Malatesta family, which ruled for a couple of centuries until Cesare Borgia took over in 1500. Sigismondo was the worst of a pretty bad lot, condemned to hell by Pope Pius II, who burned an effigy of him in Rome because of his shameful crimes, which included rape, murder, incest, adultery and

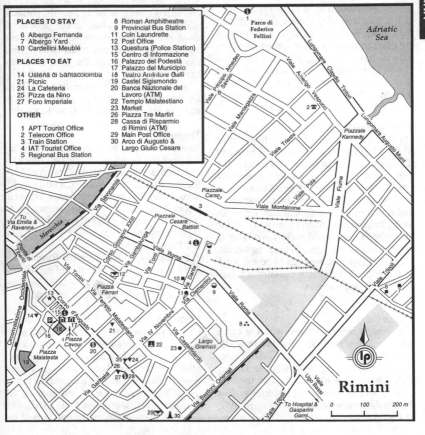

PLACES TO STAY
6 Albergo Fernanda
7 Albergo Yard
10 Cardellini Meublé

PLACES TO EAT
14 Osteria di Santacolomba
21 Picnic
24 La Cafeteria
25 Pizza da Nino
27 Foro Imperiale

OTHER
1 APT Tourist Office
2 Telecom Office
3 Train Station
4 IAT Tourist Office
5 Regional Bus Station
8 Roman Amphitheatre
9 Provincial Bus Station
11 Coin Laundrette
12 Post Office
13 Questura (Police Station)
15 Centro di Informazione
16 Palazzo del Podestà
17 Palazzo del Municipio
18 Teatro Amintore Galli
19 Castel Sigismondo
20 Banca Nazionale del Lavoro (ATM)
22 Tempio Malatestiano
23 Market
26 Piazza Tre Martiri
28 Cassa di Risparmio di Rimini (ATM)
29 Main Post Office
30 Arco di Augusto & Largo Giulio Cesare

Rimini

severe oppression of his people – the usual stuff.

Otherwise known as the Rocca Malatestiana, the building houses the **Museo delle Culture Extraeuropee**, a collection of African, Asian and pre-Columbian art. It is open Monday to Friday from 8 am to 1.30 pm and on Tuesday and Thursday afternoons from 3.30 to 6 pm. Admission is L4000.

Roman Remains

About the only evidence left of the Roman presence in the city is the crumbly **Arco di Augusto** (Arch of Augustus) built in 27 BC, at the east end of Corso d'Augusto, and the modest **Ponte di Tiberio** (Tiberius' Bridge), at the west end of the same thoroughfare, built in the 1st century AD as testimony to the city's importance to the empire. Archaeologists have also dug up half of Piazza L Ferrari to get at a possible Roman villa. The Roman forum lay where Piazza Tre Martiri is today.

Tempio Malatestiano

On Via IV Novembre, this so-called temple of the Malatesta clan is the city's grandest monument. Dedicated to St Francis, the 13th-century church was transformed into a personal chapel for the evil Sigismondo Malatesta and his beloved, Isotta degli Atti, and is one of the more significant creations of the Renaissance. Most of the work on the unfinished façade was done by Leon Battista Alberti, one of the period's great architects. A crucifix inside is believed to be the work of Giotto, and the church contains a fresco by Piero della Francesca.

Piazza Cavour

This central square is lined with the city's finest palaces, including the **Palazzo del Municipio**, built in 1562 and rebuilt after being razed during WW II. The Gothic **Palazzo del Podestà** was built in the 14th century and is undergoing restoration. The **Teatro Amintore Galli** only went up in 1857, in the feverish years leading to unification.

Beaches

Most of the beaches along the coast are either rented to private companies that in turn rent space to bathers, or connected to the many nearby hotels. The average daily charge for a deck chair is L6000. Being the kind of resort it is, many people hire change facilities and chairs for a week or more. Two deck chairs and an umbrella in the front row with cabin facilities would cost L170,000 a week! Head for the parts of the beach without the ubiquitous umbrellas (there are three small areas near Piazzale di Federico Fellini) or sit close to the shore in front of the rows of paying beach-goers. They can't stop you unless you try to erect your own umbrella.

The Po river pumps its heavily polluted waters into the Adriatic north of Rimini and this occasionally results in green algae washing onto the shores. Beaches have been closed over summer in the past, so check before you swim.

Sailboards can be hired from Bagno Nettuno on the beach near Piazzale Kennedy. Bicycles can also be hired at Piazzale Kennedy.

Theme Parks

Rimini is not just for sunlovers and socialites; there are numerous theme parks for kids and their suffering parents. You could try Italia in Miniatura in Viserba, a fairly ambitious collection of reproductions of, well, bits of Italy – like the 6600 sq metres given over to 1:5 scale models of some 120 buildings facing the Serenissima's Grand Canal and Piazza San Marco.

Fiabilandia, in Rivazzura di Rimini, is a fantasy park full of weird and wonderful characters. There are also several dolphinariums. Ask at the IAT office for details.

Places to Stay

Unless you have booked well in advance, accommodation can be difficult to find and very expensive in summer, as proprietors often make full board compulsory. In winter, many of the 1500 hotels close and the city is dead. Your only hope in summer is the room-hawkers, sanctioned by the IAT, who frequent intersections on the outskirts of the city and offer rooms at so-called 'bargain' rates, which can be excessive. For booking ahead, you could try Rimini Tourist Information (☎ 5 33 99), Parco Fellini 6. Adria Hotel Reservation (☎ 39 05 30) can also help. Other organisations will book hotels, but charge commission.

The camping ground *Maximum Internazionale* (☎ 37 26 02), on Viale Principe Piemonte at Miramare, south-east of the city, is accessible by bus No 10 or 11 and is near the water. *Camping Italia* (☎ 73 28 82), Via Toscanelli 112, is north-west of the centre at Viserba and can be reached by bus No 4.

The youth hostel, the *Ostello Urland* (☎ 37 32 16), Via Flaminia 300, is near the airport south-east of the city centre. Take bus No 124 from the train station, or the train to Stazione FS Miramare. B&B is L14,000 and a meal costs L12,000. The hostel is open from late April to the end of September.

The great majority of hotels close outside the main season. Those listed below are open all year.

The *Cardellini Meublé* (☎ 2 64 12), Via Dante 50, near the train station, has singles/doubles from L33,000/66,000 or L45,000/90,000 with a bathroom. *Gasparini Garni* (☎ 38 12 77), Via Boiardo 3, has rooms from L30,000/70,000.

Albergo Fernanda (☎ 39 11 00), Via Griffa 2, on the eastern side of town across Viale Tripoli, has rooms starting at L30,000/50,000. Nearby, *Albergo Yard* (☎ 39 05 50), Via Carducci 47, offers rooms starting at L30,000/50,000 with a bathroom and breakfast included.

As a rule of thumb, you can add up to 50% to these prices in high season.

Places to Eat

The city is not noted for its culinary contribution to the Italian table and many restaurants offer cheap tourist menus. The produce market, Mercato Centrale Coperto, is at Via Castelfidardo. The self-service restaurant *Picnic*, Via Tempio Malatestiano 32, is one of the better budget deals. Or you can pick up cheap takeaway pizza at *Pizza da Nino*, Via IV Novembre 9. *La Cafeteria*, No 11 on the same street, has good snacks.

Osteria di Santacolomba, Via di Duccio 2, off Piazza Malatesta, is located in the former bell tower of an 8th-century church and serves traditional cuisine, with dishes starting at about L10,000.

A good place for people-watching and even a moderately priced meal is the *Foro Imperiale*, on Piazza Tre Martiri.

Entertainment

The city's clubs and bars are mainly located along the waterfront, many of them to the north and south of Rimini proper. Ask at the tourist office for your type of club – they range from strip and sleazy cabaret to vaguely groovy. One of the best known is the Paradiso Club at Via Covignano 260.

Getting There & Away

Air The city's Aeroporto Civile (☎ 37 31 32), Via Flaminia, is served by flights from Rome and Milan.

Bus Ferrovie Padane operates buses to towns in the province from the station on Viale Roma. Bustturs has three daily buses to Urbino (two hours) from the station just outside the train station. There are also up to nine daily services to San Marino from here and a direct bus to Rome.

Train Trains (☎ 5 35 12) run frequently down the coast to Ancona, Bari, Lecce and Taranto, and up the line through Bologna and on to Milan and Turin.

Car & Motorbike You have a choice of the A14 (south into the Marches or north-west towards Bologna and Milan) or the toll-free but often clogged SS16.

Getting Around

TRAM buses (☎ 2 45 42) operate services throughout the city and to the airport. Buses Nos 10 and 11 pass the station and go through Piazza Tre Martiri, before heading

EMILIA-ROMAGNA

for Piazzale di Federico Fellini. Bus No 124 runs between the train station and the airport.

From the end of July to mid-September, TRAM operates the Blue Line, a late night bus service connecting the nightclubs with the city centre, train station and camping grounds. The buses run from about 10.30 pm to 4.30 am, after which you'll have to stay in the clubs or walk. In August there is also a Blue Train (Treno Azzurro) to Ravenna.

Taxis (☎ 5 00 20) charge a minimum of L7000, then L1700 a km. You can hire bicycles at Piazzale Kennedy, on the waterfront.

San Marino

What did King Arthur say of Camelot in Monty Python's *The Holy Grail*? 'It's a silly place.' Lying 657 metres above sea level and only 10 km from the Adriatic as the crow flies, the 61-sq-km Repubblica di San Marino is a little silly (one can only speculate as to what Mexico's consul does here!). Everybody is down on this place but this is perhaps a little unfair. True, you are unlikely to see a greater density of kitsch souvenir stands in many other tourist centres. But San Marino is not alone in selling kitsch and, although there isn't an awful lot to see, the old town is pleasant and the views all around quite spectacular.

If you're in Rimini, think of it as just another of the beach resort's theme parks. You can take pictures of the republic's soldiers, buy local coinage (the lira in a San Marino version) and send mail with San Marino stamps. Be warned that at weekends, in summer especially, central San Marino can be choked with visitors.

History
There are innumerable legends describing the founding of this hilly city-state, including the one about a stone-cutter who was given the land on top of Monte Titano by a rich Roman woman whose son he had cured. At any rate, the 25,000 inhabitants of the mountain republic are the inheritors of 1700

years of revolution-free liberty, as the blurbs point out. Welcome to the country of freedom, the signs proclaim. Everybody has left San Marino alone. Well almost. Cesare Borgia waltzed in early in the 16th century, but his own demise was just around the corner and his rule short-lived. In 1739 one Cardinal Giulio Alberoni took over the republic, but the Pope backed San Marino's independence and that was that. During WW II, the 'neutral' republic played host to 100,000 refugees until the Allies marched in, in 1944. San Marino joined the European Council in 1988 and the United Nations in 1992.

Information
Tourist Offices The Ufficio di Stato per il Turismo (☎ 88 29 98), Palazzo del Turismo, Contrada Omagnano 20, is open daily from 8.15 am to 2.15 pm, as well as Monday and Thursday afternoons. Two other offices, one at Contrada del Collegio 40 and the other just inside Porta di San Francesco, are open daily. The latter two will stamp your passport for a fee.

Post & Telecommunications The main post office is at Viale Antonio Onofri 87 and is open from Monday to Friday from 8.15 am to 4.30 pm. The post code is 47031. There are telephones at the information offices. The telephone code is 0549.

Emergency For police emergency call ☎ 113, and for an ambulance or medical assistance call ☎ 118.

Things to See
The best thing to do is wander along the well-kept city walls and drop in at the two fortresses, **La Rocca o Guaita** and the **Cesta o Fratta**. Otherwise there are a couple of small **musems** containing ancient weapons, torture instruments and wax dummies. Below the city, on the road to Rimini in Borgo Maggiore, is the small **Museo di Auto d'Epoca** (L5000), OK if you like looking at cars old and new.

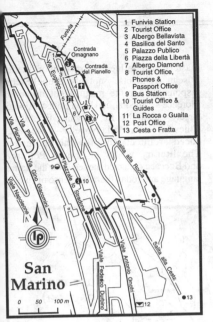

1 Funivia Station
2 Tourist Office
3 Albergo Bellavista
4 Basilica del Santo
5 Palazzo Publico
6 Piazza della Libertà
7 Albergo Diamond
8 Tourist Office,
Phones &
Passport Office
9 Bus Station
10 Tourist Office &
Guides
11 La Rocca o Guaita
12 Post Office
13 Cesta o Fratta

San Marino

0   50   100 m

SAN MARINO

Places to Stay & Eat

There are camping grounds signposted off the main road (SS72) through the republic from Rimini. San Marino city has quite a few hotels should you decide to stay. Cheapest is the *Albergo Bellavista* (☎ 99 12 12), Con-

trada del Pianello 42-44, with rooms starting at L40,000/50,000. It's just by the funivia. Only a short walk away is the *Albergo Diamond* (☎ 99 10 03), Contrada del Collegio 50, with rooms starting at L50,000/70,000. Prices increase about 20% in the high season.

It seems unfair to select single restaurants. The city centre is dotted with places offering set meals for L22,000 to L25,000. The best thing about some of the cafés and snack bars is the views.

Things to Buy

Nothing is probably the best advice. Liquor stores claim to sell cut price alcohol, but you would want to be sure about what your poison is worth in Italy before buying here in the belief you are getting duty-free bargains.

Getting There & Away

Up to nine buses run daily to Rimini. Busturs has a daily service to Urbino. Buses arrive at parking station No 1, in Piazzale Calcigni. There are no trains. If you are driving, the SS72 leads into the city centre from Rimini. If all the car parks in the city fill up, you are obliged to park near the funivia (cable car), and catch the latter to the centre (L5000 return). A nice trip is along the winding roads south to Urbino in the Marches.

Tuscany

The people of Tuscany (Toscana) can rightly claim to have just about the best of everything – art, architecture, beautiful countryside bathed in soft pink hues, and some of Italy's best fresh produce and most well-known wines. It was in Tuscany about 600 years ago that the Renaissance began and it has had a long-lasting effect on European culture. The works of Michelangelo, Donatello, da Vinci and other 15th and 16th-century Tuscan masters still influence artists worldwide. Tuscan architects – notably Brunelleschi, responsible for the magnificent dome of Florence's cathedral, and Leon Battista Alberti, largely responsible for designing the façade Chiesa di Santa Maria Novella – have influenced architects through the centuries. The literary works of Dante, Petrarch and Boccaccio planted the seeds for the Italian language and today there is a sense of rivalry

between the Sienese and the Florentines as to who speaks the purest Italian.

Most people are drawn to Tuscany by the artistic splendour of Florence and Siena or to view the leaning tower in Pisa. While these cities are the draw cards, Tuscany also features some of Italy's most impressive hill towns, including San Gimignano, Volterra, Cortona and Montepulciano. The Etruscan sites in the south – around Saturnia and Sovana – will take you away from the mainstream tourist itinerary. Southern Tuscany also contains some of the country's best beaches, on the Monte Argentario and on the island of Elba, and walkers and nature lovers can enjoy the Alpi Apuane, the Garfagnana, the Mugello (north-east of Florence) and the Parco Naturale della Maremma, near Grossetto.

Tuscan cuisine is dominated by bread and the extra virgin olive oil, which is produced in the region's hills and is close to Italy's finest. Bread features in every course, including dessert, where it can be topped with egg yolk and orange rind and sprinkled with a heavy layer of powdered sugar. *Crostini*, minced chicken liver canapés, and *fettunta*, a slab of toasted bread rubbed with garlic and dipped in oil, are popular antipasti, and hearty soups, such as *ribollita*, thickened with bread, are common starters. Meat and poultry are grilled, roasted or fried, and may come simply with a slice of lemon which the Tuscans refer to as sauce. Traditional desserts are simple, such as biscuits flavoured with nuts or spices and served with a glass of the dessert wine *vin santo*.

The region's wines are among the country's best known: Chianti, *vino nobile*, Brunello di Montalcino and Vernaccia. Traditionally, most Tuscan wines are red but in recent years the vineyards around San Gimignano have produced Vernaccia, a crisp white that is becoming more popular.

Travelling in Tuscany is easy. The A1 and the main north-south train line ensure good north-south connections and there are excellent train and bus services within the region. Most areas are easily accessible by public transport, but a car would provide flexibility

Olives: the ripe fruit is used to produce Italy's finest virgin olive oil

and enable you to get to parts of Tuscany few tourists see. Many of the cities have hotel associations which will book a room for you, although at certain times of the year – such as when the Medieval-inspired Palio festival is being held in Siena – finding a room is almost impossible unless you have booked months in advance.

Florence (Firenze)

Situated on the banks of the Arno river and set among low hills covered with olive groves and vineyards, Florence is immediately captivating. Cradle of the Renaissance and home of Dante, Machiavelli, Michelangelo and the Medici, the city is almost overwhelming in its wealth of art, culture and history. Despite the traffic, the intense and unrelenting summer heat, the pollution and the industrial sprawl on the city's outskirts, Florence still attracts millions of tourists each year who come to view Michelangelo's *David* and the treasures of the Uffizi Gallery. The French writer Stendhal expressed a feeling of culture shock – a giddy faintness that left him unable to walk after he was dazzled by the magnificence of Chiesa di Santa Croce. This condition is now known as Stendhalismo, or Stendhal's Disease, and Florentine doctors treat up to 12 cases a year.

You will need at least four or five days if you want more than a superficial impression of Florence. You could spend at least one day in the Uffizi Gallery, and then there is the Galleria dell'Accademia, the sculpture collection in the Museo Nazionale del Bargello and the many richly embellished churches and palaces. Many people leave the city unsatisfied, perhaps expecting a pristine Renaissance museum. In fact, Florence is a functioning city, complete with run-down palaces, chaotic traffic, pollution and street litter.

If possible, avoid visiting Florence during August when the weather is extremely hot, still and unrelenting, and when most Florentines depart for the coast. The best times to visit are May, June, September and October.

Etruscan Sculpture - *Medusa di Portonaccio*

HISTORY

Florence was founded as a colony of the Etruscan city of Fiesole in about 200 BC. The town later became the Roman Florentia, a strategic garrison settlement whose purpose was to control the Via Flaminia, which linked Rome to northern Italy and Gaul. The city suffered, with the rest of northern Italy, during the barbarian invasions of the Dark Ages. In the early 12th century the city became a free *comune* and by 1138 it was ruled by 12 consuls who were assisted by the Council of One Hundred, drawn mainly from the prosperous merchant class. Agitation among differing factions in the city led to the appointment of a foreign head of state in 1207, known as the *podestà*, who replaced the council.

The first conflicts between the pro-papal Guelphs and the pro-imperial Ghibellines started towards the middle of the 13th century, with power passing from one faction to another for almost a century. The Guelphs eventually formed their own government, known as the Primo Popolo and overseen by a body of merchants called the Capitano del Popolo. In 1260, the Guelphs were ousted after Florence was defeated by the Ghibell-ine Siena at the battle of Montaperti, but the Guelphs regained control of the city in 1289.

By 1292, the increasingly turbulent nobility had been excluded from government, and by the turn of the century, factions among upper-class Guelphs were grouped into two parties, the Neri (Blacks) and the antipapal Bianchi (Whites). When the latter were defeated, one of the many members driven into exile in 1302 was Dante, who established the use of the Italian vernacular in a number of his works and helped to supplant it as the language of writers.

In the period leading up to the mid-14th century, the system of government was further democratised until Florence became a commercial republic controlled by the merchant class, which was strongly Guelph.

The great plague of 1348 cut the city's population by almost half. Subsequent financial problems caused great discontent among workers, who were eventually granted representation on the city's government. However, their representation was short-lived, as from 1382 an alliance between the Guelphs and the city's wealthiest merchants seized power for the next 40-odd years.

During the latter part of the 14th century, Florence was ruled by a caucus of Guelphs under the leadership of the Albizzi family. Opposed to them were the Ricci, Alberti and Medici families, who had the support of the lower classes. During this period, the Medici consolidated their influence and eventually became the papal bankers, with branches in 16 cities. After making claims to the leadership of the party in opposition to the Albizzi, Cosimo de Medici was banished.

But Cosimo's political fortunes improved in his absence, mostly because of the sympathy the Medici enjoyed among the lower classes. He returned to Florence a year later and became the city's ruler. He was described by contemporaries as serious but unassuming, had a deep understanding of the arts and letters and was an extraordinarily generous patron. His eye for talent and his tact in dealing with artists saw the likes of Alberti, Brunelleschi, Lorenzo Ghiberti, Donatello, Fra Angelico and Filippo Lippi flourish under his patronage, and many of the city's finest buildings are testimony to his tastes.

Upon Cosimo's death in 1464, rule was assumed by his son, Peter the Gouty, and then his grandson, Lorenzo Il Magnifico.

Lorenzo's rule (1469-92) ushered in the most glorious period of Florentine civilisation and of the Italian Renaissance. His court oversaw a great flowering of art, music and poetry and Florence became the cultural capital of Italy. Lorenzo favoured philosophers, but he maintained family tradition and also sponsored artists including Botticelli and Domenico Ghirlandaio, and encouraged da Vinci and the young Michelangelo, who was working under Giovanni di Bertoldo, Donatello's pupil.

Not long before Lorenzo's death in 1492, the Medici bank failed and, two years later, the Medici were driven out of Florence. The city fell under the control of Girolamo Savonarola, a Dominican monk who led a puritanical republic until he fell from public favour and was burned as a heretic in 1498. See the Aside in this chapter.

After Florence's defeat by the Spanish in 1512, the Medici returned to the city but were once again expelled, this time by Emperor Charles V in 1527. The family made peace with Charles two years later; he not only permitted their return to Florence, but married his daughter to Alessandro de

Savonarola

The Renaissance was a time of extraordinary contrasts. Artists, writers and philosophers of great talent flourished against a backdrop of violence, war, plague and extreme poverty. In Florence, the court of Lorenzo de Medici was among the most splendid and enlightened in Europe. Yet, in the streets and increasingly in Lorenzo's court itself, there were people who had begun to listen very intently to the fanatical preachings of a Dominican monk named Girolamo Savonarola. Born in Ferrara in 1452, Savonarola moved to Florence in the last years of Lorenzo the Magnificent's rule. An inspired and eloquent orator, he preached against luxury, greed, the corruption of the clergy and against the Renaissance itself. To him both the church and the world were corrupt and he accused the ruling class of thinking only 'of new taxes, to suck the blood of the people'. When the Medici were expelled from Florence after the French invasion of Italy in 1494 and a republic was proclaimed, Savonarola was appointed its legislator and under his severe, moralistic lead the city underwent a type of religious reform. His followers numbered some of the city's greatest humanist philosophers, as well as many of its most successful artists, but his enemies were numerous and powerful – not least the exiled Medici and the corrupt Pope Alexander VI, against whom the monk preached. The pope consequently excommunicated Savonarola in 1497. In the ensuing year, the Florentine public began to turn cold on the evangelistic preacher, he came under attack from the Franciscan monks and began to lose the support of political allies. After refusing to undergo the challenge of an ordeal by fire, Savonarola was arrested and on May 22, 1498, was hanged and burned at the stake for heresy in Piazza della Signoria. His ashes were thrown into the Arno river. ■

Medici, great-grandson of Lorenzo Il Magnifico, and made him Duke of Florence in 1530. The Medici then ruled the city until 1737, gaining control of all Tuscany in the period.

After the Medici, the Grand Duchy of Tuscany passed to the House of Lorraine, and from 1799 to the French under Napoleon. In 1814, it returned to the Lorraines, who retained control until Florence was incorporated into the Kingdom of Italy in 1860. It became the capital a year later, remaining so until Rome assumed the mantle in 1875.

Florence was badly damaged during WW II by the retreating Germans, who bombed all bridges except the Ponte Vecchio. Devastating floods ravaged the city in 1966, causing inestimable damage to its buildings and artworks, some of which are still being restored. However, the cleanup programme after the floods led to the widespread use of present-day restoration techniques which have saved artworks throughout the country.

In 1993, the world-famous Uffizi Gallery was damaged by a car-bomb explosion. See the following Things to See section for details about the gallery and the explosion.

ORIENTATION

Whether you arrive by train, bus or car, the central train station, Santa Maria Novella, is a good reference point. The main thoroughfare to the city centre is Via de' Panzani and then Via de' Cerretani, about a 10-minute walk from the train station. You will know you've arrived when you first glimpse the duomo.

Once at the Piazza del Duomo you will find Florence easy to negotiate. Most of the major sights are within easy walking distance, and you can walk from one end of the city centre to the other in about 30 minutes. From Piazza San Giovanni around the baptistry, Via Roma leads to Piazza della Repubblica and continues as Via Calimala to the Ponte Vecchio. Take Via de' Calzaiuoli from Piazza del Duomo for Piazza della Signoria, the historic seat of government – don't be fooled by the lookalike of

Michelangelo's *David* outside the Palazzo Vecchio; the real one is housed in the Galleria dell'Accademia. The Uffizi Gallery is at the piazza's southern edge, near the Arno river. Cross the Ponte Vecchio, or the Ponte alle Grazie farther east, to reach Piazzale Michelangelo in the south-east for a view over the city, one of the best views in Italy.

The imposing Fortezza da Basso, where there is a reasonably priced public car park, is just north of the train station, and a brisk 10-minute walk from the historic centre along Via XXVII Aprile and Via Cavour. The HI youth hostel is on the city's north-eastern fringe, accessible by bus No 17B from the station.

Florence has two street-numbering systems: red or brown numbers indicate a commercial premises and black or blue numbers denote a private residence. When they are written, black or blue addresses are denoted by the number only, while red or brown addresses usually carry an 'r' after the number. Of course, there are exceptions, but check the colouring if you are trying to find an address.

INFORMATION
Tourist Offices

There are several tourist offices in the city. The main APT office (☎ 055-29 08 32; fax 276 03 83) is just north of the duomo at Via Cavour 1r. It has extensive information and helpful staff, some of whom speak English. Much of the more practical information on hotels, language and art courses, car and bike rental etc is contained in a large ring binder on the counter. The office is open Monday to Saturday from 8 am to 2 pm. The APT also offers a special service known as Firenze SOS Turista (☎ 276 03 82). Tourists needing guidance on matters such as disputes over hotel fees etc can phone Monday to Saturday from 9.30 am to 12.30 pm and 3 to 6 pm.

The city council, known as the Comune di Firenze, operates an excellent tourist office (☎ 21 22 45) at Stazione di Santa Maria Novella. It is just outside the station in the covered area where local buses stop. There is another small office (☎ 230 21 24) at Chiasso Baroncelli 17, just south of Piazza della

Signoria. Both offices are open Monday to Saturday from 8 am to 7.30 pm.

All tourist offices offer similar information, including the very useful free APT City of Florence map, which contains a directory of street names. You can also go to any of the city's better hotels or bars for one of the invaluable booklets available at the counter, in particular the quarterly *Florence Concierge Information* or *Firenze Oggi*, which should also be available from tourist offices. None of the tourist offices will book you a room, but see the Florence Places to Stay section for details about the Consorzio ITA office at the train station, which will do so.

There is an Informa Giovani office (☎ 21 83 10) at Vicolo Santa Maria Maggiore 1.

Money

Most of the main banks are concentrated around Piazza della Repubblica. Thomas Cook has an exchange office (☎ 055-28 97 81) at Lungarno Acciaioli 6r, near the Ponte Vecchio. From March to October it is open Monday to Saturday from 9 am to 7 pm and Sunday from 9 am to 1 pm. In other months it closes on weekdays at 6 pm and is closed Sunday. There's a full American Express office and travel service (☎ 055-28 87 51) at Via de' Guicciardini 49r in the Oltrarno on the way to Palazzo Pitti. Another branch is at Via Dante Alighieri 22r.

Post & Telecommunications

The main post office is in Via Pellicceria, off Piazza della Repubblica, and is open Monday to Friday from 8.15 am to 7 pm and Saturday to midday. Poste restante mail can be addressed to 50100 Firenze.

The Telecom office is at the post office and is open 24 hours a day. There is another office at Stazione di Santa Maria Novella, open Monday to Saturday from 8 am to 9.45 pm.

Foreign Consulates

The US Consulate (☎ 239 82 76) is at Lungarno Vespucci 38 and operates the US Information Service (USIS, ☎ 29 49 21) Monday to Friday from 8.30 am to 1.30 pm and 2 to 5.30 pm. You can only visit the USIS office by appointment. The British Consulate (☎ 28 41 33) is at Lungarno Corsini 2. Other English-speaking nationalities can choose between embassies in Rome or consulates in Milan. The French Consulate (☎ 230 25 56) is at Piazza Ognissanti 2.

Travel Agencies

The Sestante CIT office (☎ 29 43 06), Via Cavour 56r, is central Italy's main office. A smaller branch office (☎ 28 41 45) is at Piazza della Stazione 51r.

Bookshops

The Paperback Exchange, Via Fiesolana 31r, has a vast selection of new and second-hand books, including classics, contemporary literature, reference books and best sellers, as well as travel guides. It is closed Sunday. Internazionale Seeber, Via de' Tornabuoni 70r, also has a good selection of English and American classics and contemporary literature and a reasonable range of books by Australian authors. Opposite the APT office in Via Cavour is Feltrinelli, which has novels, travel guides and children's books in English.

Gay & Lesbian Information

Arci Gay (☎ 28 81 26), Via Montebello 6, operates a phone information service from 5 to 7 pm. The Edicola Balsanelli newspaper stand in Piazza Santa Maria Novella is open late and has most Babilonia publications.

Other Information

Lost property (☎ 36 79 43) can be collected (if you're lucky) from Via Circondaria 19.

If you park illegally in Florence your car will be towed away and you risk incurring a large fine. Impounded cars can be collected at Via dell'Arcovata 6 (☎ 35 52 31).

Coin laundrettes include Lavamatic, Via degli Alfani 44r, which charges L8000 for 4.8 kg.

Medical Services

The main public hospital is Ospedale Careggi (☎ 427 71 11), Viale Morgagni 85, north of

TUSCANY

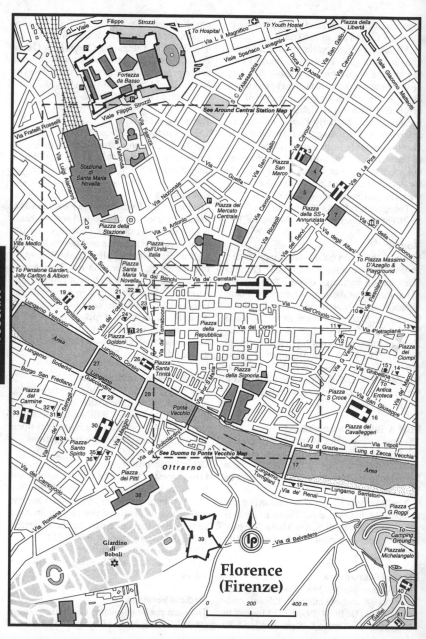

Florence (Firenze)

0   200   400 m

PLACES TO STAY						
21	Pensione Ottaviani & Albergo Visconti	22	Fiddler's Elbow	10	Paperback Exchange Bookshop	
23	Pensione Toscana & Pensione Sole	24	Da il Latini	15	Casa Buonarroti	
31	Ostello Santa Monaca	29	Angelino	16	Chiesa di Santa Croce	
34	Istituto Gould	32	Trattoria I Raddi	17	Ponte alle Grazie	
		35	Cabiria	19	Chiesa di Ognissanti	
		36	Borgo Antico	25	Palazzo Rucellai	
PLACES TO EAT		37	Trattoria Casalinga	26	Chiesa di Santa Trinità	
				27	Ponte alla Carraia	
		OTHER		28	Ponte Santa Trinità	
9	Rex Caffè	1	Tourist Medical Service	30	Chiesa di Santo Spirito	
11	Antico Noè	2	Questura (Police Station)	33	Chiesa di Santa Maria del Carmine	
12	Natalino	3	Museo di San Marco	38	Palazzo Pitti	
13	Sant'Ambrogio Caffè	4	University	39	Forte di Belvedere	
14	Enoteca Pinchiorri	5	Galleria dell'Accademia	40	Chiesa di San Salvatore al Monte	
18	I Tarrocchi	6	Chiesa di SS Annunziata	41	Chiesa di San Miniato al Monte	
20	Sostanza	7	Spedale degli Innocenti			
		8	Museo Archeologico			

TUSCANY

the city centre. There is also the Ospedale Santa Maria Nuova (☎ 2 75 81), Piazza Santa Maria Nuova 1, just east of the duomo.

An organisation of volunteer translators (English, French and German) called the Associazione Volontari Ospedalieri (☎ 234 45 67) can provide free translation once you've found a doctor. All public hospitals have a list of volunteers, but you may need to ask for it. The Tourist Medical Service (☎ 47 54 11) at Via Lorenzo il Magnifico 59 is open 24 hours a day and doctors speak English, French and German.

All-night pharmacies include the Farmacia Comunale (☎ 28 94 35) inside Stazione di Santa Maria Novella, and Molteni (☎ 28 94 90) in the city centre at Via Calzaiuoli 7r.

Emergency
For police emergency, call ☎ 113. The questura (☎ 4 97 71) is at Via Zara 2. There is an office for foreigners, where you can report thefts etc. There is an ambulance station (☎ 21 22 22) in Piazza del Duomo.

Dangers & Annoyances
The most annoying aspect of Florence is the crowds, closely followed by the summer heat. Pickpockets are very active in crowds and particularly on buses. Beware also of the numerous bands of dishevelled women and children carrying newspapers or cardboard. A few will distract you while the others rifle your bag and pockets. Carry a money pouch or wear a money belt and never carry money in your pockets. The city has a small problem with moped bandits who will try and grab handbags.

Traffic in the city centre is heavy and chaotic, so watch out for aggressive, fast drivers in the narrow streets. Air pollution can be a serious problem in Florence, particularly in summer, when locals are often warned to keep small children, people with respiratory problems and the elderly inside. If you fit one of these categories, it might be an idea to stay informed of pollution levels through the tourist office or your hotel proprietor.

THINGS TO SEE
Any list of 'must sees' in Florence is going to incite cries of protest. How can you recommend that a tour cover the Uffizi Gallery, the duomo and the baptistry, without including the Museo del Bargello, the Convento di San Marco and the churches of Santa Maria Novella, Santa Croce and SS Annunziata ? And what about Massaccio's fresco cycle in Chiesa di Santa Maria del Carmine? Or Michelangelo's *David* in the Galleria dell'Accademia and his Medici

tombs in the family chapel attached to Chiesa di San Lorenzo? You will need to combine careful planning with some ruthless choices if you want to make the most of your time. Make sure you carry plenty of L100, L200 and L500 coins for the machines to illuminate the frescoes in the churches.

Walking Tour

Here is a suggested tour of churches which are important both architecturally and for the art treasures they contain. The walk is divided into two groups of four churches, one group for the morning and one for the afternoon, since most churches close for three to four hours in the middle of the day. The APT office at Via Cavour 1r has an updated list of opening hours.

Start at **Chiesa di Santa Maria Novella**, in the piazza of the same name, just south of the main train station. Begun in the late 13th century as the Florentine base for the Dominican order, the church was largely completed by around 1360, but work continued until well into the 15th century on its façade and the embellishment of its interior. The lower section of the lovely green and white marble façade is Gothic-Romanesque, while the upper section and the main doorway were designed by Alberti and completed around 1470. The highlight of the Gothic interior is Masaccio's superb fresco of the **Trinity** (1428), one of the first artworks to use the then newly discovered techniques of perspective and proportion. It is about halfway along the north aisle.

The first chapel to the right of the choir, the Cappella di Filippo Strozzi, features lively frescoes by Filippino Lippi depicting the lives of St John the Evangelist and St Philip the Apostle. Another important work is Domenico Ghirlandaio's series of frescoes behind the main altar, painted with the help of artists who may have included the young student, Michelangelo. Relating the lives of the Virgin Mary, St John the Baptist and others, the frescoes are particularly notable for their depiction of Florentine life during the Renaissance. Brunelleschi's famous cru-

cifix hangs above the altar in the Capella Gondi, the first chapel on the left of the choir.

The cloisters (entrance on the left of the façade) feature some of the city's best frescoes. The Chiostro Verde (Green Cloisters) is so named because green is the predominant colour of the fresco cycle by Paolo Uccello. The impressive Cappellone degli Spagnuoli (Spanish Chapel) contains frescoes by Andrea di Bonaiuto which depict significant religious events. The church is open daily, except Sunday morning, from 7 to 11.30 am and 3.30 to 6 pm. The cloister is open daily, except Friday, from 9 am to 2 pm. Admission is L5000.

From the Piazza Santa Maria Novella head east along Via dei Banchi and take the first street on the left, Via del Giglio. Cross Via de' Panzani and continue straight ahead until you reach the Piazza Madonna degli Aldobrandini (the entrance to the Cappelle Medicee is here, at the rear of Basilica di San Lorenzo). The streets in this area are lined with market stalls specialising in leather goods and knitwear.

The Medici commissioned Brunelleschi to rebuild the **Basilica di San Lorenzo** in 1425 on the site of a 4th-century basilica. It is considered one of the most harmonious examples of Renaissance architecture. Michelangelo prepared a design for the façade which was never executed. It was the Medici parish church and many of the family members are buried here. The two bronze pulpits are by Donatello, who died before they were completed. He is buried in the chapel featuring Filippo Lippi's *Annunciation*. The entrance to the basilica is in the busy Piazza San Lorenzo. It is open daily from 7 am to midday and 3.30 to 5.30 pm. The adjoining **Sagrestia Vecchia** (Old Sacristy) was also designed by Brunelleschi and its interior was largely decorated by Donatello.

Visit the **Biblioteca Laurenziana**, reached through the cloister. It was commissioned by Cosimo de Medici to house the Medici library and contains 10,000 volumes. The magnificent staircase was designed by Michelangelo. It is open daily, except Sunday, from 9 am to 1 pm. Admission is free.

The **Cappelle Medicee** are entered via Piazza Madonna degli Aldobrandini. The **Cappella dei Principi** (Princes' Chapel), sumptuously decorated with precious marble and semiprecious stones, was the principal burial place of the Medici rulers. The graceful and simple **Sagrestia Nuova** (New Sacristy) was designed by Michelangelo and was his first architectural work, although he left Florence for Rome before its completion. It contains his beautiful sculptures *Night & Day*, *Dawn & Dusk* and the *Madonna with Child*, which adorn the Medici tombs. The chapels are open Tuesday to Sunday from 9 am to 2 pm. Admission is L8000.

Next stop is the **Chiesa di SS Annunziata** in the piazza of the same name. From Piazza San Lorenzo walk east along Via dei Gori to reach Via Cavour, turn left and walk until you reach Piazza San Marco (two to three minutes), then turn right into Via Cesare Battisti to reach the Piazza SS Annunziata. The church was established in 1250 by the founders of the Servite order and rebuilt by Michelozzo and others in the mid-15th century. It is dedicated to the Virgin Mary and in the ornate tabernacle, to your left as you enter the church from the atrium, is a so-called miraculous painting of the Virgin. The painting, which is no longer on public view, is attributed to a 14th-century friar, and legend says it was completed by an angel. Also of note is the ceiling, frescoes by Andrea del Castagno in the first two chapels on the left of the church, a fresco by Perugino in the fifth chapel and the frescoes in Michelozzo's atrium, particularly the *Birth of the Virgin* by Andrea del Sarto and the *Visitation* by Jacopo Pontormo. The church is open daily from 7.30 am to 12.30 pm and 4 to 7 pm.

Head back to Piazza San Marco for the **Museo di San Marco** in the now deconsecrated Dominican convent and Chiesa di San Marco. The piazza is the centre of the university area and is one of the most pleasant squares in the city. The church was founded in 1299, rebuilt by Michelozzo in 1437, and again remodelled by Giambologna some years later. It features several paintings, but they pale in comparison to the treasures contained in the adjoining convent.

Famous Florentines who called the convent home include the painters Fra Angelico and Fra Bartolomeo, as well as St Antoninus and Girolamo Savonarola. See the Aside on Savonarola earlier in this chapter. It is interesting to contemplate that Fra Angelico, who painted the radiant, imaginative and joyous frescoes which adorn the walls of the convent, and Savonarola were of the same religious order – the latter arriving in Florence almost 30 years after the painter's death in 1455. The convent is a museum of Fra Angelico's works, many of which were moved there from other locations in Florence in the 1860s. The Ospizio dei Pellegrini (Pilgrim's Hospice) contains a number of his works, notably the *Tabernacolo dei Linaioli*, the *Last Judgment* (painted with his students) and *Descent from the Cross*. The chapterhouse features more works by Fra Angelico, including one of his greatest masterpieces, a fresco of the *Crucifixion*.

Upstairs are the monks' dormitory cells, all decorated with frescoes by Fra Angelico and his assistants. At the top of the stairs is another of his masterpieces, a fresco of the *Annunciation*. Along the left corridor, in the cells on the left side, are several frescoes by the master (cells 1, 3, 4, 6, 7 and 9). The museum is open Tuesday to Sunday from 9 am to 2 pm. Admission is L8000.

The first tour ends here. If you want to stop for a quick snack, head for Bondi, Via dell'Ariento 85, in the San Lorenzo market area, near Via Nazionale. It specialises in focaccia and pizza by the slice. For something more substantial you could try Caffè Za Za, Piazza del Mercato Centrale 20 or, a few doors down, Mario's at Via Rosina 2r.

The **second tour** starts at the remarkable **duomo**, with its pink, white and green marble façade, and Brunelleschi's famous dome, which dominates the Florence skyline. No matter how many times you have visited the city, the duomo will take your breath away. Named the Cattedrale di Santa Maria del Fiore, it was begun in 1296 by the Sienese architect Arnolfo di Cambio but took almost

150 years to complete. It is the fourth-largest cathedral in the world.

Brunelleschi won a public competition to design the enormous dome, the first of its kind since antiquity. Although now severely cracked and under restoration, it remains a remarkable achievement of design. When Michelangelo went to Rome to work on the construction of St Peter's Basilica he is reported to have said, 'I go to build a greater dome, but not a fairer one.' The dome is decorated with frescoes by Vasari and Frederico Zuccari, and stained glass windows by Donatello, Andrea del Castagno, Paolo Uccello and Lorenzo Ghiberti. However, the scaffolding erected for the restoration more than 20 years ago now obscures the artistic works, and you must climb into the dome to see them. Enter to the left as you face the altar. The view from the summit over Florence is unparalleled. The dome is open Monday to Saturday from 10 am to 5 pm and the climb costs L5000.

The duomo's vast interior, about 155 metres long and 90 metres wide, and its sparse decoration comes as a surprise after the visually tumultuous façade. The sacristies on each side of the altar feature enamelled terracotta lunettes over their doorways by Luca della Robbia. Lorenzo de Medici hid in the north sacristy after his brother, Giuliano, was stabbed and killed by the Pazzi conspirators. See the Aside.

Also of note are the two frescoes in the north aisle commemorating the condottieri, Sir John Hawkwood and Niccolò da Tolentino, who fought for Florence. The former was painted by Paolo Uccello and the latter by Andrea del Castagno. Also in the north aisle is a painting of Dante with a depiction of the Divine Comedy, painted by Domenico di Michelino. A stairway near the main entrance of the duomo leads to the crypt, where excavations have unearthed parts of the 5th-century Basilica di Santa Reparata, which originally stood on the site, and Brunelleschi's tomb. The duomo's marble façade in white, green and red marble was built in the 19th century in Gothic style to replace the original, uncompleted façade designed by Arnolfo di Cambio, which was pulled down in the 16th century. The duomo is open Monday to Saturday from 8.30 am to 6.30 pm and Sunday from 1 to 5 pm. Strict dress standards are enforced.

Giotto designed and began building the graceful and unusual **bell tower** next to the duomo in 1334, but died before it was completed. His work was continued by Andrea Pisano and Francesco Talenti. The first tier of bas-reliefs around the base of the tower depicts the Creation of Man and the Arts and Industries, and was carved by Andrea Pisano, although believed to have been designed by Giotto. Those on the second tier depict the planets, cardinal virtues, the arts

---

Lorenzo de Medici & the Pazzi Conspiracy

Plots to ruin the Medici family were nothing new to Florence, but in 1478 Lorenzo de Medici lost his brother, Giuliano, and almost his own life in an incident known as the Pazzi conspiracy. The Pazzi was a wealthy Florentine family which had been denied the benefits of public office by the Medici. Jealous and bitter, Francesco de' Pazzi, who was actually a Catholic priest, formed a plan backed by Pope Sixtus IV to kill the Medici brothers and take power in Florence. The audacious plan was put into effect in the Duomo during High Mass. When all heads were bowed as the host was raised, Francesco and an accomplice struck, stabbing Giuliano to death. Lorenzo escaped into the sacristy and survived the attack, but the city was in an uproar. A mob spent days hunting down the conspirators and anyone else believed to have been associated with the incident. Hundreds died, including most members of the Pazzi family. Surviving members were imprisoned or exiled, the Pazzi name was proscibed and female members of the family were forbidden to marry and have children (Lorenzo later revoked this order).■

and the seven sacraments. The sculptures of the Prophets and Sybils in the niches of the upper storeys are actually copies of works by Donatello and others – the originals are in the duomo's museum. The bell tower is 82 metres high and you can climb its stairs daily between 9 am and 7.30 pm. Admission is L5000.

The Romanesque-style **baptistry** is generally believed to have been built from the 5th to 11th centuries on the site of a Roman temple. It is the oldest building in Florence and is dedicated to St John the Baptist. The octagonal building is decorated with stripes of white and green marble and is famous for its gilded bronze doors, particularly the celebrated east doors facing the duomo, the *Gates of Paradise* by Lorenzo Ghiberti. The bas-reliefs on its 10 panels depict scenes from the Old Testament. The south door, executed by Andrea Pisano and completed in 1336, is the oldest. The bas-reliefs on its 28 compartments deal predominantly with the life of St John the Baptist. The north door is also by Ghiberti, who won a public competition in 1401 to design it. The design was based on Pisano's earlier door and its main theme is also St John the Baptist. The *Gates of Paradise*, however, remain his consummate masterpiece. Dante was baptised in the baptistry. Most of the doors are copies – the original panels are being gradually removed for restoration and placed in the Museo dell' Opera del Duomo as work is completed. The baptistry is open Monday to Saturday from 1.30 to 6.30 pm and Sunday from 9 am to 1 pm. Admission is free.

The **Museo dell'Opera del Duomo**, behind the cathedral at Piazza del Duomo 9, features most of the art treasures from the duomo, baptistry and bell tower and is definitely worth a visit. Displays include the equipment used by Brunelleschi to build the dome, as well as his death mask. Perhaps its best piece is Michelangelo's *Pietà*, which he intended for his own tomb. Vasari recorded in his *Lives of the Artists* that, unsatisfied with the quality of the marble or his own work, Michelangelo broke up the unfinished sculpture, destroying the arm and left leg of

the figure of Christ. A student of Michelangelo later restored the arm and completed the figure of Mary Magdalene. The collection of sculpture is considered the city's second-best after that in the Museo Bargello. Note in particular Donatello's carving of the prophet Habakkuk (taken from the bell tower) and his wooden impression of Mary Magdalene. The museum is open daily, except Sunday, from 9 am to 7.30 pm (5.30 pm in winter). Admission is L5000.

From the Piazza del Duomo walk south along Via del Proconsolo and turn left into Borgo degli Albizi and the area known as Santa Croce. When you reach Piazza S Pier Maggiore turn right and walk along Via M Palmieri. Across Via Ghibellina you will pass Gelateria Vivoli in Via dell'Isola delle Stinche, one of the city's best gelaterie, where you can stop for an after lunch pick-me-up.

Continue straight ahead and turn left into Borgo de' Greci to reach the Franciscan **Chiesa di Santa Croce** in the piazza of the same name. In Savonarola's day, the piazza was used for the execution of heretics but today it is lined with souvenir shops. Attributed to Arnolfo di Cambio, Santa Croce was started in 1294 on the site of a Franciscan chapel, although the façade and bell tower were added in the 19th century. The three-nave interior of the church · is grand, but austere. The floor is paved with the tombstones of famous Florentines of the past 500 years and monuments to the particularly notable were added along the walls from the mid-16th century.

Along the south wall (to your right as you enter the church) is Michelangelo's tomb, designed by Vasari, and a cenotaph dedicated to Dante, who is buried in Ravenna. Farther along is a monument to the 18th-century dramatist and poet Vittorio Alfieri by Antonio Canova, a monument to Machiavelli and a bas-relief, *Annunciation*, by Donatello.

The Cappella Castellani, in the right transept, was completely covered with frescoes by Agnolo Gaddi. In the Cappella Baroncelli at the end of the transept frescoes by his father Taddeo Gaddi depict the life of the Virgin.

Agnolo Gaddi also painted the frescoes above and behind the altar. Adjoining the sacristy is a corridor by Michelozzo which leads to a Medici chapel, featuring a large altarpiece by Andrea della Robbia. The Bardi and Peruzzi chapels, to the right of the chancel, are completely covered in frescoes by Giotto. In the central chapel of the north transept (also a Bardi chapel) hangs a wooden crucifix by Donatello.

The **cloisters** were designed by Brunelleschi just before his death in 1446 and are noted for their serenity. Brunelleschi's Cappella Pazzi, at the end of the first cloister, is a masterpiece of Renaissance architecture. The **Museo dell'Opera di Santa Croce**, off the first cloister, features a crucifix by Cimabue, which was badly damaged during the disastrous 1966 flood when more than four metres of water inundated the Santa Croce area. The crucifix was almost completely destroyed and lost much of its paint. It has been partially restored.

In summer, the church is open Monday to Saturday from 8 am to 6.30 pm and Sunday from 8 am to 12.30 pm and 3 to 6.30 pm. In winter it is open Monday to Saturday from 8 am to 12.30 pm and 3 to 6.30 pm and Sunday from 3 to 6.30 pm. The museum is open daily, except Wednesday, from 10 am to 12.30 pm and 2.30 to 6.30 pm. In winter opening hours are shorter in the afternoon, from 3 to 5 pm. Admission is L4000.

The walking tour now heads for two churches in the **Oltrarno**, meaning literally 'the other side of the Arno'. From the top end of the piazza go left into Via dei Benci and follow it to the river. Either cross here at the Ponte alle Grazie or follow the river to your right to reach the Ponte Vecchio. Take Borgo S Jacopo, on your right after you cross Ponte Vecchio, and continue along it as it becomes Via Santo Spirito. Cross Via de' Serragli and take the first left to reach Piazza del Carmine and **Chiesa di Santa Maria del Carmine**. This 13th-century church was almost completely destroyed by a fire in the late 18th century. Fortunately the fire spared the magnificent frescoes by Masaccio in the Cappella Brancacci. Considered the painter's master-

piece, the frescoes had an enormous influence on Florentine art in the 15th century. Masaccio painted them in his early 20s and interrupted the task to go to Rome, where he died aged only 28 years. The cycle was completed some 60 years later by Filippino Lippi. Earlier frescoes in the cycle were painted by Masolino da Panicale. The frescoes were recently restored and their vibrant colours combined with Masaccio's vigorous style create a strong visual impact. Masaccio's work includes the famous *Expulsion of Adam and Eve from Paradise*, and *The Tribute Money* on the upper left wall. The chapel is open Monday to Saturday, except from 10 am to 4.30 pm (closed Tuesday) and on Sunday from 1 to 4.30 pm. Admission is L5000.

Head back in the direction of the Ponte Vecchio, but take Via Santa Monica. Cross Via de' Serragli and continue along Via Sant'Agostino until you come to Piazza Santo Spirito and **Chiesa di Santo Spirito**. One of Brunelleschi's last commissions, the church is beautifully planned, with a colonnade of 35 columns and a series of semicircular chapels. Contained in the chapels are works of art including a *Madonna & Saints* by Filippino Lippi in the right transept. Santo Spirito is open daily, except Wednesday afternoon, from 8 am to midday and 4 to 7 pm. The piazza outside has developed somewhat of a bohemian feel and one of the most popular cafés for young people, Cabiria, is to your left as you leave the church.

Around Piazza della Signoria

The hub of the city's political life through the centuries and surrounded by some of its most celebrated buildings, the piazza has the appearance of an outdoor sculpture gallery. Ammannati's huge Fountain of Neptune sits beside the Palazzo Vecchio and, flanking the entrance to the palace, are copies of Michelangelo's *David* (original in the Galleria dell'Accademia) and Donatello's *Marzocco*, the heraldic Florentine lion (the original is in the Museo Bargello). An equestrian statue of Cosimo de Medici by Giambologna stands towards the centre of the piazza. A bronze plaque marks the spot where Savonarola was hanged and burned at the stake in 1498.

The **Loggia della Signoria** was built in the late 14th century as a platform for public ceremonies and eventually became a showcase for sculptures. To the left of the steps is Benvenuto Cellini's magnificent statue of Perseus holding the head of Medusa. To the right is Giambologna's (Giovanni da Bologna) *Rape of the Sabine Women*, his final work and a famous Mannerist sculpture.

The **Palazzo Vecchio**, built by Arnolfo di Cambio between 1298 and 1314, is the traditional seat of Florentine government. Its **Torre d'Arnolfo** is 94 metres high and, with its striking crenellations, is as much a symbol

Giambologna's *Rape of the Sabine Women* was intended by the artist only as an interesting composition in form and was named by the critics of the day after a story from mythic Roman history.

of the city as the duomo. Built for the *signoria*, the highest level of Florentine republican government, it became the palace of Cosimo de Medici in the mid-16th century, before he moved to the Palazzo Pitti. Vasari was commissioned by the Medici to reorganise the interior and created a series of sumptuous rooms. There is a beautiful courtyard by Michelozzo just inside the entrance and lavishly decorated apartments upstairs. The Salone dei Cinquecento was the meeting room of the Consiglio della Repubblica (Great Council) during Savonarola's time. It was later used for banquets and festivities and features frescoes by Vasari and Michelangelo's *Genius of Victory*, originally destined for Rome and Pope Julius II's tomb. The Studiolo, which was the study of Francesco I, was designed by Vasari and decorated by several Florentine mannerist artists. Farther on is the Cappella di Signoria, decorated by Domenico Ghirlandaio in 1514. The palace is open Monday to Saturday from 9 am to 7 pm (closed Thursday) and Sunday from 8 am to 1 pm. Admission is L8000.

The **Palazzo Gondi** is a 15th-century Renaissance palace designed by G de Sangallo. It faces on to Piazza Firenze.

Uffizi Gallery (Galleria degli Uffizi)

Designed and built by Vasari in the second half of the 16th century at the request of Cosimo de Medici, the Uffizi is located in the **Palazzo degli Uffizi**, which originally housed the city's administrators, judiciary and guilds. It was, in effect an office building (uffizi means offices). Vasari also designed the private corridor which links the Palazzo Vecchio and the Palazzo Pitti, through the Uffizi Gallery and across the Ponte Vecchio. Known as the **Corridoio Vasariano**, it is lined with paintings and can be seen only on a guided tour. Cosimo's successor, Francesco I, commissioned the architect Buontalenti to modify the upper floor of the Palazzo degli Uffizi to house the Medici's growing art collection. The gallery now houses the family's private collection, which was bequeathed to the city in 1737 by the last of the Medici,

Anna Maria Ludovica, on condition that it never leave the city.

Although over the years sections of the collection have been moved to the Museo Bargello and the city's Museo Archeologico, the Uffizi Gallery still houses the world's greatest collection of Italian and Florentine art. Paintings from Florence's churches have also been moved to the gallery. Sadly, several of its artworks were destroyed and others badly damaged when a car bomb exploded outside the gallery's western wing in May 1993. Six people died in the explosion. The Mafia was blamed for the attack (although it did not claim responsibility), which was widely seen as payback for the Italian government's ongoing purge of the organisation. Among the paintings destroyed were Gerrit van Honthorst's *Birth of Christ* and *Good Fortune*, and *Scenes of Life* by Bartolomeo Manfredi. Documents cataloguing the collection were also destroyed. A massive clean-up enabled the gallery to reopen quickly, but restoration work continues on damaged paintings.

The gallery is arranged to illustrate the evolving story of Italian and, in particular, Florentine art. However, the gallery has its problems: poor funding (despite the incredible box-office takings) means that rooms have to be closed every day, and many paintings are hung in unsuitable locations or inadequately lit. To avoid the crowds go when the gallery first opens, during lunchtime or late afternoon.

The extraordinary wealth of the collection and the sheer number of famous works means one visit is not enough – if you are going to come down with Stendhalismo, it will be here! If you are in Florence for three or four days and can afford the additional cost, try to spend at least two blocks of three or so hours in the gallery, spread over a few days. Several guidebooks to the gallery are on sale at vendors all over the city, and outside the entrance.

Before heading upstairs, visit the recently restored remains of the 11th-century Chiesa di San Piero Scheraggio, which was largely destroyed during the construction of the

gallery, and its apse incorporated into the structure of the palace. Upstairs in the gallery proper, the first rooms feature works by Tuscan masters of the 13th and early 14th centuries. Room 2 is dominated by three paintings of the *Maesta* by Cimabue, Giotto and Duccio di Buoninsegna. All three were altarpieces in Florentine churches before being placed in the gallery. Also in the room is Giotto's polyptych *Virgin and Child with Angels and Saints*. Room 3 traces the Sienese school of the 14th century. Of particular note is Simone Martini's shimmering *Annunciation*, considered a masterpiece of the school, and Ambrogio Lorenzetti's triptych *Madonna and Child with Saints*. Rooms 5 and 6 house examples of the international Gothic style, among them *Adoration of the Magi* by Gentile da Fabiano. Room 7 features works by painters of the early 15th-century Florentine school, which pioneered the Renaissance. There is one panel from Paolo Uccello's *Battle of San Romano* (the other two are in the Louvre and London's National Gallery), as well as Piero della Francesca's *Portraits of Battista Sforza and Federico da Montefeltro*, and *Madonna and Child* painted jointly by Masaccio and Masolino. In the next room is Filippo Lippi's delightful *Madonna and Child with Two Angels*.

The Botticelli rooms, Nos 10 to 14, are considered the gallery's most spectacular. Highlights are the famous *Birth of Venus* and *Primavera*. Room 15 features da Vinci's *Annunciation*, painted when he was a student of Verrocchio. Room 18, known as the Tribuna, houses the celebrated *Medici Venus*, a 1st-century BC copy of a 4th-century BC sculpture by Praxiteles. The room also contains portraits of various members of the Medici. The great Umbrian painter, Perugino, who studied under Piero della Francesca and later became Raphael's master, is represented in Room 19. Room 20 features works from the German Renaissance, including Dürer's *Adoration of the Magi*. Room 21 is devoted to Giovanni Bellini and his pupil, Giorgione. Peek

Botticelli's *Birth of Venus*, inspired by a poem by Politan, depicts Venus blown by the Zephyrs to Cyprus where Pomona meets her and covers her with an embroidered cloak.

through the railings to see the 15th to 19th-century works in the Miniatures Room and then cross into the western wing, which houses works of Italian masters dating from the 16th century.

Room 25 features Michelangelo's *Holy Family* and in the next room is Raphael's *Leo X*. Room 28 features Titian's *Urbino Venus*, and in rooms 31 to 35 are works by Venetian artists, including Paolo Veronese, whose *Holy Family with St Barbara* is hung in Room 34. Canaletto features in Room 42 and Caravaggio's *Bacchus as a Youth* is in Room 43. Room 44 is dedicated to Dutch painters and features two Rembrandts. The gallery is open Tuesday to Saturday from 9 am to 7 pm and Sunday to 2 pm. Admission is L12,000.

Around Ponte Santa Trinità

From the Uffizi head west along the Arno to the **Ponte Santa Trinità**, rebuilt after being destroyed by Nazi bombing. The original plan is believed to have been drawn by Michelangelo; the bridge itself was built by Ammannati. Head north along Via de' Tor-

nabuoni, one of the city's most fashionable streets and lined with Renaissance palaces and high-class shops including Ferragamo, Gucci and Armani.

The 13th-century **Chiesa di Santa Trinità**, in the piazza of the same name, features several significant works, including frescoes depicting the life of St Francis of Assisi by Domenico Ghirlandaio in the Cappella Sassetti (in the right transept). The altarpiece of the Annunciation in the fourth chapel of the south isle is by Lorenzo Monaco, Fra Angelico's master. Monaco also painted the frescoes adorning the walls of the chapel. After leaving the church, turn right into Via Porta Rossa to visit the Palazzo Davanzati, a well-preserved 14th-century mansion that now houses the **Museo dell'Antica Casa Fiorentina** (Florentine House Museum), featuring many of the original fittings. It is open Tuesday to Sunday from 9 am to 2 pm. Admission is L4000. Just past the palace is the **Mercato Nuovo**, a loggia built in the mid-16th century to house the city's gold and silver trade and which today houses souvenir stalls and leather work vendors.

Return to Via de' Tornabuoni and head north for the **Palazzo Strozzi**, one of the most impressive Renaissance palaces in Florence. The palace is used for art exhibitions. The beautiful **Palazzo Rucellai**, designed by Alberti, is in Via della Vigna Nuova which branches off to the south-west. The palace houses a photographic museum dedicated to the vast collection compiled by the Alinari brothers. It is open Tuesday to Sunday from 10 am to 7.30 pm. Admission is L5000.

Continue along Via della Vigna Nuova to reach Piazza Goldoni and then turn right into Borgo Ognissanti to reach the 13th-century **Chiesa di Ognissanti**. The church was much altered in the 17th century and has a Baroque façade, but inside are 15th-century works by Domenico Ghirlandaio and Botticelli. Of interest is Ghirlandaio's fresco above the second altar on the right of the Madonna della Misericordia, protectress of the Vespucci family. Amerigo Vespucci, who gave his name to the American continent, is supposed to be the young boy whose head appears between the Madonna and the old man. Ghirlandaio's masterpiece, the *Last Supper*, covers most of a wall in the former

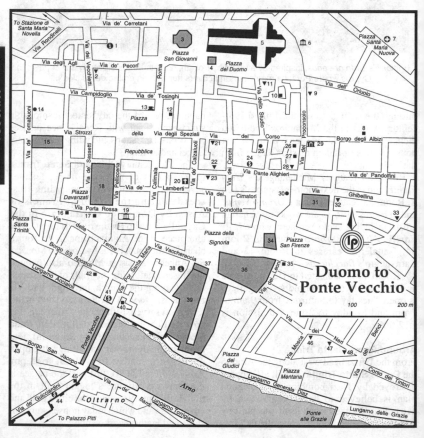

TUSCANY

monastery's refectory. The church is open daily from 8 am to midday and 4 to 7 pm.

From the Duomo towards the Arno

Take Via de' Calzaiuoli from Piazza del Duomo to reach **Chiesa di Orsanmichele**. Originally a grain market, the church was formed when the arcades of the market building were walled in the 14th century. The exterior is decorated with statues of the patron saints of the guilds of the city, commissioned over a period of 200 years and representing the work of many Renaissance artists. Some of the statues are now in the Museo Bargello. However, many splendid pieces remain, including *John the Baptist* by Lorenzo Ghiberti and a copy of Donatello's *St George*. The main feature of the interior is the splendid Gothic tabernacle, decorated with coloured marble, by Andrea Orcagna.

Just west along Via degli Speziali is the Piazza della Repubblica. Originally the site of a Roman forum, it is now home to Florence's most fashionable and expensive cafés.

Return to Piazza del Duomo, a little to the north-east of Piazza della Repubblica, and take Via del Proconsolo in the direction of the Arno. Near the intersection of Borgo degli Albizi is the **Palazzo Pazzi**, which is attributed to Brunelleschi and now houses offices. You can wander into the courtyard. From here, head west along Via del Corso for Via Santa Margherita and **Casa di Dante** at No 1, which has a small museum tracing Dante's life. It is open Monday to Friday, except Wednesday, from 9.30 am to 12.30 pm and 3.30 to 6.30 pm and on weekends to 12.30 pm. Admission is free.

Palazzo Bargello Return to Via del Proconsolo and head towards the Arno for Palazzo Bargello, also known as the Palazzo del Podestà. Started in 1254, the palace was originally the residence of the chief magistrate and then a police station. During its days as a police complex, many people were tortured near the well in the centre of the medieval courtyard. It now houses the **Museo Nazionale del Bargello** and the most comprehensive collection of Tuscan Renaissance sculpture in Italy. The museum is absolutely not to be missed. There are several works by Michelangelo on the ground floor, notably his drunken *Bacchus*, executed when the artist was 22-years-old, a marble bust of *Brutus*, a tondo of the *Madonna and Child* with the infant

TUSCANY

PLACES TO STAY					
8	Albergo Bavaria	22	Ristorante Paoli	18	Post Office & Telecom Office
10	Albergo Firenze	23	Gelateria Perchè No?	19	Museo dell' Antica Casa Fiorentina
12	Maxim	28	Trattoria il Pennello	20	Chiesa di Orsanmichele
16	Hotel Porta Rossa	32	Osteria del Gallo e Volpe	24	American Express
17	Pensione TeTi & Prestige	33	Gelateria Vivoli	25	Casa di Dante
26	Pensione Maria Luisa de Medici	43	Osteria del Cinghiale Bianco	29	Palazzo Pazzi
27	Brunori	46	Trattoria da Benvenuto	30	Badia
35	Bernini Palace	47	Angie's Pub	31	Palazzo del Bargello & Museo Nazionale del Bargello
40	Aily Home	48	Fiaschetteria	34	Palazzo Gondi
42	Pensione Alessandra			36	Palazzo Vecchio
45	Pensione la Scaletta	**OTHER**		37	Loggia della Signoria
		1	Informa Giovani Office	38	Comune di Firenze Tourist Office
PLACES TO EAT		3	Baptistry	39	Uffizi Gallery
2	Self Service Leonardo	4	Bell Tower	41	Thomas Cook Exchange Office
9	Trattoria Le Mossacce	5	Duomo	44	American Express
11	Osteria il Caminetto	6	Museo dell' Opera del Duomo		
13	Gilli	7	Hospital		
21	Festival del Gelato	14	Internazionale Seeber		
		15	Palazzo Strozzi		

StJohn, and a David (or Apollo). Also on the ground floor are many works by Benvenuto Cellini. Don't miss Donatello's stunning bronze *David* on the 1st floor, the first free-standing sculpture since antiquity to depict a fully nude man. Among the many other works by Donatello are a statue of St George, removed from the façade of Chiesa di Orsanmichele and was also replaced there with a copy, and the Marzocco, which once stood in the Piazza della Signoria and also replaced with a copy.

The museum is less popular than the Uffizi and Accademia galleries and attracts smaller crowds. It is open Tuesday to Sunday from 9 am to 2 pm. Admission is L8000.

The 10th-century **Badia**, opposite Palazzo Bargello on Via del Proconsolo, was the church of a Benedictine monastery. It is worth a visit to see Filippino Lippi's *Appearance of the Virgin to St Bernard*, to the left of the entrance. Wander into the Renaissance cloister.

Around Piazza della SS Annunziata

Return to the duomo and head north-east along Via dei Servi for the Piazza della SS Annunziata, often described as the most beautiful piazza in Florence. Located in the university district, the piazza is usually filled with students rather than tourists. In its centre is Giambologna's equestrian statue of the Grand Duke Ferdinand I de Medici.

The **Spedale degli Innocenti** on the south -east side of the piazza was founded in 1421 as Europe's first orphanage. Its portico was designed by Brunelleschi and decorated with terracotta medallions of a baby in swaddling cloths by Andrea della Robbia. Under the portico to the left of the entrance is the small revolving door where unwanted children were left. A good number of people in Florence with surnames such as degli Innocenti, Innocenti and Nocentini, can trace their family tree only as far back as the orphanage. A small gallery inside features works by Florentine artists, including Luca della Robbia and Domenico Ghirlandaio. It is open Monday to Saturday from 8.30 am to

2 pm (closed Wednesday) and Sunday from 8 am to 1 pm. Admission is L3000.

About 100 metres south-east of the church along Via della Colonna is the **Museo Archeologico**, considered to be one of Italy's best. Most of the Medici collection of antiquities is on show including the museum's highlight, an collection of Etruscan artefacts. The museum also features an impressive collection of Egyptian, Greek and Roman items. Many exhibits were badly damaged in the 1966 floods and the museum is still undergoing renovation. It is open Tuesday to Saturday from 8.30 am to 2 pm and Sunday from 8.30 am to 1 pm. Admission is L8000.

Galleria dell'Accademia Take Via Cesare Battisti from Piazza della SS Annunziata to Piazza San Marco. The entrance to the gallery is to the left on Via Ricasoli. No tour of Florence could be complete without the inclusion of this gallery. It houses paintings by Florentine artists from the 13th to 16th centuries, but its main draw card is Michelangelo's *David*. Carved from a single block of marble when the artist was only 29 years old, the *David* was originally placed in the Piazza della Signoria. The colossal statue is now situated in an alcove at the end of the main hall on the gallery's ground floor. Also in the hall are Michelangelo's celebrated unfinished *Prisoners* (or Slaves), intended for the tomb of Pope Julius II, and his *Pietà di Palestrina*, also unfinished.

The gallery is open Tuesday to Saturday from 9 am to 7 pm and Sunday to 2 pm in summer (check at the tourist office to ensure the extended hours are still in force) and, for the rest of the year, Tuesday to Saturday from 9 am to 2 pm and Sunday until 1 pm. Admission is L12,000.

Palazzo Medici-Riccardi Heading back towards the duomo, you will find this extraordinary palace on Via Cavour, just off Piazza San Lorenzo. It is typical of the Florentine Renaissance style and was started by Michelozzo for Cosimo de Medici in 1444. The Medici residence from 1459 to 1540, it was the prototype for other buildings in the city, such as the Palazzo Pitti. It was remodelled in the 17th century by the Riccardi family. The chapel upstairs has beautiful frescoes by Benozzo Gozzoli, with regal scenes featuring members of the Medici clan. The Sala di Luca Giordano was built by the Riccardi family and is sumptuously decorated. The palace is open Monday to Friday, except Wednesday, from 9 am to 1 pm and 3 to 5 pm and on weekends to midday. Admission is free.

Ponte Vecchio This famous 14th-century bridge, lined with the shops of gold and silversmiths, was the only one to survive the bombs of the retreating Nazis. The shops originally housed butchers, but Cosimo de Medici ordered them removed in favour of jewellers, whose trade was considered more appropriate and certainly more hygienic, since the butchers threw their leftovers directly into the river. Walk a few hundred metres along the Arno in either direction and then look back at the Ponte Vecchio for what has to be one of the most evocative views in Florence. The view from the small piazza in the centre of the bridge is also impressive.

Palazzo Pitti This immense and imposing palace, south of the Arno on Via de' Guicciardini, was designed by Brunelleschi for the wealthy merchant family, the Pitti, which was a great rival of the Medici. Construction started in 1458 and almost a century later, in 1549, it was bought by Eleanora di Toledo, wife of Cosimo de Medici, who had it expanded by adding two wings. The Medici, followed by the grand dukes of Lorraine, lived in the palace. In the late 19th century it became a residence of the Savoy royal family, who presented it to the state in 1919.

The palace now houses four museums. The **Galleria Palatina** (Palatine Gallery) houses paintings from the 16th to 18th centuries, which are hung in lavishly decorated rooms. The works were collected by the Medici and artists including Raphael, Filippo Lippi,

Tintoretto, Paolo Veronese and Rubens are represented. It is a large collection and if visits to the Uffizi, Accademia and Bargello haven't yet worn you out, try to spend at least half a day in the Palatina. The apartments of the Medici, and later of the Savoy, show the splendour in which the rulers lived. The other three galleries are worth a look only if you have plenty of time. The Galleria d'Arte Moderna (Modern Art Gallery, admission L4000) covers Tuscan works from the 18th until the mid-20th century, and the Museo degli Argenti (Silver Museum, admission L8000), entered from the garden courtyard, has a collection of glassware, silver and semiprecious stones from the Medici collections. The Galleria del Costume (Costume Gallery, admission L6000) has costumes from the 18th and 19th centuries. All the galleries have the same opening hours: Tuesday to Sunday from 9 am to 2 pm. Admission to the Galleria Palatina and the apartments is L12,000.

Take a break in the palace's Renaissance **Giardino di Boboli**, which were laid out in the mid-16th century and based on a design by the architect known as Il Tribolo. Buontalenti's noted artificial grotto, with a *Venus* by Giambologna, is worth a look. The star-shaped **Forte di Belvedere**, built in 1590 at the southern end of the gardens, is worth wandering past on your way east to Piazzale Michelangelo.

Piazzale Michelangelo Via di Belvedere eventually leads to the piazzale from the Palazzo Pitti, but the road has been closed for some time. Rather than catch a bus, you can head back up Via de' Guicciardini to the river and then make the long, uphill walk along Costa San Giorgio. The view from Piazzale Michelangelo makes it worth the effort, and should not be missed at any cost. Behind the piazzale is the austere Chiesa di San Salvatore al Monte.

Chiesa di San Miniato al Monte Along from Piazzale Michelangelo, this church with its green and white marble façade, is one of the best examples of the Tuscan Romanesque style. The church was started in the early 11th century, and the façade features a mosaic which was added 200 years later and depicts Christ between the Virgin and St Minius. Inside, above the altar, is a crucifix by Luca della Robbia and a tabernacle by Michelozzo. The Capella del Cardinale del Portogallo features a tomb by Antonio Rossellino and a ceiling decorated in terracotta by Luca della Robbia. It is possible to wander through the cemetery outside.

Casa Buonarroti

North from Piazza Santa Croce along Via de' Pepi is the **Casa Buonarroti**, Via Ghibellina 70, which Michelangelo owned but never lived in. Upon his death, the house went to his nephew and eventually became a museum in the mid-1850s. The collection of memorabilia is mostly copies of Michelangelo's works and portraits of the master. On the 2nd floor is Michelangelo's earliest known work, *The Madonna of the Steps*. The museum is open daily, except Tuesday, from 9.30 am to 1.30 pm. Admission is L5000.

CYCLING

I Bike Italy (☎ 234 23 71) offers reasonably priced full and half-day guided mountain-bike rides in the countryside around Florence, including in the picturesque hills around Fiesole, north-east of the city. All you need is a reasonable amount of energy and a hardy backside. I Bike Italy also offers eight-day bike tours in Tuscany and Umbria, with agriturismo accommodation.

The Globetrotter's Club in Florence (☎ 24 59 22) arranges cycling holidays around the city each spring, with most tours taking in Siena and stopping for accommodation at agriturismo farms. If you are interested in cycling, pick up a copy of *Viaggio in Toscana – Discovering Tuscany by Bike* from the APT office. It is produced by the Tuscan regional government and details this increasingly popular sport. For where to rent a bike, see Car & Motorbike in the following Getting Around section.

FAMILY ACTIVITIES

The tourist offices have information about child day care services, courses and special activities for kids (organised for local youngsters, not tourists, so ask for advice on the most suitable for your children). These options might come in handy if you are planning a few days of hectic sightseeing and your children have had enough of museums etc.

There is a small playground in Piazza Massimo d'Azeglio, about five to 10 minutes walk east of the duomo. Beside the Arno river, about 15 minutes walk to the west of Stazione di Santa Maria Novella, is a massive public park called Parco delle Cascine. Older children might find the Museo Stibbert entertaining. It features a large collection of antique costumes and armaments from Europe, the Middle East and Asia. It is at Via Stibbert 26 and is open daily from 9 am to 1 pm. Admission is L5000.

COURSES

Florence has more than 30 schools offering courses in Italian language and culture. Numerous other schools offer courses in art, including painting, drawing and sculpture, as well as art history.

While Florence is one of the most attractive cities in which to study Italian language or art, it is one of the more expensive. Perugia, Siena and Urbino offer good courses at much lower prices.

The cost of language courses in Florence ranges from about L450,000 to L900,000, depending on the school and the length of the course (one month is usually the minimum duration).

Listed here are the addresses of some language courses available in Florence:

Dante Alighieri School for Foreigners
   Via dei Bardi 12, 50125, Florence
   (☎ 234 29 84)
Istituto Europeo
   Piazzale delle Pallottole 1, 50122 Florence (☎ 28 91 45)
Istituto di Lingua e Cultura Italiana per Stranieri Michelangelo
   Via Ghibellina 88, 50122 Florence (☎ 24 09 75)

TUSCANY

Art courses range from one-month summer workshops (costing from L500,000 to more than L1,000,000) to longer term professional diploma courses. These can be expensive; some cost more than L6,500,000 a year. Schools will organise accommodation for students, upon request, either in private apartments or with Italian families.

Two art schools you might like to consider are:

The Art Institute of Florence
    Via Faenza 43, 50122 Florence (☎ 28 71 43)
Istituto per l'Arte e il Restauro
    Palazzo Spinelli, Borgo Santa Croce 10, 50122 Florence (☎ 234 58 98)

Brochures detailing courses and prices are available at Italian cultural institutes throughout the world. The Florence APT also has lists of schools and courses and will mail them on request. A brief list of schools is included here. You can write in English to request information and enrolment forms – letters should be addressed to the segretaria.

Remember that many nationalities are required to apply for a visa to study in Italy, so check with the Italian consulate in your country.

ORGANISED TOURS
CIT and American Express offer tours of the city. Call into one of their offices for information. Guides can be contacted through the APT office.

FESTIVALS
The major festivals include the Scoppio del Carro (Explosion of the Cart), when a cart full of fireworks is exploded in front of the duomo on Easter Sunday; the Festa del Patrono (the Feast of St John the Baptist) on 24 June; and the lively Calcio Storico (Football in Costume), featuring football matches played in 16th-century costume, held in June in Piazza della Signoria and ending with a fireworks display over Piazzale Michelangelo.

Florence hosts the Internazionale Antiquariato, a biennial antique fair attracting exhibitors from across Europe, at the Palazzo Strozzi, Via de' Tornabuoni. Call ☎ 28 26 35 for information.

Concerts, opera and dance are performed year-round at the Teatro Comunale, Corso Italia 16, with the main seasons running from September to December and from January to April. Contact the theatre's box office (☎ 277 92 36). The Centro Culturale Dantesco (☎ 21 50 44) stages organ concerts each April, May and June at Chiesa di Dante, Via Santa Margherita 2, and Chiesa di Santa Maria de' Ricci, Via del Corso.

Ballet is generally performed at the Verdi Theatre (☎ 21 23 20), Via a series of classical music concerts at the Teatro Municipale and Teatro Pergola, featuring musicians from around the world. Book at the festival box office (☎ 24 23 61), Via della Pergola 10Ar.

PLACES TO STAY
The city has hundreds of hotels in all categories and a good range of alternatives, including hostels and private rooms. There are more than 150 budget hotels in Florence, so even in the peak season when the city is packed with tourists, it is generally possible to find a room. However, it is advisable throughout the year to make a booking and arrive by late morning to claim your room. Hotels and pensioni are concentrated in three main areas: near the main train station, near Piazza Santa Maria Novella and in the old city between the duomo and the river.

If you arrive at Stazione di Santa Maria Novella without a hotel booking, head for ITA, the Consorzio Informazioni Turistiche e Alberghiere (☎ 28 28 93), inside the station on the main concourse. Using a computer network, the office can check the availability of rooms and book you a night for a small fee. The office is open daily from 8.30 am to 9 pm.

Contact the APT for a list of private rooms, which generally charge from L22,000 per person in a shared room and from L30,000 per person in a single room. Most fill with students during the school year (from October to June), but are a good option if you are staying for a week or longer.

When you arrive at a hotel, always ask for the full price of a room before putting your bags down. Florentine hotels and pensioni are notorious for their bill-padding, particularly in summer. Some may require an extra L5000 for a compulsory breakfast and will charge L3000 or more for a shower. By law they can charge no more than the prices posted in the rooms and theoretically you can complain to the APT if a hotel overcharges.

Prices listed here are for the high season and, unless otherwise indicated, are for rooms without a bathroom. A bathroom will cost from L10,000 to L20,000 extra. During the low season (usually from mid-October to March, with exceptions for periods including Christmas) prices drop dramatically.

Bottom End

Camping The closest camping ground to the city centre is *Italiani e Stranieri* (☎ 681 19 77), Viale Michelangelo 80, just off Piazzale Michelangelo south of the Arno. Take bus No 13 from the main train station. *Villa Camerata* (☎ 60 14 51), Viale Augusto Righi 2-4, is next to the HI hostel (take bus No 17B from the main train station, 30 minutes). Both grounds are open from April to October. There is a camping ground at Fiesole, *Campeggio Panorama* (☎ 59 90 69) at Via Peramonda 1, which also has bungalows. Take bus No 7 to Fiesole from the main train station.

Hostels The HI *Ostello Villa Camerata* (☎ 60 14 51), Viale Augusto Righi 2-4, is considered one of the most beautiful in Europe. B&B is L18,000, dinner L12,000 and there is a bar. Only members are accepted and reservations can be made by mail (essential in summer). Daytime closing is 9 am to 2 pm. Take bus No 17B, which leaves from the right of the main train station as you leave the platforms. The trip takes 30 minutes.

The private *Ostello Santa Monaca* (☎ 26 83 38), Via Santa Monaca 6, is a 15 to 20-minute walk south from the train station, through Piazza Santa Maria Novella, along Via de' Fossi, across the Ponte alla Carraia and directly ahead along Via de' Serragli. Via

Santa Monaca is a few blocks from the river, on the right. A bed costs L18,000 and sheets and hot shower are included.

The *Ostello Spirito Santo* (☎ 239 82 02), Via Nazionale 8, is a religious institution near the main train station. The nuns accept only women and families and charge L40,000 per person or L60,000 for a double. Call ahead to book. The hostel is open from July to October.

Istituto Gould (☎ 21 25 76), Via de' Serragli 49, has clean doubles for L35,000.

Hotels – east of Stazione SM Novella
Many of the hotels in this area are very well run, clean and safe, but there is also a fair number of seedy one-star establishments. The area includes the streets around Piazza della Stazione and east to Via Cavour.

Some of the cheapest rooms in Florence are at the *Daniel* (☎ 21 12 93), Via Nazionale 22. Basic singles/doubles cost L25,000/ 40,000 and rooms for three and four are L70,000/90,000. There is an extra charge to use the communal bathroom. The hotel is pleasant but dark, and the owner will not take bookings, so arrive very early. In the same building is *Soggiorno Nazionale* (☎ 238 22 03), which has singles/doubles for up to L50,000 /78,000, or for up to L60,000/88,000 with a shower.

The *Pensione Ausonia & Rimini* (☎ 49 65 47), run by a young couple who go out of their way to help travellers, is nearby at Via Nazionale 24. It has singles/doubles for L45,000/69,000 and a triple is L90,000. The price includes breakfast and use of the communal bathroom. Add about L20,000 for rooms with a bathroom.

Albergo Azzi (☎ 21 38 06), Via Faenza 56, has a very helpful management, which will arrange accommodation for you in other Italian cities. Simple, comfortable singles/doubles are L50,000/70,000. Dormitory beds cost L25,000 per person. Ask for a room away from the noisy Via Faenza and enjoy breakfast on the hotel's terrace. The same management runs *Albergo Anna* upstairs. There are several other budget pensioni in the same building and all are habitable. Across Via Nazionale is the *Pensione Accademia* (☎ 29 34 51) at Via Faenza 7. It has very pleasant rooms and incorporates an 18th-century palace with magnificent stained glass doors and carved wooden ceilings. Singles/doubles cost L40,000/65,000. A triple, including a bathroom and breakfast, is L104,000.

The *Pensione Bellavista* (☎ 28 45 28), Largo Alinari 15, at the start of Via Nazionale, is small, but a knockout bargain if you can manage to book one of the two double rooms with balconies and a view of the duomo and Palazzo Vecchio. Singles/doubles cost L45,000/60,500, although you will be hit for L3500 to use the bathroom.

Albergo Roxy (☎ 47 29 28), Piazza della Indipendenza 5, has views over the gardens in the piazza and large, modern rooms cost L45,000/70,000. *Albergo Mary* (☎ 49 63 10) in the same building has rooms for about the same price.

Hotels – around Piazza Santa Maria Novella This area is just south of the Stazione di Santa Maria Novella and includes Piazza Santa Maria Novella, the streets running south to the Arno and east to Via de' Tornabuoni.

La Mia Casa (☎ 21 30 61) at Piazza Santa Maria Novella 25 is a rambling place, filled with antiques and backpackers. The owner is helpful, speaks English and keeps his prices down. Basic singles/doubles are L30,000/45,000 and triples/quads L60,000/76,000.

Via della Scala, which runs north-west off the piazza, is lined with pensioni. *La Romagnola* (☎ 21 15 97) at No 40 has large, clean rooms and a helpful management. Singles/doubles are L42,000/64,000. A triple room is a good deal at L78,000. The same family runs *La Gigliola* (☎ 28 79 81) upstairs, with rooms for about the same price. *La Scala* (☎ 21 26 29) at No 21 is small and has singles/doubles for L40,000/60,000, slightly more with a bathroom. Rooms for three and four people cost L28,000 per person. There is a midnight curfew.

The *Pensione Margareth* (☎ 21 01 38) at No 25 has pleasantly furnished, but expensive singles/doubles for L50,000/80,000. *Pensione Montreal* (☎ 238 23 31) at No 43 has singles/doubles from L40,000/63,000.

Pensione Sole (☎ 239 60 94), Via del Sole 8, is on the 3rd floor and there is no lift. Singles/doubles are L40,000/60,000, plus L2000 to use the communal shower. A double with a bathroom costs L75,000 and triples/quads are L78,000/92,000. Ask for a quiet room. The *Pensione Toscana* (☎ 21 31 56) is at the same address. Its eccentrically decorated rooms cost L47,000/65,000 with a bathroom. *Pensione Ottaviani* (☎ 239 62 23), Piazza degli Ottaviani 1, just off Piazza Santa Maria Novella, has singles/doubles for L40,000/60,000 including breakfast. In the same building is *Albergo Visconti* (☎ 21 38 77), with décor featuring royal blue walls and statues. It has a pleasant terrace garden where you can have breakfast. Singles/doubles are L37,000/54,000 and a triple is L79,000. At Piazza Vittorio Veneto 8, a five-minute walk west of the main train station and next to the Parco delle Cascine, is the *Garden* (☎ 21 26 69), which has doubles for L68,000. Most rooms overlook a pleasant garden.

Hotels – between the Duomo & the Arno This area is a 15-minute walk south from Stazione di Santa Maria Novella in the heart of old Florence. One of the best deals is the small *Aily Home* (☎ 239 65 05), Piazza Santo Stefano 81, just near the Ponte Vecchio. Doubles cost L50,000. It has five large rooms, three overlooking the bridge, and accepts bookings.

Albergo Firenze (☎ 21 42 03), Piazza dei Donati 4, just south of the duomo, has singles/doubles for L46,000/70,000 and breakfast is included. The helpful owners of *Brunori* (☎ 28 96 48), Via del Proconsolo 5, charge L33,000/59,000 for singles/doubles and an extra L5000 for showers. *Albergo Bavaria* (☎ 234 03 13), Borgo Albizi 26, has singles/doubles for up to L60,000/70,000. A double with a bathroom is L80,000. The *Pensione TeTi & Prestige* (☎ 239 84 35), Via Porta Rossa 5, has singles/doubles for L40,000/L65,000 and charges an extra L12,000 per person for breakfast. The *Maxim* (☎ 21 74 74), Via dei Medici

TUSCANY

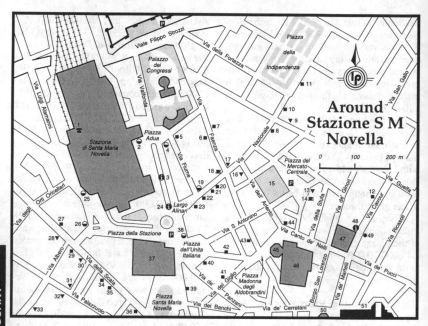

Around Stazione S M Novella

0   100   200 m

4, has singles/doubles from L45,000/75,000 and offers substantial discounts in the low season. The *Pensione Maria Luisa de Medici* (☎ 28 00 48), Via del Corso 1, is in a 17th-century palace. It has no singles – with large rooms for up to five people, the management caters for families. A double is L65,000, or L76,000 with a bathroom and a triple is L95,000, or L110,000 with a bathroom. Family rooms for four or five are reasonably priced. Prices drop in the low season. The management is accommodating and speaks English.

Middle

East of Stazione SM Novella The *Pensione Le Cascine* (☎ 21 10 66), Largo Alinari 15, near the train station, is a two-star hotel with nicely furnished rooms, some with balconies. Singles/doubles are L60,000/90,000, including use of the communal bathroom. A double with a bathroom costs up to L120,000. *Albergo Ester* (☎ 21 27 41) is

accessible by the same entrance and offers rooms for around the same price. A shower costs L2000.

Tony's Inn (☎ 21 79 75) and *Hotel Apollo* (☎ 28 41 19), at Via Faenza 77, have the same owners. The obliging owners speak English and will make bookings on request at hotels throughout Italy. Renovations are underway which will mean that both hotels will become three-star and consequently more expensive. For now Tony's Inn has singles/doubles with a bathroom and breakfast for L100,000/120,000. Hotel Apollo is a bit more expensive.

Hotel Desirèe (☎ 238 23 82), Via Fiume 20, close to the train station, has been recently renovated. Its very pleasant rooms all have a bathroom and cost up to L95,000/140,000.

Around Basilica di San Lorenzo The *Giotto* (☎ 28 98 64), Via del Giglio 13, has doubles with a bathroom for L109,000. The *Giada* (☎ 21 53 17) is in the middle of the open air

PLACES TO STAY		36	Croce di Malta	OTHER	
		39	La Mia Casa		
5	Hotel Desirèe	40	Grand Hotel	1	Telecom Office
6	Tony's Inn & Hotel Apollo		Baglioni	2	ATAF Local Bus Station
7	Albergo Azzi &	41	Giotto	3	Urban Bus Ticket &
	Albergo Anna	42	Albergo Majestic		Information Office
8	Daniel & Soggiorno	43	Pensione	4	Lazzi Bus Station &
	Nazionale		Accademia		Ticket Office
10	Pensione Kursaal &	44	Giada	15	Market
	Pensione Ausonia &			19	CAT, CAP &
	Rimini	PLACES TO EAT			COPIT Bus Station
11	Albergo Roxy &			24	Comune di Firenze
	Albergo Mary	9	Trattoria da Giovanni		Tourist Office
12	Albergo Tina	13	Mario's	25	ATAF Local Bus Station
20	Atlantic Palace	14	Caffè Za Za	26	SITA Bus Station
21	Machiavelli Palace	16	Bondi	37	Chiesa di Santa
22	Ostello Santo Spirito	17	Il Triangolo di		Maria Novella
23	Pensione Bellavista,		Bermudao	38	ATAF Local Bus Station
	Albergo Ester &	18	Caffé degli Innocenti	45	Cappelle Medicee
	Pensione Le Cascine	28	Trattoria il Giardino	46	Basilica di San Lorenzo
27	La Romagnola &	30	La Grotta di Leo	47	Palazzo Medici-Riccardi
	La Gigliola	31	Trattoria da Giorgio	48	APT Tourist Office
29	Pensione Montreal	32	Trattoria il	49	Feltrinelli Bookshop
34	Pensione Margareth		Contadino	50	Baptistry
35	La Scala	33	Ristorante Dino	51	Duomo

TUSCANY

leather market at Via Canto de' Nelli 2. Its singles/doubles with a bathroom are expensive for what you get at L100,000/140,000. *Hotel Le Casci* (☎ 21 16 86), Via Cavour 13, has good rooms for L80,000/120,000 with a bathroom.

Between the Duomo & the Arno The *Pensione Alessandra* (☎ 28 34 38), Borgo SS Apostoli 17, has lots of character. Singles/doubles are L60,000/92,000 or, with a bathroom, L80,000/116,000.

The Oltrarno *Pensione la Scaletta* (☎ 28 30 28), Via de' Guicciardini 13, is a good choice if you want to stay south of the river. It has a terrace with great views. A double is L95,000 and singles/doubles with a bathroom are L75,000/125,000.

Top End
Around Stazione SM Novella The *Hotel Albion* (☎ 21 41 71), Via il Prato 22r, just west of the train station, has very comfortable singles/doubles for L150,000/180,000. The *Atlantic Palace* (☎ 21 30 31), Via Nazio-

nale 12, has singles/doubles for up to L165,000/280,000 with breakfast included.

The *Machiavelli Palace* (☎ 236 00 08), Via Nazionale 10, is in a 17th-century palace. Many of its beautiful rooms have terraces. Singles/doubles are worth the price at L160,000/250,000. The *Jolly Carlton* (☎ 27 70), Piazza Vittorio Veneto 4A, has rooms from L160,000/250,000.

Around Piazza Santa Maria Novella The four-star *Albergo Majestic* (☎ 26 40 21), Via del Melarancio 1, has very comfortable singles/doubles from L240,000/330,000. *Grand Hotel Baglioni* (☎ 21 84 41), Piazza dell'Unità Italiana 6, has good rooms from about the same price.

Between the Duomo & the Arno The *Bernini Palace* (☎ 28 86 21), Piazza San Firenze 29, is an excellent hotel in an historic building. Its luxurious rooms are L270,000/380,000 for singles/doubles. The *Porta Rossa* (☎ 28 75 51), Via Porta Rossa 19, has large singles/doubles for L110,000/165,000.

Rental Accommodation
If you want an apartment in Florence, save

your pennies and start looking well before you arrive, as apartments are difficult to come by and can be very expensive. A one-room apartment with kitchenette in the city centre will cost from L600,000 to L1,000,000 a month. Florence & Abroad (☎ 48 70 04), Via Zanobi 58, handles rental accommodation. Florence House-finding (☎ 247 66 20) also arranges apartments. Another option is to check the notice board at the university for people looking for someone to share a flat.

PLACES TO EAT
Simplicity and quality describe the cuisine of Tuscany. In a country where the various regional styles and traditions have provided a rich and diverse cuisine, Tuscany is known for its fine cooking. The rich green olive oil of Tuscany, fresh fruit and vegetables, tender meat and, of course, the classic wine, Chianti, are the basics of a good meal in Florence.

You could start a meal with *fettunta* (known elsewhere in Italy as bruschetta), a thick slice of toasted bread rubbed with garlic and soaked with olive oil. Try the *ribollita*, a very filling soup traditionally eaten by the poor of Florence. It is basically a minestrone with lots of white beans which is reboiled with chunks of old bread and then garnished with olive oil. Another traditional dish is the deliciously simple *fagiolini alla Fiorentina* (green beans and olive oil). Florence is noted for its excellent quality beefsteak, known as *bistecca Fiorentina* – thick, juicy and big enough for two people.

Eating at a good trattoria can be surprisingly economical, but many tourists fall into the trap of eating at the self-service restaurants which line the streets of the main shopping district between the duomo and the river. Be adventurous and seek out the little eating places in the Oltrarno and near Piazza del Mercato Centrale in the San Lorenzo area where you'll eat more authentic Italian food. The market, open Monday to Saturday from 7 am to 2 pm (also Saturday from 4 to 8 pm), has fresh produce, cheeses and meat at reasonable prices.

Near Stazione SM Novella & Basilica di San Lorenzo
Mario's, a small bar and trattoria at Via Rosina 2r, near Piazza del Mercato Centrale, is open only for lunch and serves pasta for around L6000 to L8000 and mains for L7000 to L9000. It is very popular. A few doors down, at Piazza del Mercato Centrale 20, is *Caffè Za Za*, another popular eating place. Prices are around the same as at Mario's.

Bondi, Via dell'Ariento 85, specialises in focaccia and offers a variety of toppings. They start at L2500 and pizza by the slice is also L2500.

Trattoria da Giovanni, Via Guelfa 94r, offers a L15,000 set menu or entrées from L2000 and pasta from L4000.

Around SM Novella & Ognissanti
La Grotta di Leo, Via della Scala 41, is a pleasant trattoria with an L18,000 set menu or pizzas and pasta from L7000. *Trattoria il Giardino* at No 67 in the same street has a L20,000 set menu and serves good, hearty Tuscan dishes and cheap wine.

Nearby is the *Trattoria il Contadino*, Via Palazzuolo 55, with a L13,000 set menu, including wine. *Trattoria da Giorgio*, at No 54, also has a L13,000 set menu and the food is very good.

Ristorante Dino, Via Maso Finiguerra 6-8, is a good little trattoria, with pasta from L6000 and main courses from L10,000. The L2500 cover charge bumps up the price.

Da il Latini, Via dei Palchetti 4, just off Via del Moro, is an attractive trattoria serving pasta from L6000 and main courses from L12,000.

Sostanza, Via della Porcellana 25r, offers traditional Tuscan cooking and is one of the best spots in town for bistecca fiorentina. A full meal will cost around L60,000 a head.

City Centre & Towards Santa Croce
The streets between the duomo and the Arno harbour many pizzerias where you can buy takeaway pizza by the slice for around L2000 to L3000, depending on the weight.

Osteria il Caminetto, Via dello Studio 34, south of the duomo, has a small, vine-covered terrace. Pasta costs around L7000 and a main from L9000 to L10,000. The L2000 cover charge plus a 10% service charge bumps up the price of a meal. *Trattoria Le Mossacce*, Via del Proconsolo 55r, serves pasta for around L9000 and a full meal with wine will cost up to L30,000.

Trattoria il Pennello, Via Dante Alighieri 4, is popular and quite cheap. Pasta starts at L5000 and a set meal costs L20,000. *Ristorante Paoli*, Via dei Tavolini 12, has magnificent vaulted ceilings and walls covered with frescoes, and food to match. It offers a L28,000 set menu and pasta from L8000 and the cover charge is L2500.

Trattoria da Benvenuto, Via Mosca 16r, on the corner of Via dei Neri, is excellent. Its menu changes regularly and a full meal will cost under L25,000. A quick meal of pasta, bread and wine will cost around L12,000. It is wise to reserve a table. Among the great undiscovered treasures of Florence is *Angie's Pub*, Via dei Neri 35r, east of the Palazzo Vecchio, which offers a vast array of panini and focaccia, as well as hamburgers, Italian-style with mozzarella and spinach, and hot dogs with cheese and mushrooms. A menu lists the panini, but you can design your own from the extensive selection of fillings; try one with artichoke, mozzarella and mushroom cream. Prices start at around L4000. There is a good range of beers and no extra charge to sit down.

At *Fiaschetteria*, Via dei Neri 17r, you are even less likely to find a tourist. Try the excellent ribollita for L10,000. Another option for a light lunch is *Antico Noè*, a legendary sandwich bar through the Arco di San Piero, just off Piazza San Pier Maggiore. It is takeaway only. In the piazza is a pleasant, reasonably priced little trattoria, *Natalino*.

Osteria del Gallo e Volpe, on the corner of Via Ghibellina and Via de' Giraldi, has pizzas from L5000 and pasta from L6000, and the cover charge is L2500. The *Sant' Ambrogio Caffè* at Piazza Sant'Ambrogio 7 is a bar and restaurant, where you can get a sandwich from L3000 or pasta from L7000.

One of the city's finest restaurants, *Enoteca Pinchiorri*, Via Ghibellina 87, is noted for its nouvelle cuisine Italian-style. A meal will cost around L150,000 a head.

Oltrarno
Osteria del Cinghiale Bianco, Borgo San Jacopo 43, to the right as you cross Ponte Vecchio, specialises in Florentine food and offers a delicious onion soup and wild boar with polenta. Pasta starts at L7000 and main courses from L10,000 and the cover charge is L1500. *Angelino*, Via Santo Spirito 36, is an excellent trattoria where you can eat a meal, including bistecca, for around L35,000. In Piazza Santo Spirito is the pizzeria *Borgo Antico*, a great location in summer, when you can sit at an outside table and enjoy the atmosphere in the piazza.

Five minutes walk farther west will take you to Piazza Torquarto Tasso and the small restaurant *Tranvai*. The great food and good value for money makes it worth the hike. A full meal will cost under L20,000.

Trattoria Casalinga, Via dei Michelozzi 9r, is a bustling, popular eating place. The food is great and a filling meal of pasta, meat or vegetables plus wine will cost under L25,000. Don't expect to linger over a meal, as there is usually a queue of people waiting for your table. *Trattoria I Raddi*, Via Ardiglione 47, just near Via de' Serragli, serves traditional Florentine meals and has pasta from L7000 and main courses from L12,000.

I Tarocchi, Via de' Renai 12-14r, is a popular pizzeria/trattoria serving excellent pizzas from L7000, regional dishes, including a good range of pasta, from L7000 to L10,000 and plenty of salads and vegetable dishes from L4000 to L7000.

Bars, Cafés & Snacks
Caffè degli Innocenti, Via Nazionale 57, near the leather market around Piazza del Mercato Centrale, has a great selection of prepared panini and cakes for around L3000 to L4000. The *Antica Enoteca*, Via Ghibellina 142, is one of the city's oldest bars and features hundreds of wines. The owners will gladly open any bottle and engage in a chat if you have the time. Wines start at L1500 a glass. The *Fiddler's Elbow*, Piazza

TUSCANY

Santa Maria Novella, is open from 4 pm to 1 am and is a popular spot for UK and US expatriates. *Rex Caffè*, Via Fiesolana 25r, in the Sant'Antonio area, is popular with the arts community.

Gilli, Piazza della Repubblica, is one of the city's finest cafés, and is reasonably cheap if you stand at the bar: a coffee at the bar is L1500, but at a table outside it is L5000.

Il Cantinone di Gatto Nero, Via di Santo Spirito 6r, specialises in crostini, starting at L3500. Pasta is from L4500 and the cover charge is 1500. *Cabiria*, Piazza Santo Spirito, is a very popular bar among local young people, particularly in summer.

Gelati

People queue outside *Gelateria Vivoli*, Via dell'Isola delle Stinche, near Via Torta, to delight in the gelati that is widely considered the city's best. *Il Triangolo di Bermude*, Via Nazionale 61, near the leather market, and *Perché No?*, Via dei Tavolini 19r, off Via de' Calzaiuoli, are both excellent. *Festival del Gelato*, Via del Corso 75, just off Via de' Calzaiuoli, offers 90 flavours, including a good selection of semifrozen ice creams.

ENTERTAINMENT

There are several publications which list the theatrical and musical events and festivals held in the city and surrounding areas. The free, bimonthly *Florence Today*, the monthly *Firenze Information* and *Firenze Avvenimenti*, a monthly brochure distributed by the comune, are all available at the tourist offices. *Firenze Spettacolo*, the city's definitive entertainment publication, is available every 15 days for L2500 at newspaper stands. Posters at the tourist offices, the university and in Piazza della Repubblica advertise current concerts and other events.

The Astro Cinema in Piazza San Simone, near Santa Croce, runs films in English every night except Monday. There is no telephone, so check with the APT, or watch for street posters advertising upcoming movies.

As for nightclubs, La Dolce Vita, Piazza del Carmine, south of the Arno, is frequented by foreigners and Italians alike. Circus, Via delle Oche 17, is one of the better nightclubs. The Café Be Bop, Via dei Servi 76r, is a bit tacky; your feet will stick to the carpet but it really jumps from 11 pm. Both charge L10,000 admission, but the price includes one drink. Dr No, Via dei Benci 19r, is a popular club and features rock bands, flamenco and other types of live music.

A more sedate pastime is the evening stroll in Piazzale Michelangelo, overlooking the city (take bus No 13 from the station or the duomo). In May, visit the nearby iris garden, when the irises are in full bloom. The city has many small art galleries and hosts travelling art shows. Check with the APT. The area around Piazza Sant'Ambrogio has many small galleries.

THINGS TO BUY

It is said that Milan has the best clothes and Rome the best shoes, but Florence without doubt has the greatest variety of goods. The main shopping area is between the duomo and the Arno, with boutiques concentrated along Via Roma, Via de' Calzaiuoli and Via Por Santa Maria, leading to the goldsmiths lining the Ponte Vecchio. Window-shop along Via de' Tornabuoni, where the top designers, including Gucci, Saint-Laurent and Pucci, sell their wares.

The open air market (Monday to Saturday) near Piazza del Mercato Centrale offers leather goods, clothing and jewellery at low prices, but quality can vary greatly. You could pick up the bargain of a lifetime here, but check the item carefully before paying. It is possible to bargain, but not if you want to use a credit card. The flea market (Monday to Saturday) at Piazza dei Ciompi, off Borgo Allegri near Piazza di Santa Croce, is not as extensive, but there are great bargains.

Florence is famous for its beautifully patterned paper, which is stocked in the many stationery and speciality shops throughout the city and at the markets.

GETTING THERE & AWAY
Air

Florence is served by two airports, Amerigo

Vespucci (☎ 37 34 98), a few km north-west of the city centre at Via del Termine 11, and Galileo Galilei (☎ 21 60 73), near Pisa and about an hour by train or car from Florence. Vespucci serves domestic flights only; there are services to Bari, Milan, Naples, Palermo, Rome and Turin. Galileo Galilei is one of northern Italy's main international and domestic airports and has regular connections to London, Paris, Zürich, Frankfurt and major Italian cities.

Most major European and some US airlines are represented in the city. Alitalia (☎ 2 78 88) is at Lungarno Acciaiuoli 10-12r; British Airways (☎ 21 86 55) is at Via Vigna Nuova 36r; and TWA (☎ 239 68 56) is at Via dei Vecchietti 4.

Bus

The SITA bus station (☎ 21 47 21), Via Santa Caterina da Siena, is just to the west of Stazione di Santa Maria Novella. There is a direct, rapid service to Siena. Buses leave for Poggibonsi, where there are connecting buses for San Gimignano and Volterra. There are also buses for Arezzo, Castellina in the Chianti region, Faenza, Marina di Grosseto and other smaller cities throughout Tuscany. Several bus companies, including CAP and COPIT, operate from Largo Alinari, at the southern end of Via Nazionale, with services to towns including Prato and Pistoia.

Lazzi (☎ 21 51 55), Piazza Adua 1, next to Stazione di Santa Maria Novella, runs services to Rome, Pistoia and Lucca. Lazzi forms part of the Eurolines network of international bus services. You can, for instance, catch a bus to Paris, Prague or Barcelona from Florence. A detailed brochure of all Eurolines services is available from Lazzi. In collaboration with SITA, it operates a service called Alpi Bus, which runs extensive routes to the Alps. See the Getting Around chapter at the beginning of this book for further details. The buses depart from numerous cities and towns throughout Lazio, Umbria, Tuscany and Emilia-Romagna for most main resorts in the Alps. A brochure detailing the services is available at the Lazzi office.

Train

Florence is on the Rome-Milan line, which means that most of the trains for Rome, Bologna and Milan are the fast Intercities, for which you have to pay a supplement. There are also regular trains to and from Venice (three hours) and Trieste. For Verona you will generally need to change at Bologna. To get to Genoa and Turin, a change at Pisa is necessary. For train information, ring ☎ 27 87 85, or pick up the handy train timetable booklet available at Stazione di Santa Maria Novella. There is a porter service operating from the train station. Porters will escort you to your hotel and charge L2500 per article.

Car & Motorbike

Florence is connected by the A1 to Bologna and Milan in the north, and Rome and Naples in the south. The Autostrada del Mare (A11) connects Florence with Prato, Lucca, Pisa and the Mediterranean coast, and a superstrada joins the city to Siena. Exits from the autostradas into Florence are well signposted and there are tourist offices on the A1 to both the north and south of the city. If you are coming from the north on the A1, exit at Firenze Nord and then simply follow the bulls-eye 'centro' signs. If approaching from Rome, exit at Firenze Sud.

The more picturesque SS67 connects the city with Pisa to the west and Forlì and Ravenna to the east. Hitchhikers from the south can follow the SS71, which runs parallel to the A1.

For car rental details, see the following Getting Around section.

GETTING AROUND
To/From the Airports

SITA operates direct buses daily between Amerigo Vespucci airport and the company's station west of Stazione di Santa Maria Novella. The service from the airport runs from 6.10 am to 5.45 pm. From the bus station it runs from 10.15 am to 10.25 pm. The trip takes 15 minutes.

The best way to get to Galileo Galilei airport at Pisa is to check in at the air terminal

(☎ 21 60 73) inside Stazione di Santa Maria Novella near platform No 5. Check in your luggage 15 minutes before the train departs. Hourly services begin at 5.55 am, with the last train leaving at 8 pm.

Alitalia and the state railways operate an airport train which connects Florence with Rome's Fiumicino airport.

Bus

ATAF buses service the city centre and Fiesole, and the station for the most useful buses is in a small piazza to the left as you exit from Stazione di Santa Maria Novella onto Via Valfonda. Bus No 7 leaves from here for Fiesole, also stopping at the duomo. Bus No 91 Notturno connects Stazione di Santa Maria Novella, the duomo and Via Ghibellina from midnight to 6 am at half-hourly intervals. ATAF tickets must be bought at tobacconists or automatic vending machines at major bus stops before you get on the bus and must be validated in the machine as you enter. There is a small ticket booth near the train station exit on Via Valfonda where you can pick up a brochure detailing bus routes. Tickets cost L1300 for 60 minutes and L1800 for 120 minutes. A block of four tickets costs L5000 and there are 24-hour tourist tickets for L5000.

The Carta Arancio is a seven-day tourist ticket allowing unlimited travel throughout the province of Florence on trains and buses (not sightseeing buses). Tickets are available at any of the bus-ticket offices around the station.

Car & Motorbike

Traffic is restricted in the city centre. There are several major car parks and numerous smaller parking areas around the fringes of the city centre. If you are planning to spend the day in Florence, your best option is to park at the Fortezza da Basso, which costs L1500 per hour. If you are arriving by car from the north you will eventually end up at the Fortezza – you just park your car on the street and pay the attendant in advance. From here it is a brisk 10-minute walk to the duomo. Closer to the centre are more expensive underground car parks at Piazza del Mercato Centrale (much too expensive for periods longer than a few hours) and Piazza della Stazione (L1500 first hour and L3000 for each consecutive hour – it's open 24 hours). For shorter visits, there are several parking areas along the Arno river, which cost L2000 for the first hour and L3000 for each consecutive hour.

Rental Avis (☎ 21 36 29) is at Borgognissanti 128r, Europcar (☎ 29 34 44) at Borgognissanti 53r, and Hertz (☎ 28 22 60), Via Finiguerra 33r. Alinari (☎ 28 05 00) rents scooters, larger mopeds and bicycles from: Via Guelfa 85r, Via de' Bardi 35 (south of the Arno river, near Ponte Vecchio) and Piazza dei Cavalleggeri (south of Santa Croce). Mopeds/scooters cost L35,000/50,000 for five hours, or L55,000/70,000 per day. You can rent a bike for L8000 for five hours or L15,000 per day. A mountain bike costs L20,000 for five hours, L30,000 per day or L50,000 for a weekend.

Taxi

You can find taxis outside Stazione di Santa Maria Novella, or call ☎ 47 98 or 43 90. The flagfall is L3500 and then it is L1300 per km.

AROUND FLORENCE

Fiesole

Perched in hills about eight km north-east of Florence, between the valleys of the Arno and Mugnone rivers, Fiesole has attracted the likes of Boccaccio, Carducci, Giovanni Dupré, Marcel Proust, Gertrude Stein and Frank Lloyd Wright, all drawn by the lush olive groves and valleys – not to mention the spectacular view of Florence. Fiesole was founded in the 7th century BC by the Etruscans and remained the most important city in northern Etruria. It is well worth visiting for the views and is a fabulous spot for a picnic and short walk.

Fiesole is easily reached from Florence. ATAF bus No 7 from the Stazione di Santa Maria Novella in Florence passes through the city centre and connects with Piazza Mino da Fiesole, the centre of this small town. If you are driving, find your way to Piazza della Libertà north of the duomo and then follow the signs to Fiesole. The APT in Florence, or in Fiesole (☎ 055-59 87 20), Piazza Mino da Fiesole 37, can assist with information about the town and can advise on accommodation, walks and other activities. Most other services are located around the tourist office.

Things to See & Do Opposite the tourist office in Piazza Mino da Fiesole is the **duomo**, started in the 11th century and altered in the 13th century, although a 19th-century renovation has eradicated many earlier features. Behind the duomo is the **Museo Bandini**, featuring an impressive collection of early Tuscan Renaissance works, including Taddeo Gaddi's *Annunciation* and Petrarch's beautifully illustrated *Triumphs*.

Opposite the entrance to the museum on Via Portigiana, the **Zona Archeologico** features a 1st-century BC Roman theatre which is used during July and August for the Estate Fiesolana, a series of concerts and performances. Also in the complex are a small Etruscan temple and Roman baths, which date from the same period as the theatre. The small archaeological museum is worth a look if you have time, as it includes exhibits from the Bronze Age to the Roman period. A cumulative ticket costing L6000 allows you admission to the archaeological zone and museum and the Museo Bandini. Check with the APT, as opening times for all sites vary considerably during the year.

If you are planning a picnic, or just want a refreshing walk, head uphill along the main street from Piazza Mino da Fiesole to Via Corsica. Take Via Pelagaccio, which eventually becomes a dirt track as it weaves around the mountain overlooking Florence and winds back into Fiesole. Don't worry if you get lost; there is no shortage of locals to redirect you. The APT advises that you camp in designated areas.

Places to Stay & Eat There is a camping ground at Fiesole, the *Campeggio Panoramico* (☎ 055-59 90 69), Via Peramonda 1,

which also has bungalows. Take bus No 70 from Piazza Mino da Fiesole to reach the ground.

The city has several hotels but most are quite expensive. The *Bencistà* (☎ 055-5 91 63), Via Benedetto da Maiano 4, about one km from Fiesole on the road to Florence, is an old villa and from its terrace there is a magnificent view of Florence. Half board is compulsory at L74,000 per person, or L90,000 with a bathroom. It might bust the budget, but for one or two days is well worth it.

The *Casa del Popolo di Fiesole*, Via Antonio Gramsci 25, up the hill from Piazza Mino da Fiesole, is a cheap pizzeria with great views from the terrace to the mountains to the north and east. Piazza Mino da Fiesole is full of expensive bars. The *Blu Bar* is one of the more popular.

Getting There & Away Fiesole is easily reached from Florence. ATAF bus No 7 from the Stazione di Santa Maria Novella in Florence passes through the city centre and connects with Piazza Mino da Fiesole, the centre of this small town. If you are driving, find your way to Piazza della Libertà north of the duomo and then follow the signs to Fiesole. The APT in Florence, or in Fiesole (☎ 055-59 87 20), Piazza Mino da Fiesole 37, can assist with information about the town and can advise on accommodation, walks and other activities. Most other services are located around the tourist office.

The Medici Villas
The Medici built several opulent villas in the Florence countryside as their wealth and prosperity grew during the 15th and 16th centuries. Most are now enclosed by the city's suburbs and its industrial sprawl and are easily reached by taking ATAF buses from the train station. Ask for details at the APT in Florence about bus numbers and opening times.

The **Villa della Petraia**, about 3.5 km north of the city, is one of the finest. Commissioned by Cardinal Ferdinand de Medici in 1576, this former castle was converted by Buontalenti and features a magnificent garden. The **Villa di Castello**, farther north of the city, was the summer home of Lorenzo the Magnificent, while the **Villa di Poggio a Caiano**, about 15 km from Florence on the road to Pistoia, was built for Lorenzo – and it shows.

The Mugello

The area north-east of Florence leading up to Firenzuola, near the border with Emilia-Romagna, is known as the Mugello and features some of the most traditional villages in Tuscany. The Sieve river winds through the area and its valley is one of Tuscany's premier wine areas.

Start with the APT in Florence, or contact the Comunità Montana del Mugello (☎ 055-849 53 46) or the Consorzio Turistico Mugello (☎ 055-845 80 45) for information. The APT should have several brochures, including *Sorgenti di Firenze Trekking*, which details 22 walks in the area. Apart from trekking, the area is popular with free climbers and offers plenty of trails for horse riders. The Sieve's rapids are also popular with canoeists.

North & West Tuscany

PRATO

Virtually enclosed in the urban and industrial sprawl of Florence, Prato is 17 km north-west of the city and is one of Italy's main centres for textile production. Founded by the Ligurians, the city fell to the Etruscans and later the Romans, and by the 11th century was an important centre for wool production. It is worth visiting on your way to the more picturesque cities of Pistoia, Lucca and Pisa to the west.

Orientation

The old city centre is small and surrounded by the city wall. The main train station, in Piazza della Stazione, is to the east of the city centre.

Information

The APT tourist office (☎ 0574-2 41 12) is at Via Cairoli 48-52 and is open Monday to Saturday from 9 am to 1 pm. The office is also open during summer from 4 to 7 pm.

The main post office and Telecom office are at Via Arcivesco Martini 8. The post code for Prato is 51100 and the telephone code 0574.

The questura (☎ 113 or 2 77 77) is at Via Baldinucci. For medical emergencies, the Ospedale Misericordia e Dolce (☎ 49 42 54) is in Piazza dell'Ospedale, south-west of Piazza del Comune.

Things to See

Invest in the special L5000 ticket, which allows admission to three museums: including the Museo Civico, the Museo dell'Opera del Duomo.

In the Piazza del Comune is the **Museo Civico**, with a small but impressive collection of paintings. Among those represented are Filippo Lippi and Vasari. The museum is open Tuesday to Saturday from 9.30 am to 12.30 pm and 3 to 6.30 pm and on Sunday morning.

Along Via Mazzoni is the Piazza del Duomo and the 12th **duomo**. The Pisan-Romanesque façade features a lunette by Andrea della Robbia and the Pergamo del Sacro Cingolo (Pulpit of the Holy Girdle), on the right-hand side of the façade as you face the main entrance. The eroded panels of the pulpit, designed by Donatello and Michelozzo, are in the **Museo dell'Opera del Duomo** next door. Five times a year (Easter, 1 May, 15 August, 8 September and 25 December) the Holy Girdle is displayed from the pulpit (the girdle is held to have been given to St Thomas by the Virgin, and brought to the city from Jerusalem after the Second Crusade). The interior of the church features magnificent frescoes, including those behind the high altar by Filippo Lippi, which depict the martyrdoms of John the Baptist and St Stephen, and Agnolo Gaddi's *Legend of the Holy Girdle* in the chapel to the left of the entrance.

One of the main reasons for a visit to Prato is **Chiesa di Santa Maria delle Carceri**, built by Guglielmo da Sangello. Its magnificent interior is considered a Renaissance masterpiece and features a frieze and medallions of the Evangelists by the workshop of Andrea della Robbia. The **Castello d'Imperatore** was built in the 13th century by the Holy Roman emperor Frederick II. The castle is open daily, except Tuesday, from 9.30 to 11.30 am and 3 to 5.30 pm and is closed on Sunday afternoons.

Places to Stay & Eat

The *Albergo Stella d'Italia* (☎ 2 79 10), overlooking the duomo at Piazza del Duomo 8, has singles/doubles from L45,000/88,000, while the *Albergo Roma* (☎ 3 17 77), Via Carradori 1, has rooms from L56,000/75,000. *Albergo Il Giglio* (☎ 3 70 49), Piazza San Marco 14, has rooms from L66,000/87,000.

There is a produce market in Piazza Lippi, open daily, except Sunday, from 8 am to 1 pm. If you want good, cheap food, head for *Brunch One Fast Food*, Via F Ferrucci 43A, which has pasta from L4000. *Zio Tom*, Via Roma 75, has pizzas from L7000, and *San Domenico*, Via Guasti 62, is a good trattoria where a meal could cost L30,000.

Getting There & Around

CAP and Lazzi buses operate regular services to Florence and Pistoia. The train station is in Piazza della Stazione, and Prato is on the Florence-Bologna and Florence-Lucca lines. By car, take the A1 from Florence and exit at Calenzano, or the A11 and exit at Prato Est or Ovest. The SS325 connects the city with Bologna. Several buses, including No 5, connect the train station with the duomo.

PISTOIA

A pleasant city, Pistoia is surprisingly not overshadowed as a tourist destination by Florence, about 30 minutes away by train. At the foot of the Apennines, the city has grown beyond its well-preserved medieval ramparts and is today one of the world centres for the manufacture of trains. In the 16th century the city's metalworkers created the pistol, named after the city.

Orientation & Information

The old city centre is quite large, but easy to negotiate. From the train station in Piazza Dante Alighieri, head north along Via XX Settembre through Piazza Treviso and turn right into Via Cavour. Via Roma, branching off the north side of Via Cavour, takes you to Piazza del Duomo and the APT tourist office (0573-2 16 22), which is open daily from 9 am to 1 pm and 3 to 6 pm. In summer, it is open on Sunday only.

The main post office is at Via Roma 5. There are Telecom offices in Via del Molinuzzo and on Corso Gramsci, near Via della Madonna. The telephone code for Pistoia is 0573.

In an emergency, call ☎ 113. For medical emergencies, call ☎ 36 36. The public hospital is in Viale Matteotti, behind the old Ospedale del Ceppo.

Things to See

The **duomo** has a Pisan Romanesque façade decorated with a lunette of the Madonna and Child by Andrea della Robbia, who also made the terracotta tiles which line the barrel vault of the main porch. Inside, in the Cappella di San Jacopo, is the incredible **Altarpiece of St James**, made of silver. It was started in the 13th century and added to over the ensuing two centuries. Brunelleschi added the final touch with the two half-figures on the left side. The **baptistry**, elegantly banded in green-and-white marble, was started in 1337 to a design by Andrea Pisano.

On the east side of the piazza is the Gothic **Palazzo del Comune**, which houses the **Museo Civico**, with works by Tuscan artists from the 13th to the 19th centuries. The museum is open Tuesday to Saturday from 9 am to 1 pm and 3 to 7 pm as well as Sunday morning. Admission is L6000 but is free on Saturday afternoon.

Adorning the portico of the **Ospedale del Ceppo** is a remarkable terracotta frieze by Giovanni della Robbia, which depicts the

Pistoia

1	Hospital
2	Telecom Office
3	Bus Station
4	Tonino
5	Hotel Firenze
6	Hospital
7	Piazza Spirito Santo
8	Il Duomo
9	Piazza del Duomo
10	Palazzo del Comune & Museo Civico
11	Duomo & Baptistry
12	APT Tourist Office
13	Telecom Office
14	Post Office
15	Leon Rosso
16	Lazzi Bus Station
17	Train Station

Theological Virtues and the *Seven Works of Mercy*.

Places to Stay & Eat

Accommodation is reasonably cheap and generally easy to find in peak months. *Hotel Firenze* (☎ 2 31 41), Via Curtatone e Montanara, has singles/doubles for L45,000/75,000, or L60,000/92,000 with a bathroom.

There is a produce market open most days in Piazza della Sala, west of the cathedral. *Tonino*, Corso Gramsci 159, is a pleasant trattoria where a meal could cost L25,000. *Leon Rosso*, Via Panciatichi 4, is very good

and slightly more expensive, with pasta from L7000. *Il Duomo*, Via Bracciolini 5, has main courses from L8000.

Getting There & Around

Buses connect the city with most towns in Tuscany. Lazzi buses serve Prato, Florence and Pisa from Viale Vittorio Veneto, east of the train station. COPIT also serves Florence, from Via del Molinuzzo, off Piazza San Francesco d'Assisi.

Trains connect the city with Florence, Bologna, Lucca and Viareggio. By car, the city is on the A11, and the SS64 and

SS66, which head north-east for Bologna and north-west for Parma respectively. Bus Nos 10 and 12 connect the train station with the cathedral, although the city is easily explored on foot.

LUCCA

Hidden behind imposing Renaissance walls, Lucca is a pleasant place to visit and certainly a good base from which to explore the Alpi Apuane and the Garfagnana.

Founded by the Etruscans, Lucca became a Roman colony in 180 BC and a free *comune* during the 12th century, setting off a period of prosperity based on the silk trade. In 1314 it fell under the control of Pisa, but, under the leadership of local adventurer Castruccio Castracani degli Anterminelli, it regained its independence and began to amass territories in western Tuscany. Although Castruccio died in 1325, Lucca remained an independent republic for almost 500 years. The city was taken by Napoleon in 1805, who created the principality of Lucca and placed his sister, Elisa, in control. In 1817 the city became a Bourbon duchy before it was incorporated into the Kingdom of Italy. Lucca remains a strong agricultural centre. The long periods of peace enjoyed by Lucca explain the almost perfect preservation of the city walls: they were in fact rarely called on to protect against attack.

Orientation

From the train station in Piazza Ricasoli, just outside the walls to the south, walk to Piazza Risorgimento and through the Porta San Pietro. Take Via Vittorio Veneto to the huge Piazza Napoleone then walk across to Piazza San Michele – the centre of the city.

Information

The tourist office (☎ 0583-41 96 89) is in Piazzale Verdi, at the western edge of the walled city in an old city gate, the Vecchia Porta San Donato. It is open daily from 9 am to 6.45 pm (during winter it is closed Sundays and holidays).

The main post office is in Via Vallisneri, just north of the duomo, and the Telecom office is at Via Cenami 15. The city's telephone code is 0583 and the post code is 55100.

For police emergencies, call ☎ 113, or head for the questura on Viale Cavour, near the train station. The main hospital (☎ 97 01) is on Via dell'Ospedale, outside the walls to the east.

Duomo

Lucca's Romanesque duomo is dedicated to St Martin and is located in Piazza San Martino. Dating from the 11th century, the church has an impressive façade in the Lucca-Pisan style, which was designed to accommodate the pre-existing bell tower. Note the columns in the upper part of the façade: each was carved by a local artisan and each is different from the other. The reliefs over the left doorway of the portico are believed to be by Nicola Pisano. The interior was rebuilt in the 14th and 15th centuries in the Gothic style. In the north aisle is a 15th-century tempietto by Matteo Civitali, who also designed the pulpit. The tempietto houses the *Volto Santo*, an image of Christ on a wooden crucifix, said to have been carved by Nicodemused, who witness the crucifixion. It is a major object of pilgrimage and each year on 13 September is carried through the streets in a procession at dusk. In the north transept is the tomb of Ilaria del Carretto, wife of the 15th-century Lord of Lucca, Paolo Guinigi, which was carved by Jacopo della Quercia and is recognised as a masterpiece of funerary sculpture. The church also contains other artworks, including a magnificent *Last Supper* by Tintoretto, over the third altar of the south aisle.

Chiesa di San Michele in Foro

Return to Piazza Napoleone and head north along Via Vittorio Veneto for Piazza San Michele. This Romanesque church has a magnificent façade, topped by a figure of the Archangel Michael slaying a dragon. Look for Andrea della Robbia's *Madonna and Child* in the south aisle.

Opposite the church, off Via di Poggio, is the **Casa di Puccini**, where the composer

TUSCANY

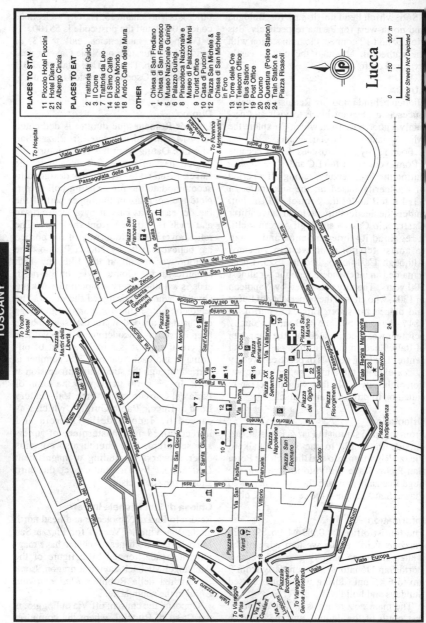

PLACES TO STAY

11 Piccolo Hotel Puccini
21 Hotel Diana
22 Albergo Cinzia

PLACES TO EAT

2 Trattoria da Guido
3 Il Cuore
7 Trattoria da Leo
14 Di Simo Caffè
16 Piccolo Mondo
18 Antico Caffè delle Mura

OTHER

1 Chiesa di San Frediano
4 Chiesa di San Francesco
5 Museo Nazionale Guinigi
6 Palazzo Guinigi
8 Pinacoteca Nazionale e
   Museo di Palazzo Mansi
9 Tourist Office
10 Casa di Puccini
12 Piazza San Michele &
   Chiesa di San Michele
   in Foro
13 Torre delle Ore
15 Telecom Office
17 Bus Station
19 Post Office
20 Duomo
23 Questura (Police Station)
24 Train Station &
   Piazza Ricasoli

Lucca

0   150   300 m

Minor Streets Not Depicted

TUSCANY

was born. It houses a small museum dedicated to his life, which is open daily, except Monday, from 10 am to 1 pm and 3 to 5 pm. Admission is L3000.

Via Fillungo

This street traverses the city's medieval section and it is interesting to wander its length, taking time to look at the centuries-old buildings which line it. The **Torre delle Ore**, the city's clock tower, is about halfway along.

East of Via Fillungo Piazza Scarpellini, at the northern end of Via Fillungo, leads into the oval-shaped **Piazza Anfiteatro**, whose buildings were constructed on the foundations of a Roman amphitheatre.

A short walk east is Piazza San Francesco and the attractive 13th-century church of the same name. Along Via della Quarquonia is the Villa Guinigi, which houses the **Museo Nazionale Guinigi** and the city's collection of paintings and sculpture. It is open daily, except Monday, from 9 am to 2 pm. Admission is L4000.

West of Via Fillungo Another example of Lucca's adaptation of the Pisan Romanesque style, the façade of **Chiesa di San Frediano** features a much-restored 13th-century mosaic. The main feature of the beautiful basilican interior is the **Fonta Lustrale**, a 12th-century font decorated with sculpted reliefs. Behind it is an *Annunciation* by Andrea della Robbia.

Of some interest is the **Pinacoteca Nazionale e Museo di Palazzo Mansi**, Via Galli Tassi. It is open daily, except Monday, from 9 am to 2 pm. Admission is a bit expensive at L8000.

If you have the time, do the four-km walk along the top of the city walls.

Courses

The Centro Koinè (☎ 49 30 40), Via Mordini 60, offers Italian courses for foreigners. A two-week summer course is L560,000, while month-long courses, available all year, cost L760,000. The school can also arrange accommodation. Write to request an information booklet, which contains an enrolment form.

Places to Stay

It is always advisable to book ahead, but if you're in a spot, try the city's hotel association, the Sindicato Lucchese Albergatori (☎ 4 41 81), Via Fillungo 121, which will help you find a room. The city's HI youth hostel, the *Ostello Il Serchio* (☎ 34 18 11), Via del Brennero 673, is outside the walls to the north. Take CLAP bus No 1 or 2 from Piazzale Verdi. B&B is L14,000. It is open from March 10 to October 10.

Albergo Cinzia (☎ 49 13 23), Via della Dogana 9, has singles/doubles for L31,000 /45,000. *Hotel Diana* (☎ 49 22 02), Via del Molinetto 11, has singles for L42,000 and doubles with a bathroom for up to L85,000. The three-star *Piccolo Hotel Puccini* (☎ 5 54 21), Via di Poggio 9, has singles/doubles with a bathroom for up to L78,000/113,000.

Places to Eat

Food shops are easily found around Piazza San Michele. The city also has a good selection of relatively cheap trattorias. For pizza -by-the-slice, there is a small takeaway at Via Fillungo 5. *Piccolo Mondo*, Piazza dei Cocomeri 5, is a good spot for a cheap meal, with pasta from L4000. *Trattoria da Leo*, Via Tegrimi 1, is quite cheap; a meal could cost L20,000. *Il Cuore*, Piazza Sant'Agostino 10, offers a reasonably priced tourist menu. At *Antico Caffè delle Mura*, Piazzale Vittorio Emanuele II, you can enjoy the view as well as the good food. A full meal will cost around L55,000. *Di Simo Caffè*, Via Fillungo 58, is a grand bar and gelateria serving local specialities including buccellato cakes.

Getting There & Away

CLAP buses (☎ 58 78 97) serve the Province of Lucca, including the Garfagnana. Lazzi (☎ 58 48 76) operates buses to Florence, La Spezia, Carrara, Pisa, Turin and Rome. Both companies operate from Piazzale Verdi.

Lucca is on the Florence-Viareggio-Pisa train line, and there are also services into the Garfagnana. By car, the A11 passes to the

TUSCANY

south of the city, connecting it with Pisa and Viareggio. The SS445 connects the city with the Garfagnana.

Getting Around

Most cars are banned from the city centre, although tourists are allowed to drive into the walled city. There are parking areas in piazzas Bernardini, San Martino and Napoleone.

The city is best seen on foot. While CLAP buses connect the train station, Piazza del Giglio and Piazzale Verdi, it is just as easy to walk.

For a taxi, call ☎ 4 49 89.

THE GARFAGNANA

This is an excellent area for trekking, horse riding and a host of other outdoor pursuits. The Garfagnana is based around the valley formed by the Serchio river and its tributaries, and its tourist infrastructure is highly organised. The tourist offices in Lucca or Pisa can provide a range of information. In the Garfagnana, the most useful organisation is the Consorzio Garfagnana Turistica, at the Comunità Montana (☎ 0583-6 51 69), Via Vittorio Emanuele 9, in Castelnuovo di Garfagnana. Many small towns have Pro Loco tourist offices which can give details about accommodation and the mountain rifugi dotted throughout the mountains.

If you are interested in walking, pick up a copy of *Garfagnana Trekking*, which details a 10-day walk. Another booklet, *Garfagnana a Cavallo*, lists details of guided horse-riding treks which can cost L18,000 an hour or L90,000 a day. Details of these and other aspects of the mountains, including agriturismo, are available from the Azienda Agrituristica La Garfagnana (☎ 0583-6 87 05), Le Prade 25, in Castiglione di Garfagnana.

The Alpi Apuane

This mountain range is bordered on one side by the stretch of coastline known as the Versilia Riviera, and on the other by the vast valley of the Garfagnana. Altitudes are relatively low, in comparison to the Alps farther

north, but the Alpi Apuane are certainly not lacking in great walking possibilities: some trails afford spectacular views to the coastline and the Ligurian Sea. The landscape in some areas is utterly destroyed by marble mining, an industry which has exploited these mountains since Roman times. No environmental laws have been in place to prevent mining companies from literally removing entire peaks in some places. But, in the end, the extent of interference in the natural landscape has created a new environment which has a certain aesthetic appeal. There is a good network of marked trails, as well as several rifugi in the Alpi Apuane. A good map is the 1:25,000 *Carta dei Sentieri e Rifugi*, published by Multigraphic, of Florence.

Information can be obtained from the Comunità Montana in Castiglione di Garfagnana.

MASSA & CARRARA

These two towns in the northern reaches of Tuscany don't really warrant a visit unless you are interested in seeing Italy's famous marble quarries. Massa is the administrative centre of the province and is rather unattractive, although the beachfront extension, Marina di Massa, is very popular with holidaying Italians. You might wonder why, if you happen to stumble onto the overpopulated shores.

Carrara, however, is quite picturesque. At the foothills of the Alpi Apuane, the town appears to be dominated by snow-capped mountains – an illusion created by limestone formations and the vast quarries which virtually cover the hills. The texture and purity of Carrara's white marble is unrivalled and was chosen by Michelangelo for many of his masterpieces. He often travelled to the quarries to personally select blocks.

The APT has offices at Marina di Massa (☎ 0585-24 00 46), Viale Vespucci 24, at Carrara (☎ 0585-84 33 70), Viale XX Settembre, and at Marina di Carrara (☎ 0585-63 22 18), Piazza Menconi 5B. The hotel association in Massa, the Associazione Commercianti (☎ 0585-4 17 96), Viale Chiesa, will help you find a room. There is a youth hostel on the coast at Marina di Massa, the *Ostello della Gioventù* (☎ 0585-78 00 34), Via delle Pinete, which charges L10,000 for a bed.

Both towns are accessible from the A12 and the SS1 Via Aurelia, and signs direct you to quarries you can visit and other attractions, such as museums.

PISA

Once a maritime power to rival Genoa and Venice, Pisa now draws its fame from an architectural project gone terribly wrong: its leaning tower. It is just about impossible to think of Pisa without the tilting bell tower and its graceful arcaded galleries leaping to mind, but the city does offer lots more. For instance, the bell tower is only one element of the fabulous trio of Romanesque buildings in the city's beautiful **Campo dei Miracoli**: along with Piazza San Marco in Venice, one of Italy's most memorable squares.

For centuries the site of one of Italy's major universities, Pisa is still an important university town and is full of young students. It is a very pleasant place to visit and really deserves more than the usual one-day stopover planned by most tourists.

History

Possibly a settlement of Greek origin, Pisa became an important naval base during Roman times and remained a significant port for many centuries. The city's greatest period, its so-called Golden Days, began late in the 9th century when it became an independent maritime republic and a rival of Genoa and Venice. This dominance peaked during the 12th and 13th centuries when Pisa controlled Corsica, Sardinia and most of the Italian coast as far south as Civitavecchia. Most of the city's finest buildings date from this period, as well as the distinctive Pisan-Romanesque architectural style.

Pisa supported the Ghibellines during the tussles between the Holy Roman emperor and the pope when much of Tuscany supported the Guelphs. As such, the city came into conflict with Siena, Lucca, Florence and Genoa, whose fleet inflicted a devastating defeat on Pisa during the naval battle of Meloria in 1284. The city fell to Florence in 1406, and the Medici encouraged great artistic, literary and scientific endeavour and re-established Pisa's university. The city's most famous son, Galileo Galilei, was later a teacher at the university. See the Aside in this section.

Orientation

By train you'll arrive at Stazione Pisa Centrale, at the southern edge of the old city centre. The main intercity bus station is in Piazza Vittorio Emanuele II, a short walk north along Viale Gramsci. The Campo dei Miracoli (also referred to as Piazza del Duomo) and the old centre is about 20 minutes walk straight ahead along Corso Italia and across the Ponte di Mezzo over the Arno river. It is quicker and easier to catch a city bus from outside the station. See the Getting Around section under Pisa.

Information

Tourist Offices There are offices in the Campo dei Miracoli (☎ 56 04 64), just behind the leaning tower, and outside the train station (☎ 4 22 91). Both offices are open Monday to Saturday from 8 am to 8 pm in summer and Monday to Saturday from 9.30 am to midday and 3 to 5.30 pm in the off season.

Money Avoid the exchange booths near the duomo. Change money at banks along Corso Italia, or at the train station.

Post & Telecommunications The main post office is in Piazza Vittorio Emanuele II. Poste restante mail can be addressed to 56100 Pisa.

There are telephones at the train station and a Telecom office at Via Carducci 15 which stays open late. The city's telephone code is 050.

Emergency For police emergency, call ☎ 113. The questura (☎ 58 35 11) is at Via Mario Lalli. For medical emergencies, contact the Ospedale Riuniti di Santa Chiara (☎ 59 21 11) at Via Roma 67.

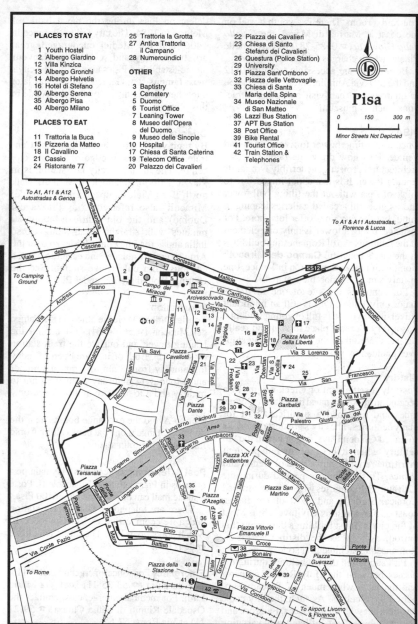

PLACES TO STAY

1 Youth Hostel
2 Albergo Giardino
12 Villa Kinzica
13 Albergo Gronchi
14 Albergo Helvetia
16 Hotel di Stefano
30 Albergo Serena
35 Albergo Pisa
40 Albergo Milano

PLACES TO EAT

11 Trattoria la Buca
15 Pizzeria da Matteo
18 Il Cavallino
21 Cassio
24 Ristorante 77
25 Trattoria la Grotta
27 Antica Trattoria
   il Campano
28 Numeroundici

OTHER

3 Baptistry
4 Cemetery
5 Duomo
6 Tourist Office
7 Leaning Tower
8 Museo dell'Opera
   del Duomo
9 Museo delle Sinopie
10 Hospital
17 Chiesa di Santa Caterina
19 Telecom Office
20 Palazzo dei Cavalieri
22 Piazza dei Cavalieri
23 Chiesa di Santo
   Stefano dei Cavalieri
26 Questura (Police Station)
29 University
31 Piazza Sant'Ombono
32 Piazza delle Vettovaglie
33 Chiesa di Santa
   Maria della Spina
34 Museo Nazionale
   di San Matteo
36 Lazzi Bus Station
37 APT Bus Station
38 Post Office
39 Bike Rental
41 Tourist Office
42 Train Station &
   Telephones

Pisa

0   150   300 m

Minor Streets Not Depicted

Things to See

The Pisans can justly claim that the Campo dei Miracoli is one of the most beautiful squares in the world. Set in its sprawling lawns is the famous group of Romanesque buildings – the duomo, the baptistry and the leaning tower. On any day the piazza is teeming with people – students studying or playing, tourists wandering and Pisan workers eating their lunch.

There is a staggered pricing system for tickets to enter one or more of the monuments in and around the square. It costs L2000 for the duomo only; L10,000 for the duomo plus one monument; L12,000 for the duomo, baptistry and one more monument; L15,000 for the baptistry, cemetery and two museums; and L17,000 for three monuments and two museums.

Duomo Pisa's cathedral is one of the most impressive and majestic Romanesque churches and was, in fact, a model for Romanesque churches throughout Tuscany and even in Sardinia. Begun in 1064, it is covered inside and out with the alternating bands of dark green and cream marble which were characteristic of the Pisan Romanesque style. Its beautiful façade has four tiers of columns and its huge interior is lined with 68 columns, most of which are antique. The bronze doors of the transept, facing the leaning tower, are by Bonanno Pisano. The 16th-century bronze doors of the main entrance are by the school of Giambologna and were made to replace the original doors, which were destroyed in a fire in 1596. The interior was much redecorated after this devastating fire. Important works which survived include Giovanni Pisano's early 14th-century pulpit and an apse mosaic of *Christ in Majesty* completed by Cimabue in 1302. The duomo is open daily from 7.45 am to 1 pm and 3 pm to sunset.

Leaning Tower The duomo's bell tower was in trouble from the start. Its architect, Bonanno Pisano, managed to complete only three tiers before the tower started to lean. The problem is generally believed to have

been caused by shifting soil, and the tower has continued to lean by an average of one mm a year ever since. Galileo climbed its 294 steps to experiment with gravity. Today it is no longer possible to follow in his footsteps. The tower has been closed for some years while the Italians have been trying to work out how to stop its inexorable lean towards the ground – it now leans five metres off the perpendicular. Finally, in 1994, they found a solution – 600 tons of lead ingots which anchor the north foundation. The lean

TUSCANY

The Leaning Tower of Pisa, now five metres off the perpendicular

stopped and the tower even began to straighten. However, in September 1995 the tower moved 2.5 mm in one night, representing 10% of the total amount that had been corrected! While no-one has any intention of turning the leaning tower into a straight tower, many still believe it will fall down eventually. The controversial Italian art historian, Vittorio Sgarbi, has noted that it would be 'better to see it fall and remember it leaning than see it straightened by mistake'.

Baptistry This unusual round building was started in 1153 by Diotisalvi, whose work was remodelled and continued by Nicola and Giovanni Pisano more than a century later, and finally completed in the 14th century – which explains the mix of architectural styles. The lower level of arcades is in the Pisan-Romanesque style and the pinnacled upper section and dome are Gothic. Inside, the beautiful pulpit was carved by Nicola Pisano and signed in 1260, and the white marble font was carved by Guido da Como in 1246. The baptistry is open from 9 am to sunset.

Cemetery Located behind the white wall to the north of the duomo, this is said to be one of the most beautiful cemeteries in the world. Its soil is said to have been brought by the shipload from Calvary during the Crusades. Many precious frescoes in the cloisters were badly damaged or destroyed during WW II Allied bombing raids.

Among those saved were the *Triumph of Death* and *Last Judgment*, attributed to an anonymous 14th-century painter known as 'The Master of the Triumph of Death'. The cemetery is open daily from 9 am to sunset.

Around Campo dei Miracoli The **Museo delle Sinopie** houses the sinopias, reddish-brown sketches drawn onto walls as the base for frescoes, which were discovered in the cemetery after the WW II bombing raids. They have been restored and provide a fascinating insight into the process of creating a fresco, although it is really only worth

visiting if you have a particular interest in the subject. The museum is open daily from 9 am to 1 pm and 3 pm to sunset.

The **Museo dell'Opera del Duomo** in Piazza Arcivescovado, near the Leaning Tower, features many artworks from the tower, duomo and baptistry, including a magnificent ivory carving, the *Madonna & Crucifix*, by Giovanni Pisano. Another highlight is the bust known as the *Madonna del Colloquio*, by the same artist, taken from the exterior of the baptistry. It is open daily from 9 am to 1 pm and 3 pm to sunset.

The City Head south along Via Santa Maria from the Campo dei Miracoli and turn left at Piazza Cavallotti for the splendid **Piazza dei Cavalieri**, which was remodelled by Vasari in the 16th century. The **Palazzo dell'Orologio**, on the north side of the piazza, occupies the site of a tower where, in 1288, Count Ugolino della Gherardesca, his sons and grandsons, were starved to death on suspicion of having helped the Genoese enemy at the battle of Meloria. The incident was recorded in Dante's *Inferno*. The **Palazzo dei Cavalieri** on the north-east side of the piazza was redesigned by Vasari and features graffiti decoration. The piazza and palace are named for the Knights of St Stephen, a religious and military order founded by Cosimo de Medici. Their church, **Santo Stefano dei Cavalieri**, was also designed by Vasari. **Chiesa di Santa Caterina**, to the east along Via San Lorenzo on Piazza Martiri della Libertà, is a fine example of Pisan Gothic architecture and contains works by Nino Pisano.

Wander south to the area around **Borgo Stretto**, the city's most authentic medieval section. East along the waterfront boulevard, the Lungarno Mediceo, is the **Museo Nazionale di San Matteo**, one of Tuscany's finest galleries. It features works by Giovanni and Nicola Pisano, Masaccio and Donatello. The gallery is open Tuesday to Saturday from 9 am to 7 pm and Sunday to 1 pm. Admission is L8000.

Cross the **Ponte di Mezzo** and head west to reach the **Chiesa di Santa Maria della**

Spina, built in the early 14th century to house a thorn from Christ's crown.

Places to Stay

Pisa has a reasonable number of budget hotels for a small town, but many double as residences for students during the school year, so it can be difficult to find a cheap room. A camping ground, the *Camping Torre Pendente* (☎ 56 06 65), Via delle Cascine 86, is west of the duomo. There is a youth hostel, the non-HI *Ostello per la Gioventù* (☎ 89 06 22), north-west of the duomo on Via Pietrasantina 15. A bed costs L12,000. Take bus No 3 from the train station.

The *Albergo Serena* (☎ 58 08 09), Via D Cavalca 45, just off Piazza Dante, has singles/doubles for up to L30,000/44,000. The *Albergo Helvetia* (☎ 55 30 84), Via Don Gaetano Boschi 31, near the duomo, has rooms for up to L36,000/48,000. *Hotel di Stefano* (☎ 55 35 59), Via Sant'Apollonia 35, near Via Carducci, has rooms for the same price.

The *Albergo Gronchi* (☎ 56 18 23), Piazza Arcivescovado 1, is a great bargain offering singles/doubles for L30,000/48,000. The *Albergo Giardino* (☎ 56 21 01), Piazza Manin 1, just west of Campo dei Miracoli, has rooms for L40,000/55,000.

More up-market is the *Villa Kinzica* (☎ 56 04 19), Piazza Arcivescovado 2, with views of the Leaning Tower and rooms with a bathroom for L100,000/135,000.

Near the train station is the *Albergo Milano* (☎ 2 31 62), Via Mascagni 14, with comfortable rooms and a friendly owner. Singles/doubles cost L40,000/50,000. The two-star *Albergo Pisa* (☎ 4 45 51), Via Manzoni 22, near Via Crispi, has rooms from L40,000/55,000.

Places to Eat

Being a university town, Pisa has a good range of cheap eating places. Head for the area around Borgo Stretto and the university. There is an open air food market in Piazza delle Vettovaglie, off Borgo Stretto.

For a lunch-time snack, *Numeroundici*, Via Domenica Cavalca 11, has a range of reasonably priced snacks, as well as full meals. *Trattoria La Mescita*, Piazza delle Vettovaglie is appealing, reasonably cheap and features a menu loaded with Pisan dishes. The *Antica Trattoria il Campano*, in an old tower at Vicolo Santa Margherita near Piazza Sant'Ombono, is slightly more expensive and a meal could cost about L30,000. *Trattoria la Grotta*, Via San Francesco 103, is another good choice and more expensive at around L30,000/40,000 a full meal.

Heading north, the *Ristorante 77*, Via Santa Cecilia 34, is reasonably expensive but the food is considered excellent. *Trattoria la Buca* in Campo dei Miracoli has pizzas from L6000. *Cassio*, Piazza Cavallotti, is a pizzeria/bar with pizzas from L5000 and pasta from L6000. *Pizzeria da Matteo*, Via Santa Maria 20, is another good choice.

One of the city's finest bars is the *Caffè Federico Salza*, Borgo Stretto 46, with cakes, gelati and chocolates. Prices inside are one-third of those charged if you eat at the tables outside. Another is *Bar Duomo*, facing the Leaning Tower and very expensive. For a great gelati, head for *La Bottega del Gelato* in Piazza Garibaldi, near the river.

Entertainment

The tourist office has a list of nightclubs and events in the city. Opera and ballet are staged at the Teatro Verdi (☎ 94 11 11), Via Palestro 40, from September to November. Cultural and historic events include the Gioco del Ponte, a festival of traditional costume held on the last Sunday in June. On 17 June, the Arno river comes to life with the Regata Storica di San Ranieri, a rowing competition commemorating the city's patron saint.

Getting There & Away

Air The city's Aeroporto Galileo Galilei (☎ 50 07 07), about two km south of the city centre, is Tuscany's main international airport and handles flights to major cities in Europe.

Alitalia (☎ 2 00 62), British Airways (☎ 50 18 38) and other major airlines are all based at the airport.

Bus Lazzi (☎ 4 62 88), Piazza Vittorio Emanuele II, operates services to Lucca, Florence, Prato,

Pistoia, Massa and Carrara. APT (☎ 2 33 84), Piazza Sant'Antonio, near the train station, serves Volterra, Livorno and Lucca.

Train The train station is in Piazza della Stazione (☎ 4 13 85) at the southern edge of town. The city is connected to Florence and is also on the Rome-La Spezia line, with frequent services running in all directions.

Car & Motorbike The city is close to the A12, which connects Livorno to Parma. It is currently being extended to Rome, but that will take several years to complete. The city is also close to the A11, connecting it with Florence. The north-south SS1, the Via Aurelia, connects the city with La Spezia and Rome, while the SS67 connects it with Florence.

Large car parks are all around Pisa, with one just north of the duomo perfect for day-trippers.

Getting Around
To get to the airport, take a train from the main station for the four-minute journey to the Stazione FS Pisa Aeroporto, or take city bus No 7, which passes through the city centre on its way to the airport. For a taxi to the airport, call ☎ 2 85 42.

To get from the train station to the duomo, take city bus No 1 or walk the 1.5 km.

If you want to hire a bike or scooter while in Pisa, try the rental outlet at Via della Spina 25 (☎ 2 02 00).

LIVORNO
Tuscany's second-largest city, Livorno (also known as Leghorn in English) is not worth a visit unless you are catching a ferry to Sardinia, Corsica, Sicily or Spain. The city is a modern industrial centre and was heavily bombed during WW II.

Orientation & Information
From the train station in Piazza Dante at the eastern edge of the city centre, walk west along Viale Carducci and then Via Grande into the central Piazza Grande. The main

APT office (☎ 0586-89 81 11) is at Piazza Cavour 6 to the south. From Piazza Grande, continue west towards the waterfront, through Piazza Micheli, Piazza Arsenale and a smaller APT (☎ 0586-89 53 20). A third office is near the main ferry terminal, known as Calata Carrara, near Stazione Marittima. The main office is open Monday to Friday from 9 am to 2 pm and Saturday to 1 pm. The smaller offices are open mornings and afternoons during summer only.

The main post office is at Via Cairoli 46 and there are Telecom offices at Largo Duomo and Scali A Saffi 21. The city's post code is 57100 and the telephone code is 0586.

For police emergency, call ☎ 113, or go to the questura (☎ 89 86 11) in the Palazzo del Governo, Piazza Unità d'Italia. The Ospedale Civile (☎ 40 33 51) is on Viale Alfieri near the main train station.

Things to See
The city does have a few worthy sights. The **Fortezza Nuova**, in the area known as Piccola Venezia because of its small canals, was built for the Medici in the late 16th century. Close to the waterfront is the city's other fort, the **Fortezza Vecchia**, built 60 years earlier on the site of an 11th-century building.

The city has two galleries of note: the **Museo Civico Giovanni Fattori**, Viale della Libertà 30, which features works by a 19th-century Livorno-based movement led by the artist Giovanni Fattori; and the **Museo Progressivo d'Arte Contemporanea**, also known as the Centro di Documentazione Visiva, Via Redi 22, which has a smattering of well-known 20th-century works. Both galleries are open Tuesday to Sunday from 9 am to 1 pm. Admission is L6000 at each. The city's unspectacular cathedral is just off Piazza Grande.

Places to Stay & Eat
Finding accommodation shouldn't be a problem. The *Albergo Stazione* (☎ 40 23 07), Viale Carducci 301, is near the main train station and has singles/doubles from L32,000/ 43,000. *Albergo L'Amico Fritz*

PLACES TO STAY

11 Pensione Dante

PLACES TO EAT

7 Pizzeria Tavola Calda
20 Cantina Senese
21 L'Angiolo d'Oro

OTHER

1 Stazione Marittima
  (Train Station)
2 Stazione Marittima
  (Ferry Terminal)
3 Tourist Office
  (Summer Only)
4 Ferries to
  Sardinia & Corsica
5 Fortezza Nuova
6 Fortezza Vecchia
8 Questura (Police Station)
9 Molo Mediceo
  (Ferry Terminal)
10 Tourist Office
  (Summer Only)
12 Cathedral
13 ATL Bus Station
14 Market
15 Telecom Office
16 Post Office
17 Telecom Office
18 Tourist Office
19 Lazzi Bus Station

TUSCANY

Livorno

0   200   400 m

Minor Streets Not Depicted

(☎ 40 11 49) is nearby at Viale Carducci 180 and has rooms for the same price, as does the *Pensione Dante* (☎ 89 34 61), near the waterfront at Scali d'Azeglio 28.

For produce, the market is on Via Buontalenti, and the area around Piazza XX Settembre is great for bars and cafés. *Pizzeria Tavola Calda*, Via dell'Angiolo 12, has pizzas from L4000 and is a good place for a cheap lunch. *L'Angiolo d'Oro*, Piazza Mazzini 15, is an inexpensive trattoria with pasta from L6000. The *Cantina Senese*, Borgo dei Cappuccini, is also cheap and serves some local dishes.

Getting There & Away

Bus ATL buses (☎ 89 61 11) depart from Piazza Grande for Cecina, Piombino and Pisa, and Lazzi buses (☎ 89 95 62) depart from Piazza Manin for Florence, Pisa, Lucca and Viareggio.

Train The main train station in Piazza Dante is on the Rome-La Spezia line and the city is also connected to Florence and Pisa. There is a second station, called Stazione Marittima, near the main port area, but trains are less frequent. It is usually easier to catch a train to the main train station and then a bus to the ports.

Car The A12 passes through the city and the SS1 connects Livorno with Rome. There are several car parks near the waterfront.

Boat Livorno is one of the main ferry ports on the west coast. The city has two main ferry terminals: the major terminal, the Stazione Marittima, is in an area called Calata Carrara and is just north of Fortezza Vecchia; the smaller ferry terminal is near Piazza Arsenale and is called the Molo Mediceo. Both can be reached by bus from the main train station. There is a third ferry terminal, known as the Porto Nuovo, at Calata Tripoli, several km north of the city along Via Sant'Orlando. It is not easily reached by public transport. Ask at the tourist office for directions.

Ferry companies operating from Livorno are:

Alimar (☎ 88 07 33), which serves Barcelona and Sicily from the Stazione Marittima.
Compagnia Sarda Navigazione Marittima (☎ 40 99 25), at Varco Galvani, Calata Tripoli, which operates ferries to Olbia.
Corsica Ferries (☎ 88 13 80), at the Stazione Marittima on Calata Carrara, which operates regular services to Bastia.
Navarma (☎ 89 33 27), Via Veneto 24, which serves Bastia, Bonifacio and Santa Teresa di Gallura from the Stazione Marittima.
Sardinia Ferries (☎ 88 13 80), in the Stazione Marittima building operates services to Olbia.
Sicil Ferry (☎ 40 98 04), at the Porto Nuovo, Calata Tripoli, which serves Palermo.

Getting Around
To get from the train station to Piazza Arsenale and the Porto Mediceo, take ATL bus No 1. To reach the Stazione Marittima, take bus No 18. To reach the city centre, take bus No 1, 2 or 8.

ELBA
Made famous by Napoleon, who spent a year in exile on the island from May 1814, Elba now attracts more than one million tourists a year who come to swim in its glorious blue waters or lie on its beaches. One of the great attractions is the range of beaches: sandy pebbly or rocky, crowded and serviced, or quiet and secluded. During August, however the island is so crowded with tourists that even the most isolated beaches can get pretty crowded. Elba is also growing in popularity among walkers, and its mountainous terrain can provide some tough treks – although there are better places to walk in Tuscany.

Just 28 km long and 19 km across at its widest point, Elba is well-geared for tourists, with plenty of hotels and camping grounds. The tourist hordes have only arrived in recent years, so the island is not (as yet) overdeveloped. Prior to the advent of tourism, its main industry was iron ore mining. The main towns are Portoferraio on the north side and Marina di Campo on the south side.

Orientation & Information
Most ferries arrive at Portoferraio, Elba's capital and its main transport hub. Ferries from Piombino arrive less frequently at Rio Marina, Marina di Campo and Porto Azzurro. The main APT office for the island (☎ 0565-91 46 71) is at Portoferraio, at Calata Italia 26, and can assist with accommodation information. If you plan to visit during the summer months, book well in advance. The local hotel association, the Associazione Albergatori Isola d'Elba (☎ 0565-91 47 54), Calata Italia 20, will find you a room.

If you're planning a walk, pick up a copy of *Trekking all'Elba*, a publication that lists walking trails and details each itinerary. For more information about walking, contact Il Genio del Bosco – Centro Trekking Isola d'Elba (☎ 0565-93 03 35) at Portoferraio. Also, the Comunità Montana at Viale Manzoni 4 in the town has contour maps of the island, with paths clearly marked.

The post code for the island is 57037, and the telephone code is 0565.

Getting There & Away
Unless you have your own boat, the only way to get to Elba is by ferry from Piombino. If you arrive in town by train, there's a connecting train to the port. There

op: View of Bologna, Emilia Romagna
m: Palazzo Vecchio with Michelangelo's *David*, Florence, Tuscany

ROB FLYNN

JOHN GILLMAN

RICHARD STEWART

Top: View from San Gimignano, Tuscany
Middle: Sunflowers near Scorgiano, Tuscany
Bottom: Florence as seen from Forte di Belvedere, Tuscany

are several companies: Toremar, Navarma and Elba Ferries and all have offices at the port. Unless it is the middle of August, you shouldn't have any trouble buying a ticket at the port. Prices are competitive, around L900 per person and L30,000 for a small car. All lines offer a special deal on certain runs (indicated in timetables). The best deal is L39,000 for two people and a car.

Getting Around
The best way to get around Elba is to rent a mountain bike, scooter or motorcycle from Rent Ghiaie, which has offices in all main towns. The Portoferraio office is Via Elba 32; in Porto Azzurro go to Viale Italia 48 and in Marciana Marina go to Via G Dussol 45. In high season mountain bikes start at L20,000 a day and L98,000 for one week; mopeds are L35,000 a day and L202,000 per week; and Vespa scooters cost L55,000 per day and 327,000 per week.

The island's bus company, ATL, runs regular services between the main towns. From Portoferraio, for instance, you can reach all of the main towns, including Marciana Marina, Marina di Campo, Capoliveri, Porto Azzurro, as well as smaller resorts and beaches such as Sant'Andrea, Cavo and Fetovaia. Ask at the tourist office for an updated timetable.

Portoferraio
Portoferraio is divided in two; the new section includes the port, but the old part, enclosed by a medieval wall, is much more interesting. It contains the **Palazzina dei Mulini**, which was one of the residences where Napoleon lived in exile. It features a splendid terraced garden and his library and is open Tuesday to Saturday from 9 am to 5 pm. Admission is L5000.

The ticket also allows you admission to the **Villa Napoleonica di San Martino**, Napoleon's summer residence, set in hills about five km south-west of the town. Take bus No 1 to reach the villa, which houses a modest collection of Napoleonic paraphernalia and also hosts an annual exhibition based on a Napoleonic theme. The villa is open the same hours as the museum.

Places to Stay & Eat If you plan on staying in Portoferraio, the closest camping grounds are about four km west of the town in Acquaviva. *Campeggio La Sorgente* (☎ 91 71 39) and *Acquaviva* (☎ 91 55 92) are easily found. The *Villa Ombrosa* (☎ 91 43 63), Via De Gasperi 3, has singles/doubles for L55,000/78,000, or L78,000/140,000 with a bathroom. The *Ape Elbana* (☎ 91 42 45), Salita de' Medici 2, in the old town, has singles/doubles with a bathroom for up to L70,000/90,000.

Restaurants are expensive, but bars selling panini and other snacks are popular. The *Ristorante Villa Ombrosa* on Viale de' Gasperi serves Tuscan dishes and a full meal could cost L30,000. Try the *Osteria Libertaria* at the port, on Calata Matteotti near the Torre della Lingua. It offers reasonably priced meals and you can sit outside with a view of the port, or in an internal courtyard garden.

Marciana Marina
About 15 km west of Portoferraio, Marciana Marina is slightly less popular with tourists and is fronted by some fabulous pebble beaches. This town is also a perfect base for walking in the island's western region, where many of the best walking tracks are to be found. The inland villages of Marciana and Poggio are easily visited (jump on the only bus). From Marciana you can take the cable car to the summit of Monte Capanne, from where you can see across Elba and as far as Corsica to the west.

In Marciana Marina, the *Albergo Villa Maria* (☎ 9 90 20), Piazza Sanzio, has rooms from L60,000/85,000. Farther west along the coast is the small resort town of **Sant'Andrea**, which remains unspoiled by the tourist hordes. It has a lovely sandy beach from where you can walk along the coast over rock formations, taking a swim if you get hot. Try the *Bellavista* (☎ 90 80 15), which has singles /doubles with a bathroom from L60,000/80,000.

Marina di Campo
Elba's second-largest town, Marina di Campo, is on Campo Bay on the island's southern

side. The beaches are among Elba's best and most crowded. Many camping grounds are located around the town and along the coastline, which means you shouldn't have too much trouble finding a site, except in the middle of summer. The *Albergo Thomas* (☎ 97 77 32), Viale degli Etruschi, is one of the cheapest hotels here and has doubles from 80,000. The *Elba* (☎ 97 62 24), Via Mascagni, has singles/doubles for L58,000/85,000. There are many cheap eateries near the beach, including a couple of decent self-service restaurants.

Porto Azzurro & Capoliveri

Dominated by its fort, built in 1603 by Philip III of Spain and now a prison, Porto Azzurro is a pleasant resort town, close to some excellent beaches. *Albergo Villa Italia* (☎ 9 51 19), Viale Italia, has doubles from L73,000. For a good meal, try the *Ristorante Delfino Verde*, on the waterfront. A meal will cost around L30,000. From Porto Azzurro, take a short trip south to Capoliveri, certainly in the island's most picturesque spot. Nearby are some great beaches: Barabarca, accessible only by a steep track which winds down a cliff, and Zuccale, more easily accessible and perfect for families.

Central & Southern Tuscany

SIENA

Italy's best-preserved medieval town, Siena is built on three hills and is still surrounded by its historic ramparts. Its medieval centre is bristling with majestic Gothic buildings, such as the Palazzo Pubblico in the campo, Siena's main square, and there is a wealth of art works contained in its numerous churches and small museums. Like Florence, Siena offers an incredible concentration of things to see, which simply can't be appreciated in a day trip. Try to plan at least an overnight stay, or better still allow yourself a few days

to appreciate the Gothic architecture and the art of the Sienese school.

Siena also makes a good base from which to explore central Tuscany, in particular the medieval towns of San Gimigano and Volterra. It is worth noting that it can be difficult year-round to find budget accommodation in Siena unless you book ahead. In August and during the city's famous twice-yearly festival, the Palio, it is impossible to find any accommodation unless you book well in advance.

History

According to legend, Siena was founded by the son of Remus and the symbol of the wolf feeding the twins Romulus and Remus is as ubiquitous in Siena as in Rome. In reality the city was probably of Etruscan origin, although it wasn't until the 1st century BC, when the Romans established a military colony called Sena Julia, that it began to grow into a proper town.

In the 12th century the wealth, size and power of the city grew with its involvement in commerce, banking and trade in European markets. Consequently, its rivalry with neighbouring Florence also grew and led to numerous wars during the first half of the 13th century between Guelph (supporters of the pope) Florence and Ghibelline (supporters of the emperor) Siena. The conflict culminated in the victory of Siena over Florence at the Battle of Montaperti in 1260. But it was a short-lived victory – only 10 years later the Tuscan Ghibellines were defeated by Charles of Anjou and for almost a century Siena was allied to Florence, the chief town of the Tuscan Guelph League.

During this period Siena reached its peak under the rule of the Council of Nine, a group dominated by the middle class. Many of the fine buildings in the Sienese Gothic style, which give the city its striking appearance, were constructed under the direction of the Council of Nine, including the cathedral, the Palazzo Pubblico and the campo. The Sienese school of painting had its beginnings at this time with Guido da Siena and reached its peak in the early 14th century with the works of artists including Duccio di Buoninsegna, Simone Martini and Pietro and Ambrogio Lorenzetti.

The outbreak of the plague in 1348 left the cathedral unfinished, killed 65,000 of the city's 100,000 people and led to a period of decline. At the end of the 14th century, Siena came under the control of Milan's Visconti family and in the 15th century was ruled by the autocratic patrician Pandolfo Petrucci, a period marked by a revival of the city's waning fortunes. Holy Roman Emperor Charles V conquered Siena in 1555 after a two-year siege that left thousands dead. Consequently, the city was handed over to Cosimo de Medici, who barred the inhabitants from operating banks and thus curtailed Siena's power for good.

Siena was home to two of Italy's most famous saints, Catherine and Bernardino.

Today the city relies heavily on tourism and on the success of its Monte dei Paschi di Siena bank, founded in 1472 and now one of the city's largest employers.

Orientation

Historic Siena, still largely surrounded by its medieval walls, is small and easily tackled by tourists on foot, even if the way in which streets swirl around the campo in semi-circles will confuse you for much of your stay. The fabulous campo is the city's heart and the main streets are the Banchi di Sopra, Via di Città and Banchi di Sotto. By bus you will arrive at Piazza San Domenico, which affords a panoramic view of the city. Walk east along Via della Sapienza and turn right into Banchi di Sopra to reach the campo.

From the train station you will need to catch a bus to Piazza Matteotti. Walk southeast out of the piazza on Via Pianigiani to reach Banchi di Sopra, turn right and follow it to the campo. Drivers should note that streets within the walls are blocked to normal traffic – even if you are staying at a hotel in the centre of town you will be required to leave the car in a car park after dropping off your bags. There are eight porta through which you can enter the city; probably the best one to use is Porta San Marco, southwest of the city centre, as it has a well-signposted route to the centre. See Getting Around in this section for details.

Information

Tourist Office The APT office (☎ 0577-28 05 51; fax 27 06 76) is at Il Campo 56 and is open Monday to Saturday from 8.30 am to 7.30 pm in summer and from 9 am to 1 pm and 3.30 to 7 pm for the rest of the year. There is another office at Via di Città 43 (☎ 0577-4 22 09). The APT publishes its information in English, French, German and Italian. Ask for a guide to the hotels, an information booklet and a map of the city.

Money There are several banks near the campo in Piazza Tolomei, Banchi di Sopra, Banchi di Sotto and Via di Città. The main branch of the Monte dei Paschi di Siena bank is in Piazza Salimbeni. The bank has an automatic exchange service at Via Banchi di Sopra 92.

Post & Telecommunications The main post office is at Piazza Matteotti 1. Poste restante mail can be addressed to 53100 Siena. The Telecom office is at Via dei Termini 40. Siena's telephone code is 0577.

Emergency For police emergency, call ☎ 113. The questura (open 24 hours a day) is at Via del Castoro, between the duomo and Via di Città. The Foreigners' Office is in Piazza Jacopo della Quercia and is open Monday to Saturday from 10 am to midday. In a medical emergency call ☎ 2 99 11, or for an ambulance call ☎ 28 01 10. The public hospital (☎ 29 08 07) is in Viale Bracci, just north of Siena at Le Scotte.

Other Services At the Onda Blu Laundry, Casato di Sotto 17, you can wash and dry six kilos for L12,000.

Il Campo

This magnificent, shell-shaped, slanting square has been the city's civic centre since it was laid out by the Council of Nine in the

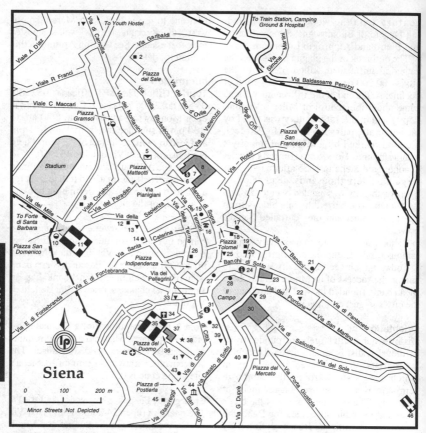

TUSCANY

Siena

0   100   200 m

Minor Streets Not Depicted

mid-14th century. Tourists gather in the square to take a break from sightseeing – backpackers lounge on the pavement in the piazza's centre, while the more well-heeled drink expensive coffees or beers at the outdoor cafés around the periphery.

The square's paving is divided into nine sectors, representing the members of the Council of Nine. At the upper part of the square is the 15th-century **Fonte Gaia** (Gay Fountain). The panels of the fountain are reproductions – the originals, by Jacopo della Quercia, can be seen in the Palazzo Pubblico.

Palazzo Pubblico

At the lowest point of the piazza is the **Palazzo Pubblico** (also known as the Palazzo Comunale, or town hall). Its bell tower, the **Torre del Mangia**, is 102 metres high. Dating from 1297, the palace is considered one of the most graceful Gothic buildings in Italy. The lower level of its façade features a characteristic Sienese Gothic arcade. Inside is the **Museo Civico**, based on a series of rooms with frescoes by artists of the Sienese school. Of particular note is Simone Martini's famous *Maestà* in the Sala del Mappamondo. Completed and signed in

1315, it features the Madonna beneath a canopy, surrounded by saints and angels. It is one of the most important works of the Sienese school. In the Sala dei Nove is Ambrogio Lorenzetti's fresco series depicting *Allegories of Good & Bad Government*, which are among the most significant to survive from the Middle Ages. There is also a chapel with frescoes by Taddeo di Bartolo. The Palazzo Pubblico and museum are open from mid-March to mid-November, Monday to Saturday from 9.30 am to 7.45 pm and Sunday from 9.30 am to 1.45 pm. For the rest of the year it closes daily at 1.45 pm. Admission is L6000, or L3000 for students. Climb to the top of the bell tower for a spectacular view (admission L4000). Opening hours for the tower vary during the year but are roughly 10 am to 6 pm in summer and 10 am to 1.30 pm in winter.

Duomo

Although its has some Romanesque elements, the duomo is one of Italy's great Gothic churches. Begun in 1196, it was largely completed by 1215, although work continued on features such as the apse and dome well into the century. Work then began on changing, enlarging and embellishing the structure. The magnificent façade of white, green and red polychrome marble was begun by Giovanni Pisano, who completed only the lower section, and was finished towards the end of the 14th century. The mosaics in the gables were added in the 19th century. The statues of philosophers and prophets by Giovanni Pisano above the lower section are copies, the originals being preserved in the adjacent Museo dell'Opera Metropolitana.

In 1339, the city's leaders launched a plan to enlarge the cathedral and create one of Italy's largest churches. Known as the New Cathedral, the remains of this unrealised project can be seen in Piazza Jacopo della Quercia, on the east side of the duomo. The plan was to build an immense new nave and the present church would have become the new transept. As it turned out, the plague of 1348, which decimated Siena, also put a stop to this ambitious plan.

The duomo's interior is incredibly rich with artworks and warrants an hour or more of your time. Its most precious feature is the inlaid-marble floor, which is decorated with 56 panels depicting historical, biblical and other subjects. The earliest panels are the graffiti designs in simple black and white marble, dating from the mid-14th century. The latest panels were completed in the 16th century. Most are roped off, while the most valuable are kept covered and revealed to the public only from 7-22 August annually.

TUSCANY

The beautiful pulpit was carved in marble and porphyry by Nicola Pisano. Other artworks include a bronze statue of St John the Baptist by Donatello, in the north transept.

Through a door from the north aisle is another of the duomo's great treasures, the **Libreria Piccolomini**, which Pope Pius III (pope during 1503) had built to house the books of his uncle, Enea Silvio Piccolomini, who became Pope Pius II. The walls of the small hall are covered by an impressive series of frescoes by Bernardino Pinturicchio, depicting events in the life of Piccolomini. In the centre of the hall is a group of statues known as the *Three Graces*, a 3rd century AD Roman copy of an earlier Hellenistic work. Admission is L2000.

On the south-west side of Piazza del Duomo is the **Ospedale Santa Maria della Scala**, a former pilgrims' hospital, with frescoes by Domenico di Bartolo in the main ward. The building houses the **Museo Archeologico**, which has an impressive collection of Roman and Etruscan remains. It is open daily from 9 am to 1.30 pm and Sunday from 9 am to 12.30 pm and is closed the first and third Mondays of the month. Admission is L4000.

Museo dell'Opera Metropolitana

This museum is next to the duomo, in what would have been the south aisle of the nave of the new cathedral. Its great art works formerly adorned the duomo, including the 12 statues of prophets and philosophers by Giovanni Pisano which decorated the façade. However, the museum's main draw card is Duccio di Buoninsegna's striking early 14th-century *Maestà*, painted on both sides as a screen for the duomo's high altar. The front and back have now been separated and the panels depicting the Story of the Passion hang opposite the Maestà. It is interesting to compare Buoninsegna's work with Martini's slightly later *Maestà* in the Palazzo Pubblico. Other artists represented in the museum are Ambrogio Lorenzetti, Simone Martini and Taddeo di Bartolo. The collection also includes tapestries and manuscripts. The museum is open daily from 16 March to 30 September from 9 am to 7.30 pm, in

October until 6 pm and for the rest of the year until 1.30 pm. Admission is L5000.

Baptistry

Behind the duomo and down a flight of stairs is the **baptistry**, with an unfinished Gothic façade. Its interior is heavily decorated with frescoes but the real attraction is a marble font by Jacopo della Quercia, decorated with bronze panels in relief depicting the life of the St John the Baptist by artists including Lorenzo Ghiberti *(Baptism of Christ* and *St John in Prison)* and Donatello *(Herod's Feast)*.

Pinacoteca Nazionale

Located in the 15th-century Palazzo Buonsignori, a short walk south of the duomo at Via San Pietro 29, the **Pinacoteca Nazionale** houses numerous masterpieces by Sienese artists. Look for Duccio di Buoninsegna's *Madonna dei Francescani*, the *Madonna col Bambino* by Simone Martini and a series of Madonnas by Ambrogio Lorenzetti. In summer, the gallery is open Tuesday to Saturday from 9 am to 7 pm, Sunday from 8 am to 1 pm and Monday from 8.30 am to 1.30 pm. In winter it is open Monday to Saturday from 8.30 am to 1.30 pm and Sunday from 8 am to 1 pm. Admission is L8000.

Chiesa di San Domenico

This imposing Gothic church was started in the early 13th century, but has been much altered over the centuries. It is famous for its association with St Catherine of Siena, who took her vows in its Cappella delle Volte. In the chapel is a portrait of the saint painted during her lifetime. In the Cappella di Santa Caterina, on the south side of the church, are frescoes by Sodoma depicting events in the saint's life. St Catherine died in Rome and her body is preserved there in Chiesa di Santa Maria sopra Minerva. In line with the bizarre practice of collecting relics of dead saints, her head was given back to Siena. It is contained in a tabernacle on the altar of the Cappella di Santa Caterina.

The **Casa di Santa Caterina**, the house where St Catherine was born, is on Costa di

Sant'Antonio, off Via della Sapienza. The rooms of the house were converted into small chapels in the 15th century and are decorated with frescoes and paintings by Sienese artists, including Sodoma. The house is open daily from 9.30 am to 12.30 pm and 3.30 to 6 pm. Admission is free.

Other Churches & Palaces

From the Loggia dei Mercanti north of the campo, take Banchi di Sotto to the east for the **Palazzo Piccolomini**, regarded as the city's finest Renaissance palace. The building houses the city's archives and a small museum which is open Monday to Saturday from 9 am to 1 pm. Admission is free. Farther east are the 13th-century **Basilica di Santa Maria dei Servi**, with a fresco by Pietro Lorenzetti, and the 14th-century **Porta Romana**.

Return to the Loggia dei Mercanti and head north along Banchi di Sopra and past Piazza Tolomei, dominated by the 13th-century **Palazzo Tolomei**. Farther along Banchi di Sopra is the Piazza Salimbeni featuring the **Palazzo Tantucci** to the north, the Gothic **Palazzo Salimbeni** to the east, the head office of the Monte dei Paschi di Siena bank and the Renaissance **Palazzo Spannocchi**. North-east of here, along Via Rossi, is **Chiesa di San Francesco**.

West along Via del Paradiso is Piazza San Domenico, from where you can see the massive **Forte di Santa Barbara** built for Cosimo de Medici.

Courses

Language It is generally held that the Sienese speak the purest form of Italian and Siena is a popular place to study the language. The Università per Stranieri (School of Italian Language & Culture for Foreigners) (☎ 4 92 60) is in Piazzetta Grassi 2, Siena 53100. The school is open all year and the only requirement for enrolment is a high-school graduation /pass certificate. There are language courses for beginners and more advanced students, as well as courses in Italian culture, covering three areas of study: Italian language and literature; archaeology and the history of art;

and Italian history and institutions. Courses cost L600,000 for 10 weeks and brochures can be obtained by making a request by letter or telephone to the secretary of the university.

It is important to remember that citizens of many countries are required to apply for a permit to study in Italy. See the Facts for the Visitor chapter for more details.

Music The Accademia Musicale Chigiana (☎ 4 61 52), Via di Città 89, offers classical music classes every summer, as well as seminars and concerts performed by visiting musicians, teachers and students as part of the Settimana Musicale Senese. Classes are offered for most classical instruments and start at L100,000. Enrolments must be completed by 4 April.

The Associazione Siena Jazz (☎ 27 14 01), Strada di Santa Regina 6, offers courses in jazz which start at L380,000; it's one of Europe's foremost institutions of its type.

Festivals

The Accademia Musicale Chigiana holds the Settimana Musicale Senese each July and November and concerts are frequently held at the San Galgano Abbey, a former abbey about 20 km south-west of the city and regarded as one of Italy's finest Gothic buildings. For information, call ☎ 4 61 52. See also the Abbazia di San Galgano section in this chapter.

The city hosts Siena Jazz, an international festival each July and August, at the Fortezza Medici. For information, call ☎ 27 14 01.

Places to Stay

Siena offers a good range of accommodation, but budget hotels generally fill quickly, so it is advisable year-round to book in advance if you want to pay less than L100,000 a double. Forget about finding a room during the Palio unless you have a booking. For assistance in finding a room, contact Siena Hotels Promotion (☎ 28 80 84; fax 28 02 90), Piazza San Domenico, which is open Monday to Saturday from 9 am to 8 pm in summer and 9 am to 7 pm in winter. Agriturismo is well organised around Siena.

Il Palio

This spectacular event, held twice-yearly on 2 July and 16 August in honour of the Virgin Mary, dates to the Middle Ages and features a series of colourful pageants, a wild horse race around the Campo and much eating, drinking and celebrating in the streets. Ten of Siena's 17 town districts, or *contrade*, compete for the coveted *palio*, a silk banner. Each of the contrade has its own traditions, symbol and colours, and its own church and palio museum. The local rivalries which explode with each palio date back centuries and make the festival very much an event for the Sienese, even though the horse race and pageantry have, in recent years, attracted ever larger crowds of tourists. On the festival days the Campo literally becomes a racetrack, with a ring of packed dirt around its perimeter serving as the course. From about 5

TARTUGA   DRAGO

Two of the traditional banners of the *contrade*, districts of Siena which compete in il Palio.

pm there are parades of contrade representatives in historical costume, each bearing their individual banners. The race is run at 7.45 pm in July and 7 pm in August. For not much more than one exhilarating minute, the 10 bareback horses and their riders tear three times around the Campo with a speed and violence that makes your hair stand on end. Even if a horse loses its rider it is still eligible to win and since many riders fall each year, it is the horses in the end who are the focus of the event. There is only one rule, that riders are not to interfere with the reins of other horses. Efforts by Benetton to sponsor the race have been unsuccessful, and the Sienese place incredible demands on the national TV network, RAI, for rights to televise the event. Book well in advance if you want to stay in Siena for the event, and join the crowds in the centre of the Campo at least four hours before the event, even earlier if you want a place on the barrier lining the track. If you can't find a good vantage point, don't despair – the race is televised live and then repeated throughout the evening on TV. ■

The tourist office has a list of more than 60 establishments which rent rooms by the week or month.

The *Colleverde* camping ground (☎ 28 00 44) is north of the historical centre at Strada di Scacciapensieri 47 (take bus No 8 from Piazza Gramsci near the city centre). The cost for one night is L10,000 for adults and L5000 for children. The HI youth hostel *Guidoriccio* (☎ 5 22 12), Via Fiorentina, Località Stellino, is about two km north-west of the city centre. Leave the city by Via Vittorio Emanuele II, which is an extension of Via di Camollia. B&B is L19,000 and a full meal is L13,000. Take bus No 15 from Piazza Gramsci.

In town, try the *Tre Donzelle* (☎ 28 03 58), Via delle Donzelle 5, off Banchi di Sotto north of the campo, which has clean, simple

singles/doubles for L32,000/53,000, or L50,000/67,000 with a bathroom. The *Piccolo Hotel Etruria* (☎ 28 80 88), close by at Via delle Donzelle 1, has pleasant rooms for up to L58,000/85,000 with a bathroom. It does have some cheaper rooms. The *Locanda Garibaldi* (☎ 28 42 04), Via Giovanni Dupré 18, just to the south of the campo, has doubles only for up to L60,000. It also has a small trattoria with a cheap tourist menu.

Albergo Bernini (☎ 28 90 47), Via della Sapienza 15, has clean, simple singles/doubles with shower for up to L55,000/70,000. *Albergo la Perla* (☎ 4 71 44) is on the 2nd floor at Via delle Terme 25, a short walk north-west of the campo. Small but clean rooms with shower are L45,000/75,000.

The *Piccolo Hotel il Palio* (☎ 28 11 31), Piazza del Sale 19, a good 15-minute walk from the campo, has singles/doubles with a bathroom for L75,000/100,000. *La Toscana* (☎ 4 60 97), at Via Cecco Angiolieri 12, has singles/doubles for L48,000/72,000, or L68,000/ 100,000 with a bathroom. It could be cleaner for the price, but is fine if other places are full. The three-star *Albergo Duomo* (☎ 28 90 88), Via Stalloreggi 34, has good singles doubles from L110,000/150,000. Just off Piazza San Domenico at Viale Curtatone 15 is the *Chiusarelli* (☎ 28 05 62), with very pleasant singles/doubles with a bathroom for L68,000/ 105,000.

Places to Eat

The Sienese claim that most Tuscan cuisine has its origins in Siena, and that the locals are still using methods introduced to the area by the Etruscans, namely simple cooking methods and the use of herbs. Among the city's many traditional dishes are soups such as ribollita; *panzanella*, a summer salad of soaked bread, basil, onion and tomatoes; *papparedelle*, pasta with hare; and the succulent steaks of the Chianina, cooked over a charcoal grill. Bread is made without salt, as throughout Tuscany. *Panforte*, a rich cake of almonds, honey and candied melon or citrus fruit, has its origins in the city. Loosely translated, panforte is heavy bread, and it was created as sustenance for the crusaders to the Holy Land.

Il Barbero in the campo is a cheap self-service restaurant, where a pasta costs from L6000. *Hostaria il Carroccio*, Via Casato di Sotto 32, off the campo, has excellent pasta for around L7000 and the bistecca is priced at L4000 an etto. *Pizzeria del Gallo Nero*, Via del Porrione 67, also off the campo, has good pizzas from L7000 and there is no cover or service charge.

La Chiacchiera, Costa di Sant'Antonio 4, off Via Santa Caterina, is very small, but it has a good menu with local specialities. Pasta costs from L6000 and a litre of house wine is L5000. A full meal will cost about L25,000. *Al Marsili*, Via del Castoro 3, is one of the city's best restaurants and has dishes from L7000 for a first course and L14,000 for a second. The 15 per cent service charge

and L4000 cover charge bump up the price of a meal. *Ristorante da Mugulone*, Via dei Pellegrini 8, is another excellent restaurant, with lots of local specialities on the menu. It is a good place to try the bistecca (L4500 an etto). Pasta costs around L10,000 and second courses cost between 10,000 and L40,000. Service and cover charges are high.

About 10-minutes walk north of the campo, in a less frenetic neighbourhood, are several trattorias and alimentari. *Da Titti*, Via di Camollia 193, is a no-frills establishment with big wooden bench-tables where full meals with wine cost around L20,000. *Pizzeria Il Riccio*, nearby at Via Malta 44, has pasta for around L7000 and big pizzas from L6000.

There are several *Crai* supermarkets scattered around the town centre, including at Via di Città 152-156, and in Via Cecco Angiolieri opposite the Hotel La Toscana. *Nannini*, Banchi di Sopra 22, is one of the city's finest cafés and pasticcerie.

Things to Buy

Ricama, a shop at Via di Città 61, promotes the crafts of Siena in particular embroidery and is worth a visit.

Getting There & Away

Regular Tra-in buses leave from Piazza San Domenico for Florence, San Gimignano, Volterra and other main cities in Tuscany. Daily buses also connect Siena with Perugia and Rome, leaving from Piazza San Domenico. Siena is not on a major train line, so from Rome it is necessary to change at Chiusi, and from Florence at Empoli, making buses a better alternative. Trains arrive at Piazza F Rosselli, north of the city centre. By car, there is a branch of the A1 connecting Florence with Siena, or, alternatively, take the SS2 which runs between Florence and Rome. From the Florence-Siena autostrada, the best exit to take is San Marco and then follow the signs marked 'centro'.

Getting Around

Tra-in (☎ 22 12 21) operates city bus services from a base in Piazza Gramsci. From the train station, catch bus No 2, 4 or 15 to Piazza Matteotti, from where it takes about 10 minutes to walk to the campo. From the bus station in Piazza San Domenico it's also a 10-minute walk. No cars, apart from those of residents, are allowed in the city centre. There are large car parks at the Stadio Comunale and around the Fortezza Medici; both are just north of Piazza San Domenico. Technically, even to just drop off your luggage at your hotel it is necessary to get a special permit to enter the city by car. This can be obtained from the vigili in Piazza San Domenico, but only if you have a hotel booking. Otherwise, phone your hotel for advice. For a taxi, call ☎ 4 92 22, or after 9 pm, ☎ 28 93 50.

ABBAZIA DI SAN GALGANO

About 20 km south-west of Siena on the SS73 is the ruined 13th-century San Galgano abbey, one of the country's finest Gothic buildings in its day and now a very romantic ruin. A former Cistercian abbey, its monks were among Tuscany's most powerful, forming the judiciary and acting as accountants for the *comuni* of Volterra and Siena. They ruled over disputes between the cities, played a significant role in the construction of the duomo in Siena and built for themselves an opulent church. By the 16th century the monks' wealth and importance had declined and the church had deteriorated to the point of ruin. The walls remain standing but the roof collapsed long ago. The abbey is definitely worth a diversion if you are driving, but visiting by public transport is quite difficult. The best option is the bus service between Siena and Massa Marittima, a little farther south-west. The Accademia Musicale Chigiana in Siena sponsors concerts at the abbey during summer. See Festivals in the Siena section.

On a hill overlooking the abbey is the tiny, round Romanesque Cappella di Monte Siepi. Inside are very badly preserved frescoes by Ambrogio Lorenzetti, which depict the life of St Galgano, a local soldier who had a vision of St Michael on this site. A real-life 'sword in the stone' is under glass in the floor of the chapel, put there, legend has it, by San Galgano.

CHIANTI

The beautiful hill country between Florence and Siena forms the area known as Chianti. The Monti del Chianti, which rise into the Apennines, form Chianti's eastern boundary and comprise some of Tuscany's most beautiful countryside. The area is famous for its internationally known wines, particularly the Chianti Classico, recognisable by the Gallo Nero (Black Cockerel) symbol. This was the original Chianti wine, produced in the last century by the Baron Bettino Ricasoli. Other Chianti wines include the excellent Colli Fiorentini and the Colli Senesi.

The stunning landscape of the Chianti area, a patchwork of forests, olive groves and vineyards dotted with castles and villas, has attracted many foreigners, who now call the area home.

Getting information about the area is easy. Virtually every tourist office in Tuscany has good information, but the best are the APTs in Florence, Siena, San Gimignano and other main centres. Also check with these tourist offices for accommodation and restaurants. Available at most tourist offices and other locations throughout the area is the newspa-

Chianti is known for its dry red and white wines.

per *Chianti News*, which lists itineraries, transport information, accommodation and tourist highlights by district. It is also a valuable source of information if you are planning to visit vineyards and gives details of visiting times. Pick up a copy of the *Map of Tuscan Wines*, which identifies the main growing areas and details 10 itineraries.

While in the Chianti area, make the effort to visit the town of **San Giovanni Valdarno**. Housed in a tiny museum attached to the town's cathedral is a stunningly beautiful *Annunciation* by Fra Angelico. Formerly located in the Convento di Montecarlo, just out of town, the painting was moved into the museum for security reasons. The town is also accessible by bus from Arezzo. See the Getting There & Away section for Arezzo.

The area is accessible by SITA bus from Florence, but it is really best to see the area by car, taking a long, slow drive along the Chiantigiana (the SS222 which connects Florence and Siena).

SAN GIMIGNANO

From a distance, the towers of San Gimignano dominate the Val d'Elsa, a lush landscape of wheat fields, olive groves and vineyards. The towers, symbols of the power and wealth of the city's medieval families, once numbered as many as 76. Today, only 13 remain, but the city still carries the name San Gimignano delle Belle Torri (of the Fine Towers).

Originally an Etruscan village, the town later took its name from the Bishop of Modena, St Gimignano, who is said to have saved the city from the barbarians. It became a *comune* in 1199, but it fought frequently with neighbouring Volterra and the internal battles between the Ardinghelli family (Guelph) and the Salvucci family (Ghibelline) over the next two centuries caused deep divisions. Most towers were built during this period as status symbols, the height depending on the family's wealth and power, although in the 13th century one particular podestà introduced a law which prohibited the building of towers higher than his (51 metres).

The town came under the control of Florence in 1353, but its importance as a stop on the Francigena (the road to France) ensured continued prosperity. Today, San Gimignano is one of Europe's best-preserved medieval cities and has the feel of a museum. In summer and at weekends year-round it is crowded with tourists.

Orientation

The manicured gardens of Piazzale dei Martiri di Montemaggio, at the southern end of San Gimignano, are outside the medieval wall and next to the main gate, the Porta San Giovanni. From the gate, Via San Giovanni heads north until it meets Piazza Cisterna and the connecting Piazza del Duomo, in the city centre. The other major thoroughfare, Via San Matteo, leaves Piazza del Duomo for the main northern gate, Porta San Matteo. The walled city is small and dominated by the cathedral, also known as the Collegiata, in Piazza del Duomo.

Information

Tourist Office The Associazione Pro Loco (☎ 94 00 08) is at Piazza del Duomo 1, on the left as you approach the cathedral. It is open daily from 9 am to 1 pm and 3 to 7 pm.

Post & Telecommunications The post office is in Piazza delle Erbe 8, on the north side of the cathedral. Poste restante mail can be addressed to 53037 San Gimignano.

A Telecom office is at Via San Matteo 15 and is open 24 hours a day. The telephone code for San Gimignano is 0577.

Emergency & Medical Services For police emergency, call ☎ 113. The carabinieri office (☎ 94 03 13) is behind the bus stop in Piazzale dei Martiri di Montemaggio. For medical assistance, call the Confraternita della Misericordia (☎ 94 03 67), Via San Matteo. The Farmacia Comunale is in Piazza della Cisterna, or call ☎ 95 50 80 for the night chemist.

Things to See

Before you set out, buy the L15,000 ticket at the ticket offices of any of the city's sights, which allows admission into most of San Gimignano's museums.

Start in the triangular Piazza Cisterna, named after the 13th-century cistern in its centre. The piazza is lined with houses and towers dating from the 13th and 14th centuries. Adjoining it to the north is Piazza del Duomo, dominated by the duomo, and facing it the late 13th-century **Palazzo del Podestà** and its tower, known as the **Torre della Rognosa**. To the left of the duomo is the Palazzo del Popolo, still the town's town hall (see below).

The Collegiata Up a flight of steps from the piazza is the town's Romanesque cathedral, its simple façade belying the remarkable frescoes which cover the walls of its interior. There are five main cycles. On the left wall as you enter are scenes from the Old Testament by Bartolo di Fredi, dating from around 1367. On the right wall are scenes from the New Testament, by Barna da Siena, completed in 1381. On the inside wall of the façade, as well as an adjoining wall, is a gruesome depiction of the Last Judgment by Taddeo di Bartolo (1393). It is fascinating to think of the impact the images of punishment for the seven deadly sins must have had on the pious of the 14th century. In the **Capella di Santa Fina** are beautiful frescoes by Domenico Ghirlandaio depicting events in the life of the saint. Without the L15,000 general ticket, it costs L3000 to enter the chapel.

The cathedral and chapel are open daily from 9 am to 12.30 pm and 3 to 6 pm, but tourists cannot enter during mass times.

Palazzo del Popolo From the internal courtyard, climb the stairs to the **Museo Civico**, which features paintings from the 12th to 15th-century Sienese and Florentine schools. Dante addressed the locals in 1299 in the Sala del Consiglio, urging them to support the Guelph cause. The room contains an early 14th-century fresco of the *Maestà*, by Lippo Memmi. Climb the palazzo's **Torre**

Grossa for a spectacular view of the town and surrounding countryside.

The palace, tower and museum are open from Tuesday to Sunday from 9.30 am to 7.30 pm in summer, with shorter hours during the rest of the year.

Other Sights The **Rocca**, a short walk to the west of Piazza del Duomo, is the atmospheric ruin of the town's fortress and there are great views across the valley.

At the northern end of the town is **Chiesa di Sant'Agostino**, whose main attraction is the fresco cycle by Benozzo Gozzoli in the apse, depicting the life of St Augustine.

Places to Stay

San Gimignano has only a handful of hotels with eye-popping prices. However, the hostel, a camping ground and the Sant' Agostino convent, with cheap rooms in the city centre, come to the rescue. The well-organised Cooperativa Hotels Promotion (☎ 94 08 09), Via San Giovanni, just inside the gate of the same name, can place you in one of the dozens of private rooms, flats or villas in and around the city. It will make arrangements months in advance and charges no fee.

The camping ground, *Il Boschetto di Piemma* (☎ 94 03 52), is at Santa Lucia, a couple of km south of the Porta San Giovanni, and is open only in summer. Buses leave from Piazzale dei Martiri di Montemaggio. The non-HI *Ostello della Gioventù* (☎ 94 19 91), Via delle Fonti 1, is at the northern edge of town inside the wall. B&B is L15,000.

The best room deal is at the *Foresteria Convento di Sant'Agostino* (☎ 94 03 83), Piazza Sant'Agostino 4, with singles/doubles for L25,000/35,000. Some of the rooms are pretty shabby, but the price is hard to beat. The hotel *Locanda Il Pino* (☎ 94 04 15), Via San Matteo 102, has doubles for L60,000, or L70,000 with a bathroom. *Hotel La Cisterna* (☎ 94 03 28), in the magnificent Piazza Cisterna, has singles/doubles from L80,000/125,000. Ask for a room in the medieval section, with a view across the valley.

Places to Eat

A produce market is held on Thursday mornings in Piazza Cisterna. Try the Vernaccia white wine or the red Brunello from the hills of Montalcino. Try wines at *Il Castello*, Via del Castello 20, a wine bar and restaurant which stays open until midnight. Pasta starts at L5000. For sandwiches and snacks try *Antica Taverna*; just follow the signs from Via San Matteo.

Pizzeria Pizzoteca, Via dei Fossi, outside the walls to the left of Porta San Matteo, is one of the cheapest in town. The pizzas are fine, but the pasta can leave a lot to be desired. *La Stella*, Via San Matteo 77, has reasonable food, although they tend to exploit the tourists by providing small serves. A meal could cost L25,000. *Trattoria La Mangiatoia*, Via Mainardi 5, is one of the city's better restaurants, with pasta from about L9000.

At the other end of town is *Trattoria Chiribiri*, Piazzetta della Madonna 1, with pastas for around L8000. Nearby is *Pizza a Taglio*, with pizza by the slice.

Gelati Giulebbe, Via San Giovanni 113, and *Gelateria di Piazza*, Piazza della Cisterna 4, are great; the latter turns the local wine, Vernaccia, into a delicious ice cream.

Getting There & Around

San Gimignano is accessible from Florence and Siena by regular buses, but you need to change at Poggibonsi. For Rome and areas such as Perugia and Assisi, you need to get to Siena and catch a bus from there. There is a direct bus to Volterra. Bus timetables are posted on a pillar to the left as you face the Pro Loco office. Buses arrive in Piazzale dei Martiri di Montemaggio at the Porta San Giovanni. The closest train station is in Poggibonsi.

To reach San Gimignano by car, take the SS68 from Colle di Val d'Elsa, which is on the SS2 between Florence and Siena, and follow the signs. The city is small and easily seen on foot. Signs direct you to large car parks outside the Porta San Giovanni.

VOLTERRA

The Etruscan settlement of Velathri was an important trading centre, a status that continued under the Romans, who renamed the city Volaterrae. A long period of conflict with Florence starting in the 12th century ended when the Medici took possession of the city in the 15th century.

Perched on top of a huge rocky plateau, the city looks almost forbidding because of its well-preserved medieval ramparts. The city has long had a strong alabaster industry.

Orientation & Information

If you arrive by car, head for the main car park in Piazza Martiri della Libertà, on the south side of the city, where all buses arrive. From here it is only a short walk to the central Piazza dei Priori.

There is a small tourist office (☎ 0588-8 61 50) at Via Turazza 2, which offers only an incomplete hotel list and little information about the town. The post office and Telecom office on the northern side of Piazza dei Priori. The city's post code is 56048, and the telephone code is 0588. For emergencies, call ☎ 113. The questura is in the Palazzo Pretorio in Piazza dei Priori.

Piazza dei Priori & the Duomo

The Piazza dei Priori is recognised as one of Italy's finest medieval squares and is surrounded by austere palaces. The 13th-century **Palazzo dei Priori** is the oldest communal palace in Tuscany and is believed to have been a model for Florence's Palazzo Vecchio. The **Palazzo Pretorio**, also dating from the 13th century, is dominated by the Piglet's Tower, so named because of the wild boar sculpted on its upper section.

Behind the Palazzo dei Priori, along Via Turazza, is the **duomo**, built in the 12th and 13th centuries. Inside, highlights include a small fresco by Benozzo Gozzoli, the *Adoration of the Magi*, behind a nativity group in the oratory at the beginning of the left aisle. The 15th-century tabernacle on the high altar is by Mino da Fiesole. The 13th-century **baptistry** features a font by Andrea Sansovino. There is an interesting small collection of local art in the **Pinacoteca Comunale** in the Palazzo Minucci Solaini,

TUSCANY

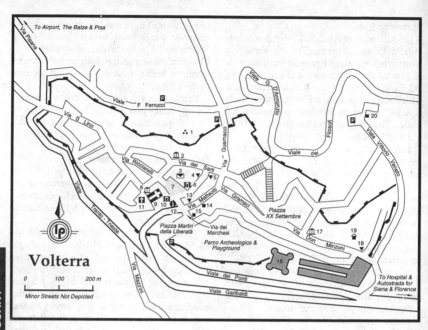

Volterra

0   100   200 m

Minor Streets Not Depicted

PLACES TO STAY

14   Albergo Etruria
15   Albergo Nazionale
19   Youth Hostel
20   Monastero di Sant'Andrea

PLACES TO EAT

4   Da Beppino

5   Pizzeria da Nanni
13   Taverna dei Priori
18   Ristorante la Pace

OTHER

1   Roman Theatre
2   Pinacoteca
3   Post Office & Telephones
6   Palazzo Pretorio &

Questura (Police Station)
7   Piazza dei Priori
8   Museo dell'Opera del
     Duomo
9   Duomo
10   Palazzo dei Priori
11   Baptistry
12   Tourist Office
16   Fortezza Medicea
17   Museo Etrusco Guarnacci

Via dei Sarti 1. The Pinacoteca Comunale is open Tuesday to Sunday from 9.30 am to 6.30 pm, with slightly shorter hours during the winter months.

A special L10,000 ticket covers visits to this museum, as well as the Museo Etrusco Guarnacci, the Roman theatre and the Acropli/Necropoli area in the Parco Archeologico.

The Museo dell'Opera del Duomo is located next to the duomo.

The Museo Etrusco Guarnacci

All the exhibits in this fascinating Etruscan museum were unearthed locally, including a vast collection of some 600 funerary urns carved from alabaster, tufo and other materials. The urns are divided by the subjects which their bas-reliefs depict and the period from which they date. It probably pays to be a bit choosy about which rooms to linger in, because one starts to merge into another after a while. Basically they get better as you go higher, with the best examples – those dating from later periods – on the 2nd and 3rd floors. The museum also houses two famous Etruscan relics: the **Ombra della Sera**, a strange elongated nude figure, which would fit in well in any museum of modern art; and the urn of the **Sposi**, featuring an elderly couple, their faces depicted in portrait fashion, rather than the stylised method usually employed by the Etruscans.

The museum is open Tuesday to Sunday from 9.30 am to 1 pm and 3 to 6.30 pm in summer and from 10 am to 4 pm in winter. Admission is L8000.

Fortezza Medicea & Parco Archeologico

Farther along Via Minzoni is the entrance to the **Fortezza Medicea**, built in the 14th century and altered by Lorenzo the Magnificent, which is now used as a prison. Near the fort is the pleasant **Parco Archeologico**, whose archaeological remains have suffered with the passage of time. Little remains, but it's a good place for a picnic. If you have small children, you can bring them here to play on the swings and slide.

Other Sights

At the city's northern edge is a **Roman theatre**, a well-preserved complex which includes a Roman bath.

The **Balze**, a deep ravine created by erosion, about a 20-minute walk north-west of the city centre, has claimed several churches since the Middle Ages, which have fallen into the deep gullies. A 14th-century monastery is perched close to the precipice and is in danger of collapsing into the ravine.

Places to Stay & Eat

The best deal is at the non-HI *Ostello della Gioventù* (☎ 8 55 77), Via Don Minzoni, near the Museo Etrusco Guarnacci, which has beds for L14,000. The *Casa per Ferie Seminario* (☎ 8 60 28), in the Monastero di Sant'Andrea, Viale Vittorio Veneto, is an excellent deal. Rooms are large, clean and have bathrooms. They cost around L50,000 for a double. The *Albergo Etruria* (☎ 8 73 77), Via Matteotti 32, has singles/doubles

from L50,000/75,000, and the *Albergo Nazionale* (☎ 8 62 84), Via dei Marchesi 7, has rooms with a bathroom from L70,000/98,000.

The restaurant *Da Beppino*, Via delle Prigioni 13, has good pasta from L8000 but hits you with a L2500 cover charge. *Pizzeria da Nanni*, opposite at No 40, has pizzas from L7000. *La Taverna dei Priori*, Via Giacomo Matteotti 19, is a self-service restaurant with pasta from L6000. A lovely restaurant with a friendly atmosphere and great food is *Ristorante la Pace*, Via Don Minzoni 55, near the town walls. A full meal will cost around L30,000.

Getting There & Around

Buses connect the city with Pisa, Siena, Florence, Cecina and San Gimignano from Piazza Martiri della Libertà. There is a small train station in the nearby town of Saline, nine km to the south-west, which is connected to Volterra by bus. Trains run to Cecina, where you can catch trains on the main Rome-Pisa line. By car, take the SS68 which runs between Cecina and Colle di Val d'Elsa. The easiest way to get around Volterra is to walk. Cars are banned from the city centre and car parks are clearly marked.

MONTEPULCIANO

Set atop a narrow ridge of volcanic rock, Montepulciano combines Tuscany's superb countryside with some of the region's finest wines. This medieval town is extremely beautiful and is the perfect place to spend a few quiet days. Stop by the various enoteche to sample the local wines.

Orientation & Information

However you arrive at Montepulciano, you will probably end up at the Porta al Prato at the town's northern edge. From here, buses take you through the town to Piazza Grande. The 15-minute walk is mostly uphill but well worth the exercise. The tourist office (☎ 0578-75 86 87) is at Via Ricci 9, just off Piazza Grande, where you can pick up *Montepulciano Perla del Cinquecento*, a useful guide to the town. The office is open Tuesday to Sunday from 10.30 am to 1 pm and 3.30

to 6.30 pm. Montepulciano's telephone code is 0578.

Things to See

Most of the main sights are clustered around Piazza Grande, although the town's streets provide a wealth of palaces and other fine buildings. It is virtually impossible to get lost, so go for a wander.

To the left as you enter the Porta al Prato, designed by the Florentine Antonio da Sangallo the Elder, is the 18th-century **Chiesa di San Bernardo**. Nearby is the **Palazzo Avignonesi** by Giacomo da Vignola. Several other palaces line the street, including the **Palazzo Bucelli** at No 73, whose façade features Etruscan and Latin inscriptions. Sangallo also designed the **Palazzo Cocconi** at No 70.

Piazza Michelozzo features Michelozzo's **Chiesa di Sant' Agostino** and a medieval tower house, topped by the town clock and the bizarre figure Pulcinella (Punch, of Punch and Judy fame) which strikes the hours.

Continue up the hill and take the first left past the **Loggia di Mercato** for Via del Poggiolo, which eventually becomes Via Ricci. The tourist office is on one side, in the Renaissance **Palazzo Ricci**, and the town's **Museo Civico** is opposite in the Gothic **Palazzo Neri-Orselli**. The small collection features terracotta reliefs by the della Robbia family and some Gothic and Renaissance paintings. It is open daily from 9 am to 1 pm and Sunday to 2 pm. Admission is L3000.

Piazza Grande marks the highest point of the town and features the austere **Palazzo Comunale**, a 13th-century Gothic building remodelled in the 15th century by Michelozzo. From the top of the 14th-century tower, on a clear day you can see the Monti Sibillini to the east and the Gran Sasso to the south. The tower is open Monday to Saturday from 8 am to 1.30 pm and the climb is free.

The other palaces in the piazza are the **Palazzo Contucci**, used as a cantina, and the **Palazzo Tarugi** attributed to Giacomo da Vignola, near the fountain. The **duomo**, dating from the 16th century, has an unfinished façade. Inside are sculptures by Michelozzo and a lovely triptych on the high altar by Taddeo da Bartolo.

Outside the town wall, about one km from the Porta al Prato, is the pilgrimage **Chiesa di San Biagio**, a fine Renaissance church built by Antonio da Sangallo the Elder and consecrated in 1529 by the Medici pope Clement VII.

Places to Stay & Eat

You might consider visiting Montepulciano on a day trip when you discover the hotel prices. The *Albergo Il Marzocco* (☎ 0578-75 72 62), Piazza Savonarola 18, has singles/doubles with a bathroom from L62,000/92,000. The *Albergo Il Borghetto* (☎ 0578-75 75 35), Via Borgo Buio 5, is very appealing and has rooms for L85,000/125,000.

Lo Spuntino, Via Roma 25, sells pizza by the slice. The *Caffè Poliziano* is a great place for breakfast, lunch or dinner and offers superb views to the north of the town. *Ristorante Dal Cittino* (☎ 0578-75 73 35), Vicolo della Via Nuova, off the Corso, has pasta from L5000 and main dishes from L8000. The owners also have rooms at L20,000 per person.

Of the many wine cellars, the *Cantine di Fognano*, Via del Sasso 3, is worth a look because it bottles on site. You can also try the local wines at *Le Cantine Contucci*, in the Palazzo Contucci on Piazza Grande. *Cantine del Redi* is also in Piazza Grande. The *Fattoria Azienda Agricola Pulcino*, Via di Gracciano nel Corso 96, offers free tastings of wines, sheep's-milk cheese and salamis. There is a restaurant next door specialising in local dishes. The local wines include the excellent Nobile di Montepulciano and the Chianti Colli Senesi.

Getting There & Around

By bus, Tra-in operates eight services daily between the town and Siena, via Pienza. LFE buses connect the town with Chiusi.

The most convenient train station is at Chiusi-Chianciano Terme, 10 km south-east, which is on the main Rome-Florence line.

Buses for Montepulciano meet each train, so it is the best way to get there from Florence or Rome. Another station, at Stazione di Montepulciano about five km to the northeast, has less frequent services, including into Montepulciano.

By car, exit the A1 at Chianciano Terme and follow the SS166 for the 18-km trip to Montepulciano. Most cars are banned from the town centre and there are car parks near the Porta al Prato. Small town buses weave their way from here to Piazza Grande, or take a taxi (☎ 0578-75 78 05).

Southern Tuscany

THE MAREMMA & ETRUSCAN SITES
The area known as the Maremma extends along the Tuscan coast from just north of Grosseto and south to the border with Lazio, incorporating the Parco Naturale della Maremma, also known as Parco dell' Uccellina, and Monte Argentario. It also extends inland to the towns of Sovana, Terme di Saturnia and Pitigliano, important because of their Etruscan remains.

Information
Grosseto is the main town in the Maremma area, so the APT there (☎ 0564-45 45 10), Via Monterosa 206, is the best place to start. Information about the Parco Naturale della Maremma can be obtained at the Grosseto APT, or at Alberese, where there is an information office for the park (☎ 0564-40 70 98). Other useful organisations are the Associazione Albergatori (☎ 0564-2 63 15), Via Matteotti 55, the local hotel association which can help you find a bed in the province.

Pick up a copy of *Gli Etruschi in Maremma* from the APT in Grosseto, a series of brochures enclosed in a folder, which provides comprehensive information and itineraries and also describes the history of the Etruscans in the Maremma area.

Things to See & Do
Definitely the main attraction in the area, the **Parco Naturale della Maremma** incorporates the Monti dell'Uccellina and a magnificent stretch of unspoiled coastline. Entry to the park is limited and cars must be left in designated parking areas. Certain areas can be visited only on certain days and excursions into the park are always limited to set itineraries. Depending on your chosen route, you may see plenty of native animals (including deer, wild boar, foxes and hawkes) and can might be able to gain access to the beach. It is necessary to buy a ticket at the Visitor's Centre in Alberese. The tickets vary in price from L4500 to L7500, according to your itinerary. There are no shelters, bars etc within the park, so make sure you carry water and are properly dressed.

The tourist office at Alberese is open Wednesday, Saturday and Sunday from 6.30 am to 6 pm and on Monday, Tuesday, Thursday and Friday from 7.30 am to 6 pm.

If the Etruscan sites take your fancy, head inland from Grosseto for the town of **Marsiliana**, where archaeologists have unearthed several significant Etruscan burial sites.

Follow the road east and then head north on the SS322 for **Terme di Saturnia**. The town is more famous for its sulphur spring and baths, but its Etruscan remains, including part of the town wall, are worth a diversion. A tomb at Sede di Carlo, just north-east of the town, is one of the area's best-preserved.

Follow the signs east for **Sovana**. Situated on the banks of the Fiora river, Sovana was a major centre during Etruscan times and features some impressive tombs. The medieval centre was built over much of the Roman and Etruscan remains, although several Etruscan features can still be seen. **Chiesa di San Mamiliano** in Piazza del Pretorio was built over a Roman temple, which itself was built over an Etruscan temple. Parts of the Etruscan wall are visible in the medieval structure.

About one km to the south of the town are a set of Etruscan tombs, the best-preserved being the **Tomba Ildebranda**. Take a flashlight (torch) if you are serious about visiting the tomb. In the town, be sure to visit the Romanesque cathedral. Sovana is also famous as the birthplace of Pope Gregory VII, whose family built the Castello Aldobrandesco, which sits outside the town wall.

About nine km to the south is the small town of **Pitigliano**, built on a tufa outcrop and featuring an incredible aqueduct. An important Etruscan burial site was discovered just outside the town walls, and features several types of tombs. Parts of the old Etruscan wall are visible near the Porta Capisotto.

Getting Around

Buses leave from Grosseto for Terme di Saturnia, Pitigliano and Sovana, as well as for Alberese, although these services are fairly sparse. Trains connect Grosseto and Alberese, but the Alberese station is about four km out of town.

MONTE ARGENTARIO
Orbetello

Situated on an isthmus some 120 km northwest of Rome, and the central one of three narrow bands of sand connecting the peninsula to the mainland, Orbetello is a pleasant place popular with Romans deserting the metropolis on weekends.

Orbetello's main attraction is its **cathedral**, which has retained its 14th-century Gothic façade despite being remodelled in the Spanish style in the 16th century. Other reminders of the Spanish garrison stationed in the city during the 16th century include the fort and city wall, parts of which are the original Etruscan wall. But the main attraction is the increasingly popular Monte Argentario and its two harbour towns, Port'Ercole and Porto Santo Stefano, both crammed with incredibly expensive boats and yachts.

Around the Peninsula

The Monte Argentario is popular with Romans, but not many tourists make the trek out. Both Porto Santo Stefano and Port' Ercole are resort towns for the wealthy: but

Port'Ercole, in a picturesque position between two forts, retains some of its fishing village character. The main tourist office (☎ 0564-81 42 08) is in Porto Santo Stefano, in the Monte dei Paschi di Siena building, Corso Umberto 55.

For a pleasant drive, follow the signs to Il Telegrafo, one of the highest mountains in the region, and turn off at the **Convento dei Frati Passionisti**, a church and convent with sensational views across to the mainland.

There are plenty of good beaches, usually of the pebble or rocky (rather than sandy) variety. One of the most popular is the long sandy strip of Feniglia, between Orbetello and Port'Ercole. Near Port'Ercole the beach is serviced, which means it's clean but cluttered with deck chairs and umbrellas for rent. As you get farther away from this area, the beach is less crowded but, as with most public beaches in Italy, it also gets more dirty.

Places to Stay & Eat

Accommodation on the peninsula is generally expensive, although there is a *camping ground* (☎ 0564-83 10 90) near Port'Ercole, on the northern fringe at the Feniglia beach.

In Orbetello, there's a very decent pensione Tony & Judy (☎ 0564-8 61 09), Corso Italia.

In Porto Santo Stefano, *Pensione Weekend* (☎ 0564-81 25 80), Via Martiri d'Ungheria 3, is a cosy place with singles/doubles from L60,000/85,000. *Albergo Belvedere* (☎ 0564-81 26 34), Via del Fortino 51, is a luxurious complex overlooking the water, with rooms from L100,000/150,000 in the high season. It also has a private beach. Also at Porto Santo Stefano is *Il Veliero*, Strada Panoramica 149, where an excellent meal will cost around L50,000. At Port'Ercole try *Il Pirata*, a good pizzeria on Lungomare Andrea Doria.

Trattoria Da Sirio, Via del Molo 5, on the waterfront in Porto Santo Stefano, has pizzas and pasta from L7000, and *Pizzeria Rossi* at Via del Molo 9 has pizza by the slice from L1500 apiece.

Getting There & Away

Rama buses (☎ 0564-86 70 57) connect most towns on the Monte Argentario with Orbetello and Grosseto. Follow the signs to Monte Argentario from the SS1, which connects Grosseto with Rome.

Eastern Tuscany

AREZZO

This city is one of the real surprises of Tuscany. Famous among art lovers for the fresco cycle by Piero della Francesca in Chiesa di San Francesco, Arezzo has a well-preserved medieval centre, featuring one of the most beautiful Romanesque churches in Italy, the Pieve di Santa Maria. An important Etruscan town, it was later absorbed into the Roman Empire. A free republic from the 10th century, Arezzo supported the Ghibelline cause in the awful battles between pope and emperor and was eventually subjugated by the Guelph Florence in 1384. During WW II, the city was heavily bombed due to its tactical importance as a road junction and many important buildings were damaged. Famous natives include the poet, Petrarch, the writer, Pietro Arentino, and Vasari, most famous for his book *Lives of the Artists*.

A widely known antiques fair is held in Piazza Grande and surrounding streets on the first weekend of every month, which means accommodation can be difficult to find unless you book well ahead.

Orientation & Information

From the train station at the southern edge of the walled city, walk north-east along Via Guido Monaco to the garden piazza of the same name. The old city is to the north-east and the modern part to the south-east along Via Roma.

The APT office (0575-37 76 78) near the train station in Piazza della Repubblica, is open daily from 8.15 am to 8 pm in summer and Monday to Friday from 8.30 am to 6 pm and Saturday from 8.30 am to 1 pm for the rest of the year.

The post office is at Via Guido Monaco 34, and the city's post code is 52100. A Telecom office is in Piazza Guido Monaco and is open late. There is another at the bottom end of Via Margaritone. The telephone code for Arezzo is 0575.

For police emergencies, call ☎ 113 or head for the questura on Via Fra Guittone. The Ospedale Civile (☎ 30 54 40) is outside the city walls on Via A De Gasperi. There is a special medical service for tourists in summer. Ask at the APT for the phone number.

Chiesa di San Francesco

This 14th-century church houses, in its apse, one of the greatest works of Italian art, Piero della Francesca's fresco cycle of the *Legend of the True Cross*. This is the artist's masterpiece, painted between 1452 and 1456, and relates in 10 episodes the story of Christ's death on the cross. Unfortunately, the frescoes have been badly damaged by damp and have been under restoration for some years. Large sections are covered, but the magnificent results of the restoration work are slowly being revealed.

Pieve di Santa Maria

This 12th-century church has a magnificent Romanesque arcaded façade, which has been recently restored and is reminiscent of the cathedral at Pisa. Each column is different from the other. Over the central doorway are reliefs of the months. The bell tower, erected in the 14th century, has 40 windows and has become something of an emblem for the city. The stark, beautiful interior of the church shows a Gothic influence. The only colour comes from the polyptych by Pietro Lorenzetti at the rear of the church on the raised sanctuary.

Piazza Grande & Around

This sloping piazza is lined with some interesting buildings, including some well-preserved palazzi from the medieval period. The **Palazzo della Fraternità dei Laici** dates from 1375. It was started in

TUSCANY

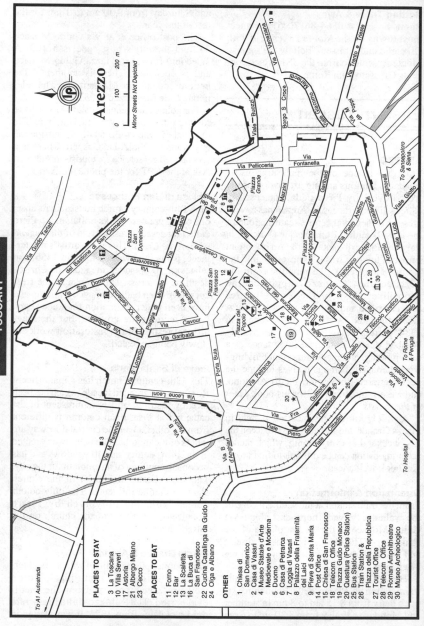

Arezzo

0   100   200 m

Minor Streets Not Depicted

PLACES TO STAY

3   La Toscana
10 Villa Severi
17 Astoria
21 Albergo Milano
23 Cecco

PLACES TO EAT

11 Forno
12 Bar
13 La Scaletta
16 La Buca di
    San Francesco
22 Cucina Casalinga da Guido
24 Olga e Albano

OTHER

1   Chiesa di
    San Domenico
2   Casa di Vasari
4   Museo Statale d'Arte
    Medioevale e Moderna
5   Duomo
6   Casa di Petrarca
7   Loggia di Vasari
8   Palazzo della Fraternità
    dei Laici
9   Pieve di Santa Maria
14 Post Office
15 Chiesa di San Francesco
18 Telecom Office
19 Piazza Guido Monaco
20 Questura (Police Station)
25 Bus Station
26 Train Station &
    Piazza della Repubblica
27 Tourist Office
28 Telecom Office
29 Roman Amphitheatre
30 Museo Archeologico

To A1 Autostrada

To Sansepolcro
& Siena

To Rome
& Perugia

To Hospital

the Gothic style and was finished after the onset of the Renaissance. On the north-eastern side of the piazza is Vasari's loggia, built in 1573.

Via dei Pileati leads to **Casa di Petrarca**, former home of the poet, which contains a small museum and the Accademia Petrarca.

Duomo

At the top of the hill on Via Ricasoli is the duomo, started in the 13th century and not completed until the 15th century. The Gothic interior houses several art works of note, including della Francesca's fresco of Mary Magdalene, just after the tomb of Bishop Guido Tarlati, in the left aisle.

Chiesa di San Domenico & Around

It is worth the walk to see the crucifix painted by Cimabue, which hangs above the main altar in this church on Via Sassoverde. South on Via XX Settembre is the **Casa di Vasari**, built and sumptuously decorated by the architect himself. The house is open Monday to Saturday from 9 am to 7 pm and Sunday to 1 pm. Entry is free. Down the hill on Via San Lorentino is the **Museo Statale d'Arte Medioevale e Moderna**, which has a collection of works by local artists spanning the 13th to 18th centuries, including Luca Signorelli and Vasari. The gallery is open from 9 am to 2 pm (closed Monday). Entry is L5000.

Museo Archeologico & Roman Amphitheatre

Not far from the train station, the museum is in a convent overlooking the remains of the Roman amphitheatre. It houses an interesting collection of Etruscan and Roman artefacts, including locally produced craftwork. The museum is open Tuesday to Saturday from 9 am to 2 pm. Admission is L5000.

Places to Stay

The closest camping ground is *Camping Michelangelo* (☎ 0575-79 38 86) in Caprese Michelangelo, 20 km north-east of Arezzo, and charges L4300 per person and L5600 for

a site. The non-HI youth hostel, the *Villa Severi* (☎ 2 90 47), Via F Redi 13, offers B&B for up to L20,000 in a wonderfully restored villa overlooking the countryside.

La Toscana (☎ 2 16 92), Via M Perennio 56, has simple rooms from L32,000/52,000. *Astoria* (☎ 2 43 61), Via Guido Monaco 54, has OK rooms for L40,000/60,000. The two-star *Cecco* (☎ 2 09 86), on the pedestrian-only Corso Italia, near the train station, has singles/doubles for 40,000/60,000, or L53,000/78,000 with a bathroom. *Albergo Milano* (☎ 2 68 36), Via della Madonna del Prato 83, is between the train station and the old centre, near Piazza Guido Monaco. Recently renovated, it has good singles/doubles for L80,000/120,000, breakfast included.

Places to Eat

Piazza Sant'Agostino comes to life each Tuesday, Thursday and Saturday with the city's produce market. There is an excellent forno in Corso Italia, just before Santa Maria della Pieve, where you can pick up interesting breads and cakes. There is a bar opposite Chiesa di San Francesco, which has tables outside in summer. One of the best-value trattorie in town is the unassuming *Cucina Casalinga Da Guido*, Via della Madonna del Prato 85, next to Albergo Milano. Here you'll eat excellent, home-style food at very reasonable prices. A full meal should come to less than L25,000. Don't be alarmed if the place is full of boys with skinhead-style haircuts – the trattoria gives the local army cadets a special deal. *Olga e Albano*, Via Crispi 32, has pizzas from L8000, as well as a full menu. *La Scaletta*, Piazza del Popolo 11, has pizzas and traditional Tuscan dishes such as ribollita. A meal will cost around L25,000. *La Buca di San Franceso*, Via San Francesco 1, near the church of the same name, is one of the city's better restaurants, where you'll pay up to L50,000 for a full meal; it offers some local specialities.

Getting There & Away

Buses depart from and arrive at Piazza della Repubblica, serving Cortona, Sansepolcro, Monterchi, Siena, San Giovanni Valdarno,

TUSCANY

Florence and many other local towns. The city is on the Florence-Rome train line. By car, Arezzo is a few km east of the A1, and the SS71 heads east to Sansepolcro. Cars are banned from parts of the old city centre, and there are car parks near the train station and in Piazza del Popolo. The staff at the APT can advise on transport to neighbouring towns.

Getting Around

The easiest way is to walk, but some of the hills might get the better of you. Several city buses weave their way from the train station, past Piazza Guido Monaco, along Via Roma and into the old centre.

SANSEPOLCRO

This town, along with Arezzo and nearby **Monterchi**, forms the key stop on an itinerary of Piero della Francesca's work. Both towns are easy to reach from Arezzo in a day. See Getting There & Away in the Arezzo section of this chapter. The reason to visit Monterchi is the artist's famous fresco *Madonna del Parto* (a pregnant Madonna). It was removed from its original home in the local cemetery for restoration and is on display in a former primary school in Via Reglia. Opening hours are 9 am to 1 pm and 2 to 7 pm daily, except Monday. Admission is L5000.

About 20 km north-east of Arezzo, Sansepolcro is the birthplace of the artist. He left the town when he was quite young and returned when he was in his 70s to work on his treatises, which included *On Perspective in Painting*.

There is a small tourist office (☎ 0575-73 02 31) at Via della Fonte 5, which can assist with some local information. The itinerary of della Francesca's work takes in other towns in Tuscany and the Marches, including Rimini, Urbino, Perugia and Florence. Pick up a copy of *Following in Piero della Francesca's Footsteps in Tuscany, Marches, Umbria & Romagna*, while in Arezzo or Sansepolcro.

The **Museo Civico**, Via Aggiunti 65, is the pride of the town. Occupying rooms in the former town hall, it features the Renaissance masterpiece, della Francesca's *Resurrection*.

If you need to stay in the town, there are several hotels, including the budget *Orfeo* (☎ 0575-74 22 87), Viale A Diaz 12, and the more expensive *Fiorentino* (☎ 0575-74 03 50), Via L Pacioli 60.

CAT buses connect Arezzo with Sansepolcro hourly, and the town is on the Terni-Perugia train line. By car, take the SS71 or SS73 from Arezzo, or the SS3b from Perugia.

CORTONA

Set into the side of a hill covered with olive groves, Cortona has changed little since the Middle Ages. From the city, there are stunning views across the Tuscan countryside. Cortona was a small settlement when the Etruscans moved in during the 8th century BC and it later became a Roman town. In the late 14th century, it attracted the likes of Fra Angelico, who lived and worked in the city for about 10 years. Luca Signorelli and the artist known as Pietro da Cortona were born here. The city is small, easily seen in a couple of hours and well worth visiting for the sensational view.

Orientation & Information

Piazzale Garibaldi, at the southern edge of the walled city, is where buses arrive and has a large car park. It also offers some of the best views in the city. From the piazza, walk straight up Via Nazionale to Piazza della Repubblica, the centre of town.

The APT (☎ 0575-63 03 52), Via Nazionale 42, can assist with a hotel list and the useful *Cortona*, a complete guide to tourist essentials. It is open Monday to Saturday from 8 am to 1 pm and 3 to 6 pm and on Sunday from 9 am to 1 pm from July to September. The town's telephone code is 0575. In an emergency, call ☎ 113.

Things to See

Start in Piazza della Repubblica with the crenellated **Palazzo Comunale**, which was renovated in the 16th century. To the north is Piazza Signorelli, named after the artist and dominated by the 13th-century **Palazzo Pretorio**, also known as the Casanova Palace, whose façade was added in the 17th century. Inside is the **Museo dell'Accademia Etrusca**, which displays substantial local Etruscan finds, including an elaborate 5th-century BC oil lamp. The museum is open daily, except Monday, from 10 am to 1 pm and 4 to 7 pm. Admission is L5000.

Little is left of the Romanesque character of the **duomo** north-west of Piazza Signorelli, which was completely rebuilt late in the Renaissance and again in the 18th century. Opposite is the **Museo Diocesano** in the former church of the Gesù. Its fine collection includes works by Luca Signorelli and a beautiful *Annunciation* by Fra Angelico.

At the eastern edge of the city centre is **Chiesa di Santa Margherita**, which features the magnificent Gothic tomb of St Margaret. Farther up the hill is the 16th-century **fortezza**, built for the Medici by Laparelli, the architect who built the fortress city of Valletta in Malta.

Places to Stay & Eat

The city has several cheap hotels and a hostel, and finding a room shouldn't be a problem at any time of the year. The HI *Ostello San Marco* (☎ 60 13 92), Via Maffei 57, just a short walk east of Piazzale Garibaldi, has B&B for L15,000. It is open from March 1 to October 15. The *Betania* (☎ 0575-6 28 29), Via Severini 50, is a monastery which offers rooms from L24,000 a person. The *Albergo Italia* (☎ 0575-63 02 54), Via Ghibellina 5, just off Piazza della Repubblica, is in an old palace and has singles/doubles from L40,000/55,000, or L60,000/80,000 with a bathroom.

There is a produce market in Piazza della Repubblica each Saturday and there are several grocery shops around the area. *Trattoria Dardano*, Via Dardano 24, is a good trattoria where you can eat a meal for around L20,000. *Il Cacciatore*, Via Roma 11, is one of the city's better restaurants and offers local specialities. A meal could cost around L35,000.

Getting There & Away

LFI buses connect the city with Arezzo from Piazzale Garibaldi at regular intervals. The city is served by two train stations. Trains from Arezzo stop at the Camucia-Cortona station, in the valley below Cortona, and trains for Rome stop at Terontola, about five km to the south of the Camucia/Cortona station. Shuttle buses connect both stations with Piazzale Garibaldi, and a board opposite the APT entrance details schedules. By car, the city is on the north-south SS71 which runs to Arezzo, and it is close to the superstrada that connects Perugia to the A1.

TUSCANY

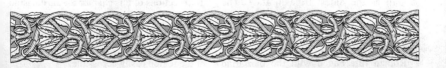

Umbria & the Marches

Dotted with splendid medieval hill towns, and offering a chance to really get away from it all in isolated valleys or mountains, the regions of Umbria and the Marches need to be explored rather then simply visited. Umbria certainly offers some star attractions – the beautifully preserved medieval town of Perugia, St Francis' home town of Assisi, and the extraordinary cathedral at Orvieto. The main attraction of the Marches is the Renaissance town of Urbino, home of the painter Raphael and Duca Federico de Montefeltro. But in both regions there is a host of smaller, lesser known towns and villages and plenty of opportunities for nature lovers, walkers and mountain bikers to escape from the tourist attractions and expend some energy.

Umbria

One of the few landlocked Italian regions, Umbria is Italy's green heart. In spring the countryside is splashed with the red, pink, yellow, purple and blue of wildflowers and in summer it explodes with the vibrant yellow of the sunflowers harvested to make cooking oil. The rolling mountains of the Apennines in the north and east descend into hills, many of which are topped by medieval towns, and eventually flatten out into lush valleys along the Tiber river. With the exception of the industrial blight around Terni in the south, most towns are unspoilt and have conserved their medieval centres.

The Romans named Umbria after the Umbrii, the Iron Age tribe which occupied the region. Little is known about them, except that the Roman naturalist Pliny described the Umbrii as the oldest tribe in Italy. The Etruscans later settled the west bank of the Tiber river, founding the towns of Perugia and Orvieto, and they eventually created 12 powerful city-states.

Roman rule ended with the barbarian invasions of the 5th and 6th centuries AD, when the Umbrians retreated to the hill towns that gave rise to fortified medieval cities such as Gubbio and Todi. Domination by the Goths, the Lombards and various ruling families, as well as centuries of Guelph-Ghibelline rivalry, led to a long decline that left Umbria ripe for papal domination from the early 16th century.

St Francis, one of the world's most famous saints, was born in Assisi in the east of the region, and after his death, the town was transformed with the construction of St Francis' Basilica and its stupendous frescoes by Giotto, Cimabue and Simone Martini. Perugia, a short distance west and the region's capital, is a stunning city, and its university for foreigners ensures a lively nightlife. Spoleto's internationally renowned Festival dei Due Mondi (Festival of the Two Worlds), the beauty of the Valnerina area in the southeast of the region, and Lago di Trasimeno, the Italian peninsula's largest lake, are added reasons to visit.

As a rule, Umbrian cuisine is very simple, and most dishes contain only three or four ingredients. *Tartufo*, a type of truffle, is a local delicacy used in pasta and rice dishes and Umbria's *funghi porcini*, a type of mushroom, are truly delicious. They are used in pasta and rice, but are best eaten as 'steaks', an experience not to be missed. *Porchetta* (roast piglet) and salami are typical foods. The golden wines from around Orvieto are popular throughout Italy.

Umbria is also noted for its extensive range of agriturismo destinations. Several organisations can suggest destinations, and the APT in each town can provide a list of farms. See Places to Stay in the Perugia and Todi sections of this chapter for agriturismo organisations.

Extensive bus routes, state train services and the private Ferrovia Centrale Umbra (Umbrian Central Railway) make most areas of the region easily accessible.

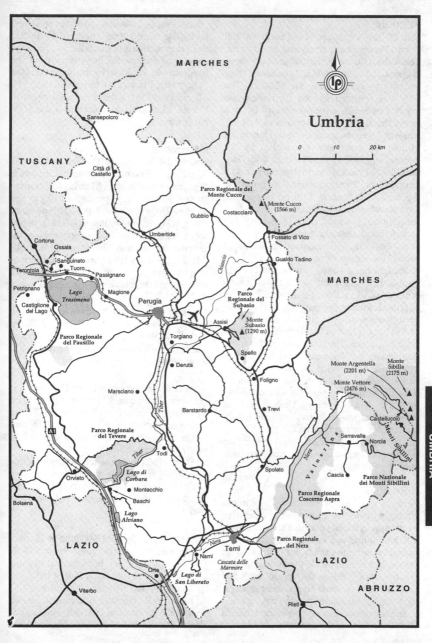

PERUGIA

One of Italy's best preserved medieval hill towns, Perugia has a lively and bloody past. The Umbrii tribe inhabited the surrounding area and controlled land stretching from present-day Tuscany into the Marches. The city was founded by the Etruscans and reached its zenith in the 6th century BC as a city-state. It fell to the Romans in 310 BC and was given the name Perusia. During the Middle Ages the city was racked by the internal feuding of the Baglioni and Oddi families and violent external wars against its neighbours. Perugia was also home in the mid-13th century to the Flagellants, a curious breed who whipped themselves for religious penance. In 1538, the city was incorporated into the Papal States under Pope Paul III, and remained under papal control for almost three centuries.

Perugia has a strong artistic and cultural tradition. It was home to the fresco painters Bernardino Pinturicchio and Pietro Vannucci, known as Perugino. Raphael was Perugino's pupil. The city also attracted the great Tuscan painters Fra Angelico and Piero della Francesca. The Università per Stranieri (University for Foreigners), established in 1925, offers courses in the Italian language and attracts thousands of students from all over the world. The city is at its most lively for 10 days in July during Umbria Jazz, an international music festival which usually features top jazz performers.

The town is also the home of *Baci*, the mouth-watering chocolate-coated hazelnuts made by Perugino.

Orientation

Perugia's medieval centre is, like most Umbrian towns, on top of a hill. If you arrive by train, you'll find yourself a few km downhill, and unless you're very energetic you'll probably prefer to catch a bus to the historic centre, rather than tackle the steep climb. If you are driving, follow the 'centro' signs and park in one of the well-signposted car parks, then take an escalator up to the city centre.

Perugia's main strip, Corso Vannucci (named after Perugino), is the focus for the old city centre. Piazza Italia at its southern end overlooks the surrounding countryside, Piazza della Repubblica is towards the middle of the street and Piazza IV Novembre is at the northern end, enclosed by the duomo and the Palazzo dei Priori. City buses will drop you off either at Piazza della Repubblica, or in Piazza Matteotti, just east of Piazza IV Novembre.

Information

Tourist Office The APT office (☎ 075-572 33 27) is in Piazza IV Novembre, opposite the duomo, and is open Monday to Saturday from 8.30 am to 1.30 pm and 4 to 7 pm and Sunday from 9 am to 1 pm. The monthly *Perugia What, Where, When* (L1000 at newspaper stands) lists all events and useful information. Informa Giovani (☎ 075-576 17 24), Piazza Italia 1, can assist with information for young or disabled travellers and with educational and cultural information.

Money The exchange booth at the main train station is open daily from 6.30 am to 8.30 pm and Corso Vannucci is lined with banks. The Cassa di Risparmio di Perugia at No 39 has an automatic exchange machine.

Post & Telecommunications The main post office is in Piazza Matteotti and is open Monday to Friday from 8.10 am to 7.25 pm and Saturday from 8.10 am to 1.25 pm. Poste restante mail can be addressed to 06100 Perugia.

There is a Telecom office in the post office open daily from 8 am to 8 pm, and another at Corso Vannucci 76, open daily from 8 am to 10 pm. The telephone code for Perugia is 075.

Emergency & Medical Services In an emergency, call ☎ 113. The questura (☎ 572 80 00) is in Piazza dei Partigiani, down the escalators in the fortress at Piazza Italia.

The Ospedale Riuniti-Policlinico (☎ 57 81) is at Viale Bonacci Brunamonti, northeast of the city centre. For night and holiday doctor service, call ☎ 3 40 24. The Farmacia

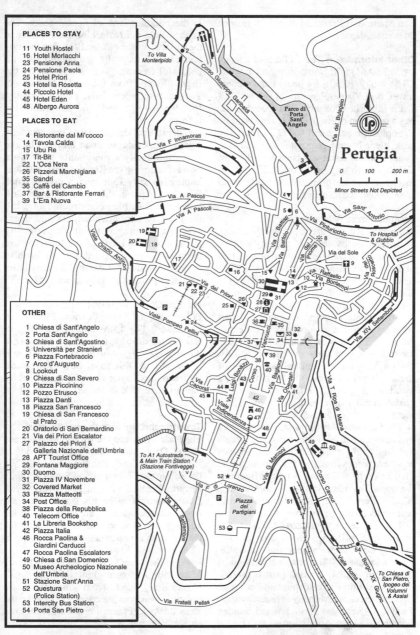

PLACES TO STAY

11 Youth Hostel
16 Hotel Morlacchi
23 Pensione Anna
24 Pensione Paola
25 Hotel Priori
43 Hotel la Rosetta
44 Piccolo Hotel
45 Hotel Eden
48 Albergo Aurora

PLACES TO EAT

4 Ristorante dal Mi'cocco
14 Tavola Calda
15 Ubu Re
17 Tit-Bit
22 L'Oca Nera
26 Pizzeria Marchigiana
35 Sandri
36 Caffè del Cambio
37 Bar & Ristorante Ferrari
39 L'Era Nuova

OTHER

1 Chiesa di Sant'Angelo
2 Porta Sant'Angelo
3 Chiesa di Sant'Agostino
5 Università per Stranieri
6 Piazza Fortebraccio
7 Arco d'Augusto
8 Lookout
9 Chiesa di San Severo
10 Piazza Piccinino
12 Pozzo Etrusco
13 Piazza Danti
18 Piazza San Francesco
19 Chiesa di San Francesco
   al Prato
20 Oratorio di San Bernardino
21 Via dei Priori Escalator
27 Palazzo dei Priori &
   Galleria Nazionale dell'Umbria
28 APT Tourist Office
29 Fontana Maggiore
30 Duomo
31 Piazza IV Novembre
32 Covered Market
33 Piazza Matteotti
34 Post Office
38 Piazza della Repubblica
40 Telecom Office
41 La Libreria Bookshop
42 Piazza Italia
46 Rocca Paolina &
   Giardini Carducci
47 Rocca Paolina Escalators
49 Chiesa di San Domenico
50 Museo Archeologico Nazionale
   dell'Umbria
51 Stazione Sant'Anna
52 Questura
   (Police Station)
53 Intercity Bus Station
54 Porta San Pietro

Perugia

0   100   200 m

Minor Streets Not Depicted

UMBRIA

San Martino at Piazza Matteotti 26 is open 24 hours a day.

Other Information The CIT travel agency (☎ 572 60 61) is at Corso Vannucci 2, while CTS (☎ 572 70 50), for budget and student travel, is at Via del Roscetto 21.

La Libreria bookshop, Via Oberdan 52, has a selection of English-language books.

For lost property, call ☎ 577 35 73. If you park illegally and return to find your car gone, chances are it has been towed away. Call the Auto Impound Lot (☎ 577 53 75) to check and be prepared to pay around L200,000 to retrieve a car.

Around Piazza IV Novembre

The piazza, at the north end of Corso Vannucci, is surrounded by some of the city's finest buildings. The austere **duomo** was started in 1345 and completed in 1430, although its red and white marble façade was never finished. The Gothic cathedral's impressive size is about its main attribute – there is little inside to cause excitement, apart from the 16th-century doorway by Galeazzo Alessi, which faces the Fontana Maggiore in the square. If you are in the city on 30 July, grab a pew for the annual unveiling of the city's prized relic: the Virgin Mary's wedding ring, which is locked away in 15 boxes, fitted inside each other for added security.

The **Fontana Maggiore** was designed by Fra Bevignate in 1278 and carved by Nicola and Giovanni Pisano. The bas-relief statues represent scenes from the Old Testament and the 12 months of the year. A female figure on the upper basin and facing Corso Vannucci is called Perugia, because the fruit she bears represents fertility, a symbol of the city.

The 13th-century **Palazzo dei Priori** is an impressive building which now houses the city's municipal offices and the **Galleria Nazionale dell'Umbria**, a collection of paintings by mainly Umbrian artists including Bernardino Pinturicchio and Perugino. Opening times are Monday to Saturday from 9 am to 1.45 pm and 3 to 7 pm and Sunday from 9 am to 1 pm. Admission is L8000. Also

in the building is a science museum. The vaulted **Sala dei Notari**, on the 1st floor of the palace, was built in 1296 for the city council and its walls are decorated with colourful frescoes. It is accessible by the flight of steps from Piazza IV Novembre. The room is open daily, except Monday, from 9 am to 1 pm and 3 to 7 pm. Admission is free.

Still in the palace, but on the Corso Vannucci side, is the **Collegio della Mercanzia**, the seat of the city's merchants who were powerful during the Renaissance. Inside is impressive early 15th-century carved-wood panelling. Also in the building is the **Collegio del Cambio**, constructed in 1450 for the city's moneychangers and decorated with magnificent frescoes by Perugino. Both parts of the building are open Tuesday to Saturday from 9 am to 12.30 pm and 3 to 7 pm and Sunday from 9 am to 1 pm. Admission to both is L2000.

West of Corso Vannucci

Follow Via dei Priori down to Piazza San Francesco. The 15th-century **Oratorio di San Bernardino** has a façade decorated with bas-reliefs by Agostino di Duccio. Next to it is the ruined **Chiesa di San Francesco al Prato**, destroyed over the centuries by various natural disasters. It is used as an atmospheric location for concerts.

Towards the Università per Stranieri

The **Pozzo Etrusco** (Etruscan Well) between Piazza Danti and Piazza Piccinino, dating from the 3rd century BC. From here take Via del Sole to the **Chiesa di San Severo**, which features Raphael's magnificent *Trinity with Saints*, thought to be his first fresco, and frescoes by Perugino. There is a L3000 ticket which admits you to both the well and the church. Both are open daily from 10.30 am to 12.30 pm and 2.30 to 6.30 pm.

From the church, walk back into Piazza Michelotti and turn right into the small Piazza Rossi Scotti, from which there is a lovely view across the countryside. Take the steps down to Piazza Fortebraccio and the **Università per Stranieri**, housed in the

Baroque Palazzo Gallenga. To the left is the **Arco d'Augusto**, one of the ancient gates to the city. Its lower section is Etruscan, dating from the 3rd century BC, and the upper part is Roman and bears the inscription 'Augusta Perusia'. On top is a loggia dating from the Renaissance.

Around Corso Garibaldi

North along Corso G Garibaldi is the **Chiesa di Sant'Agostino**, with a beautiful 16th-century choir by Baccio d'Agnolo. Small signs denote the many artworks which were carried off to France by Napoleon. At the end of Via del Tempio, off Corso G Garibaldi to the north, is the Romanesque **Chiesa di Sant'Angelo**, said to stand on the site of an ancient temple. The antique columns inside the round church were taken from earlier buildings. Corso Garibaldi continues through the 14th-century wall by way of the **Porta Sant'Angelo**. A 10-minute walk takes you to the **Villa Monteripido**, home of the Giuditta Brozzetti fabric company where you can buy hand-woven linens, that are produced using centuries-old techniques.

South of the Centre

At the end of Corso Vannucci are the tiny **Giardini Carducci**, with lovely views of the countryside. The gardens stand on top a once massive 16th-century fortress, now known as the **Rocca Paolina**, which was built by Pope Paul III over a medieval quarter formerly inhabited by some of the city's most powerful families. Destroyed by the Perugini after Italian unification, the ruins remain a symbol of defiance against oppression. A series of escalators runs through the Rocca and you can wander around inside and explore the ruins. Exhibitions are often held here.

Along Corso Cavour is the massive **Chiesa di San Domenico**, the city's largest church. It dates from the early 14th century, but its Romanesque interior was replaced by austere Gothic fittings in the 16th century. It houses the tomb of Pope Benedict XI, who died after eating poisoned figs in 1325, and has immense stained glass windows. The convent houses the **Museo Archeologico Nazionale dell'Umbria** which has an excellent collection of Etruscan pieces and a prehistoric section. It is open Monday to Saturday from 9 am to 1.30 pm and 3 to 7 pm and Sunday to 1 pm. Admission is L4000.

Continuing along Corso Cavour you come to the Porta San Pietro. Keep going along Borgo XX Giugno for the 10th-century **Chiesa di San Pietro**, reached through a fresco-decorated doorway in the first courtyard. The interior is an incredible mix of gilt and marble, and contains a *Pietà* by Perugino.

About five km south-east of the city, at Ponte San Giovanni, is the **Ipogeo dei Volumni**, a 2nd-century BC Etruscan burial site discovered in 1840. It features an underground chamber with a series of recesses holding the funerary urns of the Volumnio family. Unless you're a big fan of the Etruscans, you'll probably find the tombs at Cerveteri or Tarquinia in Lazio more interesting. It is open Monday to Saturday from 9.30 am to 12.30 pm and 4.30 to 6.30 pm and Sunday to 12.30 pm. Admission is L4000 and visits are limited to five people at a time, so there can be delays. Take the ASP bus from Piazza Italia to Ponte San Giovanni and walk the short distance from there.

Courses

The Università per Stranieri (☎ 5 74 61) is Italy's foremost academic institution for foreigners and offers courses in language, literature, history, art and other fields. It runs a series of degree courses as well as one, two, three-month and intensive courses. The basic language course costs L240,000 per month. For information, write to the Università per Stranieri, Palazzo Gallenga, Piazza Fortebraccio 4, Perugia 06100.

The Istituto Europea di Arti Operative (☎ 6 50 22), Via dei Priori, runs courses for foreigners in graphic design, drawing, painting, fashion and industrial and interior design.

To study at either institution, you may need to apply for a student visa in your country before arriving in Italy. See the Visas

& Embassies section in the Facts for the Visitor chapter.

Festivals
The Umbria Jazz Festival attracts international performers for 10 days each July, usually around the middle of the month. Check with the APT for details.

Places to Stay
Perugia has a good selection of reasonably priced hotels, but if you arrive unannounced during Umbria Jazz, or during August, expect problems. For agriturismo throughout Umbria try Agriturist Umbria (☎ 3 20 28), Via Savonarola 38; Terranostra Umbria (☎ 7 45 59), Via Campo di Marte 10; or Turismo Verde Umbria (☎ 500 29 53), Via Campo di Marte.

Camping The city has two camping grounds, both in Colle della Trinità, five km north-west of the city and reached by bus No 36. They are *Paradise d'Etè* (☎ 517 21 17) and *Il Rocolo* (☎ 517 85 50).

The non-HI youth hostel, the *Centro Internazionale per la Gioventù* (☎ 572 28 80), Via Bontempi 13, charges L15,000 a night. Sheets (for the entire stay) are an extra L1000. Its TV room has a fresco-decorated ceiling and its terrace has fantastic views.

Pensione Anna (☎ 573 63 04), Via dei Priori 48, has very simple singles/doubles for L35,000/48,000. *Pensione Paola* (☎ 572 38 16), Via della Canapina 5, is five minutes from the centre, down the escalator from Via dei Priori; it has rooms for L38,000/60,000. Just off Corso Vannucci, at Via Bonazzi 25, is the *Piccolo Hotel* (☎ 572 29 87), with doubles only, for L50,000, or L70,000 with a bathroom; showers cost an extra L3000.

The two-star *Albergo Aurora* (☎ 572 48 19), Viale Indipendenza 21, has singles/doubles with a bathroom for L68,000/88,000. *Hotel Morlacchi* (☎ 572 03 19), Via Tiberi 2, has singles/doubles for L60,000/80,000 or L110,000 for a triple with a bathroom.

Hotel Priori (☎ 572 33 78), Via Vermiglioli 3, at the corner of Via dei Priori, is in a great location and has very pleasant singles/doubles for L85,000/115,000 with a bathroom. *Hotel Eden* (☎ 572 81 02), Via Caporali 9, has bright, clean singles/doubles for L55,000/75,000. *Hotel la Rosetta* (☎ 572 08 41), Piazza Italia 19, is one of Perugia's better hotels. Its singles/doubles cost up to L100,000/235,000.

Rental Accommodation If you are planning to study in Perugia, the Università per Stranieri will organise accommodation for L300,000 to L800,000 a month, depending on your needs. The weekly *Cerco e Trovo* (L2000 at newspaper stands) lists all available rental accommodation, and the APT publishes a list of *Casa per Ferie* and affittacamere, rooms rented on a weekly or monthly basis.

Places to Eat
Being a student city, Perugia offers many budget eating options. For great pizza by the slice, there is a small outlet, *Pizzeria Marchigiana*, at Via dei Priori 3, just below Corso Vannucci.

Good places for a sit-down pizza are *L'Era Nuova*, Via Baldo 6, and *Tit-Bit*, Via dei Priori 105. A pizza will cost from L6000 to L12,000 at either restaurant.

For a cheap meal, try the tavola calda in Piazza Danti. *L'Oca Nera*, Via dei Priori 80, has a big range of pizzas, including vegetarian, and also offers good hamburgers. Salads start at L4000 and burgers at L5000. *Il Segreto di Pulcinella*, Via Larga 8, is another good place for a cheap meal.

For a traditional Umbrian meal and lots of vegetables, try *Ubu Re*, Via Baldeschi 17, where a full meal will cost around L35,000. *Ristorante dal Mi'Cocco*, Corso G Garibaldi 12, has a L20,000 set menu featuring local specialities and is a popular student restaurant. *Ferrari*, downstairs from the bar of the same name at Corso Vannucci 43, has excellent antipasto, good pizzas and a three-course menu. A meal will cost around L30,000.

There is a covered market downstairs from Piazza Matteotti which is open daily, except Sunday, from 7 am to 1.30 pm. You can buy fresh produce, bread, cheese and meat.

Cafés & Bars *Sandri*, Corso Vannucci 32, retains a medieval air and is the city's finest café. Prices are very reasonable. *Café del Cambio* at No 29 is a trendy bar. Another is *Medio Evo* on Corso Vannucci at Piazza della Repubblica. For great ice cream, try *La Fonte Maggiore*, Piazza IV Novembre, beside the APT office.

Entertainment
The Estate Perugina programme features concerts during August. The box office is in Piazza della Repubblica and is open daily from 5 pm to 8 pm. Venues are near by. The Contrappunto Jazz Club, in Via Scortici 4, is one of the best clubs.

Getting There & Away
Bus Buses arrive at and leave from Piazza dei Partigiani, just downhill from Piazza Italia at the end of the Rocca Paolina escalators, for Rome and Fiumicino airport, Florence, Siena and cities throughout Umbria, including Assisi, Gubbio and nearby Lago di Trasimeno. The bus to Rome is faster and cheaper than the train. The bus station is also more convenient to the historic centre than the train station. Full timetables for all trains and buses are available at the tourist office.

Train The main train station, Stazione Fontivegge, is in Piazza Vittorio Veneto, a few km downhill from the city centre and easily accessible by frequent buses. The city is not on the main Rome-Florence train line, so you generally need to change at Foligno for Rome or at Terontola for Florence and the north. There are one or two direct trains each day to Rome and Florence.

The private Ferrovia Centrale Umbra railway operates from Stazione Sant'Anna in Piazzale G Bellucci and serves Umbertide, Sansepolcro, Terni and Todi. It is very close to the city centre, near Piazza Partigiani.

Car & Motorbike From Rome, leave the A1 at the Orte exit and follow the signs for Terni. Once there, take the SS3bis for Perugia. From the north, exit the A1 at Valdichiana and take the dual-carriageway SS75b for Perugia. The SS75 to the east connects the city with Assisi. Hertz (☎ 500 24 39) is at Stazione Fontivegge.

Getting Around
From Stazione Fontivegge catch any bus heading for Piazza Matteotti or Piazza Italia (including Nos 20, 21, 26, 27, 28, 29 and 33) to get to the centre. Tickets cost L1200 and must be bought before you get on the bus and then validated in the machine as you enter.

If you arrive in Perugia by car, be prepared to be confused. Roads leading to the centre wind around a hill top by the old medieval town, and the normal driving time from the base of the hill to the top is around 10 minutes. By following the clearly marked 'centro' signs you should arrive at Piazza Italia, where you can leave your car and walk along Corso Vannucci to the tourist office.

Most of the city centre is closed to normal traffic, although tourists are allowed to drive to their hotels. Escalators from the historical centre will take you to large car parks downhill, including the escalator in Via dei Priori which leads to the car parks in Piazza della Cupa and Via Pellini, and the series of escalators which take you down through the Rocca Paolina to Piazza dei Partigiani. The supervised car park at Piazza dei Partigiani costs L10,000 for the first day and then L7500 a day. The escalators operate from around 6.15 am to 12.30 am.

LAGO DI TRASIMENO
The fourth-largest lake in Italy, Lago di Trasimeno is a good alternative to the northern lakes. The lake is very beautiful, although this can't be said for the autostrada along its northern shore. Because tourism is the economic mainstay of the area, the lake and its surrounds are kept clean, and swimming, fishing and other water sports are possible.

The lake's northern fringe was the site of one of the bloodiest battles in Roman history when in 217 BC Carthaginian forces led by Hannibal routed Roman troops under the command of Consul Flaminius, killing 16,000. The battlefield extended from Cortona and Ossaia ('the place of bones'), in Tuscany, to the small town of Sanguineto ('the bloody'), just north of the lake.

Passignano (its full name is Passignano sul Trasimeno) is the most popular spot by the lake for holidaying Italians, so call ahead for a room in summer months. The nicest and most picturesque town is Castiglione del Lago, situated on a chalky promontory on the lake's western side, dotted with olive trees and dominated by a 14th-century castle.

Information

In Passignano, the tourist office (☎ 075-82 76 35), Via Roma 36, can assist with accommodation and water sports and has a multitude of publications on the lake. In Castiglione del Lago, the tourist office (☎ 075-95 21 84), Piazza Mazzini 10, is open Monday to Friday from 8.30 am to 1 pm and 3 to 7 pm, as well as Saturday and Sunday mornings. It can advise on the many agriturismo options and point out good walking tracks.

The telephone code for the lake region is 075.

Things to See & Do

Water sports, walking and horse riding are the main reasons to visit the lake. Apart from the beautiful scenery, the only other attraction is Castiglione del Lago's **cathedral**, featuring several frescoes by Perugino.

The lake's only inhabited island, **Isola Maggiore**, near Passignano, was reputedly a favourite spot of St Francis. It can be reached by boat from the main towns, and although there are no camping grounds, you can pitch a tent. The island is noted for the production of lace and embroidery.

Ask at any of the tourist offices in the area for *Tourist Itineraries in the Trasimeno District*, a booklet of walking and horse riding tracks. If you want to go horse riding, you could contact the Maneggio Trasimeno (☎ 82 79 50) in San Donato about one km east of Passignano, or Poggio del

Belveduto (☎ 84 52 29) at Passignano. Both offer lessons and guided tours.

Places to Stay

Passignano Two camping grounds, the *Europa* (☎ 82 74 05) in San Donato, and the *Kursaal* (☎ 82 71 82), are near Passignano, and both charge L8000 per person and L8000 for a tent. *Del Pescatore* (☎ 82 71 65), Via San Bernardino 5, has singles/doubles from L45,000/65,000.

Castiglione del Lago The *Listro* camping ground (☎ 95 11 93), Via Lungolago, is open from April to September and has sites for L5500 per person and L6000 for a tent. Try *Elvira* (☎ 958 91 32), Via Trasimeno 192, which has doubles from L60,000. The *Vittoria* (☎ 95 10 71), Via della Stazione 5, has rooms from L55,000/75,000.

Getting There & Away

Passignano is close to the autostrada and is served by regular trains from Perugia and Terontola, making it the most accessible part of the lake. The ASP bus from Perugia to Tuoro, a few km west of Passignano, also stops here.

Castiglione del Lago is on the Florence-Rome train line, but make sure you board a local train as the Intercities don't stop there. You can also take the ASP bus from Perugia bound for Passignano.

Getting Around

SPNT (☎ 82 71 57) operates regular ferry services between the main towns. The company has information offices on the waterfront at each town, where you can pick up a timetable.

DERUTA

About 15 km south of Perugia, on the SS3bis connecting the city with Terni, is Deruta. The town is famed for its pottery, known for the richness of its colours and the intensity of its patterns. The Etruscans and later the Romans worked the clay around Deruta, but it was not until the majolica glazing technique, with its bright blue and yellow metallic oxides,

TONY WHEELER

TONY WHEELER

Top: Via Acqouedutto, Perugia, Umbria
om: Corso Vannucci, Perugia, Umbria

JOHN GILLMAN

DAMIEN SIMONIS

DAMIEN SIMONIS

JOHN GILLMAN

Top Left: Rooftops, Urbino, The Marches
Top Right: View of Piazza della Repubblica from Via V Veneto, Urbino, The Marches
Bottom Left: Piazza della Repubblica, Urbino, The Marches
Bottom Right: Wildflowers in the Monti Sibillini, The Marches

was imported from Majorca in the 15th century that the ceramics industry took off.

Commercialism has created a downside: many pieces are mass-produced and can be of poor quality. However, the pottery is still beautiful and Deruta is the place to buy it, as prices are lower than in Perugia and other towns. It is best to head into the town and browse through the large showrooms of the various pottery workshops.

ASP buses connect the town with Perugia.

TODI

Todi's reputation as one of the best-preserved medieval towns in Italy is well deserved. The small city was originally an Etruscan frontier settlement, then Roman, and then a *comune* in the early Middle Ages. It prospered during this period and boasts a perfect medieval square, the Piazza del Popolo.

Set atop a craggy hill, Todi seems to have ignored the 20th century, although tourist numbers are growing. The city is worth visiting, although getting there by public transport can be quite a slog.

Information

The APT del Tuderte (☎ 075-894 33 95) in Piazza Umberto I is open morning and late afternoon, and has information about the city and surrounding area.

The town's telephone code is 075.

Things to See

The 13th-century **Palazzo del Capitano** in Piazza del Popolo features an elegant triple window and houses the city's Pinacoteca and Museo Archeologico (both have been closed for restoration since 1977, and were expected to be reopened in late 1995). The square also features the 13th-century **Palazzo del Popolo** and the gloomy-looking **Palazzo dei Priori**.

The **duomo** at the north-western end of the square has a magnificent rose window and intricately decorated doorway. The 8th-century crypt is worth visiting for the inlaid wooden stalls in the chancel. The city has several churches worth visiting; spend an hour or so wandering through the medieval labyrinth.

Festivals

The Todi Festival, held each August and September, is a mixture of classical and jazz concerts, theatre, ballet and cinema.

Places to Stay & Eat

If you are planning to stay, expect to spend a lot of money on accommodation. For agriturismo, contact Agritop-Umbria (☎ 075-894 26 27), Via Paolo Rolli 3. The cheapest hotel in Todi is the *Tuder* (☎ 894 21 84), Via Maeta' dei Lombardi 13, with singles/doubles from L80,000/95,000. The *Villa Luisa* (☎ 894 85 71), Via A Cortesi 147, has rooms for L90,000/130,000.

The *Ristorante Umbria*, Via Santa Bonaventura 13, behind the tourist office, is reasonably expensive but worth it for the view from the terrace over the countryside.

Getting There & Away

ASP buses from Perugia terminate in Piazza Iacopone, just south of Piazza del Popolo. The city is on the Ferrovia Centrale Umbra line. The train station is inconveniently located three km from the town centre in the valley, although city bus No B makes connections. By road, the city is easily reached by taking the SS3bis between Perugia and Terni.

ASSISI

Despite the millions of tourists and pilgrims it attracts every year, the home town of St Francis manages to remain a beautiful and tranquil refuge. From Roman times its inhabitants have been aware of the visual impact of the city, perched halfway up Monte Subasio. From the valley its pink and white marble buildings shimmer in the sunlight.

St Francis was born here in 1182 and his spirit hovers over every aspect of the city's life. He renounced his father's wealth in his late teens to pursue a life of chastity and poverty, founding the order of mendicant friars known as the Order of Minors (the Franciscans after his death), which gained a huge following in Europe. One of his disciples, St Clare, born in 1193, was the founder

UMBRIA

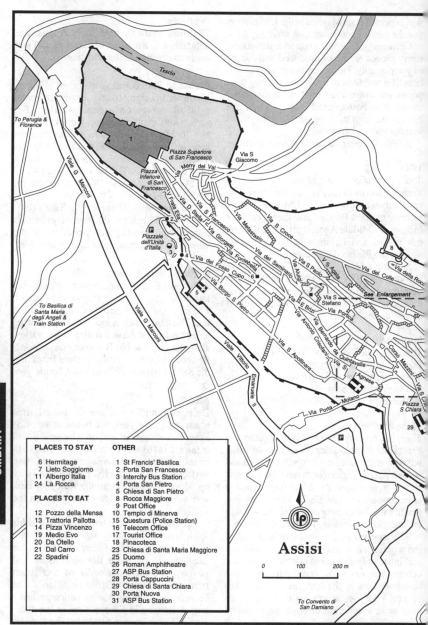

UMBRIA

PLACES TO STAY

6 Hermitage
7 Lieto Soggiorno
11 Albergo Italia
24 La Rocca

PLACES TO EAT

12 Pozzo della Mensa
13 Trattoria Pallotta
14 Pizza Vincenzo
19 Medio Evo
20 Da Otello
21 Dal Carro
22 Spadini

OTHER

1 St Francis' Basilica
2 Porta San Francesco
3 Intercity Bus Station
4 Porta San Pietro
5 Chiesa di San Pietro
8 Rocca Maggiore
9 Post Office
10 Tempio di Minerva
15 Questura (Police Station)
16 Telecom Office
17 Tourist Office
18 Pinacoteca
23 Chiesa di Santa Maria Maggiore
25 Duomo
26 Roman Amphitheatre
27 ASP Bus Station
28 Porta Cappuccini
29 Chiesa di Santa Chiara
30 Porta Nuova
31 ASP Bus Station

Assisi

0   100   200 m

To Convento di
San Damiano

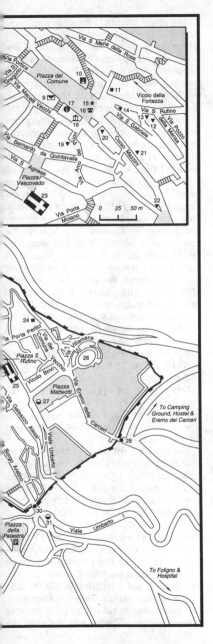

of the Franciscans' female Order of the Poor Clares.

St Francis' Basilica, started in 1228, two years after the saint's death, is the city's, and possibly Umbria's, main draw card. Don't be put off by the prospect of huge crowds: the basilica is definitely worth a visit. However, check before you visit Assisi that your trip doesn't coincide with a religious celebration, when hotels are likely to be booked out by pilgrims.

Orientation

Piazza del Comune is the centre of Assisi. At the north-western edge of this square, Via San Paolo and Via Portica eventually lead to St Francis' Basilica, although Via Portica is slightly more direct. Via Portica also leads to the Porta San Pietro and the Piazzale dell'Unità d'Italia, where most intercity buses stop, although ASP buses from smaller towns in the area terminate at Piazza Matteotti. In a southerly direction from Piazza del Comune, Corso Mazzini leads to Piazza Santa Chiara and eventually the Porta Nuova, while Via San Rufino leads to the duomo. The train station is four km south-west of the city, in Santa Maria degli Angeli; a shuttle-bus service runs every 30 minutes.

Information

Tourist Office The APT office (☎ 075-81 25 34), Piazza del Comune 12, is open Monday to Friday from 8 am to 2 pm and 3.30 to 6.30 pm and Saturday from 9 am to 1 pm and 3.30 to 6.30 pm and Sunday from 9 am to 1 pm. It has all the information you need on hotels, sights and events. There is a small branch office in Piazzale dell'Unità d'Italia.

Post & Telecommunications The main post office is in Piazza del Comune and is open Monday to Friday from 8.10 am to 6.25 pm and weekends to 1 pm. Poste restante mail can be addressed to 06081 Assisi.

A Telecom office, open daily from 8 am to 8 pm, is in the post office, and another is in Piazza del Comune, open daily from 8 am to 10 pm. The telephone code for Assisi is 075.

Emergency In an emergency, call ☎ 113. The questura (☎ 81 22 15) is in Piazza del Comune. The Ospedale di Assisi (☎ 813 91) is about one km south-east of the Porta Nuova, in Fuori Porta.

Things to See

Pilgrims and tourists crowd into Assisi year-round, but even in the busiest periods it is possible to escape the crush, which is usually confined to the main thorough-fares between the principal sights. Head into the back streets and you'll find yourself almost alone with the locals.

St Francis' Basilica (Basilica di San Francesco) The basilica comprises two churches, one built on top of the other. The lower church was started in 1228 and the upper church two years later, on a patch of land formerly know as the Hill of Hell because death sentences were carried out there. The two churches were erected as a compromise after dissent among the Franciscans, who protested against plans to build an enormous monument. Appropriately, the name of the hill was changed to Paradise Hill.

Entering the **upper church** from the picturesque Piazza Superiore di San Francesco, you are immediately overwhelmed by Giotto's famous sequence of 28 frescoes depicting the life of St Francis. There is actually strong disagreement among art scholars about whether or not the frescoes were painted by Giotto or by close followers of his style. Starting on the right wall near the altar and running clockwise around the church, the frescoes open with a young St Francis and finish with his ascension to heaven. Above the cycle is a series of 32 frescoes depicting scenes from the Old Testament, attributed to Pietro Cavallini.

Frescoes by Cimabue in the apse and transepts have badly deteriorated (a recent clean improved them only slightly), and the poor choice of pigment has left some looking like photographic negatives. They include the *Crucifixion*, *Visions of the Apocalypse*, *Life of the Virgin* and *Scenes from the Life of St Peter*.

The **lower church** is even more splendid than the upper, although quite poorly lit. Bring along quite a few L100, L200 and L500 coins for the slot machine to provide illumination. Its walls are also covered with frescoes. Those by Simone Martini showing the Life of St Martin, in the first chapel on the left as you face the altar, are the highlight.

Along the left wall of the left transept are celebrated frescoes by Pietro Lorenzetti depicting scenes of the Crucifixion and the life of St Francis. Above the main altar are beautiful frescoes depicting the virtues on which St Francis founded the Franciscan order – poverty, chastity and obedience. Originally thought to have been by Giotto, they are now attributed to one of his followers, dubbed the Maestro delle Vele. In the right transept are works by Cimabue, and below, more scenes by Simone Martini. A small chapel, reached by stairs on the right side of the church, features various artefacts of St Francis' life, including his shirt and sandals, and fragments of his famous *Canticle of the Creatures*. Descend the stairs in the middle of the church for the crypt with St Francis' tomb and those of four of his companions. The crypt was rediscovered in 1818; the coffin had been hidden in the 15th century for fear of desecration.

Dress rules are applied rigidly in the churches – absolutely no shorts, miniskirts or low-cut dresses. The complex is open daily from 6.30 am to 7 pm, although it is closed on religious holidays.

The Basilica's **Tesoreria** (Treasury), accessible from the lower church, contains a rich collection of relics given to the Franciscans over the years. It is open Monday to Saturday from 9.30 am to midday and 2 to 6 pm, April to October. Admission is L3000.

Other Sights From the basilica, take Via San Francesco back to Piazza del Comune, which was the site of the **Foro Romano**, parts of which have been excavated. Access is from Via Portica, and admission is L3000. The piazza also contains the **Tempio di Minerva**. It is now a church, but retains its impressive pillared façade. Wander into some of the shops on the piazza, which open their basements to reveal Roman ruins. The city's **Pinacoteca**, in the town hall on the southern side of the piazza, features Umbrian Renaissance art and frescoes from Giotto's school. It is open Monday to Saturday from 9.30 am to 1 pm and 3 to 7 pm, with slightly shorter hours on Sunday. Admission is L3000.

Off Via Bernardo da Quintavalle is Piazza Vescovado and the Romanesque **Chiesa di Santa Maria Maggiore**, formerly the city's cathedral and interesting for its rose window. South of Piazza del Comune along Corso Mazzini and Via Santa Chiara is the pink-and-white 13th-century Romanesque **Chiesa di Santa Chiara**, with a deteriorating but nonetheless impressive façade. The gruesome, blackened body of St Clare is in the crypt. Also in the church is the Byzantine crucifix said to have told St Francis to re-establish the moral foundations of the Church.

North-east of the church, in Piazza San Rufino, is the 13th-century Romanesque **duomo**, remodelled by Galeazzo Alessi in the 16th century and containing the font at which St Francis was baptised. The façade is decorated with grotesque figures and fantastic animals typical of this architectural style.

Dominating the city is the massive 14th-century **Rocca Maggiore**, a hill fortress offering fabulous views over the valley and Perugia. It is open daily from 9 am to 8 pm and admission is L3000, although most of the fortress is closed for a long restoration that will eventually create an immense art gallery.

A good 30-minute walk south from the Porta Nuova, or accessible by car from the Porta San Pietro, is the **Convento di San Damiano**, built on the spot where the crucifix spoke to St Francis and where he wrote his *Canticle of the Creatures*. The convent on the site was founded by St Clare.

About four km east of the city and reached via the Porta Cappuccini is the **Eremo dei Carceri** to which St Francis retreated after hearing the word of God. The carceri (prisons) are the caves which functioned as hermits' retreats for St Francis and

his followers. Apart from a few fences and tourist paths, everything has remained as it was in St Francis' time, and a few Franciscans actually live here.

In the valley south-west of the city, near the train station, is the **Basilica di Santa Maria degli Angeli**, a huge church built around the first Franciscan monastery. It features the **Cappella Transito**, where St Francis died in 1226.

Activities
The APT office has a map produced by the CAI of walks on nearby Monte Subasio (1290 metres). None is too demanding, and the smattering of religious shrines and camping grounds could make for an enjoyable couple of days.

Festivals
The Festival of St Francis falls on 3 and 4 October and is the main religious event of the city's calendar. Easter week is celebrated with processions and performances. The Ars Nova Musica festival is held from late August to mid-September and features local and national performers. The Festa di Calendimaggio celebrates May Day and the coming of spring.

Places to Stay
Assisi is well geared for tourists and there are numerous budget hotels and private rooms. Peak periods, when you will need to book well in advance, are Easter, August/September and the Festival of St Francis on 3 and 4 October. The tourist office has a full list of private rooms and religious institutions.

It is possible to stay at the Eremo dei Carceri and share the austere conditions with the Franciscan monks who live there. Call the hermitage on ☎ 81 23 01 before you arrive in Italy. You must have a letter of recommendation from your parish priest. They usually accept only one or two people at a time.

There is a non-HI *hostel* and *camping ground* just east of town at Fontemaggio (☎ 81 36 36 for both), reached by walking about two km uphill along Via Eremo delle

UMBRIA

Carceri. Beds at the hostel are L16,000 and sites start at L6000 a person. The HI youth hostel, the *Ostello della Pace* (☎ 81 67 67), Via Valecchie 171, is open all year. B&B is L18,000, or L19,000 in family rooms. It is on the bus line between Santa Maria degli Angeli and Assisi.

La Rocca (☎ 81 22 84), Via Porta Perlici 27, has singles/doubles for L30,000/46,000 and half board for up to L58,000 per person. *Albergo Italia* (☎ 81 26 25), Vicolo della Fortezza, just off Piazza del Comune, has singles/doubles for L30,000/44,000, or L40,000/60,000 with a bathroom. The two-star *Lieto Soggiorno* (☎ 81 61 91), Via A Fortini 26, near Piazza del Comune, has singles for L38,000 and doubles with a bathroom for L90,000. The three-star *Hermitage* (☎ 81 27 64), Via degli Aromatari 1, off Via Fontebella, has rooms from L70,000/110,000 and offers car parking.

Places to Eat
For pizza by the slice head for *Pizza Vincenzo*, Via San Rufino 1a. In the same complex as the camping ground at Fontemaggio is *La Stalla*, where you can eat a filling meal under an arbour for about L25,000. The restaurant at La Rocca hotel has home-made pasta from L6000. *Dal Carro*, Vicolo Nepis 2, off Corso Mazzini, has cheap pasta, while *Da Otello*, Piazzetta Chiesa Nuova, has the cheapest pizzas in town. For some traditional cooking, try *Spadini*, Via Sant' Agnese 6, where a good meal will cost L25,000. Try also *Trattoria Pallotta*, Via San Rufino 4, where a meal will cost from L25,000 to L30,000. *Pozzo della Mensa*, Via Pozzo della Mensa 11, also specialises in Umbrian food. One of the better restaurants is *Medio Evo*, Via Arco dei Priori 4, where an excellent meal will cost about L50,000.

Getting There & Away
ASP buses connect Assisi with Perugia, Foligno and other local towns, leaving from Piazza Matteotti. ASP buses also terminate in Piazza Matteotti and most of them also stop in Largo Properzio, just outside the Porta Nuova. Piazzale dell'Unità d'Italia is the terminus for buses for Rome, Florence and other major cities.

Assisi's train station is in the valley at Santa Maria degli Angeli, four km southwest of the city. It is on the Foligno-Terontola line and is about 35 minutes from Perugia. Change at Terontola for Florence and at Foligno for Rome.

By car, take the SS75 from Perugia, exit at Ospedalicchio and follow the signs. The largest and most convenient car park is near the Porta San Pietro.

Getting Around
A shuttle-bus service operates between Assisi and the train station, with departures every 30 minutes. Normal traffic is banned from the city centre, and buses depart every 20 minutes from all external parking areas to the major monuments.

SPELLO
Spello's proximity to both Perugia and Assisi makes it well worth a quick morning or afternoon trip. Emperor Augustus developed much of the land in the valley, but the Roman ruins are some distance from the town and your time would be better spent wandering Spello's narrow cobbled streets.

There is a small tourist office at Via Garibaldi 17, although if you are coming from Assisi, you can pick up better information from the APT office there.

The Augustan gate, the **Porta Venere**, leads to the **Chiesa di Sant'Andrea**, with frescoes by Bernardino Pinturicchio. Nearby is the 12th-century **Chiesa di Santa Maria Maggiore**, and the town's main sight, Pinturicchio's beautiful frescoes in the Cappella Baglioni and a pavement (dating from 1566) made of tiles from Deruta.

The people of Spello celebrate the feast of Corpus Domini on 21 July by decorating a long stretch of the main street with fresh flowers in colourful designs.

Hotels tend to be expensive and there are cheaper options in Assisi and Perugia. Try *Il Cacciatore* (☎ 65 11 41), Via Giulia 42, which has singles/doubles with a bathroom for

L65,000/85,000. It also has a restaurant with a large terrazza, perfect for a summer lunch.

ASP buses running between Perugia and Foligno serve the town, and there are also connections to Assisi. An irregular train service connects the town with Perugia and Terni, and buses operate between the station in the valley and the town. By car, Spello is on the SS75 which runs between Perugia and Foligno.

GUBBIO

Perched on the steep slopes of Monte Ingino, overlooking a picturesque valley, Gubbio looks as if time has passed it by. The ochre colouring of its stone buildings, the tint of the Romanesque tiled roofs and the absence of trees from the paved streets make it possible to imagine you have just stepped into the Middle Ages.

The city is famous for its Eugubian Tables, which date from the 3rd century BC and feature the best existing example of ancient Umbrian script. The city was an important ally of imperial Rome and a key stop on the Via Flaminia, but declined during the barbarian invasions. In the 14th century it fell into the hands of the Montefeltro family of Urbino and was later incorporated into the Papal States.

One of the town's main attractions is the Corsa dei Ceri, an annual religious event in which local men carry huge wooden candles *(ceri)* in a frenetic race uphill. Like many other hill towns in Tuscany and the Marches, Gubbio has taken on the feel of a museum. The city is worth visiting, although there is not a lot to keep you here for more than a day trip.

Orientation

The city is small and easy to explore. The immense traffic circle known as Piazza Quaranta Martiri, at the base of the hill, is where buses to the city terminate, and it also has a large car park. It was named in honour of 40 local people who were killed by the Nazis during the war. From here, it is a short walk along Via della Repubblica for the main square, Piazza Grande, also known as the

Piazza della Signoria, which is set like a ledge into the hill. Corso Garibaldi and Piazza Oderisi are to your right as you head up the hill.

Information

The APT tourist office (☎ 075-922 06 93) in Piazza Oderisi produces a good street map and can assist with accommodation. It is open Monday to Saturday from 8 am to midday and 3.30 to 6.30 pm and Sunday from 9.30 am to 12.30 pm. There is also an information office on Via della Repubblica, near Piazza Quaranta Martiri.

The main post office is at Via Cairoli 11 and is open Monday to Saturday from 8.15 am to 7 pm. The Telecom office is at Easy Gubbio, Via della Repubblica 13, and the telephone code for Gubbio is 075.

For police emergencies, call ☎ 113, or contact the questura (☎ 927 37 31) at Via Perugina. The Ospedale Civile (☎ 9 23 91) is in Piazza Quaranta Martiri.

Things to See

The **Chiesa di San Francesco**, in Piazza Quaranta Martiri is attributed to Perugia's Fra Bevignate and features impressive frescoes by a local artist, Ottaviano Nelli. The **museum** in the adjoining convent features a collection of sacred art, as well as Greek and Apulian ceramics. Ask one of the attendants to let you in. Admission is free.

From the piazza, follow Via della Repubblica up the hill to **Piazza Grande**, also known as Piazza della Signoria, which features the city's grandest group of buildings. It's dominated by the 14th-century **Palazzo dei Consoli**, attributed to Gattapone. The crenellated façade and tower can be seen from most parts of the city.

The building houses the **Museo Civico**, with the *Eugubian Tables*, discovered in 1444 near the Roman theatre west of Piazza Quaranta Martiri. The seven bronze tablets date from 300 to 100 BC and are the main source for research into the ancient Umbrian language. Upstairs is the picture gallery, which features works from the Gubbian school. The museum and gallery

UMBRIA

are open daily from 9 am to 1 pm and 3 to 7 pm from October to March, with slightly shorter hours for the rest of the year. Admission is L5000. Across the square is the **Palazzo Pretorio**, built along similar lines to its grander counterpart the Palazzo dei Consoli and now the city's town hall.

Via Ducale leads up to the 13th-century pink **duomo**, featuring a fine 12th-century stained glass window, and a fresco attributed to Bernardino Pinturicchio. The **Palazzo Ducale** opposite was built by the Montefeltro family as a scaled-down version of their grand palace in Urbino, and features an impressive Renaissance courtyard. It should reopen in late 1993 after restoration.

From Piazza Grande, Via dei Consoli leads north-west to the 13th-century **Palazzo del Bargello**, the city's medieval police station and prison, and in front of it is the **Fontana dei Pazzi**, so named because of a traditional belief that if you walk around it three times, you will go mad. At Via San Giuliano 3, just south of Palazzo Bargello, is the **Antica Fabbrica Artigiana**, a former palace and now a gallery-cum-shop for ceramic artisans – one of Gubbio's main industries during the Middle Ages.

South of Piazza Quaranta Martiri, off Viale del Teatro Romano, are the remains of a 1st-century AD **Roman theatre**. Not much of this reconstructed edifice is original, but it's still an impressive sight.

There is a funicular station in Via San Gerolamo from which you can ride the curious birdcage funicular to the **Basilica di Sant'Ubaldo**, an uninspiring church which houses the three candles used during the Corsa dei Ceri.

Festivals

The Corsa dei Ceri is held each year on 15 May. The event starts at 5.30 am and involves three teams, each carrying a *cero* (these 'candles' are actually massive wooden pillars) and racing through the city's streets. It is all very complicated, but there is lots of festivity, all intended to commemorate the city's patron saint, St Ubaldo.

This is one of Italy's most lively festivals and certainly warrants inclusion in your itinerary, but be wary if you have small children with you as the crowd can become very excited and scuffles between the supporters of the three 'competitors' are quite common.

Places to Stay

Many locals rent rooms to tourists, so ask at the APT office about private rooms. For camping, try the *Città di Gubbio* (☎ 927 20 37) in Ortoguidone, a southern suburb of Gubbio, about three km south of Piazza Quaranta Martiri along the SS298 (the Via Perugina).

The cheapest hotel is *Galletti* (☎ 927 77 53), Via Piccardi 1, which has singles/doubles from L38,000/60,000. The *Grotta dell'Angelo* (☎ 927 17 47), Via Gioia 47, has rooms from L49,000/75,000, as does the *Dei Consoli* (☎ 927 33 35), Via dei Consoli 59. The *San Marco* (☎ 922 02 34), Via Perugina 5, has rooms from L85,000/110,000.

Out of town on the state road connecting Gubbio and Perugia is *Oasi Verde Mengara* (☎ 92 01 56). It's an agriturismo establishment, where half board costs L65,000 and full board L75,000. Its fine restaurant is open to the public and you can eat a memorable and very filling meal for around L30,000. Oasi Verdi Mengara is easily accessible from Gubbio on the regular ASP bus which connects Gubbio and Perugia. It stops right outside the hotel/restaurant.

Places to Eat

If you want to try some local specialities, *Ristorante San Martino*, Piazza Giordano Bruno, occasionally features traditional dishes at a reasonable price. Pasta starts at L6000. *Il Giardino*, Piazza Quaranta Martiri, is also quite cheap and a meal could cost L25,000. *Fabiani*, in the same piazza, is a good, traditional trattoria and a meal will cost L30,000.

One of the better restaurants, *Alla Fornace di Maestro Giorgio*, in Via Maestro Giorgio, is also one of the more expensive, with main courses starting at L15,000.

The *Tipici Prodotti Gastronomici* shop, Via dei Consoli 41, features a wide range of locally produced foods and wines.

Getting There & Away

ASP buses (☎ 927 15 44) connect the city with Perugia (nine a day), Fossato di Vico, Gualdo Tadino and Umbertide, and the company operates daily services to Rome and Florence. Most buses stop in Piazza Quaranta Martiri, but some terminate at the bus station (☎ 927 39 27) in Via San Lazzaro.

Gubbio is not on a train line; the closest station is at Fossato di Vico, about 20 km south-east of the city. Trains connect with Rome and Ancona, Perugia, Terontola, Arezzo and Florence. ASP buses connect Gubbio with the station, usually an hour before each train.

By car and motorbike, take the SS298 from Perugia, or the SS76 from Ancona, and follow the signs. There is a large car park in Piazza Quaranta Martiri, which costs L1000 an hour.

Getting Around

The easiest way is to walk around this small city, although ASP buses connect Piazza Quaranta Martiri with the funicular station and most main sights.

AROUND GUBBIO

The area east of Gubbio, the **Parco Regionale del Monte Cucco** , is a veritable haven for outdoor activities and is dotted with caves, many of which can be explored. It is well set up for walkers, rock climbers and horse riders and has many hotels and mountain rifugi. **Costacciaro**, reached by bus from Gubbio, is a good base for exploring the area, and is the starting point for a walk to the summit of Monte Cucco (1566 metres).

Information is available from the APT office in Gubbio. The Centro Operativo della Scuola Nazionale di Speleologia del Club Alpino Italiano (☎ 075-917 02 36), Corso Mazzini 9, in Costacciaro, can help with information about exploring local caves. The CAI also produces a walking map entitled *Carta dei Sentieri Massiccio del Monte Cucco*.

It is possible to rent mountain bikes in Costacciaro at the local swimming pool (☎ 075-917 06 18) from L25,000 a day.

There are several horse-riding schools around Gubbio that arrange lessons or treks. Rio Verde (☎ 075-917 01 38) is just north of the city in a small town called Fornace. A farm where you can stay is the *Azienda Agraria Allevamento San Giovanni* (☎ 075-925 66 46), south-east at Torre Calzolari. Ask for directions when you arrive in these towns.

SPOLETO

Each June and July, this normally quiet medieval hill town takes centre stage for a parade of cultural and often snobbish sophistication, the Festival dei Due Mondi. The Italian-American composer Gian Carlo Menotti, with his Amercian Thomas Schippers, set up the festival in Spoleto in 1958 after inspecting more than 30 other towns for their suitability. It has given the city a worldwide reputation and has brought great wealth to the small population who bask in the glory of this international celebration of drama, music and dance.

If you are planning to visit Spoleto during the festival, ensure that you book accommodation and tickets months in advance. If you want to make day trips during the festival, the only problem you will have is finding a place to park your car. See the following Festivals section for more details.

The town is enchanting and is well worth a visit for its medieval architecture, well-preserved Roman remains and many art treasures.

Orientation

The older part of the city is the most interesting and there is no real reason to wander into the newer section, unless you arrive by train. The main train station is half a km north of the city wall, in the centre of the newer area. Buses connect the train station with the older areas and walking between the two sections will mean an uphill climb along Viale Trento e Trieste. Jump on a bus to Piazza della Libertà near the southern end of the old city,

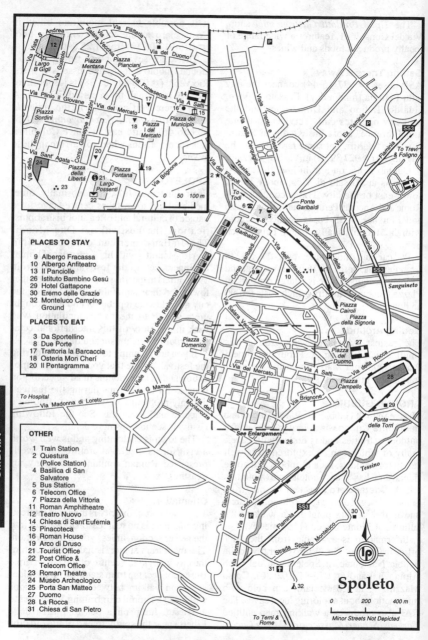

PLACES TO STAY

9 Albergo Fracassa
10 Albergo Anfiteatro
13 Il Panciolle
26 Istituto Bambino Gesú
29 Hotel Gattapone
30 Eremo delle Grazie
32 Monteluco Camping Ground

PLACES TO EAT

3 Da Sportellino
8 Due Porte
17 Trattoria la Barcaccia
18 Osteria Mon Cherí
20 Il Pentagramma

OTHER

1 Train Station
2 Questura (Police Station)
4 Basilica di San Salvatore
5 Bus Station
6 Telecom Office
7 Piazza della Vittoria
11 Roman Amphitheatre
12 Teatro Nuovo
14 Chiesa di Sant'Eufemia
15 Pinacoteca
16 Roman House
19 Arco di Druso
21 Tourist Office
22 Post Office & Telecom Office
23 Roman Theatre
24 Museo Archeologico
25 Porta San Matteo
27 Duomo
28 La Rocca
31 Chiesa di San Pietro

Spoleto

where you can buy a map of the city's confusing jumble of medieval streets and lanes.

From Piazza della Libertà, Corso Giuseppe Mazzini heads north to Piazza Mentana and the adjacent Piazza Pianciani. South-east along Via Fontesecca and Via A Saffi are a cluster of piazzas: Piazza del Mercato to the south and Piazza del Duomo and Piazza della Signoria to the east. Although the city lacks a distinct central square, Piazza del Mercato is a hub for social activities and features many food shops with a variety of local products.

Information

Tourist Office The APT office (☎ 0743-22 03 11), Piazza della Libertà 7, has loads of information about the town and surrounding area. It is open Monday to Saturday from 9 am to 1 pm and 3.30 to 6.30 pm (opening one hour later on Saturday) and Sunday from 10 am to 1 pm.

Post & Telecommunications The main post office faces Piazza della Libertà, although the entrance is off Viale Giacomo Matteotti. It is open Monday to Saturday from 8.30 am to 12.30 pm and 3 to 7 pm. The post code for the town centre is 06049.

The Telecom office is at Via dei Filosofi and there are telephones in most of the city's bars and at the post office. The telephone code for Spoleto is 0743.

Emergency In an emergency, call ☎ 113. The questura (☎ 4 90 44) is at Via dei Filosofi 57. The Ospedale di Madonna di Loreto (☎ 60 11) is on Via Madonna di Loreto, west of the Porta San Matteo.

Things to See

Pick up a map and walking itinerary from the APT office, and make the **Roman theatre** on the western edge of Piazza della Libertà your first stop. The 1st-century theatre has been rebuilt many times and is used for performances in summer. The **Museo Archeologico** next to the theatre is worth visiting, mainly because it's free, but also for its ceramic collection. The theatre and museum are open Monday to Saturday from 9 am to 1.30 pm and 3 to 7 pm and Sunday to 1 pm.

East of Piazza della Libertà, around Piazza Fontana, are more Roman ruins, including the **Arco di Druso**, which marked the entrance to the old forum. On Via di Visiale is an excavated **Roman house** dating from the 1st century AD. The house is open daily, except Monday, from 10 am to 1 pm and 3 to 6 pm and admission is L1000. The city also boasts a **Roman amphitheatre**, one of the country's largest, although it is enclosed within a military barracks and is closed to the public. Wander along Via dell' Anfiteatro, off Piazza Garibaldi, for a glimpse.

A short walk through Piazza del Municipio takes you to the 12th-century **Chiesa di Sant'Eufemia** in the grounds of the Archbishop's palace. The church is notable for its *matronea*, women's galleries set high above the main body of the church to segregate women from the congregation. It features frescoes by artists from the 15th-century Sienese school.

From here, it is a short stroll to the **duomo**, which was consecrated in 1198 and remodelled in the 17th century. The Romanesque façade is fronted by a Renaissance porch, and the central rose window is framed by the symbols of the Evangelists. Huge blocks of stone to the left of the church were salvaged from Roman buildings and used during the 11th century to build the unassuming bell tower. Inside, the first chapel to the right of the nave was decorated by Bernardino Pinturicchio, and Annibale Carracci completed an impressive fresco in the right transept. The domed apse features frescoes by Filippo Lippi and his assistants. Lippi died before completing the work, and Lorenzo de Medici travelled to Spoleto from Florence and ordered Lippi's son, Filippino, to build a mausoleum for the artist. This now stands in the right transept of the cathedral.

A couple of other features in Piazza del Duomo are the Spoleto Shop, which opens during the festival and sells posters, T-shirts etc and, at No 8, the house where composer Gian Carlo Menotti was born.

The **Pinacoteca** is in the town hall in Piazza del Municipio and was recently renovated. Unfortunately, you must be guided around the gallery, although the sumptuous building and some impressive works by Umbrian artists make a visit worthwhile. It is open daily, except Tuesday, from 10 am to 1 pm and 3 to 6 pm. Admission is L5000.

Dominating the city is **La Rocca**, a former papal fortress which, until recently, was one of the country's highest security prisons, housing such notables as Pope John Paul II's attempted assassin, Ali Agca. It is currently closed for restorations that started around 1976 and are expected to keep the building off limits for several more years.

Along Via del Ponte is the **Ponte delle Torri**, which dates from the 14th century although it was built on the foundations of a Roman aqueduct. The bridge is named after the towers on the far side.

If you feel like a walk, cross the bridge and follow the lower path, Strada di Monteluco, for the **Chiesa di San Pietro**. If a long walk doesn't appeal to you, follow Via del Ponte around La Rocca and back into Spoleto. San Pietro's 13th-century façade, the church's main attraction, features many sculpted animals.

Festivals

Events at the Festival dei Due Mondi, held in June and July, range from cinema and theatre to ballet and art exhibitions. Tickets cost from L10,000 to L200,000, depending on the performance and whether you want luxury seats or standing room, and generally sell out by March.

The festival has a ticket office in Rome (☎ 06-323 48 90) at Piazza Gentile da Fabriano 15, as well as a general office (☎ 321 02 88), Via Cesare Beccaria 18; in Spoleto, tickets can be purchased at the Teatro Nuovo (☎ 4 40 97) in Largo B Gigli.

Bookings can be made outside Italy, by writing to the Spoleto office: Biglietteria Festival dei Due Mondi, c/o Teatro Nuovo, 06049 Spoleto, Italy. You will first need to contact the office for a programme.

Places to Stay

The city is well served with cheap hotels, private rooms, hostels and camping grounds, although if you're going for the festival you will need to book a room months in advance. At other times, when the town reverts to its normal self as a sleepy medieval hill town, you should have no problem.

The closest camping ground is *Monteluco* (☎ 0743-22 03 58), just behind the Chiesa di San Pietro, open from April to September. It charges L5000 per person and L6500 for a tent. *Camping Il Girasole* (☎ 0743-5 13 35) is about 10 km north-west of Spoleto in Petrognano. Buses connect with the town from Spoleto's train station.

There are also agriturismo options around Spoleto. The tourist office has a booklet with all the details.

The *Istituto Bambino Gesù* (☎ 4 02 32) is a religious hostel, just behind the APT at Via Monterone 4; it has singles/doubles for L40,000/80,000.

The best hotel is *Albergo Fracassa* (☎ 22 11 77), Via Focaroli 15, which has singles/doubles for L30,000/40,000. *Albergo Anfiteatro* (☎ 4 98 53), Via dell'Anfiteatro 14, has rooms from L43,000/60,000. *Il Panciolle* (☎ 4 55 98), Via del Duomo 3, is in a good location and has rooms with a bathroom from L55,000/80,000.

One of the best located hotels is *Hotel Gattapone* (☎ 22 34 47) at Via del Ponte 6, overlooking Ponte delle Torri, which has rooms from L130,000/160,000.

Places to Eat

Spoleto is one of Umbria's main producers of tartufo nero (black truffles), and they are used in a variety of dishes. However, trying them can be a costly exercise. *Due Porte*, Piazza della Vittoria 14, is a good, cheap restaurant which serves local dishes. Pasta costs from L7000. *Taverna dei Duchi*, Via A Saffi 1, offers a L25,000 tourist menu, as well as a set menu of local dishes for L40,000 and a menu al tartufo for L70,000. It also serves pizzas. Da Sportellino, Viale della Cerquiglia 4, has main courses from L5000.

Trattoria la Barcaccia, Piazza Fratelli Bandiera 2, offers a L20,000 tourist menu.

You can get pizza by the slice from *Pizzeria dell'Orologia* in Piazza del Mercato and a great ice cream from *Gelateria Primavera*, opposite at No 6. The *American Bar* in Piazza del Duomo is one of the city's best bars.

Getting There & Away
Società Spoletina Trasporti (SSIT) buses (☎ 21 22 11) depart from Piazza della Vittoria for Monteluco, Foligno, Terni, Rome, Bastardo, Assisi, Perugia and dozens of smaller towns. Trains from the main station (☎ 4 85 16), Piazza Polvani, connect with Rome, Ancona and Perugia. The city is on the SS3 which runs from Terni to Foligno, basically the old Roman Via Flaminia. From Terni, it's a short trip to the A1. Car parks are located at all main approaches to the city.

Getting Around
The city is easily seen on foot, although local buses weave through the streets. Bus Circolare C connects the train station with Piazza della Libertà and Circolare D runs between the station and Piazza Garibaldi.

THE VALNERINA
Incorporating most of the lower eastern parts of Umbria, along the Nera river, the Valnerina is a beautiful area. Stretching north to the barren summit of Monte Sibilla (2175 metres) in the neighbouring Marches, the

The European wild boar: while not usually aggressive, they can be dangerous.

area is a haven for walkers. It also offers a couple of hang-gliding schools in one of the best areas in Europe to learn.

If you want to spend a few quiet days wandering around the valley, try the hotel *Agli Scacchi* (☎ 0743-9 92 21), a pleasant little establishment at the pretty medieval village of **Preci**. It has doubles for L75,000 and half board for L65,000 per person.

The area is crisscrossed by walking trails and you might try to pick up a copy of the aptly titled *20 Sentieri Ragionati in Valnerina* (20 Well-Thought-Out Routes in Valnerina).

If you are driving, the APT Valnerina-Cascia (☎ 0743-7 14 01), Via Vespasia Polla 1, in Cascia, is a good place to start. Tourist bodies in Umbria and the Marches have erected road signs on the roadside which identify driving itineraries.

Getting There & Away
Spoleto is the best point from which to head into the Valnerina. Spoleto's SSIT bus company (☎ 0743-21 22 11) operates several buses a day to the terminal at Via della Stazione in Norcia, which then have connecting bus services along the Valnerina to Preci and Cascia. Getting to Castelluccio is not so easy. There are services from Norcia on Monday and Saturday only and then only two per day.

By car, the SS395 from Spoleto and SS209 from Terni connect with the SS320 and then the SS396, which passes through Norcia. The area can also be reached from Ascoli Piceno in the Marches.

Norcia
This fortified medieval village is the main town in the valley and a transport hub of sorts. Like the rest of the Valnerina, it has suffered badly from earthquakes over the centuries. It produces what is considered to be the country's best salami. There is a small tourist office in the central Piazza San Benedetto.

Activities Fly Castellucci (☎ 0743-87 02 09), Via del Pian Perduto, can arrange hang-gliding, mountain trekking and winter skiing, and can rent mountain bikes and horses. On offer is a five-day hang-gliding course from L550,000 for beginners or more advanced gliders, and the school can arrange high flights. Pupils can also get accommodation on site for L10,000 a night, with their own sleeping bag.

Places to Stay *Da Benito* (☎ 0743-81 66 70), Via Marconi 5, has rooms from L45,000 /70,000. The *Garden* (☎ 81 67 26), Via XX Settembre 2, has rooms for L70,000/100,000.

Around Norcia

If you have a car, don't miss the opportunity to visit the vast **Piano Grande** north-east of Norcia, under Monte Vettore (2476 metres). It becomes a sea of colour as flowers bloom in early spring.

Perched above the plain is the tiny hilltop village of **Castelluccio**. If you want to stay overnight, there is a small hotel here, the *Sibilla* (☎ 0743-87 01 13), Via Piano Grande 2. Singles/doubles are L50,000/70,000. There is also a free camping ground just outside Castelluccio at Monte Prata (☎ 0737-98 28), which opens from 15 June for the summer months.

The area forms part of the new Parco Nazionale dei Monti Sibillini and there are lots of activities in the area. You can buy a map of walking trails (Kompass 1:50,000, No 666, Monti Sibillini) and head into the Monti Sibillini. If you want to learn hang-gliding, contact the Scuola di volo libero Pro Delta (☎ 0743-87 01 57). It is a very popular area for mountain-bike riding.

TERNI

Terni is a major industrial city, and as such, was virtually obliterated in WW II bombing raids. The city is also the birthplace of St Valentine, who was bishop of Terni until his martyrdom in 273 AD. If you're travelling by public transport, you may need to pass through here on your way to the Valnerina, Norcia and the Monti Sibillini.

Terni's tourist office (☎ 0744-4 30 47) is south of the main train station, on Viale della Stazione and just west of Piazza C Tacito at Viale Cesare Battisti 7, near Largo Don Minzoni. It is closed during the middle of the day and is not open on Sundays.

If you arrive in Terni by train and need to get to the bus station in Piazza Europa, or vice versa, catch bus No 1 or 2.

Cascate delle Marmore

About six km east of Terni, this waterfall was created by the Romans in 270 BC when they diverted the Velino river into the Nera river. These days, the waterfall provides hydroelectric power and its flow is confined to certain times of the day. It is worth catching a bus to see it, particularly to witness the arrival of the water after it has been switched on. The falls operate most nights between 5 and 6.30 pm, and a sound-and-light show has been installed which illuminates the water. Whenever the fall is switched on, the SS79 road connecting Terni with Rome resembles a car park as drivers stop to watch the spectacle. It is a good idea to check with the Terni tourist office on the operating times of the falls. Catch local bus No 24 to get to the falls.

ORVIETO

Orvieto's magnificent duomo is one of Italy's finest Gothic buildings and the town's main tourist attraction. The town is perched on top of a craggy cliff, pretty much in the same spot as its Etruscan precursor, Velsina, which was an Etruscan League city. It is picturesque but gets very crowded with tourists in the high season, especially at weekends. As well as the attraction of the duomo and medieval town, there are Etruscan tombs.

Orientation

The modern town at the base of the hill, known as Orvieto Scalo, offers little more than the train station. From here you can catch bus No 1 up to the old town, or catch the funicular railway which connects the station with Piazza Cahen, from where you can walk straight ahead along Corso Cavour, turning left into Via del Duomo to reach the duomo. It is possible to drive up to the old city and park in the large parking areas outside the city wall. There's also plenty of parking in Piazza Cahen.

Information

The APT office (☎ 0763-4 17 72) is at Piazza del Duomo 24 and is open Monday to Saturday from 10 am to 2 pm and 4 to 7 pm and Sunday from 10 am to midday and 4 to 6 pm. The post office is at Via Cesare Nebbia, off Corso Cavour, and is open Monday to Saturday from 8.30 am to 6.30 pm. The post code for the town centre is 05018. Telecom card dispensers and phones are west of the entrance to the Museo dell'Opera del Duomo, beside the APT. The telephone code for Orvieto is 0763.

In an emergency, call ☎ 113, or contact the questura (☎ 4 00 88) in Piazza Cahen. The hospital (☎ 4 20 71) is in Piazza del Duomo.

Duomo

This memorable building has a remarkable façade, so colourful and precisely decorated that it has been compared to a giant altar screen. Started in 1290, the cathedral was originally planned in the Romanesque style, but as work proceeded and architects changed, Gothic features were incorporated into the structure.

Pope Urban IV ordered the cathedral built after the so-called 'Miracle of Bolsena', which occurred in 1263 in the nearby town of Bolsena. A Bohemian priest, who was passing through the town, had doubts about transubstantiation but, while celebrating Mass, his uncertainty was dispelled when blood started dripping from the Host onto the altar linen. The linen was presented to Pope Urban IV, in Orvieto at the time, who declared the event a miracle and set the wheels in motion for the construction of the cathedral. He also declared the new feast day of Corpus Domini.

The building took 30 years to plan and three centuries to complete. It was probably started by Perugia's Fra Bevignate and continued by Lorenzo Maitani – responsible for Florence's duomo – Andrea Pisano, Nino Pisano, Andrea Orcagna and Michele Sammichelli.

The **façade** was unveiled in 1995 after restoration work. With its colourful mosaics and spiky pinnacles, it really is a remarkable sight and appears completely unrelated to the black-and-white striped marble church behind it. The three huge doorways are separated by fluted columns and the gables are decorated with mosaics which, although mostly reproductions, are stunning, particularly when the sun is shining on the façade, or at night under spotlights. The area between the doorways features 14th-century bas-reliefs of scriptural scenes by Maitani and his pupils. The rose window is by Andrea Orcagna.

After the splendour of the exterior, the interior can be something of a disappointment. Banded by black and white marble, the cathedral features impressive 14th-century stained glass windows. The **Cappella del Corporale** houses the blood-stained linen, preserved in a silver reliquary, decorated by artists of the Sienese school. The walls feature frescoes by Ugolino di Prete Ilario depicting the miracle. In the **Cappella Nuova** is Luca Signorelli's magnificent fresco of the *Last Judgment*. Signorelli worked on it from 1499, and it's believed it had a great influence on Michelangelo, who painted the Sistine Chapel cycle 40 years later. Restoration is expected to be completed by early 1996. Also in the chapel are ceiling frescoes by Fra Angelico. The cathedral closes during the middle of the day.

Other Sights

Next to the cathedral, in the **Palazzo dei Papi**, is the **Museo dell'Opera del Duomo**, which features religious relics from the cathedral, as well as Etruscan antiquities and works by artists such as Simone Martini and the three Pisanos: Andrea, Nono and Giovanni. The museum is closed indefinitely for restoration works. Also in the palace is the **Museo di Emilio Greco**, a museum of modern art which is well worth a visit. It was at this palace, in 1527, that Pope Clement VII rejected Henry VIII's plea for divorce from Catherine of Aragon and inadvertently set

UMBRIA

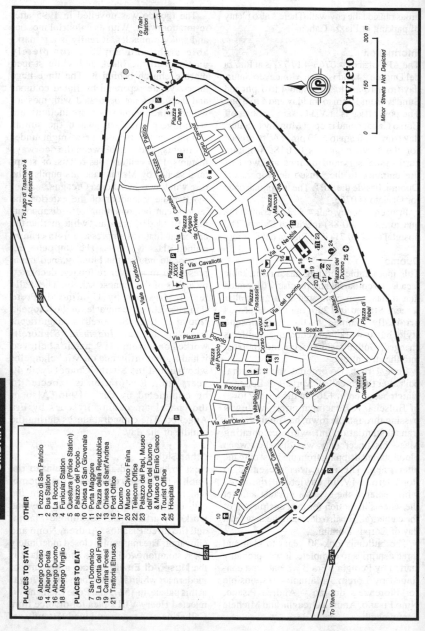

PLACES TO STAY

6 Albergo Corso
14 Albergo Posta
16 Albergo Duomo
18 Albergo Virgilio

PLACES TO EAT

7 San Domenico
9 La Grotta del Funaro
19 Cantina Foresi
21 Trattoria Etrusca

OTHER

1 Pozzo di San Patrizio
2 Bus Station
3 La Rocca
4 Funicular Station
5 Questura (Police Station)
8 Palazzo del Popolo
10 Chiesa di San Giovenale
11 Porta Maggiore
12 Piazza della Repubblica
13 Chiesa di Sant'Andrea
15 Post Office
17 Duomo
20 Museo Civico Faina
22 Telecom Office
23 Palazzo dei Papi, Museo
    dell'Opera del Duomo
    & Museo di Emilio Greco
24 Tourist Office
25 Hospital

Orvieto

0   150   300 m

Minor Streets Not Depicted

To Train Station

To Lago di Trasimeno &
A1 Autostrada

SS71

SS71

To Viterbo

in motion the foundation of the Church of England.

The **Museo Civico Faina**, in the nearby Palazzo Faina, has a collection of Etruscan vases and other relics, found in 6th-century BC tombs near Piazza Cahen. It was also closed in 1995 for restoration, but was expected to be reopened by the end of the year.

Head back to Corso Cavour and turn left for Piazza della Repubblica. On the way is the 12th-century **Chiesa di Sant'Andrea**. As with many Italian churches, it was built over a Roman structure, which in turn had incorporated an Etruscan building. It is possible to head down into the crypt to take a look at these ancient foundations. The piazza was the site of the ancient Roman forum, and the surrounding area is Orvieto's most authentic medieval quarter.

North of Corso Cavour is the Piazza del Popolo and the 13th-century **Palazzo del Popolo**, built in the Romanesque-Gothic style. At the north-western end of town is the 11th-century **Chiesa di San Giovenale**, its interior decorated with 13th and 14th-century frescoes by local artists.

At the town's easternmost tip is the 14th-century **Rocca**, part of which is now a public garden. Below the fortress is the **Pozzo di San Patrizio**, a well sunk in 1527 on the orders of Pope Clement VII to ensure the city had a supply of water in case of siege. It is open daily from 10 am to 7 pm and admission is L5000.

Places to Stay

You should have no trouble getting a room here at any time of the year, but it is always a good idea to book ahead in summer and at weekends. The closest camping grounds are about 10 km east of the town, on Lago di Corbara, near Baschi. Try the *Orvieto* (☎ 0744-95 02 40) which charges L8500 per person and L7500 a tent.

In Orvieto, one of the best deals is *Albergo Duomo* (☎ 4 18 87), Via di Maurizio 7, where singles/doubles are L38,000/50,000 or L50,000/76,000 with a bathroom; some rooms overlook the duomo. *Albergo Posta* (☎ 4 19 09), Via L Signorelli 18, has rooms for about the same price. *Albergo Corso* (☎ 4 20 20), Corso Cavour 343, has singles/doubles from L60,000/80,000, and the three-star *Albergo Virgilio* (☎ 4 18 82), Piazza del Duomo 5, overlooks the duomo and has rooms for L95,000/134,000.

Places to Eat

One of the most pleasant places for a snack is *Cantina Foresi*, Piazza del Duomo, a wine cellar with local wines and tables in the piazza, as well as good sandwiches and snacks. *San Domenico* is a pizzeria at Piazza XXIX Marzo 18, with pizzas from L5000. *La Grotta del Funaro* is an excellent little trattoria at Via Ripa Serancia 41, on Piazza della Repubblica. A meal will cost around L20,000. *Trattoria Etrusca*, Via Lorenzo Maitani, is another good and reasonably priced place to eat.

L'Archetto, Piazza del Duomo 14, has good gelati.

Getting There & Away

All buses depart from Piazza Cahen. COTRAL (☎ 0761-22 65 92 in Viterbo) connects the city with Viterbo and Bagnoregio. ATC buses (☎ 4 22 65), Piazza Cahen, connect with Baschi, Montecchio, Bolsena, Perugia and Todi. SIRA (☎ 06-4173 00 83) runs a daily service to Rome.

Trains run to Rome and Florence, and you can change at Terontola for Perugia. By car, the city is on the A1, and the SS71 heads north for Lago di Trasimeno. Make sure you have plenty of coins for the parking metres in Piazza Cahen.

Getting Around

A funicular railway connects Piazza Cahen with the train station, with carriages leaving daily every 15 minutes from 7.15 am to 8.30 pm. Once in the city, the easiest way to see it is on foot, although ATC bus No A connects Piazza Cahen with Piazza del Duomo, and No B with Piazza della Repubblica.

AROUND ORVIETO

The Etruscans produced wine in the district, the Romans continued the tradition, and today the Orvieto Classico wines are among the country's most popular. You can visit 17 vineyards and sample the produce. Unfortunately, you need a car, as ATC bus services to most small towns near the vineyards are not regular.

Grab a copy of *Andar per Vigne* from the APT office, or pop into the Consorzio Tutela Vino Orvieto Classico e Orvieto (☎ 4 37 90), Corso Cavour 36, for details of its driving tour of the local vineyards.

The Marches

Characterised by undulating countryside and peppered with barely 'discovered' medieval towns and villages, the Marches form a narrow and little travelled band between the Apennines and the Adriatic Sea. Most visitors come for the Renaissance splendour of Urbino, or to catch a ferry from Ancona, but the rest of the region deserves at least a few days exploration.

In the south-west, the treeless Monti Sibillini form an impressive and, in parts,

THE MARCHES

The Marches (Le Marche)

forbidding stretch of the Apennines, with plenty to keep even the most die-hard walker busy for days.

Much of the coastline has been overdeveloped, with rows of characterless seaside hotels and the sand swamped with beach umbrellas in summer, but some of the nooks and crannies outside Ancona and around Senigallia and Pesaro are among the best the Adriatic has to offer.

The small hill towns, however, are the region's most enchanting feature. Urbino and Macerata are the better known, but the hilly countryside is littered with curious little towns and villages, often crowned by an ancient castle or medieval monastery, quiet and always ripe for poking around. In the south, Ascoli Piceno boasts an historic centre of elegant squares and several grand monuments in a web of narrow cobbled lanes.

And now that Tuscany has outpriced itself and Umbria is well on the road to doing the same, the Marches are becoming increasingly popular with Romans and foreigners intent on buying old farm houses for renovation.

One of Italy's earliest tribes, the Piceni, was the first inhabitant of the area, which later fell under Roman control. The region prospered in the Middle Ages and boomed during the 15th and 16th centuries, when the powerful Montefeltro family ruled Urbino. The Marches attracted great Renaissance architects and painters, and Urbino gave the world the genius of Raphael and Donato Bramante.

Local cuisine draws inspiration from two sources. Inland mountain dishes comprise freshwater fish, beef, lamb, mushrooms and truffles, while on the coast, sole and prawns resembling lobsters are popular. *Brodetto* is a tempting fish stew common along the coast, while *vincisgrassi*, a rich lasagne with meat sauce, chicken livers and black truffles, is popular inland. The region is a small wine producer, with one of the best drops being the Vernaccia di Serrapetrona, a sparkling red.

The A14 and SS16 (Via Adriatica) hug the coastline, while the inland roads are good and provide easy access to all towns. Bus services inland are frequent and regular trains ply the coast on the Bologna-Lecce line.

ANCONA

Most visitors to Ancona only go there in order to head off elsewhere, namely by ferry to Greece, Turkey or even the former Yugoslavia. A major point of trade with the East since the Middle Ages, Ancona remains the mid-Adriatic's largest port, doing a healthy business in tourists as well as road freight. Heavily bombed in WW II, the old centre still has a few faded gems to offer the listless voyager waiting for a boat.

Founded in 400 BC by settlers from Syracuse, Ancona's crescent-shaped natural harbour soon attracted Rome's attention. Under Emperor Trajan it developed as an imperial port and commercial centre. It was a free city, with occasional breaks, for four centuries from 1100. In 1860 it took up arms to convince the townsfolk to join the new Italian kingdom. Wars have always been bad news for Ancona. The Austrians bombarded the city in WW I and in the last war the Allies hammered it steadily from 1943 until mid-1944, when Polish units dislodged the Germans.

Orientation

All trains arrive at the main station in Piazza Nello e Carlo Rosselli, and some continue the 1.5 km north to the ferry terminal, Stazione Marittima (or Molo Santa Maria). In any case, buses connect the two. From Largo Dogana, near the ferry terminal, walk uphill to the central Piazza Roma and on to the city's grand Piazza Cavour. There are several hotels near Piazza Roma, and a cluster around the main train station. What remains of the old town stretches in an arc around the waterfront.

Information

Tourist Offices The main APT office (☎ 3 49 38) is remarkably unhandily placed at the eastern end of town at Via Thaon de Revel 4. It is open Monday to Friday from 8 am to 2 pm, as well as Tuesday and Thursday from 3.30 to 6.30 pm. Branch offices are open at the train station and Stazione Marittima daily, morning and afternoon, in summer only.

Money There are exchange booths at the main train station and Stazione Marittima, but rates are not especially good. There is also an ATM good for Visa and MasterCard at the ferry terminal.

Post & Telecommunications The main post office is on Largo XXIV Maggio, and is open

Monday to Saturday from 8.15 am to 7 pm. Poste restante mail can be addressed to 60100 Ancona. There is a branch office on the corner of Via Pizzecolli and Via della Catena. The Telecom office is opposite the train station and is open from 8 am to 9.45 pm. There is another office at Piazza Roma 26. The telephone code for Ancona is 071.

Consulate France has a consulate (☎ 20 68 66) at Via Marsala 12.

Travel Agency CTS (☎ 87 13 27) has an office at Corso Alberto 83.

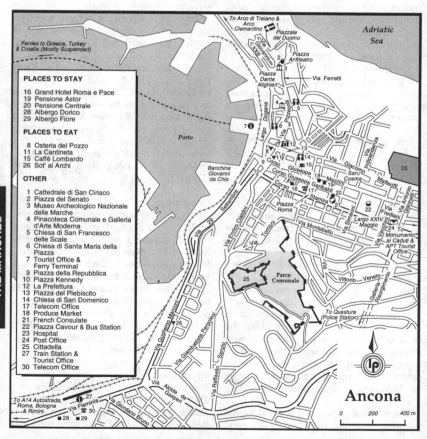

PLACES TO STAY
16 Grand Hotel Roma e Pace
19 Pensione Astor
20 Pensione Centrale
28 Albergo Dorico
29 Albergo Fiore

PLACES TO EAT
8 Osteria del Pozzo
11 La Cantineta
15 Caffè Lombardo
26 Sot' ai Archi

OTHER
1 Cattedrale di San Ciriaco
2 Piazza del Senato
3 Museo Archeologico Nazionale delle Marche
4 Pinacoteca Comunale e Galleria d'Arte Moderna
5 Chiesa di San Francesco delle Scale
6 Chiesa di Santa Maria della Piazza
7 Tourist Office & Ferry Terminal
9 Piazza della Repubblica
10 Piazza Kennedy
12 La Prefettura
13 Piazza del Plebiscito
14 Chiesa di San Domenico
17 Telecom Office
18 Produce Market
21 French Consulate
22 Piazza Cavour & Bus Station
23 Hospital
24 Post Office
25 Cittadella
27 Train Station & Tourist Office
30 Telecom Office

Ancona

0   200   400 m

Emergency For police emergency, call ☎ 113, or contact the questura (☎ 2 28 81), Via Gervasoni 19, south of the city centre. The Ospedale Generale Regionale Umberto I (☎ 59 61) is at Largo Cappelli 1. In a medical emergency call ☎ 20 28 80 or ☎ 5 56 22. The Farmacia Centrale on the corner of Corso Mazzini and Via Gramsci has an emergency night service.

Piazza del Plebiscito
This elegant piazza was medieval Ancona's main square, since overtaken by grander, if less atmospheric, piazzas in the modern town. **La Prefettura**, the former police station, is housed in a 15th-century palace noted for its beautiful courtyard and dominates the piazza. At its eastern end stands the Baroque **Chiesa di San Domenico**, containing the superb *Crucifixion* by Titian and *Annunciation* by Guercino. Near the church is the 13th-century city gate, the **Arco Ferretti**. Most of the buildings overlooking the piazza went up in the 18th century, largely replacing their medieval precursors.

Museums & Churches
From the Prefettura take Via Pizzecolli north through the old city's ramparts to the Palazzo Bosdari at No 17, which houses the **Pinacoteca Comunale** and **Galleria d'Arte Moderna**. Search out Titian's *Madonna and Saints*; the remaining works spanning some six centuries include pieces by Guercino, Carlo Crivelli and Lorenzo Lotto. The gallery is open Tuesday to Saturday from 10 am to 7 pm, when admission is L3000, and Sunday to 1 pm, when admission is free.

Farther along Via Pizzecolli and off to the right is the **Chiesa di San Francesco delle Scale**, noteworthy for its 15th-century Venetian Gothic doorway by Orsini. Beyond San Francesco is Vanvitelli's Chiesa del Gesù, and nearby, the economics faculty of the city's 13th-century **university** in the Palazzo degli Anziani.

On Via Ferretti is the **Museo Archeologico Nazionale delle Marche**, housed in the Palazzo Ferretti, which has been restored twice this century, once after WW II

bombing and again after an earthquake in 1972. It includes impressive collections of Greek vases and artefacts from the Iron Age as well as Celtic and Roman remnants.

It is open daily from 8.30 am to 1.30 pm in winter and from 10 am to 7 pm in summer. Admission is L4000.

Cattedrale di San Ciriaco
Via Giovanni XXIII leads up Monte Guasco to the cathedral, on Piazzale del Duomo – the best spot for sweeping views of the city and across the port. The Romanesque cathedral was built on the site of a Roman temple and has Byzantine and Gothic features. The small museum adjoining the church contains the 4th-century sarcophagus of Flavius Gorgonius, a masterpiece of early Christian art. The museum is open for guided visits on Sundays only, at 11.15 am and at 6.30 pm. Tickets cost L5000.

Waterfront
North of Piazza Dante Alighieri along the esplanade of Lungomare Luigi Vanvitelli is the **Arco di Traiano** (Trajan's Arch), erected in 115 AD. Vanvitelli's **Arco Clementino** (Clementine Arch), dedicated to Pope Clement XII, is farther on. South of Piazza Dante Alighieri you'll hit the small Piazza Santa Maria and the disused, oddly tumbledown looking **Chiesa di Santa Maria della Piazza**, which retains a few scraps of 5th and 6th-century pavement mosaics.

Places to Stay
Many people bunk down at the ferry terminal, although the city has many cheap hotels. *Albergo Dorico* (☎ 4 27 61), opposite the train station at Via Flaminia 8, has rooms with a bathroom for L33,000/50,000. *Albergo Fiore* (☎ 4 33 90), a few doors down at Piazza Rosselli 24, is similar. In the centre of town, *Pensione Astor* (☎ 20 27 76), Corso Mazzini 142, has simple rooms from L30,000/46,000. *Pensione Centrale* (☎ 5 43 88), Via Marsala 10, has rooms for L30,000/40,000 or doubles with a bathroom for L60,000. The three-star *Grand Hotel Roma e Pace* (☎ 20 20 07; fax 207 47 36), Via Leopardi 1, has

rooms with all mod cons and breakfast for L85,000/145,000.

Places to Eat

The produce market at Corso Mazzini 130 has fresh fruit, vegetables and other food. *Osteria del Pozzo*, Via Bonda 2, just of Piazza del Plebiscito, has good, reasonably priced food and a meal should come in under L20,000. *La Cantineta*, Via Gramsci 1, is a popular and simple trattoria near the old centre, where pasta starts at L6000. For seafood (Ancona is a port after all), try *Sot' ai Archi*, Via Marconi 95. A full meal will relieve you of about L30,000 per head. *Caffè Lombardo*, Corso Mazzini 59, is a pleasant spot with tables spilling out onto the street.

Getting There & Away

Air Flights from Rome, Milan and Perugia and the odd European charter land at Falconara airport (☎ 5 62 57), 10 km north-west of Ancona.

Bus Most provincial and regional buses depart from Piazza Cavour. COTRAN has buses to provincial towns such as Loreto, Recanati and Osimo. Other companies run buses to Macerata, Senigallia, Fano and Pesaro (the last three are run by Bucci). Bucci buses leave for Urbino daily at 11 am and 2 pm. Reni (☎ 20 25 96) operates a service to Milan Monday to Friday at 7.30 am. A daily bus for Rome leaves from in front of Stazione Marittima at 9.25 am (arrives 2.30 pm).

Train Ancona is on the Bologna-Lecce line and regular services link it with Milan, Turin, Rome, Bologna, Lecce and most main stops in between. For information, call ☎ 4 39 33.

Car & Motorbike Ancona is on the A14, which links Bologna and Bari. The SS16 coastal road runs parallel to the autostrada and is a more pleasant (toll-free) alternative. The SS76 connects Ancona with Perugia and Rome.

Boat Ferry operators have booths at the Stazione Marittima. Timetables are subject to change, prices fluctuate with the season, and some lines come and go – check at the APT office or at the terminal. Most lines offer discounts on return fares, and the boats are generally roll-on roll-off car ferries. Prices listed here are for one-way deck class in the high season:

Minoan Lines (☎ 5 67 89) operates about five ferries a week to Igoumenitsa, Corfu, Cefalonia and Patras (Greece) for L114,000, as well as Heraklion (Crete) for L184,000 and Çesme (Turkey) for L266,000. Most services stop over winter.

Marlines (☎ 20 25 66) has several services a week to Corfu, Igoumenitsa, Patras (L108,000 each) and Heraklion (L171,000; summer only).

Strintzis Lines (☎ 286 44 31) goes to Corfu, Igoumenitsa and Patras, virtually every day in summer (L114,000).

Adriatica (☎ 20 49 15) operates two ferries a week to Split in Croatia (L70,000 in high season) and Durres in Albania (L155,000). The internal situation in these countries could mean rapid reappraisal of the service.

Jadrolinija (☎ 20 28 05) runs regularly to Zadar (L47,000) and Split (L52,000).

Anek Lines (☎ 20 20 33) operates several services each week to Corfu, Igoumenitsa and Patras (L82,000) and charges L172,000 for a small car.

SMC (☎ 20 40 90) has three runs a week to Split (L50,000). It operates through the Mauro agency.

Topas (☎ 20 28 06) has a ferry through to Izmir (Turkey) in summer only. The fare is about L300,000.

Other companies that may operate in summer include: Kvarner Expres (☎ 20 45 16) for Zadar in Croatia; Hellenic Mediterranean Lines (☎ 20 40 41) for Croatia; and Navigazione Aquila (☎ 20 23 91) for Croatia and Albania. There is a L5000 port tax to Albania and Croatia and L10,000 to Greece.

Getting Around

About six ATMA buses, including No 1, connect the train station (look for the bus stop with the big sign displaying Centro and Porto) with Stazione Marittima and the city centre. For a taxi, call ☎ 4 33 21.

AROUND ANCONA

Loreto

The story goes that angels transferred the house of the Virgin Mary from Palestine to this spot towards the end of the 13th century. Why the angels should have done such a thing is unclear, but a church was soon built over the site and later expanded to become today's **Santuario della Santa Casa**. Restoration began in 1468, and additions have been made ever since, and the place is an important goal for Christian pilgrims. The house itself, whatever its origin, is beneath the dome inside the sanctuary and is open all day. Loreto lies about 28 km south of Ancona and can be reached easily by bus from there. The train station (Bologna-Lecce line) is a few km away, but shuttle buses connect it with the town centre.

Beaches

If you are hanging about Ancona for any length of time, head about 20 km south on the coast road (buses from Piazza Cavour) for Sirolo and Numana, below Monte Conero. These beaches are among the Adriatic's more appealing, although they fill up in summer.

URBINO

Jewel of the Marches and one of the best preserved and most beautiful hill towns in Italy, Urbino enjoyed a period of great splendour under the Montefeltro family from the 12th century. It reached its zenith under Duca Federico da Montefeltro, who hired some of the greatest Renaissance artists and architects to construct and decorate his palace and other parts of the town. The architects Donato Bramante, born in Urbino, and Francesco di Giorgio were among his favourites. Painters in particularly good grace with the duke included Piero della Francesca, who developed his theories on mathematical perspective in Urbino, Paolo Uccello, Justus of Ghent and Giovanni Santi. The latter was the father of Raffaello d'Urbino, the great Raphael, who was born in the city.

After Duca Federico lost his right eye and had his nose broken in a tournament, he insisted on being portrayed only in profile. The most famous result of this caprice was executed in 1466 by della Francesca and hangs in the Uffizi Gallery in Florence.

The city can be a pain to reach by public transport, but should not be missed. The area to the north, particularly the winding road to San Marino and on into Emilia-Romagna, is a treat, and there are plenty of hotels in the small towns along the way.

Orientation

Buses arrive at Borgo Mercatale on the walled city's western edge. From there it is a short walk along Via G Mazzini to Piazza della Repubblica and then back south to Via Veneto for Piazza Duca Federico and the sprawling Piazza del Rinascimento. Drivers will most likely arrive at Piazzale Roma on the city's northern edge. Via Raffaello connects the piazza with Piazza della Repubblica.

Information

Tourist Office The APT (☎ 24 41), Piazza Duca Federico 35, is open Monday to Saturday from 9 am to 1 pm.

Post & Telecommunications The main post office is at Via Bramante 18 and is open Monday to Saturday from 8.30 am to 5.30 pm. The post code for the town centre is 61029.

The Telecom office, at Via Puccinotti 4, opposite the Palazzo Ducale, is open from 8 am to 10 pm. There's another office at Piazza di San Francesco 1. The telephone code for Urbino is 0722.

Emergency & Medical Services Call the police on ☎ 113 or ☎ 27 25. For medical assistance, call ☎ 118 or ☎ 32 80 89. The Ospedale Civile (☎ 30 11) is at Via B da Montefeltro. There is a pharmacy at Piazza della Repubblica 9.

Palazzo Ducale

Completed in 1482, the grand residence of Urbino's ruling dynasty, with its courtyards, towers and loggias, dominates the heights of Urbino. Luciano Laurana drew up the original design, but several masters had a hand in its construction, including the ruling Duca Federico who had commissioned it. The best

THE MARCHES

PLACES TO STAY

1 Pensione Fosca
3 Hotel Raffaello
15 Albergo Italia
30 Albergo Panoramic

PLACES TO EAT

5 Il Coppiere
7 Gelateria Arcobaleno
10 Trattoria del Leone
13 Caffè Centrale
14 Caffè Belpassi
26 Ristorante da Franco
29 Ristorante Fosca

OTHER

2 Fortezza Albornoz
4 Casa di Raffaello
6 Telecom Office
8 Post Office
9 Piazza di San Francesco
11 Oratorio di San Giovanni Battista
12 Coin Laundrette
16 Teatro Sanzio
17 Bus Station
18 Basilica Metropolitana
19 Banca Nazionale del Lavoro
20 The Bosom Pub
21 Cassa di Risparmio
22 Tourist Office
23 Palazzo Ducale
24 University
25 Piazza del Rinascimento
27 Telecom Office
28 Chiesa di San Domenico

Urbino

0   100   200 m

Minor Streets Not Depicted

external view of the complex is from Corso Garibaldi to the north.

The palace now houses the **Galleria Nazionale delle Marche**, a formidable art collection, and the less inspiring **Museo Archeologico**.

In Room 9 of the galleria is a remarkable portrait of Federico and his son Guidobaldo, possibly by Justus of Ghent or Pedro Berruguete. Look out for della Francesca's masterpiece, *Flagellation*, in the Ducal Apartments. The collection also features two Titians – the *Last Supper* and *Resurrection* – and farther on is Raphael's *Portrait of a Lady*, which is behind glass and hard to see.

Along the way you will pass through Duca Federico's **Studiolo** which features exquisite inlaid wood panelling where cupboard doors seem to be hanging open, the books look real and a letter even appears to be lying on a desk.

The mildly interesting archaeological museum, on the far side of the Cortile d'Onore, the palace courtyard, is worth a look-in – you may as well, as admission is included in the L8000 ticket. The palace is open daily from 9 am to 2 pm.

Basilica Metropolitana

Rebuilt in the early 1800s in the neoclassical style after an earthquake destroyed Francesco di Giorgio Martini's original Renaissance building, the interior of Urbino's cathedral commands greater interest than its austere façade. Particularly memorable is Frederico Barocci's *Last Supper*. The cathedral's **Museo Albani** contains further paintings, including Andrea da Bologna's *Madonna del Latte*, along with an engaging assortment of articles collected from Urbino's churches over the centuries. The basilica is downhill from the Palazzo Ducale. It's open daily from 9.30 am to midday and 3 to 6 pm. Admission is L2000.

Churches & Oratories

Opposite the Palazzo Ducale, the medieval **Chiesa di San Domenico** is notable for its lunette, the panel above the 15th-century doorway by Luca della Robbia.

The 14th-century **Oratorio di San Giovanni Battista** on Via Barocci features brightly coloured frescoes by Lorenzo and Giacomo Salimbeni. It's open Monday to Saturday from 10 am to midday and 3 to 5 pm and Sunday to 12.30 pm. Admission is L3000. A few steps away, the **Oratorio di San Giuseppe** (same hours, admission L2000) boasts a stucco Nativity by Federico Brandani.

The **Chiesa di San Bernardino**, outside the city walls to the east along Viale Giuseppe di Vittorio, houses the mausoleum of the Dukes of Urbino, designed by Donato Bramante and Francesco di Giorgio. It's open daily from 8.30 am to 12.30 pm and 2.30 to 7 pm.

Casa di Raffaello

If you want to have a look at where Raphael first saw the light of day, the house of his birth is north of Piazza della Repubblica at Via Raffaello 57. It is open Monday to Saturday from 9 am to 1 pm and 2 to 5 pm and Sunday morning. Admission is L5000.

Courses

The university offers an intensive course in language and culture for foreigners during August at a cost of L500,000, and can arrange accommodation for L250,000 for the month. For information call ☎ 30 52 50 or write to the Segreteria dell'Università, Via Saffi 2, Urbino 61029. You can get details and book in from about March to May.

Places to Stay

The tourist office has a full list of private rooms. *Campeggio Pineta* (☎ 47 10), the only camping ground, is two km east of the city in San Donato. *Pensione Fosca* (☎ 32 96 22), Via Raffaello 67, has singles/doubles for L35,000/49,000. *Albergo Italia* (☎ 27 01), Corso Garibaldi 32, is behind the Palazzo Ducale and has singles/doubles from L37,000/ 50,000, or L48,000/65,000 with a bathroom. *Albergo Panoramic* (☎ 26 00), outside the city just off the Strada Nazionale, has rooms from L35,000/50,000 but is awkward to reach without your own transport – and charges an extra L3800 per shower. Heading up the scale in price, *Hotel Raffaello* (☎ 47 84), Via Santa Margherita 40, charges around L100,000/150,000 for singles/doubles.

Places to Eat

There are numerous bars around Piazza della Repubblica and near the Palazzo Ducale that sell good panini. Try *Pizzeria Galli*, Via Vittorio Veneto 19, for takeaway pizza by the slice. *Bar Europa*, at No 34, also sells pizza slices. *Ristorante da Franco*, just off Piazza Rinascimento and next to the university, has a self-service section for lunch, where you can eat for less than L20,000. *Trattoria del Leone*, Via Cesare Battisti 5, offers traditional dishes and a set meal will cost L20,000. You can eat well at *Ristorante Fosca*, Via F Budassi 64, for around L25,000 a head. Try the strozzapreti al pesto, worm-like shreds of pasta designed to choke priests – sounds horrid but they're delicious. For more elegant dining, head for *Il Coppiere* at Via Santa Margherita 1 – a meal in the cosy 1st-floor restaurant will cost about L40,000.

Entertainment

The Teatro Sanzio hosts a variety of drama and concerts, particularly from July to September. Pick up a brochure at the tourist office.

Getting There & Away

Bus The bus station is in Borgo Mercatale. SAPUM and Bucci operate up to 10 services a day between Urbino and Pesaro. Busturs has a bus a day to San Marino, and there are two daily runs to Ancona and one to Arezzo. Check with the APT office or consult the board under the portico near Caffè Belpassi, Piazza della Repubblica, for schedules.

Train Take the bus for Pesaro to pick up trains there.

Car & Motorbike A superstrada and the SS423 connect the city with Pesaro, and the SS73 connects the city with the SS3 for Rome.

Getting Around

Most vehicles are banned from the walled city. Small shuttle buses operate between Piazzale Roma, Borgo Mercatale and Piazza Rinascimento. Taxis (☎ 25 50) operate from Piazza della Repubblica. There are car parks outside the city gates. Your car will be towed away on Saturday mornings from Piazzale Roma, as that is market day.

AROUND URBINO
San Leo

Machiavelli, who knew a thing or two about such matters, thought the fortress of San Leo, about 60 km north-west of Urbino, quite 'impregnable'. He was probably right – it is difficult to see how the walls perched defiantly on a high outcrop of stone could be assailed.

Without a car, San Leo is a little difficult to reach. Although in the Marches, the most reliable bus route is actually from Rimini, in Emilia-Romagna. Part of the Montefeltro duchy, San Leo was first fortified by the Romans, who erected a temple to Jupiter here. The temple was later replaced by the 12th-century **duomo**, and nearby you can also admire the pre-Romanesque **Pieve**, an 11th-century basilica. The Papal States converted the fort into a prison and the Fascists used it as an aircraft-spotting post during WW II.

PESARO

Like other resort towns on the Adriatic, Pesaro offers an expanse of beach, the remains of a medieval centre and not much else. In mid-summer you can't move for the crowds, and out of season the waterfront has a sad air about it – maybe it's all the tacky concrete hotel blocks boarded up for the winter. It is, however, a handy transport junction, and the best place to get a bus for Urbino, an hour's drive inland.

Orientation

The train station is at the southern edge of the centre, away from the beach. Walk along Viale del Risorgimento, through Piazza Lazzarini and continue to Piazza del Popolo, the town's main square. Via Rossini takes you to Piazza della Libertà and the waterfront.

Information

The main APT office (☎ 6 93 41), at Via Rossini 41 near Piazza del Popolo, is open daily from 8 am to 7 pm in season (April to September) and Monday to Friday from 9 am to 1 pm (also Tuesdays and Thursdays from 4 to 7 pm) for the rest of the year. Branch offices at the train station (☎ 6 83 78) and Piazzale della Libertà (☎ 6 43 02) are open in summer only.

Money There are plenty of banks. The Banca Nazionale del Lavoro on Piazza del Popolo has an ATM good for several cards including Visa.

Post & Telecommunications The main post office is in Piazza del Popolo and is open Monday to Saturday from 8.15 am to 7.40 pm. The post code for the town centre is 61100. The Telecom office is in Piazza Matteotti, south-east of Piazza del Popolo, and is open daily from 7 am to 11 pm. The telephone code for Pesaro is 0721.

Emergency For the police, call ☎ 113, or contact the questura (☎ 38 61 11) at Via Bruno 5. For an ambulance, call ☎ 41 12 22; or try pronto soccorso on ☎ 3 29 57. Ospedale San Salvatore (☎ 36 11) is at Piazza Cinelli 4.

Things to See

The 15th-century **Palazzo Ducale**, dominating Piazza del Popolo, housed the ruling Della Rovere family. Today it houses bureaucracy and is closed to the public. The splendid

windows that grace its façade are by Domenico Rosselli.

Head north-west along Corso XI Settembre for Via Toschi Mosca and the town's **Musei Civici**, which also contains the **Pinacoteca**. The museum has a worthy collection of ceramics, the production of which has long been a speciality of Pesaro, while the gallery's prize is Giovanni Bellini's magnificent altarpiece depicting the *Coronation of the Virgin*. The complex is open Tuesday to Sunday from 8.30 am to 1 pm, and admission is L5000. The **Chiesa di Sant' Agostino** on Corso XI Settembre features

PLACES TO STAY
1 Albergo Guglielmo Tell
3 Hotel Holiday
4 Villa Olga

PLACES TO EAT
5 Ristorante il Castiglione
7 Taverna delle Sfingi
18 Ristorante C'era Una Volta
19 Black & Blue

OTHER
2 Associazione Pesarese di Albergatori
6 APT Branch Office
8 Chiesa di Sant'Agostino
9 Musei Civici
10 APT Tourist Office
11 Palazzo Ducale
12 Casa Natale di Rossini
13 Banca Nazionale del Lavoro
14 Post Office
15 Market
16 Bus Station
17 Telecom Office
20 Train Station
21 CAI Office

Pesaro

THE MARCHES

intricate 15th-century inlaid-wood choir stalls.

Music buffs may be interested in the **Casa Natale di Rossini**, on Piazza Olivieri, off Via Branca. The composer was born in Pesaro in 1792, and the small museum in the house contains various personal effects and his spinet. It's open Tuesday to Sunday from 10 am to 1 pm. Admission is L2000.

The modest **Museo Oliveriano** on Via Mazza contains archaeological finds from the area, including an Iron Age child's tomb, complete with miniature utensils, such as eating implements. Apply for admission at the adjoining library, which has a collection of ancient coins, manuscripts and medals.

Activities

The Società Canottieri Pesaro (☎ 40 00 10), Calata Caio Duilio 101, can help with the hire of sailboards and canoes, while the Club Nautico (☎ 2 56 57), Molo Strada Tra i due Porti 20, can arrange sailing lessons. The CAI (☎ 3 48 05), Viale Bramante 21, can help with trekking information in the Marches. If horse riding is your thing, ask at the APT office or try the Centro Ippico 'Da Zorigo' (☎ 28 13 13), Via Fontesecco 103.

Places to Stay

The town's hotel association, the Associazione Pesarese di Albergatori (☎ 6 79 59), has an office at Viale Dante Alighieri 40 and will help you find a room. The APT office has a lengthy list of apartments, although most are more expensive than hotels. From October to April, many hotels close, and the camping grounds may well do the same. If you can, go first to the APT office to find out what's still open.

The closest camping grounds are about five km south of the town centre at Fosso Sejore. The *Marinella* (☎ 5 08 76) on the SS16 has sites for up to L10,000 a person and L21,000 a tent, and the nearby *Norina* (☎ 5 57 92) has similar prices.

The HI *Ardizio* hostel (☎ 5 57 98), Strada Panoramica dell'Ardizio, is also at Fosso Sejore and has B&B for L14,000. It is open from April to mid-September. Take

the AMANUP bus to Fano for the camping grounds and the hostel.

One of the more attractive cheap hotel deals is *Villa Olga* (☎ 6 27 83). It has simple rooms for L30,000/48,000 in an old building virtually on the waterfront.

Hotel Holiday (☎ 3 48 51), Via Trento 159, if you're lucky, has singles going as cheaply as L23,000, but they're more likely to be around L40,000. Doubles go for L66,000. *Albergo Guglielmo Tell* (☎ 3 24 45), up the road at No 195, has rooms from L30,000/60,000 (L45,000/70,000 in the high season). Both close out of season.

Hotel Aurora (☎ 3 44 59), Viale Trieste 147 – the heart of the belt of squat, concrete blocks of buildings – has rooms for much the same prices. The *Excelsior* (☎ 3 27 20), right on the beach at Lungomare N Sauro, has rooms from L65,000/80,000.

Places to Eat

There is a produce market and several food shops on Via Branca, just behind the post office. *Black & Blue*, a takeaway joint at Viale XI Febbraio 11, has pizza slices from L1100.

Ristorante C'Era Una Volta, Via Cattaneo 26, is a good pizzeria, with pizzas from L6000. *Taverna delle Sfingi*, Viale Trieste 219, is one of the better restaurants near the beach, and a meal will set you back about L30,000. At about the same price, *La Tartaruga*, Viale Trieste 31, serves typical local dishes. If you're prepared to part with about L50,000, you could eat at *Ristorante il Castiglione*, Via Trento 148, a posh place with the air of a small castle set in rambling gardens.

Entertainment

In honour of Rossini, the town hosts a series of concerts each August at the theatre bearing his name in Piazza Lazzarini. The APT office has programmes.

Getting There & Away

Bus The main bus station is in Piazza Matteotti. AMANUP buses (☎ 3 47 68) connect the town with Gradara, Cattolica, Carpegna,

Fosso Sejore, Fano, Ancona, Senigallia and most small towns in the region. There are up to 10 buses a day to Urbino.

Train The town is on the Bologna-Lecce line and you can connect for Rome by changing trains at Falconara Marittima, just before Ancona; for information, call ☎ 3 30 09.

Car & Motorbike Pesaro is on the A14 and the SS16.

Getting Around

Most AMANUP buses connect the train station with Piazza Matteotti, including buses No 1, 3, 4, 5, CD and CS.

For a taxi in the centre, call ☎ 3 14 30, and at the train station, ☎ 3 11 11.

AROUND PESARO

If you want slightly more secluded beaches than the Pesaro waterfront, the Strada Panoramica Adriatica, the coast road north from Pesaro to Cattolica in Emilia-Romagna, will take you to them. The walled, hilltop town of **Gradara** boasts an impressive 14th-century castle, but its beaches can be as crowded as Pesaro. The smaller fishing towns of **Castel di Mezzo** and **Fiorenzuola** are appealing and quieter, even during summer. Fighting in WW II was heavy around here, as the Allies struggled to break the Germans' Gothic Line, which ran from Pesaro to La Spezia, on Italy's western coast. There is a British war cemetery two km east of Gradara.

FANO

Only 12 km south of Pesaro, Fano is a fairly sedate beach resort that nevertheless fills up in the summer rush. An ancient village that took its name from the Fanum, the Temple of Fortune, it retains several reminders of its Roman and medieval past in the pleasant historic centre, and warrants a brief stop if you're passing through.

Information

The APT office (☎ 80 35 34) is at Viale Cesare Battisti 10 in Fano, and other offices

(summer only) are in the smaller towns of Torrette (☎ 88 47 79), Via Boscomarina 10, and Marotta (☎ 96 591), Viale Colombo 31. The telephone code is 0721.

Things to See

A **triumphal arch** built in 2 AD for Augustus still stands despite losing part of its masonry to surrounding buildings over the centuries. Sections of the Roman and medieval **walls** also remain. The 16th-century **Corte Malatestiano** contains a museum with works by local artists over the centuries.

Places to Stay

Cheap accommodation is in short supply along this stretch of coastline, making Pesaro a more economical base. Five campsites on the southern end of Fano's seashore all charge L5000 to L7000 per person and up to L15,000 per tent. Try the *Fano* (☎ 80 26 52), or pick up the accommodation list from the APT office.

AROUND FANO

If you're staying a while, a couple of excursions inland are worth considering. **Mondavio** is a charming Renaissance town about 35 km south of Fano. Several buses run from Fano; if driving, take the SS16 south to Marotta, from where you head inland to San Michele. Mondavio is a few km to the north. Some 38 km south-west of Fano is **Mombaroccio**, a pleasant 15th-century hill town. The main attraction is the view from the old castle walls. Take the SS3 west from Fano and turn north at Calcinelli.

SENIGALLIA

Senigallia's aptly named Spiaggia di Velluto (Velvet Beach) is reputedly one of the Adriatic's best lidos.

The APT office (☎ 792 27 25), Piazzale Morandi 2, is between the beach and the train station. The telephone code is 071.

Apart from sea and sand, the main draw is the **Rocca Roveresca**, whose four stout, crenellated towers make it hard to miss. Built for Duca Federico da Montefeltro's son-in-law, its plush Renaissance interior makes a visit well worthwhile if you have a spare hour or two.

Places to Stay

If you're having trouble finding a room, which in summer would come as no surprise, try the hotel and camping association (☎ 6 53 43) at Via Brofferio 4 for assistance.

The *Helios* camping ground (☎ 69 87 31), Lungomare Italia 3, has sites from L3500 per person and L13,000 per tent in the low season. The *Liana* (☎ 6 52 06), Lungomare Leonardo da Vinci 54, is about the same price. The *Albergo Villa Serena* (☎ 792 22 04), Via Sardegna 4, is one of the better cheap deals, with singles/doubles from L35,000/40,000. *Albergo del Sole* (☎ 6 34 67), on the waterfront at Lungomare Alighieri 118, has rooms from L40,000/50,000.

Getting There & Away

Autolinee Bucci buses operate along the SS16 road to Ancona, Fano and Pesaro, but there are also plenty of trains on the same stretch.

GROTTE DI FRASASSI

In September 1971 a team of climbers stumbled across an aperture in hill country around Genga, about 40 km south-west of Ancona, and decided to drop in. What they found were the biggest known caves in Europe – a spectacle of stalactites and stalagmites – some of them 1.4 million years old.

Three years later they were opened to the public, with a 1.5-km-long trail carefully laid through five chambers. The first chamber, the Ancona Abyss, is almost 200 metres high, 180 metres wide and 120 metres long, and could easily accommodate Milan's duomo.

Groups are taken through the caves every couple of hours for about an hour, and tickets cost L12,000. The ticket area and car park are just outside San Vittore Terme, and the entrance to the caves is 600 metres farther west. For L30,000, you can get rigged up in caving gear to explore the remaining chambers. This has to be booked well in advance however. Call the Consorzio Frasassi (☎ 0732-9 00 80). Should you need to stay, there are a couple of hotels in San Vittore Terme and Genga.

Take the SS76 from Ancona, or the train for Genga (Rome-Ancona line), about two km from the ticket area (a shuttle bus runs from the train station in summer).

MACERATA

This bustling provincial capital is one of Italy's better kept secrets. Situated atop a rise between the Potenza river valley to the north and the Chienti river in the south, Macerata was established in the 10th century. It is as impressive as many Umbrian and Tuscan hill towns but lacks the tourists, and makes a good base for exploring the surrounding countryside – some of the region's most picturesque.

Orientation

Piazza della Libertà is the focal point of the medieval city, contained within 14th-century walls above the sprawl of the more modern development. Buses arrive at the huge Giardini Diaz, a stone's throw from the Porta Romana (the main gate) and the tourist office. A shuttle bus links the train station, which is west of the city centre, to Piazza della Libertà. There is parking virtually right around the walls and you may even get away with it on one of the main squares inside the old city.

Information

Tourist Office The main APT office (☎ 23 15 47) is at Via Garibaldi 87, above the Standa supermarket, and is open Monday to Friday from 9 am to midday and as well as from 4 to 6 pm on Tuesdays and Thursdays. A second office is in Piazza della Libertà (☎ 23 48 07), open all day in summer and otherwise mornings only.

Post & Telecommunications The Telecom office is at Galleria del Commercio 33. The city's post code is 62100 and the telephone code is 0733.

Emergency For police call ☎ 113, and for an ambulance call ☎ 23 14 44.

Things to See

Piazza della Libertà is adorned by one of the city's finest buildings, the 16th-century Renaissance **Loggia dei Mercanti**, built by the Farnese pope, Paul III. In the courtyard of the **Palazzo del Comune** are archaeological remains from Helvia Ricina, a Roman town five km from Macerata, which was destroyed by the Goths.

Corso della Repubblica, the main boulevard where locals take their late-afternoon strolls, spills into Piazza Vittorio Veneto. Here you will find the **Pinacoteca**, with a good collection of early Renaissance works, including a 15th-century *Madonna* by Carlo Crivelli. The gallery is open Tuesday to Sunday from 9 am to midday and 4.30 to 7.30 pm.

The rather ordinary Baroque **duomo** is unfinished and worth visiting only if you have some spare time.

Places to Stay & Eat

The cheapest option is *Albergo San Giorgio* (☎ 23 23 76), Via T Lauri 6, with rooms starting at L25,000/48,000. *Albergo Arena* (☎ 23 09 31), Vicolo Sferisterio 16, has singles/doubles from L40,000/650,000.

There are several pizzerias for quick takeaway food, including *Rusticanella Romana*, Corso della Repubblica 13, and *Pizzeria da Luciano*, Vicolo Ferrari 12. One of the better restaurants in town is *Da Secondo*, Via Pescheria Vecchia 26, where you are looking at about L35,000 for a full meal.

Entertainment

The Stagione Lirica (Lyric Festival) is one of Italy's most prestigious musical events, attracting big names to the superb open air Arena Sferisterio, off Piazza Mazzini, from July 15 to August 15 every year. At the same time, the private Palazzo Ricci Pinacoteca, in the street of the same name, organises a national exhibition of 20th-century Italian art.

Getting There & Away

The city is served by several bus companies operating services to Rome, Florence, Siena, Ancona, Ascoli Piceno, Civitanova Marche and Foligno. The train station (☎ 24 03 54) is in Via Corridoni. The SS77 connects the city with the A14 to the east and with roads for Rome in the west.

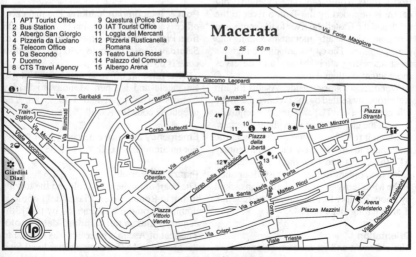

1 APT Tourist Office
2 Bus Station
3 Albergo San Giorgio
4 Pizzeria da Luciano
5 Telecom Office
6 Da Secondo
7 Duomo
8 CTS Travel Agency
9 Questura (Police Station)
10 IAT Tourist Office
11 Loggia dei Mercanti
12 Pizzeria Rusticanella Romana
13 Teatro Lauro Rossi
14 Palazzo del Comune
15 Albergo Arena

Macerata

0   25   50 m

THE MARCHES

Giacomo Leopardi
Born in Recanati on 29 June, 1798 of well-to-do parents, Giacomo Leopardi became the greatest romantic poet to emerge from Italy. From 1822, when he left home for the first time, Leopardi travelled extensively through Italy until his death in Naples in 1837, although he returned to Recanati regularly during his life. The most penetrating of his poetry, often erudite and always demanding, reflects the pain, anxiety and fragile, bitter-sweet moments of joy or simple remembrance that seem to have been the substance of the man's life. Leopardi was steeped in a classical education from a precocious age and his verse, however much it belongs to the stormy age of the romantics, remains firmly planted in the disciplined framework of classicism. The pick of his work is the *Canti*, first published between 1824 and 1835, and now a standard element of Italian literary education. ∎

AROUND MACERATA

About 20 km north-east on the road to Ancona rises the pretty little town of **Recanati**, straggling out along a high ridge. A pleasant enough stop, the town owes a special place in Italian literary history to its most famous son – the early 19th-century poet Giacomo Leopardi. A small museum is dedicated to his life in the Palazzo Leopardi.

ASCOLI PICENO

Legend has it that a woodpecker was responsible for the founding of this southern Marches town by leading its prehistoric first settlers to the site. The extensive old centre is bounded by the Tronto river to the north and the Castellano river to the south, and is dominated by nearby mountains leading into the Apennines. The city is among the region's most interesting after Urbino, and deserves more attention than it gets.

Woodpecker stories aside, Ascoli Piceno was probably settled by the Piceni tribe in the 6th century BC. The salt trade eventually brought the city into contact with the Romans, to whom it fell after clamorous defeats in the battlefield in 268 BC. By the sixth century AD, the Goths and then the Lombards had come to supplant Rome. The city flourished in the Middle Ages, despite being ransacked by troops of Holy Roman Emperor Frederick II after a long siege in 1242.

Orientation

The old town and its modern extension are separated by the Castellano river. The train station is in the new part, east of the river. From here head west across the Ponte Maggiore and along Corso Vittorio Emanuele and past the duomo. Any of the narrow cobbled lanes north will eventually take you to Piazza del Popolo, the heart of the medieval city.

Information

Tourist Office The AAST (☎ 25 72 88), at Piazza del Popolo 1, is open Monday to Friday from 8 am to 1.45 pm and 3 to 6.30 pm; the morning hours are slightly reduced on Saturday.

Post & Telecommunications The main post office is at Via Crispi, east along Corso Mazzini from Piazza del Popolo. It is open Monday to Saturday from 8.15 am to 7.40 pm. The post code is 63100.

The Telecom office is on Corso Vittorio Emanuele and is open Monday to Friday from 9 am to 1 pm and 4 to 7 pm. The telephone code for Ascoli Piceno is 0736.

Emergency In police emergency, call ☎ 113. For an ambulance, call ☎ 34 12 33.

Piazza del Popolo

The heart of medieval Ascoli and the town's forum in Roman times, Piazza del Popolo is dominated on the western side by the 13th-century **Palazzo dei Capitani del Popolo**. The seat of Ascoli's rulers, it was burned to the ground in 1535 during a bitter local feud and rebuilt 10 years later. The statue of Pope Paul III above the main entrance was erected in recognition of his efforts to bring peace to the town. The building's colourful history did not end there. Headquarters for the local branch of the Fascists from 1938, it became the seat of the partisan Comitato di Liberazione in 1945.

Closing off the piazza to the north, the **Chiesa di San Francesco** was started in 1262 and features a 15th-century wooden crucifix and 16th-century works by Cola dell'Amatrice. Virtually annexed to the church is the **Loggia dei Mercanti**. It looks suspiciously Tuscan, but was in fact built by Lombard masons in the 16th century. Merchants hawk their wares there to this day.

Pinacoteca
Inside the 17th-century Palazzo Comunale on Piazza Arringo, south of Piazza del Popolo, lies the Marches' largest art gallery. The Pinacoteca boasts 400 works, including some

by Van Dyck, Titian and Carlo Crivelli, and even a Turner. Among the prints and drawings is an etching by Rembrandt. The gallery was founded in 1861 with works taken from churches and religious orders that were suppressed in the wake of Italian unification. It is open Tuesday to Saturday from 9 am to 1 pm and Sunday from 10 am to 1 pm. Admission is L2500. In summer it is open also in the afternoon. Across Piazza Arringo, the **Museo Archeologico** has a collection of implements used by the ancient Piceni tribe. It is open about the same hours as the gallery and admission is free.

Duomo
Standing on the eastern flank of the same square, Ascoli's cathedral is a lavish example of Baroque fulsomeness, embellished in what some connoisseurs consider a less than tasteful manner. In compensation for the overkill, you will encounter what is possibly Carlo Crivelli's best work, *Virgin & Saints*, in the

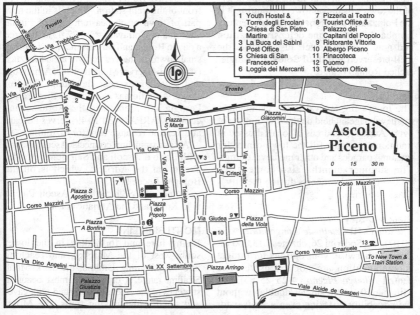

1 Youth Hostel & Torre degli Ercolani
2 Chiesa di San Pietro Martire
3 La Buca dei Sabini
4 Post Office
5 Chiesa di San Francesco
6 Loggia dei Mercanti
7 Pizzeria al Teatro
8 Tourist Office & Palazzo dei Capitani del Popolo
9 Ristorante Vittoria
10 Albergo Piceno
11 Pinacoteca
12 Duomo
13 Telecom Office

THE MARCHES

Cappella del Sacramento. The baptistry next to the cathedral, something of a traffic barrier today, has remained unchanged since it was constructed in the 11th century.

Vecchio Quartiere

The town's Old Quarter stretches from Corso Mazzini (the main thoroughfare, or decumanus, of the Roman-era settlement) to the Tronto river. Its main street is the picturesque Via delle Torri, which eventually becomes Via Solestà. This is a perfect spot to put away the guidebooks and just wander where your whim takes you. Worth watching for on the curiously named Via delle Donne (Women Street) is the 14th-century **Chiesa di San Pietro Martire**, dedicated to the saint who founded the Dominican community at Ascoli. The chunky Gothic structure houses the Reliquario della Santa Spina, containing what is said to be a thorn from Christ's crown of thorns. The church is one of about a dozen dating at least to the 15th century.

The **Torre degli Ercolani** in Via Soderini, west of San Pietro, is, at 40 metres, the tallest of the town's medieval towers. Abutting it is the **Palazzetto Longobardo**, a 12th-century Lombard-Romanesque defensive position and now a youth hostel. Just north is the well-preserved **Ponte di Solestà**, a single-arched Roman bridge.

Festivals

The town's big festival is the Quintana, a medieval pageant held on the first Sunday of every August. Hundreds of locals dressed in traditional costume fill the town centre for jousting, parades and other medieval doings. The summer months also come alive with shows and concerts during the city's Stagione Lirica.

Places to Stay

The town's HI *Ostello de' Longobardi* (☎ 25 90 07), Via Soderini 26, charges L13,000 for B&B. Otherwise, your options for budget accommodation are not extensive. The central *Albergo Piceno* (☎ 25 25 53), Via Minucia 10, offers singles/doubles without the possibility of taking even a shower for L40,000/60,000. If you want that shower, you are looking at L50,000/70,000. Five km out of town in Marino del Tronco is *Albergo Pavoni* (☎ 34 25 75), Via Navicella 135. Bus No 3 goes there from Piazza Arringo. Rooms are L35,000/60,000.

Places to Eat

Ascoli is responsible for a delicious idea for a starter. Olive all'ascolana are olives stuffed with meat and deep-fried.

There is an outdoor market in Piazza San Francesco, near Piazza del Popolo, every morning except Sunday.

For abundant serves of good local cuisine, try *La Buca dei Sabini*, Via dei Sabini 10. A full meal will come to about L20,000, and there is a cheap, self-service lunch. *Pizzeria al Teatro*, Via delle Sette Sogli 1, has pizzas from L5000 and mains from about L10,000. A full meal at *Ristorante Vittoria*, Via dei Bonaccorsi 7, will come to L30,000 a head.

Getting There & Away

Buses leave from Piazzale della Stazione, in front of the train station, which is in the new part of town on the eastern side of Fiume Castellano. Cotravat (☎ 34 22 43) has three a day to Rome, and serves Ancona as well as small towns in the Tronto river area. Mazzuca (☎ 40 35 64) serves Montemonaco, Amandola and other towns near the Monti Sibillini range. Amadio has a service to Firenze via Perugia and Siena, and the Abruzzo bus company ARPA (☎ 34 10 49) serves Pescara and Teramo (change here for L'Aquila).

A spur train line connects Ascoli Piceno with Porto d'Ascoli and San Benedetto del Tronto on the Adriatic, which is on the Bologna-Lecce line.

By car, the SS4 connects Ascoli Piceno with Rome and the Adriatic coast.

MONTI SIBILLINI

Rising bare and forbidding in the lower south-west of the Marches, and reaching into neighbouring Umbria, the stark Monti Sibillini range is one of the most beautiful stretches of the Apennines. Dotted with caves and lined with walking trails, the Monti

---

The Sibyls

Known and feared throughout the Greek world as oracles with awesome power, it is unclear if the Sibyls played any direct role in the mythology of Roman Ascoli. If nothing else, they left behind their name in the nearby mountain range, the Monti Sibillini.

The Sibyls held permanent court in locations throughout the ancient world. If Virgil's account of Aeneas' meeting with the Sibyl of Cumae is anything to go by, those requesting prophecies from a Sibyl witnessed her possessed by the god Apollo, who would utter his words through the medium of the prophetess. The problem with such pronouncements was their 'sibylline' nature, often so obscure as to be enigmatic and causing no uncertain anxiety in those trying to sort out their meaning.

Even if no Sibyl was ever resident in the Monti Sibillini in the Marches, the association was kept alive well into the Christian era. Various churches throughout the region contain frescoes depicting the oracles. In Ascoli Piceno itself, Tommaso Nardini decorated a vault of the ancient Chiesa di Sant'Angelo Magno with images of eight Sibyls, including the famous Delphic oracle and that of Cumae. ■

Sibillini are also the scene of more energetic sporting activities such as hang-gliding and horse riding. To reach the range, take the SS4 from Ascoli Piceno and follow the signs. Buses connect the area with Ascoli Piceno and various cities throughout the Marches. See also the Valnerina section in the Umbria chapter for details about hang-gliding and how to get to the mountains from Umbria.

Information

If approaching from the north, along the SS78 from Ancona, stop at the AAST in Sarnano (☎ 0733-65 71 95) in Piazza Perfetti 17. They may have limited walking and climbing information. There is nothing at the AAST in Ascoli Piceno. The CAI publishes a detailed guide in Italian to the mountains, complete with maps, *Parco Nazionale dei Sibillini – Le Più Belle Escursioni*, by Alberico Alesi and Maurizio Calibani.

Activities

Amandola makes a good base to explore the area, but lacks cheap accommodation. It is one of the prettiest villages in the Marches and is just north of Montefortino, which is a good base for walking. Montefortino is rea-

sonably close to the serious walking areas around Montemonaco, at the base of Monte Sibilla.

Montemonaco is an out-of-the-way town and not easily reached by public transport, although you'll be surprised by the number of tourists in summer. Many are there for the Gola dell'Infernaccio (Gorge of Hell), one of the easiest and most scenic walks in the Marches. The range is littered with rifugi and offers reasonable skiing in winter.

Places to Stay

There is a camping ground just south of Montefortino at Cerrentana. The *Montespino* (☎ 0736-85 92 38) has sites for L6000 a person and L9000 a tent, and opens from June 1 to September 30. Go straight to Montemonaco for accommodation, as there are quite a few rooms at good rates. The *Rifugio della Montagna* (☎ 0736-85 63 27), in Foce, just near the town, has singles/doubles from L30,000/60,000. The *Albergo Sibilla* (☎ 0736-85 61 44), Via Roma 52, has rooms for slightly more. The *Albergo Simoni* (☎ 0736-84 42 88), Via Campo Sportivo, in the town of Comunanza, near Amandola, has cheap rooms.

Abruzzo & Molise

Abruzzo, and neighbouring Molise, is one of the few parts of Italy to be spared the influx of mass tourism. Although neither region is as rich in artistic and cultural heritage as their more illustrious neighbours to the west, north and south, there is still plenty to explore, particularly in Abruzzo.

Until administratively divided in 1963, Abruzzo and Molise were known as the Abruzzi, a term still commonly used to describe the two. The earthquake-prone region was particularly hard-hit in 1915, when a massive jolt left 30,000 people dead.

Abruzzo

The wild beauty of Abruzzo's mountain terrain is captivating – the bald, craggy peaks of the Gran Sasso d'Italia, capped by the Corno Grande (at 2914 metres the highest mountain in the Apennines), have perilous drops of up to 1000 metres. Farther south, wolves and bears still roam protected in the forests of the Parco Nazionale d'Abruzzo.

The region is not just for nature-lovers. The medieval towns of L'Aquila and Sulmona are well worth visiting, and the countryside is spattered, much like the Marches to the north, with an array of castles and isolated, hilltop *borghi* – cluttered towns and villages little changed over hundreds of years.

Abruzzo's ancient fame is for witches, wizards and snake-charmers – members of a tribe known as the Marsi, who lived around modern Avezzano. Even today, snakes feature in a bizarre annual religious festival in the mountain village of Cocullo, near Sulmona.

Traditionally farm and grazing territory, Abruzzo's sheep farmers still play an important role in the local economy. A key agricultural area is the Piana del Fucino,

south of L'Aquila, which was created by draining the vast Lago Fucino in the late 19th century. Prince Torlonia undertook the project on condition that he would have title to the land, and it was completed during the Fascist period. It was not until the 1950s that the Italian government took over the plain and parcelled it out to local peasants.

Torlonia's efforts were not a first. The ancient Romans had a shot at draining the lake in what proved a remarkable, yet disastrous, feat of engineering. Under the orders of Emperor Claudius, the Romans built a tunnel about 10 km long to drain the lake into a neighbouring valley. Unfortunately, when the outlet tunnel was opened it proved too small for the massive volume of water in the lake and thousands of spectators, including the emperor himself, almost drowned.

L'AQUILA

The evening sun casts an opaque rose light across the Gran Sasso d'Italia just to the north of L'Aquila, an encouraging counterpoint to the somewhat gloomy regional capital. In spite of repeated earthquakes, the medieval core of the city remains an interesting place to explore, but L'Aquila's curious beginnings are perhaps more intriguing still. Emperor Frederick II founded the town in 1240, it is said, by drawing together the citizens of 99 villages. Whether true or not, the number 99 became a symbol. The citizens of L'Aquila ('the Eagle', a reference to the eagle in the imperial coat of arms) established 99 churches and 99 piazzas, as well as a fountain with (almost) 99 spouts. Earthquakes, especially one in 1703, have destroyed most of the churches and piazzas, but the medieval fountain survives and, every evening, the town hall bell chimes 99 times.

L'Aquila's people have a rebellious spirit but have frequently backed the wrong horse. King Manfred destroyed the city in 1266 because the people supported the Pope, and

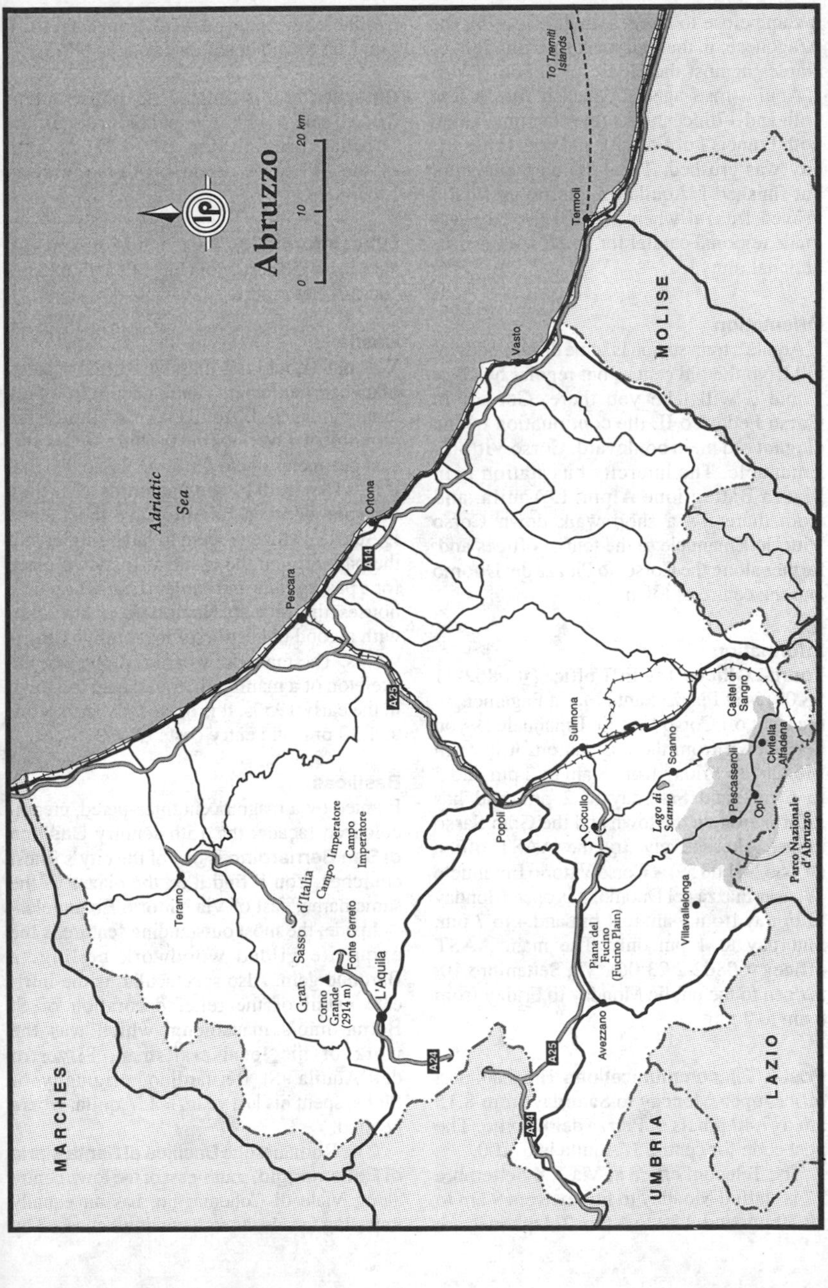

Abruzzo

0   10   20 km

MARCHES

Adriatic
Sea

To Tremiti
Islands

Termoli

Vasto

Ortona

Pescara

MOLISE

A14

A25

Teramo

Gran Sasso d'Italia

Campo Imperatore
Campo Imperatore

Corno
Grande
(2914 m)

Fonte Cerreto

L'Aquila

A24

Popoli

Sulmona

Castel di
Sangro

Scanno

Cocullo

Lago di
Scanno

Pescasseroli

Civitella
Alfadena

Opi

Parco Nazionale
d'Abruzzo

A24

Avezzano

Piana del
Fucino
(Fucino Plain)

A25

Villavallelonga

UMBRIA

LAZIO

it came close to a repeat under siege by the Aragonese, in the fight over the Kingdom of Naples against the House of Anjou. Twice L'Aquila rose against Spanish rule in the 16th and 17th centuries (the first time allied with Francis I of France), and both times the city was crushed. The 1703 earthquake all but finished L'Aquila off, but revolt finally proved fruitful when in 1860 the city was made regional capital for its efforts towards national unity.

Orientation

L'Aquila's train station is some distance downhill from the old centre, but regular bus Nos 1 and 3 will take you there. Get off in Corso Federico II, the continuation of the elegant old main boulevard, Corso Vittorio Emanuele. The intercity bus station is in Piazza Battaglione Alpini L'Aquila, and from there it's a short walk down Corso Vittorio Emanuele to the tourist offices and, farther along the Corso, to Piazza del Duomo and the centre of town.

Information

Tourist Offices The EPT office (☎ 0862-41 08 08) is at Piazza Santa Maria Paganica, to the right off Corso Vittorio Emanuele as you head down from the bus station. It is open Monday to Friday from 8 am to 2 pm and 5 to 6 pm, and Saturday to 2 pm, and has information on the town and the Gran Sasso range. Alternatively, try the AAST office (☎ 0862-41 08 59) at Corso Vittorio Emanuele 49, near Piazza del Duomo. It is open Monday to Friday from 9 am to 1 pm and 4 to 7 pm, Saturday to 1 pm only. The main AAST office (☎ 0862-2 23 06), Via Settembre 10, is open to the public Monday to Friday from 8 am to 2 pm.

Post & Telecommunications The main post office, open Monday to Saturday from 8.15 am to 7.40 pm, is in Piazza del Duomo. The post code for central L'Aquila is 67100.

The Telecom office at Via XX Settembre 77 is staffed Monday to Friday from 9 am to 12.30 pm and 2.30 to 6 pm. Telephones are available seven days a week from 8 am to 10 pm. The town's telephone code is 0862.

Emergency For immediate police attendance, call ☎ 113. The public hospital, the Ospedale San Salvatore (☎ 77 81), is north of the old town centre on Corso Vittorio Emanuele.

Other Information There is a 24-hour petrol station on the corner of Corso Federico II and Via XX Settembre.

Castle

Without a doubt this massive edifice of steep blanched battlements sunk deep into a now empty moat is L'Aquila's most impressive monument. Overlooking the old city's northeast perimeter out to the Gran Sasso d'Italia, it was first built by the Spaniards after they had put down a rebellion by the locals. L'Aquila's citizens seem to have singled out the path around the castle as the ideal place for a passeggiata and endless chat. The castle houses the **Museo Nazionale d'Abruzzo**, with a good collection of local religious artworks. The main draw card is, however, the skeleton of a mammoth, found near the town in the early 1950s. It is open daily from 9 am to 1.30 pm, and entry costs L8000.

Basilicas

Fronted by a magnificent three-tiered, cream-coloured façade, the 15th-century **Basilica di San Bernardino** is one of the city's finest churches. You'll find it on the piazza of the same name, east of Via Vittorio Emanuele.

Inside, the most outstanding feature is the exquisite gilded woodwork ceiling, a Baroque gem. Also spectacular is the intricate detail of the relief decoration of St Bernardino's mausoleum which was the work of the local craftsman, Silvestro dell'Aquila. St Bernardino, originally of Siena, spent his last years in L'Aquila, where he died.

The Romanesque **Basilica di Santa Maria di Collemaggio**, south-east of the town centre along Viale di Collemaggio, has an equally imposing façade, its rose windows encased by

L'Aquila

0   150   300 m

To Rieti & A24 Autostrada

To Fonte Cerreto

PLACES TO STAY		23	Ristorante L'Angogli Scardassieri	8	Piazza Santa Maria Paganica
2	Locanda Orazi	24	Sorelle Nuria	13	Porta Castello
3	Hotel Castello	28	Ristorante Renato	14	Basilica di San Bernadino
30	Hotel Duomo	29	Pasticceria Fratelli Nurzia	15	Piazza San Bernardino
31	Albergo Aurora			16	AAST Tourist Office
				18	Train Station
				19	Porta Rivera
		OTHER		20	Fontana della 99 Cannelle
				22	Piazza San Biagio
PLACES TO EAT		1	Hospital	25	Duomo
		4	Intercity Bus Station	26	Post Office
9	Ristorante la Mimosa	5	Piazza Battaglione Alpini L'Aquila	27	Telecom Office
10	Trattoria del Giaguaro	6	Castle &	32	BNL Bank (ATM)
11	Pizza Marchigiana		Museo Nazionale d'Abruzzo	33	24-Hour Petrol Station
12	Pizzeria Due Mari	7	EPT Tourist Office	34	Basilica di Santa Maria di Collemaggio
17	Gran Caffè Eden				
21	Trattoria San Biagio				

ABRUZZO

a quilt pattern of pink and white marble. The basilica was built at the instigation of a hermit, Pietro da Morrone, who was elected pope at the age of 80 in 1294, two years after the death of his predecessor, Pope Nicholas IV. Pietro took the name Celestine V, but this unworldly and trusting man was no match for the machinations of courtiers and politicians and eventually was forced to abdicate. His successor, Pope Boniface VIII, saw Celestine as a threat and threw him into prison, where he died. As founder of the Celestine order, he was canonised seven years later and his tomb is inside the basilica.

Fontana delle 99 Cannelle

A symbol of the city, the 'Fountain of the 99 Spouts' was erected in the late 13th century. No-one knows where the water originates, but until well into this century it was the town's life blood. Count up the various stone faces, gargoyles and the like – they do not in fact appear to add up to the magic number!

Places to Stay

The only central and cheap place is the basic *Albergo Aurora* (☎ 2 20 53), just off Piazza del Duomo at Via Cimino 21. When singles are available they cost L35,000, while doubles/triples cost L46,000/48,000. You could also try the *Locanda Orazi* (☎ 41 28 89), Via Roma 175, which has singles/doubles for L30,000/46,000.

The pleasant *Hotel Duomo* (☎ 41 08 93; fax 41 30 58), Via Dragonetti 6, the next street along from Via Cimino, has singles/doubles with bathroom, telephone and TV for L80,000/120,000. The less inspiring *Hotel Castello* (☎ 41 91 47) in Piazza Battaglione Alpini L'Aquila has rooms with the same facilities for around the same price.

Places to Eat

Traditional local dishes include *maccheroni alla chitarra*, thick macaroni cut with an instrument resembling a guitar, and lamb, either roasted or grilled. Produce is sold in the market held most days in Piazza del Duomo.

For snacks, you can try pizza slices at *Pizza Marchigiana*, Via Vittorio Emanuele 117, or *Pizzeria Due Mari* at No 109. The *Ristorante L'Angoli Scardassieri*, Via Sassa 11, just north-west off Piazza del Duomo, has a good set lunch for L15,000.

Nearby, at *Trattoria San Biagio*, Piazza San Biagio, along Via Sassa from Piazza del Duomo, you can dine well on local specialities for around L25,000. Another good choice for a low-priced meal is *Trattoria del Giaguaro*, Piazza Santa Maria Paganica 4. *Ristorante la Mimosa*, tucked away at Via Navelli 22, is more expensive at around L35,000 for a full meal, but offers excellent food. Another, more expensive option is *Ristorante Renato*, Via dell' Indipendenza 9.

Cafés & Sweets *Gran Caffè Eden* is one of the more elegant bars along Via Vittorio Emanuele, but for sweet food you should make straight for *Sorelle Nuria*, at No 38. They specialise in a chocolate variety of *torrone*, a scrumptious nougat confection. For the competition, try the *Pasticceria Fratelli Nurzia* (sic!) at Piazza del Duomo 51. They've been getting sticky fingers since 1835.

Entertainment

There is an annual season of concerts from October to May run by, among others, the Società Aquilana dei Concerti. The AAST office can provide information. If you're in town in summer, ask about the special summer concert, ballet and drama performances.

Getting There & Away

ARPA buses for Rome (L14,100; terminates at Piazzale Tiburtina) and Pescara (L11,000) leave from Piazza Battaglione Alpini L'Aquila. ARPA buses also connect L'Aquila with Avezzano and Sulmona. By train, the town is accessible from Rome via Sulmona or Terni, and from Pescara via Sulmona. From the train station, take local

ASM bus No 1 or 3 to the town centre. The A24 connects L'Aquila with Rome, and the A25 leads to Pescara.

GRAN SASSO D'ITALIA

The rocky peaks of the Gran Sasso d'Italia are close by L'Aquila. Try the city's tourist offices for details on walking trails and rifugi. A cable car leaves Fonte Cerreto every 30 minutes for Campo Imperatore (2117 metres), providing access to decent walking trails and a small but popular ski resort of the same name. Chair and ski lifts operate on the runs at Campo Imperatore and there is more skiing at nearby Monte Cristo, as well as Campo Felice.

There is a camping ground, the *Funivia del Gran Sasso* (☎ 60 61 63), at Fonte Cerreto, and a network of mountain rifugi in the area. Hotel accommodation at Fonte Cerreto and Campo Imperatore is limited to the relatively expensive three-star category, and includes the *Nido dell'Aquila* (☎ 60 66 43; fax 60 63 36) at Fonte Cerreto, which has singles/doubles starting at L90,000/120,000, and the *Campo Imperatore* (☎ 40 00 00; fax 41 32 01) at Campo Imperatore, which has doubles for L160,000.

From L'Aquila, take bus No 6 (six daily) from Via Castello to the cable car at Fonte Cerreto.

SULMONA

Sulmona, the birthplace of Ovid, is an understated but charming little town, hemmed in by mountains. The medieval centre invites one to wander, and the town is well placed to serve as a base for exploring southern Abruzzo.

Its modern claim to fame is the *confetti* industry – the making of elaborate flower-shaped arrangements of sugar almonds, a must at traditional Italian weddings.

Orientation & Information

The town's main street, Corso Ovidio, runs from the small park at Piazzale Tresca to the vast Piazza Garibaldi, a five-minute walk.

Sulmona's AAST office (☎ 0864-5 32 76), Corso Ovidio 108, is open Monday to Saturday from 8 am to 2 pm. The town's telephone code is 0864.

Things to See

Sulmona's main attraction is the **Palazzo dell'Annunziata** on Corso Ovidio, which combines Gothic and Renaissance styles. Note the beautifully carved frieze halfway up the façade. The building houses a small museum dedicated to the work of Sulmona's Renaissance goldsmiths. Next to the palace is a Baroque church of the same name, rebuilt after the 1703 earthquake. Also along Corso Ovidio, in Piazza XX Settembre, is a statue of Ovid.

Piazza Garibaldi is the scene of a colourful market every Wednesday and Saturday morning. When the bustle of the market clears, you can take a closer look at the austere Renaissance **Fontana del Vecchio**

Ovid

The image of the Augustan poet, considered by some second only to Virgil, is mixed and not altogether flattering. Born in Sulmona in 43 BC and sent at an early age to Rome to study rhetoric and make himself a comfortable career in the cesspit of Roman politics, he preferred to write poetry instead. His early erotic verse, such as *Amores* and *Ars Amatoria* gained him quick popularity in Roman high society. Possibly his most ambitious work was the *Metamorphosis*, a kind of extended cover version of a whole gamut of Greek myth culminating in descriptions of Caesar's transformation into a star and the apotheosis of Augustus, ruler at the time. This last piece of sycophancy did not stop the emperor from banishing him to the Black Sea in 8 AD for reasons not entirely clear. He died in Tomi, in modern Romania, 10 years later. ■

ABRUZZO

and the medieval **aqueduct**, which borders the piazza on two sides. The most interesting feature of the **Chiesa di San Martino**, also on the square, is its Gothic entrance. In the adjacent Piazza del Carmine, the Romanesque portal is all that remains of the **Chiesa di San Francesco della Scarpa**, destroyed in the 1703 earthquake.

Places to Stay & Eat
The *Locanda di Giovanni* (☎ 5 13 97) at Via Peligna 8, along Via Mazara from Corso Ovidio, has singles/doubles for L30,000/50,000. The pleasant *Hotel Italia* (☎ 5 23 08) in Piazza San Tommaso, through Piazza XX Settembre from Corso Ovidio, has rooms with a bathroom for L50,000/60,000. *Hotel Artù* (☎ 5 27 58) is at the entrance to the old town, just before the park, in Viale Roosevelt. It has clean, modern rooms for L40,000/55,000, or L50,000/65,000 with a bathroom.

For a square meal with no frills (about L20,000 a head), try the *Ristorante Stella* in Via Mazara. For more ambience and with more money, head for the *Ristorante Italia*, Piazza XX Settembre 22.

Getting There & Away
ARPA buses link Sulmona to L'Aquila (nine daily), Pescara (five daily), Naples (two daily), Scanno (10 daily) and other nearby towns. From Piazza Tresca, walk along Via di Circonvallazione Orientale to reach the bus station, off Via Japasseri. ARPA buses also head for Castel di Sangro and Pescasseroli in the Parco Nazionale d'Abruzzo.

Regular trains connect the town with Rome and Pescara. The train station is about two km downhill from the historic centre, and half-hourly buses (bus No A) will take you between the two.

AROUND SULMONA
Cocullo
The tiny mountain village of Cocullo warrants a visit only on one day of the year – the first Thursday in May, when its inhabitants celebrate the feast day of St Dominic in original and weird fashion. A statue of the saint is draped with live snakes and carried

in procession through the town, accompanied by townspeople also carrying live snakes. Known as the Processione dei Serpari (Procession of the Snake-Charmers), the festival has pagan origins and is an unforgettable experience.

The village has no accommodation, but is close to Sulmona and Scanno and linked to both by ARPA bus. Plan to arrive in the village early on the day of the festival, as it has attracted increasingly large crowds in recent years. Festivities usually start around 10 am, culminating in the procession at midday and then continuing throughout the afternoon.

Ask at the tourist offices in Sulmona or Scanno for details on buses to Cocullo, since services are augmented for the event.

Scanno
This village was assaulted by various photographers after WW II, and made into an example of traditionalism in the modern world. As a result, Scanno has become something of a minor tourist mecca for Italians. The handful of elderly women who still skittle about in traditional costume must, you can't help thinking, take some affront at having become individual mobile tourist 'sights'.

Scanno was long a centre of wool production, and for centuries an exclusive supplier to the Franciscan order. Today the cheerfully jumbled medieval village is surrounded by an outcrop of uninspired modern 'suburbia', not a little of which is given over to hotel space.

The place is worth the effort, especially if you have made it this far into Abruzzo. The drive south from Sulmona through the Gole di Saggitario (the Saggitarius Gorges) and past the peaceful Lago di Scanno is delightful, and beyond Scanno the road takes you right into the Parco Nazionale d'Abruzzo.

Information The AAST office (☎ 7 43 17), Via Santa Maria della Valle 12, is at the edge of the medieval town centre. The telephone code for Scanno is 0864.

Places to Stay & Eat If you plan to stay overnight, there is a camping ground at the Lago di Scanno, the *Camping I Lupi* (☎ 74 01 00), which opens from June to September. The town is crammed with hotels. Try the *Pensione Nilde* (☎ 7 43 59), Via Dela Lago, which has singles/doubles for L35,000/55,000, or the *Pensione Margherita* (☎ 7 43 53), Via Tanturri, which has rooms for L45,000/70,000. The *Hotel Vittoria* (☎ 74 71 79), Via Domenico di Rienzo 46, is a more upmarket option at L80,000/100,000.

For a meal, *Ristorante Gli Archetti* and the *Trattoria Lo Sgabello*, both in the medieval village, are decent spots.

Getting There & Away ARPA buses connect Scanno with Sulmona. An ARPA bus leaves Piazza della Repubblica in Rome for Scanno. Contact the EPT office in Via Parigi, Rome, for information.

PARCO NAZIONALE D'ABRUZZO
Established in 1923 with a former royal hunting reserve as its nucleus, the Parco Nazionale d'Abruzzo now incorporates about 40,000 hectares of the Apennines (plus an external protected area of 60,000 hectares). It is the last refuge in Italy of the Marsican brown bear and the Apennine wolf, although it is difficult to spot one of

The Apennine wolf is now rarely seen.

these now rare native animals. The park is also home to golden eagles, a herd of chamois and the odd wildcat. There are plans to reintroduce the lynx, which became extinct in this area around the turn of the century. The park's forests and meadows are perfect for family excursions and long-distance walks, but it is prohibited to leave the marked trails.

Orientation & Information
The most convenient base is the town of **Pescasseroli** (telephone code 0863), in the centre of the park, where there is a visitor's centre and tourist office, as well as accommodation. The visitor's centre, open daily from 10 am to midday and 3 to 6 pm (entrance L5000), features a museum and small zoo, where some of the park's native animals including a wolf, a Marsican brown bear and a lynx are housed in depressingly small enclosures.

The tourist office (☎ 91 27 60), at Via Piave 9, can provide information on accommodation and transport. It is open daily from 9 am to 1 pm and 4.30 to 6.30 pm. Before setting off, you should buy a detailed map of the park, which includes the walking trails and locations of rifugi, available at the Ufficio di Zona (☎ 9 19 55), Viale Gabriele d'Annunzio, just off the town's main square, the Piazza Sant'Antonio.

Another possible base is the small mountain village of **Civitella Alfadena**, on the park's eastern edge. Less touristy and more laid-back than Pescasseroli, it has a visitor's centre and a large enclosure housing six wolves. In a smaller enclosure (*area faunistica lince*) lurks a pair of lynx, under observation since 1991 to determine their suitability for release into the park.

Places to Stay
Free-camping is forbidden in the park, but there are several camping grounds, including the *Campeggio dell'Orso* (☎ 9 19 55), near the village of Opi. There are also rifugi in the park, but few are open and you must obtain permission and a key, from the Ufficio di Zona at Villavallelonga (☎ 94 92 61). Try the

visitor's centre in Pescasseroli for information.

Hotel Pinguino (☎ 91 25 80), Via Collachi 2, has singles/doubles with a bathroom for L60,000/80,000, and the *Hotel Cristiana* (☎ 91 07 95), just outside the town in Collachi, has doubles for L70,000 with a bathroom and breakfast included.

The best place to eat in Pescasseroli is the *Ristorante Pizzeria Picchio*, Via Lungo Sangro, where a full meal will cost up to L35,000. The *fast-food* outlet at Via Vittorio Veneto 11, near Piazza Sant'Antonio, opens for lunch and serves good pasta and panini.

If you want to stay overnight in Civitella Alfadena, the best choice is the *Albergo La Torre* (☎ 0864-89 01 21), in the centre of the old town, which has rooms for L25,000 per person. There is a couple of affittacamere too.

Getting There & Away
Pescasseroli, Civitella Alfadena and other villages in the park are linked by ARPA bus to Avezzano (and from there to L'Aquila), or from Castel di Sangro (reached from Sulmona by bus or train). In summer an ARPA bus leaves from Piazza della Repubblica in Rome for Pescasseroli (go to the EPT office in Via Parigi, Rome, for information).

PESCARA
A heavily developed beach resort and commercial centre, Pescara's only attraction is the beach and even that is nothing to write home about. However, travellers to Abruzzo are likely to pass through Pescara since it is also the main transport hub of the region, with trains connecting it to Bologna, Ancona, Rome and Bari, and buses running to towns throughout Abruzzo.

There is a jazz festival in the second half of July at the Teatro D'Annunzio, in the public park by the beach east of the city centre. The tourist office can provide information. Museo Ittico is a fishery museum on the waterfront at Via Raffaele Paolucci, but you'd have to be pretty desperate for something to do.

Orientation & Information
From the train station and intercity bus station in Piazzale della Repubblica, the beach is a short walk north-east down Corso Umberto I.

There is an EPT office (☎ 085-421 17 07) at Via Nicola Fabrizi 10, a few blocks in from the beach. It is open Monday to Saturday from 8 am to noon and 5 to 7 pm. Hours are usually extended in summer.

Post & Telecommunications The post office is at Corso Vittorio Emanuele II 106, to the right off Piazzale della Repubblica, and open Monday to Saturday from 8.15 am to 7.40 pm. The post code for central Pescara is 65100.

The Telecom office is at Piazza del Sacro Cuore 20 and is open daily from 8 am to 10 pm. The telephone code for Pescara is 085.

In a police emergency, call ☎ 113. The public hospital, the Ospedale Civile (☎ 37 31 11), is at Via Renato Paolini, south-west of the train station, off Via del Circuito.

Places to Stay & Eat
The *Internazionale* camping ground (☎ 6 56 53) is by the beach on Lungomare Cristoforo Colombo (take bus No 10 from the train station). Near the station, at Via Michelangelo Forti 14, is *Hotel Alba* (☎ 2 82 58), which has singles/doubles with a bathroom for L50,000/75,000. The *Hotel Natale* (☎ 421 21 80), Via del Circuito 175, has pleasant singles/doubles for L42,000/75,000, but bargaining is possible. The *Hotel Ambra* (☎ 37 82 47), Via Quarto dei Mille 28, off Via M Forti, has singles/doubles for L50,000/75,000. Prices tend to rise marginally in summer.

For a reasonably priced meal, try the *Pinguino*, Corso Manthonè, across the Pescara river. A meal at *Cantina di Jooz*, in the parallel Via delle Caserme, will cost around L40,000.

Getting There & Away
Bus ARPA buses leave from Piazzale

della Repubblica for L'Aquila, Sulmona and virtually all other possible destinations in Abruzzo. SATAM has a daily service to Naples (about five hours) while Eagle Lines buses pass through twice a week on the long haul trip from Taranto in Apulia to Udine in Friuli. Timetables are posted at the ticket office in the piazza.

Train Pescara is on the main train line along the Adriatic coast and is easily accessible to and from towns such as Bologna, Ancona, Foggia and points farther south, as well as L'Aquila, Sulmona and Rome.

Car & Motorbike You can choose between the A14 and often busy SS16 heading north or south along the coast. Those heading for Rome, L'Aquila or Sulmona should take the A25 or SS5.

Ferry A ferry to Split in Croatia may be operating again by the time you read this. Check with Agenzia Sanmar (☎ 6 52 47) at the ferry terminal, just south of the Pescara river.

Molise

Hived off in 1963 from its bigger northern sibling, Abruzzo, Molise is a small, hilly and rather undistinguished region. A kind of cultural bridge from north to south, it has a low ranking on the tourist trail.

Largely rural and repeatedly shaken by devastating earthquakes, its towns are prosaic and of little interest. In fact, the traveller moving north to south will notice, perhaps for the first time, those great clumps of hideous concrete blocks that seem to pass for a kind of standard in modern Mediterranean 'architecture' (some misnomer!), whether in southern Italy, Spain, Morocco or Egypt.

It's not all bad news. You can wander through the Roman provincial town, Saepinum, south-west of Campobasso, and there are good walking opportunities in the Monti del Matese. Excavations in Isernia have unearthed what is believed to be the oldest village in Europe, and the small beach resort of Termoli is a jumping-off point for the Tremiti Islands, bunched together off the coast of northern Apulia (see the Apulia section of the Apulia, Basilicata & Calabria chapters).

CAMPOBASSO
The regional capital, Campobasso is predominantly modern and basically unappealing, but makes a good base for exploring nearby Saepinum. The national carabinieri training school is here, as is a high-security prison.

The EPT office (0874-41 56 62) is at Piazza della Vittoria 14, open Monday to Saturday from 8.30 am to about 1.30 pm. From the train station, turn left into Via Cavour, right into Via Gazzani and left again into Corso Vittorio Emanuele to reach the office. The telephone code is 0874.

You can kill a couple of hours wandering up into the older part of town to take a look at the Romanesque churches of **San Bartolomeo** (13th century) and **San Giorgio** (12th century). The castle you can see from a distance looks impressive until you get close.

If you need a bed for the night, try the *Albergo Belvedere* (☎ 6 27 24), Via Colle delle Api 32, which has singles/doubles for L28,000/48,000 and triples for L65,000. From the train station, take bus No 1N and ask the driver to let you off at the hotel.

Campobasso is connected by bus to Termoli, Isernia and Pescara. By train it can be reached from Rome via Sulmona, or from Naples via Benevento.

AROUND CAMPOBASSO
One of the least visited Roman ruins in Italy, **Saepinum** is handy to Campobasso and worth a visit. An unimportant provincial town, it survived into the 9th century before being sacked by Arab invaders. Surrounded by small farms, the ruins are quite well preserved and include the town walls, a temple,

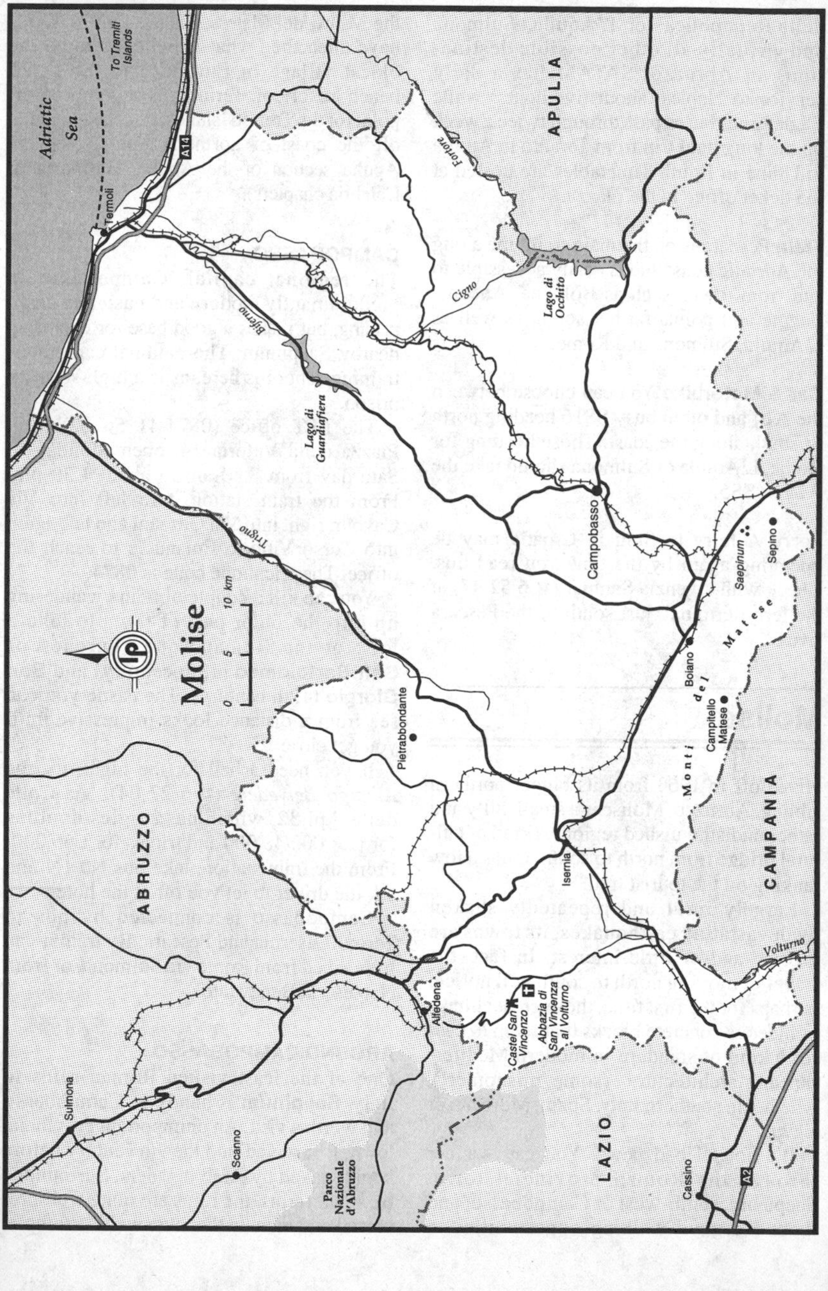
Molise
0
5
10 km
Adriatic Sea
To Tremiti Islands
Termoli
A14
Biferno
Lago di Guardiafiera
Trigno
Cigno
Fortore
APULIA
Lago di Occhito
Campobasso
Saepinum
Sepino
Bojano
Monti del Matese
Campitello Matese
CAMPANIA
Volturno
Pietrabbondante
ABRUZZO
Isernia
Alfedena
Castel San Vincenzo
Abbazia di San Vincenzo al Volturno
Sulmona
Scanno
Parco Nazionale d'Abruzzo
LAZIO
Cassino
A2

a triumphal arch and the foundations of numerous houses.

To reach Saepinum by public transport, you will need to take one of the infrequent provincial buses to Altilia, next to the archaeological zone, or Sepino, a three-km walk away.

The **Monti del Matese** south-west of Campobasso offer good hiking in summer and adequate skiing in winter. Take a bus from Campobasso to Campitello Matese, or a train from Campobasso or Isernia to Boiano. From either point there are trails into the mountains.

Campitello Matese is the centre for winter sports and has several hotels, but there's nothing cheap about them. *Lo Sciatore* (☎ 0874-78 41 37) charges L110,000 a person, including full board. They have no single rooms and will charge more if you want a room to yourself. On the other hand, they give discounts for groups and stays longer than one night.

ISERNIA

If you want to see what a town held together by scaffolding looks like, then the earthquake battered old centre of Isernia is the place for you. Otherwise it's modern and dull. In 1979 evidence of a village thought to be up to 700,000 years old, possibly the most ancient settlement in Europe, was discovered here, but this is unlikely to make your stay any more exciting. Excavations continue, and stone tools discovered at the site are on display at the town's small **Museo Nazionale**, Corso Marcelli 48 (head to the left along Corso Garibaldi from the train station).

Isernia's EPT office (☎ 0865-39 92) is at Via Farinacci 9, a short walk from the station (turn left into Corso Garibaldi and right into Via Farinacci). It is open Monday to Saturday from 8 am to 2 pm. The town's telephone code is 0865.

For a place to stay, try the *Hotel Sayonara* (☎ 5 09 92), Via G Berta 131, which has singles/doubles with a bathroom for L45,000/60,000. Try bargaining if you plan to stay for several nights.

Isernia is easily reached by bus from Campobasso and Termoli and by train from Sulmona, Pescara and Campobasso.

AROUND ISERNIA

Provincial buses will take you to local hill-top villages. Of interest are the remains of a pre-Roman village just outside **Pietrabbondante**, about 30 km north-east of Isernia. It was settled by the Samnites, who controlled the area of Molise before Roman domination. Three buses a day connect Isernia and Pietrabbondante.

Near Castel San Vincenzo, about 20 km north-west of Isernia, is the **Abbazia di San Vincenzo al Volturno** (take the bus for Castel San Vincenzo from Isernia and then walk one km to the abbey). Founded in the 8th century, this Benedictine abbey was destroyed by Arabs and rebuilt several times afterwards. However, a cycle of 9th-century Byzantine frescoes survived in the crypt and these merit a visit. Isernia's tourist office can advise on the abbey's irregular opening hours.

TERMOLI

Considerably lower in key compared to some of its northern rivals, Termoli makes a relaxing if unexciting beach stop. The tiny medieval *borgo* will keep you occupied for a wee while with its 12th-century **cathedral** and 13th-century Swabian **castle**, built by Frederick II. Termoli is also a year-round jumping-off point for the Tremiti Islands. The town is filled with holiday-makers in summer and accommodation, especially for the budget conscious, is tight. Things don't improve in winter, as much of it shuts down.

The AAST office (☎ 70 67 54) is in Piazza Bega, a short walk along Corso Umberto I from the train station. It opens Monday to Saturday from 8.15 am to 1 pm. The town's telephone code is 0875.

Places to Stay & Eat

There are camping facilities at *Cala Saracena* (☎ 5 21 93), Via SS Europa 2, No 174 (also known as SS16 to Pescara). It can be reached by local bus from the train station.

The *Affittacamere Porreca* (☎ 70 42 48), Via Mascilongo 34, has singles/doubles for L30,000/ 50,000 – don't let the abrupt manner of the staff put you off.

Hotel Meridiano (☎ 70 59 46) overlooks the beach on Lungomare Cristoforo Colombo and has singles/doubles with a bathroom for L60,000/80,000. It often closes in winter.

For a reasonable fish meal and some rough wine, try *Da Antonio* at Corso Umberto I 59. A very full meal will cost about L30,000.

Getting There & Away

Bus SATI buses connect Termoli to Campobasso and Pescara, and Isernia can be reached with the Cerella company. The main intercity bus station is in Piazza Bega. Buses also connect the town with Rome,

Milan and Naples (the tourist office has full details on bus timetables).

Train Termoli is on the main Bologna-Lecce train line along the Adriatic coast.

Car & Motorbike Termoli is on the A14 and SS16 that follow the coast north to Pescara and beyond and south to Bari.

Boat Termoli is the only place from where you can get a daily ferry all year round to the Tremiti Islands (see Apulia section of the Apulia, Basilicata & Calabria chapter). Bookings can be made through Intercontinental Viaggi (☎ 70 53 41), or at ticket booths at the ferry terminal. There is at least one departure a day (7 or 9 am), and tickets are L11,800 one way. Hydrofoils run from April to September.

Campania

Presided over by the magnificent, chaotic capital of the south, Naples, Campania has everything the traveller could want. Apart from the only true metropolis in the Mezzogiorno (literally midday, the evocative name for the country's south), Campania is blessed with some of the country's most dramatic coastline, a sprinkling of magical islands and a rich heritage in ancient ruins.

Better news still, the lion's share of Campania's jewels are concentrated in a comparatively small area around Naples. You could conceivably sample the cream of the offerings in a week, although the less time-conscious traveller could easily linger a month.

In the shadow of Mt Vesuvius lie the ruins of Pompeii and Herculaneum, Roman cities

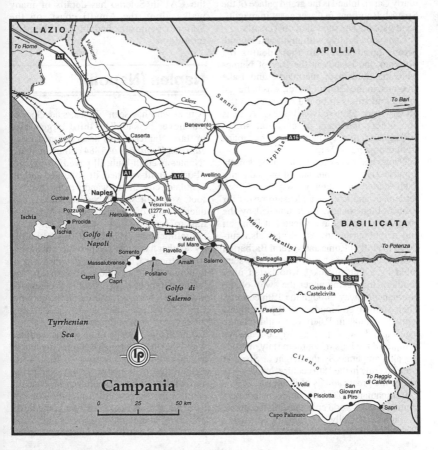

Campania

extinguished by the volcano and so preserved for posterity – both a short excursion south of Naples. For the classicist, there is plenty more to explore, including the Campi Flegrei (Phlegraean Fields) to the north of the capital, where you can still find sparse reminders of the world celebrated in the writings of Homer and Virgil. In the region's south stand the Greek temples of Paestum, among the best preserved in the world.

Rivers of ink have been spilled in the attempt to do justice to the natural beauty of the Amalfi coast, farther south of Pompeii, and the islands in the Bay of Naples, particularly Capri. Inland is the grand palace of the Spanish Bourbons in Caserta, set in magnificent gardens and modelled on Versailles.

Campania is alive with myth and legend. Sirens lured sailors to their deaths off Sorrento, the islands in the Bay of Naples were the domain of mermaids, and Lake Avernus, in the Campi Flegrei, was believed in ancient times to be the entrance to the underworld. Odysseus (Ulysses), Aeneas and other characters of classical storytelling and history have left their mark (real or imagined) here.

Naples and its bay remain the most densely populated area of Campania, although the city itself started life humbly, first as a Greek settlement and later as a pleasure resort for Rome's high society. Little touched by the eruption of 79 AD that wiped out Pompeii and neighbouring towns, Naples also survived the fall of Rome and several Barbarian assaults to become an independent city state ruled by a line of dukes who lasted until southern Italy came under the sway of the Normans midway through the 12th century. Their short-lived kingdom of the Normans, with its capital in Palermo, would change hands and dimensions regularly, but always comprised the bulk of southern Italy, including all Campania. By the height of Spanish Bourbon rule in the 18th century, Naples was one of the great capitals of Europe.

Campanian cooking is simple, its greatest contribution to world cuisine being the pizza. In Naples especially, you can pick up a quick pizza with its unmistakable, rich tomato sauce on just about any street corner. Campania produces a number of decent wines, including various tipples under the name of Greco di Tufo. More likely to leap to the eyes is the bright yellow lemon liqueur *(Limoncello)* produced along the Sorrento and Amalfi coasts and on Capri. Best taken in small doses in summer, it's an acquired taste.

Naples is on the main train line from Rome and is a regional transport hub, making travel easy and cheap. Most places of interest in Campania are accessible by train, an advantage as tracking down buses can be tiresome. For the more adventurous, the CAI in Salerno has details of many walks along the Amalfi coast, on the Sorrento peninsula and in the Picentini mountains.

Naples (Napoli)

A man who has seen Naples, said Goethe, can never be sad. The third-largest city in Italy, Naples defies description. *Cook's Tourist's Handbook* of 1884 commented that 'Naples is an ill-built, ill-paved, ill-lighted, ill-drained, ill-watched, ill-governed and ill-ventilated city...if you wander extensively on foot, you will say of Naples what is frequently said of Constantinople'. Which, it has to be assumed, was nothing very complimentary. Istanbul (Constantinople by another name) and Naples have made big strides forward, but to many people's way of thinking, the observations of a century ago retain a grain of truth. There is another side to the coin, however, and for all the carping, Cook's concludes that the city 'is, perhaps, the loveliest spot in Europe'.

The life and vitality of its people, coupled with its own identity, give Naples the feel of a 'real city' – Italy's version of New York. Beautifully positioned on the bay, Naples has a bit of everything. The old centre, once the heart of the Neapolis of Antiquity and now jammed with ancient churches, a medieval university and countless eateries and cafés, pulsates to the life of noisy street markets and their clientele, swarms of people darting about on mopeds, and the general chaos of a city at work. To the south and west extend the broad boulevards and majestic squares that lead to Santa Lucia and chic Mergellina, while above it all, the city's upper middle class sits back in the relative calm of the Vomero district, a kind of natural balcony with grand views across the city and bay to Mt Vesuvius.

Less salubrious is the area around the main train station, east of the city centre, while in the endless peripheral sprawl of what have become Naples' suburbs, such as Pozzuoli, people eke out an existence in a dense concentration of tenement housing.

Nothing is orderly and regulation is observed with absolute discretion. Traffic lights – what few there are – are routinely ignored, as are one-way signs and just about every other road rule. When it became mandatory in Italy to wear seatbelts, it was in Naples that someone thought up the idea of a T-shirt with an imprint of a seatbelt sash. It is not unusual to see a whole family aboard a single Vespa, or children buzzing around dangerously fast on mopeds.

Naples is the centre of a booming clothing counterfeiting racket and the base for most of Italy's contraband cigarette smuggling. This industry involves the Camorra, Naples' brand of the Mafia, whose specialities are bank hold-ups, controlling the local fruit and vegetable markets, and the massive *toto nero* (illegal football pools). Ironically, most of its activities are unofficially sanctioned because of the employment they bring to the city.

The benevolence of Naples' monarchs, notably 'Good King' Robert of Anjou of the early 14th century, attracted poets and artists from all over Italy including Boccaccio, Petrarch and Giotto. After his arrival in 1607, Caravaggio inspired the founding of the Neapolitan school of painting, and regarded Naples as his new home. The city's Baroque architecture is among the country's grandest.

HISTORY

Soon after founding Cumae in 1000 BC,

colonists from Rhodes established a settlement on the west side of Mt Vesuvius and, according to legend, named it after the siren Parthenope. Several centuries later, Phoenician traders and Greeks from Athens, attracted by the splendour of the coast, expanded the settlement and christened it Neapolis (new city). It prospered as a centre of Greek culture and later, under Roman rule, became a favourite for such notables as Pompey, Caesar and Tiberius.

After successive waves of invasion by the Goths and a couple of spells in loose association with Byzantium, Naples remained an independent dukedom for about 400 years until taken by the Normans in 1139. They, in turn, were overthrown by the German Hohenstaufens, whose Swabian dynasty lasted until 1266 and gave the city many new institutions, including the university. After the defeat and death of Manfred in the battle of Benevento, Charles I of Anjou took control of the Kingdom of Sicily and turned Naples into its de facto capital. The Angevins were in turn succeeded, after a period of disorder, by the Spanish house of Aragon, under whom the city later prospered. Alfonso I of Aragon in particular introduced new laws and a more modern concept of justice, as well as promoting the arts and sciences.

In 1503, Naples and the Kingdom of Sicily were absorbed by the Spanish Empire, which sent viceroys to rule as virtual dictators. Notwithstanding their heavy-handed rule, Naples flourished artistically and acquired much of its splendour, and indeed continued to do so when the Spanish Bourbons re-established Naples as capital of the Kingdom of the Two Sicilies in 1734. Aside from a Napoleonic interlude under Joachim Murat from 1806 to 1815, the Bourbons remained in the saddle until unseated by the arrival of Garibaldi and the Kingdom of Italy. One of Europe's greatest cities, Naples was a serious, but unsuccessful, contender for capital of the new nation.

The city sustained heavy damage during WW II in more than 100 bombing raids, and

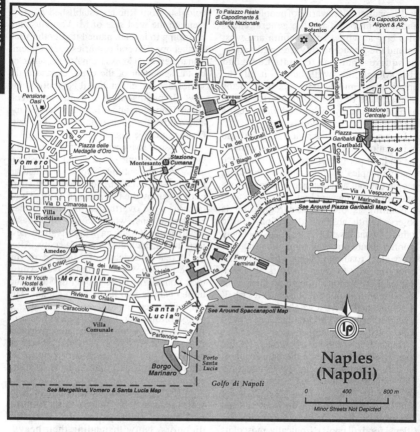

Naples
(Napoli)

0   400   800 m

Minor Streets Not Depicted

marks can still be seen on many monuments. The Allies subsequently presided over a fairly disastrous period of transition from war to peace, and not a few observers have attributed, at least in part, the initial bloom in the city's organised crime to connivance by less scrupulous members of the occupying forces. A severe earthquake in 1980 and a dormant, but not extinct, Mt Vesuvius looming to the east, remind Neapolitans of their city's vulnerability.

ORIENTATION

Naples stretches along the waterfront and is divided into *quartieri* (quarters) – most street signs bear the name of the quarter as well. The main train station, Stazione Centrale, and bus station are off Piazza Garibaldi, just east of Spaccanapoli, the old city. The piazza and its side streets form an enormous and unwelcoming transport terminus and street market. The area is distinctly seedy. Quite a few of the cheaper hotels, some of which double as brothels, and restaurants are here.

A wide shopping street, Corso Umberto I, skirts the southern edge of Spaccanapoli, the ancient heart of Naples, on its way southwest from Piazza Garibaldi to Piazza Bovio and on to the huge Piazza Municipio, which is dominated by the unmistakable Castel Nuovo. From the waterfront directly behind the castle you can find boats to the bay islands, Palermo and other long-distance destinations.

The Palazzo Reale, the former royal palace, is next to the castle. From the palace, head north for Naples' main street, Via Toledo, which becomes Via Roma for a short stretch after it crosses Piazza Carità, and you will reach Piazza Dante, on the western boundary of Spaccanapoli. The road continues as Via Santa Teresa degli Scalzi and then Corso Amedeo di Savoia before reaching the Parco di Capodimonte north of the centre.

The extensions of two of Naples' more original streets, Via Benedetto Croce (which becomes Via San Biagio dei Librai) and Via dei Tribunali, eventually meet Via Roma. Most street life, many of the city's artisans and a host of good, cheap restaurants can be found in this area. Via San Biagio dei Librai is part of an almost straight run from near Stazione Centrale through Spaccanapoli to the foot of the hilltop Vomero district.

On the bay to the south-west are the more fashionable areas of Santa Lucia and Mergellina, with its semi-grand waterfront boulevard, Via Caracciolo (from where more boats head for the islands). Rising up from Mergellina is the up-market Vomero district, dominated by the Castel Sant'Elmo and the Certosa di San Martino, a Carthusian monastery which can be seen from all over the city.

INFORMATION
Tourist Offices
Naples has several tourist offices, which provide *Qui Napoli*, a monthly listings brochure. The offices have a good map and guides to the city's monuments.

The most central, the AAST office (☎ 552 33 28), is in Piazza del Gesù Nuovo and opens Monday to Saturday from 9 am to 6 pm (although it sometimes closes in the afternoon), and Sundays to 2 pm. Other tourist offices at the Mergellina hydrofoil terminal and the entrance to the Borgo Marinari, the little island off Santa Lucia, open in summer if personnel and funds are available.

Staff at the EPT office at Stazione Centrale (☎ 26 87 79) are helpful and will book hotel rooms. The main EPT office (☎ 40 53 11) is at Piazza dei Martiri 58 (open Monday to Friday from 8.30 am to 2.30 pm), with branches at the Mergellina train station and the airport. The Stazione Centrale and airport tourist offices are open Monday to Friday from about 8.30 am to 8 pm, and Saturday morning.

Money
The city is full of exchange booths, although the rates offered are usually lower than at banks. Some banks charge commission to change travellers' cheques, so ask first. Visa, Eurocheque or MasterCard can be used at many banks with ATMs, including the Banca Nazionale del Lavoro at Via Firenze 39 and Monte dei Paschi di Siena, around the corner on Corso Novara. Banks open Monday to Friday from about 8 am to 1 pm and then 3 to 4.30 pm. American Express is represented by Every Tour (☎ 551 85 64), Piazza Municipio 5-6.

Post & Telecommunications
The main post office is at Piazza G Matteotti, off Via A Diaz, in a grand, Fascist-era building. It is open Monday to Friday from 8.15 am to 7.30 pm, and on Saturday to midday. The post code for central Naples is 80100.

The main Telecom office is at Via Depretis 40, and is open daily from 9 am to 10 pm. The telephone code is 081.

Foreign Consulates
Many countries have consulates in Naples, including Britain (☎ 66 35 11), Via Crispi 122 (☎ 0337-86 02 70 for after-hours emergencies); the USA (☎ 583 81 11), Piazza della Repubblica and France (☎ 761 22 75), also Piazza della Repubblica.

Other Information
The student travel centre, CTS (☎ 552 79 60), is at Via Mezzocannone 25.

There's a decent newspaper stand selling foreign language newspapers and magazines downstairs from Stazione Centrale, before the turnstyles to the Metropolitana.

Arci Gay Antinoo (☎ 552 88 15), Vico San Geronimo 17-20, provides information of interest to gay travellers, but the telephones are generally staffed only from 6 to 9 pm. Naples has a big lesbian community, and Orchidea Blu (same address and telephone number as Arci Gay) provides details.

Emergency & Medical Services

For police emergency, ☎ 113. The questura (☎ 794 11 11) is at Via Medina 75, off Via A Diaz. It has an office for foreigners where you can report thefts etc. To report a stolen car, ring ☎ 794 14 35.

For an ambulance, call ☎ 752 06 96. Each city quarter has a Guardia Medica. The Ospedale Monaldi (☎ 545 50 51), Vico L Bianchi, is centrally located, a short walk from the duomo. The pharmacy at Stazione Centrale is open daily from 8 am to 8 pm, or check listings in the daily *Il Tempo di Napoli*.

Dangers & Annoyances

Petty crime is a problem in Naples, so a few precautions are indispensable. Carry your money and documents in a money belt and never carry a bag or purse if you can help it – moped bandits just love them.

Women should be careful about walking alone in the streets at night, particularly near Stazione Centrale and Piazza Dante. Never venture into the dark side streets at night unless you are in a group. The area west of Via Toledo and as far north as Piazza Carità can be particularly threatening.

Take care when crossing roads. There are few functioning traffic lights and pedestrian crossings, and Neapolitans rarely stop at them anyway. When facing a green light they drive with caution, believing that those facing the red light will not stop. Vehicles and pedestrians simply slip around each other in a kind of unwritten code of road 'courtesy' that can be a little unnerving at first.

Car and motorbike theft are also problems in Naples, so think twice before bringing a vehicle to the city.

THINGS TO SEE

Most museums open daily except Monday from 9 am to 2 pm. All churches, chapels and the like are open daily but tend to close from noon to about 4 or 5 pm.

Walking Tour

You'll never walk all of Naples in a day, but the following itinerary will take you through the heart of it and help you get your bearings. Use the public transport during your stay. Even if you don't trust yourself with the buses, the Metropolitana and funiculars are simple to use and will save some shoe leather.

Starting from Piazza Garibaldi, head a short way down Corso Umberto I before veering right into Via Egiziaca a Forcella. Cross Via P Colletta and follow the main street as it veers to the left. Where this runs into the busy cross street Via Duomo, you have the **Chiesa di San Giorgio Maggiore** on your left, and two blocks north up Via Duomo, the **duomo** itself. Virtually opposite is the **Chiesa dei Girolamini**. Walk back south to where you emerged on Via Duomo. The continuation west of Via Duomo is Via San Biagio dei Librai, one of the liveliest roads in Spaccanapoli. As you stroll along, you'll pass the **Ospedale delle Bambole** and the churches of **SS Filippo e Giacomo** and **Sant'Angelo a Nilo**.

On Piazza San Domenico Maggiore stands the church of the same name. Note that the not-to-be-missed **Cappella di San Severo** is just off this square in a lane east of the church. Here you are faced with at least two choices:

You could head south along Via Mezzocannone past the **university** and rejoin Corso Umberto I, turning right and following it into Piazza Bovio. From here, Via A Depretis leads south-west to Piazza Municipio and the round-towered **Castel Nuovo**. West from here you will come to an elegant series of squares and the surrounding **Palazzo Reale**, the **Teatro San Carlo**, the **Galleria Umberto I** and the **Chiesa di San Francesco di Paola**. From here you could follow the waterside around to Santa Lucia and beyond to Mergellina, or turn north up **Via Toledo** (named after the Spanish Viceroy who had it laid out as part of his urban expansion programme in the mid-16th century) from Piazza Trento e Trieste, leading back to Spaccanapoli.

Alternatively, from Piazza San Domenico Maggiore you could continue west along Via B Croce past the **Palazzo Filomarino** and the **Basilica de Santa Chiara** as far as Piazza del Gesù Nuovo, on which are located the **Chiesa del Gesù Nuovo** and the main AAST office. Then backtrack to the first intersection, and turn left (north) along Via S Sebastiano. At the next intersection on your left a short street leads down to the **Port'Alba**, a city gate built in 1625, and Piazza Dante. Ahead of you is Piazza Bellini and to your right Piazza Luigi Miraglia. The latter becomes Via dei Tribunali and heads east to Via Duomo. It was the **decumanus**, or main street, of the original Greek and later Roman town. Two-thirds along stood the Greek **agora**, or central market and meeting place, in what is now Piazza San Gaetano.

Piazza Bellini, by the way, is a good place to rest your weary feet in one of several cafés, and while you're at it you could inspect the remains of the ancient Greek city walls under the square. You could then proceed farther north along Via Santa Maria di Costantinopoli up to the grand **Museo Archeologico Nazionale**.

Spaccanapoli

Duomo Built on the site of earlier churches, themselves preceded by a temple of Neptune, this grand cathedral was begun by Charles I of Anjou in 1272. Largely destroyed in 1456 by an earthquake, it has undergone numerous alterations. The neo-Gothic façade is the result of late 19th-century cosmetic surgery. Above the wide central nave inside hangs an ornately decorated panel ceiling.

Of central importance to Naples' religious (some would say superstitious) life is the 17th-century Baroque **Cappella di San Gennaro** (also known as the Cappella del Tesoro, or Chapel of the Treasury), to the right after you enter the church. Now under restoration, the chapel houses two phials of St Januarius' congealed blood, kept behind the opulent high altar. St Januarius (San Gennaro), the city's patron saint, was martyred at Pozzuoli, near Naples, in 305 AD, and tradition holds that two phials of his congealed blood liquefied in his hands when his body was transferred back to Naples. He is said to have saved the city from disaster on numerous occasions, although the miracle failed to occur in 1941 when Mt Vesuvius erupted. See the Festival section later in the chapter for more information.

The next chapel contains an urn with the saint's bones and various other relics. Below the cathedral high altar lies the so-called Confessio, a Renaissance chapel built to house St Januarius' relics, closed to the public since 1992.

To the left and rear of the cathedral, a passageway leads to what is effectively a separate church, the 10th-century Basilica di Santa Restituta. Also much altered over time, it is now part of the duomo's so-called archaeological zone, to which entrance costs L4000. It's open daily from 9 am to noon and 4 to 6 pm.

Around the Duomo Virtually across the road from the duomo, the **Chiesa dei Girolamini**, or San Filippo Neri, is a rich Baroque church with a beautiful façade. The gallery inside features works from the 16th and 18th centuries, and is open from 9.30 am to 12.30 pm and 2 to 5.30 pm (entrance is free).

Duck around the corner into Via dei Tribunali, and you soon have the **Chiesa di San Lorenzo Maggiore** before you, to the left in Piazza San Gaetano. The piazza is laid over what was originally the Greek **agora** and then the Roman **forum**, the centre of the ancient city. The interior of the church, begun by Provençal architects under the Franciscans in the 13th century, is French Gothic. Catherine of Austria, who died in 1323, was buried here, and her mosaic-covered tomb is among the most eye-catching of the church's adornments. You can pass through to the cloisters of the

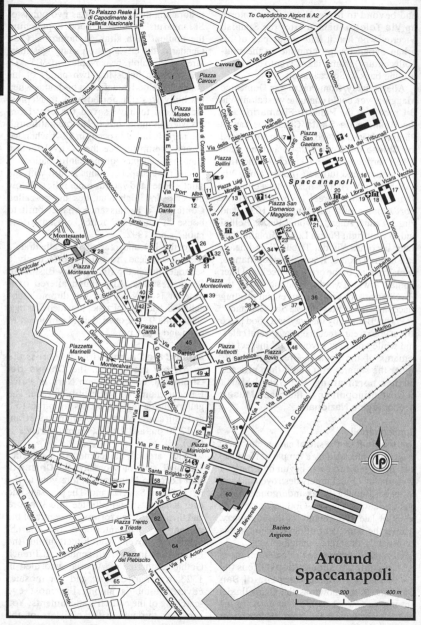

To Palazzo Reale
di Capodimente &
Galleria Nazionale

To Capodichino Airport & A2

Cavour Ⓜ

Piazza
Cavour

Piazza
Museo
Nazionale

Via Santa Teresa degli Scalzi

Via Foria

Via Duomo

Via Salvatore Rosa

Salita Tarsia

Salita Tarsia

Pontecorvo

Via E Pessina

Via Santa Maria di Constantinopoli

Viale L de Crecchio

Via della Sapienza

Viale del Sole

Via Pisanelli

Via San Paolo

Piazza
San Gaetano

Via del Tribunali

Piazza
Bellini

Via Atri

Via Port'
Alba

Piazza Luigi
Miraglia

Piazza
Dante

Via S Sebastiano

Via B Croce

Piazza San
Domenico
Maggiore

Spaccanapoli

dei Librai

Via Vicaria Vecchia

Via San Biagio

Via Duomo

Montesanto Ⓜ

Funicular

Piazza
Montesanto

Via Roma

Via P Scura

Via D Capitelli

Piazza
Monteoliveto

Via Santa Chiara

Via Mezzocannone

Corso Umberto

Via Toledo

Via F Girardi

Piazzetta
Marinelli

Via A
Montecalvan

Piazza
Carità

Piazza
degli Artisti

Piazza
Matteotti

Piazza
Bovio

Corso Umberto

Nuovo Marino

Via G Oberdan

Via A Diaz

Via R Bracco

Via A Depretis

Via de Gasperi

Via G Sanfelice

Via C Colombo

Via Medina

Via P E Imbriani

Piazza
Municipio

Via Santa Brigida

Via Emanuele III

Piazza
Trento
e Trieste

Via S Carlo

Piazza
del Plebiscito

Via A F Acton

Molo Beverello

Bacino
Angiono

Via Chiaia

Via Monte

Via G Nicotera

Funicular

Via Cesario Console

Around
Spaccanapoli

0   200   400 m

PLACES TO STAY		OTHER		35	Museo della
7	Bellini	1	Museo Archeologico		Mineralogia &
8	Alloggio Fiamma		Nazionale		Museo Zoologico
13	Soggiorno Imperia	2	Hospital	36	University
16	Duomo	3	Duomo	37	CTS Travel Agency
39	Candy	4	Chiesa dei Girolamini	44	Chiesa di Sant'Anna dei
46	Hotel Orchidea	14	Cappella di San Severo		Lombardi
48	Oriente Grand Hotel	15	Chiesa di San Lorenzo	45	Main Post Office
			Maggiore	47	Tourcar Travel Agency
PLACES TO EAT		17	Chiesa di San Giorgio	49	Questura (Police Station)
			Maggiore	50	Telecom Office
5	Pizzeria di Matteo	18	Palazzo Cuomo	51	Gastaldi Travel Agency
6	Trattoria da Carmine	19	Hospital	52	Alitalia
9	Intra Moenia	20	Palazzo Marigliano	53	CIT Travel Agency
10	Caffè dell'Epoca	21	Chiesa di SS Filippo e	54	Every Tour
11	Ristorante Bellini		Giacomo		(American Express)
12	Pizzeria Port'Alba	22	Chiesa di Sant'Angelo a	55	SITA Bus Station
23	La Campagnola		Nilo	56	Otto Jazz Club
27	Ristorante Hong Kong	24	Chiesa di San	57	Funicular to Vomero
28	Friggitoria Fiorenzano		Domenico Maggiore		(Closed)
34	Il Pizzicotto	25	Palazzo Filomarino	58	Galleria Umberto I
38	Minipizza	26	Chiesa del Gesù Nuovo	59	Box Office (Ticket Sales)
40	La Taverna del	29	Stazione Cumana	60	Castel Nuovo &
	Buongustaio	30	Piazza del Gesù Nuovo		Museo Cirico
41	Pizzeria al 22	31	AAST Tourist Office	61	Stazione Marittima
42	Lo Sfizietto	32	Basilica di	62	Teatro San Carlo
43	Gelateria della Scimmia		Santa Chiara	64	Palazzo Reale
63	Gambrinus	33	ArciGay Antinoo	65	Chiesa di San
					Francesco di Paola

neighbouring convent, where Petrarch sojourned in 1345. There is also a museum housing relics, dating back as far as Greek Neapolis, which was discovered during excavations. Entrance is free. Across Via dei Tribunali is the **Chiesa di San Paolo Maggiore**, built in the late 16th century on the site of a temple of the Dioscuri. The opulent interior houses the tomb of St Gaetano (St Cajetan).

While you're in the area, the **Chiesa di San Giorgio Maggiore**, where Via San Biagio dei Librai meets Via Duomo, is worth a quick look for its austere interior.

Across the road is the 15th-century **Palazzo Cuomo**, built by Tuscan artists. The building was moved several metres in 1881 when the street was being widened. It now contains the Museo Gaetano Filangieri, with an extensive collection of arms, furniture and china, as well as paintings of the Neapolitan school. It opens Tuesday to Saturday from 9 am to 2 pm and until 1 pm on Sunday, and entrance is L5000.

Via San Biagio dei Librai As you enter Via San Biagio dei Librai, you'll soon arrive at the **Ospedale delle Bambole**, at No 81. This 'dolls' hospital' looks a little macabre with dolls' heads piled up in the windows, but you'd be hard pressed to find too many places like it anywhere in the world for buying or repairing dolls. In fact this whole street, and its continuation, Via B Croce, the parallel Via dei Tribunali to the north and the labyrinth of side alleys throngs with craftspeople of all sorts. Here you'll find not only goldsmiths and other jewellers, but the makers of the famous Neapolitan *presepi* (Christmas nativity scenes) – some of them extraordinarily elaborate.

Farther along from the dolls' hospital, the **Palazzo Marigliano**, over Via San Gregorio Armeno, features a magnificent Renaissance entrance hall and façade. You then pass the **Palazzo di Carafa di Maddaloni** and **Chiesa di SS Filippo e Giacomo** with their contrasting Renaissance and Rococo styles.

The grand **Cappella di Monte di Pietà** boasts a fresco-decorated vault and façade.

The entrance to the **Chiesa di Sant" Angelo a Nilo** is on Vico Donnaromita 15, off Via San Biagio dei Librai. Built in 1385 and remodelled in the 18th century, the church contains the monumental Renaissance tomb of one Cardinal Brancaccio, to which Donatello contributed.

The **Chiesa di San Domenico Maggiore**, along Via B Croce in the piazza bearing its name, was built in the 14th century by the Dominican order and was favoured by the Aragonese nobility. Inside the church, a cross between Baroque and 19th-century neo-Gothic, lie 45 coffins of the princes of Aragon.

The deceptive simplicity of the **Cappella di San Severo**, in Via de Sanctis, a narrow lane east of the church, stands in dazzling contrast to the treasure chest of sculpture inside. Giuseppe Sanmartino's *Veiled Christ*, for instance, still confounds experts, who cannot agree on how he created the apparently translucent veil. Similarly baffling is Corradini's *Pudicizia* (Modesty) that, if anything, appeals directly to the erotic rather than hiding it. The chapel is open from 10 am to 5 pm, except Tuesdays, Sundays and holidays, when it closes at 1.30 pm. Entrance is L5000.

To Piazza del Gesù Nuovo From Piazza San Domenico Maggiore the road continues west, following the course of the old Roman main street under the name of Via Benedetto Croce. Croce, Italy's foremost philosopher and historian in the first half of this century, lived and died in the **Palazzo Filomarino**, a grand Renaissance building on the right just before you reach Via San Sebastiano.

Across Via San Sebastiano you come to the **Basilica di Santa Chiara**, a church and convent partly incorporating a Roman wall that was extended around the convent to protect the nuns. Built between 1310 and 1328 under the Angevin dynasty, it suffered from earthquakes, Baroque alterations in the 18th century ('overloaded with excessive ornamentation' according to one British

observer late last century) and bombing in 1943. Since the end of the war it has been returned more or less to its original spare Gothic appearance, and is one of Naples' principal medieval monuments. The **nuns' cloisters** behind the church consist of four paths that form a cross, bordered by a long parapet entirely covered in decorative ceramic tiles, depicting 64 landscapes and scenes from the nuns' lives.

A few steps west and Piazza del Gesù Nuovo opens up before you, with its *guglia*, a kind of ground-level Baroque steeple, dripping with opulent sculptural decoration. You'll see several of these around the city. The 16th-century **Chiesa del Gesù Nuovo** on the north side of the piazza is one of the city's greatest examples of Renaissance architecture, particularly the lozenge -shaped rustication of its façade. The interior was fully redecorated in the Neapolitan Baroque style by Cosimo Fanzango after a fire in 1639.

Churches

The **Chiesa di Sant'Anna dei Lombardi**, south-west of Piazza del Gesù Nuovo, was founded in 1414 by Origlia and features fine Renaissance sculpture, including a superb terracotta *Pietà* (1492) by Guido Mazzoni.

Near the train station, the **Basilica del Carmine Maggiore**, on the waterfront in Piazza del Carmine, was the scene of the 1647 Neapolitan Revolution led by Masaniello. Inside is the much-worshipped *Madonna Bruna* (Brown Madonna), and each year on 16 July a fireworks display celebrates the festival of the Madonna del Carmine by simulating the burning of the church – the *incendio simolato del campanile*.

Museums

Museo Archeologico Nazionale Housed in a vast red building that dominates the northern fringe of Spaccanapoli, on Piazza Museo Nazionale, the archaeological treasures of Naples' principal museum form one of the most comprehensive collections of Graeco-Roman artefacts in the world. You could easily lose yourself in here for several hours. Originally a cavalry barracks and later seat of the city's university, Charles of Bourbon established this museum late in the 18th century to house a rich collection of antiquities he had inherited from his mother, Elizabeth Farnese. It also contains the Borgia collection of Etruscan and Egyptian relics.

Many items from the Farnese collection of classical sculpture are featured on the ground floor, including the impressive *Farnese Bull* in the room of the same name. It is most likely a Roman copy of a Greek original dating from 150 BC, and is an enormous group depicting the death of Dirce, a figure in Greek mythology who was tied to a bull and torn apart over rocks. The whole group was carved from a single block of marble and was later restored by Michelangelo.

The 1st floor is largely devoted to discoveries from Pompeii, Herculaneum, Stabiae and Cumae. The displays range from numerous murals and frescoes rescued from the sites, through to gladiators' helmets, household items, ceramics and glassware. One room is dedicated to an extraordinary collection of vases of mixed origins, many of them carefully reassembled.

On the mezzanine floor is a gallery of mosaics, mostly from Pompeii, including the *Battle of Alexander*, the best known depiction of the great Macedonian emperor. It once paved the floor in the Casa del Fauno at Pompeii, and is just one of a series of remarkably detailed and lifelike pieces depicting animals, scenes from daily life, musicians and even Plato with his students. In all, the mosaics are an eloquent expression of ancient artistic genius.

The Egyptian collection is in the basement but has been closed to the public for years. The museum is open Tuesday to Saturday from 9 am to 2 pm and Sunday until 1 pm, and entrance is L12,000. In summer it often stays open to 7 pm.

Other Museums About one km along the waterfront east of the Piazza Garibaldi area, in a restored railway building, is the **Museo Nazionale Ferroviario** at Corso San Giovanni a Teduccio, in Pietrarsa. It was founded by Ferdinand II of Bourbon to house his collection of railway memorabilia and opens from 9 am to 2 pm. Entrance is free.

Back in the town centre, the **Museo della Mineralogia** on Via Mezzocannone 8, between Via B Croce and Corso Umberto I, features minerals, meteorites and quartz crystals collected from the Mt Vesuvius region. It is open daily from 9 am to 1 pm and entrance is free. The building also contains the **Museo Zoologico**.

City Centre & Santa Lucia
Castel Nuovo When Charles I of Anjou took over Naples and the Swabians' Sicilian kingdom, he found himself in control not only of his new southern Italian acquisitions, but possessions in Tuscany, northern Italy and Provence. It made sense to base the new dynasty in Naples rather than Palermo, and Charles launched an ambitious construction programme to expand the port and city walls. His plans included converting a Franciscan convent into the castle that still stands in Piazza Municipio. Also dubbed the Maschio Angioino, its crenellated round towers make it one of the most striking buildings in Naples. The 'New Castle' was erected in three years from 1279, but what you see today was the result of renovations by the Aragonese two centuries later, as well as a meticulous restoration effort prior to WW II. The heavy grey stone that dominates was imported from Majorca. The two-storey triumphal arch at the entrance, the Torre della Guardia, built in 1467, depicts the triumphal entry of Alfonso I of Aragon into Naples.

Spread across several halls on the ground, 1st and 2nd floors is the **Museo Civico**. Frescoes and sculpture from the 14th and 15th century, on the ground floor, are of most interest. The other two floors offer a range of paintings, either by Neapolitan artists or overwhelmingly with Naples or Campania as subjects, covering the 17th through to the early 20th centuries. The castle is open daily from 9 am to dusk, but the museum until 2 pm only (closed Mondays). Entrance to the museum is L6000.

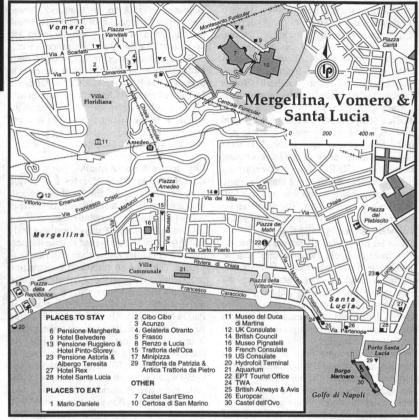

Mergellina, Vomero &
Santa Lucia

0   200   400 m

PLACES TO STAY

6 Pensione Margherita
9 Hotel Belvedere
13 Pensione Ruggiero &
   Hotel Pinto-Storey
23 Pensione Astoria &
   Albergo Teresita
27 Hotel Rex
28 Hotel Santa Lucia

PLACES TO EAT

1 Mario Daniele

2 Cibo Cibo
3 Acunzo
4 Gelateria Otranto
5 Frasco
8 Renzo e Lucia
15 Trattoria dell'Oca
17 Minipizza
29 Trattoria da Patrizia &
   Antica Trattoria da Pietro

OTHER

7 Castel Sant'Elmo
10 Certosa di San Marino

11 Museo del Duca
   di Martina
12 UK Consulate
14 British Council
16 Museo Pignatelli
18 French Consulate
19 US Consulate
20 Hydrofoil Terminal
21 Aquarium
22 EPT Tourist Office
24 TWA
25 British Airways & Avis
26 Europcar
30 Castel dell'Ovo

North-east of the Castel Nuovo on Piazza
Bovio is the **Fontana di Nettuno**. Dating
from 1601, Bernini sculpted its sea creatures
and Naccherini the figure of Neptune.

Piazza Trieste e Trento A short walk south-
west of the Castel Nuovo along Via San
Carlo leads to one of Naples' more elegant
squares, the Piazza Trieste e Trento. It's
fronted on the north-eastern side by the
Teatro San Carlo, famed for its perfect
acoustics. Built in 1737 by Charles of
Bourbon (40 years before La Scala, locals

proudly boast), San Carlo was destroyed by
fire in 1816. Restored since, it is home to one
of the oldest ballet schools in Italy. Stendhal
wrote, 'There is nothing in Europe to
compare with it, or even give the faintest
idea of what it is like.' It is open in the early
morning and mid-afternoon, although an attendant might show you through at other times.

Across Via San Carlo is one of the four
entrances to the imposing but somewhat-
worse-for-wear glass atrium of the **Galleria
Umberto I**. Built in 1890, it seems a rather
humble cousin of Milan's truly impressive
Galleria Vittorio Emanuele II.

Piazza del Plebiscito This grand square, watched over by equestrian statues of Charles III and Ferdinand I of Bourbon, is fronted on the western side by the magnificent late-Renaissance façade of the **Palazzo Reale** (Royal Palace). Built around 1600, it was completely renovated in 1841, but suffered extensive damage during WW II. The statues of the eight most important kings of Naples were inserted into niches in the façade in 1888.

After entering the courtyard, a huge double staircase under a dome leads to the **Museo del Palazzo Reale**, housed in the former royal apartments. Inside you'll get an idea of the pomp in which the Bourbon rulers lived in the 19th century, with a rich collection of furnishings, porcelain, tapestries, statues and paintings. Works by Filippino Lippi, Titian and Vasari can be seen in the rooms next to the museum, which is open Tuesday to Saturday from 9 am to 2 pm and Sunday to 1 pm. Entrance to the museum is L6000.

The palace has also, since 1925, been home to the **Biblioteca Nazionale**, which includes the vast Farnese collection brought to Naples by Charles of Bourbon, with more than 2000 papyri discovered at Herculaneum and fragments of a 5th-century Coptic Bible. Entry is free.

Closing off the eastern end of the square, the **Chiesa di San Francesco di Paola** was begun by Ferdinand I in 1817 to celebrate the restoration of his kingdom after the Napoleonic interlude. Flanked by semicircular colonnades, the church is based on Rome's Pantheon and is a popular wedding spot.

Castel dell'Ovo The so-called Castle of the Egg is on the small rocky island off Santa Lucia known as Borgo Marinaro and connected by bridge from Via Partenope. Folklore has it that the name came about after part of the island collapsed, likened by locals to Virgil's story of the breaking of an egg. The castle occupies the site of a Roman villa. Built in the 12th century by the Norman king, William I, the castle became a key fortress in the defence of Campania. You can wander through the small lanes on the island (mostly occupied by restaurants), but the castle, restored in the 1970s, is opened only for special exhibitions.

The **Fontana dell'Immacolatella**, where Via Partenope meets Via N Sauro on the way from Santa Lucia to Piazza del Plebiscito, dates from the 17th century and features statues by Bernini and Naccherini.

Mergellina

West of Santa Lucia, Via Partenope spills into Piazza della Vittoria, marking the beginning of the so-called Riviera di Chiaia, which runs along the northern edge of the **Villa Comunale**, a large park marked off on the seaward side by Via Caracciolo. An **aquarium** in the park was founded in the late 19th century by German naturalist Anton Dohrn. Its 30 tanks contain specimens of sea life exclusively from the Bay of Naples area. It opens Monday to Saturday from 9 am to 5 pm, to 6 pm on Sundays in summer and until 2 pm in winter, and entrance is L3000.

Close by at Riviera di Chiaia 200 is the **Museo Pignatelli**, an old patrician residence containing mostly 19th-century furnishings, china and other nick-nacks. A pavilion set in gardens houses a coach museum and contains English and French carriages. Both museums are open Tuesday to Saturday from 9 am to 2 pm and Sundays to 1 pm. Entrance is L5000.

Farther west, a short stroll from Piazza Sannazzaro and the Mergellina train station, is the **Tomba di Giacomo Leopardi**, the 19th-century poet who died in Naples in 1837, and an Augustan age Roman monument that has come to be known as the **Tomba di Virgilio**, although it has nothing to do with the ancient poet, who died in Brindisi in 19 BC. The tombs lie behind the Chiesa di Santa Maria di Piedigrotta, and can be visited daily from 9 am to sunset.

Vomero

Visible from all over the city, the Vomero hill (pronounced Vómero) is a bit of a world apart, a serene and well-to-do residential quarter that rises above all the chaos of the great metropolis below, connected to it by several funicular lines.

Castel Sant'Elmo Commanding views across the city and bay, this austere, star-shaped castle was built over a stronghold first established in 1329. The present structure was built under Spanish vice-regal rule in 1538. Impressive though it is, the castle has seen little real action, serving more often than not as a prison. It opens Monday to Saturday from 9 am to 2 pm and until 1 pm Sunday; entrance is L10,000. These details can vary when temporary exhibitions are being held.

Certosa di San Martino Barely 100 metres down the road from the castle lies this 14th-century Carthusian monastery. Rebuilt in the 17th century by Fanzango in Neapolitan Baroque style, it now houses the Museo Nazionale di San Martino, featuring a section on naval history, an area dedicated to the history of the Kingdom of Naples, and other interesting collections. Not all of the monastery is open to the public, but you can enjoy the tranquil Baroque Chiostro Grande, or main cloisters, whose manicured gardens are ringed by elegant porticoes. Adjacent is the monastery's church, virtually an art gallery in itself, whose original Gothic character is still evident. It contains exquisite marblework, a good number of frescoes and paintings, particularly by 17th-century Neapolitan artists. There is a magnificent view from the terraced gardens, and from Largo San Martino (the car park) outside. The monastery is open Monday to Saturday from 9 am to 2 pm and Sunday until 1 pm, and entrance is L6000.

Villa Floridiana The verdant grounds of this public park spread down the slopes from Via Domenico Cimarosa in Vomero to Mergellina. The stately home at the bottom end of the gardens was built in 1817 by Ferdinand I for his wife, the Duchess of Floridia. Today it contains the **Museo del Duca di Martina** (Museo Nazionale della Ceramica), which holds collections of Euro-

pean, Chinese and Japanese china, ivory, enamels and majolica (Renaissance Italian earthenware). The museum opens Tuesday to Saturday from 9 am to 2 pm and Sundays to 1 pm. Entrance is L4000. The park is open daily except Monday from 9 am to one hour before sunset, and entrance is free.

Capodimonte

Palazzo Reale di Capodimonte A royal estate built by Charles of Bourbon on the northern edge of the city, the palace is set in extensive parklands that formed the nobles' hunting grounds. It now houses the **Galleria Nazionale**, which consists mostly of the lavish Farnese collection. Featured are several Titians and works by Goya, Botticelli and Caravaggio, as well as an impressive range from the 18th-century Neapolitan school. The museum, housed in the royal apartments, has an extensive collection of arms, ivories, bronzes, porcelain (including more than 3000 pieces from the palace's original porcelain factory) and other works of art. It's open Tuesday to Saturday from 9 am to 2 pm (in summer sometimes to as late as 7 pm) and until 1 pm on Sunday, and entrance is L8000. Entrance to the gardens is free and they are open from 9 am to one hour before sunset.

Catacombe di San Gennaro The catacombs are just below the palace – enter from Via di Capodimonte and down an alley running beside the Chiesa di Madre del Buon Consiglio. Dating from the 2nd century, they are quite a different experience from the dark, claustrophobic catacombs characteristic of Rome: a mix of tombs, corridors and broad vestibules held up by columns and arches. St Januarius, was buried here. The walls are decorated in part with images of the deceased, including several of St Januarius executed over the centuries. Guided tours begin daily at 9.30, 10.15, 11 and 11.45 am, and cost L3000.

The **Catacombe di San Severo** (☎ 45 46 84), Piazzetta San Severo e Capodimonte, is near those of San Gennaro but can only be visited by appointment.

Orto Botanico

Head north along Via Duomo to Via Foria and turn right to reach the Orto Botanico (☎ 44 97 59) at No 223, near Piazza Carlo III. The botanical gardens were founded in 1807 by Joseph Bonaparte and are part of the Naples university. Visits are by appointment.

ACTIVITIES

If you want to go diving, contact the Diving Club Fiorito (☎ 66 61 61), Via Caracciolo 15, for details.

For sailing, the Club Nautico (☎ 764 58 29), Borgo Marinari, is a private club but the staff should be able to suggest where you can hire equipment.

ORGANISED TOURS

Excursions to the bay islands and inland to Pompeii and Mt Vesuvius are organised by CIT (☎ 552 54 26), Piazza Municipio 70; Cima Tours (☎ 554 06 46), Piazza Garibaldi 114; and Tourcar (☎ 552 33 10), Piazza Matteotti 1. A half-day tour to Pompeii is about L50,000. The AAST organises free tours of city sights every Sunday at 10.30 am.

For something completely different, you could head underground. A warren of cisterns, wells and stone quarries lies below the city's surface splendour, and can be visited with the Libera Associazione Escursionisti Sottosuolo (☎ 40 02 56), Via Santa Teresella degli Spagnoli 24. At the time of writing they met at Bar Gambrinus (Piazza Trieste e Trento) on Saturdays and Sundays at 10 am and Thursdays at 9 pm.

FESTIVALS

The big festival surrounds St Januarius, when throngs gather in the chapel bearing his name to see his blood liquefy. On the first Sunday in May, on 19 September and on 16 December each year, thousands gather to pray for a repeat of the miracle to save the city from any potential disaster. Get there early, as police turn back the crowds when the duomo is full. See the Things to See section for more information.

Other important festivals are the Madonna del Carmine on 16 July, held in Piazza del Carmine, which culminates in a fireworks display, and the Madonna di Piedigrotta (5-12 September). Around Christmas, thousands of elaborate nativity scenes are erected around the city.

WORK

The Centro di Lingua e Cultura Italiana (☎ 551 33 61), Vico Santa Maria dell'Aiuto 17, is one of several language schools in the city. If you want to teach English, start your enquiries at the British Council (☎ 41 48 76), Via dei Mille.

PLACES TO STAY

Naples is surprisingly cheap compared with the north of the country, although most of the budget hotels are clustered around Stazione Centrale in a rather unsavoury area. The EPT office at Stazione Centrale will recommend and book hotels, and you should avoid the hawkers who may harass you around the station – they are on commission and generally pushing less reputable establishments. Many of the cheaper hotels double as brothels.

Room prices should always be read in Italy as a guide rather than gospel truth, but this is even more the case in Naples. The following prices are a fair indication. Some hotels unfortunately only have doubles, and are not always willing to knock down prices for single travellers. The closest camping ground is in Pozzuoli – see the Pozzuoli section.

Hostel

The HI *Ostello Mergellina Napoli* (☎ 761 23 46), Salita della Grotta 23, in Mergellina, is modern and safe. B&B is L18,000 and a meal L12,000. It is open all year and imposes a minimum three-night stay in summer. Take bus No 152 from Stazione Centrale or the Metropolitana to Mergellina and follow the signs.

Around Stazione Centrale

The *Hotel Zara* (☎ 28 71 25), Via Firenze 81, is clean and safe with singles/doubles from L25,000/45,000. Via Firenze is off Corso

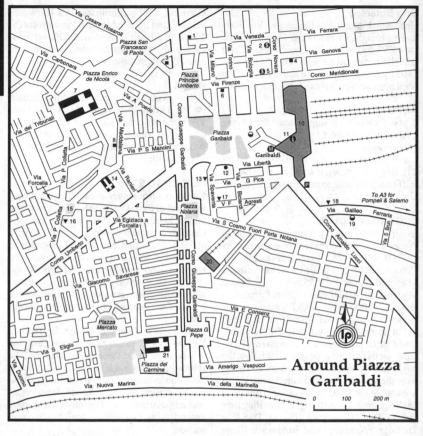

Around Piazza Garibaldi

0   100   200 m

Novara, to the right as you exit the station. The *Albergo Ginevra* (☎ 28 32 10), Via Genova 116, the second street to the right off Corso Novara, is another reliable hotel with doubles only, starting at L50,000. The *Casanova Hotel* (☎ 26 82 87), Via Venezia 2, through Piazza Garibaldi and past Piazza Principe Umberto in a small side street off Corso Garibaldi, has singles/doubles for about L30,000/55,000 and triples with a shower for L75,000. At the *Hotel Centrale* (☎ 553 74 45), Via Maddalena 40, decent, safe doubles with a bathroom go for L50,000. A pokey single costs L27,000.

Moving up the price scale, the three-star *Prati* (☎ 554 18 02), Via C Rosaroll 4, has singles/doubles from L90,000/140,000 up. It is one of the area's best hotels.

Around Spaccanapoli
Many hotels in this area are near Piazza Dante, which you can reach by bus No 185 on the Circo Sinistra (CS) line or by a Circo Destra (CD) bus from Stazione Centrale. (See the Getting Around section for more information.) You could easily miss *Soggiorno Imperia* (☎ 45 93 47), Piazza Luigi Miraglia 386, as it isn't signposted. It

PLACES TO STAY	17	Trattoria Avellinese		Urban Bus Station
	18	Bar Pietruccio	10	Stazione Centrale
1 Casanova Hotel		(SITA Tickets)	11	EPT Tourist Office
3 Prati			12	Cima Tours
4 Albergo Ginevra			14	Chiesa della
6 Hotel Zara	OTHER			Santissima
8 Hotel Centrale				Annunziata
	2	Monte dei Paschi	15	Piazza V Calenda
		di Siena	19	SITA Bus Station
PLACES TO EAT	5	Banca Nazionale del	20	Stazione
		Lavoro		Circumvesuviana
13 La Brace	7	Castel Capuano	21	Basilica del
16 Trianon	9	Intercity &		Carmine Maggiore

is through the Port'Alba from Piazza Dante. Spacious if spartan singles/doubles are L28,000/40,000. *Alloggio Fiamma* (☎ 45 91 87), Via Francesco del Giudice 13, is nearby. It has basic rooms at L25,000 a head and is really only recommendable in terms of price. An acceptable deal is *Candy* (☎ 552 13 59), Via Carrozzieri a Monteoliveto 13, south of Piazza del Gesù Nuovo. It has basic singles/doubles for L30,000/40,000.

A popular spot tucked away in the heart of Spaccanapoli is the *Bellini* (☎ 45 69 96), Via San Paolo 44, with singles/doubles for L30,000/50,000. Just down from the cathedral is the *Duomo* (☎ 26 59 88), Via Duomo 228, with doubles/triples for L60,000/90,000. Don't be put off by the entrance.

Hotel Orchidea (☎ 551 07 21), Corso Umberto 7, is just outside the rabbit warren of Spaccanapoli and has good doubles with a bathroom, some overlooking the bay, for L80,000.

For the looser wallet, the *Oriente Grand Hotel* (☎ 551 21 33), Via A Diaz 44, is one of the city's finest hotels, with singles/doubles starting at L140,000/170,000 and spiralling upwards.

Mergellina, Vomero & Santa Lucia

Near the bridge to Borgo Marinari is *Pensione Astoria* (☎ 764 99 03), Via Santa Lucia 90, which has singles/doubles from L13,000/23,000, or L23,000/26,000 with a bathroom – don't expect much in the line of comfort.

In the same building is *Albergo Teresita* (☎ 764 01 05) with singles/doubles from L30,000/50,000.

Pensione Ausonia (☎ 68 22 78), Via F Caracciolo 11, is considerably more expensive at L60,000/70,000, or slightly more for a room with full bathroom. Prices rocket in summer, making it a bit of a last-ditch alternative in high season.

At Vomero, *Pensione Margherita* (☎ 556 70 44), Via Domenico Cimarosa 29, is a few doors from the funicular station. Singles/doubles are L45,000/80,000 and triples are L110,000, including breakfast. Take a L50 coin for the lift.

Farther out (if everything is full), try *Pensione Oasi* (☎ 578 74 56), Via Mariano d'Amelio 63, with singles/ doubles for L45,000/70,000.

Just off Piazza Amedeo, *Pensione Ruggiero* (☎ 66 35 36), Via Martucci 72, is clean and bright. singles/doubles with a shower start from L65,000/95,000. It's a good location for restaurants and bars. In the same building is the pricier *Hotel Pinto-Storey*, which starts at L80,000/130,000 for singles/doubles.

Getting more expensive is the *Hotel Rex* (☎ 764 93 89), Via Palepoli 12, close to the waterfront, with singles/doubles starting at L70,000/110,000. One of Naples' better hotels, the *Santa Lucia* (☎ 764 06 66), Via Partenope 46, overlooks the bay and Mt Vesuvius in sumptuous style. Singles/doubles cost from L125,000/180,000 depending on the view. For even better views, the *Hotel Belvedere* (☎ 578 81 69), Via Tito Angelini 51, stands below the walls of the Castel Sant'Elmo and has sweeping vistas of the city and bay.

PLACES TO EAT

Neapolitan street food is among Italy's best. The pizza with mozzarella cheese and fresh tomato sauce is standard fare, as is the related *calzone*, a puffed up version with the topping becoming a filling instead. *Misto di frittura* – deep-fried potato, eggplant and zucchini flowers – tempt from tiny stalls in tiny streets, as does *mozzarella in carozza* – mozzarella deep-fried in bread. Seafood, in particular clams, is a speciality (although it is best to avoid uncooked shellfish as the bay is extremely polluted).

Pick up *Locali Veraci*, a booklet available at the AAST in Piazza del Gesù Nuovo. In Italian only, it gives the rundown on some of Naples' better and well-known restaurants, pizzerias, cafés and bars.

Spaccanapoli & City Centre

The *Trattoria da Carmine*, Via dei Tribunali 92, is one of dozens of small family trattorie in this area. It has pasta from L3000, main dishes from L4000, and cheap alcohol. It is open for lunch but, unfortunately, closes around 8 pm. *Pizzeria di Matteo*, Via dei Tribunali 94, is one of the city's best with pizzas from L3000 – try the pizza lasagne with ricotta, and the misto di frittura. It also does takeaway. *La Campagnola*, Piazzetta del Nilo, is a cosy little family run place where pasta starts at L5000 and main dishes cost L6000 and up. *Il Pizzicotto*, Via Mezzocannone 129, is a bigger, brighter place with similarly priced food. For a quick pizza, try *Minipizza*, on the corner of Via Santa Chiara and Largo Banchi Nuovi. There is another branch in the Mergellina area at Via Bausan 1a.

The *Trianon*, Via Pietro Colletta 46, has a wide selection of pizzas from L5000 and is close to Stazione Centrale. It's been going since 1925 and was for a long time a favourite with Italian celebrities such as film director Vittorio de Sica and comic actor Totò. *Trattoria Avellinese*, Via Silvio Spaventa 31-35, is just off Piazza Garibaldi and specialises in cheap seafood. Just up the road, *La Brace* at No 14 is a recommended no-nonsense eatery where you can fill up for not more than L25,000.

Ristorante Bellini, Via Santa Maria di Costantinopoli 79-80, is one of Naples' better restaurants and a full meal will cost upwards of L35,000. Seafood is a house speciality. Virtually around the corner is *Pizzeria Port'Alba*, Via Port'Alba 18. Founded in 1830, it is one of the oldest pizzerias in Naples.

La Taverna del Buongustaio, tucked in west of Via Toledo at Vico Basilico Puoti 8, is about as basic a place as you'll find. It specialises in seafood and is cheap. It's closed Sunday. *Pizzeria al 22*, off Piazza Carità at Via Pignasecca 22, has takeaway pizzas from L4000.

If you want something other than Italian, *Ristorante Hong Kong*, Vico Quercia 5A, off Via Roma near Piazza Dante, does good Chinese for about L15,000 a head.

Santa Lucia

The restaurants on Borgo Marinari are generally overpriced, but try *Trattoria da Patrizia*, Via Luculliana, with the red Coke chairs, which offers pasta from L6000. *Antica Trattoria da Pietro* is a couple of doors down and is much the same.

Mergellina & Vomero

Head for the area around Piazza Amedeo. The surrounding streets down to the waterfront are filled with bars, cafés and restaurants of varying descriptions, as well as some of Neapolitan nightlife. A full meal at *Trattoria dell'Oca*, Via Santa Teresa 11, will come in at about L15,000. For Spanish and Latin American fare, try *El Bocadillo*, Via Martucci 50.

In front of the Certosa di San Martino, *Renzo e Lucia*, Via Tito Angelini 33a, offers spectacular views over the city and lofty prices to match. Pasta costs from L10,000 and pizza from L7000, with a L3000 cover charge. To reach the restaurant, you could go for a 30-minute uphill walk (not recommended at night) from Via Roma or take bus No VS, VD or V3 from Piazza Vanvitelli.

The *Acunzo*, Via Domenico Cimarosa 60, has pizzas and pasta, and a full meal can cost L16,000. *Frasco*, nearby at Via Morghen 12, is one of Vomero's more popular spots, with pizzas and pasta from about L8000. It has a pleasant garden for al fresco dining in summer and pasta from L6000. *Mario Daniele*, Via A Scarlatti 104, is a bar with a restaurant upstairs. For a light meal in a bright new place, or just a drink at the bar, *Cibo Cibo*, Via Cimarosa 150, is a good spot.

Food Stalls

Friggitoria Fiorenzano in Piazza Montesanto is one of several food stalls scattered throughout the Spaccanapoli area that sells deep-fried vegetables for L200 apiece – the eggplant slices are especially good. For more substantial snacks and deep fried food, *Lo Sfizietto*, on the corner of Vico Basilico Puoti and Via Pignasecca, has goodies for under L1000.

Cafés

If sitting around in a bar is your idea of fun, one of the more interesting is *Intra Moenia*, Piazza Bellini 69-70, an arty/gay/leftist café/bookshop in one of the city's more beautiful piazzas. Virtually across the road at Via Constantinopoli 81, the *Caffè dell' Epoca* has been going since 1886. For something more elegant, head for *Gambrinus*, where Via Chiaia runs into Piazza Trento e Trieste.

Gelati & Sweets

For good gelati, head for *Gelateria della Scimmia*, Piazza Carità 4, or *Gelati Otranto*, in Vomero at Via M Kerbaker 43. A local tip for the best gelati in Naples is *Remy Gelo* in Mergellina.

Sfogliatelle are the great Neapolitan pastry, a vaguely sweet ricotta-filled number that tastes best straight out of the oven. *Attanasio*, Vico Ferroviario 1-4, near Stazione Centrale, is famous throughout Campania for them. Just ask around for shops selling pastries.

ENTERTAINMENT

The monthly *Qui Napoli* and the local newspapers are the only real guides to what's on. Box Office (☎ 551 91 88), Galleria Umberto I 16, sells tickets for most sporting and cultural events. Enquire there or at the tourist office about what is happening during your stay.

Cinema

Finding films in English is not easy, but you might have luck at Cinema Amedeo, Via Martucci 69, something of an art-house place with lots of classics.

Theatre & Music

The Teatro San Carlo has year-round performances of opera, ballet and concerts. Tickets start at L15,000 and spiral upwards, and always sell quickly. The booking office is at the theatre (☎ 797 21 11). Adjacent to the theatre in the Palazzo Reale (to the left of the main entrance and up the grand staircase) is the Teatro di Corte, which is slightly avant-garde but still expensive. Watch out for posters and book at the theatre.

In July, there is a series of free concerts called Luglio Musicale a Capodimonte outside the Capodimonte Palace.

Bars & Nightclubs

Young, hip Neapolitans stand around their cars and mopeds eating gelati at Piazza Amedeo, which can be fun to watch, and the city jumps with jazz joints and trendy (some might say tacky) clubs. Some clubs charge hefty entrance or membership fees (say L80,000), which usually include a drink.

The area around Piazza Amedeo is worth investigating, as there are several watering holes, clubs and live music venues sprinkled in among the trattorie and cafés. Try Via Martucci, where you'll find the Jam Club (No 87), Il Picaro (No 81), Wonky Club (No 43), New Callegher (No 39), Baboon Club (No 32) and Kafafà (No 49).

The Otto Jazz Club, Piazzetta Cariati 23, features Neapolitan jazz.

Exclusive, also known as Kiss Kiss, Via Sgambati 59, in Vomero is a well-established and expensive club, while La Belle Epoque, Via Andrea d'Isernia 33, near the Riviera di Chiaia, has rock, blues, jazz and soul on different nights.

There are several venues for live music. The Palapartenope (☎ 570 68 06), Via Barbagallo, gets Italian and international acts. Heading out of town, Havana (exit No 12 from the Tangenziale to Pozzuoli) hosts live acts and also the plastic stuff, mostly garage and underground material. Similar is Dynamik Area, on the Strada Provinciale Grumo/Sant'Arpino in Frattamaggiore.

Soccer

Matches are played at the Stadio San Paolo in the western suburb of Mostra d'Oltremare. Call ☎ 61 56 23 for details.

THINGS TO BUY

They say you can buy anything in Naples, and you can see why after a little time spent wandering around the city centre. From designer stores to improvised stalls with goods fresh off the back of a truck, Naples certainly seems to have it all.

In particular, Naples is renowned for its gold and Christmas items such as nativity scenes and *pastori* (shepherds). The former can take on enormous proportions, becoming fantastic models of all Bethlehem. Most artisans are in Spaccanapoli, in particular along Via dei Tribunali, Via B Croce and the side streets and lanes. Many goldsmiths and *gioiellerie* (jewellery shops) are clustered around Via San Biagio dei Librai, and their wares are well advertised. Be warned, some inflate prices for tourists. If you like old dolls, head for the Ospedale delle Bambole, Via San Biagio dei Librai 81.

The city's more exclusive shops are in Santa Lucia, behind Piazza del Plebiscito, along Via Chiaia to Piazza dei Martiri and down towards the waterfront. Young people shop along Via Roma and Via Toledo.

Street markets selling just about everything are scattered across the city centre, including Piazza Garibaldi and along Via Pignasecca, off Piazza Carità.

GETTING THERE & AWAY

Air

Capodichino airport (☎ 789 62 28), Viale Maddalena, about five km north-east of the city centre, is southern Italy's main airport and links Naples with most Italian and several major European cities.

Airlines represented in Naples include:

Alitalia (☎ 542 53 33), Via Medina 41-42
British Airways (☎ 780 29 52), at the airport
TWA (☎ 764 58 28), Via Partenope 23
Qantas, handled by Gastaldi Travel (☎ 552 30 01), Via Depretis 108

Bus

Buses leave for Italian and some European cities from Piazza Garibaldi in front of Stazione Centrale. Look carefully or ask, because there are no signs.

SITA (☎ 552 21 76) has a daily bus to Bari from Salerno via Napoli. Marino (☎ 871 23 72) has two buses to Bari. Miccolis (☎ 521 23 04) has three buses to Taranto, Lecce and Brindisi, while CLP (☎ 531 17 06) has four buses to Foggia.

Within Campania, SITA runs buses from Via G Ferraris to Pompeii, Herculaneum, Eboli, Salerno, the Amalfi coast and Salerno. You can pick up tickets and buses either from the main office at Via Pisanelli (near Piazza Municipio), or from Via G Ferraris, near Stazione Centrale (tickets at Bar Pietruccio, Via G Ferraris 5). CPTC has buses to Caserta and FBN to Benevento, and other companies run to Avellino every 20 minutes.

Curreri (☎ 801 54 20) has a Capodichino Airport-Sorrento bus.

Train

Naples is the hub for the south, and many trains originating in the north pass through Rome and terminate here. The city is served by regionale, diretto, espresso, Intercity, EuroCity and the superfast Pendolino (ETR 500) trains. They arrive and depart from Stazione Centrale (☎ 554 31 88) at Piazza Garibaldi. There are up to 30 trains a day to Rome.

Car & Motorbike

Naples is on the major north-south Autostrada del Sole, known as the A1 to Rome and Milan and the A3 to Salerno and Reggio di Calabria. The A30 acts as a ring road through Campania, while the A16 heads east to Bari.

When approaching the city, the autostradas meet the Tangenziale di Napoli (L1000 toll), a major ring road around the city. The multi-lane ring road, Tangenziale Ovest di Napoli, hugs the city's northern fringe, meeting the A1 for Rome and the A2 to Capodichino Airport in the east, and continues for Pozzuoli and the Phlegraean Fields to the west. The A3 for Salerno and Calabria can be reached from Corso Arnaldo Lucci, south-east of Piazza Garibaldi.

For rental information, see the following Getting Around section.

Boat

Ferries and hydrofoils leave for Capri, Sorrento, Ischia, Procida, Forio and Casamicciola from the Molo Beverello in front of the Castel Nuovo. Ferries to Palermo, Cagliari, Milazzo and the Aeolian Islands leave from Stazione Marittima, next to the Molo Beverello. Some hydrofoils leave for the bay islands from Mergellina, and Alilauro and SNAV also operate to most destinations from Mergellina.

Ferry companies and the routes they service are as follows:

SNAV (☎ 761 23 48), Via Caracciolo 10 (Mergellina), runs hydrofoils to Capri (L15,000 one way), Procida (L13,000) and Casamicciola, in Ischia (L15,500). In summer there are daily services to the Aeolian Islands.

Alilauro (☎ 761 10 04), Via Caracciolo 11 (Mergellina), operates boats and hydrofoils to Ischia (L7700 and L14,100 one way respectively) and hydrofoils to Sorrento (L12,000 one way).

Caremar (☎ 551 38 82), Molo Beverello, serves Capri (L7600 one way by ferry; L14,000 one way by hydrofoil), Ischia (same fares) and Procida (L6400 return by ferry).

Navigazione Libera del Golfo (☎ 552 72 09), Molo Beverello, services Capri (L27,000 return) and Sorrento (once daily).

Tirrenia (☎ 551 21 81) has a daily service to Palermo at 8 pm (high season fare is L68,400 one way in airline-style seat), and to Cagliari (L54,900 one way) on Thursday. From Palermo and Cagliari there are connections to Trapani and on to Tunisia.

Siremar (☎ 761 36 88), part of the Tirrenia group, operates a service to the Aeolian Islands and Milazzo on Monday and Thursday in the off-season, and up to five days a week in the high season.

Linee Lauro (☎ 551 33 52), linked with Alilauro, has summer boat services direct from Naples to Trapani (Sicily) and Tunis. One-way deck-class fares are L50,000 and L100,000 respectively. They also sometimes have direct runs to Sardinia and Corsica in high season.

GETTING AROUND
To/From the Airport

Take bus No 14 from Stazione Centrale, or CLP's airport bus (☎ 531 17 06) every 30 minutes from Via Marina, Piazza Municipio, Via Depretis, Piazza Borsa or Piazza Garibaldi (L3000).

Bus & Tram

Most city ATAN buses operating in the central area depart from and terminate in front of Stazione Centrale, although the bus stops there are not well signposted. The city does not prepare a bus map, and it is impossible to find decent information. There is an ATAN bus information office at Stazione Centrale and another at Piazza Dante. Tickets (L1000) can be bought from ATAN booths and tobacconists. They are good for buses, trams and funicular services, but not the Metropolitana.

A useful bus is the No CA, which starts and terminates at Stazione Centrale and passes Via Diaz, Via Toledo and Corso Umberto I in the city centre. Other buses and their routes include:

CD & CS: round trips in opposite directions from Stazione Centrale through the city centre to Piazza Dante

C1: from Piazza Gesù to Corso Umberto and back

C4: around Mergellina, along the waterfront to the city centre, Piazza Diaz, Piazza Amedeo and back to Mergellina

104: from Stazione Centrale through the city centre and Chiaia to Mergellina

14 & 14R: from Piazza Garibaldi to the airport and the city's north

24: from the Parco Castello and Piazza Trieste e Trento along Via Toledo, Via Roma to Capodimonte

102, 112 & 112RB: from Parco Castello, along the Riviera di Chiaia and westwards, past Mergellina

109: from Parco Castello through Piazza Dante past the museum, Capodimonte and farther north

110: from Stazione Centrale to the museum and Capodimonte

127R: from Stazione Centrale to Piazza Cavour, the museum, Capodimonte and Marianella

137R: from Piazza Dante north to Capodimonte, farther north and then back to Piazza Dante

Night buses include:

401: connects Stazione Centrale with the Riviera di Chiaia, through the city centre, and returns to the station

403S: operates from Stazione Centrale to Mergellina through the city centre, and returns along the same route

404S, 406D & 406S: operate round trips from Stazione Centrale through the city centre

Trams No 1 and 1B operate from east of Stazione Centrale, through Piazza Garibaldi, the city centre and along the waterfront to Riviera di Chiaia. Tram No 2B travels from Stazione Centrale to the city centre along Corso Garibaldi.

Train
The city has four train systems. For a long time the only Metropolitana (underground railway) line has been little more than an ordinary train running from Gianturco, east of Stazione Centrale, with stops at Stazione Centrale, Piazza Cavour, Piazza Amedeo, Mergellina, Fuorigrotta, Campi Flegrei (the Phlegraean Fields), Pozzuoli and Solfatara. Tickets (L1500) on this line are good for one trip only. A new underground line has been partly completed with EU funds. It runs north from Piazza Vanvitelli to Piazza Medaglie d'Oro and seven stops beyond, but will only become truly useful to travellers when the extension connecting Piazza Garibaldi, the duomo, Piazzas Bovio, Carità & Dante, the Museo Archeologico Nazionale

and on up to Piazza Vanvitelli is completed. Tickets on the new stretch cost L1000.

The Circumvesuviana (☎ 779 21 11), about 400 metres south-west of Stazione Centrale in Corso Garibaldi (take the underpass from Stazione Centrale), operates trains to Sorrento via Pompeii (L2500), Herculaneum and other towns along the coast. There are about 40 trains a day between 5 am and 11 pm.

The Ferrovia Cumana and the Circumflegrea (☎ 551 33 28), based at Stazione Cumana in Piazza Montesanto, 300 metres south-west of Piazza Dante, operate services to Pozzuoli and Cumae every 20 minutes.

Funicular Railway
The Funicolare Centrale from Via Toledo connects the city centre with Vomero (Piazza Fuga). The Funicolare di Chiaia (closed at the time of writing) travels from Via del Parco Margherita to Via Domenico Cimarosa, also in Vomero. The Funicolare di Montesanto travels from Piazza Montesanto to Via Morghen. All three can be used to reach the Certosa di San Martino and the Vomero area. The Funicolare di Mergellina connects the waterfront at Via Mergellina with Via Manzoni. Tickets cost L1000.

Taxi
Taxis generally ignore kerb-side arm wavers. You can arrange one through Radiotaxi (☎ 556 44 44) or else at taxi stands on most piazzas in the city. The minimum fare is L6000, and a short trip can cost up to L20,000 because of traffic delays.

Car & Motorbike
Forget it unless you have a death wish. Park your car at one of the car parks, most of which are staffed, and walk around the city centre. Try Supergarage, Via Shelley 11, in the city centre.

Apart from the headaches you will suffer trying to negotiate the city's chaotic traffic, car theft is a major problem in Naples. Although it is said that Neapolitans observe some caution when driving behind or near cars with foreign numberplates, the risk of being in an accident is quite high if you fail to deal with the local system of not (necessarily) stopping at traffic lights.

Rental Avis has offices at Via Partenope 33 (☎ 764 56 00) and Stazione Centrale (☎ 554 30 20); and Europcar (☎ 764 58 59) is at Via artenope 38. Both have offices at the airport.

It is impossible to rent a moped in Naples for reasons of theft. You can hire them at Sorrento.

Around Naples

PHLEGRAEAN FIELDS (CAMPI FLEGREI)
The area west of Naples is known as the Phlegraean ('Fiery') Fields, a classical term for the volcanic activity that has made it one of the globe's most geologically unstable areas. It includes the towns of Pozzuoli, Baia and Cumae, and it was partly through this region that Greek civilisation arrived in Italy. Homer believed the area to be the entrance to Hades, and Virgil too wrote of it in *The Aeneid*. Now part of suburban Naples, it is dirty and overdeveloped, but bears some reminders of the Greeks and Romans, is easily accessible and worth a half-day trip.

Getting There & Away
Although there is an ATAN bus from Piazza Garibaldi in Naples, and also CTP and SEPSA buses from near Stazione Centrale, train is a more straightforward bet. See the Naples Getting Around section for details of the Metropolitana, Ferrovia Cumana and Circumflegrea rail services.

The Tangenziale di Napoli runs through the area. Exit at Pozzuoli. Alternatively, take Via Caracciolo along the Naples waterfront for Posillipo.

Traghetti Pozzuoli (526 77 36) has frequent boats to Ischia from Pozzuoli (L5800 one way) and also to Procida (L3500). If you miss out with them, you could try Caremar (☎ 526 13 35), which in addition to normal boats, also has a daily hydrofoil to Procida. You can take your car across on most of the services.

Pozzuoli
Now a grubby-looking suburb of Naples, Pozzuoli still contains some impressive Roman ruins. The tourist office (☎ 081-526 24 19), Via Campi Flegrei 3, is about one km uphill from the train station and has a reasonable map.

Things to See Close to the remains of the Roman port of Puteoli is the **Tempio di Serapide** (Temple of Serapis), which was simply a market of shops and, according to some sources, skilfully designed toilets. It has been badly damaged over the centuries by the seismic activity known as bradyseism (literally 'slow earthquake') which raises and lowers the ground level over long periods. The nearby church of Santa Maria delle Grazie, along Via Roma, is sinking at a rate of about two cm a year because of this.

The **duomo** is also known as a temple of Augustus, upon which the Christian cathedral was built. Earthquake activity and excavation have revealed six columns from the temple.

North-east along Via Rosini are the substantial ruins of the **Anfiteatro Flavio**, which had seating for 40,000 people and could be flooded for mock naval battles. It's open from 9 am to 2.30 pm (sometimes later in summer) and entrance is L4000.

Farther along, Via Rosini becomes Via Solfatara and continues to the **Solfatara Crater**, about a two-km walk (or jump on any city bus heading uphill). Known to the Romans as the Forum Vulcani and bearing some remnants of ancient spa buildings, the crater occasionally ejects steam jets and bubbling mud. The entire crater is a layer of rock supported by the steam pressure beneath. Pick up a boulder, cast it into the air and listen to the rumblings as it hits the ground. Entrance to the site is L4000. The crater area includes a crowded *camping ground* (☎ 526 74 13) at Via Solfatara 47. Sites cost L10,000 per person in high season and up to L17,400 for tent space, plus car fees.

To the south of the crater is the **Chiesa di San Gennaro**, where Naples' patron saint was beheaded in 305 AD.

Baia & Cumae

Twenty minutes north-west of Pozzuoli, on the Ferrovia Cumana or by SEPSA bus, is Baia, once a fashionable Roman bathing resort, the remains of which are now submerged about 100 metres from the shore. On a clear day, ask one of the local fishers to take you out. They might charge up to L10,000, but the remains are quite extensive and worth a look.

Beyond Baia is Bacoli with more Roman remains, and Cumae, the site, according to Virgil's account, where Aeneas, the legendary Trojan prince said to have laid Rome's grew, landed in Italy. A visit to **Sibyl's Cave**, home of one of the ancient world's greatest oracles, is a must. Inland is **Lake Avernus**, the mythical entrance to the underworld where Aeneas descended to meet his father.

CASERTA

Probably founded by the Lombards in the 8th century on the site of a Roman emplacement atop Monte Tifata, the town spread into the plains below from the 12th century on. The construction of the Bourbons' grand palace assured the town a certain grandeur it otherwise would never have known.

The tourist office (☎ 32 11 37) in the palace produces a guide to the palace. The telephone code is 0823.

Palazzo Reale

Also known as the Reggia di Caserta, this splendid palace was built by the Bourbons of Naples and modelled on Versailles. Work started in 1752 after Charles III of Bourbon decided he would build himself a palace similar to Versailles. Neapolitan Luigi Vanvitelli, commissioned for the job, established his reputation as one of the leading architects of the time after working on the palace.

Covering 51,000 sq metres, with a façade stretching 250 metres, the building is of massive proportions, with 1200 rooms, 1790 windows and 34 staircases. After entering by Vanvitelli's immense staircase, you follow a path through the royal apartments, most of them richly decorated with tapestries, furniture, mirrors and crystal. After the library is a room containing a vast collection of Nativity scenes played out in several huge cabinets, featuring hundreds of hand-carved characters.

A walk in the elegant landscaped **gardens** is a must. Some three km long, the best bet is probably to take the special bus to the far end (L1500 return), marked by a waterfall and the so-called fountain of Diana, and amble your way back. Guides take groups through one garden, **Giardino Inglese**, which is sprinkled with rare plants, little lakes and fake Roman ruins – all very much the taste of the day.

Entrance to the apartments costs L8000 and they are generally open daily from 9 am to 1.30 pm. The gardens, to which entry costs L4000, are open until at least 2.30 pm.

Getting There & Away

CPTC buses connect Caserta with Naples (Piazza Garibaldi) about every half-hour from 8 am to 8 pm. Some Benevento services also stop in Caserta. Trains serve Caserta from Naples. Drivers can the A1 or SS87.

AROUND CASERTA

About two km north-west of the palace (buses run from the train station), is the **San Leucio silk factory**, built by Ferdinand IV and still operating today. A few km to the west in Capua (take a CPTC bus) are the still impressive ruins of **Arco d'Adriano** (Hadrian's Arch), under which passed the Via Appia, and the nearby **amphitheatre**, restored in 119 AD by Emperor Hadrian. About 10 km to the north-east lies **Caserta Vecchia** (CPTC bus), the decayed nucleus of the original town, where you can see the remains of the 9th-century castle and the 13th-century cathedral.

BENEVENTO

A provincial capital about 60 km from Naples, Benevento is on the Via Appia. After a period as a Lombard duchy, when it controlled much of southern Italy, the town was transferred to the control of the papacy in the 11th century and remained mostly under papal rule until 1860.

Information

The tourist office (☎ 31 06 61), Via Sala 31, has information about the town and the region. Another tourist office is located at Piazza Roma 11 (☎ 2 54 24).

The telephone code is 0824.

Things to See

The town was heavily bombed in WW II and the **Duomo** had to be largely rebuilt. Its 13th-century Pisan façade has been preserved and there are a number of Roman stones used in its construction. South-west of the cathedral is a Roman theatre, dating from Hadrian's time but oft restored since. The **Arco di Traiano** (Trajan's Arch), built in 114 AD, commemorated the opening of the Via Traiana. It was covered in scaffolding at the time of writing. The **obelisk** in Piazza Matteotti is a reminder of the Napoleonic period. The **Chiesa di Santa Sofia**, near the piazza, adjoins what was once a Benedictine abbey. Founded in 762, its main entrance dates to the 12th century. The abbey contains the **Museo del Sannio**, which houses remnants of a temple dedicated to Isis, dating from 88 AD, along with a gallery devoted to medieval paintings.

Places to Stay

Should you need to stick around overnight, the *Albergo Genova* (☎ 42 926), Via Principe di Napoli 103, is the cheapest hotel at L20,000/35,000 for a single/double and close to the train station.

Getting There & Away

Infrequent FBN trains (L6400) and buses (L6000) operate from Naples along the Valle Caudina, and FS trains operate via Caserta. Buses also link Benevento with Rome and Campobasso. Benevento is on the SS7 (the Via Appia) and close to the A16.

The Battle of Benevento

At the close of 1250, Emperor Frederick II died in Apulia, leaving his kingdom in southern Italy to his son Conrad, at the time in Germany. For the next eight years, Conrad and his son fought the papacy for control of the kingdom, until Manfred, a bastard son of Frederick, finally took the reins. In the following years, he asserted his mastery over the entire kingdom, but Rome was not idle, and in 1265 reached an agreement with Charles I of Anjou, brother of King Louis IX of France, under which the Frenchman would have the kingdom in the name of the Church, in exchange for extirpating Manfred and his Swabians.

Manfred assembled an army to meet the threat, and on 25 February he was waiting for the French in the Grandella plain north of Benevento. Charles had hoped to take the city by surprise and so have control of the road to Naples. His 30,000 troops exhausted by the long march, he now decided to stay put. Manfred, with only half that number of men, calculated his only real chance was to attack immediately, abandoning his favourable defensive position. At dawn the following day, his Saracen archers and German cavalry stormed Charles' camp, but when the latter's French horsemen entered the fight, things began to go awry. Manfred, seeing his chances of victory dwindle, charged into the mêlée, but at this vital instant was abandoned by many of his barons, who simply turned about and led their men away from the carnage. Manfred and a handful of diehards pressed on, falling to a man. Manfred was 34, and with him passed the brief but illustrious Swabian line. ■

AVELLINO

About 60 km east of Naples and connected by buses every 20 minutes, Avellino is a largely modern town of 60,000 inhabitants. The EPT office (☎ 74 732) is at Piazza Libertà 50. The telephone code is 0825.

The attraction in the area is the vertiginous summit of **Monte Vergine** and the sanctuary devoted to the Virgin Mary, north of the city. A young pilgrim, Guglielmo di Vercelli, erected a church here in the 12th century, and so began a tradition of pilgrimage that continues to the present day. His remains were finally laid to rest in the crypt of a modern basilica here in 1807. From the summit (1493 metres) you can see Naples on a clear day, and the twisting drive up from Avellino is pleasant. If you are in the province in winter, skiing is possible, but not great, at Lago Laceno, south-east of Avellino.

Although best done with your own transport, buses do run from Avellino to the sanctuary daily in summer. There is a funicular that links the sanctuary from the town of Mercogliano. A day excursion from Naples is the best idea, as accommodation options in Avellino are poor.

The Bay of Naples

CAPRI

Despite the boatloads of tourists who pour onto the Marina Grande each day and restaurants that boast *würstl* (German sausages), real English butter and Maxwell House coffee, Capri remains an enchanting island haven in the Bay of Naples. Its breathtaking caves, luxuriant vegetation and the charming narrow laneways of its small towns have attracted visitors for centuries. The best time to visit is spring (April to early June), or mid-autumn (October) after the summer crowds have ebbed away.

History

Already inhabited in the Old Stone Age, Capri was eventually occupied by the Greeks.

Rome's Emperor Augustus made it his private playground, and his successor Tiberius retired there in 27 AD. Augustus is believed to have founded the world's first palaeontological museum, in the Villa Augustus, to house fossils and Stone Age artefacts unearthed by his workers.

Tiberius, a victim of Tacitus' pen, has gone down in history as something of a porn king on the island, although there is little evidence to back the lurid claims concerning the emperor's orgies. The mud stuck however, and until modern times his name has been equated by the islanders with evil. When the eccentric Swedish doctor Axel Munthe first began picking about the ruins of Roman palaces and villas on the island late last century, locals would observe it was all *'roba di Timberio'* (Tiberius' stuff) and that *'Timberio cattivo'* – Tiberius bad.

Despite their sleepy bucolic appearances, the people of Capri and Anacapri have always been at loggerheads, and always ready to trot out their respective patron saints to ward off the Evil Eye *(malocchio)* of their rivals.

Orientation

About five km from the mainland, Capri is a mere six km long and 2.7 km wide. As you approach, there is a lovely view of the town of Capri, with the dramatic slopes of Monte Solaro (589 metres) to the west hiding the village, Anacapri.

All hydrofoils and ferries arrive at Marina Grande, a small settlement that is virtually part of Capri. Buses connect the port with Capri and Anacapri, departing from Via Marina Grande (L1500), just to the right as you leave the pier. A funicular (L1500) also connects the marina with Capri. Otherwise, follow Via Marina Grande for a three-km uphill hike.

Via Marina Grande reaches a junction at Capri with Via Roma, which, to the left, is the town's main strip and leads to Piazza Umberto I and the centre. To the right of the junction is Via Provinciale di Anacapri, which eventually becomes Via G Orlandi as it reaches Piazza Vittoria.

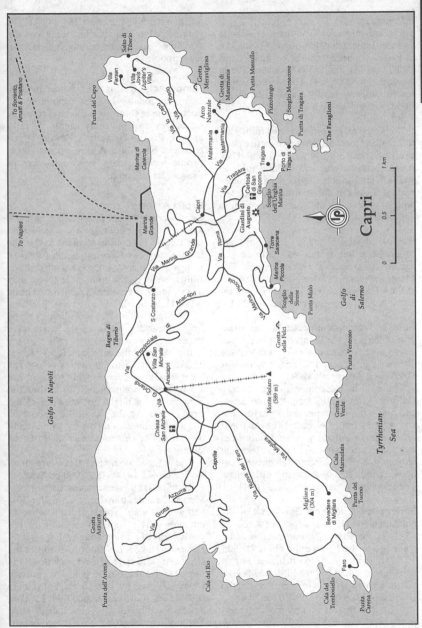

Capri

Information

There are three AAST offices: at Marina Grande, Banchina del Porto (☎ 837 06 34); at Piazza Umberto I, in the centre of Capri (☎ 837 06 86); and at Via G Orlandi 19a in Anacapri (☎ 837 15 24). The Marina Grande tourist office generally opens daily except Sunday from 9 am to midday and about 3 to 7 pm.

The Capri tourist office is open from 9 am to 7 pm, and the Anacapri tourist office daily except Sunday from 9 am to 3 pm. They provide a vague map and walking guide as well as a publication, *Capri È*, listing restaurants and other useful information. *A Capri*, with historical and cultural information, is available periodically.

Money Official exchange operations are everywhere, but watch the charges and usually unfavourable exchange rates. The Monte dei Paschi di Siena bank has branches at Via V Emanuele in Capri and Piazza Vittoria 12 in Anacapri. The latter has an ATM.

Post & Telecommunications The main post office is on Via Roma, to the left as you enter Capri. Another post office is at Viale de Tommaso in Anacapri. Capri's post code is 80073, and Anacapri's 80071.

There is a Telecom office at Piazza Umberto I, open daily from 8 am to 1 pm, and 3 to 8 pm in winter; and 8 am to 2 pm and 4 to 11 pm in summer. The Anacapri office, Piazza Vittoria 4, is open daily from 8 am to 1 pm and 3 to 10 pm in the high season (to 8 pm in winter). Telephone locations are indicated on the tourist office map. The telephone code for the island is 081.

Emergency & Medical Services For the police, call ☎ 113. The questura (☎ 837 72 45) is at Via Roma 70. For medical assistance, go to the USL public clinic (☎ 825 35 09) in Corso Vittorio Emanuele. For an ambulance, call ☎ 837 00 14. If you need a doctor's home visit out of normal hours, the Guardia Medica (☎ 837 50 19) can oblige.

In summer there is a tourist medical emergency service on ☎ 837 20 91. There is also a helicopter ambulance (☎ 584 14 81). The pharmacy, Farmacia Barile, Piazza Vittoria, Anacapri, has a night service but only for prescriptions.

Annoyances During the summer months, and occasionally in winter, hundreds of young people flock to the island to party on Friday and Saturday nights, usually around Piazza Umberto I. Beware if you choose a hotel in that area, because these people tend to make noisy nuisances of themselves all night.

Grotta Azzurra

Capri's craggy coast is studded with more than a dozen grottoes, most accessible and spectacular, but none as stunning as this, the Blue Grotto. Two Germans, writer Augustus Kopisch and painter Ernst Fries, are credited with discovering the grotto in 1826, but they merely rediscovered and renamed the Grotta Gradola, as locals had known it. Remains of Roman work inside, including a carved ledge towards the rear of the cave, were found later.

It is believed the cave sank to its present height, about 15 to 20 metres below sea level, blocking every opening except the 1.3-metre-high entrance. This causes the refraction of sunlight off the sides of the cavity, creating the magical blue colour and a reflection of light off the white sandy bottom, giving anything below the surface a silvery glow.

The inflated combined transport/admission price of L18,000 (L20,000 on Sundays and holidays) includes a motorboat trip from Marina Grande, transfer to a smaller boat and a short visit. The visit itself is worth the money. The 'captains' expect a tip, but you've already paid enough. It is slightly cheaper to take a bus from Anacapri to the Grotta Azzurra (L1500) and walk down the steps behind the bus stop to the entrance where you meet the small boats, but you are still up for L10,000 admission (plus L500 on Sundays and holidays). Tours start at 9 am. The grotto is closed if the sea is too choppy, so before making your way there, check with the tourist office that it's open.

Although frowned upon, it is not illegal to swim into the grotto. You can do it only after the last tourist boat at about 5 pm, if the water is extremely calm. Because of tidal flows through the small entrance, it is quite dangerous, but locals, despite their fear of the dragons and witches believed to inhabit the cave, have swum in it for centuries.

Around Capri Town

From Piazza Umberto I, in the centre of Capri, an afternoon can be whiled away wandering through the narrow laneways with their tiny houses and villas. In the square itself, the 17th-century **Chiesa di Santo Stefano** contains remnants from the Roman villas. Head down Via D Birago, or Via V Emanuele, for the **Certosa di San Giacomo**, a Carthusian monastery with cloisters dating from the 14th century. It is open Tuesday to Sunday from 9 am to 2 pm. The nearby **Giardini di Augusto** (Gardens of Augustus) command one of the better views of the **Faraglioni**, the rock stacks along the south coast.

The **Museo del Centro Caprese I Cerio** at Piazzetta Cerio 8a houses a collection of Neolithic and Palaeolithic fossils discovered on the island. It is open Tuesday to Sunday from 9 am to 2 pm and entry costs L5000.

Villa Jovis (Jupiter's Villa)

East of the town centre, an hour's walk along Via Tiberio leads to Villa Jovis, the residence of Emperor Tiberius. The largest and best preserved of the Roman villas on the island, it was in its heyday a vast complex including imperial quarters, entertainment areas, baths, grand halls, gardens and woodland. It is open from 9 am to one hour before sunset and entry costs L5000.

The stairway behind the villa leads to **Salto di Tiberio** (Tiberius' Leap), a cliff from where he is believed to have had out-of-favour subjects pitched into the sea. A pleasant walk down Via Matermania passes the **Arco Naturale**, a rock arch formed by the pounding sea. From there you can head farther down a long series of steps and follow the path south and back east into town, passing Punta di Tragara and the Faraglioni on the way.

Anacapri

Villa San Michele Not a few of the island's visitors are lured here, above all by the words of one of its most troubled inhabitants, Doctor Axel Munthe (see the special information box for more details). The house he built here on the ruined site of a Roman villa remains immortalised in his book *The Story of San Michele*. The villa houses Roman sculptures from the period of Tiberius' rule and is a short walk north of Piazza Vittoria in Anacapri. Opening hours are daily from 9 am to 6 pm in summer, 10.30 am to 3.30 pm in winter, and entrance is L4000. The pathway behind the villa offers superb views over Capri, and the (usually closed) stairway of 800 steps was the only link between Anacapri and the rest of the island until the mountain road was built in the 1950s.

Monte Solaro

From Piazza Vittoria in Anacapri, take the chair lift to the top of Monte Solaro (L5000 one way, L6000 return, from 9 am to two hours before sunset) where on a (rare) clear day you can see for miles. From Anacapri, take a bus to Faro (L1500), a less crowded spot with one of Italy's tallest lighthouses.

Activities

For scuba diving, try Servizi al Mare (Sea Service Centre; ☎ 837 02 21), Marina Piccola, Via Mulo 63, which represents a host of companies, including the Capri Diving Club (☎ 837 34 87). The club runs NAUI certificate courses.

The centre hires out canoes and motorised dinghies, and can take you water-skiing. Alberino Gennaro (☎ 83771 18), Via Colombo, also rents scuba equipment. For sailboards and Hobie Cats, contact Banana Sport (☎ 837 51 88) at Marina Grande. For a real treat, ask about submarine voyages around the island aboard the *Tritone*. You can book

The Story of Axel Munthe

Born in Sweden in 1857, Axel Munthe proved something of a medical prodigy, and ended up studying in Paris. His studies successfully completed, Munthe went on to lead a 'double' life, attending to the imagined ills of high society dames and plumbing the miserable depths of some of the city's poorest public hospitals. In later days he had few opportunities to return to his native land, turning his attention rather to Italy. In between summer stints working on his dream villa on Capri, Munthe was either repeating his Paris experience in Rome (living in the building by the Spanish Steps where Keats had earlier occupied rooms) or treating the ill of the disease-ridden poor quarters of Naples. He devoted much of his later time on the island to protecting migratory birds for long decimated by the local populace for food and export.

Even before finishing his Paris studies, a youthful Munthe had discovered the site of what he would one day turn into his part-time home and write about in his book *The Story of San Michele*:

Just over our heads, riveted to the steep rock like an eagle's nest, stood a little ruined chapel. Its vaulted roof had fallen in, but huge blocks of masonry shaped into an unknown pattern of symmetrical network, still supported its crumbling walls.

'Roba di Timberio,' explained old Maria.

'What is the name of the little chapel?' I asked eagerly.

'San Michele.'

'San Michele, San Michele!' echoed in my heart. ∎

in at the SNAV ticket booth at the Marina Grande, or call ☎ 837 56 46 for information. You're looking at L70,000 for an hour, and it operates from May to September only.

The main places to swim are at a small inlet west of Marina Grande; Bagno di Tiberio, where the emperor dipped; a rocky area at Marina Piccola; off concrete ledges at the Blue Grotto (only after 5 pm); and, farther west of the grotto, below the restaurants. There are no private beaches on the island, and the best areas can only be reached by hired boat or by traversing tracks, particularly around Pizzolungo.

Places to Stay

Hotel rooms are at a premium in summer, and many close during winter. There are few really cheap rooms at any time of year. Beware of the compulsory breakfast in summer, and haggle for a better price in the low season.

Camping is forbidden and offenders are either prosecuted or 'asked' to relocate to a hotel. You might want to enquire at the tourist office about renting a room in a private home.

Marina Grande The *Italia* (☎ 837 06 02), Via Marina Grande, has singles/doubles from L48,000/58,000 and ranging up to L140,000 for some doubles with shower. Nearby, the *Belvedere e Tre Re* (☎ 837 03 45), Via Marina Grande, has good views, with singles/doubles from L40,000/65,000.

Capri All rooms have views over the bay at *ABC* (☎ 837 06 83), Via M Serafina, at L45,000/75,000, with breakfast included. *Stella Maris* (☎ 837 04 52), Via Roma, also has views from every room, with prices starting at L50,000/65,000 for singles/doubles. Facing the south side, the Liberty-style *Esperia* (☎ 837 02 62), Via Sopramonte, is a crumbling villa with spectacular views. Singles/doubles start at about L50,000/80,000, but you'll probably have to pay for breakfast too. *La Reginella* (☎ 837 05 00) is pleasantly located on Via Matermania and has singles/doubles with a bathroom starting at L50,000/90,000.

Anacapri The *Loreley* (☎ 837 14 40), Via G Orlandi, is one of the better deals, starting at L30,000/60,000 for singles/doubles with a bathroom, with views towards Naples from some rooms. *Caesar Augustus* (☎ 837 14 21), Via G Orlandi, has the best view in town, with a terrace overlooking the bay. The hotel is generally not cheap, but occasionally may discount smaller vacant singles/doubles to L40,000/60,000. *Biancamaria* (☎ 837 10 00), Via G Orlandi, has rooms from L60,000/80,000. Anacapri virtually closes during winter.

Places to Eat

Food is good and reasonably priced, and even the expensive-looking bread and cheese shops aren't exorbitant. *Insalata caprese*, a delicious salad of fresh tomato, basil and mozzarella, has its origins here. Some of the local wines are a bit rough but generally good. The *Sfizi di Pane*, Via le Botteghe 4, has local breads and cakes, and the cheese shop opposite sells caprese cheese, a cross between mozzarella and ricotta.

Capri *Ristorante Settanni*, Via Longano 5, has a bay view and pasta from about L8000. *La Cisterna*, Via M Serafina 5, is one of several cosy restaurants in the alleys off Piazza Umberto I and has pizza from L5000. Another nearby is *Il Tinello*, Via l'Abate 1-3. *Da Giorgio* and *Moscardino*, virtually beside each other at Via Roma 34 and 28, have the best views in town and a cover charge to match (L3000). A full meal at either is likely to set you back about L40,000. One of the island's best traditional restaurants is *La Capannina*, Via le Botteghe 12, but a meal could cost up to L70,000 a person.

On the way to Arco Naturale, *Ristorante le Grottelle*, Via Arco Naturale, has pasta from L7000 and mains from L9000. Locals do their fruit and vegetable shopping at the small market, the *mercatino*, below the Capri bus stop (take the stairs).

Anacapri *Il Solitario*, Via G Orlandi 54, set in a garden, has pasta from L7000. *Trattoria Il Saraceno*, Via Trieste e Trento 18, serves ravioli caprese at L7000, and the owners serve their own wine. *Pizzeria Materita*, Via G Orlandi 140, has pizzas from L7000 and faces onto Piazza Diaz, as does *Mamma*

Giovanna, Via Boffe 3-5, with pasta from L6000.

Entertainment

For a drink you could head for Guarracino, Via Castello 7. In Anacapri, sit on Piazza Diaz or shoot pool at Bar Materita, Via G Orlandi 140. Nightlife is a bit thin on the ground. In Capri, try Atmosphere or Number Two, Via Camerelle 61b and 1, and the slightly more modern (if that is possible) Pentothal, Via Vittorio Emanuele 45. In Anacapri, the Zeus and New Planet discos, at Via G Orlandi 103 and 101, might get your blood rushing. The only other option is Underground, at No 259.

The main non-religious festival is from 1 to 6 January when local folk groups perform in Piazza Diaz and Piazza Umberto I.

Things to Buy

The island is covered with ceramic tiles displaying street names and numbers and romantic scenes. Massimo Goderecci, Via P Serafino Cimino 8, just off Piazza Umberto I, takes credit for most of these and will bake you a tile for about L100,000.

The island is famous for its perfume and Limoncello. The former smells like lemons and the latter tastes like vodka. Visit Limoncello Capri, Via Capodimonte 27, in Anacapri, and taste the liqueur. The perfumeries are ubiquitous.

Getting There & Away

See the Naples & Sorrento Getting There & Away sections for details of ferries and hydrofoils. Call Eli Ambassador (☎ 789 62 73) for helicopter flights between the island and Naples, which can cost several hundred thousand lira.

Getting Around

You can take your car or moped to Capri, but there is no hire service on the island. The best way to get around is by bus, with most tickets costing L1500 on the main runs between Marina Grande, Capri, Anacapri, Grotta Azzurra and Faro. Buses run between Capri and Anacapri until past midnight. A funicular links Marina Grande with Capri (L1500).

A taxi ride between any of the villages can cost up to L20,000, and from the Marina to Capri about L12,000 – the open-topped 1950s Fiats are very inviting. For a taxi in Capri, call ☎ 837 05 43; and in Anacapri, call ☎ 837 11 75.

ISCHIA

With 45,000 inhabitants and the largest and most developed of the islands in the Bay of Naples, Ischia manages to retain some sense of its past, despite its 300 or so hotels. Away from the uglier towns, people still work the land as if they'd never seen a tourist, itself an improbable proposition. Especially loved by Germans today, it was the Greeks who first colonised the island in the 8th century BC, calling it Pithecusa. The largely volcanic island is noted for its thermal springs and 'curative' muds.

The main centres are the touristy town of Ischia and Ischia Porto, Casamicciola Terme, Forio and Lacco Ameno, all fairly unattractive and overcrowded compared to the picturesque towns of Ischia Ponte, Serrara Fontana, Barano d'Ischia and Sant'Angelo. Hotel prices and camping make the island affordable, and its size means you might just be able to get away from the August crowds.

Orientation & Information

Ferries dock at Ischia Porto, the main tourist centre. It is about a half-hour walk from the pier to Ischia Ponte, an attractive older centre that culminates in the islet bearing the castle.

The tourist office (☎ 99 11 46), Via Iasolino (Banchina Porto Salvo) at the main port, is open Monday to Saturday from 8.30 am to 9 pm and until 1 pm on Sunday in summer. The times are flexible and in winter they tend to open in the mornings only. Expect to find it closed from 1.30 to about 3.30 pm for the lunch break. Get a hotel list, which has the tourist office's best attempt at a map.

There are several banks and exchange booths around the island. The Monte dei Paschi di Siena, Via Sogliuzzo 50, has an ATM.

For police, call ☎ 99 13 36, and for an ambulance call ☎ 99 40 44. The telephone code for the island is 081.

Things to See & Do

The ruins of the **Castello d'Ischia**, an Aragonese castle complex on a small islet that includes a 14th-century cathedral and several smaller churches, make for an interesting visit while in Ischia Ponte (L5000, plus L1000 for the lift).

Monte Epomeo (788 metres) is the island's highest mountain and can be reached on foot from Panza and Serrara Fontana (about 1½ hours). It offers superb views of the Bay of Naples.

Among the better beaches is the Lido dei Maronti, south of Barano. If you're interested in diving, Dimensione Blu (☎ 98 56 08), Via Iasolina 106, in Ischia Porto hires out equipment and runs courses.

Places to Stay & Eat

Call the tourist office in advance for room availability during summer. From October to May, prices can drop considerably, but beware that few hotels open at all in winter. During the peak period, watch for the compulsory breakfast and extra charge for showers.

Camping There are at least three camping grounds on the island, open in high season only. Perhaps the best placed is *Mirage* (☎ 99 05 51), at Lido dei Maronti 37 on the beach south of Barano. The others are *La Valle dell'Eden* (☎ 98 01 58) in Casamicciola Terme and *Eurocamping dei Pini* (☎ 98 20 69), Via delle Ginestre 28, Ischia.

Ischia The simple *Locanda Sul Mare* (☎ 99 15 08), Via Iasolino 68, is handy for boats off the island and has singles/doubles from L30,000/L40,000. *Villa Antonio* (☎ 98 26 60), Via San Giuseppe della Croce, has singles/doubles for L70,000/L120,000, but you might be able to bargain them down out of the peak summer months.

Cicco e Domingo, Via Luigi Mazzella 80, is a pleasant trattoria with solid seafood dishes and pasta. A full meal with wine will cost you about L25,000 a person. *Pirozzi*, Via Seminario 53, Ischia Ponte, has pizzas from L7000.

Sant'Angelo & Barano *Conchiglia* (☎ 99 92 70), Via Chiaia delle Rose, is perched over the water and has singles/doubles starting at L40,000/80,000, but increasing in high season. They also have a decent restaurant. On the promontory of Sant'Angelo, the *Pensione Francesco* (☎ 99 93 76), Via Nazario Sauro 42, has doubles only for L80,000, including breakfast.

In Barano, *Da Franceschina* (☎ 99 01 09), Via Corrado Buono 51, has singles/doubles for L40,000/65,000, and obligatory half board for L40,000 per person in August.

Getting There & Away See the Naples Getting There & Away section for details. You can get ferries direct to Capri and Procida from Ischia.

Getting Around The main bus station is at Ischia Porto, and the most useful lines are the CS (Circo Sinistra, Left Circle) and CD (Circo Destra, Right Circle), which circle the island in opposite directions, passing through each town, and leaving every 30 minutes. All hotels and camping grounds can be reached by these buses, but ask the driver for the closest stop. Taxis and microtaxis (Ape three-wheelers) are also available.

The best way to see the island is by car or moped. You can either bring your own on to the island, or rent them. Autonoleggio Ischia (☎ 99 24 44), Via A De Luca 61, has Fiats from L40,000 and scooters from L35,000 a day, with free helmets. Fratelli del Franco (☎ 99 13 34), Via A De Luca 121, rents out mopeds. Both also have mountain bikes. The vehicles cannot be taken off the island.

PROCIDA

The pinks, whites and yellows of Procida's tiny cubic houses cluttered along the waterfront make for a colourful introduction to the island. The beauty of the Bay of Naples' smallest island is immediately apparent.

There are only three hotels and six camping grounds, making it attractive for backpackers, particularly during the peak tourist season in July/August when the other islands are crowded.

The 16th-century Palazzo Reale d'Avalos, more recently a prison, dominates the island and is worth exploring. Vivara, a smaller island reached by bridge, is now a nature reserve and good for bird-watching or simply strolling.

Orientation & Information

Marina Grande is the hop-off point for ferries and hydrofoils, and forms most of the tourist showcase. There is an information office (☎ 810 19 68) right by the boat ticket office on Via Roma. If it's closed, you could try the Ente Turistico (☎ 896 99 62) at Via Principe Umberto I (closed January to March). You can call an ambulance on ☎ 896 90 58. The telephone code for the island is 081.

Places to Stay & Eat

Camping grounds are dotted around the island. The *Vivara* (☎ 896 92 42), Via IV Novembre, and *La Caravella* (☎ 896 92 30) are on the eastern side of the island, while *Privato Lubrano* (☎ 896 94 01) and *Graziella* (☎ 896 77 47), both in Via Salette, are near the better beaches of Ciraccio on the western side.

For a hotel, try the *Riviera* (☎ 896 71 97) at Chiaiolella, which has singles/doubles for L40,000/70,000, or the *Savoia* (☎ 896 76 16) near Centane, where doubles start at L55,000. Another possibility if you have a big group is *La Rosa dei Venti* (☎ 896 83 85), Via Vincenzo Rinaldi 32. It's a collection of self-contained cottages sleeping up to six people. They are set in parkland a quick walk from a beach and can cost as little as L30,000 per person if you fill a cottage. Ask at the port, or ask the bus driver, for directions.

Cheap restaurants can be found along the waterfront near the port, and grocery shops are in the area around Via Vittorio Emanuele.

Getting There & Away

Procida is linked by boat and hydrofoil to

Naples, Pozzuoli and Ischia. See the Naples and Pozzuoli Getting There & Away sections for details.

Getting Around

SEPSA runs a limited bus service, with the L2 and C1 buses making return trips to most parts of the island from the port, where the ferries and hydrofoils arrive. L1 buses connect the port and Chiaiolella. The small Ape open micro-taxis can be hired for two to three hours for about L20,000 or L30,000, depending on how hard you bargain. You can hire boats from Barcheggiando (☎ 810 19 34), although the local fishers will take you out for L10,000 to L20,000 per person, depending on the size of your group.

South of Naples

HERCULANEUM (ERCOLANO)

According to the legend, this Greek settlement was founded by Hercules (hence the name). Whatever the truth of this, it later passed to the Samnites before becoming a Roman town in 89 BC. Twelve km south of Naples, modern Ercolano is a congested, tangled suburb of the city, but Herculaneum is a peaceful fishing and port town of about 4000, and something of a resort for wealthy Romans and Campanians.

History

The fate of the city paralleled that of nearby Pompeii. Destroyed by earthquake in 63 AD, it was completely submerged in the 79 AD eruption of Mt Vesuvius. The difference was that Herculaneum was buried by a river of volcanic mud, not the tufa stone and ash that rained on Pompeii. The mud helped preserve the town for posterity. Rediscovered in 1709, amateur excavations were carried out intermittently until 1874 and much of the material found was carted off to Naples to decorate the houses of the well-to-do or end up in museums. Serious archaeological work was begun in 1927, and excavation continues today.

Orientation

Ercolano's main street, Via IV Novembre, leads from the Stazione Circumvesuviana at the modern town's eastern edge to Piazza Scavi and the main ticket office for the excavations – an easy walk.

Information

There is a tourist office (☎ 081-788 12 34) at Via IV Novembre 84, but they have little more to offer than a brochure with a map of the ruined city. The *Amedeo Maiuri* guide to Herculaneum sells at some tourist stands for L10,000, and is considered one of the better ones.

The Ruins

The site is divided into 11 islands or *insulae*, carved up in a classic Roman grid pattern. From the main entrance and ticket office you follow a path above and around the site until you arrive at the entrance to the ruins proper in the south-west corner. To leave the site, you must go all the way back to the ticket office. After your tickets have been checked, you will probably be gently assailed by would-be guides – if you really want one, make sure you understand what kind of fee or 'gift' is expected at the end. Some of the houses are closed, but an attendant may be able to open them on request. The two main streets, the *decumani*, are crossed by several *cardos*. On entering, you first encounter the **Casa di Aristide** on your left on Cardo III. Immediately next door is the **Casa d'Argo**, a well preserved example of a Roman noble family's house, equipped with a porticoed garden, *triclinium* (dining area) and a partly excavated peristyle hall.

The most extraordinary mosaic to survive intact is in the *nyphaeum* (fountain and bath) in the **Casa del Nettuno ed Anfitrite**, on Cardo IV. Neptune and Amphitrite are depicted in colours so rich they make you realise what the interior of other well-to-do households must have been like. If mosaics are your thing, make your way to the city's public baths, **Terme del Foro**, with separate sections for men and women. The floor mosaics are in pristine condition. While

1 Casa di Aristide
2 Casa d'Argo
3 Casa del Genio
4 Casa di Galba
5 Sacello degli Augustali
6 Casa del Salone Nero
7 Casa dei Due Atri
8 Terme del Foro
9 Casa del Tramezzo di Legno
10 Casa della Scheletro
11 Casa a Graticcio
12 Casa dell'Erma di Bronzo
13 Casa dell'Albergo
14 Casa con Botteghe
15 Casa del Bincentenario
16 Casa con Botteghe
17 Casa del Bel Cortile
18 Casa di Nettuno ed Anfitrite
19 Casa dell'Attrio Corinzio
20 Casa del Mobilio Carbonizz
21 Casa del Sacello in Legno

22 Casa del Gran Portale
23 Casa del Telaio
24 Casa Sannitica
25 Abitazione e Bottega
26 Casa dell'Alcova
27 Casa del Atrio o Mosaico
28 Casa dei Cervi
29 Terme Suburbane
30 Casa della Gemma
31 Casa del Rilievo di Telefo
32 Abitazione con Tabernae
33 Vestibolo Palestra
34 Bottega e Tabernae
35 Palestra

Herculaneum

0   25   50 m

women passed from the *apodyterium* (changing rooms; note the naked figure of Triton adorning the mosaic floor) through the *tepidarium* to the *calidarium* (steam bath), men had the added bracing option of the *frigidarium* – a cold bath. You can still see the benches where bathers sat, and the wall shelves for clothing.

The **Casa del Atrio Mosaico**, an impressive mansion on Cardo IV, also has extensive floor mosaics – time and nature have left the floor uneven to say the least.

Behind it, and accessible from Cardo V, the **Casa dei Cervi** (House of the Deer) is

probably the most imposing of the nobles' dwellings. The two-storey villa, built around a central courtyard, contains various murals and still-life paintings, as well as the marble groups of deer assailed by dogs. In one of the rooms stands a statue of a drunken Hercules.

On the corner of the Decumanus Inferior and Cardo V is **Casa del Gran Portale**, named after the elegant brick Corinthian columns that flank its main entrance. Inside are some well-preserved wall-paintings.

Off the main street, the Decumanus Maximus, is the **Casa del Bicentenario**, so named because it was excavated 200 years after digging at Herculaneum first began. A room upstairs contains a crucifix, indicating that there might have been Christians in the town before 79 AD. As you exit the ruins, to the left along Corso Ercolano, are the remains of a **theatre**, dating from the Augustan period.

The archaeological area is open daily from 9 am to one hour before sunset in summer, but closes as early as 2.45 pm in winter. Entrance is L12,000.

Places to Stay & Eat

Like Pompeii, Herculaneum is a convenient day trip from Naples. Otherwise, the *Albergo Belvedere* (☎ 081-739 07 44) is close to the train station and has decent singles/doubles for L45,000/60,000. There are several bars around the entrance where you can buy panini and other snacks – the one across the road from the ancient site, on the right-hand corner of Via IV Novembre, is fine.

Getting There & Away

SITA buses stop at Herculaneum on the Naples-Pompeii route. However, the easiest way to get from central Naples or Sorrento to Herculaneum is by train on the Circumvesuviana (see the Naples Getting Around section). By car, take the A3 from Naples, exit at Ercolano Portici, and follow the signs to car parks near the main entrance to the site.

MT VESUVIUS

The still active volcano dominates the landscape, looming ominously over Naples. The last eruption in 1944 blasted open the cone, and the plume of smoke that had long been a constant reminder of the peril also disappeared. This may have eased the minds of some, but living in the shadow of Vesuvius is akin to staying on the fault line in Los Angeles – scientists consider more eruptions a sure thing.

Its name is probably derived from the Greek *besubios* or *besbios*, which means fire. The volcano erupted with such ferocity on 24 August 79 AD that it all but destroyed the towns of Pompeii and Herculaneum, and

pushed the coastline out several km. The subsequent 2000 years have witnessed regular displays of the mountain's wrath, the more destructive being those of 1631, 1794 (when the town of Torre del Greco was destroyed), 1906 and most recently 1944, when poverty-stricken Naples was struggling back onto its feet under Allied occupation.

To reach Mt Vesuvius by car, take the A3 and exit at Ercolano Portici. You can follow the signs through the town, but a road map is handy. By train, get off the Circumvesuviana line from Naples at Herculaneum and await the SITA bus (L2000 one way), which runs services from the train station to the volcano. The first bus leaves the station at 8.15 am and the last leaves the mountain at 5.45 pm. They run about every two hours. A taxi ride up and back could cost L150,000.

The bus takes you to the summit car park, from where you walk a distance of about 1.5 km (it takes 30 minutes if you're quick). Work on a funicular railway to replace the long out-of-service chair lift was due to restart in early 1995. You must pay L3000 to enter the summit area and visit with a guide, although it is possible to sneak through unaccompanied. Once there, you can walk around the top of the crater. There are several bars at the summit car park. Those with cars can drive on past the turn-off for the summit car park and head closer up to the crater.

The **Vesuvius Observatory**, on the road to the summit, was commissioned by Ferdinand II of Bourbon in 1841 and is open to the public. Seismologists monitor the volcano around the clock.

POMPEII (POMPEI)

Ever since Pliny the Younger wrote his moving letters to Tacitus describing the eruption of Mt Vesuvius that buried the city in 79 AD, Pompeii has been the stuff of books learned and frivolous, and equally a perfect subject for the big screen. Much of the site, the richest insight into a Roman's daily life, is open to the public and requires at least three or four hours to visit.

History

Founded in the 7th century BC by the Campanian Oscans on a prehistoric lava flow of Mt Vesuvius, Pompeii eventually fell to the Greeks, and later, in the 5th century BC, came under the influence of the Samnites, a southern Italian people related to the Oscans. It became a Roman colony in 80 BC and prospered as a major port and trading town, adorned with grand temples, villas and palaces, until it was devastated by an earthquake in 63 AD. Pompeii had been largely rebuilt when Mt Vesuvius, overshadowing the town to the north, erupted in 79 AD and buried it under a layer of lapilli (burning fragments of pumice stone). Although the town was completely covered by the shower, only about 2000 of its 20,000 inhabitants are believed to have perished. In later years, Emperor Titus briefly considered rebuilding the city, and Severus carried out a little plundering, but Pompeii gradually receded from the public eye.

The Pompeii area was completely abandoned during the period of Saracen raids and its remains were further shaken by subsequent earthquakes. In 1594, the architect Domenico Fontana stumbled across the ruins during the construction of a canal. The discovery was recorded but substantial excavation was not conducted until 1748, in the time of Charles of Bourbon, who was interested above all in retrieving items of value. Credit for most of the major discoveries belongs to Giuseppe Fiorelli, who worked under the auspices of the Italian government from 1860.

Work continues, but most of the ancient city has been uncovered. Many of the mosaics and murals have been removed to the Museo Archeologico Nazionale in Naples and other museums around the world. The exception is the Villa dei Misteri (Villa of the Mysteries), whose frescoes remain *in situ*. They are the single most important series on the site.

Orientation

Arriving by train, you are deposited at either of the main entrances to the site; by car, signs direct you to the excavations and car parks. There are several camp sites, hotels and none-too-cheap restaurants in the vicinity, although the choice is better in and near the modern town of Pompeii itself.

Information

Tourist Offices & Guides There are two AAST offices, one in modern Pompeii at Via Sacra 1 (☎ 850 72 55), and the other just outside the excavations at Piazza Porta Marina Inferiore 12 (☎ 861 09 13), near the Porta Marina entrance. Pick up a map and a copy of the handy *NTR (Notiziario Turistico Regionale)*.

A good guidebook is essential as it is easy to miss important sites. *How to Visit Pompeii* (L7000) is small but comprehensive. The *Guide d'Agostini – Pompeii* (L12,000) is probably the best.

The tourist offices warn against the dozens of unauthorised guides who swoop at tourists, charging exorbitant prices for brief and generally inaccurate tours. Authorised guides wear identification tags and belong to one of two cooperatives, Coop Touring (☎ 536 91 01) and Gata (☎ 861 56 61). A group of up to 20 people can take a guide from the latter company for two hours at a cost of L115,000 (L3000 more for each person extra). Also be warned that some of the official attendants on the site, who should open many of the closed sites upon request, are more than keen to escort women on their own to out-of-the-way ruins, a situation that could turn nasty.

Other Information The post office is near Piazza Esedra, close to the Porta Marina entrance. The telephone code for the area is 081.

In police emergency, call ☎ 113; for the Polizia Municipale tourist section, go to the booth on Piazza Esedra or call ☎ 861 40 98. Medical first aid (☎ 850 61 93) is available at the medical centre on the corner of Via Ravellese and Via Colle San Bartolomeo, near the Piazza Anfiteatro entrance.

The Ruins

The town was surrounded by a wall with towers and eight gates, through several of

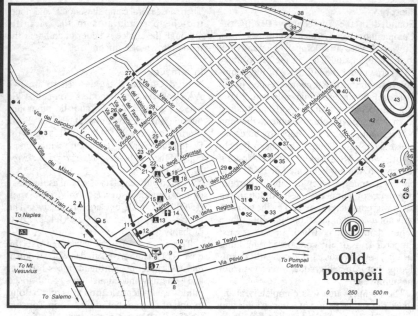

Old Pompeii

0   250   500 m

which you can now gain access to the town. The western sea gate, the **Porta Marina**, was considerably closer to the water before the eruption. Immediately as you enter you see on the right the remains of an imperial villa with long porticoes. The **antiquarium** above it contains remnants gathered from the city and, in one room, body casts formed by hollows left in the hardened tufa by decayed corpses, depicting their final moments of horror.

Farther along Via Marina you pass the striking **Tempio di Apollo**, built originally by the Samnites in the Doric style, and enter the **forum**, the centre of the city's life. To the right as you enter is the **basilica**, the city's law courts and exchange. Dating back to the 2nd century BC, it was one of Pompeii's greatest buildings. Among the fenced-off ruins to the left as you enter are more gruesome body casts. The various buildings around the forum include the **Tempio di Giove** (Temple of Jupiter), one of whose

two flanking triumphal arches remains, the **market**, where you can see the remains of a series of shops, and the **Edificio di Eumachia**, which features an imposing marble doorway.

Taking the street to the right of the Edificio di Eumachia, Via dell'Abbondanza, wander

Casts of the fleeing residents were left in the hardened tufa after their corpses decayed.

along and turn right into Via dei Teatri and enter the **Triangular Forum**, which is surrounded by the remains of a Doric colonnade. To your left is the entrance to the **Great Theatre**, originally built in the 2nd century AD and capable of seating 5000. Adjoining it is the more recent **Small Theatre**, also known as the Odeon, used for music and mime. The **Caserma dei Gladiatori** (Gladiators' Barracks) behind the theatres are surrounded by a portico of about 70 columns. You may wander around the theatres, but the attendants become testy if they see you climbing on the ruins.

From the pre-Roman **Tempio di Iside** (Temple of Isis), rebuilt after the 63 AD earthquake and dedicated to the Egyptian goddess, return to Via dell'Abbondanza, which intersects Via Stabiana. The **Terme Stabiane** is a large complex with many rooms, some featuring original tiling and murals. Several body casts are located here. Farther along Via dell'Abbondanza are the newer excavations. An attempt has been made in this area to keep frescoes (now behind glass) and artefacts exactly where they were found in some of these buildings. Look for the **Casa di Cryptoportico**, the **Casa di Sacerdote Amandus** (House of the Priest Amandus) and the **Casa di Menandro**, all well preserved.

Towards the eastern end of Via dell'Abbondanza, the **Casa di Venere** (House of Venus) stands out because of its remarkable fresco of the goddess standing in her conch shell. The next block is occupied by the so-called **Villa di Giulia Felice**, a rambling affair that includes her private residence, a public bath, various shops and an inn. Behind it lies the **amphitheatre**, the oldest such Roman theatre known and at one time capable of holding an audience of 12,000. The **Great Palaestra** close by, is an athletic field with an impressive portico and the remains of a swimming pool in its centre.

Return along Via dell'Abbondanza and turn right into Via Stabiana (which becomes Via Vesuvio) to see some of Pompeii's grandest houses. The **Casa del Fauno**, one of the best, featured a magnificent mosaic now in Naples' Museo Archeologico. A couple of blocks south-west along Via della Fortuna, the **Casa del Poeta Tragico** still contains some decent mosaics. The nearby **Casa dei Vettii**, on Vicolo di Mercurio, sports some well preserved paintings and statues. Across the road from the Casa del Fauno along Vicolo Storto was the

Lupanaro, a brothel with eye-opening murals. A good place for Pompeii's rakes to make for after the Lupanaro were probably the **forum baths**, a short walk away in Via Terme.

From the baths you could continue to the end of Via della Fortuna and turn right into Via Consolare, which takes you out of the town through the Porta Ercolano at Pompeii's north-western edge. Once past the gate, you pass the Villa di Diomede and come to the **Villa dei Misteri**, one of the most complete structures left standing in Pompeii. The Dionysiac Frieze around the walls of the large dining room, one of the largest paintings to have come to us from the ancient world, depicts the initiation of a bride-to-be into the cult of Dionysus (the Greek god of wine).

The **Museo Vesuviano**, Via San Bartolomeo, south-east of the excavations, contains an interesting array of artefacts.

Opening times of the archaeological zone change monthly, but are roughly daily from 9 am to 3 pm in winter, and to 7 pm in summer. Entrance is L12,000.

Places to Stay

Pompeii is best visited on a day trip from Naples, Sorrento or Salerno as, apart from the excavations, there is little else to do.

Camping Zeus (☎ 861 53 20) is near the Stazione Pompeii-Villa dei Misteri and has sites from L6000 per person and L10,000 for tent space. *Camping Pompei* (☎ 862 28 82), Via Plinio, has bungalows from L50,000 a double. There are some 25 hotels around the site and in the nearby modern town. *Pensione Minerva* (☎ 863 25 86), Via Plinio 23, has simple rooms with a bathroom for L45,000. The *Motel Villa dei Misteri* (861 35 93), near the villa itself, has doubles for L60,000. Heading up the scale, the *Albergo Vittoria* (☎ 536 81 66), is a pleasant old building a short walk from the entrance, and has singles/doubles for L70,000/110,000.

Places to Eat

For meals, you are best off making the effort to get into town. Via Roma, the continuation of Via Plinio, is a busy street with several options. *Á Dó Giardiniello*, at No 89, is a no-nonsense pizzeria with prices starting at L4000. *Sale e Pepe*, No 109, is a moderately-priced place with a buzzy atmosphere. A meal here will cost about L25,000 a head. *Ristorante Tiberius*, Villa dei Misteri 1B, near the villa, has pasta from L6000.

Getting There & Away

Bus SITA (see the Naples Getting There & Away section) operates regular services between Naples and Pompeii, while ATACS (see the Salerno Getting There & Away section) runs from Salerno. CIAT (see the Salerno Getting There & Away section) runs services between Pompeii and Rome. Buses arrive at the Stazione Pompeii-Villa dei Misteri.

Train The quickest route from Naples is with the Circumvesuviana (see the Naples Getting Around section) to Sorrento. Tickets to Pompeii cost L2500. Get off at Pompeii-Villa dei Misteri, near the Porta Marina entrance. Alternatively, take the Circumvesuviana for Poggiomarino, exiting at Pompeii-Santuario. A less frequent service, operated by the state railways from Stazione Centrale in Naples, goes to the new town.

Car & Motorbike Take the A3 from Naples, a trip of about 23 km, otherwise you could spend hours weaving through narrow streets and traffic snarls all the way. Use the Pompeii exit, and follow the signs to Pompei Scavi. Car parks are clearly marked. Hitchhikers should leave Naples from around Piazza Duca dell'Abruzzi and follow signs for the SS268, which goes inland and reaches Pompeii. Alternatively, follow the SS145, which hugs the coast.

SORRENTO

Back in 1884, *Cook's Tourist's Handbook* to southern Italy noted soberly that Sorrento, birthplace of the great 16th-century poet Torquato Tasso, 'is a good stopping place', adding that the surrounding ravines make for charming walks 'especially in the evening, when they have such a weirdness and gloominess, that the people light the lamps in the oratories perched on the rocks, to keep away hobgoblins and foul fiends'.

The foul fiends have long since been replaced by reliable hordes of British and German tourists, who, it appears, concur with Cook's century-old assessment. A pleasant enough town, Sorrento is handy for Capri (15 minutes away) and the Amalfi coast. The road to Pompeii is pretty in parts but has unfortunately been spoiled by expanding residential and industrial sprawl.

To the ancient Greeks, the area around Sorrento was the Temple of the Sirens. Sailors of Antiquity were powerless to resist the beautiful song of these maidens-cum-monsters, who without fail would lure them and their vessels to their doom on reefs. Homer's Odysseus (Ulysses) was determined to hear the other-worldly melodies, and so strapped himself to the mast of his ship as he sailed past the fatal place.

Orientation

Piazza Tasso, bisected by Sorrento's main street, Corso Italia, is the centre of town. The train station is about 250 metres east of the piazza, along Corso Italia, while the Marina Piccola, where ferries and hydrofoils arrive, is a similar distance northwards along Via Luigi de Maio. A walk from the port involves climbing about 200 steps to reach the piazza. Corso Italia becomes the SS145 on the way east to Naples, and changes name to Via del Capo heading west.

Information

Tourist Office The AAST office (☎ 878 22 29), Via Luigi de Maio 35, is inside the Circolo dei Forestieri (Foreigners' Club) office/restaurant complex. Pick up *Surrentum*, for a guide to what's on in the town. The tourist office is open Monday to Saturday from 8.30 am to 2 pm and 4.45 to 7.15 pm in summer; and 3.45 to 6.15 pm in winter.

Money The Deutsche Bank, Piazza Angelina Lauro, has an ATM that accepts credit cards.

American Express is represented by Acampora Travel (☎ 807 23 63), Piazza A Lauro 12.

Post & Telecommunications The post office at Corso Italia 210 is open Monday to Saturday from 8.15 am to 7.20 pm. Central Sorrento's post code is 80067. The Telecom office is in Piazza Tasso, near Via Correale. It's open daily from 8 am to 2 pm and 4 to 11 pm (summer); and 3 to 8 pm (winter). The telephone code for Sorrento is 081.

Emergency For police emergency, ring ☎ 113. The questura (☎ 807 30 90) is at Vico III Rota, near Viale Nizza. The staff speak English. Medical assistance is available at the Ospedale Civile (☎ 533 11 11).

Things to See & Do

The **cathedral** on Corso Italia bears a Romanesque façade, and its rather odd bell tower rests on an archway with four ancient columns. The 18th-century **Palazzo Correale** features some interesting murals and is home to the **Museo Correale**, which contains a small collection of secondary artists of the 17th and 18th-century Neapolitan schools, as well as an odd assortment of Greek and Roman artefacts. The gardens offer wide views of the bay, and steps lead down to the water.

The **Chiesa di San Francesco**, near the Villa Comunale park and the tourist office, boasts a beautiful if modest cloister and is set in lovely gardens – the views up and down the coast are breathtaking.

If you want a **beach**, head for Marina Grande, a 15-minute walk west from Piazza Tasso, which has small strips of sand and is very popular. The jetties nearby with the ubiquitous umbrellas and deck chairs will cost you up to L15,000 a day. Bagni Regina Giovanna, a 20-minute walk west along Via del Capo (or catch the bus for Massalubrense), is more picturesque, set among the ruins of the Roman Villa Pollio Felix. To the east is a small beach at Marinella. It is possible to hire pedal cars at Marina Grande.

CAMPANIA

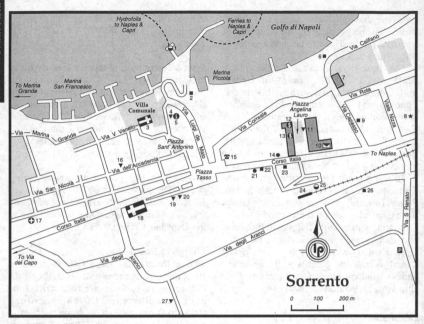

Sorrento

0   100   200 m

PLACES TO STAY

2   Excelsior Grand
     Hotel Vittoria
6   Loreley et Londres
9   Ostello Surriento
22   Albergo City
23   Albergo Nice
26   Albergo Linda

PLACES TO EAT

4   Foreigners' Club

11   Self Service
     Angelina Lauro
16   Giardinello
19   Gatto Nero
20   Osteria la Stalla
27   Caruso

OTHER

1   Hydrofoil Terminal
3   Chiesa di San
     Francesco
5   Tourist Office

7   Palazzo Correale
8   Questura
     (Police Station)
10   Post Office
12   Deutsche Bank (ATM)
13   American Express
14   Sorrento Rentacar
15   Telecom Office
17   Hospital
18   Cathedral
21   Cinema Armida
24   Train Station
25   Bus Station

From May to October, Forza 7 (☎ 878 90 08) at Marina Piccola hires out a variety of boats, starting at L25,000 an hour (or L20,000 if three hours or more) and organises boat cruises. Goldentours International (☎ 878 10 42), Corso Italia 38E, offers package tours to the Amalfi coast, Pompeii, Capri and other destinations.

Festivals

The Sorrento Film Festival, regarded as the most important in the country for Italian-produced cinema, is usually held each September/October. The city's patron, Sant' Antonio, is remembered on 5 February each year with processions and huge markets. The saint is credited with having saved Sorrento during WW II when Salerno and Naples were heavily bombed.

To encourage people to visit the city during the winter months, the town organises dozens of free events from December to March, a period known as Sorrento Inverno. Details are available from the tourist office.

Places to Stay
Most accommodation is either in the town centre or clustered along Via del Capo about three km west of the centre (many with views over the bay). To reach this area, catch the SITA buses for Sant'Agata or Massalubrense from the train station. Book early for summer.

Camping & Hostel The *Campogaio – Santa Fortunata* (☎ 807 35 79), Via del Capo 39A, has camp sites from L8000 to L15,000 and charges L8500 per person. Nearby is the *Nube d'Argento* (☎ 878 13 44), Via del Capo 21, which is slightly dearer. Catch the SITA bus for both camping grounds.

The HI *Ostello Surriento* (☎ 878 17 83), Via Capasso 5 (as you leave the train station, turn right along Corso Italia and then left), opens from March to November and B&B is L15,000. Meals cost L12,000.

Hotels The *Albergo City* (☎ 877 22 10), Corso Italia 221, has singles/doubles from L45,000/62,000. *Albergo Nice* (☎ 878 16 50), Corso Italia 257, has singles/doubles for L45,000/67,000 with a bathroom, and charges an extra L6000 per person for breakfast during summer. *Albergo Linda* (☎ 878 29 16), Via degli Aranci 125, has singles/doubles for L40,000/60,000. *Loreley et Londres* (☎ 807 31 87), Via Califano 12, overlooks the water and has doubles with a bathroom from L60,000 to L70,000. They also have a few singles for L35,000.

Near Marina Grande is *Elios* (☎ 878 18 12), Via del Capo 33, which has singles/doubles with views from L35,000/55,000. *Desirée* (☎ 878 15 63), next door at Via del Capo 31, has singles/doubles from L52,000/94,000 and triples/quads from L120,000/145,000, all with bathrooms and including

breakfast. The hotel has an elevator to its private beach. *La Tonnarella* (☎ 878 11 53), at the same address, has only doubles, starting at L70,000.

For a touch of Sorrento's former glory, you could try the venerable old *Excelsior Grand Hotel Vittoria* (☎ 807 10 44), taking up a huge block overlooking the ferry terminal. Rooms here start at about L250,000.

Places to Eat
One of the cheapest options is *Self Service Angelina Lauro*, Piazza Angelina Lauro, with pasta from L5000. It is one of several snack places on the square. *Giardiniello*, Via dell'Accademia 7, has pizzas from about L6000. *Osteria la Stalla*, Via Pietà 30, has main courses from L10,000. *Gatto Nero*, a cosy little place a couple of doors down will do you a full meal with wine for about L25,000. *Caruso*, Via Sant'Antonio 12, one of the town's best restaurants, is also one of the more expensive, and you could easily go through L45,000 per person.

The *Foreigners' Club* is at Via Luigi de Maio 35, in the same building as the AAST. It offers bay views and cheap food.

Entertainment
Outdoor concerts are held during the summer months in the cloisters of San Francesco. Nightclubs include the Kan Kan, Piazza Sant'Antonino 1, which is about the best of a bad bunch and is not overrun by the tourist hordes.

Getting There & Away
SITA buses leave from outside the train station, and their office is located near the bar in the station. They service the Amalfi coast, Naples and Sant'Agata. It is possible to catch the buses throughout the town, although you must buy tickets from shops bearing the blue SITA sign.

For more details on bus and train, see the Naples Getting There & Away and Getting Around sections.

The city can be reached by the SS145, which meets a spur from the A3 at

Castellammare. See the following section for information on rental cars in Sorrento.

Navigazione Libera del Golfo (☎ 807 18 12) and Alilauro (☎ 807 30 24) run high-speed boats to Capri, while Caremar (☎ 807 30 77) has ferries. The 15-minute run in the fast boats costs L7000 one way or L13,000 return. Alilauro has up to six boats a day to Naples (L12,000 one way), and Navigazione Libera del Golfo has one.

Getting Around

Sorrento Rentacar (☎ 878 13 86), Corso Italia 210, rents scooters from L45,000 for 24 hours or L260,000 for a week. Their cheapest car, a Fiat Uno, will set you back L116,000 a day plus petrol. They are one of several rental companies, and it is worth shopping around. For a taxi, call ☎ 878 22 04.

THE AMALFI COAST (COSTIERA AMALFITANA)

The 50-km stretch of coastline from Sorrento to Salerno is one of the most beautiful in Europe. A narrow asphalt ribbon bends and winds along cliffs that drop into crystal-clear blue waters, connecting the beautiful towns of Positano, Amalfi and the hillside village of Ravello. The coast is jam-packed with wealthy tourists in summer, prices are inflated and finding a room is impossible. The moral is that you are much better off coming during spring and autumn. The coast all but shuts down over winter. The area is famous for its ceramics.

Getting There & Away

Bus SITA operates a service along the Amalfi coast from the Sorrento train station to Salerno and vice versa, with buses leaving every 50 minutes. Tickets must be bought in advance from the bar at the Sorrento train station or the SITA bus station in Salerno, or else in bars near the bus stations in the towns along the coast (Piazza Flavio Gioia in Amalfi and Via G Marconi in Positano). Buses also leave from Rome for the Amalfi coast, terminating at Salerno (see the Rome Getting There & Away section for details).

Train Take the Circumvesuviana from Naples to Sorrento or the train to Salerno, and then the SITA bus along the coast.

Car & Motorbike The road is breathtakingly beautiful, if a little hairy at times as buses from each direction crawl past each other on narrow sections. In summer, it becomes a 50-km traffic jam and can take hours to navigate as the hordes flock to the coast. From Naples, take the A3 and exit near Castellammare, or follow the signs to Sorrento. The coast road, the SS145, passes through Sorrento and becomes the SS163 Amalfitana. A short cut over the hills beyond Meta can save about 30 minutes. Follow the signs to Vietri sul Mare or Amalfi if you approach from Salerno. Hitching is generally quite easy.

Boat Navigazione Libera Del Golfo (☎ 081-552 72 09), based in Naples, operates hydrofoils between Amalfi, Positano and Capri, and Alilauro (☎ 081-761 10 04) serves the coast from both Salerno and Naples. Amalfi Navigazione (☎ 089-87 31 90), Via Nazionale 17, Amalfi, operates services between Amalfi and Positano, Capri and Salerno, as does Avenire (☎ 089-87 76 19), also in Amalfi. Most companies operate in summer only.

Positano

Exuding a rather Moorish flavour, Positano is the most picturesque of the coast towns, and some might think the most precious, with its cute houses and expensive shops.

Positano is virtually divided in two by the cliff bearing the Torre Trasita tower. West is the smaller and more pleasant Spiaggia del Fornillo beach area and the less expensive side of town, and east is the Spiaggia Grande, which gives way to the village centre.

Navigating is easy, if steep. Via G Marconi, part of the Amalfitana coast road, runs north around and above the town, which itself cascades inside this fold in the mountain down to the water. The one-way Viale Pasitea winds down off Via G Marconi from the west to the centre, and changes name to Via Cristoforo Colombo as it climbs back up to the main road on the east side.

Information The small APT office (☎ 089-87 50 67), Via del Saraceno 4, near Spiaggia Grande, caters mainly to Italians and Germans, but their map is printed in English too. It is open daily from 8 am to 2 pm all year.

For changing money, the Ufficio Cambio is in Piazza dei Mulini, although the Deutsche Bank, Via C Colombo 75, may offer better rates and has an ATM.

The post office is on Via G Marconi where it meets Viale Pasitea. It's open Monday to Saturday from 8.20 am to 2 pm.

The post code is 84017.

You'll find telephones scattered about the town centre. Positano's telephone code is 089.

In a police emergency, call ☎ 113. The carabinieri (☎ 87 50 11) are on Via G Marconi where it intersects with Viale Pasitea.

For medical emergencies at night, on Sundays or holidays, ring the Guardia Medica on ☎ 81 14 44. Their headquarters are on Via G Marconi, near Via Cristoforo Colombo.

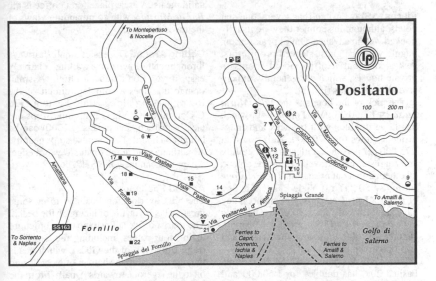

Positano

PLACES TO STAY					
15	Villa Nettuno	10	Chez Black	3	Bus Station to Montepertuso
17	Villa delle Palme	12	O'Capurale	4	Post Office
18	Pensione Italia	14	Bar de Martino	5	SITA Bus Station
19	Villa Maria Luisa	16	Il Saraceno d'Oro	6	Carabinieri (Police Station)
22	Hotel Pupetto	20	Lo Guarracino	8	Guardia Medica
				9	SITA Bus Station
PLACES TO EAT		OTHER		11	Chiesa di Santa Maria Assunta
7	Trattoria Giardino degli Aranci	1	Agip Petrol Station	13	Tourist Office
		2	Deutsche Bank	21	Torre Trasita

CAMPANIA

Things to See & Do Positano's main sight is the **Chiesa di Santa Maria Assunta**, just back from Spiagga Grande. Inside you'll find a 13th-century Byzantine *Black Madonna*. The church is closed in the afternoons.

Boating isn't cheap. Head for the 'To Rent' signs on the Spiaggia Grande, and expect to pay from L15,000 an hour for a rowing boat or L30,000 an hour for a small motor boat, both cheaper by the half or full day.

Hiring a chair and umbrella on the fenced-off beaches can cost L10,000, but the crowded public areas are free.

Places to Stay Positano has several one-star hotels, although in summer they are usually booked well in advance. Out of peak season, haggle with the guest-starved proprietors. Ask at the tourist office about rooms in private houses, which are generally expensive, or apartments for rent.

The pick of the hotels is the *Villa Maria Luisa* (☎ 87 50 23), Via Fornillo 40, which has large doubles with terraces and magnificent views for L70,000. Half board at L75,000 per person is obligatory in late July and August. Single travellers may be able to talk them down out of season. The *Pensione Italia* (87 50 24), off Viale Pasitea, is one of about 20 affittacamere in Positano. They have doubles only for L70,000. The *Villa delle Palme* (☎ 87 51 62), around the corner, charges L65,000 a double in low season and L75,000 in the peak period.

The *Villa Nettuno* (☎ 87 54 01), Viale Pasitea 208, has doubles for L60,000 and L80,000 in the high season and most rooms have balconies. It closes out of season. *Hotel Pupetto* (☎ 87 50 87), overlooking the beach at Fornillo, has doubles for L70,000 in the low season and L104,000 in the high season, and all rooms have views.

Places to Eat Most restaurants are overpriced for the food they serve, and you should always check the cover and service charges before you sit down. Many restaurants close over winter, making a brief

reappearance for Christmas and New Year. *Il Saraceno d'Oro*, Viale Pasitea 254, has pizzas from L5000, and is close to most of the cheaper hotels. *Lo Guarracino*, Via Positanesi d'America, on the waterfront path connecting the two beaches, has pasta from about L7000.

Near the main beach, *O'Capurale*, Via Regina Giovanna, serves local dishes, with pasta from L8000. Overlooking the beach is *Chez Black*, Spiaggia Grande, a popular spot specialising in seafood. A full meal could cost up to L45,000. *Trattoria Giardino degli Aranci*, Via dei Mulini 22, although still not cheap, is a little more modest and serves solid meals. A great place for a coffee is the *Bar de Martino*, with commanding views of the town and sea.

Getting Around Dozens of small stairways throughout the town make walking relatively easy, if you don't mind a climb. A small orange bus does a complete circuit of the town, passing along Viale Pasitea, Via C Colombo and Via G Marconi. Stops are clearly marked, and tickets (L1000) can be bought on board. The bus also stops near the Amalfitana road at the town's western edge, where you can meet the SITA bus.

Around Positano
The hills overlooking Positano offer some great walks if you tire of lazing on the beach. The tourist office at Positano has a brochure listing four routes, including the **Sentiero degli Dei** (Trail of the Gods), which heads into the hills from the hamlet of Nocelle and on to the Agerola, towards Amalfi. From the small village of Montepertuso, you can reach Santa Maria al Castello and Monte Sant' Angelo e Tre Pizzi (1444 metres). The latter is quite a hike.

Visit Nocelle, a tiny and still relatively isolated village above Positano, accessible by a short walking track from the end of the road from Positano. Have lunch at *Trattoria Santa Croce* (☎ 089-87 53 19), which has a terrace with panoramic views. It is open for lunch and dinner in summer, but at other times of the year it is best to phone and check in advance. Nocelle is accessible by local bus from Positano, via Montepertuso; buses run roughly every half-hour in summer from 7.50 am to midnight.

Praiano is not as scenic as Amalfi, but has more budget options, including the only camping ground on the Amalfi coast. The camping ground, *La Tranquillità* (☎ 87 40 84), is along the coastal road on the Amalfi side of Praiano and has a pensione and bungalows, as well as a small camping ground, a restaurant and a swimming pool. A camping site for two people costs L30,000, and a double room or bungalow costs L80,000. In August half board is compulsory at L65,000 per person. The SITA bus stops outside the pensione.

Amalfi

At its peak in the 11th century, Amalfi was a supreme naval power, a bitter enemy of the northern maritime republics, Pisa and Genoa, and had a population of 70,000. Its navigation tables, the *Tavole Amalfitane*, formed the world's first maritime code and governed all shipping in the Mediterranean for centuries.

Amalfi was founded in the 9th century and soon came under the rule of a doge. Fruit of its connections with the Orient, the city claims to have introduced to Italy such modern wonders as paper, coffee and carpets. The small resort still bears many reminders of its seafaring and trading heyday and is now one of Italy's most popular seaside spots.

Orientation & Information Most hotels and restaurants are located around Piazza Duomo, or along Via Genova and its continuation, Via Capuano, which snakes north from the duomo.

The AST office (☎ 87 11 07), at Corso Roma 19 on the waterfront, opens Monday to Friday from 8 am to 2 pm (it closes an hour earlier on Saturdays). In summer it tends to open from about 4.30 to 7 pm too.

The post office is at Corso Roma 29. It's open Monday to Friday from 8.15 am to 6.30 pm, and Saturday to 12.15 pm. Amalfi's post

code is 84011 and the telephone code is 089. The Deutsche Bank on the Marina Grande has an ATM.

Emergency If you need the police ring ☎ 113, or go to the questura (☎ 87 10 22) at Via Casamare 19. For medical treatment, go to the Municipio Pronto Soccorso (☎ 87 27 85), Piazza Municipio, near the tourist office.

Things to See The **Duomo Sant'Andrea**, an imposing sight at the top of a sweeping flight of stairs, dates from early in the 10th century, although the façade has been rebuilt twice. Although a hybrid, it is the Arab-Norman style of Sicily that predominates, particularly in the two-tone masonry and the bell tower. The interior is mainly Baroque and the altar features statues believed to be by Gianlorenzo Bernini and Naccherini, along with 12th and 13th-century mosaics.

The **Chiostro del Paradiso** next door was built in the 13th century in Arabic style to house the tombs of noted citizens. It opens from 9 am to 8 pm, with a break of about two hours from 1 pm. Entrance is L1000.

The **Museo Civico**, behind Corso Roma in the town hall building, contains the *Tavole Amalfitane* and other historical documents. It opens Monday to Friday from 8 am to 2 pm. The restored **Arsenale** of the former republic, the only ship building depot of its kind in Italy, is to the left of Porta della Marina.

Two paper mills still operate in Amalfi – one at Via Cartoleria 2, and another farther away from Piazza Duomo, also on Via Cartoleria, called the Cartier d'Amatruda, which still makes paper in the traditional way. The latter can be visited. The city's **paper museum** in Valle dei Mulini is situated in a 13th-century paper mill (the oldest in Amalfi), and opens daily except Monday and Friday from 9 am to 1 pm.

The many ceramics shops, mostly clustered around Piazza Duomo, testify to Amalfi's traditional promotion of this art. Visit the Bottega d'Arte in Piazza Duomo and see items being made and glazed.

About six km along the coast towards Positano is the **Grotta dello Smeraldo**, so-called for the emerald colour of its sandy bottom. Just a shadow of the Blue Grotto at Capri, it can be reached by SITA bus from either direction along the Amalfi coast, and entrance is L5000. On 24 December and 6 January, skin divers make their traditional pilgrimage to the ceramic crib in the grotto.

The Regatta of the Four Ancient Maritime Republics, rotating between Amalfi, Venice, Pisa and Genoa, is held on the first Sunday in June. Amalfi last hosted it in 1993 and will next host it in 1997.

Activities In the hills above Amalfi, on the way to Ravello, are dozens of small paths and stairways connecting the towns with mountainside villages. The CAI in Salerno publishes a map with eight long walks in the area stretching from Salerno to Sorrento. A book titled *Walks from Amalfi – The Guide to a Web of Ancient Italian Pathways*

(L10,000) is available from most bookshops in the town.

Boats can be hired in summer at the Marina Grande area, the Spiaggia Santa Croce and the Grotta dello Smeraldo.

Places to Stay The HI *Ostello Beata Solitudo* (☎ 802 50 48), Piazza G Avitabile, in Agerola (off the road to Positano) is open all year. A bed costs L13,000. *A'Scalinatella* (☎ 87 14 92), on Piazza Umberto I in Atrani, a 15-minute walk south of Amalfi, also has hostel-style accommodation for L15,000 per person (L20,000 in August).

In Amalfi itself, the *Albergo Proto* (☎ 87 10 03), Salita dei Curiali 4, is about as cheap as you'll find with singles/doubles starting at L25,000/38,000 in high season. You'll be expected to take breakfast in high season at L8000. Room rates drop marginally out of season. *Hotel Lidomare* (☎ 87 13 32), in Piazza Piccolomini off Piazza Duomo, has spacious and homey singles/doubles from L45,000/60,000, including breakfast. Rates can rise to L60,000/100,000 in high season. *Hotel Amalfi* (☎ 87 24 40), Via dei Pastai 3, has singles/doubles for about L50,000/80,000, cheaper in the low season. Full board is obligatory in summer. The *Albergo Sant' Andrea* (☎ 87 10 23), off Piazza Duomo, has singles/doubles for L45,000/65,000, and half board is compulsory in summer. *Il Nido* (☎ 87 11 45), about two km west of the centre, has attractive doubles for L90,000, but no singles. Compulsory half board in high season costs a steep L80,000 per person.

Places to Eat The *Green Bar*, Via Capuana 46, is a cheap takeaway place where you can pick up a decent slice of pizza for L2000. *Pizzeria da Maria*, Via Lorenzo d'Amalfi, has pizzas from L5000. *Trattoria San Giuseppe*, Salita Ruggiero II 4, off Via Amalfi has excellent pasta and decent second courses for around L25,000 all up. *Trattoria da Baracca*, overlooking Piazza dei Dogi, is almost as good, and prices are similar. For a sitdown pizza, you could do worse than *Ristorante al Teatro*, Via Marini 19, where you're looking at about L8000. *La*

To
Valle dei Mulini
& Paper Mills

Amalfi

0   250   500 m

To Positano,
Sorrento &
Albergo Il
Nido

Corso Roma

Marina Grande

To
Ravello &
Salerno

Amendola

*Golfo
di
Salerno*

Ferries to Salerno,
Positano & Capri

1 Green Bar	11 Albergo Sant'Andrea
2 Ristorante al Teatro	12 Deutsche Bank
3 Trattoria San Giuseppe	13 Tourist Office
4 Albergo Proto	14 Museo Civico
5 Pizzeria da Maria	15 Piazza Municipio
6 Duomo Sant'Andrea	16 Post Office
7 Piazza Duomo	17 Piazza Flavio Gioia
8 Ristorante da Baracca	18 Bus Station
9 La Caravella	19 Ferry Terminal
10 Hotel Lidomare	

Positano, Amalfi Coast, Campania

ROB FLYNN

ROB FLYNN

LAUREN SUNSTEIN

Top Left: Detail of Dionysiac Frieze, Villa dei Misteri, Pompeii, Campania
Top Right: Detail of Dionysiac Frieze, Pompeii, Campania
Bottom: Greek ruins at Paestum, Campania

Caravella, Via Matteo Camera 12, is one of Amalfi's finest restaurants, but L50,000 per person is about the minimum you'll pay.

Ravello

Ravello sits like a natural balcony overlooking the Golfo di Salerno, from where you can peer down on Amalfi and the nearby towns of Minori and Maiori. The seven-km drive from Amalfi along the Valle del Dragone passes through the soaring mountains and deep ravines that characterise the area – watch the hairpin turns. You can continue inland across the mountains and down to Nocera to link up with the A3 to Naples and Salerno. Ravello perhaps blows its trumpet a little too loudly and any claim that the town lives from anything but tourism rings rather hollow.

Ravello's tourist office (☎ 85 79 77) in Piazza Vescovado is open Monday to Saturday from 8 am to 8 pm , and has limited information. The town's telephone code is 089.

Things to See & Do The **duomo** in Piazza Vescovado dates from the 11th century and features an impressive marble pulpit with six lions carved at its base. There is a free museum in the crypt containing religious artefacts. Overlooking the piazza is the **Villa Rufolo**. Its last resident was the German composer Wagner, who wrote the third act of *Parsifal* there. The villa was built in the 13th century for the wealthy Rufolos and housed several popes, as well as Charles I of Anjou. From the terraces there is a magnificent view over the gulf. The villa's gardens are the setting for the Festivale Musicale di Ravello each July, when international orchestras and guests play a selection that always features Wagner. Tickets start at L15,000, and the festival is the centrepiece of a summer series of musical events. The city hosts a smaller Wagner festival in early July, and the patron saint, San Pantaleon, is celebrated with fireworks in late July.

Away from the Piazza Vescovado is the **Villa Cimbrone**, built this century and set in beautiful gardens.

You can visit the city's vineyards: the Casa Vinicola Caruso, Via della Marra; Vini Episopio, at the Hotel Palumbo, Via Toro; and Vini Sammarco, Via Nazionale. Or you can arrange to visit places where Limoncello is produced – ask at the tourist office.

Places to Stay & Eat Accommodation and food are too expensive to make Ravello an overnight option for most budget travellers. The small *Toro* (☎ 85 72 11), Viale Wagner 3, has singles/doubles from L48,000/80,000. *Parsifal* (☎ 85 71 44), Via d'Anna 5, in a former convent, has singles/doubles for L77,000/ 134,000 in high season.

The *Pizzeria la Colonna*, Via Roma 20, serves regional cuisine, with pasta from L8000. *Cumpà Cosimo*, Via Roma 42-44, is a little more expensive and a meal will cost L30,000.

Getting There & Away To reach the town by car, take the Amalfitana for Salerno and turn off about two km after Amalfi. SITA operates about 15 buses in each direction daily from Piazza Flavio Gioia in Amalfi, departing from 6 am to about 9 pm. Cars are not permitted in the town centre, but there is adequate parking in supervised car parks.

From Amalfi to Salerno

If you're coming from the north, life on the Amalfi coast doesn't end at the town of Amalfi. The 20 km drive on to Salerno, although marginally less exciting than the 16 km stretch to Positano and beyond, is dotted with a series of little towns that could make useful alternative bases.

Atrani, a bare km away round a point, is a pretty extension of Amalfi with a little beach. Farther on are the towns of **Minori** and **Maiori**. Although lacking much of the charm of its better-known partners up the road, both have plenty of hotels and Maiori has a fairly decent-sized beach. Perhaps most attractive on this run is the fishing village of **Cetara**. Shortly before you hit Salerno (see the following Salerno section), you pass through **Vietri sul Mare**, set on a rise commanding views over Salerno. If all else fails, you could

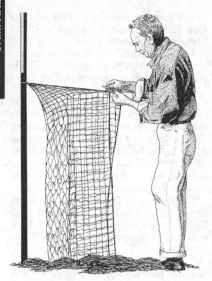

Fishing is still a traditional way of life in the coastal towns south of Naples.

even use this as a local base without really feeling cheated. It is also a good place to buy the local ceramics. The town has plenty of workshops and showrooms and, if you shop around, you'll find some good buys.

SALERNO

After the picturesque little towns of the Amalfi, the urban sweep of Salerno and its port along the Bay of Salerno (Baia di Salerno) might come as a shock. One of southern Italy's many victims of earth tremors and even landslides, Salerno was left in tatters by heavy fighting that followed landings by the American 5th Army just to the south of the city in 1943. With the exception of a mildly charming tumbledown medieval quarter, the city today is largely unexciting. It is, however, an important transport junction and a possible base for exploring the Amalfi coast to the north and Paestum and the Cilento coast to the south.

Originally an Etruscan and later a Roman colony, Salerno flourished with the arrival of the Normans in the 11th century. Robert Guiscard made it the capital of his dukedom in 1076 and under his patronage the Scuola Medica Salernitana gained fame as one of medieval Europe's greatest medical institutes.

Orientation

The train station is in Piazza Vittorio Veneto, at the eastern end of town. You'll find most intercity buses and a number of hotels in this area too. Salerno's main shopping strip, the car-free Corso Vittorio Emanuele, leads off to the north-west to the medieval part of town. Running parallel and closer to the sea is Corso Garibaldi, which becomes Via Roma as it heads north-west out of the city for the Amalfi coast. The tree-lined Lungomare Trieste on the unattractive waterfront changes name to Lungomare Marconi at the massive Piazza della Concordia on its way south-east out of town towards Paestum.

Information

Tourist Office The EPT office (☎ 089-23 14 32), near the train station in Piazza Vittorio Veneto, distributes the useful weekly *Memo*, with a host of information. There is another tourist office (☎ 089-22 47 44) at the other end of town, at Via Roma 258. Both are open daily except Sunday from 9 am to 1.30 pm and 2.30 to 8 pm.

Money The Banca Nazionale del Lavoro, at Corso Garibaldi 208 has an ATM, as do branches of Monte dei Paschi di Siena at Via Roma 118 and in Corso Vittorio Emanuele.

Post & Telecommunications The main post office is at Corso Garibaldi 203 and is open Monday to Saturday from 8.15 am to 7.15 pm. The post code for central Salerno is 84100.

The Telecom office is at Corso Garibaldi 31 and is open Monday to Friday from 9.30 am to 1 pm and 2 to 5.30 pm. The telephone code for Salerno is 089.

Emergency In an emergency, call the police on ☎ 113. The questura (☎ 61 31 11) is on Piazza Amendola. The Ospedale Ruggi d'Aragona is at Via San Leonardo. For medical emergencies, ring ☎ 24 12 33 or 67 11 11; ring ☎ 23 33 30 for an ambulance.

Things to See

You will probably enter the old town from

the east along Via dei Mercanti, its main street (conveniently, if tackily marked, by a McDonald's), off which you can duck down a brief series of narrow lanes and blind alleys.

Duomo The city's cathedral, in Piazza Alfano north of Via dei Mercanti, is dedicated to St Matthew the Evangelist, whose

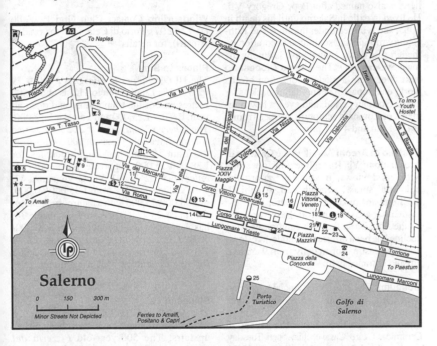

Salerno

0   150   300 m

Minor Streets Not Depicted

To Naples

To Imo Youth Hostel

To Amalfi

To Paestum

Ferries to Amalfi, Positano & Capri

Porto Turistico

Golfo di Salerno

PLACES TO STAY

16 Albergo Cinzia
18 Albergo Santa Rosa
22 Albergo Salerno
23 Plaza Hotel

PLACES TO EAT

2   Hostaria Il Brigante
3   Ristorante al Duomo
7   U Fleku

8   Pomodori & Cornetti
9   Vicolo delle Neve
21 Trattoria da Italia

OTHER

1   Castello di Arechi
4   Duomo
5   Tourist Office
6   Questura (Police Station)
10 Museo Provinciale
11 Piazza Matteotti

12 Monte dei Paschi di Siena (ATM)
13 Banca Nazionale del Lavoro (ATM)
14 Post Office
15 Monte dei Paschi di Siena (ATM)
17 Train Station
19 EPT Tourist Office
20 SITA Bus Station
24 Telecom Office
25 Ferry Terminal

remains were brought to the city in 954 and later buried in the crypt. Flanked by a Romanesque bell tower and an atrium featuring 28 Roman columns, the church was erected by the Normans under Robert Guiscard in the 11th century and remodelled in the 18th century. It sustained severe damage in the 1980 earthquake. The Cappella delle Crociate (Chapel of the Crusades), so called because crusaders' weapons were blessed here, is also named after Pope Gregory VII. He lived in exile in Salerno until his death in 1085, and is buried under the altar. The 12th-century mosaic and sculptural decoration on the left side of the central nave is among the most eye-catching. The **Museo Diocesano** next door, with a modest collection of artworks encompassing items dating back as far as the Norman period, and even a few fragments of Lombard sculpture, is open from 9 am to 1 pm and 4 to 7 pm.

Castello di Arechi A walk to the Castello di Arechi along Via Risorgimento is rewarded with good views, if you can ignore the industrial sprawl beneath you. Arechi II, the Lombard duke of Benevento, built the castle over a Byzantine fort. Last renovated by the Spanish in the 16th century, its slow decline has been arrested by modern restoration. The castle is open daily from 9 am to 2 pm and entrance is free.

Museums The Museo Provinciale, Via San Benedetto 28, contains archaeological finds from the region and opens from 9 am to 1 pm. Also worth a visit is the Museo di Ceramica, Largo Casavecchia, open Tuesday, Thursday and Saturday from 9 am to 12.30 pm.

Activities
Check with the tourist office about the myriad activities on offer in and around Salerno. The following are just a few of them.

Walking CAI (☎ 25 27 88), Via Porta di Mare 26, and *Memo*, the city's free what's-on magazine, publish details of walking excursions around Salerno, along the Amalfi coast and in the nearby Picentini mountain range. The CAI also arranges mountain-climbing expeditions.

The Centro Documentazione Trekking (☎ 86 34 14), Via G de Caro 47, can provide information and assistance with treks.

Free Climbing Contact Fly Surf (☎ 33 93 16), Via R Cocchia 181-185, for details.

Windsurfing Contact Club Gigi Pezzullo (☎ 72 32 97), Porto di Cetara (on the road to Amalfi), for details.

Places to Stay
The HI *Ostello per la Gioventù Irno* (☎ 79 02 51), Via Luigi Guercio 112, is about 500 metres east of the train station and open all year. B&B is L15,000 and a meal is L12,000. The *Albergo Santa Rosa* (☎ 22 53 46), Corso Vittorio Emanuele 14, about 200 metres from the train station, has singles/doubles for L38,000/55,000. Opposite is the *Albergo Salerno* (☎ 22 42 11), Via G Vicinanza 42, with singles/doubles from L35,000/60,000, or L55,000/75,000 with a bathroom. *Albergo Cinzia* (☎ 23 27 73), Corso V Emanuele 74, has very basic singles/doubles for L30,000/50,000. Pricier is the *Plaza Hotel* (☎ 22 44 77), Piazza Ferrovia 42, at L75,000/115,000 for singles/doubles with a bathroom, telephone and TV.

Places to Eat
The *Trattoria da Italia*, Via Vicinanza, is a takeaway restaurant but serves cheap dishes upstairs. The 500-year-old *Pizzeria del Vicolo delle Neve*, Vicolo delle Neve 24, off Via Mercanti, serves traditional fare, and a meal could cost about L20,000. For a soothing ale afterwards, you could try the *U Fleku* beerhouse at No 5.

The *Ristorante al Duomo* has a terrace overlooking Piazza al Duomo, but you're looking at about L30,000 for two courses and wine. A little more modest is the nearby *Hostaria il Brigante*, about 20 paces away at Via Fratelli Minguiti 2. For a snack, there's *Pomodori & Cornetti*, Via Mercanti 119.

Getting There & Away
Bus The SITA bus station (☎ 22 66 04) is at Corso Garibaldi 117. Buses for the Amalfi coast depart from Piazza della Concordia, usually every hour or so, while buses for Naples depart from outside the SITA bus station every 15 minutes (L4600). ATACS (☎ 24 10 43) operates buses No 4 and 41 to Pompeii from outside the train station, and also services to Paestum (catch the bus for Sapri) and other towns along the southern coast from Piazza della Concordia. BAT runs an express service to Rome's Fiumicino airport from Monday to Friday at 5.45 am (arriving around 10.30 am; pay on the bus). It departs from Piazza della Concordia. There is also a bus service to Rome which goes via the Amalfi coast, Sorrento and Pompeii (see the Rome Getting There & Away section for details).

Train Salerno is a major stop between Rome/Naples and Calabria and is served by all types of trains. It also has good services to the Adriatic coast and inland.

Car & Motorbike Salerno is on the A3 between Naples and Calabria, which at the time of writing was toll free from Salerno south. From Rome, you can bypass Naples by taking the A30.

Boat In summer only, ferries and hydrofoils run to Amalfi (L5000), Positano, Sorrento, Ischia and Capri. The trip to Agropoli costs about L6000, and other towns on the Cilento coast can also be reached this way. Contact the tourist office for latest details.

Helicopter Elicampania (☎ 738 72 57) flies helicopters to the islands in the Bay of Naples, starting at L190,000 a person.

Getting Around
Most hotels are around the train station, and Corso Vittorio Emanuele, the main drag, is a mall, so walking is the most sensible option. ATACS buses run from the train station through the town centre.

PAESTUM
The evocative image of three Greek temples standing in fields of poppies is not easily forgotten and makes the trek to this archaeological site well worth the effort. The temples are among the world's best preserved monuments of the ancient Greek world, remnants of Magna Graecia, as the Greeks called their colonies in southern Italy and Sicily. The small town is close to some of Italy's better beaches and just south of where US forces landed in 1943. The modern town of Capaccio, about three km from the site, is supposed to be renamed Paestum some time this decade.

Paestum, or Poseidonia as the city was originally known, was founded in the 6th century BC by Greek settlers from Sybaris, on the Golfo di Taranto farther south. Conquered by the Lucanians from Basilicata in the 4th century BC, it came under Roman control in 273 BC and became an important trading port. The town was gradually abandoned after the fall of the Roman Empire, periodic outbreaks of malaria and savage raids by the Saracens in 871. The temples were rediscovered in the late 18th century by road builders who subsequently ploughed right through the ruins. The road did little to alter the state of the surrounding area, which remained full of malarial swamps and teeming with snakes and scorpions until well into the 20th century.

This state of affairs belongs to the past and the site is now easily traversed by foot. All public transport is within walking distance. The tourist office (☎ 0828-81 10 16), Via Aquilia, opposite the main site, has maps.

The Ruins
The first temple you come across entering the site from the northern end, near the tourist office, is the **Temple of Ceres** (Tempio de Cerere), which dates from the 6th century BC. It is the smallest of the three and was used as a Christian church for a time. The basic outline of the **forum** is evident as you head south. Among the buildings, parts of which remain, are the Italic temple, the Greek theatre, the Bouleuterion, where the

CAMPANIA

senate met, and farther south, the amphi-theatre, through which the road was built.

The **Temple of Neptune** (Tempio di Nettuno), dating from about 450 BC, is the most impressive of the remains, the largest and best preserved with only parts of the inside walls and roof missing. From a dis-tance, its structure gives the impression that the columns are leaning outward. Virtually next door, the so-called **basilica** is the oldest surviving monument in Paestum, dating from the middle of the 6th century BC. With nine columns across and 18 along the sides, it is a majestic building. In the front of the build-ing you can make out remains of a sacrificial altar.

The city was ringed by 4.7 km of walls, built and rebuilt by Lucanians and Romans. The most intact section is west of the ruins, but the area to the east makes for a pleasant walk through the local farmland.

The **Museo di Paestum**, opposite the site, houses a collection of metopes, including 33 of the original 36 from the **Temple of Argive Hera** (Tempio di Argive Hera), nine km north of Paestum, making up one of the best collections of ancient architecture in the world. It also features wall paintings from tombs on the site. Entrance to both the museum (closed Mondays) and the ruins is L8000. Both open daily, except Monday, at 9 am and close about an hour before sunset (this means 3 pm in winter).

Places to Stay & Eat

Paestum is a short trip from Salerno, which has a better range of accommodation. There are more than 20 camping grounds in the area, including *Intercamping Apollo* (☎ 0828-81 11 78), Via Principe di Piemonte 2, close to the ruins and near the beach. *Albergo Villa Rita* (☎ 0828-81 10 81), Via Principe di Piemonte 39, is pleas-antly located back from the main road but close to the ruins. Smart singles/doubles cost L54,000/78,000 including breakfast. There are a few cafés and snack bars near the temples, or you could eat at the *Ristorante Museo* or *Ristorante delle Rose* on Via

Metope relief from the Temple of Argive Hera.

Magna Grecia, which runs between the temples and the museum.

Getting There & Away

Bus ATACS runs buses from Salerno to Paestum (catch the Sapri bus), usually departing every 35 minutes from 8.15 am to 8.15 pm. There is no marked bus stop near the ruins – just ask the driver to drop you off. When you want to leave, simply hail the bus driver.

Train Paestum is on the train line from Naples through Salerno to Reggio di Cala-bria. Many trains stop at the Stazione di Capaccio, nearer the new town (about three km from the site), and less frequently at the Stazione di Paestum, a short walk from the temples.

Car & Motorbike Take the A3 from Salerno and exit for the SS18 at Battipaglia, or follow the coast road out of Salerno. Paestum is 36 km from Salerno.

AROUND PAESTUM
The World Wide Fund for Nature has a wildlife sanctuary about 12 km inland from Paestum on the Sele river, one of the few protected natural environments in the south of Italy. It consists mainly of wetlands and is home to a wide variety of birds. The area is known as the **Woods of Diana**, after the Roman goddess of the hunt. Virgil wrote about the area, describing the roses of Paestum and the woodlands. The sanctuary (☎ 0828-97 46 84) is open from September to April, and signs direct you there from the SS18.

Forty km east of Paestum, the **Grotte di Castelcivita** were discovered late last century, and are heavily promoted as a tourist destination. You can wander for about 1700 metres through the labyrinth of chambers, shafts, stalagmites and stalactites. The **Grande Cascata** (Great Waterfall) is magnificent. The caves can be reached via the SS166, which leaves the SS18 north of Paestum, and are open all year. For information, call ☎ 0828-77 23 97.

THE CILENTO COAST (COSTIERA CILENTANA)
South of the Golfo di Salerno, the coastal plains begin to give way to more rugged territory, a foretaste of what lies farther on in the stark hills and mountains of Basilicata and the more heavily wooded peaks of Calabria. This southernmost tract of the Campania littoral is known as the Costiera Cilentina and, with some exceptions, lends itself little to summer seaside frolics, although skin-divers will perhaps appreciate some of the rocky points. Despite a desultory spattering of camp sites and the like, the beaches are not as popular as those farther north or south, into Basilicata and Calabria. ATACS buses leave Salerno for Sapri, on the regional boundary marking off Campania from Basilicata, and trains south from Salerno also stop at most towns. By car, take the SS18 which connects Agropoli with Velia

via the inland route, or the SS267, which hugs the coast.

Agropoli
The modern sprawl of this coastal town south of Paestum does not augur well at first sight, but the small medieval core of Agropoli, perched on a high promontory overlooking the sea and topped by a crumbling old castle, makes a rewarding stop. If you can find a place to stay, it could even serve as a base for travel to the temples at Paestum and also to the clean, sandy beaches to the north.

Should you want to join cycling excursions in the area around Agropoli, contact Amici della Bicicletta, Via Salerno 14 (☎ 0974-82 34 90).

The *Camping Villaggio Arco delle Rose* (☎ 0974-83 82 27), Via Isca Solofrone, is a tacky tourist resort village but has camping sites. The *Hotel Carola* (☎ 0974-82 30 05), Via Pisacane 1, near the harbour, has singles/doubles for L65,000/85,000, but closes from November to March.

The *Ristorante U Sghizu*, Piazza Umberto I, the main square in the old town, bakes a pizza for L4500 or more. A full meal will cost around L20,000.

Velia
The ruins of the Greek settlement of Elea, founded in the mid-6th century BC and later a popular spot for wealthy Romans, are worth a visit if you have the time. Its decline matches that of Paestum, but as the town was never an important trading centre, it was considerably smaller than its northern rival and its ruins are in a far worse state.

The closest town with accommodation is Ascea, which has several camping grounds and hotels. *Camping Alba* (0974-97 23 31) is near Marina di Ascea, close to the sea and a few km downhill from the main town. The *Albergo Elea* (☎ 0974-97 15 77) has singles/doubles for L40,000/60,000 and is near the water.

The train station for Ascea is at Ascea Marina. To get to the ruins, you will need to wait for a local bus to Castellamare di Velia or hitchhike.

South to Sapri

If you've made it as far as Ascea, consider pursuing the coast road south into Basilicata (see the Maratea section in the Apulia, Basilicata & Calabria chapter). From Ascea to Sapri, a dowdy seaside town a few km short of Basilicata, the road climbs, dips and curves its way through country that, while not Italy's prettiest, is rarely dull. **Pisciotta**, 12 km south of Ascea, is an attractive medieval village and another 25 km or so farther on are some striking white sandy **beaches** south of Palinuro (in and around which you can find camp sites and the odd hotel should you want to hang around). A little farther on you reach Marina di Camerota, from where the road turns steeply inland to pass through San Giovanni a Piro, with a small medieval centre. From there it's another 25 km to Sapri. If you get this far you should really make the effort to continue the short distance into Basilicata.

Apulia, Basilicata & Calabria

A good number of visitors to Italy, drawn by the beauty of the Amalfi coast and Capri, summon up the gumption to proceed south of Rome to Naples, but few venture much beyond the boundaries of Campania. The regions of Italy's 'deep south' are a world away from the industrious north, so ready to scorn its poorer cousins down the peninsula.

While you won't find the sumptuous artistic treasures of Rome or Florence in these southern regions, the Mezzogiorno beyond Campania nevertheless retains many reminders of the march past of several civilisations since the Greeks first established the colonies of Magna Graecia along the coast of Calabria, Basilicata and Apulia.

Of the three, Apulia came out best from the eras of Norman, Swabian, Angevin and Spanish rule, all of which left behind a surprisingly diverse heritage in churches, fortresses and other monuments. The same rulers pretty much left Basilicata and Calabria to their own devices. That sense of abandon created a vacuum that has all too often allowed petty overlords to maintain an often violent grip on their local territories. The 'Ndrangheta of Calabria, a vicious organised-crime syndicate keeps much of the region's population obedient with fear, and even today is an eloquent expression of that abandon.

Although great strides towards improving living standards have been made since the end of WW II, especially in Apulia, much remains to be done. These regions present on occasion a dramatic natural beauty, and foreign travellers are a definite minority – a welcome change from other more heavily trodden tourist trails.

Apulia (Puglia)

Encompassing the 'spur' and 'heel' of Italy's boot, Apulia (Puglia) is bordered by two seas, the Adriatic to the east and the Ionian (known here as the Golfo di Taranto), to the south. Its strategic position as the peninsula's gateway to the east made Apulia an important thoroughfare and a target for colonisers and invaders.

The ancient Greeks founded Magna Graecia in a string of settlements on the Ionian coast, including Taranto, which was settled by Spartan exiles; Brindisi marks the end of the Roman Appian Way; the Norman legacy is seen in the magnificent Romanesque churches across the region; Foggia and its province were favoured by the great Swabian king, Frederick II, several of whose castles remain; and Lecce, the Florence of Baroque, bears the architectural mark of the Spanish colonisers.

Coloured by its diverse history, the region holds many surprises in store, including the fascinating sanctuary dedicated to St Michael the Archangel at Monte Sant'Angelo; the *trulli*, conical-roofed, stone houses of Alberobello; the strange tradition of tarantism, from which evolved the tarantella folk dance (see the Galatina section); and the extraordinary floor mosaic in Otranto's cathedral. Then there are the Isole Tremiti, which remain unspoiled by tourism, the ancient Foresta Umbra on the Promontorio del Gargano, and the pleasant beaches of the Salentine Peninsula at the tip of the heel.

Intensive efforts to crank up industry, improve communications and education and so spur economic growth over the past 30 years have made Apulia the richest of Italy's southern regions, but high unemployment remains a grinding problem. The latter may have had a hand in the growth of mafia-style

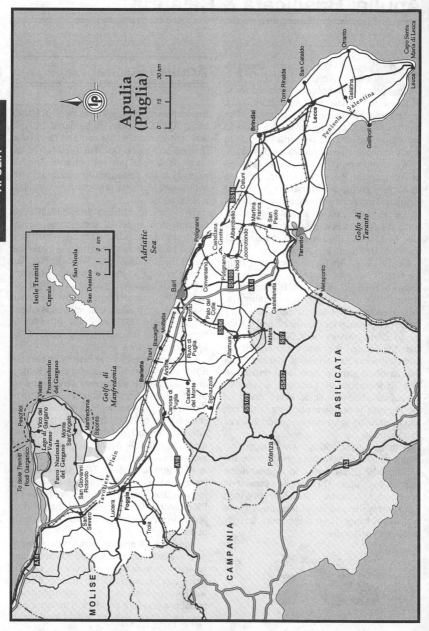

Apulia
(Puglia)

0   15   30 km

Isole Tremiti

Capraia

San Nicola

San Domino

0   1   2 km

organised crime run by the Sacra Corona Unita in the south and La Rosa in the north.

If you want to explore Apulia, you will need your own transport or lots of time, since many sights are in or near small towns and villages not always well serviced by public transport. The best option is to base yourself in the main towns and set out on daily expeditions. For instance, many of the more important Romanesque churches are reasonably close to Bari.

FOGGIA

Set in northern Apulia's patchwork landscape of the broad Tavoliere Plain, Foggia is an important transport junction and a not unlikeable place, but with little to hold the traveller up for long. Foggia came into its own in the 12th century as one of Frederick II's favourite cities, but later began to decline under the rule of the Spanish house of Aragon. Like much of the region, Foggia has been a frequent victim of earthquakes, and what these left standing of the old city centre was efficiently flattened under Allied bombardment in WW II. Its location makes it a possible launch pad for excursions to the forest and beaches of the Promontorio del Gargano, and to a couple of small towns worth visiting to the west: Troia for its beautiful Apulian-Romanesque cathedral, and Lucera for its Swabian-Angevin castle.

Orientation

The basically modern town can be a little confusing for the first timer arriving by car; otherwise it's pretty straightforward. The train station and bus station are on Piazzale Vittorio Veneto in the northern rim of town. Viale XXIV Maggio leads directly south into Piazza Cavour and the main shopping area. Several hotels, restaurants, as well as the post and telephone offices, can all be found on and around Viale XXIV Maggio.

Information

Tourist Office The EPT office (☎ 0881-67 68 64) is a good half-hour hike from the train station. It has limited information, including hotel lists, and is at Via Senatore Emilio Perrone 17. From the station, walk straight ahead along Viale XXIV Maggio to Piazza Cavour and continue along Corso P Giannone. Turn left into Via Cirillo (which becomes Via Bari) and follow it to Piazza Puglia – Via Perrone is on the right. Otherwise, take bus MD from the station. It is open Monday to Friday from 8 am to 2 pm, and on Tuesday afternoon from 5 to 7 pm.

Post & Telecommunications Foggia's post office is on Viale XXIV Maggio, and there is a telephone office (open from 8 am to 9 pm seven days a week) at Via Piave 29 (off Viale XXIV Maggio). The post code is 71100, and the telephone code 0881.

Money Plan to go to a bank in the morning (opening hours are generally 8.30 am to 1 pm) as the ATMs seem uniformly useless.

Things to See

The **Duomo**, off Corso Vittorio Emanuele, is about the only noteworthy sight. Built in the 12th century, the lower section remains true to the original Romanesque style. The top half, the noticeably different Baroque of six centuries later, was grafted on after an earthquake. Most of the cathedral's treasures were lost in the quake, but you can see a Byzantine icon preserved in a chapel inside the church. The icon was supposedly discovered in the 11th century by shepherds, in a pond over which burned three flames. The flames are now the symbol of the city.

The **Museo Civico** in Piazza Nigri (take Via Arpi to the right off Corso Vittorio Emanuele) houses archaeological finds from the province, including relics from the Roman and medieval town of Siponto. Three portals incorporated into the side of the building, one featuring two suspended eagles, are all that remains of Frederick II's local palace.

Places to Stay & Eat

A few hotels have bitten the dust in recent years, making the budget choice anything but wide. The first week of May is a good

APULIA

time to stay away, as Foggia hosts an international agriculture fair then.

Near the station, *Albergo Venezia* (☎ 67 09 03), Via Piave 40, is basic, with singles starting at L20,000 without bath and top-of-the-range doubles going for L55,000. A little farther away and a little more expensive is the *Albergo Centrale* (☎ 67 18 62), Corso Cairoli 5. The *Hotel Europa* (☎ 72 67 83), Via Monfalcone 52, has more upmarket singles/doubles starting at L110,000/165,000.

For a snack, try *Tuttopizzapanini* on the corner of Viale XXIV Maggio and Piazzale Vittorio Veneto. There are several little trattorie in the side streets to the right off Viale XXIV Maggio (walking away from the station). *Ristorante Margutta*, Via Piave 33, has pizzas starting from L5000. A bright new place is the *Ristorante L'Angolo Preferito* at Via Trieste 21. Try the seafood pasta. You can eat well for about L20,000.

Getting There & Away

Bus Buses leave from Piazzale Vittorio Veneto, in front of the train station, for towns throughout the province of Foggia. SITA has buses to Vieste on the Promontorio del Gargano (up to six daily), Monte Sant' Angelo (eight a day), Lucera (five a day), Manfredonia and Campobasso (in Molise; twice daily). Four direct services also connect Foggia with Naples. Tickets are available at window 10 in the train station, except for Naples (buy tickets on the bus). ATAF runs buses to Manfredonia, Vieste, Troia and Barletta (tickets from the tobacconist's at the station). Ferrovie dello Stato (FS) buses also connect Foggia and Lucera.

Train Foggia is connected by train to other major towns in Apulia, including Bari, Brindisi and Lecce. The town is easily accessible from points along the Adriatic coast, including Ancona and Pescara.

Car & Motorbike Take the SS16 south for Bari or north for the Adriatic coast to Termoli, Pescara and beyond. The Bologna-to-Bari A14 also passes Foggia. The SS90 south-west will put you on the road to Naples.

Central Foggia is a confusing tangle of one-way streets. Follow the 'stazione' signs for the train station and get oriented from there, especially if you are planning to stay.

LUCERA

Less than 20 km west of Foggia (and, by the way, a much more pleasant place to spend the night), Lucera has the distinction of having been re-created as an Arab city by Frederick II.

Surrounded, like Foggia, by the flat plains of the Tavoliere, the site was first settled by Rome in the 4th century BC and named Luceria Augusta. The fall of empire meant decay for the town, but Frederick II resuscitated it in the 13th century. Arab bandits had become a growing problem in Sicily, and Frederick decided to remove the thorn from his side by relocating all of them to Apulia. Some 20,000 ended up in Lucera, where the emperor allowed them to build mosques and practise Islam freely. He recruited his famous Saracen bodyguard from the Arabs of Lucera, who accompanied him loyally on his journeys between castles and even to the crusades.

Charles I of Anjou conquered Lucera in the late 13th century, and the new French arrivals replaced many of the town's mosques with Gothic churches. Both sides got along tolerably well until Charles II decided to have the Arabs slaughtered in 1300.

Things to See

The imposing **castle** was built by Frederick II in 1223, and its external walls were later added by Charles of Anjou, forming a pentagon topped by 24 towers. What is left of Frederick's castle stands in the north-east corner of the enclosure. Excavations in the centre have revealed the remains of Roman buildings. The castle is open daily until dusk. Admission is free, but the guard will expect a small tip.

The **duomo**, in the centre of the old town, was started by Charles of Anjou in 1300 and

---

Frederick II's Moveable Feast

In *A Traveller in Southern Italy*, H V Morton wrote of the 'half oriental life of the most luxurious and civilised court in Europe':

'Frederick's passage from castle to castle, from Palermo through the Calabrian mountains into Apulia, must have resembled the progress of Barnum and Bailey. The imperial elephant had been taught to bear the standard of the Hohenstaufen; the imperial treasure was carried upon the backs of camels and dromedaries; the covered litters of the harem were guarded by mounted archers of the Saracen guard; the emperor's hawks and hounds travelled like Princes, and so did the hunting leopards, riding on horseback behind their keepers.' ■

---

is considered the best example of Angevin architecture in southern Italy. He also erected the Gothic **Chiesa di San Francesco**.

On the town's eastern outskirts is a poorly maintained 1st-century BC **Roman amphitheatre**, open from 7 am to 1 pm and 2 pm until dusk. Admission is free, but tip the guard.

Places to Stay

The pick here is the *Albergo Al Passetto* (☎ 0881-52 08 21), next to the old city gate at Piazza del Popolo. Singles/doubles with bath cost L30,000/50,000, and it has a restaurant downstairs.

Getting There & Away

Lucera is easily accessible from Foggia (a 30-minute trip) by SITA and FS buses, which terminate in Piazza del Popolo.

TROIA

The village of Troia, 18 km south of Lucera, has nothing to do with the Troy of legend. However, its beautiful Apulian-Romanesque **cathedral** merits the (hardly strenuous) effort of getting here. The façade is splendidly decorated with a rose window, and in among the gargoyles and other creatures that adorn the exterior of the church are hints of Oriental influence – look particularly for the geometrical designs across the top of the eastern façade. The bronze doors are also of particular note.

If you want to stay, try the *Albergo Alba d'Oro* (☎ 0881-97 09 40) at Viale Kennedy 30, on the way out of town towards Lucera.

It has singles/doubles with bathroom for L30,000/50,000.

MANFREDONIA

Founded by the Swabian king Manfred, Frederick II's illegitimate son, this port town has little to attract tourists, other than its usefulness as a transport junction on the way to the Promontorio del Gargano. Intercity buses terminate in Piazza Marconi, a short walk along Corso Manfredi from the AAST office (☎ 0884-58 19 98) at No 26. It opens Monday to Saturday from 8.30 am to 1.30 pm, and you can get limited information on the promontory. The telephone code is 0884.

Things to See

If you have time to kill, head to the other end of Corso Manfredi for a look at the majestic **castle** started by Manfred and completed by Charles of Anjou (open daily except Monday from 9 am to 1 pm and 5 to 7 pm). The Museo Nazionale inside has a display of ancient artefacts discovered in the area around Manfredonia.

About two km south of town is **Siponto**, an important port from Roman to medieval times, but abandoned in favour of Manfredonia because of earthquakes and malaria. Apart from the **beaches**, the only thing of interest is the distinctly Byzantine looking 11th-century Romanesque **Chiesa di Santa Maria di Siponto**.

Places to Stay & Eat

There are four camp sites south of town. Of the hotels in town, the *Albergo Sipontum*

(☎ 54 29 16), Viale di Vittorio 229, is the cheapest at L30,000/60,000. Rooms at the *Hotel Azzurro* (☎ 58 14 98), at No 56, start at L44,000/70,000. For a good meal, try *Al Fuego*, Via dei Celestini, just off Corso Manfredi.

Getting There & Away
SITA buses connect Manfredonia with Foggia, Vieste and Monte Sant'Angelo, leaving from Piazza Marconi. Tickets and timetable information are available at Bar Impero in Piazza Marconi, near the corner of Corso Manfredi.

PROMONTORIO DEL GARGANO
The 'spur' of the Italian boot is made up of limestone mountains, ancient forest and beautiful beaches. For centuries an important destination for religious pilgrims, the Promontorio del Gargano (Gargano Promontory) has more recently become a popular tourist playground. Its beach resorts, including Vieste and Peschici, are developing rapidly to accommodate the annual influx of sun-and-fun seekers.

The ancient beeches and oaks of the **Foresta Umbra** in the promontory's mountainous interior make up one of Italy's last remaining original forests. Walkers will find plenty of well-marked trails and there are several picnic areas. The visitors' centre comes complete with stuffed examples of the forest's wildlife. Public transport to and from the forest can be tricky, but not impossible.

The promontory also has two important religious sanctuaries: that of the Archangel Michael at Monte Sant'Angelo, and the burial place of Padre Pio at San Giovanni Rotondo.

Monte Sant'Angelo
For centuries this isolated mountain ridge town overlooking the south coast of the Gargano has been the last stop on a gruelling pilgrimage route. The object of such devotion was and remains the Santuario di San Michele. For here in 490 AD the Archangel Michael is said to have appeared in a grotto

before the Bishop of Siponto. The legend goes that a local man who had lost his prize bull eventually found it standing at the entrance to a cave. When he could not make the animal move, he shot an arrow at it. Instead of hitting the bull, the arrow turned and hit the man, who then went to the bishop for advice. St Michael later appeared to the bishop at the grotto, ordering him to consecrate a Christian altar there. The grotto had previously been a pagan shrine with an oracle that performed dream cures.

During the Middle Ages, the sanctuary marked the end of the pilgrim Route of the Angel, which began in Normandy, passed through Rome and led to Monte Sant'Angelo. In 999 AD, Holy Roman Emperor Otto III made a pilgrimage to the sanctuary to pray that prophecies of the world coming to an end in the year 1000 would not be fulfilled. The sanctuary's fame grew after the much-predicted apocalypse did not eventuate.

Information There is a Pro Loco tourist office in the town's main street, Via Reale Basilica, which can provide limited information about the town. It's open from 9 am to 1 pm and 2.30 to 5 pm Monday to Saturday.

Things to See Like so many great destinations of pilgrimage, the **Santuario di San Michele** has lately become big tourist business. Those forgetting the religious nature of the place are quickly reminded: dress rules are strictly enforced (absolutely no shorts, miniskirts or revealing tops – even bare arms are frowned upon), and don't be surprised if you are asked to put on a special coat to cover offending exposed skin. You enter through a double archway, above which is carved in Latin: 'This is an awesome place; it is the House of God and the Gate of Heaven'.

Once inside, a flight of stone steps leads down to the grotto. As you descend, note the graffiti that fills the walls, some of it the work of 17th-century pilgrims. Archangel Michael is said to have left a footprint in stone inside the grotto, so it became customary for pilgrims to carve outlines of their feet and hands and leave accompanying messages. Magnificent Byzantine bronze and silver doors open onto the grotto itself.

Inside, a 16th-century statue of the archangel covers the spot where he is said to have left his footprint. The main altar stands at the site of the first altar consecrated by the bishop of Siponto to St Michael, and behind it is a small fountain of legendary 'healing' waters, which you can no longer drink. Also in the grotto is a beautiful marble bishop's chair, resting on two lions.

Once outside, head down the short flight of steps opposite the sanctuary to the **Tomba di Rotari**, once thought to be the tomb of a 7th-century Lombard king, but more likely a 12th-century baptistry. Little more than the façade and rose window remain of the **Chiesa di San Pietro** next door, destroyed by an earthquake in the 19th century. The adjacent 11th-century **Chiesa di Santa Maria Maggiore** is closed to the public.

Commanding the highest point of the town is a Norman **castle**, long closed for restoration.

The serpentine alleyways and jumbled houses of this town are perfect for a little aimless ambling. Take the time to head for the belvedere for sweeping views of the coast to the south.

Places to Stay & Eat Finding rooms can be decidedly difficult in Monte Sant'Angelo. Ask at the tobacconist's near the sanctuary if there are any cheap beds to be had. Accommodation for pilgrims was shut at the time of writing. If this remains the case, the only option is the comfortable if charmless three-star *Rotary Hotel* (☎ 0884-6 21 46), Via Pulsano, one km downhill from town, which has rooms for L50,000/70,000.

Via Reale Basilica is lined with takeaways and trattorie, including the *Trattoria San Michele* at No 59, and *Ristorante Garden Paradise* at No 51. While in town, try the local sweets, ostie ripiene (literally, 'stuffed Hosts') – two wafers (like Hosts used in the Catholic Communion) with a filling of almonds and honey.

Getting There & Away Monte Sant'Angelo is accessible from Foggia, Manfredonia, Vieste and San Giovanni Rotondo by SITA bus. If you have your own transport, you can take the road to/from Vico del Gargano, which cuts through the Foresta Umbra.

San Giovanni Rotondo

When Padre Pio, an ailing Capuchin priest in need of a cooler climate, arrived in 1916, San Giovanni Rotondo was a tiny, isolated medieval village in the heart of the Gargano.

Padre Pio

Padre Pio da Pietrelcina died in September 1968 at the age of 81, more than 50 years after doctors first announced that his demise was imminent because of weak health. Son of Campanian peasants, he joined the strict Capuchin order at the age of 16. Sent to San Giovanni Rotondo 13 years later to rest up, he stayed for the remainder of his life, a growing object of pilgrimage because of the many miracles attributed to him and the permanent appearance of the stigmata on his hands, feet and side. His greatest project was the construction of the Casa Sollievo della Sofferenza, a hospital where he wanted patients not only to be cured but to feel at home. Its existence is something of a miracle in itself, since Pio relied largely on offerings to finance the project.

Padre Pio was not always to the Church's taste, and on various occasions he was ordered by Rome not to say Mass any more, in an attempt to dampen public enthusiasm for the man. In 1924 a decree was issued exhorting the faithful not to go to San Giovanni Rotondo, a call that fell on deaf ears. Padre Pio is a candidate for canonisation as a saint, and the list being compiled in Rome of miracles and cures that people claim he has worked continues to grow, almost 30 years after his death. ■

In the following years, Pio gained a reputation as a mystic and miracle-worker, and San Giovanni Rotondo underwent something of a miraculous transformation itself, expanding well beyond its original limits. Up to 200,000 pilgrims crowd into the town every year to pay homage to the priest and spend up in the souvenir shops. Aside from the 14th-century Chiesa di Sant'Onofrio, a baptistery and the 16th-century Chiesa di Santa Maria delle Grazie, you can visit the tomb of Padre Pio in the modern church (Santuario) nearby.

If you want to stay, there are more than 20 hotels, although pilgrims can fill a good number of them early.

SITA buses run five times daily to and from Monte Sant'Angelo, and hourly from Manfredonia.

Vieste

The most popular seaside resort on the promontory and the best equipped with tourist facilities, Vieste is a bright little place. The better beaches are away from town, between Vieste and Peschici, particularly in the area known as La Salata, where there are three camping grounds.

Orientation & Information Intercity buses terminate in Piazza Manzoni, a few minutes walk along Via XXIV Maggio from the entrance to the old town and the AAST office (☎ 0884-70 74 95), Corso Fazzini 8, near Piazza Kennedy by the sea. The office is open in summer from 8 am to 10 pm Monday to Saturday. Out of season it supposedly opens Monday to Saturday from 8 am to 8 pm, but these rules seem to be interpreted creatively.

The post office is in Piazza Vittorio Veneto, and there are rows of public telephones there too. The town's telephone code is 0884.

Things to See & Do The old town, with its whitewashed houses and winding medieval streets, offers a couple of sights of interest, although tourists come here for the beaches rather than the history. The **duomo** is Apulian-Romanesque, but underwent alterations in the 18th century.

Head down Via Cimaglia to the **Chianca Amara** (Bitter Stone), on which thousands of citizens were beheaded when the Turks sacked Vieste in the 16th century. Nearby, at the town's highest point, is a **castle**, built by Frederick II, now occupied by the military and closed to the public.

If you want to head for a beach and don't have your own transport, the **Spiaggia del Castello** is just south of the town.

Places to Stay Most of Vieste's many hotels and pensioni are scattered along the beachfront roads to the north and south of town. Camping grounds (more than 70) abound, particularly along Lungomare E Mattei to the south. A good one is *Campeggio Capo Vieste* (☎ 70 63 26), at La Salata on the road between Vieste and Peschici. It is accessible by Ferrovie del Gargano bus.

The *Pensione al Centro Storico* (☎ 70 70 30) is at Via Mafrolla 32 in the medieval centre (from Via XXIV Maggio, walk through Piazza Vittorio Emanuele and then follow Via Pola). It has singles/doubles for up to L50,000/82,000. The *Vela Velo Club* (☎ 79 63 03) is at Lungomare Europa 19, north of the old town. It charges by the person, up to L68,000 in the high season, which covers B&B, use of the private beach and a bicycle; out of season you should be able to pay for the room only. The *Hotel del Seggio* (☎ 70 81 23) is at Via Vieste 7, in the old town. A pleasant hotel, it has a private pool and sunbathing terraces. It charges up to L120,000 a double in the high season.

Places to Eat For a snack, try *Il Fornaio*, Piazza della Libertà, at the end of Via Fazzini near the entrance to the old town, which serves pizza by the slice. A panoramic spot for a cool drink is *Sapori di Mare*, overlooking the sea in Piazzetta Petrone, downhill along Via Cimaglia. *La Ripa*, Via Cimaglia 16, is a pleasant little rustic trattoria, where a full meal will cost about L20,000. Otherwise try *Taverna al Cantinone*, on the corner of Vico Caruso and Via Mafrolla, where a good meal will cost L30,000. A cosy place is the *Locanda La Macina*, Via Alessandro III 49, near the duomo. Also close by is the *Enoteca Vesta*, Via Duomo 14, for those wanting to sip local vintages.

Getting There & Away SITA buses connect Vieste with Foggia and Manfredonia, while the Ferrovie del Gargano bus and train network connects the town with Peschici and Rodi Garganico, as well as other towns on the promontory. Buses terminate in Piazza Manzoni and timetables are posted outside the town hall nearby.

Vieste's port is just north of the old town, about five minutes' walk from the tourist office. Boats to the Isole Tremiti are run by two companies, Adriatica and Motonave, both of which have ticket offices at the port (L19,000 one way). It is also possible to make a boat tour of the coast near Vieste, which includes visits to some of the area's grottoes. Enquire at the port for timetables and tickets.

Peschici

A short, pretty drive just in from the coast separates Vieste from the next popular stop. Bunched up on a rocky outcrop above a sparkling bay, Peschici is a fast-developing resort, but to date remains relatively unspoiled.

Strongly recalling villages of the Greek islands, with its little whitewashed houses and sunny aspect, Peschici's cobbled alleyways sport some suggestive names – Vico Purgatorio (Purgatory Lane) and the parallel Via Malconsiglio and Via Buonconsiglio (Bad Advice and Good Advice Streets). Their origins are anyone's guess; Vico Stretto (Narrow Lane) is more straightforward.

Peschici's sandy beaches and hotels fill up in summer, so book well in advance.

Orientation & Information While the medieval part of town clings to the clifftop at the point of the bay, the newer parts of town extend inland and around the bay. Buses arrive at the sports ground uphill from the town's main street, Corso Garibaldi. Turn right into the Corso and walk straight ahead to reach the old town.

The Pro Loco tourist office (☎ 96 44 25), Corso Garibaldi 57, near the entrance to the old town, can provide information about accommodation, but little else. The town's telephone code is 0884.

Places to Stay Peschici has several hotels and pensioni, but prices are usually on the expensive side, particularly in summer. Numerous camp sites dot the coast on either side of Peschici. Try the *Baia San Nicola* (☎ 96 42 31), close to town, or *Camping Parco degli Ulivi* (☎ 96 34 04), a few km west on the road to Rodi Garganico.

The pick in old Peschici is the *Locanda al Castello* (☎ 96 40 38), Via Castello 29, right by the seaward cliffs. It has singles/doubles with bath starting at L40,000/75,000. *Albergo La Pineta* (☎ 96 41 26), Via Libetta 77, has rooms for L35,000/60,000, while the *Hotel Timiana* (☎ 96 43 21) next door has rooms for L40,000/80,000. These two are in the new town.

Places to Eat To stock up on supplies, shop at the Supermercato Crai at the far end of Corso Garibaldi from the medieval section. The *Locanda al Castello* has a good, reasonably priced pizzeria and trattoria. Other restaurants in the old part of town include *Ristorante La Taverna*, at Via Malconsiglio 6 off Via Castello, where a full meal will cost up to L30,000, and *Ristorante Vecchia Peschici*, Via Roma 31, where an excellent meal on the terrace overlooking the sea is worth around L35,000.

Getting There & Away Peschici is accessible by Ferrovie del Gargano buses from Vieste and Rodi Garganico. From April to September, daily boats leave Peschici's port for the Isole Tremiti at 9.15 am, getting back to Peschici at 6.15 pm. For information and tickets, go to Ondazzurra (☎ 9 42 34) at Corso Umberto I.

Rodi Garganico

Closing off the stretch of beach resorts in the north-west of the promontory is what was once a simple fishing village. Rodi Garganico and the beach stretching east to the hamlet of San Menaio are rapidly filling up with hotels, camp sites and apartments, and the area is the least agreeable of the resorts. Should you really want to go, Ferrovie del Gargano buses link it with Peschici and other towns in the promontory.

ISOLE TREMITI

This small archipelago about 40 km north of the Promontorio del Gargano consists of three main islands: San Domino, San Nicola and Capraia. Until the 1930s a convict station, the islands are becoming increasingly popular, but for now remain relatively lowkey. Out of season most of the islands' tourist facilities close down and the 370 or so permanent residents resume their isolated, quiet lives.

The islands have an ancient history. Legend says that Diomedes, a Greek hero of the Trojan War, was buried here and that a rare local species of bird, the Diomedee, continues to mourn his death. Early in the 11th century, the Abbey of Santa Maria (Abbazia e Chiesa di Santa Maria) was founded on San Nicola by Benedictine monks, who wielded power in the region until the arrival of the Spanish Bourbons in the 18th century. King Ferdinand IV used the abbey as a jail, a tradition continued by the Fascists, who sent political exiles to the islands in the 1920s and 1930s.

Easily defensible, San Nicola was always the administrative and residential centre of the islands, while the lusher San Domino was used to grow crops. With the risk of pirate attack no longer a preoccupation, you will find most of the islands' accommodation and other facilities on San Domino.

Depending on the boat you catch, you will arrive on either San Domino or San Nicola. Don't panic if you think you have been dropped off on the wrong island, since small boats regularly make the brief crossing (L1500 one way – no exact timetable, you just have to wait). Confirm the departure point of your boat. The telephone code on the islands is 0882.

Things to See & Do

San Nicola It is interesting to wander around the abbey on San Nicola, noting in particular the **Chiesa di Santa Maria**, which features an 11th-century floor mosaic, a painted wooden Byzantine crucifix brought to the island in 747 AD, and a black Madonna, which was almost certainly transported here from Constantinople in the Middle Ages.

San Domino San Domino has the only sandy beach on the islands, and it becomes extremely crowded in summer. However, numerous small coves where you can swim off the rocks dot the coastline. Some are accessible on foot, while others can be reached only by boat.

If you are feeling energetic, a walking track around the island starts at the far end of San Domino village, past Pensione Nassa. Alternatively, you could hire a bicycle from IBIS Cicli at Piazzetta San Domino. Motorised rubber dinghies are available for hire at the port for about L120,000 a day (go to the Il Piràta bar). Boats leave from San Domino's small port on tours of the island's grottoes; tickets cost L15,000.

Places to Stay & Eat

You will need to book well in advance for summer. If you intend to arrive out of season, phone to check that hotels are open. In the high season, most hotels require that you pay for full board – a good idea, since the options for eating out are not extensive.

On San Domino, *Al Faro* (☎ 66 34 24), Via della Cantina Sperimentale, has singles/doubles for around L50,000/70,000, while *Locanda La Nassa* (☎ 66 33 45) has doubles for up to L100,000. *Hotel Gabbiano* (☎ 66 34 10) has a terrace restaurant overlooking San Nicola from San Domino, and very pleasant rooms for around L130,000 a double, or L105,000 per head for full board.

On San Nicola, you could eat at *Diomedea*, where a simple meal will cost around L20,000.

Getting There & Away

Adriatica Navigazione runs a year-round daily ferry between the islands and Termoli (in Molise). From October to April the same ferry calls in at Vieste once a week. The one-way fare is L11,800. From late May to late September, *aliscafi* (hydrofoils) also run between Termoli and the islands, with occasional runs to Ortona (in Abruzzo). The one-way fare Termoli to Tremiti is L20,700, and L29,400 for the Ortona service.

All the Gargano connections can be made in the peak summer period only, generally by the so-called *monostab*, a sleek high-speed cruise boat. It links Manfredonia to Vieste, Rodi Garganico and the Isole Tremiti (Tremiti Islands). The longest trip is between Manfredonia and the islands (L29,400); the shortest is the hop between Vieste and Rodi (not touching the islands; L11,100).

Tickets can be purchased at the ports (preferably 24 hours in advance) or at the following agents:

Manfredonia
  Antonio Galli e Figlio (☎ 0884-2 28 88), Corso Manfredi 4
Vieste
  Gargano Viaggi (☎ 0884-70 85 01), Piazza Roma 7
Peschici
  Ondazzurra (☎ 0884-9 42 34), Corso Umberto I
Rodi Garganico
  Agenzia Marittima VI.Pl.Sas (☎ 0884-96 63 57), Corso Madonna della Libera 22
Tremiti
  Ditta P Domenichelli (☎ 0882-66 30 08), Via degli Abbati 10
Termoli (Molise)
  Intercontinental Viaggi (☎ 0875-70 53 41), Corso Umberto I 93
Ortona (Abruzzo)
  Agenzia Marittima Fratino e Figli (☎ 0859-06 38 55), Via Porto 34
Vasto (Abruzzo)
  Massacesi – Agenzia Viaggi e Marittima (☎ 0873-36 26 80), Piazza Diomede 3

TRANI

A vigorous facelift and a magnificent portside cathedral have made Trani one of those little jewels that turn up where you least expect to find them. Some 40 km north-west along the coast from Bari, this compact and easily manageable town makes a good base for exploring this part of Apulia. Barletta, Molfetta and the Castel del Monte, to name a few, are all in easy striking distance.

Trani was important in the Middle Ages – the modern world's oldest written maritime code, the Ordinamenta Maris, was drawn up here – and it flourished during the rule of Frederick II. The medieval harbour, long in a poor state of repair, has undergone a rejuvenation cure over the past 15 years, leaving it the most attractive and animated part of town.

Orientation

The train and bus stations are in Piazza XX Settembre. From here, Via Cavour leads past the tourist office to the main central square, the tree-lined Piazza della Repubblica. Continue along Via Cavour to Piazza Plebiscito and the public gardens and, to the left, the port area. Across the small harbour is the cathedral, spectacularly located on a small promontory.

Information

A few metres down Via Cavour from the train station is the AAST office (☎ 0883-58 88 25) at No 140, open Monday to Friday from 8.30 am to 12.30 pm and 3.30 to 5.30 pm (until noon only on Saturday). A booth on Piazza della Repubblica, when staffed, has similar hours. The town's telephone code is 0883.

Cathedral

Started in 1097 on the site of a Byzantine church, the cathedral was not completed until the 13th century. Dedicated to St Nicholas the Pilgrim (San Nicola Pellegrino), it is one of the most beautiful churches in Italy. Its simple but imposing façade is decorated with blind arches. The bronze doors of the main portal were cast in 1180 by Barisano da

Trani, an accomplished artisan of whom little is known, other than that he also cast the bronze doors of the cathedral at Ravallo and the side doors of the cathedral at Monreale.

The grand interior of the cathedral was recently restored to its original Norman austerity. Light shines through alabaster windows, giving the interior an eerie glow. Near the main altar, take a look at the remains of a 12th-century floor mosaic, similar in style to the one at Otranto. Below the church is the crypt, a forest of ancient columns, where the bones of St Nicholas are kept beneath the altar.

Around the Cathedral

The cathedral crypt opens onto the Byzantine **Chiesa di Santa Maria della Scala**. Of note here is the *Madonna Dolorata*, a life-size statue of the Madonna, dressed in black velvet, a dagger protruding from her heart. Down another flight of stairs is the **Tomba di San Leucio**, a chamber believed to date back to the 6th century.

Near the cathedral is the 13th-century **castle**, built by Frederick II. It was altered by the Angevins and until recently was used as a prison.

Around the Port

Several interesting palaces and churches are sprinkled over the port area. Note the 15th-century Gothic **Palazzo Caccetta** and the nearby 12th-century **Chiesa di Ognissanti** (All Saints' Church), both in Via Ognissanti close to the cathedral. The Templars built the church as part of a hospital complex used for knights injured in the crusades. Also worth searching out is the **Palazzo della Quercia**, in Piazza Quercia at the other end of the port zone.

Places to Stay

By far the most evocative place to spend a night is the *Hotel Regia* (☎ 58 45 27), Piazza Duomo 2, in the 18th-century Palazzo Filisio just across the road from the cathedral. Singles/doubles with bathroom cost L40,000/75,000. About three km out of

town (accessible by blue bus for Corato from the station) is the *Hotel Capirro* (☎ 58 07 12), a characterless place with secure singles/doubles for L35,000/55,000 (with TV and telephone). Further upmarket, the *Hotel Royal* (☎ 58 87 77), Via De Roberts 24, has rooms starting at L60,000/100,000.

Places to Eat

To pick up supplies, shop at the market, held every morning Monday to Saturday in Piazza della Libertà, to the left along Via Pagano from Piazza della Repubblica.

Attached to the Hotel Regia is a restaurant/pizzeria, where you can eat a reasonably priced meal.

Pizzeria Al Faro, Via Statuti Marittimi 50, at the port, is a good choice – try their seafood pizza. *La Darsena*, in the 18th-century Palazzo Palumbo at the port, is more expensive.

The *Caffè Nautico Club*, Via Statuti Marittimi 18, is actually a private club but also an excellent little restaurant. If you are lucky, you might find that the owner/chef is willing to whip up a delightful seafood meal for around L35,000.

Closer to the centre of town, the *Ristorante La Nicchia*, Corso Imbriani 22, serves up some very decent nosh for around L25,000.

Getting There & Away

Bus AMET buses connect Trani with points along the coast and inland, including Barletta, Canosa di Puglia, Ruvo di Puglia and Andria. Timetables and tickets are available at Agenzia Sprint, opposite the train station in Piazza XX Settembre, and at the tourist office.

Three buses from Trani leave in time to connect with the 8.30 am service from Andria to Castel del Monte (see the next section). The return run to Andria leaves the castle at 3 pm. Check with the tourist office for updated times.

Train Trani is on the main train line between Bari and Foggia and is easily reached from towns along the coast.

Car & Motorbike The SS16 runs through Trani, linking it to Bari and Foggia, or you can hook up with the A14 Bologna-Bari autostrada.

AROUND TRANI
Barletta
About 13 km north-west along the coast from Trani, Barletta is more faithful to the stereotype of a grubby neglected port town. It is worth a quick visit for its cathedral, castle and the so-called *Colossus*, a rather stout Roman-era bronze statue in the town centre.

Orientation & Information From the train station, turn right into Corso Garibaldi to reach Barletta's centre. From the bus station in Via Manfredi, walk to Piazza Plebiscito and turn left into Corso Vittorio Emanuele. The AAST office (☎ 53 13 73) is on Piazza Roma. The town's telephone code is 0883.

Things to See The 12th-century Apulian-Romanesque **duomo**, along Corso Garibaldi from the town centre, is among the region's better preserved examples of this architectural style. Restoration work that was due to end in 1993 is still underway and the cathedral is closed.

Virtually across the road is the imposing waterside **castle**, built initially by the Normans, rebuilt by Frederick II and fortified by Charles of Anjou. It is supposedly open from 9 am to 1 pm and 4 to 7 pm (summer) or 3 to 4 pm (winter). Entry costs L3000.

Back in the town centre, just off Corso Garibaldi in Corso Vittorio Emanuele, is the **Colossus**, a 4.5-metre-high Roman statue believed to be of Emperor Valentinian I. The statue was plundered during the sack of Constantinople in 1203 and snapped up by Barletta after the ship carrying it sank off the Apulian coast. The statue stands next to the 12th-century **Basilica of the Holy Sepulchre** (Basilica del Santo Sepolcro). Originally Romanesque, this church subsequently underwent Gothic and Baroque facelifts. The manner in which it appears to have sunk below the level of the square is uncannily reminiscent of the duomo in Modena (Emilia-Romagna).

Festival The main event on the town's calendar is the Disfida (Challenge) of Barletta, held annually on the last Sunday in July. One of Italy's best known medieval pageants, it re-enacts a duel between 13 Italian and 13 French knights on 13 February 1503, when the town was besieged by the French. The Italians won, and in return the chivalrous French decamped.

Getting There & Away From the bus station in Via Manfredi, ATAF buses connect Barletta with Foggia; there are regular AMET buses to Trani and Molfetta; and SITA buses head for Manfredonia and Bari. Barletta is on both the Bari-Foggia coastal train line and the Bari-Nord line and is easily accessible from Trani and other points along the coast, as well as inland towns.

Castel del Monte
The Castel del Monte, standing like a royal crown on a hilltop, is one of Apulia's most prominent landmarks and visible for miles around. It is situated in the Murge, a long limestone plateau stretching west and south of Bari. You have to be fairly enthusiastic to make the journey to the castle without your own transport, but it is worth the effort.

The stronghold was built by Frederick II, probably for his own pleasure and to his own design, in the early 13th century during the last 10 years of his life. It appears its most bellicose use was as a hunting lodge – in Frederick's day the surrounding country was heavily forested and teeming with game.

The castle is built on an octagonal base, each corner equipped with an octagonal tower. There is no moat or other system of defence, apart from its high walls and slit windows. Completely restored some years ago, its interconnecting rooms have decorative marble columns and fireplaces, and the doorways and window frames are adorned with corallite stone. The castle is open in summer from 8.30 am to 7 pm Monday to

Saturday, and from 9 am to 1 pm Sunday. From October to March it opens from 8.30 am to 2 pm Monday to Saturday, and from 9 am to 1 pm Sunday, although opening times can vary slightly at the whim of the guardians. Admission costs L4000.

Getting There & Away The easiest way to get to the castle is via Andria. A bus leaves Piazza Municipio in Andria at 8.30 am Monday to Saturday for the castle, returning at 3 pm, and the town is an easy trip by bus from Trani, or on the Bari-Nord train line from Bari. The Andria-Spinazzola bus (several a day) passes close to the castle – ask the driver to let you off at the right spot. See also the Getting There & Away section under Trani.

BARI

Unless you are planning to catch a ferry to Greece, Bari won't be high on your destination list. For all that, it does offer a handful of interesting sights and can make a good base for exploring neighbouring towns such as Ruvo di Puglia, Molfetta, Bitonto, Altamura and even Alberobello and the trulli area. The city's Stop Over in Bari programme makes it still more attractive for under-30s (see Information below).

Capital of Apulia and the second most important city in the south after Naples, it can be a frenetic sort of place – the peak-hour traffic is choking. It was an important Byzantine town and flourished under the Normans and later under Frederick II. Bari is a long way from the North Pole, but it is here that St Nicholas of Myra, otherwise known as Father Christmas, was finally laid to rest. His remains, contained in a liquid known as the manna that is said to have miraculous powers, were stolen from Turkey in 1087 and interred in the Basilica di San Nicola, built especially for the purpose. It is still an important place of pilgrimage.

Occupied by the Allies during WW II, the port city was heavily bombed by the Germans.

Orientation

Bari is surprisingly easy to negotiate. The FS and Bari-Nord train stations are at the vast Piazza Aldo Moro, in the newer (19th-century) section of the city, about 10 minutes' walk south of the old town, or Bari Vecchia. The main tourist office is off the same square. Via Crisanzio, a block north of Piazza Aldo Moro and running east to west, has a fair choice of hotels.

This newer part of Bari is on a grid plan and any of the streets heading north from Piazza Aldo Moro, including Via Sparano, will take you to Corso Vittorio Emanuele II, which separates the old and new cities. Corso Cavour is the main shopping strip.

Information

Tourist Offices The EPT office (☎ 080-524 22 44) is to the right as you leave the train station, just off Piazza Aldo Moro, and opens from 9 am to 1 pm and 4 to 8 pm Monday to Saturday (from October to April mornings and Tuesday evenings only).

If you are under 30, you can take advantage of Stop Over in Bari, an initiative that aims to attract youth tourism to the city. The programme operates from June to September, offering a package that includes low-priced accommodation in small hotels or private homes, or free accommodation in the Pineta San Francesco camping ground; free use of the city's buses; free admission to museums; cut-rate meals; a free bike service; and information centres for young travellers. The package, including two nights' accommodation, costs L30,000.

Stop Over's main office, OTE (☎ 080-521 45 38), is at Via Dante Alighieri 111, and there is an information booth on Piazza Aldo Moro. The staff are helpful, speak English and have loads of information about the town. While only under-30s can take advantage of the package, anyone is welcome to seek information. Ring the above number to make a booking, or go to one of Stop Over's outlets when you arrive.

Money There is no shortage of banks, many with ATMs that will accept Visa, MasterCard

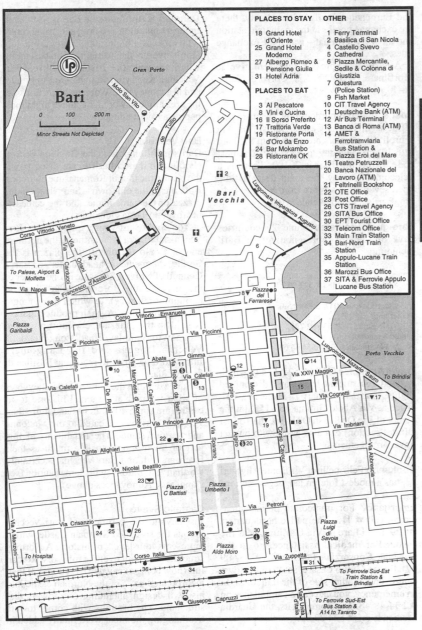

APULIA

Bari

0   100   200 m

Minor Streets Not Depicted

Gran Porto

Bari Vecchia

To Palese, Airport & Molfetta

Piazza Garibaldi

To Hospital

To Brindisi

Porto Vecchio

To Ferrovie Sud-Est Train Station & Brindisi

To Ferrovie Sud-Est Bus Station & A14 to Taranto

PLACES TO STAY

18 Grand Hotel d'Oriente
25 Grand Hotel Moderno
27 Albergo Romeo & Pensione Giulia
31 Hotel Adria

PLACES TO EAT

3   Al Pescatore
8   Vini e Cucina
16 Il Sorso Preferito
17 Trattoria Verde
19 Ristorante Porta d'Oro da Enzo
24 Bar Mokambo
28 Ristorante OK

OTHER

1   Ferry Terminal
2   Basilica di San Nicola
4   Castello Svevo
5   Cathedral
6   Piazza Mercantile, Sedile & Colonna di Giustizia
7   Questura (Police Station)
9   Fish Market
10 CIT Travel Agency
11 Deutsche Bank (ATM)
12 Air Bus Terminal
13 Banca di Roma (ATM)
14 AMET & Ferrotramviaria Bus Station & Piazza Eroi del Mare
15 Teatro Petruzzelli
20 Banca Nazionale del Lavoro (ATM)
21 Feltrinelli Bookshop
22 OTE Office
23 Post Office
26 CTS Travel Agency
29 SITA Bus Office
30 EPT Tourist Office
32 Telecom Office
33 Main Train Station
34 Bari-Nord Train Station
35 Appulo-Lucane Train Station
36 Marozzi Bus Office
37 SITA & Ferrovie Appulo Lucane Bus Station

and Eurocheque cards. Alternatively, there are exchange booths at the main train station and the ferry terminal – watch the exchange rates.

American Express's representative is Morfimare (☎ 521 00 22), Corso di Tullio 36-40.

Post & Telecommunications The main post office is in Piazza Cesare Battisti, on Via Cairoli. Its counters are open from 8.20 am to 6.30 pm, Monday to Saturday. The post code for central Bari is 70100. There is a Telecom office by the main train station, open seven days a week from 8 am to 9.45 pm. Bari's telephone code is 080.

Foreign Consulates Some 26 countries have diplomatic representatives in Bari, including:

France
      Via Amendola 138 (☎ 521 00 17)
Germany
      Corso Cavour 40 (☎ 524 40 59)
Netherlands
      Viale Ennio 2 (☎ 536 92 22)
United Kingdom
      Via Dalmazia 127 (☎ 554 36 68)

Travel Agencies CTS (☎ 521 32 44), which is good for student travel and discounted flights, is at Via Fornari 7. There is a CIT office at Via Abate Gimma 150-152, on the corner of Via De Rossi. OTE (see the Tourist Offices section) can also assist with budget travel arrangements.

Bookshop Feltrinelli, at Via Dante Alighieri 93, has a modest foreign languages section.

Emergency For immediate police attendance, call ☎ 113. The police headquarters (☎ 29 11 11) are at Via G Murat, near the castle. For medical assistance, go to the Ospedale Consorziale Policlinico (☎ 537 09 07), Piazza Giulio Cesare, south of the town centre, on the other side of the train lines. In an emergency, you can call an ambulance on ☎ 534 48 48. For home visits, the Guardia Medica is on ☎ 524 23 89.

Dangers & Annoyances Bari is fast developing a reputation as a drug and crime centre – this means a high rate of petty crime too. Don't overdo the paranoia, but be careful when visiting the historic centre (Bari Vecchia). Keep your valuables to a minimum and in a money belt. Women should not enter the area alone day or night, and at night most people avoid it altogether.

Bari Vecchia

Bari's main churches, the **Basilica di San Nicola** and the **cathedral**, are discussed in the box on the tour of Romanesque churches. Both are in the old town – San Nicola in the piazza of the same name, and the cathedral nearby, on Piazza Odegitria.

You could start your exploration of Bari Vecchia at Piazza Mercantile, at the northern end of Corso Cavour. In the piazza is the **Sedile**, the medieval headquarters of Bari's Council of Nobles. Set aside in one corner of the piazza is the **Colonna della Giustizia** (Column of Justice), to which it is thought debtors were tied. A fresh produce market is held in the piazza every morning from Monday to Saturday. Head along Via della Vecchia Dogana and the Lungomare Imperatore Augusto to reach the Basilica di San Nicola.

Squeezed into the uneven little alleyways of what is, after all, a small historic town centre, are some 40 churches and more than 120 little shrines dedicated to the Madonna and various saints. The inhabitants of this part of town appear to live much as their forebears did, and Bari Vecchia is certainly worth investigation – with some caution (see Dangers & Annoyances above).

Castello Svevo

Just beyond the perimeter of Bari Vecchia broods the so-called Swabian Castle, which represents four levels of history. A Norman structure was built over the ruins of a Roman fort (now being excavated). Frederick II then incorporated parts of the Norman castle into his own design, including two towers that still stand. The bastions with corner towers overhanging the moat were finally added in the 16th century during Spanish rule. Inside you'll find the **Gipsoteca**, a collection of plaster copies of Romanesque monumental decoration from throughout the region – an odd sort of idea really. The castle is open Tuesday to Sunday from 9 am to 1 pm and 4 to 7 pm (in summer at least), and admission costs L5000. Most of the castle is, however, closed to the public.

Festival
Bari's big annual event is the Festival of St Nicholas during the first weekend in May. If you can manage to be in town at the time, it is quite a spectacle. On the Saturday evening a procession of people in Norman costume leaves the castle for the Basilica di San Nicola, where they re-enact the delivery of the saint's bones to the Dominican friars. The next day, with a statue of the saint in pride of place, a procession of boats sets off along the coast.

Places to Stay
If you are aged under 30, profit from the Stop Over programme (see the Information section above). If not, there are several reasonably priced options. The HI youth hostel, the *Ostello del Levante* (☎ 32 02 82), is just west of Bari by the sea at Palese. Bed and breakfast is L14,000 a night and a meal costs L12,000. The hostel closes from 20 December to 15 January. The No 1 bus goes there from outside Teatro Petruzzelli on Corso Cavour.

If you choose to stay in a hotel, it is best to pay a bit more for security. The following are all reliable. *Albergo Romeo* (☎ 523 72 53), Via Crisanzio 12, has singles /doubles for L42,000/65,000 and triples for L75,000, all with bathroom. In the same building is *Pensione Giulia* (☎ 521 66 30), where rooms cost L45,000/70,000 or L65,000/80,000 with own bath.

Hotel Adria (☎ 52 66 99), Via L Zuppetta 10, to the right of the station, has rooms for L51,000/92,000 without bathroom, or L76,000/120,000 with. Back on Via Crisanzio, the *Albergo Moderno* (☎ 521 33 13), No 60, has rooms for L80,000/125,000. The *Grand Hotel d'Oriente* (☎ 524 40 11), Corso Cavour 32, is a lovely old-style hotel, with grand prices: L130,000/200,000. It does have a couple of small singles without bath for L85,000.

Places to Eat
You will find it difficult to eat a meal more cheaply in Bari than at *Vini e Cucina*, Strada Vallisa, just off Piazza del Ferrarese in the old city. It's hard to get much more basic than its cave-like atmosphere and paper tablecloths, though you come close at *Ristorante OK*, Via de Cesare 19, off Piazza Aldo Moro. A two-course lunch with wine here costs around L15,000.

Trattoria Verde, Via Cognetti 18, has excellent pizzas and very reasonably priced pasta and main dishes. A full meal will come to under L25,000. Nearby, *Il Sorso Preferito*, Via Vito Nicola de Nicolò 40, is a roomy old restaurant with loads of character. Again, you're looking at about L25,000.

Ristorante Porta d'Oro da Enzo, Via Principe Amedeo 12, off Corso Cavour, has excellent food for less than L25,000 for a full meal. *Al Pescatore*, Piazza Federico II di Svevia 8, is next to the castle and specialises in seafood and Apulian dishes. A full meal will cost around L40,000.

For excellent ice cream, head for *Bar Mokambo*, Via Crisanzio 72.

Getting There & Away
Air Bari's airport (☎ 538 23 70) is several km west of the city centre and services domestic flights. You can get there on the Bari-Nord train line. There is also an Alitalia airport bus, which leaves from a terminal at Via Calefati 37.

Bus Intercity buses leave from several locations around the town, depending on where you are going and with which company. SITA buses (☎ 521 37 14) depart from Via Capruzzi, on the south side of the main train station, but the ticket office is at Piazza Aldo Moro 15.

Buses serve towns including Andria, Bitonto, Castellana and Ruvo di Puglia.

APULIA

Ferrovie Appulo-Lucane buses (☎ 521 69 80) serve Altamura, also from Via Capruzzi.

Ferrovie del Sud-Est (FSE) buses (☎ 522 65 82) leave from Largo Ciaia, south of Piazza Aldo Moro, for places including Polignano, Ostuni and Taranto.

AMET buses leave Piazza Eroi del Mare for Andria, Barletta, Molfetta and Trani, and Ferrotramviaria buses leave from the same piazza for Barletta, Ruvo di Puglia, Trani and Bitonto.

Marozzi buses (☎ 521 60 04) for Rome leave from Piazza Aldo Moro. The company's office is at Corso Italia 32.

Note: It is not unheard of for enterprising locals to organise private buses in summer to ferry tourists direct to Castel del Monte (see Around Trani above) from Bari – check with the tourist office.

Train As with buses, an array of train lines connects Bari with the outside world.

From the main station (☎ 521 68 01) national FS trains go to Milan, Bologna, Pescara, Rome and cities throughout Apulia, including Foggia, Brindisi, Lecce and Taranto.

There are also private train lines. The Bari-Nord line connects the city with the airport, Bitonto, Andria and Barletta, and the station is next to the main station in Piazza Aldo Moro. The Appulo-Lucane line links Bari with Altamura, Matera and Potenza in Basilicata. The station is in Corso Italia, just off Piazza Aldo Moro.

FSE trains head for Alberobello, Castellana, Locorotondo, Martina Franca and Taranto, leaving from the station in Via Oberdan – cross under the train tracks south of Piazza Luigi di Savoia and head east along Via Giuseppe Capruzzi for about half a km. You can also pick up an FSE train for Martina Franca from the main station on platform 10.

Car & Motorbike Bari is on the A14 autostrada, which heads north-west to Foggia and south to Taranto and connects with the A16 to Naples at Canosa di Puglia. Exit at Bari-Nord to reach the centre of town. The easiest way to orient yourself is to follow the 'centro' signs to the centre and then the 'stazione' signs for the main train station and Piazza Aldo Moro.

Boat Ferry traffic to and from Bari is busy year-round, especially to Greece, but also to Albania, Croatia and Egypt. All ferry companies have offices at the ferry terminal, accessible from the train station on bus Nos 1 and 20.

Despite rumours to the contrary, you'll be lucky to find cheaper fares to Greece from Bari than Brindisi, and the trip is two hours longer.

Once you have bought your ticket and paid the embarkation tax, you will be given a boarding card, which must be stamped by the police at the ferry terminal.

The main companies and routes they served at the time of writing were:

Adriatica (☎ 553 03 60), c/o Agestea at the ferry terminal or Via Liside 4. It has boats to Durrës on Monday, Wednesday and Saturday. The one-way high season fare is L110,000.

European Seaways (☎ 521 91 68), ferry terminal, has two boats a week to Çesme (Turkey) via Greece from June to early October.

Jadrolinija (☎ 521 28 40), c/o P Lorusso & Co at the ferry terminal and at Via Piccinni 133. It runs a weekly ferry to Dubrovnik on Saturdays (L36,400 there; L27,300 back). Obviously, events in ex-Yugoslavia could at any time put an end to the service.

Poseidon Lines (☎ 521 00 22), c/o Morfimare at the ferry terminal and 36-40 Corso de Tullio. Also has frequent ferries to Patras and Igoumenitsa, charging fares on a par with those of Ventouris. Poseidon has onward links to Israel and Cyprus.

Ventouris Ferries (☎ 524 43 88), c/o Pan Travel at the ferry terminal, or at Via San Francesco d'Assisi 95. It has regular services to Corfu and Igoumenitsa (deck class L85,000; airline-type chair L105,000) and to Patras (deck class L95,000; airline-type chair L120,000). These are high season (roughly July-September) fares; they come down L15,000 for the rest of the year.

Yasco Yalta (☎ 523 88 10), at the ferry terminal, is one of several lines competing for business on the Bari-Durrës trip to Albania. Their one-way fare is L70,000 deck class. La Vikinga (agents Portrans; ☎ 523 24 29) is another line working this run.

Note: There is a L10,000 embarkation fee to Greece and L5000 to Albania and Croatia. It may be possible to get boats to Bar in Montenegro.

Getting Around

Central Bari is compact – a 15-minute walk will take you from Piazza Aldo Moro to the old town. Useful city buses are No 20 from the train station to the ferry terminal, and No 1 from Teatro Petruzzelli to the youth hostel.

THE TRULLI AREA

Trulli are unusual, circular houses made of whitewashed stone without mortar, with conical roofs. The roofs, topped with pinnacles, are tiled with concentric rows of grey slate, locally known as *chiancarella*. Many trulli have astrological or religious symbols painted on the roof.

The trulli area, in the Itria Valley, extends from Conversano and Goia del Colle in the west to Ostuni and Martina Franca in the east, but the greatest concentration of these houses is in and around Alberobello.

Alberobello

This pretty town virtually exists for tourism these days but, with whole quarters covered by nothing but trulli, it is quite unique. Declared a zone of historical importance in 1924, many of the trulli are no longer private dwellings, given over rather to souvenir and wine shops, boutiques and restaurants.

The Pro Loco tourist office is just off Piazza del Popolo at Corso Vittorio Emanuele 15 in the town centre. A private organisation, MTG (☎ 080-932 34 62), at Via C Acquaviva 11, can assist with information on accommodation, as well as excursions in the area. The telephone code is 080.

A few km west of the town is the **Chiesa di Santa Maria di Barsento**, accessible only if you have a vehicle (or by hitching). Founded in 591 AD as an abbey, the small complex features one of the oldest churches in Apulia. It is now part of a farm, but the owner is proud to show tourists around the property – which he makes available for wedding receptions. Take the road from

Alberobello to Putignano, and after six km turn left into the road for Noci. After three km you will see Barsento (signposted) to your right.

Places to Stay *Camping dei Trulli* (☎ 932 36 99) is just out of town on Via Castellana Grotte. Charges are L5000 per person and L8000 to L13,000 for a site. In the town centre, at Piazza Ferdinando IV 31, is *Hotel Lanzillotta* (☎ 72 15 11), which has singles/doubles for L33,000/50,000. The town's top hotel is the *Hotel dei Trulli* (☎ 932 35 55; fax 932 35 60), Via Cadore 32, which is a complex of trulli. They are self-contained, with bathroom and living area, and cost from L100,000 for a single to L220,000 for a double.

Trulli are also available for rent through various agencies, with charges ranging from around L100,000 a day to L600,000 a week. For further information contact Agenzia Immobiliare Fittatrulli (☎ 72 27 17), Via Duca d'Aosta 14, Alberobello.

Getting There & Away The easiest way to get to Alberobello is on the FSE private train line (Bari-Taranto). From the station, walk straight ahead along Via Mazzini, which becomes Via Garibaldi, to reach Piazza del Popolo.

Castellana Grotte

These spectacular limestone caves are among Apulia's prime attractions, and justifiably so. The series of subterranean caves, with their at times breathtaking formations of stalactites and stalagmites, were known as far back as the 17th century and were probably partially investigated in the 18th century. In the 1930s Italian speleologist Franco Anelli explored about three km of the caves, and today tourists can follow his path with a guide. After descending by elevator to a huge cavern known as La Grave, you are taken on a tour through several caves, culminating in the magnificent **Caverna Bianca**.

The caves are open all year (only in the morning from October to March) and tours leave roughly every hour. You can enter only with a guide, but in the low season they are usually prepared to make the tour even for one person only. There are two tours: a one-km, one-hour trip (L10,000) that does not include the Caverna Bianca, and the full three-km, two-hour trip (L20,000). At the time of writing the caves had been indefinitely closed for repair work to installations.

You can reach them on the FSE train line (Bari-Taranto). The station is about 150 metres from the entrance.

Martina Franca

Founded in the 10th century by refugees fleeing the Arab invasion of Taranto, Martina Franca flourished in the 14th century after it was granted tax exemptions (*franchigie*), hence the name Franca) by Philip of Anjou.

The town is at the edge of the trulli area and you'll see few of the conical constructions here, but it has an interesting historical centre, with a medieval quarter and several specimens of Baroque architecture.

A Little Romanesque Tour in Apulia

Of 18 important Romanesque churches in Apulia, only nine have been preserved in the original style. These include the cathedrals at Bari, Altamura, Barletta, Bitonto, Molfetta, Ruvo di Puglia and Trani. Another church that should be added to the list is the Basilica di San Nicola in Bari, used as a model for many of the churches built in the Apulian-Romanesque style and of exceptional architectural value.

With some careful planning, you can visit all these churches on day trips from Bari, although the town of Trani is worth a visit in its own right. If you want to make a full tour of the towns and cities where the churches are located, consider hiring a car for two or three days. This would also enable you to take in a couple of the less important Romanesque churches in the province, and include a trip to the Castel del Monte, the stunning octagonal castle of Frederick II of Swabia, about 40 km west of Bari.

The itinerary starts in **Bari** with the Basilica di San Nicola, built in the 11th century on the ruins of a Byzantine palace to house the miracle-working bones of St Nicholas, stolen by Bari mariners from their resting place in Myra (in what is now Turkey). The basilica has a stark, imposing façade, simply decorated with blind arches and mullioned windows, and flanked by two bell towers. Look for the Lion's Doorway on the basilica's north side, decorated with beautiful sculptures and bas-reliefs depicting chivalric scenes. Inside the three-naved interior there is a splendid 12th-century tabernacle, as well as a bishop's throne, known as Elia's Pulpit, sculpted in the second half of the 12th century. The remains of St Nicholas are housed in the crypt, under the transept.

Bari's 12th-century cathedral was built on the remains of a Byzantine cathedral. It retains its elegant Romanesque shape and bell tower, but has been much altered and added to over the centuries.

The cathedrals of Bitonto, Ruvo di Puglia and Molfetta lie west of Bari and can be reached easily by public transport. **Trani** and **Barletta** are farther along the coast, and Trani is a better base for seeing the cathedral there and in Barletta – see the Trani and Around Trani sections for more details. If you have the time, take a look also at the cathedrals in **Conversano** and **Palo del Colle**.

The cathedral of **Bitonto** is a particularly stunning example of Apulian-Romanesque architecture and one of the most beautiful in the region. Built in the late 12th century on the model of San Nicola in Bari, it is dedicated to St Valentine. Note the carved animals and plants that decorate the capitals on the side walls. The cathedral has been closed for some time and is not expected to reopen in the foreseeable future because of works under its main pavement. While in Bitonto, spare a moment to inspect the 17th-century Chiesa di Purgatorio, near the cathedral. Above the main door are people depicted burning in purgatory, and to the sides are two large figures of Death, dancing in what seems to be delight at these poor souls' fate. You can get to Bitonto from Bari on the private Bari-Nord train line. From the station, walk directly ahead along Via Matteotti (about one km) until you reach the medieval part of town. You'll see an Angevin tower and there are signs directing you to the cathedral, with tourist maps posted at various points.

Orientation & Information The FSE train station is downhill from the historic centre. City buses go to Piazza XX Settembre and the entrance to the old town, or you can walk to the right along Viale della Stazione, continuing along Via Alessandro Fighera to Corso Italia; continue to the left along Corso Italia to Piazza XX Settembre. The tourist office (☎ 080-70 57 02) is at Piazza Roma 37, where you can get a map of the town and advice on accommodation. The telephone code is 080.

Things to See Next to the tourist office on Piazza Roma is the 17th-century **Palazzo Ducale**, a vast edifice now used as the municipal offices. Several frescoed rooms on the 3rd floor are open to the public (free entry).

From the piazza, follow the narrow Corso Vittorio Emanuele into Piazza Plebiscito and the heart of the historic centre. Of note here is the Baroque façade of the 18th-century **Chiesa di San Martino**.

The graceful cathedral in **Ruvo di Puglia** has a particularly striking façade and boasts a fine rose window and three portals. The delicately carved central portal features columns supported by griffins, resting on (now very worn) lions, themselves supported by telamons. Ruvo is on the Bari-Nord train line. Otherwise you can take a Ferrotramviaria bus from Bari's Piazza Eroi del Mare (approximately every half-hour daily, except Sunday), which arrives at Cortugno, just off Ruvo's main piazza. The same bus also goes to Bitonto, Andria and Barletta. From the bus stop, walk to the left through the piazza and turn right into Corso Giovanni Jatta. Once you reach the park, turn right and then right again when you reach the tower, which is at the rear of the cathedral.

Molfetta is worth a stop not only for its impressively simple cathedral, but also for its largely abandoned, tumbledown medieval centre. Known as the Duomo Vecchio, the

Rose window from the
Cattedrale di Ruvo di Puglia.

cathedral was started in 1150 and completed at the end of the 13th century. It has a stark white, undecorated façade flanked by two bell towers. The interior is a mix of Romanesque, Byzantine and Muslim architecture. The medieval quarter, or Borgo Vecchio, stretches out behind the cathedral and is in a state of great disrepair, although sections are being restored. Molfetta is on the main Bari-Foggia train line, about 20 minutes from Bari. From the station, ask for directions to Via Dante and the port, near which you'll find the cathedral at Via Chiesa Vecchia.

Altamura is about 45 minutes south-west of Bari and easily accessible on the Appulo-Lucane train line (see the Getting There & Away section under Bari). Its 13th-century cathedral was erected during the reign of Frederick II but was badly damaged by an earthquake in 1316, later suffering some Baroque additions. The beautiful medieval main portal and elegant rose window were moved from their original position to what had been the apse. Both survived with little or no ill-effect and can be admired today. The cathedral is in the old town's main street, Via Federico II di Svevia. From the train station, walk straight ahead along Viale Regina Margherita to Piazza Unità d'Italia and enter the old town through Porta Bari. Ferrovie Appulo-Lucane buses also connect Bari and Altamura, arriving in Piazza Santa Teresa. From the piazza, turn right and walk to Piazza Unità d'Italia. ■

Festival The town stages the annual Festival of the Itria Valley in July and August, with concerts and opera. Information and tickets are available through the tourist office.

Places to Stay & Eat The cheapest accommodation options are both out of the town. *La Cremaillere* (☎ 70 00 52) is about six km away at San Paolo on the road to Taranto. It charges L60,000 to L70,000 for doubles with bathroom. *Da Luigi* (☎ 90 13 24) is about three km out on the road to Taranto and charges L40,000/60,000 for rooms with bathroom. Both are accessible by FSE bus from Piazza Crispi.

In town all hotels are expensive, including the *Park Hotel San Michele* (☎ 880 70 53), Viale Carella 9, which charges L130,000/200,000.

For a meal, try *Trattoria La Tavernetta*, Corso Vittorio Emanuele 30.

Getting There & Away The easiest way to reach the town is on the FSE train line (Bari-Taranto). FSE buses also connect the town with Taranto, Alberobello, Castellana Grotte and Bari, arriving in Piazza Crispi, off Corso Italia.

Ostuni

This stunning town of stark, whitewashed buildings is set on three hills east of Martina Franca and about 40 km north-west of Brindisi. The seemingly disordered tangle of narrow cobblestone streets, many little more than arched stairways between the houses, is strongly reminiscent of a North African Arab *medina*. Rising above it all in sombre brown stone is the 15th-century Gothic cathedral. Its distinctive cupolas, covered in green, yellow and white slate tiles, act like a beacon among the surrounding buildings. At night, the cathedral and parts of the medieval *borgo* are lit up in evocative fashion.

Ostuni's AAST office (☎ 0831-97 12 68) is in Piazza della Libertà, downhill from the cathedral in the newer part of town. It is open Monday to Friday from 9.30 am to 12.30 pm and 6.30 to 9 pm.

From Piazza della Libertà, take the narrow Via Cattedrale uphill to the cathedral. From the tiny piazza in front of the cathedral, turn right for a view across to the Adriatic, or turn left to get lost in Ostuni's whitewashed lanes.

Places to Stay & Eat Ostuni is an easy day trip from Brindisi, but if you want to stay, try the *Albergo Tre Torri* (☎ 33 11 14), Corso Vittorio Emanuele 298. It has rooms for L41,000/62,000. *Hotel Orchidea Nera* (☎ 30 13 66), Via Mazzini, has singles/doubles for L40,000/60,000.

There are some excellent eating places in the old town. The *Osteria del Tempo Perso* is tucked away behind the cathedral. To find it, head up Via Cattedrale and, when you reach the wall of the cathedral, turn right through the archway into Largo Giuseppe Spennati and follow the signs to the restaurant.

Getting There & Away Società Trasporti Pubblici (STP) buses run between Ostuni and Brindisi about every two hours, arriving in Piazza Italia in the newer part of Ostuni. STP buses also connect the town with Martina Franca. However, the easiest way to reach Ostuni is on the main train line from Brindisi or Bari. The No 1 city bus will take you from the station into the centre.

BRINDISI

Travellers associate Brindisi with waiting. The major embarkation point for ferries from Italy to Greece, the city swarms with people in transit. What's more, there really is very little to do here other than wait. Most backpackers gather at the train station, at the port in the ferry terminal, or in Piazza Cairoli in between the two. If your budget extends beyond minimum rations, you could while away a few hours in a trattoria.

Settled in ancient times and taken over by Rome in 3 BC, Brindisi is a natural safe harbour that prospered under the Romans and retained its importance until after the period of the crusades. Invasion, plague and earthquake brought about decline, but today it is again a busy merchant and passenger port.

Orientation
The port is about 10 minutes' walk from the train station along Corso Umberto I, which becomes Corso Garibaldi. There are numerous take-away food outlets along the route, as well as a bewildering array of ferry companies and travel agents.

Information
Tourist Office The EPT office (☎ 0831-52 19 44) is at Viale Regina Margherita 12, a short walk from the end of Corso Garibaldi and the ferry terminal (turn left once you reach the waterfront). It is open Monday to Saturday from 8.30 am to 12.30 pm and 4.30 to 7.30 pm.

Money There are numerous exchange offices between the station and the port. Check the rates and choose the best. Otherwise, good old-fashioned banks abound. The Banco Ambrosiano Veneto next to the post office has an ATM that accepts Visa, MasterCard and some other cards, as does Monte dei Paschi di Siena at Corso Garibaldi 112.

If you need an emergency injection of funds from home (and you're an American), you could try Mail Boxes Etc, Via Palestro 9, which is hooked up with the Western Union money transfer group.

Post & Telecommunications The main post office is in Piazza Mercato Coperto, off Corso Garibaldi. It's open Monday to Saturday from 8.15 am to 7.40 pm. The post code for central Brindisi is 72100.

The Telecom office is at Via XX Settembre 6. It opens from 9.15 am to 12.50 pm and 3.30 to 6.30 pm. The telephone code is 0831.

Emergency For police attendance, call ☎ 113. For medical attention, go to the public hospital, the Ospedale Generale Antonio di Summa (☎ 52 14 10), Piazza Antonio di Summa, west of the train station, off Via Appia. The same number is good for ambulances.

Dangers & Annoyances Brindisi is a thieves' paradise – try not to be an angel to them. Valuables should be carried in a money belt, and nothing of remote interest should be left unattended in your car. Women are advised not to walk through the town alone at night.

Brindisi is extremely busy in summer, so if you arrive by car, allow extra time for the eternal traffic jam around the port.

One word on taxis – you do not need one. Travellers arriving late in the evening are perfect victims for the line that, 'If you get a taxi, you might just make the last ferry'. Keep your cool, and walk right down to the port (if your bags will allow it), as the roundabout ride in the taxi will probably take longer. When you arrive and the ferry has inevitably left, you will of course be offered further rides to hotels.

Things to See & Do
For the Romans, Brindisi was the end of the line, or more specifically of the Via Appia. For centuries, two great columns marked the end of the imperial highway. One remains, near the waterfront (the other was removed to Lecce and only its pedestal remains). Tradition has it that the Roman poet Virgil died in a house near here after returning from a voyage to Greece.

A little farther in from the waterfront, the modest **duomo** was originally built in the 11th century but substantially remodelled about 700 years later. Next door is a small **Museo Archeologico**. Across the quiet little square is Palazzo Balsamo, an otherwise undistinguished building that sports a noteworthy **loggia**.

If you are hanging around Brindisi for any length of time, you might eye over the **Castello Svevo**, another of Frederick II's monuments to militarism. Turn left from the train station and walk straight on to get there.

The town's main sight is the **Chiesa di Santa Maria del Casale**, four km north of

APULIA

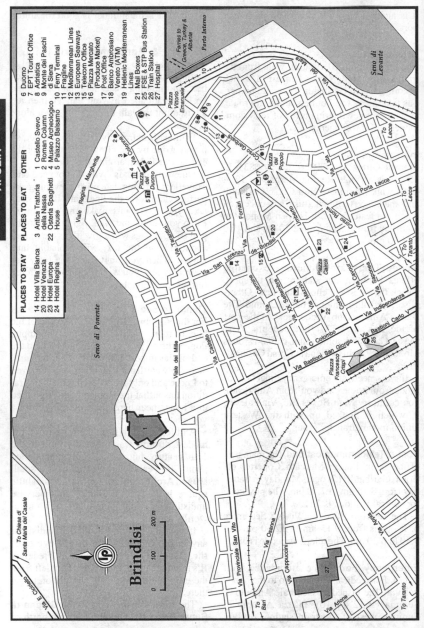

Brindisi

0   100   200 m

PLACES TO STAY
14 Hotel Villa Bianca
20 Hotel Venezia
23 Hotel Europa
24 Hotel Regina

PLACES TO EAT
3 Antica Trattoria della Nassa
22 Osteria Spaghetti House

OTHER
1 Castello Svevo
2 Roman Column
4 Museo Archeologico
5 Palazzo Balsamo
6 Duomo
7 EPT Tourist Office
8 Adriatica
9 Monte dei Paschi di Siena
10 Ferry Terminal
11 Fragline
12 Mediterranean Lines
13 European Seaways
15 Telecom Office
16 Piazza Mercato (Produce Market)
17 Post Office
18 Banco Ambrosiano Veneto (ATM)
19 Hellenic Mediterranean Lines
21 Mail Boxes
25 FSE & STP Bus Station
26 Train Station
27 Hospital

LAUREN SUNSTEIN

DAMIEN SIMONIS

DAMIEN SIMONIS

Top: Trulli outside Alberobello, Apulia
ttom Left: Trulli, Alberobello, Apulia
om Right: Scanno, Abruzzo

Top Left: Detail of the Baroque Basilica della Santa Croce, Lecce, Apulia
Top Right: Medieval harbour, Trani, Apulia
Bottom Left: Street vendor of home-made eucalyptus cough drops, Altamura, Apulia
Bottom Right: Detail of the Chiesa di San Michele, Ruvo di Apulia

the centre. Built by Prince Philip of Taranto around 1300, it is a Romanesque church with Gothic and Byzantine touches. To get there, follow Via Provinciale San Vito round the Seno di Ponente bay. The road becomes first Via E Ciciriello and then Via R de Simone.

Places to Stay
The non-HI *Ostello per la Gioventù* (☎ 41 31 23) is about two km out of town at Via N Brandi 2. B&B costs L15,000 a night (or 10% less if you happen to have a train ticket – a strange deal). Take bus No 3 or 4 from Via Cristoforo Colombo near the train station.

Hotel Venezia (☎ 52 75 11), Via Pisanelli 4, has singles/doubles for L25,000/40,000. Turn left off Corso Umberto I onto Via San Lorenzo da Brindisi. The *Hotel Villa Bianca* (☎ 2 54 38), Via Armengol 21 (farther on along Via San Lorenzo da Brindisi), has rooms for L28,000/40,000, and doubles with bathroom for L44,000. The *Hotel Europa* (☎ 52 85 46), Piazza Cairoli, has clean, basic rooms for L30,000/45,000, and L45,000/70,000 with bathroom. More upmarket is the *Hotel Regina* (☎ 56 20 01), Via Cavour 5 (take Via Cappellini off Piazza Cairoli and turn left), which charges L85,000/110,000.

Places to Eat
To pick up supplies for the boat trip, shop at the Sidis supermarket in Piazza Cairoli. A colourful fresh food market is held every morning from Monday to Saturday in Piazza Mercato, just around the corner from the post office. There are plenty of take-away outlets between the train station and port.

For a proper feed, head for the side streets off this route. The *Osteria Spaghetti House*, Via Mazzini 57, near the station, has down-to-earth meals for around L20,000. *Pizzeria/Ristorante Carlo V* in Piazzetta Ignazio Falconieri has good pizzas, served at outdoor tables. The *Antica Trattoria della Nassa*, Via Colonne 49, has good meals for around L30,000.

Entertainment
Musical and cultural events are held in Brindisi throughout the year, including Estate Insieme in July and August. Get a brochure from the tourist office if you are in town for a while.

Getting There & Away
Bus STP (☎ 52 37 31) and FSE buses connect Brindisi with Ostuni and towns throughout the Salentine Peninsula. Most leave from Via Bastioni Carlo V in front of the train station.

Marozzi has three daily express buses to Rome (Stazione Tiburtina). Two leave at 11 am and the other at 10.30 pm from Viale Regina Margherita. Tickets cost L49,000 or L53,000, depending on the speed of the service. The trip takes up to nine hours. Appia Travel (☎ 52 16 84), Viale Regina Margherita 8-9, sells tickets.

Train Brindisi is on the main FS train line, with regular services to Bari, Lecce and Taranto, as well as to Ancona, Bologna, Milan, Naples and Rome.

Car & Motorbike Brindisi is easy to reach by road. Watch out for the superstrada exit for the 'porto' or 'Grecia' (Greece). In summer the port area becomes one big traffic jam, so allow plenty of time to board your ferry.

Boat Ferries leave Brindisi for Greek destinations including Corfu (nine hours), Igoumenitsa (10½ hours), Patras (approximately 17 hours) and Cefalonia (approximately 16 hours). From Patras there is a bus to Athens. Ferries also service Turkey and Albania. The main companies are given below:

Adriatica (☎ 52 38 25), Corso Garibaldi 85-87, is one of only two companies to run ferries to Greece all year round

European Seaways (☎ 52 76 67), c/o Discovery, Corso Garibaldi 49, has departures from Brindisi for Çesme (Turkey) on Tuesdays and Wednesdays from June to early October. Deck class starts at L200,000

APULIA

Fragline (☎ 52 95 61), Corso Garibaldi 88; stops running ships from November to the end of February

Hellenic Mediterranean Lines (☎ 52 85 31), Corso Garibaldi 8, has boats from March to October, and offers a wide range of destinations in Greece

Illyria Lines (☎ 52 83 33), c/o Agenzia Marittima Silver, Corso Garibaldi 95, has three services a week to Durrës and four a week to Vlora

Mediterranean Lines (☎ 22 23 77), c/o Agenzia Marittima Angelo Titi, Corso Garibaldi 83, has ferries from April through to the end of September

Vergina Ferries (☎ 52 83 33), c/o Agenzia Marittima Silver, Corso Garibaldi 95, operates boats in the off season

Companies sometimes change hands or names, and many only operate in summer. When you get to Brindisi, shop around. Most agents can sell tickets for most lines – ask to see the company brochures if you are in any doubt about what you are paying.

Adriatica and Hellenic are the most expensive, but also the most reliable. They are the only lines that can officially accept Eurail passes and Inter-Rail passes, which means you pay nothing to go deck class, a L29,000 supplement for an airline-style seat or L45,000 for a cabin bed. If you want to use your Eurail or Inter-Rail pass, you may need to reserve some weeks in advance, particularly in summer. Holders of the Italian Tourist Ticket and the Italy Flexi Railcard are entitled to a 30% reduction. You can usually get a discount (up to about 20%) on the return leg if you buy it with the out-going trip.

You must check in at least two hours prior to departure, or risk losing your reservation (a strong possibility in the high season). You have to pay a L10,000 port tax.

Fares increase by up to 40% in July and August (ferry services also increase during this period). At the time of writing, July/August prices for Adriatica ferries to Patras were L100,000 (deck class), L120,000 (airline-type chair), L195,000 (shared cabin), or L240,000 (2nd-class, two-bed cabin). Adriatica charges the same regardless of your destination in Greece. Other companies differentiate fares according to where you're going.

Bring warm clothing and a sleeping bag if you are planning to travel deck class. The airline-type chairs are packed into rooms that are generally noisy and smoky. First-class cabins are also available with private services. All boats have snack bars and restaurants but, to save money, buy supplies in Brindisi.

Bicycles can usually be taken free of charge. At the time of writing, Adriatica's fares for other vehicles to Corfu/Igoumenitsa were L50,000 for motorbikes and L115,000 for cars. Hellenic charged L215,000 for caravans and minibuses.

LECCE

Baroque architecture can be grotesque, but never in Lecce. The style here is so refined and particular to the city that the Italians call it *barocco leccese*, Lecce Baroque. There is a more prosaic explanation for why the Leccesi went to such ornate lengths. The local stone is particularly malleable, but after it's been quarried it hardens – the perfect building and sculpting material.

A graceful and intellectual city, close to both the Adriatic and Ionian seas, Lecce makes an agreeable base from which to explore the Salentine Peninsula.

It is worth whiling away a few days in Lecce. Certainly there are enough Baroque churches and palazzi to keep you busy, and the numerous bars and restaurants are a pleasant surprise in such a small city.

History

A settlement of ancient origins, Lecce was overrun in the 3rd century BC by the Romans, who named it Lupiae. While relatively little is known of this period, Lecce boasts the remains of an imposing Roman amphitheatre, which stand in the main square, Piazza Sant'Oronzo. The city passed to the Byzantines, Normans and Swabians, but it was in the 16th to 18th centuries that it really came into its own, when it was embellished with splendid Renaissance and, most notably, Baroque buildings.

Orientation

The train station is about one km south-west of Lecce's historic centre. To get to the centre, walk straight ahead from the station and turn right into Viale Gallipoli, then left at Piazza Argento into Viale Francesco Lo Re. At the end of this street, turn left again to reach Piazza Sant'Oronzo and the city centre. Regular local buses run from the station to Viale Marconi (get off when you see the castle). From the bus station in Via Adua, turn left and walk to the Porta Napoli. Turn right and follow Via G Palmieri, turn left into Via Vittorio Emanuele and continue until you reach Piazza Sant'Oronzo.

If you have a car, the easiest point to enter the city centre is through the Porta Napoli, a 16th-century gate into the old city, just off the ring road. From the gate, follow Via Principe di Savoia and turn right into Corso Umberto I to reach Piazza Sant'Oronzo.

Information

Tourist Office The EPT office (☎ 0832-30 44 43) is in Piazza Sant'Oronzo, in the building known as Il Sedile. It is open Monday to Friday from 9 am to 1 pm and 5.30 to 7.30 pm, Saturday to 1 pm only.

Money Branches of the main banks are in Piazza Sant'Oronzo, including the Banca Nazionale del Lavoro at No 39, which has an ATM friendly to Visa and MasterCards.

Post & Telecommunications The main post office is in Piazza Libertini, along Via Salvatore Trinchese from Piazza Sant' Oronzo. The post code for central Lecce is 73100.

There is a Telecom office, with telephones outside at Via Oberdan 13. The telephone code for Lecce is 0832.

Travel Agency CTS (☎ 30 18 62) has an office at Via Palmieri 91.

Emergency For immediate police attendance, call ☎ 113. The public hospital, the Ospedale Vito Fazzi (☎ 68 51), is in Piazza F Bottazzi, south-east of the centre off Viale XX Settembre. For an ambulance, call ☎ 66 54 11.

Basilica della Santa Croce

Little can prepare you for the opulence of the most celebrated example of Lecce Baroque. Artists including Cesare Penna, Francesco Antonio Zimbalo and Giuseppe Zimbalo worked for 150 years through the 16th and 17th centuries to decorate the building, creating an extraordinarily ornate façade, divided in two by a large balcony supported by 13 caryatids and fantastic figures. The interior is more faithful to the Renaissance style, but merits a look if you can recover from the impact of the exterior. Giuseppe Zimbalo also left his mark in the two-storey **Palazzo del Governo** stretching to the left of the Basilica, formerly a convent.

Piazza del Duomo

Although it falls short of the Basilica della Santa Croce, the Baroque feast continues in Piazza del Duomo. The almost unassuming 12th-century **duomo** was completely restored in the Baroque style by Giuseppe Zimbalo, who was also responsible for the 70-metre-high **bell tower**. Also in the piazza is the 15th-century **Palazzo Vescovile** (Episcopal Palace), which was reconstructed in 1632. Of note is its beautiful 1st-floor loggia. Opposite the cathedral is the **Seminario** (seminary), designed by Giuseppe Cino and completed in 1709. Its elegant façade features two levels of windows balanced by a fine portal. Cino also designed the well in the seminary courtyard.

Other Churches

On the way from the duomo to Piazza Sant' Oronzo, in Corso Vittorio Emanuele, is another example of Lecce Baroque, the **Chiesa di Sant'Irene**, completed in 1639. Other Baroque churches of interest include the **Santa Teresa** and the **Rosario** (the last work of Giuseppe Zimbalo) in Via Libertini, and the **Santa Chiara** in Piazza Vittorio Emanuele. The **Chiesa di SS Nicolò e Cataldo** was built by the Normans in 1180

APULIA

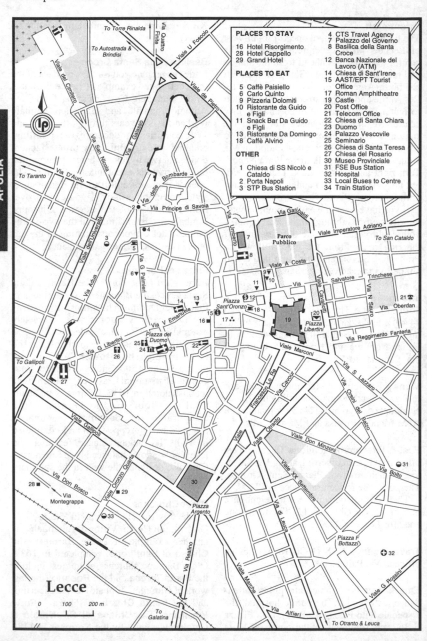

PLACES TO STAY
16 Hotel Risorgimento
28 Hotel Cappello
29 Grand Hotel

PLACES TO EAT
5 Caffè Paisiello
6 Carlo Quinto
9 Pizzeria Dolomiti
10 Ristorante da Guido e Figli
11 Snack Bar Da Guido e Figli
13 Ristorante Da Domingo
18 Caffè Alvino

OTHER
1 Chiesa di SS Nicolò e Cataldo
2 Porta Napoli
3 STP Bus Station

4 CTS Travel Agency
7 Palazzo del Governo
8 Basilica della Santa Croce
12 Banca Nazionale del Lavoro (ATM)
14 Chiesa di Sant'Irene
15 AAST/EPT Tourist Office
17 Roman Amphitheatre
19 Castle
20 Post Office
21 Telecom Office
22 Chiesa di Santa Chiara
23 Duomo
24 Palazzo Vescovile
25 Seminario
26 Chiesa di Santa Teresa
27 Chiesa del Rosario
30 Museo Provinciale
31 Hospital
32 FSE Bus Station
33 Local Buses to Centre
34 Train Station

Lecce

0   100   200 m

and rebuilt in 1716 by Cino. The Romanesque rose window and portal were retained in his new design. It is along Via San Nicola from the Porta Napoli.

Roman Remains
Excavated below the level of Piazza Sant'Oronzo is the 2nd century AD **Roman amphitheatre**, discovered in the 1930s. It's in reasonable condition, and open from 8.30 am to 4 pm (to 2 pm on Sunday). Admission is free. Virtually next door stands the **Colonna di Sant'Oronzo**, one of the two columns that marked the end of the Via Appia at Brindisi. It was moved to Lecce and a statue of the city's patron saint placed on top.

Museo Provinciale
The museum, in Viale Gallipoli near the train station, houses a collection of Roman artefacts and religious treasures from later periods. The museum is open Monday to Friday from 9 am to 1.30 pm and 2.30 to 7.30 pm, Sunday from 9 am to 1.30 pm (closed Saturdays). Admission is free.

Places to Stay
Cheap accommodation is non-existent in Lecce, but you could try campsites elsewhere in the Salentine Peninsula. Near Lecce is *Torre Rinalda* (☎ 65 21 61), near the sea at Torre Rinalda. It costs up to L9000 per person and L10,000 for a site. You can get there by STP bus from the terminal in Via Adua.

In town, try the *Hotel Cappello* (☎ 30 88 81), Via Montegrappa 4, near the station. Singles/doubles are L50,000/80,000 with bathroom. The *Grand Hotel* (☎ 30 94 05), near the station at Viale Oronzo Quarta 28, has rooms for L65,000/115,000 with bathroom and breakfast – frankly too much. *Hotel Risorgimento* (☎ 24 21 25), Via Imperatore Augusto 19, is just off Piazza Sant'Oronzo. Its very pleasant rooms cost L80,000/150,000 with bathroom.

Places to Eat
Eating in Lecce is a pleasure and needn't be expensive. There is a fresh produce market every morning from Monday to Saturday in Piazza Libertini, off Via Salvatore Trinchese. A good café for breakfast is *Caffè Alvino* at Piazza Sant'Oronzo 30, and *Caffè Paisiello*, on Piazzetta Bonifacio IX, is another of many good cafés around town.

The *Snack Bar Da Guido e Figlio*, Via Trinchese 10, is popular for a quick bite. The restaurant of the same name around the corner at Via XXV Luglio 14 serves good local food at around L8000 for pasta and L10,000 for a main. For a decent pizza, eat in or take-away, try *Pizzeria Dolomiti*, Viale A Costa 5. A cheerful, moderately priced place with a garden dining area is the *Ristorante Da Domingo*, Viale Vittorio Emanuele 48.

Carlo Quinto, Via G Palmieri 46, is one of the town's better restaurants and a full meal will cost from L50,000 to L70,000.

Entertainment
In summer there are numerous musical and cultural events, notably the Estate Musicale Leccese in July and August, and a series of classical concerts in August and September. Seasons of theatre and music continue throughout the year and information is available at the EPT office.

Getting There & Away
Bus STP buses connect Lecce with towns throughout the Salentine Peninsula, including Galatina and Leuca, from the terminal in Via Adua. FSE buses leave from Via Boito, the continuation of Viale Don Minzoni, off Viale Otranto, for towns including Gallipoli, Otranto and Taranto.

Train Lecce is directly linked by train to Bari, Brindisi, Rome, Naples and Bologna. FSE trains also depart from the main station for Taranto, Bari, Otranto, Gallipoli and Martina Franca.

Car & Motorbike Brindisi is 30 minutes away from Lecce by superstrada, and the SS7 ter goes to Taranto.

APULIA

The Spider Dance

Tarantism, a ritual that had its roots in the mass manias that swept Europe during the Middle Ages, survives in the small town of Galatina. While many will know of the folk dance known as the tarantella, few would be aware that it developed from this dance ritual performed by people known as *tarantolati*, victims of a spider bite. The bite was thought to be that of a tarantula, but in reality was probably inflicted by one of two smaller spiders found in the region, whose bite can produce pain, fear, vomiting and hallucinations.

Once a person believed they had been bitten, the only way to rid themselves of the poison was to perform a frenzied dance. Victims would go into a trance, sometimes dancing for days before collapsing in exhaustion. The phenomenon gave rise to travelling troupes of musicians, who would arrive to provide the musical accompaniment. Professor Ernesto de Martino, an expert on the subject, published the classic *La Terra del Rimorso* (The Land of Remorse) after studying the phenomenon in the Salentine Peninsula in the late 1950s. ∎

Getting Around

The historic centre of Lecce is easily seen on foot. However, useful buses include Nos 1, 3 and 4, which run from the train station to Viale G Marconi. Ask the bus driver to let you off near Piazza Sant'Oronzo.

GALATINA

The small town of Galatina, 18 km south of Lecce, is almost the only place where the ritual of tarantism is still practised (see the boxed information about The Spider Dance). Each year, on the feast day of Sts Peter & Paul (29 June), the ritual is performed at the church dedicated to the saints (now deconsecrated).

Galatina is accessible by STP bus from Lecce.

OTRANTO

Founded in antiquity and long a base of Byzantine power in Italy, Otranto is the easternmost settlement in Italy. In 1480, the Byzantines' successors in Constantinople, the Turks, landed in Otranto and took the place apart, massacring the inhabitants: an event known to history as the Sack of Otranto.

Otranto makes a good place to start a coastal tour of the Salentine Peninsula. It's obviously easier for those with their own transport, but travellers without wheels will find that local bus companies manage to link all the towns in the peninsula. Otranto itself is overrun in summer with Italian holiday-makers.

Information

The tourist office is at Via Pantaleone 12, near the Guardia Medica (first-aid clinic). The telephone code in Otranto is 0836.

Things to See

First built by the Normans in the 11th century and subsequently subjected to several face-lifts, the Romanesque cathedral, or **Basilica**, has several attractions, including a restored 12th-century floor mosaic. Depicting the tree of life and other scenes of myth and legend, it is a masterpiece unrivalled in southern Italy. 'Rex Arturis', or King Arthur as he is more commonly known to Anglo-Saxons, is depicted on horseback near the top of the mosaic. An earlier mosaic from the 4th century, discovered 40 cm below the surface, is to be put on display.

In the chapel to the right of the altar is one of the south's more bizarre sights. The walls are lined with glass cases filled with hundreds of skulls and other bones, the remains of the victims (they say there were 800) of the terrible Sack of Otranto. It is said that the town never really recovered from the slaughter. The cathedral is open from 8 am to noon and 3 pm to sunset. Next door is a small museum, open from 10 am to 1 pm and 3 to 5 pm.

The tiny Byzantine **Chiesa di San Pietro** contains some well-preserved Byzantine paintings.

The Aragonese **castle**, at the eastern edge of town beside the port, is typical of the squat, thick-walled forts you'll find in coastal towns throughout Apulia. Built in the late 15th century, it is characterised by cylindrical towers that widen towards the base. The castle is in the process of restoration.

Places to Stay & Eat

There are several camp sites in or near Otranto. The *Hydrusa* (☎ 80 12 55) near the port is basic and cheap. Of the dozen or so hotels in the area, *Il Gabbiano* (☎ 80 12 51), Via Porto Craulo 5, is one of the cheapest at L50,000/L80,000 for singles/doubles. The *Bellavista* (☎ 80 10 58), Via Vittorio Emanuele 19, has rooms for around the same price.

There are fruit and grocery shops along Corso Garibaldi, on the way from the port to the town centre. A bright place for a meal or just a drink is *La Duchesca* on the cheery square in front of the castle.

Getting There & Away

A Marozzi bus runs daily from Rome to Brindisi, Lecce and Otranto, arriving at the port. Enquire at Ellade Viaggi (☎ 80 15 78) at the port for information. Otranto can be reached from Lecce by FSE train or bus.

Ferries leave from here for Corfu and Igoumenitsa in Greece. For information and reservations, go to Ellade Viaggi at the port. Linee Lauro (☎ 90 10 05) has boats to Vlora in Albania on Mondays, Wednesdays and Saturdays. The one-way fare is L60,000.

AROUND OTRANTO

The road south from Otranto takes you along a wild coastline. The land here is rocky, and when the sea wind is up you can see why it is largely treeless. This is no Costa Azzura or Amalfi coast, but it gives you a rare feeling

in Italy, that of being well off the beaten tourist track. Many of the towns here started life as Greek settlements, and the older folk still speak Greek in some parts. There are few monuments to be seen, but the occasional solitary tower appears looking out to sea. When you reach **Santa Maria di Leuca**, you've hit the bottom of the heel of Italy, and the dividing line between the Adriatic and Ionian seas. Here as in other small Salentine towns, summer sees an influx of Italians in search of seaside relaxation, and the Ionian side of the Salentine Peninsula in particular is spattered with reasonable beaches. There are few cheap hotels in the area, but you'll stumble across a lot of camp sites around the coast.

GALLIPOLI

Jutting out almost cheekily into the Ionian Sea 50 km north-west of Santa Maria di Leuca, the picturesque old town of Gallipoli is actually an island connected to the mainland and modern city by a bridge. An important fishing centre, it has a history of strong-willed independence, being the last Salentine settlement to succumb to the Normans in the 11th century.

The entrance to the medieval island-town is guarded by an Angevin **castle**. On the other side of the bridge, in the modern part of the town, is the so-called **Fontana Ellenistica**. Reconstructed in the 16th century, it is doubtful that any of what you see is truly Hellenistic. Through the maze of narrow lanes in the old town, you will find the 17th-century Baroque **cathedral**, crammed with paintings by local artists. A little farther west, the **Museo Civico** contains a mixed bag of ancient artefacts, paintings and other odds and ends. A walk around the town perimeter is a pleasant diversion.

Should you want to stay, the pick is the *Pensione Al Pescatore* (☎ 0833-26 43 31), Riviera Colombo, in the old town. Spacious, modern rooms cost L50,000/80,000. For food, you could try *Trattoria La Tonnara*, Via Garibaldi 7, near the cathedral. It is one of several restaurants in the old town.

APULIA

FSE buses and trains link Gallipoli to Lecce. The station is in the modern town at Via XX Settembre.

TARANTO

An ideal location for a protected port, Taranto has always looked to the sea. It is Italy's second naval port after La Spezia, and during WW II the bulk of Italy's fleet was bottled up here by the British. The city was also bombed, but the present state of decline of the Città Vecchia (old town) seems more the result of neglect than enemy shellfire.

One of the city's more interesting claims to fame is that it was allegedly the point where the first cat landed on European shores.

History

Founded around the beginning of the 7th century BC by exiles from Sparta, Taras, as it was then known, became one of the wealthiest and most important colonies of Magna Graecia. At the height of its power, the city was home to some 300,000 people. In the 3rd century BC, growing friction between powerful Taras and the rising might of Rome culminated in the conquest of the city in 272 BC after a long war. The Romans changed its name to Tarentum, although Greek customs and laws were maintained.

During the Second Punic War, part of Tarentum's populace sided with Hannibal's Carthaginians, who in fact occupied the city. Unfortunately, they backed the wrong horse. After Hannibal's defeat the Romans returned, promptly punishing the traitors, pillaging the city's treasures and sending many of its people into slavery. In following centuries the city was subject, as was much of the rest of southern Italy, to invasion and foreign domination.

In WW II, when Italy was stepping up pressure on Greece, Taranto was Italy's main fleet base. British aircraft-carriers launched a torpedo-bomber strike on 11 November 1940 that sank three vessels, including the new battleship *Littorio*, for one British plane lost – a blow from which the Italian war effort never recovered.

Orientation

Taranto can be divided in two. The old city is on an island between the port and train station to the west and the new city to the east. You'll find the more expensive hotels, tourist office and banks in the modern grid of the new city.

From the train station, take bus Nos 1/2 or 8 to the centre of the new town. It is really not advisable to walk through the old city with a backpack or luggage, but if you want to take the risk, walk straight ahead from the station along Viale Duca d'Aosta, cross the bridge (Ponte Porta Napoli) and the Piazza Fontana and continue along the waterfront on Via Cariati, which becomes Via Garibaldi. At the end of the street, turn right to reach the bridge to the new city.

If you arrive in Taranto by car, particularly from the east, you will find the drive from the state road into the centre of town a long one. Simply follow the familiar 'centro' signs and aim to reach Lungomare Vittorio Emanuele III, a good point of reference.

Information

Tourist Office Taranto's EPT office (☎ 099-453 23 92) is at Corso Umberto I 113, on the corner of Via Acclavio. It is open Monday to Friday from 9.30 am to 1 pm and 5 to 7 pm (4.30 to 6.30 pm in winter), Saturday from 9.30 am to 1 pm.

Post & Telecommunications The main post office is on Lungomare Vittorio Emanuele III, a short distance from the Canale Navigabile that separates the new and old cities. The post code is 74100.

There is a public Telecom office slightly farther along the Lungomare, open Monday to Friday from 9.15 am to 12.30 pm and 4 to 7.15 pm. The telephone code is 099.

Travel Agency There is a CTS office (☎ 453 33 50) at Via Matteotti 1, near the bridge to the old city.

Emergency For immediate police attendance, call ☎ 113. The public hospital, the Ospedale SS Annunziata (☎ 98 51), is on

Via Bruno. Follow the Lungomare Vittorio Emanuele III and turn left at Via de Noto.

Dangers & Annoyances Travellers need to be alert in Taranto, particularly in the old city. Carry all valuables in a money belt and be especially cautious at night in the old city. Women should try to be indoors before the evening crowds disperse.

Città Vecchia

Taranto's old city is in an extremely dilapidated state, although recent years have seen

some efforts to renovate its palaces and churches. The **Castello Aragonese**, at the island's southern extreme on the Canale Navigabile, was completed in 1492. It is occupied by the Italian navy.

The 11th-century **duomo**, in the centre of the old city on Via del Duomo, is one of the oldest Romanesque churches in Apulia. Remodelled in the 18th century, its three-nave interior is divided by 16 ancient marble columns with Romanesque and Byzantine capitals. Its Cappella di San Cataldo is a fine example of Baroque architecture and is decorated with frescoes and inlaid marble. The

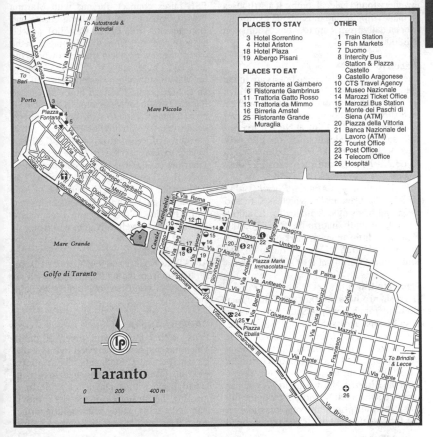

PLACES TO STAY
3 Hotel Sorrentino
4 Hotel Ariston
18 Hotel Plaza
19 Albergo Pisani

PLACES TO EAT
2 Ristorante al Gambero
6 Ristorante Gambrinus
11 Trattoria Gatto Rosso
13 Trattoria da Mimmo
16 Birreria Amstel
25 Ristorante Grande Muraglia

OTHER
1 Train Station
5 Fish Markets
7 Duomo
8 Intercity Bus Station & Piazza Castello
9 Castello Aragonese
10 CTS Travel Agency
12 Museo Nazionale
14 Marozzi Ticket Office
15 Marozzi Bus Station
17 Monte dei Paschi di Siena (ATM)
20 Piazza della Vittoria
21 Banca Nazionale del Lavoro (ATM)
22 Tourist Office
23 Post Office
24 Telecom Office
26 Hospital

Taranto

whole cathedral is dedicated to San Cataldo, Taranto's patron saint.

Visit the **fish markets** on Via Cariati, where the morning's remarkably varied catch is on display. Taranto has been famous since antiquity for its seafood, in particular its shellfish.

Museo Nazionale

In the new city, the archaeological museum at Corso Umberto I 41 is one of the most important in Italy. It houses a fascinating collection that traces the development of Greek Taras, including sculpture and pottery, as well as a display of magnificent gold jewellery found in local tombs. It also houses Roman sculpture and mosaics. The museum is open daily from 9 am to 2 pm. Admission is L8000.

Places to Stay

The city's only really cheap hotels are in the old city, on Piazza Fontana near the bridge leading to the train station. Women on their own should not stay in this area. The *Hotel Sorrentino* (☎ 470 74 56), at No 7, is reasonable and has singles/doubles for L25,000/ 50,000. Next door is the *Hotel Ariston* (☎ 470 75 63), at No 15, with rooms for L27,000/ 42,000.

In the new city is *Albergo Pisani* (☎ 453 40 87), Via Cavour 43, which is safe and clean and has singles/doubles for L38,000/ 73,000, or with bathroom for L70,000/ 95,000. A little more upmarket, the *Hotel Plaza* (☎ 459 07 75), Via D'Aquino 46, has better rooms starting at L100,000/140,000.

Places to Eat

A fresh-produce market is held every morning from Monday to Saturday in Piazza Castello, just across the Canale Navigabile. For a meal, try the *Trattoria da Mimmo*, Via Giovinazzi, or the *Trattoria Gatto Rosso* at Via Cavour 2. Both offer good food for under L25,000 a full meal.

At the *Birreria*, Via d'Aquino 27, you can choose between self-service, pizza or the full menu, and all prices are very reasonable. For fresh seafood at moderate prices, head

straight for *Ristorante Gambrinus*, Via Cariati 24. A dish costs L8000, and with the fish markets just opposite, how can you go wrong?

Ristorante al Gambero in Piazzale Democrate, across the Ponte Porta Napoli overlooking the old city, is the pricey version. You won't get away for under L50,000 for a full meal.

There are a couple of Chinese restaurants in town, including the *Grande Muraglia*, Via Berardi 64, which has a set menu for L13,500.

Getting There & Away

FSE buses connect Taranto with Martina Franca, Alberobello, Castellana Grotte and Bari (leaving from Piazza Castello), as well as Ostuni (leaving from Via Magnaghi, in the east of the new city) and smaller towns in the area. SITA buses leave from Piazza Castello for Matera, stopping at Castellaneta, and also go to Metaponto. Chiruzzi buses also leave Piazza Castello for Metaponto. STP and FSE buses connect Taranto with Lecce. For full details on other intercity bus services, ask at the tourist office. Marozzi (☎ 459 40 89) has several express services to Rome's Stazione Tiburtina (L60,000), or you can pick them up for Bari. They leave from Via Cavour. The ticket office is at Corso Umberto I 67.

Trains (both FS and FSE) connect Taranto with Brindisi, Bari, Martina Franca and Alberobello, as well as Naples and Rome.

Getting Around

AMAT bus Nos 1, 2 and 8 will come in useful for the trip from the station to the new city if you want to avoid carrying luggage through the old city.

CASTELLANETA

Fans of that great Latin lover, Rudolph Valentino, might be interested to know that he was born at Castellaneta, about 40 km west of Taranto. The town had long contented itself with a plaque on Via Roma marking the birthplace of the silent movie star, and a short, gaudy statue a little farther down the road. Oh, and they named a street and a park after him. In 1994 the town authorities saw fit to open a memorabilia museum to him. The museum is at Via Municipio 19 and opens from 10 am to 1 pm and 4 pm to 6 pm.

The whitewashed houses and flagstone lanes of the old town are not entirely without charm, and you can get there from Taranto by the SITA bus for Matera (from Piazza Castello). It is also on the FSE train line.

Basilicata

This small and much neglected region stretches across Italy's 'instep', incorporating the provinces of Potenza and Matera and brief strips of coastline on the Tyrrhenian and Ionian seas. No longer the desolate, malaria-ridden land of poverty-stricken peasants so powerfully described by Carlo Levi in his novel *Christ Stopped at Eboli*, Basilicata retains a strong sense of isolation and is still one of Italy's poorest regions.

Known to the Romans as Lucania (a name revived by Mussolini during the Fascist period), Basilicata is a mountainous region with large tracts of barren and eroded wasteland, the result of systematic deforestation over the centuries. Government subsidies and industrialisation programmes since the boom of the 1960s have rid Basilicata of disease and have improved communications, but economic progress has been slow. You don't have to wander far off the main arteries to see peasants still working this ungiving land or driving small raggedy herds of sheep across the stony hills in much the same way as they always have.

Don't come to Basilicata expecting to find a treasure chest of art, architecture and ancient history. The region's dramatic landscape, particularly the Tyrrhenian coast, and its close connection with the peasant culture of which Levi wrote are its main attractions,

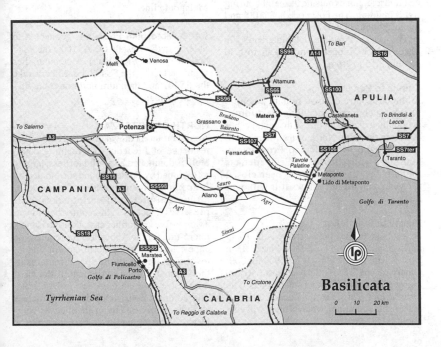

along with the strange and fascinating city of Matera.

POTENZA

Basilicata's regional capital is not the most lovely of places, but if you're travelling in the region you may well end up passing through at some point. Badly damaged in repeated earthquakes, especially that of 1980, Potenza has lost most of its medieval buildings. Its altitude makes it cloyingly hot in summer and it can be bitterly cold in winter.

The centre of town straggles east to west across a high ridge. To the south lie the main FS and FCL train stations, and local buses make the run up to the centre.

Information

The EPT office (☎ 0971-2 18 12) is at Via Alianelli 4, just off the main square, Piazza Pagano.

The post office is at Via Pretoria 255. You can find telephones outside the neighbouring INPS building. The post code is 85100, and the telephone code 0971.

The Banca Popolare del Materano, Via Vescovado 30, is open from 8.30 am to 1.30 pm and 3.15 to 4 pm.

Things to See

In the old centre of town remain a couple of modest churches, including the **duomo**, originally erected in the 12th century but rebuilt in the 18th. North of the town centre is the **Museo Archeologico Provinciale**, housing a collection of ancient artefacts found in the region, but it has been closed for years and no-one knows if it will ever reopen.

Places to Stay & Eat

About the cheapest place to stay is *La Casa dello Studente* (☎ 44 27 08), Piazza Don Bosco, with basic rooms at L25,000/35,000. Otherwise you'll have to pay at least L40,000 a single in a couple of other small hotels. The *Monticchio*, Via Caserma Lucana 21, is a reasonable restaurant, where a meal will cost about L25,000.

Getting There & Away

Bus Various companies operate out of several places, and getting sensible information can be a trial. SITA (☎ 2 29 39) has an office at Corso Umberto I 69. Its buses leave from Via Crispi. It has one service a day to Matera, and several buses a day to Venosa, Melfi and Metaponto. Grassani has two buses to Matera, leaving at 6.25 am and 2.30 pm. Otherwise, Ferrovie Appulo-Lucane has a bus to Matera at 5.45 am which goes from the Ferrovie Calabro-Lucane train and bus station, near the FS Potenzà Inferiore station.

Train To pick up a train on the main FS line from Taranto to Naples, go to Potenza Inferiore or Superiore stations, respectively south and north of the town. There are regular services to Taranto, Metaponto, Salerno and Foggia (a different line) and occasionally direct to Naples. To get to Matera, change at Ferrandina on the Metaponto line.

Car & Motorbike Potenza is connected to Salerno in the west by the A3 (take the e847 branch east at Sicignano). Metaponto lies south-east along the SS407. For Matera, take the SS407 and then turn north onto the SS7 at Ferrandina.

NORTH OF POTENZA

An important medieval town and a favourite residence of Frederick II's roaming court, **Melfi** is dominated by a solid fortress, largely refashioned by Frederick, and surrounded by four km of Norman walls. The duomo, a repeated victim of earthquakes, still preserves intact its 12th-century bell tower. Twenty-five km farther east, **Venosa** is most interesting for the Abbazia della Trinità. The abbey, located at the north-eastern end of town surrounded by the sparse remains of the original Roman settlement, is the most impressive Norman mark left in Basilicata. The complex consists of the abbey palace and two churches, one of them never completed. The Aragonese castle contains a small archaeological museum. Melfi and Venosa can be reached by bus from Potenza.

MATERA
This ancient city evokes powerful images of a peasant culture that lasted until well after WW II. Its famous *sassi* – the stone houses built in the two ravines that slice through Matera – were home to more than half of the populace (about 20,000 people) until local government built new residential areas in the late 1950s and relocated the entire population. Probably the most striking account of how these people lived is given in Carlo Levi's *Christ Stopped at Eboli*.

Levi quotes the reactions of his sister to the conditions she observed while passing through Matera on her way to visit him in nearby Aliano. Describing the stone dwellings of Sasso Caveoso and Sasso Barisano as 'a schoolboy's idea of Dante's Inferno', she went on to say:

The houses were open on account of the heat, and as I went by I could see into the caves, whose only light came in through the front doors. Some of them had no entrance but a trapdoor and ladder. In these dark holes with walls cut out of the earth I saw a few pieces of miserable furniture, beds, and some ragged clothes hanging up to dry. On the floor lay dogs, sheep, goats, and pigs. Most families have just one cave to live in and there they sleep all together; men, women, children, and animals. This is how twenty thousand people live.

She depicted children suffering from trachoma or 'with the wizened faces of old men, their bodies reduced by starvation almost to skeletons, their heads crawling with lice and covered with scabs. Most of them had enormous, dilated stomachs, and faces yellow and worn with malaria.'

This and other accounts in Levi's book of the extreme poverty and appalling conditions suffered by the people of the south came as a shock to the more affluent north. It has taken more than 50 years and vast amounts of development funds to eradicate malaria and starvation in Basilicata. Today, people are returning to live in the sassi – but now it is a trend, rather than a necessity.

Many of the primitive stone dwellings are being renovated, with a new population of artists, writers and other 'interesting' types moving in.

Orientation
The centre of the new city is Piazza Vittorio Veneto, a short walk down Via Roma from the train station and intercity bus station off Piazza Matteotti. The ravine housing the sassi zone opens up to the east of Piazza V Veneto.

Information
Tourist Office The APT office (☎ 0835-33 19 83) is in Via Viti de Marco 9, off Via Roma. It is open Monday to Saturday from 8 am to 2 pm and, if you're lucky, 4 to 7 pm. The office can put you in contact with one of several groups that provide guides to the sassi (about L25,000 an hour). One such organisation, the Coop Amici del Turista (☎ 0835-31 01 13), operates an office in Piazza San Pietro in Sasso Caveoso. It will organise guided tours for groups of up to four people for L40,000 an hour and L100,000 for three hours. For groups of five to 10 people the cost is L50,000 an hour.

If you would like to read about the sassi, an excellent book is *Sassi e Secoli* (*Stones and Centuries*) by R Guira Longa. It is available in English from Libreria dell'Arco, Via Ridola 36, near Sasso Caveoso.

Post & Telecommunications The main post office is in Via del Corso, off Piazza Vittorio Veneto. The post code is 75100.

The Telecom office, just before the post office, is open Monday to Friday from 9 am to 12.30 pm and 2.30 to 6 pm. The telephone code is 0835.

Money The Banca di Roma, Via Roma 57, has a fairly reliable ATM that accepts Visa and MasterCard.

Emergency For police attendance, call ☎ 113. The public hospital (☎ 24 32 12) is in Via del Castello, south-west of the city

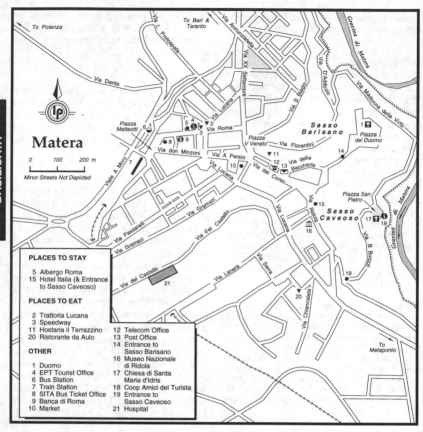

Matera

0   100   200 m

Minor Streets Not Depicted

PLACES TO STAY

5 Albergo Roma
15 Hotel Italia (& Entrance
     to Sasso Caveoso)

PLACES TO EAT

2 Trattoria Lucana
3 Speedway
11 Hostaria il Terrazzino
20 Ristorante da Aulo

OTHER

1 Duomo
4 EPT Tourist Office
6 Bus Station
7 Train Station
8 SITA Bus Ticket Office
9 Banca di Roma
10 Market

12 Telecom Office
13 Post Office
14 Entrance to
     Sasso Barisano
16 Museo Nazionale
     di Ridola
17 Chiesa di Santa
     Maria d'Idris
18 Coop Amici del Turista
19 Entrance to
     Sasso Caveoso
21 Hospital

centre. If you need a doctor to come to you, call the Guardia Medica on ☎ 24 35 38.

The Sassi

The two Sassi wards, known as **Barisano** and **Caveoso**, had no electricity, running water or sewerage system until well into this century. The oldest sassi are at the top of the ravine, and the dwellings in the lower sections of the ravine, which appear to be the oldest, were in fact established this century. As space ran out in the 1920s, the population started moving into hand-hewn or natural caves, an extraordinary example of civilisation in reverse.

The sassi zones are accessible from several points around the centre of Matera. There is an entrance just off Piazza Vittorio Veneto, or follow Via delle Beccherie to Piazza del Duomo and follow the tourist itinerary signs to enter either Barisano or Caveoso. Sasso Caveoso is also accessible from Via Ridola, by the stairs next to the Hotel Italia.

Caveoso is the most picturesque area to wander around, and the most important rock churches are here, including **Santa Maria** d'Idris and **Santa Lucia alla Malve**, both with amazingly well-preserved Byzantine frescoes. As you enter Caveoso, you might be approached by young boys wanting to act as tour guides. They generally don't speak any English, but for a few thousand lire will lead you to some of the more interesting sassi. You can take a formal tour too if you wish (see the Tourist Office section).

Town Centre

Recent excavations in Piazza Vittorio Veneto have yielded some remarkable discoveries. Beneath the piazza lie the ruins of parts of Byzantine Matera, including a rock church with frescoes, a castle, a large cistern and numerous houses. Access to the excavations is restricted.

The 13th-century Apulian-Romanesque **cathedral**, in Piazza del Duomo, overlooking Sasso Barisano, is also worth a visit.

The **Museo Nazionale Ridola** at Via Ridola 24 is in the ex-convent of Santa Chiara, dating from the 17th century, and houses an interesting collection of prehistoric and classical artefacts. It is open from 9 am to 7 pm every day, and entry costs L4000.

Festival

Matera celebrates the feast day of Santa Maria della Bruna (the city's patron saint) on 2 July. The festival culminates in a colourful procession from the cathedral. A statue of the Madonna is carried in an ornately decorated cart and, when the procession ends (and the statue has been removed), the crowd descends on the cart in a ceremony known as the *assalto al carro*, tearing it to pieces in order to take away relics.

Places to Stay & Eat

There are few budget options here. Try the *Albergo Roma* (☎ 33 39 12), Via Roma 62, which has simple but clean singles/doubles for L35,000/50,000. The pleasant *Hotel Italia* (☎ 33 35 61), Via Ridola 5, has rooms with bathroom for L95,000/120,000.

The local fare is simple and the focus is on vegetables. There is a Divella supermarket

virtually opposite the APT office, or you can pick up supplies in Piazza Vittorio Veneto at the *Casa del Pane*. A fresh produce market is held daily just south off Piazza Vittorio Veneto. For a quick snack and a beer, try *Speedway*, Via Roma 50.

Ristorante da Aulo, Via Anza di Lucana, is economical and serves cuisine typical of Basilicata. *Trattoria Lucana*, Via Lucana, has a good selection of vegetables and a full meal will cost around L30,000. Try the house specialities, such as orecchiette alla materana, a fresh pasta with a tomato, eggplant and courgette sauce. *Hostaria il Terrazzino* is in Vico San Giuseppe. It has an excellent reputation and the typical local food is excellent. A full meal will cost L30,000 plus.

Getting There & Away

Bus SITA (☎ 33 28 62) buses connect Matera with Taranto (six a day), Potenza (leaves at 2.10 pm and costs L8800) and Metaponto (up to five daily services to the beach in summer; only one in winter), as well as the many small towns in the province. Grassani (☎ 72 14 43) has two buses a day to Potenza.

A Marozzi bus connects Rome and Matera twice daily. SITA and Marozzi run a joint special service leaving for the northern cities of Siena, Florence, Pisa and others via Potenza. It leaves at 10.35 pm and booking is essential.

Train The city is on the private Ferrovie Appulo-Lucane line, which connects with Bari and Altamura. FAL runs regular trains and buses to Bari (L4400) from its station off Piazza Matteotti. To get to Potenza, you can take an FAL bus to Ferrandina and connect with an FS train, or go to Altamura to link up with FAL's Bari-Potenza run.

Car & Motorbike The city is easily accessible by road from Bari (65 km) and from Taranto (77 km). If arriving from Bari or Taranto, follow Via Nazionale, which becomes Via Annunziatella, until you reach Via XX Settembre, which connects with Piazza Vittorio Veneto and the city centre.

BASILICATA

From Metaponto, follow Via Lucana into the city centre.

ALIANO

Not one of Italy's, or even Basilicata's, great tourist stopovers, this tiny hilltop village south of Matera might attract those who have read Carlo Levi's *Christ Stopped at Eboli* and have their own transport. Levi was exiled to Basilicata during the 1930s for his opposition to Fascism, living first in Grassano and then in Aliano. He called the town Gagliano, and little has changed since he was interned here during the 1930s. The landscape is still as he described it, an 'endless sweep of clay, with the white dots of villages, stretching out as far as the invisible sea'.

Wander to the edge of the old village to see the house where he stayed (any local will point it out for you). Although the town's inhabitants are no longer stricken with poverty and malaria, the wheels of progress have turned slowly and you are just as likely to see the locals riding a donkey as driving a car. For the extra keen, Aliano is accessible by a SITA bus that leaves from Matera at 2.15 pm.

METAPONTO

Founded on the Ionian coast between the 8th and 7th centuries BC by Greek colonisers, Metaponto prospered as a grain-producing and commercial centre. One of the city's most famous residents was Pythagoras, who established a school here after being banished from Crotone (in what is now Calabria) towards the end of the 6th century BC.

After the death of Pythagoras, his house and school were incorporated into a Temple of Hera. The remains of the temple – 15 columns and sections of pavement – are known as the Tavole Palatine (Palatine Tables), since knights, or paladins, are said to have gathered there before heading off to the crusades. The columns were thought to be the legs of their giant tables.

Overtaken politically and economically by Rome, Metaponto met its end as a result of the Second Punic War. Hannibal had made it his headquarters after Rome retook Tarentum (Taranto) in 207 BC, and he is said to have relocated the town's population to spare it the fate of the people of Tarentum – sold into slavery by the Romans for having backed the Carthaginians.

Modern Metaponto's only real attraction is a sandy beach, Lido di Metaponto, that attracts loads of summer holiday-makers. It's about three km east of the train station.

Information

In summer an EPT tourist booth (☎ 74 19 33) opens at Piazzale Lido, behind the beach. The telephone code is 0835.

Things to See

You either have to be keen on ancient ruins or have your own transport to make traipsing around the sparse ruins worth your while. From the train station walk straight ahead for about two km. Signposted to your right is the so-called **Parco Archeologico**; to the left is the **Museo Archeologico Nazionale**. It's a one km walk to each. The park is actually the site of ancient Metapontum, where you can see what little remains of a **Greek theatre** and the Doric **Temple of Apollo Licius**. The museum is a modern and well presented collection of artefacts from the site. It opens daily from 9 am to 7 pm (officially at least) and admission costs L4000.

Once back on the main road between Metapontum and the museum, you have a three km trek to the most memorable reminder of this ancient city-state, the **Tavole Palatine** described above. Follow the slip road for Taranto onto the SS107 highway. The temple ruins are located north just off the highway, behind the old Antiquarium that used to house the museum.

Places to Stay

There are several camping grounds and the tourist office can point you to private rooms. Be aware that virtually nothing opens over winter. *Camping Magna Grecia* (☎ 0835-74 18 55), Via Lido, is close to the sea. *Hotel Kennedy* (☎ 0835-74 19 60), Viale Ionio, has rooms for L40,000/60,000. The *Oase*

(☎ 0835-74 19 30), Via Olimpia 12, charges about L20,000 a person.

Getting There & Away

Metaponto is accessible from Taranto's Piazza Castello by SITA or Chiruzzi buses, and from Matera by SITA bus. Metaponto is on the Taranto-Reggio di Calabria line, and trains also connect with Potenza, Salerno and occasionally Naples. The station is three km west of the Lido di Metaponto. If you don't want to walk, you could wait for one of the SITA or Chiruzzi buses to pass by on the way to the beach.

TYRRHENIAN COAST

Basilicata's Tyrrhenian coast is short (about 20 km) but sweet. The SS18 threads its way between craggy mountains on the inland side and cliffs that drop away into the sea to the west, making for one of the prettiest drives on the Tyrrhenian coast – one that curiously peters out virtually as soon as you leave Basilicata in either direction.

About halfway between the Campanian and Calabrian frontiers and a short, steep ride up from the coast lies the small town of **Maratea**. Watched over by a 22-metre tall statue of Christ (at the Santuario di San Biagio), Maratea has been done no harm by tourism. The high part of town, as so often along the south Tyrrhenian coast, forms the historic core, below which has spread an as yet unobtrusive extension.

Maratea is the administrative centre of a series of coastal villages, the prettiest of which are probably **Fiumicello** and **Porto**. Most of the accommodation is down in these coastal settlements, and each has at least one small protected beach.

The AAST office (☎ 87 69 08) is at Piazza Gesù 32 in Maratea. A booth (☎ 87 60 50) also opens in Porto during summer. The telephone code in Maratea is 0973.

One of the cheapest places is the fairly simple *Albergo Cesarino* (☎ 87 69 20) in Fiumicello. Prettier is the *Villa degli Aranci* (☎ 87 63 44), but rooms start at about L75,000/85,000.

SITA buses link Maratea to Potenza. They also run up the coast to Sapri, in Campania, and south to Praia a Mare, in Calabria. All-stops trains on the Salerno-Reggio di Calabria line call in at Maratea train station, below the town, and several of the coastal settlements. Local buses connect the coastal towns and Maratea train station with the old centre of Maratea.

Calabria

With some of the country's better beaches, and a brooding, mountainous interior, the 'toe' of the Italian boot represents for many travellers little more than a train ride down the Tyrrhenian coast on the way to or from Sicily. Although it may not loom large on the average visitor's list of Italian destinations, Calabria is worth a little exploration. The beaches are among the cleanest in Italy, and ancient history lovers can explore the sparse reminders of the civilisation of Magna Graecia. The downside is the spread of ugly holiday villages along parts of the Ionian and Tyrrhenian coasts, and sometimes you have to settle for pebbles rather than sand. Along the roads heading inland you'll encounter some magnificent natural beauty and, every now and then, picturesque and long ignored medieval villages huddled on hilltops.

Sparsely inhabited in Paleolithic times, the area was first settled by Greeks from Sicily who founded a colony at modern Reggio di Calabria. The process of colonisation spread along the Ionian coast, with Sibari and Crotone the most important settlements. Siding with Hannibal against Rome turned out to be a mistake, and with his departure for Carthage in 202 BC, the cities of Magna Graecia came under Rome's permanent control. Later, as Rome faded away, the Byzantines took superficial control. Their ineffectual rule, and the appearance of Arab raiders (the so-called Saracens) off the coast, favoured a decline in the area which was never really arrested subsequently; Calabria continued to be a

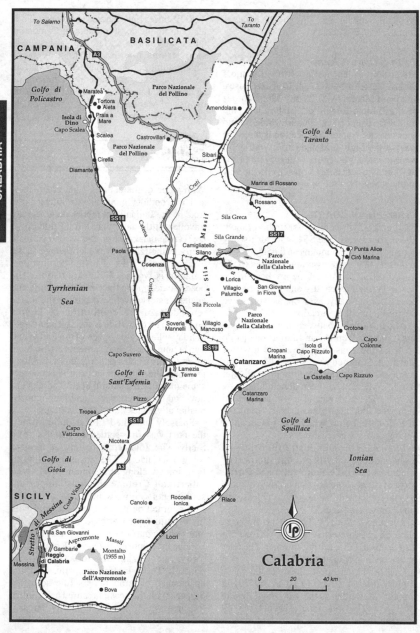

Calabria

0   20   40 km

backwater for a succession of Norman, Swabian, Aragonese, Spanish and Bourbon rulers based in Naples. Although the brief Napoleonic interregnum at the end of the 18th century and the arrival of Garibaldi and Italian unification inspired hope for change, Calabria remained chained to a virtually feudal treadmill.

The province's history of misery has sparked numerous revolts. It also caused, from the 1870s onwards, the rise of highway robbery, which has slowly grown into pervasive organised crime. For many, the only answer has been to get out, and for at least a century, Calabria has seen its young emigrate to the north or abroad in search of work.

While mostly tacky, the many tourist villages along the coast can offer excellent package deals and should not be rejected out of hand. There are plenty of camping grounds along the coast, but with the exception of some of the more popular coastal towns, budget accommodation is thin on the ground, and much of it closes from October to April. Where possible, arm yourself with provincial hotel lists from tourist offices before venturing off into the backblocks. If you plan to visit in summer, book in advance or at least try to turn up early.

The food is simple peasant fare and relies heavily on what is produced in the region. It would not be unusual to eat in a restaurant where the owners themselves have produced the salami, cheese, vegetables and the grapes for the wine.

You can get pretty much anywhere by public transport, but it is not always fast or easy. The national FS railway operates between the main cities and around the coast. The private Ferrovie della Calabria links Catanzaro and Cosenza, and serves smaller towns between the two by train and bus. Blue provincial buses, belonging to a plethora of small private companies, connect most towns – sooner or later.

CATANZARO

Long the hub of Calabria, Catanzaro replaced Reggio di Calabria as the regional capital in the early 1970s. Despite this, it is

overlooked by tourists – and it is not difficult to see why. Set atop a rocky peak 13 km in from the Ionian coast on the way north to the Sila Massif, it can be pleasant enough wandering the heart of the old city, but there is precious little to draw you to Catanzaro apart from its transport connections.

Evidence of the city's Byzantine origins is virtually non-existent. Positioned to deter raiders and prevent the spread of malaria, Catanzaro has suffered repeatedly from a different natural curse – earthquake. The severe jolts of 1688, 1783 and 1832 have left nothing much of historical interest standing.

Orientation
The train station for the private Calabrian railway, Ferrovie della Calabria, is just north of the city centre. Walk south along Via Indipendenza for Piazza Matteotti, the main square. Corso Mazzini takes you farther south through the middle of old Catanzaro. The FS station is about two km south and downhill from the centre – you'll need to take a local bus.

Information
The APT administration office (☎ 0961-85 11) in the Galleria Mancuso, just north of Piazza Prefettura, can help with information, but you're better off going to the APT office in Piazza Prefettura (☎ 0961-74 17 64). Both open from 9 am to 2 pm Monday to Friday and about 3 to 5 pm on Monday afternoon.

The main post office, in Piazza Prefettura, opens from 8.30 am to 1.30 pm Monday to Saturday. The city's post code is 88100. The public telephone office is on Via Buccarelli and the telephone code is 0961.

There is a CTS travel agency (☎ 72 45 30) at Via E Scalfaro 5.

In a police emergency, call ☎ 113, or contact the police headquarters (☎ 72 05 57) in Piazza Cavour. The main hospital (☎ 74 58 51) is on Viale Pio X, north of the Ferrovie della Calabria train station.

Things to See
Wander south along Corso Mazzini for the older and more interesting parts of the city.

CALABRIA

Of its churches, the Baroque **Basilica dell'Immacolata** is the most impressive. The **duomo**, farther south, was almost completely rebuilt after the last war and is quite ordinary. The **Chiesa di San Domenico** (also known as the Chiesa del Rosario) nearby contains several attractive Renaissance paintings by comparative unknowns.

The city's **Museo Provinciale** is inside the Villa Trieste, a large garden on the eastern edge of town near Via Jannoni. The museum has a large collection of coins and some local archaeological finds, but has been closed for some time and seems set to stay that way.

Places to Stay & Eat

If you are coming from Cosenza, there is an HI *youth hostel* (☎ 0968-66 60 79) at Soveria Mannelli on the SS19 inland Catanzaro-Cosenza road, 43 km north of Catanzaro. It is set in woodlands within striking distance of the Sila Massif. B&B costs L12,000. It's four km from the nearest train station but buses between Cosenza and Catanzaro can drop you nearby.

Catanzaro has few hotels and they are generally expensive. The *Albergo Belvedere* (☎ 72 05 91), Via Italia 33, has rooms from L38,000/50,000. It's in a decent location if

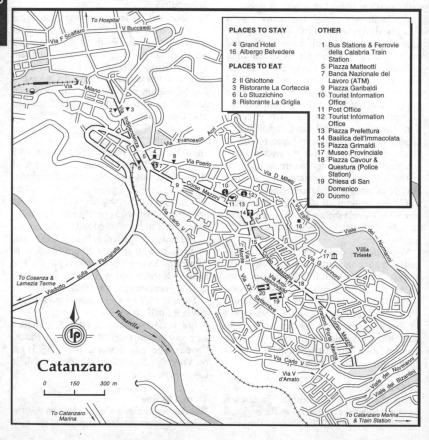

PLACES TO STAY
4 Grand Hotel
16 Albergo Belvedere

PLACES TO EAT
2 Il Ghiottone
3 Ristorante La Corteccia
6 Lo Stuzzichino
8 Ristorante La Griglia

OTHER
1 Bus Stations & Ferrovie della Calabria Train Station
5 Piazza Matteotti
7 Banca Nazionale del Lavoro (ATM)
9 Piazza Garibaldi
10 Tourist Information Office
11 Post Office
12 Tourist Information Office
13 Piazza Prefettura
14 Basilica dell'Immacolata
15 Piazza Grimaldi
17 Museo Provinciale
18 Piazza Cavour & Questura (Police Station)
19 Chiesa di San Domenico
20 Duomo

Catanzaro

you can get a room with a view. The *Grand Hotel* (☎ 70 12 56), Piazza Matteotti, has bland but comfortable rooms for L120,000/170,000 with breakfast.

The best bets for cheap food are the city's bars, where you can grab a cheap sandwich. The self-service *Lo Stuzzichino*, Piazza Matteotti, has pasta from about L5000. More substantial meals can be had at *Ristorante La Griglia*, at Via Poerio 26, off Piazza Garibaldi. *Ristorante la Corteccia*, Via Indipendenza 30, is in much the same league, while *Il Ghiottone*, across the road, is not a bad bar and pizzeria.

Getting There & Away
Air The airport, Sant'Eufemia Lamezia, is at Lamezia Terme (☎ 0968-41 41 11), about 35 km west of Catanzaro. It links the region with major Italian cities and a small number of flights serve international destinations like Paris, London and Frankfurt.

Bus FC buses depart from the Ferrovie della Calabria train station to towns throughout the province, Catanzaro Marina, other cities on the Ionian coast and into the Sila Massif. Various other small companies have terminals throughout the town.

Train The FC railway runs trains between the city and Catanzaro Marina (also known as Catanzaro Lido), where you can pick up an FS train to Reggio di Calabria or north-east along the Ionian coast. From the Catanzaro city FS station trains connect with Lamezia Terme, Reggio di Calabria, Cosenza and even Naples, Rome, Milan and Turin.

Car & Motorbike By car, leave the A3 autostrada at Lamezia Terme and head east on the SS280 for the city. If approaching from along the Ionian coast, follow the 'centro' signs off the SS106.

Getting Around
City buses connect the FS train station with the city centre, including Nos 10, 11, 12 and 13. The Circolare Lido line connects the city

centre, the FS train station and Catanzaro Marina.

IONIAN COAST
Wilder and less crowded than the Tyrrhenian seaboard, the Ionian coast nevertheless has its fair share of tourist villages – unappealing resorts that fill up in the summer months. There is something brooding and resistant to the outsider about this territory, especially if you venture into the hills and valleys away from the coast. Much of the land near the sea is under cultivation, interspersed with ramshackle villages or, more often, the growing blight of half-built housing and holiday villas.

Most of the tourist villages, hotels and camp sites close for up to eight months of the year, so finding accommodation can be tricky. Add to that the woes of travelling on the slow trains or infrequent buses along the coast, and the area might start to seem unappealing. Don't despair. There are dozens of small hill towns to explore and some of the beaches are quite good. You can get a list of camping grounds and hotels from tourist offices in the provincial capitals. Your own vehicle is a decided advantage, but you *can* get to most places by public transport.

Locri
Locri is a small, modern and unimpressive town about 100 km south of Catanzaro, but it's a potential base for exploration into the hills. The IAT office (☎ 0964-2 96 00), Via Matteotti 90, opens from 9 am to 2 pm Monday to Saturday. The *Albergo Orientale* (☎ 0964-2 07 48), Via Tripodi 31, has singles/doubles at L35,000/60,000 in the off-season. It is one of three hotels in town.

Gerace
About 10 km inland from Locri on the SS111, Gerace is an immaculately preserved medieval hill town which, perhaps sadly, is becoming a routine stop on the tourist circuit. It boasts Calabria's largest Romanesque cathedral, high up in the town. It was first laid out in 1045, and subsequent alterations robbed it of none of its majesty. There is a

Pro Loco tourist office (☎ 0964-35 68 88) at Piazza Tribuna 10. *Ristorante a Squella*, Viale della Resistenza 8, is an excellent traditional restaurant, and a meal will cost about L25,000.

Farther inland still is the town of **Canolo**, a small hamlet seemingly untouched by the 20th century. Buses connect Gerace with Locri.

Catanzaro Marina

Also known as Catanzaro Lido, this is the city's access to the sea and one of the Ionian coast's major resorts. Although heavily developed, it is less tacky than others, and the beaches stretching off in both directions are among the best on the coast. The *Hotel King* (☎ (3 17 11), Via Torrazzo 15, has singles/doubles without bath for L35,000/50,000 or L50,000/60,000 with bath.

Isola di Capo Rizzuto

Forty km north-east of Catanzaro Marina is Isola di Capo Rizzuto, one of the best locations along the Ionian coast for camping. *La Fattoria* (☎ 0962-79 11 65), Via del Faro, is one of about 15 grounds near the small town. The *Pensione Aragonese* (☎ 0962-79 50 13), Via Scesa Marina, about 10 km south-west of town on the waterfront and opposite a rather lonely looking Aragonese castle at Le Castella, has rooms from L30,000/50,000 in the off-season, rising to L100,000 full board per person in July and August.

At the northern tip of this zone, whose shore was declared a marine reserve in 1991, is **Capo Colonna**, marking the site of the Greek fortress complex of Hera Lacinia. Only a solitary column belonging to a Doric temple remains to testify to the spot's former splendour.

Crotone

About 10 km north of Isola di Capo Rizzuto, Crotone was founded by the Greeks in 710 BC and reached its zenith in the following century, when it virtually controlled all Magna Graecia. In more recent times it has regained influence as one of the region's heavyweight industrial centres and ports –

something you can hardly fail to notice as you enter the town.

The APT office (☎ 0962-2 31 85) is at Via Torino 148.

The town's **Museo Archeologico Nazionale**, Via Risorgimento, is one of Calabria's better museums. At the time of writing, however, it was closed for refurbishment. Nearby is a 15th-century **castle**, typical of the kind of fortress with cylindrical towers erected by the Aragonese in southern Italy's main coastal cities.

Albergo Italia (☎ 0962-2 39 10), Via Vittoria 12, has comfortable enough rooms ranging from L35,000 to L60,000, and is open all year round.

North of Crotone

The coastline from Crotone to Basilicata is the region's least developed, partly because the beaches are not so hot (mostly grey pebble and stone affairs), and whilst the coast road is decent (and being upgraded), public transport is generally irregular.

Cirò Marina About 30 km north of Crotone, Cirò Marina is a decent-sized town with plenty of hotel rooms and good beaches despite the huge cement breakwaters near the town. The *Albergo Atena* (☎ 0962-3 18 25), Via Bergamo, has singles/doubles from L45,000/70,000. There is a camping ground, the *Punta Alice* (☎ 0962-3 11 60) at **Punta Alice**, a couple of km north of the town.

Rossano Rossano, 56 km north of Cirò, is really two towns – Lido Sant'Angelo, the standard beach resort and coastal extension of the modern plains town of Rossano Scalo, and the original hill town itself, six km inland.

The transformation over such a short drive is remarkable. The snaking road takes you through verdant countryside, an invitation in itself to head farther inland, to a tranquil and picturesque old town, once an important link in the Byzantine empire's Italian chain.

Various reminders of Rossano's ties to the city of Constantinople remain. The **cathedral**, remodelled several times, nevertheless conserves a 9th-century Byzantine fresco of the Madonna. For more proof, try the **Museo Diocesano** next door, which houses a precious 6th-century purple-coloured codex of 188 pages. They contain the gospels of Saints Matthew and Mark in Greek. It opens from 10 am to noon and 4.30 to 6 pm Monday to Friday (entry is L2000). Ask around for the custodian if you're having trouble getting in.

The *Albergo Scigliano* (☎ 0983-51 18 46), Viale Margherita 25, has singles/doubles from L100,000/150,000 with breakfast, and there is a camping ground, the *Camping Torino* (☎ 0983-51 00 80), at Marina di Rossano.

Rossano is on the Taranto-Reggio di Calabria train line. If you want to head inland, the SS177 makes a pretty drive across the Sila Massif to Cosenza.

Sibari About 25 km farther north among reclaimed farmland is the town of Sibari, near what was the seat of the ancient Sybarites, about whose wealth and genius much ink has been spilled. This once great Greek city state was destroyed by Crotone under Pythagoras in the 6th century BC, and excavations since the 1960s have brought only a glimmer of its glory to light (there is a small museum).

COSENZA

Seated at the confluence of two rivers, the Crati and Busento, the medieval core of Cosenza is an unexpected pleasure, with its narrow *vicoletti* (alleys), some no more than steep stairways, winding past elegant, if much decayed, multi-storeyed apartment houses.

A university town since 1968, Cosenza is without doubt the most attractive of Calabria's three provincial capitals, and possibly the only one that seriously merits a stop. What's more, if you're coming from the north, it has the appeal of being a gateway into the Sila Massif and on across to the Ionian coast. As a transportation hub, the city makes a good base for the mountains.

Orientation

The main drag, Corso Mazzini, runs south off Piazza Fera (near the bus station) and intersects Viale Trieste before hitting Piazza dei Bruzi. What little there is in terms of accommodation, food, banks and tourist help is all within about a 10-minute walking radius of the intersection. Head farther south still and cross the Busento river to reach the medieval part of town.

Information

Tourist Offices There are two APT offices, one on Via P Rossi (☎ 0984-39 05 95), at the roundabout north of Viale della Repubblica (useful for drivers coming in off the A3), the other (☎ 0984-2 78 21) at Corso Mazzini 92. Among the odds and ends on offer is a guide (with map) to the agriturismo accommodation throughout the province. These places in the country, often with horse-riding facilities and similar activities, are worth considering as an alternative to the usual hotel grind. The offices open Monday to Friday from 8 am to 2 pm.

Post & Telecommunications The main post office is at Via Vittorio Veneto on the city centre's western edge. The Telecom office is at the bus station off Piazza Fera, and opens Monday to Friday from 9.30 am to 1 pm and 4 to 7.30 pm. The post code for Cosenza is 87100, and the telephone code 0984.

Emergency In a police emergency, call ☎ 113, or contact the police headquarters (☎ 3 60 01) on Piazza XV Marzo. The hospital, the Ospedale Civile (☎ 68 11), is on Via Felice Migliori, behind the post office.

Things to See

A short walk south of the Busento river along Corso Telesio is the 12th-century **duomo**, rebuilt in the Baroque style (although hardly in the most florid fashion) in the 18th century. The cathedral is unexceptional, but on the left is a Baroque chapel in the process of restoration. It contains a copy of a 13th-century Byzantine Madonna. From the cathedral you can follow Via del Seggio

CALABRIA

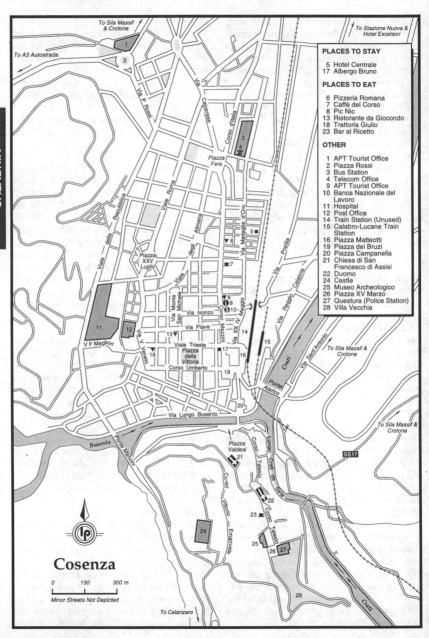

PLACES TO STAY

5 Hotel Centrale
17 Albergo Bruno

PLACES TO EAT

6 Pizzeria Romana
7 Caffè del Corso
8 Pic Nic
13 Ristorante da Giocondo
18 Trattoria Giulio
23 Bar al Ricetto

OTHER

1 APT Tourist Office
2 Piazza Rossi
3 Bus Station
4 Telecom Office
9 APT Tourist Office
10 Banca Nazionale del Lavoro
11 Hospital
12 Post Office
14 Train Station (Unused)
15 Calabro-Lucane Train Station
16 Piazza Matteotti
19 Piazza dei Bruzi
20 Piazza Campanella
21 Chiesa di San Francesco di Assisi
22 Duomo
24 Castle
25 Museo Archeologico
26 Piazza XV Marzo
27 Questura (Police Station)
28 Villa Vecchia

Cosenza

0   150   300 m

Minor Streets Not Depicted

through an enchanting little medieval quarter to the 13th century **Chiesa di San Francesco d'Assisi**, in which you'll find a chapel of the original structure behind the right transept. The cloister also bears some remnants of the first building.

Farther south along Corso Vittorio Emanuele is the **castle**, built by the Normans, rearranged by Frederick II and the Angevins in 1222 and left in disarray by several earthquakes. The views are the best part about it.

At the southern edge of the old city centre is Piazza XV Marzo, an appealing square fronted by the Accademia Cosentina, which houses the city's **Museo Civico Archeologico**, containing local finds. Entry is free and it opens Monday to Saturday from 9 am to 1 pm. South of the piazza stretches a huge public garden, the **Villa Vecchia**.

Places to Stay & Eat

Accommodation can be a prickly business in Cosenza – there are only four hotels. The cheapest option is the *Albergo Bruno* (☎ 7 38 89), Corso Mazzini 27, which has singles/doubles from L30,000/55,000. Rooms are functional and spacious, with showers outside. The *Excelsior* (☎ 7 43 83), on Piazza Stazione by the train station, has rooms without bath for L45,000/80,000. See the Information section above for agriturismo options. *Hotel Centrale* (☎ 7 38 61), Via del Tigrai, has singles/doubles starting at L88,000/118,000.

You can grab a snack at *Pic Nic*, Corso Mazzini 108 or *Pizzeria Romana*, No 190. *Trattoria Giulio*, Viale Trieste 93, is an informal place for simple meals. For something a little more substantial, head for *Ristorante da Giocondo*, Via Piave 53, where a reasonable meal will cost about L25,000. In the old town, *Bar al Ricetto*, Corso Telesio 29, is good for a quick bite. *Caffè del Corso*, on Corso Mazzini, is a bright spot for a coffee and pastry.

Getting There & Away

Bus The city's main bus station is just east of Piazza Fera. Services leave for Catanzaro, towns throughout the Sila Massif and Paola. Autolinie Preite has half a dozen buses daily along the north Tyrrhenian coast as far as Praia a Mare, and SITA goes to Maratea in Basilicata.

Train The national FS Stazione Nuova is about two km north-east of the city centre. Trains go to Reggio di Calabria, Salerno, Naples and Rome, as well as most destinations around the Calabrian coast. The Ferrovie della Calabria line serves the Sila Massif and other small towns around Cosenza.

Car & Motorbike Cosenza is off the A3 autostrada. The SS107 connects the city with Crotone and the Ionian coast, across the Sila Massif.

Getting Around

You're unlikely to need a bus in town, but it is best to get ATAC bus No 5 to or from the Stazione Nuova train station. For a taxi, call ☎ 2 88 77.

SILA MASSIF (LA SILA)

Less spectacular than many of the mountain ranges farther up the peninsula, the Sila Massif is still magnificent and offers good walking. The highest peaks are around 2000 metres, much of them covered in what amounts to a vast forest, but there is some winter skiing in the central Sila Grande. The other main areas are the Sila Greca, north of the Grande, and the Sila Piccola to the south. Sadly, there are few mountain rifugi, and camping in the national parks is forbidden.

The main towns are Camigliatello Silano and San Giovanni in Fiore, both accessible by bus along the SS107 that connects Cosenza with Crotone, or by the train running between Cosenza and San Giovanni in Fiore. You will find accommodation in various towns throughout the Sila Massif and at several tourist resorts, including the Villagio Palumbo and Villaggio Mancuso. Skiers can use lifts around Camigliatello Silano and near Lorica, on Lago Arvo.

Information

Unfortunately, the tourist offices can help you with little more than vague maps and accommodation lists. Any brochures they have will almost inevitably be in Italian only.

Camigliatello Silano

Ordinary enough in summer, Camigliatello looks quite cute under snow. It is a popular local skiing resort, but won't host any international competitions. A few lifts operate on Monte Curcio about three km to the south. One summertime activity that might interest the kids is a **steam train** excursion that runs from Camigliatello to San Giovanni in Fiore. It leaves every Saturday and costs L20,000 return. Occasionally it runs in winter too. For information, enquire at the train station.

The town has about 15 hotels including the *Miramonti* (☎ 0984-57 90 67), near the tourist office on Via Forgitelle, which has singles/doubles from L40,000/55,000. *Mancuso* (☎ 0984-57 80 82), Via del Turismo, has rooms for about the same price, while the three-star *Aquila & Edelweiss* (☎ 0984-57 80 44), Viale Stazione 11, has rooms from L60,000/90,000. You can eat well at the *Ristorante al Capriolo*, Via Camigliati 8, for less than L30,000 a head.

San Giovanni in Fiore

The biggest town in the Sila Massif, it really has little to recommend it, and although the provincial accommodation guide lists a lot of hotels as being here, most of them are scattered about small villages around – some as far away as Lorica, 20 km to the south-west.

Lorica

A peaceful little spot on Lago Arvo amidst thick woods, Lorica is a minor ski resort, with a lift operating nearby. *Camping Lorica* (☎ 0984-53 70 18), on the lake, is one of several camp sites in the area. Otherwise you could try *Albergo Trota* (☎ 0984-53 71 66), which has rooms for L50,000/80,000. You may have to pay full board in the ski season.

Villaggio Palumbo

About 15 km south of San Giovanni in Fiore, this is a tourist village resort on Lago Ampollino. It offers weekend package deals including food and accommodation, and is set up for skiing, horse-riding and the like. For information, call ☎ 0962-49 30 17.

The management has an interest in a similar venture about 25 km farther south on the road to Catanzaro, **Villaggio Mancuso**. For information, call ☎ 0961-92 20 48.

REGGIO DI CALABRIA

Gazing across the strait to the twinkling night lights of Messina in Sicily from the elegant tree-lined Lungomare Matteotti, you could almost be forgiven for thinking yourself in a rather romantic spot. Drive through miles of half-built and half lived-in concrete slum tenements, and you could hardly feel anything but pity for the bulk of this city's people. Rocked to the core repeatedly by earthquakes, the last time devastatingly in 1908, this once proud ancient Greek city has plenty of other woes, among them organised crime. You may notice an awful lot of Carabinieri and Alpine soldiers (Italy's elite troops) in the streets. Wander up to Piazza Castello where heavily armed guards surround the law courts and you begin to gauge the depth of the problem.

Orientation

The main train station is at the southern edge of town in Piazza Garibaldi, where most buses also terminate. Walk north along Corso G Garibaldi, the city's main street, for the tourist office and other services. Corso Garibaldi is a kind of de facto pedestrian zone in the evening, as streams of Reggians parade in the ritual passeggiata.

Information

Tourist Offices The APT office has branches at the train station (☎ 0965-2 71 20), the airport (☎ 0965-64 32 91) and on the autostrada near the Rosano Ovest exit. The main APT offices open to the public are at Corso Garibaldi 329 (☎ 0965-89 20 12), in the Teatro Comunale building, and tucked

CALABRIA

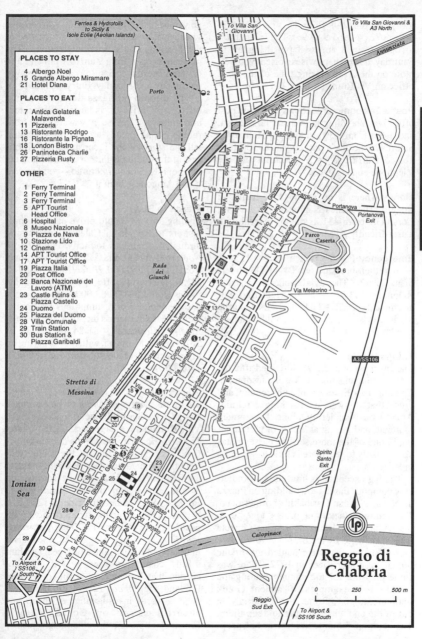

PLACES TO STAY

4 Albergo Noel
15 Grande Albergo Miramare
21 Hotel Diana

PLACES TO EAT

7 Antica Gelateria
   Malavenda
11 Pizzeria
13 Ristorante Rodrigo
16 Ristorante la Pignata
18 London Bistro
26 Paninoteca Charlie
27 Pizzeria Rusty

OTHER

1 Ferry Terminal
2 Ferry Terminal
3 Ferry Terminal
5 APT Tourist
   Head Office
6 Hospital
8 Museo Nazionale
9 Piazza de Nava
10 Stazione Lido
12 Cinema
14 APT Tourist Office
17 APT Tourist Office
19 Piazza Italia
20 Post Office
22 Banca Nazionale del
   Lavoro (ATM)
23 Castle Ruins &
   Piazza Castello
24 Duomo
25 Piazza del Duomo
28 Villa Comunale
29 Train Station
30 Bus Station &
   Piazza Garibaldi

Reggio di
Calabria

0   250   500 m

away on the 2nd floor at Via Demetrio Tripepi 72 (☎ 0965-9 84 96). They all purport to open from 8 am to 8 pm, Monday to Saturday. It is perhaps wise to orient yourself more on the 2 pm closing time of the head office on Via Roma (☎ 0965-2 11 71).

Post & Telecommunications The main post office is at Via Miraglia 14 near Piazza Italia, and opens from 8.30 am to 7 pm Monday to Saturday. The city's post code is 89100. The Telecom office is on Via Marina and the telephone code is 0965.

Money There is no shortage of banks in Reggio. The Banca Nazionale del Lavoro, Corso Garibaldi 431, is one of several with a user-friendly ATM.

Emergency For the police, call ☎ 113, or head to their headquarters (☎ 41 11) on Via Santa Caterina. The city's hospital, or Ospedali Riuniti (☎ 2 11 04), is at Via Melacrino. For an ambulance, call ☎ 2 44 44. For the Guardia Medica (visiting doctors, at night and on holidays), call ☎ 34 71 05.

Things to See
The city was completely resurrected after the 1908 earthquake that devastated southern Calabria. Few historic buildings remain, and those that do were painstakingly rebuilt. Apart from wandering along Lungomare Matteotti and gazing at Sicily, or participating in one of the more serious passeggiatas you're likely to see, there is little to see or do in Reggio.

The big exception is housed in a predictably pompous Fascist-era building on Piazza de Nava, at Corso Garibaldi's northern end. The **Museo Nazionale** brings together a wealth of finds from the Magna Graecia period, crowned by the *Bronzi di Riace*, two bronze statues that were hauled up off the Ionian coast near Riace in 1972. There was some pressure for the statues, among the world's best examples of ancient Greek sculpture, to go to Rome, but Calabria won out in the end and was able to keep them. The sculptor remains unknown, but probably lived in the 5th century BC. You can also view work by southern Italian artists, one of the Mezzogiorno's better collections. The museum is open from 9 am to 1 pm and 3 to 6.30 pm Tuesday to Saturday, mornings only on Sunday and Monday. Entry is L6000.

The **duomo** in Piazza del Duomo, just off Corso Garibaldi, is largely unspectacular until you realise it was rebuilt from rubble. Small boards around the cathedral tell the story of the reconstruction. Northeast of the duomo is Piazza Castello and the ruins of a 15th-century **castle** – you guessed it, the Aragonese built it.

Places to Stay
Finding a room should prove easy, as most visitors to Reggio di Calabria are passing through on their way to Sicily. The *Albergo Noel* (☎ 89 09 65), Via G Zerbi 13, has rooms from L45,000/60,000. *Hotel Diana* (☎ 89 15 22), Via Vitrioli 12, offers perfectly adequate rooms from L38,000/83,000 – the pricing is definitely odd. For a sumptuous stay and a view of Mt Etna across the strait, the *Grande Albergo Miramare* (☎ 81 24 44; fax 81 24 50), Via Fata Morgana, with rooms giving on to Lungomare Matteotti, starts at L80,000/140,000.

Places to Eat
There are plenty of places to buy a snack along Corso Garibaldi, including a bar in the Villa Comunale, a large park off the Corso. The *Pizzeria Rusty*, beside the duomo on Via Crocefisso, has pizza by the slice from L2000, while *Paninoteca Charlie*, next to the Red Cross on Via Generale Tommasini, is good for cheap snacks. *Ristorante la Pignata*, Via Demetrio Tripepi 122, is a bright place offering local dishes with pasta starting at around L7000. *Ristorante Rodrigo*, Via XXIV Maggio 25, specialises in Calabrian cuisine, and a full meal will hurt a little, costing in excess of L40,000. For cuisine that has nothing at all to do with England, the *London Bistro*, Via Osanna 8, is also worth investigating. A cheap and cheerful *pizzeria* on Corso Vittorio Emanuele, opposite the cinema and just up

from the Stazione Lido train station, is always busy.

For the town's richest gelati, you can't surpass the *Antica Gelateria Malavenda*, on the corner of Via Romeo and Viale Amendola.

Getting There & Away

Air The city's airport, the Aeroporto Civile Minniti (☎ 64 22 32) at Ravagnese, about four km to the south, serves two flights a day from Rome and one from Milan, as well as the occasional charter flight. Alitalia (☎ 33 14 44) is at Corso Garibaldi 521.

Bus The bus station is in Piazza Garibaldi, in front of the train station. About 10 companies operate to towns in Calabria and beyond. Saja (☎ 81 23 37) and AMA (☎ 62 01 29) serve the Aspromonte Massif, Salzone has buses to Scilla and Lirosi (☎ 0966-93 26 11) has two daily runs to Rome and one to Catanzaro.

Train Trains stop at Stazione Centrale (☎ 89 81 23), and less frequently at Stazione Lido, near the museum. Reggio is the terminus for trains from Milan, Florence, Rome and Naples.

Car & Motorbike The A3 ends at Reggio di Calabria. Heading south, the SS106 hugs the coast round the 'toe' and up along the Ionian Sea.

Boat Up to 20 hydrofoils run by SNAV (☎ 2 95 68) leave the port just north of Stazione Lido for Messina every day (L6000 one way), some of them proceeding on to the Isole Eolie (Aeolian Islands). On Sunday only three hydrofoils leave. The FS national railways run up to 12 big hydrofoils a day from the port to Messina (L4000 one way).

Car ferries cross to Messina around the clock from Villa San Giovanni, 15 minutes north up the rail line. FS railways run boats that carry cars and trains across (L1500 for foot passengers), while the private company Caronte operates car and truck ferries from a little farther north. During the day, there is usually a crossing once every 10 minutes. A standard car with Caronte costs L26,000 one way or L40,000 return (valid 60 days). Passengers don't pay; motorcycles cost L10,000 each way. The crossing takes about 20 minutes.

Tirrenia used to run a service from Reggio to Malta, calling in at several Sicilian ports on the way. At the time of writing, the service had been suspended, but it is worth enquiring in summer if it is on again.

Getting Around

Orange local buses cover most of the city. To

CALABRIA

Ancient Minorities

Possibly Calabria's richest testament to the era of Magna Graecia is to be sought not in the sparse ruins of abandoned ancient settlements along the coast, but in the hill towns east of Reggio di Calabria. For in the towns of Bova, Condofuri and Roccaforte del Greco (most easily reached from the coast road) you can still hear the older folk speaking Greek as their native tongue. Not, say some experts, a dialect of modern Greek, but rather a descendant of the ancient language of Pythagoras. Sceptics claim it is the Greek of the much later Byzantine Empire. Even so, it is remarkable to think that this linguistic island has survived for so many hundreds of years.

More numerous and more recently arrived are the Albanians, who began fleeing Muslim persecution in the mid-15th century. You'll find them mostly in small towns scattered about the Piana di Sibari, about 50 km south of the border with Basilicata on the Ionian coast. Not only have they preserved their language, but in many cases remain faithful in this bastion of Catholicism to the Greek Orthodox rite. ■

get to the airport, take bus Nos 15, 19, 111, 113, 114 or 115.

ASPROMONTE MASSIF

Inland from Reggio di Calabria rises the Aspromonte Massif, with its highest peak, Montalto, coming in at just under 2000 metres. It is dominated by a huge bronze statue of Christ and offers sweeping views across to Sicily.

The tourist office in Reggio may be able to provide information and a map of the Montalto area, now a national park. It offers some walking trails, albeit not quite as spectacular, or difficult, as those in the Sila Massif.

To reach the Aspromonte's main town of Gambarie, take city bus No 127 from Reggio di Calabria. Most of the roads inland from Reggio eventually hit the main SS183 road that runs north to the town.

TYRRHENIAN COAST

Tamer and more developed than Calabria's Ionian coast, the region's western seaboard is a striking mix of the good, the bad and the ugly. Certain stretches, particularly in the popular north, are crammed with tacky package resorts that attract holidaying Italians by the thousand each summer. By the same token, there are several small towns that make pleasant places to stay, and the odd cove with a protected sandy beach. The drive along the Costa Viola, the strip that leads from Rosarno down to Scilla and on towards Reggio di Calabria, is one of Italy's great coast drives, with breathtaking views of Sicily.

The best sources of information about the coast are the tourist offices in Reggio di Calabria and Cosenza. They will probably recommend you stay at one of the tourist villages – don't be immediately put off. Although most are reminiscent of *Carry On...* films, many offer excellent value and all have private beaches, generally some of the coast's best.

As elsewhere in Calabria, cheap accommodation can be a little problematic. Out of season, most hotels, camp sites and tourist villages close. In summer many of the hotels are full, although you should have an easier time with the camp sites.

Most coastal towns are on the main train line between Reggio and Naples, and the SS18 road hugs the coast for much of the way. The A3 from Reggio di Calabria to Salerno is farther inland.

Scilla

With the urban confusion of Reggio and Villa San Giovanni left behind, you hit one of the most striking stretches of Calabria's coastline. The highlands of the Aspromonte reach right to the coast, and the views from the cliffs across to Sicily fuel the imagination. If you're coming from the north, the drive is still better (especially if you take it slowly on the SS18). Wedged in here and arching around a small beach is the picturesque town of Scilla, its northern end dominated by the rock associated with Scylla, the mythical sea monster who drowned sailors navigating the Stretto di Messina (and if she didn't get them, Charybdis across in Sicily would).

The *Principessa Paola del Belgio* HI hostel (☎ 0965-75 40 33) is at Via Nazionale, in the castle atop Scylla's rock, and generally opens from 1 April to 30 September. At the time of writing it was closed for restoration, so call ahead to see if it has reopened. You could try the *Albergo le Sirene* (☎ 0965-75 40 19), Via Nazionale 95, with rooms for L38,000/60,000. Just north of the castle, there is a row of houses built into the water – they are worth seeing.

Nicotera

About 50 km north, Nicotera is also dominated by a medieval castle. At least one camping ground functions all year round here, *Camping Sayonara* (☎ 0963-8 19 44) at Nicotera Marina, with good ocean views. It charges about L8000 a person.

About 20 km north-west of the town at **Capo Vaticano** are several tourist villages, including the *Costa Azzurra* (☎ 0963-66 31 09). It closes in winter and generally imposes a full board arrangement.

Tropea

Just north of Capo Vaticano, Tropea is a pretty little town perched high above a small beach. The almost (but not quite) twee town centre is becoming a minor tourist drawcard in itself.

There is a Pro Loco tourist office (☎ 6 64 75) in the centre. The telephone code is 0963.

Most of the 10 or so hotels are in the higher price bracket, although *La Perla* (☎ 6 13 68), Viale Crigna, has singles/doubles from L40,000/60,000 and is open all year. The *Stromboli* tourist village (☎ 66 90 93) charges from L60,000 to L110,000 a person for full board on a sliding scale from winter to super-high season (August).

The SAV bus line operates in this area, connecting the resorts with Tropea and Pizzo, which both have train stations.

Pizzo

Farther north of Tropea, in the bars of Pizzo, you will find possibly Italy's best *tartufo*, a type of chocolate ice-cream ball.

Inside the town's **duomo** lies the tomb of Joachim Murat, king of Naples from 1808 until 1815, when he was defeated by the Austrians, and the Bourbons were restored to the Neapolitan throne. Popped there by his chum and emperor, Napoleon, and architect of various enlightened reforms, the locals seemed to prefer the Bourbon devil they had known, and showed no great concern when Murat was imprisoned and executed here after one last attempt to regain power in September 1815.

Just north of the town, the **Chiesa di Piedigrotta** was literally carved into the sandstone near the beach in the 17th century by Neapolitan shipwreck survivors. It was later added to (the statue of Fidel Castro kneeling before a medallion of Pope John XXIII is an obvious recent addition), but the place is crumbling away, and there is no move afoot to stop the rot.

Wander through Piazzetta Garibaldi, the picturesque old centre of Pizzo overlooking the water, before settling in at *Bar Ercole* for an ice-cream fix.

For a typical seafood meal, *La Nave*, in a rusting boat on the waterfront, has good main courses from L10,000.

Paola

The coast between Pizzo and Paola, about 80 km to the north, is mostly overdeveloped and ugly. Paola is the main train hub for Cosenza, about 25 km inland, and is a large, comparatively nondescript place. Watched over by a crumbling castle, its main attraction is the **Santuario di San Francesco di Paola**. St Francis was born and died in Paola in the 15th century. He was known as a miracle-worker in his lifetime, and the sanctuary he and his followers first carved out of the bare rock has for centuries been the object of pilgrimage. You can wander through these spartan chambers, but there is precious little to see. Over them have since been built a church and monastery. A chapel in the church contains a reliquary of the saint. The sanctuary is open from 6 am to 12.30 pm and 2 to 5.30 pm.

The *Albergo Elena* (☎ 0982-61 24 74), Via San Leonardo, has rooms from L30,000/45,000, although towns farther north up the coast might be preferable.

Diamante to Praia a Mare

Diamante and, five km farther north, Cirella mark the southern end of a largely uninterrupted stretch of wide, grey pebbly beach that continues for about 30 km to Praia a Mare, just short of Calabria's regional boundary with Basilicata. Although popular with the locals, it is for the most part uninspiring. Backed by rows of camp sites and growing development projects, the coast here lacks much of the scenic splendour to the north in Basilicata or indeed south towards Reggio di Calabria.

Il Fortino (☎ 0985-8 60 85), at Via Vittorio Veneto in Cirella, is one of several camp sites and so-called tourist villages along the coast here.

If you do find the coast a little flat, head for Scalea and the hills. The old centre of **Scalea**, about 15 km south of Praia, is one of the more eye-catching towns along the northern coast. Climb the stairway lanes past the muddle of tumbledown houses, or stop in Piazza de Palma for a beer at the Tarì Bar.

Back among the anonymous modern urbanscape below, you could stay at the *Camping la Pantera Rosa* (☎ 0985-2 15 46) on Corso Mediterraneo. In August it costs L10,000 for a person and a tent space, but the price drops considerably on either side of this high season.

Praia a Mare

A couple of km short of the border with Basilicata, Praia a Mare is a modern and not terribly appealing town built to serve Italian holiday-makers. At least the surrounding landscape takes a more dramatic tone here, with the SS18 coastal highway climbing away behind the town up into Basilicata. The **Isola di Dino**, just off the coast south of the town, is blessed with an easily accessible **grotto** every bit as impressive as Capri's better known Grotta Azzurra, and the grey beach is expansive enough.

If you plan to stay in Praia, *La Mantinera* (☎ 0985-7 25 84) is at the southern end of town in the Fiuzzi area. The *Hotel Rex* (☎ 0985-7 21 91), Via C Colombo, a couple of blocks back from Praia's beach, has good

rooms from L50,000/80,000. The hotel also has a decent restaurant.

Candidly, you're better off up the road in Maratea, across the regional frontier in Basilicata (see the appropriate section above).

Autolinee Preite operates five or six buses a day in each direction between Cosenza and Praia a Mare. SITA goes north to Maratea.

Aieta & Tortora

The hill villages of **Aieta** and **Tortora**, about 12 and six km inland from Praia, belong to another world. Infrequent local buses serve both villages, but this is really only a practical excursion for people with their own transport or a lot of time and patience. The towns are precariously perched upon ridges that must have been hard going before asphalt days. Aieta is higher up, and the ride constitutes much of the reward for going there. Walk up to the 16th-century Palazzo Spinello at the end of the road and take a look into the ravine behind it. The bare hills – sparsely inhabited, thinly cultivated and home to small flocks of sheep – have provided farmers with a meagre living for centuries.

Sicily (Sicilia)

Think of Sicily (Sicilia) and two things immediately come to mind: beaches and the Mafia. There is no doubt its beaches are beautiful and that organised crime has a powerful impact on Sicilian society. But the island is too diverse to be so easily summed up. It is a place of contrasts, from the crumbling grandeur of the capital, Palermo, to the up-market glitz of the tourist resort, Taormina. There are Greek ruins at Syracuse, Agrigento, Selinunte and Segesta; and the volcanic Aeolian Islands off Sicily's north coast have a wild beauty matched only by the spectacular Mt Etna on the island's east coast.

Sicily is the largest island in the Mediterranean and its strategic location made it a prize for successive waves of invaders. As well as Greek temples, there are Roman ruins, Norman churches and castles, Arab and Byzantine domes and splendid Baroque churches and palaces.

HISTORY

It is believed the earliest settlers were the Sicanians, Elymians and Siculians, who came from various points around the southern Mediterranean, followed by the Phoenicians. Greek colonisation began in the 8th century BC with the foundation of Naxos. The cities of Syracuse, Catania, Messina and Agrigento grew and still dominate the island. By 210 BC, Sicily was under Roman control, with power eventually passing to the Byzantines and then the Arabs, who had settled in by 903 AD.

Norman conquest of the island began in 1060, when Roger I of Hauteville captured Messina. Mastery of Sicily subsequently passed to the Swabians and the Holy Roman emperor Frederick II, known as Stupor Mundi (Wonder of the World). In the 13th century the French Angevins provided a period of misrule that ended with the revolt known as the Sicilian Vespers in 1282. The island was handed over to the Spanish

Aragon family and, in 1503, to the Spanish crown. After short periods of Savoy and Austrian rule in the 18th century, Sicily again came under Spanish control with the Bourbons of Naples in 1734, who united the island with southern Italy in the Kingdom of the Two Sicilies.

On 11 May 1860, Giuseppe Garibaldi landed at Marsala with his One Thousand and began the conquest that eventually set the seal on the unification of Italy. Life did not greatly improve for the people and between 1871 and 1914 more than one million Sicilians emigrated, mainly to the USA.

In 1943, some 140,000 Allied troops under General Dwight Eisenhower landed in south-eastern Sicily. Initially blocked by dogged Italian and German resistance, Eisenhower's field commanders entered Messina within six weeks, after heavy fighting had devastated many parts of the country. The Allied occupation lasted until early the following year, and in 1948 Sicily became a semi-autonomous region. Unlike other such regions in Italy, it has its own parliament and legislative powers.

ORIENTATION & INFORMATION

Although some industry has developed, the island's economy is still largely agricultural and the people remain strongly connected to the land. Along the east coast especially, there is mile upon mile of citrus groves. D H Lawrence's musings in *Sea & Sardinia* could have been penned yesterday: 'So many lemons! Think of all the lemonade crystals they will be reduced to! Think of America drinking them up next summer.'

The coastal landscape ranges from the rugged and windswept to long stretches of sandy beach, white rolling hills, mountains and dry plateaus dominate the interior. The temperate climate brings mild weather in winter, but summer is relentlessly hot and the beaches swarm with holiday-makers. The best

Sicily (Sicilia)

times to visit are spring and autumn, when it is warm enough for the beach but not too hot for sightseeing.

Sicilian food is spicy and sweet – no doubt part of the island's Oriental heritage. The focus along the coast is on seafood, notably swordfish, and fresh produce. Some say fruit and vegetables taste better in Sicily. The cakes and pastries can be works of art, but are very sweet. Try the cassata, a rich cake filled with ricotta and candied fruits (you can also buy cassata ice cream); *cannoli*, tubes of pastry filled with cream, ricotta or chocolate; and *dolci di mandorle*, the many varieties of almond cakes and pastries. Like the Spaniards, Sicilians have a penchant for marzipan, which they make just as well as their Iberian cousins. Then there is granita, a drink of crushed ice flavoured with lemon, strawberry or coffee, to name a few flavours. Perfect on a hot Sicilian day.

THE MAFIA

The overt presence of the Italian army in Sicily (you'll see armed soldiers at 'strategic' spots here and there) has done little to dent the Mafia's activities. However, since the arrest of the Sicilian 'godfather', Salvatore ('Totò') Riina, in 1993, Mafia *pentiti* (grasses) have continued to blow the whistle on fellow felons, politicians, businessmen and others, right up to former prime minister Giulio Andreotti, who went on trial in April 1995. Some fear the pentiti are inventing confessions to settle private scores, but there must be something in it, otherwise the Cosa Nostra, as the Sicilian Mafia is known, would not have opened a campaign in early 1995 to 'discourage' pentiti by bumping off their relatives. The Italian author Luigi Barzini once wrote: 'The phenomenon has deep roots in history, in the character of the Sicilians, in local habits. Its origins disappear down the dim vistas of the centuries.'

SICILY

Revolutionary for Life

The man who led the One Thousand ashore at Marsala in May 1960 was no novice in matters of arms and revolt. Giuseppe Garibaldi, born in Nice in 1807, was already a prominent agitator in Genoa by the time he reached his mid-20s. When the insurrection of 1834 in that city failed, he headed off for a more attractive source of independence wars – South America. For the next 14 years he joined various fights against Spanish hegemony, particularly in Uruguay and on the Rio Grande. It was here that he formed the Italian Legion, known also as the Red Shirts.

Back in Italy in 1849, Garibaldi fought in a vain attempt to maintain the ephemeral Republic of Rome, and was later appointed a general in Cavour's Piedmontese army in the second war of independence in the late '50s. Irritated that his native Nice was ceded in peace talks to France, he abandoned the army, only to turn up in Marsala at the head of his famous band. Five months after conquering the Kingdom of the Two

Garibaldi on an election poster, depicted as an upside-down Stalin.

Sicilies, he simply handed it over to Victor Emmanuel II, thus effectively creating Italian unity.

It didn't stop there. Garibaldi fought the Austrians in the third war of independence (1866) and several times tried to wrest Rome from papal control. In 1870 he was in France fighting the Prussians. Until he drew his last breath in 1882, he remained active in Italian politics. An unbending revolutionary to the end, he did his part to foment the organisation of workers' movements and promote the worldwide socialist movement, the First International. ■

Sicilians feel offended that the image abroad of their proud island is one written in blood. There is no need to fear you will be caught in the crossfire of a gang war while in Sicily. The 'men of honour' are little interested in the affairs of foreign tourists. (See Mafia in the Facts About the Country chapter.)

DANGERS & ANNOYANCES

Sicilians are generally welcoming and friendly, but female tourists might find the local men a little too friendly. Women especially should take a hint from local women and avoid walking around at night alone in the bigger cities such as Palermo, Catania and Messina. Exercise caution elsewhere too.

You won't have to worry about confronting the Godfather, but petty criminals abound, especially in the bigger centres. Pickpockets and motorbike-mounted snatch thieves are the worst, and the latter love handbags and small day packs. If you have to carry one of these items, keep a firm hold on it. Don't wear jewellery and keep all your valuables in a money belt or in your hotel.

Car theft is a problem in Palermo, so using private guarded car parks is advisable.

THINGS TO BUY

As in Spain and Portugal, the Arabs brought to Sicily a rich tradition of ceramic production. Although the modern product is doubtless directed at tourists, as souvenirs go they are evocative of the island. Simple designs with blues and yellows as base colours best reflect the artisanal roots of the ceramics; more luridly decorated plates, vases, pots and bowls can be found all over the island. Or you could go for a ceramic *trinacria*, a face surrounded by three legs representing the three-pointed island.

Since the 18th century, Sicily's *carretti* (carts) have been a byword for the island. Used for transport until the arrival of the motorcar, the wooden carts were lovingly sculpted and bedecked with brightly coloured illustrations of mythic events, local characters or even family histories. You'd be lucky to see one in action now, but they are occasionally hauled out as tourist attractions.

For the ultimate in memento kitsch, however, you could always buy one of the models on sale in virtually all souvenir shops.

GETTING THERE & AWAY
Air

Flights from all over Italy land at Palermo and Catania. The airports are also serviced by flights from major European cities. Palermo's airport is Punta Raisi, about 32 km out of the city, while Catania's airport is seven km out. Buses run from both airports into the respective city centres. See the Palermo and Catania Getting There & Away sections for further details. The easiest way to obtain information on flights to/from Sicily is from any CIT or Alitalia office throughout Italy. Charter flights are a possibility in and out of Palermo.

Bus

There is an SAIS bus between Rome (leaves 8 pm daily) and Sicily, arriving at Messina (4.30 am), Catania (6 am) and Agrigento (9.30 am). The bus connects in Catania with others to Palermo, Syracuse, Ragusa and Enna. Going the other way, the bus leaves Agrigento daily at 4.15 pm and Messina daily at 9.30 pm, arriving in Rome at 6.30 am. In Rome, enquire at Saistours (☎ 06-482 50 66), Piazza della Repubblica 42, or go to the bus station at Piazzale FS Tiburtina. Segesta runs a direct service between Palermo and Rome. See Palermo Getting There & Away for more details.

Train

Direct trains run from Milan, Florence, Rome, Naples and Reggio di Calabria to Messina and on to Palermo, Catania and other provincial capitals – the trains are transported from the mainland by ferry from Villa San Giovanni. Be prepared for long delays on Intercity trains on this route.

Boat

Regular car/passenger ferries cross the strait between Villa San Giovanni (Calabria) and Messina. Hydrofoils run by the railways, and snappier jobs run by SNAV, connect Messina directly with Reggio di Calabria. See the Messina and Reggio di Calabria sections for details.

Sicily is also accessible by ferry from Genoa, Livorno, Naples and Cagliari, and from Malta and Tunisia. The main company servicing the Mediterranean is Tirrenia and its services to/from Sicily include Palermo-Cagliari, Palermo-Genoa, Palermo-Naples, Catania-Livorno, Trapani-Cagliari, Trapani-Tunisia and (sometimes in summer) Naples-Reggio di Calabria-Catania-Syracuse-Malta.

Grandi Traghetti runs ferries from Livorno and Genoa to Palermo, and from there on to Malta and Tunisia. Grimaldi runs luxury cruise boats from Palermo to Genoa, Malta and Tunisia.

Alilauro runs summer ferries from Trapani to Kelibia in Tunisia (via Pantelleria) and to Naples via Ustica.

Ferry prices are determined by the season and jump considerably in summer (Tirrenia's high season varies according to destination, but is generally from July to September). Timetables can change dramatically each year. Tirrenia publishes an annual booklet listing all routes and prices, which is available at Tirrenia offices and agents throughout Italy.

In summer all routes are busy and, unless you book in advance, you may literally miss the boat. Tickets can be booked through the company concerned or travel agencies throughout Italy. Offices and telephone numbers for the ferry companies are listed in the Getting There & Away sections for the relevant cities.

The following is a guide to fares, based on high-season travel on Tirrenia at the time of writing. For an airline-type chair, fares were: Genoa-Palermo L108,100 (22 hours), Naples-Palermo L68,400 (10½ hours), Palermo-Cagliari L50,800 (14 hours) and Trapani-Tunisia L91,200 (eight hours). For a 2nd-class cabin (shared with up to three other people and often segregated by gender) fares were: Genoa-Palermo L121,900, Naples-Palermo L78,200, Palermo-Cagliari L74,700 and Trapani-Tunisia L115,500.

Fares for cars vary according to the size of the vehicle. High-season charges for the Palermo-Cagliari route ranged from L94,200 to L149,700; a small caravan cost L42,500, while motorbikes under 200 cc were L29,500 (L44,000 for 200 cc and above) and bicycles L16,200.

There are also ferry and hydrofoil services from Sicily to the small groups of islands off the coast (the Aeolian Islands, the Egadi Islands, the Pelagic Islands, Pantelleria and Ustica). See the relevant Getting There & Away sections in this chapter for details.

GETTING AROUND
Bus
The best mode of public transport in Sicily is the bus. Numerous companies run services connecting the main towns around the coast including Messina, Catania, Syracuse, Agrigento, Trapani and Palermo. Services also connect these cities with the smaller towns along the coast and in the interior. The companies with the most extensive networks are SAIS and AST. See the Getting There & Away and Getting Around sections for each town.

Train
The coastal train service between Messina and Palermo, and between Messina and Syracuse is efficient and the run between Palermo and Agrigento is also generally OK. However, train services elsewhere to the interior can be infrequent and slow, and it is best to do some research before deciding between train and bus.

Car & Motorbike
There is no substitute for the freedom your own vehicle can give you, especially for getting to places not well served by public transport. Roads are generally good and autostradas connect most major cities. It is possible to hitchhike in Sicily, but don't expect a ride in a hurry. Single women should not hitchhike under any circumstances.

SICILY

Palermo

At one time an Arab emirate and seat of a Norman kingdom, and in its heyday regarded as the grandest city in Europe, Palermo today is in a remarkable state of decay. It was heavily bombed in WW II and has been much neglected since. It is noted more for the Mafia trials of the 1980s, the assassinations in 1992 of the top anti-Mafia judges, Giovanni Falcone and Paolo Borsellino, and the upsurge in gangland killings in the mid-1990s. It was here that former prime minister Giulio Andreotti went on trial in 1995 for involvement with Cosa Nostra.

Beneath the grime enough evidence of its golden days remains for Palermo to be a compelling city to visit, if only as a crossroads between East and West. Cultural cross-fertilisation finds expression in the city's architectural mix, obvious in such monuments as the adjacent churches of La Martorana and San Cataldo.

Palermo's superb position by the sea at the foot of Monte Pellegrino, with the fertile Conca d'Oro valley behind it, has long made it a rich prize for Sicily's colonisers. The Phoenicians established the town of Ziz here, on the site of a prehistoric village around the 8th century BC. It remained a relatively minor town under Roman, and later Byzantine, domination and it was not until 831 AD, when it was conquered by the Arabs, that the city truly flourished to be become a jewel of the Islamic world.

When the Normans took control in 1072, things only improved. The seat of Roger I of Hauteville's kingdom, Palermo was hailed as one of the most magnificent and cultured cities of 12th-century Europe. For more than half a century after Roger's death the monarchy foundered, eventually passing to the German Hohenstaufens and the Holy Roman emperor Frederick II, still remembered as one of Sicily's most enlightened rulers. After his death, Palermo and all of Sicily passed to the French Anjou family, themselves later deposed following the Sicilian Vespers

revolt, which started in Palermo. By then eclipsed by Naples, Palermo's primacy gave way to a long, slow decline.

ORIENTATION

Palermo is a large but manageable city. The main streets of the historical centre are Via Roma and Via Maqueda, which extend from Stazione Centrale in the south to Piazza Castelnuovo, a vast square in the northern, modern part of town and a 20-minute walk from the train station. Around Stazione Centrale are most of the cheaper pensioni and hotels. It's a grimy and chaotic area, but behind the decaying palaces lining the main streets there is a fascinating maze of narrow lanes and tiny piazzas where you will find markets and trattorias and, unfortunately, get an even better idea of just how decrepit Palermo is.

The area around Piazza Castelnuovo seems a world away, with its malls, outdoor cafés and designer shops. Intersecting Via Maqueda and Via Roma are Via Vittorio Emanuele and Via Cavour, the main thoroughfares to the port and Stazione Marittima (about a 10-minute walk east of Via Roma).

INFORMATION
Tourist Offices

The main APT office (☎ 58 61 22) is at Piazza Castelnuovo 35. The staff speak English and you can pick up a map of the city and a monthly calendar of cultural, theatrical and musical events. Ask for the *Palermo Flash Guide* booklet. The office is open Monday to Friday from 8 am to 8 pm and Saturday to 2 pm. The branch office at Stazione Centrale is more convenient and has the same information. There are other branch offices at Stazione Marittima; in Piazza San Sepolcro, off Via Maqueda; and at Punta Raisi airport. Most of these offices were closed at the time of writing, but were due to reopen at some stage, with opening hours similar to the main APT office.

Money

The exchange office at Stazione Centrale is open daily from 8 am to 8 pm, and there's another at the airport (Banco di Sicilia). Banks are generally open from 8.30 am to 1.15 pm. Several have ATMs, including the Banca Nazionale del Lavoro, Via Roma 297, and the Monte dei Paschi di Siena off Via Sant'Oliva. American Express is represented by Ruggieri & Figli (☎ 58 71 44), Via Emerico Amari 40.

Post & Telecommunications

The main post office is at Via Roma 322. It is open from 8.10 am to 7.30 pm (on Saturday to 1.30 pm) and has fax and telex services. The post code for central Palermo is 90100.

There is a Telecom office virtually opposite Stazione Centrale in Piazza G Cesare. It is open daily from 8 am to 9.30 pm. The Telecom office on Piazzale Ungheria is open Monday to Saturday from 8 am to 8 pm. The telephone code for Palermo is 091.

Foreign Consulates

The UK consular agent (☎ 58 25 33) is at Via Cavour 117. France (☎ 58 50 73) is represented at Via Segesta 9 and Germany (☎ 58 33 77) at Via Emerico Amari 124. Although the US maintains an office (☎ 611 00 20) at Via Re Federico 18B, it mainly handles Italians' US pension problems.

Tunisia has a consulate (☎ 32 12 31) at Piazza Ignazio Florio 2. Most foreigners can travel as tourists to Tunisia visa-free, but it is worth dropping in (9 am to midday) to make sure. Australians may need a visa.

Most consulates are open Monday to Friday from about 9 am to midday (some to 1 pm).

Travel Agencies

CIT (☎ 58 63 33), where you can book train, ferry and air tickets, is at Via della Libertà 12. There is a CTS travel agent (☎ 611 07 13) at Via N Garzilli 28/G. A bit more convenient is Record Viaggi (☎ 611 09 10), Via Mariano Stabile 168 (between Via Ruggero Settimo and Via Roma). If you're looking for charter flights, shop around.

Bookshops & Newspaper Stands

Feltrinelli, Via Maqueda 459, has a small foreign language section with some books in English. There are several newspaper stands around Piazza Giuseppe Verdi selling foreign press.

Emergency & Medical Services

Ring the police on ☎ 113. The questura (☎ 21 01 11), where you should go to report thefts and other crimes, is in Piazza della Vittoria.

In a medical emergency, phone the Public Hospital (Ospedale Civico), Via Carmelo Lazzaro, on ☎ 666 11 11, or ring an ambulance on ☎ 30 66 44. There is an all-night pharmacy, Lo Cascio, near Stazione Centrale at Via Roma 1.

THINGS TO SEE

Opening times of the principal sights are constantly changing. As a vague rule of thumb, most churches open from about 8 or 9 am to midday and again for a couple of hours from 3 pm. Museums generally open only until about 1 or 2 pm.

Quattro Canti & the Centre

The busy intersection of Via Vittorio Emanuele and Via Maqueda marks the Quattro Canti (the 'Four Corners' of Palermo), the centre of the oldest part of town. Each corner is marked by a 17th-century Spanish Baroque façade decorated with a fountain and a statue. On the south-west corner is the Baroque **Chiesa di San Giuseppe dei Teatini**, its interior dripping with marble.

Across Via Maqueda, Piazza Pretoria hosts the beautiful **Fontana Pretoria**, created by Florentine sculptors in the 16th century. At the time of its unveiling, the shocked populace named it the Fountain of Shame because of its nude figures. Closing off the east side of the piazza is the Baroque **Chiesa di Santa Caterina**, while the **Palazzo del Municipio**, also known as the Palazzo delle Aquile because of the eagle sculptures that guard each corner of the roof, fronts the southern edge of the square.

On the north side of Via Vittorio Emanuele, just before it crosses Via Roma, is the Baroque **Chiesa di San Matteo**, which has a richly decorated interior. The four statues in the pilasters of the dome represent the Virtues and were carved by Giacomo Serpotta in 1728.

A few steps south of Piazza Pretoria in Piazza Bellini you will see one of Palermo's most famous churches, **La Martorana**, also known as Chiesa di Santa Maria dell'Ammiraglio. Although the original 12th-century structure has been much altered, it retains its Arab-Norman bell tower and the interior is richly decorated with Byzantine mosaics. Totally in keeping with the decoration, the Greek eastern rite Mass is

still celebrated here. Also in the piazza is the Norman **Chiesa di San Cataldo**, in the care of the Knights of the Holy Sepulchre. A small and simple church, its battlements and red domes are another fusion of Arab and Norman styles.

While wandering down Via Maqueda towards Stazione Centrale, note the Baroque palaces in various stages of decay, including the **Palazzo dei Principi di Comitini** on the corner of Via del Bosco.

The **Chiesa del Gesù**, also known as the Casa Professa, in Via Ponticello, was built in 1564 and then absorbed into another struc-

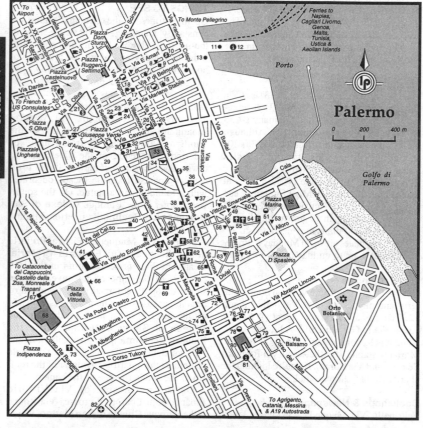

SICILY

Palermo

0   200   400 m

ture completed in 1633. Although largely destroyed by heavy bombing in 1943, most of the stucco work and frescoes have been restored. To the right of the church is a porticoed Baroque courtyard.

Duomo

Despite its hotchpotch of styles, there is little doubting the grandeur of Palermo's duomo, west of the Quattro Canti along Via Vittorio Emanuele.

Built in the second half of the 12th century, the duomo has been modified many times since, most disastrously in the 18th century when the dome was added, spoiling the architectural harmony of the building. In the same period the interior was restored. The only part conserved in purely original

Norman style is the apse, although the church overall remains an impressive example of Norman architecture. Arab influences in some of the geometric decoration are unmistakeable and the graceful Gothic towers distract the eye from that dome. Inside are royal tombs, and among those interred in porphyry sarcophagi are Roger II, Henry VI of Hohenstaufen, Constance de Hauteville and Frederick II of Hohenstaufen. The ashes of St Rosalia, patron saint of Palermo, are contained in a silver urn in one of the church's numerous chapels.

Palazzo dei Normanni & Around

Across the Piazza della Vittoria and the gardens is the **Palazzo dei Normanni**, also known as the Palazzo Reale (Royal Palace).

SICILY

PLACES TO STAY					
9	Hotel Principe di Belmonte	48	Casa del Brodo	33	Museo Archeologico Regionale
17	Grand Hotel Le Palme	49	Ristorante Vittorio Emanuele	34	Post Office
18	Hotel Petit	50	La Cambusa	35	Banca Nazionale del Lavoro
23	Albergo Libertà, Hotel Elite & Hotel Boston–Madonia	53	Trattoria Il Crudo e Il Cotto	36	Chiesa di San Domenico
		56	Antica Focacceria di San Francesco	39	Teatro Biondi
24	Hotel Liguria	63	Trattoria dai Vespri	41	Duomo
38	Hotel Moderno	64	Trattoria Stella	43	Chiesa di San Giuseppe dei Teatini
40	Albergo Columbia			44	Quattro Canti
42	Centrale Palace Hotel		**OTHER**	47	Chiesa di San Matteo
45	Grande Albergo Sole			51	AST Bus Station
46	Albergo da Luigi	1	CTS Travel Agency	52	Palazzo Chiaramonte
57	Hotel Le Terrazze	2	CIT Travel Agency	54	Chiesa di San Francesco d'Assisi
65	Albergo Corona	4	Teatro Politeama		
70	Hotel Sicilia	5	German Consulate	55	Oratorio di San Lorenzo
71	Albergos Piccadilly & Concordia	7	Pietro Barbaro (SNAV Agents)	58	Chiesa di Santa Caterina
				59	Fontana Pretoria
72	Albergo Rosalia Conca d'Oro	10	American Express	60	Palazzo del Municipio
		11	Stazione Marittima	61	Chiesa di San Cataldo
74	Pensione Vittoria	12	APT Tourist Office	62	La Martorana
75	Pensione Sud	13	Tirrenia	66	Questura (Police Station)
		14	Siremar	67	Porta Nuova
		15	Grandi Traghetti & Grimaldi	68	Palazzo dei Normanni & Cappella Palatina
	PLACES TO EAT	16	Tunisian Consulate	69	Chiesa del Gesù
3	Roney	19	APT Tourist Office	73	Chiesa di San Giovanni degli Eremiti
6	Osteria lo Bianco	21	Monte dei Paschi di Siena		
8	Hostaria Al-Duar	22	Record Viaggi Travel Agency	76	Night Pharmacy
20	Dr Jekyll Mr Hyde			77	Telecom Office
25	Hostaria la Stella	26	UK Consulate	78	Urban Bus Station
28	Ristorante Charleston	27	Telecom Office	79	Intercity Bus Station
30	Dal Pompiere	29	Teatro Massimo	80	Stazione Centrale
37	Trattoria Shanghai & Vucciria Market	31	Feltrinelli Bookshop	81	APT Tourist Office
		32	Opera dei Pupi	82	Hospital

Built by the Arabs in the 9th century, it was extended by the Normans and restructured by the Hohenstaufens. It is now the seat of Sicily's regional government.

Enter from Piazza Indipendenza to see the **Cappella Palatino**, a magnificent example of Arab-Norman artistic genius, built during the reign of Roger II and decorated with Byzantine mosaics. The chapel was once described as 'the finest religious jewel dreamt of by human thought', its mosaics rivalled only by those of Ravenna and Istanbul. While the mosaics demonstrate palpably the Byzantine influence on Palermitan art, the geometric tile designs making up a good proportion of the decoration are a clear reminder of Arab input. The carved wooden ceiling is a classic example of intricate, Arab-style stalactite design, devoid of the depiction of living beings proscribed by Islam. The chapel is open Monday to Friday from 9 am to midday and 3 to 5 pm, Saturday from 9 am to midday and Sunday from 9 to 10 am and midday to 1 pm. Admission is free.

Also worth visiting in the palace is the Sala di Ruggero (King Roger's Room), his former bedroom. It is decorated with 12th-century mosaics. It is only possible to visit the room with a guide (free of charge). Go upstairs from the Cappella Palatino.

Next to the palace is the **Porta Nuova**, built to celebrate the arrival of Charles V in Palermo in 1535.

Chiesa di San Giovanni degli Eremiti

Just south of the palace, this church is a simple and tranquil refuge from the chaos outside. Located in Via dei Benedettini, St John of the Hermits is yet another telling example of the Sicilian Arab-Norman mix. Built under Roger II, it is topped by five red domes and set in a pretty garden with cloisters. It is now deconsecrated and there is little of interest inside the church.

Museo Archeologico & Around

A block north of the main post office on Via Roma is the Museo Archeologico Regionale. To enter, turn left into Via Bara all'Olivella and into Piazza Olivella. The museum houses a collection of Greek metopes from Selinunte, the Hellenistic *Bronze Ram of Syracuse* and finds from archaeological sites throughout the island. The museum is open Monday to Saturday from 9 am to 1.30 pm (also on Tuesdays and Fridays from 3 to 5 pm) and on Sundays and holidays to 12.30 pm. Admission is L2000.

About 200 metres south on Via Roma is **Chiesa di San Domenico**. The grand 17th-century structure houses the tombs of many important Sicilians and a wealth of paintings.

Towards Piazza Marina

Plunge into the streets heading towards the waterfront from the intersection of Via Vittorio Emanuele and Via Roma, and you'll find a few more architectural gems to be examined. The **Oratorio di San Lorenzo**, Via dell'Immacolatella, is decorated with stuccoes by Giacomo Serpotta, his greatest work. Caravaggio's last known piece, a Nativity, once hung over the altar. It was stolen in 1969 and has never been recovered. Virtually next door, the 13th-century **Chiesa di San Francesco d'Assisi** features a fine rose window and Gothic portal that have survived numerous restorations and restructuring.

Farther east, on Piazza Marina itself, the 14th-century **Palazzo Chiaramonte** boasts an imposing medieval façade that served as a model for many other buildings in Sicily. The island's Grand Parliament sat here in the 16th century and for many years so did the Holy Office of the Inquisition.

Catacombs & Castle

For centuries, Sicilians of a certain social standing didn't want anyone to forget them after body and soul had finally parted company. To this end, Capuchin monks did their best to embalm the wealthy departed of Palermo. The **Catacombe dei Cappuccini** in the Capuchin convent on Piazza Cappuccino, west of the city centre, are the result. They contain the mummified bodies and skeletons of some 8000 Palermitans who died between the 17th and 19th centuries.

The bodies are lined along the walls in various attitudes, and although time has been unkind to most, a few are remarkably intact, particularly one girl who clearly got a quality embalming. The catacombs are open daily from 9 am to midday and 3 to 5 pm. Admission is free.

In the same area is the **Castello della Zisa**, a 12th-century Arab-Norman castle. The name, which means 'the Splendid', testifies to the magnificence of the palace, built for William I and completed by William II. The castle is open Monday to Saturday from 9 am to 1.30 pm (also on Tuesdays and Fridays from 3 to 5 pm) and on Sundays and holidays to 12.30 pm. Admission is free.

Markets

Palermo's historical ties with the Arab world and its proximity to North Africa are reflected in the noisy street life of the city's ancient centre. Nowhere is this more evident than in its markets, which make a truly Oriental assault on all the senses.

Several markets are spread through the tangle of lanes and alleys of central Palermo, but the most famous is the **Vucciria**, winding south from the Chiesa di San Domenico. Here you can purchase anything your stomach desires (and several items it may recoil at – slipperytripe and all sorts of fishy things) as well as a host of off-the-back-of-a-truck style bargains.

Teatro Massimo

Overlooking Piazza Giuseppe Verdi, it has been a while since the proud and haughty 19th-century Teatro Massimo played host to a stage performance. Now the show goes on around it, with restoration programmes that have supposedly been in progress for the past 20 years. Someone put the scaffolding up, but that's about it.

No-one expects the theatre to open its doors for many years to come, if ever, and millions of lira keep disappearing down a bottomless pit of building tenders. A more eloquent symbol of Sicily's problems would be difficult to find.

PLACES TO STAY

You should have little trouble finding a room in Palermo at whatever price you choose. The tourist office at Stazione Centrale will make recommendations, but not bookings.

Head for Via Maqueda or Via Roma, between the station and Quattro Canti, for the bulk of the cheap rooms, some of which are in old apartment buildings. Rooms facing onto either street will be noisy. Women on their own should be wary about staying in the area near the train station, as it is not the safest place at night. Prostitutes from time to time bring clients to many of the cheaper hotels. As a rule, this is not really a problem – it's all fairly low key. The area around Piazza Castelnuovo offers a higher standard of accommodation with fewer budget options (catch bus No 101 or 107 from the train station to Piazza Sturzo).

Bottom End

The best camping ground is *Trinacria* (☎ 53 05 90), Via Barcarello 25, by the sea at Sferracavallo. It costs L6500 per person, plus L13,000 for a tent place. Catch bus No 628 from Piazzale A De Gasperi (which can be reached by bus No 101 from Stazione Centrale).

Near the train station, try the *Albergo Orientale* (☎ 616 57 27), Via Maqueda 26, in an old and somewhat decayed building with a once grand courtyard. Basic singles/doubles are L25,000/40,000 and triples are L60,000. Just around the corner is *Albergo Rosalia Conca d'Oro* (☎ 616 45 43), Via Santa Rosalia 7, with singles/doubles for L35,000/50,000 and triples for L60,000. The *Pensione Vittoria* (☎ 616 24 37), Via Maqueda 8, is close to the station and has still more spartan singles/doubles for L32,000/44,000.

There are a few hotels in the one building at Via Roma 72. The *Albergo Piccadilly* (☎ 617 64 70) has clean rooms for L30,000/60,000, while the *Albergo Concordia* (☎ 617 15 14) is also reasonable value at L30,000/50,000. The *Albergo Corona* (☎ 616 23 40), Via Roma 118, has clean, pleasant rooms for L32,000/50,000; a double with a bathroom is L58,000. *Albergo da Luigi*

(☎ 58 50 85), Via Vittorio Emanuele 284, is next to the Quattro Canti. It has rooms for L25,000/40,000, and with a bathroom for L35,000/50,000 or more depending on the room – try for one with a view onto the Piazza Pretoria and its fountain.

Around Piazza Castelnuovo, *Hotel Petit* (☎ 32 36 16), Via Principe di Belmonte 84, has comfortable rooms for L35,000/55,000 or for L42,000/65,000 with a bathroom. The *Hotel Liguria* (☎ 58 15 88), Via Mariano Stabile 128, offers a good standard of accommodation. Rooms are L35,000/50,000 and doubles with a bathroom are L65,000.

About halfway between the train station and Piazza Castelnuovo is the *Albergo Columbia* (☎ 32 06 05), Via del Celso 31, off Via Maqueda near Via Vittorio Emanuele. It has bearable rooms costing L35,000/55,000 and doubles with a bathroom for L65,000.

Middle

Near Via Vittorio Emanuele, at Via Roma 188, *Hotel Le Terrazze* (☎ 58 63 65) is an agreeable and clean establishment with great views of the city from its terraces. Rooms are L50,000/65,000 or L60,000/80,000 with a bathroom. Farther north on Via Roma at No 276, the *Hotel Moderno* (☎ 58 86 83) offers good rooms for L60,000/85,000 and triples for L110,000 with a bathroom. *Hotel Sicilia* (☎ 616 84 60), Via Divisi 99, on the corner of Via Maqueda, has large rooms of a reasonable standard, although they can be quite noisy. Singles/doubles are L38,000/55,000 and triples are L75,000, all with a bathroom.

Near Piazza Castelnuovo is the *Albergo Libertà* (☎ 32 19 11), Via Mariano Stabile 136, which has singles/doubles for L45,000/60,000 or for L60,000/80,000 with a bathroom; triples are L95,000. There are several other hotels in the same building. The *Hotel Elite* (☎ 32 93 18) has singles/doubles for L60,000/85,000 and triples for L115,000, all with a bathroom. The *Hotel Boston-Madonia* (☎ 58 02 34) has doubles with a bathroom for L85,000, which management will let go as singles for about L60,000.

Hotel Principe di Belmonte (☎ 33 10 65), Via Principe di Belmonte 25, has rooms for L45,000/85,000 or for L70,000/90,000 with a bathroom.

Top End

The *Centrale Palace Hotel* (☎ 33 66 66; fax 33 48 81), Via Vittorio Emanuele 327, has elegantly furnished rooms and full services; breakfast is included. Singles are L120,000, doubles L180,000 and triples L220,000. The *Grande Albergo Sole* (☎ 58 18 11; fax 611 01 82), Via Vittorio Emanuele 291, has similarly attractive rooms for L115,000/170,000 and triples for L200,000.

The four-star *Grand Hotel Le Palme* (☎ 58 39 33; fax 33 15 45), Via Roma 398, at the Piazza Castelnuovo end of town, is one of the ritziest hotels in Palermo. Its beautiful rooms cost L150,000/200,000, with breakfast included.

PLACES TO EAT

With more than 300 officially listed restaurants and eateries of various categories to choose from in the city and surrounding area, you should have little trouble finding something to suit your taste and budget.

Palermo's cuisine takes advantage of the fresh produce of the sea and the fertile Conca d'Oro valley. One of its most famous dishes is pasta con le sarde, with sardines, fennel, peppers, capers and pine nuts. Swordfish is served here sliced into huge steaks. A reflection of Sicily's proximity to North Africa, couscous has infiltrated local cuisine. Basically a bowl of steamed semolina, couscous can be made or broken as a meal by the sauce ladled over it.

Palermitans are late eaters and restaurants rarely open for dinner before 8 pm.

Markets

The Vucciria market is held daily, except Sunday, in the narrow streets between Via Roma, Piazza San Domenico and Via Vittorio Emanuele. Here you can buy fresh fruit and vegetables, meat, cheese and seafood. Or you can just watch as huge, freshly caught swordfish and tuna are sliced up and sold in minutes. Numerous stalls sell steaming hot, boiled octopus. Although the

---

Gelato

It is difficult to get a bad gelato in Italy. Instead, the challenge is to find the best! It is not surprising that many travellers to Italy become obsessed with the country's ice-cream, it really is so good and comes in so many flavours that it seems a shame not to eat at least two or three a day. Serious gelato eaters should search out the *gelaterie* which make their ice-cream on the premises, particularly the few establishments which actually make their gelato from scratch, using fresh ingredients (many places use industrial powdered flavours these days). You only need to try one of the fruit flavours in order to be able to tell the difference. Most Italians would agree that the best gelato in the country is found in Sicily and if you locate a good gelateria, which makes its own ice-cream with fresh ingredients, you will realise that you have probably never before eaten a gelato *that* good! ■

---

best known, the Vucciria is far from the only such market around town. For other grocery supplies, try the Standa supermarket at Via della Libertà 30.

Inexpensive Restaurants

One of the cheapest options for a full sit-down meal is *Dr Jekyll Mr Hyde*, a self-service pizzeria/fast-food outlet next to the tourist office in Piazza Castelnuovo. A decent set menu lunch costs L12,000, and they have cheap pizza slices and the like.

Dal Pompiere, Via Bara all'Olivella 107, just up the road from the Opera dei Pupi puppet theatre, has a simple but filling set menu lunch for L10,000. The *Hostaria la Stella*, Via Cavour 97, also has a good lunch for L14,000.

If you want to try an age-old Palermo snack – a panino with milza (veal innards) and ricotta cheese – head for the *Antica Focacceria di San Francesco*, Via Paternostro 58, the street north of Piazza S Oliva. They also have pizza slices and similar snacks. The place, one of the city's oldest eating houses, is worth seeking out.

Another Palermitan institution is the *Casa del Brodo*, Via Vittorio Emanuele 173. For more than 100 years they have been serving up various broths and boiled meat dishes, all much appreciated by locals.

Osteria lo Bianco, Via E Amari 104, off Via Roma at the Castelnuovo end of town, has a menu that changes daily. A full meal will cost under L20,000. *Trattoria Stella*, Via

Alloro 104, is in the courtyard of the old Hotel Patria. In summer the entire courtyard is filled with tables. A full meal will come to around L20,000. *Trattoria dai Vespri*, Piazza Santa Croce dei Vespri 8, off Via Roma, past Chiesa di Santa Anna, has outside tables and excellent food for under L25,000 for a full meal. Meat and seafood are cooked on an outdoor barbecue in summer.

Trattoria Shanghai, right in the middle of the Vucciria market, is an atmospheric little place if you manage to get a table on the terrace overlooking the market. Despite its Chinese name, the trattoria serves typical Sicilian food, which is reasonably priced but not the best you can eat in Palermo.

La Cambusa and *Trattoria Il Crudo e Il Cotto*, both in Piazza Marina, near the port, are popular and serve good meals for around L30,000. The former sometimes has a set all-inclusive seafood menu for L35,000. Not far away, the *Ristorante Vittorio Emanuele*, at No 150 on the street of the same name, has a limited but tasty menu.

If you feel like a Tunisian night out, with couscous and other typical North African dishes, try the *Hostaria Al-Duar*, Via Ammiraglio Gravina 31A, the first street south of Via E Amari.

Expensive Restaurants

Most of the posher restaurants are on the outskirts of Palermo or in nearby towns. *I Mandarini* (☎ 671 21 99) is at Pallavicino, near Mondello beach, at Via Rosario da

SICILY

Patanna 18. The food is good and a meal will cost at least L40,000. The locals head for Mondello to eat seafood. Try *La Barcaccia* (☎ 45 40 79), Via Piano di Gallo 4. Again, you will be lucky to eat for under L40,000. A popular but pricey fish restaurant at Sferracavallo is the *Al Delfino* (☎ 53 02 82). Don't expect much change from L100,000.

The *Charleston* is one of Palermo's classiest restaurants. Its main establishment is in Palermo at Piazzale Ungheria 30. In summer it generally closes and its Mondello branch takes over, with outdoor eating on Viale Regina Elena. Expect to pay around L100,000 per head for a memorable meal.

Cafés

In Via Principe di Belmonte, which is closed to traffic between Via Ruggero Settimo and Via Roma, there are numerous cafés with outside tables, where you can linger over breakfast or lunch in summer. If you want to spend less, buy a panino in one of the many bars along Via Roma. For an expensive afternoon tea, head for *Roney*, Via della Libertà 13, Palermo's most fashionable and best known pasticceria.

ENTERTAINMENT
Theatre

For opera and ballet, the main venue is the Teatro Politeama (☎ 605 33 15) on Piazza Ruggero Settimo. If your Italian is up to it, you can see plays at the Teatro Biondi (☎ 58 87 55) on Via Roma. *Il Giornale di Sicilia* has a daily listing of what's on.

Opera dei Pupi

Something of a Sicilian speciality, the Opera dei Pupi, Via Bara all'Olivella 95, just south of Via Cavour, makes for an enchanting performance experience. A good break for young kids, the elaborate old puppets will endear themselves to adults too. You can generally expect shows to be staged on weekends. At No 40, in the same street, is one of several artisans who makes and repairs the puppets.

GETTING THERE & AWAY
Air

The airport is at Punta Raisi, 32 km west of Palermo, and is a terminal for domestic and European flights. For information about national flights, ring Alitalia on ☎ 601 91 11 and for European flights, ring ☎ 59 12 75. Alitalia has an office (☎ 601 93 33) at Via della Libertà 39. It is usually possible at any time of the year to hunt down charter flights to major European cities such as London – shop around the travel agents.

Bus

The main Intercity bus station is around Via Paolo Balsamo, to the east of the train station.

SAIS (☎ 616 60 28), Via Balsamo 16, runs services to Rome, with a change at Catania, costing L70,000 one way and L110,000 return. They leave daily at 7 am and 5 pm and take about 13 hours. SAIS also services Catania (more than 20 a day), Enna (six a day), Piazza Armerina (four a day), Syracuse (six a day), Messina (via Catania; 10 a day) and Cefalù (two a day).

Segesta (☎ 616 79 19), Via Balsamo 26, has a direct service to Rome three or four times a week. It also runs frequent buses to Trapani (two hours). For Marsala, go to Salemi (☎ 617 54 11), Via Rosario Gregorio 44. Cuffaro and Fratelli Camilleri between them have about 10 buses a day to Agrigento.

Away from the main terminal, AST (☎ 688 27 83), Piazza Marina 31, runs three daily buses to Ragusa.

Numerous other companies service points throughout Sicily and most have offices in the Via Paolo Balsamo area. Their addresses and telephone numbers, as well as destinations, are listed in *Palermo Flash Guide*, which is available at the tourist office.

Train

Regular trains leave from Stazione Centrale for Milazzo, Messina, Catania, Syracuse and Agrigento, as well as nearby towns such as Cefalù. There are also Intercity trains for Reggio di Calabria, Naples and Rome. A one-way ticket from Palermo to Rome costs

SICILY

SICILY

L78,900, plus a L23,700 supplement for Intercity trains. The trip takes about 13 hours (two hours less on the Intercity). Train timetable information (☎ 616 18 06) is available in English at the station. There is a Transalpino office inside the station, as well as baggage-storage and bathing facilities.

Car & Motorbike
Palermo is accessible by autostrada from Messina (only partially completed) and from Catania (which passes Enna). Trapani and Marsala are also easily accessible by autostrada, while Agrigento and Palermo are linked by a good state road through the interior of the island.

Rental Europcar (☎ 32 19 49) has an office at Via Cavour 77A, as well as others at Stazione Centrale (☎ 616 50 50) and the airport (☎ 59 12 27). All major rental companies are represented in Palermo.

Boat
Ferries leave from Molo Vittorio Veneto, off Via Francesco Crispi, for Cagliari (Sardinia), Naples, Livorno and Genoa (see the Getting There & Away section at the beginning of this chapter for further details). The Tirrenia office (☎ 602 11 11) is at the port in Palazzina Stella Maris. Siremar (☎ 58 24 03) runs ferries and hydrofoils to Ustica and the Aeolian Islands; its office is at Via F Crispi 118. SNAV, represented by the Pietro Barbaro agency (☎ 33 33 33) at Via Principe Belmonte 55, also runs a summer service to the Aeolian Islands.

Grandi Traghetti (☎ 58 74 04), Via Mariano Stabile 57 , has weekly ferries from Palermo to Genoa, Malta and Tunisia. They also run a direct service between Malta and Tunisia. The one-way fare for an airline-type seat from Palermo to either Malta or Tunisia is L144,000 in the high season. The trip to Malta takes 13 hours. While there is a direct ferry from Tunisia to Palermo (11 hours), the service *to* Tunisia goes via Malta – 35 hours including a nine-hour stop in Malta.

If you want to go to Tunisia, Malta, Genoa or Livorno in luxury cruise style, try

Grimaldi group, at the same address as Grandi Traghetti.

The deposito bagagli at Stazione Marittima is open daily from 7 am to 8 pm.

GETTING AROUND
To/From the Airport
Taxis to the airport cost upwards of L60,000. The cheaper option is to catch one of the regular blue buses run by Prestìa e Comandè, which leave from outside Stazione Centrale from 5.25 am to 9.15 pm roughly every hour (a timetable is posted at the bus stop, to your right as you leave the station). Buses also stop in Piazza Ruggero Settimo, in front of the Teatro Politeama. The trip takes one hour and costs L4500.

Bus
Palermo's city buses (AMAT) are efficient, and most stop in front of the train station. Tickets must be purchased before you get on the bus and are available from tobacconists or the booths at the terminal. They cost L1000 and are valid for one hour. A day pass costs L3000. Useful routes are:

No 107: from the train station along Via Roma to the Teatro Politeama, near Piazza Castelnuovo, and on to the Giardino Inglese up Via della Libertà
No 101: from the train station along Via Roma to the Politeama and on past the Giardino Inglese to Piazza A De Gasperi, from where there are connecting buses to Mondello and Sferracavallo
No 812: from near the Politeama to Monte Pellegrino
No 806: (summer only), from Piazza Don Sturzo to Mondello
No 614: from Piazza A De Gasperi to Mondello
No 628: from Piazza A De Gasperi to Sferracavallo
No 12: from Piazza Giuseppe Verde to Monte Pellegrino
No GT: from Piazza Giuseppe Verde to Mondello
No 139: from the train station to the port
No 105: from under the trees diagonally left across the piazza from the train station to Piazza dell'Indipendenza, from where there are connecting buses to Monreale and the Convento dei Cappuccini
No 389: from Piazza dell'Indipendenza to Monreale
No 327: from Piazza dell'Indipendenza to the Convento dei Cappuccini
No 124: from the Politeama to reach the Castello della Zisa

Metropolitana

Palermo's metro system won't be of much use to most people, as its 10 stations radiating out from Stazione Centrale are a good hike from any destinations of tourist interest. There is talk of expanding the system to Punta Raisi airport, which would be useful. A single trip ticket costs L1000.

Car & Motorbike

If you have dealt with Rome or Naples in your own vehicle, Palermo will present no difficulties. Theft of and from vehicles is a problem, however, and you are advised to use one of the attended car parks around town if your hotel has no parking space. You'll be looking at L15,000 to L20,000 for 24 hours.

AROUND PALERMO

There are beaches north-west of the city at Mondello and Sferracavallo. **Mondello** is popular with Palermitans, who crowd the beachfront Viale Regina Elena for the evening stroll. There are numerous seafood restaurants and snack stalls along the avenue. For bus information, see the Palermo Getting Around section.

Between Palermo and Mondello is Monte Pellegrino and the **Santuario di Santa Rosalia**. Palermo's patron saint, St Rosalia lived as a hermit in a cave on the mountain, now the site of a 17th-century shrine. The sanctuary is open daily from 7 am to 7 pm. See the Getting Around section in Palermo for bus details.

Monreale

An absolute must is a visit to the **cathedral** at Monreale, about eight km south-west of Palermo and accessible by frequent city buses. See Getting Around in the Palermo section earlier in this chapter.

The magnificent 12th-century Norman cathedral was built for William II. It is said he did not want to be inferior to his grandfather, Roger, who was responsible for the cathedral at Cefalù and the Cappella Palatino at Palermo. Considered the finest example of Norman architecture in Sicily, the cathedral in fact incorporates Norman, Arab, Byzantine and classical elements, and despite renovations over the centuries, remains substantially intact. The central doorway has bronze doors by Bonanno Pisano and its north door is by Barisano di Trani. The interior of the cathedral is almost entirely covered by dazzling gilded mosaics, the work of Byzantine artisans, representing the complete cycle of the Old and New Testaments. Over the altar is a towering mosaic of Jesus Christ.

Outside the cathedral is the entrance to the cloisters, which were part of a Benedictine abbey once attached to the church. There are 228 twin columns with polychrome ornamentation. Each of the Romanesque capitals is different, depicting plants, animals and fantastic motifs. The capital of the 19th column on the west aisle depicts William II offering the cathedral to the Madonna.

The cathedral is open daily from 8.30 am to 12.30 pm and 3.30 to 6.30 pm. The cloisters are open Monday to Saturday from 9.30 am to 7 pm and Sunday from 9 am to 12.30 pm. Admission is L2000.

Ustica

Almost 60 km north of Palermo lies the lonely island of Ustica. Its moment of fame came in 1980, when a passenger jet crashed near the island in mysterious circumstances, leaving 81 people dead. Investigators suspect the military was involved, in what way may never be known, and a dozen officers of the Italian airforce officers stand accused of a cover-up.

Ustica is otherwise a tranquil place with barely more than 1000 inhabitants, most living in the mural-bedecked village of the same name. The best months to come are June and September. To visit during August is sheer lunacy.

Parts of the rocky coast have been declared a marine reserve (Riserva Marina), and the limpid waters, kept sparkling clean by an Atlantic current through the Straits of Gibraltar, are ideal for diving.

There is an information office (☎ 844 94 56) for the Riserva Marina on Piazza della

Vittoria, part of an interlocking series of squares in the centre of the village. It is open from 8 am to 8 pm and staff can advise on activities – they have a list of the island's dive centres. The island's telephone code is 091. For police, call the carabinieri on ☎ 844 90 49. The Pronto Soccorso, for medical emergencies, is on ☎ 844 92 48.

Activities Among the most rewarding dive sites are the Secca Colombara, to the north of the island, and the Scoglio del Medico, to the west. Note that Zone A of the marine reserve, taking in a good stretch of the western coast north of Punta dello Spalmatore, is protected. Fishing, diving and even swimming are forbidden in the area without permission. The reserve's information office can organise sea-watch diving excursions into the zone. The one dive hire outlet, Ailara Rosalia (☎ 844 91 62), Banchina Barresi, operates in summer only. Otherwise you need to bring your own gear.

You can also hire a boat and cruise around the island, visiting its many grottoes and tiny beaches. Osteodes (☎ 844 92 10), Via Magazzino 5, is one of several agents who can organise boat trips, or you could try Ariston da Bartolo (☎ 844 95 42) to hire your own boat or dinghy.

Places to Stay & Eat There are eight hotels and several affittacamere on Ustica. The *Pensione Clelia* (☎ 844 94 34), Via Magazzino 7, is a decent place with rooms for L35,000/65,000. In the high season prices rocket to L88,000 per head for full board. It has a good little restaurant and the town centre has many others.

Getting There & Away From April to December there is at least one Siremar hydrofoil a day from Palermo. A car ferry runs daily throughout the year (in winter there is nothing on Sunday). The high season one-way passenger fares are L28,500 (hydrofoil) and L16,700 (ferry). The Siremar office (☎ 844 90 02) is on Piazza Capitano V di Bartolo, in the centre of Ustica.

Getting Around Orange minibuses run around the island from the village, or you could hire a moped at the Hotel Ariston in town.

NORTH COAST
Cefalù

Just over an hour by train or bus from Palermo, Cefalù is an attractive beachside village backing onto the rocky frontage to the Madonie mountains. Something of a tourist magnet, it is unspoiled and makes for a relaxing day trip from the capital.

The AAST tourist office (☎ 2 14 58) is at Corso Ruggero 77 and is open Monday to Friday from 8 am to 2 pm and 4 to 7 pm and Saturday to 2 pm. From the train station, turn right into Via Moro to reach Via Matteotti and the old town. If you are heading for the beach, turn left and walk along Via Gramsci, which becomes Via V Martoglio. Cefalù's telephone code is 0921.

Things to See & Do Roger II built the **cathedral** in the 12th century to fulfil a vow to God after his fleet was saved during a violent storm off Cefalù. The twin pyramidal towers of the cathedral stand out over the town centre, but the real beauty is inside. A towering figure of Christ Pancrator in the apse is the focal point of the elaborate Byzantine mosaics. The columns of the twin aisles support Arab-style pointed arches and have beautiful capitals.

Off Piazza del Duomo, in Via Mandralisca, is the private **Museo Mandralisca**. Its collection includes Greek ceramics and Arab pottery, as well as paintings, notably the *Portrait of an Unknown Man* by Antonello da Messina. The museum is open daily from 9 am to 12.30 pm and 3.30 to 7 pm. Admission is L4000.

From the old town's main street, Via Matteotti, look for the sign pointing uphill to the **Tempio di Diana** and make the one-hour climb to the castle. Both are ruins that can be visited, but the main attraction is the panoramic view.

SICILY

Places to Stay & Eat There are several camping grounds in the area, including *Costa Ponente Internazionale* (☎ 2 00 85), about three km west of the town at Contrada Ogliastrillo. It costs L6500 per person and up to L15,000 for a tent. Catch the bus from the train station heading for Lasari.

In town the only really cheap option is *Locanda Cangelosi* (☎ 2 15 91), Via Umberto 1, with singles/doubles for L24,000/30,000. *La Giara* (☎ 2 15 62), Via Veterani 40, uphill from the beach and off Corso Ruggero, has rooms for L56,000/86,000. *Baia del Capitano* (☎ 2 00 05) is in an olive grove near the beach at Mezzaforno, a few km out of town towards Palermo. Its pleasant rooms are L100,000/130,000.

Trattoria La Botte, Via Veterani 6, just off Corso Ruggero, serves full meals for around L25,000. Otherwise, there are plenty of restaurants and several bars along Via Vittorio Emanuele.

Getting There & Away SAIS buses leave Palermo for Cefalù twice daily (see the Palermo Getting There & Away section). Trains are more frequent, if a little slow.

Tindari
Farther along the coast towards Milazzo, at Capo Tindari, are the ruins of ancient Tyndaris, founded in 396 BC as a Greek settlement on a rocky promontory. It was later occupied by the Romans and destroyed by Arab invaders. Today fragments remain of the city's ramparts, as well as a Greek theatre and Roman buildings, including a house and public baths. A museum houses a collection of Hellenistic statues as well as Greek and Roman pottery. The site is open from 9 am to one hour before sunset.

Nearby is the **Santuario della Madonna Nera**. Built in this century to house a statue of a black Madonna revered since Byzantine times, the sanctuary is a place of pilgrimage.

To get to Tindari, catch a train to Patti (on the Palermo-Messina line) and then a bus to the site from outside the station (three a day, with increased services in summer).

Milazzo
This is not the prettiest sight in Sicily, but most people aiming for the Aeolian Islands pass through here. If you get stuck, you could head to the northern end of town for a peek at the 16th-century Spanish **Castello**, open in summer daily, except Monday, from 10 am to 7 pm, with shorter hours in winter.

There are several hotels near the port if you get stuck for the night. The *Central* (☎ 928 10 43), Via del Sole 8, has basic rooms for L30,000/53,000.

Milazzo is easy to reach by bus or train from Palermo and Messina. See Getting There & Away in the Messina section. Intercity buses terminate in Piazza della Repubblica, a five-minute walk back along Via Crispi to the port. The train station is a little farther away, connected to the port by bus No 01.

If you have your own transport, the drive north along the coast from Messina to Capo Peloro and then round to the east is pretty, and there are some reasonable **beaches** between the cape and Acquarone. Where the coast road meets the A20 heading for Milazzo, take the tollway, as the SS113 can be incredibly congested from this point.

Isole Eolie (Aeolian Islands)

The seven islands of this volcanic archipelago stretching north of Milazzo range from the developed tourist resort of Lipari and the understated jet-set haunt of Panarea, to the rugged Vulcano, the spectacular scenery of Stromboli and its fiercely active volcano, the fertile vineyards of Salina, and the solitude of outlying Alicudi and Filicudi. Also known as the Lipari Islands, they have been inhabited since the Neolithic era, when people travelled there for the valuable volcanic glass, obsidian.

The ancient Greeks believed the islands were the home of Aeolus, the god of the wind, and Homer wrote of them in his *Odyssey*. Characterised by their rich colours and volcanic activity, the rugged coastlines are at times lashed by violent seas. As attractive as all this may appear to the modern traveller, the Aeolian Islands have historically made for a difficult living environment. From the 1930s to '50s many inhabitants migrated to Australia (often referred to here as the eighth Aeolian island), virtually abandoning the outer islands and leaving behind only a small contingent on the others.

Cinema fans might like to see Nani Moretti'e *Caro Diario*. The second part of this quirky film is set in the Aeolians, and Moretti goes a long way towards capturing the essence of the islands.

You will need to book accommodation well in advance in the July-August high season. The best time to come is in May and early June or late September and into October. Ferries and hydrofoils operate all year, but winter services are much reduced and sometimes cancelled – to the outer islands at any rate – due to heavy seas.

The post code for the Aeolian Islands is 98055 and the telephone code is 090.

GETTING THERE & AWAY
Ferries and hydrofoils leave regularly from Milazzo and all the ticket offices are along Via L Rizzo, at the port. Note that there is a L1500 port fee for vehicles. All prices quoted below were one-way fares in the high season at the time of writing.

SNAV and Siremar run hydrofoils (L19,300) to Lipari and on to the other islands. SNAV hydrofoils also connect the islands with Messina (L30,500) and Reggio di Calabria (L32,700) all year round. In summer there are daily services to Cefalù (L37,000), Palermo (L58,800) and Naples (L107,500). The latter meets a bus to Rome.

Siremar runs ferries from Milazzo for about half the price of the hydrofoil (L10,600; cars from L28,700 to L67,700, depending on size), but they are slower and less regular. NGI Traghetti also runs a limited car ferry service for the same rates.

See also the Getting There & Away sections for the appropriate destination and embarkation points.

GETTING AROUND
Regular hydrofoil and ferry services operate between the islands, but they can be disrupted to the outer islands by heavy seas. Siremar and SNAV have ticket offices in the same building at Marina Corta on Lipari, at the hydrofoil pier. Siremar also has a ticket office at Marina Lunga, from where ferries depart. Full timetable information is available at all offices. On the other islands, ticket offices are at or close to the docks.

Examples of one-way fares and sailing times from Lipari are:

Alicudi: L24,900, 1½ hours (hydrofoil); L14,600, 3¼ hours (ferry)
Panarea: L11,600, 30 minutes (hydrofoil); L6400, one hour (ferry)
Stromboli: L23,200, 50 minutes (hydrofoil); L12,700, 2¾ hours (ferry)

LIPARI
The largest and most developed of the islands, Lipari is also the most popular with tourists. The main town, of the same name, is typically Mediterranean, with pastel-coloured houses huddled around its two harbours. A thriving exporter of obsidian in ancient times, it is now a centre of pumice-stone (another volcanic product) mining and the best equipped base for exploring the archipelago.

Orientation
Lipari town's two harbours, Marina Lunga and Marina Corta, are on either side of the cliff-top castle, surrounded by 16th-century walls, and the town centre extends between them. The main street, Corso Vittorio Emanuele, runs roughly north-south to the west of the castle. Hydrofoils dock at Marina Corta, from where you should walk to the right across the piazza to Via Garibaldi and follow the 'centro' signs for Corso Vittorio Emanuele.

SICILY

Information

Tourist Office The AAST office (☎ 988 00 95) is at Corso Vittorio Emanuele 233. It is the main tourist office for the archipelago, although offices open on Stromboli, Vulcano and Salina in summer. It will assist with accommodation, which is a useful service in the busy summer months. Pick up a copy of *Ospitalità in blu*, which contains details of accommodation and services on all the islands. The office is open Monday to Saturday from 8 am to 2 pm and 4.30 to 7.30 pm.

Money There are several banks in Lipari, including the Banca del Sud in Corso V Emanuele. You should have no trouble with Visa, MasterCard or Eurocheque cards for cash advances, but only the latter *might* work in the ATMs. Outside banking hours, exchange facilities can be found at the post office and several travel agencies.

Note that banking facilities on the other islands are limited, if not absent.

Post & Telecommunications The post office is at Corso V Emanuele 207, near the tourist office, and is open Monday to Friday from 8 am to 6.30 pm and on Saturday to 1 pm. Public telephones can be found throughout the township.

Emergency In a medical emergency, contact the hospital (☎ 9 88 51) or Pronto Soccorso (First Aid) on ☎ 981 10 10. The emergency number for police attendance is ☎ 113.

Things to See & Do

The **castello**, surrounded by massive walls built in the 16th century after Turkish pirates raided Lipari, stands on the site of an ancient acropolis that is now part of the **Parco Archeologico**. Buildings dating to before 1700 BC have been unearthed. Also within the castle complex is the **cathedral**, built by the Normans and sent up in flames during the 1544 pirate raid. Rebuilt a century later, the interior is Baroque. Excavations have

uncovered part of the original 12th-century Norman cloisters.

The **Museo Archeologico Eoliano** boasts well-organised exhibits that trace the volcanic and human history of the islands and include a collection of Neolithic pottery. It is open Monday to Friday from 9 am to 2 pm and Sunday to 1 pm. Admission is free.

It is worth exploring the island, in particular for views of Salina, Alicudi and Filicudi from the rugged, windy cliffs of Lipari's north-west corner. Sunbathers and swimmers head for **Canneto**, a few km north of Lipari town. The beach is accessible by a track just north of Canneto. Farther north are the pumice mines of **Pomiciazzo** and **Porticello**, where there is another beach. While cruising around the island, the village of Quattropani and the lookout known as Quattrocchi, south of Pianoconte, are good spots to drink in the views.

Scuba diving and sailing are popular. For information on courses, contact the Centro Nautico Eoliano (☎ 981 21 10), Salita San Giuseppe 8, or the tourist office.

Places to Stay

Lipari provides plenty of options for a comfortable stay, from the budget level to the luxurious. However, prices soar in summer, particularly in August. If all else fails in peak season, tourist office staff will billet new arrivals in private homes on the island. Don't reject out of hand offers by touts when you arrive, as they often have decent rooms in private houses.

To rent an apartment, contact the tourist office for a list of establishments.

Places to Stay – bottom end The island's camping ground, the *Baia Unci* (☎ 981 19 09), is at Canneto, about two km out of Lipari township and accessible by bus from the Esso service station at Marina Lunga. Once all the charges are added up, it isn't cheap – L9000 per person per night, L3000 for a car, L3000 for electric light and L8500 for your tent or caravan. The HI *youth hostel* (☎ 981 15 40), Via Castello 17, is inside the walls of the castle. B&B costs L13,000 per person and a meal L12,000 – or you can cook your own. It is open from March to October.

Cassarà Vittorio (☎ 981 15 23), Vico Sparviero 15, off Via Garibaldi near Marina Corta, is excellent value at L20,000 per person in the low season and L35,000 in the high season. There are two terraces with views, and use of the kitchen is L2000. The owner can be found (unless he finds you first) at Via Garibaldi 78, on the way from the port to the city centre. *Locanda Salina* (☎ 981 23 32), Via Garibaldi 18, is also very close to Marina Corta. It has reasonable singles/doubles for L40,000/60,000 or doubles with a bathroom for L65,000. Ask for a room with a view of the sea. *Enzo il Negro* (☎ 981 31 63) at Via Garibaldi 29 has spotless, comfortable digs for up to L45,000 per person in the high season. All rooms have a bathroom and balcony and there is a large terrace.

Places to Stay – middle *Pensione Neri* (☎ 981 14 13), Via G Marconi 43, off Corso V Emanuele, is in a lovely old, renovated villa. In the low season, a double costs L80,000 and triples/quads L100,000/ 120,000; in summer, prices jump to L110,000 a double, L140,000 a triple and L170,000 a quad. All rooms have a bathroom.

The *Hotel Oriente* (☎ 981 14 93) is next door at Via Marconi 35. It has a bar and garden and very comfortable rooms. Prices vary according to the season and range from L50,000 to L85,000 for a single, L70,000 to L150,000 for a double, L95,000 to L200,000 for a triple, and L120,000 to L250,000 for a quad. All rooms include a bathroom and breakfast.

Places to Stay – top end Lipari's top hotel is the *Villa Meligunis* (☎ 981 24 26) in Via Marte, on a hill overlooking Marina Corta. Room rates range from L150,000 to L300,000, depending on season, including breakfast.

Places to Eat
Try pasta prepared with the island's excellent capers, and be prepared to spend big to eat the day's sea catch, particularly swordfish. The waters of the archipelago abound in fish, including tuna, mullet, cuttlefish and sole, all of which end up on restaurant tables at the end of the day. The local wine is the sweet, white Malvasia.

People with access to a kitchen can shop for supplies at the grocery shops along Corso V Emanuele.

Although prices go up in the high season, you can still eat cheaply by sticking to the pizzerias along Corso V Emanuele. *Il Galeone*, Corso V Emanuele 222, has good pizzas for around L8000 or a set lunch for L17,000. *Zum Willi*, on the corner of Corso V Emanuele and Via Umberto I, is basically a bar that serves pizzas for L6000 to L10,000. For a more complete meal, eat at *Trattoria d'Oro*, Corso Umberto I 28-32. For an à la carte meal you'll pay around L25,000, and there is a good set menu.

Da Bartolo, Via Garibaldi 53, is certainly one of the island's better trattorias and a good choice for seafood. A full meal is worth around L30,000. Cheaper and just as good is *Dal Napoletano*, at No 12, where L25,000 should see you through a good meal with a glass of Malvasia on the house to finish.

Near Marina Corta, in Via Roma, there are a couple of no-nonsense trattorias, including *Nenzjna*, where you can eat for around L20,000.

Men enjoying a social drink at an outdoor café.

SICILY

Getting There & Away
See the Getting There & Away section for the Aeolian Islands.

Getting Around
Urso Guglielmo buses leave from the Esso service station at Marina Lunga for Canneto (10 a day, more frequently in summer), Porticello (seven a day) and Quattrocchi (eight a day). The company also offers special round trips of the island. Contact the tourist office for timetables.

Boats and scooters are available for hire at Foti Roberto (☎ 981 23 52), Via F Crispi 31, to the right as you leave Marina Lunga. A Vespa costs L35,000 a day and a moped is L25,000 a day. A motorised rubber dinghy costs L120,000 a day.

SEN (Società Eolie di Navigazione, ☎ 981 23 41), Corso V Emanuele 247, conducts a boat tour around Lipari and Salina (L35,000 per person), as well as to the other islands.

VULCANO
Just south of Lipari, and the first port of call for ferries and hydrofoils from Sicily, Vulcano is known for its therapeutic mud baths and hot springs. To the ancients, the island of Thermessa, Terasia or Hiera – as Vulcano was variously known – must have inspired a good deal of respect, if not downright fear. Not only did the god of fire, Vulcan, have his workshop here, but Aeolus, the god of the wind, also swirled about the place.

Of Vulcano's three volcanoes, the oldest lies on the southern tip of the island and was already extinct in ancient times. The youngest, Vulcanello, next to the mud baths at the north-east end of the island, rose from the sea in the 2nd century BC, according to Pliny. The only active volcano is the Gran Cratere, which has a number of fumaroles and whose broad, smoking crater broods over the port. A tranquil place, the Gran Cratere hasn't blown for more than four centuries but you'll notice on arrival the all-pervading stench of sulphurous gasses.

Orientation & Information
Boats dock at the Porto di Levante. To the right, as you face the island, is the small Vulcanello peninsula. All facilities are concentrated between the Porto di Levante and the Porto di Ponente, where you will find the Spiaggia Sabbia Nera (Black Sand Beach), the only smooth, sandy beach on the islands.

A tourist office (☎ 985 20 28) is open in summer only.

Things to See & Do
Climbing the **Gran Cratere** is the main attraction. Follow the signs south along Via Provinciale out of town. A track is then signposted off the road. Take the left fork and head up – about an hour's scramble. The views from the top are reward enough for the sweat.

Even if you don't need a skin cure, a wallow in the hot sulphurous mud pool of the **Laghetto di Fanghi** can be a relaxing way to pass the time, if slightly offensive to the nose. It's next to Vulcanello, and when you've had enough you can hop into the water at the adjacent beach where underwater hot springs create a natural jacuzzi effect.

Paddle boats are usually available for hire on the beach.

SEN offers a boat trip around the island for around L15,000 per person. In summer it operates a small information booth on Via Porto Levante. Otherwise information is available on Lipari.

Places to Stay & Eat
The *Pensione Agostino* (☎ 985 23 42), Via Favaloro 1, is close to the mud baths and has doubles up to L60,000 with a bathroom, depending on the season. *Pensione la Giara* (☎ 985 22 29), Via Provinciale 18, is towards the Gran Cratere. A pleasant spot, its rooms cost around L80,000 a double, although the management prefers to charge by the week. *Sea Houses Residence* (☎ 985 22 19), very close to the mud baths, is a complex of self-contained three, four and five-bed apartments in a garden setting. Prices start at

L55,000 per person per day in the off season and rise to L112,000 in August. It is open from April to October.

For a decent meal, try *Da Maurizio* or *Da Vincenzino*, both in Via Porto di Levante.

Getting There & Away
Vulcano is an intermediate stop between Milazzo and Lipari and there are a good number of vessels throughout the day going either way.

Getting Around
Scooters and bicycles are available for rent from Pino Marturano (☎ 985 24 19), Via Comunale Levante, near the Porto di Levante. The proprietor of Gioelli del Mare (☎ 985 21 70) at Porto di Levante organises bus tours around the island for groups of at least 12 people. Make a booking and hope a large enough group will form.

SALINA
Just north-west of Lipari, Salina is the most fertile of the islands and consists of two extinct volcanoes, Monte dei Porri and Monte Fosse delle Felci. Its high coastal cliffs are topped with vineyards, where most Malvasia wine is produced.

Orientation & Information
Boats dock at Santa Marina Salina, where you will find most accommodation, or at Rinella, a fishing hamlet on the south coast. The other main villages on the island are Malfa, on the north coast, and Leni, slightly inland from Rinella.

The Coop Salina '80 (☎ 984 31 90), is at Via Risorgimento 152, Santa Marina Salina. In summer there are AAST booths at Rinella, Malfa and Santa Marina Salina. For medical assistance, ring ☎ 984 40 05 and for the police, ☎ 984 30 19.

Things to See & Do
If you are feeling energetic, you could climb the Fosse delle Felci volcano. From Santa Marina Salina, head for Lingua, a small village three km south, from where paths lead up the mountain.

The **Santuario della Madonna del Terzito** at Valdichiesa, just south of Malfa, is a place of pilgrimage, particularly around the Feast of the Assumption on 15 August.

Rinella is a popular underwater fishing spot. For information, contact the tourist office or the Centro Nautico Salina (☎ 980 90 33), Via Rotabile 2, at the port, which also operates as a dive centre (week-long courses for about L500,000) and rents out motorised rubber dinghies for up to L150,000 a day. Boats are also available for rent from Centro Nautico Levante (☎ 984 31 92), Via E Gerace 13, Santa Marina Salina.

Places to Stay & Eat
The *Camping Tre Pini* (☎ 980 91 55) is on the beach at Rinella. It costs L10,000 per person, plus L8000 for your tent and L4000 for electric light. *Pensione Mamma Santina* (☎ 984 30 54) is at Via Sanità 40 in Santa Marina Salina. Head for Via Risorgimento (the narrow main street of town) and walk north for a few hundred metres. The pensione is uphill along a winding lane to your left. Singles/doubles are L35,000/55,000 and a double with a bathroom is L60,000. In summer, half board is obligatory at L75,000 per person. Two blocks farther north along Via Risorgimento and again uphill to the right is *Catena de Pasquale* (☎ 984 30 94), Via F Crispi 17. Its six rooms all have a bathroom, terrace and cooking facilities for up to L40,000 per person.

Hotel Ariana (☎ 980 90 75) is in a turn-of-the-century villa at Via Rotabile 11, overlooking the sea at Rinella. It has terraces and a bar. Half board ranges from L70,000 in the low season to L112,000 in the high season; full board is from L95,000 to L160,000.

There are several restaurants clustered around the docks at Santa Marina, or you could try the one at the Albergo Punta Barone, with views out to sea, at the northern exit of town.

SICILY

Getting There & Away

Hydrofoils and ferries service Santa Marina and Rinella. You'll find ticket offices at both.

Getting Around

Regular buses run from Santa Marina Salina to Malfa and Lingua, and from Malfa to Leni and Rinella. Timetables are posted at the ports. Motorbikes are available for rent from Antonio Bongiorno (☎ 984 33 08), Via Pozzo d'Agnello, Santa Marina Salina. A Vespa costs L30,000 a day and a moped L35,000 a day – less if you hire for more than one day.

PANAREA

Easily the most picturesque of the Aeolian Islands, tiny Panarea is three km long and two km wide. A haunt of the jet set, it is generally overpriced. Boats dock at San Pietro, where you'll find most of the accommodation.

After wandering around San Pietro, head south to Punta Milazzese, about a half-hour walk (there is a small beach along the way) to see the Bronze Age village discovered there in 1948. Pottery found at the site is now in the museum at Lipari. Rent a boat at the port to explore the coves and beaches of the island, which are otherwise inaccessible.

Your best bet for affordable accommodation (in the vicinity of L30,000/50,000) is the affittacamere in the streets of San Pietro. The *Locanda Rodà* (☎ 98 30 06) in Via San Pietro, uphill from the port and to the left, is about as close as you'll come to a cheap hotel. It charges L60,000/70,000 in the peak months, or more likely half board at L100,000. In the low season, prices can drop dramatically. It has a pizzeria/trattoria that charges average prices. *La Sirena* is also a pleasant trattoria. In the same area is *Trattoria da Nunzio*, with a terrace overlooking the sea. A meal at any of these places should cost no more than L35,000.

Hydrofoils and the occasional ferry link the island with Stromboli to the north and Salina (and on to Lipari and Milazzo) to the south.

STROMBOLI

Stromboli's almost perpetual eruptions of fiery molten rock are an unforgettable spectacle at night. Lava flow is confined to the Sciara del Fuoco (Trail of Fire) on the volcano's north-western flank, leaving the villages of San Bartolo, San Vincenzo and Scari (which merge into one town) to the east and Ginostra to the south quite safe. Until a massive eruption in 1930, some 5000 people lived on the island, but most got quite a fright and left. Permanent residents now number about 500.

The most captivating of the islands, Stromboli is inconveniently placed and boat services are prone to disruption. There's a fair choice of accommodation though and a stay is more than recommended.

Orientation & Information

Boats arrive at Scari/San Vincenzo, downhill from the township. Accommodation is a short walk up the Scalo Scari to Via Roma, or, if you plan to head straight for the crater, follow the road along the waterfront (see the following section for details).

A tourist office is open in summer. The post office is in Via Roma, and the only bank, in Via Nunziante at Ficogrande, is open only from June to September. Otherwise exchange facilities are available at the travel agency, Le Isole e Terme d'Italia, in Via Roma near the port.

Climbing the Volcano

From the port, follow the road along the waterfront, continuing straight past the beach at Ficogrande. Once past the village the path heads uphill, deviating after about 20 minutes to a bar/pizzeria and observatory. Alternatively, follow it after the village through a slightly confusing section of reeds until it starts to ascend to the crater. About halfway up, there is a good view of the Sciara del Fuoco, although in daylight the glow of the molten lava is imperceptible. The path eventually becomes quite steep and rocky. Note the warning signs at the summit and do not go too close to the edge of the crater. The round trip from the village should take about four hours.

The climb is a totally different experience at night, when darkness throws the molten lava of the Sciara del Fuoco and volcanic explosions into dramatic relief. It is possible to make the climb during the day without a guide, although the tourist office says it is forbidden, but night climbers would be wise to enlist help.

Experienced guides can be contacted through the Club Alpino Italiano office (☎ 98 62 63), just off Piazza San Vincenzo. They take groups of 10 people or more to the crater daily at 6 pm (depending on weather conditions and whether a group can be formed), returning at 11.30 pm (about L20,000 per person). Contact the office around midday to make a booking. For the night climb, you will need heavy shoes and clothing for cold, wet weather, a torch (flashlight), a good supply of water and food. Even during the day, you will need heavy, wet-weather clothing, as conditions are unpredictable.

The Società Navigazione Stromboli (☎ 98 61 35) organises nightly boat trips to view the Sciara del Fuoco from the sea. The boat, named Pippo, leaves at 10 pm from Ficogrande. SEN offers a similar boat trip, starting in Lipari and departing from the Stromboli ferry port for the Sciara del Fuoco at 8 pm. The same boat also heads out to **Strombolicchio**, a towering rock rising out of the sea north of San Vincenzo. The rock is a popular spot for underwater fishing.

Water Sports
The Centro Mare Stromboli (☎ 98 61 56), Via V Nunziante 26 (on the way to the volcano), has canoes, sailboards, catamarans and sailing boats for rent. It also offers windsurfing and sailing courses. Diving Centro Mare (☎ 98 60 18) at the Hotel Villaggio Stromboli, Via Regina Elena, on the waterfront towards Ficogrande, offers diving courses.

Alternatively, make your way to the beautiful beach of rocks and black volcanic sand at **Ficogrande** to swim and sunbathe.

Places to Stay & Eat
There's nothing much in the dirt cheap bracket on Stromboli. *Locanda Stella* (☎ 98 60 20), Via Fabio Filzi 14, has doubles for L50,000 and charges L77,000 for obligatory full board in July/August. This is about as low as prices come. You will also find a few affittacamere about, charging up to L40,000 per person for a room in the high season. A good one is *Barbablù* (☎ 98 61 18), Via Vittorio Emanuele 17, a pleasant pensione charging L90,000 to L150,000 a double, depending on the season.

Hotel Villaggio Stromboli (☎ 98 60 18) has rooms for L80,000/120,000 in the high season. It is on the beach front and has a terrace bar/restaurant.

For a reasonably priced meal, try *La Trottola* in Via Roma. The *Punta Lena* on the Lungomare, walking away from the port towards the volcano, is more expensive and has a terrace overlooking the sea. The pizzeria at the observatory, about 20 minutes walk up the volcano, is also reasonable.

Getting There & Away
Ticket offices for SNAV and Siremar are at the port. Bear in mind the cost of the trip and distance if you're considering a day visit – which in any case will rob you of the opportunity of a night climb up the volcano. Heavy seas often cause cancellation of ferry and hydrofoil services.

FILICUDI & ALICUDI
You will need a strong desire to get away from it all to stay on either of these islands west of Lipari. Facilities are limited (severely limited on Alicudi) and boats can be cancelled due to heavy seas, even in summer.

Filicudi is the larger of the two and its attractions include the Grotta del Bue Marino (Grotto of the Monk Seal) and La Canna rock pinnacle, about one km off the island towards Alicudi. On Cape Graziano, south of the port, are the hut remains of a prehistoric village dating to 1800 BC. Boats are available for rent if you want to explore the grotto, and scuba diving courses are available in summer.

The island has two hotels. *La Canna* (☎ 988 99 56), Via Rosa 43, just uphill from the port, has singles/doubles for L50,000/60,000 and half board for up to L75,000 in the high season. *Phenicusa* (☎ 988 99 46) in Via Porto has rooms for L45,000/70,000 and full board for up to L122,000.

Alicudi is the farthest from Lipari and the least developed of the Aeolian group. There is only one hotel and restaurant, the *Ericusa* (☎ 988 99 02), in Via Regina Elena. Doubles cost L90,000 and half board is L85,000. It is open only during the summer months and bookings are strongly advised.

While on the island, trek up Monte Filo dell'Arpa to see the crater of the extinct Montagnola volcano and the Timpone delle Femmine, huge fissures where women are said to have taken refuge during pirate raids.

Distance and cost make Alicudi a questionable choice for a day trip, and the accommodation situation makes staying an equally thorny option.

The East Coast

MESSINA

For most, Messina is the point of arrival in Sicily, and you could hardly imagine a less auspicious introduction. Devastated many times over the centuries, the modern city is pretty much bereft of any hint of its past. Known to the ancient Greeks as Zankle (Sickle) for its beautiful curved harbour, Messina grew into a splendid city as a Greek colony and later thrived under Roman, Byzantine and Norman patronage. Since the 18th century, Messina has been something of a disaster area, hit first by plague, then cholera and finally by earthquakes, including the massive 1908 jolt that all but destroyed the city and killed more than 80,000 people in the region. The city had barely been rebuilt

when it was flattened by bombing during WW II.

If for any reason you're stuck in Messina, don't despair. The city centre with its wide avenues is a pleasant place to wander around, and there remain a couple of vestiges of happier days.

Orientation

The FS (state) train station is on Piazza della Repubblica, at the southern end of the long waterfront. FS car and truck ferries also arrive here. The main Intercity bus station is outside the train station, to the left in the piazza. To get to the city centre from Piazza della Repubblica, walk either straight across the piazza and directly ahead along Via I Settembre to the Piazza del Duomo, or turn left into Via G La Farina and take the first right into Via Cannazzaro to reach Piazza Cairoli.

Those coming by hydrofoil from Reggio di Calabria arrive about one km north of the city on Corso Vittorio Emanuele II, while drivers on the private car ferry from Villa San Giovanni land a few km farther along, just north of the trade fair area (Fiera).

Information

Tourist Office There is a municipal office (☎ 67 29 44) in Piazza della Repubblica, to the right as you leave the train station, and an AAPIT office (☎ 67 53 56) a bit farther along at Via Calabria 301. Both have extensive information on Messina, its province and Sicily in general. The former is open Monday to Friday from 8.30 am to 2 pm and the latter Monday to Saturday from 8 am to 7 pm. Pick up the *City* brochure, which has useful information.

Money There are numerous banks in the city centre – several with ATMs – and an exchange booth at the timetable information office at the train station.

Post & Telecommunications The main post office is in Piazza Antonello, on Corso Cavour near the cathedral. It is open Monday to Saturday from 8.30 am to 6.30 pm. The post code for central Messina is 98100.

There is a Telecom office in Corso Cavour, near Via Cannazzaro, which is staffed daily from 8 am to 10 pm. The telephone code for Messina is 090.

Travel Agency The CTS student travel group has an agency (☎ 292 67 61) located at Via U Bassi 93.

Emergency & Medical Services For police attendance, call ☎ 113. The public hospital, the Ospedale Piemonte (☎ 22 21) is in Viale Europa; at night, ring ☎ 67 50 48. A booklet available at the tourist office lists pharmacies open at night on a rotation basis.

Things to See & Do

The Norman **duomo**, built in the 12th century, was almost completely destroyed by the combined effects of the 1908 earthquake and WW II bombing. Rebuilt virtually from scratch, its fine 15th-century doorway is one of the few original elements. The clock tower houses what is believed to be the world's largest astronomical clock, which strikes at midday.

In the Piazza del Duomo is the **Fontana di Orione**, an elegant 16th-century work by Angelo Montorsoli. Nearby, in Piazza Catalani, off Via Garibaldi, is the 12th-century **Chiesa della Santissima Annunziata dei Catalani**, a jewel of Arab-Norman construction. The statue in front of it is a monument to Don John of Austria, who beat the Turks at the Battle of Lepanto in 1571. Farther north, where Via Garibaldi spills into Piazza dell'Unità d'Italia, is Messina's other great fountain, the 16th-century **Fontana del Nettuno**.

The **Museo Regionale** is a long walk along Viale della Libertà (or take bus No 8 from the train station), and houses works of art including the *Virgin & Child with Saints* by Antonello da Messina, born here in 1430. It is open daily from 9 am to 1 pm and occasionally from 4 to 7 pm. Admission is L2000.

Places to Stay & Eat

The *Roma* (☎ 67 55 66), Piazza del Duomo 3 (just off Corso Cavour), has basic singles/doubles for L18,000/35,000. A warning for winter: there is no hot water.

Two OK hotels with hot water and convenient for the train station are *Touring* (☎ 293 88 51) and *Mirage* (☎ 293 88 44), at Via N Scotto 17 and 1, respectively. The latter is slightly better and charges L35,000/60,000 for singles/doubles. The Touring asks L30,000/60,000. Both have more expensive rooms with a bathroom.

Hotel Monza (☎ 67 37 55), Viale San Martino 63, is of a higher standard and charges L66,000/110,000 for singles/doubles with a bathroom. The *Hotel Excelsior* (☎ 293 14 31), Via Maddalena 32, has singles/doubles for L38,000/70,000 or L63,000/103,000 with a bathroom.

La Trappola, Via dei Verdi 39, is near the university area. Its good meals are reasonably priced, but not rock-bottom. *Trattoria al Padrino*, Via Santa Cecilia 54, is a simple place, where a meal will cost about L30,000.

Getting There & Away

Bus SAIS (☎ 77 19 14) runs a regular service (approximately every hour; last bus leaves at 8 pm) to Taormina (L5100 one way), Catania (L9500 one way) and Catania's airport. The company's office and bus station are at Piazza della Repubblica 6, to the left as you leave the train station. There is a direct connection to Rome (see Getting There & Away at the beginning of this chapter). Giuntabus (☎ 67 37 82) runs a service to Milazzo (for ferries and hydrofoils to the Aeolian Islands) roughly every hour from Via Terranova 8, on the corner of Viale San Martino.

Train Regular trains (☎ 67 52 34) connect Messina with Catania, Taormina, Syracuse, Palermo and Milazzo, but buses are generally faster. The train stations for Milazzo and Taormina are inconveniently located some distance from the city centre.

SICILY

Car & Motorbike If you arrive in Messina by FS ferry with a vehicle (see below), it is simple to make your way out of town. For Palermo (or Milazzo and the Aeolian Islands), turn right as you exit the docks and follow Viale Garibaldi along the seafront. After about one km, turn left into Viale Boccetta and follow the green autostrada (tollway) signs for Palermo. To reach Taormina, Syracuse etc, turn left from the docks into Via La Farina and follow the autostrada signs for Catania.

If you arrive by private ferry, turn right along Viale della Libertà for Palermo and Milazzo, and left for Taormina and Catania – follow the green autostrada signs. You can also take the SS114 (busy in summer).

Boat The FS railway runs car ferries to Villa San Giovanni, about 10 km north of Reggio di Calabria, from next to the train station. The private Caronte company does the same run from docks a few km up the waterfront, just north of the Fiera (trade fair centre). A standard car with Caronte costs L26,000 one way or L40,000 return (valid for 60 days) and FS prices are similar. The trip takes about 20 minutes, with departures around the clock.

There are also big FS hydrofoils to Reggio di Calabria (L4000 one way), and SNAV (☎ 36 40 44) runs up to 20 hydrofoils on weekdays to Reggio di Calabria (L6000 one way; 15 minutes). SNAV hydrofoils also connect Messina with the Aeolian Islands.

SOUTH TO TAORMINA

Those driving the Messina-Taormina route should consider a brief excursion into the foothills of the Monti Peloritani. Head for **Savoca**, four km of winding road inland from the grey pebble beaches of Santa Teresa di Riva, which take you through lemon groves and almond stands to a quiet village with a couple of medieval churches and a Capuchin monastery, which contains **catacombs**. Some eerie-looking skeletons in raggedy 18th-century rig are all that remain of local nobles who paid good money for this kind of 'immortality'. The catacombs

are open from 9 am to 1 pm and 4 to 7 pm from April to September; 9 am to midday and 3 to 5 pm the rest of the year. Admission costs L2000. STAT buses run between Savoca and Santa Teresa di Riva.

TAORMINA

Spectacularly located on a terrace of Monte Tauro, dominating the sea and with views westwards to the fuming Mt Etna, Taormina is easily Sicily's most picturesque town. From its foundation by the Siculians, Taormina remained a favourite destination for the long line of conquerors who followed. Under the Greeks, who moved in after Naxos was destroyed during colonial wars in the 5th century BC, Taormina flourished. It later came under Roman dominion and eventually became the capital of Byzantine Sicily, a period of grandeur that ended abruptly in 902 AD when the town was destroyed by Arab invaders. The town remained an important centre of art and trade throughout the subsequent periods of Norman, Spanish and French rule.

Long ago discovered by the European jet set, Taormina is an expensive and heavily touristed town. It is well served by hotels, pensioni and eating places, but some travellers might find the glitz and kitsch a little overwhelming. It would be a shame to miss this place though, as its magnificent setting, Greek theatre and nearby beaches remain as seductive as they were for the likes of Goethe and D H Lawrence.

Orientation

The train station (Taormina-Giardini) is at the bottom of Monte Tauro, and you'll need to get an SAIS bus up to the bus station (for local and Intercity buses) in Via Pirandello. A short walk uphill from there brings you to the old city entrance and Corso Umberto I, which traverses the town.

Information

Tourist Office The AAST office (☎ 2 32 43) is in the Palazzo Corvaja, just off Corso Umberto I, near Largo Santa Caterina. It has swags of information and is open Monday to Saturday from 8 am to 2 pm and 4 to 7 pm.

Money There are several banks in Taormina, mostly along Corso Umberto I. Banking hours are generally 8.30 am to 1.30 pm and 3 to 4 pm. You'll also find exchange places along the same street. Check on commissions. Several banks, such as the Monte dei Paschi di Siena on Piazza del Duomo, have user-friendly ATMs. American Express is represented by La Duca Viaggi (☎ 62 52 55), Via Don Bosco 39.

Post & Telecommunications The main post office is in Piazza Sant'Antonio, just outside the Porta Catania, at the far end of Corso Umberto I from the tourist office. There are public telephones in the Avis Rent-a-Car office, Via San Pancrazio 6, to your right off Via Pirandello at the entrance to the old town. Taormina's post code is 98039 and the telephone code is 0942.

Newspaper Stands If you're anxious for news from home, try the tobacconist at Via Bagnoli Croci 62, or the newsagent at Corso Umberto I 245, just inside Porta Catania.

Emergency There is a free night-time medical service in summer for tourists (☎ 62 54 19) in Piazza San Francesco di Paola. The hospital, the Ospedale San Vincenzo (☎ 2 35 49), is in Piazza San Vincenzo, just outside the Porta Catania. Call the same number for an ambulance; for the police, call ☎ 113, and for the carabinieri, ☎ 112.

Things to See & Do

The **Greek theatre** at the end of Via Teatro Greco, off Corso Umberto I, was built in the 3rd century BC. Later expanded and remodelled by the Romans, what you see is pretty much a Roman structure, despite its name. In the final years of the empire the amphitheatre was given over solely to gladiator fighting – the sword was mightier at the box office than the pen. The structure has been much tampered with over the centuries – the family of the Spanish Costanza

d'Aragona built its home in the 12th century over part of the theatre (to the right as you face the stage). However, it remains a most atmospheric place. The view of Mt Etna and the sea through what was once the stage area is breathtaking. Concerts are staged here in summer. The theatre is open from 9 am to 8 pm in summer and closes at 4.30 pm in winter. Admission is L2000.

From the theatre, wander down to the beautiful **villa comunale** (public gardens) on Via Bagnoli Croci. Opening hours are similar to the theatre. Take a picnic and enjoy the panorama.

Back in the town centre is the **Odeon**, a small Roman theatre, badly preserved and partly covered by the adjoining Chiesa di Santa Caterina. It was discovered and excavated in the late 19th century and is believed to have been erected on the site of a Greek temple of Apollo. Taormina's **duomo**, in the Piazza del Duomo along Corso Umberto I, was built in the early 15th century.

There are several mansions in Taormina, including the **Palazzo Corvaja**. Begun by the Arabs as a defence tower in the 11th century, it was extended several times and includes halls dating from the 14th and 15th centuries. The **Palazzo Duca di Santo Stefano**, at the other end of town, is an important example of Sicilian Gothic architecture, with a fanciful mix of Arab and Norman styles. The nearby **Badia Vecchia** (Old Abbey) is a 14th-century Gothic building, again with Norman-Arab elements.

Just wandering along the main drag, Corso Umberto I, you can see a smattering of stately old buildings, some dating to the 15th century.

The peak of Monte Tauro is adorned by the lonely, windswept ruins of the town's medieval castle, two km from the town centre along the road to Castelmola (see below) or accessible by climbing the linking stairs. The views are great.

You can reach the beaches at **Isola Bella** and **Mazzarò** directly under Taormina by cable car from Via Pirandello. It costs L2000 and runs from 8.30 am to 9 pm in winter and until 1.30 am in summer. Both beaches are largely taken up by private operators (a space with deck chairs and umbrella costs up to L18,000 a day), but there is some space for free bathing. SAIS buses also connect the beaches with the upper town.

Organised Tours

CIT (☎ 2 33 01), Corso Umberto I 101, runs excursions to various locations. Destinations include Mt Etna (L33,000), Agrigento (L70,000), Syracuse (L68,000) and Lipari (L80,000). These are winter prices; expect rises in summer. SAT (☎ 2 46 53), Corso Umberto I 73, also runs tours to Mt Etna.

Festivals

Festivals, theatre and music concerts are organised throughout the summer. The Raduno del Costume e del Carretto Siciliano, featuring parades of traditional Sicilian carts and folkloric groups, is usually held in autumn – ask at the tourist office.

Places to Stay

Taormina abounds in accommodation, but in summer you should book in advance as rooms fill rapidly, particularly during August (a good time to stay away). In winter you can sometimes get prices brought down a tad. You can camp near the beach at *Campeggio San Leo* (☎ 2 46 58), Via Nazionale, at Capo Taormina. The cost is L7000 per person per night.

There are numerous private rooms in Taormina and the tourist office has a full list. At *Pensione Ingegnere* (☎ 62 54 80), Via Timeo 8 (next to the Odeon), you will pay L35,000 per person. *Il Leone* (☎ 2 38 78), Via Bagnoli Croci 127, near the gardens, charges L29,000/43,000 for singles/doubles (including breakfast), or L61,000 per person for half board. Some rooms have terraces and great views of the sea.

Pensione Svizzera (☎ 2 37 90), Via Pirandello 26, on the way from the bus station to the town centre, has simple, pleasant singles/doubles with a bathroom for L35,000/60,000; more if you want breakfast. Farther up the same road, the *Pensione Inn*

Piero (☎ 2 31 39), at No 20, has comfortable rooms with a bathroom for L40,000/60,000.

Pensione Villa Gaia (☎ 2 31 85), Via Fazzello 34, is near the duomo and has rooms for L35,000/70,000. It is closed in winter.

Hotel Villa Carlotta (☎ 2 37 32), Via Pirandello 81, is about 10 minutes walk downhill from the town. A beautifully furnished establishment, it has rooms with terraces and bathrooms for around L70,000/100,000, including breakfast. *Villa Fiorita* (☎ 2 41 22), Via Pirandello 39, is another well-furnished, comfortable hotel, with a garden, terraces and rooms with full services. Doubles cost from L125,000.

Hotel Villa Belvedere (☎ 2 37 91), Via Bagnoli Croci 79, near the public gardens, is a three-star hotel. All rooms and terraces face Mt Etna. A single costs L88,000 and a double, with a bathroom, L140,000.

If you want to stay near the beach at Mazzarò, try the *Villa Caterina* (☎ 2 47 09), Via Nazionale 155, which has pleasant rooms for L40,000/70,000 or L101,000 per person for half board.

Places to Eat

Those on a tight budget will be limited in their choice of eating places. There are several gourmet grocery shops along Corso Umberto I, where prices are high. Alternatively, head for the side streets between Via Teatro Greco and the public gardens, where you can buy picnic supplies at several grocery and pastry shops. There is a Standa supermarket in Via Apollo Arcageta, just up from the post office. Quite a few restaurants close in winter.

For a quick takeaway, you could do worse than *Myosotis*, Corso Umberto I 113. It has pizzas, arancini (deep fried orange rice balls stuffed with meat and peas), and panini for around L3000. For a light meal try *Shelter Pub*, Via Fratelli Bandiera 10, off Corso Umberto I.

For pizza, *Mamma Rosa* at Via Naumachia 10 is a safe bet at L8000 to L10,000.

Trattoria Rosticepi, Via San Pancrazio 10, at the top of Via Pirandello, has good meals for under L25,000 per person. For an excellent meal in lovely surroundings, head for *Ristorante La Piazzetta*, Via Paladini 5, in a tiny piazza downhill from Corso Umberto I. A full meal will cost L30,000 or more. Next door is *Shatulle*, a bar/crêperie. *Il Baccanale*, on Piazzetta Filea, off Via Giovanni di Giovanni, is a popular restaurant moderately priced by Taormina standards.

For a quiet drink, head for *Arco Rosso*, Via Naumachia 7, off Corso Umberto I, or walk farther down to the busier *Da Peppe*, Via Calapitrulli 3. Many of the cafés on Corso Umberto I charge extortionately in the high season.

Getting There & Away

Bus The bus is the easiest means of reaching Taormina. SAIS (☎ 62 53 01) services leave for Messina (1½ hours; L5100) and Catania (about the same) at least hourly from about 5 am to 7 pm.

Train There are also regular trains, but the awkward location of Taormina's station is a strong disincentive. If you arrive this way, catch an SAIS bus up to the town. They run roughly every half an hour to 90 minutes (much less frequently on Sundays).

Car & Motorbike Taormina is on the A18 tollway and SS114 between Messina and Catania. Parking can be a problem in Taormina, particularly in summer.

There are several car rental agencies in Taormina, including Avis, Hertz and Maggiore. California (☎ 2 37 69), Via Bagnoli Croci 86, rents cars and motorbikes at reasonable prices. A small car will cost upwards of L300,000 a week. A Vespa costs L28,000 a day or L180,000 a week, while a moped costs L20,000 a day or L130,000 a week.

AROUND TAORMINA

Panorama fanatics should head five km up the hill to **Castelmola**, literally the high point of the area, with a ruined castle and sweeping views of, well, everything. Several buses run from Taormina.

There is an **archaeological park** south of Taormina at Giardini-Naxos (follow the 'scavi' signs), the site of the first Greek settlement in Sicily. Founded in 735 BC, it was destroyed by Dionysius, the tyrant of Syracuse, in 403 BC. There is not a lot to see, but the park is a pleasant green refuge. It is open Monday to Saturday from 9 am to one hour before sunset and Sunday to 1 pm. Admission is free. Regular buses leave from the Taormina bus station in Via Pirandello for Giardini-Naxos. Giardini's AAST tourist office (☎ 0942-5 10 10) is at Via Tysandros 76E.

Fans of Francis Ford Coppola's *The Godfather* might be interested to know that the wedding scene was shot at **Forza d'Agrò**, near Taormina (three buses a day from Taormina).

A relatively short drive (SAIS buses from Taormina at 9.15 am and 1.45 pm weekdays only) will get you to the **Gole Alcantara**, a series of modest lava gorges on the river of the same name, a few km short of Francavilla. You could stop in here on your way to Mt Etna. Admission to the gorges costs L3000, and you can hire wading boots (cost L8000), which you'll need to do anything more than peer into the gorges.

CATANIA

Catania's crumbling appearance, its chaotic traffic and its reputation as a major crime centre may make the city seem intimidating and uninviting on arrival (the ugly location of the train and bus stations doesn't help). While admittedly not Sicily's best profile, Catania merits the benefit of the doubt. You may well end up using it as a base for visiting Mt Etna, so take the time to look around its grand, if poorly maintained, Baroque palaces and churches. It is well served by hotels and pensioni, and the food is good and cheap.

A busy industrial and commercial port town, Catania has an unfortunate history. Situated at the foot of Mt Etna, it was partially destroyed in a massive eruption in 1669, and, as reconstruction proceeded, was shaken to the ground in 1693 by an earthquake that devastated much of southeastern Sicily. The 18th-century project to rebuild the city in grand Baroque style was

SICILY

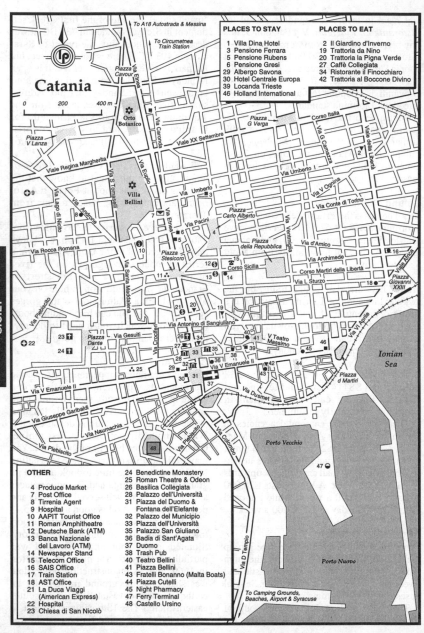

Catania

0   200   400 m

To A18 Autostrada & Messina
To Circumetnea Train Station

PLACES TO STAY
1 Villa Dina Hotel
3 Pensione Ferrara
5 Pensione Rubens
6 Pensione Gresi
29 Albergo Savona
30 Hotel Centrale Europa
39 Locanda Trieste
46 Holland International

PLACES TO EAT
2 Il Giardino d'Inverno
19 Trattoria da Nino
20 Trattoria la Pigna Verde
27 Caffè Collegiata
34 Ristorante il Finocchiaro
42 Trattoria al Boccone Divino

Ionian Sea

Porto Vecchio

Porto Nuovo

To Camping Grounds, Beaches, Airport & Syracuse

OTHER
4 Produce Market
7 Post Office
8 Tirrenia Agent
9 Hospital
10 AAPIT Tourist Office
11 Roman Amphitheatre
12 Deutsche Bank (ATM)
13 Banca Nazionale del Lavoro (ATM)
14 Newspaper Stand
15 Telecom Office
16 SAIS Office
17 Train Station
18 AST Office
21 La Duca Viaggi (American Express)
22 Hospital
23 Chiesa di San Nicolò
24 Benedictine Monastery
25 Roman Theatre & Odeon
26 Basilica Collegiata
28 Palazzo dell'Università
31 Piazza del Duomo & Fontana dell'Elefante
32 Palazzo del Municipio
33 Piazza dell'Università
35 Palazzo San Giuliano
36 Badia di Sant'Agata
37 Duomo
38 Trash Pub
40 Teatro Bellini
41 Piazza Bellini
43 Fratelli Bonanno (Malta Boats)
44 Piazza Cutelli
45 Night Pharmacy
47 Ferry Terminal
48 Castello Ursino

DAMIEN SIMONIS

LAUREN SUNSTEIN

DAMIEN SIMONIS

Top Left: Man buying onions at a market, Marsala, Sicily
Top Right: San Genaro festival, Agrigento, Sicily
Bottom: Sicilian cart, Monreale, Sicily

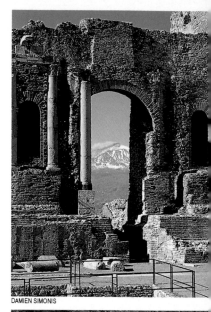

Top Left: View from Salina of Lipari, Isole Eolie (Aeolian Islands), Sicily
Top Right: Teatro Greco with Mt Etna in the background, Taormina, Sicily
Bottom Left: Temple E from Acropolis, Selinunte, Sicily
Bottom Right: Sheep, Scopello, Sicily

largely overseen by the architect Giovanni Vaccarini.

Orientation
The main train station and Intercity bus terminal are near the port at Piazza Giovanni XXIII. From here, Corso Martiri della Libertà heads west towards the city centre, about a 15-minute walk. Follow the road to Piazza della Repubblica and continue along Corso Sicilia to Via Etnea, the main thoroughfare running north off Piazza del Duomo. Most sights are concentrated around and west of Piazza del Duomo, while the commercial centre of Catania is farther north around Via Pacini and Via Umberto I.

Information
Tourist Office The AAPIT office (☎ 31 21 24) is at Largo Paisiello 5, just west of Via Etnea along Via Pacini. It is open Monday to Friday from 9 am to 1 pm and 4 to 6 pm and Saturday from 9 am to 1 pm. There are branches at the train station (☎ 53 18 02) on platform No 1, open roughly the same hours, and at the airport (☎ 34 19 00), open Monday to Friday from 8 am to 8 pm.

Money Banks are concentrated along Corso Sicilia, including the Deutsche Bank and Banca Nazionale del Lavoro, both with reliable ATMs. There is an exchange office at the train station. American Express is represented by La Duca Viaggi (☎ 31 61 55), Via Etnea 65. They have another office at Piazza Europa 1.

Post & Telecommunications The main post office is at Via Etnea 215, between Via Pacini and Via Umberto I. The Telecom office, Corso Sicilia 67, is open Monday to Saturday from 9 am to 1 pm and 4 to 7.30 pm and Sunday from 9 am to 12.30 pm. The post code for central Catania is 95100, and the telephone code is 095.

Travel Agency There is a CTS travel agent (☎ 715 04 34) at Via P Garofalo 3.

Emergency & Medical Services For the police, call ☎ 113. In a medical emergency, go to the Ospedale Vittorio Emanuele, Via Plebiscito 268, off Via Vittorio Emanuele II, or try the Ospedale Garibaldi on Viale Mario Rapisardi. There's a late night pharmacy on Via Vittorio Emanuele II, opposite Piazza Cutelli.

Piazza del Duomo & Around
Catania's most atmospheric square is easy to identify, as its centrepiece is the **Fontana dell'Elefante**, which was assembled by Vaccarini. The lava statue, carved possibly in the days of Byzantine rule, carries an Egyptian obelisk on its back. The architect worked on the entire square after the 1693 earthquake. He remodelled the 11th-century **duomo**, incorporating the original Norman apses and transept, and designed the **Palazzo del Municipio** (town hall) on the north side of the piazza. It features an elegant Baroque façade and, in keeping with a theme, is also known as the Palazzo degli Elefanti. Across Via Vittorio Emanuele II from the duomo is the **Badia di Sant'Agata** (a convent), yet another Vaccarini masterpiece whose cupola dominates the city centre.

A few blocks north-east you'll stumble into **Piazza Bellini** – the theatre of the same name is an eye-catching example of the city's architectural richness, a richness unfortunately buried beneath deep layers of grime.

North along Via Etnea from the Piazza del Duomo are several buildings of interest. Facing each other on Piazza dell' Università are two others designed by Vaccarini, the **Palazzo dell'Università** to the west and the **Palazzo San Giuliano**.

Roman Ruins & Churches
West along Via Vittorio Emanuele II, at No 226, is the entrance to the ruins of a **Roman theatre** and **odeon** (small rehearsal theatre). They are open daily from 9 am to one hour before sunset. From Piazza San Francesco, just before the entrance to the ruins, head north along Via Crociferi, which is lined with Baroque churches. Turn left into Via Gesuiti and follow it to Piazza Dante and the sombre

SICILY

Chiesa di San Niccolò. The largest church in Sicily, its façade was never completed. Next to the church is an 18th-century Benedictine monastery, the biggest in Europe after that of Mafra in Portugal, but in poor shape. It is now part of the university and slowly being restored. Wander in for a look at the cloisters – the beauty is faded, but it's there.

North of Piazza del Duomo more leftovers from Roman days include a modest **amphitheatre** in Piazza Stesicoro. For relief from the madding crowd, continue north along Via Etnea and cut in to the left behind the post office for the lovely gardens of the **Villa Bellini**, named in memory of one of Catania's most famous sons, the composer Vincenzo Bellini.

Castello Ursino
Built in the 13th century by Frederick II, one of the great castle-builders of the Middle Ages, this grim-looking fortress, surrounded by a moat, is in an equally grim neighbourhood, where it is best to travel in pairs or groups. It's south-west of Piazza del Duomo, just over the railway line. A few rooms have now been opened in the **Museo Civico** inside.

Places to Stay
Camping facilities are available at *Internazionale la Plaja* (☎ 34 08 80), Viale Kennedy 47, on the way out of the city towards Syracuse (take bus No 27 from the train station).

Budget pensioni are located around the centre, and if you are low on money, Catania is a good place to hole up. There are several places with rock-bottom prices, including the *Locanda Trieste* (☎ 32 71 05), Via Leonardi 24, near Piazza Bellini, which charges about L20,000 a person for a no-frills room.

The *Holland International* (☎ 53 27 79) is closer to the train station at Via Vittorio Emanuele II 8, just off Piazza dei Martiri, and has singles/doubles for L25,000/48,000 and doubles with a bathroom for L58,000.

A little further up-market, *Pensione Rubens* (☎ 31 70 73), Via Etnea 196, has singles/doubles for L34,000/50,000, while

Pensione Ferrara (☎ 31 60 00), Via Umberto I 66, has rooms for L33,000/54,000, or L41,000/67,000 with a bathroom. *Pensione Gresi* (☎ 32 37 09), Via Pacini 28, has singles/doubles for L37,000/58,000 and triples with a bathroom for L73,000.

Just off the Piazza del Duomo are two hotels with a little more class for those with a little more cash. The *Albergo Savona* (☎ 32 69 82), Via V Emanuele II 210, has singles/doubles for L38,000/60,000 or for L75,000/120,000 with a bathroom. *Hotel Centrale Europa* (☎ 31 13 09), Via V Emanuele II 167, comes in at L38,000/57,000 and has doubles with a bathroom for L78,000.

The *Villa Dina Hotel* (☎ 44 71 03), Via Caronda 129, is at the northern end of Via Etnea, near Piazza Cavour. It has pleasant rooms, a garden and private car park, and singles/doubles are L100,000/160,000. Take bus No 20 or 36 to the stop at Via Paleo, opposite the botanical gardens (not the Villa Bellini gardens).

Places to Eat
Every morning, except Sunday, Piazza Carlo Alberto is flooded by the chaos of a produce market, one of several in Catania, that comes close in racket to its North African counterparts. You can pick up supplies of bread, cheese, salami, fresh fruit and all manner of odd and ends.

Eating out can be a pleasant and inexpensive business in Catania. Students head for the area around Via Teatro Massimo, where there are several sandwich bars and 'pubs'. The area between here and the duomo is littered with small restaurants and trattorie – the more you look, the more you'll find. Some open only for lunch so, if you can, check first.

One eatery with a solid L15,000 lunch menu is the *Trattoria al Boccone Divino*, Via Vittorio Emanuele II 101. In the evening, you could track down the no-fuss *Trattoria la Pigna Verde*, Via Carcaci 17, where you can get local dishes and eat well for about L20,000.

Trattoria Da Nino, Via Biondi 19, has reasonably priced, good meals. Pricier but very pleasant is the *Ristorante Il Finocchiaro*, Via Cestai 8. In a similar price bracket is *Il Giardino d'Inverno*, Via Asilo Sant'Agata 34, about 500 metres north of the train station and west off Viale della Libertà. A full meal at the latter will cost about L40,000.

One of the city's better restaurants is the *Costa Azzurra*, Via de Cristoforo 4, by the sea at Ognina, north-east of the city. It specialises in seafood and is expensive. Bus No 22 leaves from Via Etnea for Ognina.

There are several decent cafés along Via Etnea, especially down the Piazza del Duomo end. For a touch of elegance, look in at the *Caffè Collegiata*, at No 3 on the street of the same name. For a Guinness, try *Trash Pub*, Piazza Scammacca 3.

Getting There & Away

Air Catania's airport, Fontanarossa, is seven km south-west of the city centre and services domestic and European flights (the latter all via Rome or Milan). In summer you may be able to dig up the odd direct charter flight to London or Paris. Take bus No 24 from outside the train station.

Bus Intercity buses terminate in the area around Piazza Giovanni XXIII, in front of the train station. SAIS (☎ 53 61 68), Via d'Amico 181, services Messina, Taormina, Noto, Syracuse, Palermo (two hours 40 minutes via autostrada; L16,000), Agrigento and Enna, and has a service to Rome. AST (☎ 53 17 56), Via Luigi Sturzo 220, also services these destinations and many smaller provincial towns around Catania, including Nicolosi and the cable car on Mt Etna. Etna Trasporti, at the same address as SAIS, runs buses to Piazza Armerina, Ragusa and Gela.

Train Frequent trains connect Catania with Messina and Syracuse (both 1½ hours) and there are less frequent services to Palermo (3¼ hours; L16,500), Enna (1¾ hours) and Agrigento (an agonisingly slow four hours). The private Circumetnea train line circles Mt Etna, stopping at the towns and villages on

the volcano's slopes. See the Mt Etna Getting There & Away section.

Car & Motorbike Catania is easily reached from Messina on the A18 and from Palermo on the A19. From the A18, signs for the centre of Catania will bring you to Via Etnea.

Boat Tirrenia (☎ 31 63 94), Via Androne 61, runs car ferries to Livorno, in Tuscany, four days a week. They may also go to Malta in summer. Other services to Reggio di Calabria and Naples were suspended at the time of writing. Gozo Channel, represented by Fratelli Bonanno (☎ 31 06 29) at Via Anzalone 7, runs boats to Malta. The ferry terminal is south of the train station along Via VI Aprile.

Getting Around

Many of the more useful AMT city buses terminate in front of the train station. These include: No 24, station-airport; Nos 29 and 36 (among others), station-Via Etnea; and No 27, station-Piazza del Duomo-Lido Plaja (beach). In summer, a special service ('D') runs to the beaches from Piazza G Verga.

MT ETNA

Dominating the landscape in eastern Sicily between Taormina and Catania, Mt Etna (approximately 3350 metres) is Europe's largest live volcano and one of the world's most active. Eruptions occur frequently, both from the four live craters at the summit (one, the Bocca Nuova, was formed in 1968) and on the slopes of the volcano, which is littered with crevices and old craters.

The volcano's most devastating eruption occurred in 1669 and lasted 122 days. A massive river of lava poured down its southern slope, engulfing a good part of Catania and dramatically altering the landscape. In 1971 an eruption destroyed the observatory at the summit, and another in 1983 finished off the old cable car and tourist centre (you can see where the lava flow stopped on that occasion). Nine people died in an explosion at the south-east crater in 1979, and two died and 10 were injured in an explosion at the crater in 1987. Its most recent eruption was in 1992, when a stream of lava pouring from a fissure in its south-eastern slope threatened to engulf the town of Zafferana Etnea. The town was saved, but not before one family lost their home and others much of their land.

The unpredictability of the volcano's activity means people are no longer allowed climb to the craters. Only a rope marks the point where it becomes unsafe, but it would be foolish to ignore the warning signs and go any farther.

On the north side of the volcano, there is a Pro Loco tourist centre at Linguaglossa (☎ 095-64 30 94), Piazza Annunziata. It has information about skiing and excursions to the craters, as well as an exhibition of the flora, fauna and rocks of the Parco Naturale dell'Etna. It is possible to hire a 4WD and guide to tour the volcano. On the south side, try the tourist office in Catania for information. The telephone code for the area is 095.

To the Craters

South With a daily bus link from Catania via Nicolosi, the south side of the volcano presents the easier option for an ascent towards the craters. From the Rifugio Sapienza, the closest the surfaced road comes to the summit, a cable car functions year-round from 9 am to 3.30 pm (L25,000 return). In summer, 4WD vehicles then take you through the eerie lava-scape close to the 3000-metre level. The all-in price for cable car, 4WD and guide was L52,500 return at the time of writing. In winter you are expected to ski back down (snow permitting) – there is no transport beyond the cable car. A day ski pass here costs L35,000.

Many tourists prefer to make the long climb from the rifugio to the top (3½ to 4 hours on a track winding up under the cable car and then following the same road used by the minibuses).

North There are several ski lifts operating at Piano Provenzana, snow permitting (a day ski pass costs up to L25,000). From the lifts you're looking at about an hour's walk to

come close to the top – a difficult proposition on snow. Enquire about hiring a guide and the feasibility of the walk in winter at the Linguaglossa Pro Loco.

In summer the lifts don't operate, but 4WDs make the same journey. Again, consider a guide for the hour's scramble from where the vehicles stop. The return trip with guide costs L55,000.

Places to Stay

There is a camping ground at Nicolosi (☎ 91 43 09), Via Goethe. The *Rifugio Sapienza* (☎ 91 10 62) near the çable car has beds for L32,000 a night and full board for L70,000 a day.

At Piano Provenzana, a small ski resort, the *Rifugio Nord-Est* (☎ 64 79 22) has beds for L30,000 a night.

There are small hotels at Piano Provenzana and in some of the towns along the Circumetnea train line, including Linguaglossa. For details, contact the Catania tourist office.

Getting There & Away

There is little doubt that your own transport will make life much easier around Mt Etna, but there are some public transport options. The easier approach is from the south.

From the South An AST bus for Rifugio Sapienza leaves from in front of the main train station in Catania at 8 am, travelling via Nicolosi. It returns from the rifugio at 4 pm. The AST office in Nicolosi (☎ 91 15 05) is at Via Etnea 32. You can also drive this route (take the Via Etnea north out of town and follow the signs for Nicolosi and Etna).

From the North SAIS and FCE buses connect Linguaglossa with Fiumefreddo on the coast (from where other SAIS buses run north to Taormina and Messina and south to Catania). Unless the FCE puts on a winter ski-season or summer bus to Piano Provenzana, your only chance from Linguaglossa is your thumb. If driving, follow the signs for Piano Provenzana out of Linguaglossa.

Around the Mountain Another option, if you are interested in circling rather than ascending Mt Etna, is to take a train on the private Circumetnea line. It runs around the mountain from Catania to the coastal town of Riposto, passing through numerous towns and villages on its slopes, including Linguaglossa. You can reach Riposto (or neighbouring Giarre) from Taormina by train or bus, if you want to make the trip from that end.

Catania-Riposto is about a 3½-hour trip, but you needn't go that far. If leaving from Catania, consider finishing the trip at **Randazzo** (two hours), a small medieval town noted for the fact that it has consistently escaped destruction despite its proximity to the summit. Randazzo is itself mildly interesting, with a couple of churches to punctuate a brief stroll along a few quiet streets, some lined with Aragonese apartments. A good example of lava architecture are the walls of the Norman Cattedrale di Santa Maria, while the Chiesa di Santa Maria della Volta preserves a squat 14th-century bell tower.

An FS railway branch line connects Randazzo with Taormina/Giardini Naxos, but services are subject to cancellation. More reliable are the infrequent SAIS buses.

The Circumetnea train station at Catania, known as Stazione Borgo, is at Via Caronda 352, off Via Etnea just after Piazza Cavour (also known as Piazza Borgo). Catch bus No 29 or 36 from the central train station to Stazione Borgo, one stop after Piazza Borgo.

You can drive a similar circuit, or catch FCE buses.

South-East Sicily

SYRACUSE (SIRACUSA)

Once a powerful Greek city to rival Athens, Syracuse is one of the highlights of a visit to Sicily. The city was founded in 734 BC by colonists from Corinth, who established their settlement on the island of Ortygia. Ruled by a succession of tyrants from the 5th century BC, Syracuse became a dominant sea power in the Mediterranean, prompting Athens to attack it in 413 BC. In one of history's great maritime battles, the Athenian fleet was sent to the bottom of the sea.

Syracuse reached its zenith under the rule of Dionysius and attracted luminaries from all around, Plato among them. He apparently so bored Dionysus with his diatribes that the tyrant ended up trying to sell the philosopher as a slave.

The Romans marched into Syracuse in 212 BC, but it remained an important and enlightened city under the new administration. Less sensitive handling came from the barbarians in the 5th century AD, later succeeded by an empire more in the old style, that of the Byzantines. Syracuse's fate subsequently followed that of much of the island, witnessing over the centuries the arrival of the Arabs, Normans, Swabians, French and Spaniards.

The Greek mathematician Archimedes was born here, and when the apostle Paul came from the Middle East to propagate the Christian faith, he dropped by. He seems to have had little trouble converting the city, but Rome was to prove a tougher nut to crack.

Orientation
The main sights of Syracuse are in two areas: on the island of Ortygia and two km across town in the Neapolis archaeological zone. From the train station, walk east along Via Francesco Crispi to Piazzale Marconi. Heading straight through the piazza to Corso Umberto will bring you to Ortygia, just a five-minute walk. Alternatively, turn left from Piazzale Marconi into Via Catania, cross the railway and follow the busy shopping street, Corso Gelone, to Viale Paolo Orsi and the archaeological zone. If you arrive by bus, you'll be dropped in or near Piazza della Posta in Ortygia. Most accommodation is in the newer part of town, to the west, while the better eating places are in Ortygia.

Information
Tourist Offices Open Monday to Saturday

SICILY

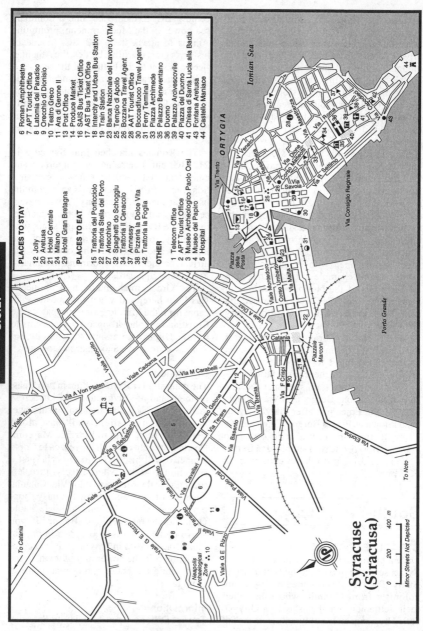

PLACES TO STAY

12 Jolly
20 Aretusa
21 Hotel Centrale
24 Milano
29 Hotel Gran Bretagna

PLACES TO EAT

15 Trattoria del Porticciolo
22 Trattoria Stella del Porto
27 Arfecchino
32 Spaghetti do Schoggiu
34 Trattoria Il Cenacolo
37 Amnessy
38 Pizzeria la Dolce Vita
42 Trattoria la Foglia

OTHER

1 Telecom Office
2 APT Tourist Office
3 Museo Archeologico Paolo Orsi
4 Museo del Papiro
5 Hospital
6 Roman Amphitheatre
7 APT Tourist Office
8 Latomia del Paradiso
9 Orecchio di Dionisio
10 Teatro Greco
11 Ara di Gerone II
13 Post Office
14 Produce Market
16 SAIS Bus Ticket Office
17 AST Bus Ticket Office
18 Intercity and Urban Bus Station
19 Train Station
23 Banca Nazionale del Lavoro (ATM)
25 Tempio di Apollo
26 Bozzanca Travel Agent
28 AAT Tourist Office
30 Boccadifuoco Travel Agent
31 Ferry Terminal
33 Piazza Archimede
35 Palazzo Beneventano
36 Duomo
39 Palazzo Arcivescovile
40 Piazza del Duomo
41 Chiesa di Santa Lucia alla Badia
43 Fontana Aretusa
44 Castello Maniace

Syracuse
(Siracusa)

0   200   400 m

Minor Streets Not Depicted

To Noto

from 8.30 am to 1.45 pm and 3 to 5 pm, the main APT office (☎ 6 77 10) is a little out of the way at Via San Sebastiano 43, in the new part of town. It has information on the city and province (including Noto). A branch office is generally open Monday to Saturday from 9 am to 1 pm at the entrance to the archaeological zone.

The AAT (☎ 6 52 01), on Ortygia at Via Maestranza 33, deals specifically with Syracuse and is probably the most convenient office at which to pick up a map and hotel list. The hours are the same as those of the main APT office.

Money Numerous banks line Corso Umberto, including the Banca Nazionale del Lavoro at No 29, which has ATMs. There are others on Corso Gelone. The rates at the train station exchange booth are generally poor.

Post & Telecommunications The post office is in Piazza della Posta, to your left as you cross the bridge to Ortygia. It is open Monday to Friday from 8 am to 7 pm and Saturday to 1 pm.

The Telecom office, Viale Teracati 46, is open Monday to Saturday from 8 am to 10 pm. The post code for Syracuse is 96100 and the telephone code is 0931.

Emergency The public hospital is in Via Testaferrata. For medical emergencies, ring ☎ 6 85 55; for immediate police assistance, ring ☎ 113.

Ortygia

The island of Ortygia is the spiritual and physical heart of the city. Its buildings are predominantly medieval, with some Baroque palaces and churches. The 7th-century **duomo** was built on top of a Greek temple of Athena, incorporating most of the original columns of the temple in its three-aisled structure. The duomo is a melting pot of architectural styles. Rebuilt after various earthquakes, it has a Gothic/Catalan ceiling, a Baroque façade and Baroque chapels and altars. The towers on the left side of the church's exterior were in fact built by the

Arabs, who used it as a mosque. Some of the columns on the left side have shifted on their bases, the result of an earthquake in 1542.

Piazza del Duomo, once the site of the Greek acropolis, is lined with Baroque palaces, including the **Palazzo Beneventano** and the **Palazzo Arcivescovile** (Archbishop's Palace), and is among the finest Baroque squares in Italy. At the southern end is the **Chiesa di Santa Lucia alla Badia**, dedicated to St Lucy, the city's patron saint, who was martyred at Syracuse during the reign of the Roman emperor Diocletian. Its Baroque façade is decorated with a wrought-iron balustrade.

Walk down Via Picherali to the waterfront and the **Fontana Aretusa**, a natural freshwater spring only metres from the sea. Greek legend says the nymph Arethusa, pursued by the river god Alpheus, was turned into a fountain by the goddess Diana in order to escape. Undeterred, Alpheus then turned himself into the river that feeds the spring. Next to the spring is the Foro Vittorio Emanuele II, where locals take their evening constitutional. At the entrance to Ortygia, in Piazza Pancali, lies the **Tempio di Apollo** (Temple of Apollo). Little remains of the 6th-century BC Doric structure, apart from the bases of a few columns. There is something rather odd about seeing the council gardener weave his way around the ruins with a lawnmower.

Parco Archeologico

For the classicist, Syracuse is summed up in one image, that of the sparkling white 5th-century BC **Greek theatre**, hewn out of the rock in what for the Greek settlers was Neapolis, or the New City. A masterwork, the ancient theatre could seat 16,000 people.

Near the theatre is the **Latomia del Paradiso** (Garden of Paradise), a former limestone quarry run by the Greeks along the lines of a concentration camp, where prisoners cut blocks of limestone in subterranean tunnels for building projects. Most of the area remained covered by a 'roof' of earth, which collapsed during the 1693 earthquake. After this, the garden of citrus and magnolia trees was created. In the garden is the **Orecchio di Dionisio** (Ear of Dionysius), a grotto 23 metres high and 65 metres deep, in the shape of an ear. It was named by Caravaggio, who during a visit in the 17th century was much impressed by its extraordinary acoustics. Caravaggio mused that the tyrant must have taken advantage of them to overhear the whispered conversations of his prisoners. Next to it, the **Grotta dei Cordari** (Cordmakers' Cave) is so named because it was used by cordmakers to practise their craft. The cave has been closed for some years.

Back outside this area and opposite the APT tourist office you'll find the entrance to the 2nd-century AD **Roman amphitheatre**. The structure was used for gladiator fighting and horse races. Roman punters used to park their chariots in the area between the amphitheatre and Viale Paolo Orsi. The Spaniards, little interested in archaeology, largely destroyed the site in the 16th century, using it as a quarry to build the city walls on Ortygia. West of the amphitheatre is the 3rd-century BC **Ara di Gerone II** (Altar of Hieron II). The monolithic sacrificial altar was a kind of giant abattoir where 450 oxen could be killed at one time.

The Parco Archeologico is open daily from 9 am to 6 pm (in the depths of winter until 3 pm). Admission is L2000, and you can remain up to an hour after the ticket window shuts. To reach it, catch a bus (No 1 and several others) from Riva della Posta on Ortygia.

Museums About 500 metres east of the archaeological zone, off Viale Teocrito, the **Museo Archeologico Paolo Orsi**, in the grounds of the Villa Landolina, contains the best organised and most interesting archaeological collection in Sicily. The museum is open Tuesday to Saturday from 9 am to 1 pm, and the first and third Sunday of every month from 9 am to 12.30 pm. Admission is L2000. Not far away, at Viale Teocrito 66, is the small **Museo del Papiro**, with exhibits including papyrus documents and other papyrus products. The plant grows in abun-

dance around the Ciane river, near Syracuse, and was used to make paper in the 18th century. It's open Tuesday to Sunday from 9 am to 2 pm.

Festivals

Since 1914, in every even-numbered year, Syracuse has hosted a festival of Greek classical drama in May and June. Performances are given in the Greek theatre and prices range from around L15,000 for unreserved seats in the rear to L60,000 for reserved seats close to the stage. Tickets are available from the APT office or at a booth at the entrance to the theatre. You can call for information on ☎ 6 53 73.

Places to Stay – bottom end

There are camping facilities at *Agriturist Rinaura* (☎ 72 12 24), about four km west of the city; catch bus No 34 from Corso Umberto. It costs L5800 per person, L8400 for a tent. *Fontane Bianche* (☎ 79 03 33) is about 18 km south-west of Syracuse, at the beach of the same name, and is open from April to October. Catch bus No 21 or 22.

The non-HI *Ostello della Gioventù* (☎ 71 11 18), Viale Epipoli 45, is eight km west of Syracuse; catch bus No 10 or 11 from Corso Umberto. Beds are L20,000 or full board L38,000.

Close to the train station is the *Hotel Centrale* (☎ 52 17 89), Corso Umberto 141. It has small, basic singles/doubles for L25,000/40,000. A little better is the *Milano* (☎ 6 69 81), Corso Umberto 10, near Ortygia, with no-frills rooms for L30,000/50,000 or L40,000/65,000 with a bathroom.

The two-star *Aretusa* (☎ 2 42 11), Via Francesco Crispi 73-81, is close to the train station and has comfortable singles/doubles for L40,000/60,000. With a bathroom, you're looking at L47,000/70,000.

The *Hotel Gran Bretagna* (☎ 6 87 65), Via Savoia 21, is the only hotel on Ortygia (pending the restoration of the more up-market Grand Hotel). A pleasant little spot, it has rooms for L46,000/76,000 or L52,000/89,000 with a bathroom.

Places to Stay – middle to top end

The *Scala Greca* (☎ 75 39 22; fax 75 37 78) is north of the archaeological zone at Via Avola 7 and has singles/doubles with a bathroom for L75,000/103,000. It is, like several other better hotels, quite a distance from the centre. The top hotel is the *Jolly* (☎ 46 11 11; fax 46 11 26), near the city centre at Corso Gelone 45. Rooms cost L190,000/220,000.

Places to Eat

In the streets near the post office, there's a produce market daily, except Sunday, until 1 pm. There are several grocery shops and supermarkets along Corso Gelone.

A lot of Syracuse restaurants are on the pricey side, but there are a few moderately priced places about. For snacks, try the excellent takeaway pizza and focaccia at *Casa del Pane*, Corso Gelone 115.

In the new part of town, the *Stella del Porto*, Via Tripoli 40, off Via Malta, is a simple trattoria with a narrow menu concentrating on seafood. Try the spaghetti with swordfish (pesce di spada). A full meal will cost about L20,000. In Ortygia, which is swarming with restaurants, you'll get similar value at the *Trattoria del Porticciolo*, Via Trento 22.

Spaghetti do Schoggiu is at Via Scinà 11, just off Piazza Archimede. It has pasta from L6000 and mains for around L10,000. *Pizzeria la Dolce Vita*, Via Roma 112, has outside tables in a small courtyard, and occasionally puts on live entertainment. *Amnessy* is a pleasant pizzeria/restaurant and bar in a corner of Piazza San Giuseppe, and charges average prices. *Trattoria Il Cenacolo* is tucked away in a tiny piazza off Via Consiglio Reginale, south of Piazza del Duomo. It serves good food at around L25,000 for a full meal. There's an atmospheric 'pub' across the square.

At *Trattoria la Foglia*, Via Capodieci 29, off Lago Aretusa, the eccentric owner/chef and her vegetarian husband serve whatever seafood and vegetables are fresh on the day, and cook their own bread. A full meal will cost around L35,000. *Arlecchino* is on the waterfront at Via dei Tolomei 5. It is one of the city's better restaurants and you'd be lucky to get away with less L45,000 a head.

Getting There & Away

Bus Unless you're coming from Catania or Messina, you'll find buses faster and more convenient than trains. SAIS buses (☎ 6 67 10) leave from Riva della Posta or near their office at Via Trieste 28, a block in. They connect with Catania and its airport, Palermo (three-four hours; L20,000), Enna and surrounding small towns, including Noto. SAIS also has a daily service to Rome, leaving Syracuse at 6.30 am and connecting with the Rome bus at Catania. A one-way ticket costs L70,000 and the trip takes 12 hours.

AST buses leave for Catania, Piazza Armerina, Noto, Modica and Ragusa from their office (☎ 46 27 11) at Riva della Posta 11.

Train More than a dozen trains daily depart for Messina (three hours) via Catania (1½ hours). Some go on to Rome, Turin, Milan and other long-distance destinations. There is only one direct connection to Palermo, leaving at 6.40 am and taking five hours. If you insist on using trains and miss this one, you'll have to go to Catania and wait for a connection. There are several slow trains to Modica and Ragusa.

Car & Motorbike By car, if arriving from the north, you will enter Syracuse on Via Scala Greca. To reach the centre of the city, turn left at Viale Teracati and follow it around to the south; it eventually becomes Corso Gelone.

Boat The question of boat services to and from Syracuse is in flux. The old Naples-Reggio di Calabria-Catania-Syracuse-Malta run seems a thing of the past, and no-one seems sure what might replace it. Maltese companies will probably continue to run summer ferry and catamaran services to Syracuse, but you'll need to hunt around the travel agencies. Try Boccadifuoco (☎ 46 38 66), Viale Mazzini 8, or Bozzanca e Figlio (☎ 46 40 00), Corso Matteotti 88. If there's nothing, ask about links between Malta and Pozzallo, south-west of Syracuse.

Getting Around

Only a few km separate the archaeological zone and Ortygia, about a 20-minute walk. Otherwise, buses Nos 1 and 2 make the trip from the Piazza della Posta.

NOTO

Flattened by the 1693 earthquake, Noto was rebuilt in grand Baroque style by its noble families. The warm gold and rose hues of the local stone tone down the heavily embellished palaces and churches, and the town is very picturesque. Noto is also good for your tastebuds, and particularly known for its cakes and pastries. Be aware that accommodation is a problem.

Orientation & Information

Intercity buses drop you in the public gardens at the main entrance to the town, the Porta Reale, at the beginning of Corso Vittorio Emanuele, the town's main street. You can get a map at the AAPIT tourist office (☎ 83 67 44), along the corso in Piazza XVI Maggio (9 am to 1 pm and 3 to 5 pm). Noto's telephone code is 0931. For police call ☎ 113. In a medical emergency call ☎ 89 02 35.

Things to See & Do

Most of the important monuments line Corso Vittorio Emanuele. Overlooking Piazza XVI Maggio are the **Chiesa di San Domenico** and the adjacent **Dominican convent**, both designed by Rosario Gagliardi, a Sicilian architect who made a big contribution to the town's reconstruction. Back towards the Porta Reale is the **Palazzo Villadorata** (also known as Palazzo Nicolaci), on Via Corrado Nicolaci. On the third Sunday in May the street is transformed into a sea of flowers for the Infiorata, a festival to welcome the spring. Each of the palace's richly sculpted balconies is different, sporting a veritable menagerie of centaurs, horses, lions, sirens and tragic masks. Once the

home of the princes of Villadorata, it is now partly used as municipal offices and some rooms are open to the public.

The **cathedral** stands at the top of a sweeping staircase overlooking Piazza Municipio. The façade is imposing, but less extravagant than most of Noto's other Baroque monuments. Next to the cathedral is the **Palazzo Landolina**, now abandoned, but belonging to Sant'Alfano, Noto's oldest noble family. Across the piazza is the **Palazzo Ducezio**, long the town hall but now buried in scaffolding.

Farther along the corso are the **Chiesa del Santissimo Salvatore** and an adjoining monastery. The interior of the church is the most impressive in Noto. The monastery was reserved for the daughters of local nobility. The fountain suspended on a wall next to the monastery was left there after Noto's streets were lowered in 1840 to facilitate the movement of carriages.

Places to Stay

There is only one hotel in Noto, the *Albergo Stella* (☎ 83 56 95), on the corner of Via F Maiore and Via Napoli, near the public gardens. It has singles/doubles for L30,000/ 50,000.

The rest of the tourist accommodation is by the sea at Noto Marina, a 15-minute drive or bus trip (although buses run only in summer). Hotels include the *Residence Korsal* (☎ 81 21 19), which has rooms for L40,000/55,000, and *Hotel Ionio* (☎ 81 20 40), with rooms for L65,000/98,000.

Places to Eat

The people of Noto are serious about their food, so take time to enjoy a meal and follow it up with a visit to the bar/pasticceria *Corrado Costanzo* at Via Silvio Spaventa 9. Signore Costanzo enjoys considerable fame worldwide for his skills as a pastry chef. He specialises in dolci di mandorle (almond cakes and sweets) and torrone (nougat). While here, try his heavenly gelati and granita made with fragolini (tiny wild strawberries). *Caffè Sicilia*, Corso V Emanuele 125, is also well known for its sweets.

Trattoria del Carmine, Via Ducezio 9, serves excellent home-style meals for about L25,000 a head, as does *Trattoria Il Giglio*, Piazza Municipio 8-10. *Ristorante Il Barocco*, off Via Cavour in Ronco Sgadari, near Via Nicolaci, is one of Noto's finest restaurants and has a lovely internal courtyard. An excellent meal will come to more than L50,000.

Getting There & Away

Noto is easily accessible by AST and SAIS buses from Catania and Syracuse (see the Getting There & Away sections for those cities). From June to August only, buses run frequently between Noto and Noto Marina.

AROUND NOTO

The beach at **Noto Marina** is pleasant and, as yet, has not been subject to the overdevelopment characteristic of most Italian resorts. Nearby, and accessible only by car or by making the 45-minute walk, is **Eloro**, the site of a Greek settlement later occupied by the Romans. Uncompleted excavations have revealed a city square and sacred area. On either side of the hill where the sparse ruins lie are long, sandy beaches comparatively free of the usual crowds.

Farther along the coast is the **Vendicari** nature reserve, a haven for water birds. Bird-watchers are well catered for by special observatories, and there is a superb, long, sandy beach that is popular in summer but never overcrowded. It is possible to reach the park by the AST bus connecting Noto and Pachino.

RAGUSA

This prosperous provincial capital is virtually two towns in one: Ragusa Ibla, a curious cocktail of medieval and Baroque, and the 18th-century 'new' town, simply known as Ragusa. This split, initially a result of the need to expand the town beyond its medieval boundaries, was accentuated after the 1693 earthquake. The upper part of the town was re-created in the grand style of the day, while the lower town clung to its medieval lines and the old name of Ibla.

Orientation

The lower town, Ibla, has most of the sights, but the transport and accommodation are in the newer upper town. The train station is in Piazza del Popolo, and the Intercity bus station in the adjacent Piazza Gramsci. From the train station, turn left and head along Viale Tenente Lena, across the bridge (Ponte Nuovo) and straight ahead along Via Roma to reach Corso Italia, the upper town's main street. Turn right on Corso Italia and follow it to the stairs to Ibla, or follow the road as it makes its winding way to the lower town.

Information

Tourist Office There is an office with a helpful staff in the Piazza del Duomo in Ibla (follow the signs). It's open Tuesday to Saturday from 8.30 am to 1.30 pm and 3 to 7.30 pm, with slightly shorter hours on Sunday. The AAPIT (☎ 62 14 21) has an office close by at Via Capitano Bocchieri 33 on the 1st floor of the Palazzo Rocca, open from 9 am to 2 pm and sometimes till later. They have more in the line of brochures.

Post & Telecommunications The main post office is in Piazza Matteotti on Corso Italia and there's a Telecom office on Via Maiorana, on the left as you approach the Ponte dei Cappuccini (the middle bridge) from Corso Italia. Ragusa's telephone code is 0932.

Emergency For police attendance, ring ☎ 113. The public hospital, the Ospedale Civile (☎ 62 39 46 for the Guardia Medica), is across Piazza del Popolo from the train station. For an ambulance, call ☎ 62 14 10.

Things to See & Do

The stairs linking the upper and lower towns are next to the **Chiesa di Santa Maria delle Scale**. The church was rebuilt after the 1693 earthquake and retains parts of the original 15th-century structure including the bell tower and doorway. Take in the panoramic view of Ibla before heading down the stairs.

The **Basilica di San Giorgio**, at the top of a flight of stairs in the Piazza del Duomo, dominates Ibla. Designed by Rosario Gagliardi and built in the late 18th century, it has the boisterous, 'wedding-cake' appearance of high Baroque.

Follow Corso XXV Aprile downhill, past the **Chiesa di San Giuseppe**, which bears similarities to San Giorgio, until you reach the **Giardino Ibleo**, the town's pleasant public gardens, where you can have a picnic.

In the upper town, visit the early 18th-century **duomo** in Piazza San Giovanni on Corso Italia, and the **Museo Archeologico Ibleo** in Via Natalelli, off Via Roma. The museum is open daily from 8.30 am to 1 pm and 3 to 7.30 pm. Admission costs L2000.

Places to Stay

All of Ragusa's accommodation is in the upper town and there are no budget hotels. *Hotel San Giovanni* (☎ 62 10 13), Via Traspontino 3, has singles/doubles for L40,000/60,000 or L60,000/96,000 with a bathroom. To get there from Piazza del Popolo, head down Viale Leonardo da Vinci, turn left at Via Ingegnere Migliorisi and follow it to the footbridge.

At Corso Italia 40 is *Hotel Rafael* (☎ 65 40 80), a pleasant establishment with rooms for L60,000/80,000. Nearby, at Corso Italia 70, is *Hotel Montreal* (☎ 62 11 33), with good singles/doubles for L75,000/100,000. Rooms at both hotels have bathrooms.

Places to Eat

There is a Standa supermarket at Via Roma 187, near the bridge. If you want to take a picnic to the park, there is a grocery shop on Corso XXV Aprile, between Piazza del Duomo and Piazza Pola in Ibla, where you can pick up supplies or have sandwiches made.

Trattoria la Bettola, Largo Camerina, downhill to the left off Piazza del Duomo, is pleasant, and meals are priced at around L25,000. *La Rusticana*, at Via XXV Aprile 68, is another reasonable little place. *U Saracinù*, Via del Convento 9, off Piazza del Duomo, has a L20,000 tourist menu; otherwise a full meal will come to around L30,000.

The *Gran Bar Puglisi*, opposite the train station, serves good coffee granitas.

Getting There & Away

Ragusa is accessible by not-so-regular trains (☎ 62 12 39) from Syracuse, Noto and Agrigento. Buses are a better bet. Etna .Trasporti, a subsidiary of SAIS (information and tickets at Gran Bar Puglisi, Via Dante 94, opposite the train station) runs eight buses per day to Catania.

AST (☎ 62 12 49) services Catania by way of Syracuse (three buses a day). It also serves Palermo (three buses a day) and runs more regularly to Noto and Syracuse (seven a day). There is an AST timetable posted at the spot in Piazza Gramsci where AST buses stop.

Getting Around

City buses Nos 1 and 3 run from Piazza del Popolo in the upper town to Piazza Pola and the gardens in the lower town.

AROUND RAGUSA
Modica

About 20 km east of Ragusa, Modica seems to be a close cousin. It has the same sun-bleached colour and is also divided into two sections: Modica Alta (High Modica) and, you guessed it, Modica Bassa (Low Modica).

The highlight is the Chiesa di San Giorgio in the upper part of town (local buses run by from the lower end), easily one of the most extraordinary Baroque churches in the province. A majestic stairway sweeps up to a daringly tall façade, erected by Rosario Gagliardi in the early 18th century, that looks like it was meant to be a tower. There are regular AST buses from Ragusa.

SICILY

Central Sicily & the South Coast

ENNA

Situated high on a commanding ridge in the sun-scorched centre of Sicily, Enna is somewhat isolated from the main tourist route around the coast. Known since Greek times as the 'umbilicus' of Sicily, the journey itself is rewarding, from whichever direction you approach. The exercise becomes more tempting still if combined with an excursion to nearby Piazza Armerina for the extraordinary mosaics of the Villa Romana (see below).

Enna, 931 metres above sea level, has been an ideal defensive position and lookout post since prehistoric times. First settled by the Sicani, Enna later became Greek, submitting to the tyranny of Syracuse in 307 BC and thereafter falling into Carthaginian and Roman hands. In Byzantine times it became a fortress and one of the main bulwarks against the Arabs, who nonetheless managed to capture the town in 859 AD. Today it is an important agricultural and mining centre.

Orientation

The principal road into the town is Via Pergusa, which eventually links with Via Roma, to the right, the main street of historic Enna. The Intercity bus station is on Viale Diaz. To get to the town centre, turn right from the terminal and follow Viale Diaz to Corso Sicilia, turn right again and follow it to Via Sant'Agata to the left, which heads down to Via Roma.

Information

The AAPIT office (☎ 52 82 28) is at Via Roma 413. The staff are helpful and you can pick up a map and information on the city and province. It is open Monday to Saturday from 9 am to 1 pm. The AAST office (☎ 50 08 75), next to the Albergo Sicilia in nearby Piazza Colajanni, has information mainly on the city itself and is open daily from 8 am to 2 pm and every evening, except Monday and Saturday, from 4 to 7 pm.

The post office is at Via Volta 1, just off Piazza Garibaldi, and the post code for Enna is 94100. Public telephones are scattered about the town, or you can try the Albergo Sicilia. The telephone code is 0935.

There are several banks on Piazza VI Dicembre, a short walk downhill from the AAPIT.

In an emergency, call the police on ☎ 113. For medical assistance, go to the Ospedale Civile Umberto I in Via Trieste, or ring ☎ 4 51 11. Out of hours, the Guardia Medica is on ☎ 50 08 96.

Castello di Lombardia

Enna's most visible monument, the medieval castle, crowns the town's highest point at the eastern end. Built by the Swabians and altered by Frederick III of Aragon, it was one of the most important defensive structures in medieval Sicily. It retains six of its original 20 towers and the views of the surrounding countryside are spectacular – you can make out Etna in the distant north-east. Closer to home and across the valley rises the town of Calascibetta, erected by the Arabs in the 9th century and forming the northern sentinel over a valley which now contains the Palermo-Catania A19 autostrada and railway. The castle, now part theatre, is open daily from 8 am to 6 pm.

Duomo

Back along Via Roma, the 14th-century duomo retains, despite remodelling in the 15th and 16th centuries, its Gothic apse and transept. Behind the duomo on Via Roma is the **Museo Alessi**, which houses the contents of the cathedral's treasury. It was closed at the time of writing. Across Via Roma in Piazza Mazzini, the **Museo Archeologico** (also known as Museo Varisano) has a small collection of ancient artefacts dug up in the area. It is open daily from 9 am to 6.30 pm and admission is free.

Towers

Farther west in Piazza Vittorio Emanuele,

the most impressive element of the **Chiesa di San Francesco** is its 15th-century bell tower, adorned with fine Gothic windows. The tower once formed part of the city's defence system. You could head over to the chunky **Torre di Federico** in the public gardens (villa comunale) in the new part of town, also part of the old system. The octagonal tower, standing 24 metres high, was once linked by a secret passage to the castle.

For a pleasant evening stroll, head for Piazza Francesco Crispi and wander along Viale Marconi to enjoy the view.

Festival

During Holy Week at Easter, Enna is the setting for colourful traditional celebrations, notably on Good Friday when thousands of people wearing hoods and capes of different colours participate in a solemn procession to the duomo.

Places to Stay & Eat

There is no cheap accommodation here, so be prepared. Enna itself has only one hotel, the *Albergo Sicilia* (☎ 2 46 22), Piazza Colajanni. Singles/doubles with breakfast come in at L79,000/119,000. For other options, catch city bus No 4 from Piazza V Emanuele to Lago di Pergusa (a small touristy lake with beaches about 10 km south). Cheapest is the *Miralago* (☎ 54 12 72), with rooms at L40,000/60,000. It is the first place you pass on the right before entering the town proper along Via Nazionale.

There is a market every morning from Monday to Saturday in Via Mercato Sant'Antonio, parallel to Via Roma off Piazza Coppola, where you can find fresh fruit, bread and cheeses etc. *Knulp*, Via Restivo 14, is a bar where snacks, including some creative sandwiches, are served. *Da Gino* is a pleasant trattoria/pizzeria on Viale Marconi. It has outdoor tables and a view, and prices are reasonable. *Ristorante Centrale*, Piazza VI Dicembre 9, is more expensive. *Al Rupe* is set into the hillside just below the castle, and serves reasonable food. It has tables on an open terrace with great views of Enna and the surrounding area.

Getting There & Away

SAIS buses (☎ 50 09 02) connect Enna with Catania (and on to Rome), Palermo and Syracuse. It is possible to reach Agrigento via Caltanisetta. Buses terminate in Viale Diaz. Regular SAIS buses also run to Piazza Armerina. Don't take a train – the station is miles away at the foot of the mountain-top town.

PIAZZA ARMERINA

A pleasant town less than an hour by bus or car south of Enna, Piazza Armerina boasts an interesting Baroque **cathedral**. This self-proclaimed *cittá dei mosaici* (mosaics city) is the nearest town to the wonderful treasure that lies in the Villa Romana del Casale, an imperial Roman villa some five km away.

The AAST tourist office (☎ 68 02 01) is at Via Cavour 15, in the town centre, uphill along Via Umberto I or Via Garibaldi from the Intercity bus stops. It is open from 8 am to 2 pm and 4.30 to 7.30 pm. Get the brochure on the villa here; it explains the layout of the ruins and the mosaics and is often unavailable at the site. SAIS buses connect Enna and Piazza Armerina (about 10 a day). There is also a daily AST bus from Syracuse.

Villa Romana del Casale

Built between the end of the 3rd and mid-4th century AD, the villa was probably the home or hunting lodge of a Roman dignitary. Buried under mud in a 12th-century flood, it remained hidden for 700 years before its magnificent floor mosaics were revealed.

Covering about 3500 sq metres, the villa was designed in line with the lie of the hill on which it stands, creating three main areas. The mosaics cover almost its entire floor space and are considered unique for their narrative style of composition, range of subjects and variety of colours – much of it clearly influenced by African themes.

The villa is well organised to cope with hordes of tourists, and by following the raised walkways, you will see all the main areas. The most captivating of the mosaics include the erotic depictions in what was probably a private apartment on the north side of the great peristyle. One of the richest mosaics in terms of colour and action, the *Little Hunt*, is in the largest room. Next door is the villa's most famous piece, illustrating 10 girls clad in what must have been the world's earliest bikinis.

The east side of the peristyle opens onto a long corridor, its floor carpeted with the splendid mosaic of the *Great Hunt*, depicting the chase for exotic wild animals. On the other side of the corridor is a series of apartments, whose floor illustrations reproduce scenes from Homer, as well as mythical subjects such as Arion playing the lyre on a dolphin's back, and Eros and Pan wrestling. There is also a lively circus scene.

The villa is open daily from 9 am to one hour before sunset. Admission is L2000. Three ATAN buses leave hourly for the villa from Piazza Generale Cascino in Piazza Armerina from 9 am, and another three from 4 pm. If driving, you will be charged L2000 to park outside the entrance.

Places to Stay & Eat
If you want to stay in Piazza Armerina, about the cheapest accommodation is the *Villa Romana* (☎ 68 29 11), Via A De Gasperi 18, which has singles/doubles starting at L40,000/60,000. *Hotel Mosaici* (☎ 68 54 53) is three km out of town on the way to the villa. It has rooms for L40,000/55,000. For a decent meal, try *Dal Goloso*, Via Garao 4, just off Piazza Garibaldi near the tourist office.

AROUND PIAZZA ARMERINA
Morgantina
About 16 km north-east of Piazza Armerina, just beyond the town of Aidone, have been unearthed the remains of what started life as a rich Sicilian town. What you see of its agora, theatre and other buildings owes more to subsequent Greek occupation than to the Sicilians, however. That the remains are not more spectacular is largely the fault of the Romans, who destroyed the town in 211 BC. Set in pleasant country with wide views to Etna, the Morgantina site is an easy detour if you have your own transport, but a difficult proposition without.

AGRIGENTO
This pleasant medieval town high on a hill overlooks the Mediterranean and the spectacular Valley of the Temples, a significant ancient Greek site. Founded in 582 BC as Akragas by settlers from Gela, themselves originally from Rhodes, the town became powerful in the 5th century BC when it was ruled by tyrants, and most of the temples date from then. The Greek poet Pindar described the town as 'the most beautiful of those inhabited by mortals'.

Sacked and destroyed by the Carthaginians in 406 BC, it was rebuilt and conquered by the Romans in the 3rd century BC. The newcomers renamed the town Agrigentum and it continued to prosper under Byzantine and Arab rule. On the road between Agrigento and Porto Empedocle is Caos, where the playwright Luigi Pirandello (1867-1936) was born.

The Greek temples are the obvious reason to come to Agrigento, but it would be a shame to overlook the town itself.

Orientation
Intercity buses arrive in the area just off the north side of Piazza Vittorio Emanuele, and the train station is slightly south in Piazza Marconi. Lying between the two is the green oasis of Piazzale Aldo Moro, at the eastern end of Via Atenea, the main street of the medieval town. Frequent city buses run to the Valley of the Temples below the town. See the Getting Around section.

Information
Tourist Office The AAST office (☎ 2 04 54), Via Cesare Battisti 15, is open Monday to Saturday from 8.30 am to 1.45 pm as well as Monday to Friday from 5.30 to 6.30 pm.

Money Banks are generally open from 8.30 am to 2 pm and the Monte dei Paschi di Siena on Piazza Vittorio Emanuele has an ATM. Out of hours there is an exchange office at the post office and another at the train station – watch the rates.

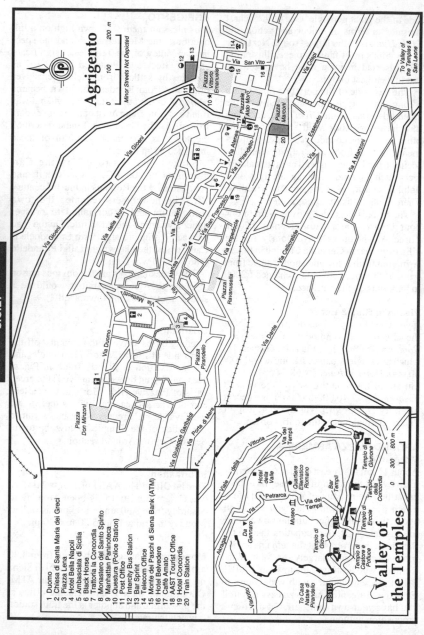

Agrigento

Minor Streets Not Depicted

0   100   200 m

1 Duomo
2 Chiesa di Santa Maria dei Greci
3 Piazza Lena
4 Hotel Bella Napoli
5 Ambasciata di Sicilia
6 Black Horse
7 Trattoria la Concordia
8 Monastero del Santo Spirito
9 Manhattan Paninoteca
10 Questura (Police Station)
11 Post Office
12 Intercity Bus Station
13 Bar Sprint
14 Telecom Office
15 Monte dei Paschi di Siena Bank (ATM)
16 Hotel Belvedere
17 Caffè Amato
18 AAST Tourist Office
19 Hotel Concordia
20 Train Station

Valley of the Temples

0   300   600 m

Post & Telecommunications The post office, Piazza Vittorio Emanuele, is open Monday to Friday from 8 am to 7 pm and Saturday to 11 am. The post code for central Agrigento is 92100.

There is a Telecom office at Via A de Gasperi 25, open Monday to Friday from 9 am to 12.30 pm and 4.30 to 7.45 pm. The telephone code is 0922.

Newspaper Stand You can get foreign newspapers and magazines near the bar in the Valley of the Temples.

Emergency For police attendance, call ☎ 113. In a medical emergency, go to the public hospital, the Ospedale San Giovanni di Dio (☎ 49 21 11), on Via Atenea, or call an ambulance (☎ 40 13 44). There is a late-night pharmacy at Via Atenea 325.

Valley of the Temples

The five main Doric temples along the 'valley' (actually a ridge) were constructed around the 5th century BC and are in various states of ruin, due to earthquakes and vandalism by early Christians.

The area is divided into two sections. East of the Via dei Templi are the most spectacular temples. The first you will come to is the **Tempio di Ercole** (Temple of Hercules), built towards the end of the 6th century BC and believed to be the oldest of the temples. Eight of its 38 columns have been raised and you can wander around the remains of the rest. The **Tempio della Concordia** (Temple of Concord) is the only one to survive relatively intact. Built around 440 BC, it was transformed into a Christian church in the 6th century AD. Its name is taken from a Roman inscription found nearby. The **Tempio di Giunone** (Temple of Juno) stands high on the edge of the ridge, a five-minute walk to the east. Part of its colonnade remains and there is an impressive sacrificial altar.

This section of the valley is not enclosed and can be visited at any time.

Across the Via dei Templi is what remains of the massive **Tempio di Giove** (Temple of Jupiter), actually never completed. Now totally in ruin, it covered an area measuring 112 metres by 56 metres, with columns 20 metres high. Between the columns stood *telamoni* (colossal statues), one of which was reconstructed and is now housed in the Museo Archeologico. A copy lies on the ground among the ruins, giving an idea of the immense size of the structure. Work began on the temple around 480 BC and it was probably destroyed during the Carthaginian invasion in 406 BC. The nearby **Tempio di Castore e Polluce** (Temple of Castor & Pollux) was partly reconstructed in the 19th century.

This area is open daily from 9 am to one hour before sunset. The temples are lit up at night.

The **Museo Archeologico**, on Via dei Templi just north of the temples, has a collection of artefacts from the area worth inspecting. It is open Monday to Saturday from 8 am to 12.30 pm as well as Tuesday and Friday from 3 to 5 pm. Admission is free.

Opposite the museum, the **Quartiere Ellenistico-Romano** (Hellenistic-Roman quarter) constituted part of urban Agrigento. Some of its structures date to the 4th century BC, while others were built as late as the 5th century AD.

West of the temples is the country house in Caos where Pirandello was born. Now a small museum, the **Casa Natale di Pirandello** is open daily from 9 am to 1 pm and 3 to 7 pm. Take bus No 1 from the station. The house is just short of Porto Empedocle, and overlooks the sea.

Medieval Agrigento

Wandering around the town's narrow, winding streets is relaxing after a day among the temples. The **Chiesa di Santa Maria dei Greci**, uphill from Piazza Lena, at the end of Via Atenea, is an 11th-century Norman church built on the site of a 5th-century BC Greek temple. Note the remains of the wooden Norman ceiling and some Byzantine frescoes.

A not so relaxing walk farther uphill is to the fragile-looking **duomo** in Via Duomo.

Built in the year 1000, the duomo has been restructured many times. The bell tower was erected in the 15th century and the panelled ceiling inside dates to the 17th century.

Back towards Piazza Vittorio Emanuele, the **Monastero del Santo Spirito** was founded by Cistercian nuns at the end of the 13th century. Giacomo Serpotta is responsible for the stuccoes in the chapel, and there is a small ethnographic museum above the old church which is open from 9 am to 1 pm. You can buy cakes and pastries from the nuns. See the Places to Eat section.

Festival

The town's big annual shindig is the Festival of the Almond Blossom, a folk festival held on the first Sunday in February in the Valley of the Temples.

Places to Stay

You can camp by the sea at San Leone, a few km south of Agrigento at *Camping Nettuno* (☎ 41 62 68), which is open all year. Take bus No 2 or 2/ from Agrigento, or drive down Via dei Templi, continue along Viale Emporium towards the sea and turn left at Lungomare Akragas.

The *Hotel Bella Napoli* (☎ 2 04 35), Piazza Lena 6, is uphill off Via Bac Bac. It has clean, basic singles/doubles for L35,000/55,000 or L40,000/60,000 with a bathroom. The *Hotel Belvedere* (☎ 2 00 51), Via San Vito 20, is in the newer part of town, uphill from Piazza Vittorio Emanuele. It has rooms for L30,000/50,000 and doubles with a bathroom for L70,000. The *Hotel Concordia* (☎ 59 62 66) is just off Via Atenea at Piazza San Francesco 11, where the daily produce market is held. It has rooms for L30,000/50,000 or L44,000/77,000 with a bathroom.

Most of Agrigento's better hotels are out of town around the Valley of the Temples or near the sea. *Hotel Akrabello* (☎ 60 62 77) is in the Parco Angeli area, east of the temples. It is modern and comfortable and has rooms for up to L120,000/160,000.

Hotel della Valle (☎ 2 69 66) is in Via dei Templi. It has lovely rooms with full services, a pool and gardens; rooms cost up to L110,000/170,000. *Hotel Kaos* (☎ 59 87 70) is by the sea, about two km from the temples. It is a large resort complex in a restored villa. Rooms cost up to L150,000/200,000.

Places to Eat

A good choice for a light lunch is the *Manhattan Paninoteca*, up Salita M Angeli from Via Atenea. *Caffè Amato*, Via Atenea 1, has a tempting selection of cakes and pastries. However, for the best pastries, and just for the experience, go to the Monastero del Santo Spirito at the end of Via Foderà. The nuns have been making heavenly cakes and pastries to a secret recipe for centuries, and their dolci di mandorle (almond cake) is particularly special (and expensive). Press the door bell and say *'Vorrei comprare qualche dolce'*, and see how you go.

The *Black Horse*, Via Celauro 8, serves good, reasonably priced meals. *Ambasciata di Sicilia*, Via Giambertoni 2, offers typical Sicilian fare, and an enjoyable meal will cost under L30,000. Another reasonable place specialising in fish is the *Trattoria la Concordia*, Via Porcello 6.

If you have a car, head for *Trattoria Kokalos*, Via C Magazzeni, east of the temples, where they dish up the area's best pizza.

One of Agrigento's better restaurants is *Le Caprice*, between the town and temples. A full meal will cost between L40,000 and L50,000. Take any bus heading for temples and get off at the Hotel Colleverde, from where it's a short walk (signposted). *Da Gennaro*, Via Petrarca, again downhill from the town, also maintains high standards. A full meal, including seafood, will cost around L70,000.

Getting There & Away

Bus For most destinations, bus is the easiest way to get to and from Agrigento. The Intercity station is in Piazza Roselli, just off Piazza Vittorio Emanuele, and timetables for most services are posted in Bar Sprint in the piazza. Autoservizi Cuffaro and Fratelli Camilleri both run buses to Palermo. SAL services Gela (where you can connect for

Ragusa), Syracuse and Porto Empedocle, while Salvatore Lumia services Marsala and Trapani.

Train Trains run to Palermo (two hours), Catania (3½ hours) and Enna. For Palermo, the train is fine, if a little slow. For anywhere else you should consider the bus.

Car & Motorbike Agrigento is easily accessible by road from all of Sicily's main towns. The SS189 links the town with Palermo, while the SS115 runs along the coast, west towards Sciacca and east for Gela and eventually Syracuse. For Enna, take the SS640 via Caltanissetta. There is plenty of parking at Piazza Vittorio Emanuele in the centre.

Getting Around
TUA city buses run down to the Valley of the Temples from in front of the train station. Take buses No 1, 1/, 2, 2/, 3 or 3/ and get off at either the museum or farther downhill at Piazzale dei Templi. The Green Line (Linea Verde) bus runs every hour from the train station to the duomo, for those who prefer not to make the uphill walk. Tickets cost L1000 and are valid for 1½ hours.

AROUND AGRIGENTO
Eraclea Minoa
A colony within a colony, Eraclea Minoa lies about halfway between Agrigento and Selinunte to the west, atop a wild bluff overlooking a splendid sandy beach. Founded by Selinunte in the 6th century BC, the ruins are comparatively spare and the 4th century theatre's seating has been covered in moulded plastic to protect the crumbling remains. Buses running between Sciacca and Agrigento will drop you at the turn-off, from where it's a four-km walk. In summer buses go from Cattolica Eraclea (which can be reached from Agrigento and Sciacca) to the site.

SCIACCA
Sciacca started life as a Roman settlement but only really took off with the arrival of the Arabs. The Normans fortified this prosper-

ous farming town, which later came to be ruled alternately by local feuding families. Today a bustling fishing port, the centre of town has a few monuments worthy of a quick look, including the **duomo**, erected by the Normans in the 12th century, the peculiar 15th-century **Steripinto** building, the neo-Gothic **Palazzo San Giacomo** and the ruins of a **castle** dominating the town. The time to come is February, when the townsfolk let their hair down for Carnevale, second on the island only to that of Acireale, near Taormina. The AAST tourist office (☎ 0925-2 27 44) is at Corso Vittorio Emanuele 84. The *Paloma Blanca* (☎ 2 51 39), Via Figuli 5 on the east side of town, has rooms for L40,000/70,000. Buses for Palermo leave from Viale della Vittoria (tickets at No 22). Others, run by the Lumia company, serve Trapani, Agrigento and destinations between from Via Agatocle.

SELINUNTE
The ancient Greek city of Selinus, founded in the 7th century BC, was long a prosperous and powerful city, but its standing rivalry with Segesta to the north was to be its undoing. In 409 BC, the latter called in a powerful ally, Carthage, whose troops utterly destroyed Selinunte. The city later recovered under the tutelage of Syracuse and then Carthage, but in 250 BC its citizens delivered the *coup de grâce* to prevent it passing to the Romans. What they left standing, mainly temples, was finished off by earthquake in the Middle Ages.

One of the more captivating ancient sites in Italy, Selinunte once fairly bristled with temples. They are known today simply by the letters A to G (and two as M and O), some huddled together in the acropolis.

Temple E, reconstructed in 1958 amid much criticism, stands out for its recently acquired completeness. Built in the 5th century BC, it is one of three next to one another at the eastern end of the site, close to the ticket office. **Temple G**, the northernmost, was built in the 6th century BC and, although never completed, was one of the largest in the Greek world. Today it is a massive pile of rubble, but evocative none-theless.

The **acropolis** is across the depression known as the Gorgo di Cottone. Here are five temples, of which **Temple C** is believed to have been the most magnificent. Some of the more outstanding metopes in Palermo's archaeological museum were taken from this temple.

Selinunte is close to the village of Marinella di Selinunte, where you can find accommodation. *Il Maggiolino* (☎ 0924-4 60 44) is one of a couple of camping grounds; charges are L6000 per person, L4000 per tent and L5000 per car. The *Pensione Costa d'Avorio* (☎ 0924-4 62 07), Via Stazione 10, has singles/doubles for L25,000/40,000 or L30,000/50,000 with a bathroom. It also has a trattoria. *Hotel Alceste* (☎ 0924-4 61 84), Via Alceste 23, has more up-market rooms for L50,000/78,000 with a bathroom.

Buses link Marinella to Castelvetrano, which can be reached by Lumia buses from Agrigento, Mazara del Vallo, Marsala and Trapani.

MAZARA DEL VALLO

A compact fishing town, Mazara del Vallo is a pleasant stopover while meandering round the coast. One of the first Greek towns to end up in Carthaginian hands in the late 5th century BC, it later fell to Romans, Byzantines and Arabs, experiencing particularly prosperous times under the latter and their Norman successors. Piazza della Repubblica forms the core of the old town, where you'll find the 11th-century **duomo**, largely remodelled in the 17th century, and flanking it the graceful 18th-century **seminario** (seminary). The tourist office (☎ 0923-94 17 27) is on the same square. You could stay at *Mediterraneo* (☎ 93 26 88), Via Valeria 36, where singles/doubles with a bathroom cost L55,000/70,000. Trains connect the town with Trapani and Palermo. Salemi buses to Palermo leave from Piazza Matteotti (tickets at La Punica travel agency, Corso Vittorio Veneto 54). Lumia buses (tickets at Bar Profiterol, Corso Vittorio Veneto 79) run to

Marsala, Trapani, Castelvetrano (for Selinunte) and Agrigento.

ISOLE PELAGIE (PELAGIC ISLANDS)

Some 240 km south of Agrigento, this tiny archipelago lies farther from mainland Sicily than Malta, and in many respects has more in common with nearby Tunisia or Libya than Italy. Indeed Libya's Colonel Gaddafi is so convinced of this that he launched a couple of wobbly missiles its way in 1987. Of the three islands, which rise on the African continental shelf, only Lampedusa is of any interest. Linosa has nothing to offer and Lampione is little more than an uninhabited pimple on the sometimes rather tempestuous surface of the Canale di Sicilia, the stretch of the Mediterranean separating Africa from Sicily.

Lampedusa, a rocky, sparsely covered and, in winter, wind-whipped place, is becoming increasingly popular with Italians looking for an early tan, and the water is enticingly limpid and warm. Of the several beaches on the south side of the 11-km-long island, the best known is the so-called Isola dei Conigli (Rabbit Island), where Caretta-Caretta turtles lay their eggs between June and August. Timid creatures, they are not stupid and generally only come in when no-one's about. There are several dive rental outlets; for more information go first to the Pro Loco tourist office (☎ 97 14 77) at Piazza Comm-Brignone 12. The telephone code is 0922. Hourly orange minibuses run from near the Pro Loco to the beach, or you could hire a Vespa from one of several outlets around town (look for the *autonoleggio* signs).

Cheap accommodation can be hard to find. The little pensioni are often full in summer and closed in winter. You could try the *Albergo Alba d'Amore* (☎ 97 02 72), west along the waterfront from the port near the expensive Hotel Medusa – a good half-hour walk that takes you past Via Roma (the main drag) and over the rise to the fishing port along Via Marconi. It has singles/doubles for L25,000/40,000, but like most places makes at least half board compulsory in summer.

A Siremar ferry leaves Porto Empedocle (seven km south-west of Agrigento) daily, except Friday, at midnight. It takes six hours to reach Linosa and another two to reach Lampedusa. The one-way fare to the latter is L47,800. A car up to 3.5 metres long costs L78,100. You can buy tickets at the Siremar booth (☎ 63 66 83) in the port. Orange buses from Agrigento arrive at Piazza Italia, from where it's a quick walk down Via Quattro Novembre to the port entrance (the last one from Porto Empedocle leaves for Agrigento about 9 pm). Boats from Lampedusa (and Linosa) leave daily, except Saturday (10 am from Lampedusa). Trips can be cancelled due to bad weather, especially in winter. There are also flights between Lampedusa and Palermo.

North-West Sicily

MARSALA

Best known for its sweet dessert wines, Marsala is not a bad place to break the journey between Agrigento and Trapani. Founded as Lilybaeon on Cape Lilibeo by Carthaginians who had fled nearby Mozia (or Motya) after its destruction by Syracuse, the city was eventually conquered by the Arabs, who renamed it Marsa Allah (Port of God). It was at Marsala that Garibaldi landed with his One Thousand in 1860.

Information

Marsala's APT tourist office (☎ 71 40 97) is at Via Garibaldi 45, in the centre of town, along Via Mazzini from the train station. It is open Monday to Saturday from 8 am to 2 pm and 3 to 7 pm. The town's telephone code is 0923. You can call the police on ☎ 113. For a medical emergency, call ☎ 95 14 10.

Things to See

Visit the **duomo** in Piazza della Repubblica, built in the 17th and 18th centuries, and its **Museo degli Arazzi**, at Via Garraffa 57. In the museum are eight 16th-century tapestries, woven for the Spanish king Philip II and depicting scenes from the war of Titus against the Jews. The **Museo Nazionale Lilibeo**, in Via Boeo by the sea (follow Via XI Maggio to Piazza Vittoria and turn left along Via N Sauro) houses a partly reconstructed Carthaginian warship, which may have seen action in the First Punic War. It was found off the coast north of Marsala in 1971. North of the museum, along Viale Vittorio Veneto, is a partly excavated archaeological zone – the **Insula Romana**, which was a 3rd-century AD Roman house.

You can also look over the site of ancient **Mozia**, situated on the island of San Pantaleo in the lagoon known as the Stagnone. Apart from excavations of the Carthaginian city (admission L1000), including the ancient

---

How Sweet it Is

The Marsala wine was 'discovered' by Englishman John Woodhouse, who after landing in the city in 1773 and tasting the local product, decided it should be marketed throughout Europe. His first competitor was Benjamin Ingham, who established his own factory in the town and began exporting the wine to the USA and Australia.

One particularly interesting figure in the Marsala-producing business was Ingham's nephew, Joseph Whitaker, who bought the island of San Pantaleo, where the ancient site Mozia was based, and built a villa there (it is still in his family today). Whitaker was responsible for renewing interest in the archaeological site of Mozia and for the few excavations carried out. His former villa is now the museum of Mozia, which houses finds from the ancient city, including the statue *Il Giovinetto di Mozia*. ∎

port and dry dock, there is a museum (admission L4000) on the island. It is about 11 km north along the coast from Marsala, a scenic drive or bus trip, and the island is accessible by boat (L3000 return; mornings only in winter). Bus No 11 from Piazza del Popolo runs in summer only; bus No 4 drops you close to the boat and runs all year.

Tipplers should head to the Florio establishment on Lungomare V Florio (bus No 16 from Piazza del Popolo). At 4 pm they open their doors to visitors to explain the process of making Marsala and give you a taste of the goods. This is the place to buy the cream of Marsala products. There are several other producers in the same area. All have an *enoteca* (wine bar), where you can select a bottle or two (usually open from about 9 am to 12.30 pm).

Places to Stay & Eat
If you want to stay in Marsala, try the *Garden* (☎ 98 23 20), near the train station at Via Gambini 36, which has singles/doubles for L50,000/75,000. The *Villa Favorita* (☎ 98 91 00) at Via Favorita 27 is two km north-east of Marsala. A tourist complex, it has rooms for L60,000/90,000. The *Trattoria Garibaldi*, Via Rubino 35, just off Piazza Addolorata, specialises in fish and a full meal will come to about L35,000. Try their homemade pasta with ragù al tonno (tuna sauce).

Getting There & Away
Buses head for Marsala from Trapani (AST or Lumia; eight a day), Agrigento (Lumia; four buses a day) and Palermo (Salemi). Palermo buses arrive at Piazza Pizzo, the others at Piazza del Popolo, off Via Mazzini, in the centre of town. The Agrigento buses generally stop at Castelvetrano, from where you can get another to Selinunte.

Trains serve Marsala from Trapani and Palermo, although from the latter you have to change at Alcamo Diramazione.

From June to September, Sandokan (☎ 71 20 60) runs a boat service to the Egadi Islands.

TRAPANI
Although not one of Sicily's top attractions, Trapani is a comfortable base from which to explore the north-west. From the ancient Greek site city of Segesta and the medieval town of Erice, to the beaches of the Golfo di Castellammare, the Riserva Naturale dello Zingaro and the Egadi Islands, this small corner is a smorgasbord of Sicily's main delights.

A Carthaginian and later a Roman city, Trapani thrived as a trading centre under Arab and Norman rule and, after the arrival of the Spanish, enjoyed a period as western Sicily's most important town. Since then, slow decline has reduced it to a coastal backwater, kept afloat by moderate sea traffic and some fishing. A handful of Baroque churches and piazzas warrant some exploration and the town's Easter celebrations (see Things to See below) mark a high point in the year.

Orientation
The main bus station is in Piazza Montalto, with the train station around the corner in Piazza Umberto I. The cheaper hotels are in the heart of the old centre, about 500 metres west. Make for Piazza Scarlatti down Corso Italia.

Information
Tourist Office The APT office (☎ 2 90 00) is in Piazzetta Saturno, off Piazza Scarlatti. It is open Monday to Saturday from 8 am to 8 pm and Sunday mornings. It is usually shut for a couple of hours from 2 pm and closes earlier in winter.

Post & Telecommunications The main post office is in Piazza Vittorio Veneto and is open Monday to Saturday from 8.20 am to 7 pm. The post code for central Trapani is 91100 and the telephone code is 0923.

Money There are several banks about the town centre. The Banca di Roma, Corso Italia, and Monte dei Paschi di Siena, Via

XXX Gennaio 80, have ATMs that take Visa and MasterCard, among others.

Emergency For police attention, call ☎ 113. The questura (☎ 5 98 11) is in Via Virgilio, off Piazza V Veneto. The public hospital, the Ospedale Sant' Antonio Abate (☎ 80 94 50), is in Via Cosenza, some distance from the centre of town. Dial the same number for an ambulance.

Things to See
The 16th-century **Palazzo Giudecca** in Via Giudecca, with its distinctive façade, stands out among the general decay of the old and run-down Jewish quarter. Cross Corso Italia

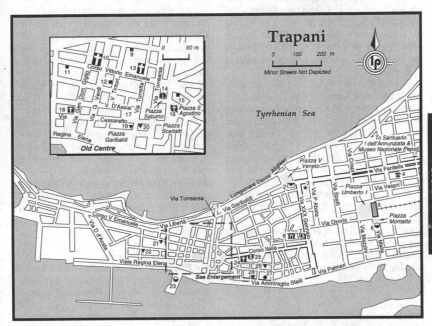

PLACES TO STAY		26	Pub	10	Cathedral
		28	Trattoria del Porto	13	Chiesa del Collegio
9	Albergo Moderno				dei Gesuiti
11	Pensione Messina	**OTHER**		14	APT Tourist Office
12	Nuovo Russo			16	Chiesa di
15	Pensione Maccotta	1	Piazza Mercato di Pesce		Sant'Agostino
		2	Post Office	17	Piazza Lucatelli
PLACES TO EAT		3	Questura (Police Station)	18	Chiesa del Purgatorio
		4	Telecom Office	23	Ferry Terminal
19	Panineria Poldo	5	Train Station	24	Chiesa di Santa
20	Chupa Chupa	6	Intercity Bus Station		Maria di Gesù
21	Pizzeria Calvino	7	Monte dei Paschi di Siena	25	Banca di Roma
22	Ristorante da Bettina	8	Palazzo Giudecca	27	Siremar

to reach the **Chiesa di Santa Maria di Gesù** in Via San Pietro, whose exterior has both Gothic and Renaissance features. The 14th-century **Chiesa di Sant'Agostino**, in Piazza Saturno, is worth a look for its fine Gothic rose window and portal. Continue along Corso Vittorio Emanuele, noting the 17th-century town hall and Chiesa del Collegio dei Gesuiti, before reaching the **cathedral**, which has a Baroque façade. Off the Corso, on Via Generale D Giglio, the **Chiesa del Purgatorio** houses the Misteri, a collection of 18th-century life-size wooden figures depicting Christ's Passion. On Good Friday, the Misteri are carried in procession around Trapani.

Trapani's major sight is the 14th-century **Santuario dell'Annunziata**, some distance from the centre in Via A Pepoli. Remodelled in Baroque style in the 17th century, the sanctuary retains its original Gothic rose window and doorway. The Cappella della Madonna, behind the high altar, contains the venerated *Madonna di Trapani*, carved, it is thought, by Nino Pisano.

The adjacent **Museo Nazionale Pepoli**, housed in a former Carmelite monastery, has an archaeological collection, statues and coral carvings. It is open Tuesday to Saturday from 9 am to 1.30 pm and also on Tuesday and Thursday from 3 to 6 pm. On Sunday it is open from 9 am to 12.30 pm. Admission is L2000.

Places to Stay

The *Pensione Messina* (☎ 2 11 98), Corso V Emanuele 71, is on the 3rd floor of a 17th-century apartment building and its rooms are very basic; the cost per person is L20,000. *Pensione Maccotta* (☎ 2 84 18), Via degli Argentieri 4, off Piazza Sant'Agostino, has higher standard singles/doubles for L30,000/55,000 or L40,000/70,000 with a bathroom.

Albergo Moderno (☎ 2 12 47), Via Genovese, which runs parallel to Corso V Emanuele, has simple rooms for L25,000/50,000 or L40,000/55,000 with a bathroom. The *Nuovo Russo* (☎ 2 21 66), Via Tintori 4, off Corso V Emanuele, has rooms, some of them classics of the 1950s, from L35,000/65,000 or L58,000/90,000 with a bathroom.

Places to Eat

Sicily's Arab heritage and Trapani's unique position on the sea route to Tunisia has made couscous (or cuscus as they spell it here), something of a speciality, particularly with a fish sauce that includes tomatoes, garlic and parsley.

The area around Piazza Lucatelli is a pleasant place for a sandwich and coffee. *Panineria Poldo* serves good sandwiches. For a decent ice cream, try *Chupa Chupa*, also in the piazza. In Piazza Scarlatti is *Kenny*, where you can eat sandwiches or crêpes. An open air market is held every morning from Monday to Saturday in Piazza Mercato di Pesce, on the north waterfront.

Pizzeria Calvino, Via N Nasi 77, towards the port off Corso V Emanuele, is the town's favourite takeaway pizza and pasta place. You can eat a set lunch at the self-service *Pub*, Via della Luce 8, for L12,000. *Trattoria del Porto*, Via Ammiraglio Staiti 45, on the south waterfront, is more upmarket, with good meals for around L35,000. Similarly priced is the *Ristorante Da Bettina*, Via San Francesco d'Assisi 69.

Getting There & Away

Air Trapani has a small airport, 16 km out of town at Birgi. Airport buses leave from outside Salvo Viaggi, Corso Italia 48, to coincide with flights. Segesta has a daily bus at 2.30 pm for the island's main airport at Punta Raisi.

Bus Express buses connect Trapani with Palermo (Segesta) and Agrigento (Lumia). They terminate in Piazza Garibaldi on the south waterfront. All other Intercity buses use Piazza Montalto, from where AST buses serve Erice (approximately every hour), Castellammare del Golfo (four a day), Castelvetrano (seven a day), Marsala and Mazara del Vallo (four a day) and San Vito Lo Capo (six a day). Autoservizi Tarantola runs a bus service from Trapani to Segesta and Calatafimi.

Train Trains connect Trapani to Palermo, Castelvetrano and Marsala. For Segesta, you can get off at Segesta (one train a day) or Calatafimi (plenty) on the way to Palermo. The stations are about equidistant from the ancient Greek site.

Car & Motorbike Having your own wheels would make it easier to explore the area around Trapani, which is linked to Palermo by the A29 autostrada.

Boat Siremar runs ferries and hydrofoils to the Egadi Islands. The high season one-way fare to the main island, Favignana, is L9100 on the hydrofoil (journey 20 minutes). Siremar's ticket office (☎ 2 77 80) is at Via Ammiraglio Staiti 61. The same company runs a daily ferry to Pantelleria at midnight. There is no service on weekends except in summer. The high season fare for the six-hour trip is L35,400. The boat returns (usually) at 11 am.

Alilauro (☎ 2 40 73) also runs hydrofoils to the Egadi Islands – tickets can be purchased on the docks.

Tirrenia runs weekly ferries to Tunisia from Trapani, leaving Mondays at 9 am. Tickets for the 7½-hour trip cost L91,200 in the high season and can be purchased at Salvo Viaggi (☎ 2 18 96), Corso Italia 48. Alilauro puts on a weekly Tunisia service in summer, to Kelibia. They also have a summer ferry for Naples via Ustica.

ERICE

This dramatic medieval town, 750 metres above the sea, is about 40 minutes from Trapani by bus and should not be missed on any account. Settled by the Elymians, an ancient mountain people who also founded Segesta, it was an important religious site associated with the goddess of fertility – first the Carthaginian Astarte, then the Greek Aphrodite and finally the Roman Venus.

Erice's tourist office (☎ 86 93 88) is at Viale Conte Pepoli 56. The telephone code is 0923.

The triangular-shaped town is best explored by pottering around its network of narrow streets and peeking through the doorways of palaces into the courtyards. At the top of the hill stands the Norman **Castello di Venere** (Castle of Venus). It was built in the 12th to 13th centuries over an ancient temple of Venus. Surrounded by the cool, green Giardino del Balio, the castle is upstaged by the panoramic vistas north-east to San Vito Lo Capo and Monte Cofano and west to Trapani.

Of the several churches and other monuments in the small, quiet town, the 14th-century **Chiesa Matrice**, in Via V Carvini just inside Porta Trapani, is probably the most interesting by virtue of its separate bell tower with mullioned windows. The interior of the church was remodelled in neo-Gothic style in the 19th century, but the 15th-century side chapels were conserved.

If you want to stay overnight, there is a HI youth hostel, *G Amodeo* (☎ 55 29 64), just out of town and open all year. B&B is L17,000 and a meal costs L12,000. Otherwise the options are acid to the pocket. The *Edelweiss* (☎ 86 91 58), Cortile P Vincenzo 5, has singles/doubles for L80,000/120,000. For a meal, the atmospheric *Ristorante La Pentolaccia*, Via G Guarnotti 17, is set inside a former 16th-century monastery.

Regular AST buses connect Erice with Trapani (Piazza Montalto).

SEGESTA

The ancient Elymians must have been great aesthetes if their choice of sites for cities is any indication. Along with Erice and Entella, they founded Segesta on and around Monte Barbaro. The Greeks later took over, and it is to them that we owe the two outstanding survivors: the theatre high up on the mountain with commanding views out to sea (how did spectators concentrate on the show with such a backdrop?) and the temple.

The city was in constant conflict with Selinunte in the south and this rivalry led it to seek assistance from a succession of allies, including Carthage, Athens, Syracuse and the Romans, and eventually it destroyed Selinunte. Time has done to Segesta what violence inflicted on Selinunte, and little remains save the theatre and the never completed Doric **temple**, the latter dating from around 430 BC and remarkably well preserved. The Hellenistic **theatre** is also in a fair state of repair and the only structure inside the old city walls to have survived intact. Nearby are ruins of a castle and church built in the Middle Ages. The site is open daily from 9 am to an hour before sunset. A shuttle bus runs every half-hour from the entrance 1.5 km uphill to the theatre.

In July and August of every odd-numbered year (alternating with Syracuse), performances of Greek plays are staged in the theatre. For information, contact the tourist office in Trapani.

Segesta is accessible by Autoservizi Tarantola bus from Piazza Montalto in Trapani, or from Palermo (Piazza Marina) by Trepanum buses (☎ 0923-51 12 32). Otherwise you can catch one of the infrequent trains from Trapani or Palermo to Segesta Tempio; the site is then a 20-minute walk away.

GOLFO DI CASTELLAMMARE

Saved from development and road projects by local protests, the tranquil and wildly beautiful **Riserva Naturale dello Zingaro** is the star attraction on the gulf. Strung out between the touristy San Vito Lo Capo to the north and the little fishing village of Scopello to the south, a stroll up the coast between the two will take about four hours along a clearly marked track; there are a few slightly tougher but even more rewarding trails away from the coast.

Camping grounds dot the coast, including *Camping Soleado* (☎ 0923-97 21 66) and *Camping La Fata* (☎ 0923-97 21 33) at San Vito Lo Capo; and *Camping Baia di Guidaloca* (☎ 0924-59 60 22) and *Camping Ciauli* (☎ 0924-3 90 49) on the coast road south of Scopello. There are numerous pensioni and hotels at San Vito and Castellammare del Golfo, a busy coastal town with an interesting medieval core 10 km south of Scopello. The tourist office at Trapani has a full list. In Scopello itself, try

the *Pensione Tranchina* (☎ 0924-59 60 63), Via Diaz 7, which has rooms for L30,000/50,000.

AST buses run to San Vito Lo Capo and Castellammare del Golfo from Trapani's Piazza Montalto. From Castellammare it is possible to catch a bus to Scopello. There is no road through the Zingaro park.

ISOLE EGADI (EGADI ISLANDS)

For centuries the Egadi islanders have lived from tuna fishing, but nowadays tourism looks set to become the main earner – even the *mattanza*, the almost ritual slaughtering of the tuna, is becoming something of a spectator sport. Made up of three islands, the archipelago is only a short hop from Trapani. Windswept Monte Santa Caterina dominates the otherwise flat main island of **Favignana**. It is pleasant to explore, with plenty of rocky coves and crystal clear water. Otherwise, there's little to it. In May the mattanza occurs in the island's last functioning *tonnara* (tuna fishing net). Schools of tuna have for centuries used the waters of western Sicily as a mating ground, and for as long this has been a bit of a mistake, as Egadi fisherman have rounded them up and slaughtered them.

Levanzo, four km north of Favignana, is known for the Grotta del Genovese, whose walls bear the 15,000-year-old graffiti of the island's prehistoric inhabitants.

Marettimo, the most distant of the islands, is also the least touched by modernity. A few hundred people live mostly in the tiny village on the east coast, and there are no roads – this is really getting away from it all. You can go with fishermen for jaunts along the coast or set off along mule tracks into the hilly interior.

There is a Pro Loco tourist office (☎ 92 16 47) at Piazza Matrice 8 in Favignana town. The telephone code for the islands is 0923. You'll find dive hire outlets and bicycles for rent around town and the small harbour.

The cheapest place to stay on Favignana is the *Bouganville* (☎ 92 20 33), Via Cimbadue 10, with singles/doubles at L33,000/55,000. Levanzo has two pensioni. The *Paradiso*

(☎ 92 40 80), on the seafront, charges L45,000/65,000 for rooms with a bathroom. There are no hotels on Marettimo, but you should be able to dig up a room with the locals. In summer, you'll probably be asked to pay full board wherever you stay.

Ferries and hydrofoils run between the islands and to Trapani. See the Trapani section for more details.

PANTELLERIA

Known to the Carthaginians as Cossyra, the island of Pantelleria fell to Rome in 217 BC and five centuries later was in Arab hands. Their presence lives on in the names they gave various localities around the island, a curious place that lies closer to Tunisia than

it does to Sicily. The draw card of sea and sunshine is balanced by the mountainous, volcanic interior, where you can find thermal springs and remnants of several ancient settlements, such as Mursia, a few km south of the main town.

There is nothing cheap about Pantelleria, especially in summer, when it is best to book ahead. The *Albergo Agadir* (☎ 91 11 00), Via Catania 1, offers simple rooms for L35,000/ 60,000. It is also possible to rent *dammusi*, the characteristic domed houses of the island. Siremar boats connect the island with Trapani (see Trapani section for more transport details). Alilauro's summer season Trapani-Tunisia boat generally calls in at Pantelleria on the way.

Sardinia (Sardegna)

The second-largest island in the Mediterranean, Sardinia (Sardegna) was colonised and invaded by the Greeks, Phoenicians and Romans, followed by the Pisans, Genoese and finally the Spanish. But it is often said that the Sardinians, known as Sardi, were never really conquered, they simply retreated into the hills.

The Romans were prompted to call the island's central-eastern mountains Barbagia (from the Latin word for barbarian) because of their views on the lifestyle of the locals. The area is still known by this name. Even today the Sardinians of the interior are a strangely insular people. Some women still wear traditional costume and shepherds still live in almost complete isolation, building enclosures of stone or wood as their ancestors did for their sheep and goats. If you venture into the interior, you will find the people incredibly gracious and hospitable, but easily offended if they sense any lack of respect.

The first inhabitants of the island were the Nuraghic people, thought to have arrived here around 2000 BC. Little is known about them, but the island is dotted with thousands of *nuraghi*, their conical-shaped stone houses and fortresses.

In 1948 Sardinia became a semiautonomous region, and the Italian government's Sardinian Rebirth Plan of 1962 had some influence on the development of tourism, industry and agriculture.

The island's cuisine is as varied as its history. Along the coast most dishes feature seafood and there are many variations of *zuppa di pesce* (fish soup). Inland you will find *porcheddu* (roast sucking pig), kid goat with olives, and even lamb's trotters in garlic sauce. The Sardi eat *pecorino* (sheep's-milk cheese) and you will rarely find Parmesan here. The preferred bread throughout the island is the paper-thin *carta musica*, also called *pane carasau*, often sprinkled with oil and salt.

The landscape of the island ranges from the 'savage, dark-bushed, sky-exposed land' described by D H Lawrence, to the incredibly beautiful gorges and valleys near Dorgali, the rugged isolation of the Gennargentu mountain range, and the hundreds of kilometres of unspoiled coastline. Although hunters have traditionally been active in Sardinia, some wildlife remains, notably albino donkeys on the island of Asinara off the north-west coast, colonies of griffon vultures on the west coast, and miniature horses in the Giara di Gesturi plain, in the south-west. The famous colony of Mediterranean monk seals at the Grotta del Bue Marino, near Cala Gonone, has not been sighted for some years.

Try to avoid the island in August, when the weather is very hot and the beaches are overcrowded. Warm weather generally continues from May to September.

GETTING THERE & AWAY
Air
Airports at Cagliari, Olbia and Alghero link Sardinia with major Italian and European cities. For information, contact the CIT or CTS offices in all major towns, or Alitalia.

Boat
The island is accessible by ferry from Genoa, Civitavecchia, Naples, Palermo, Trapani, Bonifacio (Corsica) and Tunisia, as well as Toulon and Marseille in France. The departure points in Sardinia are Olbia, Golfo Aranci and Porto Torres in the north, Arbatax on the east coast and Cagliari in the south.

The main ferry company is Tirrenia, although Ferrovie dello Stato (FS), runs a slightly cheaper ferry service between Olbia and Civitavecchia. Other companies include Moby Lines, also known as Sardegna Lines, which runs ferries between the Sardinia and Corsica, as well as from Livorno to Olbia. Brochures detailing Moby Lines and Tirrenia services are available at most travel

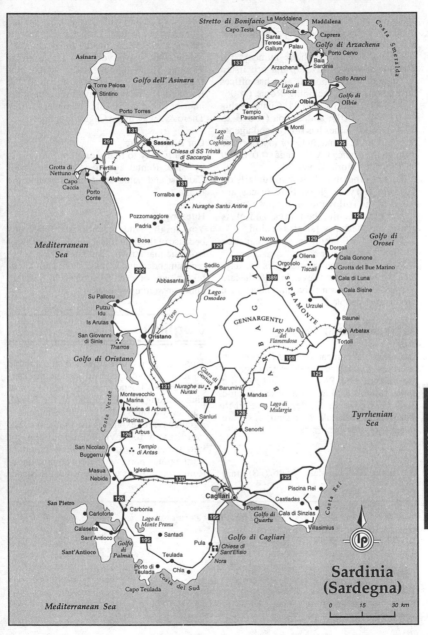

SARDINIA

Sardinia (Sardegna)

0   15   30 km

agencies. Note that timetables change dramatically every year and that prices fluctuate according to the season.

Addresses and telephone numbers for Tirrenia's offices in Sardinia are listed throughout this section. It also has offices throughout Italy, including Rome (☎ 06-474 20 41), Via Bissolati 41; Civitavecchia (☎ 0766-2 88 01); and Genoa (☎ 010-25 80 41). Moby Lines has offices and agents throughout the island. In Livorno it operates through the agency L V Ghianda (☎ 0586-89 03 25), Via Vittorio Veneto 24.

Refer to the chart below for details on Tirrenia ferry services. Fare prices are listed in the following order: poltrona in a 2nd-class cabin; bed in a 2nd-class cabin; and bed in a 1st-class cabin.

The cost of taking a small car was L139,000 on all routes.

Moby Lines offer special fares for daytime passages in low season. In 1995 the fare was L220,000 return (Livorno-Olbia) for a car and two people.

GETTING AROUND
Bus
The main bus companies are ARST, which operates extensive services throughout the island, and PANI, which links the main towns. Other companies include FDS (Ferrovie di Sardegna) and FMS (Ferrovie Meridionale Sardegna). Buses are generally faster than trains.

Train
The main Ferrovie dello Stato (FS) train lines link Cagliari with Oristano, Sassari and Olbia and are generally reliable. The private railways which link smaller towns throughout the island can be very slow. However, the Trenino Verde (Green Train) which runs from Cagliari to Arbatax through the Barbagia is a relaxing way to see part of the interior (for more details, see under Getting There & Away in the Cagliari section).

Car & Motorbike
The only way to really explore Sardinia is by road. Rental agencies are listed under Cagliari and some other towns around the island.

Hitching
You might find hitchhiking laborious because of the light traffic once you get away from the main towns. But hitchhiking is not recommended and women should not hitchhike alone, or even in groups, in Sardinia under any circumstances.

Cagliari

This is a surprisingly attractive city, notable for its interesting medieval section, its beautiful beach – Poetto – and its population of pink flamingos. The capital of the island, Cagliari warrants a day of sightseeing and is a good base for exploring the southern coast.

Believed to have been founded by Phoenicians, Cagliari became an important Carthaginian port town before coming under Roman control. As with the rest of the island,

Tirrenia Ferry Services		
Destination	*Fares*	*Duration*
Genoa-Porto Torres or Olbia	L76,700/97,600/124,700	12½ hours
Genoa-Cagliari	L102,900/129,900/170,900	19 hours
Civitavecchia-Olbia	L40,700/56,000/77,800	7 hours
Civitavecchia-Cagliari	L71,500/89,500/119,500	13½ hours
Naples-Cagliari	L52,000/72,000/93,000	15 hours
Palermo-Cagliari	L47,000/66,000/85,000	12½ hours

the city passed through the hands of various conquerors, including the Pisans, Spanish and finally the Piedmontese House of Savoy, before joining the unified Italy. The city was savagely bombed during WW II, suffering significant destruction and loss of life.

Orientation

If you arrive by bus, train or boat you will find yourself at the port area of Cagliari. The main street along the harbour is Via Roma and the old city stretches up the hill behind it to the old fortified area. At the north-western end of Via Roma, to the left as you leave the port, is Piazza Matteotti and the AAST office, the ARST intercity bus station and the train station. Most of the budget hotels and restaurants are close to the port area.

Information

Tourist Offices The AAST information booth (☎ 070-66 92 55) in Piazza Matteotti is open from 8 am to 8 pm daily during summer, and from 8 am to 2 pm in other months. It has a reasonable amount of information about the town and will advise on accommodation. There is also a provincial tourist information booth at the airport (the booth at the ferry terminal in the port has been closed indefinitely) open from 8.30 am to 1 pm and 3.30 to 9 pm daily in the high season. There is an office of the Ente Sardo Industrie Turistiche (ESIT), which covers all of Sardinia, at Via Goffredo Mameli 97. The office can be useful if you are starting your tour of the island at Cagliari.

Money There are several major banks on Largo Carlo Felice, which runs uphill from Piazza Matteotti, open from 8.30 am to 1.30 pm and 2.30 to 3.30 pm Monday to Friday. Otherwise, there is an exchange office at the train station, open daily from 7 am to 8 pm, and at the airport, open 8 am to 1 pm Monday to Saturday.

Post & Telecommunications The main post office is in Piazza del Carmine, up Via la Maddalena from Via Roma, and open from 8 am to 4.30 pm Monday to Saturday. The 24-hour Telecom office is at Via G M Angioj, off Piazza Matteotti. The post code for central Cagliari is 09100 and the telephone code is 070.

Travel Agency There is a CTS office (☎ 48 82 60) at Via Cesare Balbo 4.

Emergency For immediate police attendance, call ☎ 113, or go to the police headquarters (☎ 4 44 44), Via Amat 9. For an ambulance, call ☎ 27 23 45. For medical attention, the closest public hospital to the centre is the Ospedale Civile (☎ 601 82 67), Via Ospedale between the church of San Michele and the Anfiteatro Romano.

Things to See & Do

The **Museo Archeologico Nazionale**, Piazza Arsenale, in the new Cittadella dei Musei, has a fascinating collection of Nuraghic bronzes. It is open Monday to Saturday from 9 am to 2 pm, Sunday from 9 am to 1 pm. It opens from 3.30 to 6.30 pm on Wednesday, Friday and Saturday. Entry is L4000.

It is enjoyable to wander through the old quarter around the medieval quarter. The Pisan-Romanesque **duomo** was originally built in the 13th century, but was later remodelled. It has an interesting Romanesque pulpit.

From the **Bastione di San Remy**, which is in the centre of town in Piazza Costituzione and once formed part of the fortifications of the old city, there is a good view of Cagliari and the sea.

The Pisan **Torre di San Pancrazio**, in Piazza Indipendenza, is also worth a look. The **Anfiteatro Romano**, on Viale Buon Cammino, is considered the most important Roman monument in Sardinia. Spend the day on the **Spiaggia di Poetto** (east of the centre) and wander across to the salt lakes to see the flamingos.

Festival

The Festival of Sant'Efisio is held annually from 1 May, a colourful festival mixing the

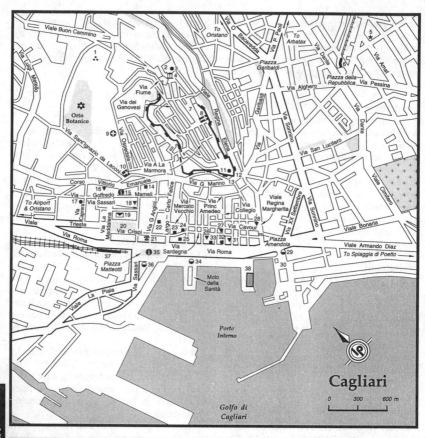

Cagliari

0   300   600 m

Golfo di Cagliari

PLACES TO STAY

14 Locanda Firenze
22 Hotel Quattro Mori
23 Albergo Centrale
24 Albergo La Perla
25 Hotel Italia
32 Locanda Miramare
33 Pensione Vittoria

PLACES TO EAT

16 Ristorante Il Corso
18 Trattoria Loddo Umberto
26 Trattoria Ci Pensa
    Cannas
27 Trattoria Gennargentu

28 Corsaro
31 Trattoria da Serafino

OTHER

1 Anfiteatro Romano
2 Piazza Indipendenza
3 Torre di San Pancrazio
4 Museo Archeologico
   Nazionale
5 Questura (Police Station)
6 Ferrovie Complementari
   della Sardegna
   Train Station
7 Piazza Palazzo
8 Duomo
9 Hospital

10 Chiesa di San Michele
11 Bastione di San Remy
12 Piazza Costituzione
13 Piazza dei Martiri
15 ESIT Tourist Office
17 Alitalia Office
19 Post Office
20 Piazza del Carmine
21 Telecom Office
29 PANI Bus Station
30 Piazza Deffenu
34 Ferry Terminal
35 AAST Tourist Office &
    Piazza Matteotti
36 ARST Bus Station
37 Train Station
38 Stazione Marittima

SARDINIA

Top: Sassi, Matera, Basilicata
ottom: Trekking in the Barbagia, Sardinia

JOHN GILLMAN

JOHN GILLMAN

COMITATO ASSISTENZA ITALIANI (COASIT)

FOTOCOLOR ESIT-CAGLIARI

Top Left:	Cliff-top housing, Calabria
Top Right:	Farmer in Gerace, Calabria
Bottom Left:	Woman hanging out peppers to dry, Basilicata
Bottom Right:	Sardinian woman weaving

secular and the religious, when an effigy of the saint is carried in procession to the small church of Sant'Efisio in the nearby town of Nora (see the Around Cagliari section).

Places to Stay

There are numerous budget hotels in the old city near the station. Try *Locanda Firenze* (☎ 65 36 78), Corso Vittorio Emanuele 50, which has a pleasant management, and singles/doubles for L35,000/42,000. *Locanda Miramare* (☎ 66 40 21), Via Roma 59, has singles/doubles for L45,000/58,000. Nearby is *Albergo Centrale* (☎ 65 47 83), Via Sardegna 4, which has rooms for L35,000/60,000, and the pleasant *Albergo la Perla* (☎ 66 94 46), Via Sardegna 16B, with rooms for L40,000/62,000.

Pensione Vittoria (☎ 65 79 70), Via Roma 75, is a very pleasant establishment, with rooms for L45,000/75,000, or L55,000/90,000 with bathroom. *Hotel Quattro Mori* (☎ 66 85 35), Via G Angioj 27, has good rooms for L65,000/90,000, or L70,000/120,000 with bathroom. The *Hotel Italia* (☎ 66 04 10), Via Sardegna 31, has more up-market, comfortable rooms for L90,000/125,000.

Places to Eat

There are several reasonably priced trattorias in the area behind Via Roma, particularly around Via Cavour and Via Sardegna. If you want to buy picnic supplies, head for Via Sardegna, where there are several good grocery shops as well as a bakery.

Trattoria da Serafino, Via Lepanto 6, on the corner of Via Sardegna, has excellent food at reasonable prices. *Trattoria Gennargentu*, Via Sardegna 60, has good pasta and seafood, and a full meal will cost around L20,000. *Trattoria Ci Pensa Cannas*, down the street at No 37, is another good choice; a full meal will cost about the same price.

A full meal at *Trattoria Loddo Umberto*, Via Sassari 86, will cost around L25,000. *Ristorante Il Corso*, Corso Vittorio Emanuele 78, specialises in seafood and a full meal will cost around L40,000.

Corsaro, Viale Regina Margherita 28, is one of the city's top seafood restaurants. During summer it transfers to the Marina Piccola at Poetto beach. A full meal will cost at least L80,000.

Getting There & Away

Air Cagliari's airport (☎ 24 00 47) is eight km north-west of the city at Elmas. ARST buses leave regularly from Piazza Matteotti to coincide with flights. The Alitalia office is at Via Caprera 14 (☎ 60 10).

Bus ARST buses leave from the bus station (☎ 409 83 24) in Piazza Matteotti for nearby towns, including Pula, the Costa del Sud and Teulada south-west of Cagliari, as well as Villasimius and the Costa Rei to the east. Granturismo PANI buses leave from farther along Via Roma at Piazza Darsena for towns such as Sassari, Nuoro, Oristano and Porto Torres. The PANI ticket office (☎ 65 23 26) is at Piazza Darsena 4.

Train Regular trains leave for Oristano, Sassari, Porto Torres and Olbia. The private Ferrovie Complementari della Sardegna station is in Piazza della Repubblica. For information about the Trenino Verde (Green Train), which runs along a scenic route between Cagliari and Arbatax, contact ESIT, the Cagliari tourist office (see under Tourist Offices), or the Ferrovie Complementari directly (☎ 58 00 76). The most interesting and scenic section of the route is between Mandas and Arbatax.

Boat Ferries arrive at the port just off Via Roma. Bookings for Tirrenia can be made at Via Campidano 1, c/o Agenave (☎ 66 60 65). There is also an office at the Stazione Marittima, which opens only before ship departures.

Ferries connect Cagliari with Palermo, Trapani, Naples, Civitavecchia and Genoa, as well as Tunisia (via Trapani). See the Getting There & Away section at the beginning of this chapter for further information.

SARDINIA

Car & Motorbike If you want to rent a car or motorbike, try Hertz (☎ 66 81 05), Piazza Matteotti 1, or Ruvioli (☎ 65 89 55), Via dei Mille 11.

Getting Around

The only reason you will need to use public transport in Cagliari is if you want to head for the beach at Poetto. Take bus P from Piazza Matteotti.

AROUND CAGLIARI
The Costa Rei

There are good beaches within day-trip distance of Cagliari. To the east is the largely undeveloped Costa Rei, dotted with camping grounds and hotels which are generally expensive.

The town of **Villasimius**, before the Costa Rei, is near reasonable beaches. Try the *Albergo Stella d'Oro* (☎ 070-79 12 55), Via Vittorio Emanuele 21. It has singles/doubles for L36,000/61,000 and half board is obligatory in August (L100,000 per person). Nearby, at the sea, is *Camping Spiaggia del Riso* (☎ 070-79 71 50); costs are L10,000 per person and L12,000 for a site. Other camping grounds include *Cala Sinzias* (☎ 070-99 50 37), on the coast near Castiadas, and, farther north, *Piscina Rei* (☎ 070-99 10 96).

Slightly farther along the coast from Villasimius is the *Hotel Cormoran* (☎ 79 81 01), in the locality of Campus, a lovely resort hotel with a private sandy beach. Prices for full board range up to L180,000 in the high season. Bungalows for two people are available for around L1,400,000 per week, for up to five people for up to L1,900,000 per week in the high season, and villas for up to seven people can be rented for up to L2,000,000 per week.

For full details on camping and other accommodation along the coast, contact the tourist office at Cagliari. Regular daily ARST buses connect Cagliari with Villasimius and places along the Costa Rei, including camping grounds.

Nora

To the west and south of Cagliari, the main points of interest are the beautiful Costa del Sud and the ruins of the Phoenician city of Nora.

Founded in the 9th century BC by the Phoenicians, Nora was considered important for its strategic position and eventually came under Roman control. The ruins of the city extend into the sea and offer evidence of both civilisations, including temples, houses, and a Roman theatre and baths. The ruins are open daily from 9 am to one hour before sunset in summer, and from 9 am to 12.30 pm and 2 to 5 pm out of season, although it is best to check with Cagliari's tourist office before setting out. To get to the ruins, take an ARST bus from Cagliari to Pula, then a local bus (Autolinee Murgia) to Nora (only three a day).

The Costa del Sud

The small town of Chia marks the start of the beautiful Costa del Sud, which is protected by special ordinances from further development – even private houses can be built only in certain zones. There is one large hotel complex which blights the coastline about halfway between Chia and Teulada, the four-star *Baia delle Ginestre* (☎ 070-927 30 05). Half board per person per week costs from L770,000, depending on the season. Apartments are also available for rent.

Those happy to settle for something simpler can camp at *Camping Comunale Portu Tramatzu* (☎ 070-927 10 22), just past Porto di Teulada. Situated by the sea, the camping ground has a supermarket, bar, pizzeria and restaurant. Costs are L9000 per person and L8000 for a site. It is open from April to October. To get to the camping ground, take the ARST Cagliari-Teulada bus, get off at Porto di Teulada and then walk the short distance from the port to the camping ground (signs will point you in the right direction).

Your only other option is the *Hotel Sebera* (☎ 070-927 00 20), a pleasant establishment in the town of Teulada, in the central piazza where buses stop. Singles/doubles with full board cost L50,000/85,000.

SARDINIA

At Porto di Teulada there is a very pleasant bar/trattoria which specialises in fresh seafood. You can enjoy lunch in a small courtyard for around L30,000 a head.

Regular ARST buses connect Cagliari with Chia, and about eight a day continue on to Teulada.

Travellers can then continue on to the island of Sant'Antioco. If you have a car, make a detour to the **Is Zuddas Caves**, near Santadi, a series of caves with interesting stalagmite and stalactite formations. There is a small, private tourist office at Santadi (☎ 0781-95 59 83), in Piazza Marconi, which organises excursions in the area, including to Is Zuddas and to the nearby **Tombe dei Giganti** (Tombs of the Giants), a type of nuraghic tomb built using upright slabs of stones.

Another deviation would include the remains of the Phoenician/Carthaginian city on **Mont Sirai**, just out of Carbonia. This 7th-century BC fort town commanded a view for miles around. Its ruins are still under excavation.

Southern Sardinia

SANT'ANTIOCO & SAN PIETRO ISLANDS

These islands, off the south-west coast of Sardinia, feature sandy beaches and quiet coves, as well as the pleasant towns of Calasetta on Sant'Antioco and Carloforte on San Pietro, both with whitewashed or pastel-coloured houses lining narrow streets. The town of Sant'Antioco is more developed.

Information

The Pro Loco tourist office (☎ 0781-8 20 31) is in the town of Sant'Antioco, at Piazza della Repubblica. It can provide information and advice on accommodation, including apartments for rent. You can request information by writing (in English) to the Associazione Turistica Pro Loco, 09017 Sant'Antioco. The telephone code for the islands is 0781.

Places to Stay

Both islands have good camping facilities. Try the *Campeggio Tonnara* (☎ 8 38 03) at Cala di Saboni on the island of Sant'Antioco, or *La Caletta* (☎ 85 47 71) on the island of San Pietro. Both grounds are by the sea, away from the towns, and are accessible by the orange FMS buses which service both islands.

In Sant'Antioco, try the *Hotel Moderno* (☎ 8 31 05), Via Nazionale 82, which has singles/doubles for L55,000/80,000 with bathroom. You will need to book well in advance. In Calasetta, the best choice is the *Fiby Hotel* (☎ 8 84 44), Via Solferino 83, a very pleasant establishment with rooms with bathroom for L50,000/75,000. It also offers half board for L70,000 per person and full board for L85,000.

At Carloforte, on San Pietro, there are few choices and only the camping grounds are cheap. The *Hieracon Hotel* (☎ 85 40 28), Corso Cavour 62, fronting the port, charges L98,000 per person for half board in the high season and L85,000 a double in other months.

Places to Eat

There is a Coop supermarket in the town of Sant'Antioco on the corner of the Lungomare and Via d'Arborea, while in Carloforte you can pick up supplies at the Mercato Super Crai in Via Diaz.

In Sant'Antioco there are several good trattorias and restaurants, including the pizzeria/restaurant *Il Cartuccio*, Viale Trento, near Piazza Repubblica. In Calasetta, try *L'Anfora*, Via Roma 121, or *Da Pasqualino*, Via Roma 99. A full meal at either will cost around L30,000. At Carloforte, the *Barone Rosso*, Via XX Settembre 26, is the place to go for a sandwich; otherwise, try *Ristorante Da Vanino*, on the waterfront a short walk from the yacht harbour.

Getting There & Away

Sant'Antioco is connected to the mainland by a land bridge. It is accessible by FMS bus from Cagliari and Iglesias. Otherwise, catch a train to Carbonia from Cagliari or Iglesias,

SARDINIA

and then an FMS bus to the island. Regular ferries connect the two islands, leaving from Calasetta and arriving at Carloforte.

Getting Around

Orange FMS buses link the small towns on Sant'Antioco and the camping grounds and localities on San Pietro. On Sant'Antioco you can rent a scooter (L65,000 a day), moped or bicycle (L48,000 a day) from in front of the Coop supermarket in the town of Sant'Antioco and make your own tour of the island. At Carloforte, go to SARINAV, Lungomare 6. Here scooters cost L100,000 a day. From both outlets you can also rent motorised rubber dinghies for around L250,000 a day.

IGLESIAS

This mining centre, slightly inland from Sardinia's south-western coast, is left off most tourist itineraries, but is, in fact, well worth a stopover. The town is in a zone rich in minerals, including lead, zinc and some silver and gold, and its mining history extends back to Roman and Carthaginian times. From the 13th century it was occupied by the Pisans, who called it Argentaria (the Place of Silver) after the rich silver deposits which were discovered there in that period. However, it was the Spanish Aragons who left a greater mark on the town.

You will have to do without tourism advice while in Iglesias because the town is unprepared for the tourists who do pass through. If you do require any information, ask at the municipal offices (from 8 am to 2 pm Monday to Saturday) in Piazza del Duomo in the centre of town. The town's telephone code is 0781.

Things to See & Do

The **duomo**, in Piazza del Duomo, opposite the municipal offices, dates from the period of Pisan domination and was built in the Romanesque-Gothic style. Nearby, in Piazza San Francesco, is the Gothic-style **Chiesa di San Francesco**. Above the old town, along Via Campidano, are remains of Pisan towers and parts of the town's fortified walls.

Places to Stay & Eat

The choice is limited to one hotel, the *Artu* (☎ 2 24 92), Piazza Quintino Sella 15, east of the old part of town. It has singles/doubles with bathroom for L60,000/90,000. There are numerous pastry shops, takeaways and grocery shops in the shopping area around Via Martini and Via Azuni, a short walk from Piazza del Duomo. For a meal, try *Stalla* in Via Musio, off Via Azuni.

Getting There & Away

Regular FMS buses link Iglesias with Cagliari, Carbonia, Sant'Antioco and Calasetta. Two FMS buses a day head for Arbus, from where you can pick up connections to the Costa Verde. The bus station is in Via Oristano, off Via XX Settembre, south-east of the old town, and tickets can be purchased at Sulcis Agenzia Viaggi, Via Roma 52 (which is parallel to Via Oristano). The town is also accessible by train from Cagliari, Carbonia and Oristano, and the train station is in Via Garibaldi, a 10 to 15-minute walk along Via Matteotti from the town centre.

AROUND IGLESIAS

About 15 km north of Iglesias towards Fluminimaggiore is the Phoenician-Roman **Tempio di Antas**. Set in a wide, picturesque valley, the small temple was dedicated by the Phoenicians to a god of fertility and hunting, while the Romans dedicated it to a local Nuraghic divinity. Six columns remain standing. If you don't have a car, take the FMS bus from Iglesias for Fluminimaggiore and get off just after the village of Sant'Angelo. The temple is then a three-km walk away along a dirt road.

Western Sardinia

THE COSTA VERDE

This magnificent stretch of coastline remains almost entirely unspoiled, despite the fact that much of the area has been extensively mined. Former mining towns such as

Buggerru, Masua and Nebida (all three are on the coast, just south of the Costa Verde) are now seeking to make their fortunes as small tourist resorts.

The actual Costa Verde, which starts just north of Buggerru and continues to Montevecchio Marina, features long, white, sandy beaches with little or no development. Laws which protect the area mean that some sections will never be subject to development, and the area remains a paradise for lovers of secluded beaches. Campers and camper-vanners who remain discreet will find that they can free-camp in the area without any hassle. The isolation of much of the coast makes it difficult, but not impossible, for people to reach without their own transport.

Buggerru, a former mining town turned minor tourist resort, is a good place to make your base. It doesn't have any hotels as yet, but there is space set aside for camping by the waterfront, and you can free-camp along the coast to the south of the town. Many residents rent out rooms and apartments and, by asking at one of the town's bars or supermarkets, you will easily find a bed for the night (although most will be booked out in August).

Between Buggerru and Portixeddu to the north is the long, sandy beach of **San Nicolao**. Something of a rarity in Italy, this is a clean public beach, where the rows of deck chairs and umbrellas characteristic of the 'privatised' beaches in other parts of Italy have never been heard of.

Buggerru is accessible by FMS bus from Iglesias, which passes San Nicolao.

In the heart of the Costa Verde is **Piscinas**, at the mouth of the Piscinas river. This magnificent beach is famous for its high sand dunes which give it the appearance of a desert. There is one hotel at the beach, *Le Dune* (☎ 070-97 71 30), in a reconstructed *colonia* (a former holiday camp for the children of mining families). Full board costs from L120,000 per person and half board is from L110,000.

To reach Piscinas from Buggerru, take the road for Ingurtosu and turn off to the left

where you see the sign for Le Dune. There is no public transport to Piscinas, but the hotel will pick you up from the airport in Cagliari if you can spare the L150,000 fare.

Marina di Arbus, also known as Gutturu Flumini, is several km north and is more developed. Accommodation possibilities here include *Camping Costa Verde* (☎ 070-97 70 09), which charges L11,000 per person and L16,000 for a site. Apartments are available for rent at *Residence Piscinas* (☎ 070-97 71 37) for a minimum of one week. A two-person apartment will cost from L510,000, and an apartment for four people over L900,000.

Getting to Marina di Arbus is not simple by public transport. You will need to catch an ARST bus from Oristano, or an FMS bus from Iglesias to Arbus, then a bus from Via della Repubblica to Marina di Arbus – which operates only in summer and only twice a day at 7.30 am and 2.30 pm, returning to Arbus in the evening.

ORISTANO

Like much of interest in Sardinia, the city of Oristano and its province should be approached with the attitude that they are to be 'discovered'. Originally inhabited by the Nuraghic people, the area around what is now Oristano was colonised by the Phoenicians, who established the port town of Tharros, later controlled by Carthaginians and then Romans.

The town of Oristano is believed to have been founded some time in the 7th century AD by the people of Tharros, who abandoned their ancient town, probably to escape raids by Moorish pirates. Oristano grew to prominence in the 14th century, particularly during the rule of Eleonora d'Arborea, who opposed the Spanish occupation of the island and drew up a body of laws known as the *Carta de Logu*, a progressive legal code which was eventually enforced throughout the island. The code is also considered important because it recorded the ancient Sardinian language, in which it was written.

Eleonora began a matriarchal, some would say feminist, tradition which has

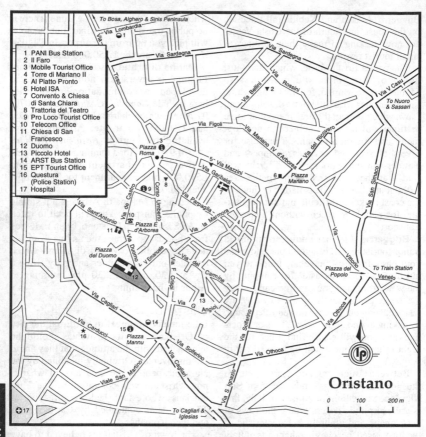

1 PANI Bus Station
2 Il Faro
3 Mobile Tourist Office
4 Torre di Mariano II
5 Al Piatto Pronto
6 Hotel ISA
7 Convento & Chiesa
   di Santa Chiara
8 Trattoria del Teatro
9 Pro Loco Tourist Office
10 Telecom Office
11 Chiesa di San
   Francesco
12 Duomo
13 Piccolo Hotel
14 ARST Bus Station
15 EPT Tourist Office
16 Questura
   (Police Station)
17 Hospital

Oristano

0   100   200 m

endured in Oristano. The town has had several women leaders, and recently the Sardinian Women's Cooperative of Sheep-Breeders (Cooperativa Allevatrici Sarde) established a highly successful agriturismo enterprise in the province (see the following Places to Stay section).

Orientation

A good point from which to orient yourself in Oristano is Piazza Roma, where, in summer, there is a tourist information caravan seven days a week from 9 am to 9 pm. The piazza is close to the PANI bus stop, off Via Tirso in Via Lombardia, and is a five-minute walk from the ARST bus station in Via Cagliari, just off Piazza Mannu. The train station is a 15 to 20-minute walk away in Piazza Ungheria. To reach Piazza Roma from here, follow Via Vittorio Veneto to Piazza Mariano and then take Via Mazzini.

Information

Tourist Office The mobile tourist office in Piazza Roma has loads of information on the town and the province and will advise on accommodation and transport. Pick up a copy of the booklet *Oristano & its Province*, available in English, which includes a map of the town. The office opens daily from 9 am to 1 pm and from 4 to 7 pm. There is a Pro Loco office (☎ 7 06 21) in Via de Castro, off Piazza Roma, open from 9 am to midday and 5 to 8 pm Monday to Friday. There is an EPT office (☎ 7 31 91), at Via Cagliari 278, open Monday to Friday from 8 am to 2 pm and also in the afternoon on Tuesday and Wednesday, from 4 to 8 pm.

Post & Telecommunications The main post office is at Via Liguria, north-west of Piazza Roma along Via Tirso, and is open Monday to Saturday from 8.15 am to 7.30 pm. There are Telecom public telephones in Piazza Eleonora d'Arborea. The post code for central Oristano is 09170 and the telephone code is 0783.

Emergency For immediate police assistance, call ☎ 113. The police headquarters are in Via Carducci. For an ambulance, call ☎ 7 82 22. There is a public hospital (☎ 7 42 61) at Via Fondazione Rockefeller, along Viale San Martino from Piazza Mannu.

Things to See

In Piazza Roma is the 13th-century **Torre di Mariano II**, also known as the Tower of San Cristoforo. From here, walk along Corso Umberto to **Piazza Eleonora d'Arborea**, where there is a 19th-century statue of Oristano's heroine. To the right is the neo-classical **Chiesa di San Francesco**. Of note inside the church is a 15th-century polychrome wooden crucifix, a 14th-century marble statue of San Basilio by Nino Pisano, and a 16th-century polyptych by Pietro Cavaro.

Follow Via Eleonora d'Arborea or Via Duomo to reach the **duomo**, built in the 13th century but completely remodelled in the 18th century. It has a Baroque bell tower, topped by a multicoloured dome. Also of interest is the 14th-century **Convento & Chiesa di Santa Chiara**, between Via Parpaglia and Via Garibaldi.

About three km south of Oristano at Santa Giusta, and easily accessible by local ARST buses, is the **Basilica di Santa Giusta**. Built around 1100, the church is Romanesque, with Pisan and Lombard influences.

Festival

The most important festival in Oristano is the colourful Sa Sartiglia, held on the last Sunday of carnival (late February or early March) and repeated on Shrove Tuesday. Arguably one of the island's most beautiful festive events, the Sartiglia had its origins in a military contest performed by the knights of the Second Crusade. It developed into a festive event during the period of Spanish domination and now involves masked, costumed riders who parade through the town before participating in a tournament, where they must pierce the centre of a silver star with their swords while riding at full speed.

Places to Stay & Eat

The town is not exactly bursting with hotels and there are no budget options. There is a camping ground, the *Camping Torregrande* (☎ 2 20 08) at Marina di Torre Grande, about seven km west of Oristano (regular ARST buses connect the two towns – see the following Getting There & Away section). It is open from May to October and may be full during August.

In town is the *Piccolo Hotel* (☎ 7 15 00), Via Martignano 19, with singles/doubles for L60,000/90,000. *Hotel ISA* (☎ 36 01 01) is half a km from the station at Piazza Mariano 50 and has singles/doubles for L70,000/110,000 with private bathroom.

Agriturismo is very well organised in the province, with B&B costing around L30,000 a head and half board around L50,000. It is organised by the Cooperativa Allevatrici Sarde (☎ 41 80 66). For details contact the tourist office or write to the cooperative at Casella Postale 107, 09170 Oristano.

For a quick snack or meal, try *Al Piatto Pronto* at Via Mazzini 21, near Piazza Roma, which has a wide range of pre-prepared dishes. *Trattoria del Teatro*, Via Parpaglia 11, has full meals for around

L30,000, while *Il Faro*, Via Bellini 25, is considered one of the town's better and more expensive restaurants.

Getting There & Away

The terminal for ARST buses, which service the province, is on Via Cagliari, opposite the EPT office. Regular buses head for Marina di Torre Grande, Putzu Idu and Su Pallosu, as well as San Giovanni di Sinis and the ruins of Tharros. Four buses a day leave for Bosa. The PANI bus stop is in Via Lombardia, outside the Blu Bar at No 30 (where you can check on timetables). There are connections to Cagliari, Sassari and Nuoro.

Oristano is accessible by train from Cagliari, Sassari and Olbia.

Getting Around

Oristano is easy to negotiate on foot, although urban bus No 2 Circolare Destra (clockwise) or Sinistra (anticlockwise) is handy for getting around.

AROUND ORISTANO

Just west of Oristano is the **Sinis Peninsula**, with some lovely sandy beaches (which have been awarded a coveted Blue Flag for cleanliness by the EC), the opportunity to see lots of flamingos, and the ruins of the ancient Phoenician port of Tharros. If you have the time, spend a few days relaxing here. There are only a couple of hotels, but rooms are available for rent and there are several places participating in the local agriturismo programme. Check at the tourist office in Oristano for details.

At the village of **San Giovanni di Sinis** is the 5th-century Byzantine church of the same name, where Mass is still celebrated. Nearby is the tiny church of San Salvatore, built over a pagan temple in a tiny village of whitewashed houses with pastel-coloured doors.

Tharros, just out of San Giovanni at the southernmost end of the peninsula, was originally a Phoenician and later a Roman port town. These important ruins, discovered in 1851 by an English archaeologist, yielded significant treasures and are well worth a visit. They are open from 9 am to 1 pm and 4 to 7 pm and entrance is free.

San Giovanni and Tharros can be reached from Oristano by regular ARST buses.

At the northern end of the peninsula are the villages of **Putzu Idu** and **Su Pallosu**, both offering peaceful surroundings and lovely beaches. Between the two villages are marshes which are home to hundreds of pink flamingos as well as other water birds. The loveliest beach on the peninsula is nearby at **Is Arutas**.

If you want to stay at Putzu Idu, try *Da Cesare* (☎ 0783-5 20 15), which has singles/doubles for around L50,000/80,000. Half board is obligatory in high season, costing L100,000 per person. A short walk away is the quieter Su Pallosu and the *Hotel Su Pallosu* (☎ 0783-5 80 21), which has rooms for L60,000/100,000. It offers special deals on half board in June.

Both villages and the beach of Is Arutas are accessible from June to September by ARST bus from Oristano.

An event of particular interest, especially for those who want to experience Sardinia's wilder side, is the Sa Ardia in **Sedilo**, a spectacular festival on 6 and 7 July in honour of St Constantine, which features a dangerous horse race through the town. Thousands of spectators crowd into Sedilo to witness the event, and some fire guns into the ground and air to excite the horses further. Needless to say, there are serious injuries every year. The race starts at 6 pm on 6 July and is repeated the following morning at about 7 am. Information about the event is available at the provincial tourist office in Oristano. Sedilo is about 50 km north-east of Oristano, near Abbasanta and Lago Omodeo.

Northern Sardinia

ALGHERO

This is one of the most popular tourist resorts in Sardinia, situated on the island's north-west coast, in the area known as the Coral Riviera. The Catalan Aragonese won the town from Genoa in 1354, and even today the locals speak a dialect strongly linked to the Catalan language. The town is a good base from which to explore the magnificent coastline that links it to Bosa in the south, and the famous Grotta di Nettuno (see the Around Alghero section).

Orientation

Alghero's historical centre is on a small promontory, jutting into the sea, with the new town stretching out behind it and along the coast to the north. Intercity buses arrive in Via Catalogna, next to a small park just outside the historic centre. The train station is about one km north, on Via Don Minzoni, and connected to the centre by a regular bus service.

Information

Tourist Office The AAST office (☎ 079-97 90 54) is at Piazza Porta Terra 9, near the port and just across the gardens from the bus station. You can pick up a map of the town and ask for assistance in finding a hotel. The old town and most hotels and restaurants are in the area west of the tourist office.

Post & Telecommunications The main post office is at Via XX Settembre 108. There is a row of public telephones on Via Vittorio Emanuele at the opposite end of the gardens from the tourist office. Poste restante mail can be addressed to 07041 Alghero. The telephone code for Alghero is 079.

Emergency For immediate police attention, call ☎ 113. From 1 July to 10 September there is a tourist medical service (☎ 93 05 33), Piazza Venezia Giulia, in Fertilia, just north of Alghero. It is open from 9 am to 12.30 pm and 4.30 to 7.30 pm, although for emergencies you can telephone 24 hours a day. Otherwise go to the Ospedale Civile (☎ 99 62 33), Via Don Minzoni.

Things to See & Do

Wander through the narrow streets of the old town and around the port. The most interesting church is the **Chiesa di San Francesco**,

Via Carlo Alberto. The town's **cathedral** has been ruined by constant remodelling, but its bell tower remains a fine example of Gothic Catalan architecture.

There are three defensive towers in the town. The **Torre del Portal**, in Piazza Porta Terra, was furnished with a drawbridge and moat, and was one of the two entrances to the walled town. The **Torre de l'Esperó Reial** was one of the bastions of Alghero's fortified wall. The octagonal **Torre de Sant Jaume** is also known as the Dog's Tower, since it was used as a pound for stray dogs.

In summer Alghero generally stages the Estate Musicale Algherese in the cloisters of the church of San Francesco. A festival, complete with fireworks display, is held annually on 15 August for the Feast of the Assumption.

Places to Stay

It is virtually impossible to find a room in August, unless you book months in advance. At other times of the year you should have little trouble. Camping facilities include *Camping Calik* (☎ 93 01 11) in Fertilia, about seven km north of town, where charges in high season are L14,000 per person and L5000 for the site. The HI *Ostello dei Giuliani* (☎ 93 03 53) is at Via Zara 1, in Fertilia. Take bus AF from Via Catalogna to Fertilia. B&B is L14,000 a night and a meal is L12,000. It is open all year.

In the old town is *Hotel San Francesco* (☎ 98 03 30), Via Ambrogio Machin 2, with singles/doubles for L50,000/85,000, with bathroom. *Pensione Normandie* (☎ 97 53 02), Via Enrico Mattei 6, is out of the centre. Follow Via Cagliari (which becomes Viale Giovanni XXIII). It has slightly shabby, but large, rooms for L27,000/50,000.

The *Miramare* (☎ 97 93 50), Via G Leopardi 9, south along the Lungomare Dante from the old town, has good rooms with bathroom for up to L60,000/90,000. *La Margherita* (☎ 97 90 06), Via Sassari 70, has good rooms with bathroom for up to L81,000/98,000.

Places to Eat

There are numerous supermarkets around

SARDINIA

the town, including a Coop in Via Lamarmora. For good sandwiches, head for *Paninoteca al Duomo*, next to the cathedral in Piazza Civica. The best ice cream is at *Paradiso 2*, through the Porta a Mare from Piazza Civica.

Ristorante La Piconia, Via Principe Umberto 29, is also a pizzeria. A full meal will cost around L25,000. *Trattoria Il Vecchio Mulino*, Via Don Deroma 3, is a pleasant establishment, where a full meal will cost about the same. A cheaper option is the *pizzeria* just off Via Roma at Vicolo Adami 17; takeaway pizza by the slice costs about L2000. At Vicolo Adami 25 is *La Posada del Mar*, which serves good pasta for around L9000 and pizzas for around L8000. *La Lepanto*, Via Carlo Alberto 135, overlooks the sea. A good full meal will cost around L45,000.

La Palafitta is a few km north of Alghero, on the way to Fertilia, literally on the beach known as Spiaggia di Maria Pia. Look for the sign and then walk through the small area of pine trees to the restaurant. A full meal will cost around L25,000 and you can follow it up with a moonlit walk along the beach.

Getting There & Away

The airport, inland from Fertilia, services domestic flights from major cities throughout Italy. Regular buses leave from Via Catalogna and also from Piazza della Mercedes to coincide with flights.

Intercity buses terminate in Via Catalogna, next to the public park. ARST buses leave for Sassari and Porto Torres; FDS buses service Sassari as well and there is a special service to Olbia to coincide with ferry departures. FDS also runs a service between Alghero and Bosa. Regular buses leave for Capocaccia and Porto Conte. Timetables are posted in the bar beside the bus stop area.

Trains connect Alghero with Sassari.

Getting Around

Urban bus No AF runs hourly between Alghero and Fertilia from 8 am to 10 pm. The more regular AP goes only as far as the Maria Pia beach. Regular FDS buses run between the port and the train station, a distance of about one km.

If you want to rent a bicycle or motorcycle to explore the coast, try Velosport (☎ 97 71 82), Via Vittorio Veneto 90. A bike will cost about L20,000 a day, a moped L45,000 and a scooter L75,000. *Cicloexpress* (☎ 97 65 92), Via Garibaldi Porto, has mountain bikes for L18,000 per day, bicycles for L12,000 per day, mopeds for L25,000 per day and Piaggio 125 cc scooters for L50,000 per day.

AROUND ALGHERO

There are good beaches north of Alghero, including the **Spiaggia di San Giovanni** and the **Spiaggia di Maria Pia**, easily accessible on the Alghero-Fertilia bus.

The **Grotta di Nettuno** (Neptune's Cave) on Capo Caccia west of Alghero, is accessible by regular boats operated by various companies from Alghero's port (L14,000), or by the SFS bus from Via Catalogna. For some services you will need to change at Porto Conte.

If you have your own means of transport, explore the Capo Caccia area and visit the **Nuraghe di Palmavera** about 10 km out of Alghero on the road to Porto Conte.

The coastline between Alghero and **Bosa**, to the south, is stunning. Rugged cliffs drop down to isolated beaches, and near Bosa is one of the last habitats of the griffon vulture. It is quite an experience if you are lucky enough to spot one of these huge birds. The only way to explore the coast is by car or motorbike. Don't leave anything in your car: thieves patrol the coast looking for easy targets like unattended cars loaded with luggage.

SASSARI

The capital of Sardinia's largest province, Sassari is also the island's second-largest city after Cagliari. It is a pleasant town, but there is really not a lot to see and it is probably best regarded as a convenient stopover on the way to the northern coast. It is certainly worth visiting in May for the Sardinian Cavalcade, one of Sardinia's most important festivals.

Orientation

Sassari has a compact medieval centre centred around its cathedral. However, most services are in the busy newer part of town, based around the vast 18th-century Piazza Italia. Most intercity buses arrive in Emiciclo Garibaldi, a piazza a few minutes walk downhill from Piazza Italia. Head up Via Brigata Sassari to Piazza Castello and turn right to reach the adjacent Piazza Italia.

The train station is about 10 minutes walk from the centre. From the station, turn left to reach Piazza Sant'Antonio and then right along Corso Vittorio Emanuele to reach Piazza Castello.

Information

Tourist Office A new AAST office was expected to open in Via Roma, next to the Museo Sanna, in late 1995. If it's not yet open, try Via Brigata Sassari 19 (☎ 079-23 13 31).

Money There is a branch of the Banca Commerciale Italiana in Piazza Italia, where you can exchange travellers' cheques and obtain cash advances on Visa and MasterCard.

Post & Telecommunications The main post office is at Via Brigata Sassari 13, just off Piazza Castello. There is a Telecom office at Viale Italia 7, across Emiciclo Garibaldi, open Monday to Friday from 9 am to 12.30 pm and 4 to 7.30 pm. Poste restante mail can be addressed to 07100 Sassari. The town's telephone code is 079.

Emergency For immediate police attendance, call ☎ 113. The public hospital, Ospedale Civile (☎ 22 05 00), is in Via E de Nicola, off Viale Italia.

Things to See

Sassari's **cathedral** is in the old town in Piazza del Duomo. Built in Romanesque style in the 13th century, it was remodelled and given a Baroque façade in the 17th century. Also worth a look is the **Chiesa di Santa Maria di Betlem**, on Viale Coppino near the station, which has a 13th-century façade and lovely 14th-century cloisters.

The town's **Museo Sanna**, Via Roma 64, is of considerable interest for its Nuraghic collection, as well as its display of traditional costumes.

Festival

The Sardinian Cavalcade (Cavalcata Sarda) is generally held on the second-last Sunday in May (although the day can change from year to year). It attracts participants from all over the island, who dress in traditional costume and participate in a large and colourful parade, followed by equestrian competitions with riders in traditional costume. If you can manage it, the town is well worth visiting for the festival.

Places to Stay

Hotels and pensioni are not abundant in Sassari and if you plan to arrive in high summer, or for the Cavalcade, it is advisable to book a room. The *Pensione Famiglia* (☎ 23 95 43), Viale Umberto 65, is run down, but singles/doubles are cheap at L25,000/ 30,000. *Hotel Giusy* (☎ 23 33 27), Piazza Sant'Antonio, is close to the station and has singles/doubles with bathroom for L48,000/ 65,000. At Via Roma 79 is the more up-market *Hotel Leonardo da Vinci* (☎ 28 07 44), which has quality singles/doubles for L95,000/147,000 and triples for L198,000, including breakfast and private bathroom.

Places to Eat

There is an outdoor fresh-produce market held every morning from Monday to Saturday in Piazza Tola, a short walk from Piazza Castello off Corso Vittorio Emanuele. Alternatively, shop at the Standa supermarket on the corner of Viale Italia and Via Sardegna. You can get good sandwiches at either of the sandwich shops in Via Turritana, off Via Brigata Sassari.

There is a *Spaghetteria* at Via Usai 10A, off Largo Felice Cavallotti, where a dish of pasta costs between L5000 and L12,000. *Ristorante/Pizzeria Al Caminetto*, Via Enrico Costa 32-34, has good food at reasonable prices. *Ristorante Liberty* is in a restored palace in Piazza Sauro, off Corso Vittorio Emanuele. A full meal will cost around L30,000. *Ristorante Florian*, off Piazza Italia at Via Bellieni 27, has a good reputation. A full meal will cost around L30,000.

Getting There & Away

ARST buses leave from outside Sarda Viaggi travel agency, Via Brigata Sassari 30, connecting with flights at Fertilia airport. Tickets can be purchased at the travel agency.

ARST buses connect Sassari with towns throughout the province, including Alghero, Bosa and Pozzomaggiore. There are also regular buses to Porto Torres (28 a day), Santa Teresa Gallura (31 a day) and Nuoro. Timetable information and tickets are available at the ARST office in the Emiciclo Garibaldi piazza, at the southern end of Via Brigata Sassari. FDS buses run to Alghero, Fertilia, Bosa, Olbia, Palau and Porto Torres. The company's ticket office, where you can check timetables, is at Emiciclo Garibaldi 26. PANI buses connect Sassari with Porto Torres, Oristano and Cagliari. They leave

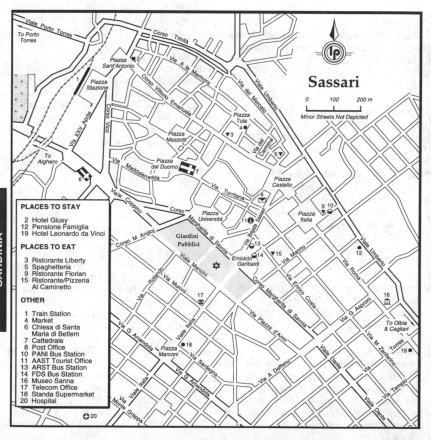

Sassari

0   100   200 m

Minor Streets Not Depicted

PLACES TO STAY
2   Hotel Giusy
12 Pensione Famiglia
19 Hotel Leonardo da Vinci

PLACES TO EAT
3   Ristorante Liberty
5   Spaghetteria
9   Ristorante Florian
15 Ristorante/Pizzeria
    Al Caminetto

OTHER
1   Train Station
4   Market
6   Chiesa di Santa
    Maria di Betlem
7   Cattedrale
8   Post Office
10 PANI Bus Station
11 AAST Tourist Office
13 ARST Bus Station
14 FDS Bus Station
16 Museo Sanna
17 Telecom Office
18 Standa Supermarket
20 Hospital

SARDINIA

from and arrive at the PANI ticket office at Via Bellieni 25, next to Ristorante Florian.

Trains connect Sassari to Porto Torres, Olbia, Oristano and Cagliari.

Getting Around

It is easy to make your way around the centre of town on foot, but a useful bus is No 8, which heads from the station to Piazza Italia, travelling along Corso Vittorio Emanuele and Via Roma. If arriving by car, you will find the familiar 'centro' signs to direct you to the centre. There are numerous supervised daytime car parks in the streets around the centre.

AROUND SASSARI

The **Chiesa di SS Trinità di Saccargia**, a splendid Romanesque Pisan church built in 1116, is set in a bare landscape near the town of Codrongianus, along the SS131 about 18 km south-east of Sassari. You should have little trouble reaching the town by ARST bus from Sassari, but then you have to walk the two km to the church.

The **Santu Antine** nuraghe, near Torralba, is just off the SS131 about 40 km south of Sassari. Said to be the most beautiful nuraghe in Sardinia, it is well worth a visit. By public transport, it can be reached from Sassari by the ARST bus heading for Padria, which stops at Torralba.

PORTO TORRES

Unless you are arriving or leaving by ferry, there is no reason to visit this port town and major petrochemical centre. To the north-west of the town is the fast-developing beach resort of Stintino, a former fishing village which has managed to retain some of the atmosphere of its past.

The town's main street is Corso Vittorio Emanuele, which is directly in front of you as you face away from the port. The tourist office (☎ 079-52 37 88) is at Via Sassari 32 and is open from 9 am to 1 pm and 5 to 9 pm (shorter hours out of season). The town's telephone code is 079.

Places to Stay & Eat

If you find it necessary to spend the night in Porto Torres, there is a hostel, the *Ostello del Comune* (☎ 51 30 01), Via Lungomare 91, on the corner of Via Balai, about three km from the port; B&B is L14,000. Otherwise, try the *Albergo Royal* (☎ 50 22 78), Via Sebastiano Satta 8, which has singles/doubles for L40,000/65,000 or with bathroom for L50,000/75,000; triples without bathroom are L90,000.

There are numerous places where you can buy sandwiches or snacks, including takeaway pizza by the slice at Via Ponte Romano 54. For a meal, try *Trattoria da Teresa*, Via Giordano Bruno, which has a very cheap set-price menu.

Getting There & Away

Regular ARST buses connect Porto Torres with Sassari, as well as with Stintino. The bus station is in Piazzale Colombo at the port and the ticket office is at Acciaro Bar, Corso Vittorio Emanuele 38. Regular trains connect the town with Sassari. Formerly, trains stopped at the port, but a new station has been built about two km west.

Tirrenia runs daily ferries to Genoa (three a day in summer). Its office (☎ 51 41 07) is in the ferry terminal at the port.

The French line SNCM runs four or five ferries per month to Toulon and Marseille, some via Bastia in Corsica, from the end of March to September. The agent for SNCM in Porto Torres is Agenzia Paglietti Petertours (☎ 51 44 77), Corso Vittorio Emanuele.

In France the company has offices in Marseille, at 61 Blvd des Dames (☎ 91 56 30 10), and in Toulon, 21 & 49 Ave de l'Infanterie de Marine (☎ 94 16 66 66). In Corsica, it can be contacted through Corsica Marittima (☎ 95 32 69 04), 15 Blvd de Gaulle, Bastia.

STINTINO

A picturesque fishing village turned tourist resort, Stintino is very crowded in summer. A few km west of the town, facing Asinara

SARDINIA

Island, is a magnificent sandy beach, the **Spiaggia di Pelosa**, at Torre Pelosa.

If you want to spend a few days in Stintino, try the *Albergo Silvestrino* (☎ 079-52 30 07), Via Sassari 12 in the centre of the village. It has doubles for L85,000, and half board for L125,000 per person (closed in January and February). The *Hotel Lina* (☎ 079-52 30 71), Via Lepanto 38, facing the village's small port, has doubles for L80,000.

The town is accessible from Porto Torres by ARST bus (five a day in summer).

SANTA TERESA GALLURA

Together with Palau, about 26 km east, this seaside resort has developed into an affordable alternative to the jet-set hang-outs on the Costa Smeralda. It is a very pleasant spot to pass a few relaxing days, particularly if the magnificent coves, rock pools and small beaches of nearby Capo Testa appeal. From the town you can see across the Stretto di Bonifacio to Corsica, or even catch one of the regular ferries which make the crossing to Bonifacio on Corsica's southern tip.

Information

Santa Teresa's AAST office (☎ 0789-75 41 27) is in the town centre at Piazza Vittorio Emanuele 24, open Monday to Saturday from 8.30 am to 1 pm and 3.30 to 6.30 pm. The helpful staff can provide loads of information and will assist in finding accommodation. It is possible to ring ahead to request information on hotels, as well as rooms and apartments for rent, or you can write (in English) to: AAST, Piazza V Emanuele 24, 07028 Santa Teresa Gallura.

You can exchange money daily from 8 am to 10 pm at the port; otherwise there is a bank in Piazza V Emanuele. The town's telephone code is 0789.

For medical attention, go to the Guardia Medica in Via Carlo Felice, on the corner of Via Eleonora d'Arborea, a short walk from the town centre.

Things to See & Do

The main reason for a visit to this area is to spend time on the beach. There is the small **Spiaggia Rena Bianca** next to the town, but it is recommended that you head for **Capo Testa**, a small cape connected to the mainland by an isthmus, about five km west of Santa Teresa. There are lovely, small beaches on either side of the cape, as well as a large rock pool. The cape is characterised by granite outcrops, worked and worn smooth by the wind and sea. The road ends just below the cape's lighthouse, from where the path to the right leads to the rock pool and the path to the left leads to a small cove and sandy beach. The area is in fact a military zone, but people move around freely.

Motorised rubber boats for up to six people are available for rent at Santa Teresa's port for L150,000 to L180,000 a day, or L90,000 for half a day. GULP, Via Nazionale 58, also rents boats, as well as bicycles and motorcycles, which are handy for exploring the area. A mountain bike costs around L25,000 a day, a moped L40,000 a day and a scooter L60,000.

Places to Stay

The town offers extensive accommodation possibilities, including rooms and apartments for rent (contact the tourist office). It is advisable to book if you plan to arrive during late July or August.

Camping facilities are all out of town. Try *La Liccia* (☎ 75 51 90), about six km from Santa Teresa towards Palau, 400 metres from the beach; charges are L13,500 per adult and up to L16,000 for a site.

In town is *Albergo Da Cecco* (☎ 75 42 20), Via Po 3 (take Via XX Settembre from the tourist office and turn right at Via Po), which has pleasant singles/doubles for L65,000/85,000 with bathroom. *Albergo Riva* (☎ 75 42 83), Via del Porto, on the corner of Via Galliano, has singles/doubles for L55,000/ 65,000 and triples for L95,000, while the *Hotel del Porto* (☎ 75 41 54), Via del Porto, on the port, has singles/doubles for L35,000/60,000, or L40,000/80,000 with bathroom.

At Capo Testa is the *Bocche di Bonifacio* (☎ 75 42 02), which has singles/doubles for

L50,000/70,000 and full board for L95,000 per person.

Places to Eat

There are plenty of good bars and sandwich shops where you can buy sandwiches, including *Poldo's Pub*, Via Garibaldi 4. For good pizza, try *Pizzeria Azzurra*, close to the port on Via del Porto. *Marinaro*, at the Hotel Marinaro, Via Angioj, has good meals for around L25,000. If visiting Capo Testa, try the trattoria at the Bocche di Bonifacio hotel.

Getting There & Away

Regular ARST buses connect Santa Teresa with Olbia, Golfo Aranci and Palau, arriving in Via Eleonora d'Arborea, off Via Nazionale, a short walk to the centre. There are also two buses a day to Sassari. Tickets can be purchased at the Bar Black & White on Via Nazionale.

Ferry services to Corsica are run by two companies, Navarma Lines (☎ 75 52 60) and Saremar (☎ 75 47 88), which both have small offices at the port. Both companies run several services a day.

PALAU, MADDALENA & CAPRERA

Close to the Costa Smeralda, Palau is little more than a conglomeration of expensive hotels and private apartment blocks and is much less pleasant than Santa Teresa. Just off the coast are the islands of **Maddalena**, site of a US navy base, and **Caprera**, which was given to the hero of Italian unification, Giuseppe Garibaldi, by King Victor Emmanuel II. Garibaldi spent his last years there and it is possible to visit his house. Most of the island is a nature reserve, which means that camping is forbidden, although it is the site of a Club Mediterranée (see the following Places to Stay section). Maddalena has an attractive main town, La Maddalena, and several good beaches, and is popular with campers. The two islands are connected by a road bridge.

Information

Palau's tourist office (☎ 0789-70 95 70) is at Via Nazionale 96. It has little tourist infor-mation, but can assist with information on accommodation, including apartments and rooms for rent. La Maddalena's tourist office (☎ 0789-73 63 21) is at Via XX Settembre 24. The telephone code for the area is 0789.

Places to Stay

Just east of Palau is *Camping Capo d'Orso* (☎ 70 81 82), on the cape of the same name. Located by the sea, its charges are L6500 per person and L13,500 for a site. It also has caravans and bungalows for rent at L110,000 and L160,000 per day respectively.

In the town there are numerous hotels and rooms for rent, but you should book ahead for July and August. The *Hotel La Serra* (☎ 70 95 19), Via Nazionale 17, has doubles for L65,000 with bathroom. *La Roccia* (☎ 70 95 28), Via dei Mille 15, has singles/doubles for L60,000/90,000. If you're looking for luxury accommodation, try the *Hotel Palau* (☎ 70 84 68), Via Baragge, which has doubles for up to L280,000.

On Maddalena there is *Villaggio Camping La Maddalena* (☎ 72 80 51) at Moneta, and *Campeggio Abbatoggia* (☎ 73 91 73) on the other side of the island at Lo Strangolato, close to a lovely beach. Both are reasonably cheap and are accessible by local bus from the town of La Maddalena. In town is *Hotel Il Gabbiano* (☎ 72 25 07), Via Giulio Cesare, which has singles/doubles for L90,000/115,000 with bathroom. The *Club Mediterranée* (☎ 72 70 78) on Caprera charges for full board by the week, at around L700,000 per person.

Places to Eat

In Palau, you can buy supplies at the Minimarket da Gemma, Via Nazionale 66. There are several decent places to eat, including *L'Uva Fragola*, Piazza Vittorio Emanuele, just off Via Nazionale near the port, which serves good pizzas, as well as salads for around L10,000. *Da Robertino*, Via Nazionale 22, is a good trattoria, where a full meal will cost around L25,000. At *La Taverna*, Via Rossini, off Via Nazionale, you can eat an excellent meal for around L50,000.

Getting There & Away

Palau is easily accessible by ARST bus from Sassari, Santa Teresa Gallura and Olbia. SFS and Autoservizi Caramelli buses connect Palau with places along the Costa Smeralda, including Baia Sardinia and Porto Cervo. Buses stop at Palau's small port. Timetables are posted inside the small ferry terminal at the port.

Getting Around

Ferries make the short crossing between Palau and La Maddalena every 20 minutes during summer, less frequently in the off season. It is not possible to take your car to La Maddalena. There is a car park just outside Palau, where you can leave the car if you want to catch a ferry to La Maddalena, and a bus shuttle service will take you to the port. While it is not obligatory to use the car park, it may be difficult to find a parking spot in town during summer.

Once on the island, catch one of the blue local buses which leave from the port every half-hour and make the round trip of the island. Buses for Caprera leave from the piazza at the end of Via Giovanni Amendola, to the right of the port.

COSTA SMERALDA

For the average tourist, the Costa Smeralda (Emerald Coast) is basically out of reach. There are no hotels of less than three stars, which means that prices for a double room start at around L120,000 a day. The coast was purchased in 1962 by a group of international investors led by Prince Karim Aga Khan, and was basically developed from scratch. Its resorts include Baia Sardinia, Liscia di Vacca and Porto Cervo, all bearing a stronger resemblance to Disneyland than seaside towns. The coastline is certainly beautiful, but it is not the real Sardinia, and unless you have money to burn, or very rich friends with an apartment, it is better to spend the day on one of its beaches and continue your journey.

Those who would like to stay on the Costa Smeralda can obtain information about

accommodation from the tourist office at Arzachena (☎ 0789-8 26 24), in Piazza Risorgimento.

The coast is accessible by ARST, SFS and Autoservizi Caramelli buses from Palau and Olbia.

OLBIA

This busy port and industrial centre will very likely be the first glimpse of Sardinia for many tourists. It is a major port for ferries arriving from Civitavecchia, Genoa and Livorno, and while it is not particularly unpleasant, it is not particularly interesting either and is best passed through quickly.

Orientation

If arriving by ferry, you will find yourself at a well-organised port complete with a new ferry terminal, and a local bus (No 3) to take you into the centre of town (only about one km). Trains also run from the main station to the port to coincide with ferry departures. Intercity buses terminate at the end of Corso Umberto at Via XX Settembre. Head to the right along Corso Umberto to reach the town centre. The train station is close by in Via Pala, off Piazza Risorgimento.

Information

Tourist Office The AAST office (☎ 0789-2 14 53) is at Via Catello Piro 1, off Corso Umberto, and open from 8 am to 2 pm and 4 to 8 pm. The staff are very keen to help and will advise on places to stay and eat, and can provide information about accommodation and places to visit throughout Sardinia.

Money There are three major banks in Corso Umberto, including the Banca Commerciale Italiana at No 191, where you can obtain cash advances on both Visa and MasterCard.

Post & Telecommunications The main post office is in Via Acquedotto, off Piazza Matteotti, and there is a Telecom office at Via de Filippi 14. Poste restante mail can be addressed to 07026 Olbia. The town's telephone code is 0789.

Emergency For immediate police attendance, call ☎ 113. For medical treatment, the public hospital, the Ospedale Civile (☎ 5 22 01), is in Viale Aldo Moro, about 15 minutes walk from the centre along Via Porto Romano and Via Gabriele d'Annunzio.

Places to Stay

The *Albergo Terranova* (☎ 2 23 95), Via Giuseppe Garibaldi 3, has singles/doubles for L38,000/60,000. The *Hotel Minerva* (☎ 2 11 90), Via Mazzini 7, has doubles for L60,000, and singles/doubles with bathroom for L45,000/70,000.

The *Hotel Gallura* (☎ 2 46 48), Corso Umberto 145, is a pleasant establishment, with singles/doubles with bathroom for L80,000 /110,000. The *Hotel Centrale* (☎ 2 30 17), Corso Umberto 85, has rooms for L100,000/140,000.

Places to Eat

If you want to stock up on food supplies, head for the Mercato Civico in Via Acquedotto. At *Gelateria Il Golosone*, Corso Umberto 41, you can buy good sandwiches, crêpes and ice cream. For an excellent meal, try *Trattoria il Gambero*, Via Lamarmora 6,

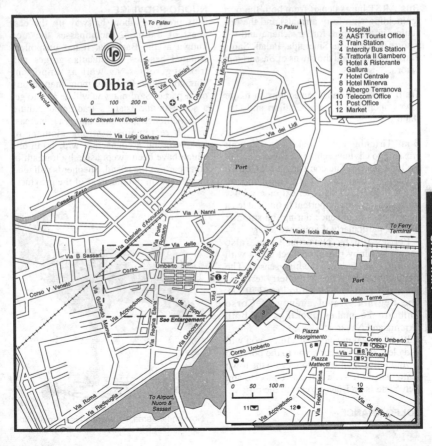

1	Hospital
2	AAST Tourist Office
3	Train Station
4	Intercity Bus Station
5	Trattoria Il Gambero
6	Hotel & Ristorante Gallura
7	Hotel Centrale
8	Hotel Minerva
9	Albergo Terranova
10	Telecom Office
11	Post Office
12	Market

SARDINIA

off Piazza Matteotti; a full meal will cost over L30,000. One of Olbia's better restaurants is the *Ristorante Gallura* at the Hotel Gallura, Corso Umberto 145; a full meal here will cost around L60,000.

Getting There & Away

Air Olbia's airport, a few km south-east of the town, services domestic flights to and from Italy's main cities. There is an airport check-in terminal in the town centre on the corner of Corso Umberto and Via XX Settembre. City bus No 2 heads from here to the airport.

Bus ARST buses depart from both the port (coinciding with ferry arrivals) and the bus station in the centre for Arzachena and the resorts of the Costa Smeralda, Palau, Santa Teresa Gallura, and the towns of Sassari and Nuoro.

Train There are train connections to major towns, including Sassari, Cagliari and Oristano.

Boat Tirrenia ferries make the 7½-hour crossing to Civitavecchia five times a day in the high season. The company has an office at the ferry terminal and at Corso Umberto 17 (☎ 2 46 91). This is an extremely busy route and it is very important to book at least three weeks in advance during the summer months, particularly if you have a car.

Ferries run by Navarma Lines (also known as Moby Lines) connect Olbia with Livorno twice a day in the high season. The company has an office at the ferry terminal and another at Corso Umberto 1 (☎ 2 79 27). The Segintur travel agency at Corso Umberto 26 makes bookings for both Tirrenia and Navarma.

If you are taking a car on a ferry, you will find clear signs directing you to the port and to your point of embarkation. From the town centre, head for Viale Principe Umberto and then Viale Isola Bianca to reach the port.

GOLFO ARANCI

This place is on the promontory north-east

of Olbia. Ferries run by the FS from Civitavecchia dock here. There is a ferry terminal from where you can catch a train directly to Olbia, or an ARST bus to Olbia, Palau or Santa Teresa Gallura. It is possible, for instance, to buy a ticket in Rome (at Stazione Termini or any Sestante CIT office) which covers the cost of the train trip to Civitavecchia, the ferry crossing and the train to Olbia.

Eastern Sardinia

NUORO PROVINCE

This province, about halfway up the east coast of Sardinia, encompasses the area known as the Barbagia. It has unspoiled, isolated beaches, spectacular gorges and trekking routes, as well as important Nuraghic sites. Probably more than in any other part of Sardinia, you will be able to get a sense of the island's traditional culture here. Although tourism in the area is increasing, there remains a strong element of isolation, and a connection with traditions which have been swept aside by tourism in other parts of the island. Shepherds still tend their flocks in remote areas of the province,

Now endangered, the Mouflon is a small wild sheep found in the mountains of Sardinia.

often living alone in stone or wooden shacks and having little contact with the outside world. It is common to see older women in the traditional black, ankle-length dresses of the area, their heads covered by Spanish-style black, fringed shawls, sometimes with beautiful coloured embroidery.

The locals remain fairly aloof and it is important when visiting the smaller, more remote towns of the area to behave respectfully. If you manage to befriend a local, you will find them incredibly hospitable and helpful.

Larger towns in the area are accessible by bus, but a car is really a necessity to explore the smaller villages and the mountains. One surprisingly cheap way to explore the area is by trekking with an organised guide.

Nuoro is the capital of the province and the gateway to areas such as: Oliena and the Sopramonte; Dorgali and the beautiful coastline around Cala Gonone; the town of Orgosolo, famous for its tradition of banditry; and the Gennargentu mountain range.

Nuoro

There is not a lot to see and do in the town, but it is a good starting point for an exploration of the Barbagia. The old centre of town is around Piazza delle Grazie, Corso Garibaldi and Via Manzoni. PANI buses stop in Via Brigata Sassari, off Piazza Italia near the tourist office. From Piazza delle Grazie walk along Via IV Novembre and Via Dante. ARST buses terminate in Via la Marmora, near the train station. The station is about 15 minutes walk from Piazza delle Grazie along Via la Marmora (turn left as you leave the station).

Information The EPT office (☎ 3 00 83) is at Piazza Italia 9 and is open Monday to Friday from 9 am to 1 pm and 4 to 7 pm. The main post office is in Piazza Crispi, between Corso Garibaldi and Piazza Dante, and there is a Telecom office at Via Brigata Sassari 6. The town's telephone code is 0784.

Things to See While in town, take a look at the neoclassical **cathedral** in Piazza Santa

Maria della Neve, and the monument and square dedicated to the local poet Sebastiano Satta. Well worth a visit is the **Museo della Vita e delle Tradizioni Popolari Sardi** (Museum of the Life & Traditions of the Sardinian People), at Via Antonio Mereu 56, south of the cathedral. Open from 9 am to 1 pm and 3 to 7 pm, the museum houses a collection of traditional costumes and masks.

Places to Stay There are no rock-bottom budget options, but you could try *Il Portico* (☎ 3 75 35) at Via Mannu 1, off Corso Garibaldi, where singles/doubles cost L40,000/50,000. *Mini Hotel* (☎ 3 31 59), Via Brofferio 13, is a pleasant little place which has singles/doubles with bathroom for L55,000/75,000. It is off Via Roma, near Piazza Sebastiano Satta). *Hotel Grillo* (☎ 3 86 78), Via Monsignor Melas 14, is in an ugly building, but its rooms are pleasant. Singles/doubles with bathroom are L65,000/87,000, and triples are L118,000.

Places to Eat To pick up supplies, shop at the Conad supermarket in Via Trieste, just near Piazza Italia, or at the great little grocery shop at Corso Garibaldi 168 and the cheese shop next door. *Pizzeria/Trattoria Da Chicchino*, Via Brofferio 31 (along Via Cattaneo from Piazza S Satta, serves good meals at reasonable prices. Otherwise try *Pizzeria del Diavolo*, Corso Garibaldi 134.

Getting There & Away ARST buses connect Nuoro with Cagliari (two a day), Olbia (six a day) and Sassari (three a day), as well as with towns throughout the province, including Oliena (hourly), Orgosolo (10 a day), Dorgali and Cala Gonone (seven a day), and Baunei (two a day). PANI buses head for Cagliari, Sassari and Oristano.

Oliena

The value of visiting Oliena, or Orgosolo farther south (see the following section), is to get a better idea of how people live in Sardinia's interior. Neither town offers much in the way of tourist facilities or sights,

SARDINIA

although both, in their own way, provide an 'alternative' travel experience.

Oliena is about 12 km south-west of Nuoro and easily accessible from there by regular ARST bus. For the more adventurous, it is a place from which to set out on a trekking exploration of the Sopramonte area to the south, and to the isolated Nuraghic site at **Tiscali**, either alone or with a guide.

For information on guided treks, contact Viaggi nel Mondo (☎ 06-581 63 65), Via Cino da Pistoia 7, in Rome. Otherwise contact one of the local guides directly by ringing ☎ 0784-28 80 24 in Oliena. Ask for Murena, a guide who operates a rifugio near Tiscali and can take you on a three-day trek from there, through the Gola di Gorropu (see the Cala Gonone section) to the beach at Cala di Luna, where you will camp for several days. He doesn't speak English, but this shouldn't be a problem, particularly if you do all the organising through the Rome office, which may be able to organise for a translator to accompany your group.

Another group organises guided tours to out-of-the-way areas in the Barbagia by Land Rover, as well as on foot. Called Barbagia Insolita, the group can be contacted on ☎ 0784-28 81 67 and has offices at Via Carducci 25, Oliena. You can choose between demanding treks or relaxing walks to places including Tiscali, the Gola di Gorropu, Monte Corrasi and the Codula di Luna.

Places to Stay Accommodation options are limited. Try *Ci Kappa* (☎ 0784-28 87 33), Via Martin Luther King, which has singles/doubles for L60,000/80,000. It also has a good pizzeria/restaurant. A few km east of town, near the beautiful Lanaittu valley, is *Su Gologone* (☎ 0784-28 75 12). In a lovely setting, the hotel is a good option for people wanting to explore the area, because it organises guided tours and treks as well as horse-riding expeditions. Singles/doubles cost L80,000/115,000 with bathroom, half board costs up to L108,000 and full board up to L140,000. Its restaurant serves excellent

traditional local dishes and is justifiably renowned throughout the island.

Orgosolo

About 18 km farther south, Orgosolo is famous for its tradition of *banditismo* (banditry), although this is not a subject you will find the locals willing to discuss openly. This tradition was immortalised by the 1963 Italian film *The Bandits of Orgosolo*. One of the town's more notorious *banditi* was released from prison in 1992 and acted as an unofficial negotiator in the much-publicised kidnapping of the son of a Costa Smeralda hotelier (and a relative of the Aga Khan). The child was eventually released in the countryside close to the town.

Orgosolo is also interesting for the series of leftist and nationalistic murals which decorate the façades of many of its buildings. The idea of a local art teacher, Francesco del Casino, a native of Siena who has lived in Orgósolo for many years, the murals started appearing in 1973. Generally designed by him, they have been painted by local students as well as other artists. Originally reflecting fairly extreme political views on a range of international issues, such as Vietnam, South Africa and the Palestinian question, the murals now deal mainly with social issues.

Orgosolo is accessible by ARST bus from Nuoro.

Places to Stay & Eat Try the *Petit Hotel* (☎ 0784-40 20 09), Via Mannu, which has singles/doubles for L40,000/55,000 with bathroom. Just out of town is *Ai Monti del Gennargentu* (☎ 0784-40 23 74), which has doubles for L55,000 with bathroom.

A local group organises lunches in the country just out of the town, where you can enjoy one of Sardinia's most traditional dishes, porcheddu (roast sucking pig). The travel agency Avitur (☎ 0789-2 43 27), Corso Vittorio Emanuele 139 in Olbia, organises guided trips by bus to Orgosolo, including the lunch, for L70,000 a head. Otherwise you can arrange to attend a lunch by contacting the organisers in Orgosolo directly (☎ 0784-

40 20 71). The cost for lunch only is L30,000 a head.

Cala Gonone & Around

This fast-developing seaside resort is an excellent base from which to explore the coves along the coastline, as well as the Nuraghic sites and rugged terrain inland.

There is a Pro Loco tourist office (☎ 0784-9 33 87) at the port, where you can pick up maps, a list of hotels, and information to help you explore the area. There is also a tourist office in the nearby town of Dorgali, which you will probably need to pass through on your way to Cala Gonone. It is in Via Lamarmora (☎ 0784-9 62 43). The telephone code for Cala Gonone is 0784.

If you are travelling by car, you will need a detailed road map of the area. One of the best is published by the Istituto Geografico de Agostini. The tourist office has maps which detail the locations of the main sights.

Things to See & Do From Cala Gonone's small port, catch a boat to the **Grotta del Bue Marino** (Cave of the Monk Seal), where a guide will take you on a one-km walk to see vast caves with stalagmites, stalactites and lakes. The caves were one of the last habitats of the rare monk seal, but the colony has not been sighted for some years. The return boat trip plus entrance to the caves costs L16,000.

Boats also leave for the beautiful **Cala di Luna** (L15,000), an isolated beach accessible only by boat or on foot, where you can spend the day on the beach (a combined return fare for the grotta and Cala di Luna is L25,000). In August the beach is crowded with day-tripping sunbathers, but at other times it is quite deserted. If the weather is unsuitable for swimming, take a walk along the **Codula di Luna**, a long valley stretching from Cala di Luna almost to Urzulei. Other boats head farther along the coast to the beach at **Cala Sisine** (this costs L21,000). There is a walking track along the coast linking Cala Gonone and Cala di Luna (about two hours).

At the Dorgali tourist office you can pick up information about walking trails in the area, including how to reach the Nuraghic village of **Tiscali** (see the section on Oliena earlier).

If you want to explore the spectacular **Gola di Gorropu** (Gorropu Gorge) about 15 km south of Dorgali, you may want to seek information from the Dorgali tourist office about hiring a guide, since it is necessary to use ropes and harnesses to traverse sections of the gorge when descending. However, it is possible to walk into the gorge from its northern entrance for about one km before it becomes impossible to proceed.

To get to the entrance, head south from Dorgali along the road for Urzulei for a couple of km. After the turn-off to the left for Cala Gonone, there is a dirt road to the right, which heads for the Hotel Sant'Elene (see under Places to Stay). Following the dirt road down into the valley for about eight km (don't head uphill for the hotel), you'll get to a small bridge where it is necessary to park the car and continue on foot. After walking for about an hour and a half, you'll reach two small lakes and the entrance to the gorge – one of the most spectacular and romantic environments in Sardinia. The huge boulders scattered around the entrance to the gorge are a reminder that nature can be harsh as well as beautiful in Sardinia. Even if you have your own car, allow a full day for the expedition, which will give you enough time for the walk, a picnic and a swim in the lakes. If you're on foot, but want to explore the gorge, you could stay at the Hotel Sant'Elene and walk to its entrance from there.

The Gruppo Ricerche Ambientali (☎ 9 34 24 at Cala Gonone and ☎ 9 61 78 at Dorgali) organises guided treks in the Gola di Gorropu, the Codula di Luna, as well as in sections of the Grotta del Bue Marino not open to the public. There are several Nuraghic sites in the area and, once again, the Dorgali tourist office can provide maps and advice on how to reach them. See also the Oliena section for information about a guided trek that approaches this area from the west.

Boat Marine Charter (☎ 9 69 52), Via Cavour 3, or at the port, runs charter-boat

SARDINIA

cruises for one day or for longer periods. If you are interested in diving courses, contact the Lupo di Mare Diving Club (☎ 9 32 33) c/o Il Bottegone, Viale Bue Marino (in summer only).

Places to Stay & Eat Try *Camping Cala Gonone* (☎ 9 31 65), Via Collodi 1, which charges up to L19,900 per person. Free camping is strictly forbidden throughout the area.

Hotels include the *Bue Marino* (☎ 9 31 30), Via Vespucci, which has singles/doubles for L45,000/60,000, and the *Gabbiano* (☎ 9 31 30) at the port, with rooms for L35,000/50,000. *Piccolo Hotel* (☎ 9 32 32), Via Cristoforo Colombo, near the port, has very pleasant rooms for L60,000/95,000 with bathroom. *Hotel La Playa* (☎ 9 35 34), Via Collodi, is more up-market; its rooms cost up to L85,000/120,000.

Just out of Dorgali, at Monte Sant'Elene, is the *Hotel Sant'Elene* (☎ 9 45 72), Località Sant'Elene, set in a panoramic position. Singles/doubles are L40,000/80,000, triples L103,000. It also has an excellent restaurant with a reasonably priced tourist menu.

Due Chiacchiere is a trattoria/pizzeria overlooking the sea at Via Acquadolce 13, near the port in Cala Gonone; a full meal will cost around L25,000. More expensive is the nearby *Ristorante Il Pescatore*, where you will pay around L35,000 or more.

Getting There & Away An ARST bus will get you from Nuoro to Cala Gonone, via Dorgali. ARST buses also connect Cala Gonone with the town of Oliena. It should be noted that services are drastically reduced to Cala Gonone out of season. From Dorgali you can also reach Baunei on an ARST bus.

Baunei

The reason for coming to this small village between Urzulei and Arbatax is to explore the high plain and valley around the ancient **Chiesa di San Pietro**. This beautiful area has an almost magical atmosphere; here you can see evidence of an ancient Mediterra-

nean civilisation. The rustic church, for centuries a place of pilgrimage, stands isolated in the countryside and is surrounded by a wall lined with pilgrims' shelters. Nearby are the Nuraghic *betili*, single, conical-shaped sacred stones which were carved to indicate feminine forms.

To get to the church from Baunei, you need to take a small dirt road north from the centre of town. A sign indicates San Pietro, but you'll probably need to ask directions. It is about 8 km to the church. On the way is *Golgo* (☎ 0337-81 18 28), a camping ground and restaurant, designed to blend into its natural surroundings. You can stay here for L7000 a day if you want to explore the area. It also has a good restaurant, where a filling, traditional-style Sardinian meal will cost up to L35,000. The complex opens from Easter to the end of September.

From the church a trail continues on for more than 10 km to Cala Sisine; otherwise head back to Golgo and take the walking trail down to the sea at Cala Goloritze (one hour). The beauty of the scenery will really take your breath away.

Baunei is accessible by ARST bus from Nuoro, Dorgali and Cagliari.

Arbatax

Not far from Baunei, towards Cagliari, is the small port town of Arbatax. If you're planning to explore the Barbagia, this is probably the most convenient place to arrive by ferry. Tirrenia ferries dock here from Civitavecchia twice a week. If you're heading north to Baunei, Cala Gonone, Dorgali, Nuoro etc, you will need to either catch an ARST bus, or walk the four km to Tortoli, from where you can catch the direct once-daily ARST bus for Nuoro. In 1995 the bus left from Tortoli at 3.30 pm, but it is probably best to check at the tourist office in Dorgali or Nuoro for precise, up-to-date information. Buses leave from Arbatax for Cagliari two or three times a day, not necessarily coinciding with ferry arrivals. Another, more interesting option, would be to take the Trenino Verde to Cagliari (see under Getting There & Away in the Cagliari section for information). If you get stuck, try the *Supersonic* hotel (☎ 0782-62 35 12), in the Porto Frailis area, a few km from Arbatax, which has doubles with bathroom for L70,000.

Central Sardinia

AROUND SU NURAXI

There are innumerable Nuraghic sites on the island, but some of the most interesting are in the interior and are often very difficult to reach without your own transport. The most important is the **Su Nuraxi** fortress, one km west of Barumini, about 60 km north of Cagliari. This vast complex consists of a castle and village. It is open from 8 am to about 6 pm, but on a day trip you will probably spend most of your time travelling if you need to use public transport.

A better option than spending hours trying to juggle bus timetables is to head for the nearby town of Gergei (10 km east of Barumini) and the delightful *Hotel Dedoni* (☎ 0782-80 80 60), Via Marconi 50. The hotel offers a very high standard of accommodation at reasonable prices: L40,000 per person for B&B, L64,000 per person for half board and L73,000 for full board. The hotel organises excursions in the area.

Although Gergei itself is a pretty anonymous place, it is a perfect base from which to explore the Su Nuraxi site, as well as the nearby plain of **Giara di Gesturi**, inhabited by wild ponies. East of Gergei is the **Giara di Serri**, a high-plain area which, like the Giara di Gesturi, is a great place for hiking. Also in this area is the Nuraghic sanctuary of **Santa Vittoria di Serri**, less well-known than Su Nuraxi, but certainly worth visiting. Of particular interest in this ancient complex is the *recinto delle feste*, a large enclosure lined with small 'rooms' where, it is believed, cult objects and other goods were displayed and sold. A few km south of Barumini, off the road for Cagliari, are the spiky ruins of a 12th-century castle, protruding from the **Las Plássas hill**.

There is an ARST bus from Cagliari to Barumini, but to return you will need to catch an FDS bus to Sanluri and then an ARST bus to Cagliari. FDS buses also serve Gergei. To avoid being stranded, check the latest bus timetables at the Cagliari tourist office. The Trenino Verde (Green Train) which runs between Cagliari and Arbatax passes nearby at Mandas. The section between Mandas and Arbatax is the most scenic part of the railway, so it might be worthwhile catching the train there if you have the time. See under Getting There & Away in the Cagliari section for information.

SARDINIA

Glossary

AAST – Azienda Autonoma di Soggiorno e Turismo, the local tourist office

acque alte – high tides (Venice)

ACI – Automobile Club Italiano, the Italian automobile club

aereo – aeroplane

affittacamere – rooms for rent (cheaper than a pensione, not part of classification system)

affresco – fresco; the painting method in which watercolour paint is applied to wet plaster

agriturismo – tourist accommodation on farms

AIG – Associazione Italiana Alberghi per la Gioventù, the Italian youth hostel association

albergo – hotel (up to five stars)

albergo diurno – day hotel, with public bathing facilities

alimentari – grocery shop

aliscafo – hydrofoil

alloggio – lodging (cheaper than a pensione, not part of the classification system)

alto – high

ambulanza – ambulance

anfiteatro – amphitheatre

appartamento – apartment, flat

apse – domed or arched area at the altar end of a church

APT – Azienda di Promozione Turistica, the provincial tourist office

arco – arch

assicurata/o – insured

atrium – forecourt of a Roman house or a Christian basilica

autobus – bus

autostazione – bus station/terminal

autostop – hitchhiking

autostrada – freeway, motorway

bagno – bathroom; also toilet

baldacchino – canopy supported by columns over the altar in a church

basilica – in ancient Rome, a building used for public administration, with a rectangular hall flanked by aisles and an apse at the end; later, a Christian church built in the same style

battistero – baptistry

benzina – petrol

bicicletta – bicycle

biglietteria – ticket office

biglietto – ticket

binario – platform

bivacco – unattended hut

borgo – ancient town/village

broletto – town hall

busta – envelope

cabinovia – two-seater cable car

CAI – Club Alpino Italiano, for information on hiking and mountain refuges

calle – street (Venice)

camera – room

camera doppia – double room with twin beds

camera singola – single bed

camera matrimoniale – double room with a double bed

campanile – bell tower

cappella – chapel

carabinieri – military police (see *polizia*)

carta marmorizzata – marbled paper

carta telefonica – telephone card

cartoleria – paper-goods shop

cartolina – postcard

casa dello studente – accommodation for students available on campus during holidays

casa religione di ospitalità – accommodation in religous institutions in cities and in monasteries in the country

castello – castle

cattedrale – cathedral

cena – evening meal

centro – centre

centro storico – (literally, historical centre) old town

chiesa – church

chiostro – cloister; covered walkway,

usually enclosed by columns, around a quadrangle

cichetti – finger food

cinquecento – sixteenth century

circo – oval or circular arena

CIT – Compagnia Italiana di Turismo, the Italian national tourist/travel agency

codice fiscale – tax number

colazione – breakfast

colonna – column

comune – equivalent to a municipality or county; town or city council; historically, a commune (self-governing town or city)

contrada – district

coperto – cover charge

corso – main street, avenue

cortile – courtyard

CTS – the student/youth travel agency, Centro Turistico Studentesco e Giovanile

cupola – dome

deposito bagagli – baggage deposit

digestivo – afgter dinner liqueur

distributore di benzina – petrol pump (see *stazione di servizio*)

duomo – cathedral

ENIT – Ente Nazionale Italiano per il Turismo, the Italian state tourist office

EPT – Ente Provinciale per il Turismo, the provincial tourist office

espresso – express mail; express train; short black coffee

farmacia – pharmacy

farmacia di turno – late-night pharmacy

ferramenta – hardware shop

ferrovia – train station

festa – festival

fiume – river

fondamenta – street beside a canal

fontana – fountain

foro – forum

francobollo – postage stamp

fresco – see *affresco*

FS – Ferrovie dello Stato, the Italian state railway

funicolare – funicular railway

funivia – cable car

gabinetto – toilet, WC

gettoni – telephone tokens

golfo – gulf

grotta – cave

intarsia – inlaid wood, marble or metal

lago – lake

largo – (small) square

lavanderia – laundrette

lavasecco – dry-cleaning

lettera – letter

lettera raccomandata – registered letter

lido – beach

locanda – inn, small hotel (cheaper than a pensione)

loggia – covered area on the side of a building; porch

lo sci – downhill skiing

lungomare – road along the seafront; promenade

malghe – Alpine huts where graziers make butter and cheese in summer

mare – sea

merceria – haberdashery shop

mercato – market

monte – mountain, mount

motorino – moped

motoscafo – motorboat

municipio – town hall

navata centrale – nave; central part of a church

navata laterale – aisle of a church

nave – ship

necropolis – (ancient) cemetery, burial site

oggetti smarriti – lost property

ospedale – hospital

ostello – hostel

osteria – snack bar/cheap restaurant

pacco – package, parcel

palazzo – palace; a large building of any type, including an apartment block

panino – bread roll with filling

parco – park

passaggio ponte – deck class

passeggiata – traditional evening stroll

pasta – cake; pasta; pastry or dough
pasticceria – shop selling cakes, pastries and biscuits
pensione – small hotel, often with board
permesso di soggiorno – work permit
piazza – square
piazzale – (large) open square
pietà – (literally, pity or compassion) sculpture, drawing or painting of the dead Christ supported by the Madonna
polizia – police
poltrona – (literally, armchair) airline-type chair on a ferry
polyptych – altarpiece consisting of more than three panels (see *triptych*)
ponte – bridge
portico – portico; covered walkway, usually attached to the outside of buildings
porto – port
posta aerea, via aerea – airmail
presepio – nativity scene
pronto soccorso – first aid, casualty ward

quattrocento – fifteenth century
questura – police station

raccomandata – recorded delivery
resentin – coffee in a grappa-rinsed cup
rifugio – mountain/Alpine refuge
rio terrà – a street following the course of a filled in canal
riva – river bank
riva alta – high river bank
rivo – a stream
rocca – fortress

sagra – festival
salumeria – delicatessen
santuario – sanctuary
sassi – stone houses
scalinata – stairway
scavi – excavations
sci di fondo – cross-country skiing
sci alpinismo – ski mountaineering
seicento – seventeenth century
Settimana Bianca – White Week: a skiing package deal combining accommodation, food and lift ticket
servizio – service fee

sestiere – city sections
sottoportego – street continuing under a building (like an extended archway)
spiaggia – beach
spiaggia libera – public beach
stazione – station
stazione di servizio – service/petrol station
stazione marittima – ferry terminal
strada – street, road
suoni e lumi – sound & light show
superstrada – expressway; highway with divided lanes

teatro – theatre
telamoni – large statues of men, used as columns in temples
telegramma – telegram
tempio – temple
terme – thermal baths
tesoro – treasury
tombaroli – tomb robbers
torre – tower
torrente – stream
traghetto – ferry
tramezzini – sandwiches
trattoria – cheap restaurant
travertino – travertine; light-coloured limestone, used extensively as a building material in both ancient and modern Rome because of large deposits in the area
treno – train
triptych – painting or carving on three panels, hinged so that the outer panels fold over the middle one, often used as an altarpiece (see *polyptych*)
trompe l'oeil – painting or other illustration designed to 'deceive the eye', creating the impression that the image is real

ufficio postale – post office
ufficio stranieri – (police) foreigners' bureau

via – street, road
via ferrata – climbing trail with permanent steel cables to aid walkers
via aerea – air mail
villa – detached house, country house; also the park surrounding the house

Index

MAPS

Thanks

We greatly appreciate the contributions of the many people who put so much effort into writing and telling us of their weird and wonderful experiences. Writers (apologies if we've misspelt your name) to whom thanks must go include:

Olle Andersson (Sw), Spiro Angeli (USA), Ro Lee Azzurri (I), Daniela Bertulu (I), Nadean & Gary Burington (USA), Peter Coppard (UK), Eda Crespan (I), Caoimhghin Croidheain (IRE), Pier D'Angelo (Aus), Lisa Ann di Fruscia (C), Patrizia Diletti (I), Andrew Edwards (UK), Linda Elliott (UK), Vindy Ghura (UK), Dair Grant (UK), James Graziano (USA), Bridget Hallam (UK), Ann Hay (UK), Theresa Hill (USA), M G Hollick (UK), Nicole Horne (Aus), Olwyn Jones (Aus), Joan Loh (I), Francesco Melillo (I), Alan Morrison (UK), Silvia Pasut (I), Eliane Ponza (I), Gilliam Price (I), Steve Ritchie, Ingino Rossi (I), Paul Rowlands (I), Jean Santacroce (I), Marco Saracino (I), Alfonso Sasson (I), Neiger Shmulik (I), Lucy Spivey (UK), Gayle Steinsdoerfer (USA), Heidi Stenning (UK), T W N (I), B Vajda (H), Libreria Il Viaggio (I), Lynda Wake (Aus), N F Whitehouse (NZ), Michael Williams (AUS), E J & Martin Williams (UK), George Winterton (Aus), Miss M Wire (UK), Janice Wittig (USA), A Quattrocchi (I), Arianna Andreani (I), Jenny Chua (HK), Kelly Noble (D), Margot Ludowici (Aus), Martin Pagel (USA), Mr J W Allen (UK), Mrs Lucille Hartshorne (Aus), Ron Edwards (UK), Ryan Spruston (UK), Sanjeev Mohan (Aus), Tom Spruetels (B), Wanda Auerbach (USA)

Aus – Australia, C – Canada, D – Denmark, I – Italy, NZ – New Zealand, Sw – Sweden, UK – United Kingdom, USA – United States of America

LONELY PLANET TV SERIES & VIDEOS

Lonely Planet travel guides have been brought to life on television screens around the world. Like our guides, the programmes are based on the joy of independent travel, and look honestly at some of the most exciting, picturesque and frustrating places in the world. Each show is presented by one of three travellers from Australia, England or the USA and combines an innovative mixture of video, Super-8 film, atmospheric soundscapes and original music.

Videos of each episode – containing additional footage not shown on television – are available from good book and video shops, but the availability of individual videos varies with regional screening schedules.

Video destinations include:
Alaska; Australia (Southeast); Brazil; Ecuador & the Galapagos Islands; Indonesia; Israel & the Sinai Desert; Japan; La Ruta Maya (Yucatan, Guatemala & Belize); Morocco; North India (Varanasi to the Himalaya); Pacific Islands; Vietnam; Zimbabwe, Botswana & Namibia.

Coming in 1996:
The Arctic (Norway & Finland); Baja California; Chile & Easter Island; China (Southeast); Costa Rica; East Africa (Tanzania & Zanzibar); Great Barrier Reef (Australia); Jamaica; Papua New Guinea; the Rockies (USA); Syria & Jordan; Turkey.

The Lonely Planet television series is produced by:
Pilot Productions
Duke of Sussex Studios
44 Uxbridge St
London W8 7TG
United Kingdom

Lonely Planet videos are distributed by:
IVN Communications Inc
2246 Camino Ramon, San Ramon
California 94583, USA

107 Power Road, Chiswick
London W4 5PL, UK

For further information on both the television series and the availability of individual videos please contact Lonely Planet.

PLANET TALK
Lonely Planet's FREE quarterly newsletter

We love hearing from you and think you'd like to hear from us.

When...*is the right time to see reindeer in Finland?*
Where...*can you hear the best palm-wine music in Ghana?*
How...*do you get from Asunción to Areguá by steam train?*
What...*is the best way to see India?*

For the answer to these and many other questions read PLANET TALK.

Every issue is packed with up-to-date travel news and advice including:

- *a letter from Lonely Planet founders Tony and Maureen Wheeler*
- *travel diary from a Lonely Planet author - find out what it's really like out on the road*
- *feature article on an important and topical travel issue*
- *a selection of recent letters from our readers*
- *the latest travel news from all over the world*
- *details on Lonely Planet's new and forthcoming releases*

To join our mailing list contact any Lonely Planet office.

Also available: Lonely Planet T-shirts. 100% heavyweight cotton (S, M, L, XL)

LONELY PLANET PUBLICATIONS
Australia: PO Box 617, Hawthorn 3122, Victoria
tel: (03) 9819 1877 fax: (03) 9819 6459 e-mail: talk2us@lonelyplanet.com.au

USA: Embarcadero West, 155 Filbert St, Suite 251, Oakland, CA 94607
tel: (510) 893 8555 TOLL FREE: 800 275-8555 fax: (510) 893 8563
e-mail: info@lonelyplanet.com

UK: 10 Barley Mow Passage, Chiswick, London W4 4PH
tel: (0181) 742 3161 fax: (0181) 742 2772 e-mail: 100413.3551@compuserve.com

France: 71 bis rue du Cardinal Lemoine – 75005 Paris
tel: 1 46 34 00 58 fax: 1 46 34 72 55 e-mail: 100560.415@compuserve.com

World Wide Web: http://www.lonelyplanet.com/

Guides to Europe

Central Europe on a shoestring
From the snow-capped peaks of the Austrian Alps, the medieval castles of Hungary and the vast forests of Poland to the festivals of Germany, the arty scene in Prague and picturesque lakes of Switzerland, this guide is packed with practical travel advice to help you make the most of your visit. This new shoestring guide covers travel in Austria, Czech Republic, Germany, Hungary, Liechtenstein, Poland, Slovakia and Switzerland.

Eastern Europe on a shoestring
This guide has opened up a whole new world for travellers – Albania, Bulgaria, Czech Republic, eastern Germany, Hungary, Poland, Romania, Slovakia and the former republics of Yugoslavia.
'...a thorough, well-researched book. Only a fool would go East without it.' – *Great Expeditions*

Mediterranean Europe on a shoestring
Details on hundreds of galleries, museums and architectural masterpieces and information on outdoor activities including hiking, sailing and skiing. Information on travelling in Albania, Andorra, Cyprus, France, Greece, Italy, Malta, Morocco, Portugal, Spain, Tunisia, Turkey and the former republics of Yugoslavia.

Scandinavian & Baltic Europe on a shoestring
A comprehensive guide to travelling in this region including details on galleries, festivals and museums, as well as outdoor activities, national parks and wildlife. Countries featured are Denmark, Estonia, the Faroe Islands, Finland, Iceland, Latvia, Lithuania, Norway and Sweden.

Western Europe on a shoestring
This long-awaited guide covers all of Western Europe's well-loved sights and provides routes for cycling and driving tours, plus details on hiking, climbing and skiing. All the travel facts on Andorra, Austria, Belgium, Britain, France, Germany, Greece, Ireland, Italy, Liechtenstein, Luxembourg, Netherlands, Portugal, Spain and Switzerland.

Baltic States & Kaliningrad – travel survival kit
The Baltic States burst on to the world scene almost from nowhere in the late 1980s. Now that travellers are free to move around the region they will discover nations with a rich and colourful history and culture, and a welcoming attitude to all travellers.

Britain – travel survival kit
Britain remains one of the most beautiful islands in the world. All the words, paintings and pictures that you have read and seen are not just romantic exaggerations. This comprehensive guide will help you to discover and enjoy this ever-popular destination.

Czech & Slovak Republics – travel survival kit
The Czech and Slovak Republics are two of the most exciting travel destinations in Europe. This guide is the essential resource for independent travellers. It's full of down-to-earth information and reliable advice for every budget – from five stars to five dollars a day.

Dublin – city guide
Where to enjoy a pint of Guinness and a plate of Irish stew, where to see spectacular Georgian architecture or experience Irish hospitality – Dublin city guide will ensure you won't miss out on anything.

Finland – travel survival kit
Finland is an intriguing blend of Swedish and Russian influences. With its medieval stone castles, picturesque wooden houses, vast forest and lake district, and interesting wildlife, it is a wonderland to delight any traveller.

France – travel survival kit
Stylish, diverse, celebrated by romantics and revolutionaries alike, France is a destination that's always in fashion. A comprehensive guide packed with invaluable advice.

Greece – travel survival kit
Famous ruins, secluded beaches, sumptuous food, sun-drenched islands, ancient pathways and much more are covered in this comprehensive guide to this ever-popular destination.

Hungary – travel survival kit
Formerly seen as the gateway to eastern Europe, Hungary is a romantic country of music, wine and folklore. This guide contains detailed background information on Hungary's cultural and historical past as well as practical advice on the many activities available to travellers.

Iceland, Greenland & the Faroe Islands – travel survival kit
Iceland, Greenland & the Faroe Islands contain some of the most beautiful wilderness areas in the world. This practical guidebook will help travellers discover the dramatic beauty of this region, no matter what their budget.

Ireland – travel survival kit
Ireland is one of Europe's least 'spoilt' countries. Green, relaxed and welcoming, it does not take travellers long before they feel at ease. An entertaining and comprehensive guide to this troubled country.

Poland – travel survival kit
With the collapse of communism, Poland has opened up to travellers, revealing a rich cultural heritage. This guide will help you make the most of this safe and friendly country.

Prague – city guide
Since the 'Velvet Revolution' in 1989, Prague and its residents have grasped their freedom with a youthful exuberance, even frenzy. This thoroughly comprehensive guide will show you the sights and hidden delights of this vivacious city.

Switzerland – travel survival kit
Ski enthusiasts and chocolate addicts know two excellent reasons for heading to Switzerland. This travel survival kit gives travellers many more: jazz, cafés, boating trips...and the Alps of course!

Trekking in Greece
Mountainous landscape, the solitude of ancient pathways and secluded beaches await those who dare to extend their horizons beyond Athens and the antiquities. Covers the main trekking regions and includes contoured maps of trekking routes.

Trekking in Spain
Aimed at both overnight trekkers and day hikers, this guidebook includes useful maps and full details on hikes in some of Spain's most beautiful wilderness areas.

Trekking in Turkey
Few people are aware that Turkey boasts mountains with walks to rival those found in Nepal. This book gives details on treks that are destined to become as popular as those further east.

Turkey – a travel survival kit
This acclaimed guide takes you from Istanbul bazaars to Mediterranean beaches, from historic battle-grounds to the stamping grounds of St Paul, Alexander the Great, Emperor Constantine and King Croesus.

USSR – travel survival kit
Invaluable advice on getting around and beating red tape for individual and group travellers alike. This comprehensive guide includes an unsanitised historical background and complete information on art and culture. Over 130 reliable maps, and all place names are given in Cyrillic script. Includes the independent states.

Vienna – city guide
There's so much to see and do in Vienna and this guide is the best way to ensure you enjoy it all.

Also available:
Central Europe phrasebook
Languages in this book cover travel in Austria, the Czech Republic, France, Germany, Hungary, Italy, Liechtenstein, Slovakia and Switzerland.

Eastern Europe phrasebook
Discover the most enjoyable way to get around and make friends in Bulgarian, Czech, Hungarian, Polish, Romanian and Slovak.

Mediterranean Europe phrasebook
Ask for directions to the galleries and museums in Albanian, Greek, Italian, Macedonian, Maltese, Serbian & Croatian and Slovene.

Scandinavian Europe phrasebook
Find your way around the ski trails and enjoy the local festivals in Danish, Finnish, Icelandic, Norwegian and Swedish.

Western Europe phrasebook
Show your appreciation for the great masters in Basque, Catalan, Dutch, French, German, Irish, Portuguese and Spanish (Castilian).

Baltic States phrasebook
Essential words and phrases in Estonian, Latvian and Lithuanian.

Greek phrasebook
Catch a *ferrybot* to the islands, laze the day away on a golden *baralia*, and say *stin iyia sas!* as you raise your glass to the setting sun... you can explore *tin acropoli* another day.

Moroccan Arabic phrasebook
Essential words and phraes for everything from finding a hotel room in Casablanca to asking for a meal of *tajine* in Marrakesh. Includes Arabic script and pronunciation guide.

Russian phrasebook
This indispensable phrasebook will help you get information, read signs and menus, and make friends along the way. Includes phonetic transcriptions and Cyrillic script.

Turkish phrasebook
Practical words and phrases that will help you to communicate effectively with local people in almost every situation. Includes pronunciation guide.

Lonely Planet Guidebooks

Lonely Planet guidebooks cover every accessible part of Asia as well as Australia, the Pacific, South America, Africa, the Middle East, Europe and parts of North America. There are six series: *travel survival kits*, covering a country for a range of budgets; *shoestring guides* with compact information for low-budget travel in a major region; *walking guides*; *city guides, travel atlases* and *phrasebooks*.

Australia & the Pacific
Australia
Australian phrasebook
Bushwalking in Australia
Islands of Australia's Great Barrier Reef
Outback Australia
Fiji
Fijian phrasebook
Melbourne city guide
Micronesia
New Caledonia
New South Wales & the ACT
New Zealand
Tramping in New Zealand
Papua New Guinea
Bushwalking in Papua New Guinea
Papua New Guinea phrasebook
Queensland
Rarotonga & the Cook Islands
Samoa
Solomon Islands
Sydney city guide
Tahiti & French Polynesia
Tonga
Vanuatu
Victoria
Western Australia

North-East Asia
Beijing city guide
China
Cantonese phrasebook
Mandarin Chinese phrasebook
Hong Kong, Macau & Canton
Japan
Japanese phrasebook
Korea
Korean phrasebook
Mongolia
Mongolian phrasebook
North-East Asia on a shoestring
Seoul city guide
Taiwan
Tibet
Tibet phrasebook
Tokyo city guide

South-East Asia
Bali & Lombok
Bangkok city guide
Cambodia
Indonesia
Indonesian phrasebook
Ho Chi Minh City city guide
Jakarta city guide
Java
Laos
Lao phrasebook
Malaysia, Singapore & Brunei
Myanmar (Burma)
Burmese phrasebook
Philippines
Pilipino phrasebook
Singapore city guide
South-East Asia on a shoestring
Thailand
Thailand travel atlas
Thai phrasebook
Thai Hill Tribes phrasebook
Vietnam
Vietnam travel atlas
Vietnamese phrasebook

Middle East
Arab Gulf States
Egypt & the Sudan
Arabic (Egyptian) phrasebook
Iran
Israel
Jordan & Syria
Middle East
Turkey
Turkish phrasebook
Trekking in Turkey
Yemen

Africa
Africa on a shoestring
Central Africa
East Africa
Trekking in East Africa
Kenya
Swahili phrasebook
Morocco
Arabic (Moroccan) phrasebook
North Africa
South Africa, Lesotho & Swaziland
West Africa
Zimbabwe, Botswana & Namibia
Zimbabwe, Botswana & Namibia travel atlas

Mail Order

Lonely Planet guidebooks are distributed worldwide. They are also available by mail order from Lonely Planet, so if you have difficulty finding a title please write to us. US and Canadian residents should write to Embarcadero West, 155 Filbert St, Suite 251, Oakland CA 94607, USA ; European residents should write to 10 Barley Mow Passage, Chiswick, London W4 4PH; and residents of other countries to PO Box 617, Hawthorn, Victoria 3122, Australia.

Indian Subcontinent
Bangladesh
India
India travel atlas
Hindi/Urdu phrasebook
Trekking in the Indian Himalaya
Karakoram Highway
Kashmir, Ladakh & Zanskar
Nepal
Trekking in the Nepal Himalaya
Nepali phrasebook
Pakistan
Sri Lanka
Sri Lanka phrasebook

Central America & the Caribbean
Baja California
Central America on a shoestring
Costa Rica
Eastern Caribbean
Guatemala, Belize & Yucatán: La Ruta Maya
Mexico

North America
Alaska
Backpacking in Alaska
Canada
Hawaii
Honolulu city guide
Pacific Northwest USA
Rocky Mountain States
Southwest USA
USA phrasebook

Europe
Baltic States & Kaliningrad
Baltics States phrasebook
Britain
Central Europe on a shoestring
Central Europe phrasebook
Czech & Slovak Republics
Dublin city guide
Eastern Europe on a shoestring
Eastern Europe phrasebook
Finland
France
Greece
Greek phrasebook
Hungary
Iceland, Greenland & the Faroe Islands
Ireland
Italy
Mediterranean Europe on a shoestring
Mediterranean Europe phrasebook
Poland
Prague city guide
Scandinavian & Baltic Europe on a shoestring
Scandinavian Europe phrasebook
Slovenia
Switzerland
Trekking in Greece
Trekking in Spain
USSR
Russian phrasebook
Vienna city guide
Western Europe on a shoestring
Western Europe phrasebook

South America
Argentina, Uruguay & Paraguay
Bolivia
Brazil
Brazilian phrasebook
Chile & Easter Island
Colombia
Ecuador & the Galápagos Islands
Latin American Spanish phrasebook
Peru
Quechua phrasebook
Rio de Janeiro city guide
South America on a shoestring
Trekking in the Patagonian Andes
Venezuela

Indian Ocean
Madagascar & Comoros
Maldives & Islands of the East Indian Ocean
Mauritius, Réunion & Seychelles

The Lonely Planet Story

Lonely Planet published its first book in 1973 in response to the numerous 'How did you do it?' questions Maureen and Tony Wheeler were asked after driving, bussing, hitching, sailing and railing their way from England to Australia.

Written at a kitchen table and hand collated, trimmed and stapled, *Across Asia on the Cheap* became an instant local bestseller, inspiring thoughts of another book.

Eighteen months in South-East Asia resulted in their second guide, *South-East Asia on a shoestring*, which they put together in a backstreet Chinese hotel in Singapore in 1975. The 'yellow bible' as it quickly became known to backpackers around the world, soon became *the* guide to the region. It has sold well over half a million copies and is now in its 8th edition, still retaining its familiar yellow cover.

Today there are over 140 Lonely Planet titles in print – books that have that same adventurous approach to travel as those early guides; books that 'assume you know how to get your luggage off the carousel' as one reviewer put it.

Although Lonely Planet initially specialised in guides to Asia, they now cover most regions of the world, including the Pacific, South America, Africa, the Middle East and Europe. The list of *walking guides* and *phrasebooks* (for 'unusual' languages such as Quechua, Swahili, Nepali and Egyptian Arabic) is also growing rapidly.

The emphasis continues to be on travel for independent travellers. Tony and Maureen still travel for several months of each year and play an active part in the writing, updating and quality control of Lonely Planet's guides.

They have been joined by over 50 authors, 110 staff – mainly editors, cartographers & designers – at our office in Melbourne, Australia, at our US office in Oakland, California and at our European office in Paris; another five at our office in London handle sales for Britain, Europe and Africa. Travellers themselves also make a valuable contribution to the guides through the feedback we receive in thousands of letters each year.

The people at Lonely Planet strongly believe that travellers can make a positive contribution to the countries they visit, both through their appreciation of the countries' culture, wildlife and natural features, and through the money they spend. In addition, the company makes a direct contribution to the countries and regions it covers. Since 1986 a percentage of the income from each book has been donated to ventures such as famine relief in Africa; aid projects in India; agricultural projects in Central America; Greenpeace's efforts to halt French nuclear testing in the Pacific; and Amnesty International.

Lonely Planet's basic travel philosophy is summed up in Tony Wheeler's comment, 'Don't worry about whether your trip will work out. Just go!'